September 9–15, 2012
Copenhagen, Denmark

Association for
Computing Machinery

Advancing Computing as a Science & Profession

Jens Olsen's World Clock, displayed in Copenhagen City Hall

ICFP'12

Proceedings of the 2012 ACM SIGPLAN
International Conference on Functional Programming

Sponsored by:

ACM SIGPLAN

Supported by:

Jane Street, Microsoft Research, NSF, Amgen, Basho, Copenhagen Finance IT Region, Standard Chartered, Facebook, Citrix, Credit Suisse, DIKU, Erlang Solutions, Galois, Google, HIPERFIT, INRIA, LexiFi, SimCorp, Twitter, Bluespec, IntelliFactory, QuviQ, Well-Typed, Northwestern University, & University of Copenhagen

Association for
Computing Machinery

Advancing Computing as a Science & Profession

The Association for Computing Machinery
2 Penn Plaza, Suite 701
New York, New York 10121-0701

ISBN: 978-1-4503-1054-3

Additional copies may be ordered prepaid from:

ACM Order Department
PO Box 30777
New York, NY 10087-0777, USA

Phone: 1-800-342-6626 (USA and Canada)
+1-212-626-0500 (Global)
Fax: +1-212-944-1318
E-mail: acmhelp@acm.org
Hours of Operation: 8:30 am – 4:30 pm ET

ACM Order Number: 565120

Printed in the USA

Cover & Title Page Image Attribution: Jens Olsen's World Clock, http://www.flickr.com/photos/demorganna/4920545863/ by Furya

Chairs' Welcome

It is our great pleasure to welcome you to Copenhagen for the 17th ACM SIGPLAN International Conference on Functional Programming: ICFP 2012.

This year's conference continues its tradition as a forum for researchers, developers, and students to hear about the latest work on the design, implementations, principles, and uses of functional programming. The conference covers the entire spectrum of work, from practice to theory, including its peripheries. The call for papers attracted 88 submissions from the Americas, Asia, Australia, and Europe. The program committee accepted 32 papers that cover a variety of topics related to functional programming. In addition, the program includes three keynote talks: "Agda-curious?" by Conor McBride, "Tales from the Jungle" by Peter Sewell, and "High Performance Embedded Domain Specific Languages" by Kunle Olukotun. This year, for the first time, ICFP hosts an ACM Student Research Competition (src.acm.org) that attracted 14 submissions. This competition is a great way for young researchers to get in touch with the community. We hope that SRC@ICFP will become an ongoing event.

As is tradition at ICFP, there was a programming contest this year, run by Kevin Hammond (co-chair), Edwin Brady (co-chair), Brian Campbell, Sam Lindley, Robert Atkey and Sam Elliott. This year 1,139 contestants participated in a three-day lambda-lifting extravaganza.

ICFP offers a record number of 13 co-located symposia, workshops, and tutorials oriented towards both academics and practitioners: the Haskell symposium, the Workshop on Cross-paradigm Language Design and Implementation (XLDI), the Workshop on Generic Programming (WGP), the Workshop on Higher-Order Programming with Effects (HOPE), the Workshop on Logical Frameworks and Meta-languages: Theory and Practice (LFMTP), the Workshop on Scheme and Functional Programming (SFP), the Workshop on ML, the OCaml Users and Developers Workshop (OUD), the Erlang Workshop, the Haskell Implementors' Workshop (HIM), the Workshop on Functional High-Performance Computing (FHPC), the Tutorial on Compiler Construction in Haskell, and the Tutorial on the Grammatical Framework. Complementing this academic program is a three-day event for Commercial Users of Functional Programming that encompasses industrial strength one- and two-day tutorials as well as a full day of experience talks about functional programming in action.

Running ICFP is a community-wide effort. Our primary thanks go to the people who joined us at the conference, submitted papers or posters, and competed in the programming contest. Special thanks go to the local organization team: Patrick Bahr, Jost Berthold, Martin Elsman, Andrzej Filinski, Fritz Henglein (chair), Ken Friis Larsen, and Jette Møller, who tirelessly prepared Copenhagen for your visit, to Andy Adams-Moran, who liaised with countless potential sponsors, to Patrik Jansson and Gabriele Keller for organizing the workshops, to Wouter Swierstra for an excellent job at beating the drum for ICFP, to Malcolm Wallace for his established video recording service, and, last but not least, to Doaitse Swierstra who agreed to chair the SRC on short notice. Thank you all, ICFP would not have been possible without your dedicated work!

We are indebted to our sponsors who made it possible to keep registration cost reasonable and who kindly supported students who would not have been able to attend the conference without financial aid. Their generosity helps our community to grow and spread.

We hope that you find the program as well as the offerings of the co-located events stimulating and thought provoking and that the ICFP week of functional programming provides you with many fruitful opportunities to meet with researchers and practitioners who share your interests.

Peter Thiemann
ICFP'12 General Chair
University of Freiburg, Germany

Robby Findler
ICFP'12 Program Chair
Northwestern University, USA

Table of Contents

ICFP 2012 Conference Organization

General Chair: Peter Thiemann *(University of Freiburg, Germany)*

Program Chair: Robby Findler *(Northwestern University, USA)*

Local Arrangements Chair: Fritz Henglein *(University of Copenhagen, Denmark)*

Workshop Chairs: Patrik Jansson *(Chalmers University of Technology, Sweden)*
Gabriele Keller *(University of New South Wales, Australia)*

Industrial Relations Chair: Andy Adams-Moran *(Galois, USA)*

Programming Contest Chairs: Kevin Hammond *(University of St. Andrews, Scotland)*
Edwin Brady *(University of St. Andrews, Scotland)*

Publicity Chair: Wouter Swierstra *(Utrecht University, The Netherlands)*

Video Chair: Malcolm Wallace *(Standard Chartered Bank, Singapore)*

Student Research Comp. Chair: Doaitse Swierstra *(Utrecht University, The Netherlands)*

Steering Committee Chair: Graham Hutton *(University of Nottingham, UK)*

Steering Committee: Amal Ahmed *(Indiana University, USA)*
Manuel Chakravarty *(University of New South Wales, Australia)*
Olivier Danvy *(Aarhus University, Denmark)*
Robby Findler *(Northwestern University, USA)*
Jeremy Gibbons *(University of Oxford, UK)*
Fritz Henglein *(University of Copenhagen, Denmark)*
Zhenjiang Hu *(National Institute of Informatics, Japan)*
Paul Hudak *(Yale University, USA)*
Graham Huttom *(University of Nottingham, UK)*
Johan Jeuring *(Utrecht University, The Netherlands)*
John Launchbury *(Galois, USA)*
Yaron Minsky *(Jane Street Capital, USA)*
Greg Morrisett *(Harvard University, USA)*
Wouter Swierstra *(Utrecht University, The Netherlands)*
Peter Thiemann *(University of Freiburg, Germany)*
Jan Vitek *(Purdue University, USA)*
Stephanie Weirich *(University of Pennsylvania, USA)*

Program Committee: Zena Ariola *(University of Oregon, USA)*
Lars Birkedal *(IT University of Copenhagen, Denmark)*
Matthias Blume *(Google, USA)*
Mariangiola Dezani-Ciancaglini *(University of Torino, Italy)*
R. Kent Dybvig *(Cisco Systems, Inc., and Indiana University, USA)*
Manuel Fähndrich *(Microsoft Research, USA)*
John Hughes *(Chalmers University of Technology, Sweden)*
Simon Marlow *(Microsoft Research, UK)*
Jan Midgaardt *(Aarhus University, Denmark)*
Brigitte Pientka *(McGill University, Canada)*
Andreas Rossberg *(Google, USA)*
Colin Runciman *(University of York, UK)*
Satnam Singh *(Google, USA)*
Eijiro Sumii *(Tohoku University, Japan)*
Sam Tobin-Hochstadt *(Northeastern University, USA)*
Andrew Tolmach *(Portland State University, USA)*

Additional reviewers:

Michael D. Adams
Kenichi Asai
Robert Atkey
Lennart Augustsson
Emil Axelsson
Jesper Bengtson
Stefano Berardi
Lars Bergstrom
Frédéric Besson
Małgorzata Biernacka
Dariusz Biernacki
Nikolaj Bjorner
Claus Brabrand
Brian Campbell
Marco Carbone
Felice Cardone
Andrew Cave
Manuel M. T. Chakravarty
James Cheney
Mario Coppo
Julien Cretin
Pierre-Evariste Dagand
Ferruccio Damiani
Thomas Dinsdale-Young
Paul Downen
Joshua Dunfield
Martin Erwig
Amr Fahmy
Francisco Ferreira
Andrzej Filinski
Pascal Fradet
Marco Gaboardi
Deepark Garg
Tony Garnock-Jones
Silvia Ghilezan
Jeremy Gibbons
Paul Govereau
Arjun Guha
John Harrison
Masahito Hasegawa
Alex Hearn
Jun Inoue
Bart Jacobs
Peter A. Jonsson
Andrew W. Keep
Naoki Kobayashi
Neelakantan R. Krishnaswami
Xavier Leroy
Ugo de Liguoro
Luke Maurer
Conor McBride
Matthew Might
Garrett Morris
Kim Nguyen
Jesper Buus Nielsen
Henrik Nilsson
Atsushi Ohori
Luca Paolini
Matthew Parkinson
Nicolas Pouillard
Willard Rafnsson
Vincent Rahli
Grigore Rosu
Didier Rémy
Sylvain Salvati
Isao Sasano
Peter Sestoft
Zhong Shao
Filip Sieczkowski
Nigel Smart
Matthew Sottile
Matthieu Sozeau
Daniel Spoonhower
Vincent St-Amour
Kasper Svendsen
Nikhil Swamy
Jacob Thamsborg
Johan Tibell
Bernardo Toninho
Takeshi Tsukada
Hiroshi Unno
Christian Urban
Viktor Vafeiadis
Germán Vidal
Philip Wadler

ICFP 2012 Sponsor & Supporters

PLATINUM PARTNERS

GOLD PARTNERS

AMGEN®
Pioneering science delivers vital medicines™

basho

CFIR
COPENHAGEN
FINANCE IT REGION

Standard Chartered

facebook

SILVER PARTNERS

CITRIX®

CREDIT SUISSE
Quantitative Strategies

DEPARTMENT OF
COMPUTER SCIENCE
UNIVERSITY OF COPENHAGEN

Erlang
SOLUTIONS

SILVER PARTNERS (Continued)

galois

Google

HIPERFIT

inria informatics mathematics

LexiFi

SimCorp

twitter

BRONZE PARTNERS

bluespec

IntelliFactory Your Functional Experts

QuviQ

Well-Typed The Haskell Consultants

INSTITUTIONAL PARTNERS AND ORGANIZERS

NORTHWESTERN UNIVERSITY | Electrical Engineering & Computer Science Department

UNIVERSITY OF COPENHAGEN

Agda-curious?

An Exploration of Programming with Dependent Types

Conor McBride

University of Strathclyde

conor.mcbride@strath.ac.uk

Abstract

I explore programming with the dependently typed functional language, AGDA. I present the progress which AGDA has made, demonstrate its usage in a small development, reflect critically on the state of the art, and speculate about the way ahead. I do not seek to persuade you to adopt AGDA as your primary tool for systems development, but argue that AGDA stimulates new useful ways to think about programming problems and deserves not just curiosity but interest, support and contribution.

Categories and Subject Descriptors D.1.1 [*Programming Techniques*]: Applicative (Functional) Programming; D.3.3 [*Language Constructs and Features*]: Data types and structures

General Terms Design, Languages, Theory

Keywords Dependent types

1. Introduction

AGDA (the Swedish form of Agatha) was implemented around the millenium by Catarina Coquand and is now in its second incarnation, implemented by Ulf Norell as part of his PhD [Norell, 2007]. Engineered to resemble HASKELL where convenient, it has gained quite some traction in the FP community, at least amongst enthusiasts for the typed frontier.

I can recommend AGDA tutorials by Norell [2008] and Bove and Dybjer [2008], but my focus here is more to investigate the issues which AGDA provokes, why you might become interested in them, and some of the ways in which there is still considerable work to be done: key questions for the Agda-curious.

2. What's the same?

At heart, AGDA is a typed λ-calculus extended with datatypes and pattern matching, very much in the mode of ML and HASKELL. It has a module system which sits nearer the package management of HASKELL than the full blown functors of ML. Whether you prefer call-by-value or something lazier, the outcome of evaluating an expression will be what you expect. Milner's 'variable rule' for specialising polymorphic types remains the means to avoid type-clutter Damas and Milner [1982]. Schematic arguments are routinely omitted at usage sites and inferred by unification.

AGDA treats types as values. However, just like all the dependent type theories in the Martin-Löf tradition, there is no 'typecase', so it is perfectly possible to erase types for run-time. We can compile by extraction to an existing functional language with its typechecker gagged, or by standard supercombinator approaches.

3. What's different?

By allowing expressions in types, identified up to computation, AGDA gains considerable powers of precision and abstraction. However, the primary mode of precision is not in the 'propositions-as-types' tradition embodied by COQ. Instead of using dependent types to build logical superstructure for ordinary datatypes and functions, an AGDA programmer usually prefers to design indexed datatypes which internalize key invariants, improving the basic hygiene of programming without recourse to proof. The gap with current FP languages is decreasing as GADTs gain adoption and more interesting kinds of index [Yorgey et al., 2012].

AGDA's typechecker can double as a proof validator, supporting integrated development of programs and proofs, the latter being programs one prefers not to run. However, the point is to shift the workload between the two, increasing the reach of typechecking the program as a broadly applicable but shallow formal method. The ability to capture requirements by indexing datatypes creates a new design space which calls for fresh insight.

AGDA is a *total* language with *codata*, as advocated by Turner [2004]. Head-normalization terminates, so the typechecker can boldly compute expressions in types, but infinitary processes such as operating systems and Turing machines can still be presented in a demand-driven way. Totality thus places no restriction on the expressable processes but rather enhances trust in their status: a type is a guarantee of a meaningful value. Termination of recursion and productivity of corecursion are checked by an oracle based on the size-change principle [Abel and Altenkirch, 2002, Lee et al., 2001].

AGDA deviates critically from the ML tradition by abandoning type inference in favour of a *bidirectional* mode of type checking: types come first. Milner's 'let rule' restricts type schemes to be machine-guessable: for the price of declaring types for definitions, we get to say what we really mean. Declared types push inward, resolving overloading and fixing types of variables. A type is an input also to the editing process, with information for missing components, mechanical splitting of patterns into cases, and type-driven search for candidate code. Types may be 'static', but they help us make programs, not just error messages.

4. What's it like?

I illustrate AGDA, and its indexing design space, by implementing a very small stack machine bytecode with two instructions.

ICFP'12, September 9–15, 2012, Copenhagen, Denmark.
ACM 978-1-4503-1054-3/12/09.

$$\textbf{data}\ \mathsf{Inst} : \mathsf{Set}\ \textbf{where}\ \mathsf{PUSH} : (v : \mathbf{N}) \to \mathsf{Inst} \qquad \mathsf{ADD} : \mathsf{Inst}$$

A first attempt to interpret a list of instructions as a function from initial to final stacks runs into the problem of *underflow*.

$$\begin{array}{lll}
\mathbf{run} : \mathsf{List\,Inst} \to \mathsf{List}\,\mathbf{N} \to \mathsf{List}\,\mathbf{N} & & \\
\mathbf{run}\ [\,]\ \ vs & = & vs \\
\mathbf{run}\ (\mathsf{PUSH}\ v, is)\ vs & = & \mathbf{run}\ is\ (v, vs) \\
\mathbf{run}\ (\mathsf{ADD}\ , is)\ [\,] & = & ? \\
\mathbf{run}\ (\mathsf{ADD}\ , is)\ (v, [\,]) & = & ? \\
\mathbf{run}\ (\mathsf{ADD}\ , is)\ (v_2, v_1, vs) & = & \mathbf{run}\ is\ (v_1 + v_2, vs)
\end{array}$$

No sensible compiler will ever deploy an ADD instruction for a short stack, so we should not need to consider the problem cases marked ?. We can nail stack usage down, indexing our instructions with 'before and after' stack heights [McKinna and Wright, 2006].

$$\begin{array}{l}
\textbf{data}\ \mathsf{Inst} : \mathbf{N} \to \mathbf{N} \to \mathsf{Set}\ \textbf{where} \\
\quad \mathsf{PUSH} : \forall \{h\} \to (v : \mathbf{N}) \to \mathsf{Inst}\ \ h\ \ (1 + h) \\
\quad \mathsf{ADD}\ \ : \forall \{h\} \to \mathsf{Inst}\ (2 + h)\ (1 + h)
\end{array}$$

Code becomes a Path of instructions with height indices fitting domino-style. A stack is a height-indexed Vector, and **run** acquires more precise type which enables an easy definition.

$$\begin{array}{lll}
\mathbf{run} : \forall \{i\,j\} \to \mathsf{Path\ Inst}\ i\ j \to \mathsf{Vec}\ \mathbf{N}\ i \to \mathsf{Vec}\ \mathbf{N}\ j & & \\
\mathbf{run}\ [\,]\ vs & = & vs \\
\mathbf{run}\ (\mathsf{PUSH}\ v, is)\ vs & = & \mathbf{run}\ is\ (v, vs) \\
\mathbf{run}\ (\mathsf{ADD}\ , is)\ (v_2, v_1, vs) & = & \mathbf{run}\ is\ (v_1 + v_2, vs)
\end{array}$$

'No underflow' is no longer a theorem to prove: it is basic. Moreover, we can index by the stack *contents*, paired with and dependent on the stack height.

$$\begin{array}{l}
\textbf{data}\ \mathsf{InstC} : \Sigma\,\mathbf{N}\,(\mathsf{Vec}\,\mathbf{N}) \to \Sigma\,\mathbf{N}\,(\mathsf{Vec}\,\mathbf{N}) \to \mathsf{Set}\ \textbf{where} \\
\quad \mathsf{PUSH} : \forall \{h\ vs\} \to (v : \mathbf{N}) \to \\
\qquad\qquad \mathsf{InstC}\ (\ \ h,\ \ vs)\ (1 + h,\ (v, vs)) \\
\quad \mathsf{ADD}\ \ : \forall \{h\ v_1\ v_2\ vs\} \to \\
\qquad\qquad \mathsf{InstC}\ (2 + h, (v_2, v_1, vs))\ (1 + h, (v_1 + v_2, vs))
\end{array}$$

The InstC type can be seen as the systematic 'ornamentation' of Inst by the behaviour of **run**. Given an expression type Expr with a reference interpreter $[\![\_]\!]$, a compiler should now map an expression e to a code sequence which effectively pushes $[\![e]\!]$.

$$\begin{array}{l}
\mathbf{compile} : \forall \{h\}\ \{vs : \mathsf{Vec}\ \mathbf{N}\ h\} \to \\
\qquad (e : \mathsf{Expr}) \to \mathsf{Path\ InstC}\ (h, vs)\ (1 + h, ([\![e]\!], vs))
\end{array}$$

It may turn out that indexing to this detail admits **compile** with not much more effort than at a simpler type, but nothing to prove, or else the detail might make the job too complex for the reward. This negotiation is what makes AGDA programming a new and fascinating skill.

5. What's the catch?

As with anything which requires a new skill, the main catch is that you need to undergo learning. The familiar-looking syntax risks stimulating misplaced entitlement, and thence frustration. More of the translation from design to execution is machine-mediated, which necessitates a clarity many of us guiltily strive to avoid. A sad omission, therefore, is machine support for rethinking failed programming attempts. It is thrilling to work from good definitions to beautiful code, but that happens only in the last cycle of a turgid process of getting stuck and propagating improvements.

Datatype indexing is not only the key contribution but the key new source of misery. This will remain true while distinct datatype declarations remain islands unconnected by exposition of common structure. Dependent types can express first class descriptions of datatypes, thus supporting abstraction over indexing schemes, but we await a language design which breaks the mould of separate generative datatype declarations and seizes this opportunity.

To deliver proven code, we also face the issue that AGDA is a much more a FP language than a theorem prover: writing proof terms is rather low-level and far from perspicuous. I agree with Adam Chlipala's warning that the certifying programmer can cope much more readily with weak programming tools than weak proof tools. If AGDA is to compete in COQ's market, it will need an investment of fresh thought about how to pick up the pieces when typechecking delivers less than the theorem required.

Meanwhile, if AGDA is to compete in HASKELL's market, it will need a much more comprehensive treatment of the stuff of 'real life', including a good compiler, primitive numeric and character types, and a broad library. These things will come with time and effort, but there is also a clear design challenge to face: how shall we program with *computational effects*?

6. What's my point?

We should relish the opportunity to think afresh about certifying program properties in a setting where it is feasible to internalize some of those properties in the types of data and functions and ensure them as part of the basic hygiene of typechecking. The fun of AGDA programming comes from the theorems you do not need to prove: it is thrilling to be drawn towards the right program by a precise type. FP has already seen one generation of languages evolve from poetry to power-tools. In the next generation, power will come from keeping the promises that let programs play *together*. AGDA is not yet the next power-tool, but it offers us new and lasting lessons about programs which keep promises. Let us learn.

References

A. Abel and T. Altenkirch. A predicative analysis of structural recursion. *J. Funct. Program.*, 12(1):1–41, 2002.

A. Bove and P. Dybjer. Dependent types at work. In A. Bove, L. S. Barbosa, A. Pardo, and J. S. Pinto, editors, *LerNet ALFA Summer School*, volume 5520 of *Lecture Notes in Computer Science*, pages 57–99. Springer, 2008. ISBN 978-3-642-03152-6.

L. Damas and R. Milner. Principal type-schemes for functional programs. In R. A. DeMillo, editor, *POPL*, pages 207–212. ACM Press, 1982. ISBN 0-89791-065-6.

C. S. Lee, N. D. Jones, and A. M. Ben-Amram. The size-change principle for program termination. In C. Hankin and D. Schmidt, editors, *POPL*, pages 81–92. ACM, 2001. ISBN 1-58113-336-7.

J. McKinna and J. Wright. A type-correct, stack-safe, provably correct, expression compiler in epigram. Submitted to the Journal of Functional Programming, 2006.

U. Norell. *Towards a Practical Programming Language based on Dependent Type Theory*. PhD thesis, Chalmers University of Technology, 2007.

U. Norell. Dependently Typed Programming in Agda. In P. W. M. Koopman, R. Plasmeijer, and S. D. Swierstra, editors, *Advanced Functional Programming*, volume 5832 of *LNCS*, pages 230–266. Springer, 2008.

D. A. Turner. Total functional programming. *J. UCS*, 10(7):751–768, 2004.

B. A. Yorgey, S. Weirich, J. Cretin, S. L. P. Jones, D. Vytiniotis, and J. P. Magalhães. Giving haskell a promotion. In B. C. Pierce, editor, *TLDI*, pages 53–66. ACM, 2012. ISBN 978-1-4503-1120-5.

Verified Heap Theorem Prover by Paramodulation

Gordon Stewart Lennart Beringer Andrew W. Appel
Princeton University, Princeton, NJ, USA
{jsseven, eberinge, appel}@cs.princeton.edu

Abstract

We present *VeriStar*, a verified theorem prover for a decidable subset of separation logic. Together with VeriSmall [3], a proved-sound Smallfoot-style program analysis for C minor, VeriStar demonstrates that fully machine-checked static analyses equipped with efficient theorem provers are now within the reach of formal methods. As a pair, VeriStar and VeriSmall represent the first application of the *Verified Software Toolchain* [4], a tightly integrated collection of machine-verified program logics and compilers giving foundational correctness guarantees.

VeriStar is (1) *purely functional*, (2) *machine-checked*, (3) *end-to-end*, (4) *efficient* and (5) *modular*. By purely functional, we mean it is implemented in Gallina, the pure functional programming language embedded in the Coq theorem prover. By machine-checked, we mean it has a proof in Coq that when the prover says "valid", the checked entailment holds in a proved-sound separation logic for C minor. By end-to-end, we mean that when the static analysis+theorem prover says a C minor program is safe, the program will be compiled to a semantically equivalent assembly program that runs on real hardware. By efficient, we mean that the prover implements a state-of-the-art algorithm for deciding heap entailments and uses highly tuned verified functional data structures. By modular, we mean that VeriStar can be retrofitted to other static analyses as a plug-compatible entailment checker and its soundness proof can easily be ported to other separation logics.

Categories and Subject Descriptors F.3.1 [*Specifying and Verifying and Reasoning about Programs*]: Mechanical verification

General Terms Verification

Keywords Separation Logic, Paramodulation, Theorem Proving

1. Introduction

Can you trust your decision procedure? When your memory analysis that calls upon this decision procedure returns "safe", how confident can you be that your C program won't dereference a null pointer? If you're writing safety- or security-critical code then such questions are crucial, but often difficult to answer: state-of-the-art theorem provers are large, intricate programs (Z3, for example, is over 300k lines of proprietary code [18]). A bug in the decision procedure might camouflage a bug in your static analysis regime, which may itself hide a disastrous bug in your safety-critical program.

ICFP'12, September 9–15, 2012, Copenhagen, Denmark.

To bridge the trust gap, you can instrument the decision procedure to produce *witnesses*—as in proof-carrying code (PCC) [5, 11, 27]—or implement and verify the decision procedure directly in a proof assistant [6, 12, 33]. Although one might suspect that separating the prover from the checker is necessary for efficiency, modern proof assistants have advanced to the point that it is now feasible to implement and verify even sophisticated analyses in a foundational way.

As evidence of this claim, we present VeriStar, an efficient *machine-verified* decision procedure for entailments in separation logic, the *de facto* standard for reasoning about shape properties of heap data. Tools based on separation logic, such as SLAyer [10], SpaceInvader [15], Infer [14] and Xisa [16], have been successfully applied to industrial code bases but have lacked foundational certification. VeriStar integrates with VeriSmall [3], a machine-checked symbolic executor, to yield a fully verified shape analysis for separation logic. When connected to the CompCert certified C compiler [23], VeriSmall+VeriStar enables end-to-end automatic verification of shape properties all the way from C to x86 or PowerPC assembly. Because CompCert's correctness theorem makes a claim directly about the generated assembly, the user of our system need trust only the Coq typechecker and CompCert's model of either x86 or PowerPC assembly.

Contributions. The VeriStar system is:

- **Purely functional.** We implemented VeriStar in Gallina, the pure functional language embedded in the interactive theorem prover Coq. The use of a pure functional implementation language gave us both an elegant programming environment and an attractive proof theory for reasoning about our code.
- **Machine-checked.** We proved VeriStar sound with a machine-checked proof in Coq. Soundness means that when the prover returns "valid", the entailment checked holds in an separation logic for C minor [22]. The separation logic is proved sound, in turn, with respect to C minor's operational semantics.
- **End-to-end.** C minor programs verified with VeriStar can be compiled to (PowerPC or x86) assembly by the semantics-preserving compiler CompCert. The end-to-end machine-checked proof ensures the absence of soundness bugs anywhere along the chain.
- **Efficient.** VeriStar implements a state-of-the-art decision procedure based on *paramodulation*, a variant of resolution (cf. Navarro Pérez and Rybalchenko [26]), and can be compiled using Coq's code extraction utility and the OCaml system to native code for nearly any architecture. It uses highly tuned verified functional data structures such as a new implementation of red-black trees to implement clause sets.
- **Modular.** Although VeriStar forms the core of the fully verified static analysis VeriSmall, its modular structure means it can be retargeted to third-party separation logics and retrofitted to ex-

isting static analysis tools such as Smallfoot [9]. As supporting evidence, we describe two alternative separation logics (Section 4) and demonstrate the integration of our prover into the original (Berdine et al.) Smallfoot system.

To the best of our knowledge, VeriStar is the first machine-checked theorem prover for separation logic that connects to a real-world operational semantics (CompCert C minor). The VeriStar architecture employs a novel abstraction of separation logic, the *Separation Logic Interface*, in order to separate the system's soundness proof from the details of the separation logic implementation, and thus increase modularity. More generally, the lessons we learned while building VeriStar—on the effectiveness of code extraction as an execution model for verified software, on the power of an elegant proof theory for reasoning about functional programs, and on the importance of modular interfaces to proofs—will inform the future construction of large, verified software toolchains from independent, machine-checked components.

We have evaluated VeriStar on a suite of separation logic entailments generated by the original Smallfoot tool during symbolic execution. On these "real-world" entailments, VeriStar's performance is comparable to that of Smallfoot's unverified entailment checker—both systems are fast enough. On a suite of artificial entailments designed to simulate the heap inconsistency checks often performed during symbolic execution, VeriStar actually outperforms Smallfoot on the majority of entailments. On the other hand, VeriStar is still a small system that lacks features found in more established theorem provers. The current implementation of VeriStar supports just four atomic predicates: the points-to predicate of separation logic describing the singleton heap, a predicate describing acyclic list segments, a predicate describing empty heaps and an equality predicate on program variables. This assertion language resembles Smallfoot's quite closely but does not yet permit general intermixing of predicates from other theories, as in SMT solvers. Finally, although VeriStar's performance is adequate for verification of small to medium-sized programs, it could be further improved by memoizing common terms in the clause database through techniques such as hash-consing, or by performing multiple inferences at once, as is done in some state-of-the-art equational theorem provers [24]. None of these limitations is insurmountable. We foresee few technical difficulties in adding support for user-defined nonspatial predicates and spatial predicates for other sorts of data structures such as trees. Switching to a more efficient term and clause representation will require straightforward engineering.

2. VeriStar by Example

Figure 1 presents the main components of the VeriStar theorem prover. To build an intuition for how the pieces fit together, consider the following (valid) VeriStar entailment

$$a \neq c \wedge b = d \wedge a \mapsto b * \mathsf{lseg}(b, c) * \mathsf{lseg}(b, d) \vdash \mathsf{lseg}(a, c)$$

which consists of two assertions separated by a *turnstile* ($\vdash$). The first assertion states that program variable a does not equal c, b equals d and the heap contains a pointer from a to b and two list segments with heads b and tails c and d, while the assertion to the right of the turnstile states that the heap is just the list segment with head a and tail c. The task of the theorem prover is either to show that this entailment is *valid*—that every model of the assertion on the left is a model of the assertion on the right—or to return a counterexample in the process.

Most existing theorem provers for separation logic (e.g., Smallfoot [9], SLAyer [10]) attack the entailment problem *top-down*, by systematically exploring proof trees rooted at the goal. Each step of a top-down proof is an entailment-level deduction justified by a validity-preserving inference rule.

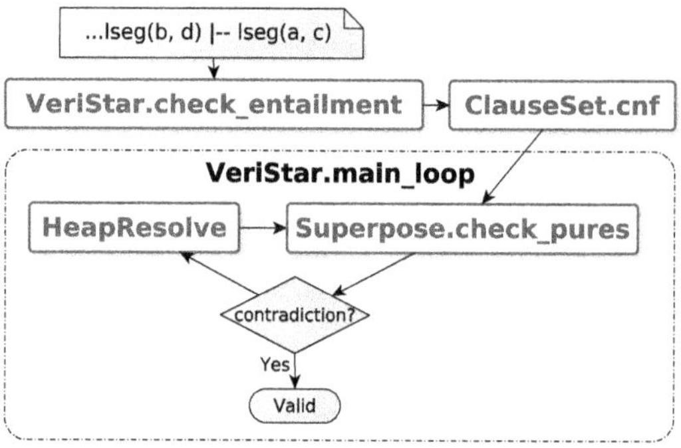

Figure 1: The main components of the VeriStar system, each of which is defined by a well-specified interface (Module Type) in Coq. Superpose and HeapResolve form the heart of the heap theorem prover, performing equational and spatial reasoning respectively. The ClauseSet module defines the clausal embedding of assertions as well as the prover's clause database using a tuned red-black tree implementation of the Coq MSets interface.

VeriStar, by contrast, is *bottom-up* and *indirect*. Instead of exploring proof trees rooted at the goal, it first decomposes the *negation* of the goal (hence indirect) into a logically equivalent set of *clauses* (its *clausal normal form*), then attempts to derive a contradiction from this set through the application of clausal inference rules. One can think of the clauses that form this initial set as a logically equivalent encoding of the original entailment into its atomic parts.

In particular, a VeriStar clause is a disjunction

$$(\pi_1 \vee \ldots \vee \pi_m) \vee (\overline{\pi'_1} \vee \ldots \vee \overline{\pi'_n}) \vee (\sigma_1 * \ldots * \sigma_r)$$

of positive pure literals π (by *pure* we mean those that are heap-independent), negated pure literals $\overline{\pi'}$ and a spatial atom Σ consisting of the star-conjoined simple spatial atoms $\sigma_1 * \ldots * \sigma_r$. The atom Σ may be negated or may occur positively but not both: we never require clauses containing two atoms Σ and Σ' of different polarities. We write positive spatial clauses (those in which Σ occurs positively) as $\Gamma \rightarrow \Delta, \Sigma$, where Γ and Δ are sets of pure atoms and Σ is a spatial atom, and use analogous notation for pure and negative spatial clauses. For example, in negative spatial clauses, Σ appears to the left of the arrow ($\Gamma, \Sigma \rightarrow \Delta$), and in pure clauses Σ does not appear at all ($\Gamma \rightarrow \Delta$). The *empty clause* $\emptyset \rightarrow \emptyset$ has no model because on the left, the conjunction of no clauses is True, and on the right, the disjunction of no clauses is False. Clauses such as $\Gamma \rightarrow a = a, \Delta$ and $\Gamma, a = b \rightarrow a = b, \Delta$ are tautologies.

To express the negation of the entailment as a set of clauses, VeriStar passes the entailment to ClauseSet.cnf (Figure 1), which takes advantage of the fact that it can encode any positive atom π as the positive unit clause $\emptyset \rightarrow \pi$ and any negative atom $\overline{\pi'}$ as the negative unit clause $\pi' \rightarrow \emptyset$. It can do the same for negative and positive spatial atoms. Since the negation of any entailment $F \vdash G$ is equivalent, classically, to $F \wedge \neg G$, the original entailment becomes:

$$a = c \rightarrow \emptyset \quad (1)$$

$$\emptyset \rightarrow b = d \quad (2)$$

$$\emptyset \rightarrow a \mapsto b * \mathsf{lseg}(b, c) * \mathsf{lseg}(b, d) \quad (3)$$

$$\mathsf{lseg}(a, c) \rightarrow \emptyset \quad (4)$$

Here the spatial atom $\mathsf{lseg}(a, c)$ appears to the left of the arrow in clause (4) since it appears in the right-hand side of the original entailment. Likewise, the spatial atom $a \mapsto b * \mathsf{lseg}(b, c) * \mathsf{lseg}(b, d)$

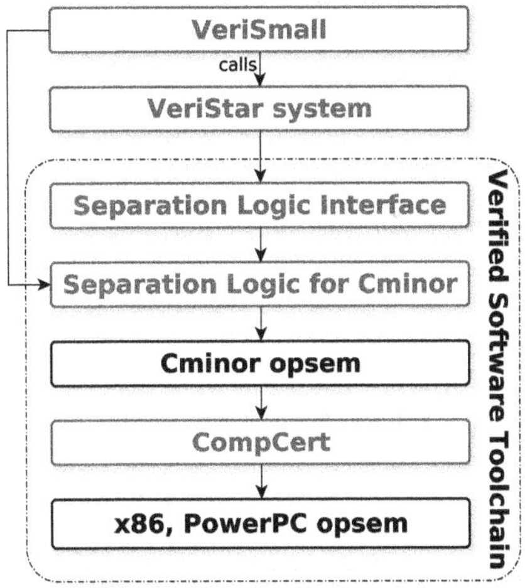

(a) Integration into the Verified Software Toolchain, yielding an end-to-end soundness proof

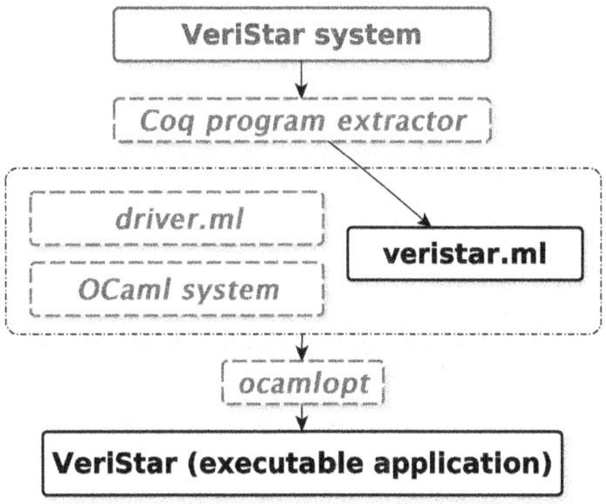

(b) Compilation toolchain

Figure 2: VeriStar's soundness proof (2a) and compilation toolchain (2b). Trusted components (dashed in red) are those that must be understood by the user to have confidence in the system. Verified components (solid in blue) have machine-checked correctness proofs. Cminor opsem and x86, PowerPC opsem are axiomatic definitions of the Cminor language and CompCert target languages respectively. When connected to the Verified Software Toolchain (2a), machine-checked proofs from VeriSmall/VeriStar through CompCert to assembly provide a foundational correctness guarantee with respect to the operational semantics of CompCert's target languages, x86 and PowerPC assembly. The modular construction of the soundness proof through the Separation Logic Interface facilitates retargeting VeriStar to third-party separation logics. VeriSmall is proved directly with respect to the C minor separation logic, and therefore is slightly less portable. In Figure 2b, we use Coq's extraction mechanism and the OCaml system to compile VeriStar to an executable application.

appears to the right of the arrow in clause (3) since it appears in the left-hand side of the original entailment.

After encoding the entailment as a set of clauses, VeriStar enters its main loop (VeriStar.main_loop in Figure 1). First, it filters the *pure* clauses from the initial clauseset (clauses (1) and (2) above), then passes these clauses to Superpose.check_pures, the pure prover. Superpose attempts to derive a contradiction from the pure clauses by equational reasoning. In this case, however, Superpose is unable to derive a contradiction, or indeed, any new clauses at all from the set, so it constructs a model of the pure clauses by setting b equal to d (completeness of the superposition calculus guarantees that this model exists) and passes the model, along with the current clauseset, to HeapResolve for spatial normalization and unfolding.

HeapResolve uses the fact that b equals d in the model as a hint to normalize the spatial clauses (3) and (4) by clause (2), resulting in the new spatial clause

$$\emptyset \rightarrow a \mapsto d * \mathsf{lseg}(d, c) * \mathsf{lseg}(d, d) \tag{5}$$

in which b has been rewritten to d and therefore no longer appears. But now the spatial prover recognizes that since list segments are acyclic, $\mathsf{lseg}(d, d)$ can hold only if it denotes the empty heap. Thus $\mathsf{lseg}(d, d)$ can be simplified to emp, resulting in the new clause

$$\emptyset \rightarrow a \mapsto d * \mathsf{lseg}(d, c). \tag{6}$$

This new clause can almost be resolved against clause (4) using *spatial resolution*—an inference rule allowing negative and positive occurrences of spatial atoms in two different clauses to be eliminated—but only if clause (4) is unfolded to accommodate the next atom $a \mapsto d$ in clause (6). Unfolding $\mathsf{lseg}(a, c)$ to $a \mapsto d * \mathsf{lseg}(d, c)$ is sound, in turn, only when $\mathsf{lseg}(a, c)$ is nonempty, i.e., when $a \neq c$. To encode this fact, HeapResolve generates the new clause

$$a \mapsto d * \mathsf{lseg}(d, c) \rightarrow a = c. \tag{7}$$

Clause (7) can then be resolved with clause (6) to produce the positive unit clause

$$\emptyset \rightarrow a = c. \tag{8}$$

Superpose now resolves clause (8) with clause (1) to derive the empty clause $\emptyset \rightarrow \emptyset$, which is unsatisfiable. Since the inference rules of the HeapResolve and Superpose systems preserve all models, the original set of clauses encoding the negation of the entailment VeriStar set out to prove is unsatisfiable; the entailment must therefore be valid.

2.1 Overview of the Rest of the Paper

In the next section, we introduce VeriStar in the context of the Verified Software Toolchain [4], a series of tightly integrated machine-verified components that connect end-to-end to yield foundational correctness guarantees. We also describe VeriStar's execution model. Sections 4 and 5 give the technical details of our model of separation logic and the VeriStar implementation and its soundness proof in Coq. Section 7 makes a case for machine-checked proofs, with examples from this case study. Section 8 describes our experience optimizing VeriStar. In Section 9, we evaluate the relative sizes in lines-of-code of the components of the prover and measure VeriStar's performance on a suite of benchmarks.

3. The Verified Software Toolchain

The Verified Software Toolchain [4] connects machine-checked program analyses to machine-checked program logics; the logics are connected to machine-checked compilers such as Leroy's CompCert, giving an end-to-end result.

Figure 2a puts VeriSmall and VeriStar in the context of the current instantiation of the Verified Software Toolchain: VeriStar is proved sound with respect to an abstract axiomatization of separation logic, the *Separation Logic Interface* (Section 4.2). VeriSmall is proved sound directly with respect to the C minor separation logic. Of course, VeriSmall's soundness proof must rely on that of VeriStar since VeriSmall frequently calls the prover to decide entailments during symbolic execution.

We instantiate the Separation Logic Interface with Hobor et al.'s separation logic for C minor [22], which has a machine-checked soundness proof in Coq with respect to CompCert C minor's operational semantics. Because CompCert preserves the semantics of safe C minor programs, properties proved at the source level using VeriSmall/VeriStar will hold of the generated assembly. Furthermore, although the operational semantics of C minor and those of CompCert's intermediate languages play a role in the end-to-end proof, only the operational semantics of the target languages, PowerPC and x86 assembly, must be trusted since the compiler's correctness theorem makes a claim directly about the behavior of the target program.

3.1 Execution via Extraction

We use Coq's extraction utility to generate OCaml code (veristar.ml, Figure 2b) for VeriStar. A small, trusted translation from Smallfoot-style entailments to VeriStar entailments (driver.ml) allows our modified Smallfoot to call VeriStar.check_entailment as a subroutine, thus replacing Smallfoot's standard entailment checker with a formally verified one and reducing the size of Smallfoot's trusted computing base by approximately 20% (modulo correctness of the Coq typechecker[1]). When connected to the machine-checked static analysis VeriSmall, VeriStar's trusted computing base is even smaller: just the Coq typechecker and CompCert's specifications of either PowerPC or x86 assembly.

4. Separation Logic Semantics

To ensure VeriStar can be retargeted to separation logics for a variety of languages and compiler frameworks, we proved the system sound with respect to an *abstract model* of separation logic. We first defined a generic Separation Logic Interface (Section 4.2) specifying the operators of separation logic on which the proof depends. We then constructed an abstract model of separation logic generically for any concrete implementation satisfying the interface (Section 4.3). We have instantiated the interface with two such implementations, Hobor et al.'s Separation Logic for C minor [22] and a bare-bones implementation (cf. Appendices B and C of the extended version of this paper [1]) but expect the interface, and hence VeriStar's soundness proof, to be general enough to be widely applicable.

4.1 The Assertion Language

Atomic assertions in VeriStar (Figure 3) denote equalities and inequalities of program variables, singleton heaps and acyclic list segments. The assertion emp denotes the empty heap. The assertion $a \mapsto b$ (Next a b in VeriStar syntax) denotes the heap containing just the value of variable b at the location given by a (and is empty everywhere else), while Lseg a b denotes the heap containing the acyclic list segment with head pointer a and tail pointer b. Equalities and inequalities of variables are *pure* assertions because they make no reference to the heap, whereas $a \mapsto b$ and Lseg are *spatial* assertions.

A complex assertion $\Pi \wedge \Sigma$ is the conjunction of the pure atoms Π with the *separating conjunction* of the spatial atoms Σ. The separating conjunction $\sigma_1 * \sigma_2$ (also called *star*) of two assertions—a notion from separation logic—is satisfied by any heap splittable into two disjoint subheaps satisfying σ_1 and σ_2, respectively. The assertion $\Pi \wedge \Sigma$ is satisfied by any environment e and heap h such

[1] and the Coq program-extractor, and the OCaml compiler that compiles both veristar.ml and driver.ml, and the C compiler that compiles OCaml's runtime system... For a discussion of these issues, see [4, Section 11].

Expressions a, b	
Nil	null pointer
Var x	Program variable
Pure Atoms π (pn_atom)	
Equ a b	Expression a equals b.
Nequ a b	Expression a does *not* equal b.
Spatial Atoms σ (space_atom)	
emp	Empty heap
Next a b	Singleton heap with $a \mapsto b$
Lseg a b	Acyclic list segment from a to b
Assertions F, G	
Assertion Π Σ	Pairs of pure atoms Π and spatial atoms Σ
Entailments ent	
Entailment F G	Assertion F implies G.

Figure 3: VeriStar syntax

that e satisfies all the assertions in Π and the pair (e, h) satisfies the separating conjunction of the assertions in Σ. Entailments $F \vdash G$ are valid whenever all the models satisfying F also satisfy G, i.e.: $\forall (e, h).\ F(e, h) \rightarrow G(e, h)$.

4.2 The Interface

We present a selection of the components of the Separation Logic Interface in Listing 1. The interface axiomatizes the types of locations loc and values val; the special values nil_val, corresponding to the `null` pointer, and empty_val, corresponding to undefined (i.e., not in the domain of a given heap); an injection val2loc from values to locations; the types of variable environments env and heaps (heap) and a points-to operator on heaps (rawnext).

We assume a *separation algebra* [20] on values (Sep_alg val), meaning that in addition to the operators on values specified in the interface (e.g., val2loc) we may use the *join* operator, written $\oplus$, to describe the union of two disjoint values. In simple separation logics, $v_1 \oplus v_2$ is defined only when either v_1 or v_2 is the empty_val (that is, two nonunit values are never disjoint). However, a more refined separation algebra on values, say with shares denoting read and write permissions, is often useful in concurrent separation logic. Our interface and the soundness proof are indifferent to the separation algebra actually used.

The parameter heap gives the type of program memories. As with val, we require a separation algebra on heaps. We also require two operators on heaps, rawnext, a low-level version of the $\mapsto$ predicate of separation logic, and emp_at $(l{:}loc)$ $(h{:}heap)$, which defines when a heap h is empty at a location l. The behavior of these operators is defined by a series of axioms. For example, the axiom rawnext_out asserts that the heap rawnext l v is empty everywhere except at location l (i.e., it is a singleton heap). The constructor mk_heap_rawnext allows one to construct new singleton heaps. In the definition of mk_heap_rawnext, comparable h h' means that h and h' share the same unit in our multi-unit separation algebras (thus they are *comparable*).[2] The assertion rawnext′ l v extends rawnext l v to any heap that contains $l \mapsto v$ as a subheap. The behavior of rawnext′ is given by a series of axioms not shown in Listing 1 but given in the code.

4.3 The Abstract Model

We defined our abstract separation logic model with respect to the opaque interface of Listing 1. In our Coq implementation, this model is literally a functor over modules satisfying the interface: we make

[2] Dockins et al. [20] describes why multi-unit separation algebras are preferable to standard, single-unit ones.

```
Module Type VERISTAR_LOGIC.
(*Locations and values*)
Parameters loc val : Type.
Declare Instance Sep_val : Sep_alg val.
Parameter val2loc : val → option loc.
Parameter nil_val : val.
Parameter empty_val : val.

(*Environments*)
Parameter env : Type.
Parameter env_get : env → var → val.
Parameter env_set : var → val → env → env.
Axiom gss_env : ∀(x : var) (v:val) (e:env),
  env_get (env_set x v e) x = v.
Axiom gso_env : ∀(x y : var) (v:val) (e:env),
  x ≠ y → env_get (env_set x v e) y = env_get e y.
Parameter empty_env : env.

(*Heaps*)
Parameter heap : Type.
Declare Instance Sep_heap: Sep_alg heap.
Parameter rawnext : ∀(x:loc) (y:val) (e:heap), Prop.
Parameter emp_at : ∀(l:loc) (h:heap), Prop.
Definition nil_or_loc (v:val) :=
  v=nil_val ∨ ∃l:loc, val2loc v = Some l.
Axiom mk_heap_rawnext : ∀h x0 x y,
  val2loc x0 = Some x → nil_or_loc y →
  ∃h', rawnext x y h' ∧ comparable h h'.
Axiom rawnext_out : ∀x x0 x' y h,
  rawnext x y h → val2loc x0 = Some x' →
  x' ≠ x → emp_at x' h.
Definition rawnext' x y h :=
  ∃h0, join_sub h0 h ∧ rawnext x y h0.

(*Further parameters and axioms are elided.*)
End VERISTAR_LOGIC.
```

Listing 1: Selected values, operators and their properties from the Separation Logic Interface. The abstract types val, loc, var, env and heap are interface parameters.

no assumptions in the proof about the underlying module beyond those defined in the interface, thus increasing portability.

States are pairs of environments e and heaps h.

```
Inductive state := State: ∀(e:env) (h:heap), state.
```

The Coq keyword **Inductive** declares a new inductively defined datatype with, in this case, a single constructor named State. State takes as parameters an environment e and a heap h. In more conventional ML-like notation, this type is equivalent to the product type State **of** (env * heap). Predicates on states, called spreds, are functions from states to Prop.

```
Notation spred := (state → Prop).
```

One can think of Prop as the type of truth values True and False, analogous to bool, except that predicates in Prop need not be decidable and are erased during program extraction. Thus, we use Prop in our proofs, but bool in the verified code. A Coq **Notation** simply defines syntactic sugar. The interpretations of expressions (expr_denote), expression equality (expr_eq) and pure atoms (pn_atom_denote) are standard.

List segments lseg are defined by an inductive type with two constructors.

```
Inductive lseg : val → val → heap → Prop :=
| lseg_nil : ∀x h, emp h → nil_or_loc x → lseg x x h
| lseg_cons : ∀x y z l h0 h1 h,
    x ≠ y → val2loc x = Some l → rawnext l z h0 →
    lseg z y h1 → join h0 h1 h → lseg x y h.
```

The lseg_nil constructor forms the trivial list segment whose head and tail pointers are equal and whose heap is emp. The lseg_cons constructor builds a list segment inductively when x does not equal y, x is injected to a location l such that $l \mapsto z$, and there is a sub-list segment from z to y.

The function space_atom_denote maps syntactic spatial assertions such as Lseg x y to their semantic counterparts (i.e., lseg x y).

```
Definition space_atom_denote (a: space_atom) : spred :=
  match a with Next x y ⇒ fun s ⇒
    match val2loc (expr_denote x s) with
    | None ⇒ False
    | Some l ⇒
        rawnext l (expr_denote y s) (hp s) ∧
        nil_or_loc (expr_denote y s)
    end
  | Lseg x y ⇒ fun s ⇒
      lseg (expr_denote x s) (expr_denote y s) (hp s)
  end.
```

For Next x y assertions, it injects the value of the variable x to a location l and requires that the heap contain just the location l with value v (that is, the heap must be the singleton $l \mapsto v$), where v is the interpretation of variable y. Coq's **match** syntax does case analysis on an inductively defined value (here the space atom a), defining a distinct result value for each constructor.

An Assertion Π Σ is the conjunction of the pure atoms $\pi \in \Pi$ with the separating conjunction of the spatial atoms $\sigma \in \Sigma$.

```
Definition assertion_denote (f:assertion) : spred :=
  match f with Assertion Π Σ ⇒
     fold pn_atom_denote andp (space_denote Σ) Π
  end.
```

The function space_denote interprets the list of spatial atoms Σ as the *fold* of space_atom_denote over the list, with unit emp. Thus (space_denote Σ) is equivalent to

$$\left(\circledast_{\sigma\in\Sigma}\mathsf{space\_atom\_denote}(\sigma)\right) * \mathsf{emp}$$

(where $\circledast$ is iterated separating conjunction) and the denotation of Assertion Π Σ is

$$\bigwedge_{\pi\in\Pi} \mathsf{pn\_atom\_denote}(\pi) \wedge \left(\circledast_{\sigma\in\Sigma}\mathsf{space\_atom\_denote}(\sigma)\right)$$

if one simplifies $P * \mathsf{emp}$ to P (recognizing that emp is the unit for $*$). Here space_denote Σ is the unit of the fold. Entailments from F to G are interpreted as the semantic entailment of the two assertions.

5. The VeriStar Algorithm

A key strength of the Navarro Pérez and Rybalchenko algorithm is that it splits the theorem prover into two modular components: the equational theorem prover for pure clauses (Superpose) and the spatial reasoning system HeapResolve, which calls Superpose as a subroutine in between rounds of spatial inference. This modular structure means well-studied techniques from equational theorem proving can be applied to the equational prover in isolation, while improving the performance of the heap theorem prover as a whole.

```
1  Function main_loop
2    (n: positive) (Σ: list space_atom) (ncl: clause) (S: M.t)
3    {measure nat_of_P n} :=
4    if Coqlib.peq n 1 then Aborted (M.elements S) else
5    match Superpose.check_pures S with
6    | (Superpose.Valid, units, _, _) ⇒ Valid
7    | (Superpose.C_example R sel, units, S*, _) ⇒
8      let Σ' := simplify_atoms units Σ in
9      let ncl' := simplify units ncl in
10     let c := norm sel (PosSpaceClause nil nil Σ') R in
11     let S1 := incorp (do_wellformed c) S* in
12     if isEq (M.compare S1 S*)
13     then if is_model_of_Π (List.rev R) ncl'
14          then let c' := norm sel ncl' in
15               let us := pures (unfolding c c') in
16               let S2 := incorp us S1 in
17               if isEq (M.compare S1 S2) then C_example R
18               else main_loop (Ppred n) Σ' ncl' S2 c
19          else C_example R
20     else main_loop (Ppred n) Σ' ncl' S1 c
21   | (Superpose.Aborted l, units, _, _) ⇒ Aborted l
22   end.
23 Proof.
24 (*Termination proof here, that n decreases*)
25 Defined.
26
27 Definition check_entailment (ent: entailment) :=
28   let S := pure_clauses (map order_eqv_clause (cnf ent)) in
29   match ent with
30   | Entailment (Assertion Π Σ) (Assertion Π' Σ') ⇒
31       match mk_pureR Π, mk_pureR Π' with
32       | (Π+, Π-), (Π'+, Π'-) ⇒
33           main_loop m Σ (NegSpaceClause Π'+ Σ' Π'-)
34               (clause_list2set S)
35       end
36   end.
```

Listing 2: The main VeriStar procedures

In this section, we describe our verified implementation of the algorithm of Navarro Pérez and Rybalchenko and give an outline of its soundness proof in Coq.

5.1 Overview of the Algorithm

Listing 2 defines the main procedures of the VeriStar system, in slightly simplified form (we have commented out the termination proof for main_loop, line 24). The first step is to encode the entailment, *ent*, as a set of clauses (its *clausal normal form*, line 28). The algorithm then enters its main loop, first calling Superpose.check_pures (line 5) on the current set of pure clauses S, a subset of the clauses that encode *ent*, and checking whether the equational prover was able to derive the empty clause from this set. If it was, the algorithm terminates with Valid (line 6). Otherwise, Superpose returns with a model R of the set of pure clauses (line 7) and a list of unit clauses *units* derived during superposition inference (also line 7). VeriStar first rewrites the spatial atoms Σ and spatial clause *ncl* by *units* (lines 8-9), then normalizes the rewritten positive spatial atom Σ' using the model R (line 10). It then adds any new pure clauses implied by the spatial wellformedness rules to the pure set (line 11). This process repeats until it converges on a fixed point (or the prover aborts abnormally; see Section 7 for details). Once a fixed point is reached, more normalization of spatial atoms is performed (line 14), and unfolding of lsegs is attempted (line 15), possibly generating new pure clauses to feed back into the loop. If no new pure clauses are generated during this process, the algorithm terminates with a counterexample.

5.2 HeapResolve for Spatial Reasoning

VeriStar divides spatial reasoning (lines 10-15 in Figure 2) into four major stages: normalization of spatial atoms, wellformedness inference, unfolding of list predicates and spatial resolution.

Normalization rules perform substitutions into spatial atoms based on pure facts inferred by the superposition system, as well as eliminate obviously redundant list segments of the form $\mathsf{lseg}(x, x)$.

Wellformedness rules generate new pure clauses from malformed spatial atoms. Consider, for example, the clause

$$\Gamma \to \Delta, \mathsf{lseg}(x, y) * \mathsf{lseg}(x, z)$$

which asserts that Γ implies the disjunction of Δ and the spatial formula $\mathsf{lseg}(x, y) * \mathsf{lseg}(x, z)$. Since the separating conjunction in the spatial part requires that the two list segments be located in disjoint subheaps, we know that the list segments cannot both start at location x unless one of the list segments is empty. However, we do not know which one is empty.[3] To formalize this line of reasoning, VeriStar generates the clause

$$\Gamma \to x = y, x = z, \Delta$$

whenever it sees a clause with two list segments of the form given above. This new clause states that Γ implies either Δ (the positive pure atoms from the original clause) or $x = y \vee x = z$. The other wellformedness rules allow VeriStar to learn entirely pure facts from spatial facts in much the same way.

The spatial *unfolding* rules formalize the notion that nonempty list segments can be unfolded into their constituent parts: a points-to fact and a sub-list segment, or in some cases, two sub-list segments. List segments should not be unfolded *ad infinitum*, however—it would be sound to do so, but our algorithm would infinite-loop. Instead, VeriStar performs unfolding only when certain other spatial facts are present in the clause database. These *hints* or triggers for rule application are key to making the proof procedure tractable.

As an example, consider Navarro Pérez and Rybalchenko's inference rule U3

$$\frac{\Gamma \to \Delta, \mathsf{lseg}(x, y) * \Sigma \qquad \Gamma', \mathsf{lseg}(x, \mathsf{nil}) * \Sigma' \to \Delta'}{\Gamma', \mathsf{lseg}(x, y) * \mathsf{lseg}(y, \mathsf{nil}) * \Sigma' \to \Delta'}$$

which states that list segments $\mathsf{lseg}(x, \mathsf{nil})$ in negative positions should be unfolded to $\mathsf{lseg}(x, y) * \mathsf{lseg}(y, \mathsf{nil})$, but only when there is a positive spatial clause somewhere in the clause database that mentions $\mathsf{lseg}(x, y)$. In this rule, the left-hand side clause $\Gamma \to \Delta, \mathsf{lseg}(x, y) * \Sigma$ is unnecessary for soundness but necessary operationally for limiting when the rule is applied.

Our Coq implementation of this rule follows the declarative version rather closely.

```
Definition unfolding3 (sc1 sc2:clause) :=
  match sc1, sc2 with
  | PosSpaceClause Γ Δ Σ, NegSpaceClause Γ' Σ' Δ' ⇒
      let l0 := unfolding3' nil Σ Σ' in
      let build_clause Σ0 := NegSpaceClause Γ' Σ0 Δ' in
        map build_clause l0
  | _, _ ⇒ nil
  end.
```

Here unfolding3' is an auxiliary function that searches for and unfolds list segments from variable x to Nil in Σ' with counterpart lists of the appropriate form in Σ.

[3] The *spooky disjunction* of Berdine et al. [9].

Finally, VeriStar performs *spatial resolution* of spatial atoms that appear both negatively and positively in two different clauses.

$$\frac{\Gamma, \Sigma \rightarrow \Delta \qquad \Gamma' \rightarrow \Delta', \Sigma}{\Gamma, \Gamma' \rightarrow \Delta, \Delta'}$$

Like the wellformedness rules, spatial resolution makes it possible to infer new pure facts from clauses with spatial atoms, in the special case in which Σ occurs both positively and negatively in two different clauses.

5.3 Superposition of Pure Clauses

In this section, we briefly describe our implementation of Bachmair and Ganzinger's System S [7], the superposition calculus with selection. We chose System S because it is a well-studied equational calculus that appears to perform well in practice but there are others (see, for instance, Nieuwenhuis and Rubio's System I [32]). System S operates by repeatedly applying inference rules of the form

$$\frac{\Gamma \rightarrow x = y, \Delta \qquad \Gamma' \rightarrow x = z, \Delta'}{\Gamma, \Gamma' \rightarrow y = z, \Delta, \Delta'}\ \text{PS}$$

to sets of clauses. The rule PS (positive superposition) implements the clausal form of replacement of equals with equals (i.e., substitution) in positive positions. System S includes rules for substitution in negative positions and equality factoring as well.

The main superposition procedure, check_pures, operates internally on two sets of clauses, the given set and the unselected set. The given set contains those clauses that were chosen to participate in superposition inference at least once in the past. The unselected set contains whichever clauses are left. At the beginning of the search, all clauses are in the unselected set and the given set is empty. At each step of the superposition procedure, a new clause is chosen from the unselected set (the given_clause). This clause may be chosen uniformly, but we instead apply a simple heuristic that greatly improves the search: choosing the smallest clause first. Intuitively, this optimization is profitable because it favors the generation of small clauses over large ones, and the ultimate goal of the search is to produce the empty clause. Once the given_clause has been chosen, we simplify it with respect to the current clauses in the given set, then perform all superposition inferences possible for c, the resulting simplified clause, and the given set extended with c. Simplification essentially rewrites the given clause by all the unit equalities in the given set. Any new clauses inferred in this process are added back to the unselected set and the process is repeated until either the empty clause is derived or a fixed point is reached.

6. Soundness End-to-end

One would hope that the modular structure of the prover lends itself to a modular soundness proof: that is, each component of the prover is shown sound in isolation and these verified modules are stitched together to prove the soundness of the entire system end-to-end. Of course, for this strategy to work the functionality and correctness of each component must be guarded by a narrow interface via a module type. Otherwise, maintenance to the prover and its soundness proof becomes overwhelming.

We employed exactly this strategy while proving the soundness of VeriStar and found that it greatly simplified the initial construction of the soundness proof and the rounds of optimizations we performed thereafter, each of which required changes both to the prover and to its soundness proof. To facilitate a modular structure, we divided the prover into the following major components:

- Clausal normal form encoding of entailments;
- Superposition;
- Spatial normalization;
- Spatial wellformedness inference rules;
- Spatial unfolding rules; and
- Model generation and selection of clauses for normalization.

Each of these components was then proved sound with respect to a minimal interface.

As an example of one such interface, the main soundness theorem for the clausal normal form encoding states that the negation of the clausal normal form of an entailment is equivalent to the original entailment before it was encoded as a clauseset.

```
Theorem cnf_correct: ∀(e:entailment),
  entailment_denote e ↔
  ∀(s:state), ¬(fold clause_denote andp TT (cnf e) s).
```

Here the notation fold f andp TT l s means $\bigwedge_{x \in l}(f\ x\ s)$. TT is the *always true* predicate. The function clause_denote defines our interpretation of *clauses*, i.e., disjunctions of pure and spatial atoms. Theorem cnf_correct is the only theorem about the clausal normal form encoding that we expose to the rest of the soundness proof, thus limiting the exposure of the rest of the proof to isolated updates to the cnf component.

Likewise, the main soundness theorem for the superposition system states that if Superpose.check_pures was able to derive the empty clause from a set of clauses $init$, then the conjunction of the clauses in $init$ entails the empty_clause.

```
Theorem check_pures_Valid_sound: ∀init units g u,
  check_pures init = (Valid, units, g, u) →
  fold clause_denote andp TT (M.elements init)
    ⊢ clause_denote empty_clause.
```

We need an additional theorem for Superpose, however, since the pure prover may return C_example for some clausesets, in addition to those for which it returns Valid. In the counterexample case, VeriStar constructs a model for the pure clauses, then uses this model to normalize spatial ones. Any clauses inferred by the pure prover while it was searching for the empty clause must therefore be entailed by the initial set of clauses.

```
Theorem check_pures_Cexample_sound:
 ∀init units final empty R sel,
 check_pures init = (C_example R sel, units, final, empty) →
 fold clause_denote andp TT (M.elements init)
   ⊢ fold clause_denote andp TT (M.elements sel) &&
       fold clause_denote andp TT (M.elements final) &&
         fold clause_denote andp TT units.
```

To prove the soundness of VeriStar.check_entailment, the main function exported by the prover (Listing 2), we made each of the components described above a functor over our abstract separation logic model, VERISTAR_MODEL. As we described in Section 4.3, our abstract model is itself a functor over modules satisfying the VERISTAR_LOGIC interface of Listing 1. VERISTAR_MODEL—and by extension, our soundness proof—is therefore entirely parametric in the low-level details of the target separation logic implementation (e.g., the definition of the *maps-to* operator).

In the main soundness proof for VeriStar.check_entailment, we imported the soundness proof for each component, instantiated each of the functors by Vsm:VERISTAR_MODEL, then composed the soundness theorems exported by each component to prove the main correctness theorem, check_entailment_sound.

```
Module VeriStarSound (Vsm:VERISTAR_MODEL).
  Module SPS := SP_Sound Vsm. (*Superposition*)
  Module NS  := Norm_Sound Vsm. (*Normalization*)
  ...
```

Module WFS := WF_Sound Vsm. *(*Wellformedness*)*
Module UFS := UF_Sound Vsm. *(*Unfolding*)*

Theorem check_entailment_sound: $\forall(ent$:entailment),
VeriStar . check_entailment ent = Valid $\rightarrow$
entailment_denote ent.
End VeriStarSound.

check_entailment_sound states that if the prover returns Valid, the original entailment is semantically valid in the Vsm model. Because of VeriStar's modular design, the proof of this theorem goes by a straightforward application of the soundness lemmas for each of the subcomponents.

6.1 Specialization to C minor

To target the soundness proof to C minor, we built an implementation of the VERISTAR_LOGIC interface for C minor addresses, values, local variable environments and heaps (CminLog). We instantiated our abstract separation logic by this module

Module Cmm:VERISTAR_MODEL:=VeriStarModel CminLog.

then applied VeriStarSound to Cmm,

Module Vss : VERISTAR_SOUND := VeriStarSound Cmm.

yielding an end-to-end proof. Here the module CminLog defines the operators and predicates on environments and heaps (env_get, env_set, rawnext, etc.) required by our soundness proof, and proves all of the required properties for these operators and predicates.

The main soundness theorem for the VeriSmall static analyzer, check_sound,

Theorem check_sound : $\forall\Gamma\ P\ c\ Q$,
check0 $P\ c\ Q$ = true $\rightarrow$
semax Γ (assertion2wpred P) (erase_stmt c)
(RET1 (assertion2wpred Q)).

relies on Vss to prove that calls made to VeriStar during symbolic execution are valid. The theorem states that when VeriSmall successfully checks a Hoare triple (check0 $P\ c\ Q$ = true), the triple is sound in our axiomatic semantics for C minor (semax).[4] The axiomatic semantics, in turn, has a machine-verified correctness proof with respect to the operational semantics of CompCert C minor. Thus we achieve an end-to-end correctness guarantee: C minor programs deemed safe by the static analyzer will be compiled by CompCert to observationally equivalent assembly programs.

7. Why bother with machine-checked proofs?

It takes some effort to encode an algorithm in a proof assistant like Coq and then prove it correct with a machine-checked proof. One might wonder whether all this effort is really worth it. That is, do we gain anything—over LaTeXproofs and unverified implementations—by formally proving an implementation of an algorithm correct?

Soundness. In this case study, we can concretely say "yes". Formal verification of VeriStar uncovered two related soundness bugs in Navarro Pérez and Rybalchenko's spatial unfolding rules (specifically, rules U4 and U5 in [26, Section 4, Fig. 1]).

It appears likely that because of the interaction of rules U4 and U5 with the spatial resolution rule, these bugs did not result in unsoundness of Navarro's implemented system. However, we have been unable to verify that this is the case since we lack access to the source code (and, of course, the absence of such bugs cannot be confirmed even by extensive testing). We *have* verified the soundness of corrected forms of U4 and U5, discovered independently by us and Navarro Pérez and Rybalchenko. We present the corrected rules here.

$$\text{U4}'\ \frac{\Gamma\rightarrow\Delta,\mathsf{lseg}(x,y)*\mathsf{next}(z,w)*\Sigma\qquad \Gamma',\mathsf{lseg}(x,z)*\Sigma'\rightarrow\Delta'}{\Gamma,\Gamma',\mathsf{lseg}(x,y)*\mathsf{lseg}(y,z)*\Sigma'\rightarrow\Delta,\Delta'}\ y\not\equiv z$$

$$\text{U5}'\ \frac{\Gamma\rightarrow\Delta,\mathsf{lseg}(x,y)*\mathsf{lseg}(z,w)*\Sigma\qquad \Gamma',\mathsf{lseg}(x,z)*\Sigma'\rightarrow\Delta'}{\Gamma,\Gamma',\mathsf{lseg}(x,y)*\mathsf{lseg}(y,z)*\Sigma'\rightarrow z=w,\Delta,\Delta'}\ y\not\equiv z$$

The new U4 and U5 rules required adding Γ and Δ to the conclusion of each rule so that the succedent of the first hypothetical clause ($\Delta,\mathsf{lseg}(x,y)*\mathsf{next}(z,w)*\Sigma$ and $\Delta,\mathsf{lseg}(x,y)*\mathsf{lseg}(z,w)*\Sigma$ resp. in U4 and U5) could be made to hold in the model. By ensuring that $\mathsf{next}(z,w)$ (resp. $\mathsf{lseg}(z,w)$) be disjoint from $\mathsf{lseg}(x,y)$, we avoid the counterexample we found for the original system (without Γ,Δ) in which $\mathsf{lseg}(x,z)$ does not hold because z points back into $\mathsf{lseg}(x,y)$ (lists must be acyclic). Appendix A of the extended version of this paper [1] presents this counterexample in more detail.

This modification to rules U4 and U5 was not obvious to us initially, before we attempted to verify the rules, since in the other unfolding rules in Navarro Pérez and Rybalchenko's system, the first hypothetical clause acts only as an operational trigger for unfolding and is never necessary for soundness.

Termination. All Coq functions are total, so a computable function implemented in Coq must terminate. One convinces the Coq system that a function terminates either by presenting a *structurally* recursive function (using Coq's **Fixpoint** notation) in which all recursive calls are clearly on substructures of the corresponding formal parameter; or by presenting a general function (using Coq's **Function** notation) along with a proof that one of the arguments decreases in some well-founded order.

Navarro Pérez and Rybalchenko state their termination proof as follows: "[T]he algorithm terminates since the growing set S is bounded by ... the finite number of distinct pure clauses which can be written with the constant symbols occurring in E." Unfortunately this proof has some weaknesses. In real implementations, including Navarro's and including our own, the set S does not grow monotonically, because optimizations are implemented to rewrite by unit equalities and remove redundant clauses. What does seem to grow is the closure of S under the addition of certain kinds of redundant clauses, but the proof of this is not at all straightforward.

We have implemented a machine-checked termination proof of the superpose loop. Termination of check_entailment is much trickier and we have not yet implemented that proof. Instead we resort to a common hack: we provide VeriStar's main loop with an additional numeric argument, and after a set number of iterations it times out. As usual when this hack is applied, it does not compromise the soundness proof: time-out does not return a result that demands soundness. Then we pass a time-out parameter that is sufficiently large for all conceivable applications. Still, even though we have not implemented a proof, we believe the algorithm does terminate, i.e. on any input, given a large enough n, it will not time out.

Completeness. Navarro Pérez and Rybalchenko [26] also proved completeness: when the algorithm returns *counterexample*, the original entailment is invalid. We have not yet done so for our Coq implementation of their algorithm. For many applications of verified software, completeness is not quite as important as soundness—an attacker could exploit a soundness bug in the verification toolset, but not a completeness bug. Nevertheless, to formally prove completeness of our implementation would confirm that we have implemented the right algorithm.

[4] Since VeriSmall and VeriStar operate on syntax, we must lift the syntactic assertions P and Q to semantic assertions operating on worlds of the program logic (assertion2wpred).

optimization	speedup	program	proof	ratio
clausesets	**1.21x**	305	4,213	13.8x
priority heuristic	**3.43**	35	50	1.43
priority caching	**1.26**	66	113	1.71
int31	**1.39**	180	471	2.62
set ops	**1.04**	183	326	1.78
redundancy elim.	**1.40**	47	45	0.96
model-based saturation	**2.09**	338	732	2.17
total:	**22.1**	1,154	5,950	5.16

Figure 4: Geomean speedups across a suite of 9,000 random separation logic entailments for the last six optimizations we performed. Columns *program* and *proof* show how many lines of code were modified to implement the improvement; *ratio* is proof/program.

8. Performance Tuning Verified Software

There is no secret to writing efficient programs [8]: (1) Take a baseline; (2) optimize; (3) evaluate the results; and (4) repeat. It is perhaps no surprise that the same methodology can be applied to verified software in much the same way, except now we are working with *machine-verified* software and must update soundness and termination proofs as we perform each optimization.

In this section, we report on some optimizations we performed while building VeriStar and measure (1) the speedup achieved by each optimization (second column of the table in Figure 4), and (2) the number of lines of code we modified—in both the program and the proof—to implement each optimization (last three columns of Figure 4). The total speedup for all optimizations was $22.1x$.

We report on these optimizations to show that verified software written in Coq is real software: when extracted and compiled with the OCaml system, it runs on real hardware, subject to the same performance constraints as all software. The corollary is that verified functional programs can be performance-tuned in predictable ways.

Clausesets. We replaced Coq's standard-library AVL-tree implementation of the MSets interface for efficient finite sets, with a new red-black tree implementation. (We use MSets to store the clause database.) This new implementation included optimized routines for set insertion, lookup, and union; and we expanded the MSets interface with optimized versions of composite operations such as with minimum-element deletion and insertion-with-membership-query. This resulted in a relative speedup over our baseline VeriStar implementation of 1.21x.

Priority Heuristic. The superpose one_inference_step picks a clause from the clauseset; any new clause will do (for soundness and completeness). An optimization is to pick the smallest new clause (see Section 5.3). This *priority* heuristic greatly winnows the size of the search space. We use the MSets not only to implement clause sets, but to simultaneously implement an efficient priority queue: the total ordering we supply for the red-black searchtree is a lexicographic ordering of clause priority and then clause content. We then use our efficient delete-min operation to pluck the smallest clause from the set in log N time. This heuristic gives speedup of $3.43x$, compared to selecting an arbitrary new clause.

Priority Caching. Caching the priorities, as integers with the clauses, yields speedup of $1.26x$.

OCaml Native Integers. Our initial implementation used Coq standard-library positive integers to represent variables and priorities. It is a data structure representing arbitrary precision binary numbers, so 101001 is xI(xO(xO(xI(xO(xI xH))))) in the datatype,

```
Inductive positive :=
| xI : positive → positive
| xO : positive → positive | xH : positive.
```

To make things faster, we now use OCaml native 31-bit integers for variables and priorities, yielding speedup of 1.39x.

When extracting to 31-bit OCaml integers, we had to be very careful about overflow. Coq positives are potentially unbounded (thus no overflow), whereas OCaml integers have mod-2^{31} addition. However, VeriStar never performs addition or multiplication of variables, and never generates new variables.[5] VeriStar does some arithmetic on *priorities*, but the soundness and completeness proofs are oblivious to the specific priority function used, so our algorithm is still correct even if priorities happen to overflow. To ensure that our machine-checked soundness proof cannot rely on properties of int31 arithmetic, we do not even axiomatize arithmetic on variables and priorities—we define $+$ and $\times$ as unaxiomatized operators.

Set Operations. Our paramodulation loop (Fig. 2) had used lists of clauses. We switched to set operations (MSets) primarily to make the code more elegant, but it also gives speedup of 1.04.

Redundancy Elimination. We remove redundant pure clauses before passing clausesets to Superpose. This yields a relatively large speedup of $1.40x$ since it often reduces the number of clauses passed to Superpose between rounds of spatial inference.

Model-based Saturation. Our main implementation of the superposition calculus uses the given-clause algorithm to saturate clausesets. As a last optimization, we rewrote the superposition engine to employ a more intelligent saturation procedure: instead of finding the smallest clause at each saturation step, we attempt to construct a model of the current clauseset (whether saturated or not). Completeness of the superposition calculus implies that this model exists whenever the clauseset is saturated (and does not contain the empty clause). Moreover, for unsaturated sets the completeness proof tells us exactly which clause to select for inference, and for which type of inference (superposition right, superposition left, etc.) in order to bring the set closer to saturation. In this optimization pass, we also improved the global propagation of unit equalities. These two optimizations together resulted in speedup of about $9x$ over our original saturation procedure (the "clausesets" version, which did not use the priority heuristic or priority caching). In the table, $2.09x$ gives the pairwise speedup of model-based saturation over the next most recent version of the prover ("redundancy elimination").

On optimization effort. Most optimizations required minimal updates to the proofs relative to the size of each change to the program (often under $2x$, see Figure 4). Figure 5 gives the total sizes, in lines-of-code, of each of the VeriStar source files.

To prove the int31 optimization sound, we had to abstract all properties of variables on which the proof depended, resulting in

[5] This is not true for VeriSmall since the static analysis must generate fresh variables during symbolic execution. But since VeriSmall—as opposed to VeriStar—is not complete in general, it can simply return "don't know" whenever generating fresh variables results in an overflow.

source file	program	proof
compare.v	-	253
variables.v	77	59
datatypes.v	60	-
superpose.v	342	-
superpose termination	-	1,904
superpose_modelsat.v	335	-
heapresolve.v	448	-
veristar.v	150	-
model_type.v	-	89
model.v	-	310
clause_lemmas.v	-	183
cclosure.v	169	-
superpose_sound.v	-	584
superpose_modelsat_sound.v	-	732
spred_lemmas.v	-	542
clausify_sound.v	-	474
wellformed_sound.v	-	399
unfold_sound.v	-	1,809
norm_sound.v	-	233
veristar_sound.v	-	354
clauses.v	308	594
list_denote.v	-	946
driver.ml	127	-
subtotals (excl. redblack.v):	2,016	9,465
ratio:	4.69	
redblack.v	281	4,110
totals:	2,297	13,575
ratio:	5.91	

Figure 5: Sizes of system components in lines-of-code. *Ratio* is proof/program.

prover	Smallfoot	VeriStar	SLP	jStar
runtime (seconds)	0.013	0.019	0.049	0.180

Figure 6: Average runtimes over 100 trials of Smallfoot, VeriStar, SLP and jStar on 209 entailments generated by Smallfoot.

more global changes. The clausesets optimization was somewhat of an outlier: to meet the existing Coq MSets interface, we had to prove many lemmas not even used by our soundness proof. On the other hand, the red-black tree implementation of Coq MSets is reusable even independently of VeriStar.

9. Measurements

We evaluated VeriStar's performance against that of jStar [19], Smallfoot and SLP on two suites of separation logic entailments. All evaluation was done on a SunFire X4100 server with two dual-core 2.2GHz Opteron 275 processors and 16GB of RAM running CentOS Linux. The first suite contains 209 separation logic entailments generated by Smallfoot during verification of 18 different list-manipulating programs found in the Smallfoot distribution. The second includes 22,000 synthetic entailments tuned from moderate to difficult. The synthetic entailments are the full suites used by Navarro Pérez and Rybalchenko to evaluate their Prolog-based theorem prover SLP against jStar and Smallfoot [26]. The Smallfoot entailments are Navarro Pérez and Rybalchenko's first *clone* set, slightly modified since our prover does not yet deal with arbitrary spatial predicates.

On the "real-world" entailments derived from programs in Smallfoot's test suite, VeriStar's performance was comparable to that of Smallfoot and SLP (on the order of hundredths of a second for the 209 entailments). jStar solved 101 of the 170 valid entailments in the suite in 0.180 seconds. We report the average runtime of each prover on these 209 entailments over 100 trials in Figure 6.

To test the provers at a finer granularity on more difficult entailments, we ran each prover on the 22,000 synthetic entailments in Navarro Pérez and Rybalchenko's Bolognesa and Spaguetti suites. The Spaguetti benchmarks consist of 11,000 entailments of the form $\Pi \wedge \Sigma \vdash \bot$, simulating the inconsistency checks that are often required during symbolic execution. The Bolognesa benchmarks consist of 11,000 general entailments of the form $\Pi \wedge \Sigma \vdash \Pi' \wedge \Sigma'$. For each prover, we measured the number of independent entailments solved within 0.01 to 5 seconds. Figure 7 shows the results of these measurements. Within 5 seconds, jStar checked 8,757 of the 22,000 entailments in the combined suites, VeriStar checked 18,610 entailments and Smallfoot checked 21,483. SLP checked 21,981 entailments within 5 seconds.

Assessment. On real-world entailments generated by Smallfoot during symbolic execution (Figure 6), VeriStar's performance is more than adequate—it solved all 209 entailments in slightly less than two hundredths of a second, three hundredths of a second faster than SLP and only slightly slower than Smallfoot. VeriStar is also the only one of the four systems with a machine-checked soundness proof. On Navarro Pérez and Rybalchenko's synthetic entailments (Figure 7), VeriStar is, in a majority of cases, faster than Smallfoot when deciding heap inconsistency entailments (those of the form $\Pi \wedge \Sigma \vdash \bot$, the Spaguetti suite) and is almost as fast SLP. On general entailments (the Bolognesa suite), VeriStar is not quite as fast as Smallfoot, and not nearly as fast as SLP. Though it is certainly fast enough for Smallfoot-like applications, there is room for improvement. We believe the main issues are:

- VeriStar is a *pure* functional program. Functional programs have a clean proof theory that makes verification a breeze (or at most, a stiff wind). But it means that we pay a log N penalty in some places, where we use red-black trees instead of arrays or hash tables. Using imperative techniques might speed things up, and yet still fit within the Coq framework [5].
- The paramodulation framework for resolution theorem-proving in its modern form is more than two decades old, and a prover such as SLP uses a large combination of time-tested heuristics. By comparison, VeriStar is still immature, and the incorporation of more of these standard techniques would likely improve performance significantly.

10. Related Work

Proof-carrying code (PCC) [27] demonstrated the effectiveness of *proof witnesses*—derivation trees in a core logic—as a means of incorporating large untrusted components into safe systems. But the problems with PCC were twofold: (1) the proof witnesses were unacceptably large in practice; and (2) the proof checkers, often running to tens of thousands of lines of code, had to be trusted.

Necula [28, 29] showed how to reduce the size of the proof by compressing common subterms and extending the proof checker to reconstruct these terms from the context. Foundational PCC [2] addressed (2) by proving the soundness of the proof checker from basic axioms but still required large proofs. In this project, we go further: the VeriStar system—when connected to VeriSmall and the rest of the Verified Software Toolchain—combines strong, foundational correctness guarantees (all the way down to the compiled assembly program) with minimal "proofs": just the program text itself, possibly annotated with light assertions such as loop invari-

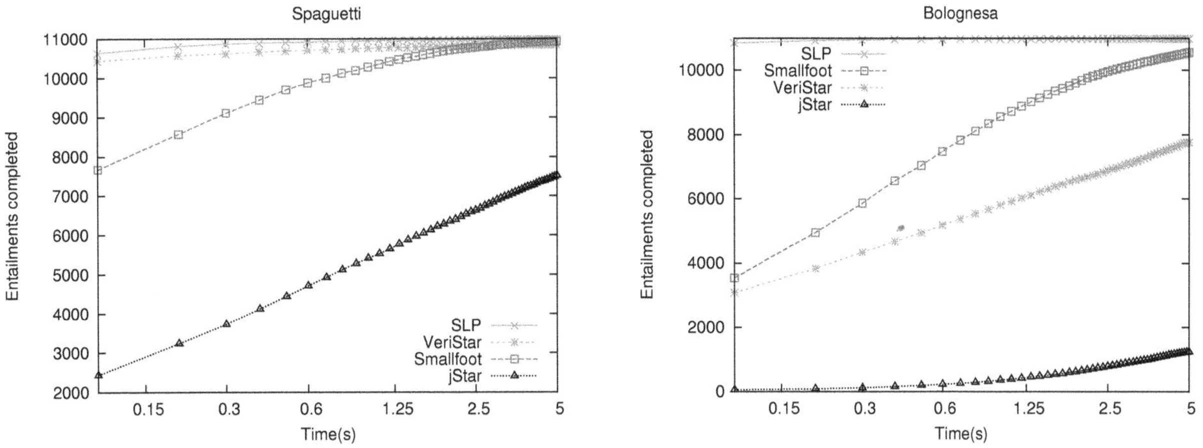

Figure 7: Number of independent entailments checked within 0.01 to 5 seconds by SLP, Smallfoot, VeriStar and jStar. (Higher is better.) The Spaguetti benchmark suite contains 11,000 entailments of the form, $\Pi \wedge \Sigma \vdash \bot$, simulating heap inconsistency checks. The Bolognesa benchmark suite contains 11,000 general separation logic entailments of the form $\Pi \wedge \Sigma \vdash \Pi' \wedge \Sigma'$.

ants. These assertions guide the proved-sound static analyzer to an appropriate safety proof.

More recent work on integrating decision procedures into trusted systems has focused on efficiently translating and checking low-level certificates. Armand et al. [5] connect SAT (ZChaff, MiniSat) and SMT solvers (VeriT) to Coq and Isabelle/HOL by translating unsat cores and boolean models to efficient certificates. These certificates are then verified through a combination of small machine-verified proof checkers for resolution chains, linear arithmetic, congruence closure and other theories. Besson et al. describe a related system [11] that permits Nelson-Oppen-style theory combination and supports additional theories besides those supported by Armand et al. In Besson's system, a significant portion of total proof time is consumed by certificate generation and checking. Although VeriStar is significantly simpler than a state-of-the-art SMT solver, it demonstrates that for certain application domains, it is possible to verify the prover, not just the checker, and thus bypass low-level certificate generation and checking completely.

Chlipala's Bedrock system [17], an impressive toolkit for proving the correctness of low-level code, includes an ad hoc simplification procedure and entailment checker for separation logic that together appear to work well in practice. One advantage of Bedrock's checker is that it works on the unencoded implications generated by verification. Errors are therefore easier to communicate to the user in a transparent way. VeriStar entailments, by contrast, are encoded and checked at the clause level, both for efficiency and for interoperability with the Superposition system, and therefore are slightly less human-friendly.

Nguyen and Chin equip a Smallfoot-style entailment checker with a mechanism to integrate user-provided lemmas, complementing the folding/unfolding lemmas that are automatically generated from inductive definitions [30].

Brotherson et al. [13] present a heap theorem prover implemented in HOL that employs a notion of *cyclic proof*. Their work opens an avenue for the integration of user-defined inductive types and auxiliary lemmas that relate such definitions, but is apparently not yet integrated with a prover for the pure part, and is not presented in clausal form. We expect that our modular architecture will allow us to explore the integration of this and other spatial theorem provers into paramodulation-based reasoning tools comparatively easily, as any such prover can be substituted for (or complement) the present unfolding rules for singly-linked lists.

THOR [25] infers invariants by combining symbolic execution with abstraction. An alternative to reimplementing invariant inference in Coq is to use THOR, or some other tool like SLAyer, to annotate loops with invariants that are then confirmed by VeriSmall+VeriStar. The HIP/SLEEK project [31] employs an interesting "shallow embedding" technique for resource use verification that might also be adapted to our setting.

11. Lessons Learned

Extraction for Execution and Profiling. Coq's code extraction facilities make it easy to write a Gallina program, extract it to OCaml (or Haskell or Scheme) and get decent performance by compiling using an optimizing compiler like `ocamlopt`. When the Gallina program is written in a straightforward functional style—forgoing extensive use of more advanced features of Coq such as dependent types[6]—code extraction followed by compilation is predictable enough even to support profiling in a traditional style, using a conventional tool like `gprof` [21]. One first extracts a verified Gallina program to OCaml, compiles the OCaml program with `ocamlopt -p`, then does a profiling run using `gprof`. Because the extracted OCaml code is very similar in structure to the Gallina source, the `gprof` profiling data can be used to optimize the Gallina program quite effectively. Figure 8 presents an excerpt of one such profiling run we performed using `gprof`, which showed us that demodulation (unit equality propagation) was a bottleneck for the prover on entailments in Navarro's Spaguetti suite.

On the Proof Theory of Functional Languages. Because Gallina programs are purely functional (one must even prove termination), Gallina has an elegant proof theory that is more tractable than that of ML or Haskell, and much nicer than that of C. This attractive proof theory made the difference, in our estimation, between a

[6] Such features are of course fair game when *proving* a Gallina program correct; Coq's type system ensures that only the program is ever extracted, never the proof.

```
time  seconds seconds     calls  name
20.81     7.63     7.63 943778606  demodulate_3526
10.42    11.45     3.82 1247887428 apply2
 9.27    14.85     3.40 343207163  pcompare_176
 5.40    16.83     1.98 297862037  pplus_111
 5.02    18.67     1.84 412584893  zplus_200
 4.12    20.18     1.51   2338512  fold_left_299
 4.09    21.68     1.50 943778606  fun_9033
 2.70    22.67     0.99 114722856  zlength_aux_322
```

Figure 8: Excerpt from the **gprof** trace of a single run of the extracted prover on 1000 entailments in the Spaguetti suite.

couple man-months to complete VeriStar's soundness proof and a couple man-years for a comparable machine-checked proof of a C implementation of the same algorithm.

The Importance of Modular Proofs. The importance of module systems for the construction of large software projects is well-known. We were surprised at just how effective conventional, ML-style module and functor systems (as implemented in Coq) were for building and evolving modular *proofs* of programs as well. By protecting the soundness proof of each component of the prover with an opaque **Module Type** in Coq (Section 6), we saved a great deal of time and energy, especially as we evolved the prover through successive rounds of optimization (Section 8).

12. Conclusion

VeriStar is the first machine-verified theorem prover for separation logic that connects to a real-world operational semantics (CompCert C minor). Together with VeriSmall, VeriStar enables automatic *foundational* checking of shape properties with respect to the compiled x86 or PowerPC assembly. VeriStar implements an efficient decision procedure for separation logic [26] using highly tuned functional data structures. VeriStar's implementation and soundness proof can be retargeted to new domains through an opaque axiomatization of separation logic. Finally, VeriStar's design, and its integration with VeriSmall and our C minor separation logic through well-defined interfaces, provides a blueprint for the design of certified end-to-end systems more generally.

Acknowledgments

Anindya Banerjee, members of the Princeton PL group and the anonymous referees provided helpful suggestions on prior drafts. Aleksandar Nanevski and David Walker gave the first author advice on appropriate venues for this work. This work was supported in part by AFOSR grant FA9550-09-1-0138 and NSF grant CNS-0910448.

References

[1] URL http://www.cs.princeton.edu/~jsseven/p/veristar.

[2] A. W. Appel. Foundational proof-carrying code. In *LICS*, 2001.

[3] A. W. Appel. VeriSmall: Verified Smallfoot shape analysis. In *First International Conf. on Certified Programs and Proofs*, Dec. 2011.

[4] A. W. Appel. Verified Software Toolchain. In *ESOP*, pages 1–17, 2011.

[5] M. Armand, G. Faure, B. Grégoire, C. Keller, L. Théry, and B. Werner. A modular integration of SAT/SMT solvers to Coq through proof witnesses. In *First International Conf. on Certified Programs and Proofs*, 2011.

[6] R. Atkey. Amortised resource analysis with separation logic. *Logical Methods in Computer Science*, 7(2:17), 2011.

[7] L. Bachmair and H. Ganzinger. Equational Reasoning in Saturation-Based Theorem Proving. In W. Bibel and P. Schmitt, editors, *Automated Deduction - A Basis for Applications*, volume I, 1998.

[8] J. L. Bentley. *Writing Efficient Programs*. Prentice-Hall, 1982.

[9] J. Berdine, C. Calcagno, and P. W. O'Hearn. Smallfoot: Modular automatic assertion checking with separation logic. In *Formal Methods for Components and Objects*, pages 115–135, 2005.

[10] J. Berdine, B. Cook, and S. Ishtiaq. SLAyer: Memory safety for systems-level code. In *CAV*, pages 178–183, 2011.

[11] F. Besson, P.-E. Cornilleau, and D. Pichardie. Modular SMT proofs for fast reflexive checking inside Coq. In *First International Conf. on Certified Programs and Proofs*, 2011.

[12] T. Braibant and D. Pous. Tactics for reasoning modulo AC in Coq. In *First International Conf. on Certified Programs and Proofs*, 2011.

[13] J. Brotherston, D. Distefano, and R. L. Petersen. Automated cyclic entailment proofs in separation logic. In *Proceedings of CADE-23*, pages 131–146, 2011.

[14] C. Calcagno and D. Distefano. Infer: an automatic program verifier for memory safety of C programs. In *Third International Conference on NASA Formal Methods*, pages 459–465, 2011.

[15] C. Calcagno, D. Distefano, P. O'Hearn, and H. Yang. Compositional shape analysis by means of bi-abduction. *SIGPLAN Not.*, 44:289–300, January 2009.

[16] B.-Y. E. Chang and X. Rival. Relational inductive shape analysis. In *POPL*, pages 247–260, 2008.

[17] A. Chlipala. Mostly-automated verification of low-level programs in computational separation logic. In *PLDI'11*, pages 234–245, 2011.

[18] L. M. de Moura and N. Bjørner. Z3: An efficient SMT solver. In *TACAS*, 2008.

[19] D. Distefano and M. J. Parkinson J. jStar: Towards practical verification for Java. In *OOPSLA*, 2008.

[20] R. Dockins, A. Hobor, and A. W. Appel. A fresh look at separation algebras and share accounting. In *APLAS: 7th Asian Symposium on Programming Languages and Systems*, pages 161–177, 2009.

[21] S. L. Graham, P. B. Kessler, and M. K. McKusick. Gprof: A call graph execution profiler. In *Proc. SIGPLAN '82 Symp. on Compiler Construction, SIGPLAN Notices*, pages 120–126. ACM Press, 1982.

[22] A. Hobor, A. W. Appel, and F. Zappa Nardelli. Oracle Semantics for Concurrent Separation Logic. In *ESOP*, pages 353 - 367, 2008.

[23] X. Leroy. A formally verified compiler back-end. *Journal of Automated Reasoning*, 43(4):363–446, 2009.

[24] B. Löchner and S. Schulz. An evaluation of shared rewriting. In *Proceedings of the Second International Workshop on Implementation of Logics, Technical Report MPI-I-2001-2-006*, pages 33–48, 2001.

[25] S. Magill, A. Nanevski, E. Clarke, and P. Lee. Inferring invariants in separation logic for imperative list-processing programs. In *Third Workshop on Semantics, Program Analysis, and Computing Environments for Memory Management (SPACE)*, 2006.

[26] J. A. Navarro Pérez and A. Rybalchenko. Separation logic + superposition calculus = heap theorem prover. In *PLDI*, pages 556–566, 2011.

[27] G. Necula. Proof-carrying code. In *POPL*, pages 106–119, 1997.

[28] G. C. Necula and P. Lee. Efficient representation and validation of proofs. In *LICS*, pages 93–104, 1998.

[29] G. C. Necula and S. P. Rahul. Oracle-based checking of untrusted software. In *POPL*, pages 142–154, 2001.

[30] H. H. Nguyen and W.-N. Chin. Enhancing program verification with lemmas. In *CAV*, pages 355–369, 2008.

[31] H. H. Nguyen, C. David, S. Qin, and W.-N. Chin. Automated verification of shape and size properties via separation logic. In *VMCAI*, pages 251–266, 2007.

[32] R. Nieuwenhuis and A. Rubio. Paramodulation-based theorem proving. In A. Robinson and A. Voronkov, editors, *Handbook of Automated Reasoning*, 2001.

[33] T. Tuerk. A formalisation of Smallfoot in HOL. In *Theorem Proving in Higher Order Logics*, pages 469–484, 2009.

Formal Verification of Monad Transformers (Abstract)

Brian Huffman
Institut für Informatik, Technische Universität München
huffman@in.tum.de

Abstract

We present techniques for reasoning about constructor classes that (like the monad class) fix polymorphic operations and assert polymorphic axioms. We do not require a logic with first-class type constructors, first-class polymorphism, or type quantification; instead, we rely on a domain-theoretic model of the type system in a universal domain to provide these features. These ideas are implemented in the Tycon library for the Isabelle theorem prover, which builds on the HOLCF library of domain theory. The Tycon library provides various axiomatic type constructor classes, including functors and monads. It also provides automation for instantiating those classes, and for defining further subclasses. We use the Tycon library to formalize three Haskell monad transformers: the error transformer, the writer transformer, and the resumption transformer. The error and writer transformers do not universally preserve the monad laws; however, we establish datatype invariants for each, showing that they are valid monads when viewed as abstract datatypes.

Categories and Subject Descriptors F.3.1 [*Logics and Meanings of Programs*]: Specifying and Verifying and Reasoning about Programs – mechanical verification.

Keywords denotational semantics, monads, polymorphism, theorem proving, type classes

1. Introduction

Much Haskell code is written with equational properties in mind: Programs, libraries, and class instances may be expected to satisfy some laws, but unfortunately, there is no formal connection between programs and properties in Haskell. One way to get around this limitation is to verify our Haskell programs in an interactive proof assistant, or theorem prover.

Isabelle/HOL (or simply "Isabelle") is a generic interactive theorem prover, with tools and automation for reasoning about inductive datatypes and terminating functions in higher-order logic [8]. Isabelle has an ML-like type system extended with axiomatic type classes, where users must supply proofs of class axioms in order to establish a class instance.

HOLCF is a library of domain theory for Isabelle/HOL, which supports denotational reasoning about programs written in pure functional languages [3, 7]. HOLCF provides tools for defining and working with (possibly lazy) recursive datatypes, general recursive functions, partial and infinite values, and least fixed-points.

ICFP'12, September 9–15, 2012, Copenhagen, Denmark.
ACM 978-1-4503-1054-3/12/09.

In addition to ordinary type classes, Haskell also supports type constructor classes like *Functor* and *Monad*, which classify type constructors of kind $* \to *$. The operations in constructor classes are often polymorphic: For example, $\mathit{fmap} :: (\mathit{Functor}\,\tau) \Rightarrow (\alpha \to \beta) \to \tau\,\alpha \to \tau\,\beta$ is polymorphic over α and β. The functor laws (identity and composition) are also polymorphic, and we expect the laws to hold at all type instances. Formal reasoning with constructor classes thus requires support for both polymorphism and type quantification, neither of which is natively supported by Isabelle. Fortunately, we can model these features in HOLCF with the help of a universal domain type.

2. Deflation model of types

HOLCF provides a universal domain type $\mathcal{U}$, which can represent a large class of cpos that includes all Haskell datatypes [2]. HOLCF formalizes representable domains with overloaded functions $\mathit{emb}_\alpha :: \alpha \to \mathcal{U}$ and $\mathit{proj}_\alpha :: \mathcal{U} \to \alpha$ which form an embedding-projection pair: $\mathit{proj}_\alpha \circ \mathit{emb}_\alpha = \mathit{id}_\alpha$ and $\mathit{emb}_\alpha \circ \mathit{proj}_\alpha \sqsubseteq \mathit{id}_{\mathcal{U}}$.

The composition $\mathit{proj}_\alpha \circ \mathit{emb}_\alpha$ yields a *deflation*, i.e., an idempotent function below *id*. HOLCF defines a type $\mathcal{D}$ of deflations over $\mathcal{U}$ as a subtype of $\mathcal{U} \to \mathcal{U}$. Deflations model types: Each representable domain type in HOLCF has a representation $[\![\alpha]\!] = \mathit{emb}_\alpha \circ \mathit{proj}_\alpha$ of type $\mathcal{D}$. Conversely, we can construct a representable domain from any given deflation, using its image set.

3. The Tycon library

The Tycon library [4] uses deflations to reason about new type system features. To model Haskell type application, we define a binary Isabelle type constructor $(- \cdot -)$ [5]. The right argument must be a representable domain, which models kind $*$. The left argument must be in a new class *Tycon*, which models kind $* \to *$.

$$\textbf{class}\ \mathit{Tycon}\ \tau\ \textbf{where}\ \{\!|\tau|\!\} :: \mathcal{D} \to \mathcal{D}$$

The Tycon library then defines type $\tau \cdot \alpha$ so that $[\![\tau \cdot \alpha]\!] = \{\!|\tau|\!\}[\![\alpha]\!]$.

Haskell's *Functor* class fixes a function $\mathit{fmap} :: (\mathit{Functor}\,\tau) \Rightarrow (\alpha \to \beta) \to (\tau\,\alpha \to \tau\,\beta)$. However, we cannot use this type for a class function in Isabelle; the extra polymorphism over α and β is not allowed. Our solution is to replace the polymorphic fmap^τ with a single, monomorphic constant $\underline{\mathit{fmap}}^\tau$ representing $\mathit{fmap}^\tau_{\mathcal{U},\mathcal{U}}$. We then define the polymorphic fmap^τ by coercion from $\underline{\mathit{fmap}}^\tau$.

$$\begin{array}{l}\textbf{class}\ (\mathit{Tycon}\,\tau) \Rightarrow \mathit{Functor}\,\tau\ \textbf{where}\\ \quad \underline{\mathit{fmap}}^\tau :: (\mathcal{U} \to \mathcal{U}) \to (\tau \cdot \mathcal{U} \to \tau \cdot \mathcal{U})\end{array}$$

$$\begin{array}{l}\mathit{fmap} :: (\mathit{Functor}\,\tau) \Rightarrow (\alpha \to \beta) \to \tau \cdot \alpha \to \tau \cdot \beta\\ \mathit{fmap}^\tau_{\alpha,\beta} = \mathit{coerce}\ \underline{\mathit{fmap}}^\tau\end{array}$$

To coerce between any two representable domains, we use the function $\mathit{coerce}_{\alpha,\beta} = \mathit{proj}_\beta \circ \mathit{emb}_\alpha$. Instances of *emb* and *proj* are defined so that *coerce* on datatypes coincides with mapping *coerce* over the elements. Similarly, coercion between function types satisfies $\mathit{coerce}\,f = \mathit{coerce} \circ f \circ \mathit{coerce}$.

The Isabelle formalization of class *Functor* also includes class axioms about $\underline{fmap}^\tau$, which are sufficient to derive the polymorphic functor laws $fmap\, id = id$ and $fmap\,(f \circ g) = fmap\, f \circ fmap\, g$. (Due to space constraints, we omit the details here.)

To facilitate *Functor* class instances, the Tycon library provides a new user-level type definition command. Its capabilities are similar to the HOLCF Domain package [3], and it reuses much of the same code. The difference is that it produces *Tycon* instances instead of ordinary representable domains. It also defines $\underline{fmap}$ and proves the identity law. (Users must prove composition.)

Users can formalize subclasses of *Functor* by a standard process involving *naturality laws*. As an example, we formalize a class *FunctorPlus* τ with an associative operation $(+\!\!+) :: \tau\alpha \to \tau\alpha \to \tau\alpha$.

$$
\begin{aligned}
&\textbf{class}\ (Functor\ \tau) \Rightarrow FunctorPlus\ \tau\ \textbf{where}\\
&\quad (\underline{+\!\!+}^\tau) :: \tau\cdot\mathcal{U} \to \tau\cdot\mathcal{U} \to \tau\cdot\mathcal{U}\\
&\quad \underline{fmap}^\tau\, f\,(x \,\underline{+\!\!+}^\tau\, y) = (\underline{fmap}^\tau\, f\, x) \,\underline{+\!\!+}^\tau\, (\underline{fmap}^\tau\, f\, y)\\
&\quad (x \,\underline{+\!\!+}^\tau\, y) \,\underline{+\!\!+}^\tau\, z \quad = x \,\underline{+\!\!+}^\tau\, (y \,\underline{+\!\!+}^\tau\, z)
\end{aligned}
$$

As above, we define the polymorphic $(+\!\!+)$ by coercion from a monomorphic class function. The class axioms include a monomorphic associativity law, as well as a naturality law whose form is derived from the polymorphic type of $(+\!\!+)$. The naturality law holds in Haskell as a consequence of parametricity [10].

We derive polymorphic versions of the class axioms by rewriting with a set of rules about *coerce*. Combinations of coercions between $\tau\cdot\mathcal{U}$ and $\tau\cdot\alpha$ yield new occurrences of $\underline{fmap}^\tau$; the naturality law then helps to complete the transfer proofs.

Monad and other constructor classes are defined similarly.

4. Verifying monad transformers

The Tycon library can easily formalize simple *Monad* instances like *List*. It can also define *Tycon* instances with additional type parameters, which may be type constructors themselves. For example, we have formalized the resumption monad transformer:

$$\textbf{data}\ ResT\ \tau\cdot\alpha = Done\ \alpha \mid More\ (\tau\cdot(ResT\ \tau\cdot\alpha))$$

(Note that although we call it a monad transformer, the class instance *Monad* $(ResT\ \tau)$ only requires τ to be a functor.)

We have also formalized the error monad transformer [6], which composes the inner monad with an ordinary error monad.

$$
\begin{aligned}
&\textbf{data}\ Error\,\varepsilon\cdot\alpha = Err\ \varepsilon \mid Ok\ \alpha\\
&\textbf{newtype}\ ErrorT\,(\varepsilon,\tau)\cdot\alpha = ErrorT\ \{\, runET :: \tau\cdot(Error\,\varepsilon\cdot\alpha)\,\}
\end{aligned}
$$

Unfortunately, proving an instance of $Monad\,(ErrorT\,(\varepsilon,\tau))$ is not possible, because not all of the class axioms hold. We define the monad operations as separate constants instead.

$$
\begin{aligned}
&unit\ a = ErrorT\,(return^\tau\,(Ok\ a))\\
&bind\ m\ k = ErrorT\,(runET\ m \gg\!\!=^\tau \lambda x.\\
&\qquad \text{case}\ x\ \text{of}\ Err\ e \to return^\tau\,(Err\ e);\ Ok\ a \to runET\,(k\ a))
\end{aligned}
$$

We can verify that the left unit law $bind\,(unit\ a)\ k = k\ a$ holds, and that *bind* satisfies the associativity law. On the other hand, the right unit monad law $bind\ m\ unit = m$ is not satisfied in general. Unless the inner monad τ has a strict *return* function, $m = ErrorT\,(return\,\bot)$ is a counterexample to the right unit law.

However, it turns out that it is impossible to construct the value $ErrorT\,(return\,\bot)$ using only the standard *ErrorT* operations *unit*, *bind*, *throw*, *catch*, and *lift*. Furthermore, we can show that for all constructible values, the monad laws do always hold. In fact, the right unit law $bind\ m\ unit = m$ is an invariant which is preserved by all of the *ErrorT* operations. So when viewed as an abstract datatype, we could still consider *ErrorT* to be a valid monad.

A similar situation occurs when formalizing the standard Haskell writer monad transformer [6]. The monad instance fails because neither the left nor the right unit laws are preserved in general. But as before, the right unit law is an invariant which is preserved by all operations; the invariant also implies the left unit law. Thus the writer monad transformer is a valid monad when viewed as an abstract datatype.

5. Related work

A different domain-theoretic model of polymorphism is presented by Amadio and Curien [1]. Here, polymorphic functions are modeled as functions from types (i.e. deflations) to values. However, this model allows non-parametric polymorphic functions that depend non-trivially on the type argument.

Sozeau and Oury [9] recently developed a type class mechanism for the Coq theorem prover. Coq has a powerful dependent type system that allows reasoning about type constructors, first-class polymorphic values and type quantification. They define a monad class with laws. However, Coq's logic of total functions does not permit all the recursive definitions possible in HOLCF.

Our earlier formalization of axiomatic constructor classes [5] could express many of the same type definitions as the current work, although the classes were defined differently. Instead of naturality laws, it used a deflation membership relation $x ::: d$ to encode polymorphic types. Some automation for the *Functor* and *Monad* classes was present, but transfer proofs for polymorphic laws were tedious, making subclass definitions impractical. Overall, the new Tycon library provides much better automation for users.

For the full version of this paper, see arXiv:1207.3208 [cs.LO].

References

[1] Roberto M. Amadio and Pierre-Louis Curien. *Domains and Lambda-Calculi*. Cambridge University Press, New York, NY, USA, 1998.

[2] Brian Huffman. A purely definitional universal domain. In Stefan Berghofer, Tobias Nipkow, Christian Urban, and Makarius Wenzel, editors, *Proceedings of the 22nd International Conference on Theorem Proving in Higher Order Logics (TPHOLs '09)*, volume 5674 of *LNCS*, pages 260–275. Springer, 2009.

[3] Brian Huffman. *HOLCF '11: A Definitional Domain Theory for Verifying Functional Programs*. Ph.D. thesis, Portland State University, 2012.

[4] Brian Huffman. Type constructor classes and monad transformers. *Archive of Formal Proofs*, June 2012. `http://afp.sf.net/entries/Tycon.shtml`, Formal proof development.

[5] Brian Huffman, John Matthews, and Peter White. Axiomatic constructor classes in Isabelle/HOLCF. In Joe Hurd and Tom Melham, editors, *Proceedings of the 18th International Conference on Theorem Proving in Higher Order Logics (TPHOLs '05)*, volume 3603 of *LNCS*, pages 147–162. Springer, 2005.

[6] Mark P. Jones. Functional programming with overloading and higher-order polymorphism. In *First International Spring School on Advanced Functional Programming Techniques*, volume 925 of *LNCS*, Båstad, Sweden, May 1995. Springer-Verlag.

[7] Olaf Müller, Tobias Nipkow, David von Oheimb, and Oskar Slotosch. HOLCF = HOL + LCF. *Journal of Functional Programming*, 9:191–223, 1999.

[8] Tobias Nipkow, Lawrence C. Paulson, and Markus Wenzel. *Isabelle/HOL — A Proof Assistant for Higher-Order Logic*, volume 2283 of *LNCS*. Springer, 2002.

[9] Matthieu Sozeau and Nicolas Oury. First-class type classes. In Otmane Ait Mohamed, César Muñoz, and Sofiène Tahar, editors, *Theorem Proving in Higher Order Logics, 21st International Conference (TPHOLs '08)*, volume 5170 of *LNCS*, pages 278–293. Springer, August 2008.

[10] Philip Wadler. Theorems for free! In *Functional Programming Languages and Computer Architecture*, pages 347–359. ACM Press, 1989.

Elaborating Intersection and Union Types

Joshua Dunfield

Max Planck Institute for Software Systems
Kaiserslautern and Saarbrücken, Germany
joshua@mpi-sws.org

Abstract

Designing and implementing typed programming languages is hard. Every new type system feature requires extending the metatheory and implementation, which are often complicated and fragile. To ease this process, we would like to provide general mechanisms that subsume many different features.

In modern type systems, parametric polymorphism is fundamental, but intersection polymorphism has gained little traction in programming languages. Most practical intersection type systems have supported only *refinement intersections*, which increase the expressiveness of types (more precise properties can be checked) without altering the expressiveness of terms; refinement intersections can simply be erased during compilation. In contrast, *unrestricted* intersections increase the expressiveness of terms, and can be used to encode diverse language features, promising an economy of both theory and implementation.

We describe a foundation for compiling unrestricted intersection and union types: an elaboration type system that generates ordinary λ-calculus terms. The key feature is a Forsythe-like merge construct. With this construct, not all reductions of the source program preserve types; however, we prove that ordinary call-by-value evaluation of the elaborated program corresponds to a type-preserving evaluation of the source program.

We also describe a prototype implementation and applications of unrestricted intersections and unions: records, operator overloading, and simulating dynamic typing.

Categories and Subject Descriptors F.3.3 [*Mathematical Logic and Formal Languages*]: Studies of Program Constructs—Type structure

Keywords intersection types

1. Introduction

In type systems, parametric polymorphism is fundamental. It enables generic programming; it supports parametric reasoning about programs. Logically, it corresponds to universal quantification.

Intersection polymorphism (the intersection type $A \wedge B$) is less well appreciated. It enables ad hoc polymorphism; it supports *irregular* generic programming. Logically, it roughly corresponds to conjunction[1]. Not surprisingly, then, intersection is remarkably versatile.

[1] In our setting, this correspondence is strong, as we will see in Sec. 2.

ICFP'12, September 9–15, 2012, Copenhagen, Denmark.

For both legitimate and historical reasons, intersection types have not been used as widely as parametric polymorphism. One of the legitimate reasons for the slow adoption of intersection types is that no major language has them. A restricted form of intersection, *refinement intersection*, was realized in two extensions of SML, SML-CIDRE (Davies 2005) and Stardust (Dunfield 2007). These type systems can express properties such as bitwise parity: after refining a type bits of bitstrings with subtypes even (an even number of ones) and odd (an odd number of ones), a bitstring concatenation function can be checked against the type

$$(\mathsf{even} * \mathsf{even} \rightarrow \mathsf{even}) \wedge (\mathsf{odd} * \mathsf{odd} \rightarrow \mathsf{even}) \\ \wedge (\mathsf{even} * \mathsf{odd} \rightarrow \mathsf{odd}) \wedge (\mathsf{odd} * \mathsf{even} \rightarrow \mathsf{odd})$$

which satisfies the refinement restriction: all the intersected types refine a single simple type, $\mathsf{bits} * \mathsf{bits} \rightarrow \mathsf{bits}$.

But these systems were only typecheckers. To *compile* a program required an ordinary Standard ML compiler. SML-CIDRE was explicitly limited to checking refinements of SML types, without affecting the expressiveness of terms. In contrast, Stardust could typecheck some kinds of programs that used general intersection and union types, but ineffectively: since ordinary SML compilers don't know about intersection types, such programs could never be run.

Refinement intersections and unions increase the expressiveness of otherwise more-or-less-conventional type systems, allowing more precise properties of programs to be verified through typechecking. The point is to make fewer programs pass the typechecker; for example, a concatenation function that didn't have the parity property expressed by its type would be rejected. In contrast, unrestricted intersections and unions, in cooperation with a term-level "merge" construct, increase the expressiveness of the term language. For example, given primitive operations `Int.+` : $\mathsf{int} * \mathsf{int} \rightarrow \mathsf{int}$ and `Real.+` : $\mathsf{real} * \mathsf{real} \rightarrow \mathsf{real}$, we can easily define an overloaded addition operation by writing a merge:

$$\textbf{val} + = \texttt{Int.+} ,, \texttt{Real.+}$$

In our type system, this function + can be checked against the type $(\mathsf{int} * \mathsf{int} \rightarrow \mathsf{int}) \wedge (\mathsf{real} * \mathsf{real} \rightarrow \mathsf{real})$.

In this paper, we consider unrestricted intersection and union types. Central to the approach is a method for elaborating programs with intersection and union types: elaborate intersections into products, and unions into sums. The resulting programs have no intersections and no unions, and can be compiled using conventional means—any SML compiler will do. The above definition of + is elaborated to a pair `(Int.+, Real.+)`; uses of + on ints become first projections of +, while uses on reals become second projections of +.

We present a three-phase design, based on this method, that supports one of our ultimate goals: to develop simpler compilers for full-featured type systems by encoding many features using intersections and unions.

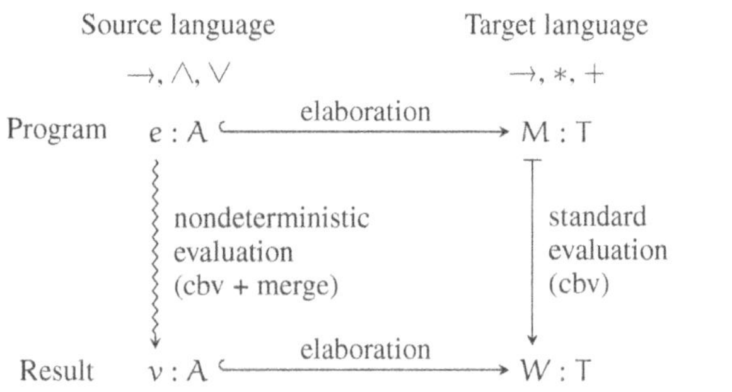

Figure 1. Elaboration and computation

1. An *encoding* phase that straightforwardly rewrites the program, for example, turning a multi-field record type into an intersection of single-field record types, and multi-field records into a "merge" of single-field records.
2. An *elaboration* phase that transforms intersections and unions into products and (disjoint) sums, and intersection and union introductions and eliminations (implicit in the source program) into their appropriate operations: tupling, projection, injection, and case analysis.
3. A *compilation* phase: a conventional compiler with no support for intersections, unions, or the features encoded by phase 1.

Contributions: Phase 2 is the main contribution of this paper. Specifically, we will:

- develop elaboration typing rules which, given a source expression e with unrestricted intersections and unions, and a "merging" construct $e_1 ,, e_2$, typecheck and transform the program into an ordinary λ-calculus term M (with sums and products);
- give a nondeterministic operational semantics ($\rightsquigarrow^*$) for source programs containing merges, in which not all reductions preserve types;
- prove a consistency (simulation) result: ordinary call-by-value evaluation ($\mapsto^*$) of the elaborated program produces a value corresponding to a value resulting from (type-preserving) reductions of the source program—that is, the diagram in Figure 1 commutes;
- describe an elaborating typechecker that, by implementing the elaboration typing rules, takes programs written in an ML-like language, with unrestricted intersection and union types, and generates Standard ML programs that can be compiled with any SML compiler.

All proofs were checked using the Twelf proof assistant (Pfenning and Schürmann 1999; Twelf 2012) (with the termination checker silenced for a few inductive cases, where the induction measure was nontrivial) and are available on the web (Dunfield 2012). For convenience, the names of Twelf source files (*.elf*) are hyperlinks.

While the idea of compiling intersections to products is not new, this paper is its first full development and practical expression. An essential twist is the source-level merging construct $e_1 ,, e_2$, which embodies several computationally distinct terms, which can be checked against various parts of an intersection type, reminiscent of Forsythe (Reynolds 1996) and (more distantly) the λ&-calculus (Castagna et al. 1995). Intersections can still be introduced *without* this construct; it is required only when no single term can describe the multiple behaviours expressed by the intersection. Remarkably, this merging construct also supports union eliminations with two computationally distinct branches (unlike markers for union elimination in work such as Pierce (1991a)). As usual, we have no source-level intersection eliminations and no source-level union introductions; elaboration puts all needed projections and injections into the target program.

Contents: In Section 2, we give some brief background on intersection types, discuss their introduction and elimination rules, introduce and discuss the merge construct, and compare intersection types to product types. Section 3 gives background on union types, discusses *their* introduction and elimination rules, and shows how the merge construct is also useful for them.

Section 4 has the details of the source language and its (unusual) operational semantics, and describes a non-elaborating type system including subsumption. Section 5 presents the target language and its (entirely standard) typing and operational semantics. Section 6 gives the elaboration typing rules, and proves several key results relating source typing, elaboration typing, the source operational semantics, and the target operational semantics.

Section 7 discusses a major caveat: the approach, at least in its present form, lacks the theoretically and practically important property of coherence, because the meaning of a target program depends on the choice of elaboration typing derivation.

Section 8 shows encodings of type system features into intersections and unions, with examples that are successfully elaborated by our prototype implementation (Section 9). Related work is discussed in Section 10, and Section 11 concludes.

2. Intersection Types

What is an intersection type? The simplistic answer is that, supposing that types describe sets of values, $A \wedge B$ describes the intersection of the sets of values of A and B. That is, $v : A \wedge B$ if $v : A$ and $v : B$.

Less simplistically, the name has been used for substantially different type constructors, though all have a conjunctive flavour. The intersection type in this paper is commutative ($A \wedge B = B \wedge A$) and idempotent ($A \wedge A = A$), following several seminal papers on intersection types (Pottinger 1980; Coppo et al. 1981) and more recent work with refinement intersections (Freeman and Pfenning 1991; Davies and Pfenning 2000; Dunfield and Pfenning 2003). Other lines of research have worked with nonlinear and/or ordered intersections, e.g. Kfoury and Wells (2004), which seem less directly applicable to practical type systems (Møller Neergaard and Mairson 2004).

For this paper, then: What is a commutative and idempotent intersection type?

One approach to this question is through the Curry-Howard correspondence. Naively, intersection should correspond to logical conjunction—but products correspond to logical conjunction, and intersections are not products, as is evident from comparing the standard[2] introduction and elimination rules for intersection to the (utterly standard) rules for product. (Throughout this paper, k is existentially quantified over $\{1, 2\}$; technically, and in the Twelf formulation, we have two rules $\wedge E_1$ and $\wedge E_2$, etc.)

$$\frac{e : A_1 \qquad e : A_2}{e : A_1 \wedge A_2}\,\wedge I \qquad\qquad \frac{e : A_1 \wedge A_2}{e : A_k}\,\wedge E_k$$

$$\frac{e_1 : A_1 \qquad e_2 : A_2}{(e_1, e_2) : A_1 * A_2}\,*I \qquad\qquad \frac{e : A_1 * A_2}{\mathbf{proj}_k\; e : A_k}\,*E_k$$

[2] For impure call-by-value languages like ML, $\wedge I$ ordinarily needs to be restricted to type a value v, for reasons analogous to the value restriction on parametric polymorphism (Davies and Pfenning 2000). Our setting, however, is not ordinary: the technique of elaboration makes the more permissive rule safe, though user-unfriendly. See Section 6.5.

Here $\wedge$I types a single term e which inhabits type A_1 *and* type A_2: via Curry-Howard, this means that a single proof term serves as witness to two propositions (the interpretations of A_1 and A_2). On the other hand, in $*$I two separate terms e_1 and e_2 witness the propositions corresponding to A_1 and A_2. This difference was suggested by Pottinger (1980), and made concrete when Hindley (1984) showed that intersection (of the form described by Coppo et al. (1981) and Pottinger (1980)) cannot correspond to conjunction because the following type, the intersection of the types of the I and S combinators, is uninhabited:

$$(A \to A) \wedge \underbrace{\big((A{\to}B{\to}C) \to (A{\to}B) \to A \to C\big)}_{\text{"D"}}$$

yet the prospectively corresponding proposition is provable in intuitionistic logic:

$$(A \supset A) \text{ and } \big((A{\supset}B{\supset}C) \supset (A{\supset}B) \supset A \supset C\big) \qquad (*)$$

Hindley notes that every term of type $A \to A$ is β-equivalent to $e_1 = \lambda x.\, x$, and every term of type D is β-equivalent to $e_2 = \lambda x.\, \lambda y.\, \lambda z.\, x\, z\, (y\, z)$, the S combinator. Any term e of type $(A \to A) \wedge D$ must therefore have two normal forms, e_1 and e_2, which is impossible.

But that impossibility holds for the *usual* λ-terms. Suppose we add a *merge* construct $e_1 ,, e_2$ that, quite brazenly, can step to two different things: $e_1 ,, e_2 \mapsto e_1$ and $e_1 ,, e_2 \mapsto e_2$. Its typing rule chooses one subterm and ignores the other (throughout this paper, the subscript k ranges over $\{1, 2\}$):

$$\frac{e_k : A}{e_1 ,, e_2 : A}\ \text{merge}_k$$

In combination with $\wedge$I, the merge_k rule allows two distinct implementations e_1 and e_2, one for each of the components A_1 and A_2 of the intersection:

$$\dfrac{\dfrac{e_1 : A_1}{e_1 ,, e_2 : A_1}\ \text{merge}_1 \qquad \dfrac{e_2 : A_2}{e_1 ,, e_2 : A_2}\ \text{merge}_2}{e_1 ,, e_2 : A_1 \wedge A_2}\ \wedge\text{I}$$

Now $(A \to A) \wedge D$ *is* inhabited:

$$e_1 ,, e_2 : (A \to A) \wedge D$$

With this construct, the "naive" hope that intersection corresponds to conjunction is realized through elaboration: we can elaborate $e_1 ,, e_2$ to $(e_1\, ,\, e_2)$, a term of type $(A \to A) * D$, which does correspond to the proposition (*). Inhabitation and provability again correspond—because we have replaced the seemingly mysterious intersections with simple products.

For source expressions, intersection still has several properties that set it apart from product. Unlike product, it has no elimination form. It also lacks an explicit introduction form; $\wedge$I is the only intro rule for $\wedge$. While the primary purpose of merge_k is to derive the premises of $\wedge$I, the merge_k rule makes no mention of intersection (or any other type constructor).

Pottinger (1980) presents intersection $A \mathbin{\widehat{\&}} B$ as a proposition with some evidence of A that is also evidence of B—unlike A & B, corresponding to $A * B$, which has two separate pieces of evidence for A and for B. In our system, though, $e_1 ,, e_2$ is a single term that provides evidence for A and B, so it is technically consistent with this view of intersection, but not necessarily consistent in spirit (since e_1 and e_2 can be very different from each other).

3. Union Types

Having discussed intersection types, we can describe union types as intersections' dual: if $v : A_1 \vee A_2$ then either $v : A_1$ or $v : A_2$ (perhaps both). This duality shows itself in several ways.

For union $\vee$, introduction is straightforward, as elimination was straightforward for $\wedge$ (again, k is either 1 or 2):

$$\frac{\Gamma \vdash e : A_k}{\Gamma \vdash e : A_1 \vee A_2}\ \vee\text{I}_k$$

Coming up with a good elimination rule is trickier. A number of appealing rules are unsound; a sound, yet acceptably strong, rule is

$$\frac{\Gamma \vdash e_0 : A_1 \vee A_2 \qquad \begin{array}{l}\Gamma, x_1 : A_1 \vdash \mathcal{E}[x_1] : C \\ \Gamma, x_2 : A_2 \vdash \mathcal{E}[x_2] : C\end{array}}{\Gamma \vdash \mathcal{E}[e_0] : C}\ \vee\text{E}$$

This rule types an expression $\mathcal{E}[e_0]$—an evaluation context $\mathcal{E}$ with e_0 in an evaluation position—where e_0 has the union type $A_1 \vee A_2$. During evaluation, e_0 will be some value v_0 such that either $v_0 : A_1$ or $v_0 : A_2$. In the former case, the premise $x_1 : A_1 \vdash \mathcal{E}[x_1] : C$ tells us that substituting v_0 for x_1 gives a well-typed expression $\mathcal{E}[v_0]$. Similarly, the premise $x_2 : A_2 \vdash \mathcal{E}[x_2] : C$ tells us we can safely substitute v_0 for x_2.

The restriction to a single occurrence of e_0 in an evaluation position is needed for soundness in many settings—generally, in any operational semantics in which e_0 might step to different expressions. One simple example is a function $f : (A \to A \to C) \wedge (B \to B \to C)$ and expression $e_0 : A \vee B$, where e_0 changes the contents pointed to by a reference of type $(A \vee B)$ ref, before returning the new value. The application $f\ e_0\ e_0$ would be well-typed by a rule allowing multiple occurrences of e_0, but unsound: the first e_0 could evaluate to an A and the second e_0 to a B.

The evaluation context $\mathcal{E}$ need not be unique, which creates some difficulties for practical typechecking (Dunfield 2011). For further discussion of this rule, see Dunfield and Pfenning (2003).

We saw in Section 2 that, in the usual λ-calculus, $\wedge$ does not correspond to conjunction; in particular, no λ-term behaves like both the I and S combinators, so the intersection $(A{\to}A) \wedge D$ (where D is the type of S) is uninhabited. In our setting, though, $(A{\to}A) \wedge D$ *is* inhabited, by the merge of I and S.

Something similar comes up when eliminating unions. Without the merge construct, certain instances of union types can't be usefully eliminated. Consider a list whose elements have type int $\vee$ string. Introducing those unions to create the list is easy enough: use $\vee\text{I}_1$ for the ints and $\vee\text{I}_2$ for the strings. Now suppose we want to print a list element x : int $\vee$ string, converting the ints to their string representation and leaving the strings alone. To do this, we need a merge; for example, given a function g : (int $\to$ string) $\wedge$ (string $\to$ string) whose body contains a merge, use rule $\vee$E on $g\ x$ with $\mathcal{E} = g\ [\,]$ and $e_0 = x$.

Like intersections, unions can be tamed by elaboration. Instead of products, we elaborate unions to products' dual, sums (*tagged* unions). Uses of $\vee\text{I}_1$ and $\vee\text{I}_2$ become left and right injections into a sum type; uses of $\vee$E become ordinary case expressions.

4. Source Language

4.1 Source Syntax

Source types	$A, B, C ::= \top \mid A \to B \mid A \wedge B \mid A \vee B$
Typing contexts	$\Gamma ::= \cdot \mid \Gamma, x : A$
Source expressions	$e ::= x \mid () \mid \lambda x.\, e \mid e_1\, e_2 \mid \textbf{fix}\ x.\, e \mid e_1 ,, e_2$
Source values	$v ::= x \mid () \mid \lambda x.\, e \mid v_1 ,, v_2$
Evaluation contexts	$\mathcal{E} ::= [\,] \mid \mathcal{E}\ e \mid v\ \mathcal{E} \mid \mathcal{E} ,, e \mid e ,, \mathcal{E}$

Figure 2. Syntax of source types, contexts and expressions

The source language expressions e are standard, except for the feature central to our approach, the merge $e_1 ,, e_2$. The types A, B, C are a "top" type $\top$ (which will be elaborated to unit), the usual function space $A \to B$, intersection $A \wedge B$ and union $A \vee B$. Values v are standard, but a merge of values $v_1 ,, v_2$ is considered a value, even though it can step! But the step it takes is pure, in the sense that even if we incorporated (say) mutable references, it would not interact with them.

4.2 Source Operational Semantics

$\boxed{e \rightsquigarrow e'}$ Source expression e steps to e' $\quad$ `step E E' in step.elf`

$$\frac{e_1 \rightsquigarrow e_1'}{e_1 e_2 \rightsquigarrow e_1' e_2}\ \text{step/app1} \qquad \frac{e_2 \rightsquigarrow e_2'}{v_1 e_2 \rightsquigarrow v_1 e_2'}\ \text{step/app2}$$

$$\frac{}{(\lambda x.\, e)v \rightsquigarrow [v/x]e}\ \text{step/beta}$$

$$\frac{}{\mathbf{fix}\, x.\, e \rightsquigarrow [(\mathbf{fix}\, x.\, e)/x]e}\ \text{step/fix}$$

$$\frac{}{e_1 ,, e_2 \rightsquigarrow e_1}\ \text{step/unmerge left} \qquad \frac{}{e_1 ,, e_2 \rightsquigarrow e_2}\ \text{step/unmerge right}$$

$$\frac{e_1 \rightsquigarrow e_1'}{e_1 ,, e_2 \rightsquigarrow e_1' ,, e_2}\ \text{step/merge1} \qquad \frac{e_2 \rightsquigarrow e_2'}{e_1 ,, e_2 \rightsquigarrow e_1 ,, e_2'}\ \text{step/merge2}$$

$$\frac{}{e \rightsquigarrow e ,, e}\ \text{step/split}$$

Figure 3. Source language operational semantics: call-by-value + merge construct

The source language operational semantics (Figure 3) is standard (call-by-value function application and a fixed point expression) except for the merge construct. This peculiar animal is a descendant of "demonic choice": by the 'step/unmerge left' and 'step/unmerge right' rules, $e_1 ,, e_2$ can step to either e_1 or e_2. Adding to its misbehaviours, it permits stepping within itself ('step/merge1' and 'step/merge2'—note that in 'step/merge2', we don't require e_1 to be a value). Worst of all, it can appear by spontaneous fission: 'step/split' turns any expression e into a merge of two copies of e.

The merge construct makes our source language operational semantics interesting. It also makes it unrealistic: $\rightsquigarrow$-reduction does not preserve types. For type preservation to hold, the operational semantics would need access to the typing derivation. Worse, since the typing rule for merges ignores the unused part of the merge, $\rightsquigarrow$-reduction can produce expressions that have no type at all, or are not even closed! The point of the source operational semantics is not to directly model computation; rather, it is a basis for checking that the elaborated program (whose operational semantics is perfectly standard) makes sense. We will show in Section 6 that, if the result M of elaborating e can step to some M', then we can step $e \rightsquigarrow^* e'$ where e' elaborates to M'.

4.3 (Source) Subtyping

Suppose we want to pass a function $f : A \to C$ to a function $g : ((A \wedge B) \to C) \to D$. This should be possible, since f requires only that its argument have type A; in all calls from g the argument to f will also have type B, but f won't mind. With only the rules discussed so far, however, the application $g\ f$ is not well-typed: we can't get inside the arrow $(A \wedge B) \to C$. For flexibility, we'll incorporate a subtyping system that can conclude, for example, $A \to C \leq (A \wedge B) \to C$.

The logic of the subtyping rules (Figure 4, top) is taken straight from Dunfield and Pfenning (2003), so we only briefly give some intuition. Roughly, $A \leq B$ is sound if every value of type A can be treated as having type B. Under a subset interpretation, this would mean that $A \leq B$ is justified if the set of A-values is a subset of the set of B-values. For example, the rule $\wedge R{\leq}$, if interpreted set-theoretically, says that if $A \subseteq B_1$ and $A \subseteq B_2$ then $A \subseteq (B_1 \cap B_2)$.

It is easy to show that subtyping is reflexive and transitive; see *sub-refl.elf* and *sub-trans.elf*. (Building transitivity into the structure of the rules makes it easy to derive an algorithm; an explicit transitivity rule would have premises $A \leq B$ and $B \leq C$, which involve an intermediate type B that does not appear in the conclusion $A \leq C$.)

Having said all that, the subsequent theoretical development is easier without subtyping. So we will show (Theorem 1) that, given a typing derivation that uses subtyping (through the usual subsumption rule), we can always construct a source expression of the same type that never applies the subsumption rule. This new expression will be the same as the original one, with a few additional coercions. For the example above, we essentially η-expand $g\ f$ to $g\ (\lambda x.\, f\ x)$, which lets us apply $\wedge E_1$ to $x : A \wedge B$. Operationally, all the coercions are identities; they serve only to "articulate" the type structure, making subsumption unnecessary.

Note that the coercion in rule $\vee L{\leq}$ is eta-expanded to allow $\vee E$ to eliminate the union in the type of x; as discussed later, the subexpression of union type must be in evaluation position.

4.4 Source Typing

The source typing rules (Figure 4) are either standard or have already been discussed in Sections 2 and 3, except for direct.

The direct rule was introduced and justified in Dunfield and Pfenning (2003, 2004). It is a 1-ary version of $\vee E$, a sort of cut: a use of the typing $e_0 : A$ within the derivation of $\mathcal{E}[e_0] : C$ is replaced by a derivations of $e_0 : A$, along with a derivation of $\mathcal{E}[x] : C$ that assumes $x : A$. Curiously, in this system of rules, direct is admissible: given $e_0 : A$, use $\vee I_1$ or $\vee I_2$ to conclude $e_0 : A \vee A$, then use two copies of the derivation $x : A \vdash \mathcal{E}[x] : C$ in the premises of $\vee E$ (α-converting x as needed). So why include it? Typing using these rules is undecidable; our implementation (Section 9) follows a bidirectional version of them (where typechecking is decidable, given a few annotations, similar to Dunfield and Pfenning (2004)), where direct is *not* admissible. (A side benefit is that direct and $\vee E$ are similar enough that it can be helpful to do the direct case of a proof before tackling $\vee E$.)

Remark. Theorem 1, and all subsequent theorems, are proved only for expressions that are closed under the appropriate context, even though merge_k does not explicitly require that the unexamined subexpression be closed; Twelf does not support proofs about objects with unknown variables.

Theorem 1 (Coercion). *If $\mathcal{D}$ derives $\Gamma \vdash e : B$ then there exists an e' such that $\mathcal{D}'$ derives $\Gamma \vdash e' : B$, where $\mathcal{D}'$ never uses rule* sub.

Proof. By induction on $\mathcal{D}$. The interesting cases are for sub and $\vee E$. In the case for sub with $A \leq B$, we show that when the coercion e_{coerce}—which always has the form $\lambda x.\, e_0$—is applied to an expression of type A, we get an expression of type B. For example, for $\wedge L_1{\leq}$ we use $\wedge E_1$. This shows that $e' = (\lambda x.\, e_0)\ e$ has type B.

For $\vee E$, the premises typing $\mathcal{E}[x_k]$ might "separate", say if the first includes subsumption (yielding the same $\mathcal{E}[x_1]$) and the second doesn't. Furthermore, inserting coercions could break evaluation positions: given $\mathcal{E} = f\ [\,]$, replacing f with an application $(e_{\text{coerce}}\ f)$

$\boxed{A \leq B ::: e}$ Source type A is a subtype of source type B, with coercion e of type $\cdot \vdash e : A \to B$ `sub A B Coe CoeTyping in typeof+sub.elf`

$$\frac{B_1 \leq A_1 ::: e \qquad A_2 \leq B_2 ::: e'}{A_1 \to A_2 \leq B_1 \to B_2 ::: \lambda f.\, \lambda x.\, e'\,(f\,(e\,x))} \to\leq \qquad \frac{}{A \leq \top ::: \lambda x.\, ()} \top R\leq$$

$$\frac{A_k \leq B ::: e}{A_1 \wedge A_2 \leq B ::: e} \wedge L_k\leq \qquad \frac{A \leq B_1 ::: e_1 \qquad A \leq B_2 ::: e_2}{A \leq B_1 \wedge B_2 ::: e_1 ,, e_2} \wedge R\leq$$

$$\frac{A_1 \leq B ::: e_1 \qquad A_2 \leq B ::: e_2}{A_1 \vee A_2 \leq B ::: \lambda x.\, (\lambda y.\, e_1\, y ,, e_2\, y)\, x} \vee L\leq \qquad \frac{A \leq B_k ::: e}{A \leq B_1 \vee B_2 ::: e} \vee R_k\leq$$

$\boxed{\Gamma \vdash e : A}$ Source expression e has source type A `typeof+sub E A in typeof+sub.elf`

$$\frac{}{\Gamma_1, x : A, \Gamma_2 \vdash x : A} \text{var} \qquad \frac{\Gamma \vdash e_k : A}{\Gamma \vdash e_1 ,, e_2 : A} \text{merge}_k \qquad \frac{\Gamma, x : A \vdash e : A}{\Gamma \vdash \textbf{fix}\, x.\, e : A} \text{fix} \qquad \frac{}{\Gamma \vdash v : \top} \top I$$

$$\frac{\Gamma, x : A \vdash e : B}{\Gamma \vdash \lambda x.\, e : A \to B} \to I \qquad \frac{\Gamma \vdash e_1 : A \to B \qquad \Gamma \vdash e_2 : A}{\Gamma \vdash e_1\, e_2 : B} \to E$$

$$\frac{\Gamma \vdash e : A_1 \qquad \Gamma \vdash e : A_2}{\Gamma \vdash e : A_1 \wedge A_2} \wedge I \qquad \frac{\Gamma \vdash e : A_1 \wedge A_2}{\Gamma \vdash e : A_k} \wedge E_k$$

$$\frac{\Gamma \vdash e_0 : A \qquad \Gamma, x : A \vdash \mathcal{E}[x] : C}{\Gamma \vdash \mathcal{E}[e_0] : C} \text{direct} \qquad \frac{\Gamma \vdash e : A_k}{\Gamma \vdash e : A_1 \vee A_2} \vee I_k \qquad \frac{\Gamma \vdash e_0 : A_1 \vee A_2 \qquad \begin{array}{c}\Gamma, x_1 : A_1 \vdash \mathcal{E}[x_1] : C \\ \Gamma, x_2 : A_2 \vdash \mathcal{E}[x_2] : C\end{array}}{\Gamma \vdash \mathcal{E}[e_0] : C} \vee E$$

$$\frac{\Gamma \vdash e : A \qquad A \leq B ::: e_{\text{coerce}}}{\Gamma \vdash e : B} \text{sub}$$

Figure 4. Source type system, with subsumption, non-elaborating

means that [] is no longer in evaluation position. To handle these issues, let $e' = (\lambda y.\, e_1' ,, e_2')\, e_0'$, where e_0' comes from applying the induction hypothesis to the derivation of $\Gamma \vdash e_0 : A_1 \vee A_2$, and e_1' and e_2' come from applying the induction hypothesis to the other two premises. Now e_0' *is* in evaluation position, because it follows a λ; the merge_k typing rule will choose the correct branch.

For details, see *coerce.elf*. We actually encode the typings for e_{coerce} as hypothetical derivations in the subtyping judgment itself (*typeof+sub.elf*), making the sub case here trivial. □

5. Target Language

Our target language is just the simply-typed call-by-value λ-calculus extended with fixed point expressions, products, and sums.

5.1 Target Syntax

Target types	$T ::= \text{unit} \mid T \to T \mid T * T \mid T + T$
Typing contexts	$G ::= \cdot \mid G, x : T$
Target terms	$M, N ::= x \mid () \mid \lambda x.\, M \mid M\, N \mid \textbf{fix}\, x.\, M$
	$\mid (M_1, M_2) \mid \textbf{proj}_k\, M$
	$\mid \textbf{inj}_k\, M \mid \textbf{case}\, M\, \textbf{of inj}_1\, x_1 \Rightarrow N_1$
	$\mid \textbf{inj}_2\, x_2 \Rightarrow N_2$
Target values	$W ::= x \mid () \mid \lambda x.\, M \mid (W_1, W_2) \mid \textbf{inj}_k\, W$

Figure 5. Target types and terms

The target types and terms (Figure 5) are completely standard.

5.2 Target Typing

The typing rules for the target language (Figure 6) lack any form of subtyping, and are completely standard.

5.3 Target Operational Semantics

The operational semantics $M \mapsto M'$ is, likewise, standard; functions are call-by-value and products are strict. As usual, we write $M \mapsto^* M'$ for a sequence of zero or more $\mapsto$s.

Naturally, a type safety result holds:

Theorem 2 (Target Type Safety). *If* $\cdot \vdash M : T$ *then either* M *is a value, or* $M \mapsto M'$ *and* $\cdot \vdash M' : T$.

Proof. By induction on the given derivation, using a few standard lemmas; see *tm-safety.elf*. (The necessary substitution lemma comes for free in Twelf.) □

And to calm any doubts about whether M might step to some other, not necessarily well-typed term:

Theorem 3 (Determinism of $\mapsto$). *If* $M \mapsto N_1$ *and* $M \mapsto N_2$ *then* $N_1 = N_2$ *(up to α-conversion).*

Proof. By simultaneous induction. See *tm-deterministic* in *tm-safety.elf*. □

6. Elaboration Typing

We elaborate source expressions e into target terms M. The source expressions, which include a "merge" construct $e_1 ,, e_2$, are typed with intersections and unions, but the result of elaboration is completely standard and can be typed with just unit, $\to$, $*$ and $+$.

$\boxed{G \vdash M : T}$ Target term M has target type T $\boxed{\texttt{typeoftm } M\ T \text{ in } \texttt{typeoftm.elf}}$

$$\frac{}{G_1, x : T, G_2 \vdash x : T}\ \text{typeoftm/var} \qquad \frac{G, x : T \vdash M : T}{G \vdash \textbf{fix}\, x.\, M : T}\ \text{typeoftm/fix} \qquad \frac{}{G \vdash () : \mathsf{unit}}\ \text{typeoftm/unitintro}$$

$$\frac{G, x : T_1 \vdash M : T_2}{G \vdash \lambda x.\, M : (T_1 \to T_2)}\ \text{typeoftm/arrintro} \qquad \frac{G \vdash M_1 : T \to T' \qquad G \vdash M_2 : T}{G \vdash M_1\, M_2 : T'}\ \text{typeoftm/arrelim}$$

$$\frac{G \vdash M_1 : T_1 \qquad G \vdash M_2 : T_2}{G \vdash (M_1, M_2) : (T_1 * T_2)}\ \text{typeoftm/prodintro} \qquad \frac{G \vdash M : (T_1 * T_2)}{G \vdash (\textbf{proj}_k\, M) : T_k}\ \text{typeoftm/prodelim}_k$$

$$\frac{G \vdash M : T_k}{G \vdash (\textbf{inj}_k\, M) : (T_1 + T_2)}\ \text{typeoftm/sumintro}_k \qquad \frac{G \vdash M : T_1 + T_2 \qquad \begin{array}{c} G, x_1 : T_1 \vdash N_1 : T \\ G, x_2 : T_2 \vdash N_2 : T \end{array}}{G \vdash (\textbf{case}\, M\, \textbf{of inj}_1\, x_1 \Rightarrow N_1 \mid \textbf{inj}_2\, x_2 \Rightarrow N_2) : T}\ \text{typeoftm/sumelim}$$

Figure 6. Target type system with functions, products and sums

$\boxed{M \mapsto M'}$ Target term M steps to M' $\boxed{\texttt{steptm } M\ M' \text{ in } \texttt{steptm.elf}}$

$$\frac{M_1 \mapsto M_1'}{M_1 M_2 \mapsto M_1' M_2} \qquad \frac{M_2 \mapsto M_2'}{W_1 M_2 \mapsto W_1 M_2'}$$

$$\frac{}{(\lambda x.\, M) W \mapsto [W/x]M} \qquad \frac{}{\textbf{fix}\, x.\, M \mapsto [(\textbf{fix}\, x.\, M)/x]M}$$

$$\frac{M \mapsto M'}{\textbf{proj}_k\, M' \mapsto \textbf{proj}_k\, M'} \qquad \frac{}{\textbf{proj}_k\, (W_1, W_2) \mapsto W_k}$$

$$\frac{M_1 \mapsto M_1'}{(M_1, M_2) \mapsto (M_1', M_2)} \qquad \frac{M_2 \mapsto M_2'}{(W_1, M_2) \mapsto (W_1, M_2')}$$

$$\frac{M \mapsto M'}{\textbf{inj}_k\, M \mapsto \textbf{inj}_k\, M'} \qquad \frac{M \mapsto M'}{\textbf{case}\, M\, \textbf{of}\, MS \mapsto \textbf{case}\, M'\, \textbf{of}\, MS}$$

$$\frac{}{\textbf{case inj}_k\, W\, \textbf{of inj}_1\, x_1 \Rightarrow N_1 \mid \textbf{inj}_2\, x_2 \Rightarrow N_2 \ \mapsto\ [W/x_k]N_k}$$

Figure 7. Target language operational semantics: call-by-value + products + sums

The elaboration judgment $\Gamma \vdash e : A \hookrightarrow M$ is read "under assumptions Γ, source expression e has type A and elaborates to target term M". While not written explicitly in the judgment, the elaboration rules ensure that M has type $|A|$, the *type translation* of A (Figure 8). For example, $|\top \wedge (\top \to \top)| = \mathsf{unit} * (\mathsf{unit} \to \mathsf{unit})$.

To simplify the technical development, the elaboration rules work only for source expressions that can be typed without using the subsumption rule sub (Figure 4). Such source expressions can always be produced (Theorem 1, above).

The rest of this section discusses the elaboration rules and proves related properties:

6.1 connects elaboration, source typing, and target typing;

6.2 gives lemmas useful for showing that target computations correspond to source computations;

6.3 states and proves that correspondence (*consistency*, Thm. 13);

6.4 summarizes the metatheory through two important corollaries of our various theorems.

Finally, Section 6.5 discusses whether we need a value restriction on $\wedge$I.

$$\begin{aligned} |\top| &= \mathsf{unit} \\ |A_1 \to A_2| &= |A_1| \to |A_2| \\ |A_1 \wedge A_2| &= |A_1| * |A_2| \\ |A_1 \vee A_2| &= |A_1| + |A_2| \end{aligned}$$

Figure 8. Type translation

6.1 Connecting Elaboration and Typing

Equivalence of elaboration and source typing: The non-elaborating type assignment system of Figure 4, minus sub, can be read off from the elaboration rules in Figure 9: simply drop the $\hookrightarrow \ldots$ part of the judgment. Consequently, given $e : A \hookrightarrow M$ we can always derive $e : A$:

Theorem 4.
If $\Gamma \vdash e : A \hookrightarrow M$ *then* $\Gamma \vdash e : A$ *(without using rule* sub*).*

Proof. By straightforward induction on the given derivation; see `typeof-erase` in `typeof-elab.elf`. □

More interestingly, given $e : A$ we can always elaborate e, so elaboration is just as expressive as typing:

Theorem 5 (Completeness of Elaboration).
If $\Gamma \vdash e : A$ *(without using rule* sub*) then* $\Gamma \vdash e : A \hookrightarrow M$.

Proof. By straightforward induction on the given derivation; see `elab-complete` in `typeof-elab.elf`. □

Elaboration produces well-typed terms: Any target term M produced by the elaboration rules has corresponding target type. In the theorem statement, we assume the obvious translation $|\Gamma|$, e.g. $|x : \top, y : \top \vee \top| = x : |\top|, y : |\top \vee \top| = x : \mathsf{unit}, y : \mathsf{unit} + \mathsf{unit}$).

Theorem 6 (Elaboration Type Soundness).
If $\Gamma \vdash e : A \hookrightarrow M$ *then* $|\Gamma| \vdash M : |A|$.

Proof. By induction on the given derivation. For example, the case for direct, which elaborates to an application, applies typeoftm/arrintro and typeoftm/arrelim. Exploiting a bijection between source types and target types, we actually prove $\Gamma \vdash M : A$, interpreting A and types in Γ as target types: $\wedge$ as $*$, etc. See `elab-type-soundness.elf`. □

$\boxed{\Gamma \vdash e : A \hookrightarrow M}$ Source expression e has source type A and elaborates to target term M (of type $|A|$) $\boxed{\textit{elab E A M} \text{ in } \textit{elab.elf}}$

$$\frac{}{\Gamma_1, x : A, \Gamma_2 \vdash x : A \hookrightarrow x}\ \text{var} \qquad \frac{\Gamma \vdash e_k : A \hookrightarrow M}{\Gamma \vdash e_1 \,,, e_2 : A \hookrightarrow M}\ \text{merge}_k \qquad \frac{\Gamma, x : A \vdash e : A \hookrightarrow M}{\Gamma \vdash \mathbf{fix}\, x.\, e : A \hookrightarrow \mathbf{fix}\, x.\, M}\ \text{fix} \qquad \frac{}{\Gamma \vdash v : \top \hookrightarrow ()}\ \top\text{I}$$

$$\frac{\Gamma, x : A \vdash e : B \hookrightarrow M}{\Gamma \vdash \lambda x.\, e : A \to B \hookrightarrow \lambda x.\, M}\ {\to}\text{I} \qquad \frac{\Gamma \vdash e_1 : A \to B \hookrightarrow M_1 \qquad \Gamma \vdash e_2 : A \hookrightarrow M_2}{\Gamma \vdash e_1\, e_2 : B \hookrightarrow M_1\, M_2}\ {\to}\text{E}$$

$$\frac{\Gamma \vdash e : A_1 \hookrightarrow M_1 \qquad \Gamma \vdash e : A_2 \hookrightarrow M_2}{\Gamma \vdash e : A_1 \wedge A_2 \hookrightarrow (M_1, M_2)}\ \wedge\text{I} \qquad \frac{\Gamma \vdash e : A_1 \wedge A_2 \hookrightarrow M}{\Gamma \vdash e : A_k \hookrightarrow \mathbf{proj}_k\, M}\ \wedge\text{E}_k$$

$$\frac{\Gamma \vdash e : A_k \hookrightarrow M}{\Gamma \vdash e : A_1 \vee A_2 \hookrightarrow \mathbf{inj}_k\, M}\ \vee\text{I}_k$$

$$\frac{\Gamma \vdash e_0 : A \hookrightarrow M_0 \qquad \Gamma, x : A \vdash \mathcal{E}[x] : C \hookrightarrow N}{\Gamma \vdash \mathcal{E}[e_0] : C \hookrightarrow (\lambda x.\, N) M_0}\ \text{direct} \qquad \frac{\Gamma \vdash e_0 : A_1 \vee A_2 \hookrightarrow M_0 \qquad \begin{array}{l}\Gamma, x_1 : A_1 \vdash \mathcal{E}[x_1] : C \hookrightarrow N_1 \\ \Gamma, x_2 : A_2 \vdash \mathcal{E}[x_2] : C \hookrightarrow N_2\end{array}}{\Gamma \vdash \mathcal{E}[e_0] : C \hookrightarrow \mathbf{case}\ M_0\ \mathbf{of}\ \mathbf{inj}_1\, x_1 \Rightarrow N_1 \mid \mathbf{inj}_2\, x_2 \Rightarrow N_2}\ \vee\text{E}$$

Figure 9. Elaboration typing rules

6.2 Relating Source Expressions to Target Terms

Elaboration produces a term that corresponds closely to the source expression: a target term is the same as a source expression, except that the intersection- and union-related aspects of the computation become explicit in the target. For instance, intersection elimination via $\wedge E_2$, implicit in the source program, becomes the explicit projection $\mathbf{proj}_2$. The target term has nearly the same structure as the source; the elaboration rules only insert operations such as $\mathbf{proj}_2$, duplicate subterms such as the e in $\wedge$I, and omit unused parts of merges.

This gives rise to a relatively simple connection between source expressions and target terms—much simpler than a logical relation, which relates all appropriately-typed terms that have the same extensional behaviour. In fact, stepping in the target *preserves elaboration typing*, provided we are allowed to step the source expression zero or more times. This consistency result, Theorem 13, needs several lemmas.

Lemma 7. *If* $e \leadsto^* e'$ *then* $\mathcal{E}[e] \leadsto^* \mathcal{E}[e']$.

Proof. By induction on the number of steps, using a lemma (*step-eval-context*) that $e \leadsto e'$ implies $\mathcal{E}[e] \leadsto \mathcal{E}[e']$. See *step*eval-context* in *step-eval-context.elf*. □

Next, we prove inversion properties of unions, intersections and arrows. Roughly, we want to say that if an expression of union type elaborates to an injection $\mathbf{inj}_k\, M_0$, it also elaborates to M_0. For intersections, the property is slightly more complicated: given an expression of intersection type that elaborates to a pair, we can step the expression to get something that elaborates to the components of the pair. Similarly, given an expression of arrow type that elaborates to a λ-abstraction, we can step the expression to a λ-abstraction.

Lemma 8 (Unions/Injections).
If $\Gamma \vdash e : A_1 \vee A_2 \hookrightarrow \mathbf{inj}_k\, M_0$ *then* $\Gamma \vdash e : A_k \hookrightarrow M_0$.

Proof. By induction on the derivation of $\Gamma \vdash e : C \hookrightarrow M$. The only possible cases are merge_k and $\vee I_k$. See *elab-inl* and *elab-inr* in *elab-union.elf*. □

Lemma 9 (Intersections/Pairs).
If $\Gamma \vdash e : A_1 \wedge A_2 \hookrightarrow (M_1, M_2)$ *then there exist* e'_1 *and* e'_2 *such that*
(1) $e \leadsto^* e'_1$ *and* $\Gamma \vdash e'_1 : A_1 \hookrightarrow M_1$, *and*
(2) $e \leadsto^* e'_2$ *and* $\Gamma \vdash e'_2 : A_2 \hookrightarrow M_2$.

Proof. By induction on the given derivation; the only possible cases are $\wedge$I and merge. See *elab-sect.elf*. □

Lemma 10 (Arrows/Lambdas).
If $\cdot \vdash e : A \to B \hookrightarrow \lambda x.\, M_0$ *then there exists* e_0 *such that* $e \leadsto^* \lambda x.\, e_0$ *and* $x : A \vdash e_0 : B \hookrightarrow M_0$.

Proof. By induction on the given derivation; the only possible cases are $\to$I and merge. See *elab-arr.elf*. □

Our last interesting lemma shows that if an expression e elaborates to a target value W, we can step e to some value v that also elaborates to W.

Lemma 11 (Value monotonicity). *If* $\Gamma \vdash e : A \hookrightarrow W$ *then* $e \leadsto^* v$ *where* $\Gamma \vdash v : A \hookrightarrow W$.

Proof. By induction on the given derivation.

The most interesting case is for $\wedge$I, where we apply the induction hypothesis to each premise (yielding v'_1, v'_2 such that $e \leadsto^* v'_1$ and $e \leadsto^* v'_2$), apply the 'step/split' rule to turn e into $(e \,,, e)$, and use the 'step/merge1' and 'step/merge2' rules to step each part of the merge, yielding $v'_1 \,,, v'_2$, which is a value.

In the merge_k case on a merge $e_1 \,,, e_2$, we apply the induction hypothesis to e_k, giving $e_k \leadsto^* v$. By rule 'step/unmerge', $e_1 \,,, e_2 \leadsto e_k$, from which $e_1 \,,, e_2 \leadsto^* v$.

See *value-mono.elf*. □

Lemma 12 (Substitution). *If* $\Gamma, x : A \vdash e : B \hookrightarrow M$ *and* $\Gamma \vdash v : A \hookrightarrow W$ *then* $\Gamma \vdash [v/x]e : B \hookrightarrow [W/x]M$.

Proof. By induction on the first derivation. As usual, Twelf gives us this substitution lemma for free. □

6.3 Consistency

This theorem is the linchpin: given e that elaborates to M, we can preserve the elaboration relationship even after stepping M, though we may have to step e some number of times as well. The expression e and term M, in general, step at different speeds:

- M steps while e doesn't—for example, if M is $\mathbf{inj}_1\ (W_1, W_2)$ and steps to W_1, there is nothing to do in e because the injection corresponds to *implicit* union introduction in rule $\vee I_1$;

- e may step *more* than M—for example, if e is $(v_1 ,, v_2)\, v$ and M is $(\lambda x.\, x)\, W$, then M β-reduces to W, but e must first 'step/unmerge' to the appropriate v_k, yielding $v_k\, v$, and *then* apply 'step/beta'.

(Note that the converse—if $e \rightsquigarrow e'$ then $M \mapsto^* M'$—does not hold: we could pick the wrong half of a merge and get a source expression with no particular relation to M.)

Theorem 13 (Consistency).
If $\cdot \vdash e : A \hookrightarrow M$ *and* $M \mapsto M'$ *then there exists* e' *such that* $e \rightsquigarrow^* e'$ *and* $\cdot \vdash e' : A \hookrightarrow M'$.

Proof. By induction on the derivation $\mathcal{D}$ of $\cdot \vdash e : A \hookrightarrow M$. We show several cases here; the full proof is in `consistency.elf`.

- **Case** var, $\top$I, $\to$I : Impossible because M cannot step.
- **Case** $\wedge$I :
$$\mathcal{D} :: \dfrac{\cdot \vdash e : A_1 \hookrightarrow M_1 \qquad \cdot \vdash e : A_2 \hookrightarrow M_2}{\cdot \vdash e : A_1 \wedge A_2 \hookrightarrow (M_1\, ,\, M_2)}$$
By inversion, either $M_1 \mapsto M_1'$ or $M_2 \mapsto M_2'$. Suppose the former (the latter is similar). By i.h., $e \rightsquigarrow^* e_1'$ and $\cdot \vdash e_1' : A_1 \hookrightarrow M_1'$. By 'step/split', $e \rightsquigarrow e ,, e$. Repeatedly applying 'step/merge1' gives $e ,, e \rightsquigarrow^* e_1' ,, e$.
For typing, apply merge_1 with premise $\cdot \vdash e_1' : A_1 \hookrightarrow M_1'$ and with premise $\cdot \vdash e : A_2 \hookrightarrow M_2$.
Finally, by $\wedge$I, we have $\cdot \vdash e_1' ,, e : A_1 \wedge A_2 \hookrightarrow (M_1'\, ,\, M_2)$.
- **Case** $\wedge E_k$:
$$\mathcal{D} :: \dfrac{\cdot \vdash e : A_1 \wedge A_2 \hookrightarrow M_0}{\cdot \vdash e : A_k \hookrightarrow \mathbf{proj}_k\, M_0}$$
If $\mathbf{proj}_k\, M_0 \mapsto \mathbf{proj}_k\, M_0'$ with $M_0 \mapsto M_0'$, use the i.h. and apply $\wedge E_k$.
If $M_0 = (W_1\, ,\, W_2)$ and $\mathbf{proj}_k\, M_0 \mapsto W_k$, use Lemma 9, yielding $e \rightsquigarrow^* e_k'$ and $\Gamma \vdash e_k' : A_k \hookrightarrow W_k$.
- **Case** merge_k :
$$\mathcal{D} :: \dfrac{\cdot \vdash e_k : A \hookrightarrow M}{\cdot \vdash e_1 ,, e_2 : A \hookrightarrow M}$$
By i.h., $e_k \rightsquigarrow^* e'$ and $\cdot \vdash e' : A$. By rule 'step/unmerge', $e_1 ,, e_2 \rightsquigarrow e_k$. Therefore $e_1 ,, e_2 \rightsquigarrow^* e'$.
- **Case** $\to$E :
$$\mathcal{D} :: \dfrac{\cdot \vdash e_1 : A \to B \hookrightarrow M_1 \qquad \cdot \vdash e_2 : A \hookrightarrow M_2}{\cdot \vdash e_1\, e_2 : B \hookrightarrow M_1\, M_2}$$
We show one of the harder subcases (`consistency/app/beta` in `consistency.elf`). In this subcase, $M_1 = \lambda x.\, M_0$ and M_2 is a value, with $M_1\, M_2 \mapsto [M_2/x]M_0$. We use several easy lemmas about stepping; for example, `step*app1` says that if $e_1 \rightsquigarrow^* e_1'$ then $e_1\, e_2 \rightsquigarrow^* e_1'\, e_2$.

Elab1 ::	$\cdot \vdash e_1 : A \to B \hookrightarrow \lambda x.\, M_0$	Subd.
ElabBody ::	$x : A \vdash e_0 : B \hookrightarrow M_0$	By Lemma 10
StepsFun ::	$e_1 \rightsquigarrow^* \lambda x.\, e_0$	"
StepsApp ::	$e_1\, e_2 \rightsquigarrow^* (\lambda x.\, e_0)e_2$	By `step*app1`
Elab2 ::	$\cdot \vdash e_2 : A \hookrightarrow M_2$	Subd.
	M_2 value	Above
Elab2′ ::	$\cdot \vdash e_2 \rightsquigarrow^* v_2$	By Lemma 11
	$\cdot \vdash v_2 : A \hookrightarrow M_2$	"
	$(\lambda x.\, e_0)e_2 \rightsquigarrow^* (\lambda x.\, e_0)v_2$	By `step*app2`
	$e_1\, e_2 \rightsquigarrow^* (\lambda x.\, e_0)v_2$	By `step*append`
	$(\lambda x.\, e_0)v_2 \rightsquigarrow [v_2/x]e_0$	By 'step/beta'
StepsAppBeta ::	$e_1\, e_2 \rightsquigarrow^* [v_2/x]e_0$	By `step*snoc`
ElabBody ::	$x : A \vdash e_0 : B \hookrightarrow M_0$	Above
	$\cdot \vdash [v_2/x]e_0 : B \hookrightarrow [M_2/x]M_0$	By Lemma 12 (Elab2′) ☐

Theorem 14 (Multi-step Consistency).
If $\cdot \vdash e : A \hookrightarrow M$ *and* $M \mapsto^* W$ *then there exists* v *such that* $e \rightsquigarrow^* v$ *and* $\cdot \vdash v : A \hookrightarrow W$.

Proof. By induction on the derivation of $M \mapsto^* W$.

If M is some value w then, by Lemma 11, e is some value v. The source expression e steps to itself in zero steps, so $v \rightsquigarrow^* v$, and $\cdot \vdash v : A \hookrightarrow W$ is given ($e = v$ and $M = W$).

Otherwise, we have $M \mapsto M'$ where $M' \mapsto^* W$. We want to show $\cdot \vdash e' : A \hookrightarrow M'$, where $e \rightsquigarrow^* e'$. By Theorem 13, either $\cdot \vdash e : A \hookrightarrow M'$, or $e \rightsquigarrow e'$ and $\cdot \vdash e' : A \hookrightarrow M'$.

- If $\cdot \vdash e : A \hookrightarrow M'$, let $e' = e$, so $\cdot \vdash e' : A \hookrightarrow M'$ and $e \rightsquigarrow^* e'$ in zero steps.
- If $e \rightsquigarrow e'$ and $\cdot \vdash e' : A \hookrightarrow M'$, we can use the i.h., showing that $e' \rightsquigarrow^* v$ and $\cdot \vdash v : A \hookrightarrow W$.

See `consistency*` in `consistency.elf`. ☐

6.4 Summing Up

Theorem 15 (Static Semantics).
If $\cdot \vdash e : A$ *(using any of the rules in Figure 4) then there exists* e' *such that* $\cdot \vdash e' : A \hookrightarrow M$ *and* $\cdot \vdash M : |A|$.

Proof. By Theorems 1 (coercion), 5 (completeness of elaboration) and 6 (elaboration type soundness). ☐

Theorem 16 (Dynamic Semantics).
If $\cdot \vdash e : A \hookrightarrow M$ *and* $M \mapsto^* W$ *then there is a source value* v *such that* $e \rightsquigarrow^* v$ *and* $\cdot \vdash v : A$.

Proof. By Theorems 14 (multi-step consistency) and 4. ☐

Recalling the diagram in Figure 1, Theorem 16 shows that it commutes.

Both theorems are stated and proved in `summary.elf`. Combined with a run of the target program ($M \mapsto^* W$), they show that elaborated programs are consistent with source programs.

6.5 The Value Restriction

Davies and Pfenning (2000) showed that the then-standard intersection introduction (that is, our $\wedge$I) was unsound in a call-by-value semantics in the presence of effects (specifically, mutable references). Here is an example (modeled on theirs). Assume a base type nat with values $0, 1, 2, \ldots$ and a type pos of strictly positive naturals with values $1, 2, \ldots$; assume pos $\leq$ nat.

```
let r = (ref 1) : (nat ref) ∧ (pos ref) in
  r := 0;
  (!r) : pos
```

Using the unrestricted $\wedge$I rule, r has type (nat ref) $\wedge$ (pos ref); using $\wedge E_1$ yields r : nat ref, so the write $r := 0$ is well-typed; using $\wedge E_2$ yields r : pos ref, so the read $!r$ produces a pos. In an unelaborated setting, this typing is unsound: (**ref** 1) creates a single cell, initially containing 1, then overwritten with 0, so $!r \rightsquigarrow 0$, which does not have type pos.

Davies and Pfenning proposed, analogously to ML's value restriction on $\forall$-introduction, an $\wedge$-introduction rule that only types values v. This rule is sound with mutable references:

$$\dfrac{v : A_1 \qquad v : A_2}{v : A_1 \wedge A_2} \wedge\text{I} \ \textit{(Davies and Pfenning)}$$

In an elaboration system like ours, however, the problematic example above is sound, because our $\wedge$I elaborates **ref** 1 to two distinct expressions, which create two unaliased cells:

$$\frac{\textbf{ref}\ 1 : \mathsf{nat\ ref} \hookrightarrow \textbf{ref}\ 1 \qquad \textbf{ref}\ 1 : \mathsf{pos\ ref} \hookrightarrow \textbf{ref}\ 1}{\textbf{ref}\ 1 : \mathsf{nat\ ref} \wedge \mathsf{pos\ ref} \hookrightarrow (\textbf{ref}\ 1\ ,\ \textbf{ref}\ 1)} \wedge\mathrm{I}$$

Thus, the example elaborates to

$$\begin{array}{l}\textbf{let}\ \mathtt{r} = (\textbf{ref}\ 1\ ,\ \textbf{ref}\ 1)\ \textbf{in} \\ \quad (\textbf{proj}_1\ \mathtt{r}) := 0; \\ \quad (!\textbf{proj}_2\ \mathtt{r}) : \mathsf{pos}\end{array}$$

which is well-typed, but does not "go wrong" in the type-safety sense: the assignment writes to the first cell ($\wedge E_1$), and the dereference reads the second cell ($\wedge E_2$), which still contains the original value 1. The restriction-free $\wedge$I thus appears sound in our setting. Being *sound* is not the same as being *useful*, though; such behaviour is less than intuitive, as we discuss in the next section.

7. Coherence

The merge construct, while simple and powerful, has serious usability issues when the parts of the merge have overlapping types. Or, more accurately, when they would have overlapping types—types with nonempty intersection—in a merge-free system: in our system, *all* intersections $A \wedge B$ of nonempty A, B are nonempty: if $v_A : A$ and $v_B : B$ then $v_A ,, v_B : A \wedge B$ by merge_k and $\wedge$I.

According to the elaboration rules, $0 ,, 1$ (checked against nat) could elaborate to either 0 or 1. Our implementation would elaborate $0 ,, 1$ to 0, because it tries the left part 0 first. Arguably, this is better behaviour than actual randomness, but hardly helpful to the programmer. Perhaps even more confusingly, suppose we are checking $0 ,, 1$ against $\mathsf{pos} \wedge \mathsf{nat}$, where pos and nat are as in Section 6.5. Our implementation would elaborate $0 ,, 1$ to `(1, 0)`, but $1 ,, 0$ to `(1, 1)`.

Since the behaviour of the target program depends on the particular elaboration typing used, the system lacks *coherence* (Reynolds 1991).

To recover a coherent semantics, we could limit merges according to their surface syntax, as Reynolds did in Forsythe, but this seems restrictive; also, crafting an appropriate syntactic restriction depends on details of the type system, which is not robust as the type system is extended. A more general approach might be to reject (or warn about) merges in which more than one part checks against the same type (or the same part of an intersection type). Implementing this seems straightforward, though it would slow typechecking since we could not skip over e_2 when e_1 checks in $e_1 ,, e_2$.

Leaving merges aside, the mere fact that $\wedge$I elaborates the expression twice creates problems with mutable references, as we saw in Section 6.5. For this, we could revive the value restriction in $\wedge$I, at least for expressions whose types might overlap.

8. Applying Intersections and Unions

8.1 Overloading

A very simple use of unrestricted intersections is to "overload" operations such as multiplication and conversion of data to printable form. SML provides overloading only for a fixed set of built-in operations; it is not possible to write a single `square` function, as we do in Figure 10. Despite its appearance, `(*[ val square : ... ]*)` is not a comment but an annotation used to guide our bidirectional typechecker (this syntax, inherited from Stardust, was intended for compatibility with SML compilers, which saw these annotations as comments and ignored them).

In its present form, this idiom is less powerful than type classes (Wadler and Blott 1989). We could extend `toString` for lists, which would handle lists of integers and lists of reals, but not lists of lists; the version of `toString` for lists would use the *earlier* occurrence of `toString`, defined for integers and reals only. Adding a mechanism for naming a type and then "unioning" it, recursively, is future work.

```
val mul = Int.*
val toString = Int.toString

val mul = mul ,, Real.*   (* shadows earlier 'mul' *)
val toString = toString ,, Real.toString

(*[ val square : (int → int) ∧ (real → real) ]*)
val square = fn x ⇒ mul (x, x)

val _ = print (toString (mul (0.5, 300.0)) ^ "; ")
val _ = print (toString (square 9) ^ "; ")
val _ = print (toString (square 0.5) ^ "\n")
```

Output of target program after elaboration: `150.0; 81; 0.25`

Figure 10. Example of overloading

8.2 Records

Reynolds (1996) developed an encoding of records using intersection types and his version of the merge construct; similar ideas appear in Castagna et al. (1995). Though straightforward, this encoding is more expressive than SML records.

The idea is to add single-field records as a primitive notion, through a type `{fld : A}` with introduction form `{fld=e}` and the usual eliminations (explicit projection and pattern matching). Once this is done, the multi-field record type `{fld1 : A1, fld2 : A2}` is simply `{fld1 : A1}` $\wedge$ `{fld2 : A2}`, and the corresponding intro form is a merge: `{fld1=A1},,{fld2=A2}`. More standard concrete syntax, such as `{fld1=A1, fld2=A2}`, can be handled trivially during parsing.

With subtyping on intersections, we get the desired behaviour of what SML calls "flex records"—records with some fields not listed—with fewer of SML's limitations. Using this encoding, a function that expects a record with fields `x` and `y` can be given *any* record that has at least those fields, whereas SML only allows one fixed set of fields. For example, the code in Figure 11 is legal in our language but not in SML.

One problem with this approach is that expressions with duplicated field names are accepted. This is part of the larger issue discussed in Section 7.

8.3 Heterogeneous Data

A common argument for dynamic typing over static typing is that heterogeneous data structures are more convenient. For example, dynamic typing makes it very easy to create and manipulate lists containing both integers and strings. The penalty is the loss of compile-time invariant checking. Perhaps the lists should contain integers and strings, but not booleans; such an invariant is not expressible in traditional dynamic typing.

A common rebuttal from advocates of static typing is that it is easy to simulate dynamic typing in static typing. Want a list of integers and strings? Just declare a datatype

```
datatype int_or_string = Int of int
                       | String of string
```

and use `int_or_string lists`. This guarantees the invariant that the list has only integers and strings, but is unwieldy: each new element must be wrapped in a constructor, and operations on the list elements must unwrap the constructor, even when those operations accept both integers and strings (such as a function of type $(\mathsf{int} \rightarrow \mathsf{string}) \wedge (\mathsf{string} \rightarrow \mathsf{string})$).

```
(*[ val get_xy : {x:int, y:int} → int*int ]*)
fun get_xy r =
  (#x(r), #y(r))

(*[ val tupleToString : int * int → string ]*)
fun tupleToString (x, y) =
  "(" ^ Int.toString x ^ "," ^ Int.toString y ^ ")"

val rec1 = {y = 11, x = 1}
val rec2 = {x = 2, y = 22, extra = 100}
val rec3 = {x = 3, y = 33, other = "a string"}

val _ = print ("get_xy rec1 = "
               ^ tupleToString (get_xy rec1) ^ "\n")
val _ = print ("get_xy rec2 = "
               ^ tupleToString (get_xy rec2)
               ^ " (extra = "
               ^ Int.toString #extra(rec2) ^ ")\n")
val _ = print ("get_xy rec3 = "
               ^ tupleToString (get_xy rec3)
               ^ " (other = " ^ #other(rec3) ^ ")\n")
```

Output of target program after elaboration:

```
    get_xy rec1 = (1,11)
    get_xy rec2 = (2,22) (extra = 100)
    get_xy rec3 = (3,33) (other = a string)
```

Figure 11. Example of flexible multi-field records

```
datatype 'a list = nil | :: of 'a * 'a list

type dyn = int ∨ real ∨ string

(*[ val toString : dyn → string ]*)
fun toString x =
  (Int.toString ,,
   (fn s ⇒ s : string) ,,
   Real.toString) x

(*[ val hetListToString : dyn list → string ]*)
fun hetListToString xs = case xs of
    nil  ⇒ "nil"
  | h::t ⇒ (toString h) ^ "::"
           ^ (hetListToString t)

val _ = print "\n\n"
val _ = print (hetListToString
                 [1, 2, "what", 3.14159, 4, "why"])
val _ = print "\n\n\n"
```

Output of target program after elaboration:

```
    1::2::what::3.14159::4::why::nil
```

Figure 12. Example of heterogeneous data

In this situation, our approach provides the compile-time invariant checking of static typing *and* the transparency of dynamic typing. The type of list elements (if we bother to declare it) is just a union type:

```
type int_union_string = int ∨ string
```

Elaboration transforms programs with `int_union_string` into programs with `int_or_string`.

Along these lines, we use in Figure 12 a type `dyn`, defined as `int ∨ real ∨ string`. It would be useful to also allow lists, but the current implementation lacks recursive types of a form that could express "`dyn = ... ∨ dyn list`".

9. Implementation

Our implementation is faithful to the spirit of the elaboration rules above, but is substantially richer. It is based on Stardust, a typechecker for a subset of core Standard ML with support for inductive datatypes, products, intersections, unions, refinement types and indexed types (Dunfield 2007), extended with support for (first-class) polymorphism (Dunfield 2009). We do not yet support all these features; support for first-class polymorphism looks hardest, since Standard ML compilers cannot even handle higher-rank predicative polymorphism. Elaborating programs that use ML-style prenex polymorphism should work, but we currently lack any proof or even significant testing to back that up.

Our implementation does currently support merges, intersections and unions, a top type, a bottom (empty) type, single-field records and encoded multi-field records (Section 8.2), and inductive datatypes (if their constructors are not of intersection type, though they can take intersections and unions as argument; removing this restriction is a high priority).

9.1 Bidirectional Typechecking

Our implementation uses *bidirectional typechecking* (Pierce and Turner 2000; Dunfield and Pfenning 2004; Dunfield 2009), an increasingly common technique in advanced type systems; see Dunfield (2009) for references. This technique offers two major benefits over Damas-Milner type inference: it works for many type systems where annotation-free inference is undecidable, and it seems to produce more localized error messages.

Bidirectional typechecking does need more type annotations. However, by following the approach of Dunfield and Pfenning (2004), annotations are never needed except on redexes. The present implementation allows some annotations on redexes to be omitted as well.

The basic idea of bidirectional typechecking is to separate the activity of checking an expression against a known type from the activity of synthesizing a type from the expression itself:

$$\Gamma \vdash e \Leftarrow A \qquad \text{e checks against known type A}$$
$$\Gamma \vdash e \Rightarrow A \qquad \text{e synthesizes type A}$$

In the checking judgment, Γ, e and A are inputs to the typing algorithm, which either succeeds or fails. In the synthesis judgment, Γ and e are inputs and A is output (assuming synthesis does not fail).

Syntactically speaking, crafting a bidirectional type system from a type assignment system (like the one in Figure 4) is a matter of taking the colons in the $\Gamma \vdash e : A$ judgments, and replacing some with "$\Leftarrow$" and some with "$\Rightarrow$". Except for merge$_k$, our typing rules can all be found in Dunfield and Pfenning (2004), who argued that introduction rules should check and elimination rules should synthesize. (Parametric polymorphism muddies this picture, but see Dunfield (2009) for an approach used by our implementation.) For functions, this leads to the bidirectional rules

$$\frac{\Gamma, x : A \vdash e \Leftarrow B}{\Gamma \vdash \lambda x.\, e \Leftarrow A \to B}\to\mathrm{I} \qquad \frac{\Gamma \vdash e_1 \Rightarrow A \to B \qquad \Gamma \vdash e_2 \Leftarrow A}{\Gamma \vdash e_1\, e_2 \Rightarrow B}\to\mathrm{E}$$

The merge rule, however, neither introduces nor eliminates. We implement the obvious checking rule (which, in practice, always tries to check against e_1 and, if that fails, against e_2):

$$\frac{\Gamma \vdash e_k \Leftarrow A}{\Gamma \vdash e_1 ,, e_2 \Leftarrow A}$$

Since it can be inconvenient to annotate merges, we also implement synthesis rules, including one that can synthesize an intersection.

$$\frac{\Gamma \vdash e_k \Rightarrow A}{\Gamma \vdash e_1 ,, e_2 \Rightarrow A} \qquad \frac{\Gamma \vdash e_1 \Rightarrow A_1 \qquad \Gamma \vdash e_2 \Rightarrow A_2}{\Gamma \vdash e_1 ,, e_2 \Rightarrow A_1 \wedge A_2}$$

Given a bidirectional typing derivation, it is generally easy to show that a corresponding type assignment exists: replace all "$\Rightarrow$" and "$\Leftarrow$" with ":" (and erase explicit type annotations from the expression).

9.2 Performance

Intersection typechecking is PSPACE-hard (Reynolds 1996). In practice, we elaborate the examples in Figures 10, 11 and 12 in less than a second, but they are very small. On somewhat larger examples, such as those discussed by Dunfield (2007), the non-elaborating version of Stardust could take minutes, thanks to heavy use of backtracking search (trying $\wedge E_1$ then $\wedge E_2$, etc.) and the need to check the same expression against different types ($\wedge$I) or with different assumptions ($\vee$E). Elaboration doesn't help with this, but it shouldn't hurt by more than a constant factor: the shapes of the derivations and the labour of backtracking remain the same.

To scale the approach to larger programs, we will need to consider how to efficiently represent elaborated intersections and unions. Like the theoretical development, the implementation has 2-way intersection and union types, so the type $A_1 \wedge A_2 \wedge A_3$ is parsed as $(A_1 \wedge A_2) \wedge A_3$, which becomes $(A_1 * A_2) * A_3$. A flattened representation $A_1 * A_2 * A_3$ would be more efficient, except when the program uses values of type $(A_1 \wedge A_2) \wedge A_3$ where values of type $A_1 \wedge A_2$ are expected; in that case, nesting the product allows the inner pair to be passed directly with no reboxing. Symmetry is also likely to be an issue: passing $v : A_1 \wedge A_2$ where $v : A_2 \wedge A_1$ is expected requires building a new pair. Here, it may be helpful to put the components of intersections into a canonical order.

The foregoing applies to unions as well—introducing a value of a three-way union may require two injections, and so on.

10. Related Work

Intersections were originally developed by Coppo et al. (1981) and Pottinger (1980), among others; Hindley (1992) gives a useful introduction and bibliography. Work on union types began later (MacQueen et al. 1986); Barbanera et al. (1995) is a key paper on type assignment for unions.

Forsythe. In the late 1980s[3], Reynolds invented Forsythe (Reynolds 1996), the first practical programming language based on intersection types. In addition to an unmarked introduction rule like $\wedge$I, the Forsythe type system includes rules for typing a construct p_1, p_2—"a construction for intersecting or 'merging' meanings" (Reynolds 1996, p. 24). Roughly analogous to $e_1 ,, e_2$, this construct is used to encode a variety of features, but can only be used unambiguously. For instance, a record and a function can be merged, but two functions cannot (actually they can, but the second phrase p_2 overrides the first). Forsythe does not have union types.

The λ&-calculus. Castagna et al. (1995) developed the λ&-calculus, which has &-terms—functions whose body is a merge, and whose type is an intersection of arrows. In their semantics, applying a &-term to some argument reduces the term to the branch of the merge with the smallest (compatible) domain. Suppose we have a &-term with two branches, one of type $\mathsf{nat} \to \mathsf{nat}$ and one of type $\mathsf{pos} \to \mathsf{pos}$. Applying that &-term to a value of type pos steps to the second branch, because its domain pos is (strictly) a subtype of nat.

Despite the presence of a merge-like construct, their work on the λ&-calculus is markedly different from ours: it gives a semantics to programs directly, and uses type information to do so, whereas we elaborate to a standard term language with no runtime type information. In their work, terms have both *compile-time types* and *run-time types* (the run-time types become more precise as the computation continues); the semantics of applying a &-term depends on the run-time type of the argument to choose the branch. The choice of the *smallest* compatible domain is consistent with notions of inheritance in object-oriented programming, where a class can override the methods of its parent.

Semantic subtyping. Following the λ&-calculus, Frisch et al. (2008) investigated a notion of purely semantic subtyping, where the definition of subtyping arises from a model of types, as opposed to the syntactic approach used in our system. They support intersections, unions, function spaces and even complement. Their language includes a *dynamic type dispatch* which, very roughly, combines a merge with a generalization of our union elimination. Again, the semantics relies on run-time type information.

Pierce's work. The earliest reference I know for the idea of compiling intersection to product is Pierce (1991b): "a language with intersection types might even provide two different object-code sequences for the two versions of + [for int and for real]" (p. 11). Pierce also developed a language with union types, including a term-level construct to explicitly eliminate them (Pierce 1991a). But this construct is only a marker for where to eliminate the union: it has only one branch, so the same term must typecheck under each assumption. Another difference is that this construct is the only way to eliminate a union type in his system, whereas our $\vee$E is marker-free. Intersections, also present in his language, have no explicit introduction construct; the introduction rule is like our $\wedge$I.

Flow types. Turbak et al. (1997) and Wells et al. (2002) use intersections in a system with flow types. They produce programs with *virtual tuples* and *virtual sums*, which correspond to the tuples and sums we produce by elaboration. However, these constructs are internal: nothing in their work corresponds to our explicit intersection and union term constructors, since their system is only intended to capture existing flow properties. They do not compile the virtual constructs into the ordinary ones.

Heterogeneous data and dynamic typing. Several approaches to combining dynamic typing's transparency and static typing's guarantees have been investigated. *Soft typing* (Cartwright and Fagan 1991; Aiken et al. 1994) adds a kind of type inference on top of dynamic typing, but provides no ironclad guarantees. Typed Scheme (Tobin-Hochstadt and Felleisen 2008), developed to retroactively type Scheme programs, has a flow-sensitive type system with union types, directly supporting heterogeneous data in the style of Section 8.3. Unlike soft typing, Typed Scheme guarantees type safety and provides genuine (even first-class) polymorphism, though programmers are expected to provide some annotations.

Type refinements. Restricting intersections and unions to refinements of a single base type simplifies many issues, and is conservative: programs can be checked against refined types, then compiled normally. This approach has been explored for intersections (Freeman and Pfenning 1991; Davies and Pfenning 2000), and for intersections and unions (Dunfield and Pfenning 2003, 2004).

11. Conclusion

We have laid a simple yet powerful foundation for compiling unrestricted intersections and unions: elaboration into a standard functional language. Rather than trying to directly understand the behaviours of source programs, we describe them via their consistency with the target programs.

The most immediate challenge is coherence: While our elaboration approach guarantees type safety of the compiled program, the

[3] The citation year 1996 is the date of the revised description of Forsythe; the core ideas are found in Reynolds (1988).

meaning of the compiled program depends on the particular elaboration typing derivation used; the meaning of the source program is actually implementation-defined.

One possible solution is to restrict typing of merges so that a merge has type A only if *exactly one* branch has type A. We could also partially revive the value restriction, giving non-values intersection type only if (to a conservative approximation) both components of the intersection are provably disjoint, in the sense that no merge-free expression has both types.

Another challenge is to reconcile, in spirit and form, the unrestricted view of intersections and unions of this paper with the refinement approach. Elaborating a refinement intersection like $(\mathsf{pos} \rightarrow \mathsf{neg}) \wedge (\mathsf{neg} \rightarrow \mathsf{pos})$ to a pair of functions seems pointless (unless it can somehow facilitate optimizations in the compiler). It will probably be necessary to have "refinement" and "unrestricted" versions of the intersection and union type constructors, at least during elaboration; it may be feasible to hide this distinction at the source level.

Acknowledgments

In 2008, Adam Megacz suggested (after I explained the idea of compiling intersection to product) that one could use an existing ML compiler "as a backend". The anonymous ICFP reviewers' suggestions have (I hope) significantly improved the presentation. Finally, I had useful discussions about this work with Yan Chen, Matthew A. Hammer, Scott Kilpatrick, Neelakantan R. Krishnaswami, and Viktor Vafeiadis.

References

Alexander Aiken, Edward L. Wimmers, and T. K. Lakshman. Soft typing with conditional types. In *Principles of Programming Languages*, pages 163–173, 1994.

Franco Barbanera, Mariangiola Dezani-Ciancaglini, and Ugo de'Liguoro. Intersection and union types: syntax and semantics. *Information and Computation*, 119:202–230, 1995.

Robert Cartwright and Mike Fagan. Soft typing. In *Programming Language Design and Implementation*, pages 278–292, 1991.

Giuseppe Castagna, Giorgio Ghelli, and Giuseppe Longo. A calculus for overloaded functions with subtyping. *Information and Computation*, 117(1):115–135, 1995.

M. Coppo, M. Dezani-Ciancaglini, and B. Venneri. Functional characters of solvable terms. *Zeitschrift f. math. Logik und Grundlagen d. Math.*, 27:45–58, 1981.

Rowan Davies. *Practical Refinement-Type Checking*. PhD thesis, Carnegie Mellon University, 2005. CMU-CS-05-110.

Rowan Davies and Frank Pfenning. Intersection types and computational effects. In *ICFP*, pages 198–208, 2000.

Joshua Dunfield. Refined typechecking with Stardust. In *Programming Languages meets Program Verification (PLPV '07)*, 2007.

Joshua Dunfield. Greedy bidirectional polymorphism. In *ML Workshop*, pages 15–26, 2009. `http://www.cs.cmu.edu/~joshuad/papers/poly/`.

Joshua Dunfield. Untangling typechecking of intersections and unions. In *2010 Workshop on Intersection Types and Related Systems*, volume 45 of *EPTCS*, pages 59–70, 2011. `arXiv: 1101.4428v1[cs.PL]`.

Joshua Dunfield. Twelf proofs accompanying this paper, March 2012. `http://www.cs.cmu.edu/~joshuad/intcomp.tar` or `http://www.cs.cmu.edu/~joshuad/intcomp/`.

Joshua Dunfield and Frank Pfenning. Type assignment for intersections and unions in call-by-value languages. In *Found. Software Science and Computation Structures (FoSSaCS '03)*, pages 250–266, 2003.

Joshua Dunfield and Frank Pfenning. Tridirectional typechecking. In *Principles of Programming Languages*, pages 281–292, 2004.

Tim Freeman and Frank Pfenning. Refinement types for ML. In *Programming Language Design and Implementation*, pages 268–277, 1991.

Alain Frisch, Giuseppe Castagna, and Véronique Benzaken. Semantic subtyping: dealing set-theoretically with function, union, intersection, and negation types. *J. ACM*, 55(4):1–64, 2008.

J. Roger Hindley. Coppo-Dezani types do not correspond to propositional logic. *Theoretical Computer Science*, 28:235–236, 1984.

J. Roger Hindley. Types with intersection: An introduction. *Formal Aspects of Computing*, 4:470–486, 1992.

Assaf J. Kfoury and J. B. Wells. Principality and type inference for intersection types using expansion variables. *Theoretical Computer Science*, 311(1–3):1–70, 2004.

David MacQueen, Gordon Plotkin, and Ravi Sethi. An ideal model for recursive polymorphic types. *Information and Control*, 71: 95–130, 1986.

Peter Møller Neergaard and Harry G. Mairson. Types, potency, and idempotency: Why nonlinearity and amnesia make a type system work. In *ICFP*, pages 138–149, 2004.

Frank Pfenning and Carsten Schürmann. System description: Twelf—a meta-logical framework for deductive systems. In *Int'l Conf. Automated Deduction (CADE-16)*, pages 202–206, 1999.

Benjamin C. Pierce. Programming with intersection types, union types, and polymorphism. Technical Report CMU-CS-91-106, Carnegie Mellon University, 1991a.

Benjamin C. Pierce. *Programming with intersection types and bounded polymorphism*. PhD thesis, Carnegie Mellon University, 1991b. Technical Report CMU-CS-91-205.

Benjamin C. Pierce and David N. Turner. Local type inference. *ACM Trans. Prog. Lang. Syst.*, 22:1–44, 2000.

Garrel Pottinger. A type assignment for the strongly normalizable lambda-terms. In *To H. B. Curry: Essays on Combinatory Logic, Lambda Calculus and Formalism*, pages 561–577. Academic Press, 1980.

John C. Reynolds. Preliminary design of the programming language Forsythe. Technical Report CMU-CS-88-159, Carnegie Mellon University, 1988. `http://doi.library.cmu.edu/10.1184/OCLC/18612825`.

John C. Reynolds. The coherence of languages with intersection types. In *Theoretical Aspects of Computer Software*, volume 526 of *LNCS*, pages 675–700. Springer, 1991.

John C. Reynolds. Design of the programming language Forsythe. Technical Report CMU-CS-96-146, Carnegie Mellon University, 1996.

Sam Tobin-Hochstadt and Matthias Felleisen. The design and implementation of Typed Scheme. In *Principles of Programming Languages*, pages 395–406, 2008.

Franklyn Turbak, Allyn Dimock, Robert Muller, and J. B. Wells. Compiling with polymorphic and polyvariant flow types. In *Int'l Workshop on Types in Compilation*, 1997.

Twelf. Twelf wiki, 2012. `http://twelf.org/wiki/Main_Page`.

Philip Wadler and Stephen Blott. How to make *ad-hoc* polymorphism less *ad hoc*. In *Principles of Programming Languages*, pages 60–76, 1989.

J.B. Wells, Allyn Dimock, Robert Muller, and Franklyn Turbak. A calculus with polymorphic and polyvariant flow types. *J. Functional Programming*, 12(3):183–227, 2002.

An Error-Tolerant Type System for Variational Lambda Calculus

Sheng Chen, Martin Erwig, Eric Walkingshaw
School of EECS, Oregon State University
{chensh,erwig,walkiner}@eecs.oregonstate.edu

Abstract

Conditional compilation and software product line technologies make it possible to generate a huge number of different programs from a single software project. Typing each of these programs individually is usually impossible due to the sheer number of possible variants. Our previous work has addressed this problem with a type system for variational lambda calculus (VLC), an extension of lambda calculus with basic constructs for introducing and organizing variation. Although our type inference algorithm is more efficient than the brute-force strategy of inferring the types of each variant individually, it is less robust since type inference will fail for the entire variational expression if any one variant contains a type error. In this work, we extend our type system to operate on VLC expressions containing type errors. This extension directly supports locating ill-typed variants and the incremental development of variational programs. It also has many subtle implications for the unification of variational types. We show that our extended type system possesses a principal typing property and that the underlying unification problem is unitary. Our unification algorithm computes partial unifiers that lead to result types that (1) contain errors in as few variants as possible and (2) are most general. Finally, we perform an empirical evaluation to determine the overhead of this extension compared to our previous work, to demonstrate the improvements over the brute-force approach, and to explore the effects of various error distributions on the inference process.

Categories and Subject Descriptors D.3.2 [*Programming Languages*]: Language Classifications – applicative (functional) languages; F.3.3 [*Logics and Meanings of Programs*]: Studies of Program Constructs – type structure

Keywords error-tolerant type systems; variational lambda calculus; variational type inference; variational types

1. Introduction

The source code of many software projects can be used to generate a huge number of distinct programs that run on different platforms and provide different sets of features. Current research on software product lines (SPLs) [20] and feature-oriented software development [2] provide processes and tools for the development of massively configurable software, suggesting that the variability of software systems will only continue to grow. Unfortunately, basic program verification tools, such as type systems, are not equipped to deal with variation on this scale. Notions of type correctness are defined in terms of single programs only, but generating all program variants and testing each one individually is usually impossible due to the sheer number of variants that can be generated.

The problem of type checking variational software is an active area of research [11, 12, 25]. Most of this work comes out of the SPL community and is therefore highly pragmatic, tool-oriented, and focused on imperative languages. Our work on this problem, begun in [5], distinguishes itself in several ways. Most significantly, while other approaches consider only type checking of programs in explicitly typed languages, we solve the more general problem of *type inference* for implicitly typed languages. Our approach begins by establishing a simple functional language, the *variational lambda calculus* (VLC), for studying variational software; it introduces a notion of *variational types* for typing variational programs; it develops a formal type system that associates variational types with VLC expressions; and it presents an algorithm that infers these types. By addressing the problem from a more theoretical and fundamental perspective, we believe our results are more reusable and extensible than others. Variational types are also a general contribution to type theory that have other potential applications; for example, they may be useful for more flexibly typing metaprograms.

A subtle difference between the problems of checking explicitly typed programs and inferring types in implicitly typed programs is that, in general, a type error encountered during inference prevents inference in the rest of the program. This means that while our solution is more general, it is less *robust*. A type error in a single variant will cause the entire inference process to fail. In this work we extend our type system and inference algorithm to allow for type errors at arbitrary positions in the inferred variational type. This extension directly supports the location of ill-typed variants, and the ability to incrementally develop variational programs by leaving some variational branches undefined or incomplete while other variants are extended and fleshed out. While the focus in [5] is on establishing a broad foundation for formal work on typing and other static analyses of variational programs, here we focus on solving a specific problem of practical importance. Solving this problem is surprisingly challenging and leads to many interesting theoretical results, summarized in Section 1.2.

1.1 Motivation

In this section we will briefly motivate this work by way of a simple example. We also motivate and explain our choice of VLC as a formal foundation for typing variational programs.

In general, there are three competing approaches to managing variational software, each with their own strengths and weaknesses. *Compositional* approaches rely on language features like mixins [4] or aspects [16] to modularize features that may or may not be included in a generated variant. This approach is mostly used in conjunction with object-oriented programming languages. *Metaprogramming*-based approaches rely on staged computations to generate program variants through the use of macros; this is especially

ICFP'12, September 9–15, 2012, Copenhagen, Denmark.

common in functional languages, for example, MetaML [24] and the Lisp family. Finally, *annotative* approaches rely on a separate annotation language to embed static variation directly within the source code. The C Preprocessor (CPP) is by far the most widely used annotative variation tool. One of the advantages of the annotative approach is that it is mostly independent of the object language and so can be applied across paradigms (and even in documentation and other non-source code). CPP annotations are frequently seen in large-scale Haskell programs, for example, GHC [9].

Although all three approaches are worthy of study, we choose the annotative approach here because it makes the variation in a program explicit, allowing us to directly traverse and manipulate the variation structure. This is not the case, for example, in metaprogramming approaches, where variability is captured only implicitly in the definition and use of macros. While our annotation language is much less powerful than metaprogramming systems, it allows us to support a much more general form of type-safe variation than is possible in, for example, MetaML.

Consider two different ways to implement a function in Haskell to find values in a lookup list of type `[(a,b)]`. In the first, we return a value of type `Maybe b`, possibly containing the first value in the lookup list associated with a given key of type `a`.

```
find x ((k,v):t) | x == k    = Just v
                 | otherwise = find x t
find _ []                    = Nothing
```

In the second, we return a list of type `[b]`, containing all of the values in the lookup list associated with the key.

```
find x ((k,v):t) | x == k    = v : find x t
                 | otherwise = find x t
find _ []                    = []
```

Based on a notation developed in [8], we can represent the variation between these two function implementations by annotating the program in-place. First, we declare a new *dimension* of variation, *Res*, representing variation in the function's result. Then we indicate the specific variation points in the code using *choices* that are bound to the *Res* dimension.

```
dim Res⟨fst,all⟩ in
find x ((k,v):t) | x == k    = Res⟨Just v,v:find x t⟩
                 | otherwise = find x t
find _ []                    = Res⟨Nothing,[]⟩
```

The *Res* dimension declaration above states that we can select one of two *tags* in the dimension: *fst*, to return the first found value, or *all*, to return all found values. The two choices in the body of the function are synchronized with these tags. For example, if we select the *fst* tag in the *Res* dimension (written *Res.fst*), the first alternative in each of the two choices in the *Res* dimension will also be selected, producing the first function definition above.

The types inferred in a variational program are also variational. For our `find` function, we infer the following *variational type* which also contains a choice in the *Res* dimension.[1]

```
find :: a -> [(a,b)] -> Res⟨Maybe b,[b]⟩
```

Using the variational type inference algorithm we have developed in [5] we can infer types like the above. A successfully inferred variational type indicates that all variants of the program are type correct. Since the typing information of shared code is reused (and for other reasons), a type-correctness result can be obtained much more efficiently in the expected case than the brute-force strategy of generating all variants and type checking them separately. For large variational programs with many dimensions of variation, the efficiency gains can make type checking all variants tractable, when otherwise it would not be.

However, variational type inference has a hidden cost relative to the brute-force strategy. While variational type inference is more efficient at *detecting errors*, it is less useful for *locating errors*. To demonstrate, suppose we add a new dimension of variation to our `find` function, *Arg*, that captures variation between looking up values based on an example key (as above) or looking up values based on a predicate on keys. We name the tags corresponding to these possibilities *val* and *pred*, respectively.

```
dim Arg⟨val,pred⟩ in
dim Res⟨fst,all⟩ in
find Arg⟨x,p⟩ ((k,v):t)
      | Arg⟨x == k,p k⟩ = Res⟨Just v,v:find x t⟩
      | otherwise       = find Arg⟨x,p⟩ t
find _ []               = Res⟨Nothing,[]⟩
```

Since we can make our selections in the *Res* and *Arg* dimensions independently, this new expression represents four total program variants. We expect variational type inference to infer the following variational type for our new implementation of `find`.

```
find :: Arg⟨a,(a -> Bool)⟩ -> [(a,b)] -> Res⟨Maybe b,[b]⟩
```

But there is an error in the above definition that causes variational type inference to fail. The error is that the variable `x` is unbound in `find x t` if we select *Arg.pred* and *Res.all*.

This can be easily fixed by replacing `x` with the choice *Arg*⟨`x`,`p`⟩. The problem is that the type inference algorithm presented in [5] provides no hint at the location of this error—it just fails, indicating that there *is* an error. The brute-force strategy is more robust. By type checking each variant individually, we can determine exactly which variant(s) contain type errors and infer types for those that are type correct. Of course, the brute-force strategy scales just as poorly for error location as it does for type checking (although it might be able to be used strategically, if one can correctly guess the variants that contain errors).

In this paper we extend variational type inference to return partially correct variational types—that is, variational types containing errors. For example, the errorful variational type of our `find` function can be written as follows, where ⊥ is a special type that indicates a type error at that location in the type.

```
find :: Arg⟨a,(a -> Bool)⟩ -> [(a,b)]
     -> Res⟨Maybe b,Arg⟨[b],⊥⟩⟩
```

This type indicates that there is a type error in the result type of the function if the second tag is chosen from each dimension (*Arg.pred* and *Res.all*). This extension therefore directly supports the location of type errors in variational programs without resorting to the brute-force strategy of typing variants individually. Similarly, it supports type inference on incomplete variational programs—programs in which only some variants are in a complete and type-correct state—a quality which is needed for incremental development.

The addition of error types is a non-trivial extension to the type system and inference algorithm presented in [5]. In particular, there are many subtle implications for the unification of variational types. In the case of an unbound variable, as above, the location of the error is obvious. However, often there are many possible candidates for the type error, depending on how we infer the surrounding types. The goal is to assign errors such that as few variants as possible are considered ill-typed, that is, to find a type that is *most-defined*. This goal is in addition to the usual goal of inferring the *most general* type possible. It is not obvious whether these two qualities of types are orthogonal. In this paper we will show that they are, and we present an inference algorithm that identifies most-defined, most-general types.

[1] To keep the following discussion simpler, we omit the `Eq` type class constraint on `a`.

1.2 Contributions and Rest of Paper

In the next section we briefly introduce the syntax and semantics of VLC, developed in [5], which is the formal foundation of this work. The structure of the rest of the paper is described relative to the major contributions of this work, which are:

1. The extension of our variational type system to support the typing of programs in which not all variants are well typed. The extension of the types themselves is discussed in Section 3, and the extension of the typing rules in Section 5. A type preservation theorem (Theorem 1) in Section 5 formally establishes the relationship between a variational type identified by our type system and the set of types or type errors produced by the brute-force force approach.

2. The concept of *typing patterns*, defined in Section 4, that indicate which variants of a variational program are well-typed, and an associated *more-defined* relation for comparing them. We use these in Section 6 to prove several results about the problem of unifying variational types containing type errors. Most significantly, we show that for any unification problem, there is a mapping that produces the most-defined result type (Theorem 2), and that among such mappings, there is a unique mapping that produces the most-general result type (Theorem 3).

3. A unification algorithm on variational types with type errors, given in Section 7, that produces unifiers that result in most-defined, most-general types. This is the core component of a type inference algorithm that implements the type system presented in this paper, given in Section 8. We show that both algorithms are sound (Theorems 4 and 6) and complete (Theorem 5 and 7).

4. A theoretical and experimental evaluation of these algorithms. In Section 7, we show that unification of variational types with errors does not increase the complexity of unifying variational types. In Section 9, we conduct experiments that demonstrate that the overhead to support error-tolerant type inference is minor and that our algorithm offers significant performance improvements over the brute-force approach. The evaluation results also reveal an interesting relationship between the distribution of type errors in an expression and the time it takes to infer a type for that expression.

Finally, in Section 10 we discuss related work and offer conclusions and directions for future work in Section 11.

The following table provides a short overview of the notation used throughout the paper. It is meant as an aid to find definitions faster (§ indicates the section(s) containing the definition).

Syntactic Categories	§	Operations	§
Expressions (e)	2.1	Selection $\lfloor e \rfloor_{D.t}$, $\lfloor T \rfloor_{D.i}$	2.2, 3
Types (T)	3	Semantics $[\![\cdot]\!]$	2.2
Typing patterns (P)	4	Masking $P \lhd T$	4
Environments (Γ, Δ)	5	Pattern union $P_1 \oplus P_2$	4
Mappings (θ)	6.2	Type matching $T_1 \bowtie T_2$	4
Partial unifiers (η)	6.2	Arrow lifting $\uparrow(T)$	5
Qual. type vars ($a_{A\tilde{B}}$)	7.1	Decision to selectors $\varphi_e(\overline{q})$	5

Relationships	§	Results	§
Equivalence $T_1 \equiv T_2$	3	Type preservation	5
Definedness $P_1 \leq P_2$	4	Principal patterns	6.2
More general $\theta_1 \sqsubseteq \theta_2$	6.1	*unify* sound & complete	7.2
		infer sound & complete	8

2. Variational Lambda Calculus

While the example from the previous section was presented in Haskell, here and in our previous work on typing variational functional programs we consider a simpler language, the *variational lambda calculus* (VLC). VLC is a conservative extension of lambda calculus with constructs for introducing and organizing static variation. Constraining the problem to VLC allows us to focus on the fundamental problem of typing variational programs and to present our solution as clearly and simply as possible. In [5] we describe how the variational type system can be extended to incorporate other, more advanced language features. In this section we briefly describe the syntax and semantics of VLC.

2.1 Syntax

VLC is based on our previous work on the *choice calculus* [8]. The choice calculus is a fundamental representation of variation in arbitrary tree structures (such as a program's abstract syntax tree), designed to serve as a general foundation for theoretical research in the field of variation management. The key features of the choice calculus were already introduced in the previous section, namely, *choices* and *dimensions*.[2] Choices specify a point of variation in a tree, while dimensions are used to synchronize and scope related choices.

The syntax of VLC is given below. The first four constructs in the syntax definition correspond to lambda calculus extended with constant values, while the dimension and choice constructs are from the choice calculus. If a VLC expression contains no dimension or choice constructs, we call the expression *plain*.

$$
\begin{array}{rcll}
e & ::= & c & \textit{Constant} \\
 & | & x & \textit{Variable} \\
 & | & \lambda x.e & \textit{Abstraction} \\
 & | & e\ e & \textit{Application} \\
 & | & \textbf{dim}\ D\langle t,t\rangle\ \textbf{in}\ e & \textit{Dimension} \\
 & | & D\langle e,e\rangle & \textit{Choice}
\end{array}
$$

Note that every dimension must contain exactly two tags and all choices must contain exactly two alternatives. This is a constraint made for presentation purposes only. Variation in dimensions with n tags can be easily simulated by $n-1$ binary dimensions. More fundamental syntactic constraints are that the tags associated with one dimension must be different (so that they can be uniquely referred to for selection), and that every choice must occur within scope of a corresponding dimension declaration.

2.2 Semantics

A VLC expression defines a set of *named variants*—a set of plain lambda calculus expressions identified by the selections that must be performed to produce them. These variants are computed *statically*. That is, the full semantics of a VLC expression consists of two distinct stages: a *selection* stage that eliminates all dimensions and choices through tag selection, and an *evaluation* stage that evaluates the resulting plain lambda calculus expression. When we speak of the semantics of a VLC expression in this paper, we refer only to the selection stage, which is briefly described below (a more thorough treatment can be found in [8]).

To select a particular plain expression from a VLC expression, we must repeatedly select tags from dimensions until we are left with an expression with no dimensions or choices. We write $\lfloor e \rfloor_{D.t}$ for the selection of tag t from dimension D in expression e. Tag selection is performed by replacing in e the topmost-leftmost dimension declaration $\textbf{dim}\ D\langle t_1,t_2\rangle\ \textbf{in}\ e'$ with a version of e' that is obtained by substituting choices bound by D with either their first or second alternatives (depending on whether $t=t_1$ or $t=t_2$). If e does not contain a dimension D, it remains unchanged.

A *decision* is a sequence of dimension-qualified tags. A decision that produces a plain expression is called a *complete decision*. The (selection) semantics $[\![e]\!]$ of an expression e is then a mapping from complete decisions to plain lambda calculus expressions.

$$
\begin{array}{c}
[\![\textbf{dim}\ A\langle t_1,t_2\rangle\ \textbf{in}\ A\langle \lambda x.x, \lambda y.\textbf{dim}\ B\langle t_3,t_4\rangle\ \textbf{in}\ B\langle 2,3\rangle\rangle]\!] = \\
\{([A.t_1],\lambda x.x),([A.t_2,B.t_3],\lambda y.2),([A.t_2,B.t_4],\lambda y.3)\}
\end{array}
$$

[2] We omit here for simplicity two constructs for sharing since they do not affect the type system in any way.

Note that tags in dimension A always occur before tags in dimension B in the domain of the mapping. Also, note that dimension B does not appear at all in the first decision since it is eliminated by the selection of the tag $A.t_1$.

3. Partial Variational Types

In Section 1 we motivated the use of *variational types* for typing variational programs. In this section we extend this representation to support *partial variational types*, that is, variational types that contain type errors. The extended representation is given below.

T	$::=$	τ	*Constant Type*
	$\mid$	a	*Type Variable*
	$\mid$	$T \to T$	*Function Type*
	$\mid$	$D\langle T,T\rangle$	*Choice Type*
	$\mid$	$\bot$	*Error Type*
	$\mid$	$\top$	*OK Type*

Constant types, type variables, and function types are as in other type systems—*plain types* contain only these three constructs.

Non-plain types may also contain *choice types*. Choice types encode variation in types in the same way that choices encode variation in expressions, with the exception that dimension names in types are globally scoped (see [5] for the rationale). Choice types often correspond directly to choice expressions; for example, the subexpression $A\langle\lambda x.\texttt{true},3\rangle$ might have the corresponding choice type $A\langle a \to \texttt{Bool},\texttt{Int}\rangle$. Since there are no tags at the type level, we extend selection to types by writing $\lfloor T\rfloor_{D.i}$, where $i \in \{1,2\}$, to represent selecting the ith alternative in all choices in dimension D. If T contains no such choices, then $\lfloor T\rfloor_{D.i} = T$. We call $D.i$ a *selector* and allow selections on types to be made in any order.

The *error type*, $\bot$, represents a type error and can appear anywhere in a variational type. We say that a variational type is *partial* if it contains one or more error types and *complete* otherwise.

Finally, the symbol $\top$ is used to represent an arbitrary complete type that also contains no type variables, that is, a type that is monomorphic and error-free. This abstraction is only used in *typing patterns*, which are described in the next section.

Many syntactically different types can be considered *equivalent* in that they represent essentially the same mapping from decisions to plain types. Type equivalency is an important concept in typing variational programs. For example, usually when applying a function of type $T \to T'$ to an argument of type T'', we require that $T = T''$, but this requirement is too strict in the variational setting. Consider the expression $\texttt{succ}\,A\langle 1,2\rangle$. The type of `succ` is $\texttt{Int} \to \texttt{Int}$ while the type of the argument is $A\langle\texttt{Int},\texttt{Int}\rangle$. Even though $\texttt{Int} \neq A\langle\texttt{Int},\texttt{Int}\rangle$, the expression should be considered well-typed because both variants (`succ 1` and `succ 2`) are well-typed. Thus, we say that the two types are *equivalent*, written $\texttt{Int} \equiv A\langle\texttt{Int},\texttt{Int}\rangle$, and require only equivalency rather equality in well-typed function applications.

Figure 1 gives the type equivalence relation in full. Most of the equivalence rules are straightforward. The FUN and CHOICE rules propagate equivalency across function types and choice types, the F-C rule commutes function types and choice types, and the two SWAP rules commute choice types in different dimensions. The three rules at the bottom of the figure make the relation reflexive, symmetric, and transitive. The two interesting cases are C-IDEMP and the MERGE rules. The C-IDEMP rule captures the property of *choice idempotency*, demonstrated in the example above. The MERGE rules capture the property of *choice domination*. For example, given the choice type $D\langle D\langle T_1,T_2\rangle,T_3\rangle$, we say that the outer choice dominates the inner since there is no way to select type T_2—the selection of the first alternative in the outer choice implies the selection of the first alternative in the inner choice. Note that choice domination only applies to nested choices *in the same dimension*.

FUN
$$\frac{T_l' \equiv T_r' \qquad T_l \equiv T_r}{T_l' \to T_l \equiv T_r' \to T_r}$$

F-C
$$D\langle T_1,T_2\rangle \to D\langle T_1',T_2'\rangle \equiv D\langle T_1 \to T_1',T_2 \to T_2'\rangle$$

C-C-SWAP1
$$D'\langle D\langle T_1,T_2\rangle,T_3\rangle \equiv D\langle D'\langle T_1,T_3\rangle,D'\langle T_2,T_3\rangle\rangle$$

C-C-SWAP2
$$D'\langle T_1,D\langle T_2,T_3\rangle\rangle \equiv D\langle D'\langle T_1,T_2\rangle,D'\langle T_1,T_3\rangle\rangle$$

C-C-MERGE1
$$D\langle D\langle T_1,T_2\rangle,T_3\rangle \equiv D\langle T_1,T_3\rangle$$

C-C-MERGE2
$$D\langle T_1,D\langle T_2,T_3\rangle\rangle \equiv D\langle T_1,T_3\rangle$$

CHOICE
$$\frac{T_1 \equiv T_1' \qquad T_2 \equiv T_2'}{D\langle T_1,T_2\rangle \equiv D\langle T_1',T_2'\rangle}$$

C-IDEMP
$$\frac{T_1 \equiv T \qquad T_2 \equiv T}{D\langle T_1,T_2\rangle \equiv T}$$

REFL
$$T \equiv T$$

SYMM
$$\frac{T \equiv T'}{T' \equiv T}$$

TRANS
$$\frac{T \equiv T' \qquad T' \equiv T''}{T \equiv T''}$$

Figure 1: Variational type equivalence.

In [5] we define a normalization process that can be used to check if two types are equivalent; this can be trivially extended to variational types containing error types. A type is in *normal form* if (1) all function types are maximally distributed into choice types, (2) choice types are nested according to a fixed ordering on dimension names, (3) the alternatives of each choice type are different, and (4) no choice type contains another choice type of the same name. For example, the types $B\langle\texttt{Int},\texttt{Int}\rangle \to A\langle\texttt{Bool},\bot\rangle$ and $\texttt{Int} \to A\langle\texttt{Bool},\bot\rangle$ are not in normal form, but $A\langle\texttt{Int} \to \texttt{Bool},\texttt{Int} \to \bot\rangle$ is.

4. Typing Patterns

A typing pattern is a variation type consisting only of $\bot$, $\top$, and choice types and is used to describe *which variants* of an expression are well-typed and which contain type errors. For example, the typing pattern $P = A\langle\top,B\langle\top,\bot\rangle\rangle$ indicates a type error in the variant corresponding to the decision $[A.2,B.2]$, and not in any other variants. A single typing pattern corresponds to an infinite number of partial variational types. Some types corresponding to P include: $A\langle\texttt{Int},B\langle\texttt{Bool},\bot\rangle\rangle$, $A\langle\texttt{Int},\texttt{Bool}\rangle \to B\langle\texttt{Int},A\langle\texttt{Bool},\bot\rangle\rangle$, and $A\langle\texttt{Int},B\langle\texttt{Bool},\bot\rangle \to B\langle\texttt{Int},\bot\rangle\rangle$. In these examples, the constant and function types are irrelevant—all that matters is that selecting $[A.2,B.2]$ produces a type containing errors, and that all other type variants are complete.

Typing patterns are not really types in the traditional sense, but rather an *abstraction* of variation types that indicate where the errors are in the variation space. They are useful for determining which types are *more defined* than others (that is, which contain errors in fewer variants) and play a crucial role in the unification of partial types (see Section 7). We conflate the representation of variational types and typing patterns because they behave similarly and doing so allows us to reuse a lot of machinery. In the rest of this section, we employ typing patterns to define a few operations that will be used throughout the paper.

We begin by defining a reflexive, transitive relation for determining which typing patterns are *more defined* than others, given in Figure 2. All typing patterns are more defined than $\bot$ and less defined than $\top$. Note that one typing pattern is not more defined

$$P \leq P \qquad P \leq \bot \qquad \top \leq P \qquad \frac{P \leq P_1 \qquad P \leq P_2}{P \leq D\langle P_1, P_2\rangle}$$

$$\frac{P_1 \leq P \qquad P_2 \leq P}{D\langle P_1, P_2\rangle \leq P} \qquad \frac{P_1 \leq P_1' \qquad P_2 \leq P_2'}{D\langle P_1, P_2\rangle \leq D\langle P_1', P_2'\rangle}$$

Figure 2: The more-defined relation on typing patterns.

than another by simply having fewer occurrences of error types. For example, the pattern $A\langle B\langle \bot, \top\rangle, B\langle \top, \bot\rangle\rangle$ is trivially more defined than $\bot$.

Next, we consider the *masking* of types with patterns. Given a pattern P and a type T, masking $P \lhd T$ potentially adds error types to T according to the position of error types in P.

$$\top \lhd T = T \qquad \bot \lhd T = \bot$$

$$D\langle P_1, P_2\rangle \lhd T = D\langle P_1 \lhd \lfloor T \rfloor_{D.1}, P_2 \lhd \lfloor T \rfloor_{D.2}\rangle$$

For example, masking type $\texttt{Int} \rightarrow A\langle \texttt{Bool}, \texttt{Int}\rangle$ with the typing pattern $A\langle \top, \bot\rangle$ yields the type $A\langle \texttt{Int} \rightarrow \texttt{Bool}, \bot\rangle$.

The *intersection* of two typing patterns P and P', written $P \otimes P'$, is a pattern that is well-typed in exactly those variants that are well-typed in both P and P'. For example, given patterns $A\langle \top, \bot\rangle$ and $B\langle \bot, \top\rangle$, their intersection is $A\langle B\langle \bot, \top\rangle, \bot\rangle$, which indicates that the only well-typed variant corresponds to the decision $[A.1, B.2]$. Intersection is just a special case of masking, where the masked type is a typing pattern: $P \otimes P' = P \lhd P'$.

The dual of intersection is pattern *union*. The union of two typing patterns P and P', written $P \oplus P'$, is well-typed in those variants that are well-typed in either P or P', or both.

$$\top \oplus P = \top \qquad \bot \oplus P = P$$

$$D\langle P_1, P_2\rangle \oplus P = D\langle P_1 \oplus \lfloor P \rfloor_{D.1}, P_2 \oplus \lfloor P \rfloor_{D.2}\rangle$$

For example, the union of $A\langle \top, \bot\rangle$ and $B\langle \bot, \top\rangle$ is $A\langle \top, B\langle \bot, \top\rangle\rangle$.

Note that the above definitions are all left-biased with regard to the nesting order of choices and the structure of the resulting type. This bias can be eliminated through the normalization process described in [5], which can be applied unaltered to typing patterns.

In the typing process, we often need to check whether two types *match*, for example, to check that the argument type of a function matches the type of the argument it is applied to. Rather than a simple boolean response, we can use typing patterns to provide a more precise account, indicating in which variants the types match ($\top$) and in which they do not ($\bot$). In the following definition of the variational type matching operation $\bowtie : T \times T \rightarrow P$ we assume both arguments are in normal form.[3]

$$\begin{aligned}
T \bowtie T &= \top \\
T_1 \rightarrow T_1' \bowtie T_2 \rightarrow T_2' &= T_1 \bowtie T_2 \otimes T_1' \bowtie T_2' \\
D\langle T_1, T_2\rangle \bowtie D\langle T_1', T_2'\rangle &= D\langle T_1 \bowtie T_1', T_2 \bowtie T_2'\rangle \\
D\langle T_1, T_2\rangle \bowtie T &= D\langle T_1 \bowtie T, T_2 \bowtie T\rangle \\
T \bowtie D\langle T_1, T_2\rangle &= D\langle T_1, T_2\rangle \bowtie T \\
\bot \bowtie T = T \bowtie \bot &= \bot \\
T \bowtie T' &= \bot \qquad \textit{(otherwise)}
\end{aligned}$$

For example, matching $\texttt{Int} \rightarrow A\langle \texttt{Bool}, \bot\rangle \bowtie B\langle \texttt{Int}, \bot\rangle \rightarrow \texttt{Bool}$ produces the typing pattern $A\langle B\langle \top, \bot\rangle, \bot\rangle$. This operation is used in the typing of applications, as we'll see in the next section.

[3] Assumed for this presentation only. Type matching is actually part of the unification algorithm, whose arguments need not be in normal form.

T-Con
$$\frac{c \text{ is a constant of type } \tau}{\Delta, \Gamma \vdash c : \tau}$$

T-Abs
$$\frac{\Delta, \Gamma; (x, T') \vdash e : T}{\Delta, \Gamma \vdash \lambda x.e : T' \rightarrow T}$$

T-Var
$$\frac{\Gamma(x) = T}{\Delta, \Gamma \vdash x : T}$$

T-App
$$\frac{\Delta, \Gamma \vdash e_1 : T_1 \qquad \Delta, \Gamma \vdash e_2 : T_2 \qquad T_2' \rightarrow T' = \uparrow(T_1) \qquad P = T_2' \bowtie T_2 \qquad T = P \lhd T'}{\Delta, \Gamma \vdash e_1\ e_2 : T}$$

T-Dim
$$\frac{\Delta; (D, D'), \Gamma \vdash e : T \qquad D' \text{ is fresh}}{\Delta, \Gamma \vdash \textbf{dim}\ D\langle t_1, t_2\rangle\ \textbf{in}\ e : T}$$

T-Choice
$$\frac{\Delta, \Gamma \vdash e_1 : T_1 \qquad \Delta, \Gamma \vdash e_2 : T_2 \qquad \Delta(D) = D'}{\Delta, \Gamma \vdash D\langle e_1, e_2\rangle : D'\langle T_1, T_2\rangle}$$

Figure 3: Typing rules mapping VLC expressions to partial types.

5. An Error-Tolerant Type System

The association of variational types with VLC expressions is determined by a set of typing rules, given in Figure 3. A VLC typing judgment has the form $\Delta, \Gamma \vdash e : T$, which states that expression e has type T in the context of environments Δ and Γ. Environments are implemented as stacks, where $E; (k, v)$ means to push the mapping (k, v) onto environment E, and $E(k) = v$ means that the topmost occurrence of k is mapped to v in E. The Γ environment maps variables to types and is the standard typing environment for lambda calculus. It is used as expected in the typing rules for variables and abstractions. The Δ environment maps expression-level dimension names to globally unique type-level dimension names. These mappings are added by the T-Dim rule and referenced by the T-Choice rule. The use of this environment also ensures that every choice is in scope of a corresponding dimension.

The focus here is on the T-App rule for typing applications, extending it to support partial types. Previously this rule required that the left argument be equivalent to a function type whose argument type is unifiable with the type of the parameter value. In the presence of partial types, we can relax these requirements, introducing error types (rather than failing) when they are not satisfied.

There are essentially two ways that error types can be introduced: (1) if we cannot convert the type of the left argument T_1 into a function type $T_2' \rightarrow T'$, and (2) if T_2' does not match the type of the parameter T_2. The introduction of errors in the second case is handled by matching the two types using the $\bowtie$ operation to produce a typing pattern P, then masking the result type T with P. In the first case, we employ a helper function $\uparrow$, which lifts a function type to the top level, introducing error types as needed.

$$\begin{aligned}
\uparrow(T_1 \rightarrow T_2) &= T_1 \rightarrow T_2 \\
\uparrow(D\langle T_1 \rightarrow T_1', T_2 \rightarrow T_2'\rangle) &= D\langle T_1, T_2\rangle \rightarrow D\langle T_1', T_2'\rangle \\
\uparrow(D\langle T_1, T_2\rangle) &= \uparrow(D\langle \uparrow(T_1), \uparrow(T_2)\rangle) \\
\uparrow(T) &= \bot \rightarrow \bot \qquad \textit{(otherwise)}
\end{aligned}$$

For example, $\uparrow(A\langle \texttt{Int} \rightarrow \texttt{Bool}, \texttt{Bool} \rightarrow \texttt{Int}\rangle) = A\langle \texttt{Int}, \texttt{Bool}\rangle \rightarrow A\langle \texttt{Bool}, \texttt{Int}\rangle$, while $\uparrow(A\langle \texttt{Int} \rightarrow \texttt{Bool}, \texttt{Int}\rangle)$ must introduce error types to lift the function type to the top: $A\langle \texttt{Int}, \bot\rangle \rightarrow A\langle \texttt{Bool}, \bot\rangle$.

To illustrate the typing of an application, consider the expression $e_1\ e_2$, where $e_1 : A\langle \texttt{Int} \rightarrow \texttt{Bool}, \texttt{Bool} \rightarrow \texttt{Bool}\rangle$ and $e_2 : \texttt{Int}$. Applying $\uparrow$ to the type of e_1 and simplifying the result type yields the type $A\langle \texttt{Int}, \texttt{Bool}\rangle \rightarrow \texttt{Bool}$. Matching $A\langle \texttt{Int}, \texttt{Bool}\rangle \bowtie \texttt{Int}$ produces the typing pattern $A\langle\top,\bot\rangle$, which we use to mask the result, $A\langle\top,\bot\rangle \lhd \texttt{Bool}$, producing the type of the application: $A\langle\texttt{Bool},\bot\rangle$.

The previous T-APP rule emerges as a special case of the generalized one. When e_1 is a function type whose argument type matches the type of e_2, then matching returns $\top$ and masking doesn't alter the return type.

The correspondence between variational types and VLC expressions is established inductively through the process of selection. Given that $e : T$, if e is plain, then T is a plain type or $\bot$. If e is not plain, then we can select a tag from e to produce $e' : T'$, and T' can be obtained by a corresponding selection from T. The inductive step is captured in the following lemma, which can be proved by induction over typing derivations.

LEMMA 1 (Variation elimination).
$\Delta,\Gamma \vdash e : T \implies \forall D,t : \Delta,\Gamma \vdash \lfloor e \rfloor_{D.t} : \lfloor T \rfloor_{\varphi_e([D.t])}$

Since tags are not present at the type level, and since expression-level dimension names may differ from type-level ones, the function φ_e is a function derived from e that maps tag sequences to the set of corresponding type-level selectors.

By induction it follows that a sequence of selections that produces a plain expression can be used to select a corresponding plain or error type. This results in the following theorem, where $\overline{q}$ is a list of dimension-qualified tags and $\overline{s}$ is a list of type-level selectors.

THEOREM 1 (Type preservation). *If* $\varnothing,\Gamma \vdash e : T$ *and* $(\overline{q}, e') \in [\![e]\!]$, *then* $\varnothing,\Gamma \vdash e' : T'$ *where* $\varphi_e(\overline{q}) = \overline{s}$ *and* $(\overline{s}, T') \in [\![T]\!]$.

This theorem demonstrates the soundness of the type systems since it establishes that from the type of a variational program we can obtain the type of each program variant it contains. We had similar type preservation results in [5], but they applied to only well-typed variational programs. The results here are stronger since they apply to *any* variational programs.

6. The Unification of Partial Types

Having extended the type system to work with and produce partial types, we now turn to the more challenging problem of inferring variational types containing type errors. By far the most difficult piece is partial type unification. In Section 6.1 we will describe the specific challenges posed. In particular, the unification algorithm must yield unifiers that produce types that are both most-general *and* most-defined, two qualities that are not obviously orthogonal. In Section 6.2 we show that such unifiers exist, and in Section 7 we present an algorithm for computing unifiers.

6.1 Reconciling Type Partiality and Generality

To support partial type inference, we must extend variational type unification to produce and extend mappings containing error types, and to identify mappings that are somehow best.

As a running example, consider the application $e\,e'$ where $e : T = A\langle\texttt{Int},\texttt{Bool}\rangle \to a$ and $e' : T' = B\langle\texttt{Int},a\rangle$. Usually we would find the most general unifier (mgu) for the problem $A\langle\texttt{Int},\texttt{Bool}\rangle \equiv^? B\langle\texttt{Int},a\rangle$, but in this case the two types are not unifiable since there is a type error in the $[A.2, B.1]$ variant. So what should we map a to? The mapping we choose should be *most-general* in the usual sense, but it should also be *most-defined*, yielding types with type errors in as few variants as possible. In this subsection we will explore the interaction of these two properties.

In Figure 4 we list several mappings we might choose to partially unify T and T' in our example. In the table, the type constants Bool, Char, and Int are shortened for space reasons. Each mapping is identified by a θ_i, for example, $\theta_2 = \{a \mapsto \texttt{Int}\}$. We also give the result of applying each mapping to each of the two types as T_i and T_i', the typing pattern P_i that results from matching the argument type of T_i to T_i', and the result type generated by masking the result type of T_i with P_i. Note that we apply mappings by adjacency and use the functions *arg* and *res* to access, respectively, the argument and result types of a function type.

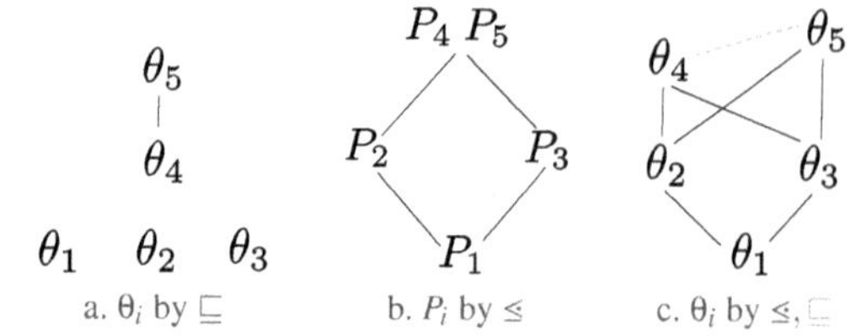

Figure 5: Orderings among patterns, result types, and mappings.

Figure 5 visualizes the more-general and more-defined relationships among mappings and typing patterns. The relations are defined for elements connected by lines, and the element higher in the graph is considered more general or more defined.

The first thing to note is that the standard more-general relation, $\sqsubseteq$, is not very helpful in selecting a mapping. A mapping θ is more general than θ', written $\theta \sqsubseteq \theta'$ if $\exists\theta''$ such that $\theta' = \theta'' \circ \theta$. But this relationship is only defined on one pair of our five mappings: $\theta_5 \sqsubseteq \theta_4$ (since $\{b \mapsto A\langle\texttt{Int},\texttt{Bool}\rangle\} \circ \theta_5 = \theta_4$). Since we are not restricted to mappings that are valid unifiers, there are many more possibilities, and many will not be ordered by the more-general relation.

More useful is the more-defined relation (see Section 4) on the match-produced typing patterns, for which many relationships are defined, as seen in Figure 5b. Using this metric, we can rule out mappings θ_1, θ_2, and θ_3 because they will produce types with errors in more variants than the mappings θ_4 and θ_5. The problem is that θ_4 and θ_5 produce the same pattern.

The solution, of course, is to use both metrics together, as demonstrated in Figure 5c. The solid lines between mappings correspond to more-defined relations between the generated typing patterns, and the dotted line corresponds to the more-general relation between the mappings directly. This reveals θ_5 as the most-defined, most-general mapping.

At this point it is not clear whether this convergence was a quirk of our example, or whether these properties will always converge in this way. In the next section we will tackle the general case, and show that a most-defined, most-general mapping always exists.

6.2 Most-General Partial Unifiers

In Section 6.1, we have illustrated how unification with partial types requires the integration of two partial orderings of types, $\leq$ and $\sqsubseteq$. In this section, we introduce the necessary machinery that enables unification to deal with this situation in general and produce most general partial unifiers.

In the following we consider a general unification problem of the form $U = T_L \equiv^? T_R$. For a given mapping θ, we write $U :: \theta$ for the typing pattern $T_L\theta \bowtie T_R\theta$ that results from θ and U. When we say that P is a typing pattern for U, we mean that there is some θ such that $P = U :: \theta$. With $vars(U)$ we refer to all type variables in U, and we use $dom(\theta)$ to denote the domain of θ. We use $\|\theta\|_U$ to normalize θ with respect to the variables in U, that is, $\|\theta\|_U$ is obtained from θ by renaming type variables such that $dom(\|\theta\|_U) = vars(U)$.

Finally, we extend selection to apply to unification problems and mappings, that is, $\lfloor U \rfloor_{D.i} = \lfloor T_L \rfloor_{D.i} \equiv^? \lfloor T_R \rfloor_{D.i}$ and $\lfloor \theta \rfloor_{D.i} = \{(a, \lfloor T \rfloor_{D.i}) \mid (a,T) \in \theta\}$. We write $\theta|_V$ for the restriction of θ by a set of variables V, which is defined as $\theta|_V = \{(a, a\theta) \mid a \in V\}$.

The first three lemmas state that selection extends in a homomorphic way across several operations.

i	θ_i	$T_i = T\theta_i$	$T'_i = T'\theta_i$	$P_i = arg(T_i) \bowtie T'_i$	$R_i = P_i \lhd res(T_i)$
1	$\{a \mapsto \mathtt{Ch}\}$	$A\langle \mathtt{In}, \mathtt{Bo}\rangle \to \mathtt{Ch}$	$B\langle \mathtt{In}, \mathtt{Ch}\rangle$	$A\langle B\langle \top, \bot\rangle, \bot\rangle$	$A\langle B\langle \mathtt{Ch}, \bot\rangle, \bot\rangle$
2	$\{a \mapsto \mathtt{In}\}$	$A\langle \mathtt{In}, \mathtt{Bo}\rangle \to \mathtt{In}$	$B\langle \mathtt{In}, \mathtt{In}\rangle$	$A\langle \top, \bot\rangle$	$A\langle \mathtt{In}, \bot\rangle$
3	$\{a \mapsto \mathtt{Bo}\}$	$A\langle \mathtt{In}, \mathtt{Bo}\rangle \to \mathtt{Bo}$	$B\langle \mathtt{In}, \mathtt{Bo}\rangle$	$A\langle B\langle \top, \bot\rangle, B\langle \bot, \top\rangle\rangle$	$A\langle B\langle \mathtt{Bo}, \bot\rangle, B\langle \bot, \mathtt{Bo}\rangle\rangle$
4	$\{a \mapsto A\langle \mathtt{In}, \mathtt{Bo}\rangle\}$	$A\langle \mathtt{In}, \mathtt{Bo}\rangle \to A\langle \mathtt{In}, \mathtt{Bo}\rangle$	$B\langle \mathtt{In}, A\langle \mathtt{In}, \mathtt{Bo}\rangle\rangle$	$A\langle \top, B\langle \bot, \top\rangle\rangle$	$A\langle \mathtt{In}, B\langle \bot, \mathtt{Bo}\rangle\rangle$
5	$\{a \mapsto B\langle b, A\langle \mathtt{In}, \mathtt{Bo}\rangle\rangle\}$	$A\langle \mathtt{In}, \mathtt{Bo}\rangle \to B\langle b, A\langle \mathtt{In}, \mathtt{Bo}\rangle\rangle$	$B\langle \mathtt{In}, A\langle \mathtt{In}, \mathtt{Bo}\rangle\rangle$	$A\langle \top, B\langle \bot, \top\rangle\rangle$	$A\langle B\langle b, \mathtt{In}\rangle, B\langle \bot, \mathtt{Bo}\rangle\rangle$

Figure 4: Some mappings for $T = A\langle \mathtt{Int}, \mathtt{Bool}\rangle \to a$ and $T' = B\langle \mathtt{Int}, a\rangle$, with the typing pattern and result types they produce.

LEMMA 2. $\lfloor T_L \bowtie T_R \rfloor_{D.i} = \lfloor T_L \rfloor_{D.i} \bowtie \lfloor T_R \rfloor_{D.i}$

The proofs for this and the following lemmas, left out for brevity, proceed by applying the definition of the operation under consideration and then performing structural induction on types.

LEMMA 3. $\lfloor T_L \oplus T_R \rfloor_{D.i} = \lfloor T_L \rfloor_{D.i} \oplus \lfloor T_R \rfloor_{D.i}$
$\lfloor T_L \otimes T_R \rfloor_{D.i} = \lfloor T_L \rfloor_{D.i} \otimes \lfloor T_R \rfloor_{D.i}$
$\lfloor P \lhd T \rfloor_{D.i} = \lfloor P \rfloor_{D.i} \lhd \lfloor T \rfloor_{D.i}$
$\lfloor T_L \to T_R \rfloor_{D.i} = \lfloor T_L \rfloor_{D.i} \to \lfloor T_R \rfloor_{D.i}$

We also have a similar result for type substitution.

LEMMA 4. $\lfloor T\theta \rfloor_{D.i} = \lfloor T \rfloor_{D.i} \lfloor \theta \rfloor_{D.i}$

The next lemma says that the computation of typing patterns can be decomposed by using selection.

LEMMA 5. $\lfloor U :: \theta \rfloor_{D.i} = \lfloor U :: \lfloor \theta \rfloor_{D.i} \rfloor_{D.i} = \lfloor U \rfloor_{D.i} :: \lfloor \theta \rfloor_{D.i}$

PROOF. The proof for the first part is as follows. Let $P = U :: \theta$ and $P' = U :: \lfloor \theta \rfloor_{D.i}$, then

$$
\begin{aligned}
\lfloor P \rfloor_{D.i} &= \lfloor T_L\theta \bowtie T_R\theta \rfloor_{D.i} & \\
&= \lfloor T_L\theta \rfloor_{D.i} \bowtie \lfloor T_R\theta \rfloor_{D.i} & \text{by Lemma 2} \\
&= \lfloor T_L \rfloor_{D.i} \lfloor \theta \rfloor_{D.i} \bowtie \lfloor T_R \rfloor_{D.i} \lfloor \theta \rfloor_{D.i} & \text{by Lemma 4} \\
\lfloor P' \rfloor_{D.i} &= \lfloor T_L \lfloor \theta \rfloor_{D.i} \bowtie T_R \lfloor \theta \rfloor_{D.i} \rfloor_{D.i} & \\
&= \lfloor T_L \lfloor \theta \rfloor_{D.i} \rfloor_{D.i} \bowtie \lfloor T_R \lfloor \theta \rfloor_{D.i} \rfloor_{D.i} & \text{by Lemma 2} \\
&= \lfloor T_L \rfloor_{D.i} \lfloor \lfloor \theta \rfloor_{D.i} \rfloor_{D.i} \bowtie \lfloor T_R \rfloor_{D.i} \lfloor \lfloor \theta \rfloor_{D.i} \rfloor_{D.i} & \text{by Lemma 4} \\
&= \lfloor T_L \rfloor_{D.i} \lfloor \theta \rfloor_{D.i} \bowtie \lfloor T_R \rfloor_{D.i} \lfloor \theta \rfloor_{D.i} &
\end{aligned}
$$

The proof for the second part is analogous. □

LEMMA 6 (Typing patterns have a join). *If P_1 and P_2 are typing patterns for U, then so is $P_1 \oplus P_2$.*

PROOF. Assume θ_1 and θ_2 are the mappings such that $P_1 = U :: \theta_1$ and $P_2 = U :: \theta_2$. The proof consists of several cases. For each case, we construct a mapping θ_3 such that $U :: \theta_3 = P_1 \oplus P_2$, which we denote as P_3. We show the proof for the case where $P_1 = D\langle P_{11}, P_{12}\rangle$ and $P_2 = D\langle P_{21}, P_{22}\rangle$ and there is no $\lesssim$ relation between P_1 and P_2. The proofs for other cases are simpler or can be transformed into this case. We assume that θ_1 and θ_2 are already normalized with respect to U. We can consider several cases.

First, if we assume $P_{21} \lesssim P_{11}$ and $P_{12} \lesssim P_{22}$, we let $\theta_3 = \{(a, D\langle \lfloor a\theta_2 \rfloor_{D.1}, \lfloor a\theta_1 \rfloor_{D.2}\rangle) \mid a \in vars(U)\}$, for which we observe the following.

$$
\begin{aligned}
U :: \theta_3 &= D\langle \lfloor U :: \theta_3 \rfloor_{D.1}, \lfloor U :: \theta_3 \rfloor_{D.2}\rangle & \\
&= D\langle \lfloor U \rfloor_{D.1} :: \lfloor \theta_3 \rfloor_{D.1}, \lfloor U \rfloor_{D.2} :: \lfloor \theta_3 \rfloor_{D.2}\rangle & \text{Lemma 5} \\
&= D\langle \lfloor U \rfloor_{D.1} :: \lfloor \theta_1 \rfloor_{D.1}, \lfloor U \rfloor_{D.2} :: \lfloor \theta_2 \rfloor_{D.2}\rangle & \text{construction} \\
&= D\langle \lfloor U :: \theta_1 \rfloor_{D.1}, \lfloor U :: \theta_2 \rfloor_{D.2}\rangle & \text{Lemma 5} \\
&= D\langle P_{21}, P_{12}\rangle & \\
&= P_1 \oplus P_2 & \text{def. of } \oplus
\end{aligned}
$$

Second, the case for $P_{11} \lesssim P_{21}$ and $P_{22} \lesssim P_{12}$ is analogous.

Third, if there is no $\lesssim$ relation between P_{21} and P_{11} or P_{12} and P_{22}, we let $U_1 = \lfloor U \rfloor_{D.1}$, $U_2 = \lfloor U \rfloor_{D.2}$, $\theta_{11} = \theta_1|_{vars(U_1)}$, $\theta_{12} = \theta_1|_{vars(U_2)}$, $\theta_{21} = \theta_2|_{vars(U_1)}$ and $\theta_{22} = \theta_2|_{vars(U_2)}$. By induction, we can construct a mapping θ_{31} from θ_{11} and θ_{21} for U_1 such that $U_1 :: \theta_{31} = P_{11} \oplus P_{21}$. Likewise, we can construct a mapping θ_{32} from θ_{12} and θ_{22} for U_2 such that $U_2 :: \theta_{32} = P_{12} \oplus P_{22}$. We can now build θ_3 based on θ_{31} and θ_{32} as follows. For each type variable $a \in vars(U)$ we define θ_3 as follows.

$$
\theta_3(a) = \begin{cases} D\langle a\theta_{31}, a\theta_{32}\rangle & \text{if } a \in vars(U_1) \wedge a \in vars(U_2) \\ a\theta_{31} & \text{if } a \in vars(U_1) \\ a\theta_{32} & \text{if } a \in vars(U_2) \end{cases}
$$

Proving that $U :: \theta_3 = D\langle P_{31}, P_{32}\rangle = D\langle P_{11}, P_{12}\rangle \oplus D\langle P_{21}, P_{22}\rangle$ is similar to the proof for the previous case. □

Combining this lemma with the rule $\top \lesssim P$ we can conclude that for any unification problem, there is an upper-bound typing pattern, which we call the *principal typing pattern*.

THEOREM 2 (Existence of principal typing patterns). *For every unification problem U there is a mapping θ with $P = U :: \theta$, such that $P \lesssim P'$ for any other mapping θ' with $P' = U :: \theta'$.*

We call a mapping that leads to the principal typing pattern a *partial unifier* and use η to denote partial unifiers. We call mappings that are not partial unifiers "non-unifiers" for short. Based on these definitions, the first example in Section 6.1 has the principal typing pattern P_4 and partial unifiers θ_4 and θ_5.

Theorem 2 only shows the existence of partial unifiers, but does not say anything about how many partial unifiers exist and how they are possibly related. It turns out that partial unifiers can be compared with respect to their generality and for each unification problem there is a *most general partial unifier* (mgpu) of which all other partial unifiers are instances.

THEOREM 3 (Partial unification is unitary). *For every unification problem U there is one partial unifier η of such that any other partial unifier η' for U is an instance of it, that is, $\eta \sqsubseteq \eta'$.*

The proof strategy is similar to that for Theorem 2, although more complex. Given any two partial unifiers, we can construct a new partial unifier that is more general than the old ones.

7. A Unification Algorithm

In this section we present a partial type unification algorithm that identifies partial unifiers that produce most-general, most-defined types. This algorithm is a conservative extension of our algorithm for unifying complete variational types, presented in [5]. That is, when the types are complete and fully unifiable, we produce the same results as before. When the types to be unified are partial and/or not unifiable, we produce partial unifiers as described in the previous section. In Section 7.1 we give a high-level overview of the process of unifying variational types, and in Section 7.2 we define the algorithm that makes up the core of this process.

7.1 Unification of Variational Types

The fundamental difference between traditional type unification [3] and variational unification is the treatment of type variables. Consider the unification problem $A\langle\texttt{Int},a\rangle \equiv^? A\langle a,\texttt{Bool}\rangle$. At first it may seem that these types are not unifiable—blithe decomposition by alternatives yields the subproblems $\texttt{Int} \equiv^? a$ and $a \equiv^? \texttt{Bool}$, but a cannot map to both `Int` and `Bool`. However, there *is* a unifier to the original problem: if we map a to $A\langle\texttt{Int},\texttt{Bool}\rangle$, then both types are equivalent to $A\langle\texttt{Int},\texttt{Bool}\rangle$ by choice domination (see Section 3). Decomposition is essential to the unification process, but decomposing by alternatives discards important context provided by the choice type. In our example, this context tells us that only one of the two a type variables will be selected in any particular variant.

As a solution, we encode the contextual information in the type variables themselves. A *qualified type variable* is a type variable marked by the choice type alternatives in which it is nested. We write $a_{A\tilde{B}}$ to indicate that type variable a is located in the first alternative of a choice type in dimension A and the second alternative of a choice type in B. Throughout most of the unification process, type variables with different qualifications are simply considered to be different type variables, but we can use the contextual information to construct the final mappings (from unqualified type variables to variational types) through a process called *completion*. In the example above, after qualification and decomposition we identify the mappings $\{a_A \mapsto \texttt{Int}, a_{\tilde{A}} \mapsto \texttt{Bool}\}$ which completes to the final result $\{a \mapsto A\langle\texttt{Int},\texttt{Bool}\rangle\}$.

Unification thus consists of three main phases: (1) the unification problem U is translated into a corresponding *qualified unification* problem Q, (2) Q is solved, and (3) the solution to Q is completed to produce a solution to U. The first step of this process is trivial. We simply traverse both types and qualify all of the type variables. Completion is also straightforward: given a list of mappings from qualified type variables, each $a_{q_i} \mapsto T_i$ describes a leaf in a tree of nested choice types that makes up the type T in the completed mapping $a \mapsto T$. We just iterate over the qualified mappings, lazily constructing and populating the resulting tree.

The difficult part is of course solving the qualified unification problem. In addition to the traditional operations of matching and decomposition, qualified unification relies on two additional operations. First, a choice type can be *hoisted* over another choice type. For example, hoisting transforms $A\langle T_1, B\langle T_2,T_3\rangle\rangle$ into $B\langle A\langle T_1,T_2\rangle, A\langle T_1,T_3\rangle\rangle$. Second, a type variable can be *split* into a choice type between two qualified versions of that variable. For example, splitting transforms a into $A\langle a_A, a_{\tilde{A}}\rangle$. These operations manipulate the types being unified so they can be further matched or decomposed. For example, the problem $A\langle\texttt{Int},a_{\tilde{A}}\rangle \equiv^? B\langle b_B, c_{\tilde{B}}\rangle$ cannot be directly decomposed. However, if we split the variable $a_{\tilde{A}}$ into $B\langle a_{\tilde{A}B}, a_{\tilde{A}\tilde{B}}\rangle$ and hoist this choice type to the top, we get the new problem $B\langle A\langle\texttt{Int},a_{\tilde{A}B}\rangle, A\langle\texttt{Int},a_{\tilde{A}\tilde{B}}\rangle\rangle \equiv^? B\langle b_B, c_{\tilde{B}}\rangle$, which can be decomposed into two trivial subproblems.

The full technical exposition of the unification of complete variational types is provided in [5]. Significantly, we also show that the unification problem is decidable and unitary. In the rest of this section we will develop the unification of *partial* variational types.

7.2 Computing the Most General Partial Unifier

In Section 6.2 we showed that for each partial unification problem, there is a unique mgpu that produces the corresponding principal typing pattern. In this section, we show how to compute each of these by extending the process described in Section 7.1. We do this first by example, then give the algorithm directly.

Consider the unification problem $A\langle\texttt{Int},a\rangle \equiv^? B\langle\texttt{Bool},b\rangle$. We begin, as described in Section 7.1, by transforming this into the corresponding qualified unification problem shown at the top of

$$A\langle\texttt{Int},a_{\tilde{A}}\rangle \equiv^? B\langle\texttt{Bool},\underline{b_{\tilde{B}}}\rangle$$
$$\downarrow_{split}$$
$$A\langle\texttt{Int},a_{\tilde{A}}\rangle \equiv^? \underline{B\langle\texttt{Bool},A\langle b_{A\tilde{B}}, b_{\tilde{A}\tilde{B}}\rangle\rangle}$$
$$\downarrow_{hoist}$$
$$A\langle\texttt{Int},a_{\tilde{A}}\rangle \equiv^? A\langle B\langle\texttt{Bool},b_{A\tilde{B}}\rangle, B\langle\texttt{Bool},b_{\tilde{A}\tilde{B}}\rangle\rangle$$

$$\dfrac{\dfrac{\texttt{Int} \equiv^? B\langle\texttt{Bool},b_{A\tilde{B}}\rangle}{\ast\,\texttt{Int} \equiv^? \texttt{Bool}\,\ast \qquad \texttt{Int} \equiv^? b_{A\tilde{B}}} \qquad a_{\tilde{A}} \equiv^? B\langle\texttt{Bool},b_{\tilde{A}\tilde{B}}\rangle}{}$$

Figure 6: Qualified unification resulting in a type error.

Figure 6. Since the top-level choice names don't match, we choose a type variable and apply the split-hoist strategy (first two steps) in order to decompose by alternatives (third step). This gives us the two subproblems at the fourth level from the top. When a plain type is unified with a choice type, we can decompose it by unifying the plain type with each alternative. This is demonstrated in the left branch, which yields two smaller subproblems, one of which, $\texttt{Int} \equiv^? \texttt{Bool}$, reveals a type error.

This decomposition contains all of the information needed to construct both the mgpu and the principal typing pattern. We construct the mgpu by composing the mappings generated at the end of every successful branch of the unification process. In this case, there were two successful branches, giving the following mgpu.

$$\{a_{\tilde{A}} \mapsto B\langle\texttt{Bool},b_{\tilde{A}\tilde{B}}\rangle, b_{A\tilde{B}} \mapsto \texttt{Int}\}$$

We construct the principal typing pattern by observing which branches of the decomposition fail and succeed. In this case, the branch corresponding to the first alternative in both A and B failed, yielding the principal error pattern $A\langle B\langle\bot,\top\rangle,\top\rangle$.

As the final step, we use completion to produce the solution to the original (unqualified) unification problem.

$$\{a \mapsto A\langle c, B\langle\texttt{Bool},d\rangle\rangle, b \mapsto B\langle f, A\langle\texttt{Int},d\rangle\rangle\}$$

Figure 7 gives the partial unification algorithm. It accepts a qualified unification problem $T_L \equiv^? T_R$ and returns a principal typing pattern P and a mgpu η. We show only the cases that differ significantly from the qualified unification algorithm presented in [5].

The algorithm relies on several helper functions. The function $choices(T)$ returns the dimension names of all choice types that occur in T. The function *splittable* returns the set of type variables that can be split into a choice type. A variable is splittable if the path from itself to the root consists only of choice types (no function types). The function $vars(T)$ returns the set of qualified variables in a type. Finally, the function $sdims(v_q, T)$ returns the set of dimension names not present in q but present in the qualifications of type variables that are more *specific* than v_q. We say that u_p is more specific than v_q if $u = v$ and p can be written as qp' for some nonempty p'. For example, $sdims(a_A, a_{A\tilde{B}} \rightarrow \texttt{Int}) = \{B\}$.

We will work through the cases of the *unify* algorithm, from top to bottom. In the body of the algorithm and in these descriptions, T_L and T_R are used to refer to the first and second arguments to *unify*, respectively. We first consider a couple of base cases. Attempting to unify any type and an error type yields an empty mapping and the fully undefined typing pattern $\bot$. This defines the propagation of errors. When unifying two plain types, we defer to the traditional *robinson* unification algorithm [21]. If it succeeds, we return the unifier and the fully defined typing pattern $\top$. If it fails, we return the empty mapping and $\bot$.

When unifying a *ground plain type* g (a type that does not contain choice types or type variables) with a choice type, we just unify g with both alternatives. This is seen in the second decomposition

$$unify : T \times T \rightarrow P \times \eta$$

$$unify(\bot, T) = (\bot, \varnothing)$$

$unify(p, p')$
$\quad | \; robinson(p, p') = \bot = (\bot, \varnothing)$
$\quad | \; \text{otherwise} = (\top, robinson(p, p'))$

$$unify(g, D\langle T_1, T_2\rangle) = unify(D\langle g, g\rangle, D\langle T_1, T_2\rangle)$$

$unify(D\langle T_1, T_2\rangle, D\langle T_1', T_2'\rangle) =$
$\quad (P_1, \eta_1) \leftarrow unify(T_1, T_1')$
$\quad (P_2, \eta_2) \leftarrow unify(T_2, T_2')$
$\quad \text{return } (D\langle P_1, P_2\rangle, \eta_1 \circ \eta_2)$

$unify(D_1\langle T_1, T_2\rangle, D_2\langle T_1', T_2'\rangle)$
$\quad | \; D_2 \notin choices(T_L) \wedge splittable(T_L) = \varnothing \wedge$
$\quad\; D_1 \notin choices(T_R) \wedge splittable(T_R) = \varnothing$
$\quad = unify(T_L, D_1\langle T_R, T_R\rangle)$

$unify(v_q, T_1' \rightarrow T_2')$
$\quad | \; v_q \in vars(T_R) = (\bot, \varnothing)$
$\quad | \; D \in sdims(v_q, T_R) = unify(D\langle v_{Dq}, v_{\tilde{D}q}\rangle, T_R)$
$\quad | \; \text{otherwise} = (\top, \{v_q \mapsto T_R\})$

$unify(T_1 \rightarrow T_2, T_1' \rightarrow T_2') =$
$\quad (P_1, \eta_1) \leftarrow unify(T_1, T_1')$
$\quad (P_2, \eta_2) \leftarrow unify(T_2\eta_1, T_2'\eta_1)$
$\quad P \leftarrow P_1 \otimes P_2$
$\quad \text{return } (P, \eta_1 \circ \eta_2)$

Figure 7: Partial unification algorithm.

in Figure 6. The first decomposition is by alternatives, which is performed when unifying two choices in the same dimension; this is captured in the fourth case of *unify*. Note that we do not need to apply the mapping η_1 to T_2 and T_2', as we might expect, because $(vars(T_1) \cup vars(T_1')) \cap (vars(T_2) \cup vars(T_2')) = \varnothing$ due to type variable qualification. We then compose the corresponding unifiers and combine the error patterns with a choice type.

The fifth case considers the unification of two choice types in different dimensions with no splittable type variables. This is not fully unifiable and so would usually represent failure. However, with partial unification we can proceed by attempting to unify all combinations of alternatives in order to locate the variants that contain errors. For example, $A\langle \texttt{Int}, \texttt{Bool}\rangle \equiv^? B\langle \texttt{Int}, \texttt{Bool}\rangle$ produces the typing pattern $A\langle B\langle \top, \bot\rangle, B\langle \bot, \top\rangle\rangle$. We reuse our existing machinery by duplicating T_R and putting it in a choice type that will be decomposed by alternatives in the recursive execution of *unify*.

Although we do not show all of the cases of unifying a qualified type variable against other types, we do show the trickiest case of unifying a type variable with a function type in the sixth case in Figure 7. There are there sub-cases to consider: (1) If v_q occurs in T_R, the unification fails. (2) If v_q does not occur in T_R but a more specific type variable v_{qr} does, then some variants may still be well-typed. So, we create a new unification problem by adding a dimension D from r to the qualification of v_q, then splitting the new variable v_{Dq} in the D dimension. (3) Finally, if v does not appear in any form in T_R, then we simply map v_q to T_R. Note that the decomposition of the unification problem is such that if there is any v_p in T_R, then either $v_p = v_q$ or v_p is more specific than v_q.

Finally, we consider the unification of two function types. We unify the corresponding argument types and result types and compose the mappings. The resulting typing pattern is the intersection of the patterns of the two subproblems since the result will be well-typed only if both the argument and result types agree.

We conclude by presenting some important properties of the unification algorithm. The first result is that the partial unification algorithm is terminating through decomposition that eventually results in either the propagation of type errors, or calls to the *robinson* algorithm, which is terminating. There are two cases that do not decompose, but rather grow the size of the types being unified, and so pose a threat to termination. The first is the splitting of type variables. The second is the fifth case shown in Figure 7. Both of these cases introduce a new choice type and duplicate one of their arguments. These cases do not prevent termination, however, for two reasons. First, both cases are followed immediately by a decomposition that produces two subproblems smaller than the original problem. Second, the number of new choice types that can be introduced is bounded by the overall number of dimensions in the unification problem. This follows from the property of choice domination and the fact that we eliminate a dimension from consideration with each decomposition by alternatives.

In [5], we did an in-depth time complexity analysis of the variational unification algorithm. We showed that if the size of T_L and T_R are l and r respectively, then the time complexity of variational unification is $O(lr(l+r))$. Since the computation of typing patterns in the unification algorithm does not exceed the time for computing partial unifiers, the run-time complexity is still $O(lr(l+r))$ for the partial unification algorithm.

The partial unification algorithm is also sound and complete. These facts are expressed in the following theorems. We use $unify'$ to refer to the entire three-part unification process described in Section 7.1 (qualification, qualified unification, completion).

THEOREM 4 (Partial unification is sound). *Given the unification problem* $T_1 \equiv^? T_2$, *if* $unify'(T_1, T_2) = (P, \eta)$, *then* $T_1\eta \bowtie T_2\eta = P$.

THEOREM 5 (Partial unification is complete, most defined, and most general). *Given the unification problem* $T_1 \equiv^? T_2$, *if* $T_1\theta \bowtie T_2\theta = P$, *then* $unify'(T_1, T_2) = (P', \eta)$ *such that* $P' \leq P$ *and if* $P' \equiv P$ *then there exists some* θ' *such that* $\theta = \theta' \circ \eta$.

8. Partial Type Inference Algorithm

Although the partial unification algorithm is quite complicated, the inference algorithm itself is simple. We define it as an extension of algorithm $\mathcal{W}$ [6] and show the most interesting case below.

$infer : \Delta \times \Gamma \times e \rightarrow \eta \times T$
$infer(\Delta, \Gamma, e_1\; e_2) =$
$\quad (\eta_1, T_1) \leftarrow infer(\Delta, \Gamma, e_1)$
$\quad (\eta_2, T_2) \leftarrow infer(\Delta, \Gamma\eta_1, e_2)$
$\quad (P, \eta) \leftarrow unify'(T_1\eta_2, T_2\eta_2 \rightarrow a) \qquad$ {- *a is a fresh variable* -}
$\quad R \leftarrow P \lhd a\eta$
$\quad \text{return } (\eta \circ \eta_2 \circ \eta_1, R)$

The algorithm takes three arguments: a dimension environment, a typing environment, and an expression. It returns a partial unifier and the inferred partial type. Traditionally, inferring the result of a function application consists of four steps: (1) infer the type of the function, (2) infer the type of the argument, (3) unify the argument type of the function with the type of the argument, and (4) instantiate the result type of the function with the returned unifier. Our algorithm adds just one more step: we must mask the result type according to the typing pattern returned by partial unification, in order to introduce error types for the cases where traditional unification would fail.

The remaining cases can be derived from the typing rules in Section 5. Variables and abstractions are treated as in $\mathcal{W}$. For a dimension declaration we extend the dimension environment and recursively infer the type of its scope. For a choice we infer the type of each alternative and build a corresponding choice type.

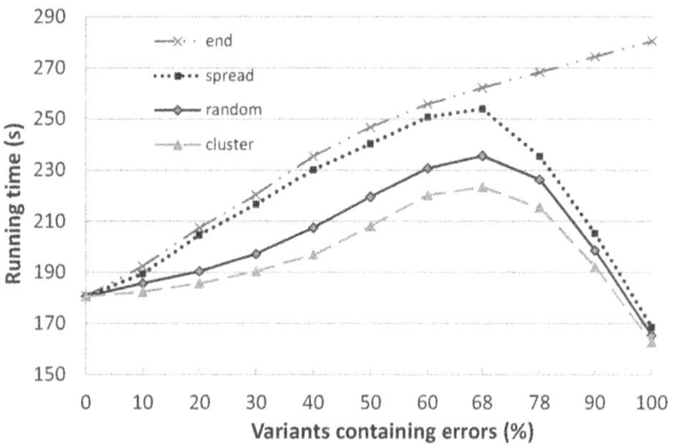

Figure 8: Running time of prototype by error distribution.

The following theorems state that our type inference algorithm is sound and complete and has the principal typing property. In the following, the symbol $\preceq$ represents a more-defined, more-general relation on variational types. That is, $T' \preceq T$ means that for every corresponding pair of (plain) variants V' and V from T' and T, respectively, either $V' \sqsubseteq V$ or $V = \bot$.

THEOREM 6 (Type inference is sound).
If $infer(\Delta, \Gamma, e) = (\eta, T)$, *then* $\Delta, \Gamma\eta \vdash e : T$.

THEOREM 7 (Type inference is complete and principal).
If $\Delta, \Gamma\eta \vdash e : T$, *then* $infer(\Delta, \Gamma, e) = (\eta', T')$ *such that* $\eta = \theta \circ \eta'$ *for some* θ *and* $T' \preceq T$.

These results mean that, for any syntactically correct VLC expression, we can infer the most general type, containing type errors in as few variants as possible, all without type annotations.

9. Evaluation

Variational type inference offers potentially huge efficiency gains over the brute-force strategy of typing each variant individually. The first opportunity is by *sharing* the typing information of code common to multiple variants. For example, in the expression $f\ A\langle e_1, e_2\rangle$ we need only type the function f once relative to e_1 and e_2. The second, more subtle opportunity is by *reducing* variability in types through choice idempotency. This is often possible because types are an abstraction of expressions. For example, in the expression $A\langle f, g\rangle\ B\langle 1, 2\rangle$, the argument type reduces to the plain type `Int`, reducing the variability in the application at the type level. While both of these cases are expected to be ubiquitous in practice, there are worst-case scenarios that fundamentally cannot be typed faster than brute-force, for example, an expression with no sharing and in which every variant has a different type, such as $A\langle B\langle T_1, T_2\rangle, B\langle T_3, T_4\rangle\rangle$ where $T_1 \ldots T_4$ are all different.

In this section we empirically evaluate the efficiency of partial type inference in a variety of ways. To do this, we have developed a prototype in Haskell that implements the contents of this paper. The prototype consists of three parts: a normalizer for variational types, the equational partial unification algorithm described in Section 7, and the type inference algorithm described in Section 8.

In the first experiment, we measure the additional cost of the extensions described in this paper, relative to [5]. To measure this overhead effectively, we intentionally induced our worst-case performance through the *cascading choice* problem. Cascading choices are long sequences of applications, where each expression is a choice in a different dimension. If the types of all alternatives are different, no solution can perform better than the brute-force strategy. The overhead of our prototype on such examples (all well-typed, with between 14 and 21 dimensions) was about 30% of the running time of the non-error-tolerant prototype described in [5].

In the second experiment, we study how the distribution of errors in an expression affects the efficiency of partial type inference. The graph in Figure 8 shows the running time of the prototype on a cascading choice problem with 21 dimensions, seeded with errors. The horizontal axis indicates the percentage of variants that were seeded with type errors, and the different lines represent different distributions of these errors. Errors can be *spread* evenly throughout the expression, *clustered* together, distributed *randomly*, or introduced at the *end* of the expression. An interesting phenomenon is that, while the running time at first increases as we introduce errors (due to the costs of maintaining and applying error patterns), in three of the four curves the running time decreases sharply as the error density increases. This is because additional errors introduce opportunities for reduction through choice idempotency ($D\langle\bot,\bot\rangle = \bot$) that are usually denied in cascading choice expressions. As expected, this feature is most pronounced when errors are clustered and least pronounced when they are spread evenly. When errors are introduced at the end of the expression, this opportunity never arises since all the work has already been done.

Finally, in the third experiment, we demonstrate the efficiency and effectiveness of partial type inference in finding type errors, relative to the brute-force approach (implemented as a prototype in the same way as our own). The results are presented in the table in Figure 9. Each row represents an artificially constructed expression that varies in the indicated number of dimensions. The size of each expression is given by the number of AST nodes. The expressions are constructed such that not all dimensions are independent (some dimensions are nested within choices), so the number of variants each expression represents is also given.

In each expression, we manually seeded the indicated number of errors according to two different distributions: errors may be *spread* evenly throughout the expression or *clustered* together. Thus, each row actually represents two expressions with different error distributions that are otherwise identical. Errors are counted relative to the variational expression, not the variants they occur in. For example, if the expression *err* produces a type error, then $A\langle err, B\langle 1,2\rangle\rangle$ is considered to contain just one type error even though that error is expressed in two variants ($[A.2, B.1]$ and $[A.2, B.2]$).

Finally, for each expression we give the percentage of errors caught and total running time in seconds (run on a 2.8GHz dual core processor with 3GB RAM) of the brute-force approach and our inference algorithm, respectively. Often the problem is intractable for the brute-force approach, so we cap the running-time at one hour and count the number of errors caught to this point. Because of this cap, and especially when errors are clustered, there is a potential for bias in which variants the brute-force algorithm sees before the time limit is reached. To mitigate this, we ran each brute-force test 10 times, starting from random variants, and averaged the results. Note that for presentation reasons we do not list the percentage of errors found for our algorithm since this value is always 100%. Similarly, we do not list the running time of the brute-force approach since this is the full 3600 seconds in all but a few cases, which are indicated by footnotes.

From the results in Figure 9 we observe that our algorithm scales well as the size, variability, and number of errors in an expression increases. Our algorithm is also more reliable for detecting errors since the ability to completely type the expressions means that it is not sensitive (in this regard) to the distribution of errors, and we do not have to consider issues like which variant the algorithm starts with.

Collectively, these results demonstrate the feasibility of error-tolerant type inference on large, complex expressions. In practice,

size	dims	variants	errors	spread		clustered	
				brute (%)	vlc (s)	brute (%)	vlc (s)
702	22	2^{16}	100	100^a	0.62	100^c	0.57
3719	22	2^{16}	100	14.90	1.09	4.10	1.02
976	24	2^{17}	200	100^b	0.71	100^d	0.68
5327	24	2^{17}	200	0.50	2.26	39.85	2.17
8412	24	2^{17}	200	0.05	3.79	0.00	3.65
1163	27	2^{21}	400	27.05	0.76	4.90	0.71
1745	33	2^{25}	500	0.42	1.31	0.00	1.19
2079	37	2^{29}	500	0.04	1.44	2.98	1.33
3505	57	2^{40}	1000	0.08	1.82	0.21	1.74
9429	215	2^{165}	1000	0.00	4.31	0.01	4.16
61345	1434	2^{892}	2000	0.00	31.45	0.99	29.44
213521	4983	2^{3073}	5000	0.02	104.61	0.00	99.37
429586	10002	2^{7455}	10000	0.00	183.75	0.10	172.52

[a] 648 s [b] 2700 s [c] 639 s [d] 2645 s

Figure 9: A comparison of the performance of the brute-force approach and our inference algorithm on large expressions containing seeded type errors. The errors are either spread evenly or clustered within the expression. Our algorithm caught 100% of the errors in all cases, so we show only the time taken to do so. The running time of the brute-force approach was capped at one hour (3600 s). For cases that completed before this cap was reached, we give the running time as a footnote. For cases that did not complete, we ran each test 10 times starting from a random variant, and averaged the results.

we expect real software to be considerably less complex (from a variational perspective) than the expressions examined in this section, and very unlikely to induce worst-case scenarios. For example, some real-world studies have suggested an average choice nesting depth of just 1.5 [13]. However, it is possible that variational complexity is artificially limited by the inadequacy of current tools, which this work directly addresses.

10. Related Work

The work presented here builds on our previous work on typing variational programs [5]. In that work, we focused on establishing VLC as a foundation for work on typing variational programs (and other static analyses), introducing the notion of variational types, and developing the fundamentals of variational typing and variational type inference. In order to be practically useful, however, variational typing must support many more features. In [5] we demonstrated how this approach can be extended to support simple typing features like sum types. The work presented in this paper represents a much more significant and challenging extension to make the type system error-tolerant. This feature is critically important for typing real-world variational programs because it directly supports tasks like error location and incremental development.

In general, our approach distinguishes itself from related work in the field of SPLs by representing variation more generally and at a finer granularity, and by solving the more general problem of type inference rather than the type- or definedness-checking of explicitly typed programs [11, 12, 25].

Choice types are similar to variant types [10], which are used to uniformly manipulate heterogeneous collection of types. A significant difference between the two is that choices (at the expression level) contain all of the information needed for inferring their corresponding choice type. Values of variant types, on the other hand, are associated with just one label, representing one branch of the larger variant type. This makes type inference very difficult. A common solution is to use explicit type annotations; whenever a variant value is used, it must be annotated with a corresponding variant type. Typing VLC does not require such annotations.

Choice types are also reminiscent of union types [7]. A union type is an agglomeration of simpler types. For example, a function `f` might accept the union of types `Int` and `Bool`. Function application is then well typed if the argument's type is an element of the union type (either `Int` or `Bool`). The biggest difference between union types and choice types is that union types are comparatively unstructured. In VLC, choices can be synchronized, allowing functions to provide different implementations for different argument types, or for different sets of functions to be defined in the context of different argument types. With union types, an applied function must be able to operate on all possible values of an argument with a union type. A major challenge in type inference with union types is union elimination, which is not syntax directed and makes type inference intractable. Therefore, as with variant types, syntactic markers are needed to support type inference.

Although they share a name, our notion of partial types differs from the work of Thatte [26]. Thatte's partial types provide a way to type certain objects that are not typable with simple types in lambda calculus, such as heterogeneous lists and persistent data. They are more similar to our typing patterns. Thatte's "untyped" type Ω represents an arbitrary well-typed expression, similar to our $\top$ type, while his inclusion relationship on partial types ($\leq$) is similar to our more-defined relationship on patterns ($\lesssim$). Type inference with Thatte's partial types was proved decidable [14, 17], a property that holds for our type system also.

Top and bottom types in subtyping [19] are also similar to the types $\top$ and $\perp$ used in typing patterns. Moreover, the subtyping relationship plays a similar role to that of $\lesssim$ on typing patterns. For example, all types are subtypes of the top type, which corresponds to the fact that all typing patterns are less or equally defined as $\top$ (similar for $\perp$ and the bottom type). However, the role of these type bounds is quite different. The top and bottom types are introduced to facilitate the proofs of certain properties and the design of type systems, for example, in bounded quantification [18], whereas the $\top$ and $\perp$ types are used as parts of larger patterns to track which variants are ill-typed, and to mask result types accordingly.

Our work is also related to the work of Siek et al. on gradual typing [22, 23]. The goal of that work is to integrate static and dynamic typing into a single type system. They use the symbol ? to represent a type that is not known statically (that is, it is a dynamic type). This is similar to our $\perp$ type in partial types and typing patterns, particularly in the way it is used to determine a notion of *informativeness*. A type is less informative if it contains more ? types (or rather, if more of the type is subsumed by ? types). This relation is similar to an inverse of our more-defined relation on typing patterns, where a pattern becomes less defined as it is subsumed by $\perp$ types. The biggest difference between this work and our own is that $\perp$ types represent parts of a variational program that are statically known to be type incorrect, whereas the parts of a program annotated with ? types may still be dynamically type correct. Also, their system isolates ? types as much as possible with respect to a plain type, while we allow $\perp$ types to propagate outward in plain types, but contain $\perp$ types to as few *variants* as possible. This is best demonstrated by the fact that (if we extend the notion of definedness to partial types) $\perp$ is equally defined as $\perp \rightarrow$ `Int`, but ? is strictly less informative than ? $\rightarrow$ `Int`.

Generating informative error messages and determining the causes and locations of type errors has been extensively studied in type systems [15, 28]. Our type system does not address this problem per se, as far as individual program variants is concerned. However, a partial type does indicate which variants contain type errors. This information can be combined with traditional, single-variant systems to improve error location in variational programs.

The unification problem for equational theories that contain distributivity and associativity is known to be undecidable [27]. However, it is decidable when an idempotency law is added [1]. Therefore, because of choice idempotency, our unification problem is decidable. As we have shown, our problem is also unitary. This is important for implementing the type inference algorithm because it is necessary for a type system that has the principal typing property.

11. Conclusion and Future Work

We have presented a type system and inference algorithm for assigning partial types to variational programs. We have shown that the addition of error types and the resulting more-defined ordering for types integrates well with a variational type system. Specifically, we were able to extend the unification and type inference algorithms to produce most-general partial types for variational lambda calculus expressions. These results are an important step toward providing type-system support for massively variational software, and for the incremental development of variational programs.

In future work we plan to explore incremental variational type inference. We expect that programmers often work on only a small subset of variants at a time, and so there is huge opportunity for efficiency gains by reusing the unchanged variational context in typing incremental changes. We expect this historical information to also be useful for producing more precise error feedback. We also plan to investigate how variational typing can be used to support strong but flexible typing in functional, staged programming languages.

Acknowledgments

This work is supported by the Air Force Office of Scientific Research under the grant FA9550-09-1-0229 and by the National Science Foundation under the grant CCF-0917092.

References

[1] S. Anantharaman, P. Narendran, and M. Rusinowitch. Unification Modulo ACUI Plus Homomorphisms/Distributivity. *Journal of Automated Reasoning*, 33:1–28, 2004.

[2] S. Apel and C. Kästner. An Overview of Feature-Oriented Software Development. *Journal of Object Technology*, 8(5):49–84, 2009.

[3] F. Baader and W. Snyder. Unification Theory. In A. Robinson and A. Voronkov, editors, *Handbook of Automated Reasoning*, chapter 8, pages 445–533. Elsevier Science Publishers, Amsterdam, NL, 2001.

[4] D. Batory, J. N. Sarvela, and A. Rauschmayer. Scaling Step-Wise Refinement. *IEEE Trans. on Software Engineering*, 30(6):355–371, 2004.

[5] S. Chen, M. Erwig, and E. Walkingshaw. Extending Type Inference to Variational Programs. Technical Report, School of EECS, Oregon State University, 2012. Available at: `http://eecs.oregonstate.edu/~erwig/ToSC/VLC-TypeSystem.pdf`.

[6] L. Damas and R. Milner. Principal Type Schemes for Functional Programming Languages. In *9th ACM Symp. on Principles of Programming Languages*, pages 207–208, 1982.

[7] M. Dezani-Ciancaglini, S. Ghilezan, and B. Venneri. The "Relevance" of Intersection and Union Types. *Notre Dame Journal of Formal Logic*, 38(2):246–269, 1997.

[8] M. Erwig and E. Walkingshaw. The Choice Calculus: A Representation for Software Variation. *ACM Trans. on Software Engineering and Methodology*, 21(1):6:1–6:27, 2011.

[9] GHC. The Glasgow Haskell Compiler. `http://haskell.org/ghc`.

[10] K. Kagawa. Polymorphic Variants in Haskell. In *ACM SIGPLAN Workshop on Haskell*, pages 37–47. ACM, 2006.

[11] C. Kästner, S. Apel, T. Thüm, and G. Saake. Type Checking Annotation-Based Product Lines. *ACM Trans. on Software Engineering and Methodology*, 2012. To appear.

[12] A. Kenner, C. Kästner, S. Haase, and T. Leich. TypeChef: Toward Type Checking #ifdef Variability in C. In *Int. Workshop on Feature-Oriented Software Development*, pages 25–32, 2010.

[13] C. H. P. Kim, C. Kästner, and D. Batory. On the Modularity of Feature Interactions. In *Int. Conf. on Generative Programming and Component Engineering*, pages 19–23, 2008.

[14] D. Kozen, J. Palsberg, and M. I. Schwartzbach. Efficient Inference of Partial Types. In *Journal of Computer and System Sciences*, pages 363–371, 1992.

[15] B. S. Lerner, M. Flower, D. Grossman, and C. Chambers. Searching for Type-Error Messages. In *ACM Conf. on Programming Language Design and Implementation*, pages 425–434, 2007.

[16] M. Mezini and K. Ostermann. Variability Management with Feature-Oriented Programming and Aspects. *ACM SIGSOFT Software Engineering Notes*, 29(6):127–136, 2004.

[17] P. M. O'Keefe and M. Wand. Type Inference for Partial Types is Decidable. In *European Symp. on Programming*, pages 408–417, 1992.

[18] B. C. Pierce. Bounded Quantification with Bottom. Technical report, Computer Science Department, Indiana University, 1997.

[19] B. C. Pierce. *Types and Programming Languages*. MIT Press, Cambridge, MA, 2002.

[20] K. Pohl, G. Böckle, and F. van der Linden. *Software Product Line Engineering: Foundations, Principles, and Techniques*. Springer-Verlang, Berlin Heidelberg, 2005.

[21] J. A. Robinson. A Machine-Oriented Logic Based on the Resolution Principle. *Journal of the ACM*, 12(1):23–41, 1965.

[22] J. G. Siek and W. Taha. Gradual Typing for Functional Languages. In *Scheme and Functional Programming Workshop*, pages 81–92, 2006.

[23] J. G. Siek and M. Vachharajani. Gradual Typing with Unification-Based Inference. In *Symp. on Dynamic Languages*, pages 7:1–7:12, 2008.

[24] W. Taha and T. Sheard. MetaML and Multi-Stage Programming with Explicit Annotations. *Theoretical Computer Science*, 248(1-2):211–242, 2000.

[25] S. Thaker, D. Batory, D. Kitchin, and W. Cook. Safe Composition of Product Lines. In *Int. Conf. on Generative Programming and Component Engineering*, pages 95–104, 2007.

[26] S. Thatte. Type Inference with Partial Types. In *Int. Colloq. on Automata, Languages and Programming*, pages 615–629, 1988.

[27] E. Tiden and S. Arnborg. Unification Problems with One-Sided Distributivity. *Journal of Symbolic Computation*, 3(1-2):183–202, 1987.

[28] M. Wand. Finding the Source of Type Errors. In *ACM Symp. on Principles of Programming Languages*, pages 38–43, 1986.

Superficially Substructural Types

Neelakantan R. Krishnaswami
MPI-SWS
neelk@mpi-sws.org

Aaron Turon
Northeastern University
turon@ccs.neu.edu

Derek Dreyer
MPI-SWS
dreyer@mpi-sws.org

Deepak Garg
MPI-SWS
dg@mpi-sws.org

Abstract

Many substructural type systems have been proposed for controlling access to shared state in higher-order languages. Central to these systems is the notion of a *resource*, which may be split into disjoint pieces that different parts of a program can manipulate independently without worrying about interfering with one another. Some systems support a *logical* notion of resource (such as permissions), under which two resources may be considered disjoint even if they govern the *same* piece of state. However, in nearly all existing systems, the notions of resource and disjointness are fixed at the outset, baked into the model of the language, and fairly coarse-grained in the kinds of sharing they enable.

In this paper, inspired by recent work on "fictional disjointness" in separation logic, we propose a simple and flexible way of enabling any module in a program to create its own custom type of splittable resource (represented as a commutative monoid), thus providing fine-grained control over how the module's private state is shared with its clients. This functionality can be incorporated into an otherwise standard substructural type system by means of a new typing rule we call *the sharing rule*, whose soundness we prove semantically via a novel resource-oriented Kripke logical relation.

Categories and Subject Descriptors D.3.1 [*Programming Languages*]: Formal Definitions and Theory; D.3.3 [*Programming Languages*]: Language Constructs and Features—Abstract data types; F.3.1 [*Logics and Meanings of Programs*]: Specifying and Verifying and Reasoning about Programs; F.3.3 [*Logics and Meanings of Programs*]: Studies of Program Constructs

General Terms Languages, Design, Theory, Verification

Keywords Substructural type systems, separation logic, sharing rule, commutative monoids, fictional disjointness, ADTs, hidden state, dependent types, capabilities, Kripke logical relations

1. Introduction

Over the past decade, many *substructural* type systems—based primarily on variants of *linear logic* [20] and *separation logic* [34]—have been proposed as a means of verifying critical semantic properties of higher-order stateful programs, ranging from basic memory safety to full functional correctness. These type systems and their key substructural elements go by a variety of names—*e.g.*, typestate [38, 11], uniqueness [8], regions [39], capabilities [42], Hoare types [27]—but one thing they all have in common is that they give programmers the ability to reason locally about the effects of their code on the state of shared resources.

The essence of this local reasoning is captured by the "frame" property: if an operation f consumes a resource satisfying the type or assertion A and produces one satisfying B, then f can also be seen to transform $A \otimes C$ to $B \otimes C$, where C is an arbitrary "frame" representing assumptions about the greater ambient environment in which f is executed. The $\otimes$ here denotes multiplicative (or "separating") conjunction, which ensures that the resource satisfying $A \otimes C$ can be split into disjoint pieces satisfying A and C, respectively; since f only consumes the resource satisfying A, it is guaranteed to leave the resource satisfying C untouched.

As this discussion suggests, a central element in substructural type systems is the notion of a *resource*, as well as the ability to split a resource into *disjoint* pieces. A resource, in essence, describes (1) the *knowledge* that the consumer of that resource has about the machine state, and (2) what *rights* they have to change the state. Two resources are then considered disjoint if they do not *interfere* with each other, that is: any operation permitted by the rights of one resource should not violate the knowledge of the other.

In some substructural type systems, such as those based on separation logic, resources take the form of entities—such as heaps—that enjoy an immediate *physical* interpretation of disjointness. When an operation consumes a heap h, it has full access to h as a physical object: it knows what h is and has the right to modify it as it pleases. In other systems, resources take the form of "permissions" or "capabilities", which are strictly *logical* descriptions of the knowledge and rights concerning some shared state. In particular, two logical resources may be considered disjoint even if they govern the *same* piece of state. For instance, "fractional" permissions [7] enable the "full" permission to a memory location ($x \mapsto v$)—which gives its consumer the knowledge that x currently points to v and the right to update x's contents—to be split into two "half" permissions ($x \overset{.5}{\mapsto} v \otimes x \overset{.5}{\mapsto} v$)—which provide their respective consumers with the knowledge that x points to v but *not* the right to update it. These half permissions are logically disjoint because they ensure that neither consumer can violate the other's knowledge that x points to v.

However, in nearly all existing systems, the notions of resource and disjointness are fixed at the outset, baked into the model of the language, and fairly coarse-grained in the kinds of sharing they enable. This is unfortunate: ideally, we would like to have a way of defining more fine-grained *custom* logical notions of resource and disjointness on a per-module or per-library basis.

1.1 Motivating Example: A Memory Manager

To take a concrete example, consider a module M implementing an explicit memory manager. M will of course maintain some private data structure representing its free list, and it will expect a certain invariant A of that data structure to hold whenever its methods are invoked. If M is simple enough that this invariant is the *only* constraint needed on its methods, we can give it an interface like:

$$\begin{array}{rcl} \mathsf{malloc} & : & A \multimap \exists X : \mathsf{Loc}.\ \mathsf{ptr}\ X \otimes \mathsf{cap}\ X\ 1 \otimes A \\ \mathsf{free} & : & \forall X : \mathsf{Loc}.\ \mathsf{ptr}\ X \otimes \mathsf{cap}\ X\ 1 \otimes A \multimap A \end{array}$$

Here, $\mathsf{ptr}\ X$ is a singleton type inhabited only by the pointer X, and $\mathsf{cap}\ X\ 1$ represents the knowledge that X points to a value of unit type 1, along with the full capability to modify it. The invariant A is threaded through the pre- and post-conditions of the operations, but in some type systems it could even be hidden entirely [32].

However, the above interface would *not* work for a more realistic memory manager that required the client to free only memory previously allocated through the manager. For instance, in the Version 7 Unix memory manager—verified (and debugged) recently by Wickerson *et al.* [43]—the implementation internally maintains a chain of pointers to the cells preceding contiguous blocks of memory, both free and allocated. In order to preserve its invariant that the blocks it maintains are contiguous, the manager must only permit its client to free a block that the manager "knows about" (has marked as allocated in its internal chain). The type of the free operation must therefore make the set of allocated blocks explicit, so that it can require the freed location to belong to that set. We can achieve this by parameterizing the manager's invariant A over the set of allocated locations L, and revising its interface as follows:

$$\begin{array}{rcl} \mathsf{malloc} & : & \forall L : \mathsf{LocSet}.\ A(L) \multimap \\ & & \quad \exists X : \mathsf{Loc}.\ \mathsf{ptr}\ X \otimes \mathsf{cap}\ X\ 1 \otimes A(L \uplus \{X\}) \\ \mathsf{free} & : & \forall L : \mathsf{LocSet}.\ \forall X : \mathsf{Loc}. \\ & & \quad \mathsf{ptr}\ X \otimes \mathsf{cap}\ X\ 1 \otimes A(L \uplus \{X\}) \multimap A(L) \end{array}$$

Unfortunately, this latter interface is problematic if the memory manager is used by multiple client modules that one would like to typecheck/verify independently. Each client module only really cares about the locations that *it* allocates/frees, but because the "global" state of the memory manager—*i.e.,* the full set of allocated locations L—is made explicit in the type $A(L)$, each client will in fact be sensitive to interference from other clients. Consequently, each client will need to pollute its own interface with explicit information about how it affects this global state, thereby leaking implementation details in the process.

Ideally, we would like a way of giving each client its own *local* view of the global state. A simple way to provide such a local view would be to allow the memory allocator's invariant to somehow be split up into (and reconstituted from) logically disjoint pieces:

$$\begin{array}{rcl} \mathsf{split} & : & \forall L_1, L_2 : \mathsf{LocSet}.\ A(L_1 \uplus L_2) \multimap A(L_1) \otimes A(L_2) \\ \mathsf{join} & : & \forall L_1, L_2 : \mathsf{LocSet}.\ A(L_1) \otimes A(L_2) \multimap A(L_1 \uplus L_2) \end{array}$$

In particular, given $A(L)$ for some initial L, we could use split to generate any number of copies of $A(\emptyset)$, each of which could be passed to a separate client, thus rendering each client completely oblivious to the existence of the others.

Intuitively, the splitting provided by the split operation is perfectly safe because L_1 and L_2 are disjoint sets, and so the only *right* granted to the owner of $A(L_1)$—namely, the right to free the locations in L_1—cannot possibly violate the *knowledge* of the owner of $A(L_2)$—namely, that the locations in L_2 are allocated. Clearly, though, if we can support such split and join operations, then $A(L)$ no longer means what it did previously: rather than asserting that L *is* the global set of allocated locations, it now asserts merely that L is some *subset* of them that the owner of $A(L)$ has the right to free. In other words, we are treating sets of locations as a kind of splittable resource, and we are using this custom resource to control the knowledge and rights that any one client module has concerning the global, shared state of the memory manager.

The question is: how can we put this intuition on a sound and flexible formal footing, thus enabling any module to develop its own custom notion of splittable resource in a safe, principled way?

1.2 Commutative Monoids to the Rescue!

The goal of this paper is to show that the above example is but one instance of a simple and general pattern, and that there is a simple and general way of supporting such custom resource management within an otherwise standard substructural type system.

The basic idea behind our approach is inspired by some very recent work on separation logic, specifically Jensen and Birkedal's *fictional separation logic* [21], Dinsdale-Young *et al.*'s *views* [12], and Ley-Wild and Nanevski's *subjective concurrent separation logic* [25]. Although these developments are all motivated by different concerns (to be described in Section 5), a common thread running through them is the idea of accounting for various custom notions of splittable resource—along with their attendant notions of *knowledge* and *rights*—in terms of *commutative monoids.*

A commutative monoid is a set S equipped with a commutative, associative *composition* operator $(\cdot) : S \times S \to S$, and a *unit* element $\epsilon \in S$ such that $\forall x \in S.\ x \cdot \epsilon = x$. If one can cast one's notion of custom resource as a commutative monoid, then one can view the global, shared state as the composition $r_L \cdot r_F$ of one's *local* resource r_L with the resource r_F of one's *frame* (*i.e.,* one's *environment*). Owning the local r_L gives one the *knowledge* that the global state must be some "extension" of r_L (*i.e.,* it must equal $r_L \cdot r_F$ for some frame resource r_F). It also gives one the *right* to update the global state however one likes, so long as the new global state satisfies $r'_L \cdot r_F$ for some r'_L. In other words, one may change one's local resource to an arbitrary r'_L, so long as the change is *frame-respecting, i.e.,* it leaves the frame resource r_F alone.

The notion of logical resource that we suggested for the memory manager module in Section 1.1 is expressible very naturally as a commutative monoid: sets of locations, with composition defined as disjoint union ($\uplus$) and $\epsilon = \emptyset$. Furthermore, the malloc and free operations are both frame-respecting, due to their universal quantification over the framing location set L.

But many other notions of splittable resource are instances of commutative monoids as well. In their work on fictional separation logic (FSL) [21], Jensen and Birkedal thus propose a way of allowing different modules in a program to specify their interfaces in terms of assertions—such as $A(L)$ in Section 1.1—about different, module-specific notions of resource, encoded as different commutative monoids. This ability to encode module-specific protocols governing shared state was in fact already present to a large extent in earlier work on *deny-guarantee reasoning* [15] and *concurrent abstract predicates* [13]; the main selling point of FSL in comparison is that it adopts a simpler and more abstract monoidal view of resource that is not bound up with concurrency-related concerns. (For a more detailed analysis, see Section 5.)

In this paper, we show how to lift the ideas of FSL and its predecessors from the first-order setting of separation logic to the higher-order setting of a substructural type system.

1.3 Contributions

We make two main contributions: one syntactic, the other semantic.

Our **syntactic** contribution is to propose a new typing rule, which we call *the sharing rule*, that gives the author of a module fine-grained control over how the module's private linear resources (*e.g.,* the full capability to access its internal data structures) are shared with its clients. In particular, as witnessed in our motivating example, the sharing rule allows the capabilities to access this shared state to be split (by $\otimes$) into pieces that are logically disjoint according to a custom commutative monoid of one's choosing. This means that our type system is only *superficially substructural*: under the hood, the A and B in $A \otimes B$ may both be capabilities to read and write *the very same* shared state, albeit in ways that are guaranteed not to interfere with each other.

We present the sharing rule in the context of a fairly standard affine type system (Section 2), supporting a combination of features from Dependent ML [45] and $\mathbf{L}^3$ [5]. While this language is not as expressive as, say, Hoare Type Theory [27]—which we would eventually like to target as well—it is nevertheless rich enough to encode interesting examples (Section 3), while simple enough to focus our attention on the sharing rule itself.

Compared with the support for custom monoids in FSL, our sharing rule is more flexible because it enables types indexed by different commutative monoids to be freely intermingled using the language's general-purpose $\otimes$ type. In contrast, FSL's "indirect Hoare triples" must be indexed explicitly by a particular monoid, and composing specifications that are indexed by different monoids requires additional, somewhat inconvenient, machinery.

However, in the face of arbitrary higher-order programs, our implementation of the sharing rule necessarily carries a dynamic cost, namely the use of a lock to protect updates to the shared state from unsafe re-entrancy. We do not believe this imposes a serious practical restriction on the use of the sharing rule in our sequential setting, but it is clear that a better approach is needed if we wish to scale to the concurrent setting. For special cases of the rule—*e.g.*, where the primitive operations on the shared state do not invoke unknown functions—it is possible to show that locking is not needed, but we leave a thorough examination of such optimizations to future work. We discuss another, more complicated but potentially more scalable approach in Section 5.

Our **semantic** contribution is a novel step-indexed Kripke logical-relations model of shared state, which facilitates a clean semantic proof of the soundness of our sharing rule (Section 4). The structure of our Kripke model directly reflects the intuition behind the sharing rule. In particular, its "possible worlds" W—which encode representation invariants on shared state—take the form of tuples of commutative monoids (think: one monoid for each application of the sharing rule). Associated with each monoid is a resource predicate that says how to interpret an element of the monoid as an invariant on some underlying resources—*e.g.*, in our motivating example, how the full set of allocated locations L maps to an invariant on the memory manager's internal state. Crucially, this resource predicate may describe invariants not only on the physical heap, but also on *logical* resources (expressed as a tuple of elements of all the monoids in W), thus enabling applications of the sharing rule to be soundly layered on top of one another.

We conclude the paper with a detailed comparison to related work (Section 5) and a discussion of future work (Section 6).

Sorts	σ	$::=$	$\mathbb{N} \mid 1 \mid \sigma \times \sigma \mid 2 \mid \mathsf{Loc} \mid \sigma \to \sigma$
		$\mid$	$\sigma_\bot \mid \mathsf{seq}\ \sigma \mid \mathcal{P}(\sigma) \mid \mathbb{Q} \mid \ldots$
Index Terms	t	$::=$	$X \mid n \mid \mathsf{tt} \mid \mathsf{ff} \mid \ldots$
Propositions	P, Q	$::=$	$\top \mid P \wedge Q \mid P \supset Q \mid \bot \mid P \vee Q$
		$\mid$	$\forall X : \sigma.\ P \mid \exists X : \sigma.\ P$
		$\mid$	$t = u \mid t > u \mid \ldots$
Kinds	κ	$::=$	$\circ \mid \sigma \to \kappa$
Types	A	$::=$	$1 \mid A \otimes B \mid A \multimap B \mid !A$
		$\mid$	$\mathsf{ptr}\ t \mid \mathsf{cap}\ t\ A$
		$\mid$	$\forall \alpha : \kappa.\ A \mid \exists \alpha : \kappa.\ A$
		$\mid$	$\forall X : \sigma :: P.\ A \mid \exists X : \sigma :: P.\ A \mid$
		$\mid$	$\mathsf{bool}\ t \mid \mathsf{nat}\ t \mid [A]$
		$\mid$	$\mathsf{if}(t, A, B) \mid \alpha \mid \lambda X : \sigma.\ A \mid A\ t$
Terms	e	$::=$	$x \mid \langle\rangle \mid \langle e, e' \rangle \mid \mathsf{let}\ \langle x, y \rangle = e\ \mathsf{in}\ e'$
		$\mid$	$\lambda x.\ e \mid e\ e' \mid !v \mid \mathsf{let}\ !x = e\ \mathsf{in}\ e'$
		$\mid$	$\mathsf{new}(e) \mid \mathsf{get}_{e'}\ e \mid e :=_{e''} e'$
		$\mid$	$\mathsf{tt} \mid \mathsf{ff} \mid \mathsf{if}(e, e_1, e_2)$
		$\mid$	$n \mid \mathsf{case}(e, 0 \to e_1, \mathsf{s}\ x \to e_2)$
		$\mid$	$\mathsf{fix}\ f(x).\ e \mid \mathsf{share}(e, \overline{v_i}) \mid \bullet$
Eval Contexts	E	$::=$	$[\,] \mid \langle E, e \rangle \mid \langle v, E \rangle \mid$
		$\mid$	$\mathsf{let}\ \langle x, y \rangle = E\ \mathsf{in}\ e \mid E\ e \mid v\ E$
		$\mid$	$!E \mid \mathsf{let}\ !x = E\ \mathsf{in}\ e$
		$\mid$	$\mathsf{new}(E) \mid \mathsf{get}_e\ E \mid \mathsf{get}_E\ v \mid E :=_{e'} e$
		$\mid$	$v :=_{e'} E \mid v :=_E v' \mid \mathsf{if}(E, e, e')$
		$\mid$	$\mathsf{case}(E, 0 \to e_1, \mathsf{s}\ x \to e_2) \mid \mathsf{share}(E, \overline{v_i})$
Values	v	$::=$	$\langle\rangle \mid \langle v, v' \rangle \mid \lambda x.\ e \mid !v$
		$\mid$	$\ell \mid \mathsf{fix}\ f(x).\ e \mid n \mid \mathsf{tt} \mid \mathsf{ff} \mid \bullet \mid x$
Heaps	h	$::=$	$\cdot \mid h, \ell : v$
Contexts			
Index/Type	Σ	$::=$	$\cdot \mid \Sigma, \alpha : \kappa \mid \Sigma, X : \sigma$
Proposition	Π	$::=$	$\cdot \mid \Pi, P$
Unrestricted	Γ	$::=$	$\cdot \mid \Gamma, x : A$
Affine	Δ	$::=$	$\cdot \mid \Delta, x : A$
Combined	Ω	$::=$	$\Sigma; \Pi; \Gamma; \Delta$

Figure 1. Syntax

$\Sigma \vdash A : \kappa$	Well-kindedness
$\Sigma \rhd t : \sigma$	Well-sortedness
$\Sigma \rhd P : \mathsf{prop}$	Well-formedness of propositions
$\Sigma \vdash \Pi\ \mathsf{ok}$	Well-formedness of propositional context
$\Sigma \vdash \Gamma\ \mathsf{ok}$	Well-formedness of hypothetical context
$\Sigma; \Pi \vdash P$	Logical entailment
$\Sigma; \Pi \vdash A \equiv B : \kappa$	Type constructor equality
$\Omega \vdash e : A$	Well-typedness

Figure 2. Judgments

2. The Core Language

Our core calculus is an implicitly-typed version of affine F_ω, extended with domains that index types. We call these domains *sorts* and their elements index terms. With a sufficiently rich language of index terms, and propositions and type-level quantification over them, we retain much of the flexibility of dependent types for giving rich type-based specifications for programs, without requiring the index terms to coincide with program terms, thus avoiding the problematic issue of affine variable occurrences in types.

Figure 1 lists the syntactic forms of the language, including sorts, index terms, propositions over index terms, kinds, types, terms, contexts (for the static semantics) and heaps (for the dynamic semantics). Judgments for checking well-formedness of kinds, index terms, propositions and contexts, as well as logical inference, type equality and typing are listed in Figure 2, but we elide the standard rules for inferring these judgments.

Sorts, Index Terms, and Propositions Sorts, ranged over by the metavariable σ, include mathematical domains such as natural numbers, tuples, functions, locations and sets, denoted by the metavariable t. Sorts are interpreted as plain mathematical sets and new sorts can be added if needed. For precise specification of properties of index terms, we allow propositions of first-order logic over the index domains to appear in our types. The standard judgment $\Sigma; \Pi \vdash P$ means that P can be inferred from the assumptions in Π, for all instances of the free variables in Σ.

Types and Terms We use a standard affine type system, whose rules are shown in Figures 4 and 5. The natural presentation of typing has four contexts; to increase the legibility of the rules, we abbreviate these with a single symbol Ω, and define notations for adding hypotheses and merging contexts in Figure 3.

As expected, the unit term $\langle\rangle : 1$ types in a context with any set of resources Δ; the typing rule for $\langle e_1, e_2 \rangle : A \otimes B$ splits its

$$
\begin{array}{lcll}
\Omega, x : A & = & \Sigma; \Pi; \Gamma; \Delta, x : A & \text{if } \Omega = \Sigma; \Pi; \Gamma; \Delta \\
\Omega, x :_! A & = & \Sigma; \Pi; \Gamma, x : A; \Delta & \text{if } \Omega = \Sigma; \Pi; \Gamma; \Delta \\
\Omega, \alpha : \kappa & = & \Sigma, \alpha : \kappa; \Pi; \Gamma; \Delta & \text{if } \Omega = \Sigma; \Pi; \Gamma; \Delta \\
\Omega, X : \sigma & = & \Sigma, X : \sigma; \Pi; \Gamma; \Delta & \text{if } \Omega = \Sigma; \Pi; \Gamma; \Delta \\
\Omega, P & = & \Sigma; \Pi, P; \Gamma; \Delta & \text{if } \Omega = \Sigma; \Pi; \Gamma; \Delta \\
\\
\Omega_1, \Omega_2 & = & \Sigma; \Pi; \Gamma; \Delta_1, \Delta_2 & \text{if } \Omega_1 = \Sigma; \Pi; \Gamma; \Delta_1 \\
 & & & \phantom{\text{if }} \Omega_2 = \Sigma; \Pi; \Gamma; \Delta_2
\end{array}
$$

Figure 3. Context Manipulation Operations

$$\boxed{\Omega \vdash e : A}$$

$$
\frac{x : A \in \Gamma}{\Sigma; \Pi; \Gamma; \Delta \vdash x : A}
\qquad
\frac{x : A \in \Delta}{\Sigma; \Pi; \Gamma; \Delta \vdash x : A}
\qquad
\frac{}{\Omega \vdash \langle\rangle : 1}
$$

$$
\frac{\Omega \vdash v : A}{\Omega \vdash \bullet : [A]}
\qquad
\frac{\Omega_1 \vdash e_1 : A \qquad \Omega_2 \vdash e_2 : B}{\Omega_1, \Omega_2 \vdash \langle e_1, e_2 \rangle : A \otimes B}
$$

$$
\frac{\Omega_1 \vdash e : A \otimes B \qquad \Omega_2, x : A, y : B \vdash e' : C}{\Omega_1, \Omega_2 \vdash \mathsf{let}\ \langle x, y \rangle = e\ \mathsf{in}\ e' : C}
$$

$$
\frac{\Omega, x : A \vdash e : B}{\Omega \vdash \lambda x.\ e : A \multimap B}
\qquad
\frac{\Omega_1 \vdash e : A \multimap B \qquad \Omega_2 \vdash e' : A}{\Omega_1, \Omega_2 \vdash e\ e' : B}
$$

$$
\frac{\Sigma; \Pi; \Gamma; \cdot \vdash v : A}{\Sigma; \Pi; \Gamma; \Delta \vdash !v : !A}
\qquad
\frac{\Omega_1 \vdash e : !A \qquad \Omega_2, x :_! A \vdash e' : C}{\Omega_1, \Omega_2 \vdash \mathsf{let}\ !x = e\ \mathsf{in}\ e' : C}
$$

$$
\frac{\Omega \vdash e : A}{\Omega \vdash \mathsf{new}(e) : \exists X : \mathsf{Loc} :: \top.\ !\mathsf{ptr}\ X \otimes \mathsf{cap}\ X\ A}
$$

$$
\frac{\Omega \vdash e : \mathsf{ptr}\ t \qquad \Omega' \vdash e' : \mathsf{cap}\ t\ A}{\Omega, \Omega' \vdash \mathsf{get}_{e'}\ e : A \otimes \mathsf{cap}\ t\ 1}
$$

$$
\frac{\Omega_1 \vdash e : \mathsf{ptr}\ t \qquad \Omega_2 \vdash e' : A \qquad \Omega_3 \vdash e'' : \mathsf{cap}\ t\ 1}{\Omega_1, \Omega_2, \Omega_3 \vdash e :=_{e''} e' : \mathsf{cap}\ t\ A}
$$

$$
\frac{\Sigma; \Pi; \Gamma, f : A \multimap B; x : A \vdash e : B}{\Sigma; \Pi; \Gamma; \cdot \vdash \mathsf{fix}\ f(x).\ e : A \multimap B}
$$

$$
\frac{}{\Omega \vdash \mathsf{tt} : \mathsf{bool}\ \mathsf{tt}}
\qquad
\frac{}{\Omega \vdash \mathsf{ff} : \mathsf{bool}\ \mathsf{ff}}
\qquad
\frac{}{\Omega \vdash n : \mathsf{nat}\ n}
$$

$$
\frac{\Omega \vdash e : \mathsf{bool}\ t \qquad \Omega', t = \mathsf{tt} \vdash e_1 : C \qquad \Omega', t = \mathsf{ff} \vdash e_2 : C}{\Omega, \Omega' \vdash \mathsf{if}(e, e_1, e_2) : C}
$$

$$
\frac{\begin{array}{c}\Omega \vdash e : \mathsf{nat}\ t \\ \Omega', t = 0 \vdash e_1 : C \qquad \Omega', X : \mathbb{N}, t = \mathsf{s}\ X, x : \mathsf{nat}\ X \vdash e_2 : C\end{array}}{\Omega, \Omega' \vdash \mathsf{case}(e, 0 \to e_1, \mathsf{s}\ x \to e_2) : C}
$$

Figure 4. Typing Rules

resource context Δ into two disjoint parts for checking subterms e_1 and e_2; and, to type the affine function $\lambda x.\ e : A \multimap B$, we add the hypothesis $x : A$ to the affine context to check the body e.

The exponential $!A$ is subject to a *value restriction* — we can type terms $!v$ at type $!A$ only when v is a value. The intuition for this restriction is that (following the standard affine interpretation) a term of type $!A$ is duplicable, so the value it evaluates to must not depend on affine resources. If v were not a value, then its evaluation could create new affine resources on which its result depended (e.g., the evaluation might allocate fresh memory and return it).

The base types bool t and nat u are *singleton* types, indexed by the Boolean sort 2 and the natural number sort $\mathbb{N}$, respectively. So,

$$\boxed{\Omega \vdash e : A}$$

$$
\frac{\Omega, \alpha : \kappa \vdash v : B}{\Omega \vdash v : \forall \alpha : \kappa.\ B}
\qquad
\frac{\Omega, X : \sigma, P \vdash v : A}{\Omega \vdash v : \forall X : \sigma :: P.\ A}
$$

$$
\frac{\begin{array}{c}\Omega \vdash e : \forall X : \sigma :: P.\ A \\ \Omega = \Sigma; \Pi; \Gamma; \Delta \qquad \Sigma \rhd t : \sigma \qquad \Sigma; \Pi \vdash [t/X]P\end{array}}{\Omega \vdash e : [t/X]A}
$$

$$
\frac{\Omega \vdash e : \forall \alpha : \kappa.\ B \qquad \Omega = \Sigma; \Pi; \Gamma; \Delta \qquad \Sigma \vdash A : \kappa}{\Omega \vdash e : [A/\alpha]B}
$$

$$
\frac{\begin{array}{c}\Omega \vdash e : [t/X]A \\ \Omega = \Sigma; \Pi; \Gamma; \Delta \qquad \Sigma \rhd t : \sigma \qquad \Sigma; \Pi \vdash [t/X]P\end{array}}{\Omega \vdash e : \exists X : \sigma :: P.\ A}
$$

$$
\frac{\begin{array}{c}\Omega \vdash v : \exists X : \sigma :: P.\ A \\ \Omega', X : \sigma, P, x : A \vdash e : C \qquad X, x \notin FV(C)\end{array}}{\Omega, \Omega' \vdash [v/x]e : C}
$$

$$
\frac{\begin{array}{c}\Omega = \Sigma; \Pi; \Gamma; \Delta \\ \Sigma \vdash A : \kappa \qquad \Sigma, \alpha : \kappa \vdash B : \circ \qquad \Omega \vdash e : [A/\alpha]B\end{array}}{\Omega \vdash e : \exists \alpha : \kappa.\ B}
$$

$$
\frac{\Omega \vdash v : \exists \alpha : \kappa.\ B \qquad \Omega', \alpha : \kappa, x : B \vdash e : C \qquad \alpha \notin FV(C)}{\Omega, \Omega' \vdash [v/x]e : C}
$$

$$
\frac{\Omega = \Sigma; \Pi; \Gamma; \Delta \qquad \Omega \vdash e : A \qquad \Sigma; \Pi \vdash A \equiv B : \circ}{\Omega \vdash e : B}
$$

$$
\frac{\begin{array}{c}\Omega = \Sigma; \Pi; \Gamma; \Delta \\ \Sigma; \Pi \vdash P \vee Q \qquad \Omega, P \vdash e : A \qquad \Omega, Q \vdash e : A\end{array}}{\Omega \vdash e : A}
$$

$$
\frac{\begin{array}{c}\Omega = \Sigma; \Pi; \Gamma; \Delta \\ \Sigma; \Pi \vdash \exists X : \sigma.\ P \qquad \Omega, X : \sigma, P \vdash e : A \qquad \Sigma \vdash A : \circ\end{array}}{\Omega \vdash e : A}
$$

$$
\frac{\Omega = \Sigma; \Pi; \Gamma; \Delta \qquad \Sigma; \Pi \vdash \bot \qquad \Sigma \vdash A : \circ}{\Omega \vdash e : A}
$$

Figure 5. Typing Rules, Continued

for example, the only value of type bool tt is tt and the only value of type nat 17 is 17.

For access to shared memory, we introduce the singleton type ptr ℓ. A term of type ptr ℓ evaluates to the location ℓ. Additionally, we have a capability type cap ℓ A, which represents the *permission* to dereference the pointer ℓ and obtain a value of type A. Intuitively, ℓ : ptr ℓ is a freely duplicable pointer, which can be shared, but the capability to use the pointer, of type cap ℓ A, is affine, and can be shared only in a controlled manner using our sharing rule. Since cap ℓ A only represents a capability, the actual value of type cap ℓ A is *computationally irrelevant*, and we write it as $\bullet$.

The two types ptr t and cap t A are tied to each other by the typing rules for reading and writing memory. For example, the $\mathsf{get}_{e'}$ e operation (see Figure 4) dereferences a pointer e of type ptr t, but it requires the capability e' of type cap t A. It returns a pair of type (cap t 1) $\otimes$ A. The operational semantics of $\mathsf{get}_\bullet$ ℓ (Figure 6), removes the current value of ℓ from the store, and replaces it with the value $\langle\rangle$. (It cannot also leave the contents of the pointer in place since doing so would violate any affine constraints on the contents. However, such behaviour is encodable for references containing a $!A$, which is duplicable.) The write

$$
\begin{array}{lcl}
\langle h; \mathsf{let}\ \langle x_1, x_2\rangle = \langle v_1, v_2\rangle\ \mathsf{in}\ e\rangle & \hookrightarrow & \langle h; [v_1/x_1, v_2/x_2]e\rangle \\
\langle h; (\lambda x.\ e)\ v\rangle & \hookrightarrow & \langle h; [v/x]e\rangle \\
\langle h; \mathsf{let}\ !x = !v\ \mathsf{in}\ e\rangle & \hookrightarrow & \langle h; [v/x]e\rangle \\
\langle h; \mathsf{new}(v)\rangle & \hookrightarrow & \langle h \uplus [\ell : v]; \langle !\ell, \bullet\rangle\rangle \\
\langle h \uplus [\ell : v]; \mathsf{get}_\bullet\ \ell\rangle & \hookrightarrow & \langle h \uplus [\ell : \langle\rangle]; \langle v, \bullet\rangle\rangle \\
\langle h \uplus [\ell : \langle\rangle]; \ell :=_\bullet v\rangle & \hookrightarrow & \langle h \uplus [\ell : v]; \bullet\rangle \\
\langle h; (\mathsf{fix}\ f(x).\ e)\ v\rangle & \hookrightarrow & \langle h; [\mathsf{fix}\ f(x).\ e/f, v/x]e\rangle \\
\langle h; \mathsf{if}(\mathsf{tt}, e, e')\rangle & \hookrightarrow & \langle h; e\rangle \\
\langle h; \mathsf{if}(\mathsf{ff}, e, e')\rangle & \hookrightarrow & \langle h; e'\rangle \\
\langle h; \mathsf{case}(0, 0 \to e, \mathsf{s}\ x \to e')\rangle & \hookrightarrow & \langle h; e\rangle \\
\langle h; \mathsf{case}(\mathsf{s}\ v, 0 \to e, \mathsf{s}\ x \to e')\rangle & \hookrightarrow & \langle h; [v/x]e'\rangle \\
\\
\langle h; \mathsf{share}(v, \overline{v_i})\rangle & \hookrightarrow & \langle h \uplus [\ell : \mathsf{ff}]; \\
 & & \quad \langle \bullet, \overline{!\mathrm{op}_i}, !\mathrm{split}, !\mathrm{join}, !\mathrm{promote}\rangle\rangle
\end{array}
$$

$$
\begin{array}{rcl}
\text{where}\quad \mathrm{op_i} & = & \lambda x.\ \mathsf{let}\ \langle \mathit{flag}, \_\rangle = \mathsf{get}_\bullet\ \ell\ \mathsf{in} \\
 & & \mathsf{let}\ \_ = \ell :=_\bullet \mathsf{tt}\ \mathsf{in} \\
 & & \mathsf{if}\ \mathit{flag}\ \mathsf{then}\ (\mathsf{fix}\ f(x).\ f\ x)\ \langle\rangle \\
 & & \qquad \mathsf{else}\ \ \mathsf{let}\ y = v_i\ x\ \mathsf{in} \\
 & & \qquad\qquad \mathsf{let}\ \_ = \ell :=_\bullet \mathsf{ff}\ \mathsf{in}\ y
\end{array}
$$

$$
\mathrm{split} = \lambda x.\ \langle \bullet, \bullet\rangle \qquad \mathrm{join} = \lambda x.\ \bullet \qquad \mathrm{promote} = \lambda x.\ !\bullet
$$

$$
\frac{\langle h; e\rangle \hookrightarrow \langle h'; e'\rangle}{\langle h; E[e]\rangle \hookrightarrow \langle h'; E[e']\rangle}
$$

Figure 6. Operational Semantics

operation $\ell :=_\bullet v'$ takes a pointer ℓ of type $\mathsf{ptr}\ \ell$, new contents v', and a capability $\bullet$ of type $\mathsf{cap}\ X\ 1$.

We generalize the idea of computational irrelevance by introducing the irrelevant type $[A]$, which is inhabited by the dummy value $\bullet$ if there is *some* value inhabiting A (see the typing rule for $[A]$ in Figure 4). The type $[A]$ is employed gainfully in our sharing rule (Section 3). Our semantic model validates several equivalances on irrelevant types, including $[\mathsf{cap}\ t\ A] \equiv \mathsf{cap}\ t\ A$ and $[A \otimes B] \equiv [B \otimes A]$, which we use freely in our examples.

Propositions over index domains are embedded in the type system at quantified types $\forall X : \sigma :: P.\ A$ and $\exists X : \sigma :: P.\ A$. Intuitively, $e : \forall X : \sigma :: P.\ A$ means that for all terms t of sort σ satisfying the proposition P, e has the type $[t/X]A$. The type $\exists X : \sigma :: P.\ A$ has the dual meaning. We also include an inconsistency rule (the last rule in Figure 5): if the propositional context Π is inconsistent (derives false), then any term is well-typed in Π. (The two prior rules give the rules for existentials and disjunctions.)

In addition, we also include type-level computation with indices with the $\mathsf{if}(t, A, B)$ type, which is equal to A if t is true, and B if t is false. There are no explicit introduction or elimination forms for this type; we simply make use of the equality judgment. To assist in this, the typing for the term-level if-then-else construct adds the appropriate equality hypotheses about its index argument in the branches of the conditional. (Similar rules apply for the other index domains, but we suppress them for space reasons.)

Kinds, κ, in our language have the forms $\circ$ (affine types) and $\sigma \to \kappa$ (dependent types). We include type-level lambda-abstraction $\lambda X : \sigma.\ A$, type-level application $A\ t$ and the universal and existential polymorphic types $\forall \alpha : \kappa.\ A$ and $\exists \alpha : \kappa.\ A$. We could also include type constructor polymorphism, but we omit it for simplicity. We need a value restriction for all quantified types because quantifiers are implicitly introduced and eliminated, and do not delay evaluation (unlike in explicit System F).

Our choice of maximal implicitness naturally makes typechecking undecidable. It should be routine to add enough type and proof annotations to make typechecking decidable, and we chose the implicit style both to make our examples more readable, and to reduce the number of clauses in the term syntax. On the whole, our language is a relatively conservative integration of the ideas of Dependent ML [45, 18] into an affine language with a type structure

$$
\frac{\Sigma \vdash A : \sigma \to \circ \qquad \Sigma; \Pi; \Gamma; \Delta \vdash e : [A\ t] \qquad \Sigma; \Pi \vdash \mathrm{monoid}_\sigma(\epsilon, (\cdot)) \qquad \forall i.\ \Sigma; \Pi; \Gamma; \cdot \vdash v_i : [A/\alpha]\mathrm{spec}_i}{\Sigma; \Pi; \Gamma; \Delta \vdash \mathsf{share}(e, \overline{v_i}) : \exists \alpha : \sigma \to \circ.\ [\alpha\ t] \otimes \overline{!\mathrm{spec}_i} \otimes !\mathsf{splitT} \otimes !\mathsf{joinT} \otimes !\mathsf{promoteT}}
$$

where

$$
\begin{array}{rcl}
\mathrm{spec}_i & = & \forall X : \sigma.\ \forall Y : \sigma'_i :: P_i.\ B_i \otimes [\alpha\ (t_i \cdot X)] \multimap \\
 & & \qquad \exists Z : \sigma''_i :: Q_i.\ C_i \otimes [\alpha\ (t'_i \cdot X)] \\
 & & \text{where } X, \alpha \notin \mathrm{FV}(P_i, Q_i, B_i, C_i, t_i, t'_i) \\
\mathsf{splitT} & = & \forall X, Y : \sigma.\ [\alpha\ (X \cdot Y)] \multimap [\alpha\ X] \otimes [\alpha\ Y] \\
\mathsf{joinT} & = & \forall X, Y : \sigma.\ [\alpha\ X] \otimes [\alpha\ Y] \multimap [\alpha\ (X \cdot Y)] \\
\mathsf{promoteT} & = & \forall X : \sigma :: X = X \cdot X.\ [\alpha\ X] \multimap ![\alpha\ X] \\
\mathrm{monoid}_\sigma(\epsilon, (\cdot)) & = & \forall X : \sigma.\ \epsilon \cdot X = X\ \wedge \\
 & & \forall X, Y : \sigma.\ X \cdot Y = Y \cdot X\ \wedge \\
 & & \forall X, Y, Z : \sigma.\ (X \cdot Y) \cdot Z = X \cdot (Y \cdot Z)
\end{array}
$$

Figure 7. The Sharing Rule

resembling that of $\mathbf{L}^3$ [5]. The primary novelty in our language is encapsulated in the *sharing rule*, which lets us put user-defined logical resources on a first-class footing. We describe this rule and its applications in the following section.

3. The Sharing Rule

A purely affine type discipline is too restrictive for most programs. In this section, we describe the *sharing rule*, our method for introducing controlled aliasing into an affine language. The intuition behind this rule is that if a library has a particular programmer-defined notion of resource, and if all the operations the programmer exposes in the interface respect the frame property for that resource, then we can treat the library's concept of resource separation as an instance of our ambient notion of separation: the tensor product.

Concretely, suppose that we have a type $A : \sigma \to \circ$, representing an affine capability indexed by a monoid σ, along with an operation $f : \forall X : \sigma.\ A(Y_1 \cdot X) \multimap A(Y_2 \cdot X)$. The type of f asserts that it can take the (logical) resource Y_1 to Y_2, and that in so doing, it preserves the frame X. If we knew that f were the only operation transforming capabilities of the form $A(t)$, then it would follow that we could split a capability $A(X \cdot Y)$ into two parts $A(X) \otimes A(Y)$, and manipulate them independently, since the only operation transforming capabilities of the form $A(t)$ is f, and f is parametric in the frame. By taking a value of type $A(X)$ and using it to construct a new abstract type, on which *only* frame-respecting operations are allowed, we can safely share an affine capability.

The sharing rule, given in Figure 7, formalizes this idea. We assert the existence of a type constructor $A : \sigma \to \circ$, where σ is a commutative monoid, and an initial resource $e : [A\ t]$, together with a family of frame-respecting, state-passing operations v_i, which take in an argument of type B_i and a state of type $[A(t_i \cdot X)]$, and return a result of type C_i and a state $[A(t'_i \cdot X)]$.[1] The full type of v_i includes additional index quantifications, which are useful for asserting propositions that connect the input and initial state or output and final state; in our examples, we suppress unused elements of this general type whenever we do not use them. The sharing operator returns a new existential type, exporting the v_i operations together with split, join and promote operations. Splitting and joining allow treating the monoidal composition as a tensor product. The promote operator takes any resource value

[1] Note that all the types of the form $A(t)$ are in proof-irrelevance brackets—this ensures that e represents a logical capability with no dynamic content, which turns out to be useful in the proof of soundness (Section 4). That said, it is possible to lift this restriction at the cost of a more complex implementation of the sharing rule. See footnote 4 in Section 4.

indexed by an idempotent value (*i.e.,* where $X = X \cdot X$), and returns a freely duplicable value.

The type constraints on the operations v_i statically ensure that $\exists X : \sigma.\ A(X)$ holds as an invariant at the beginning and ending of each call. However, if an operation v_i is passed *itself* as an argument, whether directly or indirectly, it may end up *calling* itself when its internal state does not satisfy the invariant; this is the well-known problem of *re-entrant calls* [29, 44] in higher-order imperative programs. One way to address this issue, embodied in Pottier's *anti-frame rule* [32], is to statically check that the invariant holds continuously, but this solution is often too restrictive [29]. We follow Pilkiewicz and Pottier [29] in preventing reentrancy *dynamically*, using a lock. Thus, the operational semantics of the sharing rule, given in Figure 6, is not a pure no-op, and shows how we rely on a *combination* of static and dynamic checking to enforce type safety. Sharing creates a flag variable (the lock), and wraps each operator with code to test the lock and to diverge if it is already held.

The remainder of this section gives a series of examples using our sharing rule to introduce custom notions of resource, culminating with an idealized memory allocator.

Weak References Sharing enables us to model ML-style weak references of type $!A$ that can be aliased. Suppose we have a location X : Loc, a duplicable pointer of type !ptr X and an affine capability of type cap X $!A$, and we wish to define *freely duplicable* functions to dereference and assign the location X, with types $!(1 \multimap !A)$ and $!(!A \multimap 1)$ respectively. The key idea is to use the share operator to allow these duplicable functions to close over the affine capability. First, we wrap the built-in operators $\mathsf{get}_c\ l$ and $l :=_c v$ in the following functions get_0 and set_0 whose return types resemble those of the second argument of the construct share(_, _). Typing these functions requires the equivalence $[\mathsf{cap}\ X\ !A] \equiv \mathsf{cap}\ X\ !A$, which our semantic model validates.

$$get_0 : \forall X : \mathsf{Loc}.\ !\mathsf{ptr}\ X \multimap !([\mathsf{cap}\ X\ !A] \multimap !A \otimes [\mathsf{cap}\ X\ !A])$$
$$get_0 = \lambda !l.\ !\lambda c.\ \mathsf{let}\ \langle !v, c\rangle = \mathsf{get}_c\ l\ \mathsf{in\ let}\ c = (l :=_c !v)\ \mathsf{in}\ \langle !v, c\rangle$$

$$set_0 : \forall X : \mathsf{Loc}.\ !\mathsf{ptr}\ X \multimap !(!A \otimes [\mathsf{cap}\ X\ !A] \multimap [\mathsf{cap}\ X\ !A])$$
$$set_0 = \lambda !l.\ !\lambda \langle !v, c\rangle\ .\ \mathsf{let}\ \langle !dummy, c\rangle = \mathsf{get}_c\ l\ \mathsf{in}\ l :=_c !v$$

For any expression e : !ptr X, $get_0\ e$ and $set_0\ e$ have types $!([\mathsf{cap}\ X\ !A] \multimap !A \otimes [\mathsf{cap}\ X\ !A])$ and $!(!A \otimes [\mathsf{cap}\ X\ !A] \multimap [\mathsf{cap}\ X\ !A])$, which essentially match the structure of the types spec_i in the definition of the sharing rule. Next, we define the monoid that encodes the logical state of the weak reference we are defining. Since the resource invariant for a weak reference is *fixed* and just states that the reference points to something of type $!A$, we choose the unit monoid $M = (1, \epsilon \stackrel{\text{def}}{=} \langle\rangle, (\cdot) \stackrel{\text{def}}{=} \lambda(x,y).\langle\rangle)$, and we interpret it by instantiating the capability operator A in Figure 7 with $C\ \langle\rangle \stackrel{\text{def}}{=} \mathsf{cap}\ X\ !A$. With these preliminaries, we can apply the sharing rule as follows:

$$\mathsf{share\_ref}\ \langle !l, c\rangle = \mathsf{let}\ \langle !g, !s\rangle = \langle get_0\ !l, set_0\ !l\rangle\ \mathsf{in\ share}(c, g, s)$$
$$\begin{aligned}\mathsf{share\_ref} : \forall X : \mathsf{Loc}.\ !\mathsf{ptr}\ X \otimes [\mathsf{cap}\ X\ !A] \multimap\\ \exists \alpha : 1 \to \circ.\\ [\alpha\ \langle\rangle] \otimes !\mathsf{getType} \otimes !\mathsf{setType}\\ \otimes\ !\mathsf{splitT} \otimes !\mathsf{joinT} \otimes !\mathsf{promoteT}\end{aligned}$$

where

$$\begin{aligned}\mathsf{getType} &\stackrel{\text{def}}{=} \forall X : 1.\ [\alpha\ X] \multimap !A \otimes [\alpha\ X]\\ \mathsf{setType} &\stackrel{\text{def}}{=} \forall X : 1.\ !A \otimes [\alpha\ X] \multimap [\alpha\ X]\\ \mathsf{promoteT} &\stackrel{\text{def}}{=} \forall X : 1 :: X = X \cdot X.\ [\alpha\ X] \multimap ![\alpha\ X]\end{aligned}$$

Finally, the unit monoid is idempotent by definition, so we can apply the promote operator to any value of type $[\alpha\ t]$ (for any t : 1). This allows us to construct the following function that, given a duplicable pointer and an affine capability to it, returns two duplicable functions to read and write to it:

$$\begin{aligned}&\mathsf{MLref} : \forall X : \mathsf{Loc}.\ !\mathsf{ptr}\ X \otimes [\mathsf{cap}\ X\ !A] \multimap !(1 \multimap !A) \otimes !(!A \multimap 1)\\ &\mathsf{MLref}\ \langle !l, c\rangle =\\ &\quad \mathsf{let}\ \langle q, !get, !set, \_, \_, !promote\rangle = \mathsf{share\_ref}(\langle !l, c\rangle)\ \mathsf{in}\\ &\quad \mathsf{let}\ !r = promote(q)\ \mathsf{in}\\ &\quad \mathsf{let}\ deref = !(\lambda\langle\rangle.\ \mathsf{let}\ \langle v, \_\rangle = get(r)\ \mathsf{in}\ v)\ \mathsf{in}\\ &\quad \mathsf{let}\ setref = !(\lambda a.\ \mathsf{let}\ \_ = set(a, r)\ \mathsf{in}\ \langle\rangle)\ \mathsf{in}\\ &\quad \langle deref, setref\rangle\end{aligned}$$

Monotonic Counters Next, we show how to construct shared monotonic counters that can be freely incremented by all clients. Since clients can only increment the counter, the local knowledge of each client provides a *lower bound* on the counter's actual value. Suppose our counter is stored at a location X : Loc. We start by defining a simple and standard increment function, next, that takes as argument a pointer l of type !ptr X and a capability of type cap X !(nat n), increments the counter, and returns $n+1$ and a capability of type cap X !(nat $(n+1)$). (We assume here that $+$ is a primitive operation taking unrestricted values of type nat m_1 and nat m_2 and returning an expression of type !nat $(m_1 + m_2)$.)

$$\begin{aligned}&\mathsf{next}\ \langle !l, c\rangle = \mathsf{let}\ (!n, c) = \mathsf{get}_c\ l\ \mathsf{in}\\ &\qquad\qquad\quad \mathsf{let}\ c = (l :=_c n+1)\ \mathsf{in}\ \langle n+1, c\rangle\\ &\mathsf{next} : \forall n.\ !\mathsf{ptr}\ X \otimes \mathsf{cap}\ X\ !(\mathsf{nat}\ n)\\ &\qquad \multimap !\mathsf{nat}\ (n+1) \otimes \mathsf{cap}\ X\ !(\mathsf{nat}\ (n+1))\end{aligned}$$

We wish to share the counter by passing the function next as the second argument of the share(_, _) operator. To do that, we must massage the type of next into a compatible form, capturing the fact that, once the counter is aliased, its local knowledge only provides a lower bound on its value. We define the monoid $M = (\mathbb{N}, \epsilon \stackrel{\text{def}}{=} 0, (\cdot) \stackrel{\text{def}}{=} \max)$, the type $C(n) \stackrel{\text{def}}{=} \mathsf{cap}\ X\ !(\mathsf{nat}\ n)$ (to correspond to the type A in Figure 7) and observe that next can also be given the following *weaker* type:

$$\begin{aligned}&\mathsf{next} : \mathsf{nextType}(C)\\ &\mathsf{nextType}(\alpha) = \forall Y, Z : \mathbb{N}.\ !\mathsf{ptr}\ X \otimes [\alpha(Z \cdot Y)]\\ &\qquad\qquad \multimap \exists U : \mathbb{N} :: U > Z.\ !\mathsf{nat}\ U \otimes [\alpha(U \cdot Y)]\end{aligned}$$

The weaker type, nextType(C), only asserts that if the initial value of the counter is $\max(Z, Y)$, then its value after the next operation is $\max(U, Y)$, for some $U > Z$. Intuitively, Z is the local context's initial lower bound on the counter, Y is the frame's lower bound on the counter, and U is the local context's lower bound on the counter after the increment operation. This weaker type is exactly in the form of the second argument of share(_, _), so we can define a counter sharing function that creates an abstract, shared counter from a given capability to X : Loc and the next function.

$$\begin{aligned}&\mathsf{mkCnt}\ c = \mathsf{share}(c, \mathsf{next})\\ &\mathsf{mkCnt} : \forall\ X : \mathsf{Loc}, Y : \mathbb{N}.\ [\mathsf{cap}\ X\ !(\mathsf{nat}\ Y)] \multimap\\ &\qquad \exists \alpha : \mathbb{N} \to \circ.\\ &\qquad\quad [\alpha\ Y] \otimes !\mathsf{nextType}(\alpha) \otimes !\mathsf{splitT} \otimes !\mathsf{joinT} \otimes !\mathsf{promoteT}\end{aligned}$$

Since $\max(x, x) = x$, every element of our monoid is idempotent, so we can take any counter and make it freely duplicable using the resulting function of type promoteT (as in the previous example). This permits multiple clients to make use of the same counter. Each client knows that its own use of the counter will yield monotonically increasing elements, and does not have to worry about interference with other clients of the counter.

Fractional Permissions We provide an encoding of fractional permissions that is parametric in the underlying affine resource that we wish to share. Let σ be an index sort, and let $\alpha : \sigma \to \circ$ be the type of an affine resource on top of which we want to layer a fractional permissions algebra. For example, to model fractional permissions over ref cells of type A, we could choose σ = Loc and $\alpha\ X$ = cap X A. We define a sort of fractional (rational) numbers, called Frac, and a sort of fractional permissions over σ, called FPerm(σ):

$$\begin{aligned}\mathsf{Frac} &\stackrel{\text{def}}{=} \{a \in \mathbb{Q} \mid 0 < a \leq 1\}\\ \mathsf{FPerm}(\sigma) &\stackrel{\text{def}}{=} \{\epsilon, \bot, \mathsf{Empty}\} \cup \{(a, m) \mid a \in \mathcal{S}[\![\mathsf{Frac}]\!], m \in \mathcal{S}[\![\sigma]\!]\}\end{aligned}$$

A fractional permission is either ϵ (essentially a 0 permission), $\bot$ (for an invalid permission), Empty (denoting that there is no resource currently in place to be fractionally shared), or (a, m) (denoting fractional permission a to the resource represented by m). Here, $\mathcal{S}[\![\sigma]\!]$ denotes the set of elements in the sort σ. Fractional permissions form a monoid M with unit ϵ and operation $(\cdot)$ defined on non-unit elements as follows:

$$\begin{array}{lcl} (a, m) \cdot (a', m') & = & \begin{cases} (a + a', m) & 0 < a + a' \leq 1,\ m = m' \\ \bot & \text{otherwise} \end{cases} \\ \mathsf{Empty} \cdot x & = & \begin{cases} \mathsf{Empty} & x = \epsilon \\ \bot & \text{otherwise} \end{cases} \\ \bot \cdot x & = & \bot \end{array}$$

Next, we define the affine type family FracTy_α which we actually share (this type family is called A in Figure 7). As required by the sharing rule, the type is indexed by the monoid $\mathsf{FPerm}(\sigma)$. Here, void denotes the empty type $\exists X : \mathbb{N} :: \bot.\ 1$.

$$\mathsf{FracTy}_\alpha\ \epsilon \stackrel{\text{def}}{=} \mathsf{void} \quad \mathsf{FracTy}_\alpha\ \bot \stackrel{\text{def}}{=} \mathsf{void} \quad \mathsf{FracTy}_\alpha\ \mathsf{Empty} \stackrel{\text{def}}{=} 1$$

$$\mathsf{FracTy}_\alpha\ (a, m) \stackrel{\text{def}}{=} \begin{cases} \alpha\ m & \text{when } a = 1 \\ \mathsf{void} \text{ when } a \neq 1 \end{cases}$$

Notice that this type family is uninhabitable except at the extremes. This is important because, concretely, either the whole resource will be available to the fractional permissions module as hidden state, or nothing will be, even though the fractional permissions superficially represent partial ownership.

We now show how to represent fractional permissions over the affine type α when α supports only one fractionally-shareable operation, readonlyop, that maps $\alpha\ M$ to $\alpha\ M$, possibly with auxiliary inputs and outputs (our construction generalizes very easily when there is more than one operation). Let this only operation, readonlyop, have type ReadOnlyOp defined by:

$$\begin{array}{l} \mathsf{ReadOnlyOp} \stackrel{\text{def}}{=} \\ \quad \forall X : \mathsf{FPerm}(\sigma).\ \forall Y : \sigma' \times \mathsf{Frac} :: P. \\ \quad\quad \beta\ (\pi_1(Y)) \otimes [\mathsf{FracTy}_\alpha\ ((\pi_2(Y), M) \cdot X)] \multimap \\ \quad\quad\quad \exists Z : \sigma'' :: Q.\ \gamma\ Z \otimes [\mathsf{FracTy}_\alpha\ ((\pi_2(Y), M) \cdot X)] \end{array}$$

This type has been constructed specifically to match the "spec" type for the sharing rule, and thereby provide maximal generality. We quantify over an arbitrary fraction as the second component of Y.

We can directly apply the share(_, _) operator with this operation as the second argument to obtain a shareable abstract type α' but, to make the fractional permissions useful, we would also like to provide two operations that allow clients to exchange "full" resources for "full" fractional permissions and vice versa. These two operations should have types defined below:

$$\begin{array}{lcl} \mathsf{ToFrac} & \stackrel{\text{def}}{=} & \forall X : \sigma.\ [\alpha\ X] \otimes [\alpha'\ \mathsf{Empty}] \multimap [\alpha'\ (1, X)] \\ \mathsf{FromFrac} & \stackrel{\text{def}}{=} & \forall X : \sigma.\ [\alpha'\ (1, X)] \multimap [\alpha\ X] \otimes [\alpha'\ \mathsf{Empty}] \end{array}$$

Accordingly, we would like to pass to share(_, _) two additional operations of types $\mathsf{ToFrac}[\mathsf{FracTy}_\alpha/\alpha']$ and $\mathsf{FromFrac}[\mathsf{FracTy}_\alpha/\alpha']$, respectively. Fortunately, given our definition of FracTy_α, these operations can be trivially defined as $\lambda\langle x, \langle\rangle\rangle.\ x$ and $\lambda x.\ \langle x, \langle\rangle\rangle$.

Tying everything together, we now define the following term mkFrac, a generic (polymorphic) module for layering fractional permissions over a resource α. The module provides an empty fractional permission at the outset, which can then be transferred to a full permission using ToFrac and back using FromFrac. (The type FracOp is defined as ReadOnlyOp with α' in place of FracTy_α.)

$$\begin{array}{l} \mathsf{mkFrac} = \lambda !f.\ \mathsf{share}(\langle\rangle, f, \lambda\langle x, \langle\rangle\rangle.\ x, \lambda x.\ \langle x, \langle\rangle\rangle) \\ \mathsf{mkFrac} : \\ \quad \forall \alpha : \sigma \to \mathsf{o}.\ \forall \beta : \sigma' \to \mathsf{o}.\ \forall \gamma : \sigma'' \to \mathsf{o}. \\ \quad\quad !\mathsf{ReadOnlyOp} \\ \quad\quad \multimap \exists \alpha' : \mathsf{FPerm}(\sigma) \to \mathsf{o}. \\ \quad\quad\quad [\alpha'\ \mathsf{Empty}] \otimes !\mathsf{FracOp} \otimes !\mathsf{ToFrac} \otimes !\mathsf{FromFrac} \otimes \\ \quad\quad\quad\quad !\mathsf{splitT} \otimes !\mathsf{joinT} \otimes !\mathsf{promoteT} \end{array}$$

Memory Allocator We now give a stylized memory allocator with a non-monotonic resource invariant, inspired by (but much simpler than) Wickerson *et al.*'s [43] proof of the Unix malloc function, and show how the allocator can be shared safely. The basic idea is that the memory allocator's free list is represented by an array, each entry of which contains a pair of a boolean flag and a location; the flag is true when the location is free, and false when it has been allocated to a client. For free locations, the allocator also owns a capability to access the memory of that location. For the allocated locations, it does not. To formalize this idea, we first assume a family of types for affine arrays:

$$\begin{array}{l} \mathsf{arr}_A : \mathsf{Loc} \times \mathbb{N} \times (\mathbb{N} \to \sigma) \to \mathsf{o} \\ \mathsf{alength}_A : \forall X : \mathsf{Loc}, n : \mathbb{N}, f : \mathbb{N} \to \sigma. \\ \quad\quad !\mathsf{ptr}\ X \otimes [\mathsf{arr}_A(X, n, f)] \multimap !\mathsf{nat}\ n \otimes [\mathsf{arr}_A(X, n, f)] \\ \mathsf{aswap}_A : \forall X : \mathsf{Loc}, n : \mathbb{N}, f : \mathbb{N} \to \sigma, i : \mathbb{N}, x : \sigma :: i < n. \\ \quad\quad !\mathsf{ptr}\ X \otimes !\mathsf{nat}\ i \otimes A(x) \otimes [\mathsf{arr}_A(X, n, f)] \\ \quad\quad\quad \multimap A(f\ i) \otimes [\mathsf{arr}_A(X, n, \lambda j.\ \mathsf{if}(i = j, x, f(j)))] \\ \mathsf{aread}_A : \forall X : \mathsf{Loc}, n : \mathbb{N}, f : \mathbb{N} \to \sigma, i : \mathbb{N}, x : \sigma :: i < n. \\ \quad\quad !\mathsf{ptr}\ X \otimes !\mathsf{nat}\ i \otimes (A(f\ i) \multimap B \otimes A(f\ i)) \\ \quad\quad\quad \otimes [\mathsf{arr}_A(X, n, f)] \multimap B \otimes [\mathsf{arr}_A(X, n, f)] \end{array}$$

Here, A is a σ-indexed type constructor, and the index information for the array of type $\mathsf{arr}_A(X, n, f)$ consists of its location X, its length n and a function f, such that for each $i < n$, the i-th element of the array contains a value of type $A(f\ i)$. So f serves as a representation function for the array. To modify the array, we make use of a swapping operation aswap_A, which takes an array pointer, an index, a value, and a memory capability for the array, and uses it to replace the contents of that index. In the process, it also updates the representation function f. To read the array, we make use of a reading function aread_A, which takes an array pointer, an index, an array capability, and an observer function, which takes a value at the given location and returns the array capability plus an observation of type B.

To specialize this to the memory allocator ADT we described briefly above, we choose $\sigma = 2 \times \mathsf{Loc}$, where $2 = \{\mathsf{tt}, \mathsf{ff}\}$ and $A = \mathsf{contents}$, which is defined below:

$$\begin{array}{l} \mathsf{contents} : (2 \times \mathsf{Loc}) \to \mathsf{o} \\ \mathsf{contents}(\mathsf{tt}, X) = !\mathsf{bool}\ \mathsf{tt} \otimes !\mathsf{ptr}\ X \otimes [\mathsf{cap}\ X\ 1] \\ \mathsf{contents}(\mathsf{ff}, X) = !\mathsf{bool}\ \mathsf{ff} \otimes !\mathsf{ptr}\ X \otimes 1 \end{array}$$

$$\begin{array}{l} \mathsf{freelist} : \mathsf{Loc} \times \mathbb{N} \times (\mathbb{N} \to (2 \times \mathsf{Loc})) \to \mathsf{o} \\ \mathsf{freelist}(X, n, f) = \exists\_ :: \mathsf{inj}(\pi_2 \circ f).\ [\mathsf{arr}_{\mathsf{contents}}(X, n, f)] \end{array}$$

We define the type freelist (the type of the free list of our memory allocator) as an array of contents, with the invariant that the second projection of the representation function f be injective (*i.e.,* the array has at most one entry for each location). The type operator contents takes a boolean b and a location X, where b reflects whether X is free. The capability to access X is held in the array contents only for free cells.

Next, we use the function aswap to define functions malloc_at and free_at to allocate and free locations at a particular index in the free list, respectively. The function malloc_at takes an index i in the free list, which maps to location Y, a proof that the location is free ($f(i) = (\mathsf{tt}, Y)$) and returns the capability of type $[\mathsf{cap}\ Y\ 1]$ stored in the location, swapping it with a unit value. free_at does the opposite.

$$\begin{array}{l} \mathsf{flag\_loc} : \forall b : 2, l : \mathsf{Loc}. \\ \quad\quad\quad \mathsf{contents}(b, l) \multimap (!\mathsf{bool}\ b \otimes !\mathsf{ptr}\ l) \otimes \mathsf{contents}(b, l) \\ \mathsf{flag\_loc}\ \langle !b, !l, m\rangle = \langle\langle !b, !l\rangle, \langle !b, !l, m\rangle\rangle \end{array}$$

$$\begin{array}{l} \mathsf{malloc\_at} : \\ \quad \forall X, Y : \mathsf{Loc}, n : \mathbb{N}, f : \mathbb{N} \to (2 \times \mathsf{Loc}), i : \mathbb{N} :: i < n \wedge f(i) = (\mathsf{tt}, Y). \\ \quad\quad !\mathsf{ptr}\ X \otimes !\mathsf{nat}\ i \otimes \mathsf{freelist}(X, n, f) \\ \quad\quad \multimap !\mathsf{ptr}\ Y \otimes [\mathsf{cap}\ Y\ 1] \otimes \mathsf{freelist}(X, n, \lambda j.\ \mathsf{if}(i = j, (\mathsf{ff}, Y), f(j))) \end{array}$$

$$
\begin{array}{l}
\mathsf{malloc} : \forall S : \mathcal{P}(\mathsf{Loc})_\perp, X : \mathsf{Loc}.\\
\quad\quad !\mathsf{ptr}\ X \otimes [C(S)]\\
\quad\quad \multimap \exists Y : \mathsf{Loc}.\ !\mathsf{ptr}\ Y \otimes [\mathsf{cap}\ Y\ 1] \otimes [C(S \cdot \{Y\})]\\
\mathsf{malloc}(!a, m) =\\
\quad \mathsf{let}\ (!n, m) = \mathsf{alength}(!a, m)\ \mathsf{in}\\
\quad \mathsf{let\ rec}\ loop(m, !i) =\\
\quad\quad \mathsf{if}\ i < n\ \mathsf{then}\\
\quad\quad\quad \mathsf{let}\ \langle\langle !b, !l\rangle, m\rangle = \mathsf{aread}(!a, !i, \mathsf{flag\_loc}, m)\ \mathsf{in}\\
\quad\quad\quad \mathsf{if}(b, \mathsf{malloc\_at}(!a, !i, m), loop(m, i+1))\\
\quad\quad \mathsf{else}\\
\quad\quad\quad (\mathsf{fix}\ f(x).\ f\ x)\ \langle\rangle\\
\quad \mathsf{in}\ loop(m, !0)\\
\\
\mathsf{free} : \forall S : \mathcal{P}(\mathsf{Loc})_\perp, X : \mathsf{Loc}, Y : \mathsf{Loc}.\\
\quad\quad !\mathsf{ptr}\ X \otimes !\mathsf{ptr}\ Y \otimes [\mathsf{cap}\ Y\ 1] \otimes [C(S \cdot \{Y\})] \multimap [C(S)]\\
\mathsf{free}\ (!a, !l, c, m) =\\
\quad \mathsf{let}\ (!n, m) = \mathsf{alength}(!a, m)\ \mathsf{in}\\
\quad \mathsf{let\ rec}\ loop(c, m, !i) =\\
\quad\quad \mathsf{let}\ \langle\langle !b, !l'\rangle, m\rangle = \mathsf{aread}(!a, !i, \mathsf{flag\_loc}, m)\ \mathsf{in}\\
\quad\quad \mathsf{if}(l = l', \mathsf{free\_at}(!a, !i, c, m), loop(c, m, i+1))\\
\quad \mathsf{in}\ loop(c, m, !0)
\end{array}
$$

Figure 8. The Memory Allocator

$$
\begin{array}{l}
\mathsf{malloc\_at}(!a, !i, m) =\\
\quad \mathsf{let}\ \langle\langle !b, !l\rangle, m\rangle = \mathsf{aread}(!a, !i, \mathsf{flag\_loc}, m)\ \mathsf{in}\\
\quad \mathsf{let}\ \langle\langle !b, !l, c\rangle, m\rangle = \mathsf{aswap}(!a, !i, \langle !\mathsf{ff}, !l, \langle\rangle\rangle, m)\ \mathsf{in}\ \langle !l, c, m\rangle\\
\\
\mathsf{free\_at} :\\
\quad \forall X, Y : \mathsf{Loc}, n : \mathbb{N}, f : \mathbb{N} \to (2 \times \mathsf{Loc}), i : \mathbb{N} :: i < n \wedge f(i) = (\mathsf{ff}, Y).\\
\quad\quad !\mathsf{ptr}\ X \otimes !\mathsf{nat}\ i \otimes [\mathsf{cap}\ Y\ 1] \otimes \mathsf{freelist}(X, n, f)\\
\quad\quad \multimap \mathsf{freelist}(X, n, \lambda j.\ \mathsf{if}(i = j, (\mathsf{tt}, Y), f(j)))\\
\mathsf{free\_at}(!a, !i, c, m) =\\
\quad \mathsf{let}\ \langle\langle !b, !l\rangle, m\rangle = \mathsf{aread}(!a, !i, \mathsf{flag\_loc}, m)\ \mathsf{in}\\
\quad \mathsf{let}\ \langle\langle !b, !l, \langle\rangle\rangle, m\rangle = \mathsf{aswap}(!a, !i, \langle !\mathsf{tt}, !l, c\rangle, m)\ \mathsf{in}\ m
\end{array}
$$

Next, we consider the monoid $\mathcal{P}(\mathsf{Loc})_\perp$, whose elements are sets of locations. The unit is the empty set $\epsilon = \emptyset$, and concatenation is defined by disjoint union $\uplus$, with non-disjoint sets going to $\perp$. We use this monoid to define the type $C(S)$ for a given location X pointing to the head of the free list:

$$
\begin{array}{l}
C(\perp) = \mathsf{void}\\
C(S) = \exists n : \mathbb{N}, f : \mathbb{N} \to (2 \times \mathsf{Loc}) :: S = \{l \mid \exists i < n.\ f(i) = \langle \mathsf{ff}, l\rangle\}.\\
\quad\quad\quad \mathsf{freelist}(X, n, f)
\end{array}
$$

Intuitively, for $S \neq \perp$, $C(S)$ is a free list whose allocated pointers coincide exactly with S.

Using $C(S)$, we can define operations malloc and free (Figure 8). The malloc operation traverses the free array until it finds an unallocated element, updates the flag, and returns that element. If the free list is fully allocated, then we go into an infinite loop — more realistic implementations would signal an error or resize the free list. The free operation also iterates over the array until it finds the element it was passed as an argument, but it does *not* have to perform a bounds check as it iterates: the type $C(S \cdot \{Y\})$ guarantees that the location Y will be found in the free list, and hence that i is always in bounds. Note that the type of the location comparison operation $=$ used in free is $\forall X, Y : \mathsf{Loc}.\ \mathsf{ptr}\ X \otimes \mathsf{ptr}\ Y \multimap \mathsf{bool}\ (X = Y)$.

More sophisticated versions of this pattern arise frequently in the implementation of free lists, connection pools, and other resource managers. The critical feature of our invariant is that we can only free a piece of memory if it originally came from *this* memory allocator in the first place. Furthermore, it is a non-monotonic invariant, since the same piece of memory can go in and out of the free list, which means that the size of the free list in the predicate can grow and shrink as the program executes.

However, we can nevertheless share the memory allocator, since the frame conditions on the specifications express the constraint that interference between different clients is benign—up to partial

$$
\begin{array}{rcll}
\mathrm{World}_n & \stackrel{\mathrm{def}}{=} & \left\{ W = (k, \omega) \;\middle|\; \begin{array}{l} k < n, \exists j.\ \omega \in \mathrm{Island}_k^{j+1} \\ \omega[0] = \mathrm{HIsland}_k \end{array} \right\} \\
\mathrm{Island}_n & \stackrel{\mathrm{def}}{=} & \left\{ \iota = (M, \cdot, \epsilon, I) \;\middle|\; \begin{array}{l} (M, \cdot, \epsilon)\ \text{comm. monoid}, \\ I \in M \to \mathrm{ResPred}_n \end{array} \right\} \\
\mathrm{HIsland}_n & \stackrel{\mathrm{def}}{=} & \left(\begin{array}{l} \mathrm{Heap}_\perp, \uplus, \emptyset, \\ \lambda h.\{(W, \epsilon) \mid W \in \mathrm{World}_n, h \neq \perp\} \end{array} \right) \\
\mathrm{ResPred}_n & \stackrel{\mathrm{def}}{=} & \left\{ \varphi \subseteq \mathrm{ResAtom}_n \;\middle|\; \begin{array}{l} \forall W' \sqsupseteq W.\ (W, r) \in \varphi \\ \quad\Longrightarrow\quad (W', r) \in \varphi \end{array} \right\} \\
\mathrm{ResAtom}_n & \stackrel{\mathrm{def}}{=} & \left\{ (W, r) \;\middle|\; \begin{array}{l} W \in \mathrm{World}_n,\ \forall i.\ a_i \in W.\omega[i].M, \\ r = (a_0, \ldots, a_{m-1}), m = |W.\omega| \end{array} \right\} \\
\mathrm{ValPred} & \stackrel{\mathrm{def}}{=} & \left\{ V \subseteq \mathrm{ValAtom} \;\middle|\; \begin{array}{l} \forall W' \sqsupseteq W.\ (W, (r, v)) \in V \\ \Rightarrow \forall r'.(W', (r \cdot r', v)) \in V \end{array} \right\} \\
\mathrm{ValAtom} & \stackrel{\mathrm{def}}{=} & \{(W, (r, v)) \mid \exists n.\ (W, r) \in \mathrm{ResAtom}_n \}
\end{array}
$$

$$
\begin{array}{rcl}
\triangleright(k+1, \omega) & \stackrel{\mathrm{def}}{=} & (k, \lfloor \omega \rfloor_k) \\
\lfloor (\iota_1, \ldots, \iota_n) \rfloor_k & \stackrel{\mathrm{def}}{=} & (\lfloor \iota_1 \rfloor_k, \ldots, \lfloor \iota_n \rfloor_k) \\
\lfloor (M, \cdot, \epsilon, I) \rfloor_k & \stackrel{\mathrm{def}}{=} & (M, \cdot, \epsilon, \lambda a. \lfloor I(a) \rfloor_k) \\
\lfloor \varphi \rfloor_k & \stackrel{\mathrm{def}}{=} & \{(W, r) \in \varphi \mid W.k < k\}
\end{array}
$$

$$
\begin{array}{rcl}
(\iota'_1, \ldots, \iota'_{n'}) \sqsupseteq (\iota_1, \ldots, \iota_n) & \stackrel{\mathrm{def}}{=} & n' \geq n,\ \forall i \leq n.\ \iota'_i = \iota_i \\
(k', \omega') \sqsupseteq_j (k, \omega) & \stackrel{\mathrm{def}}{=} & k' = k - j,\quad \omega' \sqsupseteq \lfloor \omega \rfloor_{k'}
\end{array}
$$

$$
\begin{array}{rcl}
(s, r) : W & \stackrel{\mathrm{def}}{=} & s = s_0 \cdot \ldots \cdot s_{m-1},\ m = |W.\omega|, \\
& & \forall i \in 0..m-1.\ (\triangleright W, s_i) \in W.\omega[i].I((s \cdot r)[i])
\end{array}
$$

Figure 9. Possible Worlds and Related Definitions

correctness, no client cares what allocations or deallocations other clients perform:

$$
\begin{array}{l}
\mathsf{mkAllocator} : \forall X, n, f, S :: S = \{l \mid \exists i < n.\ f(i) = \langle \mathsf{ff}, l\rangle\}.\\
\quad\quad\quad\quad \mathsf{freelist}(X, n, f)\\
\quad\quad\quad\quad \multimap \exists \alpha : \mathcal{P}(\mathsf{Loc})_\perp \to \mathsf{o}.\\
\quad\quad\quad\quad\quad [\alpha(S)] \otimes\ !\mathsf{mallocType} \otimes !\mathsf{freeType}\\
\quad\quad\quad\quad\quad !\mathsf{splitT} \otimes !\mathsf{joinT} \otimes !\mathsf{promoteT}\\
\mathsf{mkAllocator}\ m = \mathsf{share}(m, \mathsf{malloc}, \mathsf{free})
\end{array}
$$

The memory manager's state can be split up and shared among many different clients. The key is to observe that for any state S, we know that $\alpha(S) = \alpha(S \uplus \emptyset)$. Thus we can pass each client a copy of $\alpha(\emptyset)$, which it can use to allocate and free locally-owned memory without knowledge of the allocation behavior of other clients.

4. The Semantic Model

In this section, we justify the soundness of our type system. The main challenge, of course, is validating the sharing rule. We gain traction by characterizing the behavior of well-typed terms through a step-indexed Kripke logical relation (SKLR). While SKLRs have been used previously to give clean semantic soundness proofs of related substructural calculi [5], ours is novel in its treatment of resources. We therefore begin by laying down some conceptual groundwork and terminology concerning resources.

Physical vs. Logical Resources and the Global Store In the beginning, there is the heap: it is a primitive, *physical* notion of splittable resource, and in the absence of sharing there is little more to say. The affine heap capability $\mathsf{cap}\ \ell\ A$ gives its "owner"—*i.e.,* the term that consumes it—full control over the location ℓ and its contents, and the lack of sharing means that no other parts of the program may contain any knowledge about ℓ or its contents at all.

Each application of the sharing rule, however, introduces a new *logical* notion of splittable resource, represented as a commutative monoid $(M, \cdot, \epsilon)$, which governs access to a piece of shared state. Control over resources of type M becomes a new type of affine capability (written $[\alpha\ t]$ in the sharing rule in Figure 7), which may be consumed by or transferred between different parts of the program just as heap capabilities can.[2] Unlike the heap, which has a direct physical interpretation, M must be given an interpretation in terms of what invariants it imposes on the underlying shared state. Specifically, the capability $[A\ t]$ in Figure 7 describes the invariant that holds of the shared state when the *global store* of M (*i.e.,* the monoidal composition of all resources of type M that are currently in existence) is t. For those readers with a Hoare-logic background, it may be helpful to think of this global store of M as a kind of "ghost state" [22] that instruments the physical heap state with extra logical information.

Atomic vs. Composite Resources As a program executes, a new logical resource is created each time the sharing rule is executed, extending the resource set (which begins life with only the lone physical resouce of the heap). We will say that a resource belonging to any one of these types is an *atomic* resource.

Of course, a term may naturally own many different atomic resources, as a result of being composed from multiple different subterms. For example, it may own the heap capability cap ℓ 1 to control location ℓ, as well as the logical capability $[\alpha\ t]$ (where α is the abstract type constructor created by some application of the sharing rule). In this case, the term owns a physical heap resource ($[\ell : \langle\rangle]$), as well as a logical resource (t) of the monoidal resource type that was created along with α.

In general, a term may own resources of every type currently in existence (and later, when new types of resource are created, it can be implicitly viewed as owning the unit element of those resources). We call such a combination of resources of all the different atomic types a *composite* resource. Given that each atomic resource is a commutative monoid, observe that composite resources form a commutative monoid via the obvious product construction. For convenience, we overload $\cdot$ and write $r_1 \cdot r_2$ to denote the componentwise composition of two composite resources r_1 and r_2.

Composite resources are the fundamental currency of our model. Not only are they what terms consume and produce, but furthermore, when we apply the sharing rule to make some underlying (affine) resource shareable, that underlying resource is a composite resource, and the invariant that governs it takes the form of a predicate on composite resources.

Worlds and Islands Being a Kripke logical relation, our model (presented below) is indexed by *possible worlds*. In previous Kripke models of ML-like languages, these worlds have been used to encode invariants on the physical heap. Here, since we support logical as well as physical resources, we generalize worlds to encode (1) the knowledge of what types of logical resources have been created by applications of the sharing rule, and (2) how to interpret those logical resources as invariants on shared state.

As defined in Figure 9, worlds are tuples of *islands*, with each island describing a different type of resource.[3] (Ignore the "step indices" k and n for now; we explain them below.) An island comprises a commutative monoid $(M, \cdot, \epsilon)$, as well as a *representation invariant* I that interprets elements of M into assumptions (composite resource predicates) on the underlying shared state. Specifically, $I(t)$ denotes the invariant that holds on the shared state when the global store of the island's resource (M) is t.

[2] Note: even if the sharing rule is instantiated twice with the *same* monoid, it nevertheless generates two *distinct* types of logical resources. The distinction is enforced syntactically by the fact that each application of the sharing rule creates a fresh, existentially-quantified capability constructor α; even if two such α's (say, α_1 and α_2) are indexed by the same monoid, instantiations $[\alpha_1\ t]$ and $[\alpha_2\ t]$ will not be confused with each other.

[3] Throughout, we use dot notation like $W.k$ and $W.\omega$ to project named components from structures, and indexing notation like $\omega[i]$ to project the ith component from a tuple.

The first island (island 0) is fixed to be the built-in island for physical heaps (HIsland). Its monoid is the standard partial commutative monoid on heaps, with disjoint union as composition and the empty heap as unit, completed to a total monoid with a bottom element $\perp$. Its representation invariant $I(h)$ is trivial—it asserts no ownership of any underlying shared resource because there is none, but is only satisfied if h is a heap and not $\perp$.

In the other islands, the representation invariant I is more interesting. First and foremost, it is *world-indexed*. For those readers familiar with recent SKLRs [16, 3], which employ similarly world-indexed *heap* invariants, the reason for this world-indexing will likely be self-explanatory: it's needed to account for the presence of higher-order state. For most other readers, it may appear completely mysterious, but it is also a technical point that the reader may safely gloss over (by skipping the next paragraph).

Briefly, the reason for the world-indexing of the resource predicates is as follows: in proving the sharing rule (see the end of this section), we extend the world with a new island, and we want to define its $I(t)$ to require (roughly) that the underlying shared resource of the island must justify the capability $[A\ t]$, where A is the capability constructor in the first premise of the sharing rule (Figure 7). But for arbitrary A, the question of whether some (composite) resource r justifies the capability $[A\ t]$ depends on what the "current" world W is when the question is asked, which might be at some point in the future when new invariants have been imposed by *future* islands. Such a situation would arise, for instance, were we to apply the sharing rule to create a "weak reference" (Section 3) to a value of function type, which is (not coincidentally) the canonical example of higher-order state. The solution is thus to parameterize the resource predicate $I(t)$ over W, knowing that the W parameter will always be instantiated (in the definition of "world satisfaction" below) with the "current" world.

This parameterization trick is by now a very standard move in the SKLR playbook for building models of higher-order state [3, 17]. However, it is also a prime example of Wheeler's adage that "all problems in computer science can be solved by another level of indirection, but that usually will create another problem." Indeed, an unfortunate consequence is that it causes a "bad" circularity in the construction of worlds that cannot be solved directly in sets. The *step-indexed* approach of Ahmed *et al.* [1, 2, 3] handles this problem by stratifying the construction of worlds by $n \in \mathbb{N}$ bounding the number of execution steps for which we observe the program, with n going down by 1 in the world parameter of the resource predicate. The details of this construction are entirely standard, as are the world approximation ($\lfloor\cdot\rfloor_k$) and later ($\triangleright$) operators in Figure 9, and interested readers are referred to the literature [3, 17].

In any case, the resource predicates in the range of I are required to be *monotonic*: adding new islands to a world cannot invalidate the invariants of previous islands (see the definition of ResPred). Finally, when using a composite resource r with j atomic sub-resources in the context of a future world with $j + k$ islands, we silently assume the atomic sub-resources of the last k islands are ϵ.

Local vs. Shared Resources and World Satisfaction In reality, a term e executes under a global heap h. In our model, we think of e as executing, logically, under the *global composite store*, which comprises all the resources currently in existence: specifically, it combines the global store of every atomic resource in existence, including the heap (which is the 0-th island's resource). Some portion r of that global composite store is directly known to (and owned by) e itself—we call this e's *local resource*—while the remaining portion s constitutes the *shared resource*. The shared resource is so named because it is required to contain all the underlying shared resources needed to satisfy the representation invariants of all the islands in the world. (The *local* vs. *shared* terminology is bor-

$$
\begin{aligned}
\mathcal{K}\llbracket\circ\rrbracket &\stackrel{\text{def}}{=} \text{ValPred} \qquad \mathcal{K}\llbracket\sigma \to \kappa\rrbracket \stackrel{\text{def}}{=} \mathcal{S}\llbracket\sigma\rrbracket \to \mathcal{K}\llbracket\kappa\rrbracket \\
\mathcal{V}\llbracket B\ t\rrbracket_\rho^W &\stackrel{\text{def}}{=} \{(r, \mathcal{I}\llbracket t\rrbracket_\rho)\} \text{ for } B \in \{\mathsf{bool}, \mathsf{nat}, \mathsf{ptr}\} \\
\mathcal{V}\llbracket\mathsf{cap}\ t\ A\rrbracket_\rho^W &\stackrel{\text{def}}{=} \{(r \cdot [\mathcal{I}\llbracket t\rrbracket_\rho : v], \bullet) \mid (r, v) \in \mathcal{V}\llbracket A\rrbracket_\rho^W\} \\
\mathcal{V}\llbracket 1\rrbracket_\rho^W &\stackrel{\text{def}}{=} \{(r, \langle\rangle)\} \\
\mathcal{V}\llbracket A_1 \otimes A_2\rrbracket_\rho^W &\stackrel{\text{def}}{=} \{(r_1 \cdot r_2, \langle v_1, v_2\rangle) \mid (r_i, v_i) \in \mathcal{V}\llbracket A_i\rrbracket_\rho^W\} \\
\mathcal{V}\llbracket A \multimap B\rrbracket_\rho^W &\stackrel{\text{def}}{=} \left\{(r, v) \;\middle|\; \begin{array}{r} \forall W' \sqsupseteq W.\ (r', v') \in \mathcal{V}\llbracket A\rrbracket_\rho^{W'} \\ \Longrightarrow (r \cdot r', v\ v') \in \mathcal{E}\llbracket B\rrbracket_\rho^{W'} \end{array}\right\} \\
\mathcal{V}\llbracket !A\rrbracket_\rho^W &\stackrel{\text{def}}{=} \{(r \cdot r', !v) \mid (r, v) \in \mathcal{V}\llbracket A\rrbracket_\rho^W,\ r = r \cdot r\} \\
\mathcal{V}\llbracket\forall X{:}\sigma :: P.\, A\rrbracket_\rho^W &\stackrel{\text{def}}{=} \bigcap\left\{\mathcal{V}\llbracket A\rrbracket_{\rho[X\mapsto d]}^W \;\middle|\; \rho[X \mapsto d] \models P\right\} \\
\mathcal{V}\llbracket\exists X{:}\sigma :: P.\, A\rrbracket_\rho^W &\stackrel{\text{def}}{=} \bigcup\left\{\mathcal{V}\llbracket A\rrbracket_{\rho[X\mapsto d]}^W \;\middle|\; \rho[X \mapsto d] \models P\right\} \\
\mathcal{V}\llbracket\forall\alpha : \kappa.\ A\rrbracket_\rho^W &\stackrel{\text{def}}{=} \bigcap\left\{\mathcal{V}\llbracket A\rrbracket_{\rho[\alpha\mapsto V]}^W \;\middle|\; V \in \mathcal{K}\llbracket\kappa\rrbracket\right\} \\
\mathcal{V}\llbracket\exists\alpha : \kappa.\ A\rrbracket_\rho^W &\stackrel{\text{def}}{=} \bigcup\left\{\mathcal{V}\llbracket A\rrbracket_{\rho[\alpha\mapsto V]}^W \;\middle|\; V \in \mathcal{K}\llbracket\kappa\rrbracket\right\} \\
\mathcal{V}\llbracket\alpha\rrbracket_\rho^W &\stackrel{\text{def}}{=} \rho(\alpha) \\
\mathcal{V}\llbracket\,[A]\,\rrbracket_\rho^W &\stackrel{\text{def}}{=} \{(r, \bullet) \mid \exists v.\ (r, v) \in \mathcal{V}\llbracket A\rrbracket_\rho^W\} \\
\mathcal{V}\llbracket\mathsf{if}(t, A, B)\rrbracket_\rho^W &\stackrel{\text{def}}{=} \text{if } \mathcal{I}\llbracket t\rrbracket_\rho = \mathsf{tt} \text{ then } \mathcal{V}\llbracket A\rrbracket_\rho^W \text{ else } \mathcal{V}\llbracket B\rrbracket_\rho^W \\
\mathcal{V}\llbracket\lambda X : \sigma.\ A\rrbracket_\rho^W &\stackrel{\text{def}}{=} \lambda d \in \mathcal{S}\llbracket\sigma\rrbracket.\ \mathcal{V}\llbracket A\rrbracket_{\rho[X\mapsto d]}^W \\
\mathcal{V}\llbracket A\ t\rrbracket_\rho^W &\stackrel{\text{def}}{=} (\mathcal{V}\llbracket A\rrbracket_\rho^W)(\mathcal{I}\llbracket t\rrbracket_\rho)
\end{aligned}
$$

$$
\begin{aligned}
\mathcal{E}\llbracket A\rrbracket_\rho^W \stackrel{\text{def}}{=} \{\, (r, e) \mid\ & \forall j < W.k,\ (s, r \cdot r_{\mathrm{F}}) : W. \\
\text{if}\quad & h = (s \cdot r \cdot r_{\mathrm{F}})[0],\ \langle h; e\rangle \hookrightarrow_j \langle h'; e'\rangle \not\hookrightarrow \\
\text{then}\quad & \exists W' \sqsupseteq_j W,\ (s', r' \cdot r_{\mathrm{F}}) : W' \\
\text{with}\quad & h' = (s' \cdot r' \cdot r_{\mathrm{F}})[0],\ (r', e') \in \mathcal{V}\llbracket A\rrbracket_\rho^{W'} \,\}
\end{aligned}
$$

Figure 10. Kripke Logical Relation

rowed from Vafeiadis's work on concurrent separation logics [41], in which a closely analogous distinction arises.)

Formally, the relationship between the local and shared resources is codified by the *world satisfaction relation* $(s, r) : W$, defined in Figure 9, which asserts that s can be split into m composite resources $\overline{s_i}$ (one for each island of W) such that s_i satisfies island i's representation invariant $W.\omega[i].I$. Note that the argument passed to I is $(s \cdot r)[i]$: this is correct because I's argument is supposed to represent the global store of the i-th island, which is precisely the i-th projection of the global composite store, $s \cdot r$. Note also that the world parameter of each island's resource predicate is instantiated with $\triangleright W$, the "current" world W approximated one step-index level down.

Kripke Logical Relation Logical relations characterize program behavior by induction over type structure, lifting properties about *base* type computations to properties at *all* types: a term at a compound type is "well-behaved" if every way of eliminating it yields a "well-behaved" term at some simpler type. *Kripke logical relations* index logical relations by a world W, which places constraints on the machine states under which terms are required to behave well. Although logical relations are often *binary relations* for proving program equivalences [30], it suffices in our case to define *unary predicates*, since we are merely trying to prove safety [6].

Figure 10 presents our Kripke logical relation. We assume a semantics of sorts $\mathcal{S}\llbracket\sigma\rrbracket$, index terms $\mathcal{I}\llbracket t\rrbracket_\rho$ (where $\mathrm{fv}(t) \subseteq \mathrm{dom}(\rho)$) and propositions $\rho \models P$ (where $\mathrm{fv}(P) \subseteq \mathrm{dom}(\rho)$), all standard from multisorted first-order logic. From the semantics of sorts, we can easily build a semantics of kinds $\mathcal{K}\llbracket\kappa\rrbracket$. The value predicate $\mathcal{V}\llbracket A\rrbracket_\rho^W$ is indexed by both a world W and a semantic environment ρ, and is satisfied by pairs (r, v) of values v and their supporting (composite) resources r. Because the type system is affine, the resource r may contain some part that is irrelevant to v—and in general, if $(r, v) \in \mathcal{V}\llbracket A\rrbracket_\rho^W$ and $W' \sqsupseteq W$ then $(r \cdot r', v) \in \mathcal{V}\llbracket A\rrbracket_\rho^{W'}$, an assumption codified in the definition of ValPred. This monotonicity property means that the good behavior of a term can depend on certain islands and resources being present, but *not* on certain islands or resources being absent.

$$
\begin{aligned}
\mathrm{Env}\llbracket\cdot\rrbracket &\stackrel{\text{def}}{=} \emptyset \\
\mathrm{Env}\llbracket\Sigma, \alpha : \kappa\rrbracket &\stackrel{\text{def}}{=} \{\rho, \alpha \mapsto V \mid \rho \in \mathrm{Env}\llbracket\Sigma\rrbracket,\ V \in \mathcal{K}\llbracket\kappa\rrbracket\} \\
\mathrm{Env}\llbracket\Sigma, X : \sigma\rrbracket &\stackrel{\text{def}}{=} \{\rho, X \mapsto d \mid \rho \in \mathrm{Env}\llbracket\Sigma\rrbracket,\ d \in \mathcal{S}\llbracket\sigma\rrbracket\} \\
\mathcal{U}\llbracket\cdot\rrbracket_\rho^W &\stackrel{\text{def}}{=} \emptyset \\
\mathcal{U}\llbracket\Gamma, x : A\rrbracket_\rho^W &\stackrel{\text{def}}{=} \left\{\gamma, x \mapsto (r, v) \;\middle|\; \begin{array}{l} \gamma \in \mathcal{U}\llbracket\Gamma\rrbracket_\rho^W, (r, v) \in \mathcal{V}\llbracket A\rrbracket_\rho^W, \\ r = r \cdot r \end{array}\right\} \\
\mathcal{L}\llbracket\cdot\rrbracket_\rho^W &\stackrel{\text{def}}{=} \emptyset \\
\mathcal{L}\llbracket\Delta, x : A\rrbracket_\rho^W &\stackrel{\text{def}}{=} \{\delta, x \mapsto (r, v) \mid \delta \in \mathcal{L}\llbracket\Delta\rrbracket_\rho^W,\ (r, v) \in \mathcal{V}\llbracket A\rrbracket_\rho^W\} \\
\pi(\gamma) &\stackrel{\text{def}}{=} \bigodot\{r \mid x \in \mathrm{dom}(\gamma),\ \gamma(x) = (r, v)\} \\
\pi(\delta) &\stackrel{\text{def}}{=} \bigodot\{r \mid x \in \mathrm{dom}(\delta),\ \delta(x) = (r, v)\}
\end{aligned}
$$

$$
\begin{aligned}
\Sigma; \Pi; \Gamma; \Delta \Vdash e : A \stackrel{\text{def}}{=}\ & \forall W,\ \rho \in \mathrm{Env}\llbracket\Sigma\rrbracket, \gamma \in \mathcal{U}\llbracket\Gamma\rrbracket_\rho^W, \delta \in \mathcal{L}\llbracket\Delta\rrbracket_\rho^W. \\
& \rho \models \Pi \Longrightarrow (\pi(\gamma) \cdot \pi(\delta), \delta(\gamma(e))) \in \mathcal{E}\llbracket A\rrbracket_\rho^W
\end{aligned}
$$

Figure 11. Semantics of Open Terms

The definition of the value predicate is essentially standard—in particular, it is essentially an affine version of the model of $\mathbf{L}^3$ [5] outfitted with our monoidal worlds. One difference is our interpretation of the exponential $!A$, which is inhabited by $!v$ only when v can be supported by some *idempotent* portion of the resources—that is, some part of the resources that permits the structural rule of contraction. (In $\mathbf{L}^3$, the heap is the only resource, so only the empty heap is idempotent.) Also, since universal and existential types are introduced implicitly, they are given intersection and union semantics, respectively. The remaining differences are to do with indexed types—*e.g.*, the parameter indexing the base types bool, nat, and ptr must reflect the particular value inhabiting the type—and the computational irrelevance type $[A]$, whose interpretation records the resources needed to justify A but not the value that inhabits it.

The term predicate $\mathcal{E}\llbracket A\rrbracket_\rho^W$ captures the crucial property supporting sharing: namely, that computations are frame-respecting. Suppose that a term e owns (composite) resource r. To show e is well-behaved, we quantify over an arbitrary frame resource r_{F} representing the resource of e's evaluation context. Together, $r \cdot r_{\mathrm{F}}$ constitute the *local resource*, *i.e.*, the portion of the global composite store that the program being executed owns. We also quantify over some *shared resource* s such that $(s, r \cdot r_{\mathrm{F}}) : W$. If e reduces to an irreducible term e'—starting from the global heap that is the 0-th projection of $s \cdot r \cdot r_{\mathrm{F}}$—in j steps, where j is less than the world's step-index $W.k$, then it must (1) leave the heap in a state described by a new global composite store $s' \cdot r' \cdot r_{\mathrm{F}}$, such that (2) $(s', r' \cdot r_{\mathrm{F}}) : W'$ for some future world W' of W (whose step-index is $W.k - j$), and (3) the final term e' is in fact a value that, supported by the resource r', obeys the value predicate $\mathcal{V}\llbracket A\rrbracket_\rho^{W'}$. Note, however, that the frame resource r_{F} must remain unchanged.

The logical predicates defined in Figure 10 only describe well-behaved *closed* terms. In Figure 11, we lift these to predicates on *open* terms in the standard way: namely, we consider e to be well-behaved at the type A under context Ω, written $\Omega \Vdash e : A$, if it is well-behaved (according to $\mathcal{E}\llbracket A\rrbracket$) for all well-behaved closing instantiations of its free variables. These closing instantiations include both values and the resources supporting them; the π operator then multiplies together all the resources supporting a closing instantiation. Note that the resources accompanying the instantiations of the unrestricted variables in Γ are required to be idempotent, so that they may be safely duplicated within the proof of soundness.

Soundness of the Type System The main technical result of the paper is summed up in the following theorems:

Theorem 1 (Fundamental Theorem of Logical Relations).
If $\Omega \vdash e : A$, *then* $\Omega \Vdash e : A$.

Theorem 2 (Adequacy).
If $\emptyset \Vdash e : A$ *and* $\langle \emptyset; e \rangle \hookrightarrow_* \langle h; e' \rangle \not\hookrightarrow$, *then* e' *is a value.*

Corollary 3 (Soundness of the Type System).
If $\emptyset \vdash e : A$ *and* $\langle \emptyset; e \rangle \hookrightarrow_* \langle h; e' \rangle \not\hookrightarrow$, *then* e' *is a value.*

The proof of Adequacy is almost trivial. The proof of the Fundamental Theorem essentially proceeds by showing that each rule in our type system is *semantically* sound, *i.e.*, that it holds if all the syntactic $\vdash$'s are replaced by semantic $\Vdash$'s. The proofs for most rules follow previous developments using SKLRs [3, 17, 16]. The most interesting new case, of course, is that of the sharing rule. The proof is quite involved, so here we will just offer a rough idea of how the proof goes, focusing on the most interesting technical constructions. (For the full details, see the technical appendix [24].)

As described above, the intuition behind our worlds W is that each island in W corresponds to an application of the sharing rule. Indeed, the proof that the sharing rule is semantically sound is the only part of our proof that involves extending a given input world W with a new island to form a future world W' (as permitted in the definition of the logical term predicate). Supposing W already had n islands $(0..n-1)$, the new island will have index n.

At first glance, it would seem we want to define this new island to be $(\mathcal{S}[\![\sigma]\!], \cdot, \epsilon, I_{\mathsf{simple}})$, where $(\mathcal{S}[\![\sigma]\!], \cdot, \epsilon)$ is the monoid with which the sharing rule was instantiated, and the representation invariant I_{simple} is defined in terms of the A in the first premise of the rule (and whatever ρ we are given to interpret its free variables):

$$I_{\mathsf{simple}}(x) = \{(W, r) \mid \exists v.\ (r, v) \in \mathcal{V}[\![A]\!]^W_\rho (x)\}$$

This invariant stipulates that the shared resource of island n satisfies the capability $[A\ x]$ when the island's global store is x.

However, we must also take account of the lock ℓ that the dynamic semantics of share creates in order to protect against reentrancy. Intuitively, when the lock ℓ is released, the representation invariant of island n should be much like the above I_{simple}. But when the lock ℓ is held, it means we are in the middle of a call to one of the operations returned by share, during which the representation invariant might not hold at all. The monoid of island n must therefore reflect these two possibilities.

We define island n as $(M, +, U(\epsilon), I)$, where (in ML notation)

$$\mathsf{type}\ M = U \text{ of } \mathcal{S}[\![\sigma]\!] \mid L \text{ of } \mathcal{S}[\![\sigma]\!] \times \mathcal{S}[\![\sigma]\!] \mid \bot,$$

the composition operator $(+)$ is the commutative closure of

$$\begin{array}{rclrcl} U(x) + U(y) & = & U(x \cdot y) & L(\_) + L(\_) & = & \bot \\ L(x, y) + U(z) & = & L(x, y \cdot z) & \bot + \_ & = & \bot, \end{array}$$

and the representation invariant I is defined as

$$\begin{array}{rcl} I(U(x)) & = & \{(W, r \cdot [\ell : \mathsf{ff}]) \mid \exists v.\ (r, v) \in \mathcal{V}[\![A]\!]^W_\rho (x)\} \\ I(L(x, y)) & = & \{(W, [\ell : \mathsf{tt}]) \mid x = y\} \\ I(\bot) & = & \emptyset. \end{array}$$

The idea here is to distinguish between *unlocked* states $U(x)$, where the lock ℓ is released, and *locked* states $L(x, y)$, where ℓ is held. In the former case, I asserts that ℓ points to ff and that the rest of the island's shared resource r can satisfy $[A\ x]$, as required for invoking any of the shared operations.[4] In the latter case, I asserts that ℓ points to tt and that $x = y$ (we explain about that in a moment). Finally, we give the following interpretation for the abstract capability constructor α (returned by the share operation):

$$[\![\alpha]\!] = \lambda x \in \mathcal{S}[\![\sigma]\!].\ \{(W, (r, \bullet)) \mid r[n] = r' + U(x)\}$$

This essentially says that the owner of $[\alpha\ x]$ has control over a $U(x)$ piece of the resource on island n.

The two parameters to L are a technical trick we use to show that the shared operations of the ADT are "frame-preserving". Specifically, the monoid we have defined has the property that if we control $L(y, \epsilon)$ of the resource, then the only possible resource r that the rest of the program could have on island n, such that $I(L(y, \epsilon) + r)$ is satisfiable, is $U(y)$. To see how this is exploited in the soundness proof, suppose that a client owns $[\alpha\ t]$ (*i.e.*, she controls a $U(t)$ piece of island n's resource), and invokes one of the shared operations, whose type spec (see Figure 7) promises to transform $[\alpha\ t]$ into $[\alpha\ t']$ for some t'. (For simplicity, we'll ignore the frame X in the type of the operation. It does not add any fundamental complication.) If the lock is held, the operation will diverge and there is nothing to show. If the lock is released, the definition of I guarantees that the rest of the global store on island n must be of the form $U(y)$ for some y, and that the island's shared resource r satisfies $[A\ (t \cdot y)]$. Here, $U(y)$ represents the control the rest of the program has over the shared state of island n, and we must show that the operation we are about to execute respects it.

Now, before invoking the underlying operation, we acquire the lock, we remove r from the shared resource so that we can transfer ownership of it to the operation, and—this is the key point—we replace the client's local $U(t)$ resource with the resource $L(y, \epsilon)$, thus updating the global store of island n to $L(y, y)$. When we invoke the underlying operation, we place the $L(y, \epsilon)$ in its *frame*, which (by definition of the logical term predicate) it must preserve. Thus, when we get back control from the operation (which must be in a state such that I is satisfiable), the global store of island n must still be $L(y, y)$, of which the client controls $L(y, \epsilon)$ and the rest of the program controls $U(y)$. Also, the frame-preserving nature of the underlying operation's type tells us that it must have returned us a resource r' satisfying the capability $[A\ (t' \cdot y)]$. We can then release the lock, replace the client's $L(y, \epsilon)$ resource with $U(t')$ (which is what the client expects to control when the operation is completed), and transfer ownership of r' back to the island's shared resource, which now satisfies I at the new global store, $U(t' \cdot y)$. But crucially, despite/because of all these shenanigans, the resource $U(y)$ belonging to the rest of the program has been left untouched!

5. Related Work

Dealing with Reentrancy: Locking vs. the Anti-Frame Rule As explained in Section 3, our sharing rule uses a lock to protect against unsafe reentrancy, which can arise in our language due its support for *shared, higher-order* state. Most prior separation logics have not had to deal with such a hard problem because they are done in a first-order setting, where the possibility of reentrancy is syntactically evident; and most prior substructural type systems (*e.g.*, $\mathbf{L}^3$ [5]) have not had to deal with it because they don't support sharing/hiding of state.

One exception is Pottier's work on the *anti-frame rule* [32], which *does* account for reentrancy in the presence of shared, higher-order state. The anti-frame rule permits a group of functions to operate on a piece of hidden state described by an invariant C. Externally to the anti-frame rule, those functions may have type $!(A \multimap B)$, but internally they have roughly the form $!(A \otimes C \multimap B \otimes C)$ (but not quite, as we explain below). In a substructural setting, the rule therefore gives a way to export, *e.g.*, an affine reference with a set of operations, without treating the operations themselves as affine or forcing the client to thread the the affine reference capability through its code. The restriction to a

[4] Note that if the sharing rule did not require A to represent a *capability* (*i.e.*, to appear in proof-irrelevant brackets), then invoking any of the shared operations would require us to cough up the actual value v witnessing $A\ x$ (whereas here, v is $\exists$-quantified). This could be achieved by changing the implementation of the sharing rule so that it maintains a private reference cell ℓ storing the current witness v, and then updating I to also own $[\ell : v]$.

simple invariant has been subsequently relaxed to support hidden monotonic invariants [35], as well as monotonic "observations" about hidden state [29] (although to our knowledge the last extension has not yet been proven sound).

Pottier's approach provides a more general solution to the reentrancy problem (of which our use of locks would constitute one mode of use), but this comes at the cost of significant additional complexity in the typing rule for hiding (*i.e.*, the anti-frame rule) itself. In particular, the $\otimes$ operator that Pottier employs in the type $!(A \otimes C \multimap B \otimes C)$ above is not a simple tensor, but rather a tensoring operation, which propagates under $\rightarrow$ and ref types and comes equipped with a non-standard equational theory. Soundness proofs of the anti-frame rule using traditional syntactic techniques have consequently required years of heroic effort [33]. That said, significantly simpler semantic proofs of the anti-frame rule have also been given using Kripke logical relations [35]. Based on this experience, we chose to use a semantic model in our work, and have been very satisfied with its simplicity.

In this paper, we decided to isolate concerns by focusing on sharing and leaving an improved handling of reentrancy to future work. One possibility would be to consider synthesizing our sharing rule with the anti-frame rule, since they are complementary. The anti-frame rule offers a more general treatment of reentrancy, while the sharing rule offers a more general treatment of sharing. As demonstrated in our weak references example, simple invariants may be encoded via the sharing rule using the unit monoid, and subsequently hidden. More novel, however, is our support for a variety of interesting uses of sharing involving both monotonic state and *non-monotonic* state (*e.g.,* the memory manager example). Furthermore, our use of monoids lets clients divide, transfer, and recombine resources as they need, without restricting to a one-way increase in information as the anti-frame rule does.

Fictions of Separation From the outset, substructural reasoning about state has relied on the notion of disjointly supported assertions for local reasoning, but only gradually has the flexibility of that notion become clear. Early models of logically (but not physically) separable resources like fractional permissions [7, 10] and trees [9] treat those resources as primitive, either baking them into the operational semantics or, in simple cases, relying on a fixed interpretation into an underlying heap. To handle higher-level notions of separation, Krishnaswami *et al.* [23] embedded "domain-specific separation logics" into higher-order separation logic, and Dinsdale-Young, Gardner, and Wheelhouse named the general phenomenon "fictional disjointness" and justified its support of local reasoning by employing data refinement and axiomatic semantics [14].

Contemporaneously, *concurrent abstract predicates* (CAP, [13]) combined fictional disjointness with several other important ideas—the two most relevant being abstract predicates [28] and rights-as-resources [15]. CAP allows the specification of each module to include abstract predicates which, like the abstract data types introduced by our sharing rule, represent local knowledge and rights about a shared underlying resource. Hence, just as the tensor $\otimes$ is the all-purpose notion of separation for us, so separating conjunction $*$ is for CAP. On the other hand, CAP is built on more specific and complex forms of knowledge and rights, inherited from deny-guarantee [15] and intended for reasoning about concurrency.

In very recent work, several groups of researchers have simultaneously proposed variants of commutative monoids as an abstract way to capture fictional separation. Their original goals were quite distinct: Jensen and Birkedal's fictional separation logic (FSL) [21] is explicitly intended as a simple axiomatization of fictional disjointness within separation logic; Dinsdale-Young *et al.*'s views [12] are intended as a more abstract account of CAP (and compositional reasoning about concurrency in general); and Ley-Wild and Nanevski's subjective concurrent separation logic (SCSL) [25] is geared toward compositional reasoning about ghost state.

The three frameworks also share a shortcoming: the separating conjunction $*$ of the assertion language is tied to a single, specific monoid. With views and SCSL, this monoid is fixed at the outset, when the framework is instantiated. FSL, in contrast, is based on *indirect Hoare triples* parameterized by an *interpretation map*, which explicitly records a monoid together with its interpretation as a predicate on underlying resources. An interpretation map is akin to an island in our model (Section 4), which means that the assertions within an indirect Hoare triple must all be given in terms of a single abstract resource. While FSL enables interpretation maps to be stacked in layers or combined as a product (resembling our worlds), such structure must be explicitly managed within both assertions and proofs.

Our sharing rule also employs commutative monoids for fictional separation, but it associates a *different* monoid with each abstract data type it introduces. Consequently, our tensor product constructor $\otimes$ implicitly mediates between all resources "currently" in existence, both the physical resources and a dynamically-growing set of user-defined logical resources.

Temporarily Structural Types Most substructural type systems are not *completely* substructural: they permit, by a variety of means, linear or affine types to coexist with unrestricted types. Keeping a strict distinction between the two kinds of types is crucial for ensuring the soundness of *e.g.* strong updates, but it is also impractical for large programs with complex data structures. There have been numerous proposals for safely allowing the rules to be bent [37, 36], a well known example being Fähndrich and DeLine's *adoption and focus* [19]. At the root of these designs for "temporarily structural types" is the ability to *revoke* access to previously aliased data, providing a freshly linear view of that data. When unrestricted access is later restored, however, there must be some way of ensuring that the aliases still have an appropriate type, and the simplest way of doing that is to keep the type fixed.

Our sharing rule, on the other hand, does not commit to a particular aliasing discipline. The abstract resources supported by a shared underlying resource can be created and aliased to whatever extent their governing monoid allows, and can be strongly updated at any time without risk of invalidating non-local assertions. It remains to be seen whether our monoidal approach is flexible enough to recover the sophisticated rule-bending of the "temporarily structural" typing disciplines mentioned above.

Per-Module Notions of Resources Two recent languages—Tov's *Alms* [40] and Mazurak and Zdancewic's F° [26]—have been proposed for general-purpose, practical programming with substructural types. The generality of these languages stems from their ability to perform *substructural sealing*: they can seal an unrestricted value with an abstract type at a substructural kind, thereby preventing clients from freely aliasing the value. Substructural sealing, like our sharing construct, provides a way to introduce per-module notions of resource. But substructural sealing is used to impose a *more* restrictive interface on a *less* restrictive value, while sharing goes the other way around, allowing aliasing of affine resources. This difference is apparent in the work done by a typechecker in both cases: for substructural sealing, there is little to check, because it is always safe to tighten the interface to a value; for sharing, the exported operations must be shown to respect their frame. Ultimately, these two forms of resource introduction seem complementary, and indeed, the language we have presented supports both.

Kripke Logical Relations Kripke logical relations have long been used to reason about state in higher-order, ML-like languages [31].

Ahmed *et al.* [5, 4] have given Kripke logical relations for linear languages with state, using a simple notion of possible world corresponding to strict heap separation. The structure of our logical relation is quite similar to this earlier work, but the structure of our worlds is significantly different, since we must account for interaction between an unbounded number of abstract resource types, each of which is governed by a distinct monoid.

More recently, Ahmed *et al.* [3] and Dreyer *et al.* [16] have given models for higher-order *structural* state based on the concept of *transition systems*, which facilitate the modeling of protocol-based uses of state, as well as the "well-bracketed" state changes possible in languages without control. Since transition systems can be modeled as monoids, our current model fully supports transition systems as a mode of use. With a small extension (whose proof is in the appendix [24]), we can also model Dreyer *et al.*'s "public" vs. "private" transitions for reasoning about well-bracketed state changes, although proofs based on their techniques are arguably more direct than ours. (We plan to report on this in future work.)

6. Conclusion and Future Work

In this paper, we have shown how to put programmer-defined resource abstractions on the same footing as built-in resources such as the heap, yielding a type system that permits the flexible use of aliased data while retaining the simple intuitions of substructural logic. To do so, we combined exciting new ideas from separation logic with classical type-theoretic techniques such as refinement types and data abstraction.

An immediate direction for future work is to study how to optimize the sharing rule, both via the model (*i.e.,* proving that locks are not needed for specific implementations), and via type-theoretic extensions that we could use to avoid locking (*e.g.,* via formalizing the concept of "first-order data" as a modality, or via a sharing modality [36]). Another natural direction for future work is to examine if our methods extend to full-blown value-dependent types (*e.g.,* as in HTT [27]). This poses interesting questions, since methods based on step-indexing have historically had challenges dealing with semantic equalities (as opposed to approximation), and our sharing rule deeply connects existential types and state.

References

[1] A. Ahmed. *Semantics of Types for Mutable State.* PhD thesis, Princeton University, 2004.

[2] A. Ahmed. Step-indexed syntactic logical relations for recursive and quantified types. In *ESOP*, 2006.

[3] A. Ahmed, D. Dreyer, and A. Rossberg. State-dependent representation independence. In *POPL*, 2009.

[4] A. Ahmed, M. Fluet, and G. Morrisett. A step-indexed model of substructural state. In *ICFP*, 2005.

[5] A. Ahmed, M. Fluet, and G. Morrisett. $\mathbf{L}^3$: A linear language with locations. *Fundamenta Informaticae*, 77:397–449, 2007.

[6] A. Appel, P.-A. Melliès, C. Richards, and J. Vouillon. A very modal model of a modern, major, general type system. In *POPL*, 2007.

[7] J. Boyland. Checking interference with fractional permissions. In *SAS*, 2003.

[8] T. Brus, M. C. J. D. van Eekelen, M. van Leer, M. J. Plasmeijer, and H. P. Barendregt. Clean: A language for functional graph rewriting. In *FPCA*, 1987.

[9] C. Calcagno, P. Gardner, and U. Zarfaty. Context logic and tree update. In *POPL*, 2005.

[10] C. Calcagno, P. W. O'Hearn, and H. Yang. Local action and abstract separation logic. In *LICS*, 2007.

[11] R. DeLine and M. Fähndrich. Enforcing high-level protocols in low-level software. In *PLDI*, 2001.

[12] T. Dinsdale-Young, L. Birkedal, P. Gardner, M. Parkinson, and H. Yang. Views: Compositional reasoning for concurrency, 2012. Submitted for publication.

[13] T. Dinsdale-Young, M. Dodds, P. Gardner, M. Parkinson, and V. Vafeiadis. Concurrent abstract predicates. In *ECOOP*, 2010.

[14] T. Dinsdale-Young, P. Gardner, and M. Wheelhouse. Abstraction and refinement for local reasoning. In *VSTTE*, 2010.

[15] M. Dodds, X. Feng, M. J. Parkinson, and V. Vafeiadis. Deny-guarantee reasoning. In *ESOP*, 2009.

[16] D. Dreyer, G. Neis, and L. Birkedal. The impact of higher-order state and control effects on local relational reasoning. In *ICFP*, 2010.

[17] D. Dreyer, G. Neis, A. Rossberg, and L. Birkedal. A relational modal logic for higher-order stateful ADTs. In *POPL*, 2010.

[18] J. Dunfield. *A Unified System of Type Refinements.* PhD thesis, Carnegie Mellon University, 2007.

[19] M. Fähndrich and R. DeLine. Adoption and focus: Practical linear types for imperative programming. In *PLDI*, 2002.

[20] J.-Y. Girard. Linear logic. *TCS*, 50(1):1–102, 1987.

[21] J. Jensen and L. Birkedal. Fictional separation logic. In *ESOP*, 2012.

[22] C. B. Jones. The role of auxiliary variables in the formal development of concurrent programs. In *Reflections on the work of C.A.R. Hoare*, pages 167–188. Springer, 2010.

[23] N. R. Krishnaswami, L. Birkedal, and J. Aldrich. Verifying event-driven programs using ramified frame properties. In *TLDI*, 2010.

[24] N. R. Krishnaswami, A. Turon, D. Dreyer, and D. Garg. Superficially substructural types (Technical appendix), 2012. URL: `http://www.mpi-sws.org/~dreyer/papers/supsub/`.

[25] R. Ley-Wild and A. Nanevski. Subjective concurrent separation logic, 2012. Submitted for publication.

[26] K. Mazurak, J. Zhao, and S. Zdancewic. Lightweight linear types in System F°. In *TLDI*, 2010.

[27] A. Nanevski, G. Morrisett, and L. Birkedal. Hoare Type Theory, polymorphism and separation. *JFP*, 18(5&6):865–911, Sept. 2008.

[28] M. J. Parkinson and G. M. Bierman. Separation logic and abstraction. In *POPL*, 2005.

[29] A. Pilkiewicz and F. Pottier. The essence of monotonic state. In *TLDI*, 2011.

[30] A. Pitts. Typed operational reasoning. In B. C. Pierce, editor, *Advanced Topics in Types and Programming Languages*, chapter 7. MIT Press, 2005.

[31] A. Pitts and I. Stark. Operational reasoning for functions with local state. In *HOOTS*, 1998.

[32] F. Pottier. Hiding local state in direct style: a higher-order anti-frame rule. In *LICS*, 2008.

[33] F. Pottier. Syntactic soundness proof of a type-and-capability system with hidden state, 2011. Submitted for publication.

[34] J. C. Reynolds. Separation logic: A logic for shared mutable data structures. In *LICS*, 2002.

[35] J. Schwinghammer, L. Birkedal, F. Pottier, B. Reus, K. Støvring, and H. Yang. A step-indexed Kripke model of hidden state. *Mathematical Structures in Computer Science*, 2012. To appear.

[36] R. Shi, D. Zhu, , and H. Xi. A modality for safe resource sharing and code reentrancy. In *ICTAC*, 2010.

[37] F. Smith, D. Walker, and G. Morrisett. Alias types. In *ESOP*, 2000.

[38] R. E. Strom and S. Yemini. Typestate: A programming language concept for enhancing software reliability. *IEEE Transactions on Software Engineering*, 12(1):157–171, 1986.

[39] M. Tofte and J.-P. Talpin. Region-based memory management. *Information and Computation*, 132(2):109–176, 1997.

[40] J. Tov. *Practical Programming with Substructural Types.* PhD thesis, Northeastern University, 2012.

[41] V. Vafeiadis. *Modular fine-grained concurrency verification.* PhD thesis, University of Cambridge, 2008.

[42] D. Walker, K. Crary, and G. Morrisett. Typed memory management via static capabilities. *TOPLAS*, 22:701–771, 2000.

[43] J. Wickerson, M. Dodds, and M. Parkinson. Explicit stabilisation for modular rely-guarantee reasoning. In *ESOP*, 2010.

[44] N. Wolverson. *Game semantics for an object-oriented language.* PhD thesis, University of Edinburgh, 2008.

[45] H. Xi and F. Pfenning. Dependent types in practical programming. In *POPL*, 1999.

Shake Before Building

Replacing Make with Haskell

Neil Mitchell

ndmitchell@gmail.com

Abstract

Most complex software projects are compiled using a build tool (e.g. `make`), which runs commands in an order satisfying user-defined dependencies. Unfortunately, most build tools require all dependencies to be specified *before* the build starts. This restriction makes many dependency patterns difficult to express, especially those involving files generated at build time. We show how to eliminate this restriction, allowing additional dependencies to be specified while building. We have implemented our ideas in the Haskell library Shake, and have used Shake to write a complex build system which compiles millions of lines of code.

Categories and Subject Descriptors D.3 [*Software*]: Programming Languages

General Terms Languages

Keywords build-system, compilation, Haskell

1. Introduction

A build tool, such as `make` (Feldman 1978), takes a set of build rules, plus some input files, and produces some output files. Using `make`, a build rule can be written as:

```
result.tar : file1 file2
    tar -cf result.tar file1 file2
```

This rule says that the file result.tar depends on the inputs file1 and file2 (first line), and provides a command to build result.tar (second line). Whenever file1 or file2 change, the command will be run, and result.tar will be built.

But imagine we want to build result.tar from the list of files stored in list.txt. The dependencies of result.tar cannot be specified in advance, but depend on *the contents* of list.txt. Unfortunately, the `make` dependency system cannot express this pattern (for workarounds see §7.5). Using the build tool we describe in this paper, we can write:

```
"result.tar" *> λ_ → do
    need ["list.txt"]
    contents ← readFileLines "list.txt"
    need contents
    system' "tar" $ ["-cf", "result.tar"] ++ contents
```

This rule describes how to build result.tar. We depend on (need) the file list.txt. We read each line from list.txt into the variable contents – being a list of the files that should go into result.tar. Next, we depend on all the files in contents, and finally call the `tar` program. If either list.txt changes, or any of the files listed by list.txt change, then result.tar will be rebuilt.

The key difference from `make` (and nearly all other build tools) is that rather than specifying all dependencies *in advance*, we allow further dependencies to be specified *after* examining the results of previous dependencies. This difference is crucial to accurately describe many dependency relationships.

Consider the problem of dependencies stemming from files included by a C source file. Some build tools require these dependencies to be specified manually. Other build tools allow two separate phases, where dependencies are computed before the build starts. But if the build system generates C files and then compiles them, even a two phase system is insufficient, as the generated files are not available during the first phase. Our build tool has no such limitations – it is able to easily handle generated files, even generated files which are only necessary due to being included by other generated files.

1.1 Contributions

We have implemented our build tool as a Haskell library, named Shake, which is available online[1]. Shake provides a concise syntax for writing build systems (§3), along with a high-performance implementation (§4). By implementing Shake as a Haskell library we allow rules to be written using the full power of Haskell, including the use of modules and functions to structure large build systems.

In addition to more flexible dependencies (§2), Shake also includes the important features of `make`, such as minimal rebuilds (running only a subset of the rules when some subset of the inputs change, §2.3.2), and parallelising the build (running multiple independent rules at the same time, §4.3.2). We allow rules to operate over any values, not limited to files, allowing us to track non-file dependencies (§3.4) and properly handle commands producing multiple outputs (§6.3). We have built a number of useful tools into Shake, including build rule checking (§5.1), profiling (§5.2) and dependency analysis (§5.3).

Various versions of Shake have been used at Standard Chartered for the past three years (§6). The build system creates over 30,000 build objects, with more than a million lines of source code and a million lines of generated code, in many programming languages. We originally implemented this build system using `make`, but the result was slow to run, hard to maintain, and frequently caused spurious compile failures. Switching to Shake made our build system ten times shorter, made builds run twice as fast, and has solved our build system problems.

[1] `http://hackage.haskell.org/package/shake`

ICFP'12, September 9–15, 2012, Copenhagen, Denmark.

2. Specifying Dependencies

Most make-like build tools start by constructing a graph from the dependency information, then traverse the graph, running the rules to build the required results (or use a topological sort, giving a similar effect). However, any approach based on a static dependency graph cannot permit additional dependencies to be specified while running the rules. As we saw in §1, many examples *require* additional dependencies to be specified while running the rules. The solution is simple – we reject the idea that build tools should use a static dependency graph.

In this section we model the dependencies permitted by non-recursive make (Miller 1998), along with our enhanced dependency scheme. We describe what it means for a build system to be correct, and how to support minimal rebuilds. In §3 and §4 we show how to turn these ideas into a practical tool.

2.1 Moving Dependency Specification

While make is heavily file and IO based, we choose to model the dependencies without these distractions. Our model uses the type Key for things that can be created or are dependencies (e.g. file names), and the type Value for the values associated with a Key (i.e. file contents). With these types, we can define the main build function as:

```
build :: Set Rule → Key → Value
```

The build function takes a set of rules and the target Key to build, and returns the Value associated with that Key. We restrict our model to building only one target, while make allows multiple targets (i.e. a list of Keys to build). However, we can encode multiple targets by creating a distinguished key whose rule depends on the original targets and returns their values, and then use that key as the new target.

Using build, we can model make with the Rule type:

```
data Rule_m = Rule_m
    {creates  :: Key
    , depends :: [Key]
    , action  :: [Value] → Value
    }
```

A make Rule ($Rule_m$) can be modelled as the Key it creates, the Keys it depends on, and the action that takes the depended upon Values and produces the result Value. Note that all dependencies for a rule are specified *before* running the action.

Using the same build function, we can model our enhanced dependency scheme as:

```
data Rule_s = Rule_s
    {creates :: Key
    , action :: Action
    }

data Action = Finished Value
            | Depends Key (Value → Action)
```

A Shake Rule ($Rule_s$) can be modelled as the Key it creates, and the action that creates the result. The Action either returns the Finished Value, or requires a new dependency with Depends – specifying the Key it depends on, plus a function that takes the Value of that Key and produces a new Action.

The big difference from $Rule_m$ is the introduction of dynamic dependencies. A rule can require additional dependencies, based on the values of previous dependencies. We can easily translate $Rule_m$ to $Rule_s$, but the reverse is not possible – $Rule_s$ is strictly more powerful than $Rule_m$.

2.2 Correctness

Assuming a function which finds the Rule for a given Key, denoted by the operator (!), we can write a function to build $Rule_m$ targets as follows:

```
build_m rules target = run (rules ! target)
  where run r = action r (map (build_m rules) (depends r))
```

Starting at the target Key, we find the associated $Rule_m$, run $build_m$ on its dependencies, then run the action. A $Rule_m$ build system is able to produce the result for a given target iff the expression $build_m$ rules target is well-defined. If we assume all actions are total, then this expression is well-defined if you can build a finite dependency graph for the target with the available rules. This property can be checked without running any actions.

We can write a similar function to build $Rule_s$ targets as follows:

```
build_s rules target = run (action (rules ! target))
  where run (Finished val) = val
        run (Depends dep act) = run (act (build_s rules dep))
```

Starting at the target Key, we find the action from the associated $Rule_s$, and run it. Once we reach Finished we are done; if we encounter a Depends we run $build_m$ on that dependency before continuing. As before, a $Rule_s$ build system is able to produce a result for a given target iff the expression $build_s$ rules target is well-defined. However, unlike before, there is no obvious way to determine if the expression is well-defined in advance without detailed information about the action functions.

2.3 Minimal Rebuilds

The build functions in the previous section may evaluate one rule many times during a single run, but real build systems should minimise the number of rules run. In a single build run, any rule should be run at most once – a property that is easy to guarantee with a simple cache. Additionally, if a rule's dependencies have not changed since the last time it was run, the rule should not be rerun. In this section we describe how to avoid repeating $Rule_m$ rules whose dependencies have not changed, enhancing the scheme followed by make, then apply the same ideas to $Rule_s$.

2.3.1 Minimal Rebuilds with $Rule_m$

To avoid repeating rules whose dependencies have not changed, make does not run any rules where the dependent files have older modification times than the result file. We use a similar scheme, adapted for arbitrary Key/Value types. Whenever a rule is run, we create a $Result_m$:

```
data Result_m = Result_m
  {created :: Key
  , result  :: Value
  , built   :: Time
  }
```

$Result_m$ contains the Key the rule created, the result Value, and the Time when the result was built. We store all $Result_m$ values between build runs using a database, and skip rerunning a $Rule_m$ if the result was built more recently than its dependencies. In common with make, we assume the rules do not change between runs (see §6.2 for workarounds). To determine if we should skip, we require the result for this rule's key from the previous build run (named old) and a way to demand results for this build run (named ask):

```
skip_m :: Result_m → (Key → Result_m) → Rule_m → Bool
skip_m old ask r = all ((≤ built old) ∘ built ∘ ask) (depends r)
```

The $skip_m$ function returns True if a rule does not need running. We require the results for all dependencies, then check that they were built before this rule was last run.

The `make` approach of relying on modification times can fail if the system clock changes, if the clock resolution is too coarse, or if a file has its modification time set to a time in the past (such as when extracting a backup). Therefore, instead of using the system time for built, we use the number of runs of this build system, incrementing Time each run. This approach guarantees that Time is monotonically increasing.

A convenient property of `make` is that no additional data need be stored between runs, since the file system already stores modification times. In contrast, we must store the Time and Result_m values in a database (interestingly, an additional data store is required for many advanced build systems, see §7). However, for some types of rules, such as when Keys are filenames and Values are modification times, the Values are stored in both the Result_m database *and* the file system. If an inconsistency is detected, we must discard our stored Result_m. To detect inconsistencies, we require the following function:

```
validStored :: Key → Value → Bool
```

This function should return True if the Key's Value is not stored elsewhere, or if it is stored but the Value is consistent. As an example for files, validStored should return True only if the file exists, and has the same modification time.

2.3.2 Minimal Rebuilds with Rule_s

To achieve minimal rebuilds with Rule_m we rely on having the dependencies available without executing the action, something that is not available with Rule_s. To solve this problem, we include the list of dependencies in Result_s, and use them in skip_s:

```
data Result_s = Result_s
  {created :: Key, result :: Value, built :: Time
  , depends :: [Key]
  }

skip_s old ask r = all ((≤ built old) ∘ built ∘ ask) (depends old)
```

Compared to skip_m, we have made one small change – instead of using depends r, we use depends old. For the stored depends to be valid we rely on the rule's action not changing, and that the action is pure (see §5.1 for necessary restrictions when we allow IO actions). With this modification we are able to ensure minimal rebuilds using Rule_s. We still require the validStored check from the previous section.

2.3.3 Unchanging Results

The `make` tool has a requirement that a rule action *must* modify the file it creates, otherwise the rule will be repeatedly rerun, as the result will remain older than its dependencies. This requirement stems from using the modification time as both the result and the built time, but since we store these fields separately, we can eliminate some unnecessary rebuilds.

Instead of storing just the built time, we also store the changed time – when the result last changed. Whenever we create a result we use the current time for built, but if the result Value is the same as last time, we use the previous changed time. We can rewrite skip_s to take advantage of this additional information:

```
data Result_s = Result_s
  {created :: Key, result :: Value, built :: Time, depends :: [Key]
  , changed :: Time
  }

skip_s old ask r =
  all ((≤ built old) ∘ changed ∘ ask) (depends old)
```

```
import Development.Shake
import System.FilePath

main = shake shakeOptions $ do
  want ["Main"]

  "Main" *> \out → do
    cs ← getDirectoryFiles "." "*.c"
    let os = map (++".o") cs
    need os
    system' "gcc" $ ["-o", out] ++ os

  "*.c.o" *> \out → do
    let c = dropExtension out
    need [c]
    headers ← cIncludes c
    need headers
    system' "gcc" ["-o", out, "-c", c]

cIncludes :: FilePath → Action [FilePath]
cIncludes x = do
  (stdout, _) ← systemOutput "gcc" ["-MM", x]
  return $ drop 2 $ words stdout
```

Figure 1. A Shake build system for C code.

We have made one small change – instead of checking against the built time of the dependencies, we check against their changed time. It is important to still compare against built old because running a rule may not update its changed time, but will always update its built time, thus we avoid rebuilding repeatedly when the result does not change. Since it is always the case that changed $\leqslant$ built, skip_s will now return True more often.

In some situations, support for unchanging results can reduce rebuild times from many minutes to seconds. As an example, consider a file generated by the build system. If the generator changes it is necessary to regenerate the file, but there is a chance the result will not have changed. By supporting unchanging files we can avoid rebuilding everything depending on that file.

3. Shake in Haskell

In this section we use the theory from §2 to create a practical build tool, implemented as a Haskell library. In particular, we describe how to replace Key and Value with polymorphism, how to integrate IO actions and how to define a set of rules. We present the developer interface to Shake, but leave most implementation concerns to §4.

3.1 A Shake Example

Figure 1 shows an example build system in Shake. Running this program will build Main from all the *.c files in the current directory. If we add or remove a .c file, or change any of the .c files or the header files they `#include`, then the necessary files will be rebuilt.

The build system produces (wants) the file Main. To generate Main we list all the C files in the current directory, add the extension .o (object files), require those files to be built (need them), then call gcc to link them. To build an object file we take the associated C file and call the function cIncludes to get the headers it requires. We need those headers, then call gcc to do the compilation. The cIncludes function works by calling `gcc -MM`, causing gcc to generate the dependency information on the standard output.

This example demonstrates a number of features of Shake based build systems:

```
data ShakeOptions = ShakeOptions
    {shakeFiles    :: FilePath
    , shakeThreads :: Int
    , ...
    }
shakeOptions = ...   -- default set of options

data Rules α
instance Monad Rules
instance Monoid α ⇒ Monoid (Rules α)

data Action α
instance Monad Action
instance MonadIO Action

class (
  Typeable key, Typeable value,
  Binary   key, Binary   value,
  Eq       key, Eq       value,
  Hashable key, Hashable value,
  Show     key, Show     value,
  NFData   key, NFData   value
  ) ⇒ Rule key value where
  validStored :: key → value → IO Bool

run :: ShakeOptions → Rules () → IO ()

action :: Action () → Rules ()

rule, defaultRule :: Rule key value ⇒
  (key → Maybe (Action value)) → Rules ()

apply  :: Rule key value ⇒ [key] → Action [value]
apply1 :: Rule key value ⇒  key  → Action  value
```

Figure 2. Primitive operations in Shake

It's Haskell The main entry point can call shake directly, but it can also do command line processing (§6.1), or anything else. We have defined a local function, cIncludes, helping to split the build system into components that can be reused. We make use of the existing filepath library.

Expressive dependencies The call to getDirectoryFiles is tracked (§3.4) – adding or removing files will trigger a rebuild. We track the dependencies introduced by `#include` directives.

We use system commands We use `gcc` to compile, to link, and to determine the headers required by the C files. We can freely use both Haskell functions and system commands to generate build results.

As a practical concern, for many larger projects there are often multiple compilers that produce object files with the .o extension. We solve this problem by making the C compiler use the extension .c.o, the Haskell compiler use .hs.o etc, allowing different rules for each type of object.

3.2 Core Shake

The core interface to Shake is given in Figure 2 – everything else is defined on top. We can run the build system with run, specify targets with action, create new rules with rule/defaultRule, and express dependencies with apply/apply1.

We build the targets using the run function, which also takes an options record. Typical options include which file to use for the database (shakeFiles) and the number of processors to use (shakeThreads). To specify the targets to build we use action, specifying an action which is always run, typically calling apply to require keys to be built.

Every key/value rule pair used in Shake must be a member of the Rule class. The Rule class defines the method validStored to determine whether a value is consistent with any value stored externally (§2.3). Each key and value type must also be a member of several type classes:

Typeable We allow multiple types of rules in a single build system. To distinguish the types, we require a Typeable constraint, allowing us to obtain an explicit TypeRep (Lämmel and Peyton Jones 2003).

Binary We require Binary serialisation, allowing us to store the results between runs, to achieve minimal rebuilds (§2.3).

Eq We require equality to look up results for keys and to test if values have changed (§2.3.3).

Hashable We require Hashable to accelerate looking up results for keys. The Hashable requirement for value is currently unused, but is included for consistency.

Show We require Show for debugging messages, profiling and analysis (§4.2, §5.2).

NFData We require NFData to ensure that values are fully evaluated when they are computed, ensuring errors occur in a timely manner (§4.2).

Most rules are defined with rule, whose argument is a function which takes a single key value, and returns Nothing to indicate that this rule does not build this key, or Just with the action that builds the associated value. The function defaultRule allows a rule to be defined with a lower priority, which is used if no rules match (see §3.5). If two rules of the same priority match the same key then an error is raised.

The Rules type is a commutative Monoid, allowing two sets of rules to be joined to produce a new set of Rules. In practice, the syntactic sugar supported by Monad offers a very natural way to define rules, allowing a set of rules to be introduced with **do** and then simply written below each other. To support a Monad instance for Rules we add an additional type parameter α (almost always instantiated to ()) and make ($\gg$) join two sets of rules.

To define actions we use the Action type, which has a Monad instance to allow actions to be executed sequentially. The Action type has an instance for MonadIO, allowing users to call arbitrary IO functions using liftIO to translate IO α to Action α. Dependencies can be expressed using the function apply1 which takes a key, ensures the key is built, and returns the associated value. The apply function can be thought of as mapM apply1, but may build the necessary keys in parallel (§4.3.2).

3.3 Wildcard File Patterns

The `make` tool supports the syntax %.c to match any files ending with .c. We define a similar notation, allowing "*" to match any part of a filename and "//" to match any number of directories, using the definitions:

```
type FilePattern = String
(?≡) :: FilePattern → FilePath → Bool
```

As an example, "*.c" ?≡ "foo.c" returns True, while "*.c" ?≡ "foo.h" returns False. We reuse the FilePattern type in several of our rules.

```haskell
import qualified System.Directory as IO

data Dir = Dir FilePath FilePattern
  -- plus all necessary instances

go :: Dir → IO [FilePath]
go (Dir dir pat) =
  liftM (filter (pat?==)) $ IO.getDirectoryContents dir

instance Rule Dir [FilePath] where
  validStored q a = liftM (≡ a) $ go q

getDirectoryFiles :: FilePath → FilePattern → Action [FilePath]
getDirectoryFiles dir pat = apply1 $ Dir dir pat

defaultDir :: Rules ()
defaultDir = defaultRule $ Just ∘ liftIO ∘ go
```

Figure 3. Implementation of getDirectoryFiles.

3.4 Defining Rule Types

A typical Shake build system will use a handful of different Rule instances, usually all provided by the Shake library. To aid end users, we suggest that people defining rule types also define sugar functions, as we have done for the rule types included with Shake. As an example of defining a rule type, we give the code for getDirectoryFiles in Figure 3. This function takes a directory, and a file pattern (§3.3), and returns the list of files that match.

We start by defining a key data type (Dir), along with a function that computes the result (go). We define a Rule instance mapping from the Dir data type to the result type of [FilePath], which uses equality to check if a previous result is still valid. We define getDirectoryFiles as a strongly typed wrapper around apply1, and defaultDir as a wrapper around defaultRule. Anyone using getDirectoryFiles must include defaultDir in their rule set, so the defaultRule for Dir is available. We do not export the Dir constructor, forcing people to use the wrappers.

3.5 File Based Rules

While our build system is not restricted to rules dealing with files, in practice many build systems are file orientated. When implementing file rules, the filename is an obvious key, but value could be either modification time or a hash of the file contents (e.g. SHA1). In practice, we found that using modification time is faster (significantly faster for large files) and being able to force rebuilds using the `touch` command is highly convenient while developing build rules. Of course, our design allows anyone to define a new type of file rule, based on file content hashes.

We define file rules in Figure 4. To force files to be built, we define need and want. The need action adds a dependency on all the modification times of the files, and is typically used before performing some IO action that uses the files. We use want to specify the targets of the build system, implemented by calling need in an action that is always run.

We define defaultFile as a rule that checks if the file already exists, and if so uses it. Source files will have no associated rules to build them, so this rule just records their modification time. If a file has no rules (since any rules would be run in preference to the default rule), and does not exist, we raise an error. As with defaultDir, anyone using want/need should include defaultFile in their rule set.

We define new file rules using (?>), which takes a predicate to match against the file name and an action to run. This function

```haskell
import qualified System.Directory as IO

newtype File = File FilePath
  -- plus all necessary instances

getFileTime :: FilePath → IO (Maybe ClockTime)
getFileTime x = do
  b ← IO.doesFileExist x
  if not b then return Nothing else
    liftM Just $ IO.getModificationTime x

instance Rule File ClockTime where
  validStored (File x) t = fmap (≡ Just t) $ getFileTime x

need :: [FilePath] → Action ()
need xs = do
  apply $ map File xs :: Action [ClockTime]
  return ()

want :: [FilePath] → Rules ()
want xs = action $ need xs

defaultFile :: Rules ()
defaultFile = defaultRule $ λ(File x) → Just $ do
  res ← liftIO $ getFileTime x
  let msg = "Error, file does not exist and no rule: " ++ x
  return $ fromMaybe (error msg) res

(?>) :: (FilePath → Bool) → (FilePath → Action ()) → Rules ()
(?>) test act = rule $ λ(File x) →
  if not $ test x then Nothing else Just $ do
    liftIO $ createDirectoryIfMissing True $ takeDirectory x
    act x
    res ← liftIO $ getFileTime x
    let msg = "Error, rule failed to build the file: " ++ x
    return $ fromMaybe (error msg) res

(**>) :: [FilePattern] → (FilePath → Action ()) → Rules ()
(**>) test act = (λx → any (?==x) test) ?> act

(*>) :: FilePattern → (FilePath → Action ()) → Rules ()
(*>) test act = (test?==) ?> act
```

Figure 4. Implementation of file rules.

ensures the correct key/value types, and obtains the modification time afterwards. Before running the action we create the directory containing the output file, an idea taken from the Ninja build system (Martin 2011). We found that when running a large set of newly written rules, often one rule would create the output directory while another did not – meaning some rule execution orderings worked while others failed. Automatically creating the output directory removes this source of failure.

While (?>) is the ultimate file creation rule, we define two additional operators, using the file wildcard match operator (?==) from §3.3. We define (*>) for matching a single pattern, for example "*.c" *> ..., in a similar style to `make`. We define (**>) for matching any one of a set of patterns.

3.6 Automatically Include Default Rules

With the rule types already defined, users can write a build system using Shake. Unfortunately, if the user forgets to include the defaultFile rule, there is likely to be a runtime error. Instead of requiring the user to remember to include the default rules, we define a wrapper function shake which includes all the standard default rules:

```
shake opts rules = run opts $ do
  defaultDir   -- §3.4
  defaultFile  -- §3.5
  ...
  rules
```

In addition to the directory and file rules, we also include rules that query the existence of files, always force a rule to rerun, store arbitrary configuration data in a tracked manner and build multiple files in one action. All these rules are defined similarly to the directory and file rules.

The astute reader may be wondering why we can't specify default rules as an additional member in the Rule type class, allowing the default rule to be found from the type, and avoiding the need for the shake wrapper around run. Alas, that solution doesn't work because we need explicit rules of each type to deserialise dynamically typed values (for full details see §4.1).

3.7 Additional Functions

The IO function readFile is only safe if the file being read has previously had need called on it, tracking the dependency (for more IO safety properties see §5.1). To help build system authors, we define a safe wrapper, readFile′, which includes the call to need:

```
readFile′ :: FilePath → Action String
readFile′ x = need [x] ≫ liftIO (readFile x)
```

We also define readFileLines which is like readFile′, but splits the contents of the file into lines (therefore the first need call in the example from §1 is unnecessary, but not harmful, as readFileLines will also call need). We define writeFileLines for writing files containing a list of lines. The function writeFileChanged writes a file, but only if the contents have changed, avoiding some rebuilds due to unchanging results (§2.3.3).

We define the system′ function which runs a system command, but fails if the exit code represents failure, and also records profiling information (see §5.2). The system′ function should be used carefully, as it cannot tell which files the system command may depend on, so explicit need commands must be used. We recommend writing wrappers around system commands which insert the appropriate need calls (see §5.1 for which need calls are required).

4. Implementing Shake

We have implemented Shake, and used it extensively. In this section we sketch some of the main implementation challenges and how they can be overcome. We first describe how to handle different key/value types within a single build system, then how to deal with errors, and finally how to execute the rules efficiently and with maximum parallelism. Readers interested in more details are encouraged to download the full implementation (see §1).

4.1 Dynamically Typed Values

A single Shake program can use multiple types for keys and values. To work with heterogenous values in Haskell we define:

```
data Any = Any (∀ α •
  (Typeable α, Binary α, Eq α
  , Hashable α, Show α, NFData α) ⇒ α)
```

This definition, using existentials (Läufer and Odersky 1994), allows any type supporting all the required type classes to be stored as type Any. We define Key and Value as synonyms for Any. We can implement Eq, Hashable, Show and NFData instances for Any without difficulty, often by appealing to the TypeRep provided by the Typeable instance.

Implementing a Binary instance for Any is harder. Serialising a value is easy, we serialise the TypeRep followed by the value. However, deserialising is problematic – we can deserialise the TypeRep, but to deserialise the value we need to obtain the Binary instance for that type. Our solution is to keep a mapping from TypeRep to Any, and after deserialising the TypeRep find the associated Any and use that Binary instance. As a consequence, we cannot deserialise any file containing a TypeRep not present in our mapping. We generate the mapping from all rules defined in the Rules set. Therefore we cannot move defaultRule into the Rule type class, as then a type could be usefully used without being present in the Rules set.

When deserialising, if we encounter a type not present in the mapping, we ignore the entire database. This behaviour is pessimistic, but safe – if the set of rules has changed then the build system must have changed, which is not tracked (see §6.2).

4.2 Handling Errors

To turn Shake into a practical system, we make a number of changes from the natural implementation, designed to improve error handling.

Tracking the stack We maintain a stack while executing rules, listing the keys that cause a rule to be executed. Whenever an error occurs, either when running a rule or finding a rule, we print the stack. Whenever we execute an action, we force its result using the NFData instance, ensuring any errors are raised with the correct stack. We raise an error when trying to build a key that is already on the stack, which would indicate a key depends on itself. This last check provides a clear error message instead of executing an infinite series of rules.

Tracing and diagnostics We provide options to print every rule and system command run. Whenever a system command fails, we reprint the command line after the failure. We provide a diagnostic mode to print detailed information as the build progresses, helping to debug build systems.

Resuming after errors When running a large build system, it is common for it to fail before completing – either from a rule raising an error, or the user killing the build process. In these situations it is important that none of the work already done is lost. At startup Shake loads its database into memory, and on successful completion it saves the database to file. To ensure no results are lost, every time a rule completes we immediately store the result in a journal file. If Shake finishes successfully we delete the journal, but if a journal is present on startup, we merge its results.

4.3 Build Algorithm

The internal state of Shake includes a mapping from each key to one of six status values. Initially every key is either Loaded (was found in the database) or Missing (is not known to the build system). The build logic of Shake is implemented in a function named build, which modifies the state to ensure that a given key is either Ready (a result is available) or Error (there was an exception when running the rule). The build function is parameterised by a way to check a stored value is valid (using validStored from §3.2) and a way to build a key (appealing to the defined rules for that type). Using build, it is relatively easy to implement the core of Shake – simply run all actions and make apply call build before looking up the status of a key.

Our implementation of the build function takes 100 lines of Haskell. When implementing build there are two goals, *correctness* and *efficiency*.

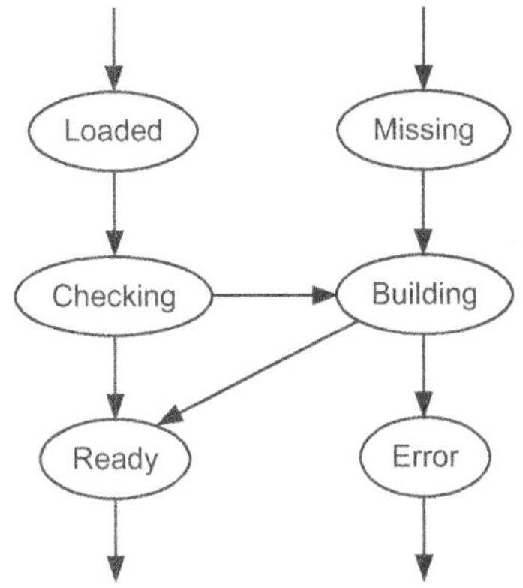

Figure 5. Building state transitions.

4.3.1 Correctness

For an implementation of build to be correct, it must always execute enough rules to ensure all results are correct, but never execute rules that could have been safely skipped. We satisfy these constraints with the status transition diagram in Figure 5. At the start of a build run all keys are either Loaded or Missing, and after calling build on a key, it is either Ready or Error. We use Checking for keys that are being checked to see if they can be skipped, and Building for rules that are currently being built. If a key is Missing and is required we have no choice but to start Building it. After Building a key, the action will either complete successfully making the result Ready, or fail producing an Error.

Most of the complexity of build comes from the Checking state, which is necessary to support unchanging results (§2.3.3). When checking a key there are two possibilities – either the check succeeds and the result is Ready, or the check fails and we start Building it. We first check the stored result using validStored, failing the check if the result is no longer valid. We then build each dependency in order, and fail the check if any dependency is Error, or has changed since we last built this key. If all dependencies are checked successfully, we transition to Ready, without running the rule.

To support unchanging results, it is necessary to build dependencies *before* running the rule requiring them – only running the rule if a dependency has changed. Since the value of earlier dependencies may change subsequent dependencies, it is important to check dependencies in the order they were required. However, if the build system has been modified, and a rule no longer requires its previous dependencies, these previous dependencies will still be built, but not used. As a consequence, even if one of these unused dependencies results in an Error, the build may still complete successfully.

4.3.2 Efficiency

When implementing build there are two separate efficiency goals. If no rules need to be run (a common case), build should strive for low overhead, as the time taken by build is likely to be a significant proportion of the total time. If rules do need running, build should start the rules as early as possible, to maximise parallelism. In order to expose parallelism we make build take a set of keys, and store depends as [[Key]] instead of just [Key] – where each item comes from one call to apply.

In some ways the goals of low overhead and high parallelism are in conflict – the first is best served by being single threaded (avoiding locks and thread contention), while the second suggests spawning many threads whenever we encounter a set of activities that could potentially be run in parallel. Our solution is to use a thread pool for running rules, a single lock to protect the state (no fine-grained locking) and a mutex for each Checking/Building state to allow other threads to wait for a result to become available. The build function takes the lock and, on a single thread, performs as many transitions as it can without waiting on a mutex or running any rules. Any waiting is performed after the state lock has been released, and any rules are run by adding them to a thread pool and waiting for the result. By using a thread pool we obtain high levels of parallelism, and by having a single state lock we can perform a build requiring no rules to be run with no thread contention.

Our thread pool obeys the shakeThreads setting (Figure 2), ensuring no more than a given maximum number of rules run in parallel. The thread pool is based around a pool of workers. If a new task is added to the pool, and less than shakeThreads workers are active, a new thread is spawned, otherwise it is queued until a worker completes. When a rule is blocked in build, waiting for dependencies to become available, we notify the thread pool to temporarily spawn another worker, ensuring maximum parallelism.

In order to reduce contention between processes, we run tasks added to the thread pool in a *random* order. Often different build rules require different resources – for example a compiler uses a lot of CPU while a linker does a lot of disk access. Running tasks in a deterministic order has the potential to always run all compilers followed by all linkers, resulting in lots of resource contention between different processes. A random ordering avoids the worst case scenario, and gives a noticeable speedup – up to 20% for some real build systems.

5. User Tools

In this section we describe three features that have been built on top of Shake – a dependency checking tool to ensure the build system is correct, a profiling tool to determine what took most time and an analysis tool to query the build dependencies.

5.1 Dependency checking

Build systems using the theory from §2 obtain dependencies using the Depends constructor, and cannot use a dependency without explicitly requesting it. However, practical build systems must integrate with IO (§3), where dependencies are not always explicit. One rule can store some IO state (e.g. create a file), and another rule can use that state (e.g. read the file) without a tracked dependency, leading to inconsistent builds. We have identified three requirements Shake build systems must follow:

Requirement 1 If an IO action makes use of some IO state, then the rule must depend on that IO state. As an example, if a rule runs the copy command `cp from to`, then the rule must depend on `from`. In practice, we weaken this requirement in two ways. Firstly, we allow modification times as a proxy for the contents of a file, which is safe assuming any changes to a file result in changes to its modification time. Secondly, we only track file system changes within a specified directory (the users project), allowing the rule calling `cp` to omit the dependency on the `cp` executable, which is rarely of interest.

Requirement 2 If an IO action makes use of some IO state that is modified by the build system, then the rule must depend on that IO state *before* performing the IO action. As an example, if a rule runs `cp from to`, and `from` is generated by the build system, then the dependency on `from` must be given before running `cp`. Looking at the build system in §3.1, this build system first calls `gcc` on the source files, then calls `need`, ensuring the header files are all dependencies (requirement 1 is satisfied). However, if we generate one of the header files, requirement 2 is violated because the `need` call comes after the first use – we show how to solve this problem in §6.4.

Requirement 3 After some IO state becomes a dependency it must not change for the rest of the build run. As a result, there cannot be two separate rules that modify the same file. Similarly, after getDirectoryFiles is called (§3.4) the build system cannot create new files matching the pattern.

Requirement 3 is simple to check – after building we run the function validStored on all Ready results in the database (§4.3.2). We have implemented this feature as an option to Shake.

To check requirements 1 and 2 requires knowing which IO state is used by an IO action. For simple IO actions (e.g. readFile) it is easy to determine which IO state will be used, but these simple actions can usually be wrapped to provide versions which are safe by construction (e.g. readFile′, §3.7). For more complex IO actions, in particular the system′ command, determining the dependencies in advance is impossible to do in a general way. The only practical approach is to *trace* which IO state is used, using a system tracing mechanism (such as `strace`). File system tracing (such as `inotify` or checking file last-access times) can provide an approximation of which IO state is used, but cannot determine if the existence of a file is tested.

The challenge when tracing IO state is cross-platform portability. Our first attempt was based around file last-access times, but on modern versions of Windows access times are turned off by default (but can be turned back on by an administrator), only accurate to one second (solvable by adding a one second delay after each IO action), and buffered for up to one hour (no feasible solution). There are no cross-platform tracing libraries, but other build systems which rely on tracing have been able to hook system libraries on Windows (Shal 2009), requiring 2000 lines of C code (more than the total size of Shake). We believe their approach could be reused in Shake, but licensing restrictions prevent us from reusing their code directly.

5.2 Profiling

Shake records two separate pieces of profiling information.

Rule execution times When running a rule we record the execution time, excluding any time building its dependencies. Execution times can be combined from different build runs, allowing us to estimate the total build time, ignoring parallelism.

Traced IO actions Most time consuming rules invoke IO actions, typically system commands. To track these actions, we provide a trace function:

traced :: String → IO α → Action α

All actions run by traced are recorded along with a human readable message (the first argument), the key being built, and the start and end times. We automatically call traced when running system commands. If we examine traced actions from a single run, we can determine how many traced actions were executing at each point in time – allowing us to produce a parallelism graph as shown in Figure 6.

We have built profiling support into the core of Shake. Since running a rule is likely to take some time (most rules will be spawning system processes), the overhead of recording profiling information is negligible. In previous versions of Shake we only recorded profiling information when explicitly asked, but found that users often wanted to profile the build run that had just finished – always recording profile information makes that possible.

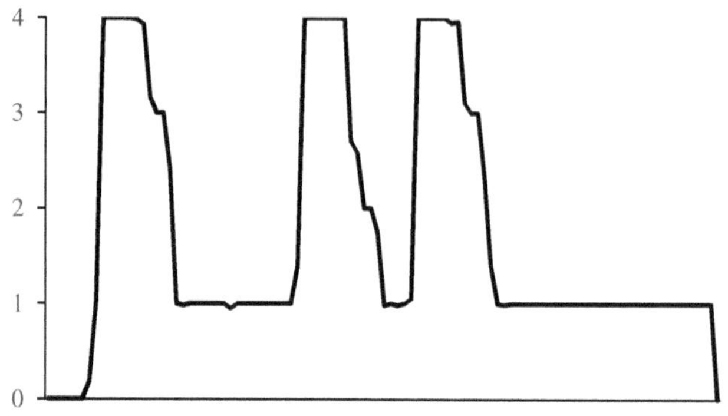

Figure 6. Build parallelism.

5.3 Analysis

The Shake database records the dependencies of each key, allowing a full dependency graph to be produced after the rules have been run. However, for any project of moderate size, a picture of the full dependency graph is rarely comprehensible – although with judicious filtering it is possible to produce something useful (see Figure 7 for an example). There has been some work on visualising large build systems, for example by Adams et al. (2007), but we have not yet tried applying it to Shake.

Our approach to analysing the database is to define queries which allow end users to answer specific questions about their build system. Some of the most useful queries include:

- Why was a particular file rebuilt? Shake shows the complete path of dependencies, including the most recently changing dependency.
- If I modify a file, what will rebuild? Shake computes the list of rules that depend on that file, including indirect dependencies, but assuming no unchanging results (§2.3.3).
- What is the most expensive file to modify? For each leaf of the graph, Shake computes all dependencies, and then uses execution times from profiling to determine which causes most rebuilding.
- Do my dependencies follow some layering principle? Many large projects are structured into isolated layers, this separation can be validated by the build system. For example, I would not expect any files outside Development.Shake.∗ to import any modules from inside that module tree, other than Development.Shake itself.

5.4 Profiling and Analysis

As an example of the profiling and analysis tools in practice, see Figures 6 and 7. Both these diagrams are produced by building the Shake library and test harness, a 24 module Haskell program, from scratch with a maximum of four processors. The entire process takes 7.41 seconds, but spends 12.91 seconds executing rules, giving a parallel speed up of 1.7 times. Executing the build system with one processor takes 11.83 seconds – the reduced rule execution time is likely due to reduced disk contention.

Figure 6 shows the number of traced system commands executing at any point during the build. We see a start up period where zero commands are running and the build system is computing dependencies, followed by three spikes of using four processors, followed by a tail of using one processor.

The dependency graph in Figure 7 shows the dependencies of the .hi files, after hiding three utility modules which are leaves in the dependency graph (they add lots of lines, obscuring the

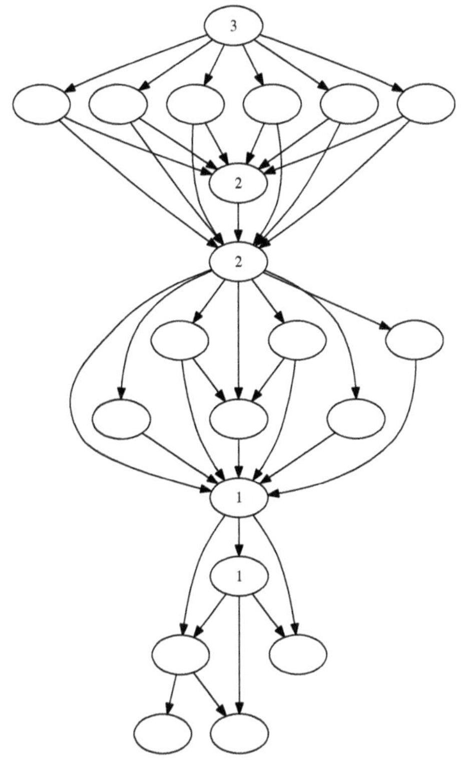

Figure 7. Dependency graph.

	ghc	Shake-1	Shake-2	make
Automatic dependencies	Yes	Yes	Yes	No
Tracks GHC installation	Yes	Yes	No	No
Build on 1 thread	7.69	11.83	11.77	11.75
Build on 4 threads	7.69	7.41	7.34	7.32
No rebuilding	0.54	0.10	0.04	0.02

All times are in seconds. Shake-1 includes a call to `ghc-pkg list` to track dependencies on GHC package versions, while Shake-2 assumes the GHC installation does not change.

Figure 8. Build time comparisons.

underlying structure). It is clear the build proceeds in three stages, with bottle-neck dependencies marked 1, 2 and 3. These three bottlenecks account for the three periods of one processor usage. The final tail of one processor includes both compilation of the main module (which profiling tells us takes 0.23 seconds) and linking (which takes 1.54 seconds).

This example shows how Shake's profiling and analysis reports can be used to improve build performance. If the bottleneck modules could be split up, or if their compilation time was reduced, the overall build time would decrease. In practice, we have found that for large build systems, where Shake is building multiple targets, parallelism usually stays at the maximum (or fractionally below it) for most of the build.

5.4.1 Comparison to `ghc --make` and `make`

Building the same project with the GHC compilation system (The GHC Team 2011), namely `ghc --make`, takes 7.69 seconds, compared to Shake with 11.83 seconds on one processor and 7.41 seconds on four processors, see Figure 8. The reason GHC is quicker on one processor is that GHC keeps all interface information and package database information in memory, whereas running separate `ghc -c` compilation commands requires reloading this information each time. However, Shake is able to use parallelism to improve the build time, while GHC cannot.

To run the build system when nothing needs compiling, GHC takes 0.54 seconds and Shake takes 0.10 seconds. Of the 0.10 seconds required by Shake, 0.06 seconds are spent checking if the GHC installation has changed (running `ghc-pkg list`) – if the GHC installation is assumed to be constant Shake requires only 0.04 seconds. Shake is faster because it reads in one file (the database) then quickly checks validStored on a small number of files. GHC must query at least the same file information, but also has to construct a dependency graph, aggregating information from many files. Of the 0.04 seconds taken by Shake, 0.03 seconds are spent writing to the database – we suspect effort spent improving the binary serialisation would reduce this overhead.

We can build the same project using `make`, generating dependency information with `ghc -M`. Unlike Shake and `ghc --make`, the end user is required to regenerate `make` rules whenever the dependencies change, and to clean the build whenever the GHC installation changes. Allowing `make` to cope with these changes would be significantly harder, and would slow `make` down by at least 0.12 seconds (`ghc-pkg` and `ghc -M` take 0.06 seconds each). In all tests, the `make` solution is about 0.08 seconds faster than Shake, or 0.02 seconds faster if Shake avoids tracking the GHC installation. The consistency in the parallel speedup between `make` and Shake suggests both systems are able to extract the maximum parallelism in this example.

6. Evaluation

At Standard Chartered we have been using build systems based on Shake for the last three years. Before Shake we used `make`, but `make` was a poor fit for our project, primarily due to a large number of generated files. In common with many large projects, we were forced to split our build system into several phases, where one phase generated some files and `make` rules which were then used by a subsequent phase. Before we switched to Shake, we had over 10,000 lines of `make` rules which were brittle and hard to extend. Our initial Shake based system was under 1,000 lines and compiled our project twice as fast – primarily due to better parallelism from removing phases, random execution order of dependencies (§4.3.2) and faster scanning for dependencies (§6.4).

Our Shake based build system has been an unqualified success – while the complexity of our project has increased (more files, more compilers, more generators and more platforms), the build system has coped well. The first version of our Shake build system was under 1000 lines and matched everything the `make` system did. Shake has been able to express all the dependencies correctly and directly, resulting in a robust build system.

From experience implementing several build systems using Shake we have learnt a number of lessons – both about best practices for structuring build systems, and how Shake can be used to deal with the complexities of real software. In this section we share some of those lessons.

6.1 Command Line Interface

While a build system can simply call shake, most systems add some command line handling, such as options to control parallelism and verbosity (see ShakeOptions in Figure 2). One common feature is a `clean` command, to delete all build results. Using Shake we could query the database to find all build results and delete them. Alternatively, deleting the database will cause a full rebuild. However, we have found the most convenient solution is to create all build objects in a directory named .make, and perform a `clean` by deleting that directory.

Using make, you can specify build targets on the command line. We have implemented an enhanced version of this feature, allowing both individual files and sets of files to be enabled/disabled. As an example, a user may write `mk !DOCS` to disable building documentation, or `mk index.html` to build only index.html. We control these targets by passing a modified version of want to the functions specifying rules, which consults the command line arguments:

```
documentation :: (String → [FilePath] → Rules ()) → Rules ()
documentation wants = do
  wants "DOCS" ["index.html"]
  "index.html" *> λout → ...
```

6.2 Build rules that change

Throughout this paper, we assume *the build rules do not change*, merely the dependencies of the rules, but that is not true in practice. We use three techniques to minimise the impact of build rule changes:

Use configuration files Most build information, such as which files a C file includes, can be computed from source files. Where such information is not available, such as which C files should be linked together to form an executable, we use configuration files to provide the information. The rule for linking can use these configuration files, which can be properly tracked. By moving any regularly changing configuration into separate files we significantly reduce the number of build system changes.

Depend on the build source We should rerun a build rule if its action has changed. Lacking equality for functions, one approach is to depend on the build system source in each of the rules, then if *any* actions change, *everything* will rebuild. While this option is safe, it causes a significant number of redundant rebuilds. As a restricted version of this technique, for a generated file we often include a dependency on the generator source and use writeFileChanged (§3.7). If the generator changes it will rerun, but typically only a few generated files will change, so little is rebuilt.

Use a version number There is a field named shakeVersion in the ShakeOptions record from Figure 2. If the build system changes in a significant and incompatible way, we increment this field to force a full rebuild. This option is a last resort, but ensures end users do not need to be aware when the build system changes, and are never required to explicitly clean their build after changes.

6.3 Multiple Outputs

Some programs, such as the Haskell compiler ghc (The GHC Team 2011), can produce two outputs with one command – compiling Foo.hs produces both Foo.o and Foo.hi. As a first approximation, the .o file depends on the entire contents of the source file, while the .hi file depends only on the type signatures. A single ghc invocation needs to do all the work to produce both, but often the .hi file will be left unchanged. Unfortunately, many build systems (including make) do not handle multiple outputs well.

In Shake, it is usually possible to describe multiple outputs in terms of single outputs – in this example we can claim that Foo.hi depends on Foo.o with no action and Foo.o depends on Foo.hs by running ghc. Thanks to support for unchanging files (§2.3.3), if the .hi file does not change then its dependencies will not be rebuilt. However, this formulation has two problems:

- If Foo.hi is deleted *without* also deleting Foo.o, then Foo.hi will not be rebuilt by running the .hi rule, and the build system will raise an error.
- If ghc updates Foo.hi, but manages to determine it does not need to update Foo.o, then Foo.hi will not be marked as dirty and the build will be incorrect.

```
data Files = Files [FilePath]
data FileTimes = FileTimes [ClockTime]

instance Rule Files FileTimes where
  validStored (Files xs) (FileTimes ys) = do
    times ← mapM getFileTime xs
    return $ map Just ys ≡ times

multipleOutputs = do
  rule $ λ(Files xs) →
    if xs ≢ ["even.txt", "odd.txt"] then Nothing else Just $ do
      need ["numbers.txt"]
      system' "number-split" []
      times ← liftIO $ mapM getFileTime xs
      return $ FileTimes $ map fromJust times

  ["even.txt", "odd.txt"] **> λ_ → do
    apply1 (Files ["even.txt", "odd.txt"]) :: Action FileTimes
    return ()
```

Figure 9. Rule type to produce multiple outputs.

Despite these limitations, a fake dependency is often sufficient in practice, provided we can assume Foo.hi is not updated independently of Foo.o. However, consider a command that reads numbers.txt containing lines of numbers, and produces even.txt and odd.txt – each containing only the even or odd numbers – but does not update an output file that does not change. In this situation there is no fake dependency that adequately captures the real dependency.

We can accurately capture the dependencies using the code in Figure 9, which introduces a new type of rule for actions producing multiple files. Inside multipleOutputs, the call to rule declares a rule that can build both even.txt and odd.txt with a single action. We call the `number-split` program, and get the file times for the results. On the **> line we define two rules to produce the output files, using the standard file creation rules from Figure 4, whose action calls apply1 with the list of files to create. If the build first requires even.txt then `number-split` will be invoked, but a subsequent requirement for odd.txt will not rerun `number-split`.

The Shake library wraps up the Files rule type, providing a simple interface using the (*>>) operator, allowing an end user to write:

```
["even.txt", "odd.txt"] *>> λ_ → do
  need ["numbers.txt"]
  system' "number-split" []
```

6.4 Transitive Dependencies

In build systems, transitive dependencies are common – where a rule depends on its children, plus their dependencies. As an example, if foo.c includes bar.h, and bar.h in turn includes baz.h, then foo.c should be recompiled if either bar.h *or* baz.h changes. In §3.1 we saw a solution to C file dependencies, using `gcc -MM` to find the transitive dependencies of a .c file then calling need on the results. This solution has two potential problems:

- If bar.h is included by many files, then both it and any headers it includes will be scanned many times. In most cases the overhead is small, but for some projects it can be significant.
- If bar.h is generated by the build system, using gcc will *not* cause bar.h to be built, since the need call is performed *after* running gcc (violating requirement 2 from §5.1). If the file is

```
"*.c.o" %> \out -> do
  need =<< readFileLines (replaceExtension out "deps")
  system' "gcc" ["-c", dropExtension out, "-o", out]

"*.deps" %> \out -> do
  dep <- readFileLines $ replaceExtension out "dep"
  deps <- mapM (readFileLines . (++".deps")) dep
  writeFileLines out $ nub $ dep ++ concat deps

["*.c.dep", "*.h.dep"] **> \out -> do
  src <- readFileLines $ dropExtension out
  let incs = [init y | x <- src
                     , Just y <- [stripPrefix "#include \"" x]]
  writeFileLines out incs
```

Figure 10. Rules to express transitive dependencies for C files.

missing gcc will fail, if it is present a stale value will be used when finding its dependencies. For projects generating header files, using `gcc -MM` to scan for headers is unworkable.

We can solve these problems by using the rule for *.c.o from Figure 10. We use a .dep file to store the immediate dependencies of a file, and a .deps file to store the transitive dependencies. For example, foo.c.dep contains the dependency bar.h while foo.c.deps contains both bar.h and baz.h. The three build rules we use are:

- The *.c.o rule depends on the associated .deps file (ensuring it is up to date) and then depends on its contents.
- The *.deps rule takes the .dep file, and all the .deps it points at, producing the transitive dependencies of its immediate dependencies. This rule can be used to find the transitive dependencies of anything with .dep rules, for example with Haskell files it would produce the set of files required for linking (namely the transitive dependencies of the imports).
- The *.c.dep/*.h.dep rule takes a source file and finds all one-level dependencies by scanning for lines starting with `#include`. This rule makes a number of assumptions about the structure of the C files which are not true in general. In particular, it assumes that includes are not skipped by `#ifdef` commands, that there is no extra whitespace, and that local includes are quoted while system includes use angle brackets. These assumptions can be relaxed, but are sufficient for many projects.

7. Related Work

Build tools can be divided into two categories – those which target single-language projects with fixed rules (e.g. `ocamlbuild`, `ghc --make`, Visual Studio projects), and those which allow user specified rules (e.g. `make` and Shake). Focusing on the second category, the defacto standard is `make`, but there are many `make` competitors (notably Ant, CMake, Jam, Scons and Waf). Most of these tools read a list of rules, generate a dependency graph, then execute commands while traversing that graph.

Since the number of build tools is vast, we focus on four build tools which take different approaches (Redo, Ninja, Tup and Fabricate). Interestingly, one thing all four systems have in common is that they require a database of build data, in addition to the rules and the file system. Unlike Shake, all these build systems are limited to files.

7.1 Redo

The Redo build system (Pennarun 2011) has a similar dependency theory to Shake. Rules are run starting at the target. A rule may call redo-ifchange (similar to need) to ensure that this rule is repeated if any of the file arguments change. A rule can build either a specific named file, or a set of files ending with a particular extension.

While Redo has similarities to Shake, the practical implementation is significantly different. Instead of a single rule store, Redo stores each rule in a separate file, and the script language is simply shell script (allowing `#!` to change the interpreter). The advantage of separate files is that Redo is able to depend on the actual rule used to build a result, meaning that build system changes are properly tracked. However, separating build rules makes it harder to reason about the build system, and eliminates many potential uses of abstraction (de Jonge 2005). Redo does not work on Windows, and has no support for unchanging files or multiple outputs.

7.2 Ninja

The Ninja build system (Martin 2011) is designed as a two-stage build system – users specify their build rules in a high-level manner, which is then translated to a set of Ninja build rules. As a result, the Ninja build system is not designed to be general purpose and configuration choices are expected to be resolved by the first level. The Ninja target language supports three dependency features beyond `make`. Firstly, a rule can depend on the list of files contained in another file, allowing additional dependencies at build time. Secondly, the command line for each rule is tracked, resulting in a rebuild if the rule itself changes. Thirdly, a rule can generate multiple outputs, which are properly tracked.

7.3 Tup

The Tup build system (Shal 2009) is designed as an incremental build system. Tup has a similar dependency structure to `make`, but a significantly different implementation. Instead of scanning all dependencies, it expects the operating system to supply a list of changed files, avoiding the overhead of checking which files have changed. For large build systems the result can be a significant speed improvement when rebuilding only a few files. We believe a similar implementation strategy could be applied to Shake.

Another difference from `make` is the treatment of dead build results. If a rule to build foo is deleted from the rule list, then Tup automatically deletes the file foo. The problem of dead build results is serious, resulting in builds succeeding that should have failed, and that will fail as soon as a clean build is performed (to reduce this risk, we suggest an overnight build which starts from scratch). However, it is often useful to have build modes which generate skeleton files which are then modified by the user – deleting these files would be most unwelcome. It would be easy to add support for deleting dead build results to Shake, but we choose not to.

7.4 Fabricate

The key innovation in the Fabricate build system (Hoyt et al. 2009) is that dependencies do not need to be stated explicitly. A build system is a Python program, which primarily executes system commands in order. While executing the commands, Fabricate uses system tracing (strace on Linux) to record which files are accessed. In future runs, if the same system command is reached but none of the files it used have changed, the command is skipped. The resulting build systems are simple, and avoid the difficulties of correctly specifying dependencies.

There are two inherent difficulties for build systems without explicit dependencies. Firstly, the system tracing mechanisms on different platforms are varied, and on Windows are somewhat fragile (see §5.1). Secondly, parallelism cannot be inferred automatically – Fabricate requires explicit grouping annotations to use parallelism.

7.5 Extending Make Dependencies

Specifying additional dependencies while building is critical for many projects. As a result, a number of techniques have been developed to specify additional dependencies in `make`. Most of these techniques rely on *generating* some portion of the `make` rules file, either before `make` starts, or invoking `make` multiple times. Taking the example from §1, we can write it with `make` as:

```
result.tar : list.txt $(shell cat list.txt)
  cat list.txt | xargs tar -cf result.tar
```

Here `make` is executing commands in two distinct phases – the first phase generates the rules file, the second runs it. In many large projects, the first phase becomes expensive or complex, resulting in specific commands such as `make depends` to update the dependencies (as required in §5.4.1 and §6). Another approach is for `make` to restart itself partway through the build, after modifying the build rules. However, multiple phases have many problems:

- There is no limit to the number of build phases required, especially when files are generated by the build system. Shake was originally designed after determining a particular build system required seven phases.
- The introduction of phases breaks compositionality, requiring build system authors to globally separate rules by phase. The above rule for result.tar fails if list.txt is itself built by the build system, whereas the Shake rule in §1 works in all cases.
- These approaches require generating `make` rules as text, which is then reinterpreted by `make`. As a result, while the Shake rule from §1 can handle spaces in file names, the `make` rule cannot.
- If all phases are run every time then there is overhead due to restarting `make`, rechecking previously checked rules and reducing parallelism opportunities. If different phases are invoked manually then the user has to be aware what has changed.

7.6 Haskell Build Libraries

There are a surprisingly large number of Haskell libraries implementing a dependency aware build system – we know of ten in addition to Shake (Abba, Blueprint, Coadjute, Cake × 2, Hake, Hmk, Nemesis, OpenShake and Zoom). Of these, the two Cake libraries and OpenShake are based on an early presentation of the principles behind Shake, before the source code was available. The primary difference from the Cake libraries is that this paper allows multiple types of build rule, while the Cake libraries only allow file rules. Compared to OpenShake (Bolingbroke 2011), we have opted to have rule/apply based on dynamic types, and then use sugared versions to regain static guarantees of type safety. In contrast, OpenShake uses type functions (Schrijvers et al. 2008) to statically track the available rule types, making serialisation simpler (§4.1), but complicating the rest of the library.

8. Conclusions and Future Work

We have presented a dependency model which allows additional dependencies to be specified *after* the build system starts running rules. This additional flexibility is essential for many build systems, especially those where source files are generated by rules. We have implemented our ideas in the Haskell library Shake, producing a user-friendly interface combined with an efficient and robust implementation. We have used Shake extensively and find it much easier to use than `make` (§6).

Functional programming is important for Shake. The theory of build systems is naturally expressed using higher-order functions, where actions are functions from dependencies to results. Moving towards a practical build system, a major consideration is the treatment of IO – we use monads to restrict where IO can be used, while also using monads to track state in a thread-safe way. We make use of the flexible syntax of Haskell to allow Shake rules to be written with minimal syntactic overhead. Laziness is not necessary for Shake, and if ignored could cause problems, but restricting laziness is simple (§4.2).

While we have optimised our build algorithms, saving the database is a noticeable bottleneck for quick builds, taking upto 75% of the time. We suspect this step could be sped up, perhaps by switching to a different binary serialisation library. We have provided some tools on top of Shake, but improvements to the analysis feature would help Shake users, as would fully implementing dependency checking. Some users have already begun work on general purpose build rules for common types of source code, which could reduce the effort required to make use of Shake.

The `make` tool has been ubiquitous for the last thirty years, specifying dependencies in advance and defining actions with shell scripting and a macro system. With Shake we offer more powerful dependencies, coupled with the Haskell language for defining actions. The dependencies allow more complex build systems to be specified in a more direct manner, while the use of Haskell allows abstraction and reuse. We hope these advantages are powerful enough to tempt many developers to consider Shake.

Acknowledgements Thanks to Standard Chartered, where Shake was initially developed, and to Raphael Montelatici for the name Shake. Thanks to Max Bolingbroke and Evan Laforge for many discussions about build systems. Thanks to Sönke Hahn, Evan Laforge, Roman Leshchinskiy and Raphael Montelatici for comments on drafts of this paper.

Neil Mitchell is employed by Standard Chartered Bank. This paper has been created in a personal capacity and Standard Chartered Bank does not accept liability for its content. Views expressed in this paper do not necessarily represent the views of Standard Chartered Bank.

References

Bram Adams, Herman Tromp, Kris De Schutter, and Wolfgang De Meuter. Design recovery and maintenance of build systems. In *Proc. ICSM '07*, pages 214–223. IEEE, October 2007.

Max Bolingbroke. OpenShake build system. `https://github.com/batterseapower/openshake`, 2011.

Merijn de Jonge. Build-level components. *IEEE Transactions on Software Engineering*, 31(7):588–600, 2005.

Stuart Feldman. Make – a program for maintaining computer programs. Technical Report 5, Bell Laboratories, 1978.

Berwyn Hoyt, Bryan Hoyt, and Ben Hoyt. fabricate – the better build tool. `http://code.google.com/p/fabricate`, 2009.

Ralf Lämmel and Simon Peyton Jones. Scrap your boilerplate: a practical design pattern for generic programming. In *Proc. TLDI '03*, pages 26–37. ACM Press, March 2003.

Konstantin Läufer and Martin Odersky. Polymorphic type inference and abstract data types. *ACM Transactions on Programming Language Systems*, 16:1411–1430, September 1994.

Evan Martin. Ninja manual. `http://martine.github.com/ninja/manual.html`, December 2011.

Peter Miller. Recursive make considered harmful. *Journal of AUUG Inc*, 19(1):14–25, 1998.

Avery Pennarun. redo: a top-down software build system. `https://github.com/apenwarr/redo`, December 2011.

Tom Schrijvers, Simon Peyton Jones, Manuel Chakravarty, and Martin Sulzmann. Type checking with open type functions. In *Proc. ICFP '08*, pages 51–62. ACM Press, 2008.

Mike Shal. Build system rules and algorithms. `http://gittup.org/tup/build_system_rules_and_algorithms.pdf`, 2009.

The GHC Team. The GHC compiler, version 7.2.2. `http://www.haskell.org/ghc/`, November 2011.

Practical Typed Lazy Contracts

Olaf Chitil
University of Kent, UK
O.Chitil@kent.ac.uk

Abstract

Until now there has been no support for specifying and enforcing contracts within a lazy functional program. That is a shame, because contracts consist of pre- and post-conditions for functions that go beyond the standard static types. This paper presents the design and implementation of a small, easy-to-use, purely functional contract library for Haskell, which, when a contract is violated, also provides more useful information than the classical blaming of one contract partner. From now on lazy functional languages can profit from the assurances in the development of correct programs that contracts provide.

Categories and Subject Descriptors D.1.1 [*Programming Techniques*]: Applicative (Functional) Programming

General Terms Languages, Reliability

Keywords purely functional, lazy, library, Haskell

1. Introduction

Pre- and post-conditions have been important tools for developing correct programs since the early days of programming. A contract for a function comprises both a pre- and a post-condition. Figure 1 shows definitions in Haskell of two functions with contracts that operate on the type `Formula`, which represents propositional logic formulae. The two functions `clausalNF'` and `clause'` have rather non-descriptive types. The function `clausalNF'` transforms a propositional formula into clausal normal form. To work correctly, the function requires its input to be in conjunctive normal form and to be "right-bracketed", that is, for example `And (Atom 'a') (And (Atom 'b') (Atom 'c'))` is used instead of `And (And (Atom 'a') (Atom 'b')) (Atom 'c')`. The output is a list of list of literals, where a literal is an atom or a negated atom. This pre-condition and post-condition are expressed in the contract `conjNF & right >-> list (list lit)`, which is attached to `clausalNF'` using the function `assert` in the definition of the contracted function variant `clausalNF`. The function `clause` has a similar contract. For any contract `c` the function `assert c` is roughly the identity function, except that it also enforces the contract. The program states the contracts and monitors them at runtime.

Since the work of Findler and Felleisen [12] on contracts for eager functional languages, contracts have become an important item in the toolbox of the Racket/Scheme programmer. Other functional languages, however, have not yet profited from the support of contracts for several reasons:

```
data Formula =
  Imp Formula Formula | And Formula Formula |
  Or Formula Formula | Not Formula | Atom Char

clausalNF =
  assert (conjNF & right >-> list (list lit))
    clausalNF'

clausalNF' :: Formula -> [[Formula]]
clausalNF' (And f1 f2) = clause f1 : clausalNF' f2
clausalNF' f           = [clause f]

clause = assert (disj & right >-> list lit) clause'

clause' :: Formula -> [Formula]
clause' (Or f1 f2) = f1 : clause' f2
clause' lit        = [lit]
```

Figure 1. Contracts of functions for clausal normal form

- Eager functional contracts were introduced as a small library of contract combinators. However, the implementation in Racket uses its powerful macro system to smoothly integrate contracts into the language[1]. Thus contracts are very easy to use, for example, do not require user-supplied program location parameters. Implementors of other programming languages, however, do not have such a powerful macro system and are wary of making the implementation effort and of extending the language.
- In contrast to dynamically typed Racket, many functional programming languages have a static type system based on Hindley-Milner types with parametric polymorphism. Thus contract combinators need to be statically typed too and it is desirable to have type-directed contract combinators such as `list :: Contract a -> Contract [a]`.

  We also have to avoid classes in types. To see why, consider the following example usage of the Haskell object observation debugger HOOD [16]:

```
length :: Observable a => [a] -> Int
length = observe "fun" length'

length' :: [a] -> Int
length' = List.length
```

[1] Recently added features concerning mutable data also required modifications of the language implementation [10].

ICFP'12, September 9–15, 2012, Copenhagen, Denmark.

Here `observe "fun"` behaves like an identity function but also records input and output of the `length'` function for debugging purposes. However, the observation function does not have the type of the identity function: the type of `length` includes the class `Observable` and thus adding an observation may require substantial changes to type annotations in the whole program. To avoid this problem, we have to ensure that contract combinators have simple parametrically polymorphic types, without class contexts.

- Eager functional contracts are strict. Let `nat` be the contract that holds only for non-negative integers. With strict contracts we would get

  ```
  assert (list nat) [4,-1,2] = error "..."
  ```

  Asserting an eager contract yields either the unchanged argument or an error/exception. In contrast, lazy functional languages demand lazy contracts. Asserting a lazy contract yields those parts of the argument data structure that meet the contract; only those parts that violate the contract are "cut off":

  ```
  assert (list nat) [4,-1,2] = [4,error "...",2]
  ```

  Because lazy evaluation generally only evaluates parts of a data structure, a computation may succeed without any contract violation error, if it only demands those data structure parts that meet the contract. Such lazy contracts preserve the lazy semantics of the program and thus ensure that we can add contracts anywhere in a program without changing its semantics, provided contracts are not violated. For example, the following definition of the infinite list of fibonacci numbers requires lazy contracts:

  ```
  fibs :: [Integer]
  fibs = assert (list nat)
           (0 : 1 : zipWith (+) fibs (tail fibs))
  ```

In this paper we develop a library for contracts in Haskell that makes the following contributions:

- The contract combinators have simple parametrically polymorphic types, such that adding a contract does not change the type of a function (Section 2).
- The library provides lazy contract combinators. Adding contracts leaves the semantics of a program unchanged, unless a contract is violated (Sections 2 and 3).
- The library is written in pure, portable Haskell, without any use of side-effecting primitives such as `unsafePerformIO` that could change the semantics of the program (Section 3).
- All data-type-dependent code is simple and thus easy to write by hand if necessary (Section 3).
- The contract combinators have a nice algebra of properties. Contract assertions are partial identities and we claim that they are idempotent too. Thus contracts are projections, like eager contracts (Section 4).
- If a contract is violated, then the raised exception does not simply blame the server (contracted expression) or its client, but provides additional information about the specific value that caused the violation (Section 5).
- The library can use Template Haskell to derive all data-type-dependent code and include source code locations. Thus the programmer can formulate contracts for new algebraic data types without any additional work (Section 6).

The contract library for Haskell is available on Hackage[2].

2. Simple Contract Combinators with a Problem

Using previous work on eager contracts [11] and typed contracts [19], we can easily design and implement most of a contract library for Haskell.

We implement a parametric type `Contract a` and a function

```
assert :: Contract a -> (a -> a)
```

that turns a contract into a partial identity, that is, `assert c` $\sqsubseteq$ `id`. Here $\sqsubseteq$ is the standard information-theoretic partial order on values with least element $\bot$. For simplicity we consider $\bot$ to be an expression. It represents both non-termination and an exception raised by a violated contract.

Most of the contract library consists of combinators for building contracts of type `Contract T`, for various types `T`.

We start with a combinator that turns a predicate into a contract:

```
prop :: Flat a => (a -> Bool) -> Contract a
```

used for example as

```
nat :: Contract Integer
nat = prop (>=0)
```

to specify natural numbers as integers greater or equal zero.

We have to restrict `prop` by a new class `Flat` to be used for flat types only. A type is flat if for all values v_1 and v_2 the ordering $v_1 \sqsubset v_2$ implies $v_1 = \bot$. We cannot use `prop` for non-flat types such as lists, because the predicate could be arbitrarily strict and thus violate our aim of building lazy contracts [2]. For example

```
nats' = prop (all (>=0)) :: Contract [Integer]
```

would not be lazy and thus would be unusable for our infinite list of fibonacci numbers.

So the class `Flat` has only a few instances such as

```
instance Flat Integer
instance Flat Float
instance Flat Char
```

In our initial example in Figure 1 we already used two combinators for building contracts:

```
(&)   :: Contract a -> Contract a -> Contract a
(>->) :: Contract a -> Contract b -> Contract (a->b)
```

The conjunction combinator `(&)` builds a contract that is violated if one of the components is violated. The combinator `(>->)` looks similar to the function type; it does *not* indicate logical implication. The function combinator combines a pre- and a post-condition to a contract for a function. For a function to be be correct, whenever the pre-condition holds, the post-condition must hold too. However, if the pre-condition is violated, then the client (caller) of the function is wrong. A function contract is an agreement between both a function and its client. So neither pre- nor post-condition should be violated. In summary, the function contract combinator is rather like the conjunction combinator, except that values of two possibly different types are monitored.

A contract that is always met is useful as component of a bigger contract to express that some values are irrelevant. The opposite contract that is never met can still be occasionally useful in a lazy functional language. We can use

```
true  :: Contract a
false :: Contract a
```

for example in

[2] `http://hackage.haskell.org`

```
type Contract a = a -> a

assert c = c

class Flat a where
  prop :: (a -> Bool) -> Contract a
  prop p = \x -> if p x then x else error "..."

pNil []    = []
pNil (_:_) = error "..."

pCons c cs [] = error "..."
pCons c cs (x:xs) = c x : cs xs

true  = id
false = const (error "...")

c1 & c2       = c2 . c1
pre >-> post = \f -> post . f . pre
```

Figure 2. A lazy contract implementation for most combinators

```
const = assert (true >-> false >-> true) const'

const' :: a -> b -> a
const' x y = x
```

to express that the second argument of the function is never demanded. Because that argument is never demanded, its contract will never be used and thus will never be violated.

Finally we need combinators to build contracts for algebraic data types, which generally are not flat. Here we introduce for each data constructor a combinator that is used like a data constructor in pattern matching.

```
pNil  :: Contract [a]
pCons :: Contract a -> Contract [a] -> Contract [a]
```

Now we can define a contract for infinite lists:

```
infinite :: Contract [a]
infinite = pCons true infinite
```

If this contract is asserted for a finite list and evaluation demands the last constructor, `[]`, of this finite list, then a contract violation exception is raised. Here we also use the contract `true` to state that we do not restrict the list elements in any way.

All our combinators can be implemented using the same contract type as for the well-known eager contracts. Even the new data constructor combinators can easily be implemented using that type. The short implementation is given in Figure 2.

However, one important combinator is still missing. On their own, data constructor combinators such as `pNil` and `pCons` are of rather limited use, the infinite list contract being one of the few examples where they suffice. We need a combinator for combining two data constructor contracts disjunctively:

```
(|>) :: Contract a -> Contract a -> Contract a
```

This combinator allows us, for example, to define the contract of a (finite or infinite) list of natural numbers as follows:

```
nats :: Contract [Integer]
nats = pNil |> pCons nat nats
```

The definition intentionally looks very similar to the definition of an algebraic data type.

We cannot define `(|>)` using the contract type definition

```
type Contract a = a -> a
```

We can combine two functions of type `a -> a` only by composition and we have done so already for the contract combinator `(&)`. For disjunction we would need to apply both functions separately and then somehow combine the two results: if one is an exception, then we should return the value of the other one. We cannot test for exceptions in a purely functional language[3].

```
type Contract a = a -> Maybe a

assert :: Contract a -> (a -> a)
assert c x = case c x of
               Just y ->y
               Nothing->error"Contract violated."

class Flat a where
  prop :: (a -> Bool) -> Contract a
  prop p x = if p x then Just x else Nothing

pNil :: Contract [a]
pNil []    = Just []
pNil (_:_) = Nothing

pCons :: Contract a -> Contract [a] -> Contract [a]
pCons c cs []     = Nothing
pCons c cs (x:xs) = Just (assert c x : assert cs xs)

true :: Contract a
true = Just

false :: Contract a
false = const Nothing

(|>) :: Contract a -> Contract a -> Contract a
c1 |> c2 = \x -> c1 x `mplus` c2 x

(&) :: Contract a -> Contract a -> Contract a
c1 & c2 = \x -> c1 x >>= c2

(>->) :: Contract a -> Contract b -> Contract (a->b)
pre >-> post =
  \f -> Just (f `seq` (assert post . f . assert pre))
```

Figure 3. Implementation of typed lazy contract combinators

3. Implementing Lazy Contract Combinators

A simple modification of our contract type definition solves our problem:

```
type Contract a = a -> Maybe a
```

The `Maybe a` type enables us to test for contract violation and then to try the next contract. The return value `Nothing` indicates that the contract is violated for the top constructor of the monitored value. The return value `Just v` indicates successful matching of the top constructor and returns the value with possibly further contracts attached to its components.

Recall that for `Maybe a` its monadic functions are defined as follows:

```
(>>=) :: Maybe a -> (a -> Maybe b)
(Just x) >>= f = f x
Nothing  >>= f = Nothing
```

[3] There is an impure solution [6] that, however, still cannot handle non-termination in one argument.

```
mplus :: Maybe a -> Maybe a -> Maybe a
(Just x) `mplus` m = Just x
Nothing  `mplus` m = m
```

Figure 3 lists the full implementation of our contract combinators.

In the definition of the function contract combinator `seq` first evaluates the function itself before returning it wrapped in assertions. This definition ensures

$$\texttt{assert (c}_1\texttt{ >-> c}_2\texttt{)}\ \bot = \bot$$

that is, function contracts are strict like all other contracts. Without `seq` the expression `assert` $(c_1$ `>->` $c_2)$ $\bot$ instead would be the function that demands no argument and always returns $\bot$, which in Haskell can be distinguished from the function $\bot$ itself. Thus the function contract combinator would change the semantics of a program even when the contract is not violated. Admittedly, we do not expect this case to ever occur in practice. The presence or absence of `seq` makes no difference for the contract properties given in the next section.

The contract type reminds of parser combinators. However, contracts are deterministic: contract application `assert c` is a function for any contract `c`. No value of a second type, e.g. a parse tree, is constructed. Hence we only need the `Maybe a` type with its two choices, not the more general list type `[a]` that would provide an arbitrary number of choices.

A pattern combinator tests only for the top constructor. If that fits, then the pattern combinator succeeds. Hence

```
assert (pCons nat pNil |> pCons true pNil) [-3] =
  [error "Contract violated."]
```

Here matching the list constructor of `pCons nat pNil` succeeds and therefore the second list contract `pCons true pNil` is never tried, even though the contract for the list element, `nat`, is violated. For all our examples the simple semantics suffices and it is easy to understand.

For example, we can define a parameterised contract for the list data type

```
list :: Contract a -> Contract [a]
list c = pNil |> pCons c (list c)
```

and use it to define the contract of list of natural numbers:

```
nats :: Contract [Integer]
nats = list nat
```

We can also define functions with non-contract parameters to construct contracts:

```
listOfLength :: Int -> Contract [a]
listOfLength 0 = pNil
listOfLength (n+1) = pCons true (listOfLength n)
```

However, in such a case we need to be sure that the parameter value is well-defined, so that it cannot introduce non-termination into the program. For example

```
lengthAtLeast :: Int -> Contract [a]
lengthAtLeast 0     = true
lengthAtLeast (n+1) = pCons true (lengthAtLeast n)

contractTake :: Int -> [a] -> [a]
contractTake n =
  assert (lengthAtLeast n >-> listOfLength n)
    (take n)
```

is only safe, because the function `take` is strict in its integer parameter, which determines how many list elements shall be returned.

```
prop p1 |> prop p2 = prop (\x -> p1 x || p2 x)
prop p1 & prop p2 = prop (\x -> p1 x && p2 x)

c1 & (c2 & c3) = (c1 & c2) & c3
true & c = c
c & true = c
false & c = false

c1 |> (c2 |> c3) = (c1 |> c2) |> c3
false |> c = c
c |> false = c
true |> c = true
c |> c = c
c1 |> (c2 |> c1) = c1 |> c2

c1 |> (c1 & c2) = c1

c1 >-> false = c2 >-> false
(c1 >-> c2) & (c3 >-> c4) = (c3 & c1) >-> (c2 & c4)
(c1 >-> c2) |> (c3 >-> c4) = c1 >-> c2
```

Figure 4. Contract properties

```
c1 & (c1 |> c2) = c1
c1 & (c2 & c1) = c1 & c2
c & c = c
```

Figure 5. Claimed contract properties

4. Properties of Contracts

Our contract type `Contract a` is a combination of the function type with the `Maybe` monad. Thus we have a rich set of known properties to work with for establishing an algebra of contracts. `Contract` itself is *not* a monad.

4.1 An Algebra of Contracts

Figure 4 lists many simple properties enjoyed by contracts. All of these can be proved by simple equational reasoning, using the monad laws of `Maybe a`.

All the properties of conjunction and disjunction of contracts also hold for conjunction and disjunction of Booleans in a lazy language. Recall that some standard properties of Boolean algebra do not hold for the Boolean type in non-strict languages. For example, `(&&)` and `||` are not commutative and the standard distribution laws do not hold. These properties do not hold for contracts either, with similar counterexamples. So the non-strict algebra of `(&&)` and `||` is a good guideline for developing the lazy contract algebra of `&` and `|>`.

The "distribution" law for conjunction and function contract may at first surprise. It holds because the function contract combinator is not some kind of implication but more a kind of conjunction. A function contract holds only if both the input and the output of a function meet the respective subcontracts. From this "distribution" law of conjunction and function plus idempotence of conjunction further laws follow:

$$(\texttt{c}_1 \texttt{ >-> c}) \texttt{ \& } (\texttt{c}_3 \texttt{ >-> c}) = (\texttt{c}_1 \texttt{ \& c}_3) \texttt{ >-> c}$$

$$(\texttt{c >-> c}_2) \texttt{ \& } (\texttt{c >-> c}_4) = \texttt{c >-> } (\texttt{c}_2 \texttt{ \& c}_4)$$

Figure 5 lists further properties of contracts that we have not proved but claim also hold. They require stronger proof methods than equational reasoning, but are linked to the idempotence of contracts discussed in the subsequent subsection. The last property in the list, idempotence of conjunction, is a corollary of the preceeding property, taking $\texttt{c}_2 = \texttt{true}$.

4.2 Contracts are Projections

Eager contracts are projections [1, 11], that is, they are idempotent and partial identities.

Lemma 4.1 (A contract is a partial identity).
For any contract c

$$\texttt{assert c} \sqsubseteq \texttt{id}$$

This can be proved using induction on the contract combinators.

Idempotence is more difficult to establish. It would follow from idempotence of conjunction, `c & c` = `c`. In practice, both properties probably need to be established in a single inductive proof. Intuitively idempotence holds because if a contract returns `Just v`, that value `v` is the same as would be returned by the eager contract type `a -> a`, and pattern contracts only test for the top constructor before returning `Just v` or `Nothing`.

Claim 4.2 (A contract is idempotent).
For any contract c

$$\texttt{assert c . assert c} = \texttt{assert c}$$

4.3 Distinct Contract Exceptions

We identified non-termination and any contract exception as the single value $\perp$. However, we might distinguish them, following [22], such that exceptions are values above $\perp$ in the information order, but still values of any type. We would change our partial order to consider exceptions as least elements, because a contract replaces some parts of values by exceptions. However, with that choice our contracts are neither partial identities, nor idempotent (the properties of Figure 4 are unaffected). The reason is that contracts such as

```
⊥ :: Contract a
prop ⊥ :: Flat a => Contract a
prop (\x->if oddx the True else ⊥) :: Contract Int
```

exist. They would still introduce $\perp$ instead of exceptions.

For related reasons other works [1, 8] restricted the definitions of contracts such that a contract can never introduce $\perp$ itself. However, the desirable freedom to use the whole language to define contracts and the fact that we are just defining a library makes this an impractical choice.

5. Informative Contract Violation

A contract is concluded between two partners, a server and a client. If a contract is violated, one of the two partners is to blame for it. A major contribution of Findler and Felleisen's functional contracts [12] is its system for choosing whom to blame. In a higher-order language function arguments can themselves be functions. If such a functional argument is used within the function such that the precondition of the functional argument is violated, then the function itself has to be blamed for contract violation, not the caller that passed the functional argument.

```
type Contract a = a -> Bool -> Either Bool a

assert :: Contract a -> (a -> a)
assert = monitor True

monitor :: Bool -> Contract a -> (a -> a)
monitor b c x =
  case c x b of
    Right x -> x
    Left b  -> error ("Contract violated. Blame "
                     ++ if b then "server."
                             else "client.")

(>->) :: Contract a -> Contract b -> Contract (a->b)
pre >-> post = \f b -> Right (f `seq`
  (monitor b post . f . monitor (not b) pre))

true :: Contract a
true = \x b -> Right x

false :: Contract a
false = \x b -> Left (not b)
```

Figure 6. Implementing blaming

5.1 Blaming

The blaming system for higher-order functional languages applies to both eager and lazy languages equally, and thus we can easily add it to our lazy contract library. For eager languages several equivalent implementations for handling blame are known [11, 12, 19]. Here we simply extend a contract by a Boolean state that indicates whether the server or the client of the contract are to blame in case of violation. The `Maybe` monad is replaced by `Either Bool a` so that blame information is available when a subcontract is violated. Figure 6 shows the most interesting extended definitions. Contract monitoring starts by potentially blaming the server, that is, the expression for which the contract is asserted. The function contract combinator `>->` negates the Boolean blame indicator for monitoring the contra-variant argument, but passes it unchanged for monitoring the co-variant result.

Now there are two different possible implementations of the contract `false` that can never be met: The contract either always blames the party indicated by the given Boolean argument, or it always blames the opposite party by negating the Boolean value. So let us look back at our example of Section 2:

```
const = assert (true >-> false >-> true) const'
```

Any client of `const` will provide some second argument, but if that second argument is actually demanded, then clearly `const'` is wrongly defined and has to be blamed. In this example `false` is in a contra-variant position of the whole contract and hence to blame the server, `false` has to negate its Boolean parameter. So on its own, `false` always blames its client, never its server. We do not provide the server-blaming variant in the library, because it does not seem to be of any practical use.

5.2 Witness Tracing

Blaming alone, however, is rather unsatisfactory. It just points the finger at one partner without providing any evidence that would explain in which way a complex contract was violated. Blaming hardly provides a good starting point for debugging. Furthermore, blaming can be misleading. Often when a contract is violated neither server nor client are wrong, but the contract itself! Specifying

```
type Contract a =
  (String->String) -> a -> Either String a

assert :: Contract a -> (a -> a)
assert = monitor id

monitor :: (String->String) -> Contract a -> (a->a)
monitor wc c x =
  case c wc x of
    Right v -> v
    Left w  -> error ("Contract violated. Witness:"
                      ++ wc ("{" ++ w ++ "}"))

(>->) :: Contract a -> Contract b -> Contract (a->b)
pre >-> post = \wc f -> Right (f `seq`
  (monitor (wc . \w->("(_->"++w++")")) post . f .
   monitor (wc . \w->("("++w++"->_)")) pre))

pNil :: Contract [a]
pNil = \wc x -> case x of
  []  -> Right x
  _:_ -> Left "_:_"

pCons :: Contract a -> Contract [a] -> Contract [a]
pCons cx cxs = \wc x -> case x of
  (y:ys) ->
    Right
      (monitor (wc . \w->("("++w++":_)")) cx y :
       monitor (wc . \w->("(_:"++w++")")) cxs ys)
  []     -> Left "[]"
```

Figure 7. Implementing witness tracing

the right contract is challenging and contract monitoring just checks whether specification and implementation agree.

Hence our lazy contracts report, when they are violated, the top data constructor, or whole flat value, that causes the contract violation, plus all data constructors in the path above it. For example

```
*Main> clausalNF form
[[Atom 'a'],[Atom 'b',Not
*** Exception: Contract violated. Witness:
((And _ (Or _ (Not {Not _})))->_)
```

Here we do not need to know the full definition of the formula `form`. The error message tells us all that we need to know: The formula contains a double-negation and therefore is not in conjunctive normal form, as the contract of `clausalNF` requires. More precisely, the contract was asserted for a function that took as argument a formula with `And` at the top, with `Or` as second argument, which has a `Not` as second argument, which has the forbidden `Not` as argument.

To trace the required information of a potential witness of contract violation, our contracts pass an additional argument that accumulates a description of the context of a monitored value, and a violated contract returns a string describing the offending value itself. The representation of the context is of type `String -> String` to easily slot another context or expression representation into the hole of the context. Figure 7 gives an outline of the implementation. The printed witness describes just the data that needs to be evaluated to notice the contract violation.

5.3 Location + Blame + Witness

Our final contract library combines blaming and witness tracing, records the source location of a contract and raises a special exception to provide the maximal information when the contract is violated. For example:

```
*Main> clausalNF form
[[Atom 'a'],[Atom 'b',Not
*** Exception: Contract at ContractTest.hs:101:3
violated by
((And _ (Or _ (Not {Not _})))->_)
The client is to blame.
```

6. Deriving Contract Combinators

For every data constructor `Con` that we want to pattern match in a contract we have to define a pattern contract `pCon`. These definitions are simple, even with handling of location, blame and witness information, but they are still tedious. Hence our contract library allows their automatic derivation using Template Haskell [23]. Template Haskell is a meta-programming extension of Haskell that the Glasgow Haskell compiler, the only Haskell system used for professional Haskell program development, provides. Template Haskell allows us to define in the contract library functions that will generate Haskell code at compile time, type check that code and compile it.

The user no longer needs to define these pattern contracts at all, but can basically derive them on demand where needed, that is, directly write

```
conjNF = $(p 'And) conjNF conjNF |> disj
disj   = $(p 'Or)  disj disj |> lit
lit    = $(p 'Not) atom |> atom
atom   = $(p 'Atom) true
```

Here `p` is a Template Haskell function that receives the name of a data constructor as argument. The `$` and the single quote in front of the data constructor are syntax required by Template Haskell. The definition of a pattern contract is short so that repeated derivation is not a problem.

Alternatively, the programmer can also write the declaration

```
$(deriveContracts ''Formula)
```

to derive all pattern contract definitions for the type `Formula`.

Finally, `assert` is also a Template Haskell function:

```
clausalNF =
  $assert (conjNF & right >-> list (list lit))
    clausalNF'
```

Template Haskell allows the definition of `assert` to determine its own location in the file and then generate code for calling the real assertion function with that location as parameter.

7. Further Contract Features

Initial experience of using contracts raises new questions and demand for additional contract combinators.

7.1 Negation

We have conjunction, `&`, and disjunction, `|>`, of contracts. However, we cannot have negation

```
neg :: Contract a -> Contract a
```

for contracts. General negation would violate basic semantic properties of contracts [2].

Nonetheless, in practice we often want to express that the top data constructor of a monitored value is *not* a specific given data constructor. Hence we introduce additional combinators such as the following for every data type.

```
pNotImp :: Contract Formula
```

```
pNotAnd :: Contract Formula
pNotOr :: Contract Formula
pNotNot :: Contract Formula
pNotAtom :: Contract Formula
```

These negated pattern contracts provide nothing new. In fact

```
pNotImp = pAnd true true |> pOr true true |>
          pNot true |> pAtom true
```

However, for types with many data constructors these combinators are certainly substantial abbreviations and they are needed frequently. Additionally, our implementation can perform an efficient single pattern match instead of many repeated ones.

We use these negated pattern contracts in the definition of contracts for our initial propositional formulae example. They substantially simplify our definition of "right-bracketedness".

```
conjNF, disj, lit, atom,
  right, rightConjNF :: Contract Formula

conjNF = pAnd conjNF conjNF |> disj
disj   = pOr disj disj |> lit
lit    = pNot atom |> atom
atom   = pAtom true

right = pImp (right & pNotImp) right |>
        pAnd (right & pNotAnd) right |>
        pOr (right & pNotOr) right |>
        pNot right |> pAtom true

rightConjNF = conjNF & right
```

Even for data types with few constructors they can express an idea more clearly. So

```
head' = assert (pNotNil >-> true) head
```

is more direct than

```
head' = assert (pCons true true >-> true) head
```

to express that the function only works on non-empty lists.

7.2 Contracts for the IO monad

We have contract combinators for flat types, algebraic data types and the function type constructor. However, a real programming language has more types, especially abstract data types. The most notorious in Haskell is the IO monad that is required for any input or output actions.

For example, we may want to write a contract for an IO action that gets a natural number from standard input:

```
getNat :: IO Integer
getNat = assert (io nat) getNat'
```

The choice of contract combinator is natural, following our general approach of type-directed contract combinators. How do we define the IO contract combinator?

```
io :: Contract a -> Contract (IO a)
io c = \io -> Just (io >>= return . assert c)
```

Our definition simply follows the scheme we are already using for the function contract combinator >->. After all, the function type is "just" an abstract data type as well[4]. With this definition our IO contract combinator also has the same properties as the function contract combinator:

$$\texttt{io}\ c_1\ \&\ \texttt{io}\ c_2 = \texttt{io}\ (c_1\ \&\ c_2)$$
$$\texttt{io}\ c_1\ |\!>\ \texttt{io}\ c_2 = \texttt{io}\ c_1$$
$$\texttt{io true} = \texttt{true}$$

Our definition of the contract combinator for the abstract data type `IO a` raises the question whether we should do the same for other data types. For example, we have

```
list :: Contract a -> Contract [a]
list c = pNil |> pCons c (list c)
```

Alternatively we could follow our definition of `io`:

```
list' c = \xs -> Just (xs >>= return . assert c)
```

which is the same as

```
list' c = \xs -> Just (map (assert c) xs)
```

It turns out that the two definitions are equivalent[5], thus confirming our original definition. Hence we prefer to define a contract combinator for a non-abstract algebraic data type such as `list` in terms of the only primitive contract combinators, the pattern contract combinators, such as `pNil` and `pCons`. For an abstract data type we define a contract combinator using the scheme above with the respective map function for the type.

7.3 Strict data types

Haskell allows the definition of strict data types. The strictness flag ! in a data type definition states that the data constructor is strict in that argument. For example,

```
data SListBool = SNil | SCons !Bool !SListBool
```

defines the type of finite Boolean lists that are either $\bot$ or fully defined.

Happily we do not need to adapt our definition of contract combinators. As usual we have

```
pSNil :: Contract SListBool
pSNil SNil = Just SNil
pSNil (SCons b bs) = Nothing

pSCons :: Contract Bool -> Contract SListBool ->
          Contract SListBool
pSCons c cs SNil = Nothing
pSCons c cs (SCons b bs) =
  Just (SCons (assert c b) (assert cs bs))
```

A contract traverses the strict list and builds a new strict list. Thus demanding the top data constructor of a contracted strict list automatically forces checking the whole list. The result will be either a contract violation ($\bot$) or the whole list. So on strict data types lazy contracts behave like eager contracts. It would be possible to define more expressive contract combinators for data types with strictness flags, that, for example, ensure that a list is ordered; but because strictness flags are rarely used in Haskell programs, such an extension does not seem worthwhile.

In the definition of `SListBool` all constructor arguments are strict and the only other types used are flat types. In such a case the data type is actually a flat type. We can declare it an instance of the class `Flat` and use expressive `prop` contracts.

[4] The forced evaluation with `seq` by the function contract combinator is required because of the peculiar semantics of functions in Haskell. It is not needed for other types. For example, if `io` = $\bot$, then also `io >>= return . assert c` = $\bot$.

[5] They are not equal, because `list` $\bot$ = $\bot$, but `list'` $\bot$ = `Just` $\bot$. However, in the context of a contract with `assert` they always yield the same result.

8. Related Work

This paper builds firmly on three sets of previous work: Findler and Felleisen's work on eager contracts for higher-order functions [12], Hinze, Jeuring and Löh's work on typed contracts for functional programming, and our own previous work on lazy functional contracts.

Eager Higher-Order Contracts Findler and Felleisen's paper on contracts for higher-order functions [12] made contracts popular for eager functional programming languages. All interesting properties of functional values, which are passed around by higher-order functions, are undecidable; it is impossible to monitor a function contract for all argument-result-pairs. However, Findler and Felleisen realised that it is sufficient to monitor both pre- and post-condition of a functional value only when this function is applied. The resulting contract system is sound.

The second major contribution of that paper is a system for correctly attributing blame in case of contract violation and its implementation. We easily added blaming to our lazy contract library. However, additionally our contracts report a witness, a partial value, that caused a contract violation.

Findler and Felleisen's contract system also provides dependent function contracts, where the contract for the function codomain can use the actual argument value. Such dependent contracts are more expressive but easily change a non-strict function into a strict function; hence our lazy contract combinators do not provide them.

Subsequent work [11, 13] stresses that contracts are projections and thus they can be implemented in a simple, modular and efficient way. Our first implementation of Figure 2 copies that work and our full implementation with disjunction is an extended variant.

The papers do not discuss algebraic data types, because in strict languages these domains are flat and hence contracts for algebraic data types are predicates like for other flat types. Consequently disjunction is not considered either. Because of the universality of predicate contracts in strict and dynamically typed functional languages, type-directed contracts such as `list` are also of little interest.

Although disjunction is not discussed in the papers, the contract system of Racket does provide a disjunctive contract combinator [14, Version 5.2.1] [15]. To support disjunction, a Racket contract for type `a` contains both a function of type `a -> a` and a function of type `a -> Bool`. Together they are used similarly to our type `a -> Maybe a`. In particular, the disjunctive combinator applies the `a -> Bool` functions of all its direct sub-contracts, checks that at most one of the results is `True` (otherwise it fails) and then applies the corresponding sub-contract further [10]. So disjunction behaves similarly to `|>` but is not sequential.

Blume et al. proposed and studied several semantic models of eager higher-order contracts [1, 11, 13]. To prove soundness, the definition of contracts is first restricted, to avoid e.g. having a contract $\perp$. Later, recursive contracts are added to regain expressivity. In a discussion of the most permissive contract, `true`, Findler and Blume point out that the contract `true`, to be the most permissive contract, should always report contract violation and blame the client. However, they also note that such a contract would be useless in practice. In contrast, our `true`, which cannot be violated, is very useful to leave parts of a contract unconstrained. Similarly, the least permissive contract should always blame the server, but we demonstrated in Section 5.1 that our definition of `false`, which always blames the client, is more useful. As a consequence in our library `false = prop (const False)` does *not* hold for flat types whereas `true = prop (const True)` does.

Typed Contracts for Functional Programming Hinze, Jeuring and Löh [19] transferred contracts for higher-order functions to the statically typed language Haskell. Hence they proposed contract combinators with parametrically polymorphic types; we have adopted all of them except for dependent contracts. Typed contracts also emphasis type-directed contract combinators such as `list`. However, the work disregards the lazy semantics of Haskell, defining contracts with a seemingly random mixture of eager and lazy monitoring. Predicate contracts can be applied to expressions of all types, not just flat types, thus breaking laziness. However, these predicate contracts are required for expressing many interesting properties, because a type-directed contract combinator such as `list` can only express a uniform property over all list elements: our pattern contracts and disjunction are missing.

Contracts are not projections, because generally they are not idempotent. Idempotence is lost because of the eagerness of predicate contracts. Hinze et al. make the point that if contract conjunction `&` was commutative, then idempotence would be a simple consequence. However, our lazy contracts demonstrate that commutativity of conjunction is not necessary for idempotence; we can have the latter without the former.

Hinze et al. also provide an interesting technique for providing more informative error messages than standard blaming. Their library provides several source locations as explanation of a single violated contract. However, these sets of source locations are still hard to understand for a programmer and the system requires a source code transformation to insert source locations into the program. Otherwise the programmer would have to do this substantial work.

Lazy Contracts for Functional Languages Lazy contracts were first discussed and several implementations presented in 2004 [5]. That paper makes the point that while eager contracts must be `True`, lazy contracts must not be `False`. This means that unevaluated parts of a data structure can never violate a lazy contract. The paper uses predicates on values of all types and hence, despite some technical tricks using concurrency, the contracts are lazy but neither idempotent nor prompt. The paper itself gives examples of where contract violations are noticed too late. This problem was later rectified [3, 4]. Both these papers implement lazy assertions as libraries that require only the commonly provided non-pure function `unsafePerformIO`, which performs side effects within a purely functional context. The first lazy and idempotent implementation [4] uses patterns contracts similar to those in this paper to express contracts over algebraic data types. However, a non-deterministic implementation of disjunction leads to semantic problems. Later [3] provided a more user-friendly language for expressing contracts and improved the internal structure of the implementation, but the implementation principles were identical and hence the non-deterministic disjunction remained.

A semantic investigation [2] developed contracts that are pure and implementable within the functional language. However, for every algebraic data type its contracts requires a different implementation type. Thus disjunction is not a parametrically polymorphic combinator but requires a class context. Furthermore, the implementations of some combinators are large and complex. Disjunction is more powerful than in the lazy contracts described in the present paper, for example

```
  assert (pCons nat pNil |> pCons true pNil) [-3]
 =assert (pCons (nat |> true) (pNil |> pNil))
 =[-3]
```

but this additional expressibility does not seem to be needed in practice.

Comparing Contracts Degen, Thiemann and Wehr [7, 8] classify existing contract systems for Haskell as eager (straight translation of [12]), semi-eager [19] and lazy [3–5]. They check whether the systems meet their desirable properties of meaning preservation and completeness. Each contract system meets at most one of these properties. The authors show that it is impossible to meet both properties. Our lazy contracts are meaning preserving but not complete. The notion of completeness seems to be biased towards a strict semantics, contradicting the principle that unevaluated parts can never violate a lazy contract. Our lazy contracts have limited expressibility, but they have a clear semantics.

Generic Programming We use Template Haskell to derive pattern contracts and to enable the assertion function to determine its own location in the source code [23]. The derivation of pattern contracts is an instance of generic programming. Many generic programming systems have been proposed and even been implemented for Haskell [17, 18, 20, 21]. All of these have two disadvantages that make them unsuitable for being used for our pattern contracts: First, they introduce one or more classes that will then appear in the type of every derived pattern contract. Thus pattern contracts will not be parametrically polymorphic. Second, they consider functions as second class values. That means that either they can only generically define code for types that do not involve function types at all, or they can recognise a functional value within an algebraic data type, but cannot do anything with it, that is, apply any transformation to it.

Template Haskell provides few static guarantees and thus requires us to ascertain that our contract library will derive typeable and correct code for any data constructor. However, Template Haskell provides all the functionalities needed in the contract library.

9. Conclusions and Future Work

This paper describes the design of a practical contract library for lazy typed functional languages and its implementation for Haskell. The library meets many essential criteria, such as combinators with simple parametric types, a lazy semantics, a rich algebra of properties, informative exceptions in case of contract violation and automatic code generation to make it easy to use.

Interestingly the resulting contract system reminds strongly of a subtyping system, especially with a definition of sub-contracts/types for algebraic data types that looks very similar to the actual type definition of algebraic data types. Defining subtypes of algebraic data types is also where we see the main application area of the contract system. Many programs require several variants of some big algebraic data types. In practice programmers then simply ignore the subtyping and define a single algebraic data type that encompasses all variants, because they want to reuse functions that work on several subtypes and have the flexibility to exchange some code without having to change between numerous similar but separate data types. The classical example is a compiler: it consists of a long sequence of passes, each of which works with a slightly differently structured abstract syntax tree, In practice, subtle differences are ignored and only a few different abstract syntax tree structures are used in one compiler. Lazy contracts provide a new solution.

Our next step is to develop the algebra of contract combinators further and thus also prove our claim that these contracts are idempotent. The main current shortcoming and thus biggest challenge for future development of the contract library is its lack of a dependent function contract combinator that allows using the function argument in the post-condition. We can define

```
(>>->) :: Contract a -> (a -> Contract b) ->
            Contract (a -> b)
pre >>-> post = \f ->
  Just (\x -> f `seq` (let y = assert pre x
                       in assert (post y) (f y)))
```

and use it for example in

```
contractTake :: Int -> [a] -> [a]
contractTake =
  assert (nat >>->
          \n -> lengthAtLeast n >-> listOfLength n)
    take
```

It is easy to extend this picky implementation to use indy monitoring [9], which may blame the contract itself, not just the server or the client. However, >>-> is not a lazy contract combinator; the post-condition may force evaluation of too much of the function argument and thus the contract may change the semantics of the program. A definition of a lazy dependent function combinator is still an open problem. Meanwhile the existing contract library can be used in practice.

Acknowledgments

I thank Simon Thompson and Stefan Kahrs for useful advice on early versions of this work and the anonymous ICFP reviewers and Robby Findler for their detailed comments.

References

[1] M. Blume and D. McAllester. Sound and complete models of contracts. *J. Funct. Program.*, 16(4-5):375–414, 2006.

[2] O. Chitil. A semantics for lazy assertions. In *Proceedings of the 20th ACM SIGPLAN workshop on Partial evaluation and program manipulation*, PEPM 2011, pages 141–150, January 2011.

[3] O. Chitil and F. Huch. Monadic, prompt lazy assertions in Haskell. In *APLAS 2007*, LNCS 4807, pages 38–53, 2007.

[4] O. Chitil and F. Huch. A pattern logic for prompt lazy assertions in Haskell. In *Implementation and Application of Functional Languages: 18th International Workshop, IFL 2006*, LNCS 4449, 2007.

[5] O. Chitil, D. McNeill, and C. Runciman. Lazy assertions. In *Implementation of Functional Languages: 15th International Workshop, IFL 2003*, LNCS 3145, pages 1–19. Springer, November 2004.

[6] N. A. Danielsson and P. Jansson. Chasing bottoms, a case study in program verification in the presence of partial and infinite values. In D. Kozen, editor, *Proceedings of the 7th International Conference on Mathematics of Program Construction, MPC 2004*, LNCS 3125, pages 85–109. Springer-Verlag, July 2004.

[7] M. Degen, P. Thiemann, and S. Wehr. True lies: Lazy contracts for lazy languages (faithfulness is better than laziness). In *4. Arbeitstagung Programmiersprachen (ATPS'09)*, Lübeck, Germany, October 2009.

[8] M. Degen, P. Thiemann, and S. Wehr. The interaction of contracts and laziness. In *Proceedings of the ACM SIGPLAN 2012 workshop on Partial evaluation and program manipulation*, PEPM '12, pages 97–106, 2012.

[9] C. Dimoulas, R. B. Findler, C. Flanagan, and M. Felleisen. Correct blame for contracts: no more scapegoating. In *Proceedings of the 38th annual ACM SIGPLAN-SIGACT symposium on Principles of programming languages*, POPL '11, pages 215–226, 2011.

[10] R. B. Findler. Comparison with Racket's contract system. Personal communication, 2012.

[11] R. B. Findler and M. Blume. Contracts as pairs of projections. In *International Symposium on Functional and Logic Programming (FLOPS)*, LNCS 3945, pages 226–241, 2006.

[12] R. B. Findler and M. Felleisen. Contracts for higher-order functions. In *ICFP '02: Proceedings of the seventh ACM SIGPLAN international conference on Functional programming*, pages 48–59, 2002.

[13] R. B. Findler, M. Blume, and M. Felleisen. An investigation of contracts as projections. Technical report, University of Chicago Computer Science Department, 2004. TR-2004-02.

[14] M. Flatt and PLT. Reference: Racket. Technical Report PLT-TR-2010-1, PLT Inc., 2010. http://docs.racket-lang.org/trl/.

[15] M. Flatt, R. B. Findler, and PLT. The Racket guide. http://docs.racket-lang.org/guide/index.html, 2012.

[16] A. Gill. Debugging Haskell by observing intermediate datastructures. *Electronic Notes in Theoretical Computer Science*, 41(1), 2001. (Proc. 2000 ACM SIGPLAN Haskell Workshop).

[17] R. Hinze. Generics for the masses. *J. Funct. Program.*, 16(4-5): 451–483, July 2006.

[18] R. Hinze and A. Löh. Generic programming in 3d. *Sci. Comput. Program.*, 74(8):590–628, June 2009.

[19] R. Hinze, J. Jeuring, and A. Löh. Typed contracts for functional programming. In *Proceedings of the 8th International Symposium on Functional and Logic Programming, FLOPS 2006*, LNCS 3945, pages 208–225, 2006.

[20] R. Lämmel and S. P. Jones. Scrap your boilerplate: a practical design pattern for generic programming. In *Proceedings of the 2003 ACM SIGPLAN international workshop on Types in languages design and implementation*, TLDI '03, pages 26–37, 2003.

[21] R. Lämmel and S. P. Jones. Scrap more boilerplate: reflection, zips, and generalised casts. In *Proceedings of the ninth ACM SIGPLAN international conference on Functional programming*, ICFP '04, pages 244–255, 2004.

[22] S. Peyton Jones, A. Reid, T. Hoare, S. Marlow, and F. Henderson. A semantics for imprecise exceptions. In *Proceedings of the ACM SIGPLAN '99 Conference on Programming Language Design and Implementation*, pages 25–36, 1999.

[23] T. Sheard and S. P. Jones. Template meta-programming for Haskell. In *Proceedings of the 2002 ACM SIGPLAN workshop on Haskell*, Haskell '02, pages 1–16, 2002.

Functional Programming with Structured Graphs

Bruno C. d. S. Oliveira
National University of Singapore
oliveira@comp.nus.edu.sg

William R. Cook
University of Texas, Austin
wcook@cs.utexas.edu

Abstract

This paper presents a new functional programming model for graph structures called *structured graphs*. Structured graphs extend conventional algebraic datatypes with explicit definition and manipulation of cycles and/or sharing, and offer a practical and convenient way to program graphs in functional programming languages like Haskell. The representation of sharing and cycles (edges) employs recursive binders and uses an encoding inspired by *parametric higher-order abstract syntax*. Unlike traditional approaches based on mutable references or node/edge lists, *well-formedness* of the graph structure is ensured statically and reasoning can be done with standard functional programming techniques. Since the binding structure is generic, we can define many useful generic combinators for manipulating structured graphs. We give applications and show how to reason about structured graphs.

Categories and Subject Descriptors D.3.2 [*Programming Languages*]: Language Classifications—Functional Languages; F.3.3 [*Logics and Meanings of Programs*]: Studies of Program Constructs

General Terms Languages

Keywords Graphs, parametric HOAS, Haskell.

1. Introduction

Functional programming languages, including Haskell [31] and ML [29], excel at manipulating *tree structures*. In those languages *algebraic datatypes* describe the structure of values, and *pattern matching* is used to define functions on such tree structured values. These mechanisms provide a high-level declarative programming model, which avoids explicit manipulation of pointers or references. Additionally algebraic datatypes facilitate reasoning about functions using standard proof methods, including *structural induction*.

However, there are many kinds of data that are more naturally represented as *graph structures* rather than trees. Some examples include: typical compiler construction concerns including control/data flow graphs or grammars [2]; entity-relational data models [8]; finite state machines; or transitions systems. Sadly, functional programming languages do not have an equally good answer when it comes to manipulating graphs as they do for trees.

In impure functional languages, including ML or OCaml [24], a combination of algebraic datatypes and mutable references can be used to model sharing and cycles. However this requires explicit manipulation of mutable references, which precludes many of the benefits of functional programming and algebraic datatypes. For example observing sharing via pointer/reference comparison breaks *referential transparency*. Even if it is possible to encapsulate the use of mutable references under a purely functional interface, reasoning about implementations remains challenging [19, 35].

In *call-by-need* functional languages, like Haskell, it is possible to construct true cyclic structures. For example:

$$ones = 1 : ones$$

creates a cyclic list where the head contains the element 1 and the tail is a reference to itself. However, sharing is not observable and, from a purely semantic perspective, $ones$ is no different from an infinite list of 1's. A drawback of this approach is that when an operation is applied to this list sharing is lost, even if it would be possible to preserve sharing. For example,

$$twos = map\ (\lambda x \rightarrow x + 1)\ ones$$

creates an infinite list of 2's instead of a cyclic list with a single 2.

To deal with the need for observable sharing some researchers have proposed approaches that use recursive binders to model cycles and sharing [14, 15, 20]. For example, $ones$ can be expressed using a recursive binder (μ) as follows:

$$ones = \mu\, x.\, (1 : x)$$

The idea is to be able to observe and manipulate the binders (μ) and variables (x), making sharing effectively explicit.

However, several questions need to be answered for this model to become effective in practice:

1. What programming language mechanisms are needed to support convenient representation and manipulation of such binders and variables? Does the approach guarantee well-formedness of cyclic structures (no unbound variables or other types of junk)?
2. Is the model expressive enough? Can it deal with general graph edges, including the back edges and cross edges which arise in non-linear graph structures?
3. Can the model deal with operations that require special treatment of fixpoint computations? For example, is it possible to exploit monotonicity to ensure termination on all inputs for an operation that checks the *nullability* [7, 28] of a grammar or regular expression?

As far as we know no approach deals with #3. Furthermore all approaches provide only partial answers to #1 and #2 (a detailed discussion is given in Section 7), and fall short in providing a practical programming model for cyclic structures.

This paper presents a new functional programming model for graph structures, called *structured graphs*, that builds on the idea of

ICFP'12, September 9–15, 2012, Copenhagen, Denmark.

using recursive binders to model sharing and cycles and provides an answer for all 3 questions. Structured graphs can be viewed as an extension of algebraic datatypes that allow explicit definition and manipulation of cycles or sharing by using recursive binders and variables to explicitly represent possible sharing points. To provide a convenient and expressive programming interface, structured graphs use a binding representation based on *parametric higher-order abstract syntax* (PHOAS) [9]. This representation not only ensures well-formedness of the binding structure, but it also allows using standard proofs methods, including structural induction, in proofs for a large class of programs. To deal with cross edges we use a recursive multi-binder inspired by *letrec* expressions in functional programming. Furthermore, the expressiveness and flexibility of our PHOAS-based representation allows us to define operations that require special treatment of fixpoint computations.

Since the binding structure is generic, it is possible to define many useful generic combinators for manipulating structured graphs. By employing some lightweight datatype-generic programming [17] techniques, we also propose a datatype-generic formulation of structured graphs. This formulation enables the definitions of useful combinators like generic folds and transformations. Using such combinators it is often possible to write programs for processing graphs that are no more difficult to write than programs on conventional algebraic datatypes.

The programming model also allows for transformations requiring complex manipulation of the binding structure, which are less easily captured in combinators. Those operations can always be defined by direct pattern matching on the binding structure (variables and binders).

To summarize, our contributions are:

- **Structured graphs:** a new programming model extending the classic notion of algebraic datatypes with cycles and sharing. This model supports the same benefits as algebraic datatypes and facilitates reasoning over cyclic structures. The binding infrastructure is conveniently defined and manipulated using a PHOAS-based representation.
- **Generic combinators and infrastructure:** Additional convenience is provided through the use of generic combinators for folds and transformations. Such generic combinators can also encapsulate the use of special fixpoints for certain operations.
- **Recursive binders using PHOAS:** We also show how to define recursive binders with PHOAS. The recursive multi-binder presented in Section 3.2 is particularly relevant, since it enables the definition of cross edges.

The presentation of our work uses Haskell. Occasionally we use some common extensions implemented in the GHC compiler. The code for this paper is available online at `http://ropas.snu.ac.kr/~bruno/papers/StructuredGraphs.zip`.

2. Parametric HOAS

This section reviews the key advantages of Parametric Higher-Order Abstract Syntax (PHOAS) [9] for representing binders. There are several approaches to binding, but PHOAS has a unique combination of advantages: 1) guaranteed *well-scopedness*; 2) *no explicit manipulation of environments*; 3) *easy to define operations*. The first two advantages are due to the fact that PHOAS is a *higher-order* approach in which the function space of the meta-language is used to encode the binders of the object language. The reuse of the meta-language function space avoids common issues with first-order approaches like α-equivalence and defining the infrastructure for capture-avoiding substitution. Other higher-order approaches like classic HOAS [34] share these advantages. However, with classic HOAS (and other higher-order approaches) many operations are non-trivial to define in languages like Haskell, whereas with PHOAS various operations are generally easier to define. This unique combination of features makes PHOAS a particularly attractive foundation for our work.

```
data PLambda a =
    Var a
  | Int Int
  | Bool Bool
  | If (PLambda a) (PLambda a) (PLambda a)
  | Add (PLambda a) (PLambda a)
  | Mult (PLambda a) (PLambda a)
  | Eq (PLambda a) (PLambda a)
  | Lam (a → PLambda a)
  | App (PLambda a) (PLambda a)
newtype Lambda = ↓ { ↑::∀a.PLambda a }
```

Figure 1. PHOAS-encoded lambda calculus with integers, booleans and some primitives.

To illustrate the advantages of PHOAS in more detail, we use the lambda calculus (with standard extensions) presented in Figure 1. Lambda terms are encoded by the newtype *Lambda*, which is defined in terms of the datatype *PLambda a*.

Well-scopedness The type argument a in *PLambda a* is supposed to be *abstract*: it should not be instantiated to a concrete type when constructing lambda terms. To enforce this, a universal quantifier ($\forall a.PLambda\ a$) is used in the definition of *Lambda*. Note that, in Haskell, the following type synonym:

```
type Lambda = ∀a.PLambda a
```

can be problematic to encode *Lambda*. This is because in Haskell all universal quantifications are pushed to the left-most position after expansion of the type synonym. This sometimes makes types less polymorphic than expected. The use of a **newtype** circumvents this problem, at the cost of introducing explicit embedding and projection functions ⇃(hide) and ↿(reveal).

Using a as an abstract type ensures that only variables *bound* by a constructor *Lam* can be used in the constructor *Var*. For example, the identity function can be defined as:

```
idLambda = ↓ (Lam (λx → Var x))
```

However the following terms are not valid, and are rejected by the type system:

```
invalid₁   = ↓ (Var 1)
invalid₂ y = ↓ (Lam (λx → Var y))
```

The first example tries to use an integer where a value of the abstract type a is expected. The second example tries to use a variable that is not (directly or indirectly) bound by a *Lam* and as such has a type different from the abstract type a.

Using *parametricity* [36, 37] it is possible to prove that PHOAS-encoded terms are well-scoped and do not allow bad values to be used in variable positions [3].

No explicit manipulation of environments Functions defined over PHOAS-based representations avoid the need for explicit manipulation of environments carrying the binding information. Instead, environments are implicitly handled by the meta-language. The evaluator for our lambda calculus presented in Figure 2 illustrates this. The type of the evaluator is simply $Lambda \rightarrow Value$: there is no need for an explicitly passed environment. The definition of the evaluator is mostly straightforward, although it is worth

```
data Value = VI Int | VB Bool | VF (Value → Value)

eval    :: Lambda → Value
eval e = [[↑ e]] where
  [[·]]           :: PLambda Value → Value
  [[Var v]]       = v
  [[Int n]]       = VI n
  [[Bool b]]      = VB b
  [[If e1 e2 e3]] = case [[e1]] of
                       VB b → if b then [[e2]] else [[e3]]
  [[Add e1 e2]]   = case ([[e1]], [[e2]]) of
                       (VI x, VI y) → VI (x + y)
  [[Mult e1 e2]]  = case ([[e1]], [[e2]]) of
                       (VI x, VI y) → VI (x * y)
  [[Eq e1 e2]]    = case ([[e1]], [[e2]]) of
                       (VI x, VI y) → VB (x ≡ y)
  [[Lam f]]       = VF ([[·]] ∘ f)
  [[App e1 e2]]   = case [[e1]] of
                       VF f → f ([[e2]])
```

Figure 2. An evaluator for the PHOAS-encoded lambda calculus.

noting that the interpreter is a partial function that can raise run-time errors from failed pattern matching. The crucial step in the interpreter is to reveal (↑) the lambda term e and instantiate the abstract type with a suitable type for defining evaluation. In the case of evaluation the obvious choice for instantiation is *Value*.

Evaluation of the lambda expression $(\lambda x \to 3 + x)\ 4$ proceeds as follows:

```
t1 = ↓ (App (Lam (λx → Add (Int 3) (Var x))) (Int 4))
test = show (eval t1)   -- returns "7"
```

The PHOAS evaluator is simpler than evaluators based on first-order binding (for example variables as strings or de Bruijn indexes), which require an explicit environment to be passed around in the evaluator. While monads [38] can encapsulate the plumbing of the environment, they also give the interpreter an imperative feel and force sequentialiality on computations that could be parallel. In contrast the PHOAS interpreter is written in a purely functional style that supports simple equational reasoning.

Easy to define operations Many operations are easier to define with PHOAS than with classic HOAS. As noted by Fegaras and Sheard [14], to evaluate a version of the lambda calculus encoded with classic HOAS, an extra function (*reify*) is needed to invert the result of evaluation:

```
data Exp = L (Exp → Exp) | A Exp Exp

evalExp :: Exp → Value
evalExp (L f)      = VF (evalExp ∘ f ∘ reify)
evalExp (A e1 e2) = case evalExp e1 of
   VF f → f (evalExp e2)

reify :: Value → Exp
reify (VF f) = L (reify ∘ f ∘ evalExp)
```

More generally, classic HOAS requires inverse functions [27], but good inverse functions do not always exist or can be significantly hard to define. For example to define a pretty print function with HOAS requires an inverse parsing function with the property $print\ (parse\ x) = x$.

```
data PLambda a = Mu1 (a → PLambda a) | ...

eval :: Lambda → Value
eval e = [[↑ e]] where
  [[·]] :: PLambda Value → Value
  ...
  [[Mu1 f]] = fix ([[·]] ∘ f)

fix :: (a → a) → a
fix f = let r = f r in r   -- f (fix f)
```

Figure 3. Extending the PHOAS-encoded lambda calculus with μ-binders.

```
data PLambda a = Mu2 ([a] → [PLambda a]) | ...

eval :: Lambda → Value
eval e = [[↑ e]] where
  [[·]] :: PLambda Value → Value
  ...
  [[Mu2 f]] = head $ fix (map [[·]] ∘ f)
```

Figure 4. Extending the interpreter with a recursive multi-binder.

3. Recursive Binders using Parametric HOAS

The traditional definition of PHOAS can be extended to model recursive binding of variables, to support single or mutual recursion.

3.1 Encoding μ-binders with Parametric HOAS

One way to support recursive functions in our lambda calculus interpreter is to extend it with a recursive binder μ. With such a μ binder the factorial function can be defined as follows.

$$\mu f.\lambda n \to \textbf{if}\ (n \equiv 0)\ \textbf{then}\ 1\ \textbf{else}\ n * f\ (n-1)$$

Figure 3 shows the extension to the calculus and interpreter in Figures 1 and 2 that is needed to encode μ binders. This extension is not very different from a conventional λ binder: it introduces a new constructor Mu_1 with the same type has Lam. However the semantics of $Mu_1\ f$ is different from a regular lambda binder: it takes the fixpoint of the composition of f with the interpreter. The fixpoint is easily encoded in Haskell by the function *fix*. The definition of *fix* exploits the call-by-need semantics of Haskell to create sharing. Another way to define fix is as $f\ (fix\ f)$, but this does not share results.

With this extension the encoding of the factorial function is:

```
fact = Mu1 (λf → Lam (λn →
   If (Eq (Var n) (Int 0))
      (Int 1)
      (Mult (Var n)
            (App (Var f) (Add (Var n) (Int (−1)))))))
test1 = ↓ (App fact (Int 7))
```

The result of running $eval\ test_1$ is 5040 (the factorial of 7).

3.2 Encoding a recursive multi-binder

A μ binder is sufficient for expressing simple recursion, but *mutual recursion* requires some additional infrastructure. Mutually recursive definitions bind several variables at once (one for each mutually recursive definition). One way to achieve this is illustrated in Figure 4. The idea is to generalize the recursive binder type in such a way that it takes as the input a list of variables and returns a list of lambda expressions. This form of multi-binder is sufficient to express the semantics of *letrec*. The *head* of the list computed by the fixpoint is the body of *letrec*.

Consider the following example of mutual recursive binding:

```
let odd  = λn → if (n ≡ 0) then False else even (n − 1)
    even = λn → if (n ≡ 0) then True else odd (n − 1)
in odd 10
```

It is encoded with a PHOAS multi-binder as follows:

```
evenodd :: Lambda
evenodd = ↓ (Mu2 (λ(~(_ : odd : even: _)) →
  [App (Var odd) (Int 10),    -- body of letrec
   Lam (λn →                  -- definition of odd
     If (Eq (Var n) (Int 0))
       (Bool False)
       (App (Var even) (Add (Var n) (Int (−1))))),
   Lam (λn →                  -- definition of even
     If (Eq (Var n) (Int 0))
       (Bool True)
       (App (Var odd) (Add (Var n) (Int (−1))))
  ]))
```

The recursive multi-binder specifies the set of mutually recursive definitions (in this case *even* and *odd*) and also the body of *letrec* (in this case *odd* 10). Therefore, there are three lambda expressions in the output list. The first element in the list is the expression representing the body of *letrec*. The other two definitions are the expressions representing the definitions of *even* and *odd*. The input list defines names that allow recursive references to each of the definitions. Finally, a *laziness annotation* (~) is necessary to ensure that the pattern matching of the input list is not stricter than it should be. Without that annotation, evaluation of the expression diverges.

Implicit assumptions Note that there are some implicit assumptions not captured by Haskell's type system. In particular, the list computed by the fixpoint must include at least one element. If the list has no elements then taking its *head* fails. The fixpoint function *fix* was assigned type $(a \rightarrow a) \rightarrow a$, but it can be generalized to $(b \rightarrow a) \rightarrow a$ where a is any *subtype* of b. Haskell does not have subtyping, but it is meaningful to consider subtyping relations between list types. For example, if a type $[T]_n$ is defined to mean lists of values of type T with at least n items, then $[T]_n$ can be viewed as a subtype of $[T]_m$ when $m \geqslant n$. Using this notation, the type of the Mu_2 constructor could be defined to allow any input list that is at least as long as the output list (which must still have at least one element).

$$[a]_m \rightarrow [PLambda\ a]_n \qquad \textbf{where } m \geqslant n \wedge n > 0$$

This more liberal assumption allows infinite lists as input. This often makes the algorithms simpler because it is not necessary to generate an input list of the exact size of the output list.

Note that these implicit assumptions can be enforced with a type system. For example, a dependently typed language or the Haskell extension for GADTs [33] can define types for fixed-size vectors. Here we prefer to keep the code simple and more accessible to the reader. However the reader interested in extensions of structured graphs that statically ensure such size constraints can look at recent work by Oliveira and Löh [30].

4. Structured Graphs

Structured graphs use the recursive binders introduced in Section 3 to describe cyclic structures. We consider two types of cyclic structures: *cyclic streams* and *cyclic binary trees*. These two types of structures are useful to illustrate two different types of edges that arise with structured graphs: *back edges* and *cross edges*. What is interesting about cyclic streams is that they only allow back edges, whereas most other types of structures (like cyclic binary trees) also allow cross edges. Back edges are modelled with simple μ binders, while cross edges require the recursive multi-binder introduced in Section 3.2.

4.1 Cyclic Streams and Back Edges

A datatype for cyclic streams can be defined as follows:

```
data PStream a v =
    Var v
  | Mu (v → PStream a v)
  | Cons a (PStream a v)
newtype Stream a = ↓ { ↑::∀v.PStream a v}
```

This datatype of streams has the usual *Cons* constructor and also PHOAS binding constructs: the variable case and the simple recursive binder. There are two possible interpretations for this datatype: an inductive and a coinductive one[1]. In the inductive interpretation, which is the one we use for most operations on streams, this datatype represents finitely representable cyclic streams such as:

$$s_1 = \downarrow (Cons\ 1\ (Mu\ (\lambda v \rightarrow Cons\ 2\ (Var\ v))))$$

$$s_2 = \downarrow (Mu\ (\lambda v \rightarrow Cons\ 1\ (Cons\ 2\ (Var\ v))))$$

Acyclic (and infinite) streams such as the stream of natural numbers are not representable under this interpretation. On the other hand the inductive interpretation allows us to define several useful operations like decidable equality procedures on cyclic streams. The coinductive interpretation admits acyclic infinite streams, but some operations are no longer be valid.

Note that the only types of cycles needed in structures like streams are *back edges*: edges that point to some previous point in the structures. This stems from the fact that streams are linear structures and "pointing back" is the only option.

A final remark is that the type *Stream a* allows values like $\downarrow (Mu\ Var)$, which do not represent any stream. Section 5 gives a representation that prevents such junk terms.

Folds on Streams The traditional notion of a *fold* on a list can be extended to cyclic streams. A cyclic fold *visits* each node only once. Classical imperative graph algorithms normally keep a list of visited nodes to avoid visiting a node twice. With our representation of streams such bookkeeping is not necessary. For example, the function *elems* visits all the elements in a stream exactly once and returns a list of visited elements.

```
elems :: Stream a → [a]
elems = pelems ∘ ↑ where    -- a fold
  pelems :: PStream a [a] → [a]
  pelems (Var v)     = v
  pelems (Mu g)      = pelems (g [])
  pelems (Cons x xs) = x : pelems xs
```

As in the evaluation function for the PHOAS-based interpreter, an auxiliary operation *pelems* is defined over the *PStream* type. The abstract type used for variables is instantiated to $[a]$. The *Cons* case is trivial and the variable case is easy too: it simply returns the list value v. Evaluation of a back edge must visit the elements only

[1] In Haskell it is not possible to convey to the compiler which interpretation to use. However other languages, including Coq, allow for such choice.

one time. To get access to the elements of the list, the generator function g must be applied somehow. Taking the fixpoint of g is wrong because it could generate an infinite list. Instead, the empty list is passed to g, so that when a variable (a back edge) is reached it returns that empty list.

More generally the recursion pattern of such fold-like operations can be captured by the following combinator:

```
foldStream :: (a → b → b) → b → Stream a → b
foldStream f k = pfoldStream ∘ ↑ where
  pfoldStream (Var x)       = x
  pfoldStream (Mu g)        = pfoldStream (g k)
  pfoldStream (Cons x xs)   = f x (pfoldStream xs)
```

which allows writing *elems* more compactly as:

```
elems' = foldStream (:) []
```

Cyclic Folds on Streams Another class of operations definable on cyclic streams are cyclic folds. Cyclic folds allow us to define operations that use cyclic streams as if they were represented as an infinite stream. A cyclic fold combinator can be defined as follows:

```
cfoldStream :: (a → b → b) → Stream a → b
cfoldStream f = pcfoldStream ∘ ↑ where
  pcfoldStream (Var x)      = x
  pcfoldStream (Mu g)       = fix (pcfoldStream ∘ g)
  pcfoldStream (Cons x xs)  = f x (pcfoldStream xs)
```

The difference to a regular fold on streams is that there is no base case. Instead, in the case for the binder the fixpoint of the function $pcfoldStream \circ g$ is provided as an argument to g and used in the variables. Examples of cyclic folds include a *toList* operation that computes an infinite list from a cyclic stream, or a pretty printing operation (*upp*) that computes an infinite string representation.

```
toList = cfoldStream (:)
upp    = cfoldStream (λx s → show x ++ " : " ++ s)
```

Sharing-preserving Transformations An example of a sharing-preserving operation is the map function (*smap*) on cyclic streams:

```
smap :: (a → b) → Stream a → Stream b
smap f s = ↓ (psmap f (↑ s)) where
  psmap f (Var v)       = Var v
  psmap f (Mu g)        = Mu (psmap f ∘ g)
  psmap f (Cons x xs)   = Cons (f x) (psmap f xs)
```

In the definition of *psmap*, variables are mapped to variables and the binders are mapped to binders. In other words the structure of the original stream is preserved. Only the elements change. Another difference to functions defined previously is that, because a new stream is produced as the final result, at the end the resulting *PStream b v* is packed into a *Stream b*.

Structural equality Cyclic (inductive) streams always have a finite representation, so they can be compared for structural equality without danger of nontermination:

```
instance Eq a ⇒ Eq (Stream a) where
  s1 ≡ s2 = peq 0 (↑ s1) (↑ s2)
peq :: Eq a ⇒
     Int → PStream a Int → PStream a Int → Bool
peq n (Var x)       (Var y)       = x ≡ y
peq n (Mu f)        (Mu g)        = peq (n + 1) (f n) (g n)
peq n (Cons x xs)   (Cons y ys)   = x ≡ y ∧ peq n xs ys
peq _ _             _             = False
```

The idea for defining structural equality is to replace each variable with a fresh label, which in this case is an integer. Then the variable case just compares whether the two labels are the same. The most interesting case is the *Mu* case. The idea is to pass the same label (n) to the generator functions f and g and to generate a new fresh label for the next time a new label is needed. Finally, the last two cases are standard.

```
stail :: Stream a → Stream a
stail s = ↓ (joinPStream (ptail (↑ s))) where
  ptail (Cons x xs) = xs
  ptail (Mu g)      = Mu (λx →
    let phead (Mu g)        = phead (g x)
        phead (Cons y ys)   = y
    in ptail (g (Cons (phead (g x)) x)))
```

Figure 5. Tail of a stream.

A Quasi-monad Structure The *PStream a* type constructor has a structure similar to a monad: it supports a *return* and *join* (or *concat*) operations. However, *PStream a* is not a functor (that is, it does not support a functorial mapping operation), failing to be a monad for this reason. The *return* of this quasi-monad is *Var*

```
retPStream :: v → PStream a v
retPStream = Var
```

and the *join* operation has a fairly straightforward definition:

```
joinPStream :: PStream a (PStream a v) → PStream a v
joinPStream (Var v)       = v
joinPStream (Mu g)        = Mu (joinPStream ∘ g ∘ Var)
joinPStream (Cons x xs)   = Cons x (joinPStream xs)
```

The *joinPStream* stream operation is useful for defining various operations on streams. For example, consider an operation *unrollStream* that unrolls a cycle once, as in these examples:

```
* Streams > unrollStream s2
1 : 2 : Mu (λa → 1 : 2 : a)
* Streams > unrollStream (unrollStream s2)
1 : 2 : 1 : 2 : Mu (λa → 1 : 2 : a)
```

This operation can be defined using *joinPStream* as follows:

```
unrollStream :: Stream a → Stream a
unrollStream s = ↓ (joinPStream (punroll (↑ s)))
punroll :: PStream a (PStream a v) →
           PStream a (PStream a v)
punroll (Mu g)        = g (joinPStream (Mu g))
punroll (Cons x xs)   = Cons x (punroll xs)
```

Note that *punroll* does not define a variable case (*Var*). This is because *punroll* is only called at the top-level structure and a variable cannot appear there because there is no variable that can be bound. In other words it is hard to fill the ... in an expression like ↓ (*Var* ...). For the recursive binder case, when *Mu g* is found, the generator function g is called to generate one level of the structure. The argument to g is the stream itself, leading to a nested stream which is collapsed using *joinPStream*. As observed by Chlipala [9] operations like *joinPStream* can be used to effectively implement substitution of variables in binders.

Tail of a Stream So far all the operations that have been presented have remarkably simple and high-level definitions in comparison with imperative algorithms on cyclic structures. However, certain operations are not as simple to define. For example Ghani et al. [15] consider defining the *tail* of a cyclic stream. They observe that a possible implementation of this function should rotate the stream when the head is part of a cycle. For example, taking the tail of s_2 should result in:

$$* \; Streams > stail \; s_2$$
$$Mu \; (\lambda a \rightarrow 2 : 1 : a)$$

The implementation of a tail of streams is presented in Figure 5. The *Cons* case is trivial, but in the *Mu* case the elements in the cycle must be rotated. The basic idea is to substitute $[x \mapsto Cons \; (phead \; (g \; x)) \; x]$ in g. This has the effect of putting the head of the original stream $(g \; x)$ in the last element before the variable. The new stream is formed by skipping the first element and using *joinPStream* in a final step to perform the substitution.

4.2 Cyclic Binary Trees and Cross Edges

The datatype for cyclic binary trees is as follows:

```
data PTree a v =
    Var v
  | Mu ([v] → [PTree a v])
  | Empty
  | Fork a (PTree a v) (PTree a v)
newtype Tree a = ↓ { ↑::∀v.PTree a v }
```

The main difference to the datatype of streams (besides the tree-specific constructors *Empty* and *Fork*) is the need for the recursive multi-binder introduced in Section 3.2. With a simple recursive binder, it is only possible to model back edges such as:

```
t1 = ↓ (Mu (λ(~(x: _)) →
    [Fork 1 (Fork 2 (Var x) Empty) (Var x)]))
```

In this case the reference x points *back* at the root.

Expressive Cross Edges Recursive multi-binders offer several expressiveness benefits over simple recursive binders. Namely it becomes possible to express: 1) cross edges between nodes in neighbouring trees and 2) cross edges in both directions (mutual recursion). As an example illustrating this expressiveness consider the following tree:

```
t2 = ↓ (Mu (λ(~(x : y: _)) →
    [Fork 1 (Var y) (Var x), Fork 2 (Var x) (Var y)]))
```

This tree has two cyclic references x and y for the subtrees *Fork* 1 (*Var* y) (*Var* x) and *Fork* 2 (*Var* x) (*Var* y). In the first subtree the reference x is a back edge because it points back at itself, whereas the reference y is a cross edge because it points at the neighbouring subtree. A similar thing happens in the second subtree, only this time in reverse: the reference x is a cross edge and the reference y is a back edge. Note that this example requires mutual recursion, because the two subtrees are defined in terms of each other.

Operations on Cyclic Binary Trees Nearly all the operations defined for cyclic streams have a corresponding definition on cyclic binary trees[2]. Figure 6 shows those definitions. Most operations are defined in a similar way to the equivalent operations on streams.

The main difference to the definitions on streams lies in the treatment of *Mu* binders. Because trees use recursive multi-binders, operations need to be generalized to account for a list of inputs and a list of outputs. To ensure that the input list has at least as many elements as the output list, we often produce an infinite list. For example, in *foldTree* the input to the generator function g is the infinite list *repeat* k_1, and in *peq* the generator functions are provided with the list *iterate succ n*.

The operation that needs a little more extra work, in comparison to the equivalent definition on streams, is structural equality. To

[2] An exception is the stream tail operation, which is specific to streams.

Fold:

```
foldTree :: (a → b → b → b) → b → b → Tree a → b
foldTree f k1 k2 s = trans (↑ s) where
  trans (Var x)      = x
  trans (Mu g)       = head (map trans (g (repeat k1)))
  trans Empty        = k2
  trans (Fork x l r) = f x (trans l) (trans r)
```

Cyclic fold:

```
cfoldTree :: (a → b → b → b) → b → Tree a → b
cfoldTree f k s = trans (↑ s) where
  trans (Var x) = x
  trans (Mu g)  = head (fix (map trans ∘ g))
  trans Empty   = k
  trans (Fork x l r) = f x (trans l) (trans r)
```

Mapping:

```
tmap :: (a → b) → Tree a → Tree b
tmap f s = ↓ (pmap f (↑ s)) where
  pmap f (Var x)      = Var x
  pmap f (Mu g)       = Mu (map (pmap f) ∘ g)
  pmap f Empty        = Empty
  pmap f (Fork x l r) = Fork (f x) (pmap f l) (pmap f r)
```

Structural Equality:

```
instance Eq a ⇒ Eq (Tree a) where
  t1 ≡ t2 = peq 0 (↑ t1) (↑ t2)

peq :: Eq a ⇒ Int → PTree a Int → PTree a Int → Bool
peq _ (Var x)        (Var y)     = x ≡ y
peq n (Mu f)         (Mu g)      =
  let l1 = f (iterate succ n)
      l2 = g (iterate succ n)
  in and $ zipWith (peq (n + length l1)) l1 l2
peq n Empty          Empty       = True
peq n (Fork x1 l1 r1) (Fork x2 l2 r2) =
  x1 ≡ x2 ∧ peq n l1 l2 ∧ peq n r1 r2
peq _ _              _           = False
```

Quasi-monadic *join* on *PTree a*:

```
pjoin :: PTree a (PTree a v) → PTree a v
pjoin (Var v)      = v
pjoin (Mu g)       = Mu (map pjoin ∘ g ∘ map Var)
pjoin Empty        = Empty
pjoin (Fork x l r) = Fork x (pjoin l) (pjoin r)
```

Unrolling:

```
unrollTree :: Tree a → Tree a
unrollTree s = ↓ (pjoin (unroll (↑ s)))

unroll :: PTree a (PTree a v) → PTree a (PTree a v)
unroll (Mu g)       = head (g (repeat (pjoin (Mu g))))
unroll Empty        = Empty
unroll (Fork x l r) = Fork x (unroll l) (unroll r)
```

Figure 6. Operations on cyclic trees.

Mapping laws:

$$smap\ id \equiv id$$
$$smap\ f \circ smap\ g \equiv smap\ (f \circ g)$$
$$tmap\ id \equiv id$$
$$tmap\ f \circ tmap\ g \equiv tmap\ (f \circ g)$$

Fold fusion (cyclic streams):
Assume f strict, $f\ a = b$ and $f\ (g\ x\ y) = h\ x\ (f\ y)$ for all $x\ y$, then:

$$f \circ foldStream\ g\ a \equiv foldStream\ h\ b$$

Figure 7. Some laws about operations on structured graphs.

account for the fact that recursive multi-binders Mu may bind several variables at once, the next fresh variable must be updated accordingly. Since an integer is used to produce fresh variables, and it is known how many new variable labels have been generated ($length\ l_1$), the next label is $n + length\ l_1$. The elements in the two output lists l_1 and l_2 are compared by zipping the two lists with $peq\ (n + length\ l_1)$ and then checking that all comparisons have returned $True$.

A final remark concerns the interpretation of the Mu binders. Here, the $head$ of the output list has a special role by being interpreted as the root of the tree. All other trees are auxiliary definitions to model the structure of the root tree. This interpretation is similar to $letrec$ in our interpreter in Section 3.2. There, the $head$ (which represented the body of $letrec$) was also treated specially. However, another alternative interpretation is to treat all trees equality, without preference for one of them. This interpretation uses a *forest* of trees, or a multi-rooted tree. Sometimes the later interpretation is useful for working with cyclic structures. An example of this is the model for grammars in Section 6.

4.3 Reasoning about Structured Graphs

One important benefit of structured graphs is that standard functional programming reasoning techniques can be used to reason about programs. In particular properties about several of operations defined in this section are provable by structural induction.

Figure 7 illustrates adaptations of typical laws for maps and folds to their corresponding structured graph operations. All these laws are proved by structural induction on the $PStream$ and $PTree$ datatypes. To do so, the definitions, including $smap$, $tmap$ and $foldStream$, must be unfolded to reveal the underlying definitions that operate on $PStream$ or $PTree$. The structural induction itself is standard, with the exception of the Mu case.

We illustrate the proof technique in more detail on the map fusion law for $Tree$:

$$tmap\ f \circ tmap\ g \equiv tmap\ (f \circ g)$$

This equation is proved in terms of the following property on $pmap$.

$$pmap\ f \circ pmap\ g \equiv pmap\ (f \circ g)$$

We rewrite this equation to pointwise form:

$$pmap\ f\ (pmap\ g\ x) \equiv pmap\ (f \circ g)\ x$$

Now structural induction on x applies. There are 4 cases. The Var and $Empty$ cases are trivial. The $Fork$ case is standard and not interesting. The only interesting case is the Mu case:

$pmap\ f\ (pmap\ g\ (Mu\ h))$
$\equiv$ {-Definition of $pmap$ -}
$pmap\ f\ (Mu\ (map\ (pmap\ g) \circ h))$
$\equiv$ {-Definition of $pmap$ -}
$Mu\ (map\ (pmap\ f) \circ map\ (pmap\ g) \circ h)$
$\equiv$ {-map-fusion (on lists) -}
$Mu\ (map\ (pmap\ f \circ pmap\ g) \circ h)$
$\equiv$ {-Induction hypothesis -}
$Mu\ (map\ (pmap\ (f \circ g)) \circ h)$
$\equiv$ {-Definition of $pmap$ -}
$pmap\ (f \circ g)\ (Mu\ h)$

Some proofs also need parametricity arguments. This is the case for the fold fusion law for $foldStream$. The proof requires a parametricity argument stating that the values appearing in the variable case must be the same as the values passed to the generator function. However, it is possible to avoid this parametricity argument with an alternative definition of $foldStream$:

```
foldStream :: (a → b → b) → b → Stream a → b
foldStream f k = pfoldStream∘ ↑ where
  pfoldStream (Var x)       = k
  pfoldStream (Mu g)        = pfoldStream (g ())
  pfoldStream (Cons x xs) = f x (pfoldStream xs)
```

By instantiating the abstract type for variables to the unit type and using k directly in the variable case, we avoid the parametricity argument. Then the proof is done with a simple structural induction proof similar to the one used in the proof for $tmap$ fusion.

Finally, note that not all operations are inductive (for example cyclic folds). Nevertheless we expect that other techniques such as coinduction or fixpoint-based reasoning techniques can be used to reason about such definitions.

5. Generic Structured Graphs

The similarity between the operations on cyclic streams and trees leads naturally to the question of whether there is a more generic way to define structured graphs. This section shows that by using some lightweight *datatype-generic programming* [17] techniques it is possible to define highly reusable combinators for manipulating structured graphs of different types. These combinators provide us with a framework which end-users can use to define their own domain-specific programs using structured graphs. Because the combinators hide most of the complexity of the PHOAS-based representation they help lowering the entry cost for users. Often, using combinators, it is possible to write programs on structured graphs that are no more complex than programs on conventional algebraic datatypes.

5.1 A Generic Representation for Structured Graphs

A generic datatype for structured graphs can be defined as follows:

```
data Rec f a =
    Var a
  | Mu ([a] → [f (Rec f a)])
  | In (f (Rec f a))
newtype Graph f = ↓{ ↑::∀a.Rec f a}
```

This representation separates the datatype-specific parts of structured graphs from the generic binding infrastructure (the constructors Var and Mu). The idea is to parametrize the datatype-specific parts with a type-constructor f, which is a similar to the functors used in various simple datatype-generic programming approaches [17, 23].

Streams Revisited To recover streams, the type-constructor f is instantiated as follows:

$$\textbf{class}\ \mathit{Functor}\ f\ \textbf{where}$$
$$\quad \mathit{fmap} :: (a \to b) \to f\ a \to f\ b$$
$$\textbf{class}\ (\mathit{Functor}\ f, \mathit{Foldable}\ f) \Rightarrow \mathit{Traversable}\ f\ \textbf{where}$$
$$\quad \mathit{traverse} :: \mathit{Applicative}\ i \Rightarrow (a \to i\ b) \to f\ a \to i\ (f\ b)$$

Figure 8. The *Functor* and *Traversable* type classes.

$$\textbf{data}\ \mathit{StreamF}\ a\ r = \mathit{Cons}\ a\ r$$
$$\quad \textbf{deriving}\ (\mathit{Functor}, \mathit{Foldable}, \mathit{Traversable})$$
$$\textbf{type}\ \mathit{Stream}\ a = \mathit{Graph}\ (\mathit{StreamF}\ a)$$

Values of this type are defined almost as those in Section 4.1. For example the cyclic stream *onetwo* $(1 : 2 : \ldots)$ is defined as follows:

$$\mathit{onetwo} = \downarrow (\mathit{Mu}\ (\lambda({\sim}(s{:}\ \_)) \to$$
$$\quad [\mathit{Cons}\ 1\ (\mathit{In}\ (\mathit{Cons}\ 2\ (\mathit{Var}\ s)))]))$$

The only difference is that additional *In* constructors are needed at each recursive step.

Trees Revisited To recover cyclic trees the functor f is instantiated as follows:

$$\textbf{data}\ \mathit{TreeF}\ a\ r = \mathit{Empty} \mid \mathit{Fork}\ a\ r\ r$$
$$\quad \textbf{deriving}\ (\mathit{Functor}, \mathit{Foldable}, \mathit{Traversable})$$
$$\textbf{type}\ \mathit{Tree}\ a = \mathit{Graph}\ (\mathit{TreeF}\ a)$$

An example of a cyclic tree is:

$$\mathit{tree} = \downarrow (\mathit{Mu}\ (\lambda({\sim}(t_1 : t_2 : t_3{:}\ \_)) \to [$$
$$\quad \mathit{Fork}\ 1\ ((\mathit{In}\ (\mathit{Fork}\ 4\ (\mathit{Var}\ t_2)\ (\mathit{In}\ \mathit{Empty})))\ (\mathit{Var}\ t_3),$$
$$\quad \mathit{Fork}\ 2\ (\mathit{Var}\ t_1)\ (\mathit{Var}\ t_3),$$
$$\quad \mathit{Fork}\ 3\ (\mathit{Var}\ t_2)\ (\mathit{Var}\ t_1)]))$$

Requirements on Functors Note that the definitions of *StreamF* and *TreeF* derive some classes. In general *Functor*, *Foldable* and *Traversable* instances are required for the functors f used in *Graph* f. These classes provide useful methods to define our generic combinators. For reference Figure 8 shows (simplified versions) of the *Functor* and *Traversable* classes. Here we only define the methods *fmap* and *traverse*, which are needed in Section 6. The function *fmap* is a generalization of the map function for containers, and *traverse* is an effectful variation of *fmap* for applicative effects [26]. The definitions of the *Foldable* and *Applicative* classes are omitted. Recent versions of the GHC compiler can derive the instances of *Functor*, *Foldable* and *Traversable* mechanically using an extension of the derivable type-classes mechanism. More information about those classes can be found in work by McBride and Paterson [26] or Gibbons and Oliveira [18].

Forbidding empty cycles An additional advantage of this representation is that it prevents empty cycles. With the datatypes used for streams and trees in Section 4, empty cycles such as:

$$\mathit{empty} = \downarrow (\mathit{Mu}\ \mathit{Var})$$

were allowed. One problem with such empty cycles is that there is no (infinite) stream or tree that corresponds to that value. Such *junk* values are not desirable and should be forbidden. Fortunately, our generic representation offers a good solution for this problem. The idea is to interleave the functor f with recursive occurrences of *Rec* f a. This is used in *Mu*, which requires a function of type $[v] \to [f\ (\mathit{Rec}\ f\ v)]$ as an argument. Meaningless expressions, e.g.

$$\mathit{empty} = \downarrow (\mathit{Mu}\ (\lambda({\sim}(x{:}\ \_)) \to [\mathit{Var}\ x])) \quad \text{-- type-error}$$

$$\mathit{gfold} :: \mathit{Functor}\ f \Rightarrow (t \to c) \to (([t] \to [c]) \to c) \to$$
$$\qquad (f\ c \to c) \to \mathit{Graph}\ f \to c$$
$$\mathit{gfold}\ v\ l\ f = \mathit{trans} \circ \uparrow \textbf{where}$$
$$\quad \mathit{trans}\ (\mathit{Var}\ x) = v\ x$$
$$\quad \mathit{trans}\ (\mathit{Mu}\ g) \ = l\ (\mathit{map}\ (f \circ \mathit{fmap}\ \mathit{trans}) \circ g)$$
$$\quad \mathit{trans}\ (\mathit{In}\ \mathit{fa}) \ = f\ (\mathit{fmap}\ \mathit{trans}\ \mathit{fa})$$
$$\mathit{fold} :: \mathit{Functor}\ f \Rightarrow (f\ c \to c) \to c \to \mathit{Graph}\ f \to c$$
$$\mathit{fold}\ \mathit{alg}\ k = \mathit{gfold}\ \mathit{id}\ (\lambda g \to \mathit{head}\ (g\ (\mathit{repeat}\ k)))\ \mathit{alg}$$
$$\mathit{cfold} :: \mathit{Functor}\ f \Rightarrow (f\ t \to t) \to \mathit{Graph}\ f \to t$$
$$\mathit{cfold} = \mathit{gfold}\ \mathit{id}\ (\mathit{head} \circ \mathit{fix})$$
$$\mathit{sfold} :: (\mathit{Eq}\ t, \mathit{Functor}\ f) \Rightarrow (f\ t \to t) \to t \to \mathit{Graph}\ f \to t$$
$$\mathit{sfold}\ \mathit{alg}\ k = \mathit{gfold}\ \mathit{id}\ (\mathit{head} \circ \mathit{fixVal}\ (\mathit{repeat}\ k))\ \mathit{alg}$$
$$\mathit{fixVal} :: \mathit{Eq}\ a \Rightarrow a \to (a \to a) \to a$$
$$\mathit{fixVal}\ v\ f = \textbf{if}\ v \equiv v'\ \textbf{then}\ v\ \textbf{else}\ \mathit{fixVal}\ v'\ f$$
$$\quad \textbf{where}\ v' = f\ v$$

Figure 9. Generic graph folds.

are not well typed because *Var* is a constructor of *Rec* f v and not of f (*Rec* f v). In other words, a constructor of the specific structure (given by the functor f) must always be used first.

5.2 Generic Operations

The operations defined on streams or trees can be made generic.

Generalizing Folds Figure 9 shows a little library of fold-like combinators. All folds described on the figure are an instance of *gfold*. The function *gfold* generalizes several fold-like functions presented in Section 4 in 2 dimensions:

- **Graph-generic:** Rather than depending on a particular graph structure like streams or trees, *gfold* is parametrized by a functor f, which abstracts over the particular graph structure. This type of generalization is a form of datatype-generic programming, which we call 'graph-generic' instead of 'datatype-generic' to emphasize the use of structured graphs rather than plain algebraic datatypes.
- **Fixpoint-parametrized:** As illustrated in Section 4, there are a few variations of folds (for example, regular and cyclic folds). The main difference lies on the treatment of the recursive binder (*Mu*). The function *gfold* generalizes such folds by parametrizing treatment of the fixpoint using the function l.

The functions *fold*, *cfold* and *sfold* are graph-generic variations of folds, but with specific treatments of the recursive binder. The function *fold* is the graph-generic version of folds like *foldStream* or *foldTree*. Correspondingly, the function *cfold* is the graph-generic version of cyclic folds like *cfoldStream* or *cfoldTree*. The more generic combinators support simpler definitions of the *elems* and *toList* functions:

$$\mathit{elems} :: \mathit{Stream}\ a \to [a]$$
$$\mathit{elems} = \mathit{fold}\ \mathit{streamf2list}\ [\,]$$
$$\mathit{toList} :: \mathit{Stream}\ a \to [a]$$
$$\mathit{toList} = \mathit{cfold}\ \mathit{streamf2list}$$
$$\mathit{streamf2list} :: \mathit{StreamF}\ a\ [a] \to [a]$$
$$\mathit{streamf2list}\ (\mathit{Cons}\ x\ \mathit{xs}) = x : \mathit{xs}$$

Finally, the *sfold* function is yet another variant of fold-like operations. It uses a special fixpoint operation *fixVal*, which works for monotonic functions and values that support a comparison operation ($\equiv$). This combinator is used in Section 6.

Generic transformations on graphs:

```
type f ⇝ g = ∀a.f a → g a

transform :: (Functor f, Functor g) ⇒
             (f ⇝ g) → Graph f → Graph g
transform f x = ↓(hmap (↑ x)) where
  hmap (Var x) = Var x
  hmap (Mu g)  = Mu (map (f ∘ fmap hmap) ∘ g)
  hmap (In x)  = In (f (fmap hmap x))
```

Generic mapping on graph containers:

```
class BiFunctor f where
  bimap :: (a → c) → (b → d) → f a b → f c d

gmap :: (BiFunctor f, Functor (f a), Functor (f b)) ⇒
        (a → b) → Graph (f a) → Graph (f b)
gmap f = transform (bimap f id)
```

Generic quasi-monadic join:

```
pjoin :: Functor f ⇒ Rec f (Rec f a) → Rec f a
pjoin (Var x) = x
pjoin (Mu g)  = Mu (map (fmap pjoin) ∘ g ∘ map Var)
pjoin (In r)  = In (fmap pjoin r)
```

Generic unrolling:

```
unrollGraph :: Functor f ⇒ Graph f → Graph f
unrollGraph g = ↓(pjoin (unroll (↑ g)))

unroll :: Functor f ⇒ Rec f (Rec f a) → Rec f (Rec f a)
unroll (Mu g) = In (head (g (repeat (pjoin (Mu g)))))
unroll (In r) = In (fmap unroll r)
```

Figure 10. Generic graph transformations

Generalizing Transformations Figure 10 shows a little library of transformation combinators. An important operation is the *transform* function. This function transforms a graph with a structure f into a graph with a structure g using a *natural transformation* $f \leadsto g$. Note that in categorical terms the auxiliary function *hmap* is a functorial map operation, but in a category with functors as objects and natural transformations as arrows. The function *transform* can be used, for example, to convert a tree or a stream into a graph structure *VGraph* that can be rendered into a graphical representation of the corresponding graph.

```
data VGraphF a = VNode String [a]
  deriving (Show, Functor, Foldable, Traversable)
type VGraph = Graph VGraphF

btree2vgraph :: Show a ⇒ Tree a → VGraph
btree2vgraph = transform trans where
  trans Empty        = VNode "" []
  trans (Fork x l r) = VNode (show x) [l, r]
```

Another operation that can be defined with *transform* is a generic mapping operation (*gmap*) on graph containers. The *gmap* function requires container-like type constructors such as *StreamF* or *TreeF* to be instances of the class *BiFunctor*. Note that such *BiFunctor* requirements are standard for this kind of container structures [23].

Finally, a different type of transformation is a generic version of the quasi-monadic join operation (*pjoin*). The function *pjoin* is a straightforward generalization of the corresponding function on streams and trees. A generic version of unrolling (*unrollGraph*) can be defined in terms of *pjoin*. Notably the *unrollGraph* transformation alters the graph-sharing shape: in the *Mu* case a value built using a *In* data constructor is returned. This is in contrast with operations of the *transform* family, which preserve the original graph-sharing structure.

5.3 Ad-hoc Generic Operations

While many operations can be captured with generic recursion pattern combinators like *gfold* and *transform*, some operations may require less common types of recursion patterns. While it is possible to add a large number of general purpose recursion patterns to our library, this introduces some additional end-user cost because users have to learn when and how to use the recursion patterns (which is not trivial). A less general, but more pragmatic approach consists of using type-classes to divide the generic processing parts of a specific operation from the structure specific parts of that operation. We illustrate this technique on two operations: generic structural equality and generic pretty printing.

Equality A generic version of structural equality can be defined by the *geq* function:

```
geq :: EqF f ⇒ Graph f → Graph f → Bool
geq g1 g2 = eqRec 0 (↑ g1) (↑ g2)

eqRec :: EqF f ⇒ Int → Rec f Int → Rec f Int → Bool
eqRec _ (Var x) (Var y) = x ≡ y
eqRec n (Mu g) (Mu h) =
  let a = g (iterate succ n)
      b = h (iterate succ n)
  in and $ zipWith (eqF (eqRec (n + length a))) a b
eqRec n (In x) (In y) = eqF (eqRec n) x y
eqRec _ _       _     = False
```

The function *eqRec* deals with the generic binding structure, while the type-class *EqF* provides equality for the structure-specific parts of the graph:

```
class Functor f ⇒ EqF f where
  eqF :: (r → r → Bool) → f r → f r → Bool
```

The type r is treated as an abstract type and the recursive call to deal with values of type r is explicitly provided. This avoids leaking implementation details of equality (dealing with fresh variables) to the code users have to write. Writing instances of equality for graphs is no more difficult than writing structural equality on conventional algebraic datatypes:

```
instance Eq a ⇒ EqF (StreamF a) where
  eqF eq (Cons x xs) (Cons y ys) = x ≡ y ∧ eq xs ys
```

Pretty Printing A generic pretty printing function can be defined as follows:

```
showGraph :: ShowF f ⇒ Graph f → String
showGraph g = showRec (iterate succ 'a') (↑ g)

showRec :: ShowF f ⇒ [Char] → Rec f Char → String
showRec _ (Var c) = [c]
showRec s (Mu f) =
  let r       = f s
      (fr, s') = splitAt (length r) s
  in "Mu (\n" ++ concat
     ["   " ++ [a] ++ " => " ++ v ++ "\n" | (a, v) ←
              zip fr (map (showF (showRec s')) r)] ++ ")\n"
showRec s (In fa) = showF (showRec s) fa
```

Like structural equality the strategy is to have an additional argument (s) which keeps track of a list of fresh variables. The *Mu* case creates the list of results based on the seed, then builds a string that maps the fresh variables to the string encoding of the results. The class $ShowF$ and the operation $showF$ deal with the structure-specific behavior.

$$\textbf{class } Functor\ f \Rightarrow ShowF\ f \textbf{ where}$$
$$showF :: (r \rightarrow String) \rightarrow f\ r \rightarrow String$$

Like in EqF the type r is treated as an abstract type and the recursive call for dealing with recursive occurrences is explicitly passed. Instances of this class look essentially the same as the corresponding operation on a conventional algebraic datatype:

```
instance Show a => ShowF (TreeF a) where
  showF sh Empty        = "Empty"
  showF sh (Fork x l r) = "Fork " ++ show x ++
    "(" ++ sh l ++ ") (" ++ sh r ++ ")"
```

6. Application: Grammars

This section shows a concrete application of structured graphs: grammar analysis and transformations. We discuss 3 different operations on grammars: nullability, first set and normalization. One interesting aspect of dealing with grammars is that some analyses, including nullability and first sets, require a special treatment for fixpoints to ensure termination for all grammars. Normalization is also interesting because it illustrates an example of a non-trivial transformation on graph structures.

6.1 Grammars

A grammar is a collection of mutually recursive productions, where each production has a name and a pattern, which can be a terminal, the empty string, a sequence of two patterns, or an alternative of two patterns. The pattern data type is defined as follows.

```
data PatternF a = Term String | E | Seq a a | Alt a a
  deriving (Functor, Foldable, Traversable)
```

A grammar is then a mutually recursive collection of patterns, where patterns can also refer to themselves or other patterns. The references between patterns are normally expressed by naming each pattern and allowing the names, called non-terminals, to be used as a pattern. We represent the same grammar structure as a graph, where the nodes are patterns and the edges are references between patterns. Binders take the place of explicit names.

Nullability One classical analysis of a grammar is nullability [7]. Nullability determines whether a given nonterminal can produce the empty string. The analysis is defined on each specific grammar expression node: terms are not nullable, ϵ is nullable, and sequence and alternative correspond to *and* and *or* respectively.

```
nullF :: PatternF Bool -> Bool
nullF (Term s)      = False
nullF E             = True
nullF (Seq g1 g2)   = g1 ∧ g2
nullF (Alt g1 g2)   = g1 ∨ g2
```

To process a complete grammar, the $nullF$ analysis is applied to each expression, such that results of analyzing a pattern are propagated to each place the pattern is used. This operation is provided by the $sfold$ combinator in Section 5.2. Using $sfold$, nullability analysis on grammars is defined by applying the $nullF$ transformation with starting value $False$.

```
nullable = sfold nullF False
```

Note that using $cfold$ instead of $sfold$ to define nullability:

```
badNullable = cfold nullF
```

is problematic, because this function does not terminate for some inputs. For example a "problematic" grammar for nullability analysis is the left-recursive grammar $a \rightarrow a \mid 'x'$, represented by:

```
g = ↓ (Mu (
  λ(~(a: _)) -> [Alt (Var a) (In (Term "x"))]))
```

Using $nullable$ nullability analysis terminates, but with $badNullable$ it doesn't. The reason for the non-termination of $badNullable$ is that it uses the generic fixpoint combinator fix, but nullability analysis requires a fixpoint operation that exploits monotonicity [28].

First Set One analysis can be reused in defining another analysis. This situation arises in defining the *first set* of a pattern. The first set is the set of terminals that can start sentences produced by a pattern.

The first set analysis takes nullability and first sets as input, and returns the first set. The only interesting case is for sequences, which include the first set of both subpatterns if the left pattern is nullable.

```
firstF :: PatternF (Bool, [String]) -> [String]
firstF (Term s)               = [s]
firstF E                      = []
firstF (Seq (b1, a1) (_, a2)) = if b1 then a1 ∪ a2 else a1
firstF (Alt (_, a1) (_, a2))  = a1 ∪ a2
```

To define a complete analysis, the nullability and first set analysis are composed.

```
nullFirstF :: PatternF (Bool, [String]) -> (Bool, [String])
nullFirstF = compose (leftPart nullF) firstF
compose f g x = (f x, g x)
leftPart :: Functor f => (f a -> a) -> f (a, b) -> a
leftPart alg = alg ∘ fmap fst
```

Finally, running the first/nullable analysis is similar to running nullability.

```
firstSet = sfold nullFirstF (False, [])
```

Normalization A more complex operation on grammars is a simple form of grammar normalization. A grammar is normalized if each node has a simple structure, where only one sequential/alternative composition may appear on the right hand side of a rule. For example, the normalized version of the grammar $a \rightarrow$ 'x' $a \mid$ 'y' a is:

```
a -> b | c
b -> 'x' a
c -> 'y' a
```

Our approach to solving this problem is to define a general mechanism for creating a new graph by writing nodes one by one. The new nodes are managed by a state monad. The state of the monad is a triple (n, i, o) where n is the number of nodes that have been defined, i is the list of referenceable node identities, and o is the list of node definitions.

```
type MGraph f a = State (Int, [a], [f (Rec f a)])
```

A helper function $addNode$ creates a new node, increments the node count and returns a reference to the new node.

```
addNode x = do (pos, inn, out) <- get
               put (pos + 1, inn, out ++ [x])
               return $ Var (inn !! pos)
```

The actual work of normalization is done by $normF$, which simply copies leaf patterns (terminals and epsilons), but creates new nodes for any composite patterns.

$$
\begin{aligned}
&\mathit{normF} :: \mathit{PatternF}\ (\mathit{Rec}\ \mathit{PatternF}\ a) \rightarrow \\
&\qquad \mathit{MGraph}\ \mathit{PatternF}\ a\ (\mathit{Rec}\ \mathit{PatternF}\ a) \\
&\mathit{normF}\ x@(\mathit{Term}\ s) = \mathit{return}\ \$\ \mathit{In}\ x \\
&\mathit{normF}\ x@E \qquad\ \ = \mathit{return}\ \$\ \mathit{In}\ x \\
&\mathit{normF}\ x \qquad\quad\ \ = \mathit{addNode}\ x
\end{aligned}
$$

The normF function is called by $\mathit{normalize}$, which traverses the actual graph.

$$
\begin{aligned}
&\mathit{normalize} :: \mathit{Graph}\ \mathit{PatternF} \rightarrow \mathit{Graph}\ \mathit{PatternF} \\
&\mathit{normalize}\ x = \downarrow (\mathit{evalState}\ (\mathit{trans}\ (\uparrow x))\ (0, [\,], [\,])) \\
&\mathit{trans}\ (\mathit{Var}\ x) = \mathit{pure}\ (\mathit{Var}\ x) \\
&\mathit{trans}\ (\mathit{Mu}\ g) = \mathit{pure}\ \$\ \mathit{Mu}\ (\lambda l \rightarrow \mathit{runIt}\ (l, g\ l)\ (\mathit{scan}\ (g\ l))) \\
&\mathit{trans}\ (\mathit{In}\ s)\ \ = \mathit{traverse}\ \mathit{trans}\ s \gg\!= \mathit{normF} \\
&\mathit{scan}\ o \qquad\ \ = \mathit{traverse}\ (\mathit{traverse}\ \mathit{trans})\ o \gg\!= \mathit{addNodes}
\end{aligned}
$$

The definitions of the auxiliary functions runIt and $\mathit{addNodes}$ are:

$$
\begin{aligned}
&\mathit{runIt}\ (l, \mathit{out})\ m = \mathit{evalState}\ m\ (\mathit{length}\ \mathit{out}, l, [\,]) \\
&\mathit{addNodes}\ \mathit{new} = \mathbf{do} \\
&\quad (\_, \_, \mathit{nodes}) \leftarrow \mathit{get} \\
&\quad \mathit{return}\ (\mathit{new} +\!\!+\ \mathit{nodes})
\end{aligned}
$$

Note that unlike nullability and first set, $\mathit{normalize}$ is defined by pattern matching on the binding structure using the auxiliary definition trans. This is because the transformation required by normalization is fairly complex and it does not fit in with common recursion schemes.

7. Related Work

Throughout the paper we have already discussed a lot of related work. In this section we make a finer comparison with the closest related work and also discuss some other related work.

Representing cyclic structures using binders In comparison to previous work, our PHOAS-based representation of binders allows a unique combination of features that:

- Ensures well-scopedeness and prevents the creation of *junk* terms;
- Allows the definition of cross edges as well as back edges;
- Makes operations easy to define and without needing to unroll cycles;
- Has fairly modest requirements from the type system;
- Can be used in dependently typed systems like Coq or Agda;
- Supports both inductive and co-inductive interpretations.

Fegaras and Sheard [14] were the first to suggest representing cyclic structures using binders. However, their mixed-variant type representation has several drawbacks that are discussed in detail by Ghani et al. [15]. The most important drawbacks, which we summarize here, are 1) their Haskell-based representation does not prevent misuses of binders and variables and there are various ways to create *junk* terms; 2) the representation forces unrolling the cycles for most operations, which significantly reduces the usefulness of the approach for preserving sharing; and 3) the representation is problematic for use in dependently typed languages like Coq or Agda, which forbid mixed-variant types. To prevent *junk*, Fegaras and Sheard propose a special-purpose type-system. This is in contrast to our PHOAS based approach, which relies in parametricity instead. Nevertheless the idea of using a placeholder constructor for variables, which (in our own representation) corresponds to Var, was first used in their approach. This placeholder constructor is important to avoid the definition of inverse functions that arise when defining functions with classic HOAS approaches to binding [27] (see also the discussion in Section 2).

Ghani et al. [15] suggest an alternative to Fegaras and Sheard's binder representation that avoids mixed-variant types. However their approach does not support cross edges and it requires *nested datatypes* [6] (which are not supported in many programming languages). The lack of support for cross edges is particularly limiting since cross edges are important for most graph structures (the exceptions are linear structures like streams). Like us, they also develop combinators and they sketch a datatype-generic programming variant of their graph library. However, the use of nested datatypes, complicates the definition of the generic combinators. Folds for cyclic stream and tree structures require *higher-ranked types* [32] (as usual for nested datatypes [5, 25]) and they suggest that in a datatype-generic version one-hole contexts [1] are also needed, adding extra complexity to the approach.

Building on Ghani et al.'s work, Hamana [20] proposes an approach that deals with cross edges. However, this representation requires a dependently typed language like Agda or, alternatively, an encoding based on *generalized algebraic datatypes* [33]. To deal with cross edges Hamana uses a *path*-based approach, where the cross edges are expressed in terms of a relative path. For example the path expression $\swarrow 11 \uparrow x$ means "go up to the node labelled x and then descent twice through the left". Dependent types are used to ensure that such paths are valid by keeping track of the shape of the structure in the types. In contrast our representation relies only on well-scoped labels to deal with cross edges. It is unclear to us that Hamana's representation extends to coinductive interpretations of cyclic structures, since this seems to require potentially infinite types to model the shapes of the structure at the level of types.

Inductive representations of unstructured graphs A different line of research concerns inductive representations of graphs in a more classical sense: *unstructured* representations of nodes and edges with no constraints on the graph structure. Erwig [13] proposes an inductive representation with two constructors: an empty graph constructor (the base case); or a graph extended with a node together with its label and edges (the inductive case). Gibbons [16] proposes an initial algebra semantics for unstructured (acyclic) graphs, but he requires 6 different types of constructors for capturing various possible configurations of nodes and edges. In contrast to structured graphs, this unstructured view does not impose strong constraints in their shape of graph structures and cannot be used to enforce constraints like: streams nodes have exactly one edge; or binary trees (Fork) nodes to have exactly two edges.

Binding With respect to binding our work builds on Chlipala's [9] Parametric HOAS approach. In contrast to us, Chlipala does not discuss applications of PHOAS to cyclic structures nor encodings of recursive binders. Instead he is focused on the applications of PHOAS to theorem proving. There are several other approaches to binding [11, 14, 21, 39], which are closely related and influenced the development of PHOAS. However PHOAS unique combination of features (which we discussed in detail in Section 2) make this approach particularly attractive for representing binders.

Other work Hughes proposes a functional programming language extension for *lazy memo functions* [22]. This extension allows functions like map to preserve the sharing of their inputs. Because it is a language-based approach it is convenient and transparent to use. Using generic combinators it is possible to approximate similar convenience with structured graphs. However, the convenience of lazy memo functions does come at a price in terms of flexibility: it is not possible to define functions that require explicit manipulation of cycles and sharing.

Analysis and transformations on grammars have been a hot topic recently [4, 10, 12, 28]. The analysis and transformations presented in Section 6 were inspired by Might et al. [28] work on Brzozowski's [7] derivative of regular expressions. Might et al. use laziness, memoization and fixed points to allow simple definitions of operations on grammars and provide guarantees of termination. However pointer equality is used in the implementation of memoization. This precludes referential transparency and complicates reasoning. In contrast we exploit call-by-need for the same effect of memoization and due to our explicit representation of variables we can avoid pointer equality.

8. Conclusion

Functional programming languages have excellent mechanisms to program with tree structures, but graph structures have always been a challenge. While traditional imperative approaches can be used to work with graphs, many nice properties are lost.

Structured graphs extend the nice mechanisms available in functional programming languages to graph structures. The purely functional nature of structured graphs means that conventional reasoning techniques can be used to reason about graph structures. Ultimately, we believe that structured graphs offer a practical programming model for graph structures without giving up the benefits of functional programming.

Acknowledgements We are especially in debt to Tijs van der Storm for many insightful discussions and providing motivation for this work. During part of the time that the first author spent at Austin, Tijs was working with the second author on a better way to write interpreters in a declarative style using graphs. It was greatly due to this work and our desire to find a purely functional way to express some of those ideas that lead to the work in this paper.

We are also grateful to Alex Loh, Andres Löh, Tom Schrijvers, the members of the IFIP WG2.1 and the anonymous reviewers for several comments and suggestions. This work was funded by the UT Austin-Portugal Colab Program.

References

[1] M. Abbott, T. Altenkirch, C. McBride, and N. Ghani. δ for data: Differentiating data structures. *Fundam. Inf.*, 65:1–28, 2004.

[2] A. V. Aho, R. Sethi, and J. D. Ullman. *Compilers: Principles, Techniques and Tools.* Addison-Wesley, 1988.

[3] R. Atkey. Syntax for free: Representing syntax with binding using parametricity. In *TLCA'09*, 2009.

[4] A. Baars, S. Doaitse Swierstra, and M. Viera. Typed transformations of typed grammars: The left corner transform. *Electron. Notes Theor. Comput. Sci.*, 253(7), 2010.

[5] R. Bird and R. Paterson. Generalised folds for nested datatypes. *Formal Aspects of Computing*, 11:11–2, 1999.

[6] R. S. Bird and L. G. L. T. Meertens. Nested datatypes. In *MPC '98*, 1998.

[7] J. A. Brzozowski. Derivatives of regular expressions. *J. ACM*, 11, 1964.

[8] P. P. Chen. The entity-relationship model–toward a unified view of data. *ACM Trans. Database Syst.*, 1(1):9–36, 1976.

[9] A. Chlipala. Parametric higher-order abstract syntax for mechanized semantics. In *ICFP'08*, 2008.

[10] N. A. Danielsson. Total parser combinators. In *ICFP'10*, 2010.

[11] J. Despeyroux, A. Felty, and A. Hirschowitz. Higher-order abstract syntax in Coq. In *TLCA'95*, 1995.

[12] D. Devriese and F. Piessens. Explicitly recursive grammar combinators - a better model for shallow parser DSLs. In *PADL 2011*, 2011.

[13] M. Erwig. Inductive graphs and functional graph algorithms. *J. Funct. Program.*, 11, 2001.

[14] L. Fegaras and T. Sheard. Revisiting catamorphisms over datatypes with embedded functions (or, programs from outer space). In *POPL'96*, 1996.

[15] N. Ghani, M. Hamana, T. Uustalu, and V Vene. Representing cyclic structures as nested datatypes. In *TFP'06*, 2006.

[16] J. Gibbons. An initial-algebra approach to directed acyclic graphs. In *MPC '95*, 1995.

[17] J. Gibbons. Datatype-generic programming. In *Spring School on Datatype-Generic Programming*, volume 4719 of *Lecture Notes in Computer Science*. Springer-Verlag, 2007.

[18] J. Gibbons and B. C. d. S. Oliveira. The essence of the iterator pattern. *J. Funct. Program.*, 19(3-4), 2009.

[19] A. Gill. Type-safe observable sharing in Haskell. In *Haskell'09*, 2009.

[20] M. Hamana. Initial algebra semantics for cyclic sharing tree structures. *Logical Methods in Computer Science*, 6(3), 2010.

[21] F. Honsell, M. Miculan, and I. Scagnetto. An axiomatic approach to metareasoning on nominal algebras in hoas. In *ICALP '01*, 2001.

[22] J. Hughes. Lazy memo-functions. In *FPCA'85*, 1985.

[23] P. Jansson and J. Jeuring. Polyp – a polytypic programming language extension. In *POPL'97*, 1997.

[24] X. Leroy, D. Doligez, A. Frisch, J. Garrigue, D. Rémy, and J. Vouillon. *The OCaml system (release 3.12): Documentation and user's manual.* Institut National de Recherche en Informatique et en Automatique, 2011.

[25] C. Martin, J. Gibbons, and I. Bayley. Disciplined, efficient, generalised folds for nested datatypes. *Form. Asp. Comput.*, 16, 2004.

[26] C. Mcbride and R. Paterson. Applicative programming with effects. *J. Funct. Program.*, 18(1), 2008.

[27] E. Meijer and G. Hutton. Bananas in space: extending fold and unfold to exponential types. In *FPCA'95*, 1995.

[28] M. Might, D. Darais, and D. Spiewak. Parsing with derivatives: a functional pearl. In *ICFP '11*, 2011.

[29] R. Milner, M. Tofte, R. Harper, and D. Macqueen. *The Definition of Standard ML - Revised.* The MIT Press, 1997.

[30] B. C. d. S. Oliveira and Andres Löh. Abstract syntax graphs for domain specific languages. Unpublished. Manuscript available at `http://ropas.snu.ac.kr/~bruno/papers/ASGDSL.pdf`, 2012.

[31] S. Peyton Jones et al. The Haskell 98 language and libraries: The revised report. *Journal of Functional Programming*, 13(1):0–255, 2003.

[32] S. Peyton Jones, D. Vytiniotis, S. Weirich, and M. Shields. Practical type inference for arbitrary-rank types. *J. Funct. Program.*, 17:1–82, 2007.

[33] S. Peyton Jones, D. Vytiniotis, S. Weirich, and G. Washburn. Simple unification-based type inference for GADTs. In *ICFP'06*, 2006.

[34] F. Pfenning and C. Elliot. Higher-order abstract syntax. In *PLDI '88*, 1988.

[35] F. Pottier. Lazy least fixed points in ML. Unpublished. Manuscript available at `http://gallium.inria.fr/~fpottier/publis/fpottier-fix.pdf`, 2009.

[36] J. C. Reynolds. Types, abstraction and parametric polymorphism. In *IFIP Congress*, pages 513–523, 1983.

[37] P. Wadler. Theorems for free! In *FPCA '89*, 1989.

[38] P. Wadler. The essence of functional programming. In *POPL'92*, 1992.

[39] G. Washburn and S. Weirich. Boxes go bananas: Encoding higher-order abstract syntax with parametric polymorphism. *Journal of Functional Programming*, 18:87–140, 2008.

Painless Programming Combining Reduction and Search

Design Principles for Embedding Decision Procedures in High-Level Languages

Tim Sheard

Portland State University

sheard@cs.pdx.edu

Abstract

We describe the Funlogic system which extends a functional language with existentially quantified declarations. An existential declaration introduces a variable and a set of constraints that its value should meet. Existential variables are bound to conforming values by a decision procedure. Funlogic embeds multiple external decision procedures using a common framework. Design principles for embedding decision procedures are developed and illustrated for three different decision procedures from widely varying domains.

Categories and Subject Descriptors D.1.0 [*Software.*]: Programming Techniques.General.

General Terms Applicative Programming, Logic Programming, Functional Programming

Keywords Search, first order logic, decision procedures

1. Introduction

There are many styles of declarative programming – functional programming (FP), logic programming (LP), and constraint based programming (CLP), to name a few. Most systems that implement a particular style fall exclusively into one of two broad computational modalities that I call *reduction* and *search*. A declarative program, in the reduction modality, consists of a set of instructions for transforming the input into the output. A declarative program, in the search modality, consists of a description of the properties of a solution using some sort of logic, and then searching a solution space for an answer that has those properties. It is important to emphasize that both kinds of systems can emulate the other (since most are Turing complete). In fact, there are some systems that combine both modalities, such as Curry[4], Ciao![10], Flora[20], AMPL[8], and Oz[24]; The most common approach is to build a general purpose language around a single search modality mechanism. These languages often call specialized external tool, such as a SAT solver (Alloy[12]), Linear-Programming libraries (AMPL), an SMT solver (DMinor[3]), or a CLP solver library (Ciao!).

Another approach is to embed a search modality into a functional language through the use of libraries or specialized data structure design. Such systems often do a competent job. But in general both kinds of systems suffer from one or more of the following problems.

ICFP'12, September 9–15, 2012, Copenhagen, Denmark.

- **Loss of generality.** Systems built around a single search based mechanisms can solve a one class of problems well, but break down on other classes.
- **Impedance mismatch.** The use of embedded libraries to broaden the class of problems amenable to solution often results in a certain unnaturalness in their use. For example they may require the user to script a bunch of library calls using a given API.
- **Sub-optimal notation.** Some problems are naturally and succinctly encoded using specialized notation. Systems built around libraries often require the user to encode their problem description in an embedded specification language using the host language's notation.
- **Poor abstraction.** Specialized systems are often very expressive, but not succinct. It matters not, that a problem can be expressed, if it requires thousands of lines to do so.
- **Loss of incremental improvement.** Through contests such as SMT-COMP [2], and the CADE ATP System Competition [25] the competition amongst implementers of specialized solvers is immense. The winning systems often make tremendous improvements over previous year's winners. Capturing these gains is important.

The author, interested in alternate ways to specify programs declaratively, tried many systems, and ran into all of the problems above. He noticed that every problem is avoided in some system. Could all the problems be avoided in a single system? He decided to try by following the design principles below.

- A good system combines both computational modalities. Search naturally describes some problems, and reduction others. The two systems complement each other in several important ways. Logic based programs are often both concise and easy to understand; while functional programs make great scripting languages, for combining things together.
- A good system should have multiple external solvers. This allows the system to be general over several classes of problems, yet benefit from specialized implementations and incremental improvements.
- A good system naturally supports alternate notations where necessary, but reuses notation where possible.
- A good abstraction that bridges between the functional and logic worlds is necessary. The abstraction should be general – it should apply to all logics. It should be both easy to use and understand.

Funlogic is a new language (not an embedded domain specific language). It has its own compiler. It reuses key ideas from many systems (set notation from Datalog, escape from one syntax to another from MetaML, relational algebra as first order logic from Alloy and KodKod, narrowing from Curry, and overloaded types from Haskell). In building Funlogic, the author learned many engineering lessons and much about combining multiple solvers. He made a number of research discoveries worth reporting.

- Search problems are best described by multiple dimensions. These include description of the search space, special cases that either shrink the search space (such as symmetries) or make its description smaller, the properties that should hold of the solution, the strategy used to search the space, and a description of the target of the search – are we looking for any solution, no solution, multiple solutions, a solution that maximizes an objective function, an approximate solution, or a solution as a probability distribution? We have found these dimensions to describe every kind of search we have studied. Additional dimensions, to add to our understanding of existing systems, are sought.
- Overloading of terms allows the same language to be used in both the reduction and search modality. A term that describes the property of a solution specifies input to an external solver. The meaning of a term in a constraint, is not the same as an identical term in another part of the program. This difference in meaning can be explained by two techniques: overloading and staging. Precise semantics can be given for the language in terms of these two techniques.

The rest of this paper is as follows: In Section 2 we describe our system. In Section 3 we solve several small problems (each with a different solver). In Section 4 we discuss the eight steps necessary to add a new solver. Then, in three large Figures (4, 5, 6), we step through the eight steps for each solver, discussing similarities and differences using real data extracted from the examples introduced in Section 3. In Section 5 we discuss a few of the many possible extensions that might make our system even more useful. In Section 6 we discuss how it is related to other systems.

2. Language description

Funlogic combines functional programming with first-order logic. A program in Funlogic consists of a sequence of *declarations*. A declaration introduces into scope one or more *names*, and each name is bound to a *value*. Values bound to newly introduced names are either primitive (like data constructors) or they are computed by either reduction or search. There are six kinds of declarations.

1. **Value.** `(twoPi,x) = (3.14159 * 2.0, not True)`
   A value declaration introduces one or more names by use of a pattern on the left-hand-side of an equation. The term on the right-hand-side is reduced to a value, and that value is matched against the pattern, binding the names in the pattern. In the example above `twoPi` is bound to `6.28318` and `x` is bound to `False`.
2. **Dimension.** `dim width#Int = [1 .. 3]`
   A dimension declaration introduces a finite subset of a base type. Base types include `Int`, `Real`, `Bool`, `String`, `Char`. Dimensions are finite sets and play a key role in describing search spaces.
3. **Data.** `data Tree a = Tip |Fork(Tree a) a (Tree a)`
   A data declaration introduces one or more *constructors* which are either functions or constants of a newly introduced type. In this example `Tree` is a new type, and `Tip` is a constant of type `Tree`, and `Fork` is a ternary function that returns a Tree. An enumeration (a data type consisting of only constants), also introduces a **Dimension** with the same name.
4. **Function.**
   ```
   len [] = 0
   len (x:xs) = 1 + len xs
   ```
   A function declaration introduces a function defined by pattern matching over one or more clauses. Functions may be recursive.
5. **Formula.**
   ```
   anc(x,y) -> person(x),person(y).
   anc(x,y) <- parent(x,y);
               parent(x,z),anc(z,y).
   ```
   A formula declaration is an alternate syntax for introducing a name that binds to a finite set. A finite set describes a relation, and the formula syntax is reminiscent of a Prolog or Datalog program. The formula is a concise way of describing complicated sets. A formula declaration has two parts: a constraint `anc(x,y) -> person(x),person(y)` and a computation: `anc(x,y) <- parent(x,y);parent(x,z),anc(z,y)`. The constraints can place arbitrary limits on what the computation can add to the set. In the example above `person` is a previously introduced dimension (playing the role of a unary predicate), and `parent` a previously introduced relation. Formula are an example of an alternate notation and are discussed in detail in Section 3.3.
6. **Search.**
   ```
   exists  ys : List 4 Int
    where  sum ys == 9
     find  First
       by  SMT
   ```
   A search declaration introduces one or more names whose values are computed by search. It contains a number of components: the name(s) being introduced (`ys`), a description of the search space (`List 4 Int`), a set of constraints (`sum ys == 9`), a strategy (`First`) and a technique (or solver) used to perform the search (`SMT`).

In the paragraphs that follow we will introduce additional features of Funlogic by introducing a number declarations, then we will explore the consequences of the declarations by showing an interaction with the read-eval-print loop of Funlogic. An interaction starts with the prompt `exp>` , which is followed on the same line with the user's input, followed on the next line with the system's response. For example

```
exp> 4+4
8:: Int
```

Here we see that the system responds with `8:: Int` when the user types `4+4` after the prompt.

Feature List. Haskell-like list syntax is supported. Lists can be constructed by enumeration, the use of constructors (`[]` for nil, and the infix `(:)` for cons), and list comprehensions. Lists also support pattern matching.

```
exp> [True,False]
[True,False]:: List Bool

exp 1:2:[]
[1,2]:: List Int

exp> [2..6]
[2,3,4,5,6]:: List Int

exp> [(i,i-j) | i <- [8,9], j <- [3,4]]
[(8,5),(8,4),(9,6),(9,5)]:: List (Int,Int)

exp> case [3,4] of { [] -> 99; (x:xs) -> x}
3:: Int
```

Feature Dimension. Finiteness plays an important role in Funlogic. Search spaces are finite n-dimensional spaces, or can be described by a finite number of logical variables. Funlogic uses the notion of *dimension* to describe this phenomena. A single dimension is introduced by the `dim` declaration, or by an enumeration.

```
dim int11#Int = [0..10]
dim int2#Int = [4,5]
data Name = Tom | Hal | Jon
```

These declarations introduce names for three dimensions.

```
exp> int11
Int#11:: Dim Int

exp> int2
Int#2:: Dim Int

exp> Name
Name#3:: Dim Name
```

In general, Funlogic uses the symbol `#` in the syntax that manipulates dimensions. Multi-dimensions are constructed from other dimensions by use of the dimension aggregate operator that consists of the `#` operator followed by a tuple of dimensions. For example.

```
pair = #(Name,int11)
triple = #(pair,int11)
```

Dimensions are flattened when they are aggregated. Note how `triple` has been flattened into sequence of 3 simpler dimensions even though it was constructed by aggregating two dimensions.

```
exp> pair
#(Name#3,Int#11):: Dim (Name,Int)

exp> triple
#(Name#3,Int#11,Int#11):: Dim (Name,Int,Int)
```

Operations on dimensions include iteration using a list comprehension, and the function `elem:: Dim a -> a -> Bool`.

```
exp> [ i | i <- #(Name,int2) ]
[(Tom,4),(Tom,5),(Hal,4),(Hal,5),(Jon,4),(Jon,5)]
:: List (Name,Int)
```

```
exp> elem pair (Tom,5)
True:: Bool
```

```
exp> elem pair (Hal,55)
False:: Bool
```

Feature Array. Array are finite aggregates with constant time access functions. An array with type: `Array d i` is indexed by values in the dimension `d` and contain elements of type `i`. Arrays are constructed by `array:: Dim d -> List i -> Array d i`.

```
twoD = array #(Name,int2) ['a','b','c','d','e','f']
oneD = array width ["red","blue","green"]
```

For 2-D arrays the elements in the initialization list appear in row-major order. It is assumed that there is an element in the list for every point in the domain `d`.

```
exp> oneD
 1      2        3
+-----+-------+--------+
|"red"| "blue"| "green"|
+-----+-------+--------+
:: Array Int String
```

```
exp> twoD
    4   5
   +---+---+
Tom|'a'|'b'|
   +---+---+
Hal|'c'|'d'|
   +---+---+
Jon|'e'|'f'|
   +---+---+
:: Array (Name,Int)
         Char
```

Arrays are accessed using `index:: Array d i -> d -> i`. The infix operator `(.)` is also bound to the same function. Dimensions of an array are accessed by `arrayDim:: Array d i -> Dim d`.

```
exp> index oneD 3
"green":: String

exp> twoD.(Jon,4)
'e':: Char

exp> arrayDim twoD
#(Name#3,Int#2):: Dim (Name,Int)
```

Feature Set. A value of type `Set(A,B,C)` stores a set of tuples of type `(A,B,C)`. A set is constructed with the function `set:: Dim d -> List d -> Set d`. Elements of a set are constrained by the domain of the set.

```
dim int3#Int = [1,2,3]
s1 = set #(int3,int3) [(1,2),(1,2),(2,3),(0,4)]
```

Set construction removes elements from the list that are outside the domain. Set construction also ignores duplicates. Note the "missing" tuples in `s1` below.

```
exp> s1
{(1,2) (2,3)}:: Set(Int,Int)
```

3. Several small problems

In Figure 1 are several small problem solutions written in Funlogic. Each illustrates a different search based paradigm. All are remarkably similar. A problem is defined. A solution is phrased in terms of an existentially declared data structure with first order constraints, and a solver is chosen. The majority of the code comprising a solution consists of a few small functions that manipulate data and express relevant boolean valued functions used to constrain which solutions are acceptable.

3.1 A production problem

In the lower-left quadrant of Figure 1 is a Funlogic program that solves a production problem using an linear-programming solver. The problem involves choosing the production level at several factories to meet estimated sales demand while minimizing transportation costs, subject to some global constraints. The existentially declared array `prod` holds production information. The value stored in `prod.(f,s)` holds the number of units produced at factory `f` destined for store `s`. Constraints include:

- Factory `A` is smaller than the others, and its total production cannot exceed 150 units.
- every `prod.(f,s)` value is positive or zero.
- The sum of production for each store is equal to estimated sales at that store.

Shipping costs vary between each factory and store, and are stored in the array `ship`. The store owners wish to minimize total shipping costs. Note that the specification of the problem is expressed in terms of ordinary user level functions: `sum`, and `and`. These and several other "library" functions are found in the lower-right quadrant of Figure 1.

3.2 An N-queens solver

In the upper-right quadrant of Figure 1 is a Funlogic program that solves the N-queens problem using an SMT solver. The problem involves placing n-queens on a $n \times n$ chessboard in a manner such that no queen can take another queen using the moves of chess.

```
rank = 2    -- Rank 2 (4x4) Soduko solver

dim size#Int = [0 .. rank*rank - 1 ]
dim digit#Int = [1.. rank*rank ]

input = set #(size,size,digit)
          [(0,3,4),(1,1,2),(1,2,1)
          ,(2,1,1),(2,2,4),(3,3,1)]

-- (i,j,n) is in the set if "ij"= n (ij in base-rank)
square = set #(size,size,size)
         [ (i,j,(div i rank) * rank + (div j rank))
         | i <- size, j <- size ]

exists grid : set #(size,size,digit) input .. universe
 where     -- every row(n) has 1-4
        and[$(full {k<-grid($n,j,k)}) | n <- size] &&
           -- every column(n) has 1-4
        and[$(full {k<-grid(i,$n,k)}) | n <- size] &&
           -- every box(n) has 1-4
        and[$(full {k<-grid(i,j,k),square(i,j,$n)})
          | n <- size ] &&
           -- each coordinate has only one digit
        $(grid(i,j,n),grid(i,j,m) -> eq#digit(n,m) )
  find First
    by SAT

ans = setToArray grid
```

```
size = 4            -- An N-Queens Solver

dim width#Int = [1 .. size]

dim i2#Int = [0,1]

rowPts i = [(i,j) | j <- width]
colPts j = [(i,j) | i <- width]
nwEdges = append (rowPts 1) (colPts 1)
swEdges = append (rowPts size) (colPts 1)

add m pts = sum [m.p | p <- pts]

downDiag(x,y) =
  (x,y):[(x+i,y+i)| i <- width, x+i <= size, y+i <= size]
upDiag  (x,y) =
  (x,y):[(x-i,y+i)| i <- width, x-i >= 1, y+i <= size]

exists  bd : Array #(width,width) i2
 where       -- every row(i) adds to 1
        and [add bd (rowPts i)    == 1 | i <- width] &&
             -- every column(i) adds to 1
        and [add bd (colPts i)    == 1 | i <- width] &&
             -- every diagonal adds to 0 or 1
        and [add bd (downDiag p) <= 1 | p <- nwEdges ] &&
        and [add bd (upDiag p)    <= 1 | p <- swEdges ]
  find  First
    by  SMT
```

```
-- Production minimization problem

data Factory = A | B | C
data Store = NYC | ATL | LA

pairs = #(Factory,Store)

ship = array pairs [2,3,5,3,2,1,3,4,2]
sales = array Store [230,140,300]

exists prod: Array #(Factory,Store) Int
 where sum[ prod.(A,s) | s <- Store ] <= 150 &&
       and [ prod.(f,s) >= 0 | (f,s) <- pairs ] &&
       and [ sales.s == sum [prod.(f,s) | f <- Factory]
           | s <- Store ]
  find Min sum[ prod.(f,s) * ship.(f,s)
              | (f,s) <- pairs ]
    by LP
```

```
-- Library functions

append :: List a -> List a -> List a
append [] ys = ys
append (x:xs) ys = x :(append xs ys)

and :: BoolLike b => [b] -> b
and [] = true
and [x] = x
and (x:xs) =  x && (and xs)

sum :: NumLike t => [t] -> t
sum [] = liftI 0
sum [x] = x
sum (x: xs) = x + (sum xs)
```

Figure 1. Solutions for several small problems

We assume the reader is familiar with this problem[1]. The program works as follows. It represents a solution by an array of integers in the range `[0..1]` A 4-queens solution looks like:

solution

	Q		
			Q
Q			
		Q	

representation

0	1	0	0
0	0	0	1
1	0	0	0
0	0	1	0

The invariant (on the representation) is that every row and column sums to exactly 1, and that the sum of every diagonal is at most 1. To compute these sums, we proceed in two steps. First we define simple functions that return a list of points, representing coordinates in the array, for rows, columns, and diagonals. It is best to visualize the points that a function returns by using a graphical representation. An `X` in a square means that coordinate is an element of the list returned. Rows (`rowPts`) and columns (`colPts`) are par-

[1] See **wikipedia.org/wiki/Eight_queens_puzzle** for a good discussion.

ticularly easy and are implemented by simple comprehensions over the size of the problem.

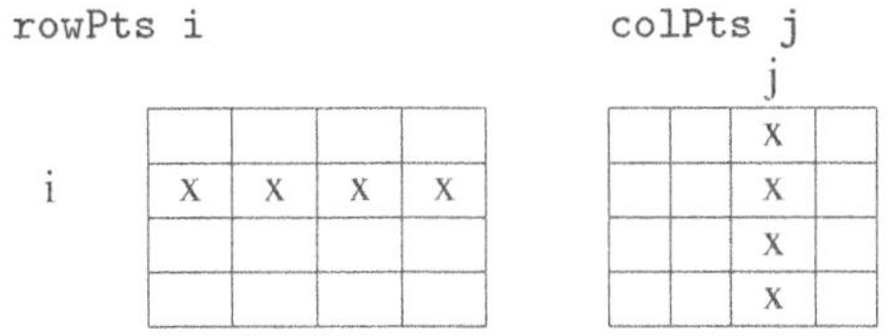

Diagonals are more complex. Given a point, (i,j), we compute the list of points on the up and down diagonals starting at that point as visualized below.

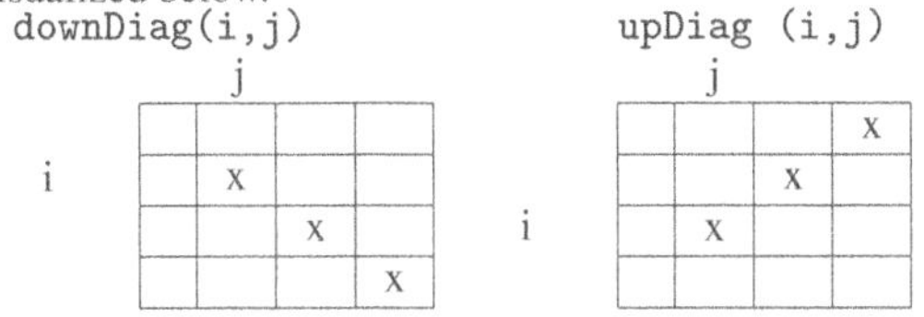

To compute all the diagonals, we see that every complete diagonal is rooted at a point on the edge of the array. Down-diagonals are rooted on points on the north and west edges, and up diagonals are rooted on points on the south and west edges.

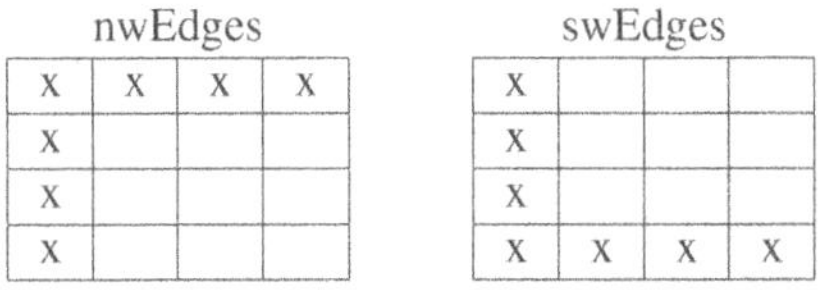

To sum the elements in an array we define the function `add`. It is given an array and a list of coordinates, and sums the elements of the array at those coordinates. Here we make use of the library function `sum` which adds all the elements in a list.

The answer we are searching for will be stored in the existentially declared array `bd`. It is a 2-D array with dimensions `#(width,width)` . It stores elements in the range of the dimension `i2 ([0..1])`.

The constraint on `bd` is a large conjunction consisting of 4 parts: rows, columns, up-diagonals, and down-diagonals. each part has the form: `and [ add bd (`*f* `i) ◇ 1 | i <-` *alphas* `]` where *alphas* is a set of elements (here, either a positive integer less than the puzzle size or a coordiate of an edge), f is a function from an element to a list of points, and ◇ is a boolean relation. For each coordinate in $(f\ i)$ we sum the element at that coordinate, and compare that sum to 1.

3.3 An exercise in alternate notation

In the upper-left quadrant of Figure 1 is a Funlogic program for solving soduko problems. It uses a SAT solver, and much of its elegance and simplicity relies on using an alternate notation for describing and manipulating sets. A set of n-tuples is an n-ary relation.

FunLog has two alternate notations for manipulating relations – *formula* and *constraints*. The simplest formula is called an atom. It is comprised of a name followed by a parenthesized list of patterns. For example $R(p_1, .., p_n)$. To be well formed R must be a set of n-tuples of type $(t_1, .., t_n)$ and each pattern p_i must have type t_i. The atom $R(p_1, .., p_n)$ denotes the largest subset of R in which every tuple matches the patterns $(p_1, .., p_n)$. Atoms are the basic building blocks of formula and constraints.

In Figure 2 are rules for constructing formula and constraints. These notations are modelled after both Prolog terms and Datalog formula (that express the relational algebra). Because I assume that

Formula syntax. let `x::Set(A,B)`, `y::Set(A,B)`, `g::Set(B,B)`, `h::Set(C,D)`, and `f::Set(C,B)`. Also let `a`, `b`, `c`, and `d` be variables, and `p` and `q` be patterns. Then we can denote operations on these sets by the following formula:

formula	*meaning*	*type*
`x(p,q)`	atomic formula, filter	`Set (A,B)`
`x(a,b); y(c,d)`	union of x and y	`Set (A,B)`
`x(a,b), y(a,b)`	intersection of x and y	`Set (A,B)`
`x(a,b), h(c,d)`	product of x and h	`Set (A,B,C,D)`
`h(c,d),f(c,b)`	join of h and f	`Set (C,D,B)`
`{ a <- y(a,b) }`	the 1st projection of y	`Set A`
`eq#n(a,b)`	equality on n	`Set (n,n)`

Constraint syntax. A constraint denotes a boolean valued function over a set of tuples. Let `r::Set d`, `s::Set d`, and `f::Set(d,e)` where `d` and `e` are finite domains as explained in Section 2, then:

formula	*meaning*
`none r(x)`	`r` is the emptyset
`full r(x)`	`r` contains every tuple in domain `d`
`some r(x)`	`r` has at least one element
`one r(x)`	`r` has exactly one element
`r(x) <= s(y)`	`r` is a subset of `s`
`f(x,y) -> r(x)`	`r` is a subset of `{ x <- f(x,y)}`
`f(x,y) | x -> y`	in `f`, `y` functionally depends on `x`

Example translation. A formula denotes a set, and a constraint denotes a boolean value. Each translates to ordinary function calls over sets. Formula translate into calls to functions that implement the relational algebra over sets of tuples. An example translation follows.

```
{ c <- x(a,"Tom"),y(a,c) }
```

First we select only those tuples of `x` whose second component is `"Tom"`, then join the resulting relation with `y` on the common component `a`. This results in a ternary relation, `z(a,"tom",c)`, which is then projected on its third component.

```
project3of3 (join (select (\(a,b)->b=="Tom") x) y)
```

Figure 2. The meaning of formula and constraints by example.

most readers are familiar with at least one of these notations[2], I only give suggestive examples for each supported construction in both notations.

Embedding alternate syntax. The default syntax of Funlogic is the expression. Any place an expression is expected a formula or a constraint can be used by *escaping* into one of the alternate syntaxes by use of the `$( ... )` operator. Consider the declarations

```
dim people#String =
   ["Anita","Barbara","Caleb","Frank","Tim"]
parent = set #(people,people)
   [("Frank","Tim"),("Tim" , "Caleb")
   ,("Anita","Tim"),("Barbara","Caleb")]
```

To create a set consisting of those tuples that include valid (child, parent, grandparent) triples, one may declare:

```
threeGen = $(parent(x,y),parent(y,z))
```

which escapes to the alternate *formula* notation to express a self-join on the `parent` relation. One can test if that set has exactly one element by escaping into the alternate *constraint* notation.

[2] if you are not, see **wikipedia.org/wiki/Datalog** for an introduction

```
exp> threeGen
{("Caleb","Tim","Anita") ("Caleb","Tim","Frank")}
: Set(String,String,String)

exp>
exp> $(one threeGen(x,y,z))
False: Bool
```

It is also possible to escape from the formula notation into the expression notation. Let the variable `n` have value `"Tim"`, then in a formula `parent(x,$n)` the `$n` indicates an escape into the expression notation, and is equivalent to the formula `parent(x,"Tim")`. This makes it possible to parameterize sets specified using the formula notation.

3.4 A Soduko solver

Soduko puzzle of rank n consists of a square matrix with edge size equal to $n \times n$ where some of the squares have been filled in with digits in the range `[1..` $n \times n$`]`. A sample puzzle of rank = 2 is given below.

	0	1	2	3	
0				4	(0,3,4)
1		2	1		(1,1,2) (1,2,1)
2		1	4		(2,1,1) (2,2,4)
3				1	(3,3,1)

To solve this problem, a number between 1 and 4 must be inserted into each empty coordinate. The invariant of a successful solution is that all the digits 1-4 must appear (in any order) in every row, in every column, and in every 2×2 box. We make the term *box* precise in our code, but note, in a rank n problem, the boxes are $n \times n$. Each coordinate in a row, column, or box is given an index (between 0 and $n-1$) as illustrated below. For example the coordinates `(1,3,i)` (in **bold** font) are in row `1`, column `3`, and box `1`.

row

0	0	0	0
1	1	1	**1**
2	2	2	2
3	3	3	3

column

0	1	2	3
0	1	2	**3**
0	1	2	3
0	1	2	3

box

0	0	1	1
0	0	1	**1**
2	2	3	3
2	2	3	3

We represent a problem as a finite set of triples. One for each filled in square in the problem description. The triples for the sample puzzle are listed to the right of the puzzle above (they are called `input` in the solution).

The interpretation of a triple `(row,col,k)` is that the value k is stored at coordinate `(row,col)`. Because both `(row,col,3)` and `(row,col,5)` could be in the set, it is possible for many numbers to be stored at each coordinate. Thus an additional invariant is that exactly one number is stored at each coordinate.

We solve the problem by computing sets of triples, which are subsets of the 3- dimensional search space. Each subset, s, contains the tuples comprising a single row, column, or box. If we project ({ `k <-` s`(i,j,k)` }) a set of tuples, like `s`, on the digit column, we obtain a set of digits, where each element is in the range 1-4 (see the `digit` dimension declaration). An invariant is met if this set is the `full` set $\{1,2,3,4\}$. Computing the projection over row n ({`k<-grid($n,j,k)`}) and column n ({`k<-grid(i,$n,k)`}) is trivial. The nth box takes some care. The set `square` assigns every coordinate to a single box index. Thus the tuple `(i,j,n)` is in the set, `square`, if coordinate `(i,j)` is assigned to box `n`. This is easy to compute by noting that $n = ij$ if we read ij as a 2 digit number in base *rank*. When rank is 2, `square` is the set:

```
{(0,0,0),(0,1,0),(0,2,1),(0,3,1),(1,0,0),(1,1,0)
,(1,2,1),(1,3,1),(2,0,2),(2,1,2),(2,2,3),(2,3,3)
,(3,0,2),(3,1,2),(3,2,3),(3,3,3)}
```

See the graphic labeled ***box*** above for a visual representation of `square` at rank 2.

4. Seven steps to adding a new solver

The steps we discuss in this section constitute a prescription of how to incorporate an external solver into a high-level language. We consider these steps to be the research results of this paper. We discuss these steps in two passes. First we introduce the steps in the abstract. Then in Figures 4, 5, and 6 we illustrate each of the steps, on each of the solvers, using actual data from the problems introduced in Figure 1.

Every solver accepts problems in a given form, the compiler must capture this form, but hide its details from the programmer. The programmer thinks in terms of data and functions supported by Funlogic. The key to "painless programming" is maintaining the programmer's view. This is done by the use of overloading. In Figure 3 are four abstract classes of operations. Three of these classes are familiar to most programmers – arithmetic, booleans, comparisons. The fourth class captures operations in the relational algebra, and will be familiar to any one who has studied data bases.

In the same figure we supply *concrete instances*. These are the functions programmers normally associate with these operations. Each solver will associate a different set of functions with these operators, and supply a mechanism to lift a concrete value to its representation type(s). This process is described in the next few paragraphs. As we look closely at each solver, keep in mind how widely their structure varies, yet they will all yield to this same process.

1. Representation types. The first step to incorporating a solver is to choose a data structure to represent problems solvable by that solver. Actual representation types appear as the first step in each of the Figures 4, 5, and 6. These come in several flavors.

- **Term representations.** The type `SAT` (figure 5) is an abstract representation of the booleans. The type `SMT` (figure 4) is an abstract representation of operations and comparisons over numeric types. These types are essentially term representations of expressions over of the concrete type they represent.
- **Structural representations.** The type `MExp` (figure 6) captures the domain of constraints over linear arithmetic expressions as used in linear-programming problems. Here the representation captures structural properties of the problem domain – that a term is a polynomial.
- **Propositional representations.** The type (`BitVector SAT t`) (figure 5) is an abstract representation of finite sets of elements of type `t`. A propositional representation stores "bits" and represents different values depending on the truth or falsity of the bits stored. Some users may be familiar with a bit-blasting propositional representation of arithmetic, where integers in the range `[0 .. n]` are represented as log_2 bits. A propositional representation "compiles" to a SAT problem.
- **Search tree.** A fourth kind of representation type is that of an explicit search tree. Overloaded operations "prune" paths in the tree that do not lead to a solution that meets the constraints. For space reasons, an example of this type of representation is not given in the paper.

2. Overloading. The second step in the process of maintaining an abstract view of solver representations is the use of overloading. Programmers write constraints using the computational mechanisms of FunLog – functions and data structures. User defined

Overloaded operators

```
class BoolLike b where
  true :: b
  false :: b
  (&&) :: b -> b -> b
  (||) :: b -> b -> b
  liftB :: Bool -> b
```

```
class NumLike t where
  liftI :: Int -> t
  liftR:: Rational -> t
  (+) :: t -> t -> t
  (*) :: t -> t -> t
```

```
class(NumLike t,BoolLike b)
  => Compare t b where
  (<=):: t -> t -> b
  (==):: t -> t -> b
```

```
class SetLike s where
  create:: Dim a -> [a] -> s a
  select:: (a -> Bool) ->
            s a -> s a
  proj3of3:: s (a,b,c) -> s c
```

Concrete instances

```
instance BoolLike Bool where
  true = P.True
  false = P.False
  x && y = x P.&& y
  x || y = x P.|| y
  liftB x = x
```

```
instance NumLike Int
 where
  liftI x = x
  liftR x =
    error "UnSupported"
  (+) x y = x P.+ y
  (*) x y = x P.* y
```

```
instance Compare Int Bool
 where
  (<=) x y = x P.<= y
  (==) x y = x P.== y
```

```
instance SetLike Set.Set where
  create dom xs =
     Set.fromList
        [ x | x <- tuples dom
            , elem x xs]
  select p xs = Set.filter p xs
  proj3of3 xs = Set.map third xs
    where third(x,y,z) = z
```

We use a Haskell-like notation to describe classes and instances. The use of the notation "P.x" indicates the concrete un-overloaded function or value. Both classes and concrete instances are abbreviated, we show only a few member functions, enough to explain the examples in Figure 1, in the implementation there are many more member functions. Note that all solvers, no matter what their representation types, will support the same abstract interfaces. For space reasons, concrete instances for `Float`, `Double`, and `Rational` are not shown.

Figure 3. Overloading with abstract and concrete instances.

functions manipulate both real data and abstract data representations through the magic of overloading. Overloading in Funlogic is similar to overloading in Haskell. Every primitive (numeric operators, boolean operators, set operations, etc.) has a standard concrete implementation and one or more overloaded abstract implementations. One for each solver that might use that operator. Abstract implementations of operators manipulate abstract representations. User written functions, through overloading, inherit multiple implementations through a library passing mechanism. Which library is passed depends upon the context. Whether the user is manipulating real data or solver representations, he uses the same functions in the same way.

3. Initialization. The third step in the process of maintaining an abstract view of solver problems is initialization. An existentially declared variable must be translated (or initialized) into the internal representation of the appropriate solver. The programmer views this internal representation as if it was an ordinary concrete value when he writes constraints. Ordinary functions and data, defined by the programmer, are used to manipulate it. Initialization chooses an abstract representation and constructs a view consistent with the programmers view of the data. An initializer looks like a type. Depending upon the solver, this type will be expanded into some abstract representation, different for each solver.

4. Staging and Resolving Overloading. The fifth step in the process of maintaining an abstract view of solver problems is handling mixed concrete and abstract data in the constraints associated with existential declarations. Data is concrete if it is a literal constant, or declared outside the existential declaration. Consider a constraint for an SMT existential declaration.

```
exists x::Int, z::Int   where   ((x + (2 + y)) == z)
```

Where (+) and (==) are overloaded, 2 is concrete, y is concrete because it is declared outside the existential, and x and z are abstract (existentially bound). We type check the program in the following environment.

```
(+):: forall n . NumLike n => n -> n -> n
(==):: forall n b . Compare n b => n -> n -> b
x:: t1     -- existentially bound x's type is unconstrained
y:: Int    -- y's type is concrete
z:: t2     -- existentially bound z's type is unconstrained
```

Type checking infers a type for a term, and reconstructs the term where overloading is made explicit, and unconstrained types my become constrained by context, and concrete sub terms are made as large as possible. The term is reconstructed with the following type, and the types of x and z are further constrained.

```
((x (+)#A (liftI#B ((liftI#C 2) (+)#D y))) (==)#E z):: t4
x:: t3;     y:: Int;      z:: t3
```

The reconstructed overloaded operators (`(+)`, `(==)`, `liftI`) are tagged with constraints (`A`, `B`, etc). We separate the constraints from the reconstructed term to make the term easier to read.

```
#A = (NumLike t3);   #B = (NumLike t3);   #C = (NumLike I)
#D = (NumLike I);    #E = (Compare t3 t4)
```

Note that the term `((liftI#C 2) (+)#D y)` is completely static, since the constraints `#C` and `#D` are completely static. Note further, that some of the others are unconstrained. This is because we make few assumptions about the variables x and z. In the next step, we use the solver context to remove this uncertainty. First, a where clause represents a boolean value, so the whole term must have the type representing SMT's version of `Bool`, which is `SMT`. Second, the existential variables have type `Int` and SMT's version of `Int` is also `SMT`. See Figure 4 for the details. So under the variable assignment {`x:: SMT, y:: Int, z:: SMT` } we check the reconstructed term.

```
((x (+)#A (liftI#B ((liftI#C 2) (+)#D y))) (==)#E z):: SMT
```

This completely fixes the types in each of the constraints

```
A# = (NumLike SMT);  B# = (NumLike SMT);  C# = (NumLike I)
D# = (NumLike I);    E# = (Compare SMT SMT)
```

This specifies an exact function for each overloaded call.

```
((x :+: LitI (id 2 P.+ y)) :=: z)
```

What we have described is a type based binding time analysis where concrete terms are static, and abstract terms are dynamic. We have used two binding time analyses, and have found them both to work well. The first is embedded in an on-line partial evaluator that uses a lazy (just in time) lifting. We have also used a static (off-line) analysis, based upon some previous work [17, 22], appropriate for a compiled semantics. See Appendix B for details of this step.

5. Constraint generation. The fourth step in the process of maintaining an abstract view of solver problems is constraint specification. The user writes a boolean valued expression involving the existentially declared variables. His constraints may also mention any other concrete data in scope. This constraint is executed using the overloading associated with the particular solver, as described above. Evaluation under the overloaded functions associated with the solver produces abstract-input appropriate for that solver.

6. Input formatting. While the representation type is meant to capture the structure of the input to a solver, there will always be some reformatting necessary to accommodate the input format of individual solvers.

7. Instantiation. Once a problem has been solved by an external solver, the solution must be used to instantiate the abstract structure of existential variables into concrete data.

4.1 The N-Queens problem

The N-Queens problem is solved by a SMT solver. The 7-step process is illustrated in Figure 4. It uses a term representation we call `SMT`. This is an untyped term algebra that builds data structures representing expressions over arithmetic, booleans, and comparisons.

Its abstract instances just build larger terms from smaller terms, by using the constructor functions from `SMT`.

The n-queens problem initializes a small vector of values, each in the range `[0..1]`. In the SMT solver, an array is initialized to a real array of abstract variables (elements of type `SMT`). The types of these abstract variables is taken from the initializer (the range `[0..1]`) and passed as input to the solver (see step 7). Functions that manipulate these variables will be overloaded and build SMT data.

To illustrate constraint generation in the queens example study one of the constraints from Figure 1.
`and [add bd (rowPts i) == 1 | i <- width]`
Binding time analysis, lifts the constant `1`, and the expression is evaluated in a context where the functions `add`, `and`, and `(==)`, are bound to their abstract instances.

Abstract variables from each row `i` are added and their sum is equated with `1`. The effect is to build `SMT` data. Inspect the abstract initialization to see that the correct variables are indeed added. The `SMT` data is then formatted to meet the input specifications of the solver.

4.2 The Soduko problem

The Soduko problem is solved by a SAT solver. The 7-step process is illustrated in Figure 5. It uses a term representation (we call `SAT`) to represent the booleans, and a propositional representation we call `BitVector` to represent sets.

The type `(BitVector SAT t)` is an abstract representation of finite sets of elements of type `t`. A `BitVector` value `(BV d xs)` stores a list of pairs, `xs`. There is one pair, `(t,b)`, in the list for each possible tuple element, `t`, of the dimension `d`. The second element, `b`, of a pair, is an abstract boolean. If that abstract boolean represents `True` then the tuple element, `t`, is in the set, otherwise it is not. When concrete booleans are used (i.e. `BitVector Bool t`), a set is a concrete bit-vector (one bit for each possible tuple). When abstract booleans are used (i.e. `BitVector SAT t`), elements can be conditionally present in a set, depending upon the assignment of truth values to logical variables (i.e. values of the form `(VarP n)`) in the abstract boolean expression.

In addition to operations over booleans, the abstract functions `create`, `select`, `proj3of3`, and `join`, that manipulate abstract sets, are defined as instances. The missing definitions appear in Appendix A, along with the functions `combine` and `mergeL`, that play important roles in explaining how abstract sets are manipulated. The function call `(combine f (x,p) pairs)` finds the pair

Step 1. Problem Representation.

```
data SMT
  = VarE String
  | LitB Bool          -- True or False
  | LitI Int           -- 23
  | SMT :&&: SMT       -- x && y
  | SMT :+: SMT        -- x + y
  | SMT :==: SMT       -- x == y
  | SMT :<=: SMT       -- x <= y
```

Step 2. Overloading.

```
instance NumLike SMT where
  liftI = LitI
  (+) x y = x :+: y
instance BoolLike SMT where
  true = LitB P.True
  false = LitB P.False
  (&&) = (:&&:)
  liftB = LitB
instance Compare SMT SMT where
  (<=) x y = x :<=: y
  (==) x y = x :==: y
```

Step 3. Initialization.
Produces an array where each element is an SMT variable.

```
bd : Array #(width,width) i2

   1     2     3     4
 +-----+-----+-----+-----+
1|'bd1 |'bd2 |'bd3 |'bd4 |
 +-----+-----+-----+-----+
2|'bd5 |'bd6 |'bd7 |'bd8 |
 +-----+-----+-----+-----+
3|'bd9 |'bd10|'bd11|'bd12|
 +-----+-----+-----+-----+
4|'bd13|'bd14|'bd15|'bd16|
 +-----+-----+-----+-----+
```

Steps 4. Binding time analysis.

```
-- user function
add m pts = sum [m.p | p <- pts]

-- one part (for brevity) of queens constraint
and [add bd (rowPts i) == 1 | i <- width]
--->
and [add bd (rowPts i) == liftI 1 | i <- width]
```

Step 5. Constraint generation. Constraint evaluates using overloaded functions `and`, `add`, and `(==)`.

```
(and (= (+ bd1  (+ bd2  (+ bd3 bd4))) 1)
     (= (+ bd5  (+ bd6  (+ bd7 bd8))) 1)
     (= (+ bd9  (+ bd10 (+ bd11 bd12))) 1)
     (= (+ bd13 (+ bd14 (+ bd15 bd16))) 1))
```

Step 6. Input formatting leads to SMT input file

```
(define bd1::(subtype (x::int) (or (= x 0)
                                   (= x 1))))
(define bd2::(subtype (x::int) (or (= x 0)
                                   (= x 1))))
...
(assert (and (= (+ bd1 (+ bd2 (+ bd3 bd4))) 1)
             (= (+ bd5 (+ bd6 (+ bd7 bd8))) 1)
             ...
```

Figure 4. N-Queens problem pipeline.

Step 1. Problem Representation.

```
data SAT =
      VarP Int
    | FalseP
    | TruthP
    | AndP SAT SAT

data BitVector b a = BV (Domain a) [(a,b)]
```

Step 2. Overloading. See Appendix A for full definitions.

```
instance BoolLike SAT where
  true = TruthP
  false = FalseP
  (&&) = AndP
  liftB True = TruthP
  liftB False = FalseP

instance BoolLike b => SetLike (BitVector b) where
  create d xs = ...
  select p (BV d xs) =
     BV d [(x, liftB (p x)) | (x,b) <- xs]
  proj3of3 (BV (D3 _ _ d) xs) = ...
  join (BV (D2 a b) xs) (BV (D2 _ c) ys) = ...
```

Step 3. Initialization.
Produces `BitVector SAT (Int,Int,Int)`

```
grid: set #(size,size,digit) input .. full

[(0,0,1)=p1  (0,0,2)=p2  (0,0,3)=p3  (0,0,4)=p4
 (0,1,1)=p5  (0,1,2)=p6  (0,1,3)=p7  (0,1,4)=p8
 (0,2,1)=p9  (0,2,2)=p10 (0,2,3)=p11 (0,2,4)=p12
 (0,3,1)=p13 (0,3,2)=p14 (0,3,3)=p15 (0,3,4)=T
 (1,0,1)=p16 (1,0,2)=p17 (1,0,3)=p18 (1,0,4)=p19
 (1,1,1)=p20 (1,1,2)=T   (1,1,3)=p21 (1,1,4)=p22
 (1,2,1)=T   (1,2,2)=p23 (1,2,3)=p24 (1,2,4)=p25
 (1,3,1)=p26 (1,3,2)=p27 (1,3,3)=p28 (1,3,4)=p29
 (2,0,1)=p30 (2,0,2)=p31 (2,0,3)=p32 (2,0,4)=p33
 (2,1,1)=T   (2,1,2)=p34 (2,1,3)=p35 (2,1,4)=p36
 (2,2,1)=p37 (2,2,2)=p38 (2,2,3)=p39 (2,2,4)=T
 (2,3,1)=p40 (2,3,2)=p41 (2,3,3)=p42 (2,3,4)=p43
 (3,0,1)=p44 (3,0,2)=p45 (3,0,3)=p46 (3,0,4)=p47
 (3,1,1)=p48 (3,1,2)=p49 (3,1,3)=p50 (3,1,4)=p51
 (3,2,1)=p52 (3,2,2)=p53 (3,2,3)=p54 (3,2,4)=p55
 (3,3,1)=T   (3,3,2)=p56 (3,3,3)=p57 (3,3,4)=p58]
```

Steps 4. Binding time analysis and alternate syntax expansion produces constraint.

```
full {k <- grid(3,j,k)}
-->
full (proj3of3 (select (\ (i,j,k)->i==3) grid))
```

Step 5. Constraint generation. Constraint evaluates using overloaded functions, `full`, `proj3of3`, and `select`.

```
(p45 \/ p49 \/ p53 \/ p56) /\
(p46 \/ p50 \/ p54 \/ p57) /\
(p47 \/ p51 \/ p55 \/ p58)
```

Step 6. Input formatting leads to .cnf file

```
p cnf 58 3
45 49 53 56 0
46 50 54 57 0
47 51 55 58 0
```

Figure 5. Soduko problem pipeline.

`(x,q)` in `pairs` (if any) and replaces its abstract boolean `q` with `(f p q)`. This can be used to effectively insert or delete elements depending upon the values of `p` and `f`, for example `(combine (||) (x,True) xs)` adds `x` and `(combine (&&) (x,False) xs)` removes `x`. The function `mergeL` iterates `combine`.

The Soduko problem initializes a finite set. An initializer for a finite set has the form: `Set #(d1,d2) s1 .. s2`. It includes a pair of concrete sets, `s1` and `s2`. The set `s1` must be a subset of the set `s2` and both must have the same dimensions as the set being initialized. Like all abstract sets, the initialized set consists of a list of pairs. The intuition for initialization can be seen in the picture below

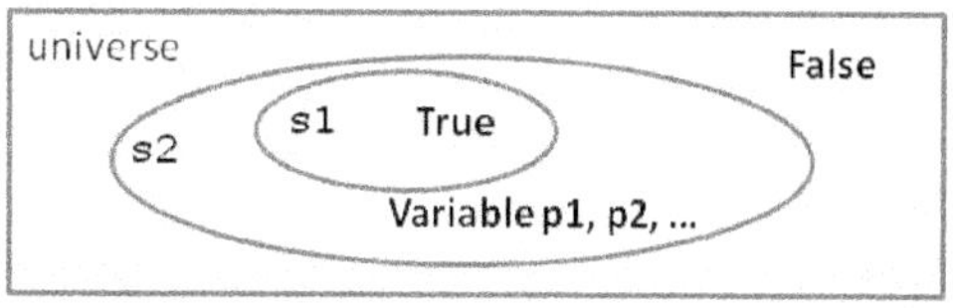

Tuples in `s1` have their `BoolLike` values set to `True`, they are definitely in the set. Tuples not in `s2` have their `BoolLike` values set to `False`, they are definitely not in the set. The others are assigned a boolean valued propositional variable. Different assignments of `True` or `False` to the propositional variables will change what is in the set.

Note that the tuples given as input to the Soduko puzzle `((0,3,4)`, `(1,1,2)`, `(1,2,1)`, `(2,1,1)`, `(2,2,4)`, and `(3,3,1))` all have their `BoolLike` value set to `True`, and all the others are assigned a propositional variable. This is because the set `s2` is the full set of tuples (the universe). It is not unusual for an initializer to be: `Set #(d1,d2) none .. universe`, which is completely unconstrained (i.e. every tuple is assigned a propositional variable). But, choosing appropriate bounds can dramatically decrease the size of the problem sent to the solver, and thus effect its efficiency. Other initializers (not shown) allow users to describe symmetries[5, 23], which also can make the search process more efficient.

In the Soduko example, one part of the constraint is: `full {k <- grid(3,j,k)}`. The alternate notation expands to a term involving the overloaded functions `full`, `proj3of3` and `select`. No binding time annotations are needed. This compares a one column projection to the full set `{1,2,3,4}`.

The term is evaluated in an overloaded context to get a `SAT` term. To see how the answer arises, consider its first conjunct `(p45 \/ p49 \/ p53 \/ p56)`. A `2` is in the set if and only if this conditions holds. The only tuples in row `3` with a `2` in the `k` position are:
`(3,0,2)=p45 (3,1,2)=p49 (3,2,2)=p53 (3,3,2)=p56`.
So, one of the variables `p45`, `p49`, `p53`, or `p56` must be true. In a similar fashion, the second and third conjuncts assure `3` and `4` are also in the set (work it out for yourself). What about `1`? Why no conjunct for `1`? Because the tuple `(3,3,1)=T` is already fixed by the input, so `1` will always in the set `{k <- grid(3,j,k)}`.

This representation is then formatted into a standard .cnf file and passed to the sat solver.

4.3 The Production problem

The Production problem is solved by a Linear Programming solver. The 7-step process is illustrated in Figure 6. It uses a structural representation (we call `Mexp`, for *M*athematical programming) to represent polynomials over several variables. For example: `3x + 2y + 1`. Operations, like `(+)`, combine polynomials. For example: `(3x + 2y + 1) + (2x + 2z + 3)` results in `(5x + 2y + 2z + 4)`.

Step 1. Problem Representation.

```
type PolyNom n = [(String,n)]
data MExp n = Term (PolyNom n) n
data Rel n                          --  true   false
  = RANGE (PolyNom n) (Range n) | TAUT | UNSAT
```

Step 2. Overloading. See Appendix A for full definitions.

```
instance NumLike (MExp Int) where
  liftI n = Term [] n
  (+) (Term [] a) (Term [] b) = ...
instance BoolLike [Rel Int] where
  liftB True = [TAUT]
  (&&) xs ys = ...
instance Compare (MExp Int) [Rel Int]  where
  (<=) (Term [] a) (Term [] b) = ...
```

Step 3. Initialization. Array filled with unit polynomials.

```
prod: Array #(Factory,Store) Int
    NYC        ATL        LA
 +---------+---------+---------+
A|‘(1a + 0)|‘(1b + 0)|‘(1c + 0)|
 +---------+---------+---------+
B|‘(1d + 0)|‘(1e + 0)|‘(1f + 0)|
 +---------+---------+---------+
C|‘(1g + 0)|‘(1h + 0)|‘(1i + 0)|
 +---------+---------+---------+
: Array (Factory,Store) (MExp Int)
```

Steps 4. Binding time analysis. Constraint is annotated.

```
and [ sales.s == sum [prod.(f,s) | f <- Factory]
    | s <- Store ]    -->
and [liftI(sales.s)==sum[prod.(f,s) | f<-Factory]
    | s <- Store ]
```

Step 5. Constraint generation. Constraint evaluates using overloaded functions. Transformed to coefficient matrix.

```
230 <= (1a + 1d + 1g) <= 230
140 <= (1b + 1e + 1h) <= 140
300 <= (1c + 1f + 1i) <= 300
         a b c d e f g h i
+----+--+-+-+-+-+-+-+-+-+----+---+
|230 |<=|1|0|0|1|0|0|1|0|0|<= |230|
+----+--+-+-+-+-+-+-+-+-+----+---+
|140 |<=|0|1|0|0|1|0|0|1|0|<= |140|
+----+--+-+-+-+-+-+-+-+-+----+---+
|300 |<=|0|0|1|0|0|1|0|0|1|<= |300|
+----+--+-+-+-+-+-+-+-+-+----+---+
```

Step 6. Input formatting leads to .mps file

```
NAME          prod
ROWS
 N  COST
 E  R1
 E  R2
 E  R3
COLUMNS
    a         COST          2
    a         R1            1  ...
ENDATA
```

Figure 6. Production Problem pipeline.

The type `[Rel n]` represents a boolean term. An element of such a list is a ternary relation, bounding a polynomial from above and below. For example: `-∞ <= (3x + 2y) <= -3`.

Comparisons build these relations. E.g. a constant comparison `(3x + 2y + 1) <= 7`, produces: `-∞ <= (3x + 2y) <= 6`.

More complex, comparing two polynomials
`(3x + 2y + 5) <=  (y + 5z + 2)` becomes
`-∞ <= (3x + y - 5z) <= -3`

Using this representation of terms, an abstract boolean is a list of ternary relations. To overload the operator `(&&)`, the two sets are unioned, by combining elements with a common polynomial, by "squeezing" the lower and upper bounds.

`{-∞ <= (3x) <= 6}` && `{ 4 <= (3x) <= 9}` becomes
`{ 4 <= (3x) <= 6 }`

The full definitions for the overloaded operations in the abstract instance step are found in Appendix A.

The production problem, like the Soduko problem, initializes to a real array storing abstract data. Here each array cell holds a unit polynomial over a different variable. A unit polynomial has only one variable (with a coefficient of 1) and an additive constant of 0.

In the production problem, we illustrate constraint generation using the last of the three constraints. Binding time analysis recognizes that the sub term `sales.s` is completely static (it will reduce to a constant, like 230) so it is annotated with `liftI`.

Each of the sums leads to a bounded polynomial. From these bounded polynomials an array of coefficients is constructed. Note that for each polynomial, only some of the coefficients are set to `1`, these correspond to the entries in `prod` for the same store (i.e. the same column in the abstract array).

The array of coefficients is formatted as a standard .mps file.

5. Possible extensions

Additional solvers. The first and most natural extension is to find and incorporate additional solvers. The linear-programming solver framework can be generalized to solve problems over real or rational numbers, or to allow non-linear constraints. We are looking for suggestions for new kinds of solvers.

Allowing programmers to add solvers. A more useful extension would be to add language features that allow programmers to add their own solvers. Currently the Funlogic compiler must be hacked to add a new solver. The design principles specify the steps necessary. To allow programmers to add solvers, each step would have to be internalized. Currently the language is a simple call by value language. Users write no type information at all, and every term is given, what appears to be a simple Hindley-Milner type.

In reality, 2-stage overloaded types are actually used. To internalize the 7 steps the language would have to be much more sophisticated. It would need overloading and classes, staging annotations, and more. All this would have to accessible to the programmer. While I believe this is possible. I have not built it, yet.

What should we search for? New solvers expand the design principles to accommodate new ideas. The linear programming solver is a case in point. The other solvers can return any solution that meets the constraints. The LP solver must find a solution that maximizes the objective function. When we first embedded the LP solver we had to generalize the notion of what we were solving for. This led us to add the `find` clause to an existential declaration. Now one can `find` the `First` (SAT,SMT,Narrowing), or the `Max` or `Min` (LP) solution. This led us to think about other possible ways of describing what we should search for. We have currently added two other `find` modes: `Many` and `Abstract`. We envision these being used as design exploration tools by the programmer. They help the programmer design his program by exploring the design space of possible constraints.

The `Abstract` mode allows the user to visualize the results of *initialization*. Rather than generate and find a solution that meets the constraint. It prints out the constraint and binds the existentially quantified variables to their initializations. This lets the programmer use the read-eval-print loop to visualize the results of potential constraints (much the way we did in Figures 4, 5, and 6, which were in fact created using the `Abstract` mode).

The `(Many x)` mode solves the constraint, and then instantiates and prints out `x` under the solution. It then pauses and goes into an interactive loop that allows the programmer to type in additional constraints. These constraints are then added to the original ones and the process is repeated. This allows the programmer to incrementally develop what constraints are necessary. Over or under constraining problem specifications is common, and using this mechanism allows exploration of the possibilities. Other possibilities of design exploration include

- **Populating large constrained data structures.** Given a data structure and a bunch of constraints one can explore questions like: Is there a value which meets all the constraints? What does a value look like? What if I add an additional constraint?
- **Model Checking.** Given a data structure and a bunch of constraints is it true that every solution (or model) has additional properties.
- **Test generation.** Find some input data that forces a computation to go down a certain path for testing purposes.

The existential declaration allows programmers to explore these design parameters from within the language. No need for an external tool or analysis.

6. Related work

Funlogic embeds multiple solvers in a general purpose language. This combination is rare. Several systems, self described as modelling languages, such as AMPL [8] and GAMS, support multiple solvers. But, they are not programming languages, just a convenient notation to write down the math that describes a problem. The solvers they support all concern minimizing or maximizing an objective under various kinds of constraints. I know of two systems that embed solvers in database languages, based upon Datalog, by using the notion of "plugin" [14, 19]. But neither provides strong scripting capability.

Recently, Kuncak et al.[16] introduced the idea of a software synthesis procedure, where code is synthesized at compile time by the use of a decision procedure. The synthesized code, when executed at runtime, will provide values for existentially defined variables. They introduce the notion of a formula, a syntactic subset of boolean valued terms, for which the decision procedure knows how to synthesize code. In this paper we demonstrate how overloading can both replace the syntactic restriction with constrained types, and broaden the class of decision procedures applicable. In more recent work[15] they have strengthened their decision procedures by extending them with a notion of symbolic evaluation of user defined functions.

While Funlogic is a unique collection of ideas, I would be remiss if I did not acknowledge many fine papers which strongly influenced my thinking in its design.

The work of Daniel Jackson[11, 29] and his student Emina Torlak[28] first opened my eyes to the fact that non-trivial specifications (all of relational algebra) could be expressed in first order logic. The thesis by Toni Mancini[18], strongly reinforced this fact.

The Curry language[9], developed by Michael Hanus and Sergio Antoy was also influential. The recent paper[4] *A New Compiler from Curry to Haskell*, explained to me exactly how Curry fits within the design principles developed in this work (though I didn't realize it at the time I first implemented a narrowing solver).

I first encountered the use of overloading to generate constraints in the paper *Logical Abstractions in Haskell*[7] by Nancy A. Day, John Launchbury, and Jeff Lewis. It took a while for me to realize that this could be generalized from boolean constraints to constraints over other domains, such as numeric domains, or even algebraic data structures. My knowledge of how to type and implement overloading comes mainly from the fine paper *Typing Haskell in Haskell*[13] by Mark Jones.

One key element necessary to use overloading as a constraint generation mechanism is effective initialization of existentially introduced variables. Good initialization abstracts over aggregates (allowing the user to declare one array, rather than many individual variables), and chooses good representations that minimize the problems to be solved. My approach to initialization was strongly influenced by the small check system[21] (which uses a type-based system to generate all "small" values of a given type) , and by conversations with Emina Torlak. Emina taught me the bounding trick for finite set initialization, and the importance of using symmetry in initialization.

Binding time analysis was the last piece of the puzzle. Experience with MetaML[26, 27] made it possible to recognize a binding time problem when I saw one. The two binding analyses I have experimented with include an interpreted approach based upon normalization by evaluation[1, 6], and an approach based on some work by a former student, Nathan Linger[22], which is outlined in Appendix B. Interesting enough, a third approach[17], outlined by Linger, performs the analysis, not by abstract interpretation, but by reducing the problem to a boolean SMT problem. So we have come full circle.

7. Performance

I built the system as a proof of concept, not to optimize performance. There are lots of possibilities. Here are a few baseline timings for the programs in the paper: 4 queens a few hundredths of a second; 8 queens in a second; 10 queens time out (the limit is 60 seconds). Rank 2 Soduko in a few hundredths of a second; Rank 3 Soduko (the normal 9x9) in about 3 seconds; Rank 4 Soduko times out.

But, by changing the initializer for SAT, and swapping in a specialized formula to CNF pass, a student solved rank 7 (49x49) puzzles. Using specialized representations makes a difference, and giving users programmers access to these is important. We leave this to future work

8. Conclusion

The existential declaration is an expressive abstraction, bridging the functional and logic worlds, for many different kinds of problems, solvable by a wide variety of decision procedures. Implementing existential declarations over a wide variety of domains requires embedding multiple decision procedures. Fortunately, the steps involved can be can be precisely described. Overloading and staging are the key ingrediants to giving precise semantics to the embedding process.

Acknowledgments

There are many people who helped me in my research. First I would like to thank Molham Aref and Emir Pasalic who got me started thinking about other ways to think about declarative programming, and LogicBlox (a great place to work in Atlanta Ga.)

which partially supported this research. I would also like to thank Jim Hook (my co-teacher) and all the class members of the Winter 2011 class *Mathematical Logic via Foundational Algorithms* at PSU that helped refine my thinking about how to combine logic and functional programming. This work was also supported in part by NSF grant 0910500.

References

[1] V. Balat and O. Danvy. Strong normalization by type-directed partial evaluation and run-time code generation. *Lecture Notes in Computer Science*, 1473:240–252, 1998. ISSN 0302-9743.

[2] C. Barrett, M. Deters, A. Oliveras, and A. Stump. Design and results of the 3rd annual satisfiability modulo theories competition (SMT-comp 2007). *International Journal on Artificial Intelligence Tools*, 17(4): 569–606, 2008.

[3] G. M. Bierman, A. D. Gordon, C. Hritc, and D. Langworthy. Semantic Subtyping with an SMT Solver. TechReport MSR-TR-2010-99, Microsoft Research, Dec. 2010. URL `http://research.microsoft.com/en-us/projects/dminor/`.

[4] B. Braßel, M. Hanus, B. Peemöller, and F. Reck. KiCS2: A new compiler from curry to haskell. In H. Kuchen, editor, *WFLP*, volume 6816 of *Lecture Notes in Computer Science*, pages 1–18. Springer, 2011. ISBN 978-3-642-22530-7. URL `http://dx.doi.org/10.1007/978-3-642-22531-4`.

[5] J. M. Crawford, M. L. Ginsberg, E. M. Luks, and A. Roy. Symmetry-breaking predicates for search problems. In *KR*, pages 148–159, 1996.

[6] O. Danvy, M. Rhiger, and K. H. Rose. Normalization by evaluation with typed abstract syntax. *J. Funct. Program*, 11(6):673–680, 2001.

[7] N. A. Day, J. Launchbury, and J. Lewis. Logical abstractions in haskell. In *Proceedings of the 1999 Haskell Workshop*. Utrecht University Department of Computer Science, Technical Report UU-CS-1999-28, October 1999.

[8] R. Fourer, D. M. Gay, and B. W. Kernighan. *AMPL – A Modeling Language for Mathematical Programming*. The Scientific Press, South San Francisco, 1993.

[9] M. Hanus. *Report on Curry (ver.0.8.2)*. Inst. fur Informatik, Christian-Albrechts Universitat, .de, 2006.

[10] M. Hermenegildo and T. CLIP Group. An Automatic Documentation Generator for (C)LP – Reference Manual. The Ciao System Documentation Series–TR CLIP5/97.3, Facultad de Informática, UPM, Aug. 1997. URL `http://clip.dia.fi.upm.es/Software/Ciao/`. Online at `http://clip.dia.fi.upm.es/Software/Ciao/`.

[11] D. Jackson. An intermediate design language and its analysis. In *Proceedings of the ACM SIGSOFT 6th International Symposium on the Foundations of Software Engineering (FSE-98)*, volume 23, 6 of *Software Engineering Notes*, pages 121–130, New York, Nov. 3–5 1998. ACM Press.

[12] D. Jackson. *Software Abstractions: Logic, Language, and Analysis*. The MIT Press, Cambridge, Mass., 2006.

[13] M. P. Jones. Typing Haskell in Haskell. In *ACM Haskell Workshop* , informal proceedings, Oct. 1999.

[14] D. Klabjan, R. Fourer, and J. Ma. Algebraic modeling in a deductive database language. In *11th INFORMS Computing Society Conference*, 2009.

[15] A. S. Koksal, V. Kuncak, and P. Suter. Constraints as control. In *POPL '12, Proceedings of the 39th annual ACM SIGPLAN-SIGACT symposium on Principles of programming languages*, pages 151–164. ACM, 2012.

[16] V. Kuncak, M. Mayer, R. Piskac, and P. Suter. Software synthesis procedures. *Communications of the ACM*, 55(2):103–111, Feb. 2012. ISSN 0001-0782 (print), 1557-7317 (electronic). doi: http://dx.doi.org/10.1145/2076450.2076472.

[17] N. Linger and T. Sheard. Binding-time analysis for metaML via type inference and constraint solving. In K. Jensen and A. Podelski, editors, *TACAS*, volume 2988 of *Lecture Notes in Computer Science*, pages 266–279. Springer, 2004. ISBN 3-540-21299-X.

[18] T. Mancini. *Declarative constraint modelling and specification-level reasoning*. Diploma thesis, Universita degli Studi di Roma 'La Sapienza', 2004.

[19] D. Z. Molham Aref and E. Pasalic. Using optimization services in datalog. In *11th INFORMS Computing Society Conference*, 2009.

[20] M. Novak, G. Gardarin, and P. Valduriez. Flora: A functional-style language for object and relational algebra. *Lecture Notes in Computer Science*, 856:37–46, 1994. ISSN 0302-9743.

[21] C. Runciman, M. Naylor, and F. Lindblad. SmallCheck and Lazy SmallCheck: automatic exhaustive testing for small values. *ACM SIGPLAN Notices*, 44(2):37–48, Feb. 2009. ISSN 0362-1340 (print), 1523-2867 (print), 1558-1160 (electronic). doi: http://doi.acm.org/10.1145/1543134.1411292.

[22] T. Sheard and N. Linger. Search-based binding time analysis using type-directed pruning. In *ASIA-PEPM*, pages 20–31, 2002. URL `http://doi.acm.org/10.1145/568173.568176`.

[23] I. Shlyakhter. Generating effective symmetry-breaking predicates for search problems. *Discrete Applied Mathematics*, 155(12):1539–1548, 2007. URL `http://dx.doi.org/10.1016/j.dam.2005.10.018`.

[24] G. Smolka. The definition of kernel oz. Technical report, Saarländische Universitäts- und Landesbibliothek; Sonstige Einrichtungen. DFKI Deutsches Forschungszentrum für Künstliche Intelligenz, 1994. URL `urn:nbn:de:bsz:291-scidok-37290`.

[25] G. Sutcliffe and C. B. Suttner. The CADE ATP system competition. In D. A. Basin and M. Rusinowitch, editors, *IJCAR*, volume 3097 of *Lecture Notes in Computer Science*, pages 490–491. Springer, 2004. ISBN 3-540-22345-2.

[26] Taha and Sheard. MetaML and multi-stage programming with explicit annotations. *TCS: Theoretical Computer Science*, 248, 2000.

[27] W. Taha and T. Sheard. MetaML and multi-stage programming with, Feb. 09 1999. URL `http://citeseer.ist.psu.edu/516106.html; http://cse.ogi.edu/ walidt/paper-2.ps`.

[28] E. Torlak and D. Jackson. Kodkod: A relational model finder. In O. Grumberg and M. Huth, editors, *TACAS*, volume 4424 of *Lecture Notes in Computer Science*, pages 632–647. Springer, 2007. ISBN 978-3-540-71208-4.

[29] E. Torlak, A. Prof, and D. Jackson. Thesis: A constraint solver for software engineering: Finding models and cores of large relational specifications., Dec. 04 2008. URL `http://stuff.mit.edu/people/emina/papers/etorlak-cv.pdf`.

A. MP abstract instance functions

In this appendix are the missing functions for the abstract instance declarations in Figures 5 and 6.

```
mergeP f [] ys = ys
mergeP f xs [] = xs
mergeP f ((x,n):xs)((y,m):ys)=
 case compare x y of
  EQ -> case (f n m) of
         0 -> mergeP f xs ys
         i -> (x,i):mergeP f xs ys
  LT -> (x,n):
        mergeP f xs ((y,m):ys)
  GT -> (y,m):
        mergeP f ((x,n):xs) ys

combine oper(t,b)[] = []
combine oper(t,m)((s,n):xs)| t==s = (t,oper m n): xs
combine oper(t,m)((s,n):xs)=(s,n):combine oper(t,m)xs

mergeL oper [] ys = ys
mergeL oper ((z,m):xs) ys =
  mergeL oper xs (combine oper (z,m) ys)

instance NumLike (MExp Int) where
  liftI n = Term [] n
```

```
  (+) (Term [] a) (Term [] b) = Term [] (a+b)
  (+) (Term [] a) (Term ys b) = Term ys (a+b)
  (+) (Term xs a) (Term [] b) = Term xs (a+b)
  (+) (Term xs a) (Term ys b)
      = Term (mergeP (+) xs ys) (a+b)

instance Compare (MExp Int) [Rel Int]  where
  (<=) (Term [] a) (Term [] b) =
       if (a <= b) then [TAUT] else [UNSAT]
  (<=) (Term [] a) (Term xs b) =
       [RANGE xs (Range (LtEQ(a-b)) PlusInf)]
  (<=) (Term xs a) (Term [] b) =
       [RANGE xs (Range MinusInf (LtEQ (b-a)))]
  (<=) (Term xs a) (Term ys b) =
       [RANGE (mergeP (+) xs (negPoly ys))
              (Range MinusInf (LtEQ (b-a)))]

instance BoolLike [Rel Int] where
  liftB True = [TAUT]
  liftB False =[UNSAT]
  true = [TAUT]
  false = [UNSAT]
  (&&) xs ys = help (sort xs) (sort ys)
       where help (UNSAT:_) ys = [UNSAT]
             help xs (UNSAT:_) = [UNSAT]
             help (TAUT: xs) ys = help xs ys
             help xs (TAUT: ys) = help xs ys
             help [] ys = ys
             help xs [] = xs
             help (RANGE x a:xs) (RANGE y b:ys)
               | x P.== y
               = RANGE x (intersectRange a b):
                 help xs ys
             help (RANGE x a:xs)(ys@(RANGE y b:_))
               | x < y
               = RANGE x a:(help xs ys)
             help (xs@(RANGE x a:_))(RANGE y b:ys)
               | x > y
               = RANGE y b:(help xs ys)


instance BoolLike b =>
         SetLike (BitVector b) where
  create d xs =
     BV d [(t,liftB(elem t xs)) | t <- tuples d]
  select p (BV d xs) =
     BV d [(x, liftB (p x)) | (x,b) <- xs]
  proj3of3 (BV (D3 _ _ d) xs) =
     BV (D1 d)
        (mergeL (||)
               [(z,b) | ((x,y,z),b) <- xs]
               [(x,false) | x <- d])
  join (BV (D2 a b) xs)(BV (D2 _ c) ys)= BV d3 ans
    where d3 = D3 a b c
          ans = mergeL (||)
                   [ ((a,b,c),p&&q)
                   | ((a,b),p) <- xs
                   , ((x,c),q) <- ys
                   , x P.== a ]
                   [(t,false)| t <- tuples d3]
```

B. Staging type inference

In this section we provide further details of the staging type-inference process discussed in Paragraph 4 of Section 4. Lets start with a description of syntax. I keep everything very simple here. The real language has more, but this simple version extends naturally.

```
constants:      i ::= {..., -1,0 +1, ...}
                b ::= {True,False}
```

```
class library: A ::= NumLike t    | BoolLike t
                   | Compare t t | SetLike t

types:         T,t ::= Int | Bool | t -> t | x

schemes:       S ::= forall xs . A => T

terms:         E,f,e ::=  v | f e | i | v#A | b
```

Each class library has a number of overloaded methods. See Figure 3 for details. In the staging type-inference process, we will need to compute a type from an overloaded operator and a class library.

```
libType:: v -> A -> T
libType (+)   (NumLike t)    = t -> (t -> t)
libType liftI (NumLike t)    = Int -> t
libType (==)  (Compare t b) = t -> (t -> t)

instan (forall xs . A => T) = (A[ts/xs],T[ts/xs])
```

Where the `ts` in `instan` are fresh type variables. The staging type-inference process is a syntax directed walk over a term in the presence of an environment, `s:: v -> S`, that maps variable names to schemes. The judgment `s |- E --> (E',T)` means, under `s` the term `E` has type `T`, and reconstructs to `E'`. The process is strongly reminiscent of type inference in the presence of class constraints[13] and search based binding time analysis[22].

```
------------------------------------------ LIB
s |-  x#A --> (X,libType x A)


fresh t
------------------------------------------ INT
s |-  i     --> (liftI#(NumLike t) i, t)


fresh t
------------------------------------------ BOOL
s |-  b     --> (liftB#(BoolLike t) b, t)


instan(s v) --> (C,t)
------------------------------------------ VAR
s |- v   -->   (v#C v,t)


fresh w
unify dom xt
s |- x --> (x',xt)
s |- f --> (f',d -> r)
t = (f' x')
------------------------------------------ APP
s |- f x --> (cast xt d r)
 where cast I d r = (liftI#(NumLike w) t,w)
       cast B d r = (liftB#(BoolLike w) t,w)
       cast n d r = (f' x',r)
```

Three points are worth making. First, in the rules `INT` and `BOOL` every constant is lifted to an overloaded type. Second, in the rule `VAR` every overloaded variable is instantiated and lifted to a fresh type. Third, in the rule `APP` if an argument of an application has a concrete type (`I` for `Int` and `B` for `Bool`), then the reconstructed call is lifted to a fresh type.

Transporting Functions across Ornaments

Pierre-Evariste Dagand Conor McBride

Mathematically Structured Programming group
University of Strathclyde
{dagand,conor}@cis.strath.ac.uk

Abstract

Programming with dependent types is a blessing and a curse. It is a blessing to be able to bake invariants into the definition of datatypes: we can finally write correct-by-construction software. However, this extreme accuracy is also a curse: a datatype is the combination of a structuring medium together with a special purpose logic. These domain-specific logics hamper any effort of code reuse among similarly structured data. In this paper, we exorcise our datatypes by adapting the notion of ornament to our universe of inductive families. We then show how code reuse can be achieved by ornamenting functions. Using these functional ornaments, we capture the relationship between functions such as the addition of natural numbers and the concatenation of lists. With this knowledge, we demonstrate how the implementation of the former informs the implementation of the latter: the user can ask the definition of addition to be lifted to lists and she will only be asked the details necessary to carry on adding lists rather than numbers. Our presentation is formalised in a type theory with a universe of datatypes and all our constructions have been implemented as generic programs, requiring no extension to the type theory.

Categories and Subject Descriptors D.1.1 [*Programming Techniques*]: Applicative (Functional) Programming

Keywords Dependent types, Datatype, Ornament

1. Introduction

Imagine designing a library for a ML-like language. For instance, we start with natural numbers and their operations, then we move to binary trees, then rose trees, etc. It is the garden of Eden: datatypes are data-*structures*, each coming with its optimised set of operations. If, tempted by a snake, we move to a language with richer datatypes, such as a dependently typed language, we enter the Augean stables. Where we used to have binary trees, now we have complete binary trees, red-black trees, AVL trees, and countless other variants. Worse, we have to duplicate code across these tree-like datatypes: because they are defined upon this common binarily branching structure, a lot of computationally identical operations will have to be duplicated for the type-checker to be satisfied.

Since the ML days, datatypes have evolved: besides providing an organising *structure* for computation, they are now offering more *control* over what is a valid result. With richer datatypes, the programmer can enforce invariants on top of the data-structures. In such a system, programmers strive to express the correctness of programs in their types: a well typed program is correct *by construction*, the proof of correctness being reduced to type-checking.

A simple yet powerful recipe to obtain these richer datatypes is to *index* the data-structure. These datatypes have originally been studied in the context of type theory under the name of *inductive families* [Dybjer 1994; Morris et al. 2009]. Inductive families made it to mainstream functional programming with Generalised Algebraic Data-Types [Xi et al. 2003], a subset of inductive families for which type inference is decidable. Refinement types [Freeman and Pfenning 1991; Swamy et al. 2011] are another technique to equip data-structures with rich invariants. Atkey et al. [2011] have shown how refinement types relate to inductive families, and Bernardy and Lasson [2011] establish a connection with realisability.

However, these carefully crafted datatypes are a threat to any library design: the same data-*structure* is used for logically incompatible purposes. This explosion of specialised datatypes is overwhelming: these objects are too specialised to fit in a global library. Yet, because they share this common structure, many operations on them are extremely similar, if not exactly the same. To address this issue, McBride [2012] developed *ornaments*, describing how one datatype can be enriched into others *with the same structure*. Such structure-preserving transformations take two forms: one can *extend* the initial type with more information – such as obtaining Maybe_A from Bool or List_A from Nat:

```
data Bool : SET where                 data Nat : SET where
  Bool ∋ true                           Nat ∋ 0
       | false                              | suc (n : Nat)

        ⇓Maybe-Orn                             ⇓List-Orn
data Maybe [A : SET] : SET where      data List [A : SET] : SET where
  Maybe_A ∋ just (a : A)                List_A ∋ nil
          | nothing                            | cons (a : A)(as : List_A)
```

Or one can *refine* the indexing of the initial type by a finer discipline – e.g., obtaining Fin by indexing Nat with a bound n:

```
data Nat : SET where
  Nat ∋ 0
      | suc (n : Nat)

        ⇓Fin-Orn
data Fin (n : Nat) : SET where
  Fin (n = suc n′) ∋ f0 (n′ : Nat)
                   | fsuc (n′ : Nat)(fn : Fin n′)
```

One can also do both at the same time – such as extending Nat into a List_A while refining the index to match the length of the list:

```
data Nat : SET where
  Nat ∋ 0
      | suc (n : Nat)

        ⇓Vec-Orn
data Vec [A : SET](n : Nat) : SET where
  Vec_A (n = 0)      ∋ nil
  Vec_A (n = suc n′) ∋ cons (n′ : Nat)(a : A)(vs : Vec_A n′)
```


ICFP'12, September 9–15, 2012, Copenhagen, Denmark.

Note that we declare datatype parameters $[A : \text{SET}]$ in brackets and datatype indices $(n : \mathsf{Nat})$ in parentheses. We make equational constraints on the latter only when needed, and explicitly.

Because of their constructive nature, ornaments are not merely identifying similar structures: they give an effective recipe to build new datatypes from old, guaranteeing by construction that the structure is preserved. Hence, we can obtain a plethora of new datatypes with minimal effort. Whilst we now have a good handle on the transformation of individual datatypes, we are still facing a major reusability issue: a datatype often comes equipped with a set of operations. Ornamenting this datatype, we have to entirely re-implement many similar operations. For example, the datatype Nat comes with operations such as addition and subtraction. When defining List_A as an ornament of Nat, it seems natural to transport some structure-preserving function of Nat to List_A, such as moving from addition of natural numbers to concatenation of lists:

$$\begin{array}{llll} (m:\mathsf{Nat}) + (n:\mathsf{Nat}) & : & \mathsf{Nat} \\ 0 \quad + \quad n & \mapsto & n \\ (\mathsf{suc}\, m) \quad + \quad n & \mapsto & \mathsf{suc}\,(m+n) \end{array}$$

$$\Downarrow$$

$$\begin{array}{lll} (xs:\mathsf{List}_A) \mathbin{+\!\!+} (ys:\mathsf{List}_A) & : & \mathsf{List}_A \\ \mathsf{nil} \quad \mathbin{+\!\!+} \quad ys & \mapsto & ys \\ (\mathsf{cons}\, a\, xs) \mathbin{+\!\!+} \quad ys & \mapsto & \mathsf{cons}\, a\, (xs \mathbin{+\!\!+} ys) \end{array}$$

Or moving from subtraction of natural numbers to dropping the prefix of a list:

$$\begin{array}{lll} (m:\mathsf{Nat}) - (n:\mathsf{Nat}) & : & \mathsf{Nat} \\ 0 \quad - \quad n & \mapsto & 0 \\ m \quad - \quad 0 & \mapsto & m \\ (\mathsf{suc}\, m) \quad - \quad (\mathsf{suc}\, n) & \mapsto & m - n \end{array}$$

$$\Downarrow$$

$$\begin{array}{lll} \mathsf{drop}\ (xs:\mathsf{List}_A)\ (n:\mathsf{Nat}) & : & \mathsf{List}_A \\ \mathsf{drop}\ \mathsf{nil}\ \quad n & \mapsto & \mathsf{nil} \\ \mathsf{drop}\ xs\ \quad 0 & \mapsto & xs \\ \mathsf{drop}\ (\mathsf{cons}\, a\, xs)\ (\mathsf{suc}\, n) & \mapsto & \mathsf{drop}\, xs\, n \end{array}$$

More interestingly, the function we start with may involve several datatypes, each of which may be ornamented differently. In this paper, we develop the notion of *functional ornament* as a generalisation of ornaments to functions:

- We adapt ornaments to our universe of datatypes [Chapman et al. 2010] in Section 3. This presentation benefits greatly from our ability to inspect indices when defining datatypes. This allows us to consider ornaments which *delete* index-determined information, yielding a key simplification in the construction of an algebraic ornament from an ornamental algebra ;
- We describe how functions can be transported through functional ornaments: 'deletion' allows us a contrasting approach to Ko and Gibbons [2011], internalising proof obligations. First, we manually work through an example in Section 2. Then, we formalise the concept of functional ornament by a universe construction in Section 4. Based on this universe, we establish the connection between a base function (such as $\_+\_$ and $\_-\_$) and its ornamented version (such as, respectively, $\_\mathbin{+\!\!+}\_$ and drop). Within this framework, we redevelop the example of Section 2 with all the automation offered by our constructions ;
- In Section 5, we provide further support to drive the computer into lifting functions semi-automatically. As we can see from our examples above, the lifted functions often follow the same recursion pattern and return similar constructors: with a few generic constructions, we shall remove further clutter and code duplication from our libraries.

$$\begin{array}{llll} (m:\mathsf{Nat}) < (n:\mathsf{Nat}) & : & \mathsf{Bool} \\ m \quad < \quad 0 & \mapsto & \mathsf{false} \\ 0 \quad < \quad \mathsf{suc}\, n & \mapsto & \mathsf{true} \\ \mathsf{suc}\, m \quad < \quad \mathsf{suc}\, n & \mapsto & m < n \end{array}$$

$$\Downarrow ?$$

$$\begin{array}{lll} \mathsf{lookup}\ (m:\mathsf{Nat})\ (xs:\mathsf{List}_A) & : & \mathsf{Maybe}_A \\ \mathsf{lookup}\ m\ \quad \mathsf{nil} & \mapsto & \mathsf{nothing} \\ \mathsf{lookup}\ 0\ \quad (\mathsf{cons}\, a\, xs) & \mapsto & \mathsf{just}\, a \\ \mathsf{lookup}\ (\mathsf{suc}\, n)\ (\mathsf{cons}\, a\, xs) & \mapsto & \mathsf{lookup}\, n\, xs \end{array}$$

Figure 1. Implementation of $\_<\_$ and lookup

This paper is an exercise in constructive mathematics: upon identifying an isomorphism, we shall look at it with our constructive glasses and obtain an effective procedure that lets us cross the isomorphism. In this paper, we put a strong emphasis on the programming aspect: we shall only hint at the isomorphisms through concrete examples and let the reader consult the companion technical report for the actual mathematical proofs.

We shall write our code in a syntax inspired by the Epigram [McBride and McKinna 2004] programming language. In particular, we make use of the *by* ($\Leftarrow$) and *return* ($\mapsto$) programming gadgets, further extending them to account for the automatic lifting of functions. For brevity, we write pattern-matching definitions when the recursion pattern is evident and unremarkable. We shall also make ample use of mathematical notations and symbols in the programming language itself (in particular, mixfix operators), hence appealing to our reader's eye for mathematics, rather than to the intricate details of a particular formal syntax. Like ML, unbound variables in type definitions are universally quantified, further abating syntactic noise. The syntax of datatype definitions draws upon the ML tradition as well: its novelty will be presented by way of examples in Section 3. All the constructions presented in this paper have been modelled in Agda, using only standard inductive definitions and two levels of universe. The formalisation and technical report are available on Dagand's website.

2. From $\_<\_$ to lookup, manually

There is an astonishing resemblance between the comparison function $\_<\_$ on natural numbers and the list lookup function (Fig. 1). The similarity is not merely at the level of types but also in their implementation: their definitions follow the same pattern of recursion (first, case analysis on the second element; then induction on the first element) and they both return a failure value (false and nothing respectively) in the first case analysis and a success value (true and just respectively) in the base case of the induction.

This raises the question: what *exactly* is the relation between $\_<\_$ and lookup? Also, could we use the implementation of $\_<\_$ to guide the construction of lookup? First, let us work out the relation at the type level. To this end, we use ornaments to explain how each individual datatype has been promoted when going from $\_<\_$ to lookup:

$$\begin{array}{lllllll} \_<\_ & : & \mathsf{Nat} & \to & \mathsf{Nat} & \to & \mathsf{Bool} \\ & & \mathsf{idO}_{\mathsf{Nat}}\Downarrow & & \mathsf{List\text{-}Orn}\Downarrow & & \mathsf{Maybe\text{-}Orn}\Downarrow \\ \mathsf{lookup} & : & \mathsf{Nat} & \to & \mathsf{List}_A & \to & \mathsf{Maybe}_A \end{array}$$

Note that the first argument is ornamented to itself, or put differently, it has been ornamented by the identity ornament.

Each of these ornaments come with a forgetful map, computed from the ornamental algebra:

$$\begin{array}{llll} \mathsf{length}\ (as : \mathsf{List}_A) & : & \mathsf{Nat} \\ \mathsf{length}\ \ \mathsf{nil} & \mapsto & 0 \\ \mathsf{length}\ (\mathsf{cons}\ a\ as) & \mapsto & \mathsf{suc}\ (\mathsf{length}\ as) \end{array} \qquad \begin{array}{llll} \mathsf{isJust}\ (m : \mathsf{Maybe}_A) & : & \mathsf{Bool} \\ \mathsf{isJust}\ \ \mathsf{nothing} & \mapsto & \mathsf{false} \\ \mathsf{isJust}\ \ (\mathsf{just}\ a) & \mapsto & \mathsf{true} \end{array}$$

Using these forgetful map, the relation, at the computational level, between $\_ < \_$ and lookup is uniquely established by their ornamentation. This relation is captured by the *coherence* property: $\forall n : \mathsf{Nat}. \forall xs : \mathsf{List}_A.\ \mathsf{isJust}\ (\mathsf{lookup}\ n\ xs) \equiv n < \mathsf{length}\ xs$.

Let us settle the vocabulary at this stage. We call the function we start with the *base function* (here, $\_ < \_$), its type being the *base type* (here, $\mathsf{Nat} \to \mathsf{Nat} \to \mathsf{Bool}$). The richer function type built by ornamenting the individual pieces is called the *functional ornament* (here, $\mathsf{Nat} \to \mathsf{List}_A \to \mathsf{Maybe}_A$). A function inhabiting this type is called a *lifting* (here, lookup). A lifting is said to be *coherent* if it satisfies the coherence property. It is crucial to understand that the coherence of a lifting is relative to a given functional ornament: the same base function ornamented differently would give rise to different coherence properties.

We now have a better grasp of the relation between the base function and its lifting. However, lookup remains to be implemented while making sure that it satisfies the coherence property. Traditionally, one would stop here: one would implement lookup and prove the coherence as a theorem. This works rather well in a system like Coq [The Coq Development Team] as it offers a powerful theorem proving environment. It does not work so well in a system like Agda [Norell 2007] that does not offer tactics to its users, forcing them to write explicit proof terms. It would not work at all in Haskell with GADTs, which has no notion of proof.

However, we are not satisfied by this laborious approach: if we have dependent types, why should we use them only for *proofs*, as an afterthought? We should rather write a lookup function *correct by construction*: by implementing a more precisely indexed version of lookup, the user can drive the index-level computations to unfold, hence making the type-checker verify the necessary invariants. We believe that this is how it should be: computers should replace proofs by computation; humans should drive computers. The other way around – where humans are coerced into computing for computers – may seem surreal, yet it corresponds to the current situation in most proof systems.

To get the computer to work for us, we would rather implement the function ilookup:

$$\begin{array}{llll} \mathsf{ilookup}\ (m : \mathsf{Nat})\ (vs : \mathsf{Vec}_A\ n) & & : & \mathsf{IMaybe}_A\ (m < n) \\ \mathsf{ilookup}\ \ m & \mathsf{nil} & \mapsto & \mathsf{nothing} \\ \mathsf{ilookup}\ \ 0 & (\mathsf{cons}\ a\ vs) & \mapsto & \mathsf{just}\ a \\ \mathsf{ilookup}\ (\mathsf{suc}\ m) & (\mathsf{cons}\ a\ vs) & \mapsto & \mathsf{ilookup}\ m\ vs \end{array}$$

Where IMaybe_A is Maybe_A indexed by its truth as computed by isJust. It is defined as follows[1]:

$$\begin{array}{l} \mathbf{data}\ \mathsf{IMaybe}\ [A : \mathrm{SET}](b : \mathsf{Bool}) : \mathrm{SET}\ \mathbf{where} \\ \quad \mathsf{IMaybe}_A\ \mathsf{true} \ni \mathsf{just}\ (a : A) \\ \quad \mathsf{IMaybe}_A\ \mathsf{false} \ni \mathsf{nothing} \end{array}$$

This comes with the following forgetful map:

$$\begin{array}{llll} \mathsf{forgetIMaybe}\ (mba : \mathsf{IMaybe}_A\ b) & & : & (ma : \mathsf{Maybe}_A) \times \mathsf{isJust}\ ma \equiv b \\ \mathsf{forgetIMaybe} & (\mathsf{just}\ a) & \mapsto & (\mathsf{just}\ a, \mathsf{refl}) \\ \mathsf{forgetIMaybe} & \mathsf{nothing} & \mapsto & (\mathsf{nothing}, \mathsf{refl}) \end{array}$$

The rationale behind ilookup is to *index* the types of lookup by their unornamented version, i.e. the arguments and result of $\_ < \_$. Hence, we can make sure that the result computed by ilookup respects the output of $\_ < \_$ on the unornamented indices: the result is correct *by indexing*! The type of ilookup is naturally derived from the ornamentation of $\_ < \_$ into lookup and is uniquely determined by the functional ornament we start with. Expounding further our vocabulary, we call *coherent liftings* these finely indexed functions that are correct by construction.

Ko and Gibbons [2011] use ornaments to specify the coherence requirements for functional liftings, but we work the other way around, using ornaments to internalise coherence requirements. From ilookup, we can extract both lookup and its proof of correctness *without having written any proof term ourselves*:

$$\begin{array}{llll} \mathsf{lookup}\ (m : \mathsf{Nat})\ (xs : \mathsf{List}_A) & & : & \mathsf{Maybe}_A \\ \mathsf{lookup}\ \ m & xs & \mapsto & \\ \quad \pi_0(\mathsf{forgetIMaybe}\ (\mathsf{ilookup}\ m\ (\mathsf{makeVec}\ xs))) \end{array}$$

$$\begin{array}{llll} \mathsf{cohLookup}\ (n : \mathsf{Nat})\ (xs : \mathsf{List}_A) & & : & \\ \quad \mathsf{isJust}\ (\mathsf{lookup}\ n\ xs) \equiv n < \mathsf{length}\ xs \\ \mathsf{cohLookup}\ \ m & xs & \mapsto & \\ \quad \pi_1(\mathsf{forgetIMaybe}\ (\mathsf{ilookup}\ m\ (\mathsf{makeVec}\ xs))) \end{array}$$

where $\mathsf{makeVec} : (xs : \mathsf{List}_A) \to \mathsf{Vec}_A\ (\mathsf{length}\ xs)$ simply turns a list into a vector of the corresponding length.

With this example, we have manually unfolded the key steps of the construction of a lifting of $\_ < \_$. Let us recapitulate each steps:

- Start with a *base function*, here $\_ < \_ : \mathsf{Nat} \to \mathsf{Nat} \to \mathsf{Bool}$
- Ornament its inductive components as desired, here Nat to List_A and Bool to Maybe_A in order to describe the desired lifting, here $\mathsf{lookup} : \mathsf{Nat} \to \mathsf{List}_A \to \mathsf{Maybe}_A$ satisfying $\forall n : \mathsf{Nat}. \forall xs : \mathsf{List}_A.\ \mathsf{isJust}\ (\mathsf{lookup}\ n\ xs) \equiv n < \mathsf{length}\ xs$
- Implement a carefully indexed version of the lifting, here $\mathsf{ilookup} : (m : \mathsf{Nat})(vs : \mathsf{Vec}_A\ n) \to \mathsf{IMaybe}_A\ (m < n)$
- Derive the lifting, here lookup, and its coherence proof, without proving any theorem

This manual unfolding of the lifting is instructive: it involves a lot of constructions on datatypes (here, the datatypes List_A and Maybe_A) as well as on functions (here, the type of ilookup, the definition of lookup and its coherence proof). Yet, it feels like a lot of these constructions could be automated. In the next Section, we shall build the machinery to describe these constructions and obtain them *within* the type theory itself.

3. A universe of datatypes and their ornaments

In dependently typed systems such as Coq or Agda, datatypes are an external entity: each datatype definition extends the type-theory with new introduction and elimination forms. The validity of datatypes is guaranteed by a positivity-checker that is part of the meta-theory of the proof system. A consequence is that, from within the type theory, it is not possible to create or manipulate datatype definitions, as they belong to the meta-theory.

3.1 A closed theory of datatypes

In our previous work [Chapman et al. 2010], we have shown how to internalise inductive families into type theory. The practical impact of this approach is that we can manipulate datatype declarations as first-class objects. We can program over datatype declarations and, in particular, we can compute new datatypes from old. This is particularly useful to formalise the notion of ornament entirely within the type theory. This also has a theoretical impact: we do not need to prove meta-theoretical properties of our constructions, we can work in our type theory and use its logic as our formal system.

Note that our results are not restricted to this setting where datatype definitions are internalised: all our constructions could be justified at the meta-level and then be syntactically presented in a language, such as, say, Agda, Coq, or Haskell with GADTs. Working with an internalised presentation, we can simply avoid these two levels of logic and work in the logic provided by the type theory itself.

[1] Note that we have overloaded the constructors of Maybe and IMaybe: for a bi-directional type-checker, there is no ambiguity as constructors are checked against their type.

$$
\begin{array}{l}
\textsf{data IDesc}\ [I : \textsc{Set}] : \textsc{Set}_1\ \textsf{where} \\
\quad \textsf{IDesc}\ I \ni \textsf{'var}\,(i : I) \\
\qquad\qquad\quad \mid \textsf{'1} \\
\qquad\qquad\quad \mid \textsf{'}\Pi\,(S : \textsc{Set})\,(T : S \to \textsf{IDesc}\ I) \\
\qquad\qquad\quad \mid \textsf{'}\Sigma\,(S : \textsc{Set})\,(T : S \to \textsf{IDesc}\ I)
\end{array}
$$

$$
\begin{array}{lll}
[\![(D : \textsf{IDesc}\ I)]\!]\ (X : I \to \textsc{Set}) & : & \textsc{Set} \\
[\![\textsf{'var}\ i]\!]\ X & \mapsto & X\ i \\
[\![\textsf{'1}]\!]\ X & \mapsto & \mathbb{1} \\
[\![\textsf{'}\Pi\ S\ T]\!]\ X & \mapsto & (s : S) \to [\![T\ s]\!]\ X \\
[\![\textsf{'}\Sigma\ S\ T]\!]\ X & \mapsto & (s : S) \times [\![T\ s]\!]\ X
\end{array}
$$

Figure 2. Universe of inductive families

For the sake of completeness, let us recall a few definitions and results from our previous work. As in previous work, our requirements on the type theory are minimal: we will need Σ-, Π-types, and at least two universes. For convenience, we require a type of finite sets, which lets us build collections of labels[2]. We also need a pre-existing notion of propositional equality, upon which we make no assumption. We internalise the inductive families by a universe construction (Fig. 2): an indexed datatype is described by a function from its index to codes. The codes are then interpreted to build the fix-point:

$$
\begin{array}{l}
\textsf{data}\ \mu\ [D : I \to \textsf{IDesc}\ I](i : I) : \textsc{Set}\ \textsf{where} \\
\quad \mu\ D\ i \ni \textsf{in}\,(xs : [\![D\ i]\!]\ (\mu\ D))
\end{array}
$$

For readability purposes, we use an informal notation to declare datatypes. This notation is strongly inspired by Agda's datatype declarations. Note that these definitions can always be turned into IDesc codes: when defining a datatype T, we will denote T-Desc the code it elaborates to. Similarly, we denote T-elim and T-case the induction principle and case analysis operators associated with T. For instance, Nat-case corresponds to case analysis over natural numbers (either 0 or suc) while Nat-elim corresponds to standard induction on natural numbers. These operations can be implemented by generic programming, along the lines of McBride et al. [2004]. Formalising the elaboration of datatypes definitions down to code is beyond the scope of this paper. However, it is simple enough to be understood with a few examples. Three key ideas are at play.

First, non-indexed datatypes definitions follow the ML tradition: we name the datatype and then comes a choice of constructors. For example, List and Brouwer ordinals would be written and elaborated as follows:

$$
\begin{array}{l}
\textsf{data List}\ [A : \textsc{Set}] : \textsc{Set}\ \textsf{where} \\
\quad \textsf{List}_A \ni \textsf{nil} \\
\qquad\qquad \mid \textsf{cons}\,(a : A)(as : \textsf{List}_A)
\end{array}
$$

$$\wr$$

$$
\begin{array}{l}
\textsf{List-Desc}\ (A : \textsc{Set})\ (x : \mathbb{1}) \ :\ \textsf{IDesc}\ \mathbb{1} \\
\textsf{List-Desc}\ A\ * \mapsto \textsf{'}\Sigma \left\{ \begin{array}{l} \textsf{'nil} \\ \textsf{'cons} \end{array} \right\} \left\{ \begin{array}{ll} \textsf{'nil} & \mapsto \textsf{'1} \\ \textsf{'cons} & \mapsto \textsf{'}\Sigma\ A\ \lambda\_.\ \textsf{'var}\ * \end{array} \right\}
\end{array}
$$

$$
\begin{array}{l}
\textsf{data Ord} : \textsc{Set}\ \textsf{where} \\
\quad \textsf{Ord} \ni \textsf{0} \\
\qquad\quad \mid \textsf{suc}\,(o : \textsf{Ord}) \\
\qquad\quad \mid \textsf{lim}\,(l : \textsf{Nat} \to \textsf{Ord})
\end{array}
$$

$$\wr$$

$$
\begin{array}{l}
\textsf{Ord-Desc}\ (x : \mathbb{1}) \ :\ \textsf{IDesc}\ \mathbb{1} \\
\textsf{Ord-Desc}\ * \mapsto \textsf{'}\Sigma \left\{ \begin{array}{l} \textsf{'0} \\ \textsf{'suc} \\ \textsf{'lim} \end{array} \right\} \left\{ \begin{array}{ll} \textsf{'0} & \mapsto \textsf{'1} \\ \textsf{'suc} & \mapsto \textsf{'var}\ * \\ \textsf{'lim} & \mapsto \textsf{'}\Pi\ \textsf{Nat}\ \lambda\_.\ \textsf{'var}\ * \end{array} \right\}
\end{array}
$$

[2] We denote finite sets of tagged elements by {'x, 'y, 'z, ...}. Their elimination principle consists of an exhaustive case enumeration and is denoted by {'x $\mapsto vx$, 'y $\mapsto vy$, 'z $\mapsto vz$, ...}. If the tags are vertically aligned, we shall skip the separating comma.

Secondly, indexed datatypes can be defined following the Agda convention: indices are *constrained* to some particular value. For example, Vec could be defined by constraining the index to be 0 in the nil case and suc n' for some n' : Nat in the cons case:

$$
\begin{array}{l}
\textsf{data Vec}\ [A : \textsc{Set}](n : \textsf{Nat}) : \textsc{Set}\ \textsf{where} \\
\quad \textsf{Vec}_A\ \ (n = 0) \quad\ \ni \textsf{nil} \\
\quad \textsf{Vec}_A\ (n = \textsf{suc}\ n') \ni \textsf{cons}\,(n' : \textsf{Nat})(a : A)(vs : \textsf{Vec}_A\ n')
\end{array}
$$

$$\wr$$

$$
\begin{array}{l}
\textsf{Vec-Desc}\ (A : \textsc{Set})\ (n : \textsf{Nat}) \ :\ \textsf{IDesc Nat} \\
\textsf{Vec-Desc}\ A\ n \mapsto \\
\quad \textsf{'}\Sigma \left\{ \begin{array}{l} \textsf{'nil} \\ \textsf{'cons} \end{array} \right\} \left\{ \begin{array}{ll} \textsf{'vnil} & \mapsto \textsf{'}\Sigma\,(n \equiv 0)\ \lambda\_.\ \textsf{'1} \\ \textsf{'vcons} & \mapsto \textsf{'}\Sigma\ \textsf{Nat}\ \lambda n'.\ \textsf{'}\Sigma\,(n \equiv \textsf{suc}\ n')\lambda\_. \\ & \qquad \textsf{'}\Sigma\ A\ \lambda\_.\ \textsf{'var}\ n' \end{array} \right\}
\end{array}
$$

The elaboration naturally captures the constraints on indices by using propositional equality. In the case of Vec, we first abstract over the index n, introduce the choice of constructors with the first 'Σ and then, once constructors have been chosen, we restrict n to its valid value(s): 0 in the first case and suc n' for some n' in the second case. Hence the placement of the equality constraints in the above definition: after the constructor is chosen, we first introduce a fresh variable and then constrain the index with it. If no fresh variable needs to be introduced, we directly constrain the index.

Thirdly, we can compute over indices: here, we make use of the crucial property that a datatype definition is a *function* from index to IDesc codes. Hence, our notation should reflect this ability to define datatypes as functions on their index. For instance, inspired by Brady et al. [2004], an alternative presentation of vector would match on the index to determine the constructor to be presented, hence removing the need for constraints:

$$
\begin{array}{l}
\textsf{data Vec}\ [A : \textsc{Set}](n : \textsf{Nat}) : \textsc{Set}\ \textsf{where} \\
\quad \textsf{Vec}_A \qquad n \quad\ \Leftarrow \textsf{Nat-case}\ n \\
\qquad \textsf{Vec}_A \quad\ 0 \qquad \ni \textsf{nil} \\
\qquad \textsf{Vec}_A\ (\textsf{suc}\ n) \ni \textsf{cons}\,(a : A)(vs : \textsf{Vec}_A\ n)
\end{array}
$$

$$\wr$$

$$
\begin{array}{l}
\textsf{Vec-Desc}\ (A : \textsc{Set})\ (n : \textsf{Nat}) \ :\ \textsf{IDesc Nat} \\
\textsf{Vec-Desc}\ A\ n \mapsto \textsf{Nat-case}\ n\ (\lambda\_.\ \textsf{IDesc Nat}) \\
\qquad\qquad\qquad\qquad\qquad \textsf{'1} \\
\qquad\qquad\qquad\qquad\qquad (\lambda n.\ \textsf{'}\Sigma\ A\ \lambda\_.\ \textsf{'var}\ n)
\end{array}
$$

In order to be fully explicit about computations, we use here the Epigram [McBride and McKinna 2004] *by* ($\Leftarrow$) programming gadget, which let us appeal to any elimination principle with a syntax close to pattern-matching. However, standard pattern-matching constructions [Coquand 1992; Norell 2007] would work just as well. Again, we shall write pattern-matching definitions when the recursion pattern is unremarkable.

Our syntax departs radically from the one adopted by Coq, Agda, and GADTs in Haskell. It is crucial to understand that this is but reflecting the actual semantics of inductive families: we can *compute* over indices, not merely constrain them to be what we would like. With our syntax, we give the user the ability to write these *functions*: the reader should now understand a datatype definition as a special kind of function definition, taking indices as arguments, potentially computing over them, and eventually emitting a choice of constructors.

3.2 Ornaments

Originally, McBride [2012] presented the notion of ornament for a universe where the indices a constructor targets could be enforced *only* by equality constraints. As a consequence, in that simpler setting, computing types from indices was impossible. We shall now adapt the original definition to our setting.

Just as the original definition, an ornament is defined upon a base datatype – specified by a function $D : I \to \textsf{IDesc}\ I$ – and indices are refined up to a reindexing function $re : J \to I$. The difference in our setting is that, just as the code of datatypes can be computed from the indices, we want the ornament to be computable from its J-index. Hence, an ornament is a function from $j : J$ to ornament codes describing the ornamentation of $D\ (re\ j)$:

$$\begin{aligned}&\mathsf{orn}(re_I : J \to I)(re_O : P \to O)(D : O \to \mathsf{IDesc}\ I) \ :\ \mathrm{SET}_1\\ &\mathsf{orn}\ re_I\ re_O\ D \ \mapsto\ (p : P) \to \mathsf{Orn}\ re_I\ (D\ (re_O\ p))\end{aligned}$$

As for the ornament codes themselves, they are similar to the original definition: we shall be able to *copy* the base datatype, *extend* it by inserting sets, or *refine* the indexing subject to the relation imposed by re. However, we also have the J-index in our context: following Brady's insight that *inductive families need not store their indices* [Brady et al. 2004], we could as well *delete* parts of a datatype definition as long as we can recover this information from the index. Hence, we obtain the following code[3]:

```
data Orn [re : J → I](D : IDesc I) : SET₁ where
  -- Extend with S:
  Orn re  D          ∋ insert (S : SET)(D⁺ : S → Orn re D)
  -- Refine index:
  Orn re  ('var i)   ∋ 'var (j : re⁻¹ i)
  -- Copy the original:
  Orn re  '1         ∋ '1
  Orn re  ('Π S T)   ∋ 'Π (T⁺ : (s : S) → Orn re (T s))
  Orn re  ('Σ S T)   ∋ 'Σ (T⁺ : (s : S) → Orn re (T s))
  -- Delete S:
                     | delete (replace : S)(T⁺ : Orn re (T replace))
```

Note that the recursive structure of the original data-type – as specified by $'\Pi$ – is preserved by the ornament: we have thus ensured, by construction, that the source datatype and its ornament have the same recursive structure. Being able to insert or delete $'\Pi$-quantifiers would defeat our purpose by making ambiguous the connection between the source datatype and its ornamented form.

Given an ornament, we can interpret it as the datatype it describes. The implementation consists in traversing the ornament code, introducing a $'\Sigma$ when inserting new data and computing the ornament at the replaced value when deleting some redundant data:

```
⟦(o : orn re_I re_O D)⟧orn (p : P)  :  IDesc J
⟦o⟧orn                      p    ↦  intOrn (D (re_O p)) (o p)        where
  intOrn(D : IDesc I)(O : Orn re D) : IDesc J
  intOrn  D   (insert S D⁺)  ↦  'Σ S λs. intOrn D (D⁺ s)
  intOrn  ('var (re j))  ('var (inv j))  ↦  'var j
  intOrn  '1  '1  ↦  '1
  intOrn  ('Π S T)  ('Π T⁺)  ↦  'Π S λs. intOrn (T s) (T⁺ s)
  intOrn  ('Σ S T)  ('Σ T⁺)  ↦  'Σ S λs. intOrn (T s) (T⁺ s)
  intOrn  ('Σ S T)  (delete replace T⁺)  ↦
      intOrn (T replace) (T⁺ replace)
```

Note that in the **delete** case, no $'\Sigma$ code is generated: the set S has been deleted from the original datatype. The witness of this existential is instead provided by replace.

Once again, we adopt an informal notation to describe ornaments conveniently. The idea is to simply mirror our **data** definition, adding **from** which datatype the ornament is defined. When specifying a constructor, we can then extend it with a new element using $[s : S]$ or delete an element originally named s by giving its value with $[s \triangleq \mathsf{value}]$. Some typical examples of extension are presented in Figure 3.

While the definition **Vec** in Figure 3 mirrors Agda's convention of constraining indices with equality, our definition of ornaments lets us define a version of **Vec** that does not store its indices:

```
data Vec [A : SET](n : Nat) from List_A where
  Vec_A   0        ∋ nil
  Vec_A   (suc n') ∋ cons (a : A)(vs : Vec_A n')
```

[3] The inverse image of a function is defined by:

```
data (⁻¹) [f : A → B](b : B) : SET where
  f⁻¹ (b = f a) ∋ inv (a : A)
```

```
data List [A : SET] from Nat where
  List_A ∋ nil
         | cons [a : A](as : List_A)

data Vec [A : SET](n : Nat) from List_A where
  Vec_A n ∋ nil [q : n ≡ 0]
          | cons [n' : Nat][q : n ≡ suc n'](a : A)(vs : Vec_A n')

data Fin (n : Nat) from Nat where
  Fin n ∋ f0 [n' : Nat][q : n ≡ suc n']
        | fsuc [n' : Nat][q : n ≡ suc n'](fn : Fin n')
```

Figure 3. Examples of ornament

Note that such a definition was unavailable in the basic presentation [McBride 2012]. Brady et al. [2004] call this operation *detagging*: the constructors of the datatype are determined by the index. The definition of **Fin** given in Figure 3 is also subject to an optimisation: by matching the index, we can avoid the duplication of n by deleting n' with the matched predecessor and deleting the resulting, obvious proof. Hence, **Fin** can be further ornamented to the optimised **Fin'**, which makes crucial use of deletion:

```
data Fin' (n : Nat) from Fin where
  Fin'  0       ∋ [b : 𝟘]                 -- no constructor
  Fin' (suc n)  ∋ f0 [n' ≜ n][q ≜ refl]
                | fsuc [n' ≜ n][q ≜ refl](fn : Fin' n')
```

Again, this definition was previously unavailable to us. Besides, we are making crucial use of the deletion ornament to avoid duplication. Brady et al. [2004] call this operation *forcing*: the content of the constructors – here n' and the constraint – are retrieved from the index, instead of being needlessly duplicated.

Just as the datatype declaration syntax was elaborated to **IDesc** codes, this high-level syntax is elaborated to ornament codes. A formal description of the translation is beyond the scope of this paper. Note that we require the order of constructors to be preserved, as their name might change from the original to the ornamented version. From the definition of an ornamented type T, we will assume the existence of its corresponding ornament code T-**Orn**.

As described by McBride [2012], every ornament induces an *ornamental algebra*: intuitively, an algebra that forgets the extra data, hence mapping the ornamented datatype back to its unornamented form. From an ornament $O : \mathsf{orn}\ re\ D$, there is a natural transformation from the ornamented functor down to the unornamented one, which we denote:

$$O\text{-}\mathsf{forgetNat} : (X : I \to \mathrm{SET})(j : J) \to [\![[\![O]\!]_{\mathsf{orn}} j]\!](X \circ re) \to [\![D(re\,j)]\!] X$$

Applied with $\mu\, D$ for X and post-composed with **in**, this natural transformation induces the ornamental algebra:

$$O\text{-}\mathsf{forgetAlg} : (j : J) \to [\![[\![O]\!]_{\mathsf{orn}}\ j]\!]\ (\mu\, D \circ re) \to \mu\, D\ (re\ j)$$

In turn, this algebra induces an ornamental forgetful map denoted:

$$O\text{-}\mathsf{forget} : (j : J) \to \mu\ [\![O]\!]_{\mathsf{orn}}\ j \to \mu\, D\ (re\ j)$$

We do not re-implement these functions here: it is straightforward to update the original definitions to our setting.

3.2.1 Algebraic ornaments

An important class of datatypes is constructed by *algebraic ornamentation* over a base datatype. The idea of an algebraic ornament is to index an inductive type by the result of a fold over the original data. From the code $D : I \to \mathsf{IDesc}\ I$ and an algebra $\alpha : (i : I) \to [\![D\ i]\!]\ X \to X\ i$, there is an ornament that defines a code $D^\alpha : (i : I) \times X\ i \to \mathsf{IDesc}\,(i : I) \times X\ i$ with the property that:

$$\mu\, D^\alpha\ (i, x) \cong (t : \mu\, D\ i) \times (\!|\alpha|\!)\ t \equiv x$$

We shall indiscriminately use D^α to refer to the ornament and the resulting datatype. Seen as a refinement type, the correctness property states that $\mu\, D^{\alpha}\,(i,x) \cong \{t \in \mu\, D\, i \mid (\!|\alpha|\!)\ t = x\}$. The type theoretic construction of D^{α} is described by McBride [2012]. We shall not reiterate it here, the implementation being essentially the same. A categorical presentation is also given in Atkey et al. [2011] that explores the connection with refinement types.

Constructively, the correctness property gives us two (mutually inverse) functions. The direction $\mu\, D^{\alpha}(i,x) \rightarrow (t : \mu\, D i) \times (\!|\alpha|\!)\ t \equiv x$ relies on the generic D^{α}-forget function to compute the first component of the pair and gives us the following theorem:

$$\mathsf{coherentOrn} : \forall t^{\alpha} : \mu\, D^{\alpha}\,(i,x).\ (\!|\alpha|\!)\ (D^{\alpha}\text{-}\mathsf{forget}\ t^{\alpha}) \equiv x$$

This corresponds to the Recomputation theorem of McBride [2012]. We shall not reprove it here, the construction being similar. In the other direction, the isomorphism gives us a function of type:

$$(t : \mu\, D\ i) \times (\!|\alpha|\!)\ t \equiv x \rightarrow \mu\, D^{\alpha}(i,x)$$

Put in full and simplifying the equation, this corresponds to the function $D^{\alpha}\text{-}\mathsf{make} : (t : \mu\, D i) \rightarrow \mu\, D^{\alpha}(i, (\!|\alpha|\!)\, t)$. This corresponds to the remember function of McBride [2012]. Again, we will assume this construction here.

A typical use-case of algebraic ornaments is the implementation of semantic-preserving operations on syntax trees [McBride 2012]. For example, let us consider arithmetic expressions, which semantics is given by interpretation in Nat:

$$\begin{array}{llll} \textbf{data}\ \mathsf{Expr} : \mathrm{SET}\ \textbf{where} & \alpha_{\mathsf{eval}}\ (es : [\![\mathsf{Expr\text{-}Desc}]\!]\ \mathsf{Nat}) & : & \mathsf{Nat} \\ \quad \mathsf{Expr} \ni \mathsf{const}\,(n : \mathsf{Nat}) & \alpha_{\mathsf{eval}}\quad (\mathsf{const}\ n) & \mapsto & n \\ \qquad\quad \mid\ \mathsf{add}\,(d\,e : \mathsf{Expr}) & \alpha_{\mathsf{eval}}\quad (\mathsf{add}\ m\ n) & \mapsto & m{+}n \end{array}$$

Using the algebra α_{eval}, we construct the algebraic ornament of Expr and obtain expressions indexed by their semantics:

$$\begin{array}{l} \textbf{data}\ \mathsf{Expr}^{\alpha_{\mathsf{eval}}}\ (k : \mathsf{Nat}) : \mathrm{SET}\ \textbf{where} \\ \quad \mathsf{Expr}^{\alpha_{\mathsf{eval}}}\quad (k = n)\ \ni \mathsf{const}\,(n : \mathsf{Nat}) \\ \quad \mathsf{Expr}^{\alpha_{\mathsf{eval}}}\ (k = m{+}n) \ni \mathsf{add}\,(m n : \mathsf{Nat}) \\ \qquad\qquad\qquad\qquad\qquad (d : \mathsf{Expr}^{\alpha_{\mathsf{eval}}}\ m)(e : \mathsf{Expr}^{\alpha_{\mathsf{eval}}}\ n) \end{array}$$

Hence, we can enforce semantics preservation by typing. For example, let us optimise away all additions of the form "$0 + e$":

$$\begin{array}{llll} \mathsf{optimize\text{-}0{+}} & (e : \mathsf{Expr}^{\alpha_{\mathsf{eval}}}\ n) & : & \mathsf{Expr}^{\alpha_{\mathsf{eval}}}\ n \\ \mathsf{optimize\text{-}0{+}} & (\mathsf{const}\ n) & \mapsto & \mathsf{const}\ n \\ \mathsf{optimize\text{-}0{+}} & (\mathsf{add}\ 0\ n\ (\mathsf{const}\ 0)\ e) & \mapsto & \mathsf{optimize\text{-}0{+}}\ e \\ \mathsf{optimize\text{-}0{+}} & (\mathsf{add}\ m\ n\ d\ e) & \mapsto & \mathsf{add}\ m\ n\ d\ e \end{array}$$

If the type-checker accepts our definition, we have that, by construction, the operation preserves the semantics. We can then prune the semantics from the types using the coherentOrn theorem and retrieve the transformation on raw syntax trees.

3.2.2 Reornaments

In this paper, we are interested in a special sub-class of algebraic ornaments. As we have seen, every ornament O induces an ornamental algebra O-forgetAlg, which forgets the extra information introduced by the ornament. Hence, given a datatype D and an ornament O_D of D, we can algebraically ornament $[\![O_D]\!]_{\mathsf{orn}}$ using the ornamental algebra O_D-forgetAlg. The resulting ornament is denoted D^{O_D}. McBride [2012] calls this object the *algebraic ornament by the ornamental algebra*. For brevity, we call it the *reornament* of O_D. Again, we shall overload D^{O_D} to denote both the ornament and the resulting datatype. A standard example of reornament is Vec: it is the reornament of List-Orn. Put otherwise, a vector is the algebraic ornament of List by the algebra computing its length, i.e. the ornamental algebra from List to Nat.

Reornaments can be implemented straightforwardly by unfolding their definition: first, compute the ornamental algebra and, second, construct the algebraic ornament by this algebra. However, such a simplistic construction introduces a lot of spurious equality constraints and duplication of information. For instance, using this naive definition of reornaments, a vector indexed by n is constructed as *any* list *as long as* it is of length n.

We can adopt a more fine-grained approach yielding an isomorphic but better structured datatype. In our setting, where we can compute over the index, a finer construction of the Vec reornament would be as follows:

- We retrieve the index, hence obtaining n ;
- By inspecting the ornament List-Orn, we obtain *exactly* the information by which n is *extended* into a list: if $n = 0$, no supplementary information is needed and if $n = \mathsf{suc}\, n'$, we need to extend it with an $a : A$. We call this the Extension of n ;
- By inspecting the ornament List-Orn again, we obtain the recursive structure of the reornament by *deleting* the data already fully determined by the index and its extension, and *refining* the indexing discipline: the tail of a vector of size $\mathsf{suc}\, n'$ is a vector of size n'. The recursive structure is denoted by Structure.

A reornament is thus the Extension of its index followed by the recursive structure as defined by Structure[4]. Based on this intuition, we define the associated reornament at index $t = \mathsf{in}\, xs : \mu\, D$ by, first, inserting the valid extensions of t with Extension, then, building the recursive structure using Structure:

$$\begin{array}{l} \mathsf{reornament}\ (O : \mathsf{orn}\ re\ D)\ :\ \mathsf{orn}\ \pi_0\ [\![O]\!]_{\mathsf{orn}} \\ \mathsf{reornament}\ O\ \mapsto\ \lambda(j, \mathsf{in}\ xs).\ \mathsf{insert}\ (\mathsf{Extension}\ (O\ j)\ xs)\ \lambda e. \\ \qquad\qquad\qquad\qquad\qquad\qquad \mathsf{Structure}\ (O\ j)\ xs\ e \end{array}$$

Applied to the reornament of List-Orn, this construction gives the fully Brady-optimised – detagged and forced – version of Vec, here written in full:

$$\begin{array}{l} \textbf{data}\ \mathsf{Vec}\ [A : \mathrm{SET}](n : \mathsf{Nat}) : \mathrm{SET}\ \textbf{where} \\ \quad \mathsf{Vec}_A\quad 0\quad \ni \mathsf{nil} \\ \quad \mathsf{Vec}_A\ (\mathsf{suc}\ n) \ni \mathsf{cons}\,(a : A)(vs : \mathsf{Vec}_A\ n) \end{array}$$

Note that our ability to *compute* over the index is crucial for this construction to work. Also, it is isomorphic to the datatype one would have obtained with the algebraic ornament of the ornamental algebra. Consequently, the correctness property of algebraic ornaments is still valid here: constructively, we get the coherentOrn theorem in one direction and the $*$-make function in the other.

In this Section, we have adapted the notion of ornament to our universe of datatypes. In doing so, we have introduced the concept of a deletion ornament, using the indexing to remove duplicated information in the datatypes. This has proved useful to simplify the definition of reornaments. We shall see how this can be turned to our advantage when we transport functions across ornaments.

4. A universe of functions and their ornaments

We are now going to generalise the notion of ornament to functions. In order to do this, we first need to be able, in type theory, to manipulate functions and especially their types. Hence, we define a universe of functions. With it, we will be able to write generic programs over the class of functions captured by our universe.

Using this technology, we define a functional ornament as a decoration over the universe of functions. The liftings implementing the functional ornament are related to the base function by a coherence property. To minimise the theorem proving burden induced by coherence proofs, we expand our system with *patches*: a patch is the type of the functions that satisfy the coherence property *by construction*. Finally, and still writing generic programs, we show how we can automatically project the lifting and its coherence certificate out of a patch.

[4] For space reasons, we shall refer the reader to the companion technical report for the type-theoretic definition of Extension and Structure. Their exact definition is not necessary for the understanding of this paper.

```
data FunOrn (T : Type) : SET₁ where
  FunOrn (μ{D i}→ T) ∋ μ⁺{(O : orn re D) (j : re⁻¹ i)}→ (T⁺ : FunOrn T)
  FunOrn (μ{D i}× T) ∋ μ⁺{(O : orn re D) (j : re⁻¹ i)}× (T⁺ : FunOrn T)
  FunOrn      1      ∋ 1
```
(a) Code

```
⟦(T⁺ : FunOrn T)⟧FunOrn           : SET
⟦μ⁺{O (inv j)}→ T⁺⟧FunOrn  ↦ μ ⟦O⟧orn j → ⟦T⁺⟧FunOrn
⟦μ⁺{O (inv j)}× T⁺⟧FunOrn  ↦ μ ⟦O⟧orn j × ⟦T⁺⟧FunOrn
⟦1⟧FunOrn                  ↦ 𝟙
```
(b) Interpretation

Figure 4. Universe of functional ornaments

4.1 A universe of functions

For clarity of exposition, we restrict our language of types to the bare minimum: a type can either be an exponential which domain is an inductive object, or a product which first component is an inductive object, or the unit type – used as a termination symbol:

```
data Type : SET₁ where
  Type ∋ μ{(D : I → IDesc I) (i : I)}→ (T : Type)
       | μ{(D : I → IDesc I) (i : I)}× (T : Type)
       | 1
```

Hence, this universe codes the function space from some (maybe none) inductive types to some (maybe none) inductive types. Concretely, the codes are interpreted as follows:

```
⟦(T : Type)⟧Type     : SET
⟦μ{D i}→ T⟧Type  ↦ μ D i → ⟦T⟧Type
⟦μ{D i}× T⟧Type  ↦ μ D i × ⟦T⟧Type
⟦1⟧Type          ↦ 𝟙
```

The constructions we develop below could be extended to a more powerful universe – such as one supporting non-inductive sets or having dependent functions and pairs. However, this would needlessly complicate our exposition.

Example 1 (Coding _<_). Written in the universe of function types, the type of _<_ is:

```
type< : Type
type< ↦ μ{Nat-Desc ∗}→ μ{Nat-Desc ∗}→ μ{Bool-Desc ∗}× 1
```

The implementation of _<_ is essentially the same as earlier, excepted that it must now return a pair of a boolean and an inhabitant of the unit type. To be explicit about the recursion pattern of this function, we make use of Epigram's *by* (⇐) construct:

```
  _      <  _      : ⟦type<⟧Type
  m      <  n      ⇐ Nat-case n
    m    <  0      ↦ (false, ∗)
    m    <  suc n  ⇐ Nat-elim m
     0   <  suc n  ↦ (true, ∗)
  suc m  <  suc n  ↦ m < n
```

That is to say: we first do a case analysis on n and then, in the successor case, we proceed by induction over m.

Example 2 (Coding _+_). Written in the universe of function types, the type of _+_ is:

```
type+ : Type
type+ ↦ μ{Nat-Desc ∗}→ μ{Nat-Desc ∗}→ μ{Nat-Desc ∗}× 1
```

Again, up to a multiplication by 𝟙, the implementation of _+_ is left unchanged.

4.2 Functional ornament

From the universe of function types, it is now straightforward to define the notion of functional ornament: we traverse the type code and ornament the inductive types as we go. Note that it is always possible to leave an object unornamented: we ornament by the identity that simply copies the original definition. Hence, we obtain the definition given in Fig. 4(a). From a functional ornament, we get the type of the liftings by interpreting each ornaments (Fig. 4(b)). This defines the universe of functional ornaments.

We will want our ornamented function to be *coherent* with the base function we started with: for a function $f : \mu\, D \rightarrow \mu\, E$, the ornamented function $f^+ : \mu\, [\![O_D]\!]_{\mathsf{orn}} \rightarrow \mu\, [\![O_E]\!]_{\mathsf{orn}}$ is said to be coherent with f if it satisfies the following equation:

$$\forall x^+ : \mu\, [\![O_D]\!]_{\mathsf{orn}} .\, f\ (O_D\text{-forget}\ x^+) \equiv O_E\text{-forget}\ (f^+\ x^+)$$

To generalise the definition of coherence to any arity, we proceed by induction over the universe of functional ornaments:

```
Coherence (T⁺ : FunOrn T) (f : ⟦T⟧Type) (f⁺ : ⟦T⁺⟧FunOrn) : SET
Coherence (μ⁺{O (inv j)}→ T⁺)  f       f⁺          ↦
    ∀x⁺ : μ ⟦O⟧orn j. Coherence T⁺ (f (forgetOrn x⁺)) (f⁺ x⁺)
Coherence (μ⁺{O (inv j)}× T⁺) (x, xs) (x⁺, xs⁺)    ↦
    x ≡ forgetOrn x⁺ × Coherence T⁺ xs xs⁺
Coherence        1             ∗       ∗           ↦ 𝟙
```

Example 3 (Ornamenting type< to describe lookup). In Section 2, we have identified the ornaments involved to transport the type of _<_ to obtain the type of lookup. From there, we give the functional ornament describing the type of the lookup function:

```
typeLookup : FunOrn type<
typeLookup ↦ μ⁺{idO_Nat ∗}→
               μ⁺{List-Orn ∗}→
                 μ⁺{Maybe-Orn ∗}× 1
```

The user can verify that $[\![\mathsf{typeLookup}]\!]_{\mathsf{FunOrn}}$ gives us the type of the lookup function, up to multiplication by 𝟙. Also, computing Coherence typeLookup (_<_) gives the expected result:

$$\lambda f^+ : [\![\mathsf{typeLookup}]\!]_{\mathsf{FunOrn}} .\ \forall n : \mathsf{Nat}. \forall xs : \mathsf{List}_A . \mathsf{isJust}\ (f^+\ n\ xs) \equiv n < \mathsf{length}\ xs$$

Note that this equation is not *specifying* the lookup function: it is only establishing a computational relation between _<_ and a candidate lifting f^+, for which lookup is a valid choice. However, one could be interested in other functions satisfying this coherence property and they would be handled by our system just as well.

Example 4 (Ornamenting type+ to describe _++_). The functional ornament of type+ makes only use of the ornamentation of Nat into List_A:

```
type++ : FunOrn type+
type++ ↦ μ⁺{List-Orn ∗}→
           μ⁺{List-Orn ∗}→
             μ⁺{List-Orn ∗}× 1
```

Again, computing $[\![\mathsf{type{+}{+}}]\!]_{\mathsf{FunOrn}}$ indeed gives us the type of _++_ while Coherence type++ (_+_) correctly captures our requirement that list append preserves the length of its arguments. As before, the list append function is not the only valid lifting: one could for example consider a function that reverts the first list and appends it to the second one.

4.3 Patches

By definition of a functional ornament, the lifting of a base function $f : [\![T]\!]_{\mathsf{Type}}$ is a function f^+ of type $[\![T^+]\!]_{\mathsf{FunOrn}}$ satisfying the coherence property Coherence $T^+\ f$. To implement a lifting that is coherent, we might ask the user to first implement the lifting f^+ and then prove it coherent. However, we find this process unsatisfactory: we fail to harness the power of dependent types when implementing f^+, this weakness being then paid off by tedious proof obligations. To overcome this limitation, we define the notion of Patch as the type of *all* the functions that are coherent by construction.

Note that we are looking for an equivalence here: we will define patches so that they are in bijection with liftings satisfying a coherence property, informally:

$$\mathsf{Patch}\; T\; T^+\; f \cong (f^+ : [\![T^+]\!]_{\mathsf{FunOrn}}) \times \mathsf{Coherence}\; T^+\; f\; f^+ \qquad (1)$$

In this paper, we constructively use this bijection in the left to right direction: having implemented a patch f^{++} of type $\mathsf{Patch}\; T\; T^+\; f$, we will show, in the next Section, how we can extract a lifting together with its coherence proof.

Before giving the generic construction of the Patch object, let us first work through the $\_ < \_$ example. After having functionally ornamented $\_ < \_$ with typeLookup, the lifting function f^+ and coherence property can be represented by the following pair:

$$(f^+ : \mathsf{Nat} \times \mathsf{List}_A \to \mathsf{Maybe}_A) \times$$
$$\forall m : \mathsf{Nat}. \forall as : \mathsf{List}_A. m < \mathsf{List\text{-}forget}\; as \equiv \mathsf{Maybe\text{-}forget}\; (f^+\; m\; as)$$

Applying dependent choice, this is equivalent to:

$$\cong (m : \mathsf{Nat}) \times (n : \mathsf{Nat}) \times (as : \mathsf{List}_A) \times \mathsf{List\text{-}forget}\; as \equiv n \to$$
$$(ma : \mathsf{Maybe}_A) \times \mathsf{Maybe\text{-}forget}\; ma \equiv m < n$$

Now, by definition of reornaments, we have that:

$$(as : \mathsf{List}_A) \times \mathsf{List\text{-}forget}\; as \equiv n \cong \mathsf{Vec}_A\; n \qquad \text{and}$$
$$(ma : \mathsf{Maybe}_A) \times \mathsf{Maybe\text{-}forget}\; ma \equiv b \cong \mathsf{IMaybe}_A\; b$$

Applying these isomorphisms, we obtain the following type, which we call the Patch of the functional ornament typeLookup:

$$\cong (m : \mathsf{Nat}) \times (n : \mathsf{Nat}) \times (vs : \mathsf{Vec}_A\; n) \to \mathsf{IMaybe}_A\; (m < n)$$

Which is thus equivalent to a pair of a lifting and its coherence.

Intuitively, the Patch construction consists in turning the pairs of data and their algebraically defined constraint into equivalent reornaments. The coherence property of reornaments tells us that projecting the ornamented function down to its unornamented components gives back the base function. By turning the projection functions into inductive datatypes, we enforce the coherence property directly by the index: we introduce a fresh index for the arguments (here, introducing m and n) and index the return types by the result of the unornamented function (here, indexing IMaybe_A by $m < n$).

To build this type generically, we simply proceed by induction over the functional ornament. Upon an argument (i.e. a $\mu^+\{O\} \mapsto$), we introduce a fresh index and the reornament of O. Upon a result (i.e. a $\mu^+\{O\} \times$), we ask for a reornament of O indexed by the result of the base function.

$$\begin{array}{l}
\mathsf{Patch}(T : \mathsf{Type})(T^+ : \mathsf{FunOrn}\; T)(f : [\![T]\!]_{\mathsf{Type}}) \;:\; \mathrm{SET} \\
\mathsf{Patch}\; (\mu\{D\,(\mathsf{re}\,j)\} \mapsto T)\; (\mu^+\{O\,(\mathsf{inv}\,j)\} \mapsto T^+)\quad f \quad\mapsto \\
\quad (x : \mu\, D\,(\mathsf{re}\,j)) \to \mu\, D^O\; (j, x) \to \mathsf{Patch}\; T\; T^+\; (f\; x) \\
\mathsf{Patch}\; (\mu\{D\,(\mathsf{re}\,j)\} \times T)\; (\mu^+\{O\,(\mathsf{inv}\,j)\} \times T^+)\; (x, xs) \mapsto \\
\quad \mu\, D^O\; (j, x) \times \mathsf{Patch}\; T\; T^+\; xs \\
\mathsf{Patch} \qquad 1 \qquad\qquad 1 \qquad\qquad * \quad \mapsto \mathbb{1}
\end{array}$$

Example 5 (Patch of typeLookup). The type of the coherent liftings of $\_ < \_$ by typeLookup, as defined by the Patch of $\_ < \_$ by typeLookup, computes to:

$$(m : \mathsf{Nat}) \to (m^+ : \mu\, \mathsf{Nat}^{\mathsf{idO}_{\mathsf{Nat}}}\; m) \to$$
$$(n : \mathsf{Nat}) \to (vs : \mu\, \mathsf{Nat}^{\mathsf{List}_A}\; n) \to \mu\, \mathsf{Bool}^{\mathsf{Maybe}_A}\; (m < n) \times \mathbb{1}$$

Note that $\mu\, \mathsf{Nat}^{\mathsf{idO}_{\mathsf{Nat}}}\; n$ is isomorphic to $\mathbb{1}$: all the content of the datatype has been forced – the recursive structure of the datatype is entirely determined by its index – and detagged – the choice of constructors is entirely determined by its index, leaving no actual data in it. Hence, we discard this argument as computationally uninteresting. On the other hand, $\mathsf{Nat}^{\mathsf{List}_A}$ and $\mathsf{Bool}^{\mathsf{Maybe}_A}$ are, respectively, the previously introduced Vec_A and IMaybe_A types.

Example 6 (Patch of type+). Similarly, the Patch of $\_ + \_$ by type+ computes to the type of the vector append function:

$$(m : \mathsf{Nat}) \to (xs : \mathsf{Nat}^{\mathsf{List}_A}\; m) \to$$
$$(n : \mathsf{Nat}) \to (ys : \mathsf{Nat}^{\mathsf{List}_A}\; m) \to \mathsf{Nat}^{\mathsf{List}_A}\; (m + n) \times \mathbb{1}$$

Discussion: While these precisely indexed functions remove the burden of theorem proving, this solution is not relevant in all situations. For instance, if we were to implement a length-preserving list reversal, our patching machinery would ask us to implement $\mathsf{vrev} : \mathsf{Vec}_A\; n \to \mathsf{Vec}_A\; n$ that will inevitably require some proving to match up the types: we must appeal to the equational theory of addition – in this case, $n + 1 \equiv \mathsf{suc}\; n$ – and this is beyond the grasp of our type-checker, which can only decide definitional identities. Unless the type-checker works up to equational theories, as done in CoqMT [Strub 2010], the programmer is certainly better off using our machinery to generate the coherence condition (Section 4.2) and implement the lifting and its coherence proof manually, rather than using patches. However, this example gives a hint as to what can be seen as a "good" coherence property: because we want the type-checker to do all the proving, the equations we rely on at the type level need to be definitionally true, either because our logic has a rich definitional equality, or because we rely on operations that satisfy these identities by definition.

4.4 Patching and coherence

At this stage, we can implement the ilookup function exactly as we did in Section 2. From there, we now want to obtain the lookup function and its coherence certificate. More generally, having implemented a function satisfying the Patch type, we want to extract the lifting and its coherence proof.

Perhaps not surprisingly, we obtain this construction by looking at the isomorphism (1) of the previous Section through our constructive glasses: indeed, as the Patch type is isomorphic to the set of liftings satisfying the coherence property, we effectively get a function taking every Patch to a lifting and its coherence proof. More precisely, we obtain the lifting by generalising the reornament-induced ∗-forget functions to functional ornaments while we obtain the coherence proof by generalising the reornament-induced coherentOrn theorem.

We call *patching* the action of projecting the coherent lifting from a Patch function. Again, it is defined by mere induction over the functional ornament. When ornamented arguments are introduced (i.e. with $\mu^+\{O\} \mapsto$), we simply patch the body of the function. This is possible because from $x^+ : \mu\, [\![O_D]\!]_{\mathsf{orn}}$, we can forget the ornament to compute $f\; (\mathsf{forgetOrn}\; x^+)$ and we can also make the reornament to compute $f^{++}\; \_\; (\mathsf{makeAlgOrn}\; x^+)$. When an ornamented result is to be returned, we simply forget the reornamentation computed by the coherent lifting:

$$\begin{array}{l}
\mathsf{patch}\; (T^+ : \mathsf{FunOrn}\; T)(f : [\![T]\!]_{\mathsf{Type}})(p : \mathsf{Patch}\; T\; T^+\; f) \;: \\
\qquad [\![T^+]\!]_{\mathsf{FunOrn}} \\
\mathsf{patch}\;\; (\mu^+\{O\,(\mathsf{inv}\,j)\} \mapsto T^+)\;\; f\;\; f^{++} \mapsto \\
\quad \lambda x^+.\, \mathsf{patch}\; (f\; (\mathsf{forgetOrn}\; x^+)) \\
\qquad\qquad (f^{++}\; (\mathsf{forgetOrn}\; x^+)\; (\mathsf{makeAlgOrn}\; x^+)) \\
\mathsf{patch}\;\; (\mu^+\{O\,(\mathsf{inv}\,j)\} \times T^+)\;\; (x, xs)\;\; (x^{++}, xs^{++}) \mapsto \\
\quad (\mathsf{forgetOrn}\; x^{++}, \mathsf{patch}\; T^+\; xs\; xs^{++}) \\
\mathsf{patch}\;\; 1\;\; *\;\; * \mapsto *
\end{array}$$

Extracting the coherence proof follows a similar pattern. We introduce arguments as we go, just as we did with patch. When we reach a result, we have to prove the coherence of the result returned by the patched function: this is a straightforward application of the coherentOrn theorem:

$$\begin{array}{l}
\mathsf{coherence}\; (T^+ : \mathsf{FunOrn}\; T)(f : [\![T]\!]_{\mathsf{Type}})(p : \mathsf{Patch}\; T\; T^+\; f) \;: \\
\qquad \mathsf{Coherence}\; T^+\; f\; (\mathsf{patch}\; T^+\; f\; p) \\
\mathsf{coherence}\;\; (\mu^+\{O\,(\mathsf{inv}\,j)\} \mapsto T^+)\;\; f\;\; p \quad \mapsto \\
\quad \lambda x^+.\, \mathsf{coherence}\, T^+\; (f\; (\mathsf{forgetOrn}\; x^+)) \\
\qquad\qquad (p\; (\mathsf{forgetOrn}\; x^+)\; (\mathsf{makeAlgOrn}\; x^+)) \\
\mathsf{coherence}\;\; (\mu^+\{O\,(\mathsf{inv}\,j)\} \times T^+)\;\; (x, xs)\;\; (x^+, p) \quad \mapsto \\
\quad (\mathsf{coherentOrn}\; x^+, \mathsf{coherence}\; T^+\; xs\; p) \\
\mathsf{coherence}\;\; 1\;\; *\;\; * \quad \mapsto *
\end{array}$$

```
_       < _      : ⟦type<⟧Type
m       < n      ⇐ Nat-case n
  m     < 0      ↦ (false, ∗)
  m     < suc n  ⇐ Nat-elim m
    0   < suc n  ↦ (true, ∗)
  suc m < suc n  ↦ m < n
```

```
ilookup     (m : Nat) (vs : Vec_A n)  : IMaybe_A (m < n)
ilookup      m         vs             ⇐ Vector-case vs
  ilookup    m         nil            ↦ nothing
  ilookup    m         (cons a vs)    ⇐ Nat-elim m
    ilookup  0         (cons a vs)    ↦ just a
    ilookup  (suc m)   (cons a vs)    ↦ ilookup m vs
```

Figure 5. Implementations of _ < _ and ilookup

Example 7 (Obtaining lookup and its coherence certificate, for free). This last step is a mere application of the patch and coherence functions. Hence, we define lookup as follows:

$$\begin{array}{lll} \mathsf{lookup} & : & [\![\mathsf{typeLookup}]\!]_{\mathsf{FunOrn}} \\ \mathsf{lookup} & \mapsto & \mathsf{patch}\ \mathsf{typeLookup}\ (\_<\_)\ \mathsf{ilookup} \end{array}$$

And we get its coherence proof, here spelled in full:

$$\begin{array}{l} \mathsf{cohLookup}\ (n : \mathsf{Nat})\ (xs : \mathsf{List}_A)\ : \\ \quad \mathsf{Maybe\text{-}forget}\ (\pi_0(\mathsf{lookup}\ n\ xs)) \equiv \pi_0(n < \mathsf{List\text{-}forget}\ xs) \\ \mathsf{cohLookup}\ \ n\ \ xs\ \ \mapsto \\ \quad \mathsf{coherence}\ \mathsf{typeLookup}\ (\_<\_)\ \mathsf{ilookup}\ n\ xs \end{array}$$

Example 8 (Obtaining _ ++ _ and its coherence certificate, for free). Assuming that we have implemented the coherent lifting vappend, we obtain concatenation of lists and its coherence proof by simply running our generic machinery:

$$\begin{array}{lll} +\!\!+ & : & [\![\mathsf{type}{+\!\!+}]\!]_{\mathsf{FunOrn}} \\ +\!\!+ & \mapsto & \mathsf{patch}\ \mathsf{type}{+\!\!+}\ (\_+\_)\ \mathsf{vappend} \end{array}$$

$$\begin{array}{l} \mathsf{coh}{+\!\!+}\ (xs : \mathsf{List}_A)\ (ys : \mathsf{List}_A)\ : \\ \quad \mathsf{List\text{-}forget}\ (\pi_0(xs +\!\!+ ys)) \equiv \pi_0((\mathsf{List\text{-}forget}\ xs) + (\mathsf{List\text{-}forget}\ ys)) \\ \mathsf{coh}{+\!\!+}\ \ xs\ \ ys\ \ \mapsto \\ \quad \mathsf{coherence}\ \mathsf{type}{+\!\!+}\ (\_+\_)\ \mathsf{vappend}\ xs\ ys \end{array}$$

Looking back at the manual construction in Section 2, we can measure the progress we have made: while we had to duplicate entirely the type signature of lookup and its coherence proof, we can now write down a functional ornament and these are generated for us. This is not just convenient: by giving a functional ornament, we establish a strong connection between two functions. By pinning down this connection with the universe of functional ornaments, we turn this knowledge into an effective object that can be manipulated and reasoned about within the type theory. We make use of this concrete object when we construct the Patch induced by a functional ornament: this is again a construction that is generic now, while we had to tediously (and perhaps painfully) construct it in Section 2. Similarly, we get patching and extraction of the coherence proof for free now, while we had to manually fiddle with several projection and injection functions.

We presented the Patch as the type of the liftings coherent by construction. As we have seen, its construction and further projection down to a lifting is now entirely automated, hence effortless. This is a significant step forward: we could either implement lookup and then prove it coherent, or we could go through the trouble of manually defining carefully indexed types and write a function correct by construction. We have now made this second alternative just as accessible as the first one. And, from a programming perspective, the second approach is much more appealing. In a word, we have made an appealing technique extremely cheap!

Finally, we shall reiterate that none of the above constructions involve extending the type theory: using our universe of datatypes, functional ornaments are internalised as a few generic programs and inductive types. For systems such as Agda, Coq, or Haskell with GADTs, this technology would need to be provided at the meta-level. However, the fact that our constructions type-check in our system suggests that adding these constructions at the meta-level is consistent with a pre-existing meta-theory.

5. Lazy programmers, clever constructors

In our journey from _ < _ to lookup, we had to implement the ilookup function. It is instructive to put _ < _ and ilookup side-by-side (Fig. 5). First, both functions follow the same recursion pattern: case analysis over n/vs followed by induction over m. Second, the returned constructors are related through the Maybe ornament: knowing that we have returned true or false when implementing _ < _, we can deduce which of just or nothing will be used in ilookup. Interestingly, the only unknown, hence the only necessary input from the user, is the a in the just case: it is precisely the information that has been introduced by the Maybe ornament.

In this Section, we are going to leverage our knowledge of the definition of the base function – such as _ < _ – to guide the implementation of the coherent lifting – such as ilookup: instead of re-implementing ilookup by duplicating most of the code of _ < _, the user indicates *what to duplicate* and only provides *strictly necessary* inputs. We are primarily interested in transporting two forms of structure:

Recursion pattern: if the base function is a fold $(\!|\alpha|\!)$ and the user provides us with a *coherent algebra* $\hat{\beta}$ of α, we automatically construct the coherent lifting $(\!|\hat{\beta}|\!)$ of $(\!|\alpha|\!)$;

Returned constructor: if the base function returns a constructor C and the user provides us with a *coherent extension* $\hat{C}$ of C, we automatically construct the coherent lifting of C

We shall formalise what we understand by being a coherent algebra and a coherent extension below. The key idea is to identify the strictly necessary inputs from the user, helped in that by the ornaments. It is then straightforward to, automatically and generically, build the lifted folds and values.

5.1 Transporting recursion patterns

When transporting a function, we are very unlikely to change the recursion pattern of the base function. Indeed, the very reason why we *can* do this transportation is that the lifting uses exactly the same structure to compute its results. Hence, in the majority of the cases, we could just ask the computer to use the induction principle induced by the base one: the only task left to the user will be to give the algebra. For clarity of exposition, we restrict ourselves to transporting folds. However, the treatment of induction is essentially the same, as hinted by the fact that induction can be reduced to folds [Fumex et al. 2011].

To illustrate this approach, we work through a concrete example: we derive $\mathsf{hd} : \mathsf{List}_A \to \mathsf{Maybe}_A$ from $\mathsf{isSuc} : \mathsf{Nat} \to \mathsf{Bool}$ by transporting the algebra. For the sake of argument, we artificially define isSuc by a fold:

$$\begin{array}{l} \mathsf{isSuc}\ (n : \mathsf{Nat})\ :\ \mathsf{Bool} \\ \mathsf{isSuc}\ \ n\ \mapsto (\!|\alpha_{\mathsf{isSuc}}|\!)\ n \quad \textbf{where} \\ \quad \alpha_{\mathsf{isSuc}}\ (xs : [\![\mathsf{Nat\text{-}Desc}]\!]\ \mathsf{Bool})\ :\ \mathsf{Bool} \\ \quad \alpha_{\mathsf{isSuc}}\ \ \text{'}0\ \mapsto \mathsf{false} \\ \quad \alpha_{\mathsf{isSuc}}\ \ (\text{'}\mathsf{suc}\ xs)\ \mapsto \mathsf{true} \end{array}$$

Our objective is thus to define the algebra for hd, which has the following type:

$$\alpha_{\mathsf{hd}} : [\![\mathsf{List\text{-}Desc}]\!]\ \mathsf{Maybe}_A \to \mathsf{Maybe}_A$$

(a) Request lifting of algebra: (user input)

```
ihd  (vs : Vec_A n)  :  IMaybe_A isSuc n
ihd                 ⇐lift  lift-fold
{?}
```

(b) Result of lifting the algebra: (system output)

```
ihd (vs : Vec_A n)  :  IMaybe_A (isSuc n)
ihd                 ⇐lift  lift-fold   where
  α_ihd (vs : ⟦Vec-Desc⟧ (λn′. IMaybe_A (isSuc n′)) n)  :  IMaybe_A (isSuc n)
  α_ihd               'nil                               {?}
  α_ihd               ('cons a xs)                       {?}
```

(c) Request lifting of constructors: (user input)

```
ihd (vs : Vec_A n)  :  IMaybe_A (isSuc n)
ihd                 ⇐lift  lift-fold   where
  α_ihd (vs : ⟦Vec-Desc⟧ (λn′. IMaybe_A (isSuc n′)) n)  :  IMaybe_A (isSuc n)
  α_ihd               'nil                               ↦lift {?}
  α_ihd               ('cons a xs)                       ↦lift {?}
```

(d) Result of lifting constructors: (system output)

```
ihd (vs : Vec_A n)  :  IMaybe_A (isSuc n)
ihd                 ⇐lift  lift-fold   where
  α_ihd (vs : ⟦Vec-Desc⟧ (λn′. IMaybe_A (isSuc n′)) n)  :  IMaybe_A (isSuc n)
  α_ihd               'nil                               ↦lift nothing {?:𝟙} [ {?:𝟙} ]
  α_ihd               ('cons a xs)                       ↦lift just {?:A} [ {?:𝟙} ]
```

(e) Type-checked term: (automatically generated from (d))

```
ihd (vs : Vec_A n)  :  IMaybe_A (isSuc n)
ihd       vs        ↦  lift-fold α_isSuc α_ihd   where
  α_ihd (vs : ⟦Vec-Desc⟧ (λn′. IMaybe_A (isSuc n′)) n)  :  IMaybe_A (isSuc n)
  α_ihd               'nil                 ↦ lift-constructor 'nil {?:𝟙} {?:𝟙} ∗
  α_ihd               ('cons a xs)         ↦ lift-constructor ('suc n) {?:A} {?:𝟙} ∗
```

Figure 6. Guided implementation of ihd

such that its fold is coherent. By the fold-fusion theorem [Bird and de Moor 1997], it is sufficient (but not necessary) for α_{hd} to satisfy the following condition:

$$\forall ms : [\![\mathsf{List\text{-}Desc}]\!]\ \mathsf{Maybe}_A .\ \mathsf{isJust}\ (\alpha_{\mathsf{hd}}\ ms) \equiv \alpha_{\mathsf{isSuc}}\ (\mathsf{List\text{-}forgetNat}([\![\mathsf{List\text{-}Desc}]\!]\ \mathsf{isJust}\ ms))$$

Following the same methodology we applied to define the Patch type, we can massage the type of α_{hd} and its coherence condition to obtain an equivalent definition enforcing the coherence by indexing. In this case, the natural candidate is:

$$\alpha_{\mathsf{ihd}} : [\![\mathsf{Vec\text{-}Desc}]\!]\ (\lambda n'.\ \mathsf{IMaybe}_A\ (\mathsf{isSuc}\ n'))\ n \rightarrow \mathsf{IMaybe}_A\ (\mathsf{isSuc}\ n)$$

This construction generalises to any functional ornament. That is, from an algebra

$$\alpha : (i : I) \rightarrow [\![D\ i]\!]\ (\lambda \_ .\ [\![T]\!]_{\mathsf{Type}}) \rightarrow [\![T]\!]_{\mathsf{Type}}$$

together with an ornament O_D : orn $re\,D$ and a functional ornament T^{+} : FunOrn T, the type of coherent algebras for α is:

$$\begin{array}{l}\hat{\beta} : (j : J)(t : \mu\, D\ (re\ j)) \rightarrow \\ \quad [\![D^{O}\ (j, t)]\!]\ (\lambda (j, t).\ \mathsf{Patch}\ T\ ((\!|\alpha|\!)\ t)\ T^{+}) \rightarrow \\ \quad\quad \mathsf{Patch}\ T\ ((\!|\alpha|\!)\ t)\ T^{+}\end{array}$$

It can formally be proved that algebras of this type capture exactly the algebras satisfying the coherence condition. Constructively, we get that such a coherent algebra induces a coherent lifting, by a mere fold of the coherent algebra:

$$\begin{array}{l}\mathsf{lift\text{-}fold}\ (\alpha : (i : I) \rightarrow [\![D\ i]\!]\ (\lambda \_ .\ [\![T]\!]_{\mathsf{Type}}) \rightarrow [\![T]\!]_{\mathsf{Type}}) \\ \quad\quad (\hat{\beta} :\ (j : J)(t : \mu\, D\ (re\ j)) \rightarrow \\ \quad\quad\quad\quad [\![D^{O}\ (j, t)]\!]\ (\lambda (j, t).\ \mathsf{Patch}\ T\ ((\!|\alpha|\!)\ t)\ T^{+}) \rightarrow \\ \quad\quad\quad\quad \mathsf{Patch}\ T\ ((\!|\alpha|\!)\ t)\ T^{+}) \\ \quad\quad :\ \mathsf{Patch}\ (\mu\{D\ (re\ j)\} \mapsto T)\ (\!|\alpha|\!)\ (\mu^{+}\{O\ j\} \mapsto T^{+}) \\ \mathsf{lift\text{-}fold}\ \alpha\ \hat{\beta}\ \mapsto\ \lambda x.\ \lambda x^{++}.\ (\!|\hat{\beta}|\!)\ x^{++}\end{array}$$

Generalising this idea, we can similarly lift induction: we denote lift-ind the corresponding clever constructor. Lifting case analysis is now simple, as case analysis is derivable from induction by stripping out the induction hypotheses [McBride et al. 2004].

Example 9 (Transporting the recursion pattern of isSuc)**.** We can now apply our generic machinery to transport isSuc to hd: in a high-level notation, we would write the command of Fig. 6(a). To this command, an interactive system would respond by automatically generating the algebra, as shown in Fig. 6(b). In the low-level type theory, this would elaborate to the following term:

```
ihd (vs : Vec_A n)  :  IMaybe_A (isSuc n)
ihd       vs        ↦  lift-fold α_isSuc α_ihd   where
  α_ihd (vs : ⟦Vec-Desc⟧ (λn′. IMaybe_A (isSuc n′)) n)  :
          IMaybe_A (isSuc n)
  α_ihd               'nil                 ↦ {?}
  α_ihd               ('cons a xs)         ↦ {?}
```

Once again, it is beyond the scope of this paper to formalise the elaboration process from the high-level notation to the low-level type theory. The reader will convince himself that the high-level notation contains all the information necessary to conduct this task. We shall now freely use the high-level syntax, with the understanding that it builds a low-level term that type-checks.

Example 10 (Transporting the recursion pattern of $\_<\_$)**.** To implement ilookup, we use lift-case to transport the case analysis on n and lift-ind to transport the induction over m. In a high-level notation, this interaction results in:

```
ilookup  :  Patch type< typeLookup _<_
ilookup     m        m^m         n         vs            ⇐lift  lift-case
  ilookup   m        m^m         0         nil           {?}
  ilookup   m        m^m         (suc n)   (cons a vs)   ⇐lift  lift-ind
    ilookup 0        0           0         nil           {?}
    ilookup (suc m)  (suc m^m)   0         nil           {?}
```

5.2 Transporting constructors

Just as the recursive structure, the returned values often simply mirror the original definition: we are in a situation where the base function returns a given constructor and we would like to return its ornamented counterpart. Informing the computer that we simply want to lift the constructor, it should fill in the parts that are already determined by the original constructor and ask only for the missing information, i.e. the data freshly introduced by the ornament.

Remember that, when implementing the coherent lifting, we are working on the reornaments of the lifting type. Hence, when returning a constructor-headed value, we are building an inhabitant of a reornament. When defining reornaments in Section 3.2.2, we have shown that, thanks to deletion ornaments, a reornament can be decomposed in two components:

- first, the extension that contains all the extra information introduced by the ornament ;
- second, the recursive structure of the refined datatype, which defines the type of the arguments of the constructor

And no additional information is required: all the information provided by indexing with the unornamented datatype is optimally used in the definition of the reornament. Thus, there is absolutely no duplication of information.

This clear separation of concerns is a blessing for us: when lifting a constructor, we only have to provide the extension and the arguments of the datatype, nothing more. In terms of implementation, this is as simple as:

$$
\begin{array}{ll}
\mathsf{lift\text{-}constructor} & (xs : [\![D\,(re\,j)]\!]\,\mu\,D) \\
 & (e : \mathsf{Extension}\,(O\,j)\,xs) \qquad\qquad \textit{– coherent extension} \\
 & (a : [\![[\![\mathsf{Structure}\,O\,xs\,e]\!]_{\mathsf{orn}}]\!]\,(\mu\,D^{O})) \quad \textit{– arguments} \\
 & (t^{++} : \mathsf{Patch}\,T\,t\,T^{+}) \\
 & : \mathsf{Patch}\,(\mu\{D\,(re\,j)\}\times\,T) \\
 & \qquad\qquad (\mathsf{in}\,xs, t) \\
 & \qquad\qquad (\mu^{+}\{O\,j\}\times\,T^{+}) \\
\mathsf{lift\text{-}constructor}\,xs\,e\,a\,t^{++} & \mapsto\ (\mathsf{in}\,(e, a), t^{++})
\end{array}
$$

Example 11 (Transporting the constructors of isSuc). Let us finish the implementation of hd from isSuc. Our task is simply to transport the true and false constructors along the Maybe ornament. In a high-level notation, we would write the command shown in Fig. 6(c). The interactive system would then respond by generating the code of Fig. 6(d). The $\mathbb{1}$ goals are trivially solved, probably automatically by the system. The only information the user has to provide is a value of type A returned by the just constructor.

Example 12 (Transporting the constructors of $\_<\_$). In the implementation of ilookup, we want to lift the returned true and false to the Maybe ornament. In a high-level notation, this would be represented as follows:

$$
\begin{array}{llllll}
\multicolumn{6}{l}{\mathsf{ilookup} : \mathsf{Patch}\ \mathsf{type}{<}\ \mathsf{typeLookup}\ \_{<}\_} \\
\mathsf{ilookup} & m & m^{m} & n & vs & \stackrel{\mathsf{lift}}{\Leftarrow}\ \mathsf{lift\text{-}case} \\
\mathsf{ilookup} & m & m^{m} & 0 & \mathsf{nil} & \stackrel{\mathsf{lift}}{\mapsto}\ \mathsf{nothing}\,*[*] \\
\mathsf{ilookup} & m & m^{m} & (\mathsf{suc}\,n) & (\mathsf{cons}\,a\,vs) & \stackrel{\mathsf{lift}}{\Leftarrow}\ \mathsf{lift\text{-}ind} \\
\mathsf{ilookup} & 0 & 0 & (\mathsf{suc}\,n) & (\mathsf{cons}\,a\,vs) & \stackrel{\mathsf{lift}}{\mapsto}\ \mathsf{just}\ \{?:A\}\,[*] \\
\mathsf{ilookup} & (\mathsf{suc}\,m) & (\mathsf{suc}\,m^{m}) & (\mathsf{suc}\,n) & (\mathsf{cons}\,a\,vs) & \{?\}
\end{array}
$$

As before, in an interactive setting, the user would instruct the machine to execute the command $\stackrel{\mathsf{lift}}{\mapsto}$ and the computer would come back with the skeleton of the expected inputs.

6. Related work

Our work is an extension of the work of McBride [2012] on ornaments, originally introduced to organise datatypes according to their common structure. This gave rise to the notion of ornamental algebras – forgetting the extra information of an ornamented datatype – and algebraic ornaments – indexing a datatype according to an algebra. This, in turn, induced the notion of algebraic ornament by ornamental algebras, which is a key ingredient for our work. However, for simplicity of exposition, these ornaments had originally been defined on a less index-aware universe of datatypes. As a consequence, computation over indices was impossible and, therefore, deletion of duplicated information was impossible. A corollary of this was that reornaments contained a lot of duplication, hence making the lifting of value from ornamented to reornamented datatype extremely tedious.

Our presentation of algebraic ornament has been greatly improved by the categorical model developed by Atkey et al. [2011]: the authors gave a conceptually clear treatment of algebraic ornament in a Lawvere fibration. At the technical level, the authors connected the definition of algebraic ornament with truth-preserving liftings, which are also used in the construction of induction principles, and op-reindexing, which models Σ-types in type theory.

Whilst the authors did not explicitly address the issue of transporting functions across ornaments, much of the infrastructure was implicitly there: for instance, lifting of folds is a trivial specialisation of induction. Also, the characterisation of the fix-point of an algebraic ornament as op-reindexing of the fold is a key ingredient to understanding index-level computations and assimilate them at the term level.

In their work on realisability and parametricity for Pure Type Systems, Bernardy and Lasson [Bernardy and Lasson 2011] have shown how to build a logic from a programming language. In such a system, terms of type theory can be precisely segregated based on their computational contribution and their logical contribution. In particular, the idea that natural numbers realise lists of the corresponding length appears in this system under the guise of vectors, the reflection of the realisability predicate. The strength of the realisability interpretation is that it is naturally defined on functions: while McBride [2012] and Atkey et al. [2011] only consider ornaments on datatypes, their work is the first, to our knowledge, to capture a general notion of functions realising – i.e. ornamenting – other functions.

Following the steps of Bernardy, Ko and Gibbons [2011] adapted the realisability interpretation to McBride's universe of datatypes and explored the other direction of the Patch equivalence, using reornaments to generate coherence properties: they describe how one could take list append together with a proof that it is coherent with respect to addition and obtain the vector append function. Their approach would shift neatly to our index-aware setting, where the treatment of reornaments is streamlined by the availability of deletion.

However, we prefer to exploit the direction of the equivalence which internalises coherence: we would rather use the full power of dependent types to avoid explicit proof. Hence, in our framework, we simultaneously induce list append and implicitly prove its coherence with addition just by defining vector append. Of course, which approach is appropriate depends on one's starting point. Moreover, our universe of functions takes a step beyond the related work by supporting the mechanised construction of liftings, leaving to the user the task of supplying a minimal patch. Our framework could easily be used to mechanise the realisability predicate constructions of Bernardy and Lasson [2011], Ko and Gibbons [2011].

7. Conclusion

In this paper, we have developed the notion of functional ornament and shown how one can achieve code reuse by transporting functions along a functional ornament. To this end, we have adapted McBride's ornaments to our universe of datatypes [Chapman et al. 2010]. This gave us the ability to compute over indices, hence introducing the deletion ornament. Deletion ornaments are a key ingredient for the internalisation of Brady's optimisation [Brady et al. 2004] over inductive families. In particular, this gave us a simpler implementation of reornaments.

We then generalised ornaments to functions: from a universe of function type, we define a functional ornament as the ornamentation of each of its inductive components. A function of the resulting type will be subject to a coherence property, akin to the ornamental forgetful map of ornaments. We have constructively presented this object, by building a small universe of functional ornaments.

Having functional ornaments, this raises the question of transporting a function to its ornamented version in such way that the coherence property holds. Instead of asking our user to write cumbersome proofs, we defined a Patch type as the type of all the functions that satisfies the coherence property by construction. Hence, we make extensive use of the dependently typed programming machinery offered by the environment: in this setting, the type-checker, that is the computer, is working with us to construct a term, not waiting for us to produce a proof.

Having implemented a function correct by construction, one then gets, for free, the lifting and its coherence certificate. This is a straightforward application of the equivalence between the Patch type and the set of coherent functions. These projection functions have been implemented in type theory by simple generic programming over the universe of functional ornaments.

To further improve code reuse, we provide two clever constructors to implement a Patch type: the idea is to use the structure of the base function to guide the implementation of the coherent lifting. Hence, if the base function uses a specific induction principle or returns a specific constructor, we make it possible for the user to specify that she wants to lift this element one level up. This way, the function is not duplicated: only the new information, as determined by the ornament, is necessary.

To conclude, we believe that this is a first yet interesting step toward code reuse for dependently typed programming systems. With ornaments, we were able to organise datatypes by their structure. With functional ornaments, we are now able to organise functions by their structure-preserving computational behaviour. Besides, we have developed some appealing automation to assist the implementation of functional ornaments, without any proving required, hence making this approach even more accessible.

7.1 Future work

Whilst we have deliberately chosen a simple universe of functions, we plan to extend it in various directions. Adding type dependency (Π- and Σ-types) but also non inductive sets is a necessary first step. Inspired by Bernardy and Lasson [2011], we would like to add a parametric quantifier: in the implementation of ilookup, we would mark the index A of Vec_A and IMaybe_A as parametric so that in the cons a case, the a could automatically be carried over.

The universe of functional ornaments could be extended as well, especially once the universe of functions has been extended with dependent quantifiers. For instance, we want to consider the introduction and deletion of quantifiers, as we are currently doing on datatypes. Whilst we have only looked at least fixed points in this paper, we also want to generalise our universe with greatest fixed points and the lifting of co-inductive definitions.

Further, our framework relies crucially on the duality between a reornament and its ornament presentation subject to a proof. We cross this isomorphism in both directions when we project the lifting from the coherent lifting. In practice, this involves a traversal of each of the input datatypes and a traversal of each of the output datatypes. However, computationally, these traversal are identities: the only purpose of these terms is at the logical level, for the type-checker to fix the types. We are looking at transforming our library of clever constructor into a proper domain-specific language (DSL). This way, implementing a coherent lifting would consists in working in a DSL for which an optimising compiler could compute away the computationally irrelevant operations.

Finally, much work remains to be done on the front of usability: for convenience, we have presented some informal notations for datatypes, their ornaments and an extension of Epigram programming facility with liftings. A formal treatment of these syntaxes and of their elaboration to the low-level type theory is underway: we are confident that a sufficiently abstract semantics can be given to these syntaxes by giving a relational specification of the elaboration process, in the style of Harper and Stone [2000] for Standard ML.

Acknowledgements We owe many thanks to the anonymous reviewer, their comments having significantly improved this paper. We are also very grateful to Guillaume Allais, Stevan Andjelkovic and Peter Hancock for their meticulous reviews of this paper. We shall also thank Edwin Brady for suggesting the study of lookup functions and Andrea Vezzosi for spotting an issue in our definition of reornaments. Finally, this paper would have remained a draft without the help and encouragement of José Pedro Magalhães. The authors are supported by the Engineering and Physical Sciences Research Council, Grant EP/G034699/1.

References

R. Atkey, P. Johann, and N. Ghani. When is a type refinement an inductive type? In *FOSSACS*, volume 6604 of *Lecture Notes in Computer Science*, pages 72–87. Springer, 2011.

J.-P. Bernardy and M. Lasson. Realizability and parametricity in pure type systems. In *FOSSACS*, volume 6604 of *Lecture Notes in Computer Science*, pages 108–122. Springer, 2011.

R. S. Bird and O. de Moor. *Algebra of programming*. Prentice Hall, 1997.

E. Brady, C. McBride, and J. McKinna. Inductive families need not store their indices. In *Types for Proofs and Programs*, pages 115–129. 2004.

J. Chapman, P.-E. Dagand, C. McBride, and P. Morris. The gentle art of levitation. *SIGPLAN Not.*, 45:3–14, September 2010.

T. Coquand. Pattern matching with dependent types. In *Types for Proofs and Programs*, 1992.

P. Dybjer. Inductive families. *Formal Asp. Comput.*, 6(4):440–465, 1994.

T. Freeman and F. Pfenning. Refinement types for ML. *SIGPLAN Not.*, 26: 268–277, May 1991.

C. Fumex, N. Ghani, and P. Johann. Indexed induction and coinduction, fibrationally. In *CALCO*, pages 176–191, 2011.

R. Harper and C. Stone. A Type-Theoretic interpretation of standard ML. In *Proof, Language, and Interaction: essays in honour of Robin Milner*, 2000.

H.-S. Ko and J. Gibbons. Modularising inductive families. In *Workshop on Generic Programming*, pages 13–24, 2011.

C. McBride. Ornamental algebras, algebraic ornaments. *Journal of Functional Programming, to appear*, 2012.

C. McBride and J. McKinna. The view from the left. *J. Funct. Program.*, 14(1):69–111, 2004.

C. McBride, H. Goguen, and J. McKinna. A few constructions on constructors. In *TYPES*, pages 186–200, 2004.

P. Morris, T. Altenkirch, and N. Ghani. A universe of strictly positive families. *Int. J. Found. Comput. Sci.*, 20(1):83–107, 2009.

U. Norell. *Towards a practical programming language based on dependent type theory*. PhD thesis, Chalmers University of Technology, 2007.

P.-Y. Strub. Coq modulo theory. In *CSL*, pages 529–543, 2010.

N. Swamy, J. Chen, C. Fournet, P.-Y. Strub, K. Bhargavan, and J. Yang. Secure distributed programming with value-dependent types. In *ICFP*, pages 266–278. ACM, 2011.

The Coq Development Team. *The Coq Proof Assistant Reference Manual*.

H. Xi, C. Chen, and G. Chen. Guarded recursive datatype constructors. In *POPL*, 2003.

Proof-Producing Synthesis of ML from Higher-Order Logic

Magnus O. Myreen Scott Owens

Computer Laboratory, University of Cambridge, UK

{magnus.myreen,scott.owens}@cl.cam.ac.uk

Abstract

The higher-order logic found in proof assistants such as Coq and various HOL systems provides a convenient setting for the development and verification of pure functional programs. However, to efficiently run these programs, they must be converted (or "extracted") to functional programs in a programming language such as ML or Haskell. With current techniques, this step, which must be trusted, relates similar looking objects that have very different semantic definitions, such as the set-theoretic model of a logic and the operational semantics of a programming language.

In this paper, we show how to increase the trustworthiness of this step with an automated technique. Given a functional program expressed in higher-order logic, our technique provides the corresponding program for a functional language defined with an operational semantics, and it provides a mechanically checked theorem relating the two. This theorem can then be used to transfer verified properties of the logical function to the program.

We have implemented our technique in the HOL4 theorem prover, translating functions to a core subset of Standard ML, and have applied it to examples including functional data structures, a parser generator, cryptographic algorithms, and a garbage collector.

Categories and Subject Descriptors D.2.4 [*Software/Program Verification*]: Formal Methods

General Terms Program Synthesis, Verification

1. Introduction

The logics of most proof assistants for higher-order logic (Coq, Isabelle/HOL, HOL4, PVS, etc.) contain subsets which closely resemble pure functional programming languages. As a result, it has become commonplace to verify functional programs by first coding up algorithms as functions in a theorem prover's logic, then using the prover to prove those logical functions correct, and then simply printing (sometimes called "extracting") these functions into the syntax of a functional programming language, typically SML, OCaml, Lisp, or Haskell. This approach is now used even in very large verification efforts such as the CompCert verified compiler [20] and several projects based on CompCert [1, 29, 38]; it has also been used in database verification [27].

However, the printing step is a potential weak link, as Harrison remarks in a survey on reflection [14]:

> " [...] the final jump from an abstract function inside the logic to a concrete implementation in a serious programming language which *appears to correspond to it* is a glaring leap of faith. "

In this paper we show how this *leap of faith* can be made into a trustworthy step. We show how the translation can be automatically performed via proof — a proof which states that (A:) the translation is semantics preserving with respect to the logic and an operational semantics of the target language. Ideally, one could then (B:) run the generated code on a platform which has been proved to implement that operational semantics. This setup provides the highest degree of trust in the executing code without any more effort on the part of programmers and prover users than the current printing/extraction approach.

In previous work, we have shown that A and B are possible for the simple case of an untyped first-order Lisp language [32], i.e. we can synthesise verified Lisp from Lisp-like functions living in higher-order logic; and achieve B by running the generated programs on a verified Lisp implementation [33] which has been proved to implement our operational semantics.

In this paper, we tackle the more complex problem of performing A for higher-order, typed ML-like functions, i.e. we show how semantics preserving translations from higher-order logic into a subset of ML can be performed inside the theorem prover. We believe our method works in general for connecting shallow and deep embeddings of functional programming languages. However, for this paper, we target a specific subset of a Standard ML language, for which we will be able to achieve B in future work with a verified compiler and runtime similar to [6], [9], or [33]. We call our ML subset MiniML and use SML syntax.

1.1 Example

To illustrate what our semantics preserving translation provides, assume that the user defines a summation function over lists using foldl as follows:[1]

$$\mathsf{sum} = \mathsf{foldl}\ (\lambda(x, y).\ x + y)\ 0$$

This sum function lives in higher-order logic but falls within the subset of the logic that corresponds directly to pure ML. As a result, we can translate sum into ML (like Poly/ML [28], our MiniML supports arbitrary precision integer arithmetic).

```
val sum = foldl (fn (x,y) => x+y) 0
```

For each run, our translation process proves a certificate theorem relating the function in the logic, sum, to the abstract syntax of the ML function, `sum`, w.r.t. an operational semantics of ML. For sum, this automatically derived certificate theorem states: when the closure that represents `sum` is applied to an argument of the right type, a list of numbers, then it will return a result, a number, which

[1] Throughout the paper we will typeset higher-order logic equations and definitions in san-serif and MiniML code in `typewriter`.

ICFP'12, September 9–15, 2012, Copenhagen, Denmark.

is exactly the same as the result of applying the HOL function sum to the same input.

The challenge is to do this translation in an easily automated, mechanical manner. In particular, one has to keep track of the relationship between shallowly embedded values, e.g., mathematical functions, and deeply embedded values in the ML semantics, e.g., closures. Our solution involves refinement/coupling invariants and combinators over refinement invariants.

1.2 Contributions

The main contribution of this paper is a new technique by which functions as defined in higher-order logic (HOL) can be translated, with proof, into pure ML equipped with an operational semantics. The ML-like subset of higher-order logic we consider includes:

- total recursive functions,
- type variables,
- functions as first-class values,
- nested pattern matching and user-defined datatypes, and
- partially specified functions, e.g. those with missing pattern match cases.

We also show how our translation technique can be extended with new translations for user-defined operations and types. As an example, we show how to add support for translation of operations over finite sets.

This work improves on the current state of the art of program synthesis from theorem provers (sometimes called program extraction, e.g. extract in Coq, emit-ML in HOL4 and code generation in Isabelle/HOL) by removing that step from the trusted computing base without requiring any additional work from the user. We prove the trustworthiness of the translation with certificate theorems stating that the generated code has exactly the behaviour (including termination) of the original logic function for all inputs where the original function is not partially specified.

We show that our technique is practical with case studies from the HOL4 examples repository, and other examples from the literature, including functional data structures, a parser generator, cryptographic algorithms, and a garbage collector.

Our translator, all of our examples, our semantics for MiniML, and its verified metatheory are all available at `http://www.cl.cam.ac.uk/~mom22/miniml/`.

2. Synthesising Quicksort: an example

Before explaining how our technique works, we first show what it does on a simple, but realistic, example: quicksort. Section 4 presents several larger and more significant examples.

One can define quicksort for lists in higher-order logic as follows.[2] Here ++ appends lists and partition splits a list into two: those elements that satisfy the given predicate, and those that do not.

$$\begin{array}{l}(\mathsf{qsort}\ R\ []\ =\ [])\ \wedge\\ (\mathsf{qsort}\ R\ (h :: t) =\\ \quad \mathsf{let}\ (l_1, l_2) = \mathsf{partition}\ (\lambda y.\ R\ y\ h)\ t\ \mathsf{in}\\ \qquad (\mathsf{qsort}\ R\ l_1){+}{+}[h]{+}{+}(\mathsf{qsort}\ R\ l_2))\end{array}$$

Given this definition of the algorithm, one can use HOL to prove the correctness of quicksort:

Theorem 1 (Quicksort correctness). *Given a transitive, total relation R and a list l, qsort returns a sorted permutation of list l.*

Proof. Mechanically verified in HOL4's library: a textbook exercise in program verification. □

Note that this definition and proof could be (and indeed were) developed in HOL4 without any reference to an intended use of the ML synthesis technique presented in this paper.

Given quicksort's definition, our translator can then generate the AST for the following MiniML function (MiniML doesn't have built-in lists; the `Nil`, `Cons`, and append constructors and function come from translating the HOL4 list library used by quicksort):

```
fun qsort r = fn l => case l of
  | Nil => Nil
  | Cons(h,t) =>
    let val x' = partition (fn y => r y h) t in
    case x' of
     | Pair(l1,l2) =>
        append (append (qsort r l1) (Cons(h,Nil)))
               (qsort r l2)
    end
```

In the process of generating the above code, the translator also establishes a correspondence between MiniML values and HOL terms and proves the following theorem stating correctness of the translation.

Theorem 2 (Certificate theorem for `qsort`). *When given an application of `qsort` to arguments corresponding to HOL terms, the MiniML operational semantics will terminate with a value that corresponds to the application of HOL function qsort to those terms.*

Proof. Automatically proved as part of the translation, the details of which are the topic of this paper. This proof uses the induction theorem that arises from the definition of qsort in HOL [39]. □

We can use this automatically proved theorem to push the verification result for qsort (Theorem 1) to also apply to the generated MiniML code `qsort`:

Theorem 3 (MiniML quicksort correctness). *If*

1. `qsort` *is bound in the MiniML environment to the implementation listed above,*
2. `leq_R` *is a value that corresponds to a transitive, total HOL relation leq, and*
3. `unsorted_l` *is a value that corresponds to HOL list l,*

then evaluation of MiniML program `qsort leq_R unsorted_l` *terminates with a list value* `sorted_l` *that corresponds to the sorted HOL list (qsort leq l).*

Proof. Trivial combination of the two theorems above. □

In summary, we have taken the quicksort algorithm, expressed as a definition in higher-order logic and verified in that setting, and we have generated a pure functional MiniML program and automatically proved that it is correct, according to the operational semantics of MiniML. Note that the meaning of HOL's qsort function is in terms of the proof theory or model theory of higher-order logic, while the MiniML `qsort` function has an operational meaning, which is understood by ML compilers.

3. Overview of approach

In this section, we give a tutorial introduction to our translation approach. Subsequent sections will provide the details (Sect. 5), case studies (Sect. 4) and formal definitions (Sect. 6) that we omit in this section.

[2] In fact, we are re-using Konrad Slind's verified quicksort algorithm from HOL4's library.

3.1 Basic judgements

Our translation from HOL to MiniML derives certificate theorems stated in terms of a predicate called Eval (which is reminiscent of a logical relation).

$$\text{Eval } \mathit{env}\ \mathit{exp}\ \mathit{post}$$

Such statements are true if MiniML expression exp evaluates in environment env to some value x and the postcondition $post$ is true for this x, i.e. $post\ x$. Here env is a list of bindings: names are bound to MiniML values (as modelled in our semantics of MiniML), exp is abstract syntax for a MiniML expression and $post$ is a function from MiniML values to $bool$.

Typically, $post$ will be instantiated with a refinement invariant relating a value from HOL to a MiniML value. An example of such an invariant is int. The relation int $n\ v$ is true if integer n is represented in MiniML as value v. With this refinement invariant we can state that the deep embedding of MiniML expression `5` evaluates to 5 in HOL, as follows. We will denote MiniML abstract syntax trees of our MiniML language using SML syntax inside $\lfloor \cdot \rfloor$.

$$\text{Eval } \mathit{env}\ \lfloor \texttt{5} \rfloor\ (\text{int } 5) \tag{1}$$

We can similarly state that MiniML variable `n` evaluates to the value held in HOL integer variable n by writing:

$$\text{Eval } \mathit{env}\ \lfloor \texttt{n} \rfloor\ (\text{int } n) \tag{2}$$

From statements such as (1) and (2), we can derive properties of compound expressions, e.g. for addition of numbers:

$$\text{Eval } \mathit{env}\ \lfloor \texttt{n+5} \rfloor\ (\text{int } (n+5)) \tag{3}$$

3.2 Refinement combinator for functions

The above examples considered simple MiniML expressions that produce concrete values. However, MiniML values can also be closures, such as produced by

```
fn n => n+5
```

To handle closures, we want to combine the refinement invariants for the input and for the output types; in this case both use invariant int. To do this, we have a refinement combinator, $\to$, which takes two invariants, a and b, as arguments:

$$a \to b$$

The statement $(a \to b)\ f\ v$ is true if the value v is a closure such that, when the closure is applied to a value satisfying refinement invariant input a, it returns a value satisfying output b; and furthermore, its input-output relation coincides with f. In other words, when evaluated v corresponds to evaluation of HOL function f. For example, $(\text{int} \to \text{int})\ (\lambda n.\ n+5)\ v$ specifies that v is a closure in MiniML which has an input-output relation corresponding to the HOL function $\lambda n.\ n+5$.

The $\to$ refinement combinator can be introduced using a rule for the MiniML closure constructor `fn`. For example, we can derive the following from statement (3) and its assumption on n, i.e. (2).

$$\text{Eval } \mathit{env}\ \lfloor \texttt{fn n => n+5} \rfloor\ ((\text{int} \to \text{int})\ (\lambda n.\ n+5)) \tag{4}$$

Closures that are specified using the $\to$ combinator can be applied to arguments of the corresponding 'input refinement invariant'. For example, we apply (4) to (1) to arrive at their combination:

$$\text{Eval } \mathit{env}\ \lfloor \texttt{(fn n => n+5) 5} \rfloor\ (\text{int } ((\lambda n.\ n+5)\ 5))$$

3.3 Type variables and functions as first-class values

The above examples used int as a fixed type/invariant. So how do we translate something that has HOL type α, i.e. a variable type? Answer: for this we use a regular HOL variable for the invariant, e.g. we can use variable a with HOL type: $\alpha \to \mathit{ml\_value} \to \mathit{bool}$ as the invariant. (Here and throughout $\mathit{ml\_value}$ is the HOL datatype which models MiniML values in HOL as a deep embedding.) The HOL type of int is $\mathit{int} \to \mathit{ml\_value} \to \mathit{bool}$, i.e. all that we did was abstract the constant int to a variable a and, similarly in its type, we abstracted the type int to α.

With this variable a ranging over all possible refinement invariants, we can state that MiniML variable `x` evaluates to HOL variable x of type α as follows.

$$\text{Eval } \mathit{env}\ \lfloor \texttt{x} \rfloor\ (a\ x)$$

Similarly, we can use the invariant combinator from above to specify that the MiniML value is some closure such that HOL function f of type $\alpha \to \alpha$ is an accurate representation in the HOL logic.

$$\text{Eval } \mathit{env}\ \lfloor \texttt{f} \rfloor\ ((a \to a)\ f)$$

Since these statements are stated in terms of refinement invariants and $\to$, we can apply the combinator rules mentioned above. For example, we can derive MiniML code corresponding to a HOL function $\lambda f\ x.\ f\ (f\ x)$ which has an abstract type involving α.

$$\begin{array}{l}\text{Eval } \mathit{env}\ \lfloor \texttt{fn f => fn x => f (f x)} \rfloor \\ \qquad (((a \to a) \to a \to a)\ (\lambda f\ x.\ f\ (f\ x)))\end{array} \tag{5}$$

Evaluation of `fn f => fn x => f (f x)` results in the following closure in our semantics of MiniML:[3]

$$\text{Closure } \mathit{env}\ \texttt{"f"}\ \lfloor \texttt{fn x => f (f x)} \rfloor$$

If we assume that MiniML variable name `"twice"` is bound to this value in the evaluation environment env then we can prove, from (5), that the MiniML code `twice` evaluates to a closure with exactly the same behaviour as a HOL function defined by $\text{twice} = \lambda f\ x.\ f\ (f\ x)$.

$$\begin{array}{l}\mathit{env}\ \texttt{"twice"} = \text{Closure } \mathit{twice\_env}\ \ldots \implies \\ \text{Eval } \mathit{env}\ \lfloor \texttt{twice} \rfloor\ (((a \to a) \to a \to a)\ \text{twice}))\end{array} \tag{6}$$

This is the way we translate non-recursive functions into MiniML.

The example above used variables in place of some refinement invariants. These variables can, of course, be instantiated when combined with Eval-theorems of more specific types. For example, we can plug together (4) and (6) to derive:

$$\begin{array}{l}\mathit{env}\ \texttt{"twice"} = \text{Closure } \ldots \implies \\ \text{Eval } \mathit{env}\ \lfloor \texttt{twice (fn n => n+5)} \rfloor \\ \qquad ((\text{int} \to \text{int})\ (\text{twice } (\lambda n.\ n+5))))\end{array}$$

3.4 Recursive functions

ML code for non-recursive functions can be derived as shown above. However, recursive functions require some additional effort. To illustrate why, consider the following definition of gcd.

$$\text{gcd } m\ n \ = \ \text{if } 0 < n \text{ then gcd } n\ (m \text{ mod } n) \text{ else } m$$

If we were to do exactly the same derivation for the right-hand side of the definition of gcd, we would get stuck. The algorithm that the examples above illustrate proceeds in a bottom-up manner: it traverses the structure of the HOL term for which we want to generate MiniML. When translating the right-hand side of a recursive function's definition, what are we to use as the Eval-description of the effect of applying the recursive call? At that stage we would like to have a theorem of the form:

$$\ldots \implies \text{Eval } \mathit{env}\ \lfloor \texttt{gcd} \rfloor\ ((\text{int} \to \text{int} \to \text{int})\ \text{gcd})$$

In other words, we would like to assume what we set out to prove.

Our solution is to make a more precise assumption: we formulate the assumption in such a way that it records for what values it

[3] We represent a closure in three parts: an environment, a parameter, and a body expression.

was applied; we then discharge these assumptions using an induction which will be explained later.

We use a new combinator eq to 'record' what values we have assumed that the recursive call is applied to. The definition of eq,

$$\mathsf{eq}\ a\ x = \lambda y\ v.\ (x = y) \wedge a\ y\ v$$

is explained in Section 6.7 together with a more thorough explanation of this example. However, for now, read the following as saying that a call to MiniML `gcd` has exactly the behaviour of HOL gcd if it is applied to int inputs m and n.

$$\mathsf{Eval}\ env\ \lfloor \mathtt{gcd} \rfloor\ ((\mathsf{eq\ int}\ m \to \mathsf{eq\ int}\ n \to \mathsf{int})\ \mathsf{gcd}) \quad (7)$$

For the rest of this example we abbreviate (7) as $\mathsf{P}\ m\ n$.

For the recursive call in gcd's right-hand side we can derive the following Eval-theorem. Note how the assumption P mentions exactly what values gcd was called with.

$$\begin{array}{l} \mathsf{P}\ n\ (m\ \mathsf{mod}\ n) \implies \\ \mathsf{Eval}\ env\ \lfloor \mathtt{gcd\ n\ (m\ mod\ n)} \rfloor\ (\mathsf{int}\ (\mathsf{gcd}\ n\ (m\ \mathsf{mod}\ n))) \end{array}$$

By making this kind of assumption at every recursive call site, we can proceed with our bottom-up derivation as before. The entire right-hand side of gcd produces the following result:

$$\begin{array}{l} (0 < n \implies \mathsf{P}\ n\ (m\ \mathsf{mod}\ n)) \implies \\ \mathsf{Eval}\ env\ \lfloor \mathtt{if\ 0\ <\ n\ then\ gcd\ \ldots} \rfloor\ (\mathsf{int}\ (\mathsf{gcd}\ m\ n)) \end{array}$$

We now proceed to package the right-hand side of gcd into a closure, very much as we did for `twice` above, except this time we need a recursive closure (which is described in Section 6.2). We omit the details regarding recursive closures here, but note that the result of this packaging is a theorem:

$$\begin{array}{l} env\ \texttt{"gcd"} = \mathsf{Recclosure}\ \ldots\ \lfloor \mathtt{if\ 0\ <\ n\ \ldots} \rfloor \implies \\ \forall m\ n.\ (0 < n \implies \mathsf{P}\ n\ (m\ \mathsf{mod}\ n)) \implies \mathsf{P}\ m\ n \end{array} \quad (8)$$

We now turn to the phase where we discharge the assumptions that were made at the call sites. For this we will use an induction principle which arises from the totality proof for gcd. All functions in HOL are total, and as a side product of definitions we get an automatically proved induction scheme that is tailored to the structure of the recursion in the definition. The induction scheme that comes out of the definition of gcd is:

$$\begin{array}{l} \forall P.\ (\forall m\ n.\ (0 < n \implies P\ n\ (m\ \mathsf{mod}\ n)) \implies P\ m\ n) \\ \quad \implies (\forall m\ n.\ P\ m\ n) \end{array} \quad (9)$$

Note that this induction scheme matches the structure of (8) precisely. This means that, by one application of modus ponens of (8) and (9), we arrive at a theorem with a right-hand side: $\forall m\ n.\ \mathsf{P}\ m\ n$. By expanding the abbreviation P (and some simplification to remove eq as explained in Section 6.8), we arrive at the desired certificate theorem for gcd:

$$\begin{array}{l} env\ \texttt{"gcd"} = \mathsf{Recclosure}\ \ldots\ \lfloor \mathtt{if\ 0\ <\ n\ \ldots} \rfloor \implies \\ \mathsf{Eval}\ env\ \lfloor \mathtt{gcd} \rfloor\ ((\mathsf{int} \to \mathsf{int} \to \mathsf{int})\ \mathsf{gcd}) \end{array}$$

To summarise: we use eq together with the custom induction scheme that HOL gives us for each recursive definition to perform translations of recursive HOL functions.

3.5 Datatypes and pattern matching

HOL provides ways of defining ML-like datatypes, e.g. the *list* type can be defined as follows:

$$\mathsf{datatype}\ \alpha\ list\ =\ \mathsf{Nil}\ \mid\ \mathsf{Cons\ of}\ \alpha \times (\alpha\ list)$$

These datatypes can be used in ML-like pattern matching. In the following text we will write Cons as :: and Nil as [ ].

We can support such datatypes in translations by defining a refinement invariant for each datatype that is encountered. For $\alpha\ list$, we define list which takes a refinement invariant a as an argument. We write application of list in post-fix notation, i.e. a list, to make it look like a type. The definition of list can be automatically produced from the datatype definition. Here Conv is a constructor-value from the MiniML semantics (as opposed to, say, a Closure value we saw previously).

$$\begin{array}{rcl} (a\ \mathsf{list})\ [\,]\ v & = & (v = \mathsf{Conv}\ \texttt{"Nil"}\ [\,]) \\ (a\ \mathsf{list})\ (x :: xs)\ v & = & \exists v_1\ v_2.\ (v = \mathsf{Conv}\ \texttt{"Cons"}\ [v_1, v_2]) \\ & & a\ x\ v_1 \wedge (a\ \mathsf{list})\ xs\ v_2 \end{array}$$

Based on this definition, we can derive lemmas (see Section 6.6) with which we can translate constructors and pattern matching for this datatype.

However, there is one trick involved: HOL functions that have pattern matching at the top-level tend to be defined as multiple equations. For example, the map function is typically defined in HOL using two equations:

$$\begin{array}{rcl} \mathsf{map}\ f\ [\,] & = & [\,] \\ \mathsf{map}\ f\ (x :: xs) & = & f\ x :: \mathsf{map}\ f\ xs \end{array}$$

In the process of defining this in HOL, the theorem prover reduces the multi-line definition to a single line with a case statement:

$$\mathsf{map}\ f\ xs\ =\ \mathsf{case}\ xs\ \mathsf{of}\ \ldots$$

It is these single-line definitions that we translate into MiniML functions with similar `case` statements. The translation of case statements will be explained in more detail in Section 6.6.

3.6 Partial functions and under specification

The use of pattern matching leads to partiality.[4] The simplest case of this partiality is the definition of hd for lists, which is defined intentionally with only one case:

$$\mathsf{hd}\ (x :: xs)\ =\ x$$

This definition could equally well have been defined in HOL as:

$$\mathsf{hd}\ xs\ =\ \mathsf{case}\ xs\ \mathsf{of}\ [\,] \Rightarrow \mathsf{ARB} \mid (x :: xs) \Rightarrow x$$

using the special ARB[5] constant in HOL, which cannot be translated into MiniML.

When translating a partial definition into MiniML, we can only prove a connection between MiniML and HOL for certain well-defined input values. For this purpose we use eq from above to restrict the possible input values. The theorem that relates hd to its MiniML counterpart includes a side-condition $xs \neq [\,]$ on the input, which is applied via eq:

$$\begin{array}{l} (env\ \texttt{"hd"} = \ldots) \wedge xs \neq [\,] \implies \\ \mathsf{Eval}\ env\ \lfloor \mathtt{hd} \rfloor\ ((\mathsf{eq}\ (a\ \mathsf{list})\ xs \to a)\ \mathsf{hd}) \end{array}$$

The generated MiniML code includes `raise Error` in the places where the translation is disconnected from the HOL function.

```
hd xs = case xs of [] => raise Error | ...
```

At the point in the derivation where we require a MiniML value corresponding to ARB, we have a trivially true theorem with false on the left-hand side of an implication.

$$\mathsf{false} \implies \mathsf{Eval}\ env\ \lfloor \mathtt{raise\ Error} \rfloor\ (a\ \mathsf{ARB})$$

This false assumption trickles up to the top level causing the side condition, $xs \neq [\,]$ for hd.

[4] All functions in HOL are total. However, their definitions can omit cases causing their equational specification to appear partial.

[5] ARB is defined non-constructively using Hilbert's arbitrary choice operator.

Translation of recursive partial functions results in recursive side conditions, e.g. the zip function is defined in HOL as:

$$\begin{array}{rcl} \mathsf{zip}\ ([\,],[\,]) & = & [\,] \\ \mathsf{zip}\ (x :: xs, y :: ys) & = & (x,y) :: \mathsf{zip}\ (xs, ys) \end{array}$$

The side condition which is produced for zip is:

$$\begin{array}{rcl} \mathsf{zip\_side}\ ([\,],[\,]) & = & \mathsf{true} \\ \mathsf{zip\_side}\ ([\,], y :: ys) & = & \mathsf{false} \\ \mathsf{zip\_side}\ (x :: xs, [\,]) & = & \mathsf{false} \\ \mathsf{zip\_side}\ (x :: xs, y :: ys) & = & \mathsf{zip\_side}\ (xs, ys) \end{array}$$

These side conditions arise in the derivation as assumptions that are not discharged when the definition-specific induction is applied.

3.7 Equality types

There is another source of partiality: equality tests. MiniML and HOL have different semantics regarding equality. In MiniML, equality of function closures cannot be tested, while equality of functions is allowed in HOL. Whenever an equality is to be translated, we use the following lemma which introduces a condition, EqualityType, on the refinement invariant a for the values that are tested. The definition of EqualityType is given in Section 6.4.

$$\begin{array}{l} \mathsf{Eval}\ env\ \lfloor \mathtt{x} \rfloor\ (a\ x) \wedge \mathsf{Eval}\ env\ \lfloor \mathtt{y} \rfloor\ (a\ y) \implies \\ \mathsf{EqualityType}\ a \implies \\ \mathsf{Eval}\ env\ \lfloor \mathtt{x = y} \rfloor\ (\mathsf{bool}\ (x = y)) \end{array}$$

In contrast to the partiality caused by missing patterns, this form of partiality is neater in that it applies to the refinement invariant, not the actual input values.

For each datatype definition we attempt to prove a lemma which simplifies such equality type constraints, e.g. for the list invariant we can automatically prove:

$$\forall a.\ \mathsf{EqualityType}\ a \implies \mathsf{EqualityType}\ (a\ \mathsf{list})$$

Such lemmas cannot always be proved, e.g. if the datatype contains a function type.

3.8 User-defined extensions

Our approach to supporting user-defined datatypes in Section 3.5 involves machinery which automatically defines new refinement invariants and proves lemmas that can be used in the translation process. The same kind of extensions can also be provided by the user with custom refinement invariants and lemmas for types defined in ways other than datatype (e.g., a quotient construction).

As a simple example, consider the following naive refinement invariant for finite sets represented as lists in MiniML:

$$(a\ \mathsf{set})\ s\ v \;=\; \exists xs.\ (a\ \mathsf{list})\ xs\ v \wedge (s = \mathsf{set\_from\_list}\ xs)$$

Using basic list operations we can prove judgements that can be used for translating basic sets and set operations, e.g. $\{\}$, $\cup$ and $\in$ are implemented by `[]`, `append` and `mem`. The last one also depends on EqualityType a.

$$\mathsf{Eval}\ env\ \lfloor \mathtt{[]} \rfloor\ ((a\ \mathsf{set})\ \{\})$$

$$\begin{array}{l} \mathsf{Eval}\ env\ \lfloor \mathtt{x} \rfloor\ ((a\ \mathsf{set})\ x) \wedge \mathsf{Eval}\ env\ \lfloor \mathtt{y} \rfloor\ ((a\ \mathsf{set})\ y) \implies \\ \mathsf{Eval}\ env\ \lfloor \mathtt{append\ x\ y} \rfloor\ ((a\ \mathsf{set})\ (x \cup y)) \end{array}$$

$$\begin{array}{l} \mathsf{Eval}\ env\ \lfloor \mathtt{r} \rfloor\ (a\ r) \wedge \mathsf{Eval}\ env\ \lfloor \mathtt{x} \rfloor\ ((a\ \mathsf{set})\ x) \implies \\ \mathsf{Eval}\ env\ \lfloor \mathtt{mem\ r\ x} \rfloor\ (\mathsf{bool}\ (r \in x)) \end{array}$$

The example above is naive and can potentially produce very inefficient code. However, the basic idea can be applied to more efficient data structures, e.g. the datatypes presented in Okasaki's book on functional data structures [36].

We have implemented extensions which can deal with finite sets, finite maps, natural numbers and n-bit machine arithmetic.

4. Case studies

Our translation is implemented (Section 5.1) as an ML program that operates over the HOL4 prover's internal representation of higher-order logic terms, producing HOL4 theorems about MiniML programs (whose semantics we have formally specified in HOL4, see Section 6.2). To demonstrate that it is robust, we have successfully applied it to the following algorithms:

- Miller-Rabin primality test (by Hurd [16])
  This example uses higher-order, recursive, and partial functions, and it requires that all three of these aspects be handled simultaneously.
- An SLR parser generator (by Barthwal [2])
  This is non-trivial algorithm with a long definition: 150 lines in HOL. Its definition makes use of pattern matching.
- AES, RC6 and TEA private key encryption/decryption algorithms (verified by Duan et al. [11])
  These algorithms operate on fixed-size word values, which we support through the technique for user-defined extensions (Section 3.8). We represent fixed-size words as integers in MiniML and use a refinement invariant to make sure the correspondence is maintained.
- McCarthy's 91 function, quicksort (by Slind [39]), and a regular expression matching function (by Owens [37])
  The 91 function and regular expression matcher both have intricate totality proofs, but our technique can easily and automatically prove termination based on the HOL-provided induction principles (which were justified by the original totality proofs).
- A copying Cheney garbage collector (by Myreen [31])
  This is a model of Cheney's algorithm for copying garbage collection — a verified algorithm used in constructing a verified Lisp runtime [33]. It models memory as a mapping from natural numbers to a datatype of abstract memory values.
- Functional data structures from Okasaki's book [36]
  - heap datatypes: leftist, pairing, lazy, splay, binomial
  - set datatypes: unbalanced, red-black
  - sorting algorithms: merge sort
  - list datatypes: binary random-access lists
  - queues datatypes: batched, bankers, physicists, real-time, implicit, Hood-Melville

The algorithms from all but the last point above have been previously verified in HOL4. We have verified 13 of the 15 functional data structures from the last point. These data structures are the examples that Charguéraud [4] uses for his characteristic formula technique (except that we omit the bootstrapped heap and catenable list whose datatypes are not supported by HOL's datatype package). Compared with Charguéraud's verification proofs, ours are similar in length. However, Charguéraud had to use special purpose tactics to deal with his characteristic formulae. In contrast, our verification proofs use only conventional HOL4 tactics. See the related work section for further comparison.

5. Algorithm

We have thus far omitted details and explained our approach through examples. Here, and in the next section, we provide formal definitions and explain that technicalities that earlier text avoided.

We start with an outline of the algorithm for translation. Our method translates one top-level function definition at a time. Each function is translated using the following automatic steps:

Information retrieval. The initial phase collects the necessary information about the function, e.g. is it a constant definition, is it recursive? If it is recursive then the induction theorem associated with its definition is fetched from the context.

Preprocessing. The next step prepares the definition for translation: the definition is collapsed to a single top-level clause, as mentioned in Section 3.5, and certain implicit pattern matching is rewritten into explicit pattern matching, e.g. $\lambda(x,y).\ body$ is expanded into $\lambda x.$ case x of $(x,y) \Rightarrow body$. For the rest of this section, assume that the definition is now of the form:

$$\mathsf{f}\ x_1\ x_2\ \ldots\ x_n = rhs$$

Bottom-up traversal. The next phase takes the right-hand side of the definition to be translated and constructs an Eval-theorem, as demonstrated in Section 3. This theorem is derived through a bottom-up traversal of the HOL expression. At each stage the proof rule or lemma which is applied introduces the corresponding MiniML syntax into the Eval-theorem. The result of this traversal is a theorem where the right-hand side of the HOL function appears together with its derived MiniML counterpart.

$$assumptions \implies \mathsf{Eval}\ env\ derived\_code\ (inv\ rhs)$$

The next phases attempt to discharge the assumptions. Trivial assumptions, such as some EqualityType assumptions, can be discharged as part of the bottom-up traversal.

Packaging. The next phase reduces the rhs to the function constant f. To do this, rules are applied which introduce a λ for each formal parameter, and then perform the following simplification on the right-hand side: the definition is collapsed and eta conversion is performed.

$$\begin{array}{ll} & \lambda x_1\ x_2\ \ldots\ x_n.\ rhs \\ = & \lambda x_1\ x_2\ \ldots\ x_n.\ \mathsf{f}\ x_1\ x_2\ \ldots\ x_n \\ = & \mathsf{f} \end{array}$$

Introduction of λ in the right-hand side of the HOL expression introduces closures on the MiniML side. For recursive functions, the final closure lemma is a special rule for introducing a recursive closure, explained in Section 6.5.

Induction. For recursive functions, the induction theorem associated with the function definition is used to discharge the assumptions that were made at the recursive call sites. The assumptions that the induction theorem fails to discharge are collected and defined to be a side-condition. Such side conditions usually arise from partiality in pattern matching (Section 3.6).

Simplification. As mentioned in Section 3.4, after the induction theorem has been applied the resulting theorem contains redundant occurrences of the eq combinator. These are removed using rewriting as explained in Section 6.8.

Future use. Once the translation is complete, the certificate theorem is stored into the translator's memory. Future translations can then use this certificate theorem in their **Bottom-up traversal** phase, when function constant f is encountered.

5.1 Implementation

Implementing the above algorithm in a HOL theorem prover is straightforward. One writes an ML program which performs the proof steps outlined above. Concretely, this involves writing ML functions that construct elements of type `thm` using the logical kernel's primitives (which correspond to axioms and inference rules of higher-order logic). Following the LCF-approach, this design ensures that all proved theorems are the result of the basic inference rules of higher-order logic.

$$\begin{array}{lcl} t & := & \alpha \mid tc \mid (t_1,\ldots,t_n)tc \mid t_1 \to t_2 \\ p & := & x \mid C\ p_1 \ldots p_n \\ e & := & x \mid \mathsf{ARB} \mid C\ e_1 \ldots e_n \mid \lambda x.e \mid e_1\ e_2 \mid e_1 = e_2 \\ & \mid & e_1 \wedge e_2 \mid e_1 \vee e_2 \\ & \mid & \mathsf{if}\ e_1\ \mathsf{then}\ e_2\ \mathsf{else}\ e_3 \mid \mathsf{let}\ x = e_1\ \mathsf{in}\ e_2 \\ & \mid & \mathsf{case}\ e\ \mathsf{of}\ p_1 \Rightarrow e_1 \mid \ldots \mid p_n \Rightarrow e_n \\ c & := & C \mid C\ \mathsf{of}\ t_1 \Rightarrow \ldots \Rightarrow t_n \\ d & := & x_1 = c_{11} \mid \ldots \mid c_{1n_1}; \ldots ; x_m = c_{m1} \mid \ldots \mid c_{mn_m} \\ & \mid & (x_1\ p_{11} \ldots p_{1n_1} = e_1) \wedge \ldots \wedge (x_m\ p_{m1} \ldots p_{mn_m} = e_m) \end{array}$$

where x ranges over identifiers, C over constructor names, and tc over type constructor names

Figure 1. Core HOL source grammar

$$\begin{array}{lcl} t & := & \ldots \mid \mathsf{bool} \mid \mathsf{int} \mid \mathsf{num} \mid \mathsf{char} \mid t_1 \times t_2 \mid t\ \mathsf{list} \mid t\ \mathsf{option} \\ p & := & \ldots \\ & \mid & \mathsf{T} \mid \mathsf{F} \mid \mathbb{Z} \mid \mathbb{N} \mid (p_1, p_2) \mid [] \mid p_1 :: p_2 \mid \mathsf{SOME}\ p_1 \mid \mathsf{NONE} \\ e & := & \ldots \\ & \mid & \mathsf{T} \mid \mathsf{F} \mid \mathbb{Z} \mid \mathbb{N} \mid (e_1, e_2) \mid [] \mid e_1 :: e_2 \mid \mathsf{SOME}\ e_1 \mid \mathsf{NONE} \end{array}$$

Figure 2. HOL source grammar after prelude extension

We have implemented our translator in the HOL4 theorem prover. Source code and examples are available at:

`http://www.cl.cam.ac.uk/~mom22/miniml/`

6. Technical details

This section dives into some technical details. We provide definitions and descriptions of the lemmas that are used as part of translations.

6.1 HOL source language

Figure 1 gives the subset of HOL definitions d that we can translate. This grammar describes a subset of the HOL4 logic, it is not deeply embedded in HOL4, nor do we formally reason about it. It includes (possibly mutually) recursive, higher-order functions that operate over (possibly mutually) recursive, user-defined datatypes. The translation will fail if it encounters a term not in this subset (e.g. universal and existential quantifiers, Hilbert's choice) in the definitions being translated. The translator comes with a standard prelude that includes support for booleans, integers, natural numbers, characters, pairs, lists, and options (Figure 2).

6.2 MiniML target language

Figure 3 gives the source grammar for MiniML types t, values v, patterns p, expressions e, type definitions td/c and top-level definitions d. The language is a mostly unsugared subset of core Standard ML. It includes mutually recursive datatype definitions; higher-order, anonymous, and mutually recursive functions; nested pattern matching; and abrupt termination (a simplified `raise`). MiniML integers are arbitrary precision (which is how the Poly/ML compiler implements integers natively, other ML implementations usually support them as a library). Unsupported features are records, mutable references, exception handling, and the module system.

We give MiniML both small-step and big-step call-by-value operational semantics, and a type system. Each of these three has an expression-level and definition-level component; here we only present the expression level, but see `http://www.cl.cam.ac.uk/~mom22/miniml/` for complete definitions as well as HOL4 proofs of the theorems below, at both levels. The type system is typical. Figure 4 gives the auxiliary definitions needed to support the semantics (in this figure we abbreviate ml_value to v), and Figure 5 gives the shapes of the various semantic relations.

$$
\begin{array}{lcl}
t & := & \alpha \mid x \mid (t_1, \ldots, t_n)x \mid t_1 \texttt{ -> } t_2 \mid \texttt{int} \mid \texttt{bool} \\
v & := & C \mid \texttt{true} \mid \texttt{false} \mid \mathbb{Z} \\
p & := & x \mid v \mid C(p_1, \ldots, p_n) \\
e & := & \texttt{raise } ex \\
  & \mid & x \mid v \mid C(e_1, \ldots, e_n) \\
  & \mid & \texttt{fn } x \texttt{ => } e \\
  & \mid & e_1\ e_2 \mid e_1\ op\ e_2 \mid e_1 \texttt{ andalso } e_2 \mid e_1 \texttt{ orelse } e_2 \\
  & \mid & \texttt{if } e_1 \texttt{ then } e_2 \texttt{ else } e_3 \\
  & \mid & \texttt{case } e \texttt{ of } p_1 \texttt{ => } e_1 \texttt{ | } \ldots \texttt{ | } p_n \texttt{ => } e_n \\
  & \mid & \texttt{let val } x \texttt{ = } e_1 \texttt{ in } e_2 \texttt{ end} \\
  & \mid & \texttt{let fun } x_1\ y_1 \texttt{ = } e_1 \texttt{ and} \ldots \texttt{and } x_n\ y_n \texttt{ = } e_n \texttt{ in } e \texttt{ end} \\
c & := & C \mid C \texttt{ of } t_1 \texttt{ * } \ldots \texttt{ * } t_n \\
td & := & (\alpha_1, \ldots, \alpha_m)\ x \texttt{ = } c_1 \texttt{ | } \ldots \texttt{ | } c_n \\
  & \mid & x \texttt{ = } c_1 \texttt{ | } \ldots \texttt{ | } c_n \\
d & := & \texttt{val } p \texttt{ = } e \\
  & \mid & \texttt{fun } x_1\ y_1 \texttt{ = } e_1 \texttt{ and} \ldots \texttt{and } x_n\ y_n \texttt{ = } e_n \\
  & \mid & \texttt{datatype } td_1 \texttt{ and} \ldots \texttt{and } td_n \\
ex & := & \texttt{Bind} \mid \texttt{Div} \\
op & := & \texttt{=} \mid \texttt{+} \mid \texttt{-} \mid \texttt{*} \mid \texttt{div} \mid \texttt{mod} \mid \texttt{<} \mid \texttt{<=} \mid \texttt{>} \mid \texttt{>=}
\end{array}
$$

where x and y range over identifiers and C over constructor names

Figure 3. MiniML source grammar

$$
\begin{array}{lcl}
v & := & C(v_1, \ldots, v_n) \\
  & \mid & \langle env, x, e \rangle \\
  & \mid & \langle env, (\texttt{fun } x_1\ y_1 \texttt{ = } e_1 \texttt{ and} \ldots \texttt{and } x_n\ y_n \texttt{ = } e_n), x \rangle \\
  & \mid & C \mid \texttt{true} \mid \texttt{false} \mid \mathbb{Z} \\
F & := & [\,]\ e \mid v\ [\,] \mid [\,]\ op\ e \mid v\ op\ [\,] \\
  & \mid & [\,] \texttt{ andalso } e \mid [\,] \texttt{ orelse } e \\
  & \mid & \texttt{if } [\,] \texttt{ then } e_2 \texttt{ else } e_3 \\
  & \mid & \texttt{case } [\,] \texttt{ of } p_1 \texttt{ => } e_1 \texttt{ | } \ldots \texttt{ | } p_n \texttt{ => } e_n \\
  & \mid & \texttt{let val } x \texttt{ = } [\,] \texttt{ in } e \texttt{ end} \\
  & \mid & C(v_1, \ldots, v_n, [\,], e_1, \ldots, e_n) \\
S & := & \langle Cenv, env, e, \langle F_1, env_1 \rangle \ldots \langle F_n, env_n \rangle \rangle \\
R_{match} & := & env \mid \texttt{no\_match} \mid \texttt{type\_error} \\
R_{step} & := & S \mid \texttt{type\_error} \mid \texttt{stuck} \\
R_{eval} & := & v \mid \texttt{raise } ex \mid \texttt{type\_error}
\end{array}
$$

where env ranges over finite maps from x to v,
$Cenv$ ranges over finite maps from C to $\langle \mathbb{N}, 2^C \rangle$,
$envT$ ranges over finite maps from x to $(\alpha_1, \ldots, \alpha_n)\ t$, *and*
$CenvT$ ranges over finite maps from C to
$\langle (\alpha_1, \ldots, \alpha_m), t_1 \ldots t_n, x \rangle$

Figure 4. Semantic auxiliaries for MiniML

The small-step semantics is a CEK-like machine [12] (see [13] for a textbook treatment) with states S (Figure 4) using a continuation stack built from frames F and environments env. Values are extended with constructed values (e.g., `Some(1)`), with closures pairing a function's environment, parameter, and body, and with recursive closures pairing an environment with a mutually recursive nest of functions. A single reduction step either gives a new state, signals a "type error", e.g., due to a misapplied primitive, or gets stuck (R_{step}). We use the small-step semantics to support a type soundness proof via preservation and progress [41], and to ensure a satisfactory treatment of divergence. Small-step evaluation and divergence are defined in terms of the transitive closure of the reduction relation.

Our technique for translating from HOL to MiniML uses a bottom-up, syntax-directed pass, and so requires a syntax-directed big-step semantics. The big-step semantics returns the same kind of things as small-step evaluation: values, exceptions and "type errors" (R_{eval}). We ensure that it gives type errors in enough cases so

Pattern matching:	$\langle Cenv, p, v, env \rangle \Downarrow R_{match}$
Small-step reduction:	$S \longrightarrow R_{step}$
Small-step evaluation:	$S \downarrow R_{eval}$
Small-step divergence:	$\langle Cenv, env, e \rangle \uparrow$
Big-step evaluation:	$\langle Cenv, env, e \rangle \Downarrow R_{eval}$
Alternate big-step evaluation:	$\langle env, e \rangle \Downarrow R_{eval}$
Typing:	$\langle CenvT, envT \rangle \vdash e : t$
Typing for environments:	$Cenv \vdash env : envT$

Figure 5. MiniML semantic relations

that only diverging expressions are not related to any result. This allows us to use (in our non-concurrent, deterministic setting) an inductive relation, instead of following a co-inductive approach [21]. Theorems 4 and 6 guarantee this property.

6.3 MiniML metatheory

Theorem 4 (Small-step/big-step equivalence). $\langle Cenv, env, e, \epsilon \rangle \downarrow R_{eval}$ *iff* $\langle Cenv, env, e \rangle \Downarrow R_{eval}$.

Proof. In HOL4.

- Forward implication:
  We first extend the big-step relation with context stack inputs, $Fs := \langle F_1, env_1 \rangle \ldots \langle F_n, env_n \rangle$. We then show that if $\langle Cenv_1, env_1, e_1, Fs_1 \rangle \longrightarrow \langle Cenv_2, env_2, e_2, Fs_2 \rangle$ and $\langle Cenv_2, env_2, e_2, Fs_2 \rangle \Downarrow R_{eval}$ then $\langle Cenv_1, env_1, e_1, Fs_1 \rangle \Downarrow R_{eval}$ by cases on the small-step relation. We then finish the proof by induction on the transitive closure of $\longrightarrow$. Note that unlike type soundness, we go backwards along the small-step trace; this is necessary to properly handle non-termination.
- Reverse implication:
  By induction on the big-step relation, with pervasive reasoning about adding context frames to the frame stacks of many-step small-step reduction sequences.

□

Theorem 5 (Big-step determinism). *If* $\langle Cenv, env, e \rangle \Downarrow R_{eval1}$ *and* $\langle Cenv, env, e \rangle \Downarrow R_{eval2}$ *then* $R_{eval1} = R_{eval2}$.

Proof. In HOL4, by induction on the big-step evaluation relation. □

Corollary 1 (Small-step determinism). *If* $\langle Cenv, env, e, \epsilon \rangle \downarrow R_{eval1}$ *and* $\langle Cenv, env, e, \epsilon \rangle \downarrow R_{eval2}$ *then* $R_{eval1} = R_{eval2}$.

Theorem 6 (Untyped safety). $\langle Cenv, env, e, \epsilon \rangle \downarrow R_{eval}$ *iff it is not the case that* $\langle Cenv, env, e \rangle \uparrow$.

Proof. In HOL4, by cases on the small-step relation. □

Theorem 7 (Type soundness). *If*

- *$Cenv$ and $CenvT$ are well-formed and consistent,*
- *$CenvT \vdash env : envT$, and*
- *$\langle CenvT, envT \rangle \vdash e : t$*

then either

- *$\langle Cenv, env, e \rangle \uparrow$, or*
- *$\langle Cenv, env, e, \epsilon \rangle \downarrow R_{eval}$ and $R_{eval} \neq$ `type_error`.*

Proof. In HOL4, a typical preservation and progress proof about the small-step semantics. □

The small- and big-step semantics are given a $Cenv$ which allows them to return `type_error` when an undefined data constructor (i.e., one not defined in a `datatype` definition) is applied, or when a data constructor is applied to the wrong number of arguments. However, we can simplify the translation from HOL by using an alternate big-step semantics that omits this argument. This alternate big-step semantics differs only in that mis-applied constructors are accepted and do not result in an error. However, they coincide on well-typed programs.

Theorem 8 (Alternate big step equivalence). *If $Cenv$ and $CenvT$ are well-formed and consistent, and $CenvT \vdash env : tenv$ and $\langle CenvT, envT\rangle \vdash e : t$ then $\langle Cenv, env, e\rangle \Downarrow R_{eval}$ iff $\langle env, e\rangle \Downarrow R_{eval}$.*

Proof. In HOL4, by induction on the big-step relation, and Theorems 6 and 7 and Corollary 1. □

6.4 Key definitions

As described in earlier sections, our translation makes statements about the semantics in terms of a predicate called Eval. We define this predicate as follows using the alternate big-step semantics evaluation relation $\Downarrow$. We define Eval $env\ exp\ post$ to be true if exp evaluates, in environment env, to some value v such that $post\ v$. The fact that it returns a value — as opposed to an error, `raise` ex — tells us that no error happened during evaluation, e.g. evaluation did not hit any missing cases while pattern matching.

$$\mathsf{Eval}\ env\ exp\ post \;=\; \exists v.\ \langle env, exp\rangle \Downarrow v \wedge post\ v$$

Here $post$ has type $ml\_value \to bool$.

The interesting part is what we instantiate $post$ with, i.e. the refinement invariants. The basic refinement invariants have the following definitions. Boolean and integer values relate to corresponding literal values in the MiniML semantics:

$$\begin{aligned} \mathsf{bool\ true} &= \lambda v.\ (v = \mathtt{true}) \\ \mathsf{bool\ false} &= \lambda v.\ (v = \mathtt{false}) \\ \mathsf{int}\ i &= \lambda v.\ (v = i) \qquad \text{where } i \in \mathbb{Z} \end{aligned}$$

We also have combinators for refinement invariants. The definition of the eq combinator was given in Section 3.4. We now turn to the $\to$ combinator which lifts refinement invariant to closures. The $\to$ combinator's definition is based on an evaluation relation for application of closures, evaluate_closure (which is defined in terms of $\Downarrow$, and applies to non-recursive and recursive closures). Read evaluate_closure $v\ cl\ u$ as saying: application of closure cl to argument v returns value u. We define a total-correctness Hoare-triple-like Spec for closure evaluation on top of this:

$$\begin{aligned} &\mathsf{Spec}\ p\ cl\ q \;= \\ &\quad \forall v.\ p\ v \implies \exists u.\ \mathsf{evaluate\_closure}\ v\ cl\ u \wedge q\ u \end{aligned}$$

The definition of the $\to$ combinator is an instance of Spec, where an abstract value x is universally quantified:

$$(a \to b)\ f \;=\; \lambda v.\ \forall x.\ \mathsf{Spec}\ (a\ x)\ v\ (b\ (f\ x))$$

Here the type of f is $\alpha \to \beta$ and the type of v is simply the type of a MiniML value in our MiniML semantics, i.e. ml_value.

The remaining definition is that of EqualityType a. A refinement invariant a supports equality if the corresponding MiniML value cannot be a closure, not_contains_closure, and testing for structural equality of MiniML values is equivalent to testing equality at the abstract level:

$$\begin{aligned} &\mathsf{EqualityType}\ a \;= \\ &\quad (\forall x\ v.\ a\ x\ v \implies \mathsf{not\_contains\_closure}\ v) \wedge \\ &\quad (\forall x\ v\ y\ w.\ a\ x\ v \wedge a\ y\ w \implies (v = w \iff x = y)) \end{aligned}$$

For example, bool and int, defined above, satisfy EqualityType.

6.5 Lemmas used in translations

In this section we present the lemmas about Eval that are used to perform the translations. All variables in these theorems are implicitly universally quantified at the top-level. The proof of these lemmas follow almost directly from the underlying definitions: none of the proofs required more than ten lines of script in HOL4.

Closure application. We start with the rule for applying a closure. A closure $a \to b$ can always be applied to an Eval-theorem with a matching refinement invariant a.

$$\begin{aligned} &\mathsf{Eval}\ env\ \lfloor \mathtt{f} \rfloor\ ((a \to b)\ f) \wedge \\ &\mathsf{Eval}\ env\ \lfloor \mathtt{x} \rfloor\ (a\ x) \implies \\ &\mathsf{Eval}\ env\ \lfloor \mathtt{f\ x} \rfloor\ (b\ (f\ x)) \end{aligned}$$

Closure introduction. Closures can be created with the following rule if the abstract and concrete values, x and v, which the body depends on can be universally quantified. Here $n \mapsto v$ extends the environment env with binding: name n maps to value v.

$$\begin{aligned} &(\forall x\ v.\ a\ x\ v \implies \mathsf{Eval}\ (env[n \mapsto v])\ \lfloor \mathtt{body} \rfloor\ (b\ (f\ x))) \implies \\ &\mathsf{Eval}\ env\ \lfloor \mathtt{fn}\ n\ \mathtt{=>}\ \mathtt{body} \rfloor\ ((a \to b)\ f) \end{aligned}$$

Alternative closure introduction. The rule above is not always applicable because side conditions restrict the variable x, i.e. the universal quantification cannot be introduced. This is an alternative rule which achieves the same without universal quantification of x — at the cost of introducing the eq combinator.

$$\begin{aligned} &(\forall v.\ a\ x\ v \implies \mathsf{Eval}\ (env[n \mapsto v])\ \lfloor \mathtt{body} \rfloor\ (b\ (f\ x))) \implies \\ &\mathsf{Eval}\ env\ \lfloor \mathtt{fn}\ n\ \mathtt{=>}\ \mathtt{body} \rfloor\ ((\mathsf{eq}\ a\ x \to b)\ f) \end{aligned}$$

Closure evaluation. The translator always returns theorems where the code is described by an assumption stating that the function name refers to the relevant code in the environment, i.e. an assumption of the form $env\ name =$ closure .... The following rule is used for deriving theorems with such assumptions for non-recursive closures:

$$\begin{aligned} &\mathsf{Eval}\ cl\_env\ \lfloor \mathtt{fn}\ n\ \mathtt{=>}\ \mathtt{body} \rfloor\ p \implies \\ &env\ name = \mathsf{Closure}\ cl\_env\ n\ \lfloor \mathtt{body} \rfloor \implies \\ &\mathsf{Eval}\ env\ \lfloor name \rfloor\ p \end{aligned}$$

Introduction of recursive closure. Our rule for introducing recursive closures, i.e. closures where the environment can refer to itself and hence perform recursive function calls to itself, is more verbose. Introduction of recursive closures is done using the following lemma. For this lemma to be applicable some name $name$ must refer to a recursive closure where $name$ is given. Let Recclosure cl_env $[(name, n, \lfloor \mathtt{body} \rfloor)]$ $name$ be abbreviated by Rec below.

$$\begin{aligned} &(\forall v.\ a\ x\ v \implies \\ &\qquad \mathsf{Eval}\ (env[n \mapsto v, name \mapsto \mathsf{Rec}])\ \lfloor \mathtt{body} \rfloor\ (b\ (f\ x))) \\ &\implies \\ &env\ name = \mathsf{Rec} \implies \\ &\mathsf{Eval}\ env\ \lfloor name \rfloor\ ((\mathsf{eq}\ a\ x \to b)\ f) \end{aligned}$$

Let introduction. Let-statements are constructed using the following lemma. Here let is HOL's internal combinator which represents let expressions. In HOL, let $f\ x = f\ x$ and the HOL printer knows to treat let as special, e.g. let $(\lambda a.\ a + 1)\ x$ is printed on the screen as let $a = x$ in $a + 1$.

$$\begin{aligned} &\mathsf{Eval}\ env\ \lfloor \mathtt{x} \rfloor\ (a\ x) \wedge \\ &(\forall v.\ a\ x\ v \implies \mathsf{Eval}\ (env[n \mapsto v])\ \lfloor \mathtt{body} \rfloor\ (b\ (f\ x))) \implies \\ &\mathsf{Eval}\ env\ \lfloor \mathtt{let\ val}\ n\ \mathtt{=\ x\ in\ body\ end} \rfloor\ (b\ (\mathsf{let}\ f\ x)) \end{aligned}$$

Variable simplification. During translation, the intermediate theorems typically contain assumptions specifying which HOL values relate to which MiniML values. It's convenient to state these as Eval env $\lfloor m \rfloor$ $(inv\ n)$, for some inv and some fixed variable name m. When variables get bound, e.g. as a result of introducing a closure, env is specialised and these assumptions can be simplified. We use the following lemma to simplify the assumptions when env gets specialised.

$$\begin{array}{l}\mathsf{Eval}\ (env[name \mapsto v])\ \lfloor m \rfloor\ p = \\ \quad \mathsf{if}\ m = name\ \mathsf{then}\ p\ v\ \mathsf{else}\ \mathsf{Eval}\ env\ \lfloor m \rfloor\ p\end{array}$$

If statements. The translation of HOL's if statements is done using the following rule. Note that the assumptions h_2 and h_3 get prefixed by the guard expression x_1.

$$\begin{array}{l}(h_1 \Longrightarrow \mathsf{Eval}\ env\ \lfloor \texttt{x1} \rfloor\ (\mathsf{bool}\ x_1)) \wedge \\ (h_2 \Longrightarrow \mathsf{Eval}\ env\ \lfloor \texttt{x2} \rfloor\ (inv\ x_2)) \wedge \\ (h_3 \Longrightarrow \mathsf{Eval}\ env\ \lfloor \texttt{x3} \rfloor\ (inv\ x_3)) \Longrightarrow \\ (h_1 \wedge (x_1 \Longrightarrow h_2) \wedge (\neg x_1 \Longrightarrow h_3)) \Longrightarrow \\ \quad \mathsf{Eval}\ env\ \lfloor \texttt{if x1 then x2 else x3} \rfloor \\ \quad\quad (inv\ (\mathsf{if}\ x_1\ \mathsf{then}\ x_2\ \mathsf{else}\ x_3))\end{array}$$

Literal values. MiniML has boolean and integer literals. The relevant lemmas for such literals:

$$\mathsf{Eval}\ env\ \lfloor \texttt{true} \rfloor\ (\mathsf{bool\ true})$$

$$\mathsf{Eval}\ env\ \lfloor \texttt{false} \rfloor\ (\mathsf{bool\ false})$$

$$\mathsf{Eval}\ env\ \lfloor i \rfloor\ (\mathsf{int}\ i) \qquad \text{where } i \in \mathbb{Z}$$

Binary operations. Each of the operations over the integers and booleans have separate lemmas. A few examples are listed below. Division and modulo have a side condition.

$$\begin{array}{l}\mathsf{Eval}\ env\ \lfloor \texttt{i} \rfloor\ (\mathsf{int}\ i) \wedge \\ \mathsf{Eval}\ env\ \lfloor \texttt{j} \rfloor\ (\mathsf{int}\ j) \Longrightarrow \\ \mathsf{Eval}\ env\ \lfloor \texttt{i + j} \rfloor\ (\mathsf{int}\ (i + j))\end{array}$$

$$\begin{array}{l}\mathsf{Eval}\ env\ \lfloor \texttt{i} \rfloor\ (\mathsf{int}\ i) \wedge \\ \mathsf{Eval}\ env\ \lfloor \texttt{j} \rfloor\ (\mathsf{int}\ j) \Longrightarrow \\ j \neq 0 \Longrightarrow \mathsf{Eval}\ env\ \lfloor \texttt{i div j} \rfloor\ (\mathsf{int}\ (i\ \mathsf{div}\ j))\end{array}$$

$$\begin{array}{l}\mathsf{Eval}\ env\ \lfloor \texttt{i} \rfloor\ (\mathsf{int}\ i) \wedge \\ \mathsf{Eval}\ env\ \lfloor \texttt{j} \rfloor\ (\mathsf{int}\ j) \Longrightarrow \\ \mathsf{Eval}\ env\ \lfloor \texttt{i < j} \rfloor\ (\mathsf{bool}\ (i < j))\end{array}$$

$$\begin{array}{l}\mathsf{Eval}\ env\ \lfloor \texttt{a} \rfloor\ (\mathsf{bool}\ a) \wedge \\ \mathsf{Eval}\ env\ \lfloor \texttt{b} \rfloor\ (\mathsf{bool}\ b) \Longrightarrow \\ \mathsf{Eval}\ env\ \lfloor \texttt{a andalso b} \rfloor\ (\mathsf{bool}\ (a \wedge b))\end{array}$$

There are also dynamically derived lemmas, e.g. each translation results in a new lemma that can be used in subsequent translations and datatype definitions result in a few lemmas (as described in the next section). Users can also manually provide additional lemmas.

6.6 Lemmas automatically proved for datatypes

For each datatype, we define a refinement invariant that relates it to ML values. Type variables cause these definitions to take refinement invariants as input. For example, for the $list$ datatype from Section 3.5 we define a refinement invariant, called list, as the following map into constructor, Conv, applications in MiniML. We write application of list in post-fix notation, i.e. a list, to make it look like a type.

$$\begin{array}{rcl}(a\ \mathsf{list})\ []\ v & = & (v = \mathsf{Conv}\ \texttt{"Nil"}\ []) \\ (a\ \mathsf{list})\ (x :: xs)\ v & = & \exists v_1\ v_2.\ (v = \mathsf{Conv}\ \texttt{"Cons"}\ [v_1, v_2]) \\ & & a\ x\ v_1 \wedge (a\ \mathsf{list})\ xs\ v_2\end{array}$$

Based on this definition we can derive lemmas that aid translation of constructor applications in HOL.

$$\mathsf{Eval}\ env\ \lfloor \texttt{Nil} \rfloor\ ((a\ \mathsf{list})\ [])$$

$$\begin{array}{l}\mathsf{Eval}\ env\ \lfloor \texttt{x} \rfloor\ (a\ x) \wedge \\ \mathsf{Eval}\ env\ \lfloor \texttt{xs} \rfloor\ ((a\ \mathsf{list})\ xs) \Longrightarrow \\ \mathsf{Eval}\ env\ \lfloor \texttt{Cons(x,xs)} \rfloor\ ((a\ \mathsf{list})\ (x :: xs))\end{array}$$

We also derive lemmas which aid in translating pattern matching over these HOL constructors. As mentioned in Section 3.5, multi-line pattern matches, i.e. HOL definitions that are defined as multiple equations, are merged into a single line definition with a case statement by the definition mechanism. By making sure translations are always performed only on these collapsed single line definitions, it is sufficient to add support for translations of case statements for the new datatype:

$$\mathsf{case}\ l\ \mathsf{of}\ [] \Rightarrow \ldots \mid (x :: xs) \Rightarrow \ldots$$

In HOL, case statements (including complicated-looking nested case statements) are internally represented as primitive 'case functions'. The case function for the $list$ datatype is defined using the following two equations:

$$\begin{array}{rcl}\mathsf{list\_case}\ []\ f_1\ f_2 & = & f_1 \\ \mathsf{list\_case}\ (x :: xs)\ f_1\ f_2 & = & f_2\ x\ xs\end{array}$$

Thus, in order to translate case statements for the $list$ datatype, it is sufficient to be able to translate any instantiation of $\mathsf{list\_case}\ l\ f_1\ f_2$. The lemma which we use for this is shown below. This lemma can be read as a generalisation of the lemma for translating closure introduction and if statements.

$$\begin{array}{l}(h_0 \Longrightarrow \mathsf{Eval}\ env\ \lfloor \texttt{l} \rfloor\ ((a\ \mathsf{list})\ l)) \wedge \\ (h_1 \Longrightarrow \mathsf{Eval}\ env\ \lfloor \texttt{y} \rfloor\ (b\ f_1)) \wedge \\ (\forall x\ xs\ v\ vs. \\ \quad a\ x\ v \wedge (a\ \mathsf{list})\ xs\ vs \wedge h_2\ x\ xs \Longrightarrow \\ \quad \mathsf{Eval}\ (env[n \mapsto v][m \mapsto vs])\ \lfloor \texttt{z} \rfloor\ (b\ (f_2\ x\ xs))) \Longrightarrow \\ (\forall x\ xs. \\ \quad h_0 \wedge ((l = []) \Longrightarrow h_1) \wedge \\ \quad ((l = x :: xs) \Longrightarrow h_2\ x\ xs)) \Longrightarrow \\ \mathsf{Eval}\ env\ \lfloor \texttt{case l of Nil => y | Cons(}n\texttt{,}m\texttt{) => z} \rfloor \\ \quad (b\ (\mathsf{list\_case}\ l\ f_1\ f_2))\end{array}$$

6.7 Translation of recursive functions

The most technical part of our approach is the details of how recursive functions are translated. In what follows, we expand on the gcd example given in Section 3.4 and explain our use of induction and eq in more detail.

$$\mathsf{gcd}\ m\ n \ = \ \mathsf{if}\ 0 < n\ \mathsf{then}\ \mathsf{gcd}\ n\ (m\ \mathsf{mod}\ n)\ \mathsf{else}\ m$$

As was already mentioned, when such a function is to be translated, we perform the bottom-up traversal (Section 5) for the right-hand side of the definition. When doing so we encounter the recursive call to gcd for which we need an Eval theorem. In this theorem we need to make explicit with what values we make the recursive call. For this purpose we use the eq combinator

$$\mathsf{eq}\ a\ x = \lambda y\ v.\ (x = y) \wedge a\ y\ v$$

which when used together with $\rightarrow$ restricts the universal quantifier that is hidden inside the $\rightarrow$ function combinator. One can informally read, refinement invariant int $\rightarrow \ldots$ as saying "for any int input, ...". Similarly, eq int $i \rightarrow \ldots$ can be read as "for any int input equal to i, ...", which is the same as "for int input i, ...".

We state the assumption we make at call sites as follows:

$$\mathsf{Eval}\ env\ \lfloor \texttt{gcd} \rfloor\ ((\mathsf{eq\ int}\ m \rightarrow \mathsf{eq\ int}\ n \rightarrow \mathsf{int})\ \mathsf{gcd}) \qquad (10)$$

For the rest of this example we abbreviate (10) as $\mathsf{P}\ m\ n$. In order to derive an Eval theorem for the expression $\mathsf{gcd}\ n\ (m\ \mathsf{mod}\ n)$, we first derive an Eval theorem argument n

$$\begin{array}{l}\mathsf{Eval}\ env\ \lfloor\mathtt{n}\rfloor\ (\mathsf{int}\ n) \implies \\ \mathsf{Eval}\ env\ \lfloor\mathtt{n}\rfloor\ (\mathsf{int}\ n)\end{array}$$

and an Eval theorem argument m mod n

$$\begin{array}{l}\mathsf{Eval}\ env\ \lfloor\mathtt{m}\rfloor\ (\mathsf{int}\ m) \wedge \\ \mathsf{Eval}\ env\ \lfloor\mathtt{n}\rfloor\ (\mathsf{int}\ n) \wedge n \neq 0 \implies \\ \mathsf{Eval}\ env\ \lfloor\mathtt{m\ mod\ n}\rfloor\ (\mathsf{int}\ (m\ \mathsf{mod}\ n))\end{array}$$

Next, we use the following rule to introduce eq combinators to the above theorems

$$\forall a\ x\ m.\ \mathsf{Eval}\ env\ m\ (a\ x) \implies \mathsf{Eval}\ env\ m\ ((\mathsf{eq}\ a\ x)\ x)$$

and then we apply to Closure application rule from Section 6.5 to get an Eval theorem for $\mathsf{gcd}\ n\ (m\ \mathsf{mod}\ n)$.

$$\begin{array}{l}\mathsf{Eval}\ env\ \lfloor\mathtt{m}\rfloor\ (\mathsf{int}\ m) \wedge \mathsf{P}\ n\ (m\ \mathsf{mod}\ n) \wedge \\ \mathsf{Eval}\ env\ \lfloor\mathtt{n}\rfloor\ (\mathsf{int}\ n) \wedge n \neq 0 \implies \\ \mathsf{Eval}\ env\ \lfloor\mathtt{gcd\ n\ (m\ mod\ n)}\rfloor\ (\mathsf{int}\ (\mathsf{gcd}\ n\ (m\ \mathsf{mod}\ n)))\end{array}$$

By then continuing the bottom-up traversal as usual and packaging up the right-hand side following the description in Section 5, we arrive at the following theorem where our abbreviation P appears both as an assumption and as the conclusion.

$$\begin{array}{l}env\ \texttt{"gcd"} = \mathsf{Recclosure}\ \ldots\ \lfloor\mathtt{if\ 0\ <\ n}\ \ldots\rfloor \implies \\ \forall m\ n.\ (0 < n \implies \mathsf{P}\ n\ (m\ \mathsf{mod}\ n)) \implies \mathsf{P}\ m\ n\end{array} \quad (11)$$

Note that the shape of the right-hand side of the implication matches the left-hand side of the following induction which HOL provides as a side product of proving totality of the gcd function.

$$\begin{array}{l}\forall P.\ (\forall m\ n.\ (0 < n \implies P\ n\ (m\ \mathsf{mod}\ n)) \implies P\ m\ n) \\ \quad \implies (\forall m\ n.\ P\ m\ n)\end{array} \quad (12)$$

By one application of modus ponens of (11) and (12), we arrive at a theorem with a right-hand side: $\forall m\ n.\ \mathsf{P}\ m\ n$. By expanding the abbreviation P and some simplification to remove eq (explained in the next section), we arrive at the desired certificate theorem for the gcd function:

$$\begin{array}{l}env\ \texttt{"gcd"} = \mathsf{Recclosure}\ \ldots\ \lfloor\mathtt{if\ 0\ <\ n}\ \ldots\rfloor \implies \\ \mathsf{Eval}\ env\ \lfloor\mathtt{gcd}\rfloor\ ((\mathsf{int} \to \mathsf{int} \to \mathsf{int})\ \mathsf{gcd})\end{array}$$

The gcd function is a very simple function. However, the technique above is exactly the same even for functions with nested recursion (e.g. as in McCarthy's 91 function) and mutual recursion (in such cases the induction has two conclusions). We always use the eq combinator to record input values, then apply the induction arising from the function's totality proof to discharge these assumptions and finally rewrite away the remaining eq combinators as described in the next section.

6.8 Simplification of eq

Our gcd example in Section 3.4 glossed over how eq combinators are removed. In this section, we expand on that detail.

When translating recursive functions, we use the eq combinator to 'record' what values we instantiate the inductive hypothesis with. Once the induction has been applied, we are left with an Eval-theorem which is cluttered with these eq combinators. The theorems have this shape:

$$\begin{array}{l}\forall x_1\ x_2\ \ldots\ x_n. \\ \quad \mathsf{Eval}\ env\ code \\ \qquad ((\mathsf{eq}\ a_1\ x_1 \to \mathsf{eq}\ a_2\ x_2 \to \ldots \to \mathsf{eq}\ a_n\ x_n \to b)\ func)\end{array}$$

Next, we show how these eq combinators can be removed by rewriting. First, we need two new combinators. The examples below will illustrate their use.

$$\begin{array}{rcl}\mathsf{A}\ a\ y\ v &=& \forall x.\ a\ x\ y\ v \\ \mathsf{E}\ a\ y\ v &=& \exists x.\ a\ x\ y\ v\end{array}$$

We use these combinators to push the external $\forall$ inwards. The following rewrite theorem shows how we can turn an external $\forall$ into an application of the A combinator. Here $(\mathsf{A}x.\ p\ x)$ is an abbreviation for $\mathsf{A}\ (\lambda x.\ p\ x)$.

$$\begin{array}{l}(\forall x.\ \mathsf{Eval}\ env\ code\ ((p\ x)\ f)) = \\ \mathsf{Eval}\ env\ code\ ((\mathsf{A}x.\ p\ x)\ f)\end{array} \quad (13)$$

Once we have introduced A, we can push it through $\to$ using the following two rewrite theorems.

$$\mathsf{A}x.\ (a \to p\ x) = (a \to (\mathsf{A}x.\ p\ x)) \quad (14)$$

$$\mathsf{A}x.\ (p\ x \to a) = ((\mathsf{E}x.\ p\ x) \to a) \quad (15)$$

These rewrites push the quantifiers all the way to the eq combinators. We arrive at a situation where each eq combinator has an E quantifier surrounding it. Such occurrences of E and eq cancel out

$$\mathsf{E}x.\ \mathsf{eq}\ a\ x = a$$

leaving us with a theorem where all of the eq, A and E combinators have been removed:

$$\mathsf{Eval}\ env\ code\ ((a_1 \to a_2 \to \ldots \to a_n \to b)\ func)$$

The proofs of (13) and (14) require that the underlying big-step operational semantics is deterministic. This requirement arises from the fact that these lemmas boil down to an equation where an existential quantifier is moved across a universal quantifier.

$$\begin{array}{l}\forall x.\ \exists v.\ \langle env, code\rangle \Downarrow v \wedge \ldots = \\ \exists v.\ \langle env, code\rangle \Downarrow v \wedge \forall x.\ \ldots\end{array}$$

Such equations can be proved if we assume that $\Downarrow$ is deterministic since then there is only one v that can be chosen by the existential quantifier. Note that the definition of Eval in Section 6.4 would not have had its intended meaning if the operational semantics had been genuinely non-deterministic.

7. Related work

There is a long tradition in interactive theorem proving of using logics that look like functional programming languages: notable examples include LCF [30], the Boyer-Moore prover [3], the Calculus of Constructions [8], and TFL [19, 39]. The logic of the Boyer-Moore prover (and it successor, ACL2 [18]) are actual programming languages with standard denotational or operational semantics. However, many other systems, including Coq [7] and various HOL systems [35] (including Isabelle/HOL [17] and HOL4 [15]), use a more mathematical logic with model-theoretic or proof-theoretic semantics that differ from standard programming languages, e.g. the logics of HOL systems include non-computational elements. However, because these logics are based on various λ-calculi, they still resemble functional languages. A contribution of our work is to make this resemblance concrete by showing how (computable) functions in these logics can be moved to a language with a straight-forward operational semantics while provably preserving their meaning.

Slind's TFL library for HOL [39] and Krauss' extensions [19] make HOL's logic (which is roughly Church's simple theory of types) look like a functional language with support for well-founded general recursive definitions and nested pattern matching. We rely on TFL to collapse multi-clause definitions and to simplify pattern matching expressions (Sections 6.6 and 3.5).

Extraction from Coq [22] has two phases. First, purely logical content (e.g., proofs about the definitions) are removed from the definitions to be extracted, then the remaining, computational context is printed to a programming language. The first step is theoretically well-justified; the second operates much as in HOL provers and is what we address in this paper.

ACL2 uses a first-order pure subset of Common Lisp as its logic, thus there is no semantic mismatch or need to perform extraction; logical terms are directly executable in the theorem prover. However, a translation technique similar to the one described in this paper can be of use when verifying the correctness of such theorem provers (including the correctness of their reflection mechanisms), as we did in previous work [10] using [32].

Proof producing synthesis has previously been used in HOL for various low-level targets including hardware [40] and assembly-like languages [24–26]. These systems implement verified compilers by term rewriting in the HOL4 logic. They apply a series of rewriting theorems to a HOL function yielding a proof that it is equivalent to a second HOL function that uses only features that have counterparts in the low-level language. Only then do they take a step relating these "low-level" HOL functions to the low-level language's operational semantics. This approach makes it easy to implement trustworthy compiler front-ends and optimisations, but significantly complicates the step that moves to the operational setting. In contrast, we move to (MiniML's) operational semantics immediately, which means that any preconditions we need to generate are understandable in terms of the original function, and not phrased in terms of a low-level intermediate language. This is why we can easily re-use the HOL-generated induction theorems to automatically prove termination.

In the other direction, proof producing decompilation techniques [23, 34] have addressed the problem of reasoning about low-level machine code by translating such code into equivalent HOL functions; however, these functions retain the low-level flavour of the machine language.

Charguéraud's characteristic formulae approach also addresses translation in the other direction, from OCaml to Coq [4], and it can support imperative features [5]. With his technique, an OCaml program is converted into a Coq formula that describes the program's behaviour, and verification is then carried out on this formula. His approach tackles the problem of verifying existing OCaml programs, which in particular requires the ability to handle partial functions and side effects. In contrast, this paper is about generating, from pure functional specifications, MiniML programs that are correct by construction. Part of our approach was inspired by Charguéraud's work, in particular our Eval predicate was inspired by his AppReturns predicate.

8. Future work

In this paper, we show how to create a verified path from the theorem prover to an operational semantics that operates on abstract syntax trees. We have not attempted to solve the problem of verified parsing or pretty printing. Ultimately, we want a verified compiler that will be able to accept abstract syntax as input, avoiding the problem altogether. However, it would still be useful to verify a translation from ASTs to concrete syntax strings for use with other compilers.

We have implemented our technique in HOL4 for translation to MiniML; however, we believe it would work for other target languages, so long as they both support ML-like features and can be given big-step semantics. Haskell support should be straightforward; laziness poses no problems because we are already proving termination under a strict semantics. We do rely on determinism of the big-step semantics for the quantifier shifting used in eq combinator removal (Section 6.8), but most languages that do not define evaluation order (e.g., Scheme, OCaml) should be able to support a deterministic semantics for the pure, total subset.

Our technique should also extend to other provers, including Isabelle/HOL and Coq. For function definitions that are in the ML-like fragment (i.e., that do not use sophisticated type classes or dependent types), including most of those in CompCert, it should be straightforward to implement our technique, although the details of the automation will vary.

Lastly, because MiniML also has a small step semantics, we hope to be able to verify complexity theoretic results about, e.g., our functional data structure case studies.

9. Conclusion

This paper's contribution is a step towards making proof assistants into trustworthy and practical program development platforms. We have shown how to give automated, verified translations of functions in higher-order logic to programs in functional languages. This increases the trustworthiness of programs that have been verified by shallowly embedding them in an interactive theorem prover, which has become a common verification strategy. We believe this is the first mechanically verified connection between HOL functions and the operational semantics of a high-level programming language. Our case studies include sophisticated data structures and algorithms, and validate the usefulness and scalability of our technique.

Acknowledgments

We thank Arthur Charguéraud, Anthony Fox, Mike Gordon, Kathy Gray, Ramana Kumar and Tom Sewell for commenting on drafts of this paper. This work was partially supported by EPSRC Research Grants EP/G007411/1, EP/F036345 and EP/H005633.

References

[1] G. Barthe, D. Demange, and D. Pichardie. A formally verified SSA-based middle-end – Single Static Assignment meets CompCert. In H. Seidl, editor, *21st European Symposium on Programming, ESOP 2012*, volume 7211 of *LNCS*, pages 47–66. Springer, 2012.

[2] A. Barthwal and M. Norrish. Verified, executable parsing. In G. Castagna, editor, *18th European Symposium on Programming, ESOP 2009*, volume 5502 of *LNCS*, pages 160–174. Springer, 2009.

[3] R. S. Boyer and J. S. Moore. Proving theorems about LISP Functions. *Journal of the Association for Computing Machinery*, 22(1):129–144, 1975.

[4] A. Charguéraud. Program verification through characteristic formulae. In *Proceeding of the 15th ACM SIGPLAN International Conference on Functional Programming, ICFP 2010*, pages 321–332. ACM, 2010.

[5] A. Charguéraud. Characteristic formulae for the verification of imperative programs. In *Proceeding of the 16th ACM SIGPLAN International Conference on Functional Programming, ICFP 2011*, pages 418–430. ACM, 2011.

[6] A. Chlipala. A verified compiler for an impure functional language. In *Proceedings of the 37th ACM SIGPLAN-SIGACT Symposium on Principles of Programming Languages, POPL 2010*, pages 93–106. ACM, 2010.

[7] Coq. The Coq home page, 2012. `http://coq.inria.fr/`.

[8] T. Coquand and G. Huet. The calculus of constructions. *Inf. Comput.*, 76(2–3):95–120, Feb. 1988.

[9] Z. Dargaye. *Vèrification formelle d'un compilateur pour langages fonctionnels*. PhD thesis, Universitè Paris 7 Diderot, July 2009.

[10] J. Davis and M. O. Myreen. The self-verifying Milawa theorem prover is sound (down to the machine code that runs it), 2012. `http://www.cl.cam.ac.uk/~mom22/jitawa/`.

[11] J. Duan, J. Hurd, G. Li, S. Owens, K. Slind, and J. Zhang. Functional correctness proofs of encryption algorithms. In G. Sutcliffe and A. Voronkov, editors, *Logic for Programming, Artificial Intelligence,*

and Reasoning: 12th International Conference, LPAR 2005, volume 3835 of *LNAI*, pages 519–533. Springer-Verlag, 2005.

[12] M. Felleisen and D. P. Friedman. Control operators, the SECD-machine, and the lambda-calculus. In *3rd Working Conference on the Formal Description of Programming Concepts*, Aug. 1986.

[13] M. Felleisen, R. B. Findler, and M. Flatt. *Semantics Engineering with PLT Redex*. MIT Press, 2009.

[14] J. Harrison. Metatheory and reflection in theorem proving: A survey and critique. Technical Report CRC-053, SRI Cambridge, Cambridge, UK, 1995.

[15] Hol. The HOL4 home page, 2012. `http://hol.sourceforge.net/`.

[16] J. Hurd. Verification of the Miller-Rabin probabilistic primality test. *J. Log. Algebr. Program.*, 56(1-2):3–21, 2003.

[17] Isabelle. The Isabelle home page, 2012. `http://www.cl.cam.ac.uk/research/hvg/isabelle/`.

[18] M. Kaufmann and J. S. Moore. The ACL2 home page, 2011. `http://www.cs.utexas.edu/users/moore/acl2/`.

[19] A. Krauss. *Automating Recursive Definitions and Termination Proofs in Higher-Order Logic*. PhD thesis, Technische Universitiät München, 2009.

[20] X. Leroy. A formally verified compiler back-end. *J. Autom. Reasoning*, 43(4):363–446, 2009.

[21] X. Leroy and H. Grall. Coinductive big-step operational semantics. *Inf. Comput.*, 207(2):284–304, 2009.

[22] P. Letouzey. A new extraction for Coq. In *Proceedings of the 2002 International Conference on Types for Proofs and Programs*, TYPES'02, pages 200–219. Springer-Verlag, 2003.

[23] G. Li. Validated compilation through logic. In M. Butler and W. Schulte, editors, *FM 2011: Formal Methods - 17th International Symposium on Formal Methods*, volume 6664 of *LNCS*, pages 169–183. Springer, 2011.

[24] G. Li and K. Slind. Compilation as rewriting in higher order logic. In F. Pfenning, editor, *Automated Deduction - CADE-21, 21st International Conference on Automated Deduction*, volume 4603 of *LNCS*, pages 19–34. Springer, 2007.

[25] G. Li and K. Slind. Trusted source translation of a total function language. In C. R. Ramakrishnan and J. Rehof, editors, *Tools and Algorithms for the Construction and Analysis of Systems, 14th International Conference, TACAS 2008*, volume 4963 of *LNCS*, pages 471–485. Springer, 2008.

[26] G. Li, S. Owens, and K. Slind. Structure of a proof-producing compiler for a subset of higher order logic. In R. D. Nicola, editor, *Programming Languages and Systems: 16th European Symposium on Programming, ESOP 2007*, volume 4421 of *LNCS*, pages 205–219. Springer, 2007.

[27] J. G. Malecha, G. Morrisett, A. Shinnar, and R. Wisnesky. Toward a verified relational database management system. In *Proceedings of the 37th ACM SIGPLAN-SIGACT Symposium on Principles of Programming Languages, POPL 2010*, pages 237–248. ACM, 2010.

[28] D. Matthews. Poly/ML home page, 2012. `http://www.polyml.org`.

[29] A. McCreight, T. Chevalier, and A. P. Tolmach. A certified framework for compiling and executing garbage-collected languages. In *Proceeding of the 15th ACM SIGPLAN International Conference on Functional Programming, ICFP 2010*, pages 273–284, 2010.

[30] R. Milner. Logic for computable functions; description of a machine implementation. Technical Report STAN-CS-72-288, A.I. Memo 169, Stanford University, 1972.

[31] M. O. Myreen. Reusable verification of a copying collector. In G. T. Leavens, P. W. O'Hearn, and S. K. Rajamani, editors, *Verified Software: Theories, Tools, Experiments, Third International Conference, VSTTE 2010*, volume 6217 of *LNCS*, pages 142–156. Springer, 2010.

[32] M. O. Myreen. Functional programs: conversions between deep and shallow embeddings. In L. Beringer and A. Felty, editors, *Interactive Theorem Proving (ITP)*, volume 7406 of *LNCS*, pages 412–418. Springer, 2012.

[33] M. O. Myreen and J. Davis. A verified runtime for a verified theorem prover. In M. C. J. D. van Eekelen, H. Geuvers, J. Schmaltz, and F. Wiedijk, editors, *Interactive Theorem Proving (ITP)*, volume 6898 of *LNCS*, pages 265–280. Springer, 2011.

[34] M. O. Myreen, K. Slind, and M. J. C. Gordon. Extensible proof-producing compilation. In O. de Moor and M. I. Schwartzbach, editors, *Compiler Construction, 18th International Conference, CC 2009*, volume 5501 of *LNCS*, pages 2–16. Springer, 2009.

[35] M. Norrish and K. Slind. A thread of HOL development. *Comput. J.*, 45(1):37–45, 2002.

[36] C. Okasaki. *Purely Functional Data Structures*. Cambridge University Press, 1998.

[37] S. Owens and K. Slind. Adapting functional programs to higher-order logic. *Higher-Order and Symbolic Computation*, 21(4):377–409, Dec. 2008.

[38] J. Ševčík , V. Vafeiadis, F. Z. Nardelli, S. Jagannathan, and P. Sewell. Relaxed-memory concurrency and verified compilation. In *Proceedings of the 38th ACM SIGPLAN-SIGACT Symposium on Principles of Programming Languages, POPL 2011*, pages 43–54. ACM, 2011.

[39] K. Slind. *Reasoning about Terminating Functional Programs*. PhD thesis, TU Munich, 1999.

[40] K. Slind, S. Owens, J. Iyoda, and M. Gordon. Proof producing synthesis of arithmetic and cryptographic hardware. *Formal Aspects of Computing*, 19(3):343–362, Aug. 2007.

[41] A. K. Wright and M. Felleisen. A syntactic approach to type soundness. *Inf. Comput.*, 115(1):38–94, 1994.

Operational Semantics Using the Partiality Monad

Nils Anders Danielsson

Chalmers University of Technology and University of Gothenburg

nad@chalmers.se

Abstract

The operational semantics of a partial, functional language is often given as a relation rather than as a function. The latter approach is arguably more natural: if the language is functional, why not take advantage of this when defining the semantics? One can immediately see that a functional semantics is deterministic and, in a constructive setting, computable.

This paper shows how one can use the coinductive partiality monad to define big-step or small-step operational semantics for lambda-calculi and virtual machines as total, computable functions (total definitional interpreters). To demonstrate that the resulting semantics are useful type soundness and compiler correctness results are also proved. The results have been implemented and checked using Agda, a dependently typed programming language and proof assistant.

Categories and Subject Descriptors F.3.2 [*Logics and Meanings of Programs*]: Semantics of Programming Languages—Operational semantics; D.1.1 [*Programming Techniques*]: Applicative (Functional) Programming; E.1 [*Data Structures*]; F.3.1 [*Logics and Meanings of Programs*]: Specifying and Verifying and Reasoning about Programs—Mechanical verification

Keywords Dependent types; mixed induction and coinduction; partiality monad

1. Introduction

Consider the untyped λ-calculus with a countably infinite set of constants c:

$$t ::= c \mid x \mid \lambda x.t \mid t_1\ t_2$$

Closed terms written in this language can compute to a value (a constant c or a closure $\lambda x.t\rho$), but they can also go wrong (crash) or fail to terminate.

How would you write down an operational semantics for this language? A common choice is to define the semantics as an inductively defined relation, either using small steps or big steps. For an example of the latter, see Figure 1: $\rho \vdash t \Downarrow v$ means that the term t can terminate with the value v when evaluated in the environment ρ. However, as noted by Leroy and Grall (2009), this definition provides no way to distinguish terms which go wrong from terms which fail to terminate. If we want to do this, then we can define two more relations, see Figure 2: $\rho \vdash t \Uparrow$, defined *coinductively*,

$$\rho \vdash c \Downarrow c \qquad \frac{\rho(x) = v}{\rho \vdash x \Downarrow v} \qquad \rho \vdash \lambda x.t \Downarrow \lambda x.t\rho$$

$$\frac{\rho \vdash t_1 \Downarrow \lambda x.t'\rho' \qquad \rho \vdash t_2 \Downarrow v' \qquad \rho', x = v' \vdash t' \Downarrow v}{\rho \vdash t_1\ t_2 \Downarrow v}$$

Figure 1. A call-by-value operational semantics for the untyped λ-calculus with constants, specifying which terms can terminate with what values (very close to a semantics given by Leroy and Grall (2009)).

$$\frac{\rho \vdash t_1 \Uparrow}{\rho \vdash t_1\ t_2 \Uparrow} \qquad \frac{\rho \vdash t_1 \Downarrow v \qquad \rho \vdash t_2 \Uparrow}{\rho \vdash t_1\ t_2 \Uparrow}$$

$$\frac{\rho \vdash t_1 \Downarrow \lambda x.t'\rho' \qquad \rho \vdash t_2 \Downarrow v' \qquad \rho', x = v' \vdash t' \Uparrow}{\rho \vdash t_1\ t_2 \Uparrow}$$

$$\rho \vdash t \lightning \quad \stackrel{\text{def}}{=} \quad \neg\,(\exists v.\ \rho \vdash t \Downarrow v) \wedge \neg\,(\rho \vdash t \Uparrow)$$

Figure 2. Two more operational semantics for the untyped λ-calculus with constants, specifying which terms can fail to terminate or go wrong. The definition written using double lines is coinductive, and is taken almost verbatim from Leroy and Grall (2009).

means that the term t can fail to terminate when evaluated in the environment ρ; and $\rho \vdash t \lightning$ means that t goes wrong.

Now we have a complete definition. However, this definition is somewhat problematic:

1. There are four separate rules which refer to application. For a small language this may be acceptable, but for large languages it seems to be easy to forget some rule, and "rule duplication" can be error-prone.
2. It is not immediately obvious whether the semantics is deterministic and/or computable: these properties need to be proved.
3. If we want to define an interpreter which is correct by construction, then the setup with three relations is awkward. Consider the following type-signature, where $\_\uplus\_$ is the sum type constructor:

$$\mathit{eval} : \forall\ \rho\ t \rightarrow (\exists v.\ \rho \vdash t \Downarrow v) \uplus \rho \vdash t \Uparrow \uplus \rho \vdash t \lightning$$

This signature states that, for any environment ρ and term t, the interpreter either returns a value v and a proof that t can terminate with this value when evaluated in the given environment; or a proof that t can fail to terminate; or a proof that t goes wrong. It should be clear that it is impossible to implement *eval*

ICFP'12, September 9–15, 2012, Copenhagen, Denmark.

in a total, constructive language, as this amounts to solving the halting problem.

The situation may have been a bit less problematic if we had defined a small-step semantics instead, but small-step semantics are not necessarily better: Leroy and Grall (2009) claim that "big-step semantics is more convenient than small-step semantics for some applications", including proving that a compiler is correct.

I suggest another approach: define the semantics as a *function* in a *total* meta-language, using the *partiality monad* (Capretta 2005) to represent non-termination, where the partiality monad is defined coinductively as $A_\bot = \nu X.\, A \uplus X$. If this approach is followed then we avoid all the problems above:

1. We have one clause for applications, and the meta-language is total, so we cannot forget a clause.
2. The semantics is a total function, and hence deterministic and computable.
3. The semantics is an interpreter, and its type signature does not imply that we solve the halting problem:

$$[\![\_]\!] \;:\; \mathit{Term} \rightarrow \mathit{Environment} \rightarrow (\mathit{Maybe\ Value})_\bot$$

An additional advantage of using a definitional interpreter is that this can make it easy to test the semantics (if the interpreter is not too inefficient). Such tests can be useful in the design of non-trivial languages (Aydemir et al. 2005).

The main technical contribution of this paper is that I show that one can prove typical meta-theoretical properties directly for a semantics defined using the partiality monad:

- A big-step, functional semantics is defined and proved to be classically equivalent to the relational semantics above (Sections 3 and 5; for simplicity well-scoped de Bruijn indices are used instead of names).
- Type soundness is proved for a simple type system with recursive types (Section 4).
- The meaning of a virtual machine is defined as a small-step, functional semantics (Section 6).
- A compiler correctness result is proved (Section 7).
- The language and the type soundness and compiler correctness results are extended to a non-deterministic setting in order to illustrate that the approach can handle languages where some details—like evaluation order—are left up to the compiler writer (Section 8).
- Finally Section 9 contains a brief discussion of term equivalences (applicative bisimilarity and contextual equivalence).

As far as I know these are the first proofs of type soundness or compiler correctness for operational semantics defined using the partiality monad. The big-step semantics avoids the rule duplication mentioned above, and this is reflected in the proofs: there is only one case for application, as opposed to four cases in some corresponding proofs for relational semantics due to Leroy and Grall (2009). Related work is discussed further in Section 1.3.

1.1 Operational?

At this point some readers may complain that $[\![\_]\!]$ does not define an operational semantics, but rather a denotational one. Perhaps a better term would be "hybrid operational/denotational", but the semantics is *not* denotational:

- It is not defined in a compositional way: $[\![\ t\ ]\!]$ is not defined by recursion on the structure of t, but rather a combination of corecursion and structural recursion (see Section 3).
- Furthermore the "semantic domain" is rather syntactic: it includes closures, and is not defined as the solution to a domain equation.

I do not see this kind of semantics as an alternative to denotational semantics, but rather as an alternative to usual operational ones. (See also the discussion of term equivalences in Section 9.)

1.2 Mechanisation

The development presented below has been formalised in the dependently typed, functional language Agda (Norell 2007; Agda Team 2012), and the code has been made available to download.

In order to give a clear picture of how the results can be mechanised Agda-like code is also used in the paper. Unfortunately Agda's support for total corecursion is somewhat limited,[1] so to avoid distracting details the code is written in an imaginary variant of Agda with a very clever productivity checker (and some other smaller changes). The accompanying code is written in actual Agda, sometimes using workarounds (Danielsson 2010) to convince Agda that the code is productive. There are also other, minor differences between the accompanying code and the code in the paper.

1.3 Related Work

Reynolds (1972) discusses definitional interpreters, and there is a large body of work on using monads to structure semantics and interpreters, going back at least to Moggi (1991) and Wadler (1992).

The toy language above is taken from Leroy and Grall (2009), who bring up some of the disadvantages of (inductive) big-step semantics mentioned above. The type system in Section 4 is also taken from Leroy and Grall, who discuss various formulations of type soundness (but not the main formulations given below). Finally the virtual machine and compiler defined in Sections 6–7 are also taken from Leroy and Grall, who give a compiler correctness proof.

Leroy and Grall also define a semantics based on approximations: First the semantics is defined (functionally) at "recursion depth" n; if $n = 0$, then the result $\bot$ is returned. This function is similar to the functional semantics $[\![\_]\!]$ defined in Section 3, but defined using recursion on n instead of corecursion and the partiality monad. The semantics of a term t is then defined (relationally) to be s if there is a recursion depth n_0 such that the semantics at recursion depth n is s for all $n \geqslant n_0$. Leroy and Grall prove that this semantics is equivalent to a relational, big-step semantics. This proof is close to the proof in Section 5 which shows that $[\![\_]\!]$ is equivalent to a relational, big-step semantics.

Further comparisons to the work of Leroy and Grall is included below.

The type soundness proof in Section 4 is close to proofs given by Tofte (1990) and Milner and Tofte (1991). They use ordinary, inductive big-step definitions to give semantics of languages with cyclic closures, define typing relations for values coinductively (as greatest fixpoints of monotone operators F), and use coinduction ($x \in \nu F$ if $x \in X$ for some $X \subseteq F(X)$) to prove that certain values have certain types. In this paper the value typing relation is defined inductively rather than coinductively. However, another typing relation, that for possibly non-terminating computations, is defined coinductively, and the proof still uses coinduction (which takes the form of corecursion, see Section 2).

Capretta (2005) discusses the partiality monad, and gives a semantics for partial recursive functions (primitive recursive functions plus minimisation) as a function of type $\forall\, n.\ (\mathbb{N}^n \rightarrow \mathbb{N}) \rightarrow ({\mathbb{N}_\bot}^n \rightarrow \mathbb{N}_\bot)$.

[1] The same applies to Coq (Coq Development Team 2011).

Nakata and Uustalu (2009) define coinductive big-step and small-step semantics, in both relational and functional style, for a while language. Their definitions do not use the partiality monad, but are trace-based, and have the property that the trace can be computed (productively) for any source term, converging or diverging. My opinion is that the *relational* big-step definition is rather technical and brittle; the authors discuss several modifications to the design which lead to absurd results, like while true do skip having an arbitrary trace. The *functional* big-step semantics avoids these issues, because the semantics is required to be a productive function from a term and an initial state to a trace. Nakata and Uustalu have extended their work to a while language with interactive input/output (2010), but in this work they use relational definitions.

Paulin-Mohring (2009) defines partial streams using (essentially) the partiality monad, shows that partial streams form a pointed CPO, and uses this CPO to define a functional semantics for (a minor variation of) Kahn networks.

Benton et al. (2009) use the partiality monad to construct a lifting operator for CPOs, and use this operator to give denotational semantics for one typed and one untyped λ-calculus; the former semantics is crash-free by construction, the latter uses $\bot$ to represent crashes. Benton and Hur (2009) define a compiler from one of these languages to a variant of the SECD machine (with a relational, small-step semantics), and prove compiler correctness.

Ghani and Uustalu (2004) introduce the partiality monad *transformer*, $\lambda M\, A.\ \nu X.\ M\ (A \uplus X)$. (In the setting of Agda M should be restricted to be strictly positive.)

Goncharov and Schröder (2011) use the partiality monad transformer (they use the term *resumption monad transformer*) to give a class of functional semantics for a concurrent language.

Rutten (1999) defines an operational semantics for a while language corecursively as a function, using a "non-constructive" variant of the partiality monad, $A_\bot = (A \times \mathbb{N}) \uplus \{\infty\}$ (where ∞ represents non-termination and the natural number stands for the number of computation steps needed to compute the value of type A). With this variant of the monad the semantics is not a *computable* function, because the semantics returns ∞ iff a program fails to terminate. Rutten also discusses weak bisimilarity and explains how to construct a compositional semantics from the operational one.

Cousot and Cousot (1992, 2009) describe *bi-inductive* definitions, which generalise inductive and coinductive definitions, and give a number of examples of their use. One of their examples is a big-step semantics for a call-by-value λ-calculus. This semantics captures both terminating and non-terminating behaviours in a single definition, with less "duplication" of rules than in Figures 1–2, but more than in Section 3. An operator F on $\wp(\mathit{Term} \times (\mathit{Term} \cup \{\bot\}))$, where *Term* stands for the set of terms and $\bot$ stands for non-termination, is first defined by the following inference rules (where v ranges over values):

$$v \Rightarrow v \qquad \frac{t_1 \Rightarrow \bot}{t_1\ t_2 \Rightarrow \bot} \qquad \frac{t_1 \Rightarrow v \qquad t_2 \Rightarrow \bot}{t_1\ t_2 \Rightarrow \bot}$$

$$\frac{t_1 \Rightarrow \lambda x.t \qquad t_2 \Rightarrow v \qquad t[x := v] \Rightarrow r}{t_1\ t_2 \Rightarrow r}$$

These rules should neither be read inductively nor coinductively. The semantics is instead obtained as the least fixpoint of F with respect to the order $\_\sqsubseteq\_$ defined by

$$X \sqsubseteq Y \quad = \quad X^+ \subseteq Y^+ \quad \wedge \quad X^- \supseteq Y^-,$$

where $Z^+ = \{\,(t, s) \in Z \mid s \neq \bot\,\}$ and $Z^- = Z \setminus Z^+$. F is not monotone with respect to $\_\sqsubseteq\_$ (which forms a complete lattice), so Cousot and Cousot give an explicit proof of the existence of a least fixpoint (for a closely related semantics).

2. The Partiality Monad

Agda is a total language (assuming that the implementation is bug-free, etc.). Ordinary data types are *inductive*. For instance, we can define the type *Fin n* of natural numbers less than n, and the type *Vec A n* of A-lists of length n, as follows:

```
data Fin : ℕ → Set where
  zero : {n : ℕ}       → Fin (1 + n)
  suc  : {n : ℕ} → Fin n → Fin (1 + n)
data Vec (A : Set) : ℕ → Set where
  []   :                      Vec A 0
  _::_ : {n : ℕ} → A → Vec A n → Vec A (1 + n)
```

(Cons is an infix operator, _::_; the underscores mark the argument positions.) Inductive types can be destructed using structural recursion. As an example we can define a safe lookup/indexing function:

```
lookup : {A : Set} {n : ℕ} → Fin n → Vec A n → A
lookup zero    (x :: xs) = x
lookup (suc i) (x :: xs) = lookup i xs
```

The arguments within braces, {...}, are *implicit*, and can be omitted if Agda can infer them. To avoid clutter most implicit argument declarations are omitted, together with a few explicit instantiations of implicit arguments.

Agda also supports "infinite" data through the use of coinduction (Coquand 1994). Coinductive types can be introduced using suspensions: $\infty\, A$ is the type of suspensions, that if forced give us something of type A. Suspensions can be forced using $\flat$, and created using $\sharp\_$:

```
♭  : ∞ A → A
♯_ : A → ∞ A
```

(Here $\sharp\_$ is a tightly binding prefix operator. In this paper nothing binds tighter except for ordinary function application.)

The partiality monad is defined coinductively as follows:

```
data _⊥ (A : Set) : Set where
  now   : A      → A⊥
  later : ∞ (A⊥) → A⊥
```

You can read this as the greatest fixpoint $\nu X.A \uplus X$.[2] The constructor now returns a value immediately, and later postpones a computation. Computations can be postponed forever:

```
never : A⊥
never = later (♯ never)
```

Here *never* is defined using *corecursion*, in a *productive* way: even though *never* can unfold forever, the next constructor can always be computed in a finite number of steps. Note that structural recursion is not supported for coinductive types, as this would allow the definition of non-productive functions.

The partiality monad is a monad, with now as its return operation, and bind defined corecursively as follows:

```
_>>=_ : A⊥ → (A → B⊥) → B⊥
now x   >>= f = f x
later x >>= f = later (♯ (♭ x >>= f))
```

If x fails to terminate, then $x \gg\!= f$ also fails to terminate, and if x terminates with a value, then f is applied to that value.

It is easy to prove the monad laws up to (strong) *bisimilarity*, which is a coinductively defined relation:

[2] This is not entirely correct in the current version of Agda (Altenkirch and Danielsson 2010), but for the purposes of this paper the differences are irrelevant.

$$
\begin{array}{l}
\textbf{data}\ \_{\cong}\_ : A_\bot \to A_\bot \to \mathit{Set}\ \textbf{where} \\
\quad \mathsf{now} : \qquad\qquad\qquad \mathsf{now}\ x \cong \mathsf{now}\ x \\
\quad \mathsf{later} : \infty\ ({\flat}\ x \cong {\flat}\ y) \to \mathsf{later}\ x \cong \mathsf{later}\ y
\end{array}
$$

(Note that the constructors have been overloaded.) This equivalence relation relates diverging computations, and it also relates computations which converge to the same value *using the same number of steps*.

Note that $\_{\cong}\_$ is a type of potentially infinite proof terms. Proving $x \cong y$ amounts to constructing a term with this type. This proof technique is quite different from the usual coinductive proof technique (where $x \in \nu F$ for a monotone F if $x \in X$ for some $X \subseteq F(X)$), so let me show in detail how one can prove that bind is associative:

$$
\begin{array}{l}
\mathit{associative} : \\
\quad (x : A_\bot)\ (f : A \to B_\bot)\ (g : B \to C_\bot) \to \\
\quad (x \gg\!= f \gg\!= g) \cong (x \gg\!= \lambda\, y \to f\ y \gg\!= g)
\end{array}
$$

We can do this using corecursion and case analysis on x:

$$
\begin{array}{l}
\mathit{associative}\ (\mathsf{now}\ x)\ f\ g = ? \\
\mathit{associative}\ (\mathsf{later}\ x)\ f\ g = ?
\end{array}
$$

We can ask Agda what types the two goals (?) have. The first one has type $f\ x \gg\!= g \cong f\ x \gg\!= g$, and can be completed by appeal to reflexivity ($\mathit{refl}\text{-}{\cong} : (x : A_\bot) \to x \cong x$ can be proved separately):

$$
\mathit{associative}\ (\mathsf{now}\ x)\ f\ g = \mathit{refl}\text{-}{\cong}\ (f\ x \gg\!= g)
$$

The second goal has type $\mathsf{later}\ s_1 \cong \mathsf{later}\ s_2$ for some suspensions s_1 and s_2, so we can refine the goal using a later constructor and a suspension:

$$
\mathit{associative}\ (\mathsf{later}\ x)\ f\ g = \mathsf{later}\ ({\sharp}\ ?)
$$

The new goal has type

$$
({\flat}\ x \gg\!= f \gg\!= g) \cong ({\flat}\ x \gg\!= \lambda\, y \to f\ y \gg\!= g),
$$

so we can conclude by appeal to the coinductive hypothesis:

$$
\mathit{associative}\ (\mathsf{later}\ x)\ f\ g = \mathsf{later}\ ({\sharp}\ \mathit{associative}\ ({\flat}\ x)\ f\ g)
$$

Note that the proof is productive. Agda can see this, because the corecursive call is *guarded* by a constructor and a suspension.

Strong bisimilarity is very strict. In many cases *weak* bisimilarity, which ignores finite differences in the number of steps, is more appropriate:[3]

$$
\begin{array}{l}
\textbf{data}\ \_{\approx}\_ : A_\bot \to A_\bot \to \mathit{Set}\ \textbf{where} \\
\quad \mathsf{now} : \qquad\qquad\qquad \mathsf{now}\ x \approx \mathsf{now}\ x \\
\quad \mathsf{later} : \infty\ ({\flat}\ x \approx {\flat}\ y) \to \mathsf{later}\ x \approx \mathsf{later}\ y \\
\quad \mathsf{later}^{\mathsf{l}} : \quad {\flat}\ x \approx y \to \mathsf{later}\ x \approx y \\
\quad \mathsf{later}^{\mathsf{r}} : \quad x \approx {\flat}\ y \to x \approx \mathsf{later}\ y
\end{array}
$$

This relation is defined using mixed induction and coinduction (induction nested inside coinduction, $\nu X.\mu Y.\ F\ X\ Y$). Note that later is coinductive, while $\mathsf{later}^{\mathsf{l}}$ and $\mathsf{later}^{\mathsf{r}}$ are inductive. An infinite sequence of later constructors is allowed, for instance to prove $\mathit{never} \approx \mathit{never}$:

$$
\begin{array}{l}
\mathit{allowed} : \mathit{never} \approx \mathit{never} \\
\mathit{allowed} = \mathsf{later}\ ({\sharp}\ \mathit{allowed})
\end{array}
$$

However, only a finite number of consecutive $\mathsf{later}^{\mathsf{l}}$ and $\mathsf{later}^{\mathsf{r}}$ constructors is allowed, because otherwise we could prove $\mathit{never} \approx \mathsf{now}\ x$:

[3] Capretta (2005) defines weak bisimilarity in a different but equivalent way.

$$
\begin{array}{l}
\mathit{disallowed} : \mathit{never} \approx \mathsf{now}\ x \\
\mathit{disallowed} = \mathsf{later}^{\mathsf{l}}\ \mathit{disallowed}
\end{array}
$$

On the other hand, because the induction is nested *inside* the coinduction it is fine to use an infinite number of $\mathsf{later}^{\mathsf{l}}$ or $\mathsf{later}^{\mathsf{r}}$ constructors if they are non-consecutive, with intervening later constructors:

$$
\begin{array}{l}
\mathit{also\text{-}allowed} : \mathit{never} \approx \mathit{never} \\
\mathit{also\text{-}allowed} = \mathsf{later}^{\mathsf{r}}\ (\mathsf{later}\ ({\sharp}\ \mathit{also\text{-}allowed}))
\end{array}
$$

If we omit the $\mathsf{later}^{\mathsf{r}}$ constructor from the definition of weak bisimilarity, then we get a preorder $\_{\gtrsim}\_$ with the property that $x \gtrsim y$ holds if y terminates in fewer steps than x (with the same value), but not if x terminates in strictly fewer steps than y, or if one of the two computations terminates and the other does not:

$$
\begin{array}{l}
\textbf{data}\ \_{\gtrsim}\_ : A_\bot \to A_\bot \to \mathit{Set}\ \textbf{where} \\
\quad \mathsf{now} : \qquad\qquad\qquad \mathsf{now}\ x \gtrsim \mathsf{now}\ x \\
\quad \mathsf{later} : \infty\ ({\flat}\ x \gtrsim {\flat}\ y) \to \mathsf{later}\ x \gtrsim \mathsf{later}\ y \\
\quad \mathsf{later}^{\mathsf{l}} : \quad {\flat}\ x \gtrsim y \to \mathsf{later}\ x \gtrsim y
\end{array}
$$

It is easy to prove that $x \cong y$ implies $x \gtrsim y$, which in turn implies $x \approx y$.

The three relations above are transitive, but one needs to be careful when using transitivity in corecursive proofs, because otherwise one can "prove" absurd things. For instance, given $\mathit{refl}\text{-}{\approx} : (x : A_\bot) \to x \approx x$ and $\mathit{trans}\text{-}{\approx} : x \approx y \to y \approx z \to x \approx z$ we can "prove" that weak bisimilarity is trivial:

$$
\begin{array}{l}
\mathit{trivial} : (x\ y : A_\bot) \to x \approx y \\
\mathit{trivial}\ x\ y = \\
\quad \mathit{trans}\text{-}{\approx}\ (\mathsf{later}^{\mathsf{r}}\ (\mathit{refl}\text{-}{\approx}\ x)) \\
\qquad\quad (\mathit{trans}\text{-}{\approx}\ (\mathsf{later}\ ({\sharp}\ \mathit{trivial}\ x\ y)) \\
\qquad\qquad\quad (\mathsf{later}^{\mathsf{l}}\ (\mathit{refl}\text{-}{\approx}\ y)))
\end{array}
$$

This "proof" uses the following equational reasoning steps: $x \approx \mathsf{later}\ ({\sharp}\ x) \approx \mathsf{later}\ ({\sharp}\ y) \approx y$. The problem is that *trivial* is not productive: $\mathit{trans}\text{-}{\approx}$ is "too strict". This issue is closely related to the problem of weak bisimulation up to weak bisimilarity (Sangiorgi and Milner 1992).

Fortunately some uses of transitivity are safe. For instance, if we are proving a weak bisimilarity, then it is safe to make use of *already proved* greater-than results, in the following way (where $y \lesssim z$ is a synonym for $z \gtrsim y$):

$$
\begin{array}{l}
x \gtrsim y \to y \approx z \to x \approx z \\
x \approx y \to y \lesssim z \to x \approx z
\end{array}
$$

(Compare Sangiorgi and Milner's "expansion up to $\lesssim$".) Agda does not provide a simple way to show that these lemmas are safe, but this could be done using sized types as implemented in MiniAgda (Abel 2010).[4] With sized types one can define $x \approx^i y$ to stand for potentially incomplete proofs of $x \approx y$ of size (at least) i, and prove the following lemma:

$$
\forall\, i.\ x \gtrsim y \to y \approx^i z \to x \approx^i z
$$

This lemma is not "too strict": the type tells us that the (bound on the) size of the incomplete definition is preserved. Unfortunately MiniAgda, which is a research prototype, is very awkward to use in larger developments.

For more details about coinduction and corecursion in Agda, and further discussion of transitivity in a coinductive setting, see Danielsson and Altenkirch (2010).

[4] The experimental implementation of sized types in Agda does not support coinduction.

3. A Functional, Operational Semantics

This section defines an operational semantics for the untyped λ-calculus with constants. Let us start by defining the syntax of the language. Just as Leroy and Grall (2009) I use de Bruijn indices to represent variables, but I use a "well-scoped" approach, using the type system to keep track of the free variables. Terms of type *Tm n* have at most *n* free variables:

```
data Tm (n : ℕ) : Set where
  con : ℕ               → Tm n  -- Constant.
  var : Fin n           → Tm n  -- Variable.
  lam : Tm (1 + n)      → Tm n  -- Abstraction.
  _·_ : Tm n → Tm n     → Tm n  -- Application.
```

Environments and values are defined mutually:

```
mutual
  Env : ℕ → Set
  Env n = Vec Value n

  data Value : Set where
    con : ℕ                        → Value  -- Constant.
    lam : Tm (1 + n) → Env n       → Value  -- Closure.
```

Note that the body of a closure has at most one free variable which is not bound in the environment.

The language supports two kinds of "effects", partiality and crashes. The partiality monad is used to represent partiality, and the maybe monad is used to represent crashes:

```
⟦_⟧ : Tm n → Env n → (Maybe Value)⊥
```

(*Maybe A* has two constructors, nothing : *Maybe A* and just : *A* → *Maybe A*.) The combined monad is the maybe monad transformer ($\lambda M\ A.\ M\ (Maybe\ A)$) applied to the partiality monad. We can define a failing computation, as well as return and bind, as follows:

```
fail : (Maybe A)⊥
fail = now nothing

return : A → (Maybe A)⊥
return x = now (just x)

_>>=_ : (Maybe A)⊥ → (A → (Maybe B)⊥) → (Maybe B)⊥
now nothing >>= f = fail
now (just x) >>= f = f x
later x      >>= f = later (♯ (♭ x >>= f))
```

It should also be possible to use the reader monad transformer to handle the environment, but I believe that this would make the code harder to follow.

With the monad in place it is easy to define the semantics using two mutually (co)recursive functions:

```
mutual
  ⟦_⟧ : Tm n → Env n → (Maybe Value)⊥
  ⟦ con i ⟧ ρ = return (con i)
  ⟦ var x ⟧ ρ = return (lookup x ρ)
  ⟦ lam t ⟧ ρ = return (lam t ρ)
  ⟦ t₁ · t₂ ⟧ ρ = ⟦ t₁ ⟧ ρ >>= λ v₁ →
                  ⟦ t₂ ⟧ ρ >>= λ v₂ →
                  v₁ • v₂

  _•_ : Value → Value → (Maybe Value)⊥
  con i₁    • v₂ = fail
  lam t₁ ρ₁ • v₂ = later (♯ (⟦ t₁ ⟧ (v₂ :: ρ₁)))
```

Constants are returned immediately, variables are looked up in the environment, and abstractions are paired up with the environment to form a closure. The interesting case is application: $t_1 \cdot t_2$ is evaluated by first evaluating t_1 to a value v_1, then (if the evaluation of t_1 terminates without a crash) t_2 to v_2, and finally evaluating the application $v_1 \bullet v_2$. If v_1 is a constant, then we crash. If v_1 is a closure, then a later constructor is emitted and the closure's body is evaluated in its environment extended by v_2. The result contains one later constructor for every β-redex that has been reduced (infinitely many in case of non-termination).

Note that this is a call-by-value semantics, with functions evaluated before arguments. Note also that the semantics is not compositional, i.e. not defined by recursion on the structure of the term, so it is not a denotational semantics. (It would be if _•_ were defined prior to ⟦_⟧; it is easy to construct a compositional semantics on top of this one.)

Agda does not accept the code above; it is not obvious to the productivity checker that ⟦_⟧ and _•_ are total (productive) functions. If bind had been a constructor, then Agda would have found that the code uses a lexicographic combination of guarded corecursion and structural recursion: every call path from ⟦_⟧ to ⟦_⟧ is either

1. guarded by one or more constructors and at least one suspension (and nothing else), or
2. guardedness is "preserved" (zero or more constructors/suspensions), and the term argument becomes strictly smaller.

Now, bind is not a constructor, but it does preserve guardedness: it takes apart its first argument, but introduces a new suspension before forcing an old one—in MiniAgda one can show that bind preserves the sizes of its arguments. For a formal explanation of totality, see the accompanying code.[5]

The semantics could also have been defined using continuation-passing style, and then we could have avoided the use of bind:

```
mutual
  ⟦_⟧CPS : Tm n → Env n → (Value → (Maybe A)⊥) →
           (Maybe A)⊥
  ⟦ con i ⟧CPS ρ k = k (con i)
  ⟦ var x ⟧CPS ρ k = k (lookup x ρ)
  ⟦ lam t ⟧CPS ρ k = k (lam t ρ)
  ⟦ t₁ · t₂ ⟧CPS ρ k = ⟦ t₁ ⟧CPS ρ (λ v₁ →
                       ⟦ t₂ ⟧CPS ρ (λ v₂ →
                       (v₁ •CPS v₂) k))

  _•CPS_ : Value → Value → (Value → (Maybe A)⊥) →
           (Maybe A)⊥
  (con i₁    •CPS v₂) k = fail
  (lam t₁ ρ₁ •CPS v₂) k = later (♯ (⟦ t₁ ⟧CPS (v₂ :: ρ₁) k))
```

This definition would not have made the productivity checker any happier (it is productive, though, see the accompanying code). However, it avoids the inefficient implementation of bind; note that bind traverses the full prefix of later constructors before encountering the now constructor, if any.

Before we leave this section, let us work out a small example. The term $(\lambda x.xx)\ (\lambda x.xx)$ can be defined as follows (writing 0 instead of zero):

```
Ω : Tm 0
Ω = lam (var 0 · var 0) · lam (var 0 · var 0)
```

It is easy to show that this term does not terminate:

[5] In the accompanying code ⟦_⟧ is defined using a data type containing the constructors return, _>>=_, fail and later, thus ensuring guardedness. These constructors are interpreted in the usual way in a second pass over the result. This technique is explained in detail by Danielsson (2010).

```
Ω-loops : ⟦ Ω ⟧ [] ≈ never
Ω-loops = later (♯ Ω-loops)
```

4. Type Soundness

To illustrate how the semantics can be used, let us define a type system and prove type soundness.

I follow Leroy and Grall (2009) and define recursive, simple types coinductively as follows:

```
data Ty : Set where
  nat  : Ty
  _⇾_ : ∞ Ty → ∞ Ty → Ty
```

Contexts can be defined as vectors of types:

```
Ctxt : ℕ → Set
Ctxt n = Vec Ty n
```

The type system can then be defined inductively. Γ ⊢ t ∈ σ means that t has type σ in context Γ:

```
data _⊢_∈_ (Γ : Ctxt n) : Tm n → Ty → Set where
  con : Γ ⊢ con i ∈ nat
  var : Γ ⊢ var x ∈ lookup x Γ
  lam : ♭ σ :: Γ ⊢ t ∈ ♭ τ  →  Γ ⊢ lam t ∈ σ ⇾ τ
  _·_ : Γ ⊢ t₁ ∈ σ ⇾ τ  →  Γ ⊢ t₂ ∈ ♭ σ  →
        Γ ⊢ t₁ · t₂ ∈ ♭ τ
```

The use of negative recursive types implies that there are well-typed terms which do not terminate. For instance, Ω is typeable with *any* type:

```
Ω-well-typed : (τ : Ty)  →  [] ⊢ Ω ∈ τ
Ω-well-typed τ  =  _·_ {σ = ♯ σ} {τ = ♯ τ}
                     (lam (var · var)) (lam (var · var))
  where σ = ♯ σ ⇾ ♯ τ
```

(Some implicit arguments which Agda could not infer have been given explicitly using the {x = ...} notation.)

Let us now prove that well-typed programs (closed terms) do not go wrong. It is easy to state what should be proved:

```
type-soundness : [] ⊢ t ∈ σ  →  ¬ (⟦ t ⟧ [] ≈ fail)
```

Here ¬_ is negation (¬ A = A → *Empty*, where *Empty* is the empty type). As noted by Leroy and Grall it is harder to state type soundness for usual big-step semantics, because such semantics do not distinguish between terms which go wrong and terms which fail to terminate.

We can start by defining a reusable predicate transformer which lifts predicates on A to predicates on $(\mathit{Maybe}\ A)_\bot$. If *Lift P x* holds, then we know both that the computation x does not crash, and that if x terminates with a value, then the value satisfies P. *Lift* is defined coinductively as follows:

```
data Lift (P : A → Set) : (Maybe A)⊥ → Set where
  now-just : P x               → Lift P (return x)
  later    : ∞ (Lift P (♭ x)) → Lift P (later x)
```

The proof below uses the fact that bind "preserves" *Lift*:

```
_>>=-cong_ : Lift P x → ({x : A} → P x → Lift Q (f x)) →
             Lift Q (x >>= f)
```

Let us now define some typing predicates for values and computations, introduced mainly as part of the proof of type soundness. $WF_V\ \sigma\ v$ means that the value v is well-formed with respect to the type σ. This relation is defined inductively, mutually with a corresponding relation for environments:

```
mutual
  data WFV : Ty → Value → Set where
    con : WFV nat (con i)
    lam : ♭ σ :: Γ ⊢ t ∈ ♭ τ → WFE Γ ρ →
          WFV (σ ⇾ τ) (lam t ρ)
  data WFE : Ctxt n → Env n → Set where
    []   :                      WFE [] []
    _::_ : WFV σ v → WFE Γ ρ → WFE (σ :: Γ) (v :: ρ)
```

The most interesting case above is that for closures. A closure lam t ρ is well-formed with respect to σ ⇾ τ if there is a context Γ such that Γ ⊢ lam t ∈ σ ⇾ τ and ρ is well-formed with respect to Γ. The predicates are related by the following unsurprising lemma:

```
lookup_wf : (x : Fin n)  →  WFE Γ ρ  →
            WFV (lookup x Γ) (lookup x ρ)
```

We can use the predicate transformer introduced above to lift WF_V to computations:

```
WF⊥ : Ty → (Maybe Value)⊥ → Set
WF⊥ σ x = Lift (WFV σ) x
```

Non-terminating computations are well-formed, and terminating computations are well-formed if they are successful (not nothing) and the value is well-formed. The following lemma implies that type soundness can be established by showing that ⟦ t ⟧ [] is well-formed:

```
does-not-go-wrong : WF⊥ σ x → ¬ (x ≈ fail)
does-not-go-wrong (now-just _) ()
does-not-go-wrong (later wf)   (later¹ eq) =
  does-not-go-wrong (♭ wf) eq
```

Recall that negation is a function into the empty type. The lemma is proved by structural recursion: induction on the structure of the proof of x ≈ *fail*. The first clause contains an "absurd pattern", (), to indicate that there is no constructor application of type *return v* ≈ *fail*.

We can now prove the main lemma, which states that the computations resulting from evaluating well-typed terms in well-formed environments are well-formed. This lemma uses the same form of nested corecursion/structural recursion as the definition of the semantics:

```
mutual
  ⟦⟧wf : Γ ⊢ t ∈ σ  →  WFE Γ ρ  →  WF⊥ σ (⟦ t ⟧ ρ)
  ⟦⟧wf con             ρwf = now-just con
  ⟦⟧wf (var {x = x})   ρwf = now-just (lookup_wf x ρwf)
  ⟦⟧wf (lam t∈)        ρwf = now-just (lam t∈ ρwf)
  ⟦⟧wf (t1∈ · t2∈)     ρwf =
    ⟦⟧wf t1∈ ρwf >>=-cong λ fwf →
    ⟦⟧wf t2∈ ρwf >>=-cong λ vwf →
    •wf fwf vwf

  •wf : WFV (σ ⇾ τ) f  →  WFV (♭ σ) v  →
        WF⊥ (♭ τ) (f • v)
  •wf (lam t1∈ ρ1wf) v2wf =
    later (♯ ⟦⟧wf t1∈ (v2wf :: ρ1wf))
```

The implicit variable pattern {x = x} is used to bind the variable x, which is used on the right-hand side.

Finally we can conclude:

```
type-soundness : [] ⊢ t ∈ σ  →  ¬ (⟦ t ⟧ [] ≈ fail)
type-soundness t∈ = does-not-go-wrong (⟦⟧wf t∈ [])
```

Note that there is only one case for application in the proof above (plus one sub-case in $\bullet_{wf}$).

The proof of type soundness is formulated for a functional semantics defined using environments and closures, whereas Leroy and Grall (2009) prove type soundness for relational semantics defined using substitutions. I have chosen to use environments and closures in this paper to avoid distracting details related to substitutions. However, given an implementation of the operation which substitutes a term for variable zero it is easy to define a substitution-based functional semantics using the partiality monad, and given a proof showing that this operation preserves types it is easy to adapt the proof above to this semantics. See the accompanying code for details.

The proof above can be compared to a typical type soundness proof formulated for a relational, substitution-based small-step semantics. Such a proof often amounts to proving progress and preservation:

$$\begin{array}{lll} \textit{progress} & : [\,] \vdash t \in \sigma & \rightarrow \textit{Value}\ t \uplus \exists\, \lambda\, t' \rightarrow t \rightsquigarrow t' \\ \textit{preservation} & : [\,] \vdash t \in \sigma & \rightarrow t \rightsquigarrow t' \rightarrow [\,] \vdash t' \in \sigma \end{array}$$

Here *Value* t means that t is a value, $\_\rightsquigarrow\_$ is the small-step relation, and $\exists\, \lambda\, t' \rightarrow \ldots$ can be read as "there exists a t' such that...". Given these two lemmas one can prove type soundness using classical reasoning (Leroy and Grall 2009):

$$\begin{array}{l} \textit{type-soundness} : [\,] \vdash t \in \sigma \rightarrow \\ \qquad t \rightsquigarrow^{\infty} \uplus \exists\, \lambda\, t' \rightarrow t \rightsquigarrow^{\star} t' \times \textit{Value}\ t' \end{array}$$

Here $\_\rightsquigarrow^{\star}\_$ is the reflexive transitive closure of $\_\rightsquigarrow\_$, $t \rightsquigarrow^{\infty}$ means that t can reduce forever, and $\_\times\_$ can be read as "and". (Note that this statement of type soundness is inappropriate for non-deterministic languages, as it does not rule out the possibility of crashes.) The lemma $[\![]\!]_{\mathrm{wf}}$ above can be seen as encompassing both progress and preservation, plus the combination of these two lemmas into type soundness. This combination does not need to involve classical reasoning, because $WF_{\perp}$ is defined coinductively.

5. The Semantics are Classically Equivalent

Let us now prove that the semantics given in Section 3 is classically equivalent to a relational semantics.

The semantics given in Figures 1–2 can be adapted to a setting with well-scoped terms and de Bruijn indices in the following way:

$$\begin{array}{l} \textbf{data}\ \_\vdash\_\Downarrow\_\ (\rho : \textit{Env}\ n) : \textit{Tm}\ n \rightarrow \textit{Value} \rightarrow \textit{Set}\ \textbf{where} \\ \quad \mathsf{con} : \rho \vdash \mathsf{con}\ i \Downarrow \mathsf{con}\ i \\ \quad \mathsf{var} : \rho \vdash \mathsf{var}\ x \Downarrow \textit{lookup}\ x\ \rho \\ \quad \mathsf{lam} : \rho \vdash \mathsf{lam}\ t \Downarrow \mathsf{lam}\ t\ \rho \\ \quad \mathsf{app} : \rho \vdash t_1 \Downarrow \mathsf{lam}\ t'\ \rho' \rightarrow \rho \vdash t_2 \Downarrow v' \rightarrow \\ \qquad\qquad v' :: \rho' \vdash t' \Downarrow v \rightarrow \rho \vdash t_1 \cdot t_2 \Downarrow v \\ \textbf{data}\ \_\vdash\_\Uparrow\ (\rho : \textit{Env}\ n) : \textit{Tm}\ n \rightarrow \textit{Set}\ \textbf{where} \\ \quad \mathsf{app}^{\mathsf{l}} : \infty\,(\rho \vdash t_1 \Uparrow) \rightarrow \rho \vdash t_1 \cdot t_2 \Uparrow \\ \quad \mathsf{app}^{\mathsf{r}} : \rho \vdash t_1 \Downarrow v \rightarrow \infty\,(\rho \vdash t_2 \Uparrow) \rightarrow \rho \vdash t_1 \cdot t_2 \Uparrow \\ \quad \mathsf{app} : \rho \vdash t_1 \Downarrow \mathsf{lam}\ t'\ \rho' \rightarrow \rho \vdash t_2 \Downarrow v' \rightarrow \\ \qquad\qquad \infty\,(v' :: \rho' \vdash t' \Uparrow) \rightarrow \rho \vdash t_1 \cdot t_2 \Uparrow \\ \_\vdash\_\lightning : \textit{Env}\ n \rightarrow \textit{Tm}\ n \rightarrow \textit{Set} \\ \rho \vdash t\ \lightning = \neg\,(\exists\,\lambda\,v \rightarrow \rho \vdash t \Downarrow v) \times \neg\,(\rho \vdash t \Uparrow) \end{array}$$

Note that $\_\vdash\_\Downarrow\_$ is defined inductively and $\_\vdash\_\Uparrow$ coinductively.

How should we state the equivalence of $\_\vdash\_\Downarrow\_/\_\vdash\_\Uparrow/\_\vdash\_\lightning$ and $[\![\_]\!]$? The following may seem like a suitable statement:

$$\begin{array}{lll} \rho \vdash t \Downarrow v & \Leftrightarrow & [\![\, t \,]\!]\ \rho \approx \textit{return}\ v \\ \rho \vdash t \Uparrow & \Leftrightarrow & [\![\, t \,]\!]\ \rho \approx \textit{never} \\ \rho \vdash t\ \lightning & \Leftrightarrow & [\![\, t \,]\!]\ \rho \approx \textit{fail} \end{array}$$

However, in a constructive setting one cannot prove that $[\![\, t \,]\!]\ \rho \approx \textit{never}$ implies $\rho \vdash t \Uparrow$. To see why, let us try. Assume that we have a proof p of type $[\![\, t_1 \cdot t_2 \,]\!]\ \rho \approx \textit{never}$. Now we need to construct a proof starting with either $\mathsf{app}^{\mathsf{l}}$, $\mathsf{app}^{\mathsf{r}}$ or app. In order to do this we need to know whether t_1 terminates or not, but this is not decidable given only the proof p. It also seems unlikely that we can prove that $\rho \vdash t\ \lightning$ implies $[\![\, t \,]\!]\ \rho \approx \textit{fail}$: one might imagine that this can be proved by just executing $[\![\, t \,]\!]\ \rho$ until it terminates and then performing a case analysis, but the fact that t does not fail to terminate is not (obviously) enough to convince Agda that it does terminate.

We can avoid these issues by assuming the following form of excluded middle, which states that everything (in *Set*) is decidable:

$$\begin{array}{l} \textit{EM} : \textit{Set}_1 \\ \textit{EM} = (A : \textit{Set}) \rightarrow A \uplus \neg A \end{array}$$

We end up with the following six proof obligations:

$$\begin{array}{llll} & \rho \vdash t \Downarrow v & \rightarrow [\![\, t \,]\!]\ \rho \approx \textit{return}\ v & (1) \\ & \rho \vdash t \Uparrow & \rightarrow [\![\, t \,]\!]\ \rho \approx \textit{never} & (2) \\ & [\![\, t \,]\!]\ \rho \approx \textit{return}\ v & \rightarrow \rho \vdash t \Downarrow v & (3) \\ \textit{EM} \rightarrow & [\![\, t \,]\!]\ \rho \approx \textit{never} & \rightarrow \rho \vdash t \Uparrow & (4) \\ \textit{EM} \rightarrow & \rho \vdash t\ \lightning & \rightarrow [\![\, t \,]\!]\ \rho \approx \textit{fail} & (5) \\ & [\![\, t \,]\!]\ \rho \approx \textit{fail} & \rightarrow \rho \vdash t\ \lightning & (6) \end{array}$$

The last two follow easily from the previous ones, so let us focus on the first four:

1. Given $p : \rho \vdash t \Downarrow v$ it is easy to prove $[\![\, t \,]\!]\ \rho \approx \textit{return}\ v$ by recursion on the structure of p.

   The only interesting case is application. Let us introduce the following abbreviation:

   $$x_1\ [\![\cdot]\!]\ x_2 = x_1 \gg\!= \lambda\, v_1 \rightarrow x_2 \gg\!= \lambda\, v_2 \rightarrow v_1 \bullet v_2$$

   We can then proceed as follows (using the same names as in the app constructor's type signature):

   $$\begin{array}{ll} [\![\, t_1 \cdot t_2 \,]\!]\ \rho & \cong \\ [\![\, t_1 \,]\!]\ \rho \quad [\![\cdot]\!]\ [\![\, t_2 \,]\!]\ \rho & \approx \\ \textit{return}\ (\mathsf{lam}\ t'\ \rho')\ [\![\cdot]\!]\ \textit{return}\ v' & \gtrsim \\ [\![\, t' \,]\!]\ (v' :: \rho') & \approx \\ \textit{return}\ v & \end{array}$$

   The inductive hypothesis is used twice in the second step and once in the last one.

2. One can prove that $\rho \vdash t \Uparrow$ implies $[\![\, t \,]\!]\ \rho \approx \textit{never}$ using corecursion plus an inner recursion on the structure of t.

   In the case of the app constructor we can proceed as follows:

   $$\begin{array}{ll} [\![\, t_1 \cdot t_2 \,]\!]\ \rho & \cong \\ [\![\, t_1 \,]\!]\ \rho \quad [\![\cdot]\!]\ [\![\, t_2 \,]\!]\ \rho & \gtrsim \\ \textit{return}\ (\mathsf{lam}\ t'\ \rho')\ [\![\cdot]\!]\ \textit{return}\ v' & \cong \\ \mathsf{later}\ (\sharp\ [\![\, t' \,]\!]\ (v' :: \rho')) & \approx \\ \textit{never} & \end{array}$$

   The second step uses (1) twice, once for $p_1 : \rho \vdash t_1 \Downarrow \mathsf{lam}\ t'\ \rho'$ and once for $p_2 : \rho \vdash t_2 \Downarrow v'$, plus the fact that $x \approx \mathsf{now}\ v$ implies that $x \gtrsim \mathsf{now}\ v$. The last step uses the coinductive hypothesis (under a guard) for $p_3 : v' :: \rho' \vdash t' \Uparrow$.

   The $\mathsf{app}^{\mathsf{l}}$ case is different:

   $$\begin{array}{ll} [\![\, t_1 \cdot t_2 \,]\!]\ \rho & \cong \\ [\![\, t_1 \,]\!]\ \rho\ [\![\cdot]\!]\ [\![\, t_2 \,]\!]\ \rho & \approx \\ \textit{never}\quad [\![\cdot]\!]\ [\![\, t_2 \,]\!]\ \rho & \cong \\ \textit{never} & \end{array}$$

   The last step uses the fact that *never* is a left zero of bind. The second step uses the *inductive* hypothesis for $p : \rho \vdash t_1 \Uparrow$; note that t_1 is structurally smaller than $t_1 \cdot t_2$, and that this call is not guarded.

The $\mathsf{app}^{\mathsf{r}}$ case is similar to the $\mathsf{app}^{\mathsf{l}}$ one, and omitted.

Note that the use of transitivity in this proof is safe, as discussed in Section 2.

3. Given $p : [\![t]\!]\ \rho \approx \mathit{return}\ v$ one can observe that p cannot contain the constructors later or $\mathsf{later}^{\mathsf{r}}$: it must have the form $\mathsf{later}^{\mathsf{l}}\ (\ldots\ (\mathsf{later}^{\mathsf{l}}\ \mathsf{now})\ \ldots)$, with a finite number of $\mathsf{later}^{\mathsf{l}}$ constructors—one for every β-reduction in the computation of $[\![t]\!]\ \rho$. Let the *size* of p be this number. One can prove that $[\![t]\!]\ \rho \approx \mathit{return}\ v$ implies $\rho \vdash t \Downarrow v$ by complete induction on this size.

   Only the application case is interesting. We can prove the following inversion lemma:

   $$\begin{array}{l}(x \gg\!= f) \approx \mathit{return}\ v \rightarrow \\ \quad \exists\ \lambda\ v' \rightarrow (x \approx \mathit{return}\ v') \times (f\ v' \approx \mathit{return}\ v)\end{array}$$

   Here the size of the left-hand proof is equal to the sum of the sizes of the two right-hand proofs. If we have $[\![t_1 \cdot t_2]\!]\ \rho \approx \mathit{return}\ v$, then we can use inversion twice plus case analysis to deduce that $[\![t_1]\!]\ \rho \approx \mathit{return}\ (\mathsf{lam}\ t'\ \rho')$ and $[\![t_2]\!]\ \rho \approx \mathit{return}\ v'$ for some t', ρ', v' such that $[\![t']\!]\ (v' :: \rho') \approx \mathit{return}\ v$. We can finish by applying app to three instances of the inductive hypothesis, after making sure that the proofs are small enough.

   This proof is a bit awkward when written out in detail, due to the use of sizes.

4. Finally we should prove that excluded middle and $[\![t]\!]\ \rho \approx \mathit{never}$ imply $\rho \vdash t \Uparrow$. This can be proved using corecursion.

   As before the only interesting case is application. We can prove the following inversion lemma by using excluded middle:

   $$\begin{array}{l}(x \gg\!= f) \approx \mathit{never} \rightarrow \\ \quad x \approx \mathit{never}\ \uplus \\ \qquad \exists\ \lambda\ v \rightarrow (x \approx \mathit{return}\ v) \times (f\ v \approx \mathit{never})\end{array}$$

   If $x \gg\!= f$ does not terminate, then either x fails to terminate, or x terminates with a value v and $f\ v$ does not terminate. Given a proof of $[\![t_1 \cdot t_2]\!]\ \rho \approx \mathit{never}$ we can use inversion twice to determine which of $\mathsf{app}^{\mathsf{l}}$, $\mathsf{app}^{\mathsf{r}}$ and app to emit, in each case continuing corecursively (and in the latter two cases also using (3)).

6. Virtual Machine

This section defines a virtual machine (VM), following Leroy and Grall (2009) but defining the semantics functionally instead of relationally, and using a well-scoped approach. (The accompanying code contains a relational semantics and a proof showing that it is equivalent to the functional one.)

The VM is stack-based, and uses the following instructions:

```
mutual
  data Instr (n : ℕ) : Set where
    var : Fin n          → Instr n   -- Push variable.
    con : ℕ              → Instr n   -- Push constant.
    clo : Code (1 + n)   → Instr n   -- Push closure.
    app :                  Instr n   -- Apply function.
    ret :                  Instr n   -- Return.

  Code : ℕ → Set
  Code n = List (Instr n)
```

Instructions of type *Instr n* have at most n free variables. The type family *Code* consists of sequences of instructions.

Values and environments (*VM-Value* and *VM-Env*) are defined as in Section 3, but using *Code* instead of *Tm* in the definition of closures. Stacks contain values and return frames:

```
data Stack-element : Set where
  val : VM-Value               → Stack-element
  ret : Code n → VM-Env n → Stack-element

Stack : Set
Stack = List Stack-element
```

The VM operates on states containing three components, the code, a stack, and an environment:

```
data State : Set where
  ⟨_,_,_⟩ : Code n → Stack → VM-Env n → State
```

The result of running the VM one step, starting in a given state, is either a new state, normal termination with a value, or abnormal termination (a crash):

```
data Result : Set where
  continue : State    → Result
  done     : VM-Value → Result
  crash    :            Result
```

The function *step* (see Figure 3) shows how the result is computed. Given *step* it is easy to define the VM's semantics corecursively:

```
exec : State → (Maybe VM-Value)⊥
exec s with step s
... | continue s′ = later (♯ exec s′)
... | done v      = return v
... | crash       = fail
```

In a state s, run *step s*. If the result is continue s', continue running from s'; if it is done v, return v; and if it is crash, fail.

The function *exec* is an example of a functional, *small-step* operational semantics. As before it is clear that the semantics is deterministic and computable, and just as with a relational small-step semantics we avoid duplication of rules. However, the use of a wild-card in the last clause of *step* means that it is possible to forget a rule. If we tried to omit one of the clauses from the definition of $[\![\_]\!]$ (Section 3), then the definition would be rejected, but this is not the case for the first six clauses of *step*.

7. Compiler Correctness

Let us now define a compiler from *Tm* to *Code* and prove that it preserves the semantics of the input program. The definition follows Leroy and Grall (2009), but uses a code continuation to avoid the use of list append and some proof overhead (Hutton 2007, Section 13.7):

```
comp : Tm n → Code n → Code n
comp (con i) c = con i :: c
comp (var x) c = var x :: c
comp (lam t) c = clo (comp t [ret]) :: c
comp (t₁ · t₂) c = comp t₁ (comp t₂ (app :: c))
```

We can also "compile" values:

```
compᵥ : Value → VM-Value
compᵥ (con i)   = con i
compᵥ (lam t ρ) = lam (comp t [ret]) (map compᵥ ρ)
```

I state compiler correctness as follows:

```
correct : (t : Tm 0) →
            exec ⟨ comp t [], [], [] ⟩ ≈
              ([[ t ]] [] >>= λ v → return (compᵥ v))
```

Given a closed term t, the result of running the corresponding compiled code (*comp t* [ ]) on the VM (starting with an empty stack and environment), should be the same as evaluating the term (in

$$
\begin{array}{llllll}
\mathit{step} : \mathit{State} \to \mathit{Result} \\
\mathit{step}\ \langle\ [\,] & ,\mathsf{val}\ v :: [\,] & ,[\,]\ \rangle & = & \mathsf{done}\ v \\
\mathit{step}\ \langle\ \mathsf{var}\ x :: c, & & s, \rho\ \rangle & = & \mathsf{continue}\ \langle\ c\ ,\mathsf{val}\ (\mathit{lookup}\ x\ \rho) :: s, & \rho\ \rangle \\
\mathit{step}\ \langle\ \mathsf{con}\ i :: c, & & s, \rho\ \rangle & = & \mathsf{continue}\ \langle\ c\ ,\mathsf{val}\ (\mathsf{con}\ i) \qquad :: s, & \rho\ \rangle \\
\mathit{step}\ \langle\ \mathsf{clo}\ c' :: c, & & s, \rho\ \rangle & = & \mathsf{continue}\ \langle\ c\ ,\mathsf{val}\ (\mathsf{lam}\ c'\ \rho) \quad :: s, & \rho\ \rangle \\
\mathit{step}\ \langle\ \mathsf{app} & :: c, \mathsf{val}\ v :: \mathsf{val}\ (\mathsf{lam}\ c'\ \rho') :: & s, \rho\ \rangle & = & \mathsf{continue}\ \langle\ c', \mathsf{ret}\ c\ \rho \qquad :: s, v :: & \rho'\ \rangle \\
\mathit{step}\ \langle\ \mathsf{ret} & :: c, \mathsf{val}\ v :: \mathsf{ret}\ c'\ \rho' & :: s, \rho\ \rangle & = & \mathsf{continue}\ \langle\ c', \mathsf{val}\ v \qquad :: s, & \rho'\ \rangle \\
\mathit{step}\ \_ & & & = & \mathsf{crash}
\end{array}
$$

Figure 3. A function which computes the result of running the virtual machine one step from a given state.

an empty environment) and, if evaluation terminates with a value, return the "compiled" variant of this value.

We can compare this statement to a corresponding statement phrased for relational semantics:

$$
\begin{array}{lll}
([\,] \vdash t \Downarrow v & \Leftrightarrow \langle\ \mathit{comp}\ t\ [\,], [\,], [\,]\ \rangle \leadsto^{\star} \\
& \qquad \langle\ [\,], \mathsf{val}\ (\mathit{comp}_{\mathsf{V}}\ v) :: [\,], [\,]\ \rangle) & \times \\
([\,] \vdash t \Uparrow & \Leftrightarrow \langle\ \mathit{comp}\ t\ [\,], [\,], [\,]\ \rangle \leadsto^{\infty}) & \times \\
([\,] \vdash t\ \lightning & \Leftrightarrow \langle\ \mathit{comp}\ t\ [\,], [\,], [\,]\ \rangle \leadsto^{\lightning})
\end{array}
$$

Here $\_\leadsto\_ : \mathit{State} \to \mathit{State} \to \mathit{Set}$ is the VM's small-step relation, $\_\leadsto^{\star}\_$ its reflexive transitive closure, $s \leadsto^{\infty}$ means that there is an infinite transition sequence starting in s, and $s \leadsto^{\lightning}$ means that there is a "stuck" transition sequence starting in s (i.e., a sequence which cannot be extended further, and which does not end with a state of the form $\langle\ [\,], \mathsf{val}\ \_ :: [\,], [\,]\ \rangle$). I prefer the statement of *correct* above: I find it easier to understand and get correct.

Let us now prove *correct*. In order to do this the statement can be generalised as follows:

$$
\begin{array}{l}
\mathit{correct}' : \\
\quad (t : \mathit{Tm}\ n)\ \{k : \mathit{Value} \to (\mathit{Maybe\ VM\text{-}Value})_{\perp}\} \\
\quad (\mathit{hyp} : (v : \mathit{Value}) \to \\
\qquad \mathit{exec}\ \langle\ c, \mathsf{val}\ (\mathit{comp}_{\mathsf{V}}\ v) :: s, \mathit{map}\ \mathit{comp}_{\mathsf{V}}\ \rho\ \rangle \approx k\ v) \to \\
\quad \mathit{exec}\ \langle\ \mathit{comp}\ t\ c, s, \mathit{map}\ \mathit{comp}_{\mathsf{V}}\ \rho\ \rangle \approx (\llbracket\ t\ \rrbracket\ \rho \gg= k)
\end{array}
$$

This statement is written in continuation-passing style to avoid some uses of transitivity (which can be problematic, as discussed in Section 2). The statement is proved mutually with the following one:

$$
\begin{array}{l}
\bullet\text{-}\mathit{correct} : \\
\quad (v_1\ v_2 : \mathit{Value})\ \{k : \mathit{Value} \to (\mathit{Maybe\ VM\text{-}Value})_{\perp}\} \\
\quad (\mathit{hyp} : (v : \mathit{Value}) \to \\
\qquad \mathit{exec}\ \langle\ c, \mathsf{val}\ (\mathit{comp}_{\mathsf{V}}\ v) :: s, \mathit{map}\ \mathit{comp}_{\mathsf{V}}\ \rho\ \rangle \approx k\ v) \to \\
\quad \mathit{exec}\ \langle\ \mathsf{app} :: c, \mathsf{val}\ (\mathit{comp}_{\mathsf{V}}\ v_2) :: \mathsf{val}\ (\mathit{comp}_{\mathsf{V}}\ v_1) :: s, \\
\qquad\quad \mathit{map}\ \mathit{comp}_{\mathsf{V}}\ \rho\ \rangle \\
\qquad \approx (v_1 \bullet v_2 \gg= k)
\end{array}
$$

The statements can be proved using the same recursion structure as $\llbracket\_\rrbracket_{\mathsf{CPS}}/\_\bullet_{\mathsf{CPS}}\_$: mixed corecursion/structural recursion.

The interesting case of *correct′* is application, where we can proceed as follows (with safe uses of transitivity):

$$
\begin{array}{ll}
\mathit{exec}\ \langle\ \mathit{comp}\ t_1\ (\mathit{comp}\ t_2\ (\mathsf{app} :: c)), s, \mathit{map}\ \mathit{comp}_{\mathsf{V}}\ \rho\ \rangle & \approx \\
\llbracket\ t_1\ \rrbracket\ \rho \gg= \lambda\, v_1 \to\ \llbracket\ t_2\ \rrbracket\ \rho \gg= \lambda\, v_2 \to v_1 \bullet v_2\ \ \gg= k & \cong \\
\llbracket\ t_1\ \rrbracket\ \rho \gg= \lambda\, v_1 \to (\llbracket\ t_2\ \rrbracket\ \rho \gg= \lambda\, v_2 \to v_1 \bullet v_2) \gg= k & \cong \\
(\llbracket\ t_1\ \rrbracket\ \rho \gg= \lambda\, v_1 \to\ \llbracket\ t_2\ \rrbracket\ \rho \gg= \lambda\, v_2 \to v_1 \bullet v_2) \gg= k & \cong \\
\llbracket\ t_1 \cdot t_2\ \rrbracket\ \rho \gg= k
\end{array}
$$

The last three steps use associativity of bind twice. (These uses of associativity could have been avoided by using continuation-passing style instead of bind when defining the semantics. See the accompanying code.) The first step is more complicated. Here is its proof term:

$$\mathit{correct}'\ t_1\ (\lambda\, v_1 \to \mathit{correct}'\ t_2\ (\lambda\, v_2 \to \bullet\text{-}\mathit{correct}\ v_1\ v_2\ \mathit{hyp}))$$

First an appeal to the inductive hypothesis (t_1 is structurally smaller than $t_1 \cdot t_2$), then, in the continuation, another appeal to the inductive hypothesis, and finally, in the nested continuation, a use of $\bullet$-*correct*.

The interesting case of $\bullet$-*correct* is when v_1 is a closure, $\mathsf{lam}\ t_1\ \rho_1$, in which case we need to prove that

$$
\begin{array}{l}
\mathit{exec}\ \langle\ \mathsf{app} :: c, \mathsf{val}\ (\mathit{comp}_{\mathsf{V}}\ v_2) :: \mathsf{val}\ (\mathit{comp}_{\mathsf{V}}\ (\mathsf{lam}\ t_1\ \rho_1)) :: s, \\
\qquad \mathit{map}\ \mathit{comp}_{\mathsf{V}}\ \rho\ \rangle
\end{array}
$$

is weakly bisimilar to

$$\mathsf{lam}\ t_1\ \rho_1 \bullet v_2 \gg= k.$$

We can start by emitting a later constructor and suspension:

$$\mathsf{later}\ (\sharp\ ?)$$

The question mark should be replaced by a proof showing that

$$
\begin{array}{l}
\mathit{exec}\ \langle\ \mathit{comp}\ t_1\ [\mathsf{ret}], \mathsf{ret}\ c\ (\mathit{map}\ \mathit{comp}_{\mathsf{V}}\ \rho) :: s, \\
\qquad \mathit{map}\ \mathit{comp}_{\mathsf{V}}\ (v_2 :: \rho_1)\ \rangle
\end{array}
$$

is weakly bisimilar to

$$\llbracket\ t_1\ \rrbracket\ (v_2 :: \rho_1) \gg= k.$$

This can be proved by appeal to the coinductive hypothesis:

$$\mathit{correct}'\ t_1\ (\lambda\, v \to \mathsf{later}^{\mathsf{l}}\ (\mathit{hyp}\ v))$$

Here the use of $\mathsf{later}^{\mathsf{l}}$ corresponds to the reduction of

$$
\begin{array}{l}
\mathit{exec}\ \langle\ [\mathsf{ret}], \mathsf{val}\ (\mathit{comp}_{\mathsf{V}}\ v) :: \mathsf{ret}\ c\ (\mathit{map}\ \mathit{comp}_{\mathsf{V}}\ \rho) :: s, \\
\qquad \mathit{map}\ \mathit{comp}_{\mathsf{V}}\ (v_2 :: \rho_1)\ \rangle
\end{array}
$$

to

$$\mathit{exec}\ \langle\ c, \mathsf{val}\ (\mathit{comp}_{\mathsf{V}}\ v) :: s, \mathit{map}\ \mathit{comp}_{\mathsf{V}}\ \rho\ \rangle,$$

which has the right form for the use of *hyp*.

The proof sketch above—and especially the compact proof terms—may look a bit bewildering. Fortunately one does not have to understand every detail of a machine-checked proof. It is more important to understand the statement of the theorem.[6] Furthermore, the writer of the proof has the support of a proof assistant, that in my case provided much help with the construction of the proof terms.

The proof above can be compared to that of Leroy and Grall (2009), who prove the following two implications (in their slightly different setting):

$$
\begin{array}{lll}
[\,] \vdash t \Downarrow v & \to & \langle\ \mathit{comp}\ t\ [\,], [\,], [\,]\ \rangle \leadsto^{\star} \\
& & \quad \langle\ [\,], \mathsf{val}\ (\mathit{comp}_{\mathsf{V}}\ v) :: [\,], [\,]\ \rangle \\
[\,] \vdash t \Uparrow & \to & \langle\ \mathit{comp}\ t\ [\,], [\,], [\,]\ \rangle \leadsto^{\infty}
\end{array}
$$

[6] With the caveat that one should not put too much trust into Agda, which is a very experimental system.

Consider application. In the proof above there is *one* case for application, with two sub-cases, one for crashes and one for closures. In the proof of the two implications there are *four* cases for application: one in case of termination and three for non-terminating applications. The rule duplication in the semantics shows up as rule duplication in the proof.

8. Non-determinism

The compiler correctness statement used above is sometimes too restrictive (Leroy 2009). For instance, evaluation order may be left up to the compiler. This section illustrates how this kind of situation can be handled by defining a non-deterministic language, and implementing a compiler that implements one out of many possible semantics for this language.

The syntax of the language defined in Section 3 is extended with a term-former for non-deterministic choice:

$$\_|\_ \;:\; Tm\; n \to Tm\; n \to Tm\; n$$

The semantic domain is now the maybe monad transformer applied to the partiality monad transformer ($\lambda M\, A.\, \nu X.\, M\,(A \uplus X)$ for strictly positive monads M) applied to a non-determinism monad ($\lambda A.\, \mu X.\, A \uplus X \times X$; Moggi (1990)), implemented monolithically as follows:

$$\begin{array}{l} \textbf{data}\; D\;(A \;:\; Set) \;:\; Set\;\textbf{where} \\ \quad \mathsf{fail} \quad\;\; : \qquad\qquad\quad D\,A \\ \quad \mathsf{return} : A \qquad\qquad \to D\,A \\ \quad \_|\_ \quad\;\, : D\,A \to D\,A \to D\,A \\ \quad \mathsf{later} \quad : \infty\,(D\,A) \quad\;\; \to D\,A \end{array}$$

$$\begin{array}{l} \_\gg\!=\_ \;:\; D\,A \to (A \to D\,B) \to D\,B \\ \mathsf{fail} \qquad\;\; \gg\!= f \;=\; \mathsf{fail} \\ \mathsf{return}\; x \;\gg\!= f \;=\; f\,x \\ (x_1 \mid x_2) \;\gg\!= f \;=\; (x_1 \gg\!= f) \mid (x_2 \gg\!= f) \\ \mathsf{later}\; x \quad \gg\!= f \;=\; \mathsf{later}\;(\sharp\;(\flat\; x \gg\!= f)) \end{array}$$

As before the monad laws hold up to strong bisimilarity, which can be defined as follows:

$$\begin{array}{l} \textbf{data}\;\_\cong\_ \;:\; D\,A \to D\,A \to Set\;\textbf{where} \\ \quad \mathsf{fail} \quad\;\; : \qquad\qquad\qquad\qquad\quad \mathsf{fail} \;\cong\; \mathsf{fail} \\ \quad \mathsf{return} : \qquad\qquad\qquad\qquad\quad \mathsf{return}\; x \;\cong\; \mathsf{return}\; x \\ \quad \_|\_ \quad\;\, : x_1 \cong y_1 \to x_2 \cong y_2 \to x_1 \mid x_2 \;\cong\; y_1 \mid y_2 \\ \quad \mathsf{later} \quad : \infty\,(\flat\; x \cong \flat\; y) \qquad\;\; \to \mathsf{later}\; x \;\cong\; \mathsf{later}\; y \end{array}$$

Finally we can extend the semantics by adding a clause for choice (note that $\_|\_$ is overloaded):

$$[\![\, t_1 \mid t_2 \,]\!]\; \rho \;=\; [\![\, t_1 \,]\!]\; \rho \mid [\![\, t_2 \,]\!]\; \rho$$

It may be worth pointing out that now the semantics is no longer deterministic, despite being defined as a function.

As an example we can define a call-by-value fixpoint combinator ($Z = \lambda f.\, (\lambda g.\, f\, (\lambda x.\, g\, g\, x))\; (\lambda g.\, f\, (\lambda x.\, g\, g\, x))$) and a non-deterministic non-terminating term ($t \;=\; Z\; (\lambda f\, x.\, f\, x \mid f\, x)\; 0$):

$$\begin{array}{l} Z \;:\; Tm\; 0 \\ Z \;=\; \mathsf{lam}\;(h \cdot h) \\ \quad \textbf{where}\; h \;=\; \mathsf{lam}\;(\mathsf{var}\; 1 \cdot \mathsf{lam}\;(\mathsf{var}\; 1 \cdot \mathsf{var}\; 1 \cdot \mathsf{var}\; 0)) \end{array}$$

$$\begin{array}{l} t \;:\; Tm\; 0 \\ t \;=\; Z \cdot \mathsf{lam}\;(\mathsf{lam}\;(\mathsf{var}\; 1 \cdot \mathsf{var}\; 0 \mid \mathsf{var}\; 1 \cdot \mathsf{var}\; 0)) \cdot \mathsf{con}\; 0 \end{array}$$

The semantics of t, $[\![\, t \,]\!]\; [\,]$, is strongly bisimilar to *t-sem*:

$$\begin{array}{l} \textit{t-sem} \;:\; D\; Value \\ \textit{t-sem} \;=\; \mathsf{later}\;(\sharp\;\mathsf{later}\;(\sharp\;\mathsf{later}\;(\sharp\;\mathsf{later}\;(\sharp\;(\textit{t-sem} \mid \textit{t-sem}))))) \end{array}$$

The virtual machine is unchanged, so the compiler correctness statement will relate deterministic and non-deterministic computations. To do this we can use the following variant of weak bisimilarity:

$$\begin{array}{l} \textbf{data}\;\_\approx^{\in}\_ \;:\; (Maybe\; A)_{\bot} \to D\,A \to Set\;\textbf{where} \\ \quad \mathsf{fail} \quad\;\; : \mathsf{now\;nothing} \;\approx^{\in}\; \mathsf{fail} \\ \quad \mathsf{return} : \mathsf{now\;(just}\; x) \;\approx^{\in}\; \mathsf{return}\; x \\ \quad |^{\mathsf{l}} \qquad\; : x \approx^{\in} y_1 \to x \approx^{\in} y_1 \mid y_2 \\ \quad |^{\mathsf{r}} \qquad\; : x \approx^{\in} y_2 \to x \approx^{\in} y_1 \mid y_2 \\ \quad \mathsf{later} \quad : \infty\,(\flat\; x \approx^{\in} \flat\; y) \to \mathsf{later}\; x \approx^{\in} \mathsf{later}\; y \\ \quad \mathsf{later}^{\mathsf{l}} \;\; : \qquad \flat\; x \approx^{\in} \quad y \to \mathsf{later}\; x \approx^{\in} \qquad y \\ \quad \mathsf{later}^{\mathsf{r}} \;\, : \qquad\;\; x \approx^{\in} \flat\; y \to \qquad\quad x \approx^{\in} \mathsf{later}\; y \end{array}$$

You can read $x \approx^{\in} y$ as "x implements one of the allowed semantics of y".

Compiler correctness can now be stated as follows:

$$\begin{array}{l} \textit{correct} \;:\; (t \;:\; Tm\; 0) \to \\ \qquad\qquad exec\; \langle\; comp\; t\; [\,], [\,], [\,]\; \rangle \;\approx^{\in} \\ \qquad\qquad\quad [\![\, t \,]\!]\; [\,] \;\gg\!=\; \lambda\, v \to \mathsf{return}\; (comp_{\mathsf{v}}\; v) \end{array}$$

If we extend the compiler in the following way, then we can prove that it is correct using an argument which is very similar to that in Section 7:

$$comp\; (t_1 \mid t_2)\; c \;=\; comp\; t_1\; c$$

We can also prove type soundness for the non-deterministic language, using the type system from Section 4 extended with the following rule:

$$\_|\_ \;:\; \Gamma \vdash t_1 \in \sigma \;\to\; \Gamma \vdash t_2 \in \sigma \;\to\; \Gamma \vdash t_1 \mid t_2 \in \sigma$$

Type soundness can be stated using $\_\approx^{\in}\_$. Type-correct terms should not crash, no matter how the non-determinism is resolved:

$$\begin{array}{l} \textit{type-soundness} \;:\; [\,] \vdash t \in \sigma \;\to \\ \qquad\qquad\qquad\quad \neg\; (\mathsf{now\;nothing} \;\approx^{\in}\; [\![\, t \,]\!]\; [\,]) \end{array}$$

It is easy to prove this statement by adapting the proof from Section 4. All it takes is to extend the *Lift* type with the constructor

$$\_|\_ \;:\; Lift\; P\; x \;\to\; Lift\; P\; y \;\to\; Lift\; P\; (x \mid y),$$

and then propagating this change through the rest of the proof. Note that the new definition of *Lift* uses induction nested inside coinduction (as do D and $\_\approx^{\in}\_$).

9. Term Equivalences

Let us now return to the deterministic language from Section 3. Weak bisimilarity as defined in Section 2 is, despite its name, a very strong notion of equality for the semantic domain $(Maybe\; Value)_{\bot}$. We can lift this equality to closed terms in the following way:

$$\begin{array}{l} \_\equiv\_ \;:\; Tm\; 0 \to Tm\; 0 \to Set \\ t_1 \;\equiv\; t_2 \;=\; [\![\, t_1 \,]\!]\; [\,] \;\approx\; [\![\, t_2 \,]\!]\; [\,] \end{array}$$

This is a very syntactic equality, which distinguishes the observationally equivalent terms $t_1 \;=\; \mathsf{lam\;(lam\;(var\;0))} \cdot \mathsf{con}\; 0$ and $t_2 \;=\; \mathsf{lam\;(var\;0)}$, because

$$\begin{array}{ll} [\![\, t_1 \,]\!]\; [\,] & \approx \\ \textit{return}\; (\mathsf{lam\;(var\;0)\;(con\;0} :: [\,])) & \not\approx \\ \textit{return}\; (\mathsf{lam\;(var\;0)} \qquad\quad\; [\,]) & \approx \\ [\![\, t_2 \,]\!]\; [\,]. & \end{array}$$

The relational big-step semantics from Section 5 is no different: $[\,] \vdash t_1 \Downarrow v$ does not imply that we have $[\,] \vdash t_2 \Downarrow v$.

This section defines some less syntactical term equivalences. Discussion of the finer points of these equivalences is out of scope for this paper; the main point is that they can be defined without too much fuss.

Let us start by defining a notion of applicative bisimilarity (Abramsky 1990). Computations are equivalent ($\_\approx_{\bot}\_$) if they are weakly bisimilar, with equivalent (rather than equal) possibly exceptional values; possibly exceptional values are equivalent ($\_\approx_{MV}\_$) if they are of the same kind and, in the case of success, contain equivalent values; and values are equivalent ($\_\approx_{V}\_$) if they are either equal constants, or closures which are equivalent when evaluated with the free variables bound to an arbitrary value:[7]

```
mutual
  data _≈⊥_ :
           (Maybe Value)⊥ → (Maybe Value)⊥ → Set where
    now    :       u ≈MV v → now u ≈⊥ now v
    later  : ∞ (♭ x ≈⊥ ♭ y) → later x ≈⊥ later y
    laterˡ :     ♭ x ≈⊥   y → later x ≈⊥       y
    laterʳ :       x ≈⊥ ♭ y →         x ≈⊥ later y

  data _≈MV_ : Maybe Value → Maybe Value → Set where
    just    : u ≈V v → just u  ≈MV just v
    nothing :          nothing ≈MV nothing

  data _≈V_ : Value → Value → Set where
    con : con i ≈V con i
    lam : (∀ v → ∞ (⟦ t₁ ⟧ (v :: ρ₁) ≈⊥ ⟦ t₂ ⟧ (v :: ρ₂))) →
          lam t₁ ρ₁ ≈V lam t₂ ρ₂
```

This is yet again a definition which uses induction nested inside coinduction. Note that the lam constructor is coinductive. If this constructor were inductive, then the relations would not be reflexive: lam (var zero) [ ] would be provably distinct from itself.

Using the relations above we can define applicative bisimilarity by stating that terms are equivalent if they are equivalent when evaluated in an arbitrary context:

```
_≈T_ : Tm n → Tm n → Set
t₁ ≈T t₂ = ∀ ρ → ⟦ t₁ ⟧ ρ ≈⊥ ⟦ t₂ ⟧ ρ
```

The definition of $\_\approx_{\bot}\_$ is very similar to the definition of weak bisimilarity in Section 2. It is possible to define a single notion of weak bisimilarity, parametrised by a relation to use for values. The accompanying code uses such a definition.

Let us now turn to contextual equivalence. Contexts with zero or more holes can be defined as follows:

```
data Context (m : ℕ) : ℕ → Set where
  hole :                                  Context m m
  con  : ℕ                              → Context m n
  var  : Fin n                          → Context m n
  lam  : Context m (1 + n)              → Context m n
  _·_  : Context m n → Context m n → Context m n
```

The type *Context m n* contains contexts whose holes expect terms of type *Tm m*. If we fill the holes, then we get a term of type *Tm n*:

```
_[_] : Context m n → Tm m → Tm n
hole       [t] = t
con i      [t] = con i
var x      [t] = var x
lam C      [t] = lam (C [t])
(C₁ · C₂) [t] = C₁ [t] · C₂ [t]
```

Contextual equivalence can be defined in two equivalent ways. The usual one states that t_1 and t_2 are contextually equivalent if $C\,[t_1]$ terminates iff $C\,[t_2]$ terminates, for any closing context C:

```
_⇓ : A⊥ → Set
x ⇓ = ∃ λ v → x ≈ now v
```

```
_≈C_ : Tm n → Tm n → Set
t₁ ≈C t₂ = ∀ C → ⟦ C [t₁] ⟧ [] ⇓ ⇔ ⟦ C [t₂] ⟧ [] ⇓
```

However, we can also define contextual equivalence using weak bisimilarity:

```
_≈′C_ : Tm n → Tm n → Set
t₁ ≈′C t₂ = ∀ C → ⟦ C [t₁] ⟧ [] ≈° ⟦ C [t₂] ⟧ []
```

Here $\_\approx^{\circ}\_$ is a notion of weak bisimilarity which identifies all terminating computations:

```
now : now u ≈° now v
```

It is easy to prove that these two notions of contextual equivalence are equivalent.

As an aside one can note that the contextual equivalences above are a bit strange, because there is no context which distinguishes con 0 from con 1. This could be fixed by extending the language with suitable constructions for observing the difference between distinct constants.

10. Conclusions

When writing down a semantics I think one of the main priorities should be to make it easy to understand. Sometimes a more complicated definition may be more convenient for certain tasks, but in that case one can define two semantics and prove that they are equivalent.

I hope I have convinced you that functional operational semantics defined using the partiality monad are easy to understand. I have also used two such semantics to state a compiler correctness result, and I find this statement to be easier to understand than a corresponding statement phrased using relational semantics (see Section 7).

The semantics also seem to be useful when it comes to proving typical meta-theoretic properties, at least for the simple languages discussed in this paper. I have proved type soundness and compiler correctness directly for the semantics given above. The type soundness proof in Section 4 is given in relatively complete, formal detail, yet it is short and should be easy to follow. Furthermore, as mentioned in Section 7, the compiler correctness proof avoids some duplication which is present in a corresponding proof for relational semantics.

As discussed above the support for total corecursion in languages like Agda and Coq is somewhat limited: definitions like $⟦\_⟧$ are often rejected. However, my experience with sized types in MiniAgda (see Section 2) is encouraging. I suspect that a more polished implementation of sized types could be quite satisfying to work with.

Finally I want to mention a drawback of this kind of semantics: proofs which proceed by induction on the structure of $\_\vdash\_\Downarrow\_$ when a relational big-step semantics is used can become somewhat awkward when transferred to this setting, as illustrated by the proof in Section 5 showing that $⟦\, t \,⟧\ \rho \approx \mathit{return}\ v$ implies $\rho \vdash t \Downarrow v$. However, it is unclear to me how often this is actually a problem. For instance, neither the type soundness proofs nor the compiler correctness proofs in this paper are affected by this drawback.

Acknowledgements

I want to thank Thorsten Altenkirch for encouraging this line of work, Peter Dybjer for useful feedback on a draft of the paper, and Tarmo Uustalu for pointing out some related work. I would also like to thank the anonymous reviewers for lots of useful feedback.

Large parts of this work were done when I was working at the University of Nottingham, with financial support from EPSRC (grant code: EP/E04350X/1). I have also received support from the

[7] $\forall\, v \rightarrow \ldots$ means the same as $(v : \_) \rightarrow \ldots$; Agda tries to infer the value of the underscore automatically.

ERC: "The research leading to these results has received funding from the European Research Council under the European Union's Seventh Framework Programme (FP7/2007-2013) / ERC grant agreement n° 247219."

References

Andreas Abel. MiniAgda: Integrating sized and dependent types. In *Proceedings Workshop on Partiality and Recursion in Interactive Theorem Provers (PAR 2010)*, volume 43 of *EPTCS*, 2010. doi:10.4204/EPTCS.43.2.

Samson Abramsky. The lazy lambda calculus. In *Research Topics in Functional Programming*. Addison-Wesley, 1990.

The Agda Team. The Agda Wiki. Available at `http://wiki.portal.chalmers.se/agda/`, 2012.

Thorsten Altenkirch and Nils Anders Danielsson. Termination checking in the presence of nested inductive and coinductive types. Short note supporting a talk given at the Workshop on Partiality and Recursion in Interactive Theorem Provers (PAR 2010), 2010.

Brian E. Aydemir, Aaron Bohannon, Matthew Fairbairn, J. Nathan Foster, Benjamin C. Pierce, Peter Sewell, Dimitrios Vytiniotis, Geoffrey Washburn, Stephanie Weirich, and Steve Zdancewic. Mechanized metatheory for the masses: The PoplMark challenge. In *Theorem Proving in Higher Order Logics, 18th International Conference, TPHOLs 2005*, volume 3603 of *LNCS*, pages 50–65, 2005. doi:10.1007/11541868_4.

Nick Benton and Chung-Kil Hur. Biorthogonality, step-indexing and compiler correctness. In *ICFP'09, Proceedings of the 2009 ACM SIGPLAN International Conference on Functional Programming*, pages 97–107, 2009. doi:10.1145/1596550.1596567.

Nick Benton, Andrew Kennedy, and Carsten Varming. Some domain theory and denotational semantics in Coq. In *Theorem Proving in Higher Order Logics, 22nd International Conference, TPHOLs 2009*, volume 5674 of *LNCS*, pages 115–130, 2009. doi:10.1007/978-3-642-03359-9_10.

Venanzio Capretta. General recursion via coinductive types. *Logical Methods in Computer Science*, 1(2):1–28, 2005. doi:10.2168/LMCS-1(2:1)2005.

The Coq Development Team. *The Coq Proof Assistant, Reference Manual, Version 8.3pl3*, 2011.

Thierry Coquand. Infinite objects in type theory. In *Types for Proofs and Programs, International Workshop TYPES '93*, volume 806 of *LNCS*, pages 62–78, 1994. doi:10.1007/3-540-58085-9_72.

Patrick Cousot and Radhia Cousot. Inductive definitions, semantics and abstract interpretations. In *POPL '92, Proceedings of the 19th ACM SIGPLAN-SIGACT symposium on Principles of programming languages*, pages 83–94, 1992. doi:10.1145/143165.143184.

Patrick Cousot and Radhia Cousot. Bi-inductive structural semantics. *Information and Computation*, 207(2):258–283, 2009. doi:10.1016/j.ic.2008.03.025.

Nils Anders Danielsson. Beating the productivity checker using embedded languages. In *Proceedings Workshop on Partiality and Recursion in Interactive Theorem Provers (PAR 2010)*, volume 43 of *EPTCS*, pages 29–48, 2010. doi:10.4204/EPTCS.43.3.

Nils Anders Danielsson and Thorsten Altenkirch. Subtyping, declaratively: An exercise in mixed induction and coinduction. In *Mathematics of Program Construction, 10th International Conference, MPC 2010*, volume 6120 of *LNCS*, pages 100–118, 2010. doi:10.1007/978-3-642-13321-3_8.

Neil Ghani and Tarmo Uustalu. Monad combinators, non-determinism and probabilistic choice. Extended abstract distributed at the workshop on Categorical Methods in Concurrency, Interaction and Mobility (CMCIM 2004), 2004.

Sergey Goncharov and Lutz Schröder. A coinductive calculus for asynchronous side-effecting processes. In *Fundamentals of Computation Theory, 18th International Symposium, FCT 2011*, volume 6914 of *LNCS*, pages 276–287, 2011. doi:10.1007/978-3-642-22953-4_24.

Graham Hutton. *Programming in Haskell*. Cambridge University Press, 2007.

Xavier Leroy. Formal verification of a realistic compiler. *Communications of the ACM*, 52:107–115, 2009. doi:10.1145/1538788.1538814.

Xavier Leroy and Hervé Grall. Coinductive big-step operational semantics. *Information and Computation*, 207(2):284–304, 2009. doi:10.1016/j.ic.2007.12.004.

Robin Milner and Mads Tofte. Co-induction in relational semantics. *Theoretical Computer Science*, 87(1):209–220, 1991. doi:10.1016/0304-3975(91)90033-X.

Eugenio Moggi. An abstract view of programming languages. Technical Report ECS-LFCS-90-113, Lab. for Found. of Comp. Sci., University of Edinburgh, 1990.

Eugenio Moggi. Notions of computation and monads. *Information and Computation*, 93(1):55–92, 1991. doi:10.1016/0890-5401(91)90052-4.

Keiko Nakata and Tarmo Uustalu. Trace-based coinductive operational semantics for While: Big-step and small-step, relational and functional styles. In *Theorem Proving in Higher Order Logics, 22nd International Conference, TPHOLs 2009*, volume 5674 of *LNCS*, pages 375–390, 2009. doi:10.1007/978-3-642-03359-9_26.

Keiko Nakata and Tarmo Uustalu. Resumptions, weak bisimilarity and big-step semantics for While with interactive I/O: An exercise in mixed induction-coinduction. In *Proceedings Seventh Workshop on Structural Operational Semantics (SOS 2010)*, volume 32 of *EPTCS*, pages 57–75, 2010. doi:10.4204/EPTCS.32.5.

Ulf Norell. *Towards a practical programming language based on dependent type theory*. PhD thesis, Chalmers University of Technology and Göteborg University, 2007.

Christine Paulin-Mohring. A constructive denotational semantics for Kahn networks in Coq. In *From Semantics to Computer Science: Essays in Honour of Gilles Kahn*, pages 383–413. Cambridge University Press, 2009.

John C. Reynolds. Definitional interpreters for higher-order programming languages. In *ACM '72, Proceedings of the ACM annual conference*, volume 2, pages 717–740, 1972. doi:10.1145/800194.805852.

J.J.M.M. Rutten. A note on coinduction and weak bisimilarity for while programs. *Theoretical Informatics and Applications*, 33:393–400, 1999. doi:10.1051/ita:1999125.

Davide Sangiorgi and Robin Milner. The problem of "weak bisimulation up to". In *CONCUR '92, Third International Conference on Concurrency Theory*, volume 630 of *LNCS*, pages 32–46, 1992. doi:10.1007/BFb0084781.

Mads Tofte. Type inference for polymorphic references. *Information and Computation*, 89(1):1–34, 1990. doi:10.1016/0890-5401(90)90018-D.

Philip Wadler. The essence of functional programming. In *POPL '92, Proceedings of the 19th ACM SIGPLAN-SIGACT symposium on Principles of programming languages*, pages 1–14, 1992. doi:10.1145/143165.143169.

High Performance Embedded Domain Specific Languages

Kunle Olukotun
Standford University
kunle@stanford.edu

Today, all high-performance computer architectures are parallel and heterogeneous; a combination of multiple CPUs, GPUs and specialized processors. This creates a complex programming problem for application developers. Domain-specific languages (DSLs) are a promising solution to this problem because they provide an avenue for application-specific abstractions to be mapped directly to low level architecture-specific programming models providing high programmer productivity and high execution performance.

In this talk I will describe our approach to building high performance DSLs, which is based on embedding in Scala, light-weight modular staging and a DSL infrastructure called Delite. I will describe how we transform impure functional programs into efficient first-order low-level code using domain specific optimization, parallelism optimization, locality optimization, scalar optimization, and architecture-specific code generation. All optimizations and transformations are implemented in an extensible DSL compiler architecture that minimizes the programmer effort required to develop a new DSL.

Categories and Subject Descriptors D.1.3 [*Concurrent Programming*]: Parallel Programming; D.3.2 [*Language Classifications*]: Specialized application languages

Keywords DSLs, Scala, Delite

ICFP'12, September 9–15, 2012, Copenhagen, Denmark.
ACM 978-1-4503-1054-3/12/09.

Pure Type Systems with Corecursion on Streams

From Finite to Infinitary Normalisation

Paula Severi
Department of Computer Science,
University of Leicester, UK
ps56@mcs.le.ac.uk

Fer-Jan de Vries
Department of Computer Science,
University of Leicester, UK
fdv1@mcs.le.ac.uk

Abstract

In this paper, we use types for ensuring that programs involving streams are well-behaved. We extend pure type systems with a type constructor for *streams*, a modal operator *next* and a fixed point operator for expressing *corecursion*. This extension is called *Pure Type Systems with Corecursion* (CoPTS). The typed lambda calculus for reactive programs defined by Krishnaswami and Benton can be obtained as a CoPTS. CoPTSs allow us to study a wide range of typed lambda calculi extended with corecursion using only one framework. In particular, we study this extension for the calculus of constructions which is the underlying formal language of Coq. We use the machinery of infinitary rewriting and formalise the idea of well-behaved programs using the concept of infinitary normalisation. The set of finite and infinite terms is defined as a metric completion. We establish a precise connection between the modal operator ($\bullet A$) and the metric at a syntactic level by relating a variable of type ($\bullet A$) with the depth of all its occurrences in a term. This syntactic connection between the modal operator and the depth is the key to the proofs of infinitary weak and strong normalisation.

Categories and Subject Descriptors F.4.1 MATHEMATICAL LOGIC AND FORMAL LANGUAGES [*Mathematical Logic*]: Lambda calculus and related systems; D.3.2 PROGRAMMING LANGUAGES [*Language Classifications*]: Applicative (functional) Programming

Keywords Typed lambda calculus, modal operator, recursion, streams, infinitary normalisation

1. Introduction

In this paper, we are interested in using types to ensure that programs involving streams defined by recursive equations are well-behaved. As an example, we consider streams in Haskell. The program zeros defined by the following corecursive equation:

```
zeros = 0:zeros
```

is well-behaved because the run-time system yields a value which is a potentially infinite normal form:

$$0 : (0 : (0 : (\ldots)))$$

ICFP'12, September 9–15, 2012, Copenhagen, Denmark.

The following three programs are not well-behaved because they do not produce any output.

```
omega = omega
omegaprime = tail (0: omegaprime)
e = filter (\x-> (x>0)) zeros
```

The last program does not produce the empty list, but it loops like the other two programs. Intuitively, the above programs are "badly behaved". The idea of badly behaved programs is formalised in infinitary rewriting: programs are deemed to be bad behaved if they are not infinitary normalisation [25–27], where a program is *infinitary (weakly) normalising* if it has either a reduction to finite or a reduction to infinite normal form. None of the above three examples are infinitary normalising. A typed lambda calculus satisfies the property of *infinitary normalisation* if all typable terms are infinitary normalising. Unfortunately, the typed lambda calculus underlying Haskell is not infinitary normalising since it allows us to type the above three non-infinitary normalising terms.

```
omega :: a
omegaprime :: [Integer]
e :: [Integer]
```

The typed lambda calculus of reactive programs defined by Krishnaswami and Benton can type some recursive programs such as zerosprime and disallows terms like omega [30]. Their system is the simply typed lambda calculus extended with corecursion on streams. In this paper, we extend their typed lambda calculus of reactive programs to the calculus of constructions which is a subset of the underlying formal language for Coq [11]. This extension will allow us to write other forms of abstractions:

1. Polymorphic functions such as map and zip.
2. Type constructors such as the following one (written in Haskell notation):

   ```
   type DoubleFun a = [a] -> [a] -> [a]
   ```

3. Properties on streams and their proofs, using the Curry Howard isomorphism [12, 13, 22]. For example, we can have a constant

   $$\mathsf{EqStr} : \Pi X{:}\mathsf{set}.(\mathsf{Stream}\ X) \to (\mathsf{Stream}\ X) \to \mathsf{prop}$$

   to represent equality between streams.

To give a more general presentation, we consider pure type systems (PTSs) [2, 4, 40]. Pure type systems are a framework to define several existing typed lambda calculi à la Church in a uniform way.[1] In particular, this includes the systems of the λ-cube and the calculus of constructions [11]. We define *Pure Type Systems with Corecursion* (CoPTSs) by extending the set of pseudoterms of a PTS with:

1. The type for *streams* (Stream A) with the constructor cons and the destructors head and tail.
2. The *next* modal type ($\bullet A$), the constructor $\circ$ which moves *one step after* and a destructor await which moves *one step before* the moment in which the term is evaluated.
3. The fixed point operator to express *corecursion* which is denoted by cofix.

The judgements of a CoPTS are written as $\Gamma \vdash a{:}_i A$ where i is an index representing *time*. A term of type ($\bullet A$) represents 'the information that is going to be displayed *later* in the future'.

CoPTSs allow us to study a wide range of typed lambda calculi extended with corecursion using only one framework. We will study the properties of infinitary (weak) normalisation and infinitary strong normalisation for CoPTSs. These notions are the analogues of weak and strong normalisation in finite rewriting. Proving infinitary weak normalisation of a typed lambda calculus is a way of ensuring that all typable programs are well-behaved. Infinitary weak normalisation expresses that typable terms have a reduction to finite or infinite normal form. Infinitary strong normalisation expresses something stronger, namely, that any reduction strategy will find the possibly infinite normal form.

What does an infinite normal form of a typable terms look like?

To describe the infinite normal forms of typable terms, we define a set $\mathcal{C}^\infty$ of finite and infinite terms as a metric completion of the set of finite terms over the given syntax using an appropriate *metric*. We will use a metric based on a notion of *depth* where only the depth of a subterm b in the contexts (cons a b) and ($\circ b$) is counted as one (level) deeper than the depth of the terms (cons a b) and ($\circ b$) themselves. This type of completion is well known from infinitary versions of term rewriting systems, lambda calculus and combinatory reduction systems [25–27].

One way of proving infinitary weak normalisation is to give a reduction strategy that finds an infinite or infinite normal form of a term if it has one.

It is well-known that in classic, finitary lambda calculus the leftmost strategy is normalising [3, Theorem 3.2.2]. However, when we allow for both finite and infinite normal forms, the leftmost strategy is not longer infinitary normalising. In the example,

```
zeross = zeros: zeross
```

the leftmost strategy does not find the infinite normal form in ω-steps.[2] For CoPTSs, we follow an infinitary normalising strategy that reaches the normal form in ω-steps which is a variation of the depth-first leftmost strategy. Figure 1 shows a tree representation of the infinite normal form of zeross that respects our notion of depth. The tree is finitely branched. The first line is at depth 0 and it should be printed first, the second line is at depth 1 and it should be printed second, and so on.

We establish a precise connection between the modal operator and the metric at a syntactic level by relating a variable of type ($\bullet A$) with the depth of its occurrences in a term. This syntactic connection between the modal operator and the depth is the key to the proofs of infinitary weak and strong normalisation. A programming language will never be able to display the whole infinite normal form $0 : (0 : (0 : (\ldots)))$ but it will display only its truncation at certain depth n (an approximant):

$$0 : (0 : \ldots (0 : \bot) \ldots))$$

The modal operator ($\bullet A$) represents the information that will appear *later* in the computation which is also the information that appears *deeper* in the infinite normal form.

The connection between the modality and the depth is formalised as follows.

If $x{:}_i(\bullet A) \vdash b{:}_i B$ then all occurrences of x in b occur at depth (strictly) greater than 0.

Similarly,

If $x{:}_{i+1} A \vdash b{:}_i B$ then all occurrences of x in b occur at depth (strictly) greater than 0.

For typing (cofix $x{:}A.b$), we require that $x{:}_{i+1}A \vdash b{:}_i A$. This means that the variable x in (cofix $x{:}A.b$) occurs in b at depth (strictly) greater than 0. In other words, the truncation of b at depth 1 contains no occurrences of x. Let's examine what happens during the computation. Let $\to_\gamma$ be the reduction that unfolds fixed points:

$$(\mathsf{cofix}\ x{:}A.b) \to_\gamma b[x := (\mathsf{cofix}\ x{:}A.b)]$$

After contracting the fixed point, we have that the truncation of $b[x := (\mathsf{cofix}\ x{:}A.b)]$ at depth 1 does not contain any residuals of the contracted redex. As an example, we consider the program zeros which is expressed in our syntax as follows.

$$\mathsf{zeros} = (\mathsf{cofix}\ xs{:}(\mathsf{Stream\ Nat}).(\mathsf{cons}\ 0\ xs))$$

The γ-redex occurs at depth 0 in zeros. We perform one γ-reduction step:

$$\mathsf{zeros} \quad \to_\gamma \quad (\mathsf{cons}\ 0\ \mathsf{zeros})$$

In the *future* of *zeros*, that is in the reduct (cons 0 zeros), the γ-redex occurs at depth 1. The truncation (cons 0 $\bot$) of (cons 0 zeros) at depth 1 represents the information that has been obtained in the first time step. The truncated subterm zeros at depth 1 in (cons 0 zeros) represents the information that will appear *later*.

This paper is organised as follows. Section 2 gives an overview of PTSs. Section 3 defines the notion of CoPTSs. Section 4 shows some basic properties, the most important one concerns $\beta\sigma$-strong normalisation. Section 5 defines the set $\mathcal{C}^\infty$ of finite and infinite terms as metric completion of the set of finite terms. Section 6 studies infinitary weak normalisation. Section 7 studies infinitary strong normalisation. Section 8 draws some conclusions and explains related work. Section 9 gives some plan for future work.

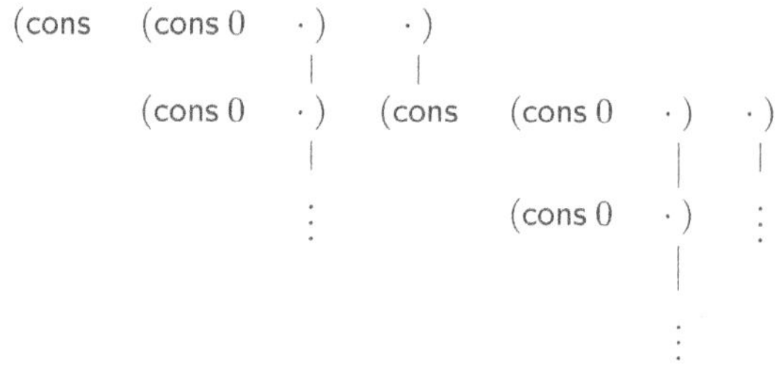

Figure 1. The infinite normal form of zeross represented as a tree

[1] By typing à la Church, we mean that abstractions are of the form $\lambda x{:}A.b$, i.e. the variable in the abstraction is provided with an explicit type declaration.

[2] In the infinitary lambda calculus, the situation is actually worse: *infinite left spines*, which are terms of the form $((\ldots)P_2)P_1$ don't have a leftmost redex, when for instance each P_i contains a redex.

2. Preliminaries on Pure Type Systems

In this section, we recall the notion of *pure type system* (PTS) [2]. Pure type systems were introduced independently by Berardi and Terlouw [4, 40] as a way of generalising the systems of the λ-cube [2]. Pure type systems consists of seven typing rules, Two of them are parametrised by what is called a *specification*: the axiom and the product rule. By instantiating the parameters, we can describe many kinds of typed lambda calculi such as the the extended calculus of constructions [35] including inconsistent systems [21]. The word *pure* stands for the fact that there is only one type constructor Π and only one reduction β.

We recall the definition of specification. The specification instantiates the parameters in the definition of pure type system.

Definition 2.1 (Specification). *A specification is a triple* $\mathcal{S} = (\mathcal{S}, \mathcal{A}, \mathcal{R})$ *such that*

1. $\mathcal{S}$ *is a set of symbols called* sorts,
2. $\mathcal{A} \subseteq \mathcal{S} \times \mathcal{S}$ *called set of* axioms,
3. $\mathcal{R} \subseteq \mathcal{S} \times \mathcal{S} \times \mathcal{S}$ *called set of* rules.

We will follow custom to abbreviate rules of the form (s_1, s_2, s_2) *by just* (s_1, s_2).

We will need the notion of single sorted specification to ensure unicity of types (Theorem 4.6) and the well-definedness of the encoding in $\lambda\omega$ (Definition 4.9).

Definition 2.2 (Single Sorted Specification). *We say that a specification is single sorted if*

1. *If* (s_1, s_2) *and* (s_1, s_2') *are in* $\mathcal{A}$, *then* $s_2 = s_2'$.
2. *If* (s_1, s_2, s_3) *and* (s_1, s_2, s_3') *are in* $\mathcal{R}$, *then* $s_3 = s_3'$.

Types and terms are defined in the same set $\mathcal{T}$.

Definition 2.3 (Pseudoterms). *The set* $\mathcal{T}_\mathcal{S}$ *(or* $\mathcal{T}$ *for short) of pseudoterms is defined as follows.*

$$\mathcal{T} ::= \mathcal{V} \mid \mathcal{S} \mid (\lambda\mathcal{V}{:}\mathcal{T}.\mathcal{T}) \mid (\mathcal{T}\ \mathcal{T}) \mid (\Pi\mathcal{V}{:}\mathcal{T}.\mathcal{T})$$

Sorts are denoted by $s, s', \ldots$, variables by $x, y, \ldots$ and pseudoterms by capital $A, B, \ldots$ and also by lower case $a, b, \ldots$. The set $\mathsf{fv}(A)$ of free variables of A is defined in the usual way and $A \to B$ is an abbreviation for $\Pi x{:}A.B$ if $x \notin \mathsf{fv}(B)$.

Definition 2.4 (β-Reduction). *We define* β*-reduction as usual:*

$$(\lambda x{:}A.b)\ a \quad \to b[x := a] \quad (\beta)$$

The relation $\to_\beta$ *is defined as the smallest relations on pseudoterms that are closed under the* β*-rule and under contexts.*

In the following section, we will define other notions of reductions such as σ and γ. We introduce the following notation which works for all of them.

Notation 2.5. *Let* ρ *be a notion of reduction.*

1. $M \to_\rho N$ *denotes a one step reduction from* M *to* N;
2. $M \twoheadrightarrow_\rho N$ *denotes a finite reduction from* M *to* N*, possibly consisting of 0 steps;*
3. $M \twoheadrightarrow_\rho^+ N$ *denotes a finite reduction from* M *to* N *consisting at least one step;*
4. $M =_\rho N$ *denotes conversion,* $(\to_\rho \cup \leftarrow_\rho)^*$

A *pseudocontext* is a finite ordered sequence of type declarations: $\Gamma = x_1{:}A_1, x_2{:}A_2, \ldots x_n{:}A_n$ where x_i are all different variables and A_i are pseudoterms for all $1 \leq i \leq n$.

Definition 2.6 (Pure Type System). *A* Pure Type System *(PTS) denoted by* $\lambda(\mathcal{S})$ *is given by the judgement* $\Gamma \vdash_\mathcal{S} a : A$ *(or just* $\Gamma \vdash a : A$*) and defined by the typing rules of Figure 2.*

(**axiom**) $\vdash s_1{:}s_2$ if $(s_1, s_2) \in \mathcal{A}$

(**start**) $\dfrac{\Gamma \vdash A{:}s}{\Gamma, x{:}A \vdash x{:}A}$ x Γ-fresh

(**weak**) $\dfrac{\Gamma \vdash A{:}s \quad \Gamma \vdash b{:}B}{\Gamma, x{:}A \vdash b{:}B}$ x Γ-fresh

(**prod**) $\dfrac{\Gamma \vdash A{:}s_1 \quad \Gamma, x{:}A \vdash B{:}s_2}{\Gamma \vdash (\Pi x{:}A.B){:}s_3}$ $(s_1, s_2, s_3) \in \mathcal{R}$

(**abs**) $\dfrac{\Gamma, x{:}A \vdash b{:}B \quad \Gamma \vdash (\Pi x{:}A.B){:}s}{\Gamma \vdash (\lambda x{:}A.b){:}(\Pi x{:}A.B)}$

(**app**) $\dfrac{\Gamma \vdash b{:}(\Pi x{:}A.B) \quad \Gamma \vdash a{:}A}{\Gamma \vdash (b\ a){:}B[x := a]}$

(β-**conv**) $\dfrac{\Gamma \vdash a{:}A \quad \Gamma \vdash A'{:}s}{\Gamma \vdash a{:}A'}$ $A =_\beta A'$

Figure 2. Pure Type Systems

Example 2.7 (Systems of the λ-cube). *The systems of the* λ*-cube are obtained from the following set of sorts and axioms [2].*

$$\mathcal{S} = \{\mathsf{type}, \mathsf{kind}\} \quad \mathcal{A} = \{(\mathsf{type}, \mathsf{kind})\}$$

Ranging the parameters s_1, s_2 *in* $(s_1, s_2) \in \mathcal{R}$ *over* $\{\mathsf{type}, \mathsf{kind}\}$ *we can represent different types of functions:*

- $(\mathsf{type}, \mathsf{type})$ *for terms depending on terms (functions),*
- $(\mathsf{kind}, \mathsf{type})$ *for terms depending on types (polymorphic functions),*
- $(\mathsf{type}, \mathsf{kind})$ *for types depending on terms (dependent types),*
- $(\mathsf{kind}, \mathsf{kind})$ *for types depending on types (type constructors).*

The set $\{(\mathsf{type}, \mathsf{type}), (\mathsf{kind}, \mathsf{type}), (\mathsf{type}, \mathsf{kind}), (\mathsf{kind}, \mathsf{kind})\}$ *has eight subsets that contain* $\{(\mathsf{type}, \mathsf{type})\}$. *This gives us Barendregt's "*λ*-cube" consisting of eight pure type systems. The smallest such subset gives rise to the simply typed lambda calculus and the biggest subset to the calculus of constructions, [11]. We show the specification of the four systems that we will use later.*

The simply typed lambda calculus $\lambda_\to$ *is obtained from the specification* $\mathcal{S}_\to$ *defined by the common sets* $\mathcal{S}$ *and* $\mathcal{A}$ *given above for the systems of the* λ*-cube and the following set of rules:*

$$\mathcal{R} = \{(\mathsf{type}, \mathsf{type})\}$$

The second order lambda calculus [21, 38] is the pure type system $\lambda 2$ *similarly obtained from the set of rules:*

$$\mathcal{R} = \{(\mathsf{type}, \mathsf{type}), (\mathsf{kind}, \mathsf{type})\}$$

The pure type system $\lambda\omega$ *corresponds to* $F\omega$ *of [21] and is obtained from the set of rules:*

$$\mathcal{R} = \{(\mathsf{type}, \mathsf{type}), (\mathsf{kind}, \mathsf{type}), (\mathsf{kind}, \mathsf{kind})\}$$

The calculus of constructions [11] is obtained from the set of rules:

$$\mathcal{R} = \{(\mathsf{type}, \mathsf{type}), (\mathsf{kind}, \mathsf{type}), (\mathsf{type}, \mathsf{kind}), (\mathsf{kind}, \mathsf{kind})\}$$

Example 2.8 (Inconsistent Pure Type Systems). *The system* λV *is given by the following specification (called* $\lambda*$ *in [2]).*

$$\mathcal{S} = \{\mathsf{type}\} \quad \mathcal{A} = \{(\mathsf{type}, \mathsf{type})\} \quad \mathcal{R} = \{(\mathsf{type}, \mathsf{type})\}$$

This system is inconsistent in the sense that all types are inhabited [2, 21]. For examples where the circularity type:type *is not necessary to derive inconsistency, see [2, Example 5.2.4].*

In any inconsistent logical pure type system, a looping combinator can be derived from any term of type $\bot = \Pi X{:}\mathsf{type}.X$

[10]. The paper [17] shows that Curry's and Turing's fixed point combinators $\mathsf{Y} = \lambda f.(\lambda x.f(xx))(\lambda x.f(xx))$ *and* $\Theta = (\lambda xf.f(xxf))(\lambda xf.f(xxf)$ *cannot be typed in* λV.

Definition 2.9 (Term and Context). *Let $\mathcal{S}$ be a specification.*

1. *A (typable) term is a pseudoterm a such that $\Gamma \vdash a{:}A$ for some Γ and A.*
2. *A (legal) context is a pseudocontext Γ such that $\Gamma \vdash a{:}A$ for some a and A.*

In the following definition, we consider an arbitrary reduction ρ. In later sections, we will define other notions of reduction besides β.

Definition 2.10 (Weak and Strong Normalisation). *Let ρ be a notion of reduction.*

1. *We say that a pseudoterm a is weakly ρ-normalising if there exists a pseudoterm b in ρ-normal form such that $a \twoheadrightarrow_\rho b$.*
2. *We say that a pseudoterm a is strongly ρ-normalising if all ρ-reduction sequences starting from a are finite.*

Definition 2.11 (Weakly and Strongly Normalizing PTS). *We say that $\lambda(\mathcal{S})$ is strongly (weakly) β-normalising iff for all $\Gamma \vdash a{:}A$ we have that a and A are strongly (weakly) β-normalising.*

Notation 2.12. *We use the notation $\lambda(\mathcal{S}) \models \rho$-SN if $\lambda(\mathcal{S})$ is strongly ρ-normalising, and $\lambda(\mathcal{S}) \models \rho$-WN if $\lambda(\mathcal{S})$ is weakly ρ-normalising.*

Obviously, $\lambda(\mathcal{S}) \models \rho$-SN implies $\lambda(\mathcal{S}) \models \rho$-WN. A proof of the following result can be found in [2].

Theorem 2.13 (Strong Normalisation of $\lambda(C)$). *We have that $\lambda(C) \models \beta$-SN.*

The following result is proved in [2, Proposition 5.2.31]. We use the abbreviation $\bot = \Pi X{:}\mathsf{type}.X$.

Theorem 2.14 (Inconsistent implies not normalizing). *Let $\lambda(\mathcal{S})$ be a PTS extending $\lambda 2$. Suppose $\Gamma \vdash a{:}\bot$. Then, a is not weakly β-normalising. Hence, $\lambda(\mathcal{S}) \not\models \beta$-WN.*

As a consequence of the previous theorem, the inconsistent pure type system λV from Example 2.8 is not weakly normalising.

3. Pure Type Systems with Corecursion

In this section, we define the notion of *pure type system with corecursion* (CoPTS). The set $\mathcal{T}$ of pseudoterms is extended to include the type constructor ($\mathsf{Stream}\ A$) for *streams* of type A, ($\bullet A$) for the modality *next* and a fixed point operator ($\mathsf{cofix}\ x{:}A.a$) for expressing *corecursion*.

Definition 3.1 (Pseudoterms with Streams and Corecursion). *The set $\mathcal{C}_\mathcal{S}$ (or $\mathcal{C}$ for short) is defined by the following grammar.*

$$\begin{aligned}\mathcal{C} ::= \ & \mathcal{V} \mid \mathcal{S} \mid (\lambda\mathcal{V}{:}\mathcal{C}.\mathcal{C}) \mid (\mathcal{C}\ \mathcal{C}) \mid (\Pi\mathcal{V}{:}\mathcal{C}.\mathcal{C})\\ & \bullet\mathcal{C} \mid \circ\mathcal{C} \mid (\mathsf{await}\ \mathcal{C}) \mid\\ & (\mathsf{Stream}\ \mathcal{C}) \mid (\mathsf{cons}\ \mathcal{C}\ \mathcal{C}) \mid (\mathsf{hd}\ \mathcal{C}) \mid (\mathsf{tl}\ \mathcal{C}) \mid\\ & (\mathsf{cofix}\ \mathcal{V}{:}\mathcal{C}.\mathcal{C})\end{aligned}$$

We introduce two other reductions besides β-reduction: γ-reduction for unfolding fixed points and σ-reduction for computing the destructors of next and stream types.

Definition 3.2 (σ and γ-Reductions). *We define the following reduction rules:*

$$\begin{array}{lll}(\mathsf{await}\ (\circ a)) & \to a & (\sigma)\\ (\mathsf{hd}\ (\mathsf{cons}\ a\ b)) & \to a & (\sigma)\\ (\mathsf{tl}\ (\mathsf{cons}\ a\ b)) & \to b & (\sigma)\\ (\mathsf{cofix}\ x{:}A.b) & \to b[x := (\mathsf{cofix}\ x{:}A.b)] & (\gamma)\end{array}$$

The relations $\to_\sigma$, $\to_\gamma$ are defined as the smallest relations on pseudoterms that are closed under the respective rules and under contexts. The relation $\to_{\beta\sigma\gamma}$ is the union of $\to_\beta$, $\to_\sigma$ and $\to_\gamma$.

Judgements of CoPTSs are of the form $\Gamma \vdash a :_i A$ where i is an index representing "time". A pseudocontext

$$\Gamma = x_1{:}_{i_1} A_1, x_2{:}_{i_2} A_2, \ldots x_n{:}_{i_n} A_n$$

for a CoPTS is a finite ordered sequence of type declarations where x_i are all different variables and A_i are pseudoterms in $\mathcal{C}$ for all $1 \le i \le n$.

We extend the typing rules of pure type systems for our extended set $\mathcal{C}$ of pseudoterms. Recall that $\mathcal{S}_\to$ is the specification for the simply typed lambda calculus defined in Example 2.7.

Definition 3.3 (Pure Type System with Corecursion). *Let $\mathcal{S}$ be a specification extending $\mathcal{S}_\to$. A* Pure Type System with Corecursion on Streams *(CoPTS) denoted by $\lambda^{\mathsf{co}}(\mathcal{S})$ is given by the judgement $\Gamma \vdash^{\mathsf{co}}_{\mathcal{S}} a :_i A$ (or just $\Gamma \vdash a{:}_i A$) for $i \in \mathbb{N}$ and defined by the typing rules of Figure 3.*

Example 3.4 (Typed λ-calculus of Reactive Programs as a CoPTS). *Krishnaswami and Benton's typed lambda calculus presented in [30] can be obtained as a CoPTS using the specification of the simply typed lambda calculus given in Example 2.7. This system will be denoted as $\lambda^{\mathsf{co}}_\to$.*

Remark 3.5 (Alternative Typing Rules for cofix using Modality). *As in [30, 31], we add a constant* cofix *to represent the fixed point combinator. The typing rule for* (**cofix**) *in Figure 3 is similar to the one presented in [31]. In this version of the rule, the variable x needs to have type A using the index $i+1$. There is another version of the rule that uses modality $\bullet A$ and it is as follows.*

$$(\textbf{cofix'})\ \frac{\Gamma, x{:}_i\bullet A \vdash b{:}_i A \quad \Gamma \vdash A{:}_i\mathsf{type}}{\Gamma \vdash \mathsf{cofix}'\ x{:}\bullet A.b{:}_i A}$$

The typing rules (cofix) *and* (cofix') *are equivalent. The rule* (cofix) *allows us to derive* (cofix$'$) *by defining* $\mathsf{cofix}'\ x{:}\bullet A.b = \mathsf{cofix}\ y{:}A.b[x := (\circ y)]$. *Conversely, we can set* $\mathsf{cofix}\ y{:}A.b = \mathsf{cofix}'\ x{:}\bullet A.b[y := (\mathsf{await}\ x)]$ *and hence both systems are equivalent. It is also easy to see that the typing rule for* cofix' *is equivalent to adding a type declaration of the form* $\mathsf{cofix}'' :_i (\bullet A \to A) \to A$ *for all i as in [30].*

In spite of the fact that the rules (**cofix**) and (**cofix'**) are equivalent, we prefer the rule (**cofix**) to (**cofix'**). The terms that will be shown later in our examples are typed using (**cofix**) and we see that in these examples the modality is not necessary. If we had defined the type system using the rule (**cofix'**), our programmes would have been burdened with modalities. For example, let's write the example of zeros given in the introduction using cofix'.

$$\mathsf{zeros}' = \quad (\mathsf{cofix}'\ xs{:}\bullet(\mathsf{Stream\ Nat}).(\mathsf{cons}\ 0\ (\mathsf{await}\ xs)))$$

The explicit type given for xs contains $\bullet$ and the recursive call needs to use await. None of this is necessary when zeros is written using cofix (see Example 3.6). This means that depending on the applications we may be able to remove the rules for modalities from our system. We include the modality to encompass the type system of reactive programs as a CoPTS [30] (examples where modalities are necessary can be found in [30–32]). Nakano's type system has modalities without indices with help of subtyping and recursive types [36]. In our current formulation, the indices cannot be removed. But this does not matter, because the indices are hidden to the programmer as they are handled by the type checker.

$$(\textbf{axiom}) \vdash s_1{:}_i s_2 \quad \text{if } (s_1, s_2) \in \mathcal{A}$$

$$(\textbf{start}) \frac{\Gamma \vdash A{:}_i s \quad j \geq i}{\Gamma, x{:}_i A \vdash x{:}_j A} \; x \; \Gamma\text{-fresh}$$

$$(\textbf{weak}) \frac{\Gamma \vdash A{:}_i s \quad \Gamma \vdash b{:}_j B}{\Gamma, x{:}_i A \vdash b{:}_j B} \; x \; \Gamma\text{-fresh}$$

$$(\textbf{prod}) \frac{\Gamma \vdash A{:}_i s_1 \quad \Gamma, x{:}_i A \vdash B{:}_i s_2}{\Gamma \vdash (\Pi x{:}A.B){:}_i s_3} \; (s_1, s_2, s_3) \in \mathcal{R}$$

$$(\textbf{abs}) \frac{\Gamma, x{:}_i A \vdash b{:}_i B \quad \Gamma \vdash (\Pi x{:}A.B){:}_i s}{\Gamma \vdash (\lambda x{:}A.b){:}_i (\Pi x{:}A.B)}$$

$$(\textbf{app}) \frac{\Gamma \vdash b{:}_i (\Pi x{:}A.B) \quad \Gamma \vdash a{:}_i A}{\Gamma \vdash (b\; a){:}_i B[x := a]}$$

$$(\beta\sigma\gamma\textbf{-conv}) \frac{\Gamma \vdash a{:}_i A \quad \Gamma \vdash A'{:}_i s}{\Gamma \vdash a{:}_i A'} \; A {=}_{\beta\sigma\gamma} A'$$

$$(\textbf{mod}) \frac{\Gamma \vdash A{:}_i \mathsf{type}}{\Gamma \vdash \bullet A{:}_i \mathsf{type}}$$

$$(\bullet I) \frac{\Gamma \vdash a{:}_{i+1} A}{\Gamma \vdash \circ a{:}_i \bullet A}$$

$$(\bullet E) \frac{\Gamma \vdash a{:}_i \bullet A}{\Gamma \vdash (\mathsf{await}\; a){:}_{i+1} A}$$

$$(\textbf{stream}) \frac{\Gamma \vdash A{:}_i \mathsf{type}}{\Gamma \vdash (\mathsf{Stream}\; A){:}_i \mathsf{type}}$$

$$(\textbf{cons}) \frac{\Gamma \vdash a{:}_i A \quad \Gamma \vdash b{:}_{i+1} (\mathsf{Stream}\; A)}{\Gamma \vdash (\mathsf{cons}\; a\; b){:}_i (\mathsf{Stream}\; A)}$$

$$(\textbf{hd}) \frac{\Gamma \vdash a{:}_i (\mathsf{Stream}\; A)}{\Gamma \vdash (\mathsf{hd}\; a){:}_i A}$$

$$(\textbf{tl}) \frac{\Gamma \vdash a{:}_i (\mathsf{Stream}\; A)}{\Gamma \vdash (\mathsf{tl}\; a){:}_{i+1} (\mathsf{Stream}\; A)}$$

$$(\textbf{cofix}) \frac{\Gamma, x{:}_{i+1} A \vdash b{:}_i A \quad \Gamma \vdash A{:}_i \mathsf{type}}{\Gamma \vdash (\mathsf{cofix}\; x{:}A.b){:}_i A}$$

Figure 3. Pure Type Systems with Corecursion on Streams

We will give examples of terms typable in CoPTSs. We define a context Γ_{Nat} containing the following type declarations:

$$\begin{array}{rl}
\mathsf{Nat} & {:}_i\; \mathsf{type} \\
0 & {:}_i\; \mathsf{Nat} \\
\mathsf{suc} & {:}_i\; \mathsf{Nat} \to \mathsf{Nat} \\
+ & {:}_i\; \mathsf{Nat} \to \mathsf{Nat} \to \mathsf{Nat} \\
* & {:}_i\; \mathsf{Nat} \to \mathsf{Nat} \to \mathsf{Nat} \\
\mathsf{Bool} & {:}_i\; \mathsf{type} \\
< & {:}_i\; \mathsf{Nat} \to \mathsf{Nat} \to \mathsf{Bool} \\
\mathsf{if} & {:}_i\; \mathsf{Bool} \to (\mathsf{Stream\ Nat}) \to (\mathsf{Stream\ Nat})
\end{array}$$

For the sake of the example, adding those constants via a context suffices, so that we can ignore the corresponding computational and typing rules that would come with this extra syntax.

Example 3.6 (Terms typable in $\lambda^{\mathsf{co}}_{\to}$). *Define the following:*

$$\begin{array}{rl}
\mathsf{FunSNat} = & (\mathsf{Stream\ Nat}) \to (\mathsf{Stream\ Nat}) \to \\
& (\mathsf{Stream\ Nat}) \\[4pt]
\mathsf{zeros} = & (\mathsf{cofix}\; xs{:}(\mathsf{Stream\ Nat}).(\mathsf{cons}\; 0\; xs)) \\[4pt]
\mathsf{interleave} = & \mathsf{cofix}\; f{:}\; \mathsf{FunSNat}. \\
& \quad \lambda xs : (\mathsf{Stream\ Nat}). \\
& \quad\quad \lambda ys : (\mathsf{Stream\ Nat}). \\
& \quad\quad\quad (\mathsf{cons}\; (\mathsf{hd}\; xs)\; (f\; ys\; (\mathsf{tl}\; xs))) \\[4pt]
\mathsf{sumlist} = & \mathsf{cofix}\; f{:}\mathsf{FunSNat}. \\
& \quad \lambda xs{:}(\mathsf{Stream\ Nat}). \\
& \quad\quad \lambda ys{:}(\mathsf{Stream\ Nat}). \\
& \quad\quad\quad \mathsf{cons}\; (+\; (\mathsf{hd}\; xs)\; (\mathsf{hd}\; ys)) \\
& \quad\quad\quad\quad\quad (f\; (\mathsf{tl}\; xs)\; (\mathsf{tl}\; ys)) \\
\mathsf{merge} = & \mathsf{cofix}\; f{:}\mathsf{FunSNat}. \\
& \quad \lambda xs{:}(\mathsf{Stream\ Nat}). \\
& \quad\quad \lambda ys{:}(\mathsf{Stream\ Nat}). \\
& \quad\quad\quad \mathsf{if}\; (\mathsf{hd}\; xs) < (\mathsf{hd}\; ys)\; \mathsf{then} \\
& \quad\quad\quad\quad (\mathsf{cons}\; (\mathsf{hd}\; xs)\; (f\; (\mathsf{tl}\; xs)\; ys)) \\
& \quad\quad\quad \mathsf{elseif}\; (\mathsf{hd}\; xs) < (\mathsf{hd}\; ys)\; \mathsf{then} \\
& \quad\quad\quad\quad (\mathsf{cons}\; (\mathsf{hd}\; ys)\; (f\; xs\; (\mathsf{tl}\; ys))) \\
& \quad\quad\quad \mathsf{else} \\
& \quad\quad\quad\quad\quad (\mathsf{cons}\; (\mathsf{hd}\; xs)\; (f\; (\mathsf{tl}\; xs)\; (\mathsf{tl}\; ys)))
\end{array}$$

We have that all the above terms can be typed in $\lambda^{\mathsf{co}}_{\to}$.

$$\begin{array}{ll}
\Gamma_{\mathsf{Nat}} & \vdash \mathsf{zeros} :_i (\mathsf{Stream\ Nat}) \\
\Gamma_{\mathsf{Nat}} & \vdash \mathsf{interleave} :_i \mathsf{FunSNat} \\
\Gamma_{\mathsf{Nat}} & \vdash \mathsf{sumlist} :_i \mathsf{FunSNat} \\
\Gamma_{\mathsf{Nat}} & \vdash \mathsf{merge} :_i \mathsf{FunSNat}
\end{array}$$

Example 3.7 (CoPTSs beyond $\lambda^{\mathsf{co}}_{\to}$). *Going beyond $\lambda^{\mathsf{co}}_{\to}$ we can type polymorphic functions, type constructors and prove properties on streams using the Curry-Howard isomorphism. The polymorphic map function:*

$$\begin{array}{rl}
\mathsf{map} = & \lambda X{:}\mathsf{type}. \\
& \quad \lambda Y{:}\mathsf{type}. \\
& \quad\quad \lambda g{:}X \to Y. \\
& \quad\quad\quad \mathsf{cofix}\; f{:}(\mathsf{Stream}\; X) \to (\mathsf{Stream}\; Y). \\
& \quad\quad\quad\quad \lambda xs : (\mathsf{Stream}\; X). \\
& \quad\quad\quad\quad\quad (\mathsf{cons}\; (g\; (\mathsf{hd}\; xs))\; (f\; (\mathsf{tl}\; xs)))
\end{array}$$

can be typed in $\lambda^{\mathsf{co}}2$, *i.e.*

$$\begin{array}{l}
\vdash \mathsf{map}{:}_i \Pi X{:}\mathsf{type}.\Pi Y{:}\mathsf{type}. \\
\quad\quad (X \to Y) \to \\
\quad\quad (\mathsf{Stream}\; X) \to (\mathsf{Stream}\; Y)
\end{array}$$

We can also write type constructors such as:

$$\begin{array}{rl}
\mathsf{DoubleFun} = & \lambda X{:}\mathsf{type}. \\
& (\mathsf{Stream}\; X) \to (\mathsf{Stream}\; X) \to (\mathsf{Stream}\; X)
\end{array}$$

which can be typed in $\lambda^{\mathsf{co}}\omega$ *as follows.*

$$\vdash \mathsf{DoubleFun} :_i \mathsf{type} \to \mathsf{type}$$

In $\lambda^{\mathsf{co}}(C)$, *we can write and prove properties on streams. For example, we can have a constant* EqStr *to represent equality between streams.*

$$\Gamma_{\mathsf{Nat}}, \mathsf{EqStr}{:}_i \Pi X{:}\mathsf{type}.(\mathsf{Stream}\; X) \to (\mathsf{Stream}\; X) \to \mathsf{type}$$

$$\vdash \mathsf{EqStr\ Nat\ zeros\ zeros}{:}_i \mathsf{type}$$

Example 3.8 (Typable Terms in CoPTS not satisfying guardedness condition). *The proof assistant Coq ensures that corecursive definitions are well-defined by means of the the guardedness condition, i.e. the recursive calls should be guarded by constructors [9, 20].*

The following programmes can all be typed in $\lambda^{\text{co}}2$ but they do not satisfy the guardedness condition. Let mapn = map Nat Nat.

$$\begin{aligned}
\text{zeros}'' &= (\text{cofix } xs{:}(\text{Stream Nat}).)\\
&\qquad (\text{cons } 0 \text{ (interleave } xs\ xs)\\
\text{fib} &= \text{cofix } xs{:}(\text{Stream Nat}).\\
&\qquad (\text{cons } 1 \text{ (cons } 1 \text{ (sumlist } xs \text{ (tl } xs))))\\
\text{hamming} &= \text{cofix } h{:}(\text{Stream Nat}).\\
&\quad \text{cons } 1\\
&\qquad (\text{merge}\\
&\qquad\ (\text{mapn } (\lambda x{:}\text{Nat}.2 * x)\ h)\\
&\qquad\ (\text{merge}\\
&\qquad\quad (\text{mapn}(\lambda x{:}\text{Nat}.3 * x)\ h)\\
&\qquad\quad (\text{mapn } (\lambda x{:}\text{Nat}.5 * x)\ h)))
\end{aligned}$$

They can all be typed in $\lambda^{\text{co}}2$ as follows.

$$\begin{aligned}
\Gamma_{\text{Nat}} &\vdash \text{zeros}'' :_i \text{Nat}\\
\Gamma_{\text{Nat}} &\vdash \text{fib} :_i \text{Nat}\\
\Gamma_{\text{Nat}} &\vdash \text{hamming} :_i \text{Nat}
\end{aligned}$$

We formalise the badly behaved Haskell programmes given in the introduction in our setting and show that they are not typable.

Example 3.9 (The Undesirables). *The badly behaved programmes shown in the introduction can be written in our syntax as follows.*

$$\begin{aligned}
\Omega &= (\text{cofix } x{:}A.x)\\
\Omega_{\text{tail}} &= (\text{cofix } xs{:}A.(\text{tl } xs))\\
\Omega' &= (\text{cofix } xs{:}A.(\text{tl (cons } 0\ xs)))\\
\Omega'' &= (\text{cofix } x{:}A.(\text{await } (\circ x)))\\
\text{E} &= \text{filter Nat } (\lambda xs{:}(\text{Stream Nat}).x > 0) \text{ zeros})
\end{aligned}$$

where the function filter *is defined as follows:*

$$\begin{aligned}
\text{filter} = \ &\lambda X : \text{type}.\lambda P : X \to \text{Bool}.\\
&\text{cofix } f{:}(\text{Stream } X) \to (\text{Stream } X).\\
&\ \lambda xs{:}(\text{Stream } X).\\
&\quad \text{if } (P \text{ (hd } xs)) \text{ then}\\
&\qquad (\text{cons (hd } xs)\ (f \text{ (tl } xs)))\\
&\quad \text{else}\\
&\qquad (f \text{ (tl } xs))
\end{aligned}$$

None of the above terms are typable in any CoPTS. More formally, we have that the following holds for all A and i:

$$\begin{array}{ll}
A :_i \text{type} \not\vdash \Omega :_i A & A :_i \text{type} \not\vdash \Omega_{\text{tail}} :_i A\\
A :_i \text{type} \not\vdash \Omega' :_i A & A :_i \text{type} \not\vdash \Omega' :_i A\\
\Gamma_{\text{Nat}} \not\vdash \text{filter} ::_i A & \Gamma_{\text{Nat}} \not\vdash \text{E} ::_i A
\end{array}$$

The terms $\Omega, \Omega_{\text{tail}}$ and filter *are not typable because the depth of the variable for the fixed point operator happens to be at depth 0 (Theorem 7.6). The terms Ω' and Ω'' are not typable because they σ-reduce to Ω which is not typable (Theorem 4.5). The term* E *is not typable because it has a subterm which is not typable.*

We define auxiliary type systems that will be used later in the proof of infinitary normalisation.

Definition 3.10 (Pure Type System with Corecursion from n). *Let $\mathcal{S}$ be a specification extending $\mathcal{S}_\to$ and $n \in \mathbb{N}$. A* Pure Type System with Corecursion on Streams from *n (CoPTSn) denoted by $\lambda^{\text{co}}_n(\mathcal{S})$ is given by the judgement $\Gamma \vdash^n_{\mathcal{S}} a :_i A$ (or just $\Gamma \vdash^n a{:}_iA$) for $i \in \mathbb{N}$ and defined by replacing the rule* (**cofix**) *from the typing rules of Figure 3 by the following one:*

$$(\textbf{cofix}^n)\ \frac{\Gamma, x{:}_{i+1}A \vdash^n b{:}_iA \quad \Gamma \vdash^n A{:}_i\text{type}}{\Gamma \vdash^n (\text{cofix } x{:}A.b){:}_iA}\ i \geq n$$

4. Basic Properties

In this section we prove some basic properties on CoPTSn's. which apply to CoPTSs as well since we have that $\Gamma \vdash a{:}_iA$ iff $\Gamma \vdash^0 a{:}_iA$.

Theorem 4.1 (Confluence). *$(\mathcal{C}, \twoheadrightarrow_{\beta\sigma\gamma})$ is confluent.*

Proof. This follows from [29, Corollary 13.6] (see also [28]) by observing that $(\mathcal{C}, \twoheadrightarrow_{\beta\sigma\gamma})$ is an orthogonal combinatory reduction system. □

Theorem 4.2 (σ-strong normalization). *Let $a \in \mathcal{C}$. Then, a is strongly σ-normalising.*

Proof. Observe that the number of symbols decreases in each σ-reduction step. □

The notation Γ_{+k} means that we add k to the index of every hypothesis in Γ.

Theorem 4.3 (Time Adjustment). *If $\Gamma, \Gamma' \vdash^n a{:}_iA$ then $\Gamma, \Gamma'_{+k} \vdash^n a{:}_{i+k}A$.*

The above theorem is proved by induction on the derivation.

Lemma 4.4 (Substitution). *If $\Gamma \vdash^n a{:}_iA$ and $\Gamma, x{:}_iA, \Gamma' \vdash^n b{:}_jB$ then $\Gamma, \Gamma'[x := a] \vdash^n b[x := a]{:}_jB[x := a]$.*

Proof. This lemma follows by induction on the derivation using Theorem 4.3 for the case of the (start)-rule. □

Theorem 4.5 (Subject Reduction). *Let $a \twoheadrightarrow_{\beta\sigma\gamma} a'$. If $\Gamma \vdash^n a{:}_iA$ then $\Gamma \vdash^n a'{:}_iA$.*

Proof. We extend the reduction to contexts $\Gamma \to_{\beta\sigma\gamma} \Gamma'$ by allowing to reduce the types in Γ. We have to prove the following two statements simultaneously:

1. If $\Gamma \vdash^n a{:}_iA$ and $a \twoheadrightarrow_{\beta\sigma\gamma} a'$ then $\Gamma \vdash^n a'{:}_iA$.
2. If $\Gamma \vdash^n a{:}_iA$ and $\Gamma \twoheadrightarrow_{\beta\sigma\gamma} \Gamma'$ then $\Gamma' \vdash^n a{:}_iA$.

We use Lemma 4.4, Theorem 4.3 and the analogon of Generation Lemma [2, Lemma 5.2.13] adapted to the typing rules for CoPTSs □

Theorem 4.6 (Uniqueness of Types). *Let $\mathcal{S}$ be single sorted. If $\Gamma \vdash^n a{:}_iA$ and $\Gamma \vdash^n a{:}_iA'$ then $A =_{\beta\sigma\gamma} A'$.*

The proof of the above theorem is similar to [2, Lemma 5.2.21].

Definition 4.7 (Strongly Normalizing CoPTS). *Let ρ be a notion of reduction. We say that $\lambda^{\text{co}}(\mathcal{S})$ is weakly (strongly) ρ-normalising if for all $\Gamma \vdash a{:}_iA$, we have that a and A are weakly (strongly) ρ-normalising.*

Notation 4.8. *$\lambda^{\text{co}}(\mathcal{S}) \models \rho$-WN (SN) if $\lambda^{\text{co}}(\mathcal{S})$ is weakly (strongly) ρ-normalising.*

We use the following abbreviations:

$$\begin{aligned}
\bot &= \Pi X{:}\text{type}.X\\
\text{S} &= \lambda X{:}\text{type}.\Pi Y{:}\text{type}.(X \to Y \to Y) \to Y
\end{aligned}$$

We consider the context Γ_0 defined as $c{:}\bot$ where c is 'fresh'.

Definition 4.9 (Encoding in $\lambda\omega$). *Let $\Gamma \vdash d{:_i}D$. We define $\{d\}$ by induction on d.*

$$\begin{array}{rl} \{x\} & = x \\ \{s\} & = s \\ \{\Pi x{:}A.B\} & = \Pi x{:}\{A\}.\{B\} \\ \{\lambda x{:}A.b\} & = \lambda x{:}\{A\}.\{b\} \\ \{(a\ b)\} & = (\{a\}\ \{b\}) \\ \{\bullet A\} & = \{A\} \\ \{\circ a\} & = \{a\} \\ \{(\mathsf{await}\ a)\} & = \{a\} \\ \{(\mathsf{Stream}\ A)\} & = \mathsf{S}\ \{A\} \\ \{(\mathsf{cons}\ a\ b)\} & = \lambda Y{:}\mathsf{type}.\lambda f{:}A_0 \to Y \to Y. \\ & \quad f\ \{a\}\ (\{b\}\ Y\ f) \\ \{(\mathsf{hd}\ a)\} & = \{a\}\ A_0\ (\lambda x{:}A_0\lambda y{:}A_0.x) \\ \{(\mathsf{tl}\ a)\} & = \{a\}(\mathsf{S}\ A_0)\ (\lambda x{:}(\mathsf{S}\ A_0)\lambda y{:}\ (\mathsf{S}\ A_0).y) \\ \{(\mathsf{cofix}\ x{:}A.b)\} & = (\lambda x{:}\{A\}.\{b\})\ (c\ \{A\}) \end{array}$$

When d is either (cons a b), (tl a) *or* (hd a), *we define the type A_0 as the β-normal form (if it exists) of $\{A\}$ where A is a type satisfying in each one of those cases:*

$$\Gamma \vdash (\mathsf{cons}\ a\ b){:_i}(\mathsf{Stream}\ A)$$

$$\Gamma \vdash (\mathsf{tl}\ a){:_i}(\mathsf{Stream}\ A)$$

$$\Gamma \vdash (\mathsf{hd}\ a){:_i}A$$

The map $\{\}$ is extended to contexts in the obvious way.

$$\{x_1{:_{i_1}}A_1, \ldots, x_n{:_{i_n}}A_n\} = x_1{:_{i_1}}\{A_1\}, \ldots, x_n{:_{i_n}}\{A_n\}$$

The following statements are not difficult to prove.

Theorem 4.10. *1. If $a \to_\beta a'$ then $\{a\} \twoheadrightarrow^+_\beta \{a'\}$.*

2. If $a \to_\sigma a'$ then $\{a\} \twoheadrightarrow_\beta \{a'\}$.

Theorem 4.11 (Encoding from $\lambda^{co}\omega$ to $\lambda\omega$). *If $\Gamma \vdash_\omega d :_i D$ then $\{\Gamma\}, \{d\}, \{D\}$ are well defined and $\Gamma_0, \{\Gamma\} \vdash_\omega \{d\} : \{D\}$.*

Proof. This follows by induction on the structure of the term using Generation Lemma. We show the case $d =$ (cons a b). Suppose $\Gamma \vdash (\mathsf{cons}\ a\ b){:_i}(\mathsf{Stream}\ A)$ and $\Gamma \vdash (\mathsf{cons}\ a\ b){:_i}(\mathsf{Stream}\ A')$. Note that in $\lambda^{co}\omega$, we only have β-conversion without $\sigma\gamma$. It follows from Theorem 4.6 that $A =_\beta A'$. By Theorem 4.10, we have that $\{A\} =_\beta \{A'\}$. Hence, $\Gamma \vdash a :_i A$ and $\Gamma \vdash a :_i A'$. By Induction Hypothesis, $\{\Gamma\} \vdash \{a\} : \{A\}$ and $\{\Gamma\} \vdash \{a\} : \{A'\}$. Since $\lambda\omega$ is strongly β-normalising, A_0 from Definition 4.9 is uniquely determined since the β-normal forms of A and A' are the same. Hence, $\{d\}$ is well defined. □

Theorem 4.12 (Strong Normalization of $\lambda^{co}\omega$ without Contracting Fixpoints). *$\lambda^{co}\omega \models \beta\sigma$-SN.*

Proof. Suppose $\Gamma \vdash a :_i A$. By Theorem 4.11, we have that $\{a\}$ is typable in $\lambda\omega$ and hence, it is β-strongly normalising. We prove that a is strongly $\beta\sigma$-normalising by contradiction. Suppose that a is not strongly $\beta\sigma$-normalising. That is, suppose there exists an infinite $\beta\sigma$-reduction sequence starting from a. Observe that the number of β-reduction steps in this sequence must be infinite because σ is strongly normalising (Theorem 4.2). Hence, the sequence is of the form:

$$a = a_0 \twoheadrightarrow_\sigma a_1 \to_\beta a_2 \twoheadrightarrow_\sigma a_3 \to_\beta a_4 \twoheadrightarrow_\sigma a_5 \to_\beta a_6 \ldots$$

By Theorem 4.10, we have that:

$$\{a\} = \{a_0\} \twoheadrightarrow_\beta \{a_1\} \to_\beta \{a_2\} \twoheadrightarrow_\beta \{a_3\} \to_\beta \{a_4\} \twoheadrightarrow_\beta \ldots$$

which contradicts the fact that $\{a\}$ is β-strongly normalising. □

In order to prove that $\lambda^{co}(C)$ is $\beta\sigma$-strongly normalising, we adapt the proof that $\lambda\omega \models \beta$-SN implies $\lambda C \models \beta$-SN given in [2] to CoPTSs.

Definition 4.13. *We consider $\lambda^{co}(C)$.*

- *We say that A is a kind if $\Gamma \vdash^{co} a$: kind for some Γ.*
- *We say that A is a type constructor if $\Gamma \vdash^{co} A : B$: kind for some Γ and B.*
- *We say that a is an object if $\Gamma \vdash^{co} a : A$: type for some Γ and A.*

We consider the context Γ_1 defined as 0:type, $c{:}\bot$. where $0, c$ are 'fresh'. As in [2], we define three mappings:

1. The mapping ρ on kinds is exactly as in [2, Definition 5.3.3].
2. The mapping τ on type constructors and kinds is the extension of [2, Definition 5.3.7] with the following clauses:

$$\begin{array}{rl} \tau(\bullet(A)) & = \bullet\tau(A) \\ \tau(\mathsf{Stream}\ A) & = \mathsf{Stream}\ \tau(A) \end{array}$$

3. The mapping $[\![\_]\!]$ on objects, type constructors and kinds is the extension of [2, Definition 5.3.10] with the following clauses:

$$\begin{array}{rl} [\![\bullet A]\!] & = c\ (0 \to 0)\ [\![A]\!] \\ [\![\circ a]\!] & = \circ[\![a]\!] \\ [\![(\mathsf{await}\ a)]\!] & = (\mathsf{await}\ [\![a]\!]) \\ [\![(\mathsf{Stream}\ A)]\!] & = c\ (0 \to 0)\ [\![A]\!] \\ [\![(\mathsf{cons}\ a\ b)]\!] & = (\mathsf{cons}\ [\![a]\!]\ [\![b]\!]) \\ [\![(\mathsf{hd}\ a)]\!] & = (\mathsf{hd}\ [\![a]\!]) \\ [\![(\mathsf{tl}\ a)]\!] & = (\mathsf{tl}\ [\![a]\!]) \\ [\![(\mathsf{cofix}\ x{:}A.b)]\!] & = (\lambda z{:}0.(\mathsf{cofix}\ x{:}\tau(A).[\![b]\!]))[\![A]\!] \end{array}$$

Lemma 4.14 (Mapping on kinds). *Let $\Gamma \vdash_C A :_i$ kind.*

1. Then $\vdash_\omega \rho(A) :_i$ kind.

2. If $A \twoheadrightarrow_{\beta\sigma\gamma} A'$ then $\rho(A) \equiv \rho(A')$.

The first statement follows by induction on the derivation. The second one follows by induction on the structure of A.

Lemma 4.15 (Mapping on type constructors and kinds). *Let $\Gamma \vdash_C A :_i B$ where $\Gamma \vdash_C B :_i$ kind or $B \equiv$ kind.*

1. Then, $\tau(\Gamma) \vdash_\omega \tau(A) :_i \rho(B)$.

2. If $A \twoheadrightarrow_{\beta\sigma\gamma} A'$ then $\tau(A) \twoheadrightarrow_\beta \tau(A')$.

The first statement follows by induction on the derivation using Lemma 4.14. The second one follows by induction on the structure of A observing that τ deletes the objects which are the only ones that can contain $\sigma\gamma$-redexes.

Lemma 4.16 (Mapping on objects, type constructors and kinds). *Let $\Gamma \vdash_C a :_i A$.*

1. $\tau(\Gamma) \vdash_\omega [\![a]\!] :_i \tau(A)$.

2. If $a \to_{\beta\sigma} a'$ then $[\![a]\!] \twoheadrightarrow^+_{\beta\sigma} [\![a']\!]$.

The first statement follows by induction on the derivation using Lemma 4.15. The second one follows by induction on the structure of a.

Theorem 4.17. *$\lambda^{co}(C) \models \beta\sigma$-SN.*

Proof. Suppose a is typable in $\lambda^{co}(C)$. By Lemma 4.16 part (1), $[\![a]\!]$ is typable in $\lambda^{co}\omega$. Suppose towards a contradiction that there exists an infinite $\beta\sigma$-reduction sequence starting from a. By Lemma 4.16 part (2), there also exists an infinite $\beta\sigma$-reduction starting from $[\![a]\!]$. This contradicts Theorem 4.12. □

Remark 4.18. *The above theorem is about $\beta\sigma$-reduction and does not mention γ, because CoPTSs are in general not γ-normalising as terms containing a fixed point may have an infinite γ-reduction.*

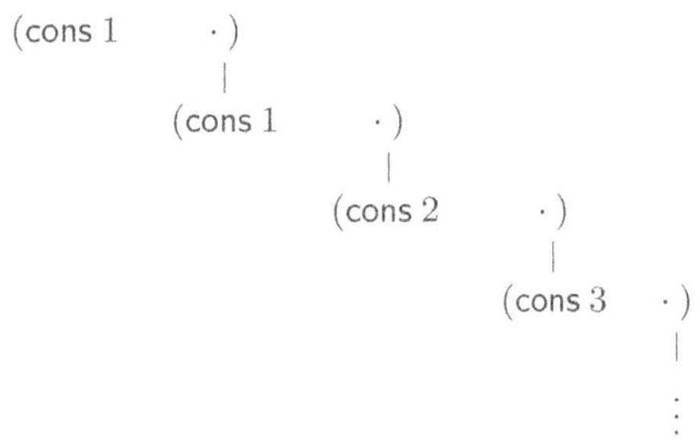

Figure 4. The term partialfib represented as a tree

5. Infinite Pseudoterms

The program fib of Example 3.8 is not finitary but infinitary normalising, i.e. the normal form of fib is the infinite term

$$(\mathsf{cons}\ 1\ (\mathsf{cons}\ 1\ (\mathsf{cons}\ 2\ (\mathsf{cons}\ 3\ (\mathsf{cons}\ 5\ \ldots)))))$$

What do infinite normal forms of typable terms look like? CoPTSs cannot type $(\mathsf{cofix}\ x{:}A.f\ x)$ but they can type $(\mathsf{cofix}\ x{:}A.f\ (\circ x))$:

$$A :_i \mathsf{type}, f :_i \bullet A \to A \vdash (\mathsf{cofix}\ x{:}A.f\ (\circ x)) :_i A$$

To describe the infinite normal forms of typable terms, we define a set $\mathcal{C}^\infty$ of finite and infinite terms as a metric completion. The infinite terms in $\mathcal{C}^\infty$ have finitely many symbols at any given depth, where we will count depth of a subterm in a term as the number of *cons* or $\circ$ operators on the path from the root of the term to the root of the subterm. We do not use any of the existing metrics defined in the literature on infinitary rewriting [25–27]. This is because we want to correlate the modal operator, the level n of a CoPTSn and the index i in $\Gamma \vdash a{:}_i A$ to the above notion of depth (Theorems 6.4 and 7.5). This connection will later be exploited in the proofs of infinitary weak and strong normalisation.

Definition 5.1 (Subterm at position p). *Let p be a sequence of 0's and 1's. The subterm at position p, denoted as $a|_p$, is defined by induction as follows.*

$$\begin{array}{rlrl}
a|_\epsilon & = a & & \\
(\Pi x{:}A.B)|_{0.p} & = A|_p & (\Pi x{:}A.B)|_{1.p} & = B|_p \\
\lambda x{:}A.b|_{0.p} & = A|_p & \lambda x{:}A.b|_{1.p} & = b|_p \\
(a\ b)|_{0.p} & = a|_p & (a\ b)|_{1.p} & = b|_p \\
(\bullet A)|_{0.p} & = A|_p & & \\
(\circ a)|_{0.p} & = a|_p & & \\
((\mathsf{await}\ a))|_{0.p} & = a|_p & & \\
(\mathsf{Stream}\ A)|_{0.p} & = A|_p & & \\
(\mathsf{cons}\ a\ b)|_{0.p} & = a|_p & (\mathsf{cons}\ a\ b)|_{1.p} & = b|_p \\
(\mathsf{hd}\ a)|_{0.p} & = a|_p & & \\
(\mathsf{tl}\ a)|_{0.p} & = a|_p & & \\
(\mathsf{cofix}\ x{:}A.b)|_{0.p} & = A|_p & (\mathsf{cofix}\ x{:}A.b)|_{1.p} & = b|_p
\end{array}$$

Let partialfib be the result of unfolding fib three times.

$$\mathsf{partialfib} = (\mathsf{cons}\ 1\ (\mathsf{cons}\ 1\ (\mathsf{cons}\ 2\ (\mathsf{cons}\ 3\ (\mathsf{cons}\ 5\ \mathsf{fib})))))$$

The subterm of partialfib at position 1.1.1 is (cons 3 (cons 5 fib)).

Let p, q be two positions, i.e. sequences of 0's and 1's. We define $p < q$ if there exists a non-empty position r such that $q = p.r$.

Definition 5.2 (Depth). *The depth of a subterm b of a is the number of subterms of a at positions $q < p$ such that $a|_q$ is either of the form* (cons c d) *or* ($\circ c$).

For example, the depth of (cons 3 (cons 5 fib)) in partialfib is three. Figure 4 illustrates our notion of depth by drawing the term as a finitely branched tree.

We will define a metric on the collection $\mathcal{C}$ of terms using truncations. To define truncations we add a new constant $\bot$ to the syntax. The idea is that we truncate a term by replacing all its subterms at depth n by $\bot$.

Definition 5.3 (Truncation). *The truncation of a at depth n is denoted by a^n and defined by induction as follows.*

$$\begin{array}{rl}
a^0 & = \bot \\
x^{n+1} & = x \\
s^{n+1} & = s \\
\Pi x{:}A.B^{n+1} & = \Pi x{:}A^{n+1}.B^{n+1} \\
\lambda x{:}A.b^{n+1} & = \lambda x{:}A^{n+1}.b^{n+1} \\
(b\ a)^{n+1} & = (a^{n+1}\ b^{n+1}) \\
(\bullet A)^{n+1} & = \bullet A^{n+1} \\
(\circ a)^{n+1} & = \circ a^n \\
((\mathsf{await}\ a))^{n+1} & = (\mathsf{await}\ a^{n+1}) \\
(\mathsf{Stream}\ A)^{n+1} & = (\mathsf{Stream}\ A^{n+1}) \\
(\mathsf{cons}\ a\ b)^{n+1} & = (\mathsf{cons}\ a^{n+1}\ b^n) \\
(\mathsf{hd}\ a)^{n+1} & = (\mathsf{hd}\ a^{n+1}) \\
(\mathsf{tl}\ a)^{n+1} & = (\mathsf{tl}\ a^{n+1}) \\
(\mathsf{cofix}\ x{:}A.b)^{n+1} & = (\mathsf{cofix}\ x{:}A^{n+1}.b^{n+1})
\end{array}$$

For example, the truncation of partialfib at depth three is

$$(\mathsf{cons}\ 1\ (\mathsf{cons}\ 1\ (\mathsf{cons}\ 2\ \bot)))$$

Definition 5.4 (Metric). *We define a(n ultra-)metric $d : \mathcal{C} \times \mathcal{C} \to [0,1]$ as follows: $d(a,b) = 0$, if $a = b$ and $d(a,b) = 2^{-m}$, where $m = max\{n \in \mathsf{Nat} \mid a^n = b^n\}$.*

Definition 5.5 (Set of Finite and Infinite Pseudoterms). *$\mathcal{C}^\infty$ is the metric completion of $(\mathcal{C}, d)$.*

Note that restricted to the subset of lambda terms in $\mathcal{C}$ the metric d is just the discrete metric. Hence $\mathcal{C}^\infty$ contains all finite lambda terms, but it does not contain the infinite lambda terms in the syntax of infinitary lambda calculus [25, 26].

Example 5.6 (Infinite Pseudoterms in $\mathcal{C}^\infty$). *The following are infinite pseudoterms belonging to $\mathcal{C}^\infty$:*

$$\begin{array}{ll}
(\mathsf{cons}\ 0\ (\mathsf{cons}\ 0\ \ldots)) & \circ(\circ(\circ\ldots)) \\
(\mathsf{cons}\ 0\ (\mathsf{tl}\ (\mathsf{cons}\ 0\ (\mathsf{tl}\ \ldots)))) & (\mathsf{await}\ (\circ(\mathsf{await}\ (\circ\ldots))))
\end{array}$$

Example 5.7 (What is not in $\mathcal{C}^\infty$?). *The following "terms" do not belong to $\mathcal{C}^\infty$.*

$$\begin{array}{l}
(f\ (f\ \ldots)) \\
\lambda x_1.\lambda x_2.\lambda x_3.\ldots \\
(((\ldots)x_3)x_2)x_1 \\
(\mathsf{tl}\ (\mathsf{tl}\ (\mathsf{tl}\ \ldots))) \\
(\mathsf{await}\ (\mathsf{await}\ (\mathsf{await}\ \ldots)))
\end{array}$$

The first three terms are characteristic examples of respectively a Böhm tree, Lévy Longo and Berarducci tree [1, 3, 5, 25, 33, 34]. These terms belong to syntax of the infinitary lambda calculus [25, 26]. The last two terms belong to the metric completions defined for infinitary term rewriting and infinitary combinatory reduction systems [25, 27].

Notation 5.8 (Reduction at depth n). *We denote $a \xrightarrow{n}_\rho b$ if the contracted ρ-redex is at depth n.*

Definition 5.9 (Strongly Converging Reductions). *A strongly convergent ρ-reduction sequence of length α (an ordinal) is a sequence $\{a_\beta \mid \beta \leq \alpha\}$ of terms in $\mathcal{C}^\infty$, such that*

1. *$a_\beta \to_\rho a_{\beta+1}$ for all $\beta < \alpha$,*
2. *$a_\lambda = \lim_{\beta<\lambda} a_\beta$ for every limit ordinal $\lambda \leq \alpha$.*

3. $\lim_{i \to \lambda} d_i = \infty$ *where* d_i *is the depth of the redex contracted at* $a_i \to_\rho a_{i+1}$ *for every limit ordinal* $\lambda \leq \alpha$.

Notation 5.10 (Strongly convergent reduction). $a \twoheadrightarrow\!\!\!\!\!\twoheadrightarrow_\rho b$ *denotes a strongly converging reduction from a to b.*

By construction, the set $\mathcal{C}^\infty$ is closed under strongly converging reduction.

Example 5.11 (Strongly Converging Reductions). *We have that* zeros $\twoheadrightarrow_\gamma$ (cons 0 (cons 0 (cons 0 ...))) *via the following strongly convergent reduction of length* ω *(we indicate the depth of the contracted redex in the superscript of the rewrite arrows):*

$$\begin{array}{ll} \mathsf{zeros} & \xrightarrow{0}_\gamma (\mathsf{cons}\ 0\ \mathsf{zeros}) \\ & \xrightarrow{1}_\gamma (\mathsf{cons}\ 0\ (\mathsf{cons}\ 0\ \mathsf{zeros})) \\ & \xrightarrow{2}_\gamma (\mathsf{cons}\ 0\ (\mathsf{cons}\ 0\ (\mathsf{cons}\ 0\ \mathsf{zeros}))) \\ & \xrightarrow{3}_\gamma \ldots \\ & \vdots \\ & (\mathsf{cons}\ 0\ (\mathsf{cons}\ 0\ (\mathsf{cons}\ 0\ \ldots))) \end{array}$$

Let nfzeros = (cons 0 (cons 0 (cons 0 ...))) *be the infinite normal form of* zeros *(see Definition 6.1). We show an example of a reduction sequence of length* ω^2.

$$\begin{array}{ll} \mathsf{zeross} & \twoheadrightarrow_\gamma (\mathsf{cons\ nfzeros\ zeross}) \\ & \twoheadrightarrow_\gamma (\mathsf{cons\ nfzeros\ (cons\ nfzeros\ zeross)}) \\ & \twoheadrightarrow_\gamma \ldots \\ & \vdots \\ & (\mathsf{cons\ nfzeros\ (cons\ nfzeros\ } (\ldots)) \end{array}$$

As we mentioned in the introduction, there exists a strongly converging reduction sequence of length ω *from* zeross *to the infinite normal form by following a depth-first-leftmost strategy.*

Example 5.12 (Non-strongly Converging Reductions). *The following infinite reduction sequences are not strongly convergent:*

$$\Omega \xrightarrow{0}_\gamma \Omega \xrightarrow{0}_\gamma \Omega \xrightarrow{0}_\gamma \ldots$$

$$\Omega_{\mathsf{tail}} \xrightarrow{0}_\gamma (\mathsf{tl}\ \Omega_{\mathsf{tail}}) \xrightarrow{0}_\gamma (\mathsf{tl}\ (\mathsf{tl}\ \Omega_{\mathsf{tail}})) \xrightarrow{0}_\gamma \ldots$$

$$\begin{array}{ll} (\mathsf{cofix}\ x{:}A.f\ x) & \xrightarrow{0}_\gamma f\ (\mathsf{cofix}\ x{:}A.f\ x) \\ & \xrightarrow{0}_\gamma f\ (f\ (\mathsf{cofix}\ x{:}A.f\ x)) \\ & \xrightarrow{0}_\gamma \ldots \end{array}$$

6. Infinitary Weak Normalisation

In this section, we introduce the concept of an infinitary weakly normalising typing system. We prove that any $\beta\sigma$-normalising CoPTS is infinitary weakly $\beta\sigma\gamma$-normalising. Proving infinitary weak normalisation encounters several concerns:

1. Contracting γ-redexes can create $\beta\sigma$-redexes.
2. Contracting $\beta\sigma$-redexes can decrease the depth of subterms.

We will overcome these concerns by using the auxiliary system $\vdash^n$ in analogy to a construction in [30].

Definition 6.1 (Infinitary Weak Normalisation). *Let* ρ *be a notion of reduction. We say that* a *is infinitary weakly* ρ*-normalising if there exists a possibly infinite* ρ*-normal form* b *such that* $a \twoheadrightarrow_\rho b$.

The undesirable terms (see Example 3.9) are not infinitary weakly $\beta\sigma\gamma$-normalising. The term (mapNat Nat id xs) is infinitary weakly $\beta\sigma\gamma$-normalising. Its normal form is depicted as a tree in Figure 5. Our way of drawing of the term as tree reflects the notion of depth.

(cons (hd xs) $\cdot$)
|
(cons (hd (tl xs)) $\cdot$)
|
$\vdots$

Figure 5. Infinite normal form of (map Nat Nat id xs) as a tree

Definition 6.2 (Infinitary Weak Normalizing CoPTS). *We say that* $\lambda^{\mathsf{co}}(\mathcal{S})$ *is infinitary weakly* ρ*-normalising if for all* $a \in \mathcal{C}$ *such that* $\Gamma \vdash a :_i A$, *we have that* a *is infinitary weakly* ρ*-normalising.*

Notation 6.3. $\lambda^{\mathsf{co}}(\mathcal{S}) \models \rho\text{-}WN^\infty$ *if* $\lambda^{\mathsf{co}}(\mathcal{S})$ *is infinitary weakly* ρ*-normalising*

In the next theorem, we relate the n of a CoPTSn with the truncation at depth n.

Theorem 6.4 (Truncation at depth n of a term in CoPTSn). *Let* $n \geq i$. *If* $\Gamma \vdash^n a{:}_i A$ *then* a^{n-i} *is in* γ*-normal form, i.e.* a^{n-i} *does not have fixed points.*

Proof. We prove this simultaneously with the statement: if $x{:}_j B$ is in Γ then B^{n-j} is in γ-normal form. □

We define a function that contracts all cofix occurrences of a pseudoterm just once.

Definition 6.5. *We define* $\lceil a \rceil$ *by induction on* a.

$$\begin{array}{rl} \lceil x \rceil & = x \\ \lceil s \rceil & = s \\ \lceil \Pi x{:}A.b \rceil & = \Pi x{:}\lceil A \rceil.\lceil b \rceil \\ \lceil \lambda x{:}A.b \rceil & = \lambda x{:}\lceil A \rceil.\lceil b \rceil \\ \lceil (a\ b) \rceil & = (\lceil a \rceil\ \lceil b \rceil) \\ \lceil \bullet A \rceil & = \bullet \lceil A \rceil \\ \lceil \circ a \rceil & = \circ \lceil a \rceil \\ \lceil (\mathsf{await}\ a) \rceil & = (\mathsf{await}\ \lceil a \rceil) \\ \lceil (\mathsf{Stream}\ A) \rceil & = (\mathsf{Stream}\ \lceil A \rceil) \\ \lceil (\mathsf{cons}\ a\ b) \rceil & = (\mathsf{cons}\ \lceil a \rceil\ \lceil b \rceil) \\ \lceil (\mathsf{hd}\ a) \rceil & = (\mathsf{hd}\ \lceil a \rceil) \\ \lceil (\mathsf{tl}\ a) \rceil & = (\mathsf{tl}\ \lceil a \rceil) \\ \lceil (\mathsf{cofix}\ x{:}A.b) \rceil & = \lceil b \rceil [x := (\mathsf{cofix}\ x{:}\lceil A \rceil.\lceil b \rceil)] \end{array}$$

The map $\lceil\ \rceil$ is extended to contexts in the obvious way.

$$\lceil x_1 :_{i_1} A_1, \ldots, x_n :_{i_n} A_n \rceil = x_1 :_{i_1} \lceil A_1 \rceil, \ldots, x_n :_{i_n} \lceil A_n \rceil$$

Note that $a \twoheadrightarrow_\gamma \lceil a \rceil$.

Theorem 6.6. *Let* $\Gamma \vdash^n a{:}_i A$. *Then* $\lceil \Gamma \rceil \vdash^{n+1} \lceil a \rceil{:}_i \lceil A \rceil$.

Proof. This is proved by induction on the derivation. We show the key case:

$$(\mathbf{cofix}^n)\ \frac{\Gamma, x{:}_{i+1} A \vdash^n b{:}_i A \quad \Gamma \vdash^n A{:}_i \mathsf{type}}{\Gamma \vdash^n (\mathsf{cofix}\ x{:}A.b){:}_i A}\ i \geq n$$

By Induction Hypothesis,

$$\lceil \Gamma \rceil, x{:}_{i+1} \lceil A \rceil \vdash^{n+1} \lceil b \rceil{:}_i \lceil A \rceil \quad (1)$$

$$\lceil \Gamma \rceil \vdash^{n+1} \lceil A \rceil{:}_i \mathsf{type} \quad (2)$$

From the above rule, we know that $i \geq n$. However, we cannot apply $\mathbf{cofix}^{n+1}$ unless $i \geq n+1$. The trick is to apply Time Adjustment (Theorem 4.3) to (1) and (2).

$$\begin{array}{l} \lceil \Gamma \rceil, x{:}_{i+2} \lceil A \rceil \vdash^{n+1} \lceil b \rceil{:}_{i+1} \lceil A \rceil \\ \lceil \Gamma \rceil \vdash^{n+1} \lceil A \rceil{:}_{i+1} \mathsf{type} \end{array}$$

Since $i+1 \geq n+1$, we can apply ($\mathbf{cofix}^{n+1}$) and obtain:

$$\lceil\Gamma\rceil \vdash^{n+1} (\mathsf{cofix}\ x{:}\lceil A\rceil.\lceil b\rceil){:}_{i+1}\lceil A\rceil \quad (3)$$

It follows from Substitution Lemma (Lemma 4.4), (1) and (3) that

$$\lceil\Gamma\rceil \vdash^{n+1} \lceil b\rceil[x := (\mathsf{cofix}\ x{:}\lceil A\rceil.\lceil b\rceil)]{:}_i\lceil A\rceil$$

Since $\lceil(\mathsf{cofix}\ x{:}A.b)\rceil = \lceil b\rceil[x := (\mathsf{cofix}\ x{:}\lceil A\rceil.\lceil b\rceil)]$, we are done. □

Theorem 6.7 (Infinitary Weak $\beta\sigma\gamma$-Normalisation). *If $\lambda^{\mathrm{co}}(\mathcal{S}) \models \beta\sigma$-WN then $\lambda^{\mathrm{co}}(\mathcal{S}) \models \beta\sigma\gamma$-WN$^\infty$. Moreover, if a term has a possibly infinite $\beta\sigma\gamma$-normal forms, it can be found in at most ω-steps.*

Proof. Suppose $\Gamma \vdash a :_i A$. Hence, $\Gamma \vdash^0 a :_i A$. We show that there exists a normalising strategy starting from a. We construct a reduction sequence of following form:

$$a = a_0 \twoheadrightarrow_\gamma a_0' \twoheadrightarrow_{\beta\sigma} a_1 \twoheadrightarrow_\gamma a_1' \twoheadrightarrow_{\beta\sigma} a_2 \ldots \quad (4)$$

We define a_0' as $\lceil a_0\rceil$. By Theorem 6.6, we have that $\lceil\Gamma\rceil \vdash^1 a_0' :_i \lceil A\rceil$. Since $\lambda^{\mathrm{co}}(\mathcal{S})$ is $\beta\sigma$-weakly normalising, so is $\lambda^{\mathrm{co}}_n(\mathcal{S})$ for all n. We can, then, define a_1 as the $\beta\sigma$-normal form of a_0'. By Theorem 4.5, $\lceil\Gamma\rceil \vdash^1 a_1 :_i \lceil A\rceil$. We repeat this process for each n. Either this process stops and we are done, or the reduction sequence (4) has the following form:

$$a = a_0 \twoheadrightarrow_{\beta\sigma\gamma} a_1 \twoheadrightarrow_{\beta\sigma\gamma} a_2 \twoheadrightarrow_{\beta\sigma\gamma} \cdots \quad (5)$$

where for all n there exist Γ_n and A_n such that $\Gamma_n \vdash^n a_n :_i A_n$. By Theorem 6.4, we have that $(a_n)^n$ is in $\beta\sigma\gamma$-normal form for all $n \geq i$. From i onwards, the sequence of truncations $a_i^0, a_{i+1}^1, a_{i+2}^2, \ldots$ is increasing (with respect to the subterm relation). Hence the reduction sequence (5) is strongly converging to an infinite limit a_ω in $\beta\sigma\gamma$-normal form. The general compression lemma [25, 27]. for left-linear rewriting systems implies that this reduction can be compressed to one of at most ω many steps. □

Corollary 6.8. *$\lambda^{\mathrm{co}}(C)$ and all the systems of the λ-cube extended with corecursion are infinitary weakly $\beta\sigma\gamma$-normalising.*

Proof. It follows from Theorems 4.17 and 6.7, that $\lambda^{\mathrm{co}}(C)$ is infinitary weakly $\beta\sigma\gamma$-normalising. Since all the systems of the λ-cube extended with corecursion are included in $\lambda^{\mathrm{co}}(C)$, we can conclude infinitary weakly $\beta\sigma\gamma$-normalisation for all of them. □

7. Infinitary Strong Normalisation

In this section, we connect the index and the modality with the depth. We also define the concept of infinitary strong normalisation and prove that CoPTSs are strongly γ-normalising.

Definition 7.1 (Infinitary Strong Normalisation). *Let ρ be a notion of reduction. We say that a is infinitary strongly ρ-normalising if we have that all ρ-reduction sequences starting from a are strongly convergent.*

For example, the term $(\lambda x{:}A.\mathsf{zeros})\Omega$ is infinitary weakly $\beta\sigma\gamma$-normalising but it is not infinitary strongly $\beta\sigma\gamma$-normalising.

Definition 7.2 (Infinitary Strongly Normalizing CoPTS). *Let ρ be a notion of reduction. We say that $\lambda^{\mathrm{co}}(\mathcal{S})$ is infinitary strongly ρ-normalising if for all $a \in \mathcal{C}$ such that $\Gamma \vdash^{\mathrm{co}} a :_i A$ we have that a is strongly ρ-normalising.*

Notation 7.3. *$\lambda^{\mathrm{co}}(\mathcal{S}) \models \rho$-SN$^\infty$ if $\lambda^{\mathrm{co}}(\mathcal{S})$ is infinitary strongly ρ-normalising*

Note that $\lambda^{\mathrm{co}}(\mathcal{S}) \models \rho$-SN$^\infty$ implies $\lambda^{\mathrm{co}}(\mathcal{S}) \models \rho$-WN$^\infty$.

Theorem 7.4 (Depth of Variables). *Let $\Gamma, x{:}_iA, \Gamma' \vdash b{:}_jB$. Then the depth of all occurrences of x in b is greater than $i-j$ if $i > j$.*

Proof. We have to prove it simultaneously with the statement: if $\Gamma, x{:}_iA, \Gamma' \vdash b{:}_jB$ and $y{:}_kC \in \Gamma'$ then all occurrences of x in C occur at depth greater than $i-k$ if $i > k$. □

Corollary 7.5 (Depth of x of type $(\bullet A)$). *If $\Gamma, x{:}_i(\bullet A) \vdash b{:}_iB$ then the depth of all occurrences of x in b is greater than 0.*

Corollary 7.6 (Depth of x in cofix). *If $\Gamma \vdash (\mathsf{cofix}\ x{:}A.b){:}_iA$ then the depth of all occurrences of x in b is greater than 0.*

As a consequence of Theorem 7.4, we have that if a fixed point occurs in a typable term at depth n then it will occur at depth $n+1$ after its contraction. Let $\mathsf{cardfix}_n(a)$ be the number of fixed points of a at depth n.

Theorem 7.7 (Strong Normalisation of γ-reduction at depth n). *Let $\Gamma \vdash a{:}_iA$.*

1. *If $a \xrightarrow{n}_\gamma b$ then* $\mathsf{cardfix}_n(a) > \mathsf{cardfix}_n(b)$.
2. *Any reduction sequence of $\xrightarrow{n}_\gamma$ steps is finite.*

Proof. The first statement is proved by induction on the structure of a using Corollary 7.6. The second one follows by absurd. Suppose there is an infinite reduction sequence starting from $a = a_0 \xrightarrow{n}_\gamma a_1 \xrightarrow{n}_\gamma a_2 \ldots$. From the first part, we would have an infinite decreasing sequence of natural numbers $\mathsf{cardfix}_n(a_0) > \mathsf{cardfix}_n(a_1) > \ldots$ This is a contradiction. This means that this reduction sequence has to be finite. □

Theorem 7.8 (Infinitary Strong γ-normalisation). *We have that $\lambda^{\mathrm{co}}(\mathcal{S}) \models \gamma$-SN$^\infty$.*

Proof. Suppose there is an infinite reduction sequence starting from $a = a_0 \rightarrow_\gamma a_1 \rightarrow_\gamma a_2 \ldots$ with an infinite number of steps at depth 0. By Theorem 7.7, the number of steps at depth 0 in that sequence must be finite. Hence, there exists a_k such that from a_k onwards, all reduction steps contract redexes at depth greater than 1. We repeat the process for $n = 1$ and then for each depth n observing that the number of fixed points of a term at depth n decreases if we only contract redexes at depth greater or equal than n. □

8. Conclusions and Related Work

Comparison with other typed lambda calculi. Nakano defines a typed lambda calculus with modality, subtyping and recursive types where Curry's and Turing's fixed point combinators Y and Θ can be typed and both have type $(\bullet A \to A) \to A$ [36]. Nakano proves that all typable terms have a Böhm tree without $\perp$ which amounts to saying that they have an infinite β-normal form in the infinitary lambda calculus with the '001' metric of [26]. Nakano's type system can type terms that CoPTSs cannot type (their infinite normal forms do not belong to $\mathcal{C}^\infty$). For example, it can type $\mathsf{Y}f$ whose infinite normal form is the following:

$$(f\ (f\ \ldots))$$

and also $\mathsf{Y}(\lambda xy.yx)$ is typable using the recursive type $\mu X.(\bullet X \to B) \to B$ whose infinite normal form is the following:

$$(\lambda y_1.y_1(\lambda y_2.y_2(\lambda y_3.y_3\ldots)))$$

Krishnaswami and Benton's typed lambda calculus of reactive programs use an equational theory instead of reduction [30]. Corollary 6.8 generalises and strengthens in several directions the result in [30] where only weak normalisation is proved for the fragment of $\lambda^{\mathrm{co}}_{\to}$ without fixed points.

Krishnaswami, Benton and Hoffman consider a variant of $\lambda^{\mathrm{co}}_{\to}$ with linearity in [32]. They define a notion of reduction and show that all typable terms reduce to some value. Since values are essentially abstractions. we can view this result as somewhat similar to weak head normalisation.

Giménez studies an extension of the calculus of constructions with inductive and coinductive types [19]. A type constructor $\widehat{A}$ is introduced that resembles a modal operator. The meaning of this operator is not the same as $\bullet A$. While $\bullet A$ can be understood as the information displayed in the *future*, $\widehat{A}$ represents the set of terms that are *guarded* by constructors.

Borghuis studies modal pure type systems (MPTSs) in [8]. CoPTSs are essentially MPTSs with fixed points and streams but without the double negation axiom. The contexts for MPTSs look a bit different because they group together type declarations with the same index $\Gamma_n, \Gamma_{n-1}, \ldots, \Gamma_0$ where $\Gamma_i = \{x_1{:}_i A_1, \ldots, x_n{:}_i A_n\}$. Judgements in a MPTS can only infer types at time 0.

Productivity. The notion of *productivity* given in [14, 42] is equivalent to our notion of weak normalisation. The notion of productivity is defined as weak normalisation but excluding terms that do not contain constructors such as (tl (tl (tl ...))). In our case, we exclude terms without constructors from the start by defining an appropriate metric on terms.

The *guardedness condition* is a criterion that ensures productivity [9]. We cannot say that the guardedness condition is more restrictive than CoPTS. On one hand, CoPTSs can type some terms that do not satisfy the guardedness condition as shown in Example 3.8. On the other hand, CoPTSs cannot type the following example which satisfies the guardedness condition:

```
pairup (a1:a2:xs) = cons (a1, a2) (pairup xs)
```

The papers [14, 42] define a decidable criterion on (first order) term rewriting systems to ensure that programs using corecursive equations are productive [14, 42]. Using this criteria, the terms given in Example 3.8 would satisfy their criterion as well as the example of pairup above.

As pointed out by Eduardo Giménez in [21], the guardedness condition (this applies to the criterion in [14, 42] as well) has the problem of being a syntactic condition that can be checked only when the proof has been completed. So, it would be desirable to have a typing mechanism that prevents the user from doing a bad recursive call while she is writing the proof and not at the end.

Other approaches to corecursion. Hutton and Jaskelioff propose a methodology that ensures that the fixed point of a function on streams is well defined [23]. In this methodology each particular case has to be treated on its own, and it is not clear how it can be automatised. Our approach with with typing treats all programs in "a uniform way" and could be automatised. However Hutton and Jaskelioff can handle functions as zeros''' that CoPTSs cannot type.

$$\begin{aligned}\mathsf{zeros}''' = \;& (\mathsf{cofix}\; xs{:}(\mathsf{Stream\ Nat}).)\\ & (\mathsf{cons}\ 0\ (\mathsf{interleave}\ xs\ (\mathsf{tl}\ xs)))\end{aligned}$$

The infinite normal form of zeros''' is

$$(\mathsf{cons}\ 0\ (\mathsf{cons}\ 0\ (\mathsf{cons}\ 0\ \ldots)))$$

Techniques to prove normalisation. In order to prove preservation of strong normalisation without contracting fixed points, we use two translations: one from $\lambda^{\mathsf{co}}\omega$ into $\lambda\omega$ (Theorem 4.12) and another one from $\lambda^{\mathsf{co}}(C)$ to $\lambda^{\mathsf{co}}\omega$ (Theorem 4.17). The translation from $\lambda^{\mathsf{co}}(C)$ to $\lambda^{\mathsf{co}}\omega$ is an adaptation of the one given by Geuvers and Nederhof in [16]. This translation preserves reduction in a way that one step is mapped into one or more steps. The translation from $\lambda^{\mathsf{co}}(C)$ to $\lambda^{\mathsf{co}}\omega$ codes the streams making use of polymorphism and 'ignores' the modality. As a consequence of this, σ-steps that contract the modal operator can be cancelled. In spite of this, we can prove preservation of strong normalisation using the fact that σ is strongly normalising on untyped terms. A similar technique has been used to prove $\lambda\mathcal{S} \models \beta$-SN implies $\lambda^{\delta}(\mathcal{S}) \models \beta\delta$-SN where $\lambda^{\delta}(\mathcal{S})$ is the extension of $\lambda(\mathcal{S})$ with definitions where the translation can cancel δ-steps [39].

In order to prove infinitary weak normalisation we used an auxiliary system $\vdash^n$ (and the unfolding $\lceil a \rceil$). This technique is used in [31] to prove that all typable terms have an m-normal form for a calculus based on $\lambda^{\mathsf{co}}_{\rightarrow}$ with linearity. The notion of m-normal form is defined in [31] in terms of the auxiliary system $\vdash^n$. This does not ensure yet that typable terms are well-behaved.

9. Future Work

Our work is closely related to the metric model introduced by Birkedal et al. in [6] (used later by Krishnaswami and Benton in [30]). It will be interesting to define a Böhm model for corecursion on streams by interpreting terms as infinite normal forms [5, 24]. Once we have a Böhm Model for corecursion on streams, we would like to find a way of integrating the syntactic model of Böhm trees which is an ultra metric space with the model of ultra metric spaces [6, 30] and the topos of trees [7].

To ensure that the Böhm model is well defined, we need to prove infinitary confluence besides infinitary weak normalisation. The problem is that $\twoheadrightarrow\!\!\!\!\!\rightarrow_{\beta\sigma\gamma}$ is not confluent on untypable terms. We construct a counter-example from the σ-rules which are hypercollapsing, i.e. they are of the form $C[x] \rightarrow x$ [25, 26].

Example 9.1 (Failure of Confluence). *We have that*

$$\Omega \;\xleftarrow{\sigma}\; \Omega' \;\xrightarrow{\gamma}\!\!\!\!\rightarrow\!\!\!\rightarrow\; (\mathsf{tl}\ (\mathsf{cons}\ 0\ (\mathsf{tl}\ (\mathsf{cons}\ 0\ \ldots))))$$

cannot be joined. The terms Ω and (tl (cons 0 (tl (cons 0 ...)))) *can only reduce to themselves.*

Ketema and Simonsen prove confluence up to hypercollapsing terms for orthogonal infinitary combinatory reduction systems [27]. However, we cannot apply their result. This is because $\mathcal{C}^{\infty}$ is strictly included in their syntax and their confluence result may give us a common reduct which is outside our syntax

We have proved that $\lambda^{\mathsf{co}}(\mathcal{S})$ is infinitary strongly γ-normalising. However, it remains open to prove it for $\beta\sigma\gamma$.

In this paper we have considered only streams which is one particular coinductive data type. It will be interesting to consider a general form of coinductive data type in the spirit of Coq and the Calculus of Inductive Constructions [18–20, 41]. This will allow us to capture other notions of infinite data apart from streams such as infinite trees or equality between infinite objects .

Consider a basic primitive recursive function such as $+$ defined as follows:

$$\begin{aligned} + = \;& (\lambda x : \mathsf{Nat}.\\ & \quad \mathsf{cofix} f{:}(\mathsf{Nat} \rightarrow \mathsf{Nat}).\\ & \quad\quad \lambda y : \mathsf{Nat}.\\ & \quad\quad\quad \mathsf{case}\ y\ \mathsf{is}\ 0 \quad \mathsf{then}\ x\\ & \quad\quad\quad\quad\quad \mathsf{is}\ (\mathsf{succ}\ z)\ \mathsf{then}\ \mathsf{succ}\ (f\ z)\end{aligned}$$

It is not typable because the variable f occurs at depth 0 (see Theorem 7.6). We think that the solution to this problem is to have two different fixed points, one for expressing recursion on inductive data types and the other one for corecursion on coinductive data types as in [18–20].

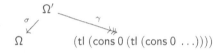

In infinitary rewriting other metrics have been considered that result in more infinite lambda terms in the completion of the finite lambda calculus [25–27]. It would be interesting to know whether there are typing systems that type the normal forms in the lambda calculi of respectively the Böhm trees, the Lévy Longo trees and the Berarducci trees. This will help us in the study of confluence and normalisation for a calculus with a general form of coinductive data type.

Finally, we did not consider a η-reduction because, as is well-known, confluence of $\beta\eta$ on untypable terms with annotated types does not hold. The counterexample due to Nederpelt is $\lambda x{:}A.(\lambda y{:}B.y)x$ for $A \neq B$ [37]. A general confluence proof for weakly $\beta\eta$-normalising PTSs is proved in [15]. It should be possible to adapt this proof to CoPTSs.

Acknowledgments

We would like to acknowledge Alexander Kurz, Tadeusz Litak and Daniela Petrişan for discussing the papers by Krishnaswami and Benton with us. We would also like to thank Neelakantan Krishnaswami for a helpful email exchange. Finally, we are grateful to the reviewers for their detailed and helpful comments and suggestions.

References

[1] S. Abramsky and C.-H. L. Ong. Full abstraction in the lazy lambda calculus. *Inform. and Comput.*, 105(2):159–267, 1993. ISSN 0890-5401.

[2] H. Barendregt. Lambda calculi with types. In S. Abramsky, D. Gabbay, and T. Maibaum, editors, *Handbook of Logic in Computer Science*, volume 2, pages 118–310. Oxford University Press, 1992.

[3] H. P. Barendregt. *The Lambda Calculus: Its Syntax and Semantics*. North-Holland, Amsterdam, Revised edition, 1984. ISBN 0-444-86748-1; 0-444-87508-5.

[4] S. Berardi. *Type Dependency and Constructive Mathematics*. PhD thesis, Carnegie Mellon University and Universitá di Torino, 1990.

[5] A. Berarducci. Infinite λ-calculus and non-sensible models. In *Logic and algebra (Pontignano, 1994)*, pages 339–377. Dekker, New York, 1996.

[6] L. Birkedal, J. Schwinghammer, and K. Støvring. A metric model of lambda calculus with guarded recursion. Presented at FICS 2010, 2010.

[7] L. Birkedal, R. E. Møgelberg, J. Schwinghammer, and K. Støvring. First steps in synthetic guarded domain theory: Step-indexing in the topos of trees. In *LICS*, pages 55–64, 2011.

[8] T. Borghuis. Modal pure type systems. *Journal of Logic, Language and Information*, 7(3):265–296, 1998.

[9] T. Coquand. Infinite objects in type theory. In *TYPES*, pages 62–78, 1993.

[10] T. Coquand and H. Herbelin. A-translation and looping combinators in pure type systems. *J. Funct. Program.*, 4(1):77–88, 1994.

[11] T. Coquand and G. P. Huet. The calculus of constructions. *Inf. Comput.*, 76(2/3):95–120, 1988.

[12] H. B. Curry and R. Feys. *Combinatory Logic*, volume I. North-Holland, 1958.

[13] N. G. de Bruijn. A survey of the AUTOMATH project. In J. R. Hindley and J. Seldin, editors, *To H.B. Curry: Essays on Combinatory Logic, Lambda Calculus and Formalism*. Academic Press, 1980.

[14] J. Endrullis, C. Grabmayer, D. Hendriks, A. Isihara, and J. W. Klop. Productivity of stream definitions. *Theor. Comput. Sci.*, 411(4-5): 765–782, 2010.

[15] H. Geuvers. The Church-Rosser property for beta-eta-reduction in typed lambda-calculi. In *LICS*, pages 453–460, 1992.

[16] H. Geuvers and M.-J. Nederhof. Modular proof of strong normalization for the calculus of constructions. *J. Funct. Program.*, 1(2): 155–189, 1991.

[17] H. Geuvers and J. Verkoelen. On fixed points and looping combinators in type theory. Note, 2009.

[18] E. Giménez. *A Calculus of Infinite constructions and its applications to the verification of communicating systems*. PhD thesis, Ecole Normale Supérieure de Lyon, 1996.

[19] E. Giménez. Structural recursive definitions in type theory. In *ICALP*, pages 397–408, 1998.

[20] E. Giménez and P. Casterán. A tutorial on [co-]inductive types in coq. Technical report, Inria, 1998.

[21] J.-Y. Girard. *Interprétation fonctionelle et élimination des coupures de l'arithmétique d'ordre supérieur*. PhD thesis, Université Paris VII, 1972.

[22] W. A. Howard. The formulae-as-types notion of construction. In J. R. Hindley and J. Seldin, editors, *To H.B. Curry: Essays on Combinatory Logic, Lambda Calculus and Formalism*. Academic Press, 1980.

[23] G. Hutton and M. Jaskelioff. Representing Contractive Functions on Streams. Submitted to the Journal of Functional Programming, 2011.

[24] J. R. Kennaway, J. W. Klop, M. R. Sleep, and F.-J. de Vries. Infinitary lambda calculi and Böhm models. In *RTA*, pages 257–270, 1995.

[25] J. R. Kennaway, J. W. Klop, M. R. Sleep, and F.-J. de Vries. Transfinite reductions in orthogonal term rewriting systems. *Inf. Comput.*, 119 (1):18–38, 1995.

[26] J. R. Kennaway, J. W. Klop, M. R. Sleep, and F.-J. de Vries. Infinitary lambda calculus. *Theor. Comput. Sci.*, 175(1):93–125, 1997.

[27] J. Ketema and J. G. Simonsen. Infinitary combinatory reduction systems. *Inf. Comput.*, 209(6):893–926, 2011.

[28] J. W. Klop. *Combinatory Reduction Systems*. PhD thesis, Rijkuniversiteit Utrecht, 1980.

[29] J. W. Klop, V. van Oostrom, and F. van Raamsdonk. Combinatory reduction systems: Introduction and survey. *Theor. Comput. Sci.*, 121 (1&2):279–308, 1993.

[30] N. R. Krishnaswami and N. Benton. Ultrametric semantics of reactive programs. In *LICS*, pages 257–266, 2011.

[31] N. R. Krishnaswami and N. Benton. A semantic model for graphical user interfaces. In *ICFP*, pages 45–57, 2011.

[32] N. R. Krishnaswami, N. Benton, and J. Hoffmann. Higher-order functional reactive programming in bounded space. In *POPL*, pages 45–58, 2012.

[33] J.-J. Lévy. An algebraic interpretation of the $\lambda\beta K$-calculus, and an application of a labelled λ-calculus. *Theoretical Computer Science*, 2 (1):97–114, 1976.

[34] G. Longo. Set-theoretical models of λ-calculus: theories, expansions, isomorphisms. *Ann. Pure Appl. Logic*, 24(2):153–188, 1983. ISSN 0168-0072.

[35] Z. Luo. ECC, an Extended Calculus of Constructions. In *LICS*, pages 386–395, 1989.

[36] H. Nakano. A modality for recursion. In *LICS*, pages 255–266, 2000.

[37] R. P. Nederpelt. *Strong Normalization in a typed lambda calculus*. PhD thesis, Technische Universiteit Eindhoven, The Netherlands, 1973.

[38] J. C. Reynolds. Towards a theory of type structure. In *Symposium on Programming*, pages 408–423, 1974.

[39] P. Severi and E. Poll. Pure type systems with definitions. In *LFCS*, pages 316–328, 1994.

[40] J. Terlouw. Een nadere bewijstheoretische analyse van GSTT's. Manuscript, 1989.

[41] B. Werner. *Une théorie des constructions inductives*. PhD thesis, Université Paris VII, 1994.

[42] H. Zantema and M. Raffelsieper. Proving productivity in infinite data structures. In *RTA*, pages 401–416, 2010.

On the Complexity of Equivalence of Specifications of Infinite Objects

Jörg Endrullis Dimitri Hendriks Rena Bakhshi

VU University Amsterdam
Department of Computer Science
De Boelelaan 1081a
1081 HV Amsterdam
The Netherlands
{j.endrullis, r.d.a.hendriks, r.r.bakhshi}@vu.nl

Abstract

We study the complexity of deciding the equality of infinite objects specified by systems of equations, and of infinite objects specified by λ-terms. For equational specifications there are several natural notions of equality: equality in all models, equality of the sets of solutions, and equality of normal forms for productive specifications. For λ-terms we investigate Böhm-tree equality and various notions of observational equality. We pinpoint the complexity of each of these notions in the arithmetical or analytical hierarchy.

We show that the complexity of deciding equality in all models subsumes the entire analytical hierarchy. This holds already for the most simple infinite objects, viz. streams over $\{0, 1\}$, and stands in sharp contrast to the low arithmetical Π^0_2-completeness of equality of equationally specified streams derived in [17] employing a different notion of equality.

Categories and Subject Descriptors F.3.2 [*Logics and Meanings of Programs*]: Semantics; F.1.3 [*Computation by Abstract Devices*]: Complexity Measures and Classes; F.1.1 [*Models of Computation*]; F.4 [*Mathematical Logic and Formal Languages*]

Keywords Infinite objects, equational specifications, lambda terms, equality, semantics, complexity.

1. Introduction

In the last two decades interest has grown towards infinite data, as witnessed by the application of type theory to infinite objects [5], as well as the emergence of coalgebraic techniques for infinite data types like streams [19], infinitary term rewriting and infinitary lambda calculus [24]. In functional programming, the use of infinite data structures dates back to 1976, see [11, 14].

We are concerned with the complexity of deciding the equality of infinite objects specified by systems of equations, and infinite objects specified by λ-terms. The equational specification of infinite objects is common practice in coalgebra, term rewriting and functional programming. Consider an example from [17]:

$$\left.\begin{array}{ll} \mathsf{zeros} = 0 : \mathsf{zeros} & \mathsf{ones} = 1 : \mathsf{ones} \\ \mathsf{blink} = 0 : 1 : \mathsf{blink} & \mathsf{zip}(x : \sigma, \tau) = x : \mathsf{zip}(\tau, \sigma) \end{array}\right\} \quad (1)$$

This is an equational specification of three infinite lists of bits, and a binary function over infinite lists.[1] Then, a typical question is whether the following equality holds:

$$\mathsf{zip}(\mathsf{zeros}, \mathsf{ones}) = \mathsf{blink} \quad (2)$$

The answer depends on the semantics we choose to interpret the equality; for example (2) is not valid in the hidden models considered in [17]; for more details we refer to Section 2. In order to answer such a question, we first need to settle on the precise semantics of equality for equational specifications; the candidates we consider in this paper are

I. Equality in all models.

II. Equality of the set of solutions.

For λ-terms we are not concerned with equality in the sense of convertibility (which is known to be Π^0_2-complete, see [1]). Instead, we are interested in *behavioral* equivalence of λ-terms in all contexts, because this corresponds to the interchangeability of expressions in purely functional languages. It is also closely related to referential transparency, and the notion of Böhm trees as values of expressions including those without normal form. Thus we consider the following equivalences for λ-terms:

III. Observational equivalences.

IV. Böhm-tree equality.

The 'right' choice of equivalence depends on the intended application. The classic semantics mentioned in items I and II above, are defined by model-theoretic means. From a algebraic perspective I and II are the most natural semantics to consider for equational reasoning. On the other hand, III and IV, are defined by means of evaluation, i.e., rewriting. In functional programming the latter are of foremost importance, because these take (lazy) evaluation strategies into account. From an evaluation perspective, two terms are equal if they have the same observable behavior, independent of the context they are in. In contrast to the model-theoretic notions, this equality is invariant under the exchange of *meaningless subterms*, that is, subterms which cannot be evaluated to a (weak) head

[0] The technical report supporting this paper can be found on `arxiv.org` under the same title.

[1] In Haskell there is $\mathsf{zip} :: [a] \to [b] \to [(a, b)]$, but we prefer to use 'zip' for the *interleaving* of lists, as defined by the equation in (1), since that is what a zipper does: it interleaves rows of teeth.

normal form. Another candidate for the semantics of equality is

V. Equality of normal forms for productive specifications.

A rewrite specification is *productive* [9, 23] if the terms under consideration can be fully evaluated, that is, (outermost-fair) rewriting yields a (possibly infinite) constructor normal form in the limit. In such a setting, equality of the normal forms is a suitable semantics for the equivalence of terms. Deciding the equality of productive specifications has been shown to be a Π^0_1-complete problem in [13]; this semantics is not considered here.

We now briefly describe the concepts I–IV.

Equality in models (I and II). The semantics I (equality in all models) is useful when the objects under consideration are specified in the same specification. This semantics interprets the objects simultaneously in each model satisfying the specification. This allows us to compare objects that depend on a common unknown, an underspecified object; see (4) below for an illustrating example. If the objects under consideration are fully specified, that is, have unique solutions, then semantics I coincides with semantics II.

In contrast to I, semantics II is more suitable for comparing objects specified by different specifications, as we explain below. The objects are compared via the set of their solutions (in their respective specifications). This semantics is well-known from equations over real (or complex) numbers, where two equations, like

$$(x-1)^2 - 1 = 0 \qquad \text{and} \qquad x^2 - 2x = 0\,,$$

are equivalent if they have the same solutions for x, here $\{0, 2\}$.

A Σ-algebra $\mathcal{A}$ consists of a carrier set A (the domain of $\mathcal{A}$) and an interpretation $[\![\cdot]\!]$ of the symbols Σ occurring in the equational specification as functions over A. Then $\mathcal{A}$ is called a *model* of an equational specification E, which we denote by $\mathcal{A} \models E$, if all equations of E respect the interpretation; that is, for every equation of E both sides have the same interpretation for every assignment of the variables. As the domain we will typically choose (a subset of) the *final coalgebra* [21] describing the class of objects we are specifying. The final coalgebra ensures that the model is *continuous*, that is, if we have a converging sequence of terms $t_1, t_2, \ldots$ with limit t_ω, then the sequence of interpretations $[\![t_1]\!], [\![t_2]\!], \ldots$ converges towards $[\![t_\omega]\!]$. For example, in a specification like

$$\mathsf{ones} = 1 : \mathsf{ones} \qquad\qquad \mathsf{ones}' = 1 : \mathsf{ones}' \tag{3}$$

the symbols ones and ones' are guaranteed to have the same interpretation. Continuity is crucial to conclude the validity of equations such as $\mathsf{ones} = \mathsf{ones}'$ which are not satisfied in non-continuous models like the *initial* algebra of the specification.

Let E be a specification of M and N. Then M is considered equal to N with respect to semantics I if every model of E is also a model of $M = N$: $\forall \mathcal{A}.\ \ \mathcal{A} \models E \ \Rightarrow\ \mathcal{A} \models M = N$. This notion is especially of interest if M and N depend on a common unknown and consequently have to be interpreted simultaneously in the same model. For example in

$$\left.\begin{array}{ll} M = \mathsf{zip}(X, X) & \mathsf{zip}(x : \sigma, \tau) = x : \mathsf{zip}(\tau, \sigma) \\ N = \mathsf{dup}(X) & \mathsf{dup}(x : \sigma) = x : x : \mathsf{dup}(\sigma) \end{array}\right\} \tag{4}$$

the streams M and N are both specified in terms of an unspecified stream X. Whatever interpretation X has, M and N are equal, and so they are equal in the sense of semantics I.

On the other hand, semantics I has the effect that an underspecified constant is not equivalent to its renamed copy. This is illustrated by the following specification:

$$M = 0 : \mathsf{tail}(M) \qquad\qquad N = 0 : \mathsf{tail}(N) \tag{5}$$

Here M and N are not equal in every model; for example, let $[\![M]\!] = 0 : 0 : \ldots$ and $[\![N]\!] = 0 : 1 : 1 : \ldots$. Nevertheless, M and N are equal in the sense that they exhibit the same behaviors. That is, they have the same set of solutions: every stream starting with a zero is a solution for M as well as for N. Thus, M and N are equal with respect to the semantics II. This paves the way for comparing objects M and N that are given by separate specifications E_M and E_N, respectively. Note that it is not always suitable to apply semantics I to the union $E_M \cup E_N$ even if the specifications have disjoint signatures (using renaming), see further Remark 2.

Two objects M and N are equal with respect to semantics II if the set of solutions of M in E_M coincides with the set of solutions of N in E_N: $\{\, [\![M]\!]^{\mathcal{A}} \mid \mathcal{A} \models E_M \,\} = \{\, [\![N]\!]^{\mathcal{A}} \mid \mathcal{A} \models E_N \,\}$. Here the set of solutions of a constant X in a specification E_X is the set of interpretations of X in all models of E_X.

Observational equivalence (III and IV). In purely functional languages based on the λ-calculus [1], the evaluation of expressions is *free of side effects*. As a consequence, an expression (or subexpression) can always be replaced by its normal form, the so-called *value* of the expression. This principle is known as *referential transparency*. This also implies that expressions can be substituted for each other if they have the same normal form.

For specifications of coinductive objects, such as infinite lists (called *streams*) or infinite trees, the value typically is an infinite term. For example in $\mathsf{ones} = 1 : \mathsf{ones}$, the term ones has as value (or infinite normal form) the infinite term $1 : 1 : 1 : \ldots$. However, it is not always guaranteed that a term can be fully evaluated. During the evaluation to the (possibly infinite) normal form, we may encounter subterms that cannot be evaluated because these subterms do not have a head normal form. In λ-calculus, such terms are known as *meaningless terms*. For example, consider:

$$\begin{array}{ll} \mathsf{natsx}(n) = n : \mathsf{g}(0) : \mathsf{natsx}(n+1) & \qquad \mathsf{g}(n) = \mathsf{g}(n) \\ \mathsf{natsx}'(n) = n : \mathsf{g}(n) : \mathsf{natsx}'(n+1) & \end{array}$$

Here $\mathsf{g}(n)$ is meaningless for every n. Consequently, $\mathsf{natsx}(0)$ evaluates to a stream in which every second element is meaningless, and therefore, undefined. An infinite value containing undefined parts can be represented by means of Böhm trees [1] introduced in 1975 by Corrado Böhm. In particular, the Böhm tree of $\mathsf{natsx}(0)$ is: $0 : \bot : 1 : \bot : 2 : \bot : 3 : \bot : 4 : \bot : \ldots$, where $\bot$ is a special symbol representing an undefined element.

In λ-calculus (or orthogonal higher-order rewriting), terms with equal Böhm trees can be exchanged (for each other) without changing the meaning of the whole expression. In the specification above, $\mathsf{natsx}(0)$ and $\mathsf{natsx}'(0)$ have the same Böhm tree, and hence are interchangeable. In contrast, from the model-theoretic perspective $\mathsf{natsx}(0)$ and $\mathsf{natsx}'(0)$ are different. In every model of $\mathsf{natsx}(0)$ all elements at odd indexes coincide, whereas $\mathsf{natsx}'(0)$ admits models that assign different interpretations to these elements. From a rewriting as well as functional programming perspective, these differences are irrelevant as they concern undefined subterms.

There are several notions of infinite values, depending on what terms are considered meaningless, including Böhm trees, Lévy-Longo trees, Berarducci trees, η-Böhm trees, η^∞-Böhm trees; see further [6]. The terms $\lambda x.xx$ and $\lambda x.x(\lambda z.xz)$, for instance, have distinct Böhm trees, but we may want to consider the terms *behaviorally*, or *observationally equivalent* as they are η-convertible. There are several natural concepts of *observational equivalence* for λ-calculus, where terms are considered *equivalent* if they yield the same observations in every context. To that end, we consider three forms of *observations*: normal forms (nf), head normal forms (hnf), and weak head normal forms (whnf). A *head normal form* is a λ-term of the form $\lambda x_1 \ldots \lambda x_n . y N_1 \ldots N_m$ with $n, m \geq 0$. A *weak head normal form* is an hnf or an abstraction, i.e., a whnf is a term of the form $x M_1 \ldots M_m$ or $\lambda x.M$. Each of the observations gives rise to an equivalence $=_{nf}$, $=_{hnf}$ or $=_{whnf}$, defined by

$$M =_{nf} N \ \text{ iff } \ (\forall C.\ C[M] \text{ has a nf iff } C[N] \text{ has a nf})$$

$$M =_{hnf} N \text{ iff } (\forall C.\, C[M] \text{ has a hnf iff } C[N] \text{ has a hnf})$$
$$M =_{whnf} N \text{ iff } (\forall C.\, C[M] \text{ has a whnf iff } C[N] \text{ has a whnf})$$

In fact, the equivalence $=_{nf}$ corresponds to η-Böhm trees, and $=_{hnf}$ to η^∞-Böhm trees. For more details we refer to [6], where it is argued that $=_{whnf}$ corresponds to evaluation strategies used by lazy functional languages. If two expressions behave the same in every context, then no functional program can distinguish them.

Contribution. We characterize for each of the semantics I–IV the complexity of deciding the equality of terms. For I and II we will focus on equational specifications of bitstreams, and for III and IV on behavioral equivalences of λ-terms and Böhm tree equality.

Each of these equivalences is undecidable, therefore we characterize their complexity by means of the arithmetical and analytical hierarchies, see Figure 1. The arithmetical hierarchy classifies the complexity of a problem P by the minimum number of quantifier alternations in first-order formulas that characterize P. The analytical hierarchy extends this classification to second-order arithmetic, then counting the alternations of set quantifiers.

(A) It turns out that the complexities of deciding the equality in all models as well as the equality of the set of solutions subsume the entire arithmetical and analytical hierarchy when the domain of the models is the set of all streams, so-called *full* models, see Theorems 3 and 5. The idea of the proof is as follows. We translate formulas of the analytical hierarchy into stream specifications by representing $\forall$ set quantifiers by equations with variables. This simulates a quantification over all streams as the models are full, and the equations have to hold for all assignments of the variables. The $\exists$ set quantifiers are eliminated in favor of Skolem functions (here stream functions). The interpretation of the functions is determined by the model, and the question whether there exists a model corresponds to an existential quantification over all Skolem functions.

(B) & (C) If we admit models whose domain does not contain all streams, then the complexity of deciding equality drops to the level Π^1_1 of the analytical hierarchy for semantics I, and to Π^1_2 for II, see Theorems 1, and 7. The reason is that equations with variables no longer have to hold for all streams, but only for the streams that exist in the model. By the Löwenheim-Skolem theorem we obtain that if there exists a model, then there exists a countable model: from an uncountable model we construct a countable one, by taking the finitely many streams "of interest" and closing them under all functions in the model. Thus, it suffices to quantify over countable models for which one single set quantifier is enough.

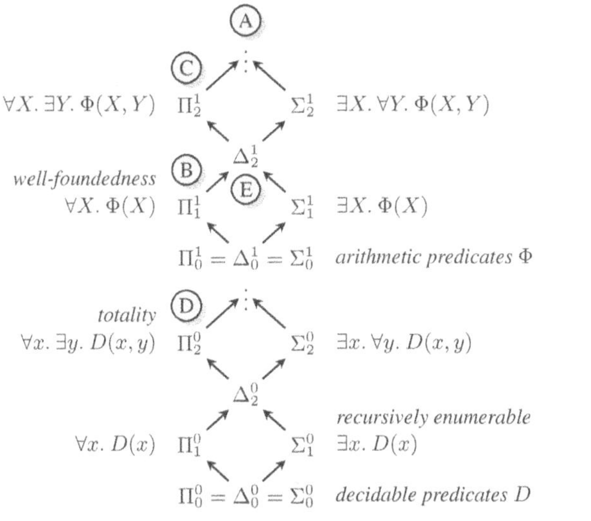

Figure 1. Arithmetical (bottom) and analytical hierarchy (top).

The aforementioned results already hold for bitstreams, one of the simplest coinductive objects, and thereby can serve as a lower bound on the hardness of the equality problem for other coinductive objects. We also study the behavioral semantics from [17]. We find that if behavioral equivalence $\equiv$ is required to be a congruence, like for example in [2], then the complexity of deciding behavioral equivalence is catapulted out of the arithmetical hierarchy, to the level Π^1_1 of the analytical hierarchy, see Theorem 8. Likewise so for the behavioural equivalence for specifications of streams of natural numbers, relaxing the congruence requirement, see Theorem 9.

(D) For the equivalences on λ-terms, we show that deciding the Böhm tree and Lévy–Longo tree equality, as well as the observational equivalences $=_{nf}$, $=_{hnf}$ and $=_{whnf}$ are Π^0_2-complete problems, see Theorem 11. (It is clear that when an object is given by a rewrite system, like the λ-calculus, then the complexity resides in the arithmetical hierarchy, since it suffices to quantify over a number steps to evaluate parts of the object.)

(E) Finally, we consider the complexity of unique solutions. A term s has a unique solution within a specification E if there exists models of E, and in all models of E, s has the same interpretation. The problem of deciding unique solvability in all full models again subsumes the analytical hierarchy, see Theorem 4. When also considering the non-full models, we find that the problem is Π^1_1- and Σ^1_1-hard, but is strictly contained in Δ^1_2, see Theorem 2.

Outline. We first discuss related work. We formally introduce bitstream specifications and stream models in Section 3, and Turing machines with oracles in Section 4. We recall the basic complexity-related notions in Section 5. We use these concepts in Section 6 to derive the complexity results for the model-theoretic notions. In Section 7 we consider a different notion of models, namely the behavioural semantics as in [17]. Finally, we investigate the observational equivalences of λ-terms in Section 8.

2. Related Work

The complexity of the equality of streams specified by systems of equations has been investigated in the ICFP paper [17, Corollary 1]; we cite: *Proving equality on streams defined equationally is a* Π^0_2*-complete problem.* This result is based on a behavioral notion of stream models [16]. We briefly summarize the main characteristics of these models:

(i) Every stream $\sigma \in \{0, 1\}^\omega$ can have multiple representatives in the model (known as *confusion*).

(ii) For every equation $\ell = r$ it is required that the interpretations $[\![\ell]\!]$ and $[\![r]\!]$ are *behaviorally equivalent*, denoted by $\equiv$, that is, equality under all $[\![\mathsf{head}]\!]([\![\mathsf{tail}]\!]^n(\square))$ experiments. In particular, it is not required that $[\![\ell]\!] = [\![r]\!]$.

(iii) Behavioral equivalence $\equiv$ is not required to be a congruence.

Behavioral models have a wide range of applications, for example for modeling computations with hidden states, or capturing certain forms of nondeterminism. For these applications it is often intended that the semantics is not preserved under equational reasoning. For example, consider the following specification from [17]

$$\mathsf{tail}(\mathsf{push}(\sigma)) = \sigma\ ,$$

specifying a function push that prefixes an element to the argument stream, while leaving unspecified which element. In the behavioral models we obtain a restricted form of nondeterminism [25], for example, the following is not behaviorally satisfied:

$$\mathsf{push}(\mathsf{tail}(\mathsf{push}(\sigma))) = \mathsf{push}(\sigma)\ , \qquad (6)$$

although derivable by pure equational reasoning. For a nondeterministic operation, it is of course desirable that (6) does not hold.

However, for function definitions employing pattern matching, behavioral models sometimes yield unexpected results; consider:

$$\mathsf{ones} = 1 : \mathsf{ones} \qquad\qquad \mathsf{f}(x : \sigma) = \sigma \tag{7}$$

Now, there are models that satisfy the specification (7), but not (8):

$$\mathsf{f}(\mathsf{ones}) = \mathsf{ones} \tag{8}$$

In these models we have that $[\![\mathsf{ones}]\!] \neq [\![1:\mathsf{ones}]\!]$ and, at the same time, that $[\![\mathsf{ones}]\!]$ cannot be constructed by the stream constructor $[\![:]\!]$, that is, $[\![\mathsf{ones}]\!] \neq [\![:]\!](x, s)$ for all $x \in \{0,1\}$ and $s \in A_S$. Consequently, the interpretation $[\![\mathsf{f}]\!]([\![\mathsf{ones}]\!])$ can be arbitrary.

Thus, behavioral reasoning is typically not sound for behavioral models, and therefore the corresponding specifications are usually referred to as *behavioral specifications*. In this paper we are interested in specifications where equational reasoning is sound.

Remark 1. We construct a behavioral model $\langle A, [\![\cdot]\!]\rangle$ in the sense of [17] where specification (1) is behaviorally satisfied but the goal equation $\mathsf{zip}(\mathsf{zeros}, \mathsf{ones}) = \mathsf{blink}$ is not. The model thereby forms a counterexample to [17, Example 2].

We define the domain by $A_B = \{0, 1\}$ and

$$A_S = \{z_w \mid w \in \{0,1\}^*\} \cup \{o_w \mid w \in \{0,1\}^*\} \cup \{0,1\}^\omega$$

Here z_ε and o_ε are alternative representations of 0^ω and 1^ω, respectively, and z_w and o_w have an additional finite prefix $w \in \{0,1\}^*$. We define the interpretations $[\![\cdot]\!]$ for every $a \in \{0,1\}, \sigma \in \{0,1\}^\omega$, $w, v \in \{0,1\}^*$ and $x, y \in A_S$. For $[\![\mathsf{head}]\!]$ and $[\![\mathsf{tail}]\!]$ we define:

$$[\![\mathsf{head}]\!](z_\varepsilon) = 0 \qquad [\![\mathsf{head}]\!](o_\varepsilon) = 1 \qquad [\![\mathsf{head}]\!](a\sigma) = a$$
$$[\![\mathsf{tail}]\!](z_\varepsilon) = z_\varepsilon \qquad [\![\mathsf{tail}]\!](o_\varepsilon) = o_\varepsilon \qquad [\![\mathsf{tail}]\!](a\sigma) = \sigma$$
$$[\![\mathsf{head}]\!](z_{aw}) = a \qquad [\![\mathsf{head}]\!](o_{aw}) = a$$
$$[\![\mathsf{tail}]\!](z_{aw}) = z_w \qquad [\![\mathsf{tail}]\!](o_{aw}) = o_w$$

We define the interpretation $[\![:]\!]$ of the stream constructor by:

$$[\![:]\!](a, z_w) = z_{aw} \qquad [\![:]\!](a, o_w) = o_{aw} \qquad [\![:]\!](a, \sigma) = a\sigma$$

Note that the elements z_ε and o_ε cannot be constructed by $[\![:]\!]$.

We interpret $[\![\mathsf{zeros}]\!]$, $[\![\mathsf{ones}]\!]$ and $[\![\mathsf{blink}]\!]$ as follows:

$$[\![\mathsf{zeros}]\!] = z_\varepsilon \qquad [\![\mathsf{ones}]\!] = o_\varepsilon \qquad [\![\mathsf{blink}]\!] = (01)^\omega$$

We define an auxiliary function $\bowtie$ that (similar to zip) interleaves the elements of finite or infinite words; for $u_1, u_2 \in \{0,1\}^{\leq\omega} = \{0,1\}^* \cup \{0,1\}^\omega$, let $au_1 \bowtie u_2 = a(u_2 \bowtie u_1)$ and $\varepsilon \bowtie u_2 = u_2$. We now define the interpretation $[\![\mathsf{zip}]\!]$ of the symbol zip as follows:

$$[\![\mathsf{zip}]\!](z_w, o_v) = \begin{cases} (w \bowtie v)0^\omega & \text{for } |w| = |v| \\ (w\, 0^\omega) \bowtie (v\, 1^\omega) & \text{otherwise} \end{cases}$$

$$[\![\mathsf{zip}]\!](o_w, z_v) = \begin{cases} (w \bowtie v)0^\omega & \text{for } |w| = |v| + 1 \\ (w\, 1^\omega) \bowtie (v\, 0^\omega) & \text{otherwise} \end{cases}$$

and in all other cases, we define $[\![\mathsf{zip}]\!](x, y) = emb(x) \bowtie emb(y)$ where $emb(z_w) = w0^\omega$, $emb(o_w) = w1^\omega$, and $emb(\sigma) = \sigma$.

It is straightforward to check that specification 1 is behaviorally satisfied, whereas $[\![\mathsf{zip}(\mathsf{zeros}, \mathsf{ones})]\!] = 0^\omega \not\equiv (01)^\omega = [\![\mathsf{blink}]\!]$.

The counterexample in Remark 1 employs the fact that the behavioral models of [17] do not require that every stream can be constructed by the (interpretation of the) stream constructor $[\![:]\!]$. As a consequence, the equation $\mathsf{zip}(x : \sigma, \tau) = x : \mathsf{zip}(\tau, \sigma)$ does not fully define $[\![\mathsf{zip}]\!]$; it defines $[\![\mathsf{zip}]\!](\sigma, \tau)$ only for those arguments σ that can be constructed by $[\![:]\!]$.

The example illustrates that the behavioral models of [17] do not go along with function definitions using pattern matching. To fully define $[\![\mathsf{zip}]\!]$, we can specify it using the stream destructors: $\mathsf{head}(\mathsf{zip}(\sigma, \tau)) = \mathsf{head}(\sigma)$, and $\mathsf{tail}(\mathsf{zip}(\sigma, \tau)) = \mathsf{zip}(\tau, \mathsf{tail}(\sigma))$. This change of the specification format resolves the problem.

Alternatively, keeping the specification format, we can adapt the notion of models. To reestablish soundness of equational reasoning one can (i) exclude confusion or (ii) require that $\equiv$ is a congruence. Note that the common models of streams are free of confusion: final coalgebras [20], one-sided infinite words A^ω, and the function space $\mathbb{N} \to A$. In hidden algebras [15], confusion is often allowed but its negative effects are prevented by restricting to behavioral models [2], in which behavioral equivalence is a congruence: $s \equiv t \Rightarrow f(\ldots, s, \ldots) \equiv f(\ldots, t, \ldots)$.

Our results show that when $\equiv$ is required to be a congruence (or confusion is eliminated), then the complexity of the equality of bitstreams that are specified equationally jumps from the low level Π^0_2 of the arithmetical hierarchy to the level Π^1_1 of the analytical hierarchy, thereby exceeding the arithmetical hierarchy. Moreover, we show that even for behavioral specifications with confusion (as in [17]), equality of *streams of natural numbers* is Π^1_1-complete. Consequently, the results of [17] are valid only for bitstreams in combination with the behavioral equality discussed above. For general behavioral specifications (not the special case of stream specifications), the Π^1_1-completeness has been shown in [3].

Term rewriting systems are closely related to equational specifications. The complexity of deciding various standard properties of term rewriting systems, such as productivity, termination and confluence (Church–Rosser), has been investigated in [8, 10].

3. Bitstream Specifications

We will focus mainly on *streams*, one-sided infinite sequences of symbols, the prime example of coinductive structures. There are various ways of introducing streams: as functions $\mathbb{N} \to A$ mapping an index n to the n-th element of the stream, as final coalgebras over the functor $X \mapsto A \times X$, using coinductive types [12], or observational models [2]. All these definitions are equivalent in the sense that the resulting coalgebras are isomorphic.

For the model-theoretic semantics of equality, we will focus on specifications of bitstreams, streams over the alphabet $\{0, 1\}$. Due to their simplicity, bitstreams can be embedded in almost every non-trivial coinductive structure. Specifications of bitstreams are inherently sorted, with a sort B for bits, and a sort S for bitstreams. To this end, we introduce sorted terms. Let $\mathcal{S}$ be a set of sorts; an *$\mathcal{S}$-sorted set* C is a family of sets $\{C_s\}_{s\in\mathcal{S}}$. Let C and D be $\mathcal{S}$-sorted sets. Then an $\mathcal{S}$-sorted *function* (or *map*) from C to D is a function $f : C \to D$ such that $f(C_s) \subseteq D_s$ for all $s \in \mathcal{S}$, that is, a function that respects the sorts.

An $\mathcal{S}$-sorted signature Σ is a set of symbols $f \in \Sigma$, each having a type $(s_1, \ldots, s_n, s) \in \mathcal{S}^{n+1}$, denoted by $f :: s_1 \times \ldots \times s_n \to s$, where n is the arity of f. Let $\mathcal{X}$ be an $\mathcal{S}$-sorted set of *variables*. The $\mathcal{S}$-sorted set of *terms* $Ter(\Sigma, \mathcal{X})$ is inductively defined by:

- $\mathcal{X}_s \subseteq Ter(\Sigma, \mathcal{X})_s$ for every $s \in \mathcal{S}$, and
- $f(t_1, \ldots, t_n) \in Ter(\Sigma, \mathcal{X})_s$ if $f :: s_1 \times \ldots \times s_n \to s$, $f \in \Sigma$, and $t_1 \in Ter(\Sigma, \mathcal{X})_{s_1}, \ldots, t_n \in Ter(\Sigma, \mathcal{X})_{s_n}$.

An $\mathcal{S}$-sorted *equation* $\ell = r$ consists of terms $\ell, r \in Ter(\Sigma, \mathcal{X})_s \times Ter(\Sigma, \mathcal{X})_s$ for some $s \in \mathcal{S}$.

Definition 1. A *bitstream signature* Σ is an $\mathcal{S}$-sorted signature with $\mathcal{S} = \{B, S\}$ such that $0, 1, : \in \Sigma$ where $0, 1 :: B$ are called *bits*, and the infix symbol ':' of type $B \times S \to S$ is the *stream constructor*. An *equational bitstream specification* over Σ is a *finite* set E of equations over Σ.

From now on we let $\mathcal{S} = \{B, S\}$.

Definition 2. A *stream algebra* $\mathcal{A} = \langle A, [\![\cdot]\!]\rangle$ consists of:

(i) an $\mathcal{S}$-sorted domain A; $A_B = \{0, 1\}$ and $\varnothing \neq A_S \subseteq \{0,1\}^{\mathbb{N}}$,

(ii) for every $f :: s_1 \times \ldots \times s_n \to s \in \Sigma$ an *interpretation* $[\![f]\!] : A_{s_1} \times \ldots A_{s_n} \to A_s$,
(iii) $: \in \Sigma$ with $[\![:]\!](x, \sigma) = x : \sigma$,
(iv) $0, 1 \in \Sigma$ with $[\![0]\!] = 0$ and $[\![1]\!] = 1$.

The clause (iv) of the definition is optional; in fact, the results in this paper are independent of its presence. We have included it since the models where $[\![0]\!] = [\![1]\!]$ are trivial, in the sense that then all bitstreams are equal.

Definition 3. Let $\mathcal{A} = \langle A, [\![\cdot]\!]\rangle$ be a stream algebra. Moreover, let $\alpha : \mathcal{X} \to A$ be a variable assignment. As usual, the *interpretation of terms* $[\![\cdot]\!]^{\mathcal{A}}_{\alpha} : Ter(\Sigma, \mathcal{X}) \to A$ is defined inductively by:

$$[\![x]\!]^{\mathcal{A}}_{\alpha} = \alpha(x) \quad [\![f(t_1, \ldots, t_n)]\!]^{\mathcal{A}}_{\alpha} = [\![f]\!]([\![t_1]\!]^{\mathcal{A}}_{\alpha}, \ldots, [\![t_n]\!]^{\mathcal{A}}_{\alpha})$$

Then $\mathcal{A}$ is called a *(stream) model* of E if $[\![\ell]\!]_{\alpha} = [\![r]\!]_{\alpha}$ for every $\ell = r \in E$ and $\alpha : \mathcal{X} \to A$. We write $[\![\cdot]\!]_{\alpha}$ for $[\![\cdot]\!]^{\mathcal{A}}_{\alpha}$ whenever $\mathcal{A}$ is clear from the context. For ground terms $t \in Ter(\Sigma, \varnothing)$, we have $[\![t]\!]_{\alpha} = [\![t]\!]_{\beta}$ for all assignments α, β; we then write $[\![t]\!]$ for short.

Thus, we interpret function symbols as functions over bits and bitstreams as imposed by their sort. In particular, terms of type S are interpreted as bitstreams. In contrast to [17], our setup does not allow for *confusion* in the models. Recall that confusion means that the models can contain multiple representatives for the same stream.

Definition 4. We say that a model $\mathcal{A} = \langle A, [\![\cdot]\!]\rangle$ is *full* if its domain contains all bitstreams, $A_S = \{0, 1\}^{\mathbb{N}}$.

4. Turing Machines as Equational Specifications

We now define a set of standard equations (for bitstream specifications) that will be used throughout this paper:

$$\left.\begin{aligned} \mathsf{zeros} &= 0 : \mathsf{zeros} \qquad \mathsf{ones} = 1 : \mathsf{ones} \\ \mathsf{zip}_1(\tau) &= \tau \\ \mathsf{zip}_2(x : \tau_1, \tau_2) &= x : \mathsf{zip}_2(\tau_2, \tau_1) \\ \mathsf{zip}_n(\tau_1, \ldots, \tau_n) &= \mathsf{zip}_2(\tau_1, \mathsf{zip}_{n-1}(\tau_2, \ldots, \tau_n)) \quad (n > 2) \end{aligned}\right\} \quad (9)$$

To give an example, $\mathsf{zip}_3(\sigma, \tau, \rho) = \sigma(0) : \tau(0) : \sigma(1) : \rho(0) : \sigma(2) : \tau(1) : \sigma(3) : \rho(1) : \sigma(4) : \tau(2) : \ldots$, writing $\sigma(i)$ for the i'th entry of the stream σ.

We emphasize that all systems of equations in this paper are finite. To that end, we extend the specifications only by those equations from (9) that are needed by the specification, that is, the equations $\mathsf{zip}_n(\ldots) = \ldots$ for which a symbol zip_m with $n \leq m$ occurs in the specification.

Lemma 1. *In every stream model $\mathcal{A} = \langle A, [\![\cdot]\!]\rangle$ of a specification including the equations from (9) we have:*

(i) $[\![\mathsf{zeros}]\!] = 0^{\omega}$ *and* $[\![\mathsf{ones}]\!] = 1^{\omega}$,
(ii) for all $\sigma_1, \ldots, \sigma_k \in A_S$, $k \geq 2$ *and* $n \in \mathbb{N}$:
$[\![\mathsf{zip}_1]\!](\sigma_1) = \sigma_1$,
$[\![\mathsf{zip}_k]\!](\sigma_1, \ldots, \sigma_k)(2n) = \sigma_1(n)$
$[\![\mathsf{zip}_k]\!](\sigma_1, \ldots, \sigma_k)(2n + 1) = [\![\mathsf{zip}_{k-1}]\!](\sigma_2, \ldots, \sigma_k)(n)$

A *Turing machine* M is a quadruple $\langle Q, \Gamma, q_0, \delta\rangle$ consisting of a finite set of states Q, an initial state $q_0 \in Q$, a finite alphabet Γ containing a designated *blank* symbol $\square$, and a partial *transition function* $\delta : Q \times \Gamma \rightharpoonup Q \times \Gamma \times \{L, R\}$.

For convenience, we restrict Γ to the alphabet $\Gamma = \{0, 1\}$ where 0 is the blank symbol $\square$, and we denote Turing machines by triples $\langle Q, q_0, \delta\rangle$. As input for the Turing machines we typically use a unary number representation $11\ldots1$ (n-times) to encode the number n. Of course, another encoding is possible, as long as the encoding is computable, and the Turing machine is able to detect the end of the input (since 0 is part of the input alphabet and it is also the blank symbol).

We define a translation of Turing machines to equational specifications of bitstream functions, based on the standard translation to term rewriting systems from [24]. However, we represent the tape using streams instead of finite lists, and have one instead of four rules for 'extending' the tape. In particular, the equation for extending the tape is the equation for zeros from (9). The terms of the shape $q(\sigma, \tau)$ represent configurations of the Turing machine, where the stream τ contains the tape content below and right of the head, and σ the tape content left of the head. Notably, the head of the machine stands on the first symbol of τ.

Definition 5. Let $\mathsf{M} = \langle Q, q_0, \delta\rangle$ be a Turing machine. We define the specification E_{M} to consist of the following equations:

$$q(x, b : y) = q'(b' : x, y) \qquad \text{for every } \delta(q, b) = \langle q', b', R\rangle$$
$$q(a : x, b : y) = q'(x, a : b' : y) \qquad \text{for every } \delta(q, b) = \langle q', b', L\rangle$$

and for halting configurations additionally:

$$q(x, b : y) = b \qquad \text{whenever } \delta(q, b) \text{ undefined}$$

with the signature $\Sigma = \{0, 1, :\} \cup Q$ with types $q :: S \times S \to B$ for every symbol $q \in Q$, and $0, 1 :: B$ and ':' of type $B \times S \to S$. Moreover, we use R_{M} to denote the term rewriting system obtained from E_{M} by orienting all equations from left to right.

Apart from the additional rule for termination, the translation R_{M} is standard, and the rewrite rules model the transition relation of Turing machines in one-to-one fashion. So we take the liberty to define input of tuples $\langle n_1, \ldots, n_k\rangle \in \mathbb{N}^k$ and oracles directly on the term representations. We pass k-tuples $\langle n_1, \ldots, n_k\rangle \in \mathbb{N}^k$ of natural numbers as input to a Turing machine by choosing the following start configuration $q_0(\mathsf{zeros}, \mathsf{zip}_{k+1}(\underline{k}, \underline{n_1}, \ldots, \underline{n_k}))$ where $\underline{n}$ stands for $(1 :)^n$ zeros. The particular encoding of tuples is not crucial, but $\mathsf{zip}_{k+1}(\underline{k}, \underline{n_1}, \ldots, \underline{n_k})$ is for equational specifications more convenient than the Gödel encoding.

We obtain machines with oracles $\xi_1, \ldots, \xi_m \subseteq \mathbb{N}$ by writing the oracles elementwise interleaved on the tape left of the head:

Notation 1. *For $n \in \mathbb{N}$ we use $\underline{n}$ to abbreviate $(1 :)^n$: zeros. For $\xi \subseteq \mathbb{N}$, we let $\underline{\xi}$ denote the stream $\chi_{\xi}(0) : \chi_{\xi}(1) : \chi_{\xi}(2) : \ldots$ where χ_{ξ} is the characteristic function of ξ. We write $\vec{\alpha}$ short for $\alpha_1, \ldots, \alpha_k$ and $\underline{\vec{\alpha}}$ for $\underline{\alpha_1}, \ldots, \underline{\alpha_k}$ if k is clear from the context.*

For a term rewriting system R, we write $\to_R$ for a rewrite step with respect to R, and $\to^*_R$ is the reflexive-transitive closure of $\to_R$.

Definition 6. Let $\mathsf{M} = \langle Q, q_0, \delta\rangle$ be a Turing machine. Then for stream terms $\xi_1, \ldots, \xi_m :: S$ and $n_1, \ldots, n_k :: S$, we define

$$\mathsf{M}(\xi_1, \ldots, \xi_m; n_1, \ldots, n_k) :=$$
$$q_0(\mathsf{zip}_m(\xi_1, \ldots, \xi_m), \mathsf{zip}_{k+1}(\underline{k}, n_1, \ldots, n_k))$$

Definition 7. A Turing machine $\mathsf{M} = \langle Q, q_0, \delta\rangle$ *halts (with output b)* on inputs $n_1, \ldots, n_k \in \mathbb{N}$ with oracles $\xi_1, \ldots, \xi_m \subseteq \mathbb{N}$ if there is a rewrite sequence $\mathsf{M}(\underline{\xi_1}, \ldots, \underline{\xi_m}; \underline{n_1}, \ldots, \underline{n_k}) \to^*_{R_{\mathsf{M}}} b$, where $b \in \{0, 1\}$. Here $\underline{\xi}$ is short for the stream $\chi_{\xi}(0) : \chi_{\xi}(1) : \chi_{\xi}(2) : \ldots$ where χ_{ξ} is the characteristic function of ξ.

Note that the initial term is infinite due to the oracles, nevertheless we consider only finite reduction sequences. Due to the rules for zip_n and zeros, there are infinite rewrite sequences even if the Turing machine halts. However, R_{M} is orthogonal and therefore outermost-fair rewriting (or lazy evaluation) is normalizing, that is, computes the (unique) normal form $b \in \{0, 1\}$ if it exists.

Definition 8. A *k-ary predicate P with m oracles* is a relation $P \subseteq \wp(\mathbb{N})^m \times \mathbb{N}^k$. Then P is called *decidable* if there is a Turing machine M such that for all $\vec{\xi} \in \wp(\mathbb{N})^m$ and $\vec{n} \in \mathbb{N}^k$: M halts on input $\vec{n}$ with oracles $\vec{\xi}$, and the output is 1 if and only if $P(\vec{\xi}, \vec{n})$.

In correspondence with Definition 6 we define for $\xi_1, \ldots, \xi_m, n_1, \ldots, n_k \in \{0,1\}^\omega$, $[\![\mathsf{M}]\!](\xi_1, \ldots, \xi_m; n_1, \ldots, n_k)$ as shorthand for $[\![q_0]\!]([\![\mathsf{zip}_m]\!](\xi_1, \ldots, \xi_m),\ [\![\mathsf{zip}_{k+1}]\!]([\![\underline{k}]\!], n_1,\ \ldots,\ n_k))$. Then for the models of Turing machine specifications we have:

Lemma 2. *Let $P \subseteq \wp(\mathbb{N})^m \times \mathbb{N}^k$ be decidable, and $\mathsf{M} = \langle Q, q_0, \delta \rangle$ the corresponding Turing machine. Then in every stream model $\mathcal{A} = \langle A, [\![\cdot]\!] \rangle$ of a specification including the equations from* (9) *and E_M we have for every $\vec{\xi} \in \wp(\mathbb{N})^m$ and $\vec{n} \in \mathbb{N}^k$: $(\vec{\xi}, \vec{n}) \in P$ if and only if $[\![\mathsf{M}]\!](\xi_1, \ldots, \xi_m; n_1,\ \ldots,\ n_k) = 1$.*

Proof. P is decidable, hence $\mathsf{M}(\underline{\xi_1}, \ldots, \underline{\xi_m}; \underline{n_1},\ \ldots,\ \underline{n_k})$ has a nf in $\{0,1\}$, and the normal form is 1 if and only if $(\vec{\xi}, \vec{n}) \in P$. □

5. Levels of Undecidability

We briefly introduce complexity related notions that are relevant for this paper: promise problems, reducibility, hardness and completeness, and the arithmetical and the analytical hierarchy. For more details, we refer to the standard textbooks [18, 22].

Definition 9. Let $A \subseteq P \subseteq \mathbb{N}$. The *promise (membership) problem for A with promise P* is the question of deciding on the input of $n \in P$ whether $n \in A$. For the case $P = \mathbb{N}$, we speak of the *membership problem for A*.

We identify the membership problem for A with the set A itself, and the promise problem for A with promise P with the pair $\langle A, P \rangle$, also denoted by $A|_P$.

Definition 10. Let $A, B, P, Q \subseteq \mathbb{N}$. Then $A|_P$ *can be (many-one) reduced to* $B|_Q$, denoted $A \leq B$, if there exists a partial recursive function $f : \mathbb{N} \rightharpoonup \mathbb{N}$ such that $P \subseteq \mathit{domain}(f)$, $f(P) \subseteq Q$, and $\forall n \in P.\, n \in A \Leftrightarrow f(n) \in B$.

Definition 11. Let $B, Q \subseteq \mathbb{N}$ and $\mathcal{P} \subseteq \wp(\mathbb{N}) \times \wp(\mathbb{N})$. Then $B|_Q$ is called *$\mathcal{P}$-hard* if every $A|_P \in \mathcal{P}$ can be reduced to $B|_Q$. Moreover, $B|_Q$ is *$\mathcal{P}$-complete* if additionally $B|_Q$ can be reduced to some $A|_P \in \mathcal{P}$.

We stress that Definition 11 does not require that a $\mathcal{P}$-complete promise problem $B|_Q$ is member of $\mathcal{P}$ itself. This allows for classifying promise problem using the usual arithmetic and analytical hierarchy (for membership problems).

Lemma 3. *If $A|_P$ can be reduced to $B|_Q$ and $A|_P$ is $\mathcal{P}$-hard, then B is $\mathcal{P}$-hard.*

We use $\langle\!\langle\cdot\rangle\!\rangle$ to denote the well-known Gödel encoding of finite *lists* of numbers as elements of $\mathbb{N}$: $\langle\!\langle n_1, \ldots, n_k \rangle\!\rangle := p_1^{n_1+1} \cdot \ldots \cdot p_k^{n_k+1}$, where $p_1 < p_2 < \ldots < p_k$ are the first k prime numbers.
We define the arithmetical and analytical hierarchies:

Definition 12. Let $\Sigma^0_0 := \Pi^0_0 := \Delta^0_0$ be the collection of recursive sets of natural numbers (the decidable problems). Then for $n \geq 1$, we define:

- Σ^0_n consists of sets $\{n \mid \exists x \in \mathbb{N}.\, \langle\!\langle x, n \rangle\!\rangle \in B\}$ with $B \in \Pi^0_{n-1}$,
- Π^0_n consists of sets $\{n \mid \forall x \in \mathbb{N}.\, \langle\!\langle x, n \rangle\!\rangle \in B\}$ with $B \in \Sigma^0_{n-1}$,
- $\Delta^0_n := \Sigma^0_n \cap \Pi^0_n$.

The *arithmetical hierarchy* consists of the classes Π^0_n, Σ^0_n and Δ^0_n for $n \in \mathbb{N}$.

For example, the membership $a \in A$ for every set $A \in \Pi^0_2$ can be defined by a formula of the form $\forall x_1.\exists x_2.\forall x_3.P(a, x_1, x_2, x_3)$ where P is a decidable predicate.

The analytical hierarchy extends this classification of sets to formulas of the language of second-order arithmetic, that is, with set (or equivalently function) quantifiers. The following definition makes use of a result from recursion theory, see [18], stating that if there is at least one set quantifier, then two number quantifiers suffice (for functions quantifiers, one number quantifier suffices).

Definition 13. Let $\Sigma^1_0 := \Pi^1_0 := \Delta^1_0 = \bigcup_{n \in \mathbb{N}} \Pi^0_n$ be the set of all arithmetic predicates. A set $A \subseteq \mathbb{N}$ is in Π^1_n for $n > 0$ if there is a decidable predicate P with m oracles such that for all $a \in \mathbb{N}$:

$$a \in A \iff \forall \xi_1.\,\exists \xi_2. \ldots \exists \xi_m.\,\forall x_1.\,\exists x_2.\; P(\xi_1, \ldots, \xi_n, a, x_1, x_2)$$
$$a \in A \iff \forall \xi_1.\,\exists \xi_2. \ldots \forall \xi_m.\,\exists x_1.\,\forall x_2.\; P(\xi_1, \ldots, \xi_n, a, x_1, x_2)$$

for n even, and n odd, respectively. Here, $\xi_1, \ldots, \xi_m \subseteq \mathbb{N}$, the corresponding quantifiers are set quantifiers, and $x_1, x_2 \in \mathbb{N}$ with number quantifiers. Then A is in Σ^1_n, if the condition holds with all $\forall$ and $\exists$ quantifiers swapped. Finally, $\Delta^1_n = \Pi^1_n \cap \Sigma^1_n$.

6. Equality in Models

In this section we study the complexity of different model-theoretic semantics of equivalence of bitstream specifications. Based on the notion of models for bitstream specifications from Section 3, we first formalize the equivalences that we consider.

For all of the following model-theoretic equivalences, we have the choice whether or not we require the models to be full, that is, their domain contains all bitstreams. For example, we can consider the equality of terms in all models or in all full models:

Definition 14. Let E be a bitstream specification over Σ, and $s, t \in \mathit{Ter}(\Sigma, \mathcal{X})$ with $s, t :: S$. Then s and t are said to be

- *equal in all models of E* if
  $\mathcal{A} \models E$ implies $\mathcal{A} \models s = t$ for all stream algebras $\mathcal{A}$,
- *equal in all full models of E* if
  $\mathcal{A} \models E$ implies $\mathcal{A} \models s = t$ for all full stream algebras $\mathcal{A}$.

The set of solutions of a term s in a specification E is the set of interpretations $[\![s]\!]$ of s in all models satisfying E:

Definition 15. Let E be a bitstream specification over Σ, and $s \in \mathit{Ter}(\Sigma, \varnothing)$ with $s :: S$. Then the set of

- *solutions of s in E with respect to all models* is
  $$[\![s]\!]_E = \{\, [\![s]\!]^\mathcal{A} \mid \mathcal{A} \models E \,\},$$
- *solutions of s in E with respect to all full models* is
  $$[\![s]\!]_{E,\,\text{full}} = \{\, [\![s]\!]^\mathcal{A} \mid \mathcal{A} \text{ full}, \mathcal{A} \models E \,\}.$$

Here it suffices to consider only ground terms $s \in \mathit{Ter}(\Sigma, \varnothing)$. For terms $t \in \mathit{Ter}(\Sigma, \mathcal{X})$ with variables, the set of solutions can be defined as $[\![t]\!]_E = \{\, [\![t]\!]^\mathcal{A}_\alpha \mid \mathcal{A} \models E, \alpha : \mathcal{X} \to A \,\}$. However, then $[\![t]\!]_E = [\![s]\!]_E$ if s is the ground term obtained from t by interpreting the variables in t as fresh constants (formally, this amounts to an extension of the signature).

Definition 16. Let E_s and E_t be bitstream specifications over Σ_s and Σ_t, respectively. Let $s \in \mathit{Ter}(\Sigma_s, \varnothing)$ and $t \in \mathit{Ter}(\Sigma_t, \varnothing)$. Then s and t have

- *equal solutions over all models* if $[\![s]\!]_{E_s} = [\![t]\!]_{E_t}$,
- *equal solutions over all full models* if $[\![s]\!]_{E_s,\,\text{full}} = [\![t]\!]_{E_t,\,\text{full}}$.

Definition 17. Let E be bitstream specifications over Σ, and $s \in \mathit{Ter}(\Sigma, \varnothing)$. Then s is said to have

- *a unique solution over all models* if $|[\![s]\!]_E| = 1$,
- *a unique solution over all full models* if $|[\![s]\!]_{E,\,\text{full}}| = 1$,
- *a solution over all models* if $|[\![s]\!]_E| \geq 1$,
- *a solution over all full models* if $|[\![s]\!]_{E,\,\text{full}}| \geq 1$,
- *at most one solution over all models* if $|[\![s]\!]_E| \leq 1$,

– *at most one solution over all full models* if $|[\![s]\!]_{E,\text{full}}| \leq 1$.

6.1 Auxiliary Definitions

First, we define a few (systems of) equations that are repeatedly used throughout this section. The following function $\mathsf{is_{zeros}}$ that maps zeros to ones and every other bitstreams to zeros:

$$\left.\begin{aligned} \mathsf{is_{zeros}}(\mathsf{zeros}) = \mathsf{ones} \quad \mathsf{is_{zeros}}(0:\sigma) &= \mathsf{is_{zeros}}(\sigma) \\ \mathsf{is_{zeros}}(1:\sigma) &= \mathsf{zeros} \end{aligned}\right\} \qquad (10)$$

This function does exactly what its name suggests; it checks whether the argument is the stream of zeros. We use the bit 0 or the stream zeros for *false*, and 1 and ones for *true*.

We focus on specifications of bitstreams, and encode streams of natural numbers as bitstreams via the sequence of run-length of ones. For instance, the stream $3 : 1 : 0 : 2 : \ldots$ is encoded as $1:1:1:0:1:0:0:1:1:0:\ldots$. We then define functions uhd and utl that are the unary counterpart for head and tail on streams of natural numbers:

$$\left.\begin{aligned} \mathsf{uhd}(0:\sigma) &= \mathsf{zeros} & \mathsf{utl}(0:\sigma) &= \sigma \\ \mathsf{uhd}(1:\sigma) &= 1:\mathsf{uhd}(\sigma) & \mathsf{utl}(1:\sigma) &= \mathsf{utl}(\sigma) \end{aligned}\right\} \qquad (11)$$

For instance, we have

$$\mathsf{uhd}(1:1:1:0:1:0:0:1:1:\ldots) = 1:1:1:\mathsf{zeros}$$
$$\mathsf{utl}(1:1:1:0:1:0:0:1:1:\ldots) = 1:0:0:1:1:\ldots$$

The following lemma summarizes these properties:

Lemma 4. *In every stream model $\mathcal{A} = \langle A, [\![\cdot]\!]\rangle$ of a specification including the equations from* (10) *and* (11) *we have:*

(i) $[\![\mathsf{is_{zeros}}]\!](0^\omega) = 1^\omega$,
$[\![\mathsf{is_{zeros}}]\!](w) = 0^\omega$ *for every* $w \in A_S \setminus \{0^\omega\}$,
(ii) $[\![\mathsf{uhd}]\!](1^n\,0\,w) = 1^n\,0^\omega$ *for every* $w \in A_S$,
$[\![\mathsf{uhd}]\!](1^\omega) = 1^\omega$,
(iii) $[\![\mathsf{utl}]\!](1^n\,0\,w) = w$ *for every* $w \in A_S$.

Note that all interpretations are uniquely defined, apart from the combination $[\![\mathsf{utl}]\!](1^\omega)$ which can be any stream depending on the model. To avoid this case, we need means to ensure that a certain bitstream is a valid encoding of a stream of natural numbers, that is, the stream contains infinitely many zeros:

$$\left.\begin{aligned} \mathsf{natstr}(\mathsf{ones}) = \mathsf{zeros} \quad \mathsf{natstr}(0:\sigma) &= 1:\mathsf{natstr}(\sigma) \\ \mathsf{natstr}(1:\sigma) &= \mathsf{natstr}(\sigma) \end{aligned}\right\} \qquad (12)$$

Then an equation $\mathsf{natstr}(X) = \mathsf{ones}$ guarantees that $[\![X]\!]$ represents a stream of natural numbers:

Lemma 5. *In every stream model $\mathcal{A} = \langle A, [\![\cdot]\!]\rangle$ of a specification including the equations from* (12) *we have:* $[\![\mathsf{natstr}]\!](w) = 1^\omega$ *if and only if w contains infinitely many zeros.*

Proof. The equations on the right 'walk' over the stream, deleting 1's and converting 0's to 1's. If the stream contains infinitely many 0's, then an infinite stream of 1's will be produced. However, if some tail of the stream contains only 1's then the equation on the left ensures that the interpretation is unequal to 1^ω. □

Definition 18. Let $\mathsf{M} = \langle Q, q_0, \delta\rangle$ be a Turing machine. Then the *canonical model* $\mathcal{A} = \langle A, [\![\cdot]\!]\rangle$ for the union of the specifications E_M, (9), (10), (11) and (12) consists of the domain $A_S = \{0,1\}^\mathbb{N}$ with interpretations $[\![\cdot]\!]$ as given in Lemmas 4 and 5, extended by

(i) $[\![\mathsf{utl}]\!](1^\omega) = 1^\omega$,
(ii) for every $\xi_1, \ldots, \xi_m, n_1, \ldots, n_k \subseteq \mathbb{N}$:
$[\![q]\!](\vec{\xi}, \vec{n}) = 1$ whenever $[\![q]\!](\vec{\xi}, \vec{\underline{n}}) \to^* 1$, and
$[\![q]\!](\vec{\xi}, \vec{n}) = 0$ otherwise.

Lemma 6. *The canonical model is a model of the union of the equational specifications R_M,* (9), (10), (11) *and* (12).

Proof. The rewrite system R_M is orthogonal, consequently we have finitary confluence and infinitary unique normal forms [24]. Hence, we can employ a normal forms semantics for $[\![q]\!]$ (where we map terms without normal forms to 0). For the remaining equations, it is easy to see that the chosen semantics forms a model. □

6.2 Equality in all Models

For the complexity of equality in all models we obtain:

Theorem 1. *The following problem is Π^1_1-complete:*
INPUT: *Bitstream specification E, terms $s, t :: S$.*
QUESTION: *Are s and t equal in all models of E?*

Proof. The well-foundedness problem for decidable binary relations is known to be Π^1_1-complete, that is, the problem of deciding on the input of a decidable binary predicate $M \subseteq \mathbb{N} \times \mathbb{N}$ (given in the form of a Turing machine), whether M is well-founded. We reduce this problem to an equality problem. Let $M \subseteq \mathbb{N}\times\mathbb{N}$ be a decidable predicate, and $\mathsf{M} = \langle Q, q_0, \delta\rangle$ the corresponding Turing machine. We define the following specification E:

$$\mathsf{S} = \mathsf{is_{zeros}}(\mathsf{run}(1,\mathsf{X})) \qquad \mathsf{natstr}(X) = \mathsf{ones}$$
$$\mathsf{run}(0,\sigma) = \mathsf{ones}$$
$$\mathsf{run}(1,\sigma) = 0 : \mathsf{run}(\overbrace{\mathsf{M}(\mathsf{zeros}; \mathsf{uhd}(\sigma), \mathsf{uhd}(\mathsf{utl}(\sigma)))}^{\Phi(\sigma)}, \mathsf{utl}(\sigma))$$

together with the equations from E_M and (9), (10), (11) and (12). We prove that: $E \models \mathsf{S} = \mathsf{zeros}$ if and only if M is well-founded.

For '⇒' let M be non-well-founded, and $n_0\ M\ n_1\ M\ n_2\ M \ldots$ be an infinite chain. We construct a Σ-algebra $\mathcal{A} = \langle A, [\![\cdot]\!]\rangle$ such that $\mathcal{A} \models E$ but not $\mathcal{A} \models \mathsf{S} = \mathsf{zeros}$. We define $\mathcal{A}$ as an extension of the canonical model (Definition 18). The values of $[\![\Phi(\sigma)]\!]$ and $[\![\mathsf{utl}(\sigma)]\!]$ are determined by the canonical model, and together with the equations for run we obtain for every stream $\xi \in \{0,1\}^\omega$: $[\![\mathsf{run}]\!](0,\xi) = 1^\omega$, and $[\![\mathsf{run}]\!](1,\xi) = 0 : [\![\mathsf{run}]\!]([\![\Phi(\xi)]\!], [\![\mathsf{utl}]\!](\xi))$. Hence, there is a unique interpretation $[\![\mathsf{run}]\!]$ that results in a model for the equations of run. We define $\kappa_i = 1^{n_i}\,0\,1^{n_{i+1}}\,0\,1^{n_{i+2}}\ldots$ and we let $\underline{n} = 1^n\,0^\omega$. Then for $i \in \mathbb{N}$ we have

$$\begin{aligned}[\![\mathsf{run}]\!](1,\kappa_i) &= 0 : [\![\mathsf{run}]\!]([\![\Phi]\!](\kappa_i), \kappa_{i+1}) \\ &= 0 : [\![\mathsf{run}]\!]([\![\mathsf{M}]\!](\underline{n_i}, \underline{n_{i+1}}), \kappa_{i+1}) = 0 : [\![\mathsf{run}]\!](1, \kappa_{i+1})\end{aligned}$$

since we have that $[\![\mathsf{uhd}]\!](\kappa_j) = \underline{n_j}$ and $[\![\mathsf{utl}]\!](\kappa_j) = \kappa_{j+1}$ for all $j \in \mathbb{N}$ by Lemma 4. Thus, $[\![\mathsf{run}]\!](1,\kappa_0) = 0^\omega$. Let $[\![\mathsf{X}]\!] = \kappa_0$ and $[\![\mathsf{S}]\!] = 1^\omega$. Then $[\![\mathsf{natstr}]\!]([\![\mathsf{X}]\!]) = [\![\mathsf{ones}]\!]$ by Lemma 5, and $[\![\mathsf{S}]\!] = [\![\mathsf{is_{zeros}}]\!]([\![\mathsf{run}]\!](1,[\![\mathsf{X}]\!]))$ by Lemma 4. We have constructed a model, where $[\![\mathsf{S}]\!] = 1^\omega$, and, hence, $E \not\models \mathsf{S} = \mathsf{zeros}$.

For '⇐' let M be well-founded. Let $\mathcal{A}$ be a Σ-algebra such that $\mathcal{A} \models E$. We show that $[\![\mathsf{S}]\!] = 0^\omega$. Since $[\![\mathsf{natstr}]\!]([\![\mathsf{X}]\!]) = [\![\mathsf{ones}]\!]$, $[\![\mathsf{X}]\!]$ contains infinitely many zeros by Lemma 5. Thus, $[\![\mathsf{X}]\!] = 1^{n_0}\,0\,1^{n_1}\,0\,1^{n_2}\ldots$ for some $n_0, n_1, n_2, \ldots \in \mathbb{N}$. Let $\kappa_i = 1^{n_i}\,0\,1^{n_{i+1}}\,0\,1^{n_{i+2}}\ldots$ for $i \in \mathbb{N}$. Then

$$\begin{aligned}[\![\mathsf{run}]\!](1,\kappa_i) &= 0 : [\![\mathsf{run}]\!]([\![\mathsf{M}]\!](\underline{n_i}, \underline{n_{i+1}}), \kappa_{i+1}) \\ &= \begin{cases} [\![\mathsf{run}]\!](1,\kappa_{i+1}) & \text{if } [\![\mathsf{M}]\!](\underline{n_i}, \underline{n_{i+1}}) = 1 \\ [\![\mathsf{run}]\!](0,\kappa_{i+1}) = 1^\omega & \text{if } [\![\mathsf{M}]\!](\underline{n_i}, \underline{n_{i+1}}) = 0 \end{cases}\end{aligned}$$

Hence, $[\![\mathsf{run}]\!](1,[\![\mathsf{X}]\!]) = 0^\omega$ if and only if $[\![\mathsf{M}]\!](\underline{n_i}, \underline{n_{i+1}}) = 1$ for all $i \in \mathbb{N}$. However, this would contradict well-foundedness of M. As a consequence, we obtain that $[\![\mathsf{run}]\!](1,[\![\mathsf{X}]\!]) \neq 0^\omega$ and $[\![\mathsf{S}]\!] = \mathsf{is_{zeros}}([\![\mathsf{run}]\!](1,[\![\mathsf{X}]\!])) = 0^\omega$ by Lemma 4. This concludes the Π^1_1-hardness proof.

To show Π^1_1-membership, we resort to the Löwenheim–Skolem theorem. It states that if a formula of first-order predicate logic has an uncountable model, then it also has a countable model. Here, we employ that the domain A_S can be encoded as an arbitrary set with functions $[\![\mathsf{head}]\!] :: A_S \to \{0,1\}$ and $[\![\mathsf{tail}]\!] :: A_S \to A_S$ together with a first-order predicate logic formula that excludes confusion, that is, elements $a, b \in A_S$ with $[\![\mathsf{head}]\!][\![\mathsf{tail}]\!]^n(a) = [\![\mathsf{head}]\!][\![\mathsf{tail}]\!]^n(b)$ for all $n \in \mathbb{N}$ are required to be equal, that is, $a = b$. Likewise, the interpretations of the symbols in Σ can be translated to first-order predicates, and validity of the equations to first-order formulas. As a consequence, $\mathcal{A} \models E \wedge [\![s]\!] \neq [\![t]\!]$ can be expressed as first-order formula, and if it has a model, then also a countable one. Hence, it suffices in $\forall \mathcal{A}.\ \mathcal{A} \models E \Rightarrow [\![s]\!] = [\![t]\!]$ to quantify over countable models. For this purpose of quantifying over countable models, a set quantifier $\forall \mathcal{A} \subseteq \mathbb{N}$ suffices. This proves Π^1_1-membership. □

The following three results are obtained by slight adaptations of the proof of Theorem 1.

Theorem 2. *The following problems:*

INPUT: *Bitstream specification E, ground term $s :: S$.*
QUESTION: *Does s have (i) at most one solution, (ii) a solution, and (iii) a unique solution over all models of E?*

are (i) Π^1_1-complete, (ii) Σ^1_1-complete, and (iii) Π^1_1-hard, Σ^1_1-hard and strictly contained in Δ^1_2.

6.3 Equality in all Full Models

In Section 6.2 we have considered models whose domain was any non-empty set of bitstreams ($A_S \subseteq \{0,1\}^\omega$). However, when writing equations such as $\mathsf{even}(x : y : \tau) = x : \mathsf{even}(\tau)$, the intended semantics is often that these equations should hold for all streams, that is, in full models with domain $A_S = \{0,1\}^\omega$. We find that the restriction to full models results in a huge jump of the complexity, which then subsumes the entire analytical hierarchy.

To prepare for the proof, we introduce some auxiliary specifications. We define nat such that an equation $\mathsf{nat}(X) = \mathsf{ones}$ guarantees that the interpretation $[\![X]\!]$ represents a natural number in unary encoding, that is, $[\![X]\!] = 1^n\, 0^\omega$ for $n \in \mathbb{N}$, as follows:

$$\left.\begin{array}{ll} \mathsf{nat}(0:1:\sigma) = \mathsf{zeros} & \mathsf{nat}(1:\sigma) = \mathsf{nat}(\sigma) \\ \mathsf{nat}(0:0:\sigma) = \mathsf{nat}(0:\sigma) & \mathsf{nat}(\mathsf{ones}) = \mathsf{zeros} \end{array}\right\} \quad (13)$$

Lemma 7. *In every stream model $\mathcal{A} = \langle A, [\![\cdot]\!]\rangle$ of a specification including the equations from (13) we have: if $[\![\mathsf{nat}]\!](w) = 1^\omega$ then $w = 1^n\, 0^\omega$ for some $n \in \mathbb{N}$.*

Proof. If a stream is not of the format $1^n\, 0^\omega$ for some $n \in \mathbb{N}$ then it is 1^ω or contains $\ldots 01 \ldots$. The last equation rules out the case 1^ω (ensures that the interpretation is not 1^ω).

The first three equations are exhaustive in the sense that every stream can be matched by one of them. The first equation rules out streams that contain a 1 after a 0, and the equations two and three 'walk' step by step over the stream (proceed with the tail). □

We moreover define a function leq such that $\mathsf{leq}(X, Y) = \mathsf{ones}$ guarantees that pointwise $[\![X]\!] \leq [\![Y]\!]$:

$$\left.\begin{array}{l} \mathsf{leq}(0:\sigma, x:\tau) = \mathsf{leq}(\sigma,\tau) \\ \mathsf{leq}(1:\sigma, 1:\tau) = \mathsf{leq}(\sigma,\tau) \\ \mathsf{leq}(1:\sigma, 0:\tau) = \mathsf{zeros} \end{array}\right\} \quad (14)$$

Lemma 8. *In every stream model $\mathcal{A} = \langle A, [\![\cdot]\!]\rangle$ of a specification including the equations from (14) we have that if $[\![\mathsf{leq}]\!](\sigma,\tau) = 1^\omega$, then σ is pointwise $\leq$ than τ (for all $\sigma, \tau \in A_S$).*

Lemmas 7 and 8 are valid for non-full models as well. As explained in the introduction, the assumption of full models is crucial to guarantee that equations with variables have to hold for all streams (assigned to the variables) and not only the streams in the model.

Theorem 3. *The following problem subsumes the analytical hierarchy:*

INPUT: *Bitstream specification E, terms $s, t :: S$.*
QUESTION: *Are s and t equal in all* full *models of E?*

The idea of the proof is as follows. We translate formulas of the analytical hierarchy into stream specifications by representing $\forall$ set quantifiers by equations with variables. This simulates a quantification over all streams as the models are *full*, and the equations have to hold for all assignments of the variables.

The $\exists$ set quantifiers are eliminated in favor of Skolem functions f, that is, axioms of the form $\forall \vec{x}.\ \exists y.\ \psi(x_1, \ldots, x_n, y)$ are replaced by $\forall \vec{x}. \psi(x_1, x_2, \ldots, x_n, f(x_1, \ldots, x_n))$. The interpretation of these functions is determined by the model, and the question whether there exists a model corresponds to an existential quantification over all Skolem functions.

Proof. For every analytical set A, we reduce the membership problem in A to an equality problem. Every set A of the analytical hierarchy can be defined by

$$a \notin A \iff \qquad (15)$$
$$\forall \xi_1.\ \exists \xi_2.\ \forall \xi_3.\ \ldots \exists \xi_n.\ \forall x_1.\ \exists x_2.\ M(\xi_1, \ldots, \xi_n, a, x_1, x_2)$$

where $n \in \mathbb{N}$ is even (without loss of generality since $\Pi^1_n \subset \Pi^1_{n+1}$) and M a decidable predicate. Let $\mathsf{M} = \langle Q, q_0, \delta\rangle$ the Turing machine corresponding to M. Let $a \in \mathbb{N}$ be given. We define E to be the following system of equations:

$$\begin{aligned}
\mathsf{S}(\tau_1, \tau_3, \ldots, \tau_{n-1}) &= \mathsf{run}(1,\ \mathsf{zip}_n(\tau_1, \mathsf{g}_2(\tau_1), \tau_3, \mathsf{g}_4(\tau_1, \tau_3), \\
&\qquad \ldots, \tau_{n-1}, \mathsf{g}_n(\tau_1, \tau_3, \ldots, \tau_{n-1})),\ \mathsf{zeros}) \\
\mathsf{S}(\tau_1, \tau_3, \ldots, \tau_{n-1}) &= \mathsf{zeros} \\
\mathsf{run}(0, \tau, \gamma_1) &= \mathsf{ones} \\
\mathsf{run}(1, \tau, \gamma_1) &= 0 : \mathsf{run}(\mathsf{M}(\tau; A, \gamma_1, \mathsf{h}_2(\tau, \gamma_1)),\ \tau,\ 1 : \gamma_1) \\
A &= (1 :)^a\ \mathsf{zeros} \\
\mathsf{nat}(\mathsf{h}_2(\tau, \gamma_1)) &= \mathsf{ones}
\end{aligned}$$

together with the equations from E_{M}, (9), and (13). The symbols g_{2i} are typed $S^i \to S$. We claim: $E \models \mathsf{zeros} = \mathsf{ones}$ if and only if $a \in A$. For this purpose it suffices to show that the specification has a model ($\exists \mathcal{A}.\ \mathcal{A} \models E$) if and only if the formula in the right-hand side of (15) is valid.

The idea is that the specification models a Skolem normal form of the analytical formula in (15). The $\forall$ set quantifiers are modeled by an equation with stream variables; recall that equations have to hold for all assignments of the variables. In particular, the variables $\tau_1, \tau_3, \ldots, \tau_{n-1}$ in the first equation $\mathsf{S}(\tau_1, \tau_3, \ldots, \tau_{n-1}) = \ldots$ model the set quantifiers $\forall \xi_1, \ldots, \forall \xi_{n-1}$, respectively. The $\exists$ set quantifiers are modeled by Skolem functions $g_2, g_4, \ldots, g_n$ which in the specification are stream functions that get the value of the preceding $\forall$ quantifiers as arguments. These stream functions g_{2i} are unspecified and can be 'freely chosen' by the model $\mathcal{A}$. Thus, the existential quantification over the Skolem functions corresponds to the existential quantification over all models in $\exists \mathcal{A}.\ \mathcal{A} \models E$.

The streams $\tau_1, g_2(\tau_i), \ldots, \tau_{n-1}, g_n(\tau_1, \tau_3, \ldots, \tau_{n-1})$ that represent the values of the set quantifiers are then interleaved by zip_n, and passed as the second argument, named τ, to run; this argument serves as the left side of the tape for every invocation of the Turing machine M.

The $\forall x_1$ number quantifier is modeled by the third argument γ_1 of run. The initial value of γ_1 is zeros, and '$1 : \square$' is prepended (corresponding to counting up) each time the Turing machine halts with output 1. The number quantifier $\exists x_2$ is modeled by the Skolem function h_2 for which the equation $\mathsf{nat}(\mathsf{h}_2(\tau, \gamma_1)) = \mathsf{ones}$ ensures by Lemma 4 that the interpretation $[\![\mathsf{h}_2(\tau,\gamma_1)]\!]$ is a unary encoding of a natural number. Then the term $\mathsf{M}(\tau; A, \gamma_1, \mathsf{h}_2(\tau,\gamma_1))$ with $\tau = \mathsf{zip}_n(\tau_1, \mathsf{g}_2(\tau_1), \tau_3, \mathsf{g}_4(\tau_1,\tau_3), \ldots, \tau_{n-1}, \mathsf{g}_n(\tau_1,\tau_3,\ldots,\tau_{n-1}))$ corresponds precisely to $M(\xi_1,\ldots,\xi_n,a,x_1,x_2)$ in (15).

For '$\Leftarrow$', assume that the formula in (15) is valid. We construct a model $\mathcal{A} = \langle A, [\![\cdot]\!]\rangle$ as an extension of the canonical model (Definition 18). For $[\![g_2]\!], [\![g_4]\!], \ldots, [\![g_n]\!], [\![h_2]\!]$ we pick the Skolem functions for the quantifiers $\exists\xi_2, \exists\xi_4, \ldots, \exists\xi_n, \exists x_2$, respectively (where $[\![h_2]\!]$ is a stream function that works on the unary encoding of natural numbers). For $\sigma \in \{0,1\}^\omega$, we define $[\![\mathsf{nat}]\!](\sigma) = 1^\omega$ if σ is of the form $1^n\,0^\omega$, and 0^ω, otherwise. The definition of $[\![\mathsf{run}]\!]$ is analogous to the proof of Theorem 1. Finally, we define $[\![\mathsf{S}]\!](\tau_1,\tau_2,\ldots,\tau_{n-1}) = 0^\omega$ for all $\tau_1,\tau_2,\ldots,\tau_{n-1} \in \{0,1\}^\omega$, and $[\![A]\!] = 1^a\,0^\omega$. Then it is straightforward to verify that $\mathcal{A}$ is a model of the specification.

For '$\Rightarrow$', let $\mathcal{A} = \langle A, [\![\cdot]\!]\rangle$ be a model of the specification. Then we let the existential quantifiers $\exists\xi_2, \exists\xi_4, \ldots, \exists\xi_n$ and $\exists x_2$ in (15) behave according to the interpretations $[\![g_2]\!], [\![g_4]\!], \ldots, [\![g_n]\!], [\![h_2]\!]$, respectively (here the translation from sets $\xi \subseteq \mathbb{N}$ to streams $\underline{\xi}$ is as usual). Assume that there exists an assignment of the $\forall$ quantifiers $\forall\xi_1, \forall\xi_2, \ldots, \forall\xi_{n-1}$ and $\forall x_2$ for which the formula in (15) is not valid, that is, $M(\xi_1,\ldots,\xi_n,a,x_1,x_2)$ does not hold where the existential choices are governed by the model as described above. We translate this 'counterexample' back to the model by considering $[\![\mathsf{S}]\!](\underline{\xi_1},\underline{\xi_3}\ldots,\underline{\xi_{n-1}})$. As in the proof of Theorem 1, it is then straightforward to show that $[\![\mathsf{S}]\!](\underline{\xi_1},\underline{\xi_3}\ldots,\underline{\xi_{n-1}}) \neq 0^\omega$. However, this contradicts the assumption of $\mathcal{A}$ being a model due to the equation $\mathsf{S}(\tau_1,\tau_3,\ldots,\tau_{n-1}) = \mathsf{zeros}$. □

The proof of Theorem 3 immediately yields the following:

Theorem 4. *Each of the following problems (i), (ii), and (iii), subsume the analytical hierarchy:*

INPUT: *Bitstream specification E, ground term $t :: S$.*
QUESTION: *Does t have: (i) a solution, (ii) a unique solution, (iii) at most one solution, over all* full *models of E?*

6.4 Equality of Solutions

In this section, we study the complexity of deciding whether terms have the same set of solutions over all (full) models. It is easy to see that the hardness of these problems is at least that of deciding equality in all (full) models. When considering all models, the problem turns out Π^1_2-complete, and, thus, higher than the degree Π^1_1 of equality in all models.

Remark 2. Let us briefly discuss the applicability of equality in all (full) models for the comparison of terms s, t that are specified in independent specifications E_s and E_t. First, we rename the symbols of one of the specifications such that $\Sigma_s \cap \Sigma_t = \{0, 1, :\}$. Thereafter, we consider the validity of $s = t$ in the union $E_s \cup E_t$.

We show on two examples that this approach does not always yield the intended results. Let E_M consist of the single equation $M = 1 : M$, and E_N of

$$N = \mathsf{inv}(N) \quad \mathsf{inv}(0 : \sigma) = 1 : \mathsf{inv}(\sigma) \quad \mathsf{inv}(1 : \sigma) = 0 : \mathsf{inv}(\sigma)$$

Then M has the stream of ones as unique solution, but N has no solution. Since E_N does not have model, the union $E_M \cup E_N$ also does not admit one. Thus, $E_M \cup E_N \models M = N$ holds for trivial reasons. Nevertheless, we would not like to consider M and N as equivalent (at least if they are given by independent specifications).

Even if the specifications have unique solutions, a similar effect can occur. Let $M = \mathsf{zeros}$ and E_M consist of the equations

$$\mathsf{is}_{\mathsf{zeros}}(\mathsf{nxor}(\sigma)) = \mathsf{zeros}$$
$$\mathsf{nxor}(0:0:\sigma) = 1 : \mathsf{nxor}(\sigma) \quad \mathsf{nxor}(0:1:\sigma) = 0 : \mathsf{nxor}(\sigma)$$
$$\mathsf{nxor}(1:0:\sigma) = 0 : \mathsf{nxor}(\sigma) \quad \mathsf{nxor}(1:1:\sigma) = 1 : \mathsf{nxor}(\sigma)$$

together with the equations (10). Let $N = \mathsf{blink}$ and E_N consist of the equation $\mathsf{blink} = 0 : 1 : \mathsf{blink}$. Both specifications have models, and zeros and blink have unique solutions. For example, E_M admits a model whose domain consists of all eventually constant streams. However, E_M rules out models for which there exist elements $\sigma \in A_S$ with $[\![\mathsf{nxor}]\!](\sigma) = 0^\omega$. In particular, the stream $0101\ldots$ is excluded from the domain A_S. As a consequence, the union $E_M \cup E_N$ has no models, and $E_M \cup E_N \models \mathsf{zeros} = \mathsf{blink}$ holds.

As a consequence of the proof of Theorem 3, we obtain:

Theorem 5. *The following problem subsumes the analytical hierarchy:*

INPUT: *Bitstream specifications E_s, E_t, ground terms $s, t :: S$.*
QUESTION: *Do s and t have equal solutions over all* full *models, that is, $[\![s]\!]_{E_s,\mathit{full}} = [\![t]\!]_{E_t,\mathit{full}}$?*

We conclude this section with an investigation of the complexity of deciding whether two terms have the same set of solutions over all models. The proof of Theorem 1 yields only Π^1_1-hardness. In order to show Π^1_2-hardness, we employ a result of [4] stating that it is a Π^1_2-complete problem to decide whether the ω-language of a non-deterministic Turing machine contains all words $\{0,1\}^\omega$.

Therefore, we consider non-deterministic Turing machines with one-sides tapes. Without loss of generality, we may restrict the non-determinism $\delta : Q \times \Gamma \to \wp(Q \times \Gamma \times \{L, R\})$ to binary choices in each step, that is, $|\delta(q, b)| \leq 2$ for every $q \in Q$ and $b \in \{0, 1\}$. (Broader choices then are simulated by sequences of binary choices.) Moreover, for our purposes, it suffices to consider Turing machines that never halt. For the ω-language, halting always corresponds to rejecting a run, and this rejection can be simulated by alternating moving forth and back eternally.

That is, a non-deterministic Turing machine $\mathsf{M} = \langle Q, q_0, \delta_0, \delta_1\rangle$ has two transition functions $\delta_0, \delta_1 : Q \times \Gamma \to Q \times \Gamma \times \{L, R\}$ and we allow a non-deterministic choice between these functions in each step. Note that, for modeling non-determinism in an equational specifications, we cannot take the union of the specifications $E_{\langle Q, q_0, \delta_0\rangle}$ and $E_{\langle Q, q_0, \delta_1\rangle}$, since multiple equations having the same left-hand side do not model choice, but additional restrictions on the models of the specification. To this end, we introduce a third argument for the binary function symbols $q \in Q$ in Definition 5. This argument then governs the non-deterministic choice. In order to model one-sided tapes, we introduce a fourth argument that stores the position on the tape, and is increased, when moving right, and decreased, when moving left. That is, we adapt Definition 5 to:

$$q(x, b : y, i : z, p) = q'(b' : x, y, z, 1 : p)$$
$$q(a : x, b : y, i : z, 1 : p) = q'(x, a : b' : y, z, p)$$

for $\delta_i(q, b) = \langle q', b', R\rangle$ and $\delta_i(q, b) = \langle q', b', L\rangle$, respectively. We use E^n_{M} to denote this specification, and R^n_{M} for the corresponding term rewriting system. In the initial configuration, the third argument should be an underspecified stream, allowing for any non-deterministic choice. We pass zeros as fourth argument, thereby ensuring that the head cannot move to negative tape indices.

A *run* of M on an ω-word $w \in \{0,1\}^\omega$ is a R^n_{M} rewrite sequence starting from a term $q_0(\mathsf{zeros}, \underline{w}, \underline{N}, \mathsf{zeros})$ where $N \in \{0,1\}^\omega$ determines the non-deterministic choices; here $\underline{w}$ is the term $w(0) : w(1) : \ldots$ A run of M is *complete* if every tape position $p \geq 0$ is visited (that is, positions right of the starting position), and it is *oscillating* if some tape position is visited infinitely often. A run is *accepting* if it is complete and not oscillating, that it, it visits every position $p \geq 0$ at least once, but only finitely often.

Definition 19. The ω-language $\mathcal{L}^\omega(\mathsf{M})$ is the set of all ω-words $w \in \{0,1\}^\omega$ such that M has an accepting run w.

We employ the following result, which follows from [4]:

Theorem 6. *The set* $\{\mathsf{M} \mid \mathcal{L}^\omega(\mathsf{M}) = \{0,1\}^\omega\}$ *is* Π^1_2*-complete.*

We are now ready for the proof of Π^1_2-completeness of equality of the set of solutions over all models. In the proof, we introduce a fifth argument for the symbol $q \in Q$ in E^n_{M} which enforces progress (productivity) and rules out exactly the oscillating runs.

Theorem 7. *The following problem is* Π^1_2*-complete:*

INPUT: *Bitstream specifications* E_s, E_t, *ground terms* $s, t :: S$.

QUESTION: *Do* s *and* t *have equal solutions over all models equal, that is,* $[\![s]\!]_{E_s} = [\![t]\!]_{E_t}$?

Proof. Let $\mathsf{M} = \langle Q, q_0, \delta_0, \delta_1 \rangle$ be a non-deterministic Turing machine. We reduce the problem in Theorem 6 to a decision problem for the equality of the set of solutions over all full models. We let $s = \mathsf{X}$ and define the specification E_s to consist of:

$$q_0(\mathsf{zeros}, \mathsf{X}, \mathsf{N}, \mathsf{zeros}, P) = \mathsf{zeros} \tag{16}$$

$$\mathsf{natstr}(P) = \mathsf{ones} \tag{17}$$

$$q(x, b : y, i : z, p, 1 : v) = q'(b' : x, y, z, 1 : p, v) \quad \text{for } \delta_i(q,b) = \langle q', b', R \rangle \tag{18}$$

$$q(a : x, b : y, i : z, 1 : p, 1 : v) = q'(x, a : b' : y, z, p, v) \quad \text{for } \delta_i(q,b) = \langle q', b', L \rangle \tag{19}$$

$$q(x, y, z, 1 : p, 0 : v) = 0 : q(x, y, z, p, v) \tag{20}$$

$$q(x, y, z, 0 : p, 0 : v) = \mathsf{ones} \tag{21}$$

$$q(a : x, b : y, i : z, 0 : p, 1 : v) = \mathsf{ones} \quad \text{for } \delta_i(q,b) = \langle q', b', L \rangle \tag{22}$$

The equation (16) starts M on the stream X with non-deterministic choices governed by N and P for enforcing progress. The streams X and N are unspecified, thus arbitrary. The equation (17) ensures that $[\![P]\!]$ contains infinitely many zeros. The equations (18) and (19) model the computation of M as discussed before, but now in each step removing the context $1 : \square$ from the fifth argument. If the fifth argument starts with a 0, then (20) decrements the position counter (the fourth argument). Recall, the position counter determines how many steps the Turing machine M is permitted to move left. Thus, always eventually decrementing the counter rules out the oscillating runs. The equations (21) and (22) rule out models where the head move left of the envisaged progress $[\![P]\!]$.

It is important to note that for any non-oscillating run σ, we can define a function $p : \mathbb{N} \to \mathbb{N}$ such that after $p(n)$ steps, M visits only tape indices $\geq n$. Then an assignment $[\![P]\!] = 1^{p(0)}\,0\,1^{p(1)}\,0\,1^{p(2)}\,0\ldots$ in the model will permit this run to happen, that is, the head will never fall behind the envisaged progress and Equations (21) and (22) do not apply.

As a consequence, we have $[\![s]\!]_{E_s} = \{0,1\}^\omega$ if and only if for every $[\![\mathsf{X}]\!] \in \{0,1\}^\omega$ there exists a non-oscillating run (that is, an appropriate choice $[\![\mathsf{N}]\!]$) of M on $[\![\mathsf{X}]\!]$. Now we define $t = \mathsf{Y}$ and $E_t = \{\mathsf{Y} = \mathsf{Y}\}$ for which obviously $[\![t]\!]_{E_t} = \{0,1\}^\omega$. Therefore, $[\![s]\!]_{E_s} = [\![t]\!]_{E_t}$ if and only if $\mathcal{L}^\omega(\mathsf{M}) = \{0,1\}^\omega$. This concludes the proof of Π^1_2-hardness.

For Π^0_2-membership, the problem can be characterized by the following analytical formula: $\forall\langle\mathcal{A}_s, \mathcal{A}_t\rangle.\exists\langle\mathcal{A}'_s, \mathcal{A}'_t\rangle.(\mathcal{A}_s \models E_s \Rightarrow \mathcal{A}'_t \models E_t \wedge [\![s]\!]^{\mathcal{A}_s} = [\![t]\!]^{\mathcal{A}'_t}) \wedge (\mathcal{A}_t \models E_t \Rightarrow \mathcal{A}'_s \models E_s \wedge [\![t]\!]^{\mathcal{A}_t} = [\![s]\!]^{\mathcal{A}'_s})$. As in the proof of Theorem 1, here, it suffices to quantify over countable models. □

7. Equality for Behavioral Specifications

In this section we consider the notion of equality from [17] which is based on hidden algebras [16]. We introduce the hidden models of bitstream specifications as employed in [17], where it has been shown that deciding the equality of (equationally defined) streams, with respect to this semantics, is a Π^0_2-complete problem. We consider the following two extensions of this semantics:

(i) extending the semantics to streams over natural numbers, or

(ii) requiring the behavioral equivalence $\equiv$ to be a congruence.

We show that both extensions lift the complexity of deciding equality to the level Π^1_1 of the analytical hierarchy. If the specifications are required to be productive (thus, separating the problem of productivity [10] from that of equality) it can be shown that the complexity resides at Π^0_1 [13]. The results in [17] (as well as the results we mention in the current paper) are based on the comparison of non-productive specifications, and the proofs inherently encode productivity problems.

Let us briefly explain why the Π^1_1-completeness for the equality of bitstreams in Theorem 1 does not directly carry over the setup of [17]. The problem is the definition of the function natstr in (12) containing the equation $\mathsf{natstr}(\mathsf{ones}) = \mathsf{zeros}$. This equation does not work if we have confusion in the models and behavioral equivalence is not a congruence. In particular, as discussed in Section 2, if $\mathsf{ones}' = 1 : \mathsf{ones}'$, we cannot conclude that $\mathsf{natstr}(\mathsf{ones}') = \mathsf{zeros}$. As a consequence, with the behavioral specifications of [17] it is not possible to enforce that a bitstream always eventually contains a zero. However, if we consider behavioral specifications of streams of natural numbers, then we no longer need natstr, hence, reestablishing the Π^1_1-completeness result for the equality of streams of natural numbers specified behaviorally. There is a similar problem with the equation $\mathsf{is}_{\mathsf{zeros}}(\mathsf{zeros}) = \mathsf{ones}$, that, however, can be overcome by discarding $\mathsf{is}_{\mathsf{zeros}}$ as in the proof of Theorem 2.

7.1 Basic Setup

In [17], every bitstream specification contains the equations

$$\mathsf{head}(x : \sigma) = x \qquad\qquad \mathsf{tail}(x : \sigma) = \sigma$$

where $\mathsf{head} :: S \to B$ and $\mathsf{tail} :: S \to S$.

Definition 20. A *hidden* Σ*-algebra* $\mathcal{A} = \langle A, [\![\cdot]\!] \rangle$ consists of

(i) an $\mathcal{S}$-sorted domain A where $A_B = \{0,1\}$,

(ii) for every $f :: s_1 \times \ldots \times s_n \to s \in \Sigma$ an *interpretation* $[\![f]\!] : A_{s_1} \times \ldots A_{s_n} \to A_s$,

(iii) $0, 1 \in \Sigma$ with $[\![0]\!] = 0$ and $[\![1]\!] = 1$.

We stress that now A_S is an *arbitrary* set.

Definition 21. Let $\mathcal{A} = \langle A, [\![\cdot]\!] \rangle$ be a hidden Σ-algebra. Then $\sigma, \tau \in A_S$ are called *behaviorally equivalent*, denoted by $\sigma \equiv \tau$, if they are indistinguishable with $\{\mathsf{head}, \mathsf{tail}\}$-experiments, that is:

$$\sigma \equiv \tau \iff \forall n \in \mathbb{N}.\ [\![\mathsf{head}]\!]([\![\mathsf{tail}]\!]^n(\sigma) = [\![\mathsf{head}]\!]([\![\mathsf{tail}]\!]^n(\tau)$$

On the domain A_B, we let $\equiv$ be the identity relation.

Note that $\equiv$ is a not a congruence (only for $[\![\mathsf{head}]\!]$ and $[\![\mathsf{tail}]\!]$).

Definition 22. Let E be a bitstream specification over Σ. A hidden Σ-algebra *behaviorally satisfies* E, denoted $\mathcal{A} \models E$, if for every equation of E, the left- and right-hand sides are behaviorally equivalent: $[\![\ell]\!]_\alpha \equiv [\![r]\!]_\alpha$ for every $\ell = r \in E$ and $\alpha : \mathcal{X} \to A$. We say that an equation $\ell = r$ is *behaviorally satisfied in all hidden models of* E, denoted $E \models \ell = r$ if $\mathcal{A} \models E$ implies $\mathcal{A} \models \ell = r$ for every hidden Σ-algebra $\mathcal{A}$.

For a discussion of this semantics, we refer to Section 2.

7.2 Behavioral Equivalence as Congruence

We now adapt the basic setup by requiring $\equiv$ to be a *congruence relation*, that is, $s \equiv t$ implies $f(\ldots, s, \ldots) \equiv f(\ldots, t, \ldots)$. The resulting models are called *behavioral* in [2].

Definition 23. A hidden Σ-algebra is called *behavioral* if $\equiv$ is a congruence relation. For a bitstream specification E over Σ, we say that $\ell = r$ *is behaviorally satisfied in all behavioral models of* E if $\mathcal{A} \models E \Rightarrow \mathcal{A} \models \ell = r$ for every behavioral hidden Σ-algebra $\mathcal{A}$.

Theorem 8. *The following problem is* Π^1_1*-complete:*

INPUT: *Bitstream specification* E*, terms* $s, t :: S$.

QUESTION: *Is* $s = t$ *satisfied in all behavioral models of* E*?*

Proof. We show: the equation $s = t$ is behaviorally satisfied in all behavioral models of E if and only if $s = t$ holds in all models of E; the latter property is Π^1_1-complete by Theorem 1.

The direction '$\Leftarrow$' follows immediately, since every Σ-algebra is a behavioral hidden Σ-algebra. For '$\Rightarrow$', let $\mathcal{A} = \langle A, [\![\cdot]\!]\rangle$ be a hidden Σ-algebra. Let $\mathcal{A}/_{\equiv} = \langle A/_{\equiv}, [\![\cdot]\!]/_{\equiv}\rangle$ be the quotient algebra. That is, $A/_{\equiv}$ are the congruence classes of A with respect to $\equiv$. For symbols $f \in \Sigma$ and $B_1, \ldots, B_{ar(f)} \in A/_{\equiv}$, we define $[\![f]\!]/_{\equiv}(B_1, \ldots, B_{ar(f)}) = B$ if $[\![f]\!](b_1, \ldots, b_{ar(f)}) = b$ for $b_1 \in B_1, \ldots, b_{ar(f)} \in B_{ar(f)}$, and B is the congruence class of b with respect to $\equiv$. The quotient algebra $\mathcal{A}/_{\equiv}$ is a behavioral hidden Σ-algebra that, due to $\equiv$ being a congruence, behaviorally satisfies the same equations as $\mathcal{A}$. Let $\mathcal{A}'$ be the Σ-algebra obtained from $\mathcal{A}/_{\equiv}$ by renaming the domain elements into the streams they represent, that is, $a \in (\mathcal{A}/_{\equiv})_S$ becomes $[\![\mathsf{head}]\!](a) : [\![\mathsf{head}]\!]([\![\mathsf{tail}]\!](a)) : \ldots$. Then $[\![:]\!](x, \sigma) = x : \sigma$, since in $\mathcal{A}/_{\equiv}$ every stream has a unique representative in the model. Hence, $\mathcal{A}'$ is a stream algebra. Moreover, for elements a, b of the domain of $\mathcal{A}/_{\equiv}$, we have $a \equiv b$ iff $a = b$. Hence, $\mathcal{A}'$ is a model of an equation $s = t$ if and only if $s = t$ is behaviorally satisfied in $\mathcal{A}$. □

7.3 Streams of Natural Numbers

We briefly study hidden models with confusion, described in Section 2, for streams of natural numbers. A $\mathbb{N}$*-stream specification* is now defined like a bitstream specification, except the sorts are $\mathcal{S} = \{N, S\}$, and the symbols are $0 :: N$, $s :: N \to N$ and ':' of type $N \times S \to S$. We adapt the definition of hidden Σ-algebras accordingly.

Definition 24. A *hidden* Σ*-algebra* $\mathcal{A} = \langle A, [\![\cdot]\!]\rangle$ consists of

(i) an $\mathcal{S}$-sorted domain A and $A_N = \mathbb{N}$,

(ii) for every $f :: s_1 \times \ldots \times s_n \to s \in \Sigma$ an *interpretation* $[\![f]\!] : A_{s_1} \times \ldots A_{s_n} \to A_s$,

(iii) $0, s \in \Sigma$ with $[\![0]\!] = 0$ and $[\![s]\!](x) = x + 1$,

(iv) for every $s \in A_S$ there are $n \in \mathbb{N}$ and $s' \in A_S$ such that we have $s = [\![:]\!](b, s')$; see further Remark ??.

The definitions of behavioral equivalence and satisfaction are the same as for bitstream specifications. A slight modification of the proof of Theorem 2 results in the following.

Theorem 9. *The following problem is* Π^1_1*-complete:*

INPUT: $\mathbb{N}$*-stream specification* E*, terms* $s, t :: S$.

QUESTION: *Does* $E \models s = t$ *hold? That is, is* $s = t$ *behaviorally satisfied in all hidden models of* E*?*

Proof. We reduce the well-foundedness problem for decidable binary relations to an equality problem. Let $M \subseteq \mathbb{N} \times \mathbb{N}$ be a decidable predicate, and $\mathsf{M} = \langle Q, q_0, \delta\rangle$ the corresponding Turing machine. We define the following specification E:

$$\mathsf{zeros} = \mathsf{run}(1, \mathsf{X}) \qquad \mathsf{unary}(0) = \mathsf{zeros}$$
$$\mathsf{run}(0, \sigma) = \mathsf{ones} \qquad \mathsf{unary}(s(x)) = 1 : \mathsf{unary}(x)$$
$$\mathsf{run}(1, \sigma) = 0 : \mathsf{run}(\mathsf{M}(\mathsf{zeros}; \mathsf{unary}(\mathsf{head}(\sigma)), \mathsf{unary}(\mathsf{head}(\mathsf{tail}(\sigma)))), \mathsf{tail}(\sigma))$$

together with the equations from E_{M} and (9). In contrast with the proof of Theorem 2, X is now a stream of natural numbers. Since X is unspecified, its interpretation in the model can be an arbitrary stream of natural numbers. As in the proofs of Theorems 1 and 2, we employ X to guess an infinite path through M. Instead of $\mathsf{uhd}(\cdot)$ and $\mathsf{utl}(\cdot)$ on bitstreams, we now take $\mathsf{unary}(\mathsf{head}(\cdot))$ and $\mathsf{tail}(\cdot)$, respectively, where the function unary converts natural numbers to unary representations in forms of streams. As in the proof of Theorem 2, it follows that there exists a hidden Σ-algebra $\mathcal{A}$ with $\mathcal{A} \models E$ if and only if M is not well-founded. Thus, $E \models \mathsf{zeros} = \mathsf{ones}$ if and only if M is well-founded. □

8. Equivalence of Lambda Terms

In this section we investigate the complexity of deciding the equality of λ-terms with respect to the observational equivalences $=_{nf}$, $=_{hnf}$ and $=_{whnf}$ as introduced in Section 1. Furthermore, we study the complexity of deciding whether two λ-terms have the same Böhm trees or Lévy–Longo trees. The interested reader is referred to [1, 7] for an introduction to Böhm trees, and to [6] for a thorough study of the observational equivalences on λ-terms.

Definition 25. Let M be a λ-term. The *Böhm tree* $\mathsf{BT}(M)$ *of* M is a potentially infinite term defined as follows. If M has no hnf, then $\mathsf{BT}(M) = \bot$. Otherwise, there is a head reduction $M \to_h^* \lambda x_1 \ldots \lambda x_n . y M_1 \ldots M_m$ to head normal form. Then we define $\mathsf{BT}(M) = \lambda x_1 \ldots \lambda x_n . y \mathsf{BT}(M_1) \ldots \mathsf{BT}(M_m)$.

Definition 26. Let M be a λ-term. The *Lévy–Longo tree* $\mathsf{LT}(M)$ *of* M is a potentially infinite term defined as follows:

$$\begin{aligned} \mathsf{LT}(M) &= \bot && \text{if } M \text{ has no whnf} \\ \mathsf{LT}(M) &= \lambda x . \mathsf{LT}(N) && \text{if } M \to_h^* \lambda x . N \\ \mathsf{LT}(M) &= x \mathsf{LT}(M_1) \ldots \mathsf{LT}(M_m) && \text{if } M \to_h^* x M_1 \ldots M_m \end{aligned}$$

For the observational equivalences we obtain:

Theorem 10. *For each* $=_? \in \{=_n, =_h, =_w\}$*, the following problem is* Π^0_2*-complete:*

INPUT: λ*-terms* M, N.

QUESTION: *Does* $M =_? N$ *hold?*

Proof. First, we show Π^0_2-membership of the problem. We consider $=_n$ ($=_h$ and $=_w$ work analogously). A λ-term Q has a normal form if and only if Q admits a standard reduction $\to_{std}^*$ to a normal form, see [1]. For a λ-term Q, and $n \in \mathbb{N}$, we write $Q \to_{std}^{\leq n} nf$ to denote that Q rewrites to a normal form within $\leq n$ steps of standard reduction. Note that this is a decidable property. Then we claim:

$$M =_n N \iff \qquad (23)$$
$$\forall C. \forall n. \exists m. \left(C[M] \to_{std}^{\leq n+m} nf \Leftrightarrow C[N] \to_{std}^{\leq n+m} nf\right)$$

For '$\Rightarrow$' in (23), assume that $M =_n N$. Let C be a context. We distinguish the following cases:

(i) Assume that $C[M]$ has a normal form. Then $C[N]$ has one, and $C[M] \to_{std}^{k} nf$ and $C[N] \to_{std}^{\ell} nf$ for some $k, \ell \in \mathbb{N}$. Then in (23) for any $n \in \mathbb{N}$ we can choose $m = \max(k, \ell)$.

(ii) The case that $C[N]$ has a normal form is symmetric to (i).

(iii) If neither $C[M]$ nor $C[N]$ have a normal form, then neither $C[M] \to_{std}^{\leq n+m} nf$ nor $C[N] \to_{std}^{\leq n+m} nf$ for any $n, m \in \mathbb{N}$.

For '$\Leftarrow$' in (23), assume $M \neq_n N$. Then there is a context C such that exactly one of the terms $C[M]$ and $C[N]$ has a normal form; without loss of generality, assume $C[M] \to_{std}^{\leq n} nf$ for some $n \in \mathbb{N}$. Hence, $C[M] \to_{std}^{\leq n+m} nf$ for every $m \in \mathbb{N}$, but $C[N] \to_{std}^{\leq n+m} nf$ for no $m \in \mathbb{N}$. Thus, the right-hand side of (23) is not satisfied.

From (23) it follows that $=_n$ is in Π^0_2, since the two quantifiers $\forall C$ and $\forall n$ can be merged into a single $\forall$-quantifier.

We now proceed with proving Π^0_2-hardness of the problem. Let T be a Turing machine, and let T be a λ-term such that for all $n, m \in \mathbb{N}$, $T\,\underline{n}\,\underline{m}$ rewrites to K if T terminates on input n within m steps, and to KI, otherwise. Here, $\mathsf{K} = \lambda xy.x$ and $\mathsf{I} = \lambda x.x$ are the usual combinators, and $\underline{k} = \lambda f.\lambda x.f^n x$ is the Church numeral representing the natural number $k \in \mathbb{N}$. The construction of such T is standard, see [1]. Now we define:

$$M = (\lambda x.\lambda a.a(xx))(\lambda x.\lambda a.a(xx))$$

$$N = N'N'\mathsf{zer} \qquad N' = \lambda xn.T'n\,\mathsf{zer}(\lambda a.a(xx(\mathsf{succ}\,n)))$$

$$T' = T''T'' \qquad T'' = \lambda xnm.Tnm\mathsf{I}(xxn(\mathsf{succ}\,m))$$

$$\mathsf{zer} = \lambda fx.x \qquad \mathsf{succ} = \lambda zfx.f(zfx)$$

We show that $M =_? N$ if and only if T halts on all $n \in \mathbb{N}$. Note that $T'\underline{n}\,\underline{m} \to^* \mathsf{I}$ if $T\underline{n}\,\underline{m} \to^* \mathsf{K}$, that is, if T terminates on input n in m steps; otherwise $T'\underline{n}\,\underline{m} \to^* T'\underline{n}\,(\underline{m+1})$. Hence, we obtain

$$T'\underline{n}\,\underline{0} \to^* \mathsf{I} \iff \mathsf{T} \text{ halts on input } n$$
$$\iff T'\underline{n}\,\underline{0} \text{ has a (weak) head normal form}$$

The Lévy–Longo tree of M is $\lambda a.a(\lambda a.a(\lambda a.a\ldots))$. If T halts on input n, we have

$$N'N'\underline{n} \to^* T'\underline{n}\,\mathsf{zer}(\lambda a.a(N'N'\underline{n+1})) \to^* \lambda a.a(N'N'\underline{n+1})$$

Thus if T terminates on all $n \in \mathbb{N}$, then the Lévy–Longo trees of M and N are equal, and, hence, by [6] we have $M =_w N$, $M =_h N$ and $M =_n N$. Otherwise, let $n \in \mathbb{N}$ be minimal such that T does not halt on n. Then by the above, we have:

$$N \to^* \underbrace{\lambda a.\,a(\lambda a.\,a(\ldots \lambda a.\,a}_{n\text{-times}}(N'N'\underline{n})\ldots))$$

Then $N\mathsf{I}^n \to^* N'N'\underline{n}$ has no (weak) head normal form, but $M\mathsf{I}^n$ has. Thus we have $M \neq_n N$, $M \neq_h N$ and $M \neq_w N$. This proves Π^0_2-hardness. □

The proof immediately yields the following result:

Theorem 11. *The following problems are Π^0_2-complete:*
INPUT: *λ-terms M, N.*
QUESTION: *(i) Do s and t have equal Böhm trees?*
(ii) Do s and t have equal Lévy–Longo trees?

Proof. Follows immediately from the proof of Theorem 10 since M and N are observationally equal if and only if they have the same Lévy–Longo tree, and for M and N the Lévy–Longo trees coincide with their Böhm trees. □

We mention that for Berarducci trees, the proof of Theorem 10 implies Π^0_2-hardness. It is not difficult to see that the problem of deciding the equality of Berarducci trees is in Π^0_3. We leave the determination of the precise complexity to future work.

9. Conclusions

We have investigated different model-theoretic and rewriting based semantics of equality of infinite objects, specified either by systems of equations or by λ-terms. It turns out that the complexities for these notions vary from the low levels of the arithmetical hierarchy Π^0_1 and Π^0_2, up to Π^1_1 and Π^1_2 of the analytical hierarchy, and some even subsume the entire arithmetical and analytical hierarchy. In particular, the observational equivalences of λ-terms, that are of interest for functional programming, are all Π^0_2-complete.

Apart from Π^0_1, none of these classes are recursively enumerable or co-recursively enumerable. Thus, there exists no complete proof systems for proving or for disproving equality. An exception is the equality of normal forms for productive specifications for which inequalities can be recursively enumerated [13].

References

[1] H. P. Barendregt. *The Lambda Calculus, its Syntax and Semantics.* North-Holland, 1984.

[2] M. Bidoit, R. Hennicker, and A. Kurz. Observational Logic, Constructor-based Logic, and Their Duality. *Theor. Comput. Sci.*, 298:471–510, 2003.

[3] S. R. Buss and G. Rosu. Incompleteness of Behavioral Logics. *ENTCS*, 33:61–79, 2000.

[4] J. Castro and F. Cucker. Nondeterministic ω-Computations and the Analytical Hierarchy. *Logik u. Grundlagen d. Math*, 35:333–342, 1989.

[5] T. Coquand. Infinite Objects in Type Theory. In *Postproc. Conf. on Types for Proofs and Programs (TYPES 1993)*, volume 806 of *LNCS*, pages 62–78. Springer, 1993.

[6] M. Dezani-Ciancaglini and E. Giovannetti. From Böhm's Theorem to Observational Equivalences: an Informal Account. In *BOTH'01*, volume 50 of *ENTCS*, 2001.

[7] M. Dezani-Ciancaglini, P. Severi, and F.-J. de Vries. Böhm's theorem for Berarducci trees. In *CATS 2000 Computing: the Australasian Theory Symposium*, volume 31 of *ENTCS*, 2000.

[8] J. Endrullis, H. Geuvers, J. G. Simonsen, and H. Zantema. Levels of Undecidability in Rewriting. *Information and Computation*, 209(2):227–245, 2011.

[9] J. Endrullis, C. Grabmayer, and D. Hendriks. Data-Oblivious Stream Productivity. In *Proc. Conf. on Logic for Programming Artificial Intelligence and Reasoning (LPAR 2008)*, number 5330 in LNCS, pages 79–96. Springer, 2008.

[10] J. Endrullis, C. Grabmayer, and D. Hendriks. Complexity of Fractran and Productivity. In *Proc. Conf. on Automated Deduction (CADE 22)*, volume 5663 of *LNCS*, pages 371–387, 2009.

[11] D. P. Friedman and D. S. Wise. CONS Should Not Evaluate its Arguments. In *ICALP*, pages 257–284, 1976.

[12] H. Geuvers. Inductive and Coinductive Types with Iteration and Recursion. In *Proc. Workshop on Types for Proofs and Programs (TYPES 1992)*, pages 193–217, 1992.

[13] C. Grabmayer, J. Endrullis, D. Hendriks, J. W. Klop, and L. S. Moss. Automatic Sequences and Zip-Specifications. In *Proc. Symp. on Logic in Computer Science (LICS 2012)*. IEEE Computer Society, 2012. To appear.

[14] P. Henderson and J. H. Morris, Jr. A Lazy Evaluator. In *Proc. ACM SIGACT-SIGPLAN Symp. on Principles on programming languages (POPL)*, pages 95–103. ACM, 1976.

[15] G. Malcolm. Hidden Algebra and Systems of Abstract Machines. In *Proc. Symp. on New Models for Software Architecture (IMSA)*, 1997.

[16] G. Roşu. *Hidden Logic.* PhD thesis, University of California, 2000.

[17] G. Roşu. Equality of Streams is a Π^0_2-complete Problem. In *Proc. ACM SIGPLAN Conf. on Functional Programming (ICFP)*, pages 184–191. ACM, 2006.

[18] H. Rogers, Jr. *Theory of Recursive Functions and Effective Computability.* McGraw-Hill, New York, 1967.

[19] J. J. M. M. Rutten. Behavioural Differential Equations: a Coinductive Calculus of Streams, Automata, and Power Series. *Theor. Comput. Sci.*, 308(1-3):1–53, 2003.

[20] J. J. M. M. Rutten. A Tutorial on Coinductive Stream Calculus and Signal Flow Graphs. *Theor. Comput. Sci.*, 343:443–481, 2005.

[21] D. Sangiorgi and J. J. M. M. Rutten. *Advanced Topics in Bisimulation and Coinduction.* Cambridge University Press, 2012.

[22] J. R. Shoenfield. *Degrees of Unsolvability.* North-Holland, 1971.

[23] B. A. Sijtsma. On the Productivity of Recursive List Definitions. *ACM Transactions on Programming Languages and Systems*, 11(4):633–649, 1989.

[24] Terese. *Term Rewriting Systems.* Cambridge University Press, 2003.

[25] M. Walicki and S. Meldal. Nondeterminism vs. underspecification. In *Proc. of the World Multiconference on Systemics, Cybernetics and Informatics*, ISAS-SCI 2001, pages 551–555. IIIS, 2001.

Automatic Amortised Analysis of Dynamic Memory Allocation for Lazy Functional Programs

Hugo Simões
Pedro Vasconcelos
Mário Florido
LIACC, Universidade do Porto,
Porto, Portugal
{hrsimoes,pbv,amf}@dcc.fc.up.pt

Steffen Jost
Ludwig Maximillians Universität,
Munich, Germany
jost@tcs.ifi.lmu.de

Kevin Hammond
University of St Andrews,
St Andrews, UK
kh@cs.st-andrews.ac.uk

Abstract

This paper describes the first successful attempt, of which we are aware, to define an automatic, type-based static analysis of resource bounds for lazy functional programs. Our analysis uses the automatic amortisation approach developed by Hofmann and Jost, which was previously restricted to eager evaluation. In this paper, we extend this work to a lazy setting by capturing the costs of unevaluated expressions in type annotations and by amortising the payment of these costs using a notion of *lazy potential*. We present our analysis as a proof system for predicting heap allocations of a minimal functional language (including higher-order functions and recursive data types) and define a formal cost model based on Launchbury's natural semantics for lazy evaluation. We prove the soundness of our analysis with respect to the cost model. Our approach is illustrated by a number of representative and non-trivial examples that have been analysed using a prototype implementation of our analysis.

Categories and Subject Descriptors D.3.2 [*Programming Languages*]: Functional Languages

Keywords lazy evaluation, resource analysis, amortisation, type systems

1. Introduction

Non-strict functional programming languages, such as Haskell [36], offer important benefits in terms of modularity and abstraction [23]. A key practical obstacle to their wider use, however, is that extra-functional properties, such as time- and space-behaviour, are often difficult to determine prior to actually running the program. Recent advances in static cost analyses, such as *sized-timed types* [43, 44] and *type-based amortisation* [18, 19] have enabled the *automatic* prediction of resource bounds for eager functional programs, including uses of higher-order functions [29]. This paper extends type-based amortisation to lazy evaluation, describing a static analysis for determining *a-priori* worst-case bounds on execution costs (specifically, dynamic memory allocations).

ICFP'12, September 9–15, 2012, Copenhagen, Denmark.

This paper makes the following novel contributions:

a) we present the first successful attempt, of which we are aware, to produce an automatic, type-based, static analysis of resource bounds for lazy evaluation;

b) we introduce a cost model for heap allocations for a minimal lazy functional language based on Launchbury's natural semantics for lazy evaluation [30], and use this as the basis for developing a resource analysis;

c) we have proved the soundness of our analysis with respect to the cost-instrumented semantics (due to space limitations, we present only a proof sketch); and

d) we provide results from a prototype implementation to show the applicability of our analysis to some non-trivial examples.*

Our amortised analysis derives costs with respect to a cost semantics for lazy evaluation that derives from Launchbury's natural operational semantics of graph reduction. It deals with both first-order and higher-order functions, but does not consider polymorphism. For simplicity, we restrict our attention to heap allocations†, but previous results have shown that the amortised analysis approach also extends to other countable resources, such as worst-case execution time [28]. In order to ensure a good separation of concerns, our analysis assumes the availability of Hindley-Milner type information. We extend Hofmann and Jost's type annotations for capturing *potential* costs [19] with information about the lazy evaluation context. The analysis produces a set of constraints over cost variables that we solve in our prototype implementation using an external LP-solver. We have thus demonstrated all the steps that are necessary to produce a fully-automatic analysis for determining bounds on resource usage for lazily-evaluated programs.

2. A Cost Model for Lazy Evaluation

Our cost model is built on Sestoft's revision [40] of Launchbury's natural semantics for lazy evaluation [30]. Launchbury's semantics forms one of the earliest and most widely-used operational accounts of lazy evaluation for the λ-calculus. De la Encina and Peña-Marí [13, 14] subsequently proved that the *Spineless Tagless G-Machine* [24] is sound and complete w.r.t. one of Sestoft's abstract machines. We therefore have a high degree of confidence that the cost model for lazy evaluation developed here is not just theo-

* The detailed soundness proof and a web version of our analysis are available at `http://www.dcc.fc.up.pt/~pbv/cgi/aalazy.cgi`.

† Note that, because we do not consider deallocation, we model total allocation but not residency.

retically sound, but also that it could, in principle, be extended to model real implementations of lazy evaluation.

2.1 Syntax

The syntax of *initial expressions* (the subject of our cost analysis) is the λ-calculus extended with local bindings, data constructors and pattern matching:

$$\begin{array}{rcl} e & ::= & x \mid \lambda x.e \mid e\,x \\ & \mid & \mathsf{let}\ x = e_1\ \mathsf{in}\ e_2 \mid \mathsf{letcons}\ x = c(\vec{y})\ \mathsf{in}\ e \\ & \mid & \mathsf{match}\ e_0\ \mathsf{with}\ c(\vec{x})\ \text{->}\ e_1\ \mathsf{otherwise}\ e_2 \end{array}$$

As in Launchbury's semantics, we restrict the arguments of applications to be variables and we require that nested applications be translated into nested let-bindings.[‡] *let*-expressions bind variables to possibly recursive terms. In line with common practice in non-strict functional languages, we do not have a separate *letrec* form, as in ML. For simplicity, we consider only single-variable let-bindings: multiple let-bindings can be encoded, if needed, using pairs and projections. Note that constructor applications $c(\vec{x})$ will never occur in the initial expression. They are only ever introduced through evaluation of *letcons*-expressions. This is the main difference between our notation and those of Launchbury or Sestoft. The difference is motivated by the need to syntactically distinguish *allocating* a new constructor from simply *referencing* an existing one. De la Encina and Peña-Marí use a similar notation. Our operational semantics is defined over *augmented expressions*, $\widehat{e}$, that include these constructor applications:

$$\widehat{e} \quad ::= \quad e \mid c(\vec{\ell})$$

An evaluation result is then an (augmented) expression w, which is in *weak head normal form* (*whnf*), i.e. it is a λ-abstraction or constructor application.

$$w \quad ::= \quad \lambda x.e \mid c(\vec{\ell})$$

In the remainder of this paper we will use lowercase letters x, y for bound variables in initial expressions and ℓ, k for "fresh" variables (designated *locations*) that are introduced through evaluation of *let*- and *letcons*-expressions.

2.2 Cost-instrumented operational semantics

Figure 1 defines an instrumented big-step operational semantics for lazy evaluation that we will use as the basis for our analysis. Our semantics is given as a relation $\mathcal{H}, \mathcal{S}, \mathcal{L} \vdash^{m}_{m'} \widehat{e} \Downarrow w, \mathcal{H}'$, where $\widehat{e}$ is an augmented expression; $\mathcal{H}$ is a *heap* mapping variables to augmented expressions (*thunks*, that may require evaluation to weak head normal form); $\mathcal{S}$ is a set of bound variables that are used to ensure the freshness condition in the $\text{LET}_{\Downarrow}$/$\text{LETCONS}_{\Downarrow}$ rules; and $\mathcal{L}$ is a set of variables used to record thunks that are under evaluation and to prevent cyclic evaluation (similar to the well-known "black-hole" technique used in [30]). The result of evaluation is an expression w in *whnf* and a final heap $\mathcal{H}'$. The parameters m, m' are non-negative integers representing the number of available heap locations before and after evaluation, respectively. The purpose of the analysis that will be developed in Section 3 is to obtain a static approximation for m that will safely allow execution to proceed. For readability, we may omit the resource information from judgements when they are not otherwise mentioned, writing simply $\mathcal{H}, \mathcal{S}, \mathcal{L} \vdash \widehat{e} \Downarrow w, \mathcal{H}'$ instead of $\mathcal{H}, \mathcal{S}, \mathcal{L} \vdash^{m}_{m'} \widehat{e} \Downarrow w, \mathcal{H}'$.

The only rules that bind variables to expressions in the heap are $\text{LET}_{\Downarrow}$ and $\text{LETCONS}_{\Downarrow}$. These are therefore the only places

$$\frac{w \text{ is in whnf}}{\mathcal{H}, \mathcal{S}, \mathcal{L} \vdash^{m}_{m} w \Downarrow w, \mathcal{H}} \quad (\text{WHNF}_{\Downarrow})$$

$$\frac{\ell \notin \mathcal{L} \qquad \mathcal{H}, \mathcal{S}, \mathcal{L} \cup \{\ell\} \vdash^{m}_{m'} \mathcal{H}(\ell) \Downarrow w, \mathcal{H}'}{\mathcal{H}, \mathcal{S}, \mathcal{L} \vdash^{m}_{m'} \ell \Downarrow w, \mathcal{H}'[\ell \mapsto w]} \quad (\text{VAR}_{\Downarrow})$$

$$\frac{\ell \text{ is fresh} \qquad e_1' = e_1[\ell/x] \qquad e_2' = e_2[\ell/x] \qquad \mathcal{H}[\ell \mapsto e_1'], \mathcal{S}, \mathcal{L} \vdash^{m}_{m'} e_2' \Downarrow w, \mathcal{H}'}{\mathcal{H}, \mathcal{S}, \mathcal{L} \vdash^{m+1}_{m'} \mathsf{let}\ x = e_1\ \mathsf{in}\ e_2 \Downarrow w, \mathcal{H}'} \quad (\text{LET}_{\Downarrow})$$

$$\frac{\ell \text{ is fresh} \qquad y_i' = y_i[\ell/x] \qquad e' = e[\ell/x] \qquad \mathcal{H}[\ell \mapsto c(\vec{y'})], \mathcal{S}, \mathcal{L} \vdash^{m}_{m'} e' \Downarrow w, \mathcal{H}'}{\mathcal{H}, \mathcal{S}, \mathcal{L} \vdash^{m+1}_{m'} \mathsf{letcons}\ x = c(\vec{y})\ \mathsf{in}\ e \Downarrow w, \mathcal{H}'} \quad (\text{LETCONS}_{\Downarrow})$$

$$\frac{\mathcal{H}, \mathcal{S}, \mathcal{L} \vdash^{m}_{m'} e \Downarrow \lambda x.e', \mathcal{H}' \qquad \mathcal{H}', \mathcal{S}, \mathcal{L} \vdash^{m'}_{m''} e'[\ell/x] \Downarrow w, \mathcal{H}''}{\mathcal{H}, \mathcal{S}, \mathcal{L} \vdash^{m}_{m''} e\,\ell \Downarrow w, \mathcal{H}''} \quad (\text{APP}_{\Downarrow})$$

$$\frac{\mathcal{H}, \mathcal{S} \cup \{\vec{x}\} \cup \mathrm{BV}(e_1) \cup \mathrm{BV}(e_2), \mathcal{L} \vdash^{m}_{m'} e_0 \Downarrow c(\vec{\ell}), \mathcal{H}' \qquad \mathcal{H}', \mathcal{S}, \mathcal{L} \vdash^{m'}_{m''} e_1[\vec{\ell}/\vec{x}] \Downarrow w, \mathcal{H}''}{\mathcal{H}, \mathcal{S}, \mathcal{L} \vdash^{m}_{m''} \mathsf{match}\ e_0\ \mathsf{with}\ c(\vec{x})\text{->}e_1\ \mathsf{otherwise}\ e_2 \Downarrow w, \mathcal{H}''} \quad (\text{MATCH}_{\Downarrow})$$

$$\frac{\mathcal{H}, \mathcal{S} \cup \{\vec{x}\} \cup \mathrm{BV}(e_1) \cup \mathrm{BV}(e_2), \mathcal{L} \vdash^{m}_{m'} e_0 \Downarrow w', \mathcal{H}' \qquad w' \neq c(\vec{\ell}) \qquad \mathcal{H}', \mathcal{S}, \mathcal{L} \vdash^{m'}_{m''} e_2 \Downarrow w, \mathcal{H}''}{\mathcal{H}, \mathcal{S}, \mathcal{L} \vdash^{m}_{m''} \mathsf{match}\ e_0\ \mathsf{with}\ c(\vec{x})\text{->}e_1\ \mathsf{otherwise}\ e_2 \Downarrow w, \mathcal{H}''} \quad (\text{FAIL}_{\Downarrow})$$

Figure 1. Cost-instrumented Operational Semantics

where new fresh locations are needed. These heap allocations may either allocate new constructors (*letcons*), or thunks or λ-abstractions (*let*). For simplicity, but without loss of generality, we choose to use a uniform cost model: evaluation will cost one (heap) unit for each fresh heap location that is needed during evaluation. Other cost models are also possible [28], modelling the usage of other countable resources such as execution time, or stack usage, for example. The $\text{WHNF}_{\Downarrow}$ rule for weak-head normal forms (λ-expressions and constructors) incurs no cost. Any costs must have been already accounted for by an initial *let*- or *letcons*-expression. The $\text{VAR}_{\Downarrow}$ and $\text{APP}_{\Downarrow}$ rules are identical to the equivalent ones in Launchbury's semantics. The $\text{VAR}_{\Downarrow}$ rule is restricted to locations that are not marked as being under evaluation (so enforcing "black-holing"). The $\text{MATCH}_{\Downarrow}$ and $\text{FAIL}_{\Downarrow}$ cases deal respectively with successful/unsuccessful pattern matches against a constructor. These rules record the bound variables in e_1 plus the new bound variables in $\vec{x}$ solely in order to ensure freshness in the $\text{LET}_{\Downarrow}$/$\text{LETCONS}_{\Downarrow}$ rules.

We now give the auxiliary definition[§] that formalises the notion of freshness of variables and a lemma regarding the preservation of locations that are marked as "black-holes".

Definition 2.1 (Freshness). A variable x is *fresh* in judgement $\mathcal{H}, \mathcal{S}, \mathcal{L} \vdash \widehat{e} \Downarrow w, \mathcal{H}'$ if x does not occur in either $\mathrm{dom}(\mathcal{H})$, $\mathcal{L}$ or $\mathcal{S}$ nor does it occur bound in either $\widehat{e}$ or $\mathrm{ran}(\mathcal{H})$.

Lemma 2.2 (Invariant Black Holes). *If* $\mathcal{H}, \mathcal{S}, \mathcal{L} \vdash \widehat{e} \Downarrow w, \mathcal{H}'$ *then for all* $\ell \in \mathcal{L}$ *we have* $\mathcal{H}'(\ell) = \mathcal{H}(\ell)$. *In other words,*

‡ This transformation does not increase worst-case costs because, in a call-by-need setting, function arguments must, in general, be heap-allocated in order to allow in-place update and sharing of normal forms.

§ Due to de La Encina and Peña-Marí [13].

heap locations that are under evaluation are preserved during intermediate evaluations.

Proof. By inspection of the operational semantics (Figure 1) we observe that $\text{VAR}_{\Downarrow}$ is the only rule that modifies an existing location ℓ and that this rule does not apply when $\ell \in \mathcal{L}$. □

2.3 Example: call-by-need versus call-by-value/call-by-name

Consider the expression below, which includes a divergent term:

$$\mathsf{let}\ z = z\ \mathsf{in}\ (\lambda x.\, \lambda y.\, y)\ z \tag{2.1}$$

Under a *call-by-value* semantics, this would fail to terminate, because z does not admit a normal form. In our *call-by-need* semantics, however, evaluation succeeds:

$$\mathcal{H}, \mathcal{S}, \mathcal{L} \vdash^{1}_{0} \mathsf{let}\ z = z\ \mathsf{in}\ (\lambda x.\, \lambda y.\, y)\ z \Downarrow \lambda y.\, y, \mathcal{H}[\ell_3 \mapsto \ell_3]$$

The final heap is augmented with a fresh location ℓ_3 whose content is a cyclic self-reference; because the argument z is discarded by the application, its evaluation is never attempted. We can see that the semantics is call-by-need rather than call-by-name by observing the sharing of normal forms. Consider,

$$\begin{aligned}&\mathsf{let}\ f = \mathsf{let}\ z = z\ \mathsf{in}\ (\lambda x.\, \lambda y.\, y)\ z \\ &\quad \mathsf{in}\ \mathsf{let}\ i = \lambda x.\, x\ \mathsf{in}\ \mathsf{let}\ v = f\ i\ \mathsf{in}\ f\ v\end{aligned} \tag{2.2}$$

where f is bound to the thunk (2.1) and applied twice to the identity function. Evaluation of $f\ v$ forces the thunk. After the thunk is evaluated, the location ℓ_0 that is associated with f is updated with the corresponding *whnf*, $\lambda y.\, y$. The second evaluation of f does not *not* re-evaluate the thunk (2.1). Starting from the empty configuration, we derive:

$$\begin{aligned}\emptyset, \emptyset, \emptyset \vdash^{4}_{0}\ & (2.2) \Downarrow \lambda x.\, x, \\ & [\ell_0 \mapsto \lambda y.\, y, \ell_1 \mapsto \lambda x.\, x, \ell_2 \mapsto \lambda x.\, x, \ell_3 \mapsto \ell_3]\end{aligned}$$

Evaluating expression (2.2) thus costs four heap cells, that is, one cell for each let-expression. Under a *call-by-name* semantics, the cost would instead be 5, since the let-expression that is bound to f would then be evaluated twice, rather than once as here.

3. An Amortised Analysis for Lazy Evaluation

Our type-based cost analysis is based on the principle of *amortisation*, that is, averaging the costs of individual operations over a sequence of such operations. It is often possible to obtain better worst-case bounds by amortisation than by reasoning about the costs of single operations. For example, we may obtain a worst-case bound of $O(n)$ for a sequence of n operations even if some of the individual operations cost more than $O(1)$. Amortisation has been successfully used in manual complexity analysis of data structures in both imperative [42] and functional settings [35] and for automatic resource analysis of strict functional languages [18, 19, 27, 29]. It has never been previously used for automatic resource analysis of lazy evaluation. One method for deriving amortised bounds starts by defining a *potential function* from data structures to real numbers. The *amortised cost* of an operation is defined as $t + \phi' - \phi$, where t is the actual cost of the operation (e.g. time or memory) and ϕ, ϕ' are the potentials of the data before and after the operation. The key objective is to choose the potential function so that it simplifies the amortised costs, e.g. so that the change in potential offsets any variation in actual costs, and the amortised costs are therefore constant.

We assign potential to data structures in a type-directed way: recursive data types are annotated with positive coefficients that specify the contribution of each constructor to the potential of the data structure. For example, if we annotate the empty list constructor with q_{nil} and the non-empty list constructor with q_{cons}, then the overall potential of a list of n elements (ignoring any potential for the list elements themselves) is $q_{\mathtt{nil}} + n \times q_{\mathtt{cons}}$, as expected. The principal advantage of this choice is that we can use efficient linear constraint solvers to automatically determine suitable type annotations. The main limitation is that we can only express potentials and costs that are linear functions of the number of constructors in a data structure. Recent work by Hoffmann et al. [18] shows that multivariate polynomial cost functions can also be efficiently inferred, however, and still only require linear constraint solving.

A crucial difference between classic amortised analysis [35, 42] and type-based amortised analysis is that the type system can keep track of data sharing through an explicit structural rule. This allows potential to be defined *per-reference* reflecting how often a data structure is accessed. The advantage is that we do not require ephemeral usage of data structures to ensure the soundness of amortisation. The disadvantage is that (fully evaluated) cyclic data can only be assigned either zero or infinite potential, and that the type system requires an extra structural rule.

It is important to note that, although we are defining a static analysis, the overall potential for any actual data structure can only be known dynamically, when the concrete data size is known. We never actually need to compute this potential, however, but rather concern ourselves with the *change* in potential along all possible computation paths.

3.1 Annotated types and contexts

The syntax of annotated types includes type variables, functions, thunks and (possibly recursive) data types over labelled sums of products, representing the types of each constructor.

$$\begin{aligned} A, B, C \quad ::= \quad & X \mid A \xrightarrow[q']{q} B \mid \mathsf{T}^{q}_{q'}(A) \\ \mid\ & \mu X.\{c_1 : (q_1, \vec{B}_1) \mid \cdots \mid c_n : (q_n, \vec{B}_n)\}\end{aligned}$$

We use meta-variables A, B, C for types, X, Y for type variables and p, q for annotations (i.e. non-negative rational numbers, representing potential). Typing contexts are *multisets* of pairs $x{:}A$ of variables and annotated types; we use multisets to allow separate potential to be accounted for in multiple references. We use Γ, Δ etc for contexts and $\Gamma\restriction_x$ for the multiset of types associated with x in Γ, i.e. $\Gamma\restriction_x = \{A \mid x{:}A \in \Gamma\}$.

The annotations q, q' in the function type $A \xrightarrow[q']{q} B$ express the resources before and after evaluation (hence its cost); similarly, the annotations q, q' in a type $\mathsf{T}^{q}_{q'}(A)$ capture the cost of evaluating a thunk (this can be zero if the thunk is known to be in *whnf*). For simplicity, we exclude *resource parametricity* [29], since this is only important for functions that are re-used in different circumstances, and not for thunks that are evaluated at most once. It is thus orthogonal to this paper.

In a (possibly recursive) data type $\mu X.\{c_1 : (q_1, \vec{B}_1) \mid \ldots \mid c_n : (q_n, \vec{B}_n)\}$ each coefficient q_i represents the potential associated with one application of constructor c_i. We consider only recursive data types that are *non-interleaving* [32], i.e. we exclude μ-types whose bound variables overlap in scope (e.g. $\mu X.\{c_1 : (\ldots, \mu Y.\{c_2 : (\ldots, X)\})\}$). This helps us prove a crucial lemma on cyclic structures in the key soundness proof (Theorem 1). Note that this restriction does *not* prohibit nested data types; e.g. the type of lists of lists of naturals is $\mu Y.\{\mathtt{nil} : (q'_n, ()), \mathtt{cons} : (q'_c, (\mathsf{LN}, Y))\}$, where $\mathsf{N} = \mu X.\{\mathtt{zero} : (q_z, ()), \mathtt{succ} : (q_s, X)\}$ is the type of naturals and $\mathsf{LN} = \mu Y.\{\mathtt{nil} : (q_n, ()), \mathtt{cons} : (q_c, (\mathsf{N}, Y))\}$ is the type of list of naturals. Note also that distinct lists can be assigned different constructor annotations in their types, thus improving the precision of the cost analysis.

$$\frac{}{\curlyvee(A \mid \emptyset)} \qquad \text{(SHAREEMPTY)}$$

$$\frac{}{\curlyvee(X \mid X, \ldots, X)} \qquad \text{(SHAREVAR)}$$

$$\frac{\begin{array}{c} B_i = \mu X.\{c_1 : (q_{i1}, \vec{B}_{i1}) \mid \cdots \mid c_m : (q_{im}, \vec{B}_{im})\} \\ \curlyvee\left(\vec{A}_j \,\middle|\, \vec{B}_{1j}, \ldots, \vec{B}_{nj}\right) \quad p_j \geq \sum_{i=1}^{n} q_{ij} \quad (1 \leq i \leq n,\ 1 \leq j \leq m) \end{array}}{\curlyvee\left(\mu X.\{c_1 : (p_1, \vec{A}_1) \mid \cdots \mid c_m : (p_m, \vec{A}_m)\} \mid B_1, \ldots, B_n\right)} \qquad \text{(SHAREDAT)}$$

$$\frac{\curlyvee(A_i \mid A) \quad \curlyvee(B \mid B_i) \quad q_i \geq q \quad q_i - q \geq q'_i - q' \quad (1 \leq i \leq n)}{\curlyvee\left(A \xrightarrow[q']{q} B \,\middle|\, A_1 \xrightarrow[q'_1]{q_1} B_1, \ldots, A_n \xrightarrow[q'_n]{q_n} B_n\right)} \qquad \text{(SHAREFUN)}$$

$$\frac{\curlyvee(A \mid A_1, \ldots, A_n) \quad q_i \geq q \quad q_i - q \geq q'_i - q' \quad (1 \leq i \leq n)}{\curlyvee\left(\mathsf{T}^{q}_{q'}(A) \,\middle|\, \mathsf{T}^{q_1}_{q'_1}(A_1), \ldots, \mathsf{T}^{q_n}_{q'_n}(A_n)\right)} \qquad \text{(SHARETHUNK)}$$

$$\frac{\curlyvee(A_j \mid B_{1j}, \ldots, B_{nj}) \quad m = |\vec{A}| = |\vec{B}_i| \quad (1 \leq i \leq n,\ 1 \leq j \leq m)}{\curlyvee\left(\vec{A} \,\middle|\, \vec{B}_1, \ldots, \vec{B}_n\right)} \qquad \text{(SHAREVEC)}$$

$$\frac{}{\curlyvee(\Gamma \mid \emptyset)} \qquad \text{(SHAREEMPTYCTX)}$$

$$\frac{\curlyvee(A \mid B_1, \ldots, B_n) \quad \curlyvee(\Gamma \mid \Delta)}{\curlyvee(x : A, \Gamma \mid x : B_1, \ldots, x : B_n, \Delta)} \qquad \text{(SHARECTX)}$$

Figure 2. Sharing Relation

3.2 Sharing and Subtyping

Figure 2 shows the syntactical rules for an auxiliary judgement $\curlyvee(A \mid B_1, \ldots, B_n)$ that is used to *share* a type A among a finite multiset of types $\{B_1, \ldots, B_n\}$. It is used to limit contraction in our type system. Datatype annotations for potential associated with A are linearly distributed by the $\curlyvee$ relation among $B_1, \ldots, B_n$, whereas cost annotations for functions and thunks are preserved. Sharing also allows the relaxing of annotations to subsume subtyping (i.e. potential annotations can decrease, cost annotations may increase). It is important to note that a *decrease* of cost annotations for thunks (possibly down to zero) can only be achieved through the PREPAY structural rule (Figure 4) and not through these sharing rules. "Pre-paying" allows us to correctly model the reduced costs of lazy evaluation by allowing costs to be accounted only once for a thunk. The SHAREEMPTY, SHAREVAR and SHAREVEC rules are trivial. The SHAREDAT rule allows potential from the data constructors that comprise A to be shared among the B_i. The SHAREFUN and SHARETHUNK rules allow any costs for functions and thunks, respectively, to be replicated. The SHARECTXEMPTY and SHARECTX rules extend the sharing relation for typing contexts in a pointwise manner: Γ shares to Δ *iff* for each type assignment $x{:}A$ in Γ there exists $x{:}B_1, \ldots, x{:}B_n$ in Δ and A shares to $B_1, \ldots, B_n$. The special case of sharing one type to a single other corresponds to a *subtyping relation*; we define the shorthand notation $A <: B$ to mean $\curlyvee(A \mid B)$. This relation expresses the relaxation of potentials and costs: informally, $A <: B$ implies that A, B have identical underlying types but B has *lower or equal potential* and *greater or equal cost* than that of A. As usual in structural subtyping, this relation is contravariant in the left argument of functions (SHAREFUN). A special case occurs when sharing a type or context to itself: because of non-negativity $\curlyvee(A \mid A, A)$ (respectively $\curlyvee(\Gamma \mid \Gamma, \Gamma)$), requires that the potential annotations in A (respectively Γ) be zero. We use this property to impose a constraint that types or contexts carry no potential. A variant of this is $\curlyvee(A \mid A, A')$, which implies that A' is a subtype of A that holds no potential.

3.3 Typing judgements

Our analysis is presented in Figures 3 and 4 as a proof system that derives judgments of the form $\Gamma \overset{p}{\underset{p'}{\vdash}} \widehat{e} : A$, where Γ is a typing context, $\widehat{e}$ is an augmented expression, A is an annotated type and p, p' are non-negative numbers approximating the resources available before and after the evaluation of $\widehat{e}$, respectively. For simplicity, we will omit these annotations whenever they are not explicitly mentioned. Because variables reference heap expressions, rules dealing with the introduction and elimination of variables also deal with the introduction and elimination of thunk types: VAR eliminates an assumption of a thunk type, i.e. of the form $x : \mathsf{T}^{q}_{q'}(A)$. Dually, LET and LETCONS introduce an assumption of a thunk type. Note that LETCONS is not simply identical to a LET rule that allows augmented expressions to be bound, since it accounts for the constructor potential q differently. In order to avoid duplicating potential where a λ-abstraction is applied more than once, ABS ensures that Γ does not carry potential, by forcing it to share with itself. APP ensures that the argument and function types match and includes the cost of the function in the final result. The CONS rule simply ensures consistency between the arguments and the result type. Since constructors cannot appear in source forms, the rule is used only when we need to assign types either to heap expressions or to evaluation results. The MATCH rule deals with pattern-matching over an expression of a (possibly recursive) data type. The rule requires that both branches admit an identical result type and that estimated resources after execution of either branch are equal; fulfilling such a condition may require relaxing type and/or cost information using the structural rules below. The matching branch uses extra resources corresponding to the potential annotation on the matched constructor. The structural rules of Figure 4 allow the analysis to be relaxed in various ways: WEAK allows the introduction of an extra hypothesis in the typing context; RELAX

$$\frac{}{x{:}\mathsf{T}^{p}_{p'}(A) \vdash^{p}_{p'} x : A} \quad \text{(VAR)}$$

$$\frac{x \notin \mathrm{dom}(\Gamma, \Delta) \qquad \curlyvee(A \mid A, A') \qquad q \geq q' \qquad \Gamma, x{:}\mathsf{T}^{0}_{0}(A') \vdash^{q}_{q'} e_1 : A \qquad \Delta, x{:}\mathsf{T}^{q}_{q'}(A) \vdash^{p}_{p'} e_2 : C}{\Gamma, \Delta \vdash^{1+p}_{p'} \mathsf{let}\ x = e_1\ \mathsf{in}\ e_2 : C} \quad \text{(LET)}$$

$$\frac{\begin{array}{c} A = \mu X.\{\cdots \mid c : (q, \vec{B}) \mid \cdots\} \qquad x \notin \mathrm{dom}(\Gamma, \Delta) \qquad \curlyvee(A \mid A, A') \\ \Gamma, x{:}\mathsf{T}^{0}_{0}(A') \vdash^{0}_{0} c(\vec{y}) : A \qquad \Delta, x{:}\mathsf{T}^{0}_{0}(A) \vdash^{p}_{p'} e : C \end{array}}{\Gamma, \Delta \vdash^{1+q+p}_{p'} \mathsf{letcons}\ x = c(\vec{y})\ \mathsf{in}\ e : C} \quad \text{(LETCONS)}$$

$$\frac{\Gamma, x{:}A \vdash^{q}_{q'} e : C \qquad x \notin \mathrm{dom}(\Gamma) \qquad \curlyvee(\Gamma \mid \Gamma, \Gamma)}{\Gamma \vdash^{0}_{0} \lambda x.e : A \xrightarrow[q']{q} C} \quad \text{(ABS)}$$

$$\frac{\Gamma \vdash^{p}_{p'} e : A \xrightarrow[q']{q} C}{\Gamma, y{:}A \vdash^{p+q}_{p'+q'} e\, y : C} \quad \text{(APP)}$$

$$\frac{B = \mu X.\{\cdots \mid c : (q, \vec{A}) \mid \cdots\}}{y_1{:}A_1[B/X], \ldots, y_k{:}A_k[B/X] \vdash^{q}_{0} c(\vec{y}) : B} \quad \text{(CONS)}$$

$$\frac{\begin{array}{c} B = \mu X.\{\cdots \mid c : (q, \vec{A}) \mid \cdots\} \qquad |\vec{A}| = |\vec{x}| = k \qquad x_i \notin \mathrm{dom}(\Delta),\ \text{for all } i \\ \Gamma \vdash^{p}_{p'} e_0 : B \qquad \Delta \vdash^{p'}_{p''} e_2 : C \qquad \Delta, x_1{:}A_1[B/X], \ldots, x_k{:}A_k[B/X] \vdash^{p'+q}_{p''} e_1 : C \end{array}}{\Gamma, \Delta \vdash^{p}_{p''} \mathsf{match}\ e_0\ \mathsf{with}\ c(\vec{x})\text{->}e_1\ \mathsf{otherwise}\ e_2 : C} \quad \text{(MATCH)}$$

Figure 3. Syntax Directed Type Rules

$$\frac{\Gamma \vdash^{p}_{p'} e : C}{\Gamma, x{:}A \vdash^{p}_{p'} e : C} \quad \text{(WEAK)}$$

$$\frac{\Gamma \vdash^{p_0}_{p'_0} e : A \qquad p \geq p_0 \qquad p - p_0 \geq p' - p'_0}{\Gamma \vdash^{p}_{p'} e : A} \quad \text{(RELAX)}$$

$$\frac{\Gamma, x{:}\mathsf{T}^{q_0}_{q'}(A) \vdash^{p}_{p'} e : C \qquad q_0 \geq q'}{\Gamma, x{:}\mathsf{T}^{q_0+q_1}_{q'}(A) \vdash^{p+q_1}_{p'} e : C} \quad \text{(PREPAY)}$$

$$\frac{\Gamma, x{:}A_1, x{:}A_2 \vdash^{p}_{p'} e : C \qquad \curlyvee(A \mid A_1, A_2)}{\Gamma, x{:}A \vdash^{p}_{p'} e : C} \quad \text{(SHARE)}$$

$$\frac{\Gamma, x : B \vdash^{p}_{p'} e : C \qquad A <: B}{\Gamma, x : A \vdash^{p}_{p'} e : C} \quad \text{(SUPERTYPE)}$$

$$\frac{\Gamma \vdash^{p}_{p'} e : B \qquad B <: C}{\Gamma \vdash^{p}_{p'} e : C} \quad \text{(SUBTYPE)}$$

Figure 4. Structural Type Rules

allows argument costs to be relaxed; PREPAY allows (part of) the cost of a thunk to be paid for, so reducing the cost of further uses; SUPERTYPE and SUBTYPE allow supertyping in a hypothesis and subtyping in the conclusion, respectively; finally, SHARE allows the use of sharing to split potential in a hypothesis.

Because our semantics does not deallocate resources, it can be expected that all the "lower" annotations in the type system can be set to zero, i.e. the p' in a type judgement, and the q' in function and thunk types (but *not* the m' in an evaluation judgement). However, fixing them to zero would increase the complexity of our soundness proof [26, Section 2.1] and we have therefore retained them.

3.4 Worked examples

We now present type derivations for the examples from Section 2.3 in order to illustrate how the type rules of Figures 3 and 4 model the costs of our operational semantics. Recall example (2.1) which demonstrates that unneeded redexes are not reduced (i.e., that the semantics is non-strict):

$$\mathsf{let}\ z = z\ \mathsf{in}\ (\lambda x.\, \lambda y.\, y)\ z$$

Evaluation of this term in our operational semantics succeeds and requires one heap cell (for allocating the thunk named by z):

$$\mathcal{H}, \mathcal{S}, \mathcal{L} \vdash^{1}_{0} \mathsf{let}\ z = z\ \mathsf{in}\ (\lambda x.\, \lambda y.\, y)\ z \Downarrow \lambda y.y, \mathcal{H}'$$

An analysis for this term is given in Figure 5 as an annotated type derivation with the following final judgement:

$$\emptyset \vdash^{1}_{0} \mathsf{let}\ z = z\ \mathsf{in}\ (\lambda x.\lambda y.y)\ z : \mathsf{T}^{q}_{q'}(B) \xrightarrow[q']{q} B$$

The annotations in the turnstile of this judgement give a cost estimate of one heap cell, matching the exact cost of the operational semantics. The result of the evaluation is the identity function, $\lambda y.y$.

$$
\dfrac{\left\{\begin{array}{l}
\dfrac{}{z{:}\mathsf{T}^0_0(A) \vdash^{0}_{0} z : A}\;\text{Var} \\[1ex]
\dfrac{\dfrac{\dfrac{\dfrac{\dfrac{}{y{:}\mathsf{T}^q_{q'}(B) \vdash^{q}_{q'} y : B}\;\text{Var}}{\emptyset \vdash^{0}_{0} \lambda y.y : \mathsf{T}^q_{q'}(B) \xrightarrow[q']{q} B}\;\text{Abs}}{x{:}\mathsf{T}^p_{p'}(A) \vdash^{0}_{0} \lambda y.y : \mathsf{T}^q_{q'}(B) \xrightarrow[q']{q} B}\;\text{Weak}}{\emptyset \vdash^{0}_{0} \lambda x.\lambda y.y : \mathsf{T}^p_{p'}(A) \xrightarrow[0]{0} \mathsf{T}^q_{q'}(B) \xrightarrow[q']{q} B}\;\text{Abs}}{z{:}\mathsf{T}^p_{p'}(A) \vdash^{0}_{0} (\lambda x.\lambda y.y)\, z : \mathsf{T}^q_{q'}(B) \xrightarrow[q']{q} B}\;\text{App}
\end{array}\right.}{\emptyset \vdash^{1}_{0} \mathsf{let}\ z = z\ \mathsf{in}\ (\lambda x.\lambda y.y)\, z : \mathsf{T}^q_{q'}(B) \xrightarrow[q']{q} B}\;\text{Let}
$$

$$\text{where } p \geq p', q \geq q', \curlyvee(A \mid A, A) \tag{3.1}$$

Figure 5. Type derivation for non-strict evaluation example (2.1).

The type annotations q, q' represent the cost of the thunk for the argument. These parameters can be arbitrary, subject only to the side conditions $q \geq q'$. The type B is similarly arbitrary.

The second example (2.2) illustrates the sharing of normal forms, i.e. lazy evaluation:

$$\begin{array}{l} \mathsf{let}\ f = \mathsf{let}\ z = z\ \mathsf{in}\ (\lambda x.\, \lambda y.\, y)\, z \\ \quad \mathsf{in}\ \mathsf{let}\ i = \lambda x.\, x\ \mathsf{in}\ \mathsf{let}\ v = f\, i\ \mathsf{in}\ f\, v \end{array}$$

Evaluating $f\ v$ forces the thunk f; following evaluation, the location associated with f is updated with the *whnf*. Subsequent evaluation of f re-uses this result. Evaluation of the overall expression therefore costs 4 cells:

$$\begin{array}{l} \emptyset, \emptyset, \emptyset \vdash^{4}_{0} (2.2) \Downarrow \lambda x.\, x, \\ \qquad [\ell_0 \mapsto \lambda y.\, y, \ell_1 \mapsto \lambda x.\, x, \ell_2 \mapsto \lambda x.\, x, \ell_3 \mapsto \ell_3] \end{array}$$

The type derivation in Figure 6 shows the analysis for this example, with the final type judgement replicating the exact operational cost of 4 heap cells. Note that we use the structural rule PREPAY to pay the cost of the thunk that is bound to f precisely once. We also employ SHARE to allow the function f to be used twice. The duplication is justified because the type of f carries no potential (i.e. it shares to itself).

4. Experimental results

We have constructed a prototype implementation of an inference algorithm for the type system of Figures 3 and 4.¶ The inference algorithm is fully automatic (it does not require type annotations from the programmer) and may either produce an admissible annotated typing or fail (meaning that cost bounds could not be found). Our analysis is therefore a *whole program* analysis. Inference is conducted in three stages:

a) We first perform Damas-Milner type inference to obtain an unannotated Hindley-Milner version of the type derivation using the syntax-directed rules in Figure 3. The unannotated types form a free algebra and can be determined using standard first-order unification.

b) We then decorate the Hindley-Milner types with fresh annotation variables for the types of thunks, arrows and data constructors and perform a traversal of the type derivation gathering linear constraints among annotations according to the sharing and subtyping conditions.

c) Finally, we feed the linear constraints to a standard linear programming solver‖ with the objective of minimizing the overall expression cost. Any solution gives rise to a valid annotated typing derivation, and hence to a concrete formula bounding evaluation costs in terms of the program's input data sizes.

The implementation allows some trivial syntactic extensions to the term language, namely, multiple constructor branches in match-expressions and omission of the default alternative. Also, as in ML or Haskell, we require that data constructors are associated with a single data type. This ensures that the use of the CONS rule is syntax-directed.

It remains to explain how to decide when to use the structural rules from Figure 4. We use SHARE to split the context Γ into two Γ_1, Γ_2 when typing sub-expressions (e.g. when typing e_1 and e_2 in $\mathsf{let}\ x = e_1\ \mathsf{in}\ e_2$); note that this does not lose precision unnecessarily, since the unused types can be assigned zero potential. We consequently delegate the task of finding the best assignment (i.e. one yielding the least cost) to the LP solver. We use WEAK depending on the remaining free variables in the sub-expressions. We allow PREPAY to be used for the body e_2 of any let-expression $\mathsf{let}\ x = e_1\ \mathsf{in}\ e_2$. Once again, this does not lose precision because the rule can be used to pay any part of the cost (possibly zero); hence, we allow the LP solver to decide how to use it for each individual thunk in order to achieve an overall optimal solution. Finally, we allow the use of RELAX at every node of the derivation and SUBTYPE at the application rule (to enforce compatibility between the function and its argument) and at the MATCH rule (to obtain a compatible result type). This may generate more constraints and variables for intermediate types than necessary; the resulting increase in size has negligible cost for current LP-solvers (in fact, all our examples were solved by a typical desktop computer in less than one second). Hoffman and Jost have shown that the LP problems that are generated for the eager amortised analysis exhibit regularities that allow lower complexity than general LP solving [19]. We conjecture that this should also be true for our analysis.

4.1 List reversal

Our first recursive example is the classical list reversal using an accumulating parameter:

```
let rev_acc = \xs ys -> match xs with
      Nil () -> ys
    | Cons(x,xs') -> letcons ys' = Cons(x,ys)
                     in rev_acc xs' ys'
```

The analysis fails to find an annotated typing for the above fragment. This is because the recursion is over the first argument of a Curried function and the ABS rule only allows potential in the last argument (since it requires the context to share to itself in order to avoid duplicating potential). Two solutions are possible: either rewrite the function to use a pair of lists instead of using Currying or simply flip the argument order. We choose the latter:

```
let rev_acc' = \ys xs -> match xs with
      Nil () -> ys
    | Cons(x,xs') -> letcons ys' = Cons(x,ys)
                     in rev_acc' ys' xs'
```

The analysis can now yield an informative type. If we abbreviate the type of lists of A as:

$$\begin{array}{l} \mathsf{L}(q_c, q_n, A) \stackrel{\text{def}}{=} \\ \qquad \mu X.\{\, \mathtt{Cons} : (q_c,\ (\mathsf{T}^0_0(A), \mathsf{T}^0_0(X)))\ \mid \mathtt{Nil} : (q_n,\ ())\,\} \end{array}$$

¶ Available at `http://www.dcc.fc.up.pt/~pbv/cgi/aalazy.cgi`.

‖ We use the GLPK library: `http://www.gnu.org/software/glpk`.

$$\cfrac{\text{(Figure 5)}}{f{:}\mathsf{T}_0^1(\mathsf{T}_0^0(B)\xrightarrow[0]{0} B)\vdash_0^0 \text{let } z = z \text{ in } (\lambda x.\lambda y.\,y)\,z : \mathsf{T}_0^0(B)\xrightarrow[0]{0} B}\;\text{Weak}$$

$$\cfrac{\cfrac{\cfrac{\cfrac{\cfrac{}{x{:}\mathsf{T}_0^0(B)\vdash_0^0 x : B}\;\text{Var}}{\emptyset\vdash_0^0 \lambda x.x : B}\;\text{Abs}}{i : \mathsf{T}_0^0(B)\vdash_0^0 \lambda x.x : B}\;\text{Weak}}{}}{}$$

$$\cfrac{\cfrac{\cfrac{\cfrac{\cfrac{f{:}\mathsf{T}_0^0(\mathsf{T}_0^0(B)\xrightarrow[0]{0} B)\vdash_0^0 f : \mathsf{T}_0^0(B)\xrightarrow[0]{0} B}{f{:}\mathsf{T}_0^0(\mathsf{T}_0^0(B)\xrightarrow[0]{0} B),\, i{:}\mathsf{T}_0^0(B)\vdash_0^0 f\,i : B}\;\substack{\text{Var}\\\text{App}}\qquad \cfrac{f{:}\mathsf{T}_0^0(\mathsf{T}_0^0(B)\xrightarrow[0]{0} B)\vdash_0^0 f : \mathsf{T}_0^0(B)\xrightarrow[0]{0} B}{f{:}\mathsf{T}_0^0(\mathsf{T}_0^0(B)\xrightarrow[0]{0} B),\, v{:}\mathsf{T}_0^0(B)\vdash_0^0 f\,v : B}\;\substack{\text{Var}\\\text{App}}}{f{:}\mathsf{T}_0^0(\mathsf{T}_0^0(B)\xrightarrow[0]{0} B),\, f{:}\mathsf{T}_0^0(\mathsf{T}_0^0(B)\xrightarrow[0]{0} B),\, i{:}\mathsf{T}_0^0(B)\vdash_0^1 \text{let } v = f\,i \text{ in } f\,v : B}\;\text{Let}}{f{:}\mathsf{T}_0^0(\mathsf{T}_0^0(B)\xrightarrow[0]{0} B),\, i{:}\mathsf{T}_0^0(B)\vdash_0^1 \text{let } v = f\,i \text{ in } f\,v : B}\;\text{Share}}{f{:}\mathsf{T}_0^0(\mathsf{T}_0^0(B)\xrightarrow[0]{0} B)\vdash_0^2 \text{let } i = \lambda x.x \text{ in } \ldots : B}\;\text{Let}}{f{:}\mathsf{T}_0^1(\mathsf{T}_0^0(B)\xrightarrow[0]{0} B)\vdash_0^3 \text{let } i = \lambda x.x \text{ in } \ldots : B}\;\text{Prepay}$$

$$\emptyset\vdash_0^4 \text{let } f = (\text{let } z = z \text{ in } (\lambda x.\lambda y.\,y)\,z) \text{ in let } i = \lambda x.x \text{ in let } v = f\,i \text{ in } f\,v : B, \quad \text{where } B = \mathsf{T}_0^0(C)\xrightarrow[0]{0} C \quad \text{Let}$$

Figure 6. Type derivation for lazy-evaluation example (2.2).

then we obtain:

$$\mathtt{rev\_acc'} : \mathsf{T}_0^0(L(0,0,A))\xrightarrow[0]{0}\mathsf{T}_0^0(L(1,0,A))\xrightarrow[0]{0} L(0,0,A)$$

This annotated type assigns a potential of 1 heap cell to each `Cons` in the recursion argument xs. The first argument ys and the result both have no potential. Thus, the analysis gives a bound of n heap cells for reversing a list of length n, which is, in fact, the exact cost.

4.2 Functional queues

We now consider Okasaki's purely functional queues, implemented as pairs of lists [35]. This data structure allows $O(1)$ amortised access time to both ends of the queue, and is commonly used as an example for deriving amortised bounds. The translation into our language is shown in Figure 7. It consists of three functions: `mkqueue` normalizes a pair of front and back lists by reversing the back list when the front list is empty, so ensuring that the front is empty *iff* the queue as a whole is empty; the `enqueue` function adds an element to the back of the queue; and the `dequeue` function returns a new queue without the front element. We omit the auxiliary definition of `reverse` which uses `rev_acc'` from Section 4.1. Assuming normalized queues, the `enqueue` function has constant worst-case cost. The `dequeue` function may involve reversing a variable-size list, so its worst-case is $O(n)$; however, the amortised cost for both operations is $O(1)$. The types inferred by our analysis are shown in Figure 8. They express amortised bounds that correspond exactly to Okasaki's analysis, which assigns 1 unit of potential for each element in the back list of the queue. More precisely:

- `mkqueue` consumes a fixed cost of 3 heap cells plus 1 cell for each node in the back list; furthermore, the result queue preserves 1 unit of potential for each node in the new back list;

- `enqueue` and `dequeue` have fixed amortised costs (5 & 3 units, respectively), preserving 1 unit of potential in the back list.

4.3 Infinite structures

Our next example concerns the use of lazy evaluation to define infinite lists (i.e. *streams*). Consider two definitions of a function that generates a stream of identical values:

```
let repeat = \x -> letcons ys = Cons(x,ys)
                   in ys
```

```
let mkqueue = \f r -> match f with
        Nil() -> let f' = reverse r
                 in letcons r' = Nil()
                 in letcons q = Pair(f',r')
                 in q
        otherwise letcons q = Pair(f,r) in q

let enqueue = \x q -> match q with
        Pair(f,r) -> letcons r' = Cons(x,r)
                     in mkqueue f r'

let dequeue = \q -> match q with
        Pair(f,b) -> match f with
            Cons(x,f') -> mkqueue f' b
```

Figure 7. Okasaki's purely functional queues.

```
let repeat' = \x -> let xs = repeat' x
                    in letcons ys = Cons(x,xs)
                    in ys
```

The two definitions yield exactly the same infinite list of values. However, the first one is more efficient: `repeat` will generate a cyclic structure occupying a single heap node, while `repeat'` will allocate many (identical) nodes as the result stream is traversed. We can observe these non-functional properties in the types that our analysis infers for the two definitions:

$$\mathtt{repeat} : \mathsf{T}_0^0(A)\xrightarrow[0]{1}\mu X.\{\mathtt{Cons} : (0, (\mathsf{T}_0^0(A), \mathsf{T}_0^0(X))) \mid \ldots\}$$

$$\mathtt{repeat'} : \mathsf{T}_0^0(A)\xrightarrow[0]{2}\mu X.\{\mathtt{Cons} : (0, (\mathsf{T}_0^0(A), \mathsf{T}_0^2(X))) \mid \ldots\}$$

First note that, because the results of both functions are infinite structures, they must have zero potential, hence the zero annotation on `Cons`. The type for `repeat` shows that it costs 1 heap cell to generate the first node and that subsequent nodes have no further cost (because the thunk annotations are zero). The type for `repeat'`, however, shows that evaluating each tail thunk of the result list costs 2 cells (plus 2 cells for the first node).

$$\texttt{mkqueue} : \mathsf{T}^0_0(\mathsf{L}(0,0,A)) \xrightarrow[0]{0} \mathsf{T}^0_0(\mathsf{L}(1,0,A)) \xrightarrow[0]{3} \mathsf{T}^0_0(\mathsf{L}(0,0,A)) \times \mathsf{T}^0_0(\mathsf{L}(1,0,A))$$

$$\texttt{enqueue} : \mathsf{T}^0_0(A) \xrightarrow[0]{0} \mathsf{T}^0_0(\mathsf{T}^0_0(\mathsf{L}(0,0,A)) \times \mathsf{T}^0_0(\mathsf{L}(1,0,A))) \xrightarrow[0]{5} \mathsf{T}^0_0(\mathsf{L}(0,0,A)) \times \mathsf{T}^0_0(\mathsf{L}(1,0,A))$$

$$\texttt{dequeue} : \mathsf{T}^0_0(\mathsf{T}^0_0(\mathsf{L}(0,0,A)) \times \mathsf{T}^0_0(\mathsf{L}(1,0,A))) \xrightarrow[0]{3} \mathsf{T}^0_0(\mathsf{L}(0,0,A)) \times \mathsf{T}^0_0(\mathsf{L}(1,0,A))$$

Figure 8. Analysis of the functional queues example.

$$\texttt{map} : \mathsf{T}^0_0(\mathsf{T}^0_0(A) \xrightarrow[0]{0} B) \xrightarrow[0]{0} \mathsf{T}^0_0(\mu X.\{\texttt{Cons} : (3, (\mathsf{T}^0_0(A), \mathsf{T}^0_0(X))) \mid \texttt{Nil} : (1, ())\}) \xrightarrow[0]{0} \mu X.\{\texttt{Cons} : (0, (\mathsf{T}^0_0(B), \mathsf{T}^0_0(X))) \mid \ldots\} \quad (4.1)$$

$$\texttt{map} : \mathsf{T}^0_0(\mathsf{T}^0_0(A) \xrightarrow[0]{1} B) \xrightarrow[0]{0} \mathsf{T}^0_0(\mu X.\{\texttt{Cons} : (3, (\mathsf{T}^0_0(A), \mathsf{T}^0_0(X))) \mid \texttt{Nil} : (1, ())\}) \xrightarrow[0]{0} \mu X.\{\texttt{Cons} : (0, (\mathsf{T}^1_0(B), \mathsf{T}^0_0(X))) \mid \ldots\} \quad (4.2)$$

$$\texttt{map} : \mathsf{T}^0_0(\mathsf{T}^0_0(A) \xrightarrow[0]{0} B) \xrightarrow[0]{0} \mathsf{T}^0_0(\mu X.\{\texttt{Cons} : (0, (\mathsf{T}^0_0(A), \mathsf{T}^0_0(X))) \mid \texttt{Nil} : (0, ())\}) \xrightarrow[0]{3} \mu X.\{\texttt{Cons} : (0, (\mathsf{T}^0_0(B), \mathsf{T}^3_0(X))) \mid \ldots\} \quad (4.3)$$

$$\texttt{map} : \mathsf{T}^0_0(\mathsf{T}^0_0(A) \xrightarrow[0]{1} B) \xrightarrow[0]{0} \mathsf{T}^0_0(\mu X.\{\texttt{Cons} : (0, (\mathsf{T}^0_0(A), \mathsf{T}^0_0(X))) \mid \texttt{Nil} : (0, ())\}) \xrightarrow[0]{3} \mu X.\{\texttt{Cons} : (0, (\mathsf{T}^1_0(B), \mathsf{T}^3_0(X))) \mid \ldots\} \quad (4.4)$$

Figure 9. Analyses of `map` for finite (4.1) (4.2) and infinite lists (4.3) (4.4).

4.4 Higher order functions over lists

Consider now the higher-order function `map` that applies a function to every element in a list:

```
let map = \f xs -> match xs with
            Nil () -> letcons nil=Nil() in nil
          | Cons(x,xs') -> let y = f x
                           in let ys' = map f xs'
                           in letcons ys = Cons(y,ys')
                           in ys
```

Figure 9 shows four distinct typings inferred depending on use: (4.1) and (4.2) were inferred for mapping over a *finite* list (which can carry potential) while (4.3) and (4.4) were inferred for mapping over an *infinite* one (which must have zero potential). Thus, the first two typings (4.1) and (4.2) offset costs with potential from the argument list (three heap cells for each `Cons` and one for each `Nil`) while (4.3) and (4.4) defer costs to the tail thunk of the result lists. Note also that (4.1) and (4.3) allow a zero-cost argument function while (4.2) and (4.4) allow a unit-cost argument function; the effect of this change is reflected on the thunk costs for the head of the result lists. Finally, we remark that the analysis chooses these typings automatically according to use.[**]

5. Soundness

This section establishes the soundness of our analysis with respect to the operational semantics of Section 2. We begin by stating some auxiliary proof lemmas and preliminary definitions, notably formalizing the notion of *potential* from Section 3. We then define the principal invariants of our system, namely, *type consistency* and *type compatibility* relations between a heap configuration of the operational semantics and global types, contexts and balance. We conclude with the soundness result proper (Theorem 1).

5.1 Auxiliary Lemmas

We now present some auxiliary proof lemmas for our type system. The first lemma allows us to replace variables in type derivations. Note that because of the lazy evaluation semantics (and unlike the usual substitution lemma for the λ-calculus), we substitute only variables but not arbitrary expressions.

Lemma 5.1 (Substitution). *If* $\Gamma, x{:}A \vdash^{p}_{p'} \widehat{e} : C$ *and* $y \notin \mathrm{dom}(\Gamma) \cup \mathrm{FV}(\widehat{e})$ *then also* $\Gamma, y{:}A \vdash^{p}_{p'} \widehat{e}[y/x] : C$.

Proof. By induction on the height of derivation of $\Gamma, x{:}A \vdash^{p}_{p'} \widehat{e} : C$, simply replacing any occurrences of x for y. □

The next two lemmas establish inversion properties for constructors and λ-abstractions.

Lemma 5.2 (Cons inversion). *If* $\Gamma \vdash c(\vec{y}) : B$ *then* $B = \mu X.\{\ldots \mid c : (q, \vec{A}) \mid \ldots\}$ *and* $\curlyvee(\Gamma \mid \vec{y}{:}\vec{A}[B/X])$.

Lemma 5.3 (Abs inversion). *If* $\Gamma \vdash \lambda x.e : A \xrightarrow[q']{q} C$ *then there exists* Γ' *such that* $\curlyvee(\Gamma \mid \Gamma')$, $\curlyvee(\Gamma' \mid \Gamma', \Gamma')$, $x \notin \mathrm{dom}(\Gamma')$ *and* $\Gamma', x{:}A \vdash^{q}_{q'} e : C$.

Proof Sketch for both lemmas. A typing with conclusion $\Gamma \vdash c(\vec{y}) : B$ must result from axiom Cons followed by (possibly zero) uses of structural rules. Similarly, a typing $\Gamma \vdash \lambda x.e : A \xrightarrow[q']{q} C$ must result from an application of the rule Abs followed by uses of structural rules. The proof follows by induction on the structural rules, considering each rule separately. □

The final auxiliary lemma allows splitting contexts used for typing expressions in *whnf* according to a split of the result type.

Lemma 5.4 (Context Splitting). *If* $\Gamma \vdash^{0}_{0} w : A$, *where* w *is an expression in whnf and* $\curlyvee(A \mid A_1, A_2)$; *then there exists* Γ_1, Γ_2 *such that* $\curlyvee(\Gamma \mid \Gamma_1, \Gamma_2)$, $\Gamma_1 \vdash^{0}_{0} w : A_1$ *and* $\Gamma_2 \vdash^{0}_{0} w : A_2$.

Proof Sketch. The proof follows from an application of Lemma 5.2 (if w is a constructor) or Lemma 5.3 (if w is an abstraction) together with the definition of sharing. □

5.2 Global Types, Contexts and Balance

We now define some auxiliary mappings that will be necessary for formulating the soundness of our type system. The mapping $\mathcal{M}$ from locations to types, written $\{\ell_1 \mapsto A_1, \ldots, \ell_n \mapsto A_n\}$, records the *global type* of a location, which accounts for all potential in all references to that location. The mapping $\mathcal{C}$ from locations to typing contexts, written $\{\ell_1 \mapsto \Gamma_1, \ldots, \ell_n \mapsto \Gamma_n\}$, associates each location with its *global context* that justifies its global type. We extend the projection operation from (local) contexts to global contexts in the natural way:

$$\mathcal{C}\restriction_\ell = \{\ell_1 \mapsto \Gamma_1, \ldots, \ell_n \mapsto \Gamma_n\}\restriction_\ell \stackrel{\text{def}}{=} (\Gamma_1, \ldots, \Gamma_n)\restriction_\ell$$

We also extend subtyping to global types in the natural way, namely $\mathcal{M} <: \mathcal{M}'$ if and only if $\mathrm{dom}(\mathcal{M}) \subseteq \mathrm{dom}(\mathcal{M}')$ and for all $\ell \in \mathrm{dom}(\mathcal{M})$ we have $\mathcal{M}(\ell) <: \mathcal{M}(\ell')$. This relation will be

[**] Note, however, that using the same definition with both finite and infinite structures would generate infeasible constraints due to the absence of *"resource parametricity"* (introduced in [29]).

used to assert that the potential assigned to global types is always non-increasing during execution. Furthermore, we introduce an auxiliary *balance* (or *lazy potential*) mapping $\mathcal{B}$ from locations to non-negative rational numbers. This keeps track of the partial costs of thunks that have been paid in advance by applications of the PREPAY rule. Note that these auxiliary mappings are needed only in the soundness proof of the analysis for bookkeeping purposes, but are *not* part of the operational semantics — in particular, they do not incur runtime costs.

5.3 Potential

We define the potential of an augmented expression with respect to a heap and an annotated type. The potential of expressions that are not *whnf*s (i.e. thunks) and λ-abstractions is always zero. For data constructors, the potential is obtained by summing the type annotation with the (recursive) potential contributed by each of the arguments. Note that for cyclic data structures, the potential is only defined if all the type annotations of all nodes encountered along a cycle are zero (the overall potential must therefore also be zero).

Definition 5.5 (Potential). The potential assigned to an augmented expression $\widehat{e}$ of type A under heap $\mathcal{H}$, written $\phi_{\mathcal{H}}(\widehat{e}{:}A)$, is defined in (5.1) within Figure 10.

Equation (5.2) extends the definition to typing contexts in the natural way. Equation (5.3) defines potential for global contexts, but considers only thunks that are not under evaluation. Finally, (5.4) defines a convenient shorthand notation for a similar summation over the balance. The next two lemmas formalize the intuition that sharing splits the potential of a type and that a supertype of a type A has potential that is no greater than A.

Lemma 5.6 (Potential Splitting). *If* $\curlyvee(A \mid A_1, \ldots, A_n)$ *then for all* $\widehat{e}$ *such that the potentials are defined, we have* $\phi_{\mathcal{H}}(\widehat{e}{:}A) \geq \sum_i \phi_{\mathcal{H}}(\widehat{e}{:}A_i)$.

This lemma has an important special case when A occurs as one of the types on the right hand side: if $\curlyvee(A \mid A, B_1, \ldots, B_n)$ then $\phi_{\mathcal{H}}(\widehat{e}{:}B_i) = 0$ for all i.

Proof Sketch. First note that the results follow immediately if $\widehat{e}$ is not in *whnf* or is a λ-abstraction (because potentials are zero in those cases). The potential is also zero if $\widehat{e}$ is a constructor that is part of a cycle (since otherwise it would be undefined). The remaining case is for a constructor with no cycles, i.e. a directed acyclic graph (DAG). The proof is then by induction on the length of the longest path. □

Lemma 5.7 (Potential Subtype). *If* $A <: B$ *then for all* $\widehat{e}$ *such that the potentials are defined, we have* $\phi_{\mathcal{H}}(\widehat{e}{:}A) \geq \phi_{\mathcal{H}}(\widehat{e}{:}B)$.

Proof. By the definition of subtyping, this is a direct corollary of Lemma 5.6 for the case when $n = 1$. □

5.4 Consistency and Compatibility

We now define the principal invariants for proving the soundness of our analysis, namely, *consistency* and *compatibility* relations between a heap configuration and the global types, contexts and balance. We proceed by first defining type consistency of a single location and then extend it to a whole heap.

Definition 5.8 (Type consistency of locations). We say that location ℓ admits type $\mathsf{T}^q_{q'}(A)$ under context Γ, balance $\mathcal{B}$, heap configuration $(\mathcal{H}, \mathcal{L})$, and write $\Gamma, \mathcal{B}; \mathcal{H}, \mathcal{L} \vdash_{\text{LOC}} \ell : \mathsf{T}^q_{q'}(A)$, if $q \geq q'$ and one of the following cases holds:

(LOC1) $\mathcal{H}(\ell)$ is in *whnf* and $\Gamma \vdash^{0}_{0} \mathcal{H}(\ell) : A$

(LOC2) $\mathcal{H}(\ell)$ not in *whnf* and $\ell \notin \mathcal{L}$ and $\Gamma \vdash^{q + \mathcal{B}(\ell)}_{q'} \mathcal{H}(\ell) : A$

(LOC3) $\mathcal{H}(\ell)$ not in *whnf* and $\ell \in \mathcal{L}$ and $\Gamma = \emptyset$

The three cases in the above definition are mutually exclusive: LOC1 applies when the expression in the heap is already in *whnf*; otherwise LOC2 and LOC3 apply, depending on whether the thunk is or is not under evaluation. For LOC2, the balance $\mathcal{B}(\ell)$ associated with location ℓ is added to the available resources for typing the thunk $\mathcal{H}(\ell)$, effectively reducing its cost by the prepaid amount. Once evaluation has begun (LOC3), or once it has completed (LOC1), the balance is considered spent. However, we never lower or reset the balance, since it is simply ignored in such cases.

Definition 5.9 (Type consistency of heaps). We say that a heap state $(\mathcal{H}, \mathcal{L})$ is consistent with global contexts, global types and balance, and write $\mathcal{C}, \mathcal{B} \vdash_{\text{MEM}} (\mathcal{H}, \mathcal{L}) : \mathcal{M}$, if and only if for all $\ell \in \text{dom}(\mathcal{H})$: $\mathcal{C}(\ell), \mathcal{B}; \mathcal{H}, \mathcal{L} \vdash_{\text{LOC}} \ell : \mathcal{M}(\ell)$ holds.

Definition 5.10 (Global compatibility). We say that a global type $\mathcal{M}$ is *compatible* with context Γ and a global context $\mathcal{C}$, written $\curlyvee(\mathcal{M} \mid \Gamma, \mathcal{C})$, if and only if $\curlyvee(\mathcal{M}(\ell) \mid \Gamma\!\upharpoonright_\ell, \mathcal{C}\!\upharpoonright_\ell)$ for all $\ell \in \text{dom}(\mathcal{M})$.

Definition 5.9 requires the type consistency of each specific location. Definition 5.10 requires that the global type of each location accounts for the joint potential of all references to it in either the local or global contexts.

5.5 Soundness of the proof system

We can now state the soundness of our analysis as an augmented type preservation result.

Theorem 1 (Soundness). *Let* $t \in \mathbb{Q}^+$ *be fixed, but arbitrary. If the following statements hold*

$$\Gamma \vdash^{p}_{p'} e : A \tag{1.A}$$

$$\mathcal{C}, \mathcal{B} \vdash_{\text{MEM}} (\mathcal{H}, \mathcal{L}) : \mathcal{M} \tag{1.B}$$

$$\curlyvee(\mathcal{M} \mid (\Gamma, \Theta), \mathcal{C}) \tag{1.C}$$

$$\mathcal{H}, \mathcal{S}, \mathcal{L} \vdash e \Downarrow w, \mathcal{H}' \tag{1.D}$$

then for all $m \in \mathbb{N}$ *such that*

$$m \geq t + p + \phi_{\mathcal{H}}(\Gamma) + \phi_{\mathcal{H}}(\Theta) + \Phi^{\mathcal{L}}_{\mathcal{H}}(\mathcal{C}) + \Phi^{\mathcal{L}}_{\mathcal{H}}(\mathcal{B}) \tag{1.E}$$

there exist m', Γ', $\mathcal{C}'$, $\mathcal{B}'$ *and* $\mathcal{M}'$ *such that*

$$\mathcal{M} <: \mathcal{M}' \tag{1.F}$$

$$\Gamma' \vdash^{0}_{0} w : A \tag{1.G}$$

$$\mathcal{C}', \mathcal{B}' \vdash_{\text{MEM}} (\mathcal{H}', \mathcal{L}) : \mathcal{M}' \tag{1.H}$$

$$\curlyvee(\mathcal{M}' \mid (\Gamma', \Theta), \mathcal{C}') \tag{1.I }$$

$$\mathcal{H}, \mathcal{S}, \mathcal{L} \;\frac{m}{m'}\; e \Downarrow w, \mathcal{H}' \tag{1.J }$$

$$m' \geq t + p' + \phi_{\mathcal{H}'}(w{:}A) + \phi_{\mathcal{H}'}(\Theta) + \Phi^{\mathcal{L}}_{\mathcal{H}'}(\mathcal{C}') + \Phi^{\mathcal{L}}_{\mathcal{H}'}(\mathcal{B}') \tag{1.K}$$

Informally, the soundness theorem reads as follows: if an expression e admits a type A (1.A), the heap can be consistently typed (1.B) (1.C) and the evaluation is successful (1.D), then the result *whnf* also admits type A (1.G). Furthermore, the resulting heap can can also be typed (1.H) (1.I) and the static bounds that are obtained from the typing of e give safe resource estimates for evaluation (1.E) (1.J) (1.K). The arbitrary value t is used to carry over excess potential which is not used for the immediate evaluation but will be needed in subsequent ones (i.e. for the argument of an application). Similarly, the context Θ is used to preserve types for variables that are not in the current scope but that are necessary for subsequent evaluations (i.e. the alternatives of the match). Because of space limitations, we present here only a proof sketch; a detailed proof is available at `http://www.dcc.fc.up.pt/~pbv/AALazyExtended.pdf`.

$$\phi_{\mathcal{H}}(\widehat{e}{:}A) \stackrel{\text{def}}{=} \begin{cases} p + \sum_i \phi_{\mathcal{H}}(\mathcal{H}(\ell_i){:}B_i[A/X]) & \text{if } A = \mu X.\{\cdots \mid c{:}(p, \vec{B}) \mid \cdots\} \text{ and } \widehat{e} = c(\vec{\ell}) \\ \phi_{\mathcal{H}}(\widehat{e}{:}B) & \text{if } A = \mathsf{T}^{q}_{q'}(B) \\ 0 & \text{otherwise} \end{cases} \tag{5.1}$$

$$\phi_{\mathcal{H}}(\Gamma) \stackrel{\text{def}}{=} \sum \{\phi_{\mathcal{H}}(\mathcal{H}(x){:}A) \mid x{:}A \in \Gamma\} \tag{5.2}$$

$$\Phi^{\mathcal{L}}_{\mathcal{H}}(\mathcal{C}) \stackrel{\text{def}}{=} \sum \{\phi_{\mathcal{H}}(\mathcal{C}(\ell)) \mid \ell \in \text{dom}(\mathcal{H}) \text{ and } \ell \notin \mathcal{L} \text{ and } \mathcal{H}(\ell) \text{ is not a whnf}\} \tag{5.3}$$

$$\Phi^{\mathcal{L}}_{\mathcal{H}}(\mathcal{B}) \stackrel{\text{def}}{=} \sum \{\ \mathcal{B}(\ell) \mid \ell \in \text{dom}(\mathcal{H}) \text{ and } \ell \notin \mathcal{L} \text{ and } \mathcal{H}(\ell) \text{ is not a whnf}\} \tag{5.4}$$

Figure 10. Potential

Proof Sketch. The proof is by induction on the lengths of the derivations of (1.D) and (1.A) ordered lexicographically, with the derivation of the evaluation taking priority over the typing derivation. We proceed by case analysis of the typing rule used in premise (1.A), considering just some representative cases.

Case VAR*:* The typing premise $\ell{:}\mathsf{T}^{p}_{p'}(A) \vdash^{p}_{p'} \ell : A$ is an axiom. By inversion of the evaluation premise, we obtain $\mathcal{H}, \mathcal{S}, \mathcal{L} \cup \{\ell\} \vdash \mathcal{H}(\ell) \Downarrow w, \mathcal{H}'$. In order to apply induction to the evaluation of the thunk $\mathcal{H}(\ell)$, we take the typing context from the hypothesis of type consistency for the location ℓ. We apply induction to a typing with the global type $\mathcal{M}(\ell)$ rather than the local type $\mathsf{T}^{p}_{p'}(A)$ in the local context. This gives us a stronger conclusion with a context that we can then split using Lemma 5.6 to justify type consistency for the heap update and the local context answer for the answer. Finally, we require an auxiliary result to ensure that if the update introduces a cycle, the locations on the cycle can be assigned a type with zero potential (a lemma contained in the full proof).

Case LET*:* The typing premise is $\Gamma, \Delta \vdash^{1+p}_{p'} \mathsf{let}\ x = e_1\ \mathsf{in}\ e_2 : C$ and evaluation premise gives $\mathcal{H}_0, \mathcal{S}, \mathcal{L} \vdash e_2[\ell/x] \Downarrow w, \mathcal{H}'$ where $\mathcal{H}_0 = \mathcal{H}[\ell \mapsto e_1[\ell/x]]$ is the heap extended with a new location ℓ and thunk. To apply induction to the evaluation of $e_2[\ell/x]$ we re-establish the consistency to the new location ℓ; this is done using Γ from the typing hypothesis together with an idempotent type for self-references to ℓ. Applying induction then yields all required conclusions.

Case MATCH*:* The typing premise is:

$$\Gamma, \Delta \vdash^{p}_{p''} \mathsf{match}\ e_0\ \mathsf{with}\ c(\vec{x})\text{->}e_1\ \mathsf{otherwise}\ e_2 : C$$

By inversion of the type rule, we get a typing $\Gamma \vdash^{p}_{p'} e_0 : B$ for e_0, where $B = \mu X.\{\cdots \mid c : (q, \vec{A}) \mid \cdots\}$ is some data type with a constructor c. We apply induction to the evaluation of e_0 and then do a case analysis on the evaluation rule used (i.e. $\text{MATCH}_{\Downarrow}$ or $\text{FAIL}_{\Downarrow}$). We then apply induction to either $e_1[\vec{\ell}/\vec{x}]$ or e_2 and obtain the proof obligation. To establish the premise (1.E) on m for the $\text{MATCH}_{\Downarrow}$ case, we use definition of potential: $\phi_{\mathcal{H}}(c(\vec{\ell}){:}B) = q + \sum_i \phi_{\mathcal{H}}(\ell_i{:}A_i[B/X])$ — i.e. the potential of the constructor is the sum of the type annotation q plus the potential of its context.

□

6. Related Work

As described above, we build heavily on Launchbury's natural semantics for lazy evaluation [30], as subsequently adapted by Sestoft, and exploit ideas that were developed by de la Encina and Peña-Marí [14, 15]. There is a significant body of other work on the semantics of call-by-need evaluation. Pre-dating Launchbury's work, Josephs [25] gave a *denotational* semantics of lazy evaluation, using a continuation-based semantics to model sharing, and including an explicit store. However, this approach doesn't fit well with standard proof techniques. Maraist et al. [31] subsequently defined both natural and reduction semantics for the call-by-need lambda calculus, so enabling equational reasoning, and a similar approach was independently described by Ariola and Felleisen [4].

Bakewell and Runciman [6] have previously defined an operational semantics for Core Haskell that gives time and space execution costs in terms of Sestoft's semantics for his Mark 1 abstract machine. The work has subsequently been extended to give a model that can be used to determine space leaks by comparing the space usage for two evaluators using a bisimulation approach [5]. Gustavsson and Sands [17] have similarly defined a space-improvement relation that guarantees that some optimisation can never lead to asymptotically worse space behaviour for call-by-need programs and Moran and Sands [33] have defined an improvement relation for call-by-need programs that can be used to determine whether one terminating program improves another in all possible contexts.

Finally, like de la Encina and Peña-Marí, Mountjoy [34] derived an operational semantics for the Spineless Tagless G-Machine from the natural semantics of Launchbury and Sestoft, including poly-applicative λ-expressions. The main differences between these approaches are that de la Encina and Peña-Marí correct some mistakes in Mountjoy's presentation, that they provide correctness proofs, that their semantics correctly deals with partial applications in the Spineless Tagless G-Machine, that they deal with partial applications as normal forms, and that they consider two distinct implementation variants, based on push/enter versus apply/eval. Our own work differs from this body of earlier work in that we not only provide an operational semantics to *model* lazy evaluation, but also provide a corresponding cost semantics from which we derive a static analysis to automatically determine upper bounds on the memory requirements of lazily evaluated programs.

Resource analysis based on profiling and manual code inspection has long formed the state-of-the-art and still is current practice in many cases. Indeed, for non-strict functional languages, such as Haskell, ad-hoc techniques, manual analysis or symbolic profiling are the only currently viable approaches: as we have seen, the dynamic *demand-driven* nature of lazy functional programming creates particular problems for resource analysis, whether manual or automatic. There has therefore been very little work on static resource analysis for lazy functional programs, and, to our knowledge, no *previous automatic analysis has ever been produced.* The most significant previous work in the area is that by Sands [37, 38], whose PhD thesis proposed a cost calculus for reasoning about sufficient and necessary execution time for lazily evaluated higher-order programs, using an approach based on *evaluation contexts* [39, 45] to capture information about evaluation degree and appropriate *projections* [47] to project this information to the required approach. Wadler [45] had earlier proposed a similar approach to that taken by Sands, but using *strictness analysis* combined with appropriate projections, rather than the *neededness analysis* that Sands uses. A primary disadvantage of such approaches lies in the complexity of the domain structure and associated projections that must be used when analysing even simple data structures such as lists. In contrast, our approach easily extends to arbitrarily complex data structures. A secondary disadvantage is that, unlike the self-contained analysis we have described, projection-based approaches rely on the existence of a complex and powerful external *neededness analysis* to determine evaluation contexts for expressions. These are serious practical disadvantages: in fact, to date, we are not aware of any fully automatic static analysis that has been produced using these techniques.

A number of authors have proposed analysis approaches based on transforming lazy programs to eager ones (e.g. Bjerner and Holmström [7], Fradet and Métayer [16]). The resulting programs may then be analysed using (simpler) techniques for eagerly evaluated programs, such as the automatic amortised analysis we have previously developed [19, 28, 29]. Unlike our work, these approaches are generally restricted to first-order programs, and suffer from the problems that they are, in general, not cost-preserving, that they lead to potentially exponential code explosion, and that, because they alter the program, they are not suitable for use with standard compilers for lazy functional languages.

Several authors have proposed *symbolic profiling* approaches, where programs are annotated with additional cost parameters. For example, Wadler [46] uses *monads* to capture execution costs through a tick-counting function; Albert et al. [1] adds additional cost parameters to each function, using logic variables to capture sharing information and so avoid cost duplication; and Hope [22] describes how to derive an instrumented function for determining time and space usage, including a simple deallocation model, for a strict functional language and outlines how this could be extended to lazy evaluation. Danielsson [12] takes this work a stage further, describing a library that can be used to annotate (lazy) functions with the time that is needed to compute their result. An annotated monad is then used to combine these time complexity annotations. This can be used to verify (but *not infer*) the time complexity of (lazy) functional data structures and algorithms against Launchbury's semantics, using a dependent type approach. Provided the cost model is sufficiently accurate, symbolic profiling approaches can give "exact" costs for specific program inputs. They are also easy to implement. However, unlike the work described here, the cost information is input-dependent, cannot give a guaranteed worst-case except in trivial cases, and transforms the program in a way that may not be cost-preserving for all metrics. Unlike our analysis, such approaches therefore cannot produce upper bounds on resource usage for all possible program inputs.

The amortised analysis approach has been previously studied by a number of authors, but has never previously been used to automatically determine the costs of lazy evaluation. Tarjan [42] first described amortised analysis, but as a manual technique. Okasaki [35] subsequently described how Tarjan's approach could be applied to (lazy) data structures, but again as a manual technique. While there has subsequently been significant interest in the use of amortised analysis for automatic resource usage analysis, using an advanced per-reference potential, none of this newer work, however, considers lazy evaluation. Hofmann and Jost [19] were the first to develop an *automatic* amortised analysis for heap consumption, exploiting a difference metric similar to that used by Crary and Weirich [11] (the latter, however, only *check* bounds, and therefore do not perform an automatic static analysis of the kind we require); Hofmann et al. have extended their method to cover a comprehensive subset of Java, including imperative updates, inheritance and type casts [20, 21]; Shkaravska et al. [41] subsequently considered heap consumption inference for first-order polymorphic lists; and Campbell [9] has developed the ideas of depth-based and temporary credit uses to give better results for stack usage. Hoffmann et al. [18] achieved another breakthrough by extending the technique to infer multivariate polynomial cost functions, still only requiring efficient LP solving. Finally, several authors have recently studied analyses for heap usage in eager languages, without considering lazy evaluation. For example, Albert et al. [2] present a fully automatic, live heap-space analysis for an object-oriented bytecode language with a scoped-memory manager, and have subsequently extended this to consider garbage collection [3], but, unlike our system, data-dependencies cannot be expressed. Braberman et al. [8] infer polynomial bounds on the live heap usage for a Java-like language with automatic memory management, but do not cover general recursive methods. Finally, Chin et al. [10] present a linearly-bounded heap and stack analysis for a low-level (assembler) language with explicit (de)-allocation, but do not cover lazy evaluation or high-level functional programming constructs.

7. Conclusions and Further Work

This paper has introduced a new automatic type-based analysis for accurately determining bounds on the execution costs of lazy (higher-order) functional programs. The analysis uses the new idea of *lazy potential* as part of an amortised analysis technique that is capable of directly analysing lazy programs without requiring defunctionalisation or other non-cost-preserving program transformations. Our analysis deals with (potentially infinite) recursive data structures, nested data structures, and cyclic data structures. It is defined for arbitrary data types (including e.g. trees). We have proved the soundness of this analysis against an operational semantics derived from Launchbury's natural semantics of graph reduction, and analysed some non-trivial examples of lazy evaluation using a prototype implementation of the analysis.

A number of extensions to this work would repay further investigation. Firstly, to reduce complexity, our system is restricted to monomorphic definitions. It should be straightforward, albeit laborious, to adapt our previous work on polymorphism [29] to also cover the lazy setting, including "resource parametricity", which allows function applications to have different costs depending on context. Secondly, we have only considered linear cost functions. Although it would increase complexity, Hoffmann et al. [18]'s approach to polynomial cost functions, which infers asymptotically tight bounds for many practical examples, should also be applicable here. Thirdly, while we have previously constructed [28, 29] analyses that are capable of dealing with arbitrary countable resources for strict languages, for simplicity, in this paper we have restricted our attention to heap allocations. Analysing time and stack usage should follow a similar structure to that presented here, but requires a richer operational semantics than that given by Launchbury. Finally, it would be interesting to extend this work to a full production abstract machine such as the Spineless Tagless G-Machine [24]. This would allow us to confirm our results against real functional programs written in non-strict languages such as Haskell.

Acknowledgements

This work is supported by EU grants SCIEnce (RII3-CT-026133), ADVANCE (IST-248828) and ParaPhrase (IST-288570), and EPSRC grant HPC-GAP (EP/G 055181). Hugo Simões would like to thank "Fundação para a Ciência e Tecnologia, Portugal" for Ph.D. grant SFRH/BD/17096/2004.

References

[1] E. Albert, J. Silva, and G. Vidal. Time Equations for Lazy Functional (Logic) Languages. In *Proc. AGP-2003: 2003 Joint Conf. on Declarative Prog., Reggio Calabria, Italy, Sept. 3-5, 2003*, pages 13–24, 2003.

[2] E. Albert, S. Genaim, and M. Gómez-Zamalloa. Live Heap Space Analysis for Languages with Garbage Collection. In *Proc. ISMM 2009: Intl. Symp. on Memory Management*, pages 129–138, Dublin, Ireland, June 2009. ACM. ISBN 978-1-60558-347-1.

[3] E. Albert, S. Genaim, and M. Gómez-Zamalloa. Parametric Inference of Memory Requirements for Garbage Collected Languages. In *Proc. 2010 International Symposium on Memory Management*, ISMM '10, pages 121–130, New York, NY, USA, 2010. ACM.

[4] Z. M. Ariola and M. Felleisen. The Call-by-Need Lambda Calculus. *J. Funct. Program.*, 7:265–301, May 1997.

[5] A. Bakewell and C. Runciman. A Model for Comparing the Space Usage of Lazy Evaluators. In *Proc. PPDP 2000: Intl. Conf. on Principles and Practice of Declarative Prog., Quebec, Canada*, pages 151–162, 2000.

[6] A. Bakewell and C. Runciman. A Space Semantics for Core Haskell. *Electr. Notes Theor. Comput. Sci.*, 41(1), 2000.

[7] B. Bjerner and S. Holmström. A Compositional Approach to Time Analysis of First Order Lazy Functional Programs. In *Proc. FPCA '89: Conf. on Functional Prog. Langs. and Comp. Arch.*, pages 157–165, 1989.

[8] V. Braberman, F. Fernández, D. Garbervetsky, and S. Yovine. Parametric Prediction of Heap Memory Requirements. In *Proc. ISMM 2008: Intl. Symp. on Memory Management*, pages 141–150, New York, NY, USA, June 2008.

[9] B. Campbell. Amortised Memory Analysis Using the Depth of Data Structures. In G. Castagna, editor, *Proc. ESOP 2009: 18th European Symposium on Programming, York, UK*, pages 190–204. Springer LNCS 5502, 2009.

[10] W.-N. Chin, H. Nguyen, C. Popeea, and S. Qin. Analysing Memory Resource Bounds for Low-Level Programs. In *Proc. ISMM'08: Intl. Symp. on Memory Management*, pages 151–160, Tucson, USA, June 2008. ACM. ISBN 978-1-60558-134-7.

[11] K. Crary and S. Weirich. Resource Bound Certification. In *Proc. POPL 2000: ACM Symp. on Principles of Prog. Langs.*, pages 184–198, Jan. 2000.

[12] N. A. Danielsson. Lightweight Semiformal Time Complexity Analysis for Purely Functional Data Structures. In *Proc. POPL 2008: Symp. on Principles of Prog. Langs., San Francisco, USA, January 7-12, 2008*, pages 133–144. ACM, 2008.

[13] A. de la Encina and R. Peña-Marí. Proving the Correctness of the STG Machine. In *Proc. IFL '01: Impl. of Functional Langs., Stockholm, Sweden, Sept. 24-26, 2001*, pages 88–104. Springer LNCS 2312, 2002.

[14] A. de la Encina and R. Peña-Marí. Formally Deriving an STG Machine. In *Proc. 5th International ACM SIGPLAN Conference on Principles and Practice of Declarative Programming, 27-29 August 2003, Uppsala, Sweden*, pages 102–112. ACM, 2003.

[15] A. de la Encina and R. Peña-Marí. From Natural Semantics to C: a Formal Derivation of two STG Machines. *J. Funct. Program.*, 19(1): 47–94, 2009.

[16] P. Fradet and D. L. Métayer. Compilation of functional languages by program transformation. *ACM Transactions on Programming Languages and Systems*, 13(1):21–51, January 1991.

[17] J. Gustavsson and D. Sands. A Foundation for Space-Safe Transformations of Call-by-Need Programs. *Electronic Notes on Theoretical Computer Science*, 26, 1999.

[18] J. Hoffmann, K. Aehlig, and M. Hofmann. Multivariate Amortized Resource Analysis. In *38th Symp. on Principles of Prog. Langs. (POPL'11)*, pages 357–370, 2011.

[19] M. Hofmann and S. Jost. Static Prediction of Heap Space Usage for First-Order Functional Programs. In *Proc. POPL 2003: ACM Symp. on Principles of Prog. Langs.*, pages 185–197, Jan. 2003.

[20] M. Hofmann and S. Jost. Type-Based Amortised Heap-Space Analysis (for an Object-Oriented Language). In *Proc. ESOP '06: European Symposium on Prog.*, pages 22–37, Mar. 2006.

[21] M. Hofmann and D. Rodriguez. Efficient type-checking for amortised heap-space analysis. In *Proc. CSL '09: 18th EACSL Annual Conf. on Computer Science Logic*, pages 317–331, 2009.

[22] C. Hope. *A Functional Semantics for Space and Time*. PhD thesis, 2008. University of Nottingham.

[23] R. Hughes. Why Functional Programming Matters. *The Computer Journal*, 32(2):98–107, 1989.

[24] S. L. P. Jones. Implementing Lazy Functional Languages on Stock Hardware: The Spineless Tagless G-Machine. *J. Funct. Program.*, 2 (2):127–202, 1992.

[25] M. B. Josephs. The semantics of lazy functional languages. *Theor. Comput. Sci.*, 68(1):105–111, 1989.

[26] S. Jost. Static Prediction of Dynamic Space Usage of Linear Functional Programs, Dipl. Thesis, Darmstadt Univ. of Tech., 2002, .

[27] S. Jost. *Automated Amortised Analysis*. PhD thesis, LMU Munich, .

[28] S. Jost, H.-W. Loidl, K. Hammond, N. Scaife, and M. Hofmann. "Carbon Credits" for Resource-Bounded Computations Using Amortised Analysis. In *Proc. FM 2009: Intl. Conf. on Formal Methods*, pages 354–369. Springer LNCS 5850, 2009.

[29] S. Jost, H.-W. Loidl, K. Hammond, and M. Hofmann. Static determination of quantitative resource usage for higher-order programs. In *Proc. POPL 2010: ACM Symp. on Principles of Prog. Langs., Madrid, Spain*, pages 223–236, Jan. 2010.

[30] J. Launchbury. A Natural Semantics for Lazy Evaluation. In *Proc. POPL '93: Symp. on Princ. of Prog. Langs.*, pages 144–154, 1993.

[31] J. Maraist, M. Odersky, and P. Wadler. The Call-by-Need Lambda Calculus. *J. Funct. Program.*, 8:275–317, May 1998.

[32] R. Matthes. *Extensions of System F by Iteration and Primitive Recursion on Monotone Induction Types*. PhD thesis, LMU Munich, 1998.

[33] A. Moran and D. Sands. Improvement in a Lazy Context: An Operational Theory for Call-by-Need. In *POPL*, pages 43–56, 1999.

[34] J. Mountjoy. The Spineless Tagless G-machine, naturally. In *Proc. ICFP '98: Intl. Conf. on Functional Prog.*, pages 163–173, 1998.

[35] C. Okasaki. *Purely Functional Data Structures*. Cambridge University Press, 1998.

[36] S. Peyton Jones (ed.), L. Augustsson, B. Boutel, F. Burton, J. Fasel, A. Gordon, K. Hammond, R. Hughes, P. Hudak, T. Johnsson, M. Jones, J. Peterson, A. Reid, and P. Wadler. Report on the Non-Strict Functional Language, Haskell (Haskell98). Technical report, Yale University, 1999.

[37] D. Sands. Complexity Analysis for a Lazy Higher-Order Language. In *Proc. ESOP '90: European Symposium on Programming, Copenhagen, Denmark*, Springer LNCS 432, pages 361–376, 1990.

[38] D. Sands. *Calculi for Time Analysis of Functional Programs*. PhD thesis, Imperial College, University of London, September 1990.

[39] D. Sands. Computing with Contexts: A Simple Approach. In *Proc. HOOTS II: Higher-Order Operational Techniques in Semantics*, Electr. Notes in Theoretical Comp. Sci. 1998.

[40] P. Sestoft. Deriving a Lazy Abstract Machine. *J. Functional Programming*, 7(3):231–264, 1997.

[41] O. Shkaravska, R. van Kesteren, and M. van Eekelen. Polynomial Size Analysis of First-Order Functions. In *Proc. TLCA 2007: Typed Lambda Calculi and Applications (TLCA 2007)*, pages 351–365, Paris, France, June 26–28, June 2007. Springer LNCS 4583.

[42] R. E. Tarjan. Amortized computational complexity. *SIAM Journal on Algebraic and Discrete Methods*, 6(2):306–318, April 1985.

[43] P. B. Vasconcelos. *Space Cost Analysis Using Sized Types*. PhD thesis, University of St Andrews, 2008.

[44] P. B. Vasconcelos and K. Hammond. Inferring Cost Equations for Recursive, Polymorphic and Higher-Order Functional Programs. In *Proc. IFL '03: Impl. of Functional Languages*, pages 86–101, Edinburgh, UK, 2004. Springer LNCS 3145.

[45] P. Wadler. Strictness Analysis aids Time Analysis. In *Proc. POPL '88: ACM Symp. on Princ. of Prog. Langs.*, pages 119–132, 1988.

[46] P. Wadler. The Essence of Functional Programming. In *Proc. POPL '92: ACM Symp. on Principles of Prog. Langs.*, pages 1–14, Jan. 1992.

[47] P. Wadler and J. Hughes. Projections for Strictness Analysis. In *Proc. FPCA'87: Intl. Conf. on Functional Prog. Langs. and Comp. Arch.*, Springer LNCS 274, pages 385–407, Sept. 1987.

Introspective Pushdown Analysis of Higher-Order Programs

Christopher Earl
University of Utah
cwearl@cs.utah.edu

Ilya Sergey
KU Leuven
ilya.sergey@cs.kuleuven.be

Matthew Might
University of Utah
might@cs.utah.edu

David Van Horn
Northeastern University
dvanhorn@ccs.neu.edu

Abstract

In the static analysis of functional programs, pushdown flow analysis and abstract garbage collection skirt just inside the boundaries of soundness and decidability. Alone, each method reduces analysis times and boosts precision by orders of magnitude. This work illuminates and conquers the theoretical challenges that stand in the way of combining the power of these techniques. The challenge in marrying these techniques is not subtle: computing the reachable control states of a pushdown system relies on limiting access during transition to the top of the stack; abstract garbage collection, on the other hand, needs full access to the entire stack to compute a root set, just as concrete collection does. *Introspective* pushdown systems resolve this conflict. Introspective pushdown systems provide enough access to the stack to allow abstract garbage collection, but they remain restricted enough to compute control-state reachability, thereby enabling the sound and precise product of pushdown analysis and abstract garbage collection. Experiments reveal synergistic interplay between the techniques, and the fusion demonstrates "better-than-both-worlds" precision.

Categories and Subject Descriptors D.3.4 [*Programming languages*]: Processors—Optimization; F.3.2 [*Logics and Meanings of Programs*]: Semantics of Programming Languages—Program analysis, Operational semantics

General Terms Languages, Theory

Keywords CFA2, pushdown systems, abstract interpretation, pushdown analysis, program analysis, abstract machines, abstract garbage collection, higher-order languages

1. Introduction

The recent development of a context-free[1] approach to control-flow analysis (CFA2) by Vardoulakis and Shivers has provoked a seismic shift in the static analysis of higher-order programs [22]. Prior to CFA2, a precise analysis of recursive behavior had been a stumbling block—even though flow analyses have an important role to play in optimization for functional languages, such as flow-driven inlining [13], interprocedural constant propagation [19] and type-check elimination [23].

While it had been possible to statically analyze recursion *soundly*, CFA2 made it possible to analyze recursion *precisely* by matching calls and returns without approximation. In its pursuit of recursion, clever engineering steered CFA2 just shy of undecidability. The payoff is an order-of-magnitude reduction in analysis time and an order-of-magnitude increase in precision.

For a visual measure of the impact, Figure 1 renders the abstract transition graph (a model of all possible traces through the program) for the toy program in Figure 2. For this example, pushdown analysis eliminates spurious return-flow from the use of recursion. But, recursion is just one problem of many for flow analysis. For instance, pushdown analysis still gets tripped up by the spurious cross-flow problem; at calls to `(id f)` and `(id g)` in the previous example, it thinks `(id g)` could be `f` *or* `g`.

Powerful techniques such as abstract garbage collection [14] were developed to solve the cross-flow problem.[2] In fact, abstract garbage collection, by itself, also delivers orders-of-magnitude improvements to analytic speed and precision. (See Figure 1 again for a visualization of that impact.)

It is natural to ask: can abstract garbage collection and pushdown anlysis work together? Can their strengths be multiplied? At first glance, the answer appears to be a disheartening *No.*

1.1 The problem: The whole stack *versus* just the top

Abstract garbage collections seems to require more than pushdown analysis can decidably provide: access to the full stack. Abstract garbage collection, like its name implies, discards unreachable values from an abstract store during the analysis. Like concrete garbage collection, abstract garbage collection also begins its sweep with a root set, and like concrete garbage collection, it must traverse the abstract stack to compute that root set. But, pushdown

[1] As in context-free language, not context-sensitivity.

[2] The cross-flow problem arises because monotonicity prevents revoking a judgment like "procedure `f` flows to `x`," or "procedure `g` flows to `x`," once it's been made.

ICFP '12 September 10–12, Copenhagen, Denmark.

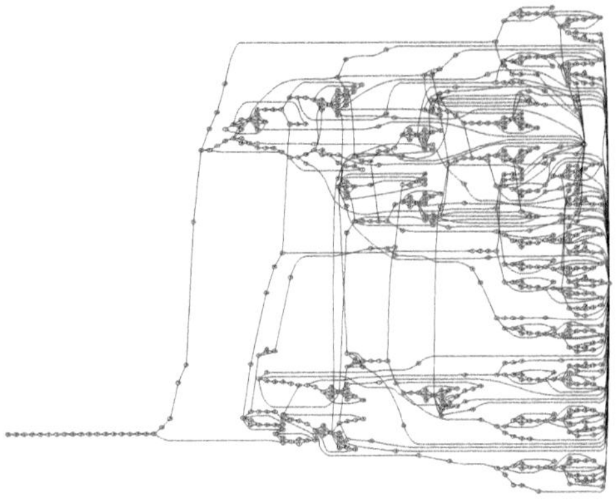

(1) without pushdown analysis or abstract GC: 653 states

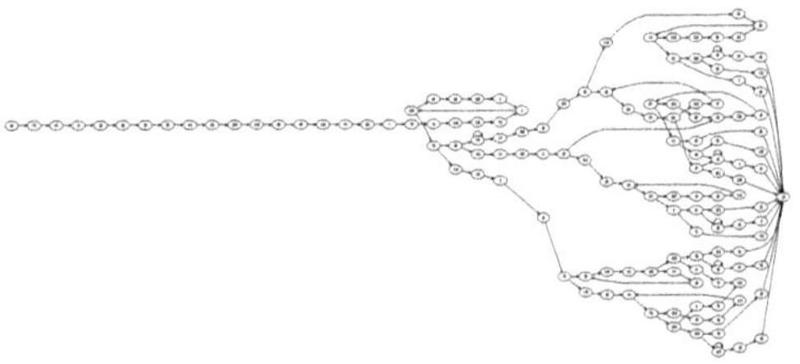

(2) with pushdown only: 139 states

(3) with GC only: 105 states

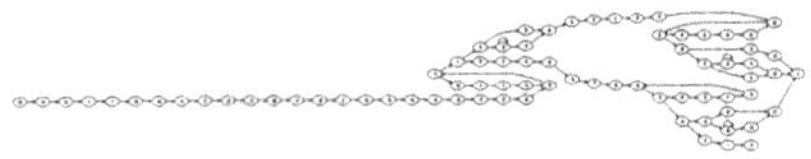

(4) with pushdown analysis and abstract GC: 77 states

Figure 1. We generated an abstract transition graph for the same program from Figure 2 four times: (1) without pushdown analysis or abstract garbage collection; (2) with only abstract garbage collection; (3) with only pushdown analysis; (4) with both pushdown analysis and abstract garbage collection. With only pushdown or abstract GC, the abstract transition graph shrinks by an order of magnitude, but in different ways. The pushdown-only analysis is confused by variables that are bound to several different higher-order functions, but for short durations. The abstract-GC-only is confused by non-tail-recursive loop structure. With both techniques enabled, the graph shrinks by nearly half yet again and fully recovers the control structure of the original program.

```
(define (id x) x)

(define (f n)
  (cond [(<= n 1)  1]
        [else      (* n (f (- n 1)))]))

(define (g n)
  (cond [(<= n 1)  1]
        [else      (+ (* n n) (g (- n 1)))]))

(print (+ ((id f) 3) ((id g) 4)))
```

Figure 2. A small example to illuminate the strengths and weaknesses of both pushdown analysis and abstract garbage collection.

systems are restricted to viewing the top of the stack (or a bounded depth)—a condition violated by this traversal.

Fortunately, abstract garbage collection does not need to arbitrarily modify the stack. In fact, it does not even need to know the order of the frames; it only needs the *set* of frames on the stack. We find a richer class of machine—*introspective* pushdown systems—which retains just enough restrictions to compute reachable control states, yet few enough to enable abstract garbage collection.

It is therefore possible to fuse the full benefits of abstract garbage collection with pushdown analysis. The dramatic reduction in abstract transition graph size from the top to the bottom in Figure 1 (and echoed by later benchmarks) conveys the impact of this fusion.

Secondary motivations There are three strong secondary motivations for this work: (1) bringing context-sensitivity to pushdown analysis; (2) exposing the context-freedom of the analysis; and (3) enabling pushdown analysis without continuation passing style.

In CFA2, monovariant (0CFA-like) context-sensitivity is etched directly into the abstract semantics, which are in turn, phrased in terms of an explicit (imperative) summarization algorithm for a partitioned continuation-passing style.

In addition, the context-freedom of the analysis is buried implicitly inside this algorithm. No pushdown system or context-free grammar is explicitly identified. A necessary precursor to our work was to make the pushdown system in CFA2 explicit.

A third motivation was to show that a transformation to continuation-passing style is unnecessary for pushdown analysis. In fact, pushdown analysis is arguably more natural over direct-style programs.

1.2 Overview

We first review preliminaries to set a consistent feel for terminology and notation, particularly with respect to pushdown systems. The derivation of the analysis begins with a concrete CESK-machine-style semantics for A-Normal Form λ-calculus. The next step is an infinite-state abstract interpretation, constructed by bounding the C(ontrol), E(nvironment) and S(tore) portions of the machine while leaving the stack—the K(ontinuation)—unbounded. A simple shift in perspective reveals that this abstract interpretation is a rooted pushdown system.

We then introduce abstract garbage collection and quickly find that it violates the pushdown model with its traversals of the stack. To prove the decidability of control-state reachability, we formulate introspective pushdown systems, and recast abstract garbage collection within this framework. We then show that control-state reachability is decidable for introspective pushdown systems as well.

We conclude with an implementation and empirical evaluation that shows strong synergies between pushdown analysis and abstract garbage collection, including significant reductions in the size of the abstract state transition graph.

1.3 Contributions

We make the following contributions:

1. Our primary contribution is demonstrating the decidability of fusing abstract garbage collection with pushdown flow analysis of higher-order programs. Proof comes in the form of a fixed-point solution for computing the reachable control-states of an introspective pushdown system and an embedding of abstract garbage collection as an introspective pushdown system.
2. We show that classical notions of context-sensitivity, such as k-CFA and poly/CFA, have direct generalizations in a pushdown setting: monovariance[3] is *not* an essential restriction, as in CFA2.
3. We make the context-free aspect of CFA2 explicit: we clearly define and identify the pushdown system. We do so by starting with a classical CESK machine and systematically abstracting until a pushdown system emerges. We also remove the orthogonal frame-local-bindings aspect of CFA2, so as to directly solely on the pushdown nature of the analysis.
4. We remove the requirement for CPS-conversion by synthesizing the analysis directly for direct-style (in the form of A-normal form lambda-calculus).
5. We empirically validate claims of improved precision on a suite of benchmarks. We find synergies between pushdown analysis and abstract garbage collection that makes the whole greater that the sum of its parts.

2. Pushdown preliminaries

The literature contains many equivalent definitions of pushdown machines, so we adapt our own definitions from Sipser [20]. *Readers familiar with pushdown theory may wish to skip ahead.*

2.1 Syntactic sugar

When a triple (x, ℓ, x') is an edge in a labeled graph:

$$x \overset{\ell}{\rightarrowtail} x' \equiv (x, \ell, x').$$

Similarly, when a pair (x, x') is a graph edge:

$$x \rightarrowtail x' \equiv (x, x').$$

We use both string and vector notation for sequences:

$$a_1 a_2 \ldots a_n \equiv \langle a_1, a_2, \ldots, a_n \rangle \equiv \vec{a}.$$

2.2 Stack actions, stack change and stack manipulation

Stacks are sequences over a stack alphabet Γ. To reason about stack manipulation concisely, we first turn stack alphabets into "stack-action" sets; each character represents a change to the stack: push, pop or no change.

For each character γ in a stack alphabet Γ, the **stack-action** set $\Gamma_\pm$ contains a push character γ_+; a pop character γ_-; and a no-stack-change indicator, ϵ:

$$\begin{aligned} g \in \Gamma_\pm ::= {} & \epsilon & & \text{[stack unchanged]} \\ \mid {} & \gamma_+ & \text{for each } \gamma \in \Gamma \quad & \text{[pushed } \gamma\text{]} \\ \mid {} & \gamma_- & \text{for each } \gamma \in \Gamma \quad & \text{[popped } \gamma\text{]}. \end{aligned}$$

In this paper, the symbol g represents some stack action.

When we develop introspective pushdown systems, we are going to need formalisms for easily manipulating stack-action strings and stacks. Given a string of stack actions, we can compact it into a minimal string describing net stack change. We do so through the operator $\lfloor \cdot \rfloor : \Gamma_\pm^* \to \Gamma_\pm^*$, which cancels out opposing adjacent push-pop stack actions:

$$\lfloor \vec{g}\ \gamma_+ \gamma_-\ \vec{g}\,' \rfloor = \lfloor \vec{g}\ \vec{g}\,' \rfloor \qquad \lfloor \vec{g}\ \epsilon\ \vec{g}\,' \rfloor = \lfloor \vec{g}\ \vec{g}\,' \rfloor,$$

so that $\lfloor \vec{g} \rfloor = \vec{g}$, if there are no cancellations to be made in the string $\vec{g}$.

We can convert a net string back into a stack by stripping off the push symbols with the stackify operator, $\lceil \cdot \rceil : \Gamma_\pm^* \rightharpoonup \Gamma^*$:

$$\lceil \gamma_+ \gamma'_+ \ldots \gamma^{(n)}_+ \rceil = \langle \gamma^{(n)}, \ldots, \gamma', \gamma \rangle,$$

and for convenience, $[\vec{g}] = \lceil \lfloor \vec{g} \rfloor \rceil$. Notice the stackify operator is defined for strings containing only push actions.

2.3 Pushdown systems

A **pushdown system** is a triple $M = (Q, \Gamma, \delta)$ where:

1. Q is a finite set of control states;
2. Γ is a stack alphabet; and
3. $\delta \subseteq Q \times \Gamma_\pm \times Q$ is a transition relation.

The set $Q \times \Gamma^*$ is called the **configuration-space** of this pushdown system. We use $\mathbb{PDS}$ to denote the class of all pushdown systems.

For the following definitions, let $M = (Q, \Gamma, \delta)$.

- The labeled **transition relation** $(\longmapsto_M) \subseteq (Q \times \Gamma^*) \times \Gamma_\pm \times (Q \times \Gamma^*)$ determines whether one configuration may transition to another while performing the given stack action:

$$\begin{aligned} (q, \vec{\gamma}) \overset{\epsilon}{\underset{M}{\longmapsto}} (q', \vec{\gamma}) &\text{ iff } q \overset{\epsilon}{\rightarrowtail} q' \in \delta & \text{[no change]} \\ (q, \gamma : \vec{\gamma}) \overset{\gamma_-}{\underset{M}{\longmapsto}} (q', \vec{\gamma}) &\text{ iff } q \overset{\gamma_-}{\rightarrowtail} q' \in \delta & \text{[pop]} \\ (q, \vec{\gamma}) \overset{\gamma_+}{\underset{M}{\longmapsto}} (q', \gamma : \vec{\gamma}) &\text{ iff } q \overset{\gamma_+}{\rightarrowtail} q' \in \delta & \text{[push].} \end{aligned}$$

- If unlabelled, the transition relation $(\longmapsto)$ checks whether *any* stack action can enable the transition:

$$c \underset{M}{\longmapsto} c' \text{ iff } c \overset{g}{\underset{M}{\longmapsto}} c' \text{ for some stack action } g.$$

- For a string of stack actions $g_1 \ldots g_n$:

$$c_0 \overset{g_1 \ldots g_n}{\underset{M}{\longmapsto}} c_n \text{ iff } c_0 \overset{g_1}{\underset{M}{\longmapsto}} c_1 \overset{g_2}{\underset{M}{\longmapsto}} \cdots \overset{g_{n-1}}{\underset{M}{\longmapsto}} c_{n-1} \overset{g_n}{\underset{M}{\longmapsto}} c_n,$$

for some configurations $c_0, \ldots, c_n$.

[3] Monovariance refers to an abstraction that groups all bindings to the same variable together: there is *one* abstract variant for all bindings to each variable.

- For the transitive closure:

$$c \underset{M}{\overset{*}{\longmapsto}} c' \text{ iff } c \underset{M}{\overset{\vec{g}}{\longmapsto}} c' \text{ for some action string } \vec{g}\,.$$

2.4 Rooted pushdown systems

A **rooted pushdown system** is a quadruple (Q, Γ, δ, q_0) in which (Q, Γ, δ) is a pushdown system and $q_0 \in Q$ is an initial (root) state. $\mathbb{RPDS}$ is the class of all rooted pushdown systems.

For a rooted pushdown system $M = (Q, \Gamma, \delta, q_0)$, we define the **reachable-from-root transition relation**:

$$c \underset{M}{\overset{g}{\longmapsto\!\!\!\rightarrow}} c' \text{ iff } (q_0, \langle\rangle) \underset{M}{\overset{*}{\longmapsto}} c \text{ and } c \underset{M}{\overset{g}{\longmapsto}} c'.$$

In other words, the root-reachable transition relation also makes sure that the root control state can actually reach the transition.

We overload the root-reachable transition relation to operate on control states:

$$q \underset{M}{\overset{g}{\longmapsto\!\!\!\rightarrow}} q' \text{ iff } (q, \vec{\gamma}) \underset{M}{\overset{g}{\longmapsto\!\!\!\rightarrow}} (q', \vec{\gamma}\,') \text{ for some stacks } \vec{\gamma}, \vec{\gamma}\,'.$$

For both root-reachable relations, if we elide the stack-action label, then, as in the un-rooted case, the transition holds if *there exists* some stack action that enables the transition:

$$q \underset{M}{\longmapsto\!\!\!\rightarrow} q' \text{ iff } q \underset{M}{\overset{g}{\longmapsto\!\!\!\rightarrow}} q' \text{ for some action } g.$$

2.5 Computing reachability in pushdown systems

A pushdown flow analysis can be construed as computing the *root-reachable* subset of control states in a rooted pushdown system, $M = (Q, \Gamma, \delta, q_0)$:

$$\left\{q : q_0 \underset{M}{\longmapsto\!\!\!\rightarrow} q\right\}$$

Reps *et. al* and many others provide a straightforward "summarization" algorithm to compute this set [1, 8, 17, 18]. Our preliminary report also offers a reachability algorithm tailored to higher-order programs [4].

2.6 Nondeterministic finite automata

In this work, we will need a finite description of all possible stacks at a given control state within a rooted pushdown system. We will exploit the fact that the set of stacks at a given control point is a regular language. Specifically, we will extract a nondeterministic finite automaton accepting that language from the structure of a rooted pushdown system. A **nondeterministic finite automaton** (NFA) is a quintuple $M = (Q, \Sigma, \delta, q_0, F)$:

- Q is a finite set of control states;
- Σ is an input alphabet;
- $\delta \subseteq Q \times (\Sigma \cup \{\epsilon\}) \times Q$ is a transition relation.
- q_0 is a distinguished start state.
- $F \subseteq Q$ is a set of accepting states.

We denote the class of all NFAs as $\mathbb{NFA}$.

3. Setting: A-Normal Form λ-calculus

Since our goal is analysis of *higher-order languages*, we operate on the λ-calculus. To simplify presentation of the concrete and abstract semantics, we choose A-Normal Form λ-calculus. (This is a strictly cosmetic choice: all of our results can be replayed *mutatis mutandis* in the standard direct-style setting as well.) ANF enforces an order of evaluation and it requires that all arguments to a function be atomic:

$$\begin{array}{rcll}
e \in \mathsf{Exp} & ::= & (\mathtt{let}\ ((v\ \mathit{call}))\ e) & \text{[non-tail call]} \\
& | & \mathit{call} & \text{[tail call]} \\
& | & æ & \text{[return]} \\
f, æ \in \mathsf{Atom} & ::= & v \mid \mathit{lam} & \text{[atomic expressions]} \\
\mathit{lam} \in \mathsf{Lam} & ::= & (\lambda\ (v)\ e) & \text{[lambda terms]} \\
\mathit{call} \in \mathsf{Call} & ::= & (f\ æ) & \text{[applications]} \\
& & v \in \mathsf{Var} \text{ is a set of identifiers} & \text{[variables].}
\end{array}$$

$$\begin{array}{rcll}
c \in \mathit{Conf} & = & \mathsf{Exp} \times \mathit{Env} \times \mathit{Store} \times \mathit{Kont} & \text{[configurations]} \\
\rho \in \mathit{Env} & = & \mathsf{Var} \rightharpoonup \mathit{Addr} & \text{[environments]} \\
\sigma \in \mathit{Store} & = & \mathit{Addr} \to \mathit{Clo} & \text{[stores]} \\
\mathit{clo} \in \mathit{Clo} & = & \mathsf{Lam} \times \mathit{Env} & \text{[closures]} \\
\kappa \in \mathit{Kont} & = & \mathit{Frame}^* & \text{[continuations]} \\
\phi \in \mathit{Frame} & = & \mathsf{Var} \times \mathsf{Exp} \times \mathit{Env} & \text{[stack frames]} \\
& & a \in \mathit{Addr} \text{ is an infinite set of addresses} & \text{[addresses].}
\end{array}$$

Figure 3. The concrete configuration-space.

We use the CESK machine of Felleisen and Friedman [5] to specify a small-step semantics for ANF. The CESK machine has an explicit stack, and under a structural abstraction, the stack component of this machine directly becomes the stack component of a pushdown system. The set of configurations (Conf) for this machine has the four expected components (Figure 3).

3.1 Semantics

To define the semantics, we need five items:

1. $\mathcal{I} : \mathsf{Exp} \to \mathit{Conf}$ injects an expression into a configuration:
$$c_0 = \mathcal{I}(e) = (e, [], [], \langle\rangle).$$
2. $\mathcal{A} : \mathsf{Atom} \times \mathit{Env} \times \mathit{Store} \rightharpoonup \mathit{Clo}$ evaluates atomic expressions:
$$\begin{array}{rcll}
\mathcal{A}(\mathit{lam}, \rho, \sigma) & = & (\mathit{lam}, \rho) & \text{[closure creation]} \\
\mathcal{A}(v, \rho, \sigma) & = & \sigma(\rho(v)) & \text{[variable look-up].}
\end{array}$$
3. $(\Rightarrow) \subseteq \mathit{Conf} \times \mathit{Conf}$ transitions between configurations. (Defined below.)
4. $\mathcal{E} : \mathsf{Exp} \to \mathcal{P}(\mathit{Conf})$ computes the set of reachable machine configurations for a given program:
$$\mathcal{E}(e) = \{c : \mathcal{I}(e) \Rightarrow^* c\}\,.$$
5. $\mathit{alloc} : \mathsf{Var} \times \mathit{Conf} \to \mathit{Addr}$ chooses fresh store addresses for newly bound variables. The address-allocation function is an opaque parameter in this semantics, so that the forthcoming abstract semantics may also parameterize allocation. This parameterization provides the knob to tune the polyvariance and context-sensitivity of the resulting analysis. For the sake of defining the concrete semantics, letting addresses be natural numbers suffices, and then the allocator can choose the lowest

unused address:

$$Addr = \mathbb{N}$$
$$alloc(v, (e, \rho, \sigma, \kappa)) = 1 + \max(dom(\sigma)).$$

Transition relation To define the transition $c \Rightarrow c'$, we need three rules. The first rule handle tail calls by evaluating the function into a closure, evaluating the argument into a value and then moving to the body of the closure's λ-term:

$$\overbrace{(\llbracket (f\ æ) \rrbracket, \rho, \sigma, \kappa)}^{c} \Rightarrow \overbrace{(e, \rho'', \sigma', \kappa)}^{c'}, \text{ where}$$
$$(\llbracket (\lambda\ (v)\ e) \rrbracket, \rho') = \mathcal{A}(f, \rho, \sigma)$$
$$a = alloc(v, c)$$
$$\rho'' = \rho'[v \mapsto a]$$
$$\sigma' = \sigma[a \mapsto \mathcal{A}(æ, \rho, \sigma)].$$

Non-tail call pushes a frame onto the stack and evaluates the call:

$$\overbrace{(\llbracket (\texttt{let}\ ((v\ call))\ e) \rrbracket, \rho, \sigma, \kappa)}^{c} \Rightarrow \overbrace{(call, \rho, \sigma, (v, e, \rho) : \kappa)}^{c'}.$$

Function return pops a stack frame:

$$\overbrace{(æ, \rho, \sigma, (v, e, \rho') : \kappa)}^{c} \Rightarrow \overbrace{(e, \rho'', \sigma', \kappa)}^{c'}, \text{ where}$$
$$a = alloc(v, c)$$
$$\rho'' = \rho'[v \mapsto a]$$
$$\sigma' = \sigma[a \mapsto \mathcal{A}(æ, \rho, \sigma)].$$

4. Pushdown abstract interpretation

Our first step toward a static analysis is an abstract interpretation into an *infinite* state-space. To achieve a pushdown analysis, we simply abstract away less than we normally would. Specifically, we leave the stack height unbounded.

Figure 4 details the abstract configuration-space. To synthesize it, we force addresses to be a finite set, but crucially, we leave the stack untouched. When we compact the set of addresses into a finite set, the machine may run out of addresses to allocate, and when it does, the pigeon-hole principle will force multiple closures to reside at the same address. As a result, we have no choice but to force the range of the store to become a power set in the abstract configuration-space. The abstract transition relation has components analogous to those from the concrete semantics:

Program injection The abstract injection function $\hat{\mathcal{I}} : \mathsf{Exp} \to \widehat{Conf}$ pairs an expression with an empty environment, an empty store and an empty stack to create the initial abstract configuration:

$$\hat{c}_0 = \hat{\mathcal{I}}(e) = (e, [], [], \langle\rangle).$$

Atomic expression evaluation The abstract atomic expression evaluator, $\hat{\mathcal{A}} : \mathsf{Atom} \times \widehat{Env} \times \widehat{Store} \to \mathcal{P}(\widehat{Clo})$, returns the value of an atomic expression in the context of an environment and a store; it returns a *set* of abstract closures:

$$\hat{\mathcal{A}}(lam, \hat{\rho}, \hat{\sigma}) = \{(lam, \hat{\rho})\} \quad \text{[closure creation]}$$
$$\hat{\mathcal{A}}(v, \hat{\rho}, \hat{\sigma}) = \hat{\sigma}(\hat{\rho}(v)) \quad \text{[variable look-up]}.$$

$\hat{c} \in \widehat{Conf} = \mathsf{Exp} \times \widehat{Env} \times \widehat{Store} \times \widehat{Kont}$	[configurations]
$\hat{\rho} \in \widehat{Env} = \mathsf{Var} \rightharpoonup \widehat{Addr}$	[environments]
$\hat{\sigma} \in \widehat{Store} = \widehat{Addr} \to \mathcal{P}\left(\widehat{Clo}\right)$	[stores]
$\widehat{clo} \in \widehat{Clo} = \mathsf{Lam} \times \widehat{Env}$	[closures]
$\hat{\kappa} \in \widehat{Kont} = \widehat{Frame}^*$	[continuations]
$\hat{\phi} \in \widehat{Frame} = \mathsf{Var} \times \mathsf{Exp} \times \widehat{Env}$	[stack frames]
$\hat{a} \in \widehat{Addr}$ is a *finite* set of addresses	[addresses].

Figure 4. The abstract configuration-space.

Reachable configurations The abstract program evaluator $\hat{\mathcal{E}} : \mathsf{Exp} \to \mathcal{P}(\widehat{Conf})$ returns all of the configurations reachable from the initial configuration:

$$\hat{\mathcal{E}}(e) = \left\{\hat{c} : \hat{\mathcal{I}}(e) \leadsto^* \hat{c}\right\}.$$

Because there are an infinite number of abstract configurations, a naïve implementation of this function may not terminate.

Transition relation The abstract transition relation $(\leadsto) \subseteq \widehat{Conf} \times \widehat{Conf}$ has three rules, one of which has become non-deterministic. A tail call may fork because there could be multiple abstract closures that it is invoking:

$$\overbrace{(\llbracket (f\ æ) \rrbracket, \hat{\rho}, \hat{\sigma}, \hat{\kappa})}^{\hat{c}} \leadsto \overbrace{(e, \hat{\rho}'', \hat{\sigma}', \hat{\kappa})}^{\hat{c}'}, \text{ where}$$
$$(\llbracket (\lambda\ (v)\ e) \rrbracket, \hat{\rho}') \in \hat{\mathcal{A}}(f, \hat{\rho}, \hat{\sigma})$$
$$\hat{a} = \widehat{alloc}(v, \hat{c})$$
$$\hat{\rho}'' = \hat{\rho}'[v \mapsto \hat{a}]$$
$$\hat{\sigma}' = \hat{\sigma} \sqcup [\hat{a} \mapsto \hat{\mathcal{A}}(æ, \hat{\rho}, \hat{\sigma})].$$

We define all of the partial orders shortly, but for stores:

$$(\hat{\sigma} \sqcup \hat{\sigma}')(\hat{a}) = \hat{\sigma}(\hat{a}) \cup \hat{\sigma}'(\hat{a}).$$

A non-tail call pushes a frame onto the stack and evaluates the call:

$$\overbrace{(\llbracket (\texttt{let}\ ((v\ call))\ e) \rrbracket, \hat{\rho}, \hat{\sigma}, \hat{\kappa})}^{\hat{c}} \leadsto \overbrace{(call, \hat{\rho}, \hat{\sigma}, (v, e, \hat{\rho}) : \hat{\kappa})}^{\hat{c}'}.$$

A function return pops a stack frame:

$$\overbrace{(æ, \hat{\rho}, \hat{\sigma}, (v, e, \hat{\rho}') : \hat{\kappa})}^{\hat{c}} \leadsto \overbrace{(e, \hat{\rho}'', \hat{\sigma}', \hat{\kappa})}^{\hat{c}'}, \text{ where}$$
$$\hat{a} = \widehat{alloc}(v, \hat{c})$$
$$\hat{\rho}'' = \hat{\rho}'[v \mapsto \hat{a}]$$
$$\hat{\sigma}' = \hat{\sigma} \sqcup [\hat{a} \mapsto \hat{\mathcal{A}}(æ, \hat{\rho}, \hat{\sigma})].$$

Allocation: Polyvariance and context-sensitivity In the abstract semantics, the abstract allocation function $\widehat{alloc} : \mathsf{Var} \times \widehat{Conf} \to \widehat{Addr}$ determines the polyvariance of the analysis. In a control-flow analysis, *polyvariance* literally refers to the number of abstract addresses (variants) there are for each variable. An advantage of this framework over CFA2 is that varying this abstract allocation function instantiates pushdown versions of classical flow analyses. All of the following allocation approaches can be used with the abstract semantics. The abstract allocation function is a parameter to the analysis.

Monovariance: Pushdown 0CFA Pushdown 0CFA uses variables themselves for abstract addresses:

$$\widehat{Addr} = \mathsf{Var}$$
$$alloc(v, \hat{c}) = v.$$

Context-sensitive: Pushdown 1CFA Pushdown 1CFA pairs the variable with the current expression to get an abstract address:

$$\widehat{Addr} = \mathsf{Var} \times \mathsf{Exp}$$
$$alloc(v, (e, \hat{\rho}, \hat{\sigma}, \hat{\kappa})) = (v, e).$$

Polymorphic splitting: Pushdown poly/CFA Assuming we compiled the program from a programming language with let-bound polymorphism and marked which functions were let-bound, we can enable polymorphic splitting:

$$\widehat{Addr} = \mathsf{Var} + \mathsf{Var} \times \mathsf{Exp}$$
$$alloc(v, (\llbracket (f\ æ) \rrbracket, \hat{\rho}, \hat{\sigma}, \hat{\kappa})) = \begin{cases} (v, \llbracket (f\ æ) \rrbracket) & f \text{ is let-bound} \\ v & \text{otherwise.} \end{cases}$$

Pushdown k-CFA For pushdown k-CFA, we need to look beyond the current state and at the last k states. By concatenating the expressions in the last k states together, and pairing this sequence with a variable we get pushdown k-CFA:

$$\widehat{Addr} = \mathsf{Var} \times \mathsf{Exp}^k$$
$$\widehat{alloc}(v, \langle (e_1, \hat{\rho}_1, \hat{\sigma}_1, \hat{\kappa}_1), \ldots \rangle) = (v, \langle e_1, \ldots, e_k \rangle).$$

4.1 Partial orders

For each set $\hat{X}$ inside the abstract configuration-space, we use the natural partial order, $(\sqsubseteq_{\hat{X}}) \subseteq \hat{X} \times \hat{X}$. Abstract addresses and syntactic sets have flat partial orders. For the other sets, the partial order lifts:

- point-wise over environments:
$$\hat{\rho} \sqsubseteq \hat{\rho}' \text{ iff } \hat{\rho}(v) = \hat{\rho}'(v) \text{ for all } v \in dom(\hat{\rho});$$
- component-wise over closures:
$$(lam, \hat{\rho}) \sqsubseteq (lam, \hat{\rho}') \text{ iff } \hat{\rho} \sqsubseteq \hat{\rho}';$$
- point-wise over stores:
$$\hat{\sigma} \sqsubseteq \hat{\sigma}' \text{ iff } \hat{\sigma}(\hat{a}) \sqsubseteq \hat{\sigma}'(\hat{a}) \text{ for all } \hat{a} \in dom(\hat{\sigma});$$
- component-wise over frames:
$$(v, e, \hat{\rho}) \sqsubseteq (v, e, \hat{\rho}') \text{ iff } \hat{\rho} \sqsubseteq \hat{\rho}';$$
- element-wise over continuations:
$$\langle \hat{\phi}_1, \ldots, \hat{\phi}_n \rangle \sqsubseteq \langle \hat{\phi}'_1, \ldots, \hat{\phi}'_n \rangle \text{ iff } \hat{\phi}_i \sqsubseteq \hat{\phi}'_i; \text{ and}$$
- component-wise across configurations:
$$(e, \hat{\rho}, \hat{\sigma}, \hat{\kappa}) \sqsubseteq (e, \hat{\rho}', \hat{\sigma}', \hat{\kappa}') \text{ iff } \hat{\rho} \sqsubseteq \hat{\rho}' \text{ and } \hat{\sigma} \sqsubseteq \hat{\sigma}' \text{ and } \hat{\kappa} \sqsubseteq \hat{\kappa}'.$$

4.2 Soundness

To prove soundness, an abstraction map α connects the concrete and abstract configuration-spaces:

$$\alpha(e, \rho, \sigma, \kappa) = (e, \alpha(\rho), \alpha(\sigma), \alpha(\kappa))$$
$$\alpha(\rho) = \lambda v.\alpha(\rho(v))$$
$$\alpha(\sigma) = \lambda \hat{a}. \bigsqcup_{\alpha(a)=\hat{a}} \{\alpha(\sigma(a))\}$$
$$\alpha\langle \phi_1, \ldots, \phi_n \rangle = \langle \alpha(\phi_1), \ldots, \alpha(\phi_n) \rangle$$
$$\alpha(v, e, \rho) = (v, e, \alpha(\rho))$$
$$\alpha(a) \text{ is determined by the allocation functions.}$$

It is then easy to prove that the abstract transition relation simulates the concrete transition relation:

Theorem 4.1. *If:*

$$\alpha(c) \sqsubseteq \hat{c} \text{ and } c \Rightarrow c',$$

then there must exist $\hat{c}' \in \widehat{Conf}$ *such that:*

$$\alpha(c') \sqsubseteq \hat{c}' \text{ and } \hat{c} \leadsto \hat{c}'.$$

Proof. The proof follows by case-wise analysis on the type of the expression in the configuration. It is a straightforward adaptation of similar proofs, such as that of [11] for k-CFA. □

5. The shift: From abstract CESK to rooted PDS

In the previous section, we constructed an infinite-state abstract interpretation of the CESK machine. The infinite-state nature of the abstraction makes it difficult to see how to answer static analysis questions. Consider, for instance, a control flow-question:

> At the call site $(f\ æ)$, may a closure over lam be called?

If the abstracted CESK machine were a finite-state machine, an algorithm could answer this question by enumerating all reachable configurations and looking for an abstract configuration $(\llbracket (f\ æ) \rrbracket, \hat{\rho}, \hat{\sigma}, \hat{\kappa})$ in which $(lam, \_) \in \hat{\mathcal{A}}(f, \hat{\rho}, \hat{\sigma})$. However, because the abstracted CESK machine may contain an infinite number of reachable configurations, enumeration is not an option.

Fortunately, a shift in perspective reveals the abstracted CESK machine to be a rooted pushdown system. This shift permits the use of a control-state reachability algorithm in place of exhaustive search of the configuration-space. In this shift, a control-state is an expression-environment-store triple, and a stack character is a frame. Figure 5 defines the program-to-RPDS conversion function $\widehat{\mathcal{PDS}} : \mathsf{Exp} \to \mathbb{RPDS}$.

At this point, we can compute the root-reachable control states using a straightforward summarization algorithm [1, 17, 18]. This is the essence of CFA2.

6. Introspection for abstract garbage collection

Abstract garbage collection [14] yields large improvements in precision by using the abstract interpretation of garbage collection to make more efficient use of the finite address space available during analysis. Because of the way abstract garbage collection operates, it

$$\widehat{\mathcal{PDS}}(e) = (Q, \Gamma, \delta, q_0), \text{ where}$$
$$Q = \mathsf{Exp} \times \widehat{Env} \times \widehat{Store}$$
$$\Gamma = \widehat{Frame}$$
$$(q, \epsilon, q') \in \delta \text{ iff } (q, \hat{\kappa}) \leadsto (q', \hat{\kappa}) \text{ for all } \hat{\kappa}$$
$$(q, \hat{\phi}_-, q') \in \delta \text{ iff } (q, \hat{\phi} : \hat{\kappa}) \leadsto (q', \hat{\kappa}) \text{ for all } \hat{\kappa}$$
$$(q, \hat{\phi}'_+, q') \in \delta \text{ iff } (q, \hat{\kappa}) \leadsto (q', \hat{\phi}' : \hat{\kappa}) \text{ for all } \hat{\kappa}$$
$$(q_0, \langle\rangle) = \hat{\mathcal{I}}(e).$$

Figure 5. $\widehat{\mathcal{PDS}} : \mathsf{Exp} \to \mathbb{RPDS}$.

grants exact precision to the flow analysis of variables whose bindings die between invocations of the same abstract context. Because pushdown analysis grants exact precision in tracking return-flow, it is clearly advantageous to combine these techniques. Unfortunately, as we shall demonstrate, abstract garbage collection breaks the pushdown model by requiring full stack inspection to discover the root set.

Abstract garbage collection modifies the transition relation to conduct a "stop-and-copy" garbage collection before each transition. To do this, we define a garbage collection function $\hat{G} : \widehat{Conf} \to \widehat{Conf}$ on configurations:

$$\hat{G}(\overbrace{e, \hat{\rho}, \hat{\sigma}, \hat{\kappa}}^{\hat{c}}) = (e, \hat{\rho}, \hat{\sigma} | \mathit{Reachable}(\hat{c}), \hat{\kappa}),$$

where the pipe operation $f|S$ yields the function f, but with inputs not in the set S mapped to bottom—the empty set. The reachability function $\mathit{Reachable} : \widehat{Conf} \to \mathcal{P}(\widehat{Addr})$ first computes the root set, and then the transitive closure of an address-to-address adjacency relation:

$$\mathit{Reachable}(\overbrace{e, \hat{\rho}, \hat{\sigma}, \hat{\kappa}}^{\hat{c}}) = \left\{ \hat{a} : \hat{a}_0 \in \mathit{Root}(\hat{c}) \text{ and } \hat{a}_0 \underset{\hat{\sigma}}{\overset{*}{\twoheadrightarrow}} \hat{a} \right\},$$

where the function $\mathit{Root} : \widehat{Conf} \to \mathcal{P}(\widehat{Addr})$ finds the root addresses:

$$\mathit{Root}(e, \hat{\rho}, \hat{\sigma}, \hat{\kappa}) = \mathit{range}(\hat{\rho}) \cup \mathit{StackRoot}(\hat{\kappa}),$$

and the $\mathit{StackRoot} : \widehat{Kont} \to \mathcal{P}(\widehat{Addr})$ function finds roots down the stack:

$$\mathit{StackRoot}\langle(v_1, e_1, \hat{\rho}_1), \ldots, (v_n, e_n, \hat{\rho}_n)\rangle = \bigcup_i \mathit{range}(\hat{\rho}_i),$$

and the relation $(\twoheadrightarrow) \subseteq \widehat{Addr} \times \widehat{Store} \times \widehat{Addr}$ connects adjacent addresses:

$$\hat{a} \underset{\hat{\sigma}}{\twoheadrightarrow} \hat{a}' \text{ iff there exists } (\mathit{lam}, \hat{\rho}) \in \hat{\sigma}(\hat{a}) \text{ such that } \hat{a}' \in \mathit{range}(\hat{\rho}).$$

The new abstract transition relation is thus the composition of abstract garbage collection with the old transition relation:

$$(\leadsto_{\mathrm{GC}}) = (\leadsto) \circ \hat{G}$$

Problem: Stack traversal violates pushdown constraint In the formulation of pushdown systems, the transition relation is restricted to looking at the top frame, and even in less restricted formulations, at most a bounded number of frames can be inspected. Thus, the relation $(\leadsto_{\mathrm{GC}})$ cannot be computed as a straightforward pushdown analysis using summarization.

Solution: Introspective pushdown systems To accomodate the richer structure of the relation $(\leadsto_{\mathrm{GC}})$, we now define *introspective* pushdown systems. Once defined, we can embed the garbage-collecting abstract interpretation within this framework, and then focus on developing a control-state reachability algorithm for these systems.

An **introspective pushdown system** is a quadruple $M = (Q, \Gamma, \delta, q_0)$:

1. Q is a finite set of control states;
2. Γ is a stack alphabet;
3. $\delta \subseteq Q \times \Gamma^* \times \Gamma_\pm \times Q$ is a transition relation; and
4. q_0 is a distinguished root control state.

The second component in the transition relation is a realizable stack at the given control-state. This realizable stack distinguishes an introspective pushdown system from a general pushdown system. $\mathbb{IPDS}$ denotes the class of all introspective pushdown systems.

Determining how (or if) a control state q transitions to a control state q', requires knowing a path taken to the state q. Thus, we need to define reachability inductively. When $M = (Q, \Gamma, \delta, q_0)$, transition from the initial control state considers only empty stacks:

$$q_0 \underset{M}{\overset{g}{\longmapsto\!\!\!\!\!\twoheadrightarrow}} q \text{ iff } (q_0, \langle\rangle, g, q) \in \delta.$$

For non-root states, the paths to that state matter, since they determine the stacks realizable with that state:

$$q \underset{M}{\overset{g}{\longmapsto\!\!\!\!\!\twoheadrightarrow}} q' \text{ iff there exists } \vec{g} \text{ such that } q_0 \underset{M}{\overset{\vec{g}}{\longmapsto\!\!\!\!\!\twoheadrightarrow}} q \text{ and } (q, \lfloor\vec{g}\rfloor, g, q') \in \delta,$$

$$\text{where } q \underset{M}{\overset{\langle g_1, \ldots, g_n\rangle}{\longmapsto\!\!\!\!\!\twoheadrightarrow}} q' \text{ iff } q \underset{M}{\overset{g_1}{\longmapsto\!\!\!\!\!\twoheadrightarrow}} q_1 \underset{M}{\overset{g_2}{\longmapsto\!\!\!\!\!\twoheadrightarrow}} \cdots \underset{M}{\overset{g_n}{\longmapsto\!\!\!\!\!\twoheadrightarrow}} q'.$$

6.1 Garbage collection in introspective pushdown systems

To convert the garbage-collecting, abstracted CESK machine into an introspective pushdown system, we use the function $\widehat{\mathcal{IPDS}} : \mathsf{Exp} \to \mathbb{IPDS}$:

$$\widehat{\mathcal{IPDS}}(e) = (Q, \Gamma, \delta, q_0)$$
$$Q = \mathsf{Exp} \times \widehat{Env} \times \widehat{Store}$$
$$\Gamma = \widehat{Frame}$$
$$(q, \hat{\kappa}, \epsilon, q') \in \delta \text{ iff } \hat{G}(q, \hat{\kappa}) \leadsto (q', \hat{\kappa})$$
$$(q, \hat{\phi} : \hat{\kappa}, \hat{\phi}_-, q') \in \delta \text{ iff } \hat{G}(q, \hat{\phi} : \hat{\kappa}) \leadsto (q', \hat{\kappa})$$
$$(q, \hat{\kappa}, \hat{\phi}_+, q') \in \delta \text{ iff } \hat{G}(q, \hat{\kappa}) \leadsto (q', \hat{\phi} : \hat{\kappa})$$
$$(q_0, \langle\rangle) = \hat{\mathcal{I}}(e).$$

7. Introspective reachability via Dyck state graphs

Having defined introspective pushdown systems and embedded our abstract, garbage-collecting semantics within them, we are ready to define control-state reachability for IDPSs.

We cast our reachability algorithm for introspective pushdown systems as finding a fixed-point, in which we incrementally accrete the reachable control states into a "Dyck state graph."

A **Dyck state graph** is a quadruple $G = (S, \Gamma, E, s_0)$, in which:

1. S is a finite set of nodes;
2. Γ is a set of frames;
3. $E \subseteq S \times \Gamma_{\pm} \times S$ is a set of stack-action edges; and
4. s_0 is an initial state;

such that for any node $s \in S$, it must be the case that:

$$(s_0, \langle\rangle) \underset{G}{\overset{*}{\longmapsto}} (s, \vec{\gamma}) \text{ for some stack } \vec{\gamma}.$$

In other words, a Dyck state graph is equivalent to a rooted pushdown system in which there is a legal path to every control state from the initial control state.[4] We use $\mathbb{DSG}$ to denote the class of Dyck state graphs. (Clearly, $\mathbb{DSG} \subset \mathbb{RPDS}$.)

Our goal is to compile an implicitly-defined introspective pushdown system into an explicited-constructed Dyck state graph. During this transformation, the per-state path considerations of an introspective pushdown are "baked into" the Dyck state graph. We can formalize this compilation process as a map, $\mathcal{DSG} : \mathbb{IPDS} \to \mathbb{DSG}$.

Given an introspective pushdown system $M = (Q, \Gamma, \delta, q_0)$, its equivalent Dyck state graph is $\mathcal{DSG}(M) = (S, \Gamma, E, q_0)$, where $s_0 = q_0$, the set S contains reachable nodes:

$$S = \left\{q : q_0 \underset{M}{\overset{\vec{g}}{\longmapsto\!\!\!\rightarrow}} q \text{ for some stack-action sequence } \vec{g}\right\},$$

and the set E contains reachable edges:

$$E = \left\{q \overset{g}{\rightarrowtail} q' : q \underset{M}{\overset{g}{\longmapsto\!\!\!\rightarrow}} q'\right\}.$$

Our goal is to find a method for computing a Dyck state graph from an introspective pushdown system.

7.1 Compiling to Dyck state graphs

We now turn our attention to compiling an introspective pushdown system (defined implicitly) into a Dyck state graph (defined explicitly). That is, we want an implementation of the function $\mathcal{DSG}$. To do so, we first phrase the Dyck state graph construction as the least fixed point of a monotonic function. This formulation provides a straightforward iterative method for computing the function $\mathcal{DSG}$.

The function $\mathcal{F} : \mathbb{IPDS} \to (\mathbb{DSG} \to \mathbb{DSG})$ generates the monotonic iteration function we need:

$$\begin{aligned}
\mathcal{F}(M) &= f, \text{ where} \\
M &= (Q, \Gamma, \delta, q_0) \\
f(S, \Gamma, E, s_0) &= (S', \Gamma, E', s_0), \text{ where} \\
S' &= S \cup \left\{s' : s \in S \text{ and } s \underset{M}{\longmapsto\!\!\!\rightarrow} s'\right\} \cup \{s_0\} \\
E' &= E \cup \left\{s \overset{g}{\rightarrowtail} s' : s \in S \text{ and } s \underset{M}{\overset{g}{\longmapsto\!\!\!\rightarrow}} s'\right\}.
\end{aligned}$$

Given an introspective pushdown system M, each application of the function $\mathcal{F}(M)$ accretes new edges at the frontier of the Dyck state graph.

[4] We chose the term *Dyck state graph* because the sequences of stack actions along valid paths through the graph correspond to substrings in Dyck languages. A **Dyck language** is a language of balanced, "colored" parentheses. In this case, each character in the stack alphabet is a color.

7.2 Computing a round of $\mathcal{F}$

The formalism obscures an important detail in the computation of an iteration: the transition relation ($\longmapsto\!\!\!\rightarrow$) for the introspective pushdown system must compute all possible stacks in determining whether or not there exists a transition. Fortunately, this is not as onerous as it seems: the set of all possible stacks for any given control-point is a regular language, and the finite automaton that encodes this language can be lifted (or read off) the structure of the Dyck state graph. The function $\mathit{Stacks} : \mathbb{DSG} \to S \to \mathbb{NFA}$ performs exactly this extraction:

$$\begin{aligned}
\mathit{Stacks}(\overbrace{S, \Gamma, E, s_0}^{M})(s) &= (S, \Gamma, \delta, s_0, \{s\}), \text{ where} \\
(s', \gamma, s'') &\in \delta \text{ if } (s', \gamma_+, s'') \in E \\
(s', \epsilon, s'') &\in \delta \text{ if } s' \underset{M}{\overset{\vec{g}}{\longmapsto\!\!\!\rightarrow}} s'' \text{ and } [\vec{g}] = \epsilon.
\end{aligned}$$

7.3 Correctness

Once the algorithm reaches a fixed point, the Dyck state graph is complete:

Theorem 7.1. $\mathcal{DSG}(M) = \text{lfp}(\mathcal{F}(M))$.

Proof. Let $M = (Q, \Gamma, \delta, q_0)$. Let $f = \mathcal{F}(M)$. Observe that $\text{lfp}(f) = f^n(\emptyset, \Gamma, \emptyset, q_0)$ for some n. When $N \subseteq M$, then it easy to show that $f(N) \subseteq M$. Hence, $\mathcal{DSG}(M) \supseteq \text{lfp}(\mathcal{F}(M))$.

To show $\mathcal{DSG}(M) \subseteq \text{lfp}(\mathcal{F}(M))$, suppose this is not the case. Then, there must be at least one edge in $\mathcal{DSG}(M)$ that is not in $\text{lfp}(\mathcal{F}(M))$. By the defintion of $\mathcal{DSG}(M)$, each edge must be part of a sequence of edges from the initial state. Let (s, g, s') be the first edge in its sequence from the initial state that is not in $\text{lfp}(\mathcal{F}(M)$. Because the proceeding edge is in $\text{lfp}(\mathcal{F}(M))$, the state s *is* in $\text{lfp}(\mathcal{F}(M))$. Let m be the lowest natural number such that s appears in $f^m(M)$. By the definition of f, this edge must appear in $f^{m+1}(M)$, which means it must also appear in $\text{lfp}(\mathcal{F}(M))$, which is a contradiction. Hence, $\mathcal{DSG}(M) \subseteq \text{lfp}(\mathcal{F}(M))$. □

7.4 Complexity

While decidability is the goal, it is straightforward to determine the complexity of this naïve fixed-point method. To determine the complexity of this algorithm, we ask two questions: how many times would the algorithm invoke the iteration function in the worst case, and how much does each invocation cost in the worst case? The size of the final Dyck state graph bounds the run-time of the algorithm. Suppose the final Dyck state graph has m states. In the worst case, the iteration function adds only a single edge each time. Between any two states, there is one ϵ-edge, one push edge, or some number of pop edges (at most $|\Gamma|$). Since there are at most $|\Gamma|m^2$ edges in the final graph, the maximum number of iterations is $|\Gamma|m^2$.

The cost of computing each iteration is harder to bound. The cost of determining whether to add a push edge is constant, as is the cost of adding an ϵ-edge. So the cost of determining all new push edges and new ϵ-edges to add is constant. Determining whether or not to add a pop edge is expensive. To add the pop edge $s \rightarrowtail^{\gamma_-} s'$, we must prove that there exists a configuration-path to the control state s, in which the character γ is on the top of the stack. This reduces to a CFL-reachability query [9] at each node, the cost of which is $O(|\Gamma_{\pm}|^3 m^3)$ [8].

To summarize, in terms of the number of reachable control states, the complexity of this naive algorithm is:

$$O((|\Gamma|m^2) \times (|\Gamma_\pm|^3 m^3)) = O(|\Gamma|^4 m^5).$$

(As with summarization, it is possible to maintain a work-list and introduce an ϵ-closure graph to avoid spurious recomputation. This ultimately reduces complexity to $O(|\Gamma|^2 m^4)$.)

8. Implementation and evaluation

We have developed an implementation to produce the Dyck state graph of an introspective pushdown system. While the fixed-point computation 7.2 could be rendered directly as functional code, extending the classical summarization-based algorithm for pushdown reachability to introspective pushdown systems yields better performance. In this section we present a variant of such an algorithm and discuss results from an implementation that can analyze a large subset of the Scheme programming language.

8.1 Iterating over a DSG: An implementor's view

To synthesize a Dyck state graph from an introspective pushdown system, it is built incrementally—node by node, edge by edge. The naïve fixed point algorithm presented earlier, if implemented literally, would (in the worst case) have to re-examine the entire DSG to add each edge. To avoid such re-examination, our implementation adds ϵ-summary edges to the DSG.

In short, an ϵ-summary edge connects two control states if there exists a path between them with no net stack change—that is, all pushes are cancelled by corresponding pops. With ϵ-summary edges available, any change to the graph can be propagated directly to where it has an effect, and then any new ϵ-summary edges that propagation implies are added.

Whereas the correspondence between CESK and an IPDS is relatively straightforward, the relationship between a DSG and its original IPDS is complicated by the fact that the IPDS keeps track of the *whole* stack, whereas the DSG distributes (the same) stack information throughout its internal structure.

A classic reachability-based analysis for a pushdown system requires two mutually-dependent pieces of information in order to add another edge:

1. The topmost frame on a stack for a given control state q. This is essential for *return* transitions, as this frame should be popped from the stack and the store and the environment of a caller should be updated respectively.
2. Whether a given control state q is reachable or not from the initial state q_0 along realizable sequences of stack actions. For example, a path from q_0 to q along edges labeled "push, pop, pop, push" is not realizable: the stack is empty after the first pop, so the second pop cannot happen—let alone the subsequent push.

These two data are enough for a classic pushdown reachability summarization to proceed one step further. However, the presence of an abstract garbage collector, and the graduation to an *introspective* pushdown system, imposes the requirement for a third item of data:

3. For a given control state q, what are *all* possible frames that could happen to be *on* the stack at the moment the IPDS is in the state q?

It is possible to recompute these frames from scratch in each iteration using the NFA-extraction technique we described. But, it is easier to maintain per-node summaries, in the same spirit as ϵ-summary edges.

A version of the classic pushdown summarization algorithm that maintains the first two items is presented in [4], so we will just outline the key differences here.

The crux of the algorithm is to maintain for each node q' in the DSG, a set of *ϵ-predecessors*, i.e., nodes q, such that $q \mapsto\!\!\!\twoheadrightarrow^{\vec{g}}_{M} q'$ and $[\vec{g}] = \epsilon$. In fact, only two out of three kinds of transitions can cause a change to the set of ϵ-predecessors for a particular node q: an addition of an ϵ-edge or a pop edge to the DSG.

It is easy to see why the second action might introduce new ϵ-paths and, therefore, new ϵ-predecessors. Consider, for example, adding the γ_--edge $q \rightarrowtail^{\gamma_-} q'$ into the following graph:

$$q_0 \xrightarrow{\gamma_+} q \qquad\qquad q' \xrightarrow{\epsilon} q_1$$

As soon this edge drops in, there becomes an "implicit" ϵ-edge between q_0 and q_1 because the net stack change between them is empty; the resulting graph looks like:

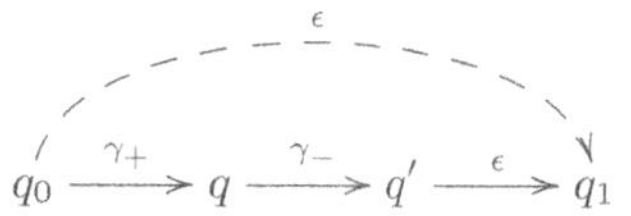

where we have illustrated the implicit ϵ-edge as a dashed line.

A little reflection on ϵ-predecessors and top frames reveals a mutual dependency between these items during the construction of a DSG. Informally:

- A *top frame* for a state q can be pushed as a direct predecessor, or as a direct predecessor to an ϵ-predecessor.
- When a new ϵ-edge $q \xrightarrow{\epsilon} q'$ is added, all ϵ-predecessors of q become also ϵ-predecessors of q'. That is, ϵ-summary edges are transitive.
- When a γ_--pop-edge $q \xrightarrow{\gamma_-} q'$ is added, new ϵ-predecessors of a state q_1 can be obtained by checking if q' is an ϵ-predecessor of q_1 and examining all existing ϵ-predecessors of q, such that γ_+ is their possible top frame: this situation is similar to the one depicted in the example above.

The third component—*all* possible frames on the stack for a state q—is straightforward to compute with ϵ-predecessors: starting from q, trace out only the edges which are labeled ϵ (summary or otherwise) or γ_+. The frame for any action γ_+ in this trace is a possible stack action. Since these sets grow monotonically, it is easy to cache the results of the trace, and in fact, propagate incremental changes to these caches when new ϵ-summary or γ_+ nodes are introduced. Our implementation directly reflects the optimizations discussed above.

8.2 Experimental results

A fair comparison between different families of analyses should compare both precision and speed. We have extended an existing

Program	Exp	Var	k	k-CFA			k-PDCFA			k-CFA + GC			k-PDCFA + GC		
mj09	19	8	0	83	107	4	38	38	4	36	39	4	33	32	4
			1	454	812	1	44	48	1	34	35	1	32	31	1
eta	21	13	0	63	74	4	34	34	6	28	27	8	28	27	8
			1	33	33	8	32	31	8	28	27	8	28	27	8
kcfa2	20	10	0	194	236	3	36	35	4	35	43	4	35	34	4
			1	970	1935	1	87	144	2	35	34	2	35	34	2
kcfa3	25	13	0	272	327	4	58	63	5	53	52	5	53	52	5
			1	> 7119	> 14201	≤ 1	1761	4046	2	53	52	2	53	52	2
blur	40	20	0	> 1419	> 2435	≤ 3	280	414	3	274	298	9	164	182	9
			1	261	340	9	177	189	9	169	189	9	167	182	9
loop2	41	14	0	228	252	4	113	122	4	86	93	4	70	74	4
			1	> 10867	> 16040	≤ 3	411	525	3	151	163	3	145	156	3
sat	63	31	0	> 5362	> 7610	≤ 6	775	979	6	1190	1567	6	321	384	6
			1	> 8395	> 12391	≤ 6	7979	10299	6	982	1330	7	107	106	13

Figure 6. Benchmark results. The first three columns provide the name of a benchmark, the number of expressions and variables in the program in the ANF, respectively. For each of eight combinations of pushdown analysis, $k \in \{0, 1\}$ and garbage collection on or off, the first two columns in a group show the number of *control states* and transitions/DSG edges computed during the analysis (for both less is better). The third column presents the amount of *singleton* variables, i.e, how many variables have a single lambda flow to them (more is better). Inequalities for some results denote the case when the analysis did not finish within 30 minutes. For such cases we can only report an upper bound of singleton variables as this number can only decrease.

implementation of k-CFA to optionally enable pushdown analysis, abstract garbage collection or both. Our implementation source and benchmarks are available:

`http://github.com/ilyasergey/reachability`

As expected, the fused analysis does at least as well as the best of either analysis alone in terms of singleton flow sets (a good metric for program optimizability) and better than both in some cases. Also worthy of note is the dramatic reduction in the size of the abstract transition graph for the fused analysis—even on top of the already large reductions achieved by abstract gabarge collection and pushdown flow analysis individually. The size of the abstract transition graph is a good heuristic measure of the temporal reasoning ability of the analysis, *e.g.*, its ability to support model-checking of safety and liveness properties [12].

In order to exercise both well-known and newly-presented instances of CESK-based CFAs, we took a series of small benchmarks exhibiting archetypal control-flow patterns (see Figure 6). Most benchmarks are taken from the CFA literature: `mj09` is a running example from the work of Midtgaard and Jensen designed to exhibit a non-trivial return-flow behavior, `eta` and `blur` test common functional idioms, mixing closures and eta-expansion, `kcfa2` and `kcfa3` are two worst-case examples extracted from Van Horn and Mairson's proof of k-CFA complexity [21], `loop2` is an example from the Might's dissertation that was used to demonstrate the impact of abstract GC [11, Section 13.3], `sat` is a brute-force SAT-solver with backtracking.

8.2.1 Comparing precision

In terms of precision, the fusion of pushdown analysis and abstract garbage collection substantially cuts abstract transition graph sizes over one technique alone.

We also measure singleton flow sets as a heuristic metric for precision. Singleton flow sets are a necessary precursor to optimizations such as flow-driven inlining, type-check elimination and constant propagation. Here again, the fused analysis prevails as the best-of- or better-than-both-worlds.

Program	0-CFA		0-PDCFA		1-CFA		1-PDCFA	
mj09	$1''$	ϵ	ϵ	$1''$	$4''$	ϵ	ϵ	ϵ
eta	ϵ	ϵ	ϵ	ϵ	$1''$	ϵ	ϵ	ϵ
kcfa2	$1''$	ϵ	ϵ	$1''$	$24''$	ϵ	$1''$	ϵ
kcfa3	$2''$	ϵ	ϵ	$1''$	∞	$1''$	$58''$	$2''$
blur	∞	$7''$	$2'$	$50''$	$4'$	$30''$	$11''$	$55''$
loop2	$36''$	$1''$	$29''$	$16''$	∞	$5''$	$13'$	$2'$
sat	∞	$45''$	$6'$	$19'$	∞	$3'$	$12'$	$37''$

Figure 7. We ran our benchmark suite on a 2 Core 2.66 GHz OS X machine with 4 Gb RAM. For each of the four analyses the left column denotes the values obtained with no abstract collection, and the right one—with GC on. The results of the analyses are presented in minutes ($'$) or seconds ($''$), where ϵ means a value less than 1 second and ∞ stands for an analysis, which has been interrupted due to the an execution time greater than 30 minutes.

Running on the benchmarks, we have revalidated hypotheses about the improvements to precision granted by both pushdown analysis [22] and abstract garbage collection [11]. The table in Figure 6 contains our detailed results on the precision of the analysis.

8.2.2 Comparing speed

In the original work on CFA2, Vardoulakis and Shivers present experimental results with a remark that the running time of the analysis is proportional to the size of the reachable states [22, Section 6]. There is a similar correlation in the fused analysis, but it is not as strong or as absolute. From examination of the results, this appears to be because small graphs can have large stores inside each state, which increases the cost of garbage collection (and thus transition) on a per-state basis, and there is some additional per-transition overhead involved in maintaining the caches inside the Dyck state graph. Table 7 collects absolute execution times for comparison.

It follows from the results that pure machine-style k-CFA is always significantly worse in terms of execution time than either with GC or push-down system. The histogram on Figure 8 presents

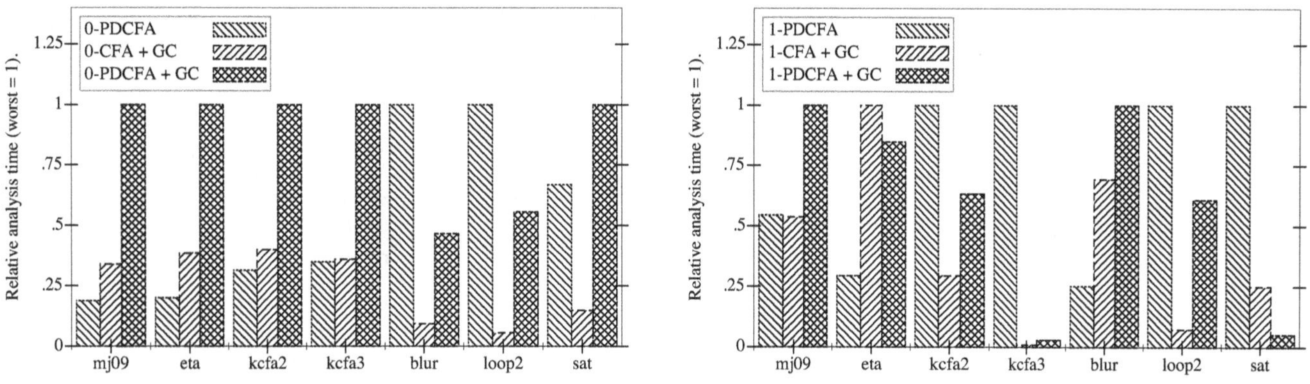

Figure 8. Analysis times relative to worst (= 1) in class; smaller is better. On the left is the monovariant 0CFA class of analyses, on the right is the polyvariant 1CFA class of analyses. (Non-GC k-CFA omitted.)

normalized relative times of analyses' executions. About half the time, the fused analysis is faster than one of pushdown analysis or abstract garbage collection. And about a tenth of the time, it is faster than both.[5] When the fused analysis is slower than both, it is generally not much worse than twice as slow as the next slowest analysis.

Given the already substantial reductions in analysis times provided by collection and pushdown anlysis, the amortized penalty is a small and acceptable price to pay for improvements to precision.

9. Related work

Garbage-collecting pushdown control-flow analysis draws on work in higher-order control-flow analysis [19], abstract machines [5] and abstract interpretation [3].

Context-free analysis of higher-order programs The motivating work for our own is Vardoulakis and Shivers very recent discovery of CFA2 [22]. CFA2 is a table-driven summarization algorithm that exploits the balanced nature of calls and returns to improve return-flow precision in a control-flow analysis. Though CFA2 exploits context-free languages, context-free languages are not explicit in its formulation in the same way that pushdown systems are explicit in our presentation of pushdown flow analysis. With respect to CFA2, our pushdown flow analysis is also polyvariant/context-sensitive (whereas CFA2 is monovariant/context-insensitive), and it covers direct-style.

On the other hand, CFA2 distinguishes stack-allocated and store-allocated variable bindings, whereas our formulation of pushdown control-flow analysis does not: it allocates all bindings in the store. If CFA2 determines a binding can be allocated on the stack, that binding will enjoy added precision during the analysis and is not subject to merging like store-allocated bindings. While we could incorporate such a feature in our formulation, it is not necessary for achieving "pushdownness," and in fact, it could be added to classical finite-state CFAs as well.

[5] The SAT-solving bechmark showed a dramatic improvement with the addition of context-sensitivity. Evaluation of the results showed that context-sensitivity provided enough fuel to eliminate most of the non-determinism from the analysis.

Calculation approach to abstract interpretation Midtgaard and Jensen [10] systematically calculate 0CFA using the Cousot-Cousot-style calculational approach to abstract interpretation [2] applied to an ANF λ-calculus. Like the present work, Midtgaard and Jensen start with the CESK machine of Flanagan *et al.* [6] and employ a reachable-states model.

The analysis is then constructed by composing well-known Galois connections to reveal a 0CFA incorporating reachability. The abstract semantics approximate the control stack component of the machine by its top element. The authors remark monomorphism materializes in two mappings: "one mapping all bindings to the same variable," the other "merging all calling contexts of the same function." Essentially, the pushdown 0CFA of Section 4 corresponds to Midtgaard and Jensen's analysis when the latter mapping is omitted and the stack component of the machine is not abstracted.

CFL- and pushdown-reachability techniques This work also draws on CFL- and pushdown-reachability analysis [1, 8, 17, 18]. For instance, ϵ-closure graphs, or equivalent variants thereof, appear in many context-free-language and pushdown reachability algorithms. For our analysis, we implicitly invoked these methods as subroutines. When we found these algorithms lacking (as with their enumeration of control states), we developed Dyck state graph construction.

CFL-reachability techniques have also been used to compute classical finite-state abstraction CFAs [9] and type-based polymorphic control-flow analysis [16]. These analyses should not be confused with pushdown control-flow analysis, which is computing a fundamentally more precise kind of CFA. Moreover, Rehof and Fahndrich's method is cubic in the size of the *typed* program, but the types may be exponential in the size of the program. Finally, our technique is not restricted to typed programs.

Model-checking higher-order recursion schemes There is terminology overlap with work by Kobayashi [7] on model-checking higher-order programs with higher-order recursion schemes, which are a generalization of context-free grammars in which productions can take higher-order arguments, so that an order-0 scheme is a context-free grammar. Kobyashi exploits a result by Ong [15] which shows that model-checking these recursion schemes is decidable (but ELEMENTARY-complete) by transforming higher-order programs into higher-order recursion schemes.

Given the generality of model-checking, Kobayashi's technique may be considered an alternate paradigm for the analysis of higher-order programs. For the case of order-0, both Kobayashi's technique and our own involve context-free languages, though ours is for control-flow analysis and his is for model-checking with respect to a temporal logic. After these surface similarities, the techniques diverge. In particular, higher-order recursions schemes are limited to model-checking programs in the simply-typed lambda-calculus with recursion.

10. Conclusion

Our motivation was to further probe the limits of decidability for pushdown flow analysis of higher-order programs by enriching it with abstract garbage collection. We found that abstract garbage collection broke the pushdown model, but not irreparably so. By casting abstract garbage collection in terms of an introspective pushdown system and synthesizing a new control-state reachability algorithm, we have demonstrated the decidability of fusing two powerful analytic techniques.

As a byproduct of our formulation, it was also easy to demonstrate how polyvariant/context-sensitive flow analyses generalize to a pushdown formulation, and we lifted the need to transform to continuation-passing style in order to perform pushdown analysis.

Our empirical evaluation is highly encouraging: it shows that the fused analysis provides further large reductions in the size of the abstract transition graph—a key metric for interprocedural control-flow precision. And, in terms of singleton flow sets—a heuristic metric for optimizability—the fused analysis proves to be a "better-than-both-worlds" combination.

Thus, we provide a sound, precise and polyvariant introspective pushdown analysis for higher-order programs.

Acknowledgments

We thank our anonymous reviewers for their detailed comments on the submitted paper. This material is based on research sponsored by DARPA under the programs Automated Program Analysis for Cybersecurity (FA8750-12-2-0106) and Clean-Slate Resilient Adaptive Hosts (CRASH). The U.S. Government is authorized to reproduce and distribute reprints for Governmental purposes notwithstanding any copyright notation thereon.

References

[1] BOUAJJANI, A., ESPARZA, J., AND MALER, O. Reachability analysis of pushdown automata: Application to Model-Checking. In *CONCUR '97: Proceedings of the 8th International Conference on Concurrency Theory* (1997), Springer-Verlag, pp. 135–150.

[2] COUSOT, P. The calculational design of a generic abstract interpreter. In *Calculational System Design*, M. Broy and R. Steinbrüggen, Eds. 1999.

[3] COUSOT, P., AND COUSOT, R. Abstract interpretation: A unified lattice model for static analysis of programs by construction or approximation of fixpoints. In *Conference Record of the Fourth ACM Symposium on Principles of Programming Languages* (1977), ACM Press, pp. 238–252.

[4] EARL, C., MIGHT, M., AND VAN HORN, D. Pushdown control-flow analysis of higher-order programs. In *Proceedings of the 2010 Workshop on Scheme and Functional Programming* (Aug. 2010).

[5] FELLEISEN, M., AND FRIEDMAN, D. P. A calculus for assignments in higher-order languages. In *POPL '87: Proceedings of the 14th ACM SIGACT-SIGPLAN Symposium on Principles of Programming Languages* (1987), ACM, pp. 314+.

[6] FLANAGAN, C., SABRY, A., DUBA, B. F., AND FELLEISEN, M. The essence of compiling with continuations. In *PLDI '93: Proceedings of the ACM SIGPLAN 1993 Conference on Programming Language Design and Implementation* (June 1993), ACM, pp. 237–247.

[7] KOBAYASHI, N. Types and higher-order recursion schemes for verification of higher-order programs. In *POPL '09: Proceedings of the 36th Annual ACM SIGPLAN-SIGACT Symposium on Principles of Programming Languages* (2009), POPL '09, ACM, pp. 416–428.

[8] KODUMAL, J., AND AIKEN, A. The set constraint/CFL reachability connection in practice. *SIGPLAN Not. 39* (June 2004), 207–218.

[9] MELSKI, D., AND REPS, T. W. Interconvertibility of a class of set constraints and context-free-language reachability. *Theoretical Computer Science 248*, 1-2 (Oct. 2000), 29–98.

[10] MIDTGAARD, J., AND JENSEN, T. P. Control-flow analysis of function calls and returns by abstract interpretation. In *ICFP '09: Proceedings of the 14th ACM SIGPLAN International Conference on Functional Programming* (2009), pp. 287–298.

[11] MIGHT, M. *Environment Analysis of Higher-Order Languages*. PhD thesis, Georgia Institute of Technology, June 2007.

[12] MIGHT, M., CHAMBERS, B., AND SHIVERS, O. Model checking via Gamma-CFA. In *Verification, Model Checking, and Abstract Interpretation* (Jan. 2007), pp. 59–73.

[13] MIGHT, M., AND SHIVERS, O. Environment analysis via Delta-CFA. In *POPL '06: Conference Record of the 33rd ACM SIGPLAN-SIGACT Symposium on Principles of Programming Languages* (2006), ACM, pp. 127–140.

[14] MIGHT, M., AND SHIVERS, O. Improving flow analyses via Gamma-CFA: Abstract garbage collection and counting. In *ICFP '06: Proceedings of the 11th ACM SIGPLAN International Conference on Functional Programming* (2006), ACM, pp. 13–25.

[15] ONG, C. H. L. On Model-Checking trees generated by Higher-Order recursion schemes. In *21st Annual IEEE Symposium on Logic in Computer Science (LICS'06)* (2006), pp. 81–90.

[16] REHOF, J., AND FÄHNDRICH, M. Type-based flow analysis: From polymorphic subtyping to CFL-reachability. In *POPL '01: Proceedings of the 28th ACM SIGPLAN-SIGACT Symposium on Principles of Programming Languages* (2001), ACM, pp. 54–66.

[17] REPS, T. Program analysis via graph reachability. *Information and Software Technology 40*, 11-12 (Dec. 1998), 701–726.

[18] REPS, T., SCHWOON, S., JHA, S., AND MELSKI, D. Weighted pushdown systems and their application to interprocedural dataflow analysis. *Science of Computer Programming 58*, 1-2 (2005), 206–263.

[19] SHIVERS, O. G. *Control-Flow Analysis of Higher-Order Languages*. PhD thesis, Carnegie Mellon University, 1991.

[20] SIPSER, M. *Introduction to the Theory of Computation*, 2 ed. Course Technology, Feb. 2005.

[21] VAN HORN, D., AND MAIRSON, H. G. Deciding *k*CFA is complete for EXPTIME. In *ICFP '08: Proceeding of the 13th ACM SIGPLAN International Conference on Functional Programming* (2008), pp. 275–282.

[22] VARDOULAKIS, D., AND SHIVERS, O. Cfa2: a Context-Free Approach to Control-Flow Analysis. In *European Symposium on Programming (ESOP)* (2010), vol. 6012 of *LNCS*, pp. 570–589.

[23] WRIGHT, A. K., AND JAGANNATHAN, S. Polymorphic splitting: An effective polyvariant flow analysis. *ACM Transactions on Programming Languages and Systems 20*, 1 (Jan. 1998), 166–207.

Efficient Lookup-Table Protocol in Secure Multiparty Computation

John Launchbury, Iavor S. Diatchki, Thomas DuBuisson, Andy Adams-Moran
Galois, Inc. *
{john, diatchki, tommd, adams-moran}@galois.com

Abstract

Secure multiparty computation (SMC) permits a collection of parties to compute a collaborative result, without any of the parties gaining any knowledge about the inputs provided by other parties. Specifications for SMC are commonly presented as boolean circuits, where optimizations come mostly from reducing the number of multiply-operations (including *and*-gates)—these are the operations which incur significant cost, either in computation overhead or in communication between the parties. Instead, we take a language-oriented approach, and consequently are able to explore many other kinds of optimizations. We present an efficient and general purpose SMC table-lookup algorithm that can serve as a direct alternative to circuits. Looking up a private (i.e. shared, or encrypted) n-bit argument in a public table requires $log(n)$ parallel-and operations. We use the advanced encryption standard algorithm (AES) as a driving motivation, and by introducing different kinds of parallelization techniques, produce the fastest current SMC implementation of AES, improving the best previously reported results by well over an order of magnitude.

Categories and Subject Descriptors D.3.2 [*PROGRAMMING LANGUAGES*]: Language Classifications: Specialized application languages

Keywords Secure Multiparty Computation, Cloud, EDSL, Haskell

1. Introduction

There is growing interest in performing computation on encrypted data, partly motivated by the challenges of cloud computing. As we lose control of the *location* of our data, we still want to retain control of the *confidentiality* and/or *integrity* of our data. If we could encrypt our data (either for confidentiality, or for integrity) and then have the cloud operators perform computations on the data in the encrypted form, then we may have the best of both worlds: the cloud supplies storage and computational resources, while the encryption provides guarantees about what happens to the data.

At first it seems quite improbable that it would be possible to perform computations on encrypted data. After all, once the data is encrypted, it is completely obscured. However, the cryptography community has long known that some kinds of computations are possible—at least in principle. This was notably demonstrated by Yao's seminal work on secure multiparty computation (SMC) [Y86], and more recently by Gentry's work on fully homomorphic encryption (FHE) [G09]. SMC computations permit a collection of parties to compute a collaborative result, without any of the parties gaining any knowledge about the inputs provided by other parties (at least, nothing more than would be derivable from the final result of the computation).

SMC protocols can be targeted to different security models, but the performance cost in establishing and maintaining the security for particular models can vary significantly. The simplest security model used for SMC is *honest but curious* [G04], where the separate parties are assumed to follow the protocol honestly, but may at the same time attempt to learn secrets by looking at internal values of the computation, including any communications. This security model is appropriate for settings such as preventing information leakage by individuals with administrator access, or after a cyber break-in. There are also fairly generic techniques for augmenting honest-but-curious protocols to provide more stringent security guarantees (such as against malicious adversaries who intend to subvert the computation), so the honest-but-curious protocol may be seen as a significant first step towards constructing more secure versions.

Honest-but-curious was exactly the security model considered sufficient for a Danish beet auction in 2008 [BCD+08]. There, 1200 Danish farmers submitted obfuscated bids to three servers that were run by distinct agencies. Each of the agencies was considered well motivated to follow the multi-party protocols honestly, and the confidentiality built into the SMC protocols provided sufficient reassurance to the farmers, 78% of whom agreed that, "it is important that my bids are kept confidential."

While Gentry-style FHE is very new and still wildly impractical, there has been significant effort in the last 10 years or so to make SMC usable in practice. The fact that a genuine commercial auction could be programmed in this style is a testament to the progress made. However, the state of the art is such that an SMC implementation of an algorithm such as the AES block cipher [NIST01] is still considered challenging, with execution times of around a few blocks per second (very, very slow compared with non-secure computation). There are two fundamental reasons for this: first, all SMC computations have to be performed generically across all possible input and internal values (otherwise information is revealed), and second, SMC schemes require significant network

* This material is based upon work supported by the Defense Advanced Research Projects Agency through the U.S. Office of Naval Research under Contract N00014-11-C-0333. The views expressed are those of the author and do not reflect the official policy or position of the Department of Defense or the U.S. Government.

ICFP'12, September 9–15, 2012, Copenhagen, Denmark.

communication, typically growing linearly with the number of and-gates in the function being evaluated.

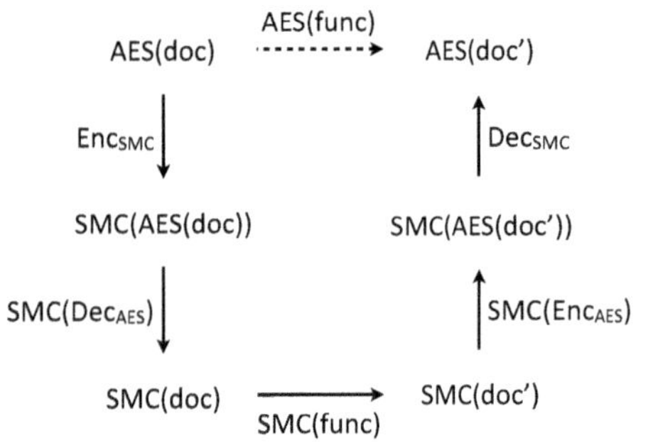

Figure 1. Lifting Secure Computation to AES

The AES block cipher is also interesting in its own right as a part of the SMC universe. Many use cases for computation on encrypted data will end up using AES to optimize one or more aspects of the data flow. Here are two example scenarios:

- A user records video on a smartphone and wants to upload it to the cloud for storage and processing (lighting adjustment, facial recognition, etc.). Encrypting the video stream directly using an encrypted computation scheme such as SMC or FHE would incur a significant communication bandwidth overhead (e.g. anything from a factor of three to factors of thousands, depending on the scheme). It would be much more desirable to encrypt the video with AES to upload it to the cloud, and then securely decrypt the video-stream as part of the SMC processing.
- Data previously stored in the cloud is more likely to be encrypted with a standard block cipher such as AES than with any given SMC scheme. Therefore, many SMC applications are likely to start with AES decrypt, perform the computation in the SMC context, and conclude with an AES encrypt to place the processed result back in the cloud.

Figure 1 shows how to lift the capability for secure computation to AES-encrypted documents. Assuming that we know how to compute the bottom arrow (i.e. that we know how to securely evaluate some function *func* with SMC), if we can also securely evaluate AES encryption and decryption, then we have created a scheme for securely computing *func* in an AES-encrypted context. Note that in this setting it makes no sense to perform the AES decryption and/or encryption in the clear, otherwise the data it is protecting would be revealed.

1.1 Contributions of this paper

The prevailing approach to SMC is to express the computation to be performed as a circuit, and then to process that circuit with cryptographic techniques. Efficiencies are gained first by optimizing the translation and processing, and then by staging the phases of circuit generation so that only portions of the circuit exist at any time.

An alternative view of SMC is to view the secure multiparty computational substrate as an *SMC-machine*—an abstract machine with highly non-standard interface and performance properties. Efficiencies are gained through minimizing expensive operations, by reducing the overheads of individual operations (through exploiting opportunities for SIMD-like parallelization if available), and by hiding residual latencies involved in network-based operations. This language-centric approach is what we describe in this paper. Our particular contributions are as follows:

- We present an innovative SMC protocol for performing table lookups. In a RAM-machine table-lookup is trivial. Not so on a SMC-machine. Our table lookup protocol minimizes the number of parallel-ands required, and provides a general mechanism for compiling many kinds of functions into a (SIMD-parallelizable) SMC framework in a regular way—any n-bit input function can be represented as a lookup table of size 2^n. The protocol presented here performs an n-bit table lookup using $log(n)$ parallel-and operations (i.e. bit-wise multiply), where each *and*-operation operates on up to 2^n individual bits.

  If n remains small enough (say below about 20), then SMC schemes may perform better by using these table lookups rather than attempting to evaluate a function directly. That is, it may be more efficient to have a table storing the pre-computed results of the function and just looking up the answer. SMC computations are often limited by the cost of communication, but with table lookup the limiting factor is most likely to be the local size of the lookup tables rather than the size or number of communications. The reason is that the size of communication is one bit per table entry, with the number of communications being the log of the log of the number of table entries.
- Using the table-lookup protocol, we present an SMC implementation of AES that is dramatically faster than anything previously reported. Depending on the specific machine configurations, we achieve speeds of over 300 AES blocks per second, compared with other SMC schemes, the fastest of which previously reported is around 17 AES blocks per second[1].

  Unlike other approaches to doing AES in SMC, we do not rely on the algebraic properties of the AES algorithm itself, but adapt a standard table-driven algorithm that is popular in both software and hardware. The table-driven approach treats the internal lookup tables of AES (called *S-boxes*) as unstructured, so the techniques we develop here carry over directly to other applications.
- To enable each of these contributions, we developed a library for SMC in Haskell which, in effect, provides an embedded domain-specific language (EDSL) for programming SMC applications. The EDSL allows us to explore multiple execution tradeoffs. In particular, we exhibit the importance of three different kinds of optimizations:
  - Structural algorithmic parallelization within the definition of SMC protocols such as table lookup;
  - Local SIMD parallelism when using specific SMC protocols; and
  - Task-level parallelism to achieve a pipelining effect.

  Interestingly, SMC implementations that use simple secret-sharing schemes are typically presented as either arithmetic sharing, or XOR sharing. Because we construct the EDSL in a type-directed way, we demonstrate that these two styles arise as endpoints in a spectrum of sharing mechanisms that naturally combine both styles.

These contributions are presented specifically in the context of a simple sharing SMC scheme, though the techniques appear to be transferrable to other SMC and FHE schemes. We provide a brief discussion of this in the conclusion.

[1] Of course, to put this in perspective we note that openSSH on similar machines computes over 7 million AES blocks per second. But the comparison would not be fair as each of our AES encryptions requires tens of thousands of openSSH AES encryptions to secure the networking, on top of tens of thousands of native AES encryptions for random number generation. It does, however, give an indication of how far SMC still has to go.

2. Background

For concreteness, we present the lookup-table protocol in the context of a particular sharing scheme, but the protocol is relatively independent of the scheme itself. We assume some familiarity with Haskell, which we use as a notation for protocols.

The SMC scheme we use is simple arithmetic/xor sharing across three peer machines acting as the compute servers. For the protocols we discuss, the three machines run the same code as each other, and communicate (and hence synchronize) between themselves in a cyclic pattern, as shown in Figure 2. Some more complex protocols require less uniform computation and communication patterns, but we won't need them here.

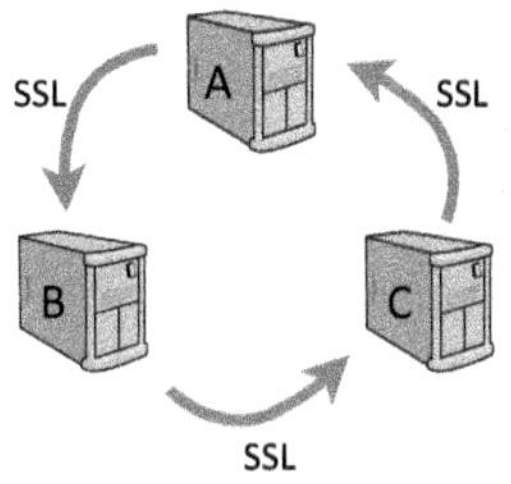

Figure 2. Machine Configuration

In a simple sharing scheme, private (secret) values never exist concretely but instead are represented by three separate *shared* values, each of which lives on one of the peer servers. A value is shared between the machines in a form that is dependent on its type. Fixed-width integer types (e.g `Int16`, `Int32`, etc) are shared *arithmetically*. Thus, a true value x in `Int16` will be shared as three randomly drawn values x_A, x_B, x_C such that $x = x_A + x_B + x_C (mod\ 2^{16})$. The initial shares can be produced by generating x_A and x_B randomly from a uniform distribution, and then defining $x_C = x - x_A - x_B$. Despite x_C being computed, all three numbers exhibit the properties of being fully random, and knowledge of any two of the numbers provides absolutely zero knowledge about the original private value—not even a single bit. Subsequently, the computational protocols will maintain this semantic share property through the calculations that are performed.

Sharing is lifted to structured types as follows: tuples of private values are shared component-wise, and fixed-length sequences of values (i.e. lists or arrays) are shared element-wise. Thus, a private value $[x, y, z]$ will be shared as three randomly drawn values $[x_A, y_A, z_A]$, $[x_B, y_B, z_B]$, $[x_C, y_C, z_C]$ such that $x = x_A + x_B + x_C$, and so on. Sequences of bits are a special case of more general sequences. They need to be handled in an efficient way (else the overhead can kill many algorithmic improvements), so we treat fixed-width bit-vectors (represented as unsigned integers in our library) as if they were sequences of individual bits (i.e. elements of `Int1`, where multiplication is just *and*, and addition is *xor*). Thus, a private value x in `Word8` (a bit-vector of length 8) will be shared as three randomly drawn values x_A, x_B, x_C such that $x = x_A \oplus x_B \oplus x_C$ (where $\oplus$ is bitwise xor).

2.1 Share Operations

To represent the code (i.e. protocol) that runs on each of the machines, we introduce the `Protocol` type (Figure 3). `Protocol` is a variant of the `IO` type, and comes with built-in information about how to communicate with the neighbors. Like `IO`, `Protocol` is a monad, so we can write sequences of operations using the `do`-notation.

Composite protocols are built from primitive protocol operations, which have distinct behaviors for each different value type.

```
type Protocol
instance Monad Protocol

class Entropy a where
  entropy :: a -> Protocol a
  (.+.) :: a -> a -> a
  (.-.) :: a -> a -> a
  (.*.) :: a -> a -> a
```

Figure 3. Primitive Share Operations

We use the type class `Entropy` to overload the protocol operations. The class name `Entropy` reflects the need to access randomness in order to share values. The `entropy` operation returns a random value (fresh entropy) of the same size and shape as its argument[2]. The `entropy` operation is a state-changing operation, so its result type is in the `Protocol` monad. The `.+.` operation is the structural arithmetic operation described above, `.-.` is its inverse, and `.*.` is the corresponding (local) multiplication i.e. multiplication modulo the word size on integer types, lifted pointwise over structural types. On sequences of bits, therefore, `.*.` is just a local parallel-and operation.

To explore the EDSL components in more detail, consider the following exemplar definitions of `Entropy` instances for `Int32`, lists, and `Word8`:

```
instance Entropy Int32 where
  entropy _ = do {r <- randomM;
                  return (fromIntegral r)}
  x .+. y = x + y
  x .-. y = x - y
  x .*. y = x * y

instance Entropy a => Entropy [a] where
  entropy v = sequence [entropy u | u <- v]
  x .+. y = zipWith (.+.) x y
  x .-. y = zipWith (.-.) x y
  x .*. y = zipWith (.*.) x y

instance Entropy Word8 where
  entropy _ = do {r <- randomM;
                  return (fromIntegral r)}
  (.+.) x y = x `xor` y
  (.-.) x y = x `xor` y
  (.*.) x y = x .&. y
```

In the `Int32` declaration, the meanings of `.+.` etc. are just the usual arithmetic operators on 32-bit integers. In the list declaration, we lift the meanings of `.+.` etc. on the element types to act pointwise on the lists. Following the principle that types such as `Word8` be viewed as sequences of bits, the `.*.` operation on `Word8` is the bitwise *and*-operation (`.&.`). Our implementation also provides declarations for other types such as characters, and tuples[3].

2.2 Share Protocols

The operations of the `Entropy` class are all local operations that operate on local shares of values. We use these operations to construct operations which are semantically correct with respect to original shared value. These operations are the *share protocols*.

[2] When the type tells us everything about the size and shape of the argument, we don't need to refer to the value itself.

[3] It is not yet known how to share other kinds of values such as floating point numbers, or value-structure recursive structures (e.g. ordered trees), or functions etc. How to do so is an open problem.

```
add :: Entropy a => a -> a -> Protocol a
mul :: Entropy a => a -> a -> Protocol a
```

The multiply (`mul`) operation is global in that it involves interactions between the machines. The add operation (`add`) is a local operation. A richer language would also have other protocols, including methods for accepting shares of private inputs from users and for distributing shares of private results back to the users. For simplicity, in the latter cases we will simply configure these actions outside the EDSL.

Protocols such as `add` and `mul` are polymorphic over the `Entropy` class, so their precise action is structurally dependent on the types to which they are applied. To add together two private numbers which are represented by shares, we can simply add together the component shares (using `.+.`) and we are done. To multiply two private numbers, we have to compute nine partial products of their shares (Table 1). Each machine already has the

	y_A	y_B	y_C
x_A	$x_A y_A$	$x_A y_B$	$x_A y_C$
x_B	$x_B y_A$	$x_B y_B$	$x_B y_C$
x_C	$x_C y_A$	$x_C y_B$	$x_C y_C$

Table 1. Multiplication with Shares

values it needs to enable it to compute one of the entries on the diagonal. If each machine also communicates its x,y shares to its neighbor (according to the pattern in Figure 2), then every partial product in the matrix can be computed by somebody. For instance, machine B can compute $x_A y_B$, $x_B y_A$, and $x_B y_B$. We describe this in Haskell as follows:

```
mul :: Entropy a => a -> a -> Protocol a
mul x y = do
  (p,q) <- rotateRight (x,y)
  return ((x .*. y) .+. (p .*. y) .+. (x .*. q))
```

The low-level operation `rotateRight` transmits its argument `(x,y)` to its right hand neighbor machine, and receives a corresponding value `(p,q)` from its left hand neighbor. Recall, all three machines are operating loosely in lockstep, so all are executing the same instruction at around the same time. On receiving the neighbor's value, each machine computes the partial products, and returns the result to the calling procedure.

We need an additional refinement. If we performed multiple multiplications, we could end up rotating particular values to all three servers. This would then reveal enough information to reconstruct a private value, and so violate security. To avoid this, we take an extra step and re-randomize the shares before communication, as follows:

```
reshare :: Entropy a => a -> Protocol a
reshare s = do
  u <- entropy s
  v <- rotateRight u
  return (s .+. u .-. v)
```

Here each machine generates local entropy of the same size and shape as its argument, passes that entropy value to the right neighbor and receives a value from the left neighbor, and then calculates a new value for the share. As each random value is both added and subtracted from one of the shares, the overall (global) sum remains unchanged[4].

We can now write a secure version of the multiply protocol as follows:

```
mul :: Entropy a => a -> a -> Protocol a
mul x y = do
  (u,v) <- reshare (x,y)
  (p,q) <- rotateRight (u,v)
  return ((u .*. v) .+. (p .*. v) .+. (u .*. q))
```

Because each use of multiply communicates re-randomized shares, no information accumulates. Cryptographically, this makes the multiply operation *universally composable*, that is, we can use it repeatedly without fear of violating security.

Note, once again, that these operations are highly polymorphic. Because the `Entropy` class provides a structural extension over the overloading of the basic operations, the `add` and `mul` protocols are able to add and multiply whatever sizes and shapes of values we shall need (including lists and tuples).

3. Lookup Tables

Now that we have constructed the EDSL for share protocols, we can start writing programs. We quickly discover that we need data structures, and many standard assumptions no longer apply. In particular, we shall want table lookup (i.e. simple array indexing) but this becomes tricky—to say the least—when no individual server actually knows what index to look up!

A simple type for the lookup protocol is as follows:

```
indexing :: [a] -> Index -> Protocol a
```

where the `Index` type is some numeric type (e.g. `Word8`).

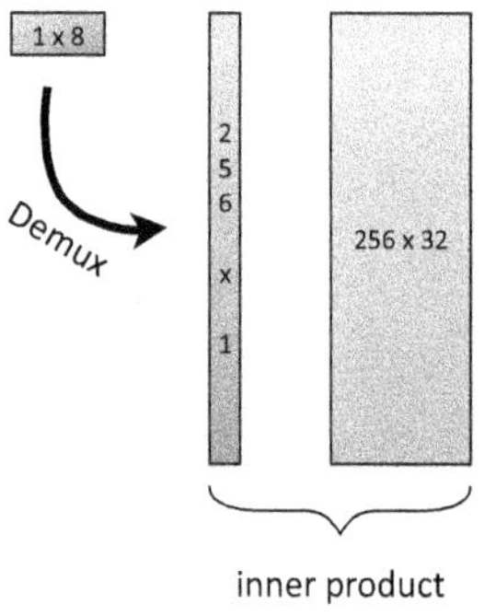

Figure 4. Inner Product with Demux

A moment's thought will convince us that the lookup algorithm has to act on all the entries of the table—otherwise we must have had *some* information as to what the index value was. Consequently, we should look to express the lookup protocol as some computation across the whole table. In fact, the form is very simple if we postulate a `demux` protocol that maps a binary representation of a value into a fixed-length, unary representation. Then the table lookup protocol is just a kind of inner product between the result of the demux protocol, and the table itself (see Figure 4). This intuition may be expressed more precisely as follows:

```
indexing :: [a] -> Index -> Protocol a
indexing table index = do
  ds <- demux index
  return (foldr1 (.+.) (zipWith mask ds table)
  where
    mask d entry = if d then entry else 0
```

[4] We actually implement a standard optimization that removes the network communication implied here. Each machine generates its entropy using pseudo-random numbers. During initialization, we pass the random seed around to the next neighbor, so each machine can locally generate the entropy stream of its predecessor.

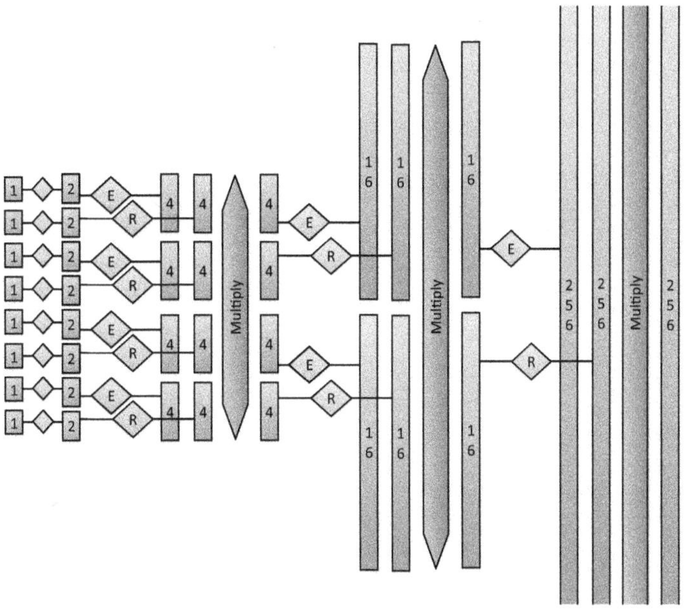

Figure 5. Parallel Manifestation of Demux Operation (for 8-bits)

A pure (i.e., non-share) demux function would map a binary representation of a value into a unary representation. For example, a 4-bit demux would take a 4-bit value and produce a 16-bit value (i.e. 2^4-bits) in which exactly one bit was set to 1, the other bits all being 0. We will adopt the convention that the demux bits are numbered from left to right. So, for example (using strings of 1's and 0's to represent lists of bits (Bools))[5],

```
demux "0000" = "1000 0000 0000 0000"
demux "0100" = "0000 0000 1000 0000"
demux "1111" = "0000 0000 0000 0001"
```

and so on. Note, we use big bit-endian representation for the binary bit-sequences, but count these unary bit-sequences from the left (consistent with Haskell practice elsewhere).

Correspondingly, a demux *protocol* would map a *share* of a 4-bit value, to a *share* of a 16-bit value. That is, if $x = x_A \oplus x_B \oplus x_C$, and if $d_i (i \in \{A, B, C\})$ is the result of running the demux protocol on the x_i, then $demux(x) = d_A \oplus d_B \oplus d_C$. For example, if we compute the demux of `0x8`, again going from 4-bits to 16-bits, then (one random outcome for) the d_i might be as follows:

```
d_A = "1011 0010 1110 1011"
d_B = "0011 0100 1100 1101"
d_C = "1000 0110 1010 0110"
```

Notice that only the 9th position (representing the value 8) has odd parity across all three shares; every other position has even parity.

Correctness of `indexing` is easy to establish. If we were dealing with pure functions (i.e. not share protocols), only one bit resulting from `demux` will be set, and this bit will select exactly the single row of the table corresponding to the original index. In the case of the share protocols, each d_i will contain a share of the true demux. That is, for each bit position j in the demux shares, $d_A(j) \oplus d_B(j) \oplus d_C(j) = 0$, except for the single bit position corresponding to the original index, in which case $d_A(j) \oplus d_B(j) \oplus d_C(j) = 1$. The `mask` function (written here as m) distributes across $\oplus$, so that $m(d_A(j) \oplus d_B(j) \oplus d_C(j), e) = m(d_A(j), e) \oplus m(d_B(j), e) \oplus m(d_C(j), e)$.

[5] Spaces are shown for ease of readability only.

3.1 Demux Protocol

All the computations involved in the definition of `index` were local (i.e. additions, or "scalar" multiplications where at least one value was known), except for those involved in the demux protocol. It is here that we shall have to work hard to minimize the number of global (multiply) operations.

As a pure function, demux can be expressed as a divide and conquer algorithm, satisfying the following equation.

```
demux (bs ++ cs)
   = [ b && c | b <- demux bs, c <- demux cs]
```

The list comprehension should be read as, "for each value `b` drawn from the list `bs`, and then for each value `c` drawn from the list `cs`, construct the value `b&c`." Thus, if `demux "10"` is given by `"0010"` and `demux "01"` is given by `"0100"`, then `demux 0b1001` is given by `"0000 0000 0100 0000"`.

Equivalently, we can express the cartesian product as a parallel multiply:

```
demux (bs ++ cs) = mul ds es
  where
    bs' = demux bs
    cs' = demux cs
    ds = expand (length cs') bs'
    es = replicate (length bs') cs'
```

where `expand n` duplicates each bit n times, and `replicate n` repeats the entire bit sequence n times. Thus, on the previous example,

```
expand 4 "0010"    = "0000 0000 1111 0000"
replicate 4 "0100" = "0100 0100 0100 0100"
```

Now a bitwise mul (&) produces `"0000 0000 0100 0000"`, i.e. 9.

We can do this fully in parallel as depicted in Figure 5. First we do a 1-bit demux (i.e. $0 \mapsto$ `"10"`, and $1 \mapsto$ `"01"`). Then we replicate and expand alternating 2-bit sequences to produce 4-bit sequences that are multiplied (i.e., anded) together. Similarly we replicate and expand 4-bit sequences into 16 bit sequences, and finally 16-bit sequences into a 256-bit sequence.

```
demux :: (Entropy word) => word -> Protocol [Bool]
demux w = demuxMerge (demuxBase (bits w))

demuxBase [] = []
demuxBase (b:bs) = [not b, b] : demuxBase bs

demuxMerge [bs] = return bs
demuxMerge bss  = do
    let (zss,odds) = chop2 bss
    let (xs,ys)    = unzip (map cartesian zss)
    zs <- mul xs ys
    demuxMerge (zs++odds)

expandReplicate (xs,ys)    = unzip [(a,b) | a <- ys, b <- xs]

chop2 []         = ([],[])
chop2 [x]        = ([],[x]) -- handles bit sizes that are not a power of 2
chop2 (x:y:xys) = case chop2 xys of (xs,ys) -> ((x,y):xs,ys)
```

Figure 6. Specification of Parallel Demux Operation (for any number of bits)

Figure 5 represents exactly the computation size and shape we need for AES. For reference, however, the code in Figure 6 provides a generic specification of the demux, even when the index word size is not a power of 2. Note, however, that the specification uses explicit lists of Booleans so, while it is fully executable, it is superficially inefficient. In practice, we re-implement the functions `demuxBase` and `demuxMerge` to work over packed representations of bits (e.g. 256 bits represented as a tuple of four 64-bit words). The definitions of these specific functions are provided in the Appendix.

The demux protocol on 8-bits requires just three multiplies (parallel-ands). But we can go one step further. The whole name of the game is to reduce the number of multiplications (because of their communication overhead), so we lift the whole definition of `demux` up to a list of indices, and return a list of results. Concretely, the version specialized to 8-bit indices is as follows:

```
demux :: [Word8] -> Protocol [Word256]
demux ws = do
    wss <- mul (map expnd4 ws) (map replt4 ws)
    yss <- mul (map expnd16 wss) (map replt16 wss)
    zss <- mul (map expnd256 yss) (map replt256 yss)
    return zss
```

Now `demux` has the same three calls to `mul` however long the input list of indices is. We can do this because the `mul` operation is overloaded on lists, and gathers together all the elements into a single packet for network communication. The corresponding type for `indexing` becomes:

```
indexing :: [a] -> [Word8] -> Protocol [a]
```

4. AES example

We are now ready to program AES in the share protocol EDSL. Figure 7 depicts the pattern of information flow, showing where information comes from and where it ends up. We assume that there is a machine which holds a plaintext version of a document (PT), and one that holds the key with which to encrypt the plain text. These machines send shares of their values (i.e. random values that—in this case—collectively xor to the originals) to the computation servers A, B and C. The servers then proceed to collaboratively encrypt the plain text—and this takes place without any individual server being able to discover anything about either the plain text or the key. Once the encryption computation is complete, the servers send their shares of the result to a machine responsible for collecting and constructing the cipher text (CT), which xors the individual shares to obtain the final result. Note that in some use cases the plain text, key, and cipher text may be on the same machine, and in others they may be on separate machines. The only security aspect we are aiming to maintain is that the computational servers A, B and C are distinct. Of course, as before, all communication is performed over SSL.

For the algorithm itself, we don't plan to give a detailed explanation of AES, partly because the main lookup protocol is so generic that we don't need to delve into the internals of the algorithm, and partly because the language aspects of what we are doing can be explained at a structural level.

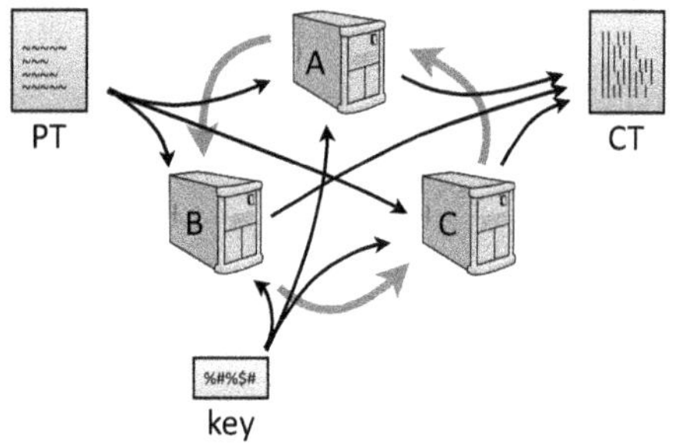

Figure 7. AES Configuration

The structure of the AES algorithm is shown in Figure 8. In the 128-bit version of AES, the plain text PT is a 16 byte chunk of the input, viewed as a 4x4 matrix of bytes. This matrix is called the *state*. In the *Key addition* phases, the bytes of the state are xor'd with key material generated from a pseudo-random generator that was seeded with the original crypto key. The *Shift row* phases rotate the individual rows of the state, and the *Mix column* phases does a column-based transformation based on modular polynomial multiplication. The *Byte substitution* phase replaces each byte in the state with a new byte, the value of which is defined by some Galois-field arithmetic, but whose software implementation is usually done by table lookup.

We decided to use a variant of the AES implementation that merges the byte substitution phase with the mix column phase, called *T-boxes*. The T-box formulation has become popular in both

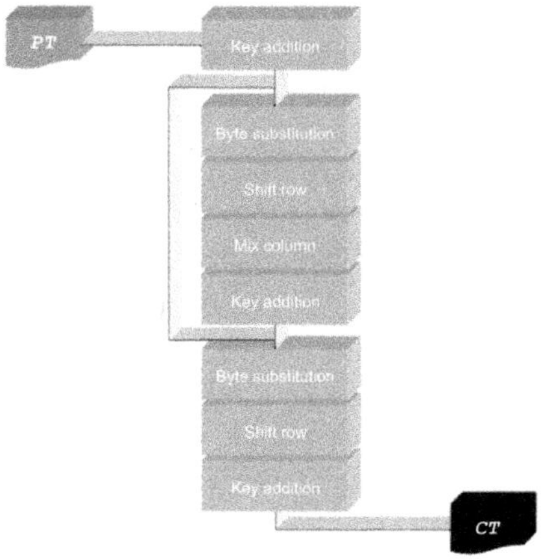

Figure 8. Structure of AES

software and hardware implementations [FM01] as it embodies all the algebraic complexity of AES in precomputed lookup tables. It was convenient for us because we had already produced an executable specification in Haskell for a different purpose. The core of the algorithm is given in Figure 9.

```
type State    = [[Word8]] -- 4x4
type RoundKey = [[Word8]] -- 4x4

encrypt :: (RoundKey,[RoundKey],RoundKey)
           -> [Word8] -> [Word8]
encrypt (key0,keys,keyN) inp = let
    input  = chop 4 inp
    first  = addRoundKey key0 input
    ending = seqMap cryptoRound keys first
    end    = finalRound keyN ending
  in  concat end

cryptoRound :: RoundKey -> State -> State
cryptoRound key u = let v = shiftRow u
                        w = map tFunc v
                    in addRoundKey key w

finalRound :: RoundKey -> State -> State
finalRound key u = let v = map (map (sbox !!)) u
                       w = shiftRow v
                   in addRoundKey key w

tFunc :: [Word8] -> [Word8]
tFunc [a,b,c,d] = let
    a' = tbox !! a
    b' = tbox !! b
    c' = tbox !! c
    d' = tbox !! d
  in (a' `xorPoly` rotLeft 3 b' `xorPoly`
      rotLeft 2 c' `xorPoly` rotLeft 1 d')
xorPoly = zipWith xor
```

Figure 9. T-Box Implementation of AES in Haskell

In this (inefficient) executable specification, the T-box is represented as a list of `Word32` with 256 elements. The T-box function `tFunc` looks up four byes in this table, and permutes and xors the result according to the T-box algorithm. The S-box table is simply a list of bytes (again specified in the definition of AES). The remaining functions such as `shiftRow` and `addRoundKey` are made up of simple rearrangements of structure and/or xor operations.

The control operator `seqMap` is a variant of `foldl` in which the arguments are flipped. For each of the round keys, `seqMap` applies the function `cryptoRound` to both the particular key in the list and the state, producing a new state for the next application. Think of `seqMap` as a kind of for-loop.

4.1 AES Share Protocol

It turns out to be simple to lift this specification into our EDSL for share protocols: the operation for table lookup is replaced by its monadic equivalent `indexing`, the `seqMap` control operator is replaced with the natural monadic equivalent, and the rest of the code is converted into monadic form in a standard manner (Figure 10).

```
encrypt :: (RoundKey,[RoundKey],RoundKey)
             -> [Word8] -> Protocol [Word8]
encrypt (key0,keys,keyN) inp = do
    let input = chop 4 inp
    let first = addRoundKey key0 input
    ending <- seqMapM cryptoRound keys first
    end    <- finalRound keyN ending
    return $ concat end

cryptoRound :: RoundKey -> State -> Protocol State
cryptoRound key u = do
    let v = shiftRow u
    w <- mapM tFunc v
    addRoundKey key w

finalRound :: RoundKey -> State -> Protocol State
finalRound key u = do
    v <- mapM (mapM (indexing sbox)) u
    let w = shiftRow v
    addRoundKey key w

tFunc :: [Word8] -> Protocol [Word8]
tFunc [a,b,c,d] = do
  a' <- indexing tbox a
  b' <- indexing tbox b
  c' <- indexing tbox c
  d' <- indexing tbox d
  return (a' `xorPoly` rotLeft 3 b' `xorPoly`
          rotLeft 2 c' `xorPoly` rotLeft 1 d')
```

Figure 10. AES as a share protocol

Already this version takes advantage of the bit-level parallelism built into the `indexing` function—within `tFunc`, four bytes of the state are looked up in parallel. However, there are four sets of the 4-byte lookups, and they are indexed sequentially. This means that this implementation of AES requires 12 (networked) multiplications (i.e. parallel-ands) per round (i.e. 4 indexing operations, each requiring 3 parallel-ands).

We can improve performance by modifying the definition of `cryptoRound` so that it does a SIMD lookup operation on all the bytes of the state at once.

```
tFunc :: [Word8] -> Protocol [Word8]
tFunc [a,b,c,d] = do
  [a',b',c',d'] <- fmap (chop 4) $
                   indexing tbox (concat [a,b,c,d])
  return (a' `xorPoly` rotLeft 3 b' `xorPoly`
          rotLeft 2 c' `xorPoly` rotLeft 1 d')
```

Now, all the indexing operations are performed together, so we have just 3 (bit-parallel) multiplies per round. More bits are being being anded each time, but the overhead of enlarging the vector of values in a single parallel-and is very small.

It would be a pity if we always had to do these kinds of performance improvements by hand. In the next section we show how we use compilation techniques to transform the direct SMC version into a more efficient implementation.

5. Automated Performance Improvements

There are a number of improvements that would lead to a more efficient SMC implementation. In particular, we would like to eliminate the list manipulations and—whenever possible—to replace sequential multiplications by grouping many together in one larger parallel SIMD-style operation. This section describes an automated approach to doing so, which may be generalized to other EDSLs. It is fairly technical and can be skipped on first reading.

We start by re-interpreting the algorithm in an environment where some of the types and operations have been replaced with *symbolic* counterparts. For example, the usual type for bytes, `Word8` is replaced by the following symbolic version (using Haskell's GADT notation for consistency later on):

```
data Word8 where
  Var8    :: Name -> Word8
  SBox    :: Word256 -> Word8
  Xor8    :: Word8 -> Word8 -> Word8
  GetByte :: Int -> Word32 -> Word8
```

The constructor `Var8` represents a completely unknown value, while the other constructors are for values constructed with the corresponding functions, thus the symbolic version of a function is simply the constructor:

```
xor = Xor8
```

Executing the algorithm in this environment essentially performs symbolic computation: types that were left concrete are evaluated away, and the final result is a symbolic description of the algorithm.

For the AES example, we left functions and lists as concrete types, while we used symbolic representations for the word types and the `Protocol` monad. Executing the `encrypt` function in this environment performs a partial evaluation, producing a residual version of the algorithm where all the loops are unrolled and there are no list manipulations. We perform additional optimizations on this data structure to derive the final efficient algorithm, which we describe later.

To represent symbolic `Protocol` computations we used a *syntactic monad* with all binds normalized to the right, so the datatype resembles a list of (appropriately typed) primitive operations, `ProtocolOp`, terminated by a `Return`:

```
type Protocol = SMonad (->)

data SMonad :: (* -> * -> *) -> * -> * where
  Return :: a -> SMonad fun a
  (:>>=) :: ProtocolOp a
         -> a `fun` SMonad fun b
         -> SMonad fun b

data ProtocolOp :: * -> * where
  Mul     :: Entropy a => a -> a -> ProtocolOp a
  LkpTBox :: Word256 -> ProtocolOp Word32
```

The type is parameterized by the function-space constructor so that we can use it with both concrete and symbolic function-spaces: the first one is useful for symbolic evaluation, while the second one is useful for analyzing `Protocol` computations. As in the case for pure symbolic evaluation, defining the symbolic functions is fairly simple, except that in this case we have to make sure that they are in the normal form that we chose:

```
instance Monad Protocol where
  return a             = Return a
  Return a     >>= f   = f a
  (op :>>= k) >>= f    = op :>>= \r -> k r >>= f

mul :: Entropy a => a -> a -> Protocol a
mul x y = Mul x y :>>= return
```

The final step before we have a representation of the algorithm that can be analyzed and optimized is to write a function that will replace the concrete functions in a monadic computation with their symbolic equivalents:

```
type Code      = SMonad (:->)
data a :-> b   = a :-> b

compile :: Supply Name -> Protocol a -> Code a
compile _     (Return a)  = Return a
compile names (op :>>= k) =
  let (n1,n2) = split2 names
      x       = case op of
                  Mul {}     -> newVar n1
                  LkpTBox {} -> newVar n1
  in op :>>= x :-> compile n2 (k x)
```

The basic idea behind `compile` is to replace a function's argument with a symbolic value, which is then used to evaluate the function's body. Symbolic values are generated by the overloaded function `newVar` (the actual name generation uses the technique described in [Aug94], thus avoiding the need to plumb the name supply around). Note the intricate interaction between generalized algebraic datatypes and overloading in the definition of the symbolic value, `x`: pattern matching on the operation reveals the type of the expected result which, in turn, allows the compiler to resolve the overloading of `newVar`[6].

At this stage, we have a completely symbolic (but still typed) representation of the algorithm, which is suitable for analysis and rewriting. Our goal is to group single multiplications into multiple-value SIMD-style multiplications. Note that the operations of the `Protocol` monad *commute* in the sense that they can be rearranged freely, only subject to data dependencies: as long as the three computational nodes operate in sync, it does not matter in what order they compute the multiplications. Using this fact, we can write a code transformation that rearranges the code by data-dependencies: first we execute instructions that only depend on the function arguments, next we execute instructions that depend on function arguments and the results of the first group, and so on. The details are presented in function `rearrange`:

```
rearrange :: [Name] -> Code a -> Code a
rearrange _ (Return x) = Return x
rearrange us p =
  let (vs, m1, m2) = pullUp us p
  in m1 (rearrange vs m2)

pullUp :: [Name] -> Code a
       -> ([Name], Code b -> Code b, Code a)
pullUp us (Return a) = (us, id, Return a)
pullUp us (op :>>= x :-> m)
  | all (`elem` us) (fvs op)
    = ( newDefs ++ vs
```

[6] In the case of multiplication, the overloading is resolved because the symbolic version of the Entropy class supports generating symbolic values.

```
      , \k -> op :>>= x :-> this k
      , next )
  | otherwise = (vs, this, op :>>= x :-> next)
  where
  (vs,this,next) = pullUp us m
  newDefs        = case op of
                     Mul {} -> fvs x
                     LkpTBox {} -> fvs x
```

Most of the work for this transformation is performed by the function pullUp which, given a set of names and a computation, splits the computation into two parts: those instructions that only depend on the names (represented in continuation-passing style) and all other instructions. While performing the analysis, pullUp also computes the new set of defined names, to be used in the following iteration of the analysis.

Having rearranged the instructions by data-dependency, all we need to do is implement another code transformation that identifies independent adjacent multiplications and combines them into a single SIMD-style multiplication. For illustration purposes the code transformation that we show uses nested (symbolic) pairs to perform multiplications in parallel. In a similar fashion we could write another code transformation that flattens the nested pairs into a more efficient data structure (e.g., an array of a fixed size):

```
joinMul :: Code a -> Code a
joinMul (Mul a b :>>= c :-> (Mul x y :>>= z :-> m))
  | all (`notElem` fvs c) (fvs x ++ fvs y)
    = joinMul
    $ Mul (Pair a x) (Pair b y) :>>= Pair c z :-> m
joinMul (op :>>= c :-> m) = op :>>= c :-> joinMul m
joinMul m = m
```

At this point we have transformed the original (somewhat inefficient) algorithm into one with a better structure for run-time performance. The approach of deriving the efficient implementation in this manner gives us some confidence in the correctness of the final efficient algorithm because (i) we used a typed representation throughout the development, and (ii) the transformation steps are small and independent, so we can can examine and evaluate them in isolation. Furthermore, while we used AES as an example, the overall idea is quite general, and can be used for other algorithms also.

Throughout this section we described how to derive an efficient algorithm for encrypting a single AES block. However, a typical use of AES involves processing many blocks, which gives rise to yet another opportunity for speeding the implementation: we can improve the performance by processing multiple AES blocks in parallel. This works well in certain encryption modes—in Galois counter mode (GCM), for example, where AES is used from a fixed starting point to produce a kind of one-time pad. Pipelining is not appropriate in other modes: in cipher-block chaining (CBC), for example, the result of one encryption is xor'd with the next block prior to its encryption, so pipelining is not possible.

When we can do multiple blocks at the same time, we can either use concurrency primitives to execute multiple encryption functions at once, and/or generate custom encryption functions that encrypt multiple blocks at once. We actually do both for different reasons, as we explain in the next section.

The technique described in this section make it extremely easy to derive such multi-block encrypting functions. For example, to generate a function that encrypts 4 blocks at once, we simply run our "compiler" on the following code:

```
keys :-> b1 :-> b2 :-> b3 :-> b4 :->
  do r1 <- encrypt keys b1
     r2 <- encrypt keys b2
     r3 <- encrypt keys b3
     r4 <- encrypt keys b4
     return (Pair4 r1 r2 r3 r4)
```

Evaluating this program symbolically unrolls all loops and groups together all multiplications. Note that because the blocks are processed independent of each other, all their multiplications end up grouped together into large SIMD-style multiplications, which helps performance.

6. Performance

The first implementation we did was extremely inefficient. Our initial focus was on the correctness of the specification of the table-lookup algorithm and avoided making any (possibly premature) commitments to particular optimizations. Consequently, the first implementations were slow, executing AES at about one block per second. We then systematically identified performance hot spots and bottlenecks, and corrected them. All of these mitigations were quite localized, so the code we ended up with is still very recognizably similar to the original specification.

The major optimization was mentioned above—to perform all 16 indexing operations from a single AES state in one go, exploiting the fact that we were able to build the indexing function with a parallel SIMD-style capability.

Laziness was both good and bad. We make extensive use of laziness in control structures built from (virtual) data structures, but at the same time we have to control laziness in the results of Protocol computations. Laziness can lead to large intermediate computations being created in the heap before consumers for the values eventually force their evaluation. In the AES example, no control decisions are ever taken on the basis of shares of private values—naturally, given their random nature—so the only evaluation-demand came from serializing intermediate values for network sends. Judicious use of seq and its more vigorous cousins (e.g. reduction to full normal form by NFData) handled this potential problem very easily.

As mentioned previously, the first version of indexing used lists of booleans to represent the result of demux. Once we were confident that the definition was correct, they weren't particularly hard to replace with packed representations. The calculations of the precise bit-manipulations are tedious however, so we have included the code in the Appendix.

We had some issues with GHC not inlining the primitive monad operators (i.e. >>=). This created a significant overhead by itself, and additionally prevented GHC from carrying out other optimizations. We traced the problem to our overloading the randomization operations to work in multiple monads (we needed IO and Protocol). Once we separated these cases, the GHC inliner was able to do its magic.

After calculating the demux of the index, the indexing function computes a masked xor of the whole table. This is such a central operation, and repeated so often that we had to ensure it was maximally efficient. We could probably have coaxed Haskell to produce optimal code, but for this simple operation it was easier to just write it in C and call the C function through Haskell's foreign function interface (FFI)—the FFI is to Haskell as asm is to C. On similar lines, we also introduced a new interface to the SSL Haskell bindings that allowed us to build Storable values directly rather than build byte strings simply to have them converted into storables.

We also upgraded the standard Haskell random number generator to be cryptographically random as well as statistically random. We used the secure RNG design based on AES, as provided by NIST [BK12]. Happily, this did not run any slower, and on machines with special AES instructions runs significantly faster than the standard randoms in Haskell.

All of these optimizations improved both space and time usage of the non-networked part of the computation. Earlier versions of the code had heap residency of 8-10MB plus a couple of space leaks. After the optimizations described here, the heap residency was stable at around 220KB. We considered that sufficiently optimized for our purposes.

6.1 Latency

With heap requirements being well-managed, the limiting factors on performance become CPU, network bandwidth, and network latency. Given that multiple network communications take place in the midst of any non-trivial share computation, the general pattern of any computation is shown in Figure 11.

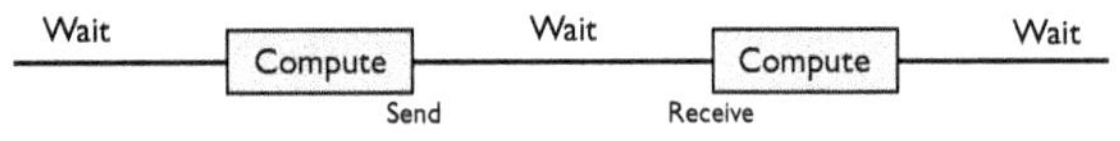

Figure 11. Effect of Network Latency

We do some work, then perform a network send to communicate values, and then wait to receive the values to come from the neighbor machine. What does this mean for AES? There are 10 rounds in the AES algorithm, each round requiring one (parallel) table lookup. Each table lookup requires three (global) parallel-and operations, and each of these parallel-and operations requires a round-robin communication between the servers. On our benchmarking setup[7], the latency of a 1kbyte SSL communication between machines is around 300 μs. Encrypting a single block, therefore, will cost 9 ms just in network latency. Indeed, we measure that computing one block of AES in isolation takes around 14.3 ms. This number is important: as we increase the opportunities for parallelism we will decrease the overall time per block, but we will never decrease the block latency below this figure. Indeed, it may increase slightly.

When encrypting a single block at a time, the network latency in every table lookup is the limiting factor—even on a fast network—as CPU loads are low, and network bandwidth is low. As described in the previous section, there are two kinds of parallelism we can introduce to reduce the impact of this network latency.

First, we can process many blocks in parallel in a single instance of the protocol. Doing two or more blocks at once increases the amount of work we do before incurring the network latency, and it does not increase the wait phase significantly (though we may start to increase the number of packets sent per operation). In effect, this form of SIMD parallelism shares the cost of network latency amongst multiple blocks, thus reducing the latency overhead on any individual block. Secondly, we can run multiple instances of the protocol in parallel, each with their own SSL connection. This parallelism is simply traditional concurrency, where concurrent execution allows the wait time in one thread to be shadowed by the compute time in another thread.

The results of varying these parameters is shown in Figure 12. Each point is the average of 10 runs. In both charts, the Y-axis is amortized encryption time (in ms per 128-bit AES block). In the upper chart, the X-axis specifies the number of blocks being processed by any single compute phase, and the different curves represent the number of concurrent threads independently processing groups of blocks. In the lower chart, the roles of these are transposed.

[7] All the benchmarks were carried out on three physically separate machines networked with gigabit ethernet. The systems are identical, running quad-core 3.1 GHz Intel Nehalem-C CPU with 16GB of memory and accelerated AES instructions (for random number generation). To ease benchmark administration, each worker runs CentOS 6.2 as a KVM virtual machine.

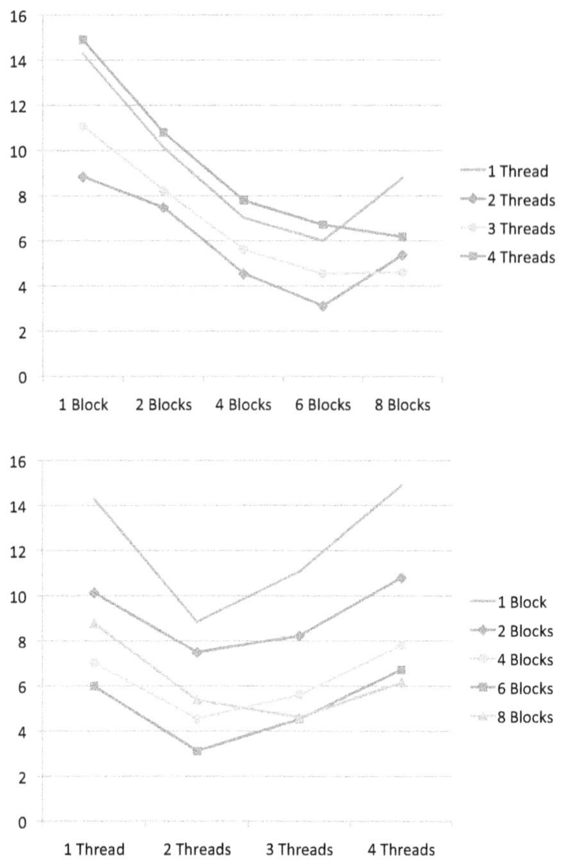

Figure 12. Time (in ms) to encrypt an AES Block

In these specific experiments, the winner is clear. Running two concurrent threads, each of which is processing 6-AES blocks in SIMD style, produces the minimum amortized time per block of 3.1 ms. This translates to 320 AES blocks per second, or a secure-encryption throughput of 41 kilobits per second.

In the lower chart, all the curves rise after two or three threads. The local network is sufficiently fast that the latency does not need many threads to become fully shadowed, and having additional threads simply introduces contention. In a different network setting, such as connecting three servers owned by different organizations across the public internet, we expect that many more threads will be required to shadow the much larger network latency that would arise.

Network bandwidth was not a limiting factor for us. In the fastest case (6 blocks, 2 threads) packet sizes ranged from 166 to 4412 bytes, with an average packet size of 784 bytes. Packets flowed at a rate of 3195 per second, translating to an average network bandwidth of 20 megabits per second. Likewise, CPU utilization was not limiting (given our 4 core machines). In the 1 block, 1 thread case, CPU utilization was 0.75. It rose to 1.45 in the 6 block, 2 threads case, and to 1.70 in the 6 blocks, 4 threads case.

7. Related Work

After the seminal work of Yao [Y86], the FairPlay system was arguably the first major leap towards practicability [MNPS04]. The Fairplay system provided a full compilation pathway from a version of C down through compilation that carried out various optimizations of the underlying Yao *garbled circuit* scheme. FairPlay had array lookup and assignment (like our table lookup) and the Fairplay compiler builds multiplexing and demultiplexing circuits as explicit boolean circuits, though there is no effort to maximize parallelism as we do here. In fact, it is an open question as to whether a SIMD-style parallelism is possible in the Yao setting.

There have been a number of implementations of AES in FairPlay and other Yao-style implementations that also assume the same honest-but-curious security model. In two-party implementations of AES, one party typically knows the key, and the other part knows the cypher text. Damgaard and Keller attempted to gain a fast AES by exploiting the algebraic structure of the algorithm itself [DK10]. They proposed several variants, the best of which required (approximately) an average of 2200 elementary operations in 70 rounds to encrypt one AES block. Their implementation with three participants in a local network showed that one block can be encrypted in 2 seconds, though they argue that this result could be improved by optimizing the implementation.

Huang *et al*'s recent USENIX paper focused on how to optimize Yao garbling to make the protocols significantly faster than before [HEKM11], in many cases faster than corresponding custom-designed protocols. In their setting—as with ours—the key-schedule is expanded outside of the crypto framework (for them, because one party knows the key entirely; for us, because the key is known by the initiator of the computation), so in neither case does key expansion contribute to the cost of the computation. The AES implementation is done on the original formulation of AES, where the mix-column is performed explicitly. This is done just using XOR's, which come pretty much for free in their framework. Large circuits still get generated, but they are produced in a pipelined fashion so never need to be stored all in one place. When table lookups are performed, the tables are viewed as circuits themselves, requiring garbled version of the tables to be generated and transmitted. AES encryption time is 0.06 seconds per block (after preprocessing). That is, about 17 blocks per second.

Pinkas et al focus on a more stringent security model, where the protocol still succeeds despite a certain proportion of malicious players who attempt to corrupt the protocol [PSSW09]. In this setting, again based on Yao garbling, a single block AES encrypt takes 8 seconds under honest-but-curious assumptions (not counting preprocessing time), and 661 seconds under malicious adversary assumptions.

The Sharemind system [BLW08] is built on the same principles as the system described here. It too has three servers, and performs arithmetic sharing. In some dimensions, the Sharemind system is more fully engineered than our EDSL, in that it comprises a stand alone input language SecreC (i.e. much of C, along with annotations for secrecy), a compiler, a low-level virtual machine interpreter, and theorem proving support for privacy proofs. On the other hand, the fact that we built an EDSL on Haskell means that we are able to bypass most of those components and inherit them from the host language directly. Consequently, we have been able to implement shares of private values for many new families of data types, and rapidly explore many different instantiations of higher level protocols. The Sharemind system has produced many advances in protocols, notably including division, and has been used for a number of real world application demonstrations. In the last couple of months, the Sharemind developers have begun work on their own version of AES.

Bain et al also constructed a language for privacy computation as an embedded DSL in Haskell [BMS+11]. Their language is agnostic about the underlying cryptographic computational substrate, and were able to hook into multiple computational backends (Shamir-sharing, Yao garbling, and FHE). Their main focus was on establishing privacy proofs rather than on algorithmic improvements, and did not attempt to optimize their implementations.

A significant breakthrough on the underlying security model has come from Gentry's *fully homomorphic encryption* (FHE) scheme [G09]. FHE doesn't rely on multiple parties, but does all the computation within crypto mathematics. In Gentry's scheme, individual bits are randomly encoded as large noisy vectors, i.e. points in a space that are close (but not too close) to the points on a regular multi-dimensional lattice. Operations of addition and multiplication on the lattice also perform corresponding calculation on the cipher texts, the results of which are revealed once the resultant cipher texts are decrypted. There is a detail to manage though: as these lattice operations are performed, the *noise* increases (i.e. the cipher texts move further and further away from the lattice points), requiring use of a *recrypt* operation to reset the noise to something like original levels. FHE schemes are currently *very* inefficient, with initial implementations requiring about two seconds to compute a single *and*-operation [GH11]. However, progress in this area is rapid, and AES may be within sight of FHE implementations relatively soon.

8. Conclusion

The programming language community has an excellent understanding of the performance profile of standard CPU RAM architectures, even though multi-cores and cache and other memory hierarchies make many things very much more complicated than they used to be. SMC-style computation on private values presents a very different execution model, and one that is only beginning to receive attention.

In all existing manifestations of computation on private values, multiplication (both arithmetic and boolean) is exceedingly expensive compared with every other operation. In arithmetic sharing (the setting of this paper) the expense comes from the entropy and network accesses required. In Yao garbling, the expense arises because multiplications create significant expansions in the size of the circuit that has to be communicated and evaluated. In fully homomorphic encryption, the expense comes from multiplications dramatically increasing the noise within the crypto value. These force the programmer to trade off between using larger security parameters or requiring more frequent reset operations, each of which entails using a homomorphic instance of the decrypt operation.

When optimizing computations in SMC or FHE computational models, we need to approach multiplications with the same mindset we use for disk accesses—how do we minimize them, block them together, and hide the latencies they incur? Some of these performance-improving techniques can be implemented within the secure computation technique itself—for example, some of the SMC and FHE approaches are moving to produce SIMD versions of the basic multiply operation (e.g. [SF11])—but that only goes so far. The rest of the optimizations have to come from programming and/or compilation techniques that are designed to optimize for this strange execution model.

This paper contains an example of the kind of algorithmic rethinking that is required. We gained well over an order of magnitude for AES based mostly on a good algorithm for table lookup and judicious use of parallelism. The field is in its infancy regarding how we do other kinds of algorithms, and progress here can have a dramatic impact.

Acknowledgments

Mark Tullsen helped with network and testing setup, and Sally Browning aided in generating benchmark figures. Abhi Shelat and John Mitchell provided helpful discussions about the security of the demux. Dan Bogdanov and Jan Willemson helped with understanding the share protocols used in this implementation.

References

[NIST01] National Institute of Standards and Technology (NIST). *FIPS 197: Advanced encryption standard, 2001.* Available at http://csrc.nist.gov/publications/fips/fips197/fips-197.pdf.

[Aug94] Lennart Augustsson, Mikael Rittri, and Dan Synek *On Generating Unique Names.* Journal of Functional Programming (1994), 4 : pp 117-123

[BLW08] D. Bogdanov, S. Laur, J. Willemson. *Sharemind: a framework for fast privacy-preserving computations.* In Proceedings of 13th European Symposium on Research in Computer Security, ESORICS 2008, LNCS, vol. 5283. Springer-Verlag, 2008.

[BCD+08] P. Bogetoft, D. L. Christensen, I. Damgaard, M. Geisler, T. Jakobsen, M. Kroeigaard, J. D. Nielsen, J. B. Nielsen, K. Nielsen, J. Pagter, M. Schwartzbach, and T. Toft, *Secure Multiparty Computation Goes Live.* Financial Cryptography and Data Security, R. Dingledine and P. Golle (eds), LNCS Vol. 5628, Springer-Verlag 2009.

[BK12] E. Barker and J. Kelsey. *Recommendation for Random Number Generation Using Deterministic Random Bit Generators.* NIST Special Publication 800-90A. http://csrc.nist.gov/publications/nistpubs/800-90A/SP800-90A.pdf

[BMS+11] A.M. Bain, J.C. Mitchell, R. Sharma, D. Stefan and J. Zimmerman. *A domain-specific language for computing on encrypted data.* Invited Talk. In Foundations of Software Technology and Theoretical Computer Science, 2011.

[DK10] I. Damgaard and M. Keller, *Secure Multiparty AES,* Financial Cryptography and Data Security, R. Sion (ed), LNCS Vol. 6052, Springer-Verlag 2010.

[FM01] Two Methods of Rijndael Implementation in Reconfigurable Hardware, *V. Fischer and M. Drutarovsk.* Cryptographic Hardware and Embedded Systems (CHES 2001). LNCS Vol. 2162. Spring-Verlag 2001.

[G09] C. Gentry, *Fully homomorphic encryption using ideal lattices.* ACM Symposium on Theory of Computing (STOC 2009), 2009.

[GH11] C. Gentry and S. Halevi. *Implementing Gentrys fully-homomorphic encryption scheme.* Advances in Cryptology (Eurocrypt 2011), LNCS Voli. 6632, Springer-Verlag, 2011.

[G04] O. Goldreich, *Foundations of Cryptography, Vol 2: Basic Applications.* Cambridge University Press, 2004.

[HEKM11] Y. Huang. D. Evans, J. Katz, L. Malka, *Faster Secure Two-Party Computation Using Garbled Circuits.* In 20th USENIX Security Symposium, San Francisco, 2011.

[MNPS04] D. Malkhi, N. Nisan, B. Pinkas, and Y. Sella, *FairPlay – a secure two party computation system.* Proceedings of the 13th conference on USENIX Security Symposium - Vol. 13, 2004.

[PSSW09] B. Pinkas, T. Schneider, N. P. Smart, and S. C. Williams. *Secure Two-Party Computation is Practical.* Proceedings of the 15th International Conference on the Theory and Application of Cryptology and Information Security: Advances in Cryptology. ASIACRYPT 09. Springer-Verlag 2009.

[SF11] N. P. Smart and F. Vercauteren. *Fully homomorphic SIMD operations.* Manuscript at http://eprint.iacr.org/2011/133, 2011.

[Y86] A. C. Yao. *How to generate and exchange secrets.* In Proceedings of the 27th IEEE Symposium on Foundations of Computer Science, 1986.

A. Appendix

Here is a listing of the functions called by `demux`. For performance, is it critical to use packed representations of the bit sequences, and while it is not trivial to work out the bit manipulations involved, they can all be derived by calculation from the general specification provided earlier.

The `expnd4` and `replt4` functions map from the original 8-bit word in Figure 5 through to the 16-bit words prior to the first multiplication. As the diagram indicates, `expnd4` operates on the odd numbered bits, and `replt4` on the even numbered bits (counting 0-7). In both functions, initially a 0 maps to 01, and a 1 maps to 10 (representing a 1-bit demux). Then, in `expnd4` these sequences are expanded bitwise, and in `replt4` they are replicated.

```
expnd4 :: Word8 -> Word16
expnd4 b  = case 8 * sel 7 b + 4 * sel 5 b
                 + 2 * sel 3 b + sel 1 b of
             0  -> 0x3333
             1  -> 0x333c
             2  -> 0x33c3
          -- etc
             15 -> 0xcccc

replt4 :: Word8 -> Word16
replt4 b = case 8 * sel 6 b + 4 * sel 4 b
               +  2 * sel 2 b + sel 0 b of
             0  -> 0x5555
             1  -> 0x555a
             2  -> 0x55a5
          -- etc
             15 -> 0xaaaa

sel :: Int -> Word8 -> Word8
sel k b = shiftR b k .&. 0x01  -- select bit k
```

In `expnd16` and `replt16` the argument represents four 4-bit words: `expnd16` operates on the odd numbered nibbles, and `replt16` on the even numbered ones (counting 0-3). In `expnd256` and `replt256` the argument represents two 16-bit words. The resulting 256-bit words are represented as four 64-bit words.

```
expnd16 :: Word16 -> Word32
expnd16 w  =  expn ((w .&. 0x00f0) `shiftR` 4) .|.
  ((expn ((w .&. 0xf000) `shiftR` 12)) `shiftL` 16)
  where  expn w4 = case w4 of
                     0  -> 0x0000
                     1  -> 0x000f
                     2  -> 0x00f0
                  -- etc
                     15 -> 0xffff

replt16 :: Word16 -> Word32
replt16 w = fromIntegral ((w .&. 0x000f) * 0x1111)
  .|. (fromIntegral (((w .&. 0x0f00) `shiftR` 8)
         * 0x1111) `shiftL` 16)

expnd256 :: Word32 -> Word256
expnd256 w
  = W256 (scale 12) (scale 8) (scale 4) (scale 0)
 where
  scale :: Int -> Word64
  scale off = scale1 off 3 .|. scale1 off 2
            .|. scale1 off 1 .|. scale1 off 0
  scale1 :: Int -> Int -> Word64
  scale1 off ix = (if x `testBit` (off + ix)
                   then 0xFFFF else 0x0000)
                           `shiftL` (ix * 16)
  x :: Word32
  x = w `shiftR` 16

replt256 :: Word32 -> Word256
replt256 w = W256 w64 w64 w64 w64
  where
    w64 = (x `shiftL` 48) .|. (x `shiftL` 32)
        .|. (x `shiftL` 16) .|. x
    x :: Word64
    x = fromIntegral (w .&. 0xffff)
```

Addressing Covert Termination and Timing Channels in Concurrent Information Flow Systems

Deian Stefan[1] Alejandro Russo[2] Pablo Buiras[2] Amit Levy[1] John C. Mitchell[1] David Mazières[1]

(1) Stanford University, Stanford, CA, USA (2) Chalmers University of Technology, Gothenburg, Sweden

Abstract

When termination of a program is observable by an adversary, confidential information may be leaked by terminating accordingly. While this termination covert channel has limited bandwidth for sequential programs, it is a more dangerous source of information leakage in concurrent settings. We address concurrent termination and timing channels by presenting a dynamic information-flow control system that mitigates and eliminates these channels while allowing termination and timing to depend on secret values. Intuitively, we leverage concurrency by placing such potentially sensitive actions in separate threads. While termination and timing of these threads may expose secret values, our system requires any thread observing these properties to raise its information-flow label accordingly, preventing leaks to lower-labeled contexts. We implement this approach in a Haskell library and demonstrate its applicability by building a web server that uses information-flow control to restrict untrusted web applications.

Categories and Subject Descriptors D.1.3 [*Programming Techniques*]: Concurrent Programming; D.4.6 [*Security and Protection*]: Information flow controls

General Terms Security, Languages, Design

Keywords Monad, Library, Covert channels

1. Introduction

Covert channels arise when programming language features are misused to leak information [30]. For example, when termination of a program is observable to an adversary, a program may intentionally or accidentally communicate a confidential bit by terminating according to the value of that bit. While this termination covert channel has limited bandwidth for sequential programs, it is a significant source of information leakage in concurrent settings. Similar issues arise with covert timing channels, which are potentially widespread because so many programs involve loops or recursive functions. These channels, based on either internal observation by portions of the system or external observation, are also effective in concurrent settings.

We present an information-flow system, in a form of an execution monitor, that mitigates and eliminates termination and timing channels in concurrent systems, while allowing timing and termination of loops and recursion to depend on secret values. Because the significance of these covert channels depends on concurrency, we fight fire with fire by leveraging concurrency to mitigate these channels: we place potentially non-terminating actions, or actions whose timing may depend on secret values, in separate threads. In our system, each thread has an associated *current label* that keeps track of the sensitivity of the data it has observed and restricts the locations to which the thread can write. Hence, while termination and timing of these threads may expose secret values, our system requires any thread observing these properties to raise its information-flow label accordingly. This prevents lower security threads from observing confidential information. We implement this approach in a Haskell library and demonstrate its applicability by building a web server that applies information-flow control to untrusted web applications. One advantage of Haskell is that the Haskell type system prevents code from circumventing our dynamic information-flow tracking. Although we do not address underlying hardware issues such as cache timing, our language-level methods can be combined with hardware-level mechanisms as needed to provide comprehensive defenses against covert channels.

Termination covert channel Askarov et al. [2] show that, for sequential programs with outputs, leakage using the termination covert channel requires exponential time in the size of the secret. Moreover, if secrets are uniformly distributed, the attacker's advantage (after observing a polynomial amount of output) is negligible in comparison with the size of the secret. Because of this relatively low risk, accepted sequential information-flow tools, such as Jif [38] and FlowCaml [48], are only designed to address termination-insensitive noninterference. In a concurrent setting, however, the termination covert channel may be exploited more significantly [18]. We therefore focus on termination covert channels in concurrent programs and present an extension to our Haskell LIO library [52], which provides dynamic tracking of labeled values. By providing labeled explicit futures with `lFork` and `lWait`, our extension removes the termination covert channel from sequential and concurrent programs while allowing loops whose termination conditions depend on secret information.

Internal timing channel Multi-threaded programs can leak information through an *internal timing covert channel* [56] when the order of public events depends on secret data. Generally, an internal timing attack can be carried out whenever a race to acquire a shared public resource may be affected by secrets. We close this covert channel by decoupling the execution of computations that produce public events from computations that manipulate secret data. Using `lFork` and `lWait`, a computation depending on secret data proceeds in a new thread; LIO asserts that the number of instructions executed by threads producing public events does not depend on secrets. Therefore, a possible race to a shared public resource does not depend on the secret, eliminating internal timing leaks.

ICFP'12, September 9–15, 2012, Copenhagen, Denmark.

External timing channel External timing covert channels, which involve externally measuring the time used to complete operations that may depend on secret information, have been used in practice to leak information [6, 15] and break cryptosystems [17, 28, 57]. While several existing mechanisms mitigate external timing channels [1, 4, 19], these covert channels are not addressed by conventional information-flow tools and, in fact, most of the previous techniques for language-based information-flow control appear to have limited application. Our contribution to external timing channels is to bring the mitigation techniques from the OS community into the language-based security setting. Generalizing previous work [3], Zhang et al. [60] propose a black-box mitigation technique that we adapt to a language-based security setting. In this approach, the source of observable events is wrapped by a timing mitigator that delays output events so that they contain only a bounded amount of information. We take advantage of Haskell's ability to identify computations that produce outputs, and implement the mitigator as part of our information flow control library. Leveraging monad transformers [33], we show how to modularly extend LIO and other Haskell libraries that perform side-effects, to provide a suitable form of Zhang et al.'s mitigator.

In summary, the main contributions of this paper are:

- We present a dynamic information flow control (IFC) system that eliminates the termination and internal timing covert channels, while mitigating external timing. While these covert channels have been addressed differently in static IFC approaches, this is the first implementation of a language-based dynamic IFC system for concurrency that does not rely on cooperative-scheduling. Our system provides support for threads, lightweight synchronization primitives, and allows loops and branches to depend on sensitive values.
- We eliminate termination and internal-timing covert channels using concurrency, with potentially sensitive actions run in separate threads. This is implemented in a Haskell library that uses labeled concurrency primitives[1].
- We provide language-based support for resource-usage mitigation using monad transformers. We use this method to implement the black-box external timing mitigation approach of Zhang et al.; the method is also applicable to other covert channels, such as storage.
- We evaluate the language implementation by building a simple server-side web application framework. In this framework, untrusted applications have access to a persistent key-value store. Moreover, requests to apps may be from malicious clients colluding with the application in order to learn sensitive information. We show several potential leaks through timing and termination and show how our library is used to address them.

Section 2 provides background on information flow, Haskell, and the `LIO` monad. We describe how to address the termination covert channel in Section 3, the internal timing covert channel in Section 4, and the external timing channel in Section 5. Labeled communication primitives are detailed in Section 6. A formalization of the library is given in Section 7, with security guarantees detailed in Section 8. The implementation and experimental evaluation are presented in Section 9. Related work is described in Section 10. We conclude in Section 11.

2. Background

We build on the Haskell dynamic information flow control library called LIO [52]. This section describes LIO and some of its relevant background.

[1] The library implementations discussed in this paper can be found at `http://www.scs.stanford.edu/~deian/concurrent_lio`

2.1 Information flow control

The goal of IFC is to track and control the propagation of information. In an IFC system, every bit has an associated *label*. Labels form a lattice [9] governed by a partial order $\sqsubseteq$ pronounced "can flow to." The value of a bit labeled L_{out} can depend on a bit labeled L_{in} only if $L_{\text{in}} \sqsubseteq L_{\text{out}}$.

In a *floating-label* system, such as LIO, every execution context has a label that can rise to accommodate reading more sensitive data. For a computation P labeled L_P to observe an object labeled L_O, P's label must rise to the least upper bound or *join* of the two labels, written $L_P \sqcup L_O$. P's label effectively "floats above" the labels of all objects it observes. Furthermore, systems frequently associate a *clearance* with each execution context that bounds its label.

Specific label formats depend on the application and are not the focus of this work. Instead, we will focus on a very simple two-point lattice with labels `Low` and `High`, where `Low` $\sqsubseteq$ `High` and `High` $\not\sqsubseteq$ `Low`. We, however, note that our implementation is polymorphic in the label type and any label format that implements a few basic relations (e.g., $\sqsubseteq$, join $\sqcup$, and meet $\sqcap$) can be used when building applications. Additionally, the LIO library supports *privileges* which are used to implement decentralized information flow control as originally presented in [37]; though we do not discuss privileges in this paper, our implementation also provides privileged-aware versions of the combinators described in later sections.

2.2 Haskell

We chose Haskell because its abstractions allow IFC to be provided by a library [31]. Building a library is far simpler than developing a programming language from scratch (or heavily modifying a compiler). Moreover, a library offers backwards compatibility with a large body of existing Haskell code.

From a security point of view, Haskell's most distinctive feature is a clear separation of pure computations from those with side-effects. Any computation with side-effects must have a type encapsulated by the monad `IO`. The main idea behind the LIO library is that untrusted actions must be specified with a new Labeled I/O monad, `LIO`, instead of `IO`. Using `LIO` ensures that all computations obey information control flow.

2.3 The `LIO` monad

LIO dynamically enforces IFC, but without the features described in this paper, provides only *termination-insensitive* IFC [2] for sequential programs. At a high level, LIO provides the `LIO` monad intended to be used in place of `IO`. The library furthermore contains a collection of `LIO` actions, many of them similar to `IO` actions from standard Haskell libraries, except that the `LIO` versions contain label checks that enforce IFC. For instance, LIO provides file operations that look like those of the standard library, except that they confine the application to a dedicated portion of the file system where they store a label along with each file.

The `LIO` monad keeps a *current label*, L_{cur}, that is effectively a ceiling over the labels of all data that the current computation may depend on. `LIO` also maintains a *current clearance*, C_{cur}, which specifies an upper bound on permissible values of L_{cur}.

LIO does not individually label definitions and bindings. Rather, all symbols in scope are identically labeled with L_{cur}. The only way to observe or modify differently labeled data is to execute actions that internally access privileged symbols. Such actions are responsible for appropriately validating and adjusting the current label. As an example, the LIO file-reading function `readFile`, when executed on a file labeled L_F, first checks that $L_F \sqsubseteq C_{\text{cur}}$, throwing an exception if not. If the check succeeds, the function raises L_{cur}

to $L_{cur} \sqcup L_F$ before returning the file content. The LIO file-writing function, `writeFile`, throws an exception if $L_{cur} \not\sqsubseteq L_F$.

As previously mentioned, allowing experimentation with different label formats, LIO actions are parameterized by the label type. For instance, simplifying slightly:

```
readFile :: (Label l) ⇒ FilePath → LIO l String
```

To be more precise, it is really `(LIO l)` that is a replacement for the `IO` monad, where `l` can be any label type. The context `(Label l)⇒` in `readFile`'s type signature restricts `l` to types that are instances of the `Label` typeclass, which abstracts the label specifics behind the basic methods $\sqsubseteq$, $\sqcup$, and $\sqcap$.

2.4 Labeled values

Since LIO protects all nameable values with L_{cur}, we need a way to manipulate differently-labeled data without monotonically increasing L_{cur}. For this purpose, LIO provides explicit references to labeled, immutable data through a polymorphic data type called `Labeled`. A locally accessible symbol (at L_{cur}) can name, say, a `Labeled l Int` (for some label type `l`), which contains an `Int` protected by a different label.

Several functions allow creating and using `Labeled` values:

- `label :: (Label l)⇒l →a → LIO l (Labeled l a)`
  Given label l : $L_{cur} \sqsubseteq l \sqsubseteq C_{cur}$ and value v, action `label` l v returns a `Labeled` value guarding v with label l.
- `unlabel :: (Label l)⇒Labeled l a →LIO l a`
  If `lv` is a `Labeled` value v with label l, `unlabel lv` raises L_{cur} to $L_{cur} \sqcup l$ (provided $L_{cur} \sqcup l \sqsubseteq C_{cur}$ holds, otherwise it throws an exception) and returns v.
- `toLabeled :: (Label l)⇒l →LIO l a → LIO l (Labeled l a)`
  The dual of `unlabel`: given a label l, and an action `m` that would raise L_{cur} to L'_{cur} where $L'_{cur} \sqsubseteq l \sqsubseteq C_{cur}$, `toLabeled` l `m` executes `m` without raising L_{cur}, and instead encapsulates `m`'s result in a `Labeled` value protected by label l.
- `labelOf :: (Label l)⇒Labeled l a →l`
  Returns the label of a `Labeled` value.

As an example, we show an `LIO` action that adds two `Labeled Int`s:

```
addLIO lA lB = do a ← unlabel lA
                  b ← unlabel lB
                  return (a + b)
```

If the inputs' labels are L_A and L_B, this action raises L_{cur} to $L_A \sqcup L_B \sqcup L_{cur}$ and returns the sum of the values. To avoid raising the current label, and instead return a `Labeled Int`, `addLIO` can be wrapped by `toLabeled`:

```
add lA lB = toLabeled (labelOf lA ⊔ labelOf lB)
                      (addLIO lA lB)
```

Implicit flows in LIO We note that in an imperative language with labeled variables, dynamic labels can lead to implicit flows [10]. The canonical example is as follows:

```
public := 0;        // public has a Low label
if (secret)         // secret has a High label
  public := 1;      // public depends on secret
```

To avoid directly leaking the `secret` bit into `public`, one should track the label of the program counter and determine that execution of the assignment `public :=1` depends on `secret`, and raise `public`'s label when assigning `public :=1`. However, since the assignment executes conditionally depending on `secret`, now `public`'s *label* leaks the `secret` bit. LIO does not suffer from implicit flows. When branching on a secret, L_{cur} becomes `High` and therefore no public events are possible.

Listing 1 Exploiting the termination channel by brute-force

```
bruteForce:: String → Int → Labeled l Int → LIO l ()
bruteForce name n secret = forM_ [0..n] $ λi → do
  toLabeled High $ do
    s ← unlabel secret
    when (s == i) ⊥
  outputLow (name ++ " ≠ " ++ show i)
```

3. The termination covert channel

As mentioned in the introduction, information-flow control results and techniques for sequential settings do not naturally generalize to concurrent settings. In this section we highlight that the sequential LIO library is, like many IFC systems, susceptible to leaks due to termination and show that a naive, but typical, extension that adds concurrency drastically amplifies this leak. We present a modification to the LIO library that eliminates the termination covert channel from both sequential and concurrent programs; our solution allows for flexible programming patterns, even writing loops whose termination condition depends on secret data.

Sequential setting As described by [2], a brute-force attack, taking exponential time in the size (# of bits) of the secret, is the most effective way to exploit the termination channel in a sequential program. Listing 1 shows an implementation of such attack. Function `bruteForce` takes three arguments: a public string (helper) message, a public upper-bound on the secret, and the secret `Int` of type `Labeled Int`. Given the three arguments `bruteForce` returns an `LIO` action which when executed returns unit `()`, but produces intermediate side-effects. Specifically, `bruteForce` writes to a `Low` labeled channel using `outputLow` while L_{cur} is `Low`. We assume that the attack is executed with initial L_{cur} = `Low`, and secret `Int` labeled `High`.

The attack consists of iterating (variable `i`) over the domain of the secret (`forM_ [0..n]`), producing a publicly-observable output at every iteration until the secret is guessed. On every iteration L_{cur} is raised to the label of the `secret` within a `toLabeled` block. As described in Section 2.4, the current label outside the `toLabeled` block remains unaffected, and so the computation can continue producing publicly-observable outputs if the computation within the `toLabeled` block does not diverge. This is the case unless guess `i` is equal to the secret, at which point the computation diverges (`when (s ==i) ⊥`) and no additional publicly-observable outputs are produced. The leak due to termination is obvious: when the attacker, observing the `Low` labeled output channel, no longer receives any data, the value of the secret can be inferred given the previous outputs. For instance, to leak a 16-bit `secret`, we execute `bruteForce "secret" 65536 secret`. Assuming the value of the secret is 3, executing the action produces the outputs "`secret ≠0`", "`secret ≠1`", and "`secret ≠2`" before diverging. The assumption here, and the rest of the paper, is that the code is untrusted (e.g., provided by the attacker) and therefore an observer that knows the implementation of `bruteForce` can directly infer that the value of the secret is 3. Observe that the code producing public outputs (`outputLow (msg ++" ≠" ++show i)`) does not inspect secret data, which makes it difficult to avoid termination leaks by simply tracking the flow of labeled data inside programs.

Concurrent setting Suppose that we (naively) add support for concurrency to LIO using a hypothetical primitive `fork`, which simply executes a given computation in a new thread. Although we can preserve termination-insensitive non-interference, we can extend the previous brute force attack to leak a secret value in linear, as opposed to exponential, time. In general, adding concurrency primitives in a straight-forward manner makes attacks that leverage the termination covert channel very effective [18]. To illustrate this point, consider the attack shown in Listing 2, which

Listing 2 A concurrent termination channel attack

```
concurrentAttack :: Int → Labeled l Int → LIO l ()
concurrentAttack k secret = forM_ [0..k] $ λi → do
  iBit ← toLabeled High $ do
           s ← unlabel secret
           return (extractBit i s) )
  fork $ bruteForce (show k ++ "-bit") 1 iBit
    where extractBit :: Int → Int → Int
          extractBit i n = (shiftR n i) .&. (bit 0)
```

leaks the bit-contents of a secret value in linear time. Given the bit-length `k` of the secret and the labeled `secret`, `concurrentAttack` returns an action which, when executed, extracts each bit of the secret (`extractBit i s`) and spawns a corresponding thread to recover the bit using the sequential brute-force attack of Listing 1 (`bruteForce (show k ++"-bit") 1 iBit`). By collecting the public outputs generated by the different threads (having the form "`0-bit` ≠ 0", "`3-bit` ≠ 0", "`1-bit` ≠ 0", etc.), it is directly possible to recover the secret value. Observe that the divergence of one thread does not affect the termination of other threads and thus does not require observations external to the program, as in the sequential case.

3.1 Removing the termination covert channel in LIO

Since LIO has floating labels, a leak to a `Low` channel due to termination *cannot* occur after the current label is raised to `High`, unless the label raise is within an enclosed `toLabeled` computation. Hence, we can deduce that a piece of LIO code can exploit the termination covert channel only when using `toLabeled`. The key insight is that `toLabeled` is the single LIO combinator that effectively allows a piece of code to temporarily raise its current label, perform a computation, and then continue with the original current label. The attack in Listing 1 is a clear example that leverages this property of `toLabeled` to leak information.

Consider the necessary conditions for eliminating the termination channel of Listing 1: the execution of the publicly-observable `outputLow` action must not depend on the data or control flow of the secret computation executed within the `toLabeled` block. Hence, one approach to close the termination covert channel is by decoupling the execution of computations enclosed by `toLabeled`. To this end, we provide an alternative to `toLabeled` that executes computations that might raise the current label (as in `toLabeled`) in a newly-spawned thread. To observe the result (or non-termination) of such a spawned computation, the current label is firstly raised to the label of the (possibly) returned result. In doing so, after observing a secret result (or non-termination) of a spawned computation, actions that produce publicly-observable side-effects can no longer be executed. In this manner, the termination channel is closed.

In Listing 1, the execution of `outputLow` depends on the termination of the computation enclosed by `toLabeled`. However, using our proposed approach of spawning a new thread when "performing a `toLabeled`", if the code following the sensitive block wishes to observe whether or not the `High` computation has terminated, it would first need to raise the current label to `High`. Thereafter, an `outputLow` action cannot be executed regardless of the result (or termination) of the `toLabeled` computation.

Concretely, we close the termination channel by removing the insecure function `toLabeled` from `LIO` and, instead, provide the following (termination sensitive) primitives.

```
lFork :: Label l ⇒ l → LIO l a → LIO l (Result l a)
lWait :: Label l ⇒ Result l a → LIO l a
```

Intuitively, `lFork` can be considered as a concurrent version of `toLabeled`. `lFork l lio` spawns a new thread to perform the computation `lio`, whose current label may rise, and whose result is a value labeled with `l`. Rather than block, immediately after spawning a new thread, the primitive returns a value of type `Result l a`, which is simply a handler to access the labeled result produced by the spawned computation. Similar to `unlabel`, we provide `lWait`, which inspects values returned by spawned computations, i.e., values of type `Result l a`. The labeled wait, `lWait`, raises the current label to the label of its argument and then proceeds to inspect it.

In principle, rather than forking threads, it would be enough to prove that computations involving secrets terminate, e.g., by writing them in Coq or Agda. However, while this idea works in theory, it is still possible to crash an Agda or Coq program at runtime: for example, with a stack overflow. Generally, abnormal termination due to resource exhaustion exploits the termination channel just as effectively. Forking threads removes the termination channel by design. Although it might seem expensive, forking threads in Haskell is a light-weight operation [25].

We note that adding concurrency to LIO is a major modification which introduces security implications beyond that of handling the termination channel. In the following section, we describe the *internal timing covert channel*, a channel that is only present in programming languages that have support for concurrency and shared-resources.

Listing 3 Internal timing leak

```
doGuess secret guess cond = do
  toLabeled High $ do v ← unlabel secret
                      when (v ≠ guess) $ loopUntil cond
  outputLow (show guess)
  broadcastCondition cond

attack :: Labeled l Bool → LIO l ()
attack secret = do cond ← mkSharedCond
 {- thread 1: -}    fork $ doGuess secret True  cond
 {- thread 2: -}    fork $ doGuess secret False cond
```

4. The Internal timing covert channel

Multi-threaded programs, wherein threads share a common (public) resource, can leak sensitive information through the *internal timing covert channel* [56]. In an internal timing attack, sensitive data can be leaked by affecting the timing behavior of threads, which consequently alters the order of events on a shared public channel.

Listing 3 shows an example of the internal timing attack in LIO with the added `fork` primitive. Here, action `mkSharedCond` creates a shared resource that is used as a "condition variable", `loopUntil` waits until the condition is satisfied, and `broadcastCondition` sets the condition to signal all the waiting threads. The shared resource may be defined in terms of language level constructs, such as mutable references: `mkSharedCond` can create a public `Bool` reference set initially to `False`, `loopUntil` loops until the dereferenced value is `True` and `broadcastCondition` assigns `True` to it. Alternatively, it can be defined in terms of an implicit state, such as the scheduler: `mkSharedCond` and `broadcastCondition` can simply return `()`, while `loopUntil` delays the running thread for a reasonable amount of time (e.g., by using `threadDelay`).

Although in isolation both threads are secure (i.e., they satisfy non-interference), by executing them concurrently it is possible to leak information about `secret`. When executing `attack secret`, if `secret` is (labeled) `True`, thread 2 will output to the public (low) channel after thread 1 regardless of which thread is executed first. In other words, the produced output will be "`True`", "`False`". The converse holds when `secret` is `False` and the program prints out "`False`", "`True`". Notice that an attacker can infer the value of `secret` by simply observing the outputs on the public channel: the order of "`True`" and "`False`" is influenced by the secret data.

Unlike other timing channel attacks, internal timing attacks do not require a powerful attacker that must measure the execution time as to deduce secret information. The interleaving of threads can directly be used to produce leaks! Additionally, we note that although the example of Listing 3 only leaks a single bit, it is easy to construct an attack that uses a loop to leak the bit-contents of a secret value in linear time of its length. Tsai et al. [54] show such an amplified attack and demonstrate its effectiveness even in settings where little information about the run-time system (e.g., the scheduler) is available.

4.1 Removing the internal timing channel

As indicated by our example, the internal timing covert channel can be exploited when the time to produce public events (e.g., writing data to a public channel) depends on secrets. In other words, leaks due to internal timing occur when there is a race to acquire a public shared resource that may be affected by secret data. To close this channel, we apply the technique used to close the termination covert channel: we decouple the execution of computations that produce public events from computations that manipulate secret data. By using `lFork` and `lWait`, computations dealing with secrets are executed in a new thread. Consequently, any possible race to a shared public resource cannot depend on sensitive data, making leaks due to internal timing infeasible.

5. The external timing covert channel

In a real-world scenario, IFC applications interact with unlabeled, publicly observable, resources. For example, a server-side IFC web application interacts with a browser, which may itself be IFC-unaware, over a public network channel. Consequently, an adversary can take measurements *external* to the application (e.g., the application response time) from which they may infer information about confidential data computed by the web application. Although our results generalize (e.g., to the storage covert channel), in this section we address the *external timing covert channel*: an application can leak information over a channel to an observer that precisely measures message-arrival timings.

Most of the language-based IFC techniques that consider external timing channels are limited. Despite the successful use of external timing attacks to leak information in web [6, 15] and cryptographic [17, 28, 57] applications, they remain widely unaddressed by mainstream, practical IFC tools, including Jif [38]. Furthermore, most techniques that provide IFC in the presence of the external timing channel [1, 4, 19] are overly restrictive, e.g., they do not allow folding over secret data. In this work, we show a modular approach of mitigating the external timing covert channel for Haskell libraries, such as LIO.

5.1 Mitigating the external timing channel

Recently, a predictive black-box mitigation technique for external timing channels has been proposed [3, 60]. The predictive mitigation technique assumes that the attacker has control of the application (computing on secret data) and can measure the time a message is placed on a channel (e.g., when a response is sent to the browser). Treating the application as a black-box event source, a mitigator is interposed between the application and system output.

Internally, the mitigator keeps a *schedule* describing when outputs are to be produced. For example, the time mitigator might keep a schedule "predicting" that the application will produce an output every 1ms. If the application delivers events according to the schedule, or at a higher rate, the mitigator will be able to produce an output at every 1ms interval, according to the schedule, and thus leak no information.

The application may fail to deliver an event to the mitigator on time, and thus render the mitigator's schedule prediction false. At this point, the mitigator must handle the misprediction by selecting, or "predicting", a new schedule for the application. In most cases, this corresponds to doubling the application's *quantum*. For instance, following a misprediction where the quantum was 1 ms, the application will subsequently be expected to produce an output every 2 ms. It is at the point of switching schedules where an attacker learns information: rather than seeing events spaced at 1 ms intervals, the attacker now observes outputs at 2 ms intervals, indicating that the application violated the predicted behavior (a decision that can be affected by secret data). Askarov et al. [3] show that the amount of information leaked by this *slow-doubling* mitigator is polylogarithmic in the application runtime.

The aspects of the predictive mitigation technique of [3, 60] that make it particularly attractive to use in LIO are:

- ▶ The mitigator can adaptively reduce the quantum, as to increase the throughput of a well-behaved application in a manner that bounds the covert channel bandwidth (though with the leakage factor slightly larger than that of the slow-doubling mitigator);
- ▶ The mitigator can leverage public factors to decide a schedule. For example, in a web application setting where responses are mitigated, the arrival of an HTTP request can be used as a "reset" event. This is particularly useful as a quiescent application would otherwise be penalized for not producing an output according to the predicted schedule. Our web application of Section 9 implements this mitigation technique.
- ▶ The amount of information leaked is bounded by a combinatorial analysis on the number of attacker observations.

Monadic approach to black-box mitigation The functionality of different monads, such as I/O and error handling, can be combined in a modular fashion using *monad transformers* [33]. A monad transformer t, when applied to a monad m, generates a new, combined monad, $t\ m$, that shares the behavior of monad m as well as the behavior of the monad encoded in the monad transformer. The modularity of monad transformers comes from the fact that they consider the underlying monad m opaque, i.e., the behavior of the monad transformer t does not depend on the internal structure of m. In this light, we adopt Zhang et al.'s system-oriented predictive black-box mitigator to a language-based security setting in the form of a monad transformer.

5.2 Language-based mitigators

We envision the implementation of mitigators that address covert channels other than external timing. For example, we prototype a mitigator for the storage covert channel, which addresses attacks in which the message length is used to encode secret information. Hence, our mitigation monad transformer `MitM s q` is polymorphic in the mitigator-specific state `s` and quantum type `q` :

```
newtype MitM s q m a = MitM ...
```

We provide the function `evalMitM`, which takes an action of type `MitM s q m a` and returns an action of type `m a`, which when executed will mitigate the computation outputs. We note that the value constructor for the mitigation monad must not be exported to untrusted code, which can use it to circumvent the mitigation.

The time-mitigation monad transformer is a special case:

```
type TimeMitM = MitM TStamp TStampDiff
```

where the internal state `TStamp` is a time stamp, and the quantum `TStampDiff` is a time difference. Superficially, a value of type `TimeMitM m a` is a monadic computation that produces a value of type `a`. Internally, a time measurement is taken whenever an output is to be emitted in the underlying monad `m`, the internal state and quantum are adjusted to reflect the output event, and the output is delayed if it was produced ahead of the predicted schedule.

Consider, for instance, a version of `hPut` executing in the time mitigated `IO` monad, where every handle is mitigated:

```
type MIO = TimeMitM IO
...
hPut :: Handle → ByteString → MIO ()
```

If `hPut h` is invoked according to the specified schedule (e.g., at least every 1 ms), the actual IO function `IO.hPut` is used to write the provided byte-string every 1 ms. Conversely, if the function does not follow the predicted schedule, the quantum will be increased, and write-throughput to the file will decrease.

The use of a monad transformer leaves the possibility to use (almost) any underlying monad `m`, not just `IO` or `LIO`. However, this generality comes with a trade-off: either every computation `m` is mitigated, or trustworthy programmers must define *what* objects (e.g., file handles, sockets, references, etc.) they wish to mitigate and *how* to mitigate them (e.g., providing a definition for `hPut`, above). Given that the former design choice would not allow for distinguishing between inputs and outputs, we implemented the latter and more explicit mitigation approach.

To define *what* is to be mitigated, we provide the data type `data Mitigated s q a`, in terms of which a time-mitigated I/O file handle (as used in `hPut`) can simply be defined as:

```
type TimeMitigated = Mitigated TStamp TStampDiff
type Handle = TimeMitigated IO.Handle
```

`Mitigated` allows us to do mitigation at very fine granularity. Specifically, the monad transformer can be used to associate a mitigator with each `Mitigated` value (henceforth "handle"). This allows an application to write to multiple files, all of which are mitigated independently, and thus may be written to, at different rates[2]. It remains for us to address *how* the mitigators are defined.

Mitigators are implemented as instances of the type class `Mitigator`, which provides two functions:

```
class MonadConcur m ⇒ Mitigator m s q where
  -- | Create a Mitigated "handle".
  mkMitigated :: Maybe s       -- ^ Internal state
              → q              -- ^ Quantum
              → m a            -- ^ Handle constructor
              → MitM s q m (Mitigated s q a)

  -- | Mitigate an operation
  mitigate :: Mitigated s q a   -- ^ Mitigated "handle"
           → (a → m ())         -- ^ Output computation
           → MitM s q m ()
```

The context `MonadConcur m` is used to impose the requirement that the underlying monad be an `IO`-like monad which allows forking new `IO` threads (as to separate the mitigator from the computation being mitigated) and operations on synchronizing variables, MVars [25] (which are internal to the `MitM` transformer). The `mkMitigated` function is used to create a mitigated handle given an initial state, quantum, and underlying constructor. The default implementation of `mkMitigated` creates the mitigator state (internal to the transformer) corresponding to the handle. A simplified version of our `openFile` operation shows how `mkMitigated` is used:

```
openFile :: FilePath → IOMode → MIO Handle
openFile f mode = mkMitigated Nothing q $ do
  h ← IO.openFile f mode    -- Handle constructor
  return h                  -- Raw handle
    where q = mkQuant 1000  -- Initial quantum of 1ms
```

Here, the constructor `IO.openFile` creates a file handle to the file at path `f`. This constructor is supplied to `mkMitigated`, in addition to the "empty" state `Nothing`, and initial quantum q = 1 ms, which creates the corresponding mitigator and `Mitigated` handle (recall `Handle` is a type alias of `TimeMitigated IO.Handle`). We note that although the default definition of `mkMitigated` creates a mitigator per handle, instances may provide a definition that is more coarse-grained (e.g., associate mitigator with all handles of a thread).

Unlike for `mkMitigated`, each mitigator must define `mitigate`, which specifies how a computation should be mitigated. The function takes two arguments: the mitigated handle and a computation that produces an output on given the underlying, "raw" handle. Our time mitigator instance

```
instance ... ⇒ Mitigator m TStamp TStampDiff where
  mitigate mH act = ... -- Actual mitigation code
```

provides a definition for `mitigate`. Using `mitigate` we define our time mitigated `hPut` function as: `hPut hPut`

```
hPut :: Handle → ByteString → MIO ()
hPut mH bs = mitigate mH (λh → IO.hPut h bs)
```

The `mitigate` function first retrieves the internal state of the mitigator corresponding to the mitigated handle `mH` and forks a new thread (allowing other mitigated actions to be executed). In the new thread, a time measurement t_1 is taken. Then, if the time difference between t_1 and the internal mitigator time stamp t_0 exceeds the quantum q, the new mitigator quantum is set to $2q$; otherwise, the computation is delayed for $t_1 - t_0$ microseconds. Following, the `IO` action is executed, and the internal timestamp is replaced with the current time. We force operations on the same handle to be sequential and thus follow the latest schedule.

We finally remark that adapting an existing program to have mitigated outputs comes almost for free: a *trustworthy* programmer needs to define the constructor functions, such as `openFile`, and output functions, such as `hPut`, and simply *lift* all the remaining operations. We provide a definition for the function `lift :: Monad m ⇒m a →MitM s q m a`, which lifts a computation in the `m` monad into the mitigation monad, without performing any actual mitigation. A simple example illustrating this is the definition of `hGet` which reads a specified number of bytes from a handle:

```
hGet :: Handle → Int → TimeMitigated IO ByteString
hGet = lift ∘ IO.hGet ∘ mitVal
```

Here, `mitVal` simply returns the underlying "raw" handle.

6. Synchronization primitives in concurrent LIO

In the presence of concurrency, synchronization is vital. This section introduces an IFC-aware version of `MVars`, which are well-established synchronization Haskell primitives [25]. As with `MVars`, `LMVars` can be used in different manners: as synchronized mutable variables, as channels of depth one, or as building blocks for more complex communication and synchronization primitives.

A value of type `LMVar l a` is mutable location that is either empty or contains a value of type `a` labeled with `l`. `LMVars` are associated with the following operations:

```
newEmptyLMVar :: (Label l) ⇒ l → LIO l (LMVar l a)
putLMVar      :: (Label l) ⇒ LMVar l a → a → LIO l ()
takeLMVar     :: (Label l) ⇒ LMVar l a → LIO l a
```

Function `newEmptyLMVar` takes a label `l` and creates an empty `LMVar l a` for any desired type `a`. The creation succeeds only if the label `l` is between the current label and clearance of the `LIO` computation that creates it. Function `putLMVar` fills an `LMVar l a` with a value of type `a` if it is empty and blocks otherwise. Dually, `takeLMVar` empties an `LMVar l a` if it is full and blocks otherwise.

Note that both `takeLMVar` and `putLMVar` observe if the `LMVar` is empty in order to proceed to modify its content. Precisely,

[2] In cases where schedule mispredictions are common, it is important to implement the *l-grace* period policy of [60]. The policy states that when there are more than l mispredictions, the new scheduling should affect all mitigators.

Listing 4 Syntax for values, expressions, and types.

Label:	l
LMVar:	m
Value:	$v ::= \texttt{true} \mid \texttt{false} \mid () \mid l \mid m \mid x \mid \lambda x.e \mid \texttt{fix}\ e$
	$\mid \texttt{Lb}\ l\ e \mid (e)^{\text{LIO}} \mid \boxdot \mid \texttt{R}\ m \mid \bullet$
Expression:	$e ::= v \mid e\ e \mid \texttt{if}\ e\ \texttt{then}\ e\ \texttt{else}\ e \mid \texttt{let}\ x = e\ \texttt{in}\ e$
	$\mid \texttt{return}\ e \mid e \texttt{ >>= } e \mid \texttt{label}\ e\ e$
	$\mid \texttt{unlabel}\ e \mid \texttt{lowerClr}\ e \mid \texttt{getLabel}$
	$\mid \texttt{getClearance} \mid \texttt{labelOf}\ e \mid \texttt{out}\ e\ e$
	$\mid \texttt{lFork}\ e\ e \mid \texttt{lWait}\ e \mid \texttt{newLMVar}\ e\ e$
	$\mid \texttt{takeLMVar}\ e \mid \texttt{putLMVar}\ e\ e$
	$\mid \texttt{labelOfLMVar}\ e$
Type:	$\tau ::= \texttt{Bool} \mid () \mid \tau \to \tau \mid \ell \mid \texttt{Labeled}\ \ell\ \tau$
	$\mid \texttt{Result}\ \ell\ \tau \mid \texttt{LMVar}\ \ell\ \tau \mid \texttt{LIO}\ \ell\ \tau$

takeLMVar and putLMVar perform a read and a write of the mutable location. Consequently, from a security point of view, operations on a given LMVar l a are executed only when the label l is below or equal to the clearance (i.e., l $\sqsubseteq C_{\text{cur}}$ due to the read) and above or equal to the current label (i.e., $L_{\text{cur}} \sqsubseteq$ l due to the write). Moreover, after either operation, L_{cur} is raised to l.

Many communication channels used in practice are similarly *bi-directional*, i.e., a read produces a write (and vice versa). For instance, reading a file may modify the access time in the inode; writing to a socket may produce an observable error if the connection is closed, etc. As described above, LMVar are bi-directional channels. If we treated them as uni-directional, observe that, a termination leak would be possible: a thread, whose current label is Low can use a LMVar labeled Low to send information to a computation whose current label is High; the High thread can then decide to empty the LMVar according to a secret value and thus leak information to the Low thread.

7. Formal semantics for LIO

In this section, we model our concurrent LIO implementation encompassing the concurrency primitives discussed in Sections 3, 4, and 6. We do not model the external timing mitigator since our monad transformer approach effectively treats computations as black-boxes. Thus, although our approach is more fine grained, the security guarantees of [3, 60] readily apply to our library.

We formalize our LIO library as a simply typed Curry-style call-by-name λ-calculus with some extensions. Listing 4 defines the formal syntax for the language. Syntactic categories v, e, and τ represent values, expressions, and types, respectively. Values are side-effect free while expressions denote (possible) side-effecting computations. Due to lack of space, we only show the reduction and typing rules for the core part of the library.

Values The syntax category v includes the symbol `true` and `false` representing Boolean values. Symbol () represents the unit value. Symbol ℓ denotes security labels. Symbol m represents LMVars. Values include variables (x), functions ($\lambda x.e$), and recursive functions (`fix` e). Special syntax nodes are added to this category: `Lb` v e, $(e)^{\text{LIO}}$, `R` m, $\boxdot$, and $\bullet$. Node `Lb` v e denotes the run-time representation of a labeled value. Similarly, node $(e)^{\text{LIO}}$ denotes the run-time result of a monadic `LIO` computation. Node $\boxdot$ denotes the run-time representation of an empty LMVar. Node `R` m is the run-time representation of a handle, implemented as a LMVar, that is used to access the result produced by spawned computations. Alternatively, `R` m can be thought of as an explicit *future*.

Listing 5 Typing rules for special syntax nodes.

$$\frac{}{\Gamma \vdash \bullet : \tau} \qquad \frac{}{\Gamma \vdash m : \texttt{LMVar}\ \ell\ \tau} \qquad \frac{\Gamma \vdash e : \tau}{\Gamma \vdash \texttt{Lb}\ l\ e : \texttt{Labeled}\ \ell\ \tau}$$

$$\frac{\Gamma \vdash e : \tau}{\Gamma \vdash (e)^{\text{LIO}} : \texttt{LIO}\ \ell\ \tau} \qquad \frac{}{\Gamma \vdash \boxdot : \tau} \qquad \frac{\Gamma \vdash m : \texttt{LMVar}\ \ell\ \tau}{\Gamma \vdash \texttt{R}\ m : \texttt{Result}\ \ell\ \tau}$$

Node $\bullet$ represents an erased term (explained in Section 8). None of these special nodes appear in programs written by users and they are merely introduced for technical reasons.

Expressions Expressions are composed of values (v), function applications (e e), conditional branches (`if` e `then` e `else` e), and local definitions (`let` x = e `in` e). Additionally, expressions may involve operations related to monadic computations in the `LIO` monad. More precisely, `return` e and e `>>=` e represent the monadic return and bind operations. Monadic operations related to the manipulation of labeled values inside the `LIO` monad are given by `label` and `unlabel`. Expression `unlabel` e acquires the content of the labeled value e while in an `LIO` computation. Expression `label` e_1 e_2 creates a labeled value, with label e_1, of the result obtained by evaluating the `LIO` computation e_2. Expression `lowerClr` e allows lowering of the current clearance to e. Expressions `getLabel` and `getClearance` return the current label and current clearance of an `LIO` computation, respectively. Expression `labelOf` e obtains the security label of labeled values. Expression `out` e_1 e_2 denotes the output of e_2 to the output channel at security level e_1. For simplicity, we assume that there is only one output channel per security level. Expression `lFork` e_1 e_2 spawns a thread that computes e_2 and returns a handle with label e_1. Expression `lWait` e inspects the value returned by the spawned computation whose result is accessed by the handle e. Non-proper morphisms related to creating, reading, and writing labeled MVars are respectively captured by expressions `newLMVar`, `takeLMVar`, and `putLMVar`.

Types We consider standard types for Booleans (`Bool`), unit (()), and function ($\tau \to \tau$) values. Type ℓ describes security labels. Type `Result` ℓ τ denotes handles used to access labeled results produced by spawned computations, where the results are of type τ and labeled with labels of type ℓ. Type `LMVar` ℓ τ describes labeled MVars, with labels of type ℓ and storing values of type τ. Type `LIO` ℓ τ represents monadic `LIO` computations, with a result type τ and the security labels of type ℓ.

The typing judgments have the standard form $\Gamma \vdash e : \tau$, such that expression e has type τ assuming the typing environment Γ; we use Γ for both variable and store typings. Typing rules for the special syntax nodes are shown in Listing 5. These rules are liberal on purpose. Recall that special syntax nodes are run-time representations of certain values, e.g., labeled MVars. Thus, they are only considered in a context where it is possible to uniquely deduce their types. The typing for the remaining terms and expressions are standard and we therefore do not describe them any further. We do not require any of the commonly used extensions to Haskell's type-system, a direct consequence of the fact that security checks are performed at run-time. Since typing rules are straightforward, we assume that the type system is sound with respect to our semantics.

The `LIO` monad is essentially implemented as a State monad. To simplify the formalization and description of expressions, without loss of generality, we make the state of the monad part of the run-time environment. More precisely, each thread is accompanied by a local security run-time environment σ, which keeps track of the current label (σ.`lbl`) and clearance (σ.`clr`) of the running `LIO` computation. Common to every thread, the symbol Σ holds the global LMVar store ($\Sigma.\phi$) and the output channels ($\Sigma.\alpha_l$, one for

Listing 6 Semantics for non-standard expressions.

$$E \ ::= \ \ldots \mid \texttt{label}\ E\ e \mid \texttt{unlabel}\ E \mid \texttt{out}\ E\ e \mid \texttt{out}\ l\ E$$
$$\mid \texttt{lFork}\ E\ e \mid \texttt{newLMVar}\ E\ e \mid \texttt{takeLMVar}\ E$$
$$\mid \texttt{putLMVar}\ E\ e \mid \texttt{labelOfLMVar}\ E$$

(LAB)
$$\frac{\sigma.\texttt{lbl} \sqsubseteq l \sqsubseteq \sigma.\texttt{clr}}{\{\Sigma, \langle\sigma, E[\texttt{label}\ l\ e]\rangle\} \longrightarrow \{\Sigma, \langle\sigma, E[\texttt{return}\ (\texttt{Lb}\ l\ e)]\rangle\}}$$

(UNLAB)
$$\frac{l' = \sigma.\texttt{lbl} \sqcup l \qquad l' \sqsubseteq \sigma.\texttt{clr} \qquad \sigma' = \sigma[\texttt{lbl} \mapsto l']}{\{\Sigma, \langle\sigma, E[\texttt{unlabel}\ (\texttt{Lb}\ l\ e)]\rangle\} \longrightarrow \{\Sigma, \langle\sigma', E[\texttt{return}\ e]\rangle\}}$$

(OUTPUT)
$$\frac{\sigma.\texttt{lbl} \sqsubseteq l \sqsubseteq \sigma.\texttt{clr} \qquad \Sigma' = \Sigma[\alpha_l \mapsto \Sigma.\alpha_l \rhd \texttt{out}(v)]}{\{\Sigma, \langle\sigma, E[\texttt{out}\ l\ v]\rangle\} \longrightarrow \{\Sigma', \langle\sigma, E[\texttt{return}\ ()]\rangle\}}$$

(LFORK)
$$\frac{\sigma.\texttt{lbl} \sqsubseteq l \sqsubseteq \sigma.\texttt{clr} \qquad \Sigma' = \Sigma[\phi \mapsto \Sigma.\phi[m \mapsto \texttt{Lb}\ l\ \boxdot]] \qquad e' = e \ \texttt{>>=}\ \lambda x.\texttt{putLMVar}\ m\ x \qquad m \text{ fresh}}{\{\Sigma, \langle\sigma, E[\texttt{lFork}\ l\ e]\rangle\} \xrightarrow{\texttt{fork}(e')} \{\Sigma', \langle\sigma, E[\texttt{return}\ (\texttt{R}\ m)]\rangle\}}$$

(LWAIT)
$$\{\Sigma, \langle\sigma, E[\texttt{lWait}\ (\texttt{R}\ m)]\rangle\} \longrightarrow \{\Sigma, \langle\sigma, E[\texttt{takeLMVar}\ m]\rangle\}$$

(NLMVAR)
$$\frac{\sigma.\texttt{lbl} \sqsubseteq l \sqsubseteq \sigma.\texttt{clr} \qquad \Sigma' = \Sigma[\phi \mapsto \Sigma.\phi[m \mapsto \texttt{Lb}\ l\ e]] \qquad m\ \textit{fresh}}{\{\Sigma, \langle\sigma, E[\texttt{newLMVar}\ l\ e]\rangle\} \longrightarrow \{\Sigma', \langle\sigma, E[\texttt{return}\ m]\rangle\}}$$

(TLMVAR)
$$\frac{\Sigma.\phi(m) = \texttt{Lb}\ l\ e \qquad e \neq \boxdot \qquad \sigma.\texttt{lbl} \sqsubseteq l \sqsubseteq \sigma.\texttt{clr} \qquad \sigma' = \sigma[\texttt{lbl} \mapsto \sigma.\texttt{lbl} \sqcup l] \qquad \Sigma' = \Sigma[\phi \mapsto \Sigma.\phi[m \mapsto \texttt{Lb}\ l\ \boxdot]]}{\{\Sigma, \langle\sigma, E[\texttt{takeLMVar}\ m]\rangle\} \longrightarrow \{\Sigma', \langle\sigma', E[\texttt{return}\ e]\rangle\}}$$

(PLMVAR)
$$\frac{\Sigma.\phi(m) = \texttt{Lb}\ l\ \boxdot \qquad \sigma.\texttt{lbl} \sqsubseteq l \sqsubseteq \sigma.\texttt{clr} \qquad \sigma' = \sigma[\texttt{lbl} \mapsto \sigma.\texttt{lbl} \sqcup l] \qquad \Sigma' = \Sigma[\phi \mapsto \Sigma.\phi[m \mapsto \texttt{Lb}\ l\ e]]}{\{\Sigma, \langle\sigma, E[\texttt{putLMVar}\ m\ e]\rangle\} \longrightarrow \{\Sigma', \langle\sigma', E[\texttt{return}\ ()]\rangle\}}$$

(GLABR)
$$\frac{e = \Sigma.\phi(m)}{\{\Sigma, \langle\sigma, E[\texttt{labelOfLMVar}\ m]\rangle\} \longrightarrow \{\Sigma, \langle\sigma, E[\texttt{labelOf}\ e]\rangle\}}$$

every security label l). A store ϕ is a mapping from LMVars to labeled values, while an output channel is a queue of events of the form out(v) (output) , for simplicity, we assume that every store contains a mapping for every possible LMVar. The run-time environments Σ, σ, and a LIO computation form a *sequential configuration* $\{\Sigma, \langle\sigma, e\rangle\}$.

The relation $\{\Sigma, \langle\sigma, e\rangle\} \xrightarrow{\gamma} \{\Sigma', \langle\sigma', e'\rangle\}$ represents a single evaluation step from expression e, under the run-time environments Σ and σ, to expression e' and run-time environments Σ' and σ'. We define this relation in terms of a structured operational semantics via evaluation contexts [14]. We say that e reduces to e' in one step. We write $\longrightarrow^*$ for the reflexive and transitive closure of $\longrightarrow$. Symbol γ ranges over the *internal* events triggered by expressions. We utilize internal events to communicate between the threads and the scheduler. Listing 6 shows the reduction rules for the core contributions in our library. Rules (LAB) and (UNLAB) impose the same security constrains as for the sequential version of LIO [52].

Listing 7 Semantics for threadpools.

(STEP)
$$\frac{\{\Sigma, t\} \longrightarrow \{\Sigma', t'\}}{\{\Sigma, t \lhd t_s\} \hookrightarrow \{\Sigma', t_s \rhd t'\}}$$

(NO-STEP)
$$\frac{\{\Sigma, t\} \not\longrightarrow \qquad t = \langle\sigma, e\rangle \qquad e \neq v}{\{\Sigma, t \lhd t_s\} \hookrightarrow \{\Sigma, t_s \rhd t\}}$$

(FORK)
$$\frac{\{\Sigma, t\} \xrightarrow{\texttt{fork}(e)} \{\Sigma', \langle\sigma, e'\rangle\} \qquad t_{\text{new}} = \langle\sigma, e\rangle}{\{\Sigma, t \lhd t_s\} \hookrightarrow \{\Sigma', t_s \rhd \langle\sigma, e'\rangle \rhd t_{\text{new}}\}}$$

(EXIT)
$$\frac{l = \sigma.\texttt{lbl}}{\{\Sigma, \langle\sigma, v\rangle \lhd t_s\} \hookrightarrow \{\Sigma', t_s\}}$$

Rule (LAB) generates a labeled value if and only if the label is between the current label and clearance of the LIO computation. Rule (UNLAB) requires that, when the content of a labeled value is "retrieved" and used in a LIO computation, the current label is raised ($\sigma' = \sigma[\texttt{lbl} \mapsto l']$, where $l' = \sigma.\texttt{lbl} \sqcup l$), thus capturing the fact that the remaining computation might depend on e. Output channels are treated as deques of events. We use a standard deque-like interface with operations ($\lhd$) and ($\rhd$) for front and back insertion (respectively), and we also allow pattern-matching in the rules as a representation of deconstruction operations. Rule (OUTPUT) adds the event $\texttt{out}(v)$ to the end of the output channel at security level l ($\Sigma.\alpha_l \rhd \texttt{out}(v)$).

The main contributions of our language are related to the primitives for concurrency and synchronization. Rule (LFORK) allows for the creation of a thread and generates the internal event $\texttt{fork}(e')$, where e' is the computation to spawn. The rule allocates a new LMVar in order to store the result produced by the spawned thread ($e \ \texttt{>>=}\ \lambda x.\texttt{putLMVar}\ m\ x$). Using that LMVar, the rule provides a handle to access to the thread's result ($\texttt{return}\ (\texttt{R}\ m)$). Rule (LWAIT) simply uses the LMVar for the handle. Rule (TLMVAR) describes the creation of a new LMVar with a label bounded by the current label and clearance ($\sigma.\texttt{lbl} \sqsubseteq l \sqsubseteq \sigma.\texttt{clr}$). As mentioned in Section 4, operations on LMVar are *bi-directional* and consequently the rules (TLMVAR), and (PLMVAR) require not only that the label of the mentioned LMVar be between the current label and current clearance of the thread ($\sigma.\texttt{lbl} \sqsubseteq l \sqsubseteq \sigma.\texttt{clr}$), but that the current label be raised appropriately. As such, considering the security level l of a LMVar, rule (TLMVAR) raises the current label ($\sigma' = \sigma[\texttt{lbl} \mapsto \sigma.\texttt{lbl} \sqcup l]$) when emptying ($\Sigma.\phi[m \mapsto \texttt{Lb}\ l\ \boxdot]$) its content ($\Sigma.\phi(m) = \texttt{Lb}\ l\ e$). Similarly, considering the security level l of a LMVar, rule (PLMVAR) raises the current label ($\sigma' = \sigma[\texttt{lbl} \mapsto \sigma.\texttt{lbl} \sqcup l]$) when filling ($\Sigma.\phi[m \mapsto \texttt{Lb}\ l\ e]$) its content ($\Sigma.\phi(m) = \texttt{Lb}\ l\ \boxdot$). Finally, rule (GLABR) fetches a labeled LMVar from the LMVar store ($e = \Sigma.\phi(m)$, i.e., a value of the form $\texttt{Lb}\ l\ e'$), and returns its label. To simplify the formalism, insecure programs "get stuck" in their evaluation. In practice, however, an exception is raised to the most outer trusted code, which handles it in an application-specific manner, e.g., in the case of a web server, the trusted code handles such exceptions by not sending a reply to the client. In some other cases, where the user is trusted, it may be desirable to display a notification explaining the source of error.

Listing 7 shows the formal semantics for threadpools. The relation $\hookrightarrow$ represents a single evaluation step for the threadpool, in contrast with $\longrightarrow$ which is only for a single thread. We write $\hookrightarrow^*$ for the reflexive and transitive closure of $\hookrightarrow$. Configurations are of

Listing 8 Erasure function.

$$\varepsilon_L(\{\Sigma, t_s\}) = \{\varepsilon_L(\Sigma), \text{filter } (\lambda\langle\sigma, e\rangle.e \not\equiv \bullet) \text{ (map } \varepsilon_L\ t_s)\}$$

$$\varepsilon_L(\langle\sigma, e\rangle) = \begin{cases} \langle\sigma, \bullet\rangle & \sigma.\texttt{lbl} \not\sqsubseteq L \\ \langle\sigma, \varepsilon_L(e)\rangle & \text{otherwise} \end{cases}$$

$$\varepsilon_L(\Sigma) = \Sigma[\phi \mapsto \varepsilon_L(\Sigma.\phi)][\alpha_l \mapsto \varepsilon_L(\alpha_l)]_{l \in \text{Labels}}$$

$$\varepsilon_L(\alpha_l) = \begin{cases} \epsilon & l \not\sqsubseteq L \\ \text{map } \varepsilon_L\ \alpha_l & \text{otherwise} \end{cases}$$

$$\varepsilon_L(\phi) = \{(x, \varepsilon_L(\phi(x))) : x \in \text{dom}(\phi)\}$$

$$\varepsilon_L(\texttt{Lb}\ l\ e) = \begin{cases} \texttt{Lb}\ l\ \bullet & l \not\sqsubseteq L \\ \texttt{Lb}\ l\ \varepsilon_L(e) & \text{otherwise} \end{cases}$$

In the rest of the cases, ε_L is homomorphic.

the form $\{\Sigma, t_s\}$, where Σ is the global runtime environment and t_s is a queue of sequential configurations. The front of the queue is the thread that is currently executing. Threads are scheduled in a round-robin fashion. The thread at the front of the queue executes one step, and it is then moved to the back of the queue (rule (STEP)). If this step involves a fork (represented by $\xrightarrow{\text{fork}(e)}$), a new thread is created at the back of the queue (rule (FORK)). The identifier t_{new} is bound in rule (FORK), and it stands for the configuration of the newly-forked thread, i.e., $t_{\text{new}} = \langle\sigma, e\rangle$ if the parent thread transition had a label $\texttt{fork}(e)$. Threads are also moved to the back of the threadpool if they are blocked, e.g., waiting to read a value from an empty `LMVar` (rule (NO-STEP) defines $\not\longrightarrow$ as the impossibility to make any progress). When a thread finishes, i.e., it can no longer reduce, the thread is removed from the queue (rule (EXIT)).

Considering IFC for a general scheduler could lead to refinements attacks (e.g., [21, 22, 39, 50, 51, 56]) or the need to severely restrict programs (e.g., [47]). By considering a deterministic scheduler, our approach is more permissive — it rejects fewer programs — and robust against refinement attacks. We remark that it is possible to generalize our work by considering a range of deterministic schedulers (e.g., those of [40]) without drastically changing our proof technique.

8. Security guarantees

In this section, we show that LIO computations satisfy termination-sensitive non-interference. As in [32, 43, 52], we prove this property by using the *term erasure* technique. The erasure function ε_L rewrites data at security levels that the attacker cannot observe into the syntax node $\bullet$.

Listing 8 defines the erasure function ε_L. This function is defined in such a way that $\varepsilon_L(e)$ contains no information above[3] level L, i.e., the function ε_L replaces all the information more sensitive than L in e with a hole ($\bullet$). In most of the cases, the erasure function is simply applied homomorphically (e.g., $\varepsilon_L(e_1\ e_2) = \varepsilon_L(e_1)\ \varepsilon_L(e_2)$). For threadpools, the erasure function is mapped into all sequential configurations; all threads with a current label above L are removed from the pool (filter $(\lambda\langle\sigma, e\rangle.e \not\equiv \bullet)$ (map $\varepsilon_L\ t_s$), where $\equiv$ denotes syntactic equivalence). The computation performed in a certain sequential configuration is erased if the current label is above L. For runtime environments and stores, we map the erasure function into their components. An output channel is erased into the empty channel (ϵ) if it is above L, otherwise the individual output events are erased according to ε_L. A labeled value is erased if the label assigned to it is above L.

[3] We loosely use the word "above" to mean $\not\sqsubseteq$, since labels may not be comparable.

Following the definition of the erasure function, we introduce a new evaluation relation $\longrightarrow_L$ as follows:

$$\frac{\{\Sigma, t_s\} \longrightarrow \{\Sigma', t_s'\}}{\{\Sigma, t_s\} \longrightarrow_L \varepsilon_L(\{\Sigma', t_s'\})}$$

The relation $\longrightarrow_L$ guarantees that confidential data, i.e., data not below level L, is erased as soon as it is created. We write $\longrightarrow_L^*$ for the reflexive and transitive closure of $\longrightarrow_L$. Similarly, we introduce a relation $\hookrightarrow_L$ as follows:

$$\frac{\{\Sigma, t_s\} \hookrightarrow \{\Sigma', t_s'\}}{\{\Sigma, t_s\} \hookrightarrow_L \varepsilon_L(\{\Sigma', t_s'\})}$$

As usual, we write $\hookrightarrow_L^*$ for the reflexive and transitive closure of $\hookrightarrow_L$. In order to prove non-interference, we will establish a simulation relation between $\hookrightarrow^*$ and $\hookrightarrow_L^*$ through the erasure function: erasing all secret data and then taking evaluation steps in $\hookrightarrow_L$ is equivalent to taking steps in $\hookrightarrow$ first, and then erasing all secret values in the resulting configuration. Note that this relation would not hold if information from some level above L was being leaked by the program. In the rest of this section, we only consider well-typed terms to ensure there are no stuck configurations.

For simplicity, we assume that the address space of the memory store is split into different security levels and that allocation is deterministic. Therefore, the address returned when creating an LMVar with label l depends only on the LMVars with label l already in the store.

We start by showing that the evaluation relations $\longrightarrow_L$ and $\hookrightarrow_L$ are deterministic.

Proposition 1 (Determinacy of $\longrightarrow_L$). *If* $\{\Sigma, t\} \longrightarrow_L \{\Sigma', t'\}$ *and* $\{\Sigma, t\} \longrightarrow_L \{\Sigma'', t''\}$, *then* $\{\Sigma', t'\} = \{\Sigma'', t''\}$.

Proof. By induction on expressions and evaluation contexts, showing there is always a unique redex in every step. □

Proposition 2 (Determinacy of $\hookrightarrow_L$). *If* $\{\Sigma, t_s\} \hookrightarrow_L \{\Sigma', t_s'\}$ *and* $\{\Sigma, t_s\} \hookrightarrow_L \{\Sigma'', t_s''\}$, *then* $\{\Sigma', t_s'\} = \{\Sigma'', t_s''\}$.

Proof. By induction on expressions and evaluation contexts, showing there is a unique redex in every step and using Lemma 1. □

The next lemma establishes a simulation between $\hookrightarrow^*$ and $\hookrightarrow_L^*$.

Lemma 1 (Many-step simulation). *If* $\{\Sigma, t_s\} \hookrightarrow^* \{\Sigma', t_s'\}$, *then* $\varepsilon_L(\{\Sigma, t_s\}) \hookrightarrow_L^* \varepsilon_L(\{\Sigma', t_s'\})$.

Proof. In order to prove this result, we rely on properties of the erasure function, such as the fact that it is idempotent and homomorphic to the application of evaluation contexts and substitution. We show that the result holds by case analysis on the rule used to derive $\{\Sigma, t_s\} \hookrightarrow^* \{\Sigma', t_s'\}$, and considering different cases for threads whose current label is below (or not) level L. □

The L-equivalence relation $\approx_L$ is an equivalence relation between configurations (and their parts), defined as the equivalence kernel of the erasure function ε_L: $\{\Sigma, t_s\} \approx_L \{\Sigma', r_s\}$ iff $\varepsilon_L(\{\Sigma, t_s\}) = \varepsilon_L(\{\Sigma', r_s\})$. If two configurations are L-equivalent, they agree on all data below or at level L, i.e., they cannot be distinguished by an attacker at level L. Note that two queues are L-equivalent iff the threads with current label that flows to L are pairwise L-equivalent in the order appearing in the queue.

The next theorem shows the non-interference property. It essentially states that if we take two executions of a program with two L-equivalent inputs, then for every intermediate step of the computation of the first run, there is a corresponding step in the computation of the second run which results in an L-equivalent configuration. Note that this also includes the termination channel, since

L-equivalence of configurations requires the same public threads to be terminated. We formulate the theorem in terms of a function since we only consider programs that receive input (represented by the argument to the function) at the beginning of their execution and then produce outputs (represented by the `out` primitive).

Theorem 1 (Termination-sensitive non-interference). *Given a function e (with no* **Lb***, m,* $()^{LIO}$*,* $\boxdot$*,* **R***, and* $\bullet$*) where* $\Gamma \vdash e : \texttt{Labeled}\ \ell\ \tau \rightarrow \texttt{LIO}\ \ell\ (\texttt{Labeled}\ \ell\ \tau')$*, an attacker at level L, an initial security context* σ*, and runtime environments* Σ_1 *and* Σ_2 *where* $\Sigma_1.\phi = \Sigma_2.\phi = \emptyset$ *and* $\Sigma_1.\alpha_k = \Sigma_2.\alpha_k = \epsilon$ *for all levels k, then*

$$\begin{aligned} &\forall e_1 e_2.(\Gamma \vdash e_i : \texttt{Labeled}\,\ell\ \tau)_{i=1,2} \wedge e_1 \approx_L e_2 \\ &\quad \wedge \{\Sigma_1, \langle\sigma, e\ e_1\rangle\} \hookrightarrow^* \{\Sigma_1', t_s^1\} \\ &\Rightarrow \exists \Sigma_2' t_s^2 . \{\Sigma_2, \langle\sigma, e\ e_2\rangle\} \hookrightarrow^* \{\Sigma_2', t_s^2\} \wedge \{\Sigma_1', t_s^1\} \approx_L \{\Sigma_2', t_s^2\} \end{aligned}$$

Proof. Since e_1 and e_2 are L-equivalent and Σ_1 and Σ_2 are initially empty, the initial configurations $\{\Sigma_1, \langle\sigma, e\ e_1\rangle\}$ and $\{\Sigma_2, \langle\sigma, e\ e_2\rangle\}$ must be L-equivalent. This implies that the erased configurations $\varepsilon_L(\{\Sigma_1, \langle\sigma, e\ e_1\rangle\})$ and $\varepsilon_L(\{\Sigma_2, \langle\sigma, e\ e_2\rangle\})$ must be syntactically equivalent. Also, by Lemma 1 (Simulation) we have $\varepsilon_L(\{\Sigma_1, \langle\sigma, e\ e_1\rangle\}) \hookrightarrow_L^* \varepsilon_L(\{\Sigma_1', t_s^1\})$, and by Proposition 2 (Determinacy), we can always find a reduction $\varepsilon_L(\{\Sigma_2, \langle\sigma, e\ e_2\rangle\}) \hookrightarrow_L^* \varepsilon_L(\{\Sigma_2', t_s^2\})$ where $\varepsilon_L(\{\Sigma_1', t_s^1\}) = \varepsilon_L(\{\Sigma_2', t_s^2\})$. By Lemma 1 again, we have $\{\Sigma_2, \langle\sigma, e\ e_2\rangle\} \hookrightarrow^* \{\Sigma_2', t_s^2\}$, and therefore $\{\Sigma_1', t_s^1\}$ and $\{\Sigma_2', t_s^2\}$ are L-equivalent. □

9. Example Application: Dating Website

We implemented the concurrency primitives discussed in Sections 3, 4, and 6 using Concurrent Haskell [25]. We rely on `forkIO` and `MVars` to implement the forking primitives, and types `Result` and `LMVar`. Similarly, we implement the time-based mitigator detailed in Section 5, and a small library that mitigates the standard I/O file handle functions. We refer the interested reader to the source code, available at `http://www.scs.stanford.edu/~deian/concurrent_lio`. In this section we evaluate the feasibility of leaking information through timing-based covert channels as well as the effectiveness of LIO in addressing these leaks.

To this end, we built a simple dating website that allows third-party developers to build applications (or apps) that interact with a common database. Our website exposes a shared key-value store to third-party apps encoding interested-in relationships. A key corresponds to a user ID and its associated value represent the users that he/she is interested in. For simplicity, we do not consider the list of users sensitive, but interested-in relationships should remain confidential. In particular, a user should be able to learn which other users are interested in them, but should not be able to learn the interested-in relationships of other users.

The website consists of two main components: 1) a trusted web server that executes apps written using LIO and 2) untrusted third-party apps that may interact with users and read and write to the database. The database is simply a list of tuples mapping keys (users) to `LMVars` storing lists of users. Apps are separated from each other by URL prefixes. For example, the URL `http://xycombinator.biz/App1` points to `App1`. Requests with a particular app's URL prefix are serviced by invoking the app's request handler in an IFC-constrained, and time-mitigated, environment. We assume a powerful, but realistic adversary. In particular, malicious app writers may themselves be users of the dating site. We stress that the considered examples discussed below were deliberately chosen to highlight a plausible attack scenario and not necessarily as a realistic example. (For a production-use system that relies on LIO, we refer the reader to `http://gitstar.com`.) We also remark that programming with the concurrent version of LIO does not impose major challenges since its interface is very similar to that of the original library [52].

Termination covert channel As detailed in Section 3, the implementation of LIO [52], with `toLabeled`, is susceptible to a termination channel attack. In the context of our dating-website, a malicious app $term$, running on behalf of an (authenticated) user a can be used to leak information on another (target) user t as follows:

- Adversary a issues a request that contains a guess that user t has an interest in g: `GET` $/term$`?target=`t`&guess=`g
- The trusted app container invokes the app $term$ and forwards the request to it.
- The app $term$ then executes the following LIO code:

```
toLabeled ⊤ $ do v ← lookupDB t
                 when (g == v) ⊥
return $ mkHtmlResp200 "Bad guess"
```

  Here, `lookupDB` t is used to perform a database lookup with key t. If g is present in the database entry, the app will not terminate, otherwise it will respond, denoting the guess was wrong.

We found the termination attack to be very effective. Specifically, we measured the time required to reconstruct a database of 10 users to be 73 seconds[4].

If `toLabeled` is prohibited and `lFork` is used instead, the termination attack cannot be mounted. This is because `lWait` first raises the label of the app request handler. An attempt to output a response to the client browser will not succeed since the current label of the handler cannot flow to the label of the client's browser. (The browser label is used to restrict apps from sending responses that the end-user, in this case a, cannot observe.) It is important to note that errors of this kind are made indistinguishable from non-terminating requests. To accomplish this, our dating site catches label violation errors and converts them to $\bot$.

Internal timing covert channel To carry out an internal timing attack, an app must execute two threads that share a common resource. Concretely, an app can use internal timing to leak information on a target user t as follows:

- Adversary a issues a request containing a guess that t is interested-in g: `GET` $/internal$`?target=`t`&guess=`g
- The trusted app container invokes the app $internal$.
- App $internal$ then executes the following LIO code:

```
varHigh ← fork $
  toLabeled ⊤ $ do
    v ← lookupDB t
    when (g == v) (sleep 5000)
  appendToAppStorage g
varLow ← fork $ do sleep 3000
                   appendToAppStore -1
wait varHigh
wait varLow
r ← readFromAppStore
return $ mkHtmlResp200 r
```

The code spawns two threads. The first reads the high value in a `toLabeled`, sleeps for 5 seconds if the guess is correct, and then write the guess to a `Low`-labeled persistent store[5] The second thread simply write a placeholder (`-1`) after waiting for 3 seconds. Here, the ordering of the data in the store reveals whether the guess is correct. If the guess is incorrect, the store will read `g,-1`; if the guess is correct, the store will read `-1,g`.

[4] All our measurements were conducted on a laptop with a Intel Core i7 2620M (2.7GHz) processor and 8GB of RAM, with GHC 7.4.1.

[5] Apps can write to the database on behalf of invoking user, we use the store notion for simplicity.

We implemented a magnified version of the attack above by sending several requests to the server. The adversary repeatedly sends requests to $internal$ for each user in the system as a guess g. As with the termination channel attack, we found that internal timing attack is feasible. For a database of 10 users we managed to recover all the database entries in 66.92 seconds.

Our modifications to LIO can be used to address the internal timing attacks described above; replacing `toLabeled` with `lFork` eliminates the internal timing leaks. We observe that by using `lFork`, the time when the app executes `appendToAppStore` cannot be influenced by sensitive data. Hence, replacing `fork` and `wait` by their LIO counterparts renders the attack futile.

External timing covert channel We consider a simple external timing attack to our dating website in which the adversary a has access to a high-precision timer. An app $external$ colluding with a can use external timing to leak a target user t's interested-in relationship as follows:

- Authenticated adversary a issues requests containing the target user t: `GET` $/external$`?target=`t`&guess=`g
- The trusted container invokes $external$ with the request.
- App $external$ then proceeds to execute the following LIO code:

```
toLabeled ⊤ $ do
  v ← lookupDB t
  when (g == v) (sleep 5000)
return $ mkHtmlResp200 "done"
```

Given a target t and guess g, if the g is correct the thread sleeps; otherwise it does nothing. In both cases the final response is public. The attacker thus simply measures the response time – recognizing a delay as a correct guess. Despite its simplicity, we also found this attack to be effective. In 33 seconds, we recovered a database of 10 users. To address the leak, we mitigated the app handler, as described in Section 5. Concretely, the response time of an app was mitigated, taking into account the arrival of a request. Although we manged to recover 3 of the 10 user entries in 64 seconds—we found that recovering the remaining user entries was infeasible. The performance of well-behaved apps is unaffected.

10. Related Work

IFC security libraries The seminal work by Li and Zdancewic [31] presents an implementation of information-flow security as a Haskell library using arrows. Russo et al. [43] show a similar IFC security library based solely on monads, that library leverages Haskell's type-system to statically enforce non-interference. Tsai et al. [54] extend [31] by considering side-effects and concurrency. Different from our approach, they provide termination-insensitive non-interference under a cooperative scheduler and no synchronization primitives. Jaskelioff and Russo [24] propose a library that enforces non-interference by executing the program as many times as security levels, known as secure multi-execution [11]. More recently, we propose the use of the `LIO` monad to track information-flow dynamically [52]. Morgenstern et al. [36] encoded an authorization- and IFC-aware programming language in Agda. Their encoding, however, does not consider computations with side-effects. Devriese and Piessens [12] used monad transformers and parametrized monads to enforce non-interference, both dynamically and statically. None of the above approaches handle the termination covert channel. Moreover, except for [54] they do not consider a concurrent language.

Internal timing covert channel In addressing the internal timing cover channel, compared to this work, other language-based approaches sacrifice standard semantics, practical enforcement, permissiveness, and language expressiveness. The works [49–51, 56] rely on an unrealistic primitive `protect(c)` which hides the timing behavior of a command `c`. However, assuming a scenario where it is possible to modify the scheduler, [5, 40] show how an interaction between threads and the scheduler can be used to implement a generalized version of `protect(c)`. To close internal timing leaks, the work in [4] makes the unlikely assumption that rolling back a transaction takes the same time as committing it. In contrast, our `forkLIO` and `waitLIO` are implemented using standard concurrency primitives available in Haskell.

Low-determinism [58] states that public outputs must be deterministic such that no race on public data is possible. This concept inherently makes enforcement mechanisms non-compositional (e.g., two parallel threads that only write to a public channel is considered insecure). A model-checking and type-system approach to enforcing low-determinism have been presented in [23], and [53], respectively. Mantel et al. [34] use synchronization barriers after branching on secret data and before producing public outputs. Different from these enforcement techniques, our library scales to a large number of threads.

With respect to permissiveness, some works do not allow publicly-observable events after branching on secrets. Specifically [7, 8] avoid internal timing leaks by disallowing public events after branching on secret data. They consider a fixed number of threads and no synchronization primitives. Conversely, we allow spawning arbitrary threads that branch (or loop) on secrets while the program continues producing public events. Several approaches consider a restrictive language where dynamic thread creation is not allowed [7, 8, 16, 50, 51, 56, 58].

Russo and Sabelfeld [41] remove internal timing leaks under a cooperative scheduling by manipulating `yield` commands. However, the termination channel is intrinsically present under cooperative scheduling. Closer to our approach, Russo et al. [42] transform sequential programs into concurrent programs that spawn new threads when executing branches and loops on secret values. Although the idea of spawning threads for sensitive computations is similar, we use the approach in a different context. Firstly, Russo et al. apply their technique for a simple sequential While-language, while we consider concurrent programs with synchronization primitives in the context of a practical language. Secondly, and different from our work, their approach does not consider leaks due to termination, i.e., their transformation only guarantees termination-insensitive non-interference. Finally, their transformation approach is conservative in preserving security and, as such, the termination behavior of a transformed program may change. Our proposal, on the other hand, guarantees that the semantics of the program is that which the programmer writes.

Termination and external covert channels There are several language-based mechanisms for addressing the termination and external timing channels. Smith and Volpano [51, 55] describe a type-system that removes the termination channel by forbidding loops whose conditional depend on secrets. This restriction is also used in [34, 47]. The work by Hedin and Sands [19] avoids the termination and external timing covert channels for sequential Java bytecode by disallowing outputs after branching on secrets. This is similar to our approach; however, we allow the spawning new threads for such sensitive tasks, while the rest of the program can still perform public events. Agat [1] describes a code transformation that removes external timing leaks by padding programs with dummy computations, and avoids the termination channel by disallowing loops on secrets. One drawback of Agat's transformation is that if there is a conditional on secret data, and only one of the branches is non-terminating the transformed program is non-terminating. Despite this, the approach has been adapted for languages with concurrency [44, 45, 47]. Moreover, the transformation has been rephrased as a unification problem [29] and implemented with transactions [4]. While targeting sequential programs, secure multi-execution [11] removes both the termination and external timing channels. However, the latter is only closed in a special configuration, e.g., if there are as many CPUs (or cores) as security levels. We refer the reader to the systematization of knowledge paper [26] for a more detailed description of possible enforcements for timing- and termination-sensitive non-interference.

Recently, Zhang et al. [61] propose a language-based mitigation approach for a simple While-language extended with a `mitigate` primitive. Their work relies on static annotations to provide information about the underlying hardware. Compared to their work, our functional approach is more general and can be extended to address other covert channels (e.g., storage). However, their attack model is more powerful in considering the effects of hardware, including caches. Nevertheless, we find their work to be complimentary: our system can leverage static annotations and the Xeon "no-fill" mode to address attacks relying on underlying hardware.

Secure operating systems and the termination channel A number of operating systems have been developed that intentionally left termination channels out of a belief that closing them was intractable, e.g., IX [35]. Another is Asbestos, whose limited their security ambitions to ensuring "that at least two cooperating processes are required to communicate information in violation of a label policy" [13]. In their seminal paper on the decentralized label model [37], which revived the operating system community's interest in information flow control, Myers and Liskov expressed skepticism the problem could ever be overcome with purely dynamic checks. HiStar [59] avoided hard-coding termination channels into the operating system. In practice, however, privileged software had to implement them anyway explicitly using privileges through untainting gates, because operating-system-level resource management requires knowing when a process has exited. By contrast, we believe that we have found abstractions that are both practical on their own, and sound with respect to non-interference.

π-calculus and information-flow Honda et al. [22] present a sophisticated type-system that addresses internal and termination covert channels in π-calculus. They classify channels into two types: *truly linear*, used exactly once, and *non-linear (nondeterministic)*, used an arbitrary number of times. The type-system allows public outputs after reading from linear channels but prevents a process from sending public outputs after receiving secret values on a non-linear channel. Without this restriction, a termination leak might occur because data might never arrive on the (non-linear) channel. The typing judgements guarantee that for every sender on a linear channel there is a corresponding receiver. Since it is not possible to have two processes writing to a common public linear channel, leaks dues to internal timing are not possible. Our library relies on essentially the same mechanism Honda et al. use to prevent leaks associated with non-linear channels. However, our approach enforces IFC dynamically rather than statically. Our systems are incomparable: we are more permissive in taking the dynamic approach [46], while Honda et al. are more permissive by allowing, in certain situations, outputs on public channels after inspecting secret data. Subsequent work [21] describes a more advanced type-system that utilizes a different classification for channels but imposes restrictions similar to [22]. Focusing on simplicity, Pottier [39] describes a type-system that disallows public outputs after reading secrets from a channel, similar to the restriction imposed by non-linear channels described above. Our work can be understood as a dynamic analog to [39] and [20]. Kobayashi [27] addresses and eliminates the termination and internal timing covert channels in addition to improving the precision of the type-system described in [21] to allow synchronization locks (similar to MVars). The semantics formulation in [27] is different from this and other related work [20–22, 39].

11. Summary

Many information flow control systems allow applications to sequence code with publicly visible side-effects after code that computes over sensitive data. Unfortunately, such sequencing leaks sensitive data through termination channels (which affect whether the public side-effects ever happen), internal timing channels (which affect the order of publicly visible side-effects), and external timing channels (which affect the response time of visible side-effects). Such leaks are far worse in the presence of concurrency, particularly when untrusted code can spawn new threads.

We demonstrate that such sequencing can be avoided by introducing additional concurrency when public values must reference the results of computations over sensitive data. We implemented this idea in an existing Haskell information flow library, LIO. In addition, we show how our library is amenable to mitigating external timing attacks by quantizing the appearance of externally visible side-effects. To evaluate our ideas, we prototyped the core of a dating web site showing that our interfaces are practical and our implementation does indeed mitigate these covert channels.

Acknowledgments We thank the anonymous reviewers for insightful comments and bringing several references to our attention. This work was funded by DARPA CRASH under contract #N66001-10-2-4088, by multiple gifts from Google, and by the Swedish research agencies VR and STINT. D. Stefan is supported by the DoD through the NDSEG Fellowship Program.

References

[1] J. Agat. Transforming out timing leaks. In *Proc. ACM Symp. on Principles of Programming Languages*, pages 40–53, Jan. 2000.

[2] A. Askarov, S. Hunt, A. Sabelfeld, and D. Sands. Termination-insensitive noninterference leaks more than just a bit. In *Proc. of the 13th ESORICS*. Springer-Verlag, 2008.

[3] A. Askarov, D. Zhang, and A. C. Myers. Predictive black-box mitigation of timing channels. In *Proc. of the 17th ACM CCS*. ACM, 2010.

[4] G. Barthe, T. Rezk, and M. Warnier. Preventing timing leaks through transactional branching instructions. *Electron. Notes Theor. Comput. Sci.*, 153, May 2006.

[5] G. Barthe, T. Rezk, A. Russo, and A. Sabelfeld. Security of multithreaded programs by compilation. In *Proc. European Symp. on Research in Computer Security*, pages 2–18, Sept. 2007.

[6] A. Bortz and D. Boneh. Exposing private information by timing web applications. In *Proc. of the 16th World Wide Web*. ACM, 2007.

[7] Boudol and Castellani. Noninterference for concurrent programs. In *Proc. ICALP'01*, volume 2076 of *LNCS*. Springer-Verlag, July 2001.

[8] G. Boudol and I. Castellani. Non-interference for concurrent programs and thread systems. *Theoretical Computer Science*, 281(1), June 2002.

[9] D. E. Denning. A lattice model of secure information flow. *Communications of the ACM*, 19(5):236–243, May 1976.

[10] D. E. Denning and P. J. Denning. Certification of programs for secure information flow. *Communications of the ACM*, 20(7):504–513, 1977.

[11] D. Devriese and F. Piessens. Noninterference through secure multi-execution. In *Proc. of the 2010 IEEE Symposium on Security and Privacy*, SP '10. IEEE Computer Society, 2010.

[12] D. Devriese and F. Piessens. Information flow enforcement in monadic libraries. In *Proc. of the 7th ACM SIGPLAN Workshop on Types in Language Design and Implementation*. ACM, 2011.

[13] P. Efstathopoulos, M. Krohn, S. VanDeBogart, C. Frey, D. Ziegler, E. Kohler, D. Mazières, F. Kaashoek, and R. Morris. Labels and event processes in the asbestos operating system. In *Proc. of the twentieth ACM symp. on Operating systems principles*, SOSP '05. ACM, 2005.

[14] M. Felleisen. The theory and practice of first-class prompts. In *Proc. of the 15th ACM SIGPLAN-SIGACT Symp. on Principles of programming languages*, pages 180–190. ACM, 1988.

[15] E. W. Felten and M. A. Schneider. Timing attacks on web privacy. In *Proc. of the 7th ACM conference on Computer and communications security*, CCS '00. ACM, 2000.

[16] G. L. Guernic. Automaton-based confidentiality monitoring of concurrent programs. In *Proc. of the 20th IEEE Computer Security Foundations Symposium*, CSF '07. IEEE Computer Society, 2007.

[17] H. Handschuh and H. M. Heys. A timing attack on RC5. In *Proc. of the Selected Areas in Cryptography*. Springer-Verlag, 1999.

[18] D. Hedin and A. Sabelfeld. A perspective on information-flow control. In *Proc. of the 2011 Marktoberdorf Summer School*. IOS Press, 2011.

[19] D. Hedin and D. Sands. Timing aware information flow security for a javacard-like bytecode. *Elec. Notes Theor. Comput. Sci.*, 141, 2005.

[20] M. Hennessy and J. Riely. Information flow vs. resource access in the asynchronous pi-calculus. *ACM Trans. Program. Lang. Syst.*, 24(5), Sept. 2002.

[21] K. Honda and N. Yoshida. A uniform type structure for secure information flow. *ACM Trans. Program. Lang. Syst.*, Oct. 2007.

[22] K. Honda, V. T. Vasconcelos, and N. Yoshida. Secure information flow as typed process behaviour. In *Proc. of the 9th European Symposium on Programming Languages and Systems*. Springer-Verlag, 2000.

[23] M. Huisman, P. Worah, and K. Sunesen. A temporal logic characterisation of observational determinism. In *Proc. IEEE Computer Sec. Foundations Workshop*, July 2006.

[24] M. Jaskelioff and A. Russo. Secure multi-execution in Haskell. In *Proc. Andrei Ershov International Conference on Perspectives of System Informatics*, LNCS. Springer-Verlag, June 2011.

[25] S. P. Jones, A. Gordon, and S. Finne. Concurrent Haskell. In *Proc. of the 23rd ACM SIGPLAN-SIGACT symposium on Principles of programming languages*. ACM, 1996.

[26] V. Kashyap, B. Wiedermann, and B. Hardekopf. Timing- and termination-sensitive secure information flow: Exploring a new approach. In *Proc. of IEEE Symposium on Sec. and Privacy*. IEEE, 2011.

[27] N. Kobayashi. Type-based information flow analysis for the π-calculus. *Acta Inf.*, 42(4), Dec. 2005.

[28] P. C. Kocher. Timing attacks on implementations of Diffie-Hellman, RSA, DSS, and other systems. In *Proc. of the 16th CRYPTO*. Springer-Verlag, 1996.

[29] B. Köpf and H. Mantel. Eliminating implicit information leaks by transformational typing and unification. In *Formal Aspects in Security and Trust, Third International Workshop (FAST'05)*, volume 3866 of *LNCS*. Springer-Verlag, July 2006.

[30] B. W. Lampson. A note on the confinement problem. *Communications of the ACM*, 16(10):613–615, 1973.

[31] P. Li and S. Zdancewic. Encoding Information Flow in Haskell. In *CSFW '06: Proc. of the 19th IEEE Workshop on Computer Security Foundations*. IEEE Computer Society, 2006.

[32] P. Li and S. Zdancewic. Arrows for secure information flow. *Theoretical Computer Science*, 411(19):1974–1994, 2010.

[33] S. Liang, P. Hudak, and M. Jones. Monad transformers and modular interpreters. In *In Proc. of the 22nd ACM Symposium on Principles of Programming Languages. ACMPress*, 1995.

[34] H. Mantel, H. Sudbrock, and T. Krausser. Combining different proof techniques for verifying information flow security. In *Proc. of the 16th international conference on Logic-based program synthesis and transformation*, LOPSTR'06. Springer-Verlag, 2007.

[35] M. D. Mcilroy and J. A. Reeds. Multilevel security in the unix tradition. *SoftwarePractice and Experience*, 22:673–694, 1992.

[36] J. Morgenstern and D. R. Licata. Security-typed programming within dependently typed programming. In *Proc. of the 15th ACM SIGPLAN International Conference on Functional Programming*. ACM, 2010.

[37] A. C. Myers and B. Liskov. A decentralized model for information flow control. In *Proc. of the 16th ACM Symp. on Operating Systems Principles*, pages 129–142, 1997.

[38] A. C. Myers, L. Zheng, S. Zdancewic, S. Chong, and N. Nystrom. Jif: Java information flow. Software release. Located at http://www.cs.cornell.edu/jif, July 2001.

[39] F. Pottier. A simple view of type-secure information flow in the π-calculus. In *In Proc. of the 15th IEEE Computer Security Foundations Workshop*, pages 320–330, 2002.

[40] A. Russo and A. Sabelfeld. Securing interaction between threads and the scheduler. In *Proc. IEEE Computer Sec. Foundations Workshop*, pages 177–189, July 2006.

[41] A. Russo and A. Sabelfeld. Security for multithreaded programs under cooperative scheduling. In *Proc. Andrei Ershov International Conference on Perspectives of System Informatics (PSI)*, LNCS. Springer-Verlag, June 2006.

[42] A. Russo, J. Hughes, D. Naumann, and A. Sabelfeld. Closing internal timing channels by transformation. In *Proc. of Asian Computing Science Conference*, LNCS. Springer-Verlag, Dec. 2006.

[43] A. Russo, K. Claessen, and J. Hughes. A library for light-weight information-flow security in Haskell. In *Proc. ACM SIGPLAN Symposium on Haskell*, pages 13–24. ACM Press, Sept. 2008.

[44] A. Sabelfeld. The impact of synchronisation on secure information flow in concurrent programs. In *Proc. Andrei Ershov International Conference on Perspectives of System Informatics*, volume 2244 of *LNCS*, pages 225–239. Springer-Verlag, July 2001.

[45] A. Sabelfeld and H. Mantel. Static confidentiality enforcement for distributed programs. In *Proc. Symp. on Static Analysis*, volume 2477 of *LNCS*, pages 376–394. Springer-Verlag, Sept. 2002.

[46] A. Sabelfeld and A. Russo. From dynamic to static and back: Riding the roller coaster of information-flow control research. In *Proc. Andrei Ershov International Conference on Perspectives of System Informatics*, LNCS. Springer-Verlag, June 2009.

[47] A. Sabelfeld and D. Sands. Probabilistic noninterference for multi-threaded programs. In *Proc. IEEE Computer Sec. Foundations Workshop*, pages 200–214, July 2000.

[48] V. Simonet. The Flow Caml system. Software release at `http://cristal.inria.fr/~simonet/soft/flowcaml/`, July 2003.

[49] Smith. Probabilistic noninterference through weak probabilistic bisimulation. In *Proc. IEEE Computer Sec. Foundations Workshop*, pages 3–13, 2003.

[50] G. Smith. A new type system for secure information flow. In *Proc. IEEE Computer Sec. Foundations Workshop*, June 2001.

[51] G. Smith and D. Volpano. Secure information flow in a multi-threaded imperative language. In *Proc. ACM Symp. on Principles of Programming Languages*, pages 355–364, Jan. 1998.

[52] D. Stefan, A. Russo, J. C. Mitchell, and D. Mazières. Flexible dynamic information flow control in Haskell. In *Haskell Symposium*. ACM SIGPLAN, September 2011.

[53] T. Terauchi. A type system for observational determinism. In *Proc. of the 2008 21st IEEE Computer Security Foundations Symposium*, pages 287–300. IEEE Computer Society, 2008.

[54] T. C. Tsai, A. Russo, and J. Hughes. A library for secure multi-threaded information flow in Haskell. In *Proc. IEEE Computer Sec. Foundations Symposium*, July 2007.

[55] D. Volpano and G. Smith. Eliminating covert flows with minimum typings. In *Proc. of the 10th IEEE workshop on Computer Security Foundations*, CSFW '97. IEEE Computer Society, 1997.

[56] D. Volpano and G. Smith. Probabilistic noninterference in a concurrent language. *J. Computer Security*, 7(2–3), Nov. 1999.

[57] W. H. Wong. Timing attacks on RSA: revealing your secrets through the fourth dimension. *Crossroads*, 11, May 2005.

[58] S. Zdancewic and A. C. Myers. Observational determinism for concurrent program security. In *Proc. IEEE Computer Sec. Foundations Workshop*, pages 29–43, June 2003.

[59] N. Zeldovich, S. Boyd-Wickizer, E. Kohler, and D. Mazières. Making information flow explicit in histar. In *Proc. of the 7th USENIX Symp. on Operating Systems Design and Implementation*. USENIX, 2006.

[60] D. Zhang, A. Askarov, and A. C. Myers. Predictive mitigation of timing channels in interactive systems. In *Proc. of the 18th ACM CCS*. ACM, 2011.

[61] D. Zhang, A. Askarov, and A. C. Myers. Language-based control and mitigation of timing channels. In *Proc. of PLDI*. ACM, 2012.

Sneaking Around *concatMap*

Efficient Combinators for Dynamic Programming

Christian Höner zu Siederdissen

Institute for Theoretical Chemistry, University of Vienna, 1090 Wien, Austria

choener@tbi.univie.ac.at

Abstract

We present a framework of dynamic programming combinators that provides a high-level environment to describe the recursions typical of dynamic programming over sequence data in a style very similar to algebraic dynamic programming (ADP). Using a combination of type-level programming and stream fusion leads to a substantial increase in performance, without sacrificing much of the convenience and theoretical underpinnings of ADP.

We draw examples from the field of computational biology, more specifically RNA secondary structure prediction, to demonstrate how to use these combinators and what differences exist between this library, ADP, and other approaches.

The final version of the combinator library allows writing algorithms with performance close to hand-optimized `C` code.

Categories and Subject Descriptors D.1.1 [*Programming Techniques*]: Applicative (Functional) Programming; D.3.4 [*Programming Languages*]: Optimization

General Terms Algorithms, Dynamic Programming

Keywords algebraic dynamic programming, program fusion, functional programming

1. Introduction

Dynamic programming (DP) is a cornerstone of modern computer science with many different applications (e.g. Cormen et al. [6, Cha. 15] or Sedgewick [34, Cha. 37] for a generic treatment). Durbin et al. [8] solve a number of problems on bio-sequences with DP and it is also used in parsing of formal grammars [15].

Despite the number of problems that have been solved using dynamic programming since its inception by Bellman [1], little on methodology has been available until recently. Algebraic dynamic programming (ADP) [10, 12, 13] was introduced to provide a formal, mathematical background as well as an implementation strategy for dynamic programming on sequence data, making DP algorithms less difficult and error-prone to write.

One reviewer of early ADP claimed [10] that *the development of successful dynamic programming recurrences is a matter of experience, talent, and luck.*

The rationale behind this sentence is that designing a dynamic programming algorithm and successfully taking care of all corner cases is non-trivial and further complicated by the fact that most implementations of such an algorithm tend to combine all development steps into a single monolithic program. ADP on the other hand separates three concerns: the construction of the search space, evaluation of each candidate (or correct parse) available within this search space, and efficiency via *tabulation* of parts of the search space using annotation [13] of the grammar.

In this work we target the same set of dynamic programming problems as ADP: dynamic programming over sequence data. In particular, we are mostly concerned with problems from the realm of computational biology, namely RNA bioinformatics, but the general idea we wish to convey, and the library based on this idea, is independent of any specific branch of dynamic programming over sequence data.

In particular, our introductory example uses the CYK algorithm [15, Cha. 4.2] to determine if the input forms part of its context-free language. In other words: our library can be used to write generic high-performance parsers.

The idea of expressing parsers for a formal language using high-level and higher-order functions has a long standing in the functional programming community. Hutton [20] designed a library for *combinator parsing* around 20 years ago. Combining simple parsers for terminal symbols using symbolic operators is now widespread. The *parsec* (see [30, Cha 16] for a tutorial) library for Haskell might be the most well-known. Combinators can be used to build complex parsers in a modular way and it is possible to design new combinators quite easily.

The crucial difference in our work is that the combinators in the ADPfusion library provide efficient code, comparable to hand-written `C`, directly in the functional programming language Haskell [19]. The work of Giegerich et al. [13] already provided an implementation of combinators in Haskell, albeit with large constants, for both space and time requirements. Translation to `C` [11], and recently a completely new language (GAP-L) [33] and compiler (GAP-C) based on the ideas of ADP were introduced as a remedy. Another recent, even more specific, approach is the Tornado language [32] for stochastic context-free grammars designed solely to parse RNA sequences.

Most of the work on domain-specific languages (DSL) for dynamic programming points out that using a DSL has a number of benefits [11], either in terms of better parser error handling, higher performance, or encapsulation from features not regarded as part of the DSL.

Designing a DSL written as part of the host language, provides a number of benefits as well, and strangely, one such benefit is being able to use features not provided by the DSL. Designing a language with a restricted set of features always poses the danger of having a potential user requiring *exactly* that feature which has not yet been made available. A direct embedding, on the other hand, simply does

ICFP'12, September 9–15, 2012, Copenhagen, Denmark.

not have this problem. If something can be expressed in the host language, it is possible to use it in the DSL.

Another point in favor of staying within an established language framework is that optimization work done on the backend is automatically available as well. One of the points made by our work is that it is not required to move to a specialized DSL compiler to achieve good performance. Furthermore, certain features of the Haskell host language yield performance-increasing code generation (almost) for free.

What we can not provide is simplified error handling, but this becomes a non-issue for us as we specifically aim for Haskell-savvy users or those interested in learning the language.

We can also determine the appropriateness of embedding the ADPfusion DSL by looking at the guidelines given by Mernik et al. [27, Sec. 2.5.2] on "When and How to Develop Domain-Specific Languages". Most advantages of the embedded approach (development effort, more powerful language, reuse of infrastructure) are ours while some disadvantages of embedding (sub-optimal syntax, operator overloading) are easily dealt with using the very flexible Haskell syntax and standards set by ADP.

Our main contributions to dynamic programming on sequence data are:

- a generic framework separating grammatical structure, semantics of parses, and automatic generation of high-performance code using stream fusion;
- removal of the need for explicit index calculations: the combinator library takes care of corner cases and allows for linked index spaces;
- performance close to C with real-world examples from the area of computational biology;
- the possibility to use the library for more general parsing problems (beyond DP algorithms) involving production rules.

"Sneaking around *concatMap*" is a play on one of the ways how to write the Cartesian product of two sets. (Non-) terminals in production rules of grammars yield sets of parses. Efficient, generic treatment of production rules in an embedded DSL requires some work as we will explain in this work.

The outline of the paper is as follows: in the next section we introduce a simple parsing problem. Using this problem as an example, we rewrite it using ADP in Sec. 3, thereby showing the benefits of an embedded DSL. A short introduction to stream fusion follows (Sec. 4).

Armed with knowledge of both ADP and stream fusion, we write DP combinators that are compiled into efficient code in Sec. 5. We expand on ADPfusion with nested productions for more efficient code (Sec. 6).

Runtime performance of ADPfusion is given for two examples from RNA bioinformatics in Sec. 7 with comparisons to C programs.

Sections 8 and 9 are on specialized topics and we conclude with remarks on further work and open questions in Sec. 10.

2. Sum of digits

To introduce the problem we want to solve, consider a string of matched brackets and digits like $((1)(3))$. We are interested in the sum of all digits, which can simply be calculated by

```
sumD = sum ∘ map readD ∘ filter isDigit
readD x = read [x] :: Int.
```

The above algorithm works, because the structure of the nesting and digits plays no role in determining the semantics (sum of digits) of the input. For the sake of a simple introductory example, we now assume that we have to solve this problem using a parser that implements the following three rules:

1. a digit may be read only if the string is of size 1, and the single character is a digit;
2. an outermost pair of brackets may be removed, these rules are then applied recursively to the remaining string;
3. the string may be split into two non-empty substrings to which these rules are applied recursively.

These rules can be written as a context-free grammar (CFG) and such a grammar is shown in Fig. 1 together with the successful parse of the string $((1)(3))$. As can be seen, the grammar describes the structure of parses, but make no mention of any kind of semantics. We simply know that a string is a *word* in the grammar but there is no meaning or semantics attached to it. This, of course, conforms to parsing of formal languages in general [15].

One way of parsing an input string is to use the CYK parser, which is a bottom-up parser using dynamic programming [15, Cha. 4.2].

We have chosen the example grammar of Fig. 1 for two reasons. First, it covers a lot of different parsing cases. The first production rule describes parsing with a single terminal on the right-hand side. The second rule includes a non-terminal bracketed by two terminal characters. The third rule requires parsing with two non-terminals. In addition, there are up to $n-1$ different successful parses for the $n-1$ different ways to split the string into two non-empty substrings. The third rule makes use of Bellman's principle of optimality. Parses of substrings are re-used in subsequent parses and optimal parses of substrings can be combined to form the optimal parse of the current string. This requires memoization.

Second, these seemingly arbitrary rules are actually very close to those used in RNA secondary structure prediction, being described in Sec. 7, conforming to hairpin structures, basepairing, and parallel structures. Furthermore, important aspects of dynamic programming (DP) and context-free grammars (CFGs) are included.

In the next section, we introduce algebraic dynamic programming (ADP), a domain-specific language (DSL) for dynamic programming over sequence data embedded in Haskell. Using the example from above, we will be able to separate structure and semantics of the algorithm.

```
S → 1 | 2 | ... | 0   -- single digit
  |   ( S )           -- '(' substring ')'
  |    S S            -- split into substrings
```

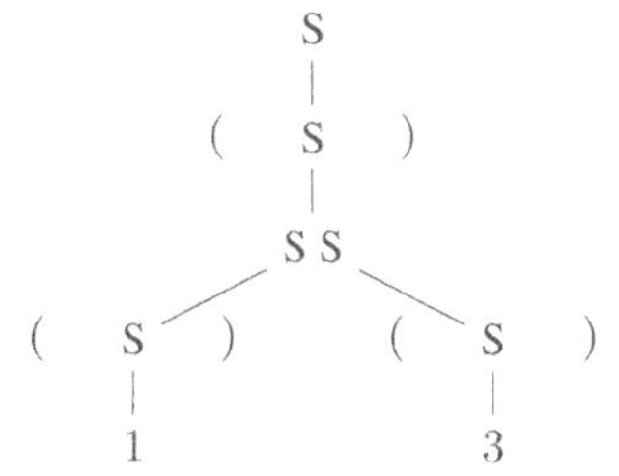

Figure 1. top: A context-free grammar for the nested-digits problem of Sec. 2. CFGs describe the structure of the search space. The semantics of a parse are completely separate.
bottom: Successful parse of the string $((1)(3))$. The semantics of this parse are 4 using the sum of digits semantics.

```
-- signature
readDigit :: Char → S
bracket   :: Char → S → Char → S
split     :: S → S → S
h         :: [S] → [S]

-- structure or grammar
sd = (
readDigit <<< char 'with' isDigit              |||
(bracket   <<< char 'cThenS' sd 'sThenC' char)
                'with' brackets                |||
split      <<< sd 'nonEmpty' sd                ... h)

-- additional structure encoding
isDigit (i,j)   = j-i≡1 && Data.Char.isDigit (inp!j)
brackets (i,j) = inp!(i+1)≡'(' && inp!j≡')'
-- (!) is the array indexing operator: array ! index

-- semantics or algebra
readDigit c = read [c] :: Int
bracket l s r = s
split l r = l+r
h xs = if null xs then [] else [maximum xs]
```

Figure 2. Signature, structure (grammar), and semantics (algebra) of the sum-of-digits example (Sec. 2). The functions cThenS, sThenC, and nonEmpty chain arguments of terminals like char and non-terminals like sd. A special case is with that filters candidate parses based on a predicate. The symbolic functions (<<<), (|||), and (...) apply a function, allow different parses, and select a parse as optimal, respectively.

3. Algebraic dynamic programming

In this section we briefly recall the basic premises of algebraic dynamic programming (ADP) as described in Giegerich et al. [13]. We need to consider four aspects. The signature, defining an interface between a grammar and algebra, the grammar which defines the structure of the problem, its algebras each giving specific semantics, and memoization.

ADP makes use of *subwords*. A subword is a pair (Int,Int) which indexes a substring of the input. Combinators, terminals, and non-terminals all carry a subword as the last argument, typically as (i,j) with the understanding that $0 \leq i \leq j \leq n$ with n being the length of the input.

3.1 Signature

We have a finite alphabet $\mathcal{A}$ of symbols over which finite strings, including the empty string ϵ can be formed. In addition, we have a sort symbol denoted S. A signature Σ in ADP is a set of functions, with each function $f_i \in \Sigma$ having a specific type $f_i :: t_{i1} \to \cdots \to t_{in} \to S$ where $t_{ik} \in \{\mathcal{A}^+, S\}$. In other words, each function within the signature has one or more arguments, and each argument is a non-empty string over the alphabet or of the sort type which in turn is also the return type of each function. It is possible to use arguments which are derivative of these types, for instance providing the length of a string instead of the string itself. Such more specific cases are optimizations which do not concern us here.

The signature Σ includes an objective function $h : \{S\} \to \{S\}$. The objective function selects from a set of possible answers those which optimize a certain criterion like minimization or maximization.

3.2 Grammar

Grammars in ADP vaguely resemble grammatical descriptions as used in text books [15] or formal methods like the Backus-Naur form. They define the structure of the search space or the set of all parses of an input. In Fig. 2 we have the grammar for the sum of digits example of Fig. 1. The grammar has one non-terminal sd, which is equivalent to S of the context-free grammar. Furthermore, we have the three rules again. There are, however, major differences in how one encodes such a rule. Consider the third rule (S → S S) which now reads (split <<<sd 'nonEmpty' sd) minus the left-hand side. From left to right, we recognize one of the function symbols of the signature (split), a combinator function (<<<) that applies the function to its left to the argument on its right, the non-terminal (sd), a second combinator function ('nonEmpty') in infix notation, and finally the non-terminal again.

What these combinators do is best explained by showing their source, which also leads us back to why we want to "sneak around *concatMap*".

```
infix 8 <<<
(<<<) :: (a→b) → (Subword→[a]) → Subword → [b]
(<<<) f xs (i,j) = map f (xs (i,j))

infixl 7 'nonEmpty'
nonEmpty :: (Subword → [y→z])
         → (Subword → [y]) → Subword → [z]
nonEmpty fs ys (i,j) = [ f y
                       | k ← [i+1..j-1]
                       , f ← fs (i,k)
                       , y ← ys (k,j) ]
```

or equivalently

```
nonEmpty fs ys (i,j) = concatMap idx [i+1..j-1]
where
idx k = concatMap (λf → map f (ys (k,j))) (fs (i,k))
```

Each combinator takes a left and a right argument and builds a list from the Cartesian product of the two inputs, with (<<<) taking care of the scalar nature of the function to be mapped over all inputs. Importantly, all first arguments are partially applied functions which has a performance impact and hinders optimization.

The third argument of each combinator is the subword index that is threaded through all arguments. (Non-) terminals are functions from a subword to a list of values. For example char returns a singleton list with the i'th character of the input when given the subword $(i, i+1)$ and an empty list otherwise.

```
char :: Subword → [Char]
char (i,j) = [inp!i | i+1≡j]
```

Similarly, the non-terminal sd is a function

```
sd :: Subword → [S]
sd = ... -- grammar as above
```

which can be memoized as required.

As a side note, in GHC Haskell, concatMap is not used in the implementation of list comprehensions, but the message stays the same: as we will see later in runtime measurements concatMap and list comprehensions are hard to optimize.

We complete the argument combinators with cThenS and sThenC (having the same type as nonEmpty):

```
infixl 7 'cThenS' 'sThenC'

cThenS fs ys (i,j) = [ f y | i<j, f ← fs (i,i+1)
                           , y ← ys (i+1,j) ]
```

```
sThenC fs ys (i,j) = [ f y | i<j, f ← fs (i,j-1)
                           , y ← ys (j-1,j) ]
```

We are still missing two combinators, (|||) and (...). Both are simple, as ADP deals solely with lists, we just need to take care of the subword index in each case.

```
infixr 6 |||
(|||) :: (Subword→[a])→(Subword→[a])→Subword→[a]
(|||) xs ys (i,j) = xs (i,j) ++ ys (i,j)
infix 5 ...
(...) :: (Subword→[a])→([a]→[a])→Subword→[a]
(...) xs h (i,j) = h (xs (i,j))
```

There is an actual difference in the grammars of Fig. 1 and Fig. 2. In Fig. 1 the terminal symbols are explicit characters like '1' or '(', while in Fig. 2 `char` matches all single characters. We use this to introduce another useful combinator (`with`) that allows us to filter parses based on a predicate:

```
with :: (Subword→[a])→(Subword→Bool)→Subword→[a]
with xs p (i,j) = if p (i,j) then xs (i,j) else []
```

3.3 Algebra

We now have the grammar describing the structure of the algorithm. The function symbols of the signature are included and can be "filled" using one of several algebras describing the semantics we are interested in. Apart from the objective function `h`, all functions describe the semantics of production rules of the grammar. In our example above (Fig. 2) we either read a single digit (`readDigit`), keep just the sum of digits of the bracketed substring (`bracket`), or add sums from a `split` operation.

The objective function (`h`) selects the optimal parse according to the semantics we are interested in. In this case the maximum over the parses.

Another possibility is to calculate some descriptive value over the search space, say its total size. As an example, the *Inside-Outside* algorithm [23],[8, Ch. 10] adds up all probabilities generated by productions in a stochastic CFG instead of selecting one.

The specialty of ADP grammars is that they form tree grammars [10], [9, Sec. 2.2.1]. While they are analogous to context-free grammars, the right-hand sides of productions form proper trees with function symbols from the signature as inner nodes and terminal and non-terminal symbols at the leaves. For the example parse in Fig. 1 (bottom) this has the effect of replacing all non-terminal symbols (`S`) with function symbols from the signature. This also means that we can, at least in principle, completely decouple the generation of each parse tree from its evaluation. While the size of the search space might be prohibitive in practice, for small inputs, an exhaustive enumeration of all parses is possible. In an implementation, data constructors can be used as functions, while the objective function is simply the identity function. This allows us to print all possible parse trees for an input.

Each such tree has at its leaf nodes a sequence of characters, a word, from the alphabet: $w \in \mathcal{A}^*$. And for each given word w there are zero or more trees representing this word. If no tree for a given word exists, then the grammar can not parse that word and if more than one tree exists then the grammar is syntactically ambiguous in this regard. This kind of ambiguity is not problematic, typically even wanted, as the objective function can be used to evaluate different tree representations of a word w and return the optimal one.

3.4 Memoization

As noted in Sec. 3.2, non-terminals in grammars can be memoized. ADP introduces a function

`tabulated :: Int →(Subword →[a]) →Subword →[a]`, used as `sd = tabulated (length input) ( productions )`, that stores the answers for each subword in an array. Depending on the algorithm, other memoization schemes, or none at all, are possible. In general, memoization is required to make use of Bellman's principle of optimality and reduce the runtime of an algorithm from exponential to polynomial.

3.5 ADP in short

To summarize, algebraic dynamic programming achieves a separation of concerns. Parsing of input strings for a given grammar is delegated to the construction of candidates which are correct parses. Evaluation of candidates is done by specifying an evaluation algebra, of which there can be more than one. Selection from all candidates based on their evaluation is done by an objective function which is part of each evaluation algebra. Memoization makes the parsing process asymptotically efficient. Giegerich et al. [13] provide a much more detailed description than given here.

As our objective is to perform parsing, evaluation and selection more efficiently, we will, in the next sections, change our view of dynamic programming over sequence data to describe our approach starting with streams as a more efficient alternative to lists.

4. Stream fusion

We introduce the basics of stream fusion here. Considering that the ADPfusion library is based around applications of `map`, `flatten` (a variant of `concatMap`, more amenable to fusion), and `fold`, these are the functions described. For advanced applications, the whole range of fusible functions may be used, but those fall outside the scope of both this introduction to stream fusion and the paper in general. In addition, here and in the description of ADPfusion, we omit that stream fusion and ADPfusion are parametrized over Monads.

Stream fusion is a short-cut fusion system for lists [7], and more recently arrays [25], that removes intermediate data structures from complicated compositions of list-manipulating functions. Ideally, the final, fused, algorithm is completely free of any temporary allocations and performs all computations efficiently in registers, apart from having to access static data structures containing data. Stream fusion is notable for fusing a larger set of functions than was previously possible, including zipping and concatenating of lists.

Stream fusion is built upon two data types, `Stream` captures a function to calculate a single step in the stream and the seed required to calculate said step. A `Step` can indicate if a stream is terminated (`Done`). If not, the current step either `Yield`s a value or `Skip`s, which can be used for filtering. One other use of `Skip` is in concatenation of streams which becomes non-recursive due to `Skip` as well. Unless a stream is `Done`, each new `Step` creates a new seed, too.

```
data Stream a = ∃ s. Stream (s → Step a s) s
data Step a s = Done
              | Yield a s
              | Skip s
```

The point of representing lists as sequence co-structures is that no function on streams is recursive (except final *folds*), permitting easy fusion to generate efficient code.

We construct a new stream of a single element using the `singleton` function. A singleton stream emits a single element `x` and is `Done` thereafter. Notably, the `step` function defined here is non-recursive.

```
singleton_S x = Stream step True where
  step True  = Yield x False
  step False = Done
```

Mapping a function over a stream is non-recursive as well, in marked contrast to how one maps a function over a list.

```
mapS f (Stream step s) = Stream nstp s where
  nstp s = case (step s) of
    Yield x s' → Yield (f x) s'
    Skip    s' → Skip s'
    Done       → Done
```

As a warm-up to stream-flattening, and because we need to concatenate two streams with (|||) anyway, we look at the stream version of (++).

```
(Stream stp1 ss) ++S (Stream stp2 tt) =
Stream step (Left ss) where
  step (Left s) = case s of
    Yield x s' → Yield x (Left s')
    Skip    s' → Skip    (Left s')
    Done       → Skip    (Right tt)
  step (Right t) = case t of
    Yield x t' → Yield x (Right t')
    Skip    t' → Skip    (Right t')
    Done       → Done
```

The `Left` and `Right` constructors encode which of the two streams is being worked on, while the jump from the first to the second stream is done via a (again non-recursive) `Skip`.

The `flatten` function takes three arguments: a function `mk` which takes a value from the input stream and produces an initial seed for the user-supplied `step` function. The user-supplied `step` then produces zero or more elements of the resulting stream for each such supplied value. Note the similarity to stream concatenation. `Left` and `Right` are state switches to either initialize a new substream or to create stream `Steps` based on this initial seed.

Again, it is important to notice that no function is recursive, the hand-off between extracting a new value from the outer stream and generating part of the new stream is done via `Skip (Right (mk a, t'))`.

```
flattenS mk step (Stream ostp s) = Stream nstp (Left s)
where
  nstp (Left t) = case (ostp s) of
    Yield a t' → Skip (Right (mk a, t'))
    Skip    t' → Skip (Left t')
    Done       → Done
  nstp (Right (b,t)) = case (step b) of
    Yield x s' → Yield x (Right (s',t))
    Skip    s' → Skip (Right (s',t))
    Done       → Left t
```

Finally, we present the only recursive part of the stream fusion, folding a stream to produce a final value.

```
foldS f z (Stream step s) = loop f z where
  loop f z = case (step s) of
    Yield x s' → loop (f z x) s'
    Skip    s' → loop z s'
    Done       → z
```

If such code is used to build larger functions like

```
foldS (+) 0 (flattenS id f (singletonS 10)) where
f x = if (x > 0)
      then Yield x (x-1)
      else Done
```

call-pattern specialization [31] of the constructors (`Yield`, `Skip`, `Done`) creates specialized functions for the different cases, and inlining merges the newly created functions, producing an efficient, tight loop. A detailed explanation can be found in Coutts et al. [7, Sec. 7] together with a worked example. The GHC compiler [36] performs all necessary optimizations.

5. Designing efficient combinators for dynamic programming

Algebraic dynamic programming is already able to provide asymptotically optimal dynamic programming recursions. A dynamic program written in ADP unfortunately comes with a rather high overhead compared to more direct implementations. Two solutions have been proposed to this problem. The first was translation of ADP code into `C` using the ADP Compiler [35] and the second a complete redesign providing a new language and compiler (GAP-L and GAP-C) [33]. Both approaches have their merit but partially different goals than ours. Here we want to show how to keep most of the benefits of ADP while staying *within* Haskell instead of having to resort to a different language.

We introduce combinators in a top-down manner, staying close to our introductory example of Fig. 2. An important difference is that functions now operate over stream fusion [7] streams instead of lists. This change in internal representation lets the compiler optimize grammar and algebra code much better than otherwise possible.

We indicate the use of stream fusion functions like `mapS` with a subscript $_S$ to differentiate between normal list-based functions and stream fusion versions.

5.1 Combining and reducing streams

Two of the combinators, the choice between different productions (|||) and the application of an objective function, stay essentially the same, except that the type of `h` is now `Stream a →b`, instead of `[a] → [b]`. The objective function returns an answer of a scalar type, say `Int`, allowing for algorithms that work solely with unboxed types, or a vector type (like lists, boxed, or unboxed vectors). This gives greater flexibility in terms of what kind of answers can be calculated and choosing the best encoding, in terms of performance, for each algorithm.

```
infixl 7 |||
(|||) xs ys ij = xs ij ++S ys ij

infixl 6 ...
(...) stream h ij = h (stream ij)
```

In addition, the index is not a tuple anymore, but rather a variable `ij` of type `DIM2`. Instead of plain pairs `(Int,Int)` we use the same indexing style as the Repa [22] library. Repa tuples are inductively defined using two data types and constructors:

```
data Z = Z
data a :. b = a :. b
type DIM1 = Z :. Int
type DIM2 = DIM1 :. Int
```

The tuple constructor `(:.)` resembles the plain tuple constructor `(,)`, with `Z` as the base case when constructing a 1-tuple `(Z:.a)`. We can generalize the library to cover higher-dimensional DP algorithms just like the Repa library does for matrix calculations. It allows for uniform handling of multiple running indices which are represented as k-dimensional inductice tuples as well, increasing k by one for each new (non-) terminal. Using plain tuples would require nesting of pairs. Also, subwords are now of type `DIM2` instead of `(Int,Int)`.

5.2 Creating streams from production rules

As of now, we can combine streams and reduce streams to a single value or a set of values of interest. As streams expose many optimization options to the compiler (cf. Sec. 4 and [7]), we can expect good performance. What is still missing is how to create a stream, given a production rule, in the first place. Rules such as `readDigit <<<char` with a single terminal or non-terminal to the right are the simplest to construct.

The combinator `(<<<)` applies a function to one or more arguments and is defined as:

```
infixl 8 <<<
(<<<) f t ij =
  map_S (λ(_,_,as) → apply f as) (streamGen t ij)
```

The `streamGen` function takes the argument `arg` on the right of `(f <<< arg)`, with `arg` of type `DIM2` $\rightarrow \alpha$, and the current subword index to create a stream of elements. If α is scalar (expressed as `DIM2` $\rightarrow$ `Scalar` β), the result is a singleton stream, containing just β, but α can also be of a vector type say $[\beta]$, in which case a stream of β arguments is generated, containing as many elements as are in the vector data structure.

We use a functional dependency to express[1] that the type of the stream `r` is completely determined by the type of the (non-) terminal(s) `t`.

```
class StreamGen t r | t → r where
  streamGen :: t → DIM2 → Stream r
```

The instance for a scalar argument (`DIM2` $\rightarrow$ `Scalar` β) follows as:

```
instance StreamGen (DIM2 → Scalar β) (DIM2,Z:.Z,Z:.β)
```

delaying the actual implementation for now.

Streams generated by `streamGen` have as element type a triple of inductively defined tuples we call "stacks", whose stack-like nature is only a type-level device, no stacks are present during runtime.

The first element of the triple is the subword index, the second gives an index into vector-like data structures, while the third element of the triple holds the actual values. We ignore the second element for now, just noting that (non-) terminals of scalar type do not need indexing, hence `Z` as type and value of the index. Arguments are encoded using inductive tuples, and as we only have one argument to the right of `(<<<)`, the tuple is `(Z:.`α`)`, as all such tuples or stacks (e.g. subword indices, indices into data structures, argument stacks) always terminate with `Z`.

The final ingredient of `(<<<)`, `apply`, is now comparatively simple to implement and takes an n-argument function `f` and applies it to n arguments `(Z:.`a_1`:.`$\cdots$`:.`a_n`)`. We introduce a type dependency between the arguments of the function to apply and the arguments on the argument stack, using an associated type synonym.

```
class Apply x where
  type Fun x :: *
  apply :: Fun x → x

instance Apply (Z:.a1:. ··· :.an → r) where
  type Fun (Z:.a1:. ··· :.an → r)
    = a1 → ··· → an → r
  apply fun (Z:.a1:. ··· :.an) = fun a1 ··· an
```

5.3 Extracting values from (non-) terminals

As a prelude to our first stream generation instance (that we still have to implement) we need to be able to extract values from terminals and non-terminals. There are three classes of arguments that act as (non-) terminals. We have already encountered the type (`DIM2` $\rightarrow$ `Scalar` β) for functions returning a single (scalar) value. A second class of functions yields multiple values of type β: (`DIM2` $\rightarrow$ `Vector` β). In this case we do not have vector-valued arguments to but rather multiple choices from which to select. Finally, we can have data structures. A data structure can again store single (scalar) results or multiple results (vector-like) for each subword. For data structures, it will be necessary to perform an indexing operation (e.g. `(!)` is used for the default Haskell arrays) to access values for a specific subword.

The `ExtractValue` type class presented below is generic enough to allow many possible styles of retrieving values for a subword and new instances can easily be written by the user of the library.

We shall restrict ourselves to the instance (`DIM2` $\rightarrow$ `Scalar` β). Instances for other common data structures are available with the library, including lazy and strict arrays of scalar and vector type.

The `ExtractValue` class itself has two associated types, `Asor` denoting the accessor type for indexing individual values within a vector-like argument and `Elem` for the type of the values being retrieved.

For, say, (`DIM2` $\rightarrow$ `[`β`]`), a possible `Asor` type is `Int` using the list index operator `(!!)`, while the `Elem` type is β.

For scalar types, the `Asor` will be `Z` as there is no need for an index operation in that case.

The type class for value extraction is:

```
class ExtractValue cnt where
  type Asor cnt :: *
  type Elem cnt :: *
  extractStream
    :: cnt → Stream (Idx3 z,as,vs)
    → Stream (Idx3 z, as:.Asor cnt,vs:.Elem cnt)
  extractStreamLast
    :: cnt → Stream (Idx2 z,as,vs)
    → Stream (Idx2 z,as:.Asor cnt,vs:.Elem cnt)

type Idx3 z = z:.Int:.Int:.Int
type Idx2 z = z:.Int:.Int
```

`extractStream` and `extractStreamLast` are required to correctly handle subword indices with multiple arguments in productions. Their use is explained below, but note that `extractStream` accesses the 2nd right-most subword (k,l), while `extractStreamLast` accesses the rightmost (l,j) one. Consider the production

```
S → x y z
   i k l j
```

where `y` would be handled by `extractStream` and `z` by `extractStreamLast`, and `x` has already been handled at this point, its value is on the `Elem` stack.

Each function takes a stream and extends the accessor (`Asor`) stack with its accessor and the value (`Elem`) stack is extended with the value of the argument.

Now to the actual instance for (`DIM2` $\rightarrow$ `Scalar` β):

```
instance ExtractValue (DIM2 → Scalar β) where
  type Asor (DIM2 → Scalar β) = Z
  type Elem (DIM2 → Scalar β) = β
  extractStream cnt s = map_S f s where
    f (z:.k:.l:.j,as,vs) =
    let Scalar v = cnt (Z:.k:.l)
    in  (z:.k:.l:.j,as:.Z,vs:.v)
  extractStreamLast cnt s = map_S f s where
    f (z:.l:.j,as,vs) =
    let Scalar v = cnt (Z:.l:.j)
    in  (z:.l:.j,as:.Z,vs:.v)
```

[1] Instead of type families for reasons explained in Sec. 9.

5.4 Streams for productions with one (non-) terminal

We can finish the implementation for streams of (DIM2 →Scalar β) arguments. The instance is quite similar to the `singleton` function presented in Sec. 4 but while `singleton` creates a single-element stream unconditionally we have to take care to only create a stream if the subword `(Z:.i:.j)` is legal. An illegal subword $i > j$ should lead to an empty stream.

```
instance
( ExtractValue (DIM2 → Scalar β)
) ⇒ StreamGen (DIM2 → Scalar β) (DIM2,Z:.Z,Z:.β)
  where
  streamGen x ij = extractStreamLast x
                   (unfoldrS step ij)
  step (Z:.i:.j)
     | i≤j = Just ((Z:.i:.j,Z,Z), (Z:.j+1:.j))
     | otherwise = Nothing
```

In this case, we use the subword `ij` as seed. If the subword is legal, a stream with this subword and empty `(Z)` `Asor` and `Elem` stacks is created. The new seed is the *illegal* subword $(j + 1, j)$ which will terminate the stream after the first element.

We then immediately extend the stream elements using `extractStreamLast` which creates the final stream of type `(DIM2,Z:.Z,Z:.β)` by adding the corresponding accessor of type `Z` and element of type β as top-most element to their stack. With one argument, the only argument is necessarily the last one, hence the use of `extractStreamLast` instead of `extractStream`.

Using the construction scheme of only creating streams if subwords are legal, we effectively take care of all corner cases. Illegal streams (due to illegal subwords) are terminated before we ever try to extract values from arguments. This means that `ExtractValue` instances typically do not have to perform costly runtime checks of subword arguments.

5.5 Handling multiple arguments

We implement a single combinator (`nonEmpty`) as this is already enough to show how productions with any number (≥ 2) of arguments can be handled. In addition, `nonEmpty` has to deal with the corner case of empty subwords ($i = j$) on both sides. That is, its left and right argument receive only subwords of at least size one.

Recall that in ADP the first argument to each combinator turns out to be a partially applied function that is immediately given its next argument with each additional combinator. Partially applied functions, however, can reduce the performance of our code and make it impossible (or at least hard) to change the subword index space dependent on arguments to the left of the current combinator as the function would already have been applied to those arguments.

By letting `nonEmpty` have a higher binding strength than `(<<<)` we can first collect all arguments and then apply the corresponding algebra function. In addition, we need to handle inserting the current running index, `Asor` indices of the arguments, and `Elem` values for a later `apply`. Hence `nonEmpty` is implemented in a completely different way than in ADP:

```
infixl 9 ‘nonEmpty‘
xs ‘nonEmpty‘ ys = Box mk step xs ys where
  mk (z:.i:.j,vs,as) = (z:.i:.i+1:.j,vs,as)
  step (z:.i:.k:.j,vs,as)
     | k+1≤j = Yield (z:.i:.k   :.j,vs,as)
                     (z:.i:.k+1:.j,vs,as)
     | otherwise = Done
```

The `nonEmpty` combinator does, in fact, not combine the arguments `xs` and `ys` at all but only prepares two functions `mk` and `step`.

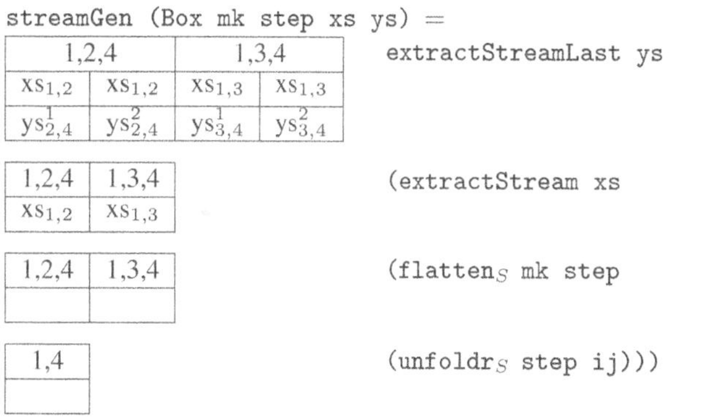

Figure 3. A stream from two arguments built step-wise bottom to top. First, a running index is inserted between the original subword $(1, 4)$ indices using `flatten`. Then, elements are extracted from the scalar argument `xs`. The vector-like argument `ys` yields two elements for each subword (indices [1] and [2]). (`step` as in Sec. 5.4)

These define the set of subwords (i, k) and (k, j) splitting the current subword (i, j) between `xs` and `ys`. Again, we make sure that any corner cases are caught. The first value for k is $i + 1$, after which k only increases. Hence `xs` is nonEmpty. In `step` we also stop creating new elements once $k + 1 > j$ meaning `ys` is never empty. Finally, should the initial subword (i, j) have size $j - i < 2$, the whole stream terminates immediately.

Of course, we are not constructing a stream at all but rather a `Box`. The implication is that two or more (non-) terminals in a production lead to nested boxes where `xs` is either another `Box` or an argument, while `ys` is always an argument. Furthermore `mk` and `step` are the two functions required by `flatten`. The `streamGen` function will receive such a nested `Box` data structure whenever two or more arguments are involved. The compiler can deconstruct even deeply nested boxes during compile time, enabling full stream fusion optimization for the production rule, completely eliminating *all* intermediate data structures just presented. We expose these optimizations to the compiler with `StreamGen` instances that are recursively applied during compilation.

5.6 Streams from productions with multiple arguments

Efficient stream generation requires deconstucting `Box`es, correct generation of subwords in streams, and extraction of values from arguments. This can be achieved with a `StreamGen` instance for `Box`es and an additional type class `PreStreamGen`.

These instances will generate the code shown in Fig. 3 (right).

The `StreamGen` instance fo the outermost `Box`

```
instance
  ( ExtractValue ys, Asor ys ∼ a, Elem ys ∼ v
  , PreStreamGen xs (idx:.Int,as,vs)
  , Idx2 undef ∼ idx
  ) ⇒ StreamGen (Box mk step xs ys)
                (idx:.Int,as:.a,vs:.v) where
  streamGen (Box mk step xs ys) ij
    = extractStreamLast ys
      (preStreamGen (Box mk step xs ys) ij)
```

handles the last argument of a production, extracting values using `extractStreamLast`. `PreStreamGen` instances handle the creation of the stream excluding the last argument recursively employing `preStreamGen`.

And we finally make use of `flatten`. This function allows us to create a stream and use each element as a seed of a substream when adding an argument further to the right – basically on the way back up from the recursion down of the nested Boxes.

The type class `PreStreamGen` follows `StreamGen` exactly:

```
class PreStreamGen s q | s → q where
  preStreamGen :: s → DIM2 → Stream q
```

To handle a total of two arguments, including the last, this `PreStreamGen` instance is sufficient[2]:

```
instance
( ExtractValue xs, Asor xs ~ a, Elem xs ~ v
, Idx2 undef ~ idx
) ⇒ PreStreamGen (Box mk step xs ys)
                 (idx:.Int,as:.a,vs:.v) where
preStreamGen (Box mk step xs ys) ij
  = extractStream xs
    (flattenS mk step
    (unfoldrS step ij))
step (Z:.i:.j)
  | i≤j = Just ((Z:.i:.j,Z,Z), Z:.j+1:.j)
  | otherwise = Nothing
```

For three or more arguments we need a final ingredient. Thanks to overlapping instances (cf. Sec. 9.1 on overlapping instances) this instance

```
instance
( PreStreamGen (Box mkI stepI xs ys) (idx,as,vs)
( ExtractValue ys, Asor ys ~ a, Elem ys ~ v
, Idx2 undef ~ idx
) ⇒ PreStreamGen (Box mk step (Box mkI stepI xs ys) zs)
                 (idx:.Int,as:.a,vs:.v) where
preStreamGen (Box mk step box@(Box _ _ _ ys) zs) ij
  = extractStream ys
    (flattenS mk step Unknown
    (preStreamGen box ij))
```

which matches two or more nested Boxes, will be used except for the final, innermost Box. Then, the above (more general) instance is chosen and recursion terminates.

As the recursion scheme is based on type class instances, the compiler will instantiate during compilation, exposing each `flatten` function to fusion. Each of those calculates subword sizes and adds to the subword stack, while `Asor` and `Elem` stacks are filled using `extractStream` and `extractStreamLast`, thereby completing the ensemble of tools required to turn production rules into efficient code.

5.7 Efficient streams from productions

Compared with ADP combinators (Sec. 3) we have traded a small amount of additional user responsibilities with the potential for enormous increases in performance.

The user needs to write an instance (of `ExtractValue`) for data structures not covered by the library or wrap such structures with (`DIM2` $\rightarrow \alpha$) accordingly.

New combinators are slightly more complex as well, requiring the `mk` and `step` function to be provided, but again several already exist. Even here, the gains outweigh the cost as each combinator has access to the partially constructed subword, `Asor`, and `Elem` stack of its stream step. One such application is found in the RNAfold algorithm (Sec. 7.2) reducing the runtime from $O(n^4)$ to $O(n^3)$ as in the reference implementation.

[2] for type inference purposes, additional type equivalence terms are required for `mk` and `step` which are omitted here

6. Applying Bellman's principle locally

All major pieces for efficient dynamic programming are now in place. A first test with a complex real-world dynamic program unfortunately revealed disappointing results. Consider the following production in grammar form:

```
S → char string S string char
     i   i+1     k l    j-1   j
```

Two single characters (`char`) bracket three arguments of variable size. A stream generated from those five arguments is quadratic in size, due to two indices, k and l, with $i+1 \leq k \leq l \leq j-1$ with k (l) to the left (right) of S. We would like to evaluate the outer arguments (the `char` terminals) only once, but due to the construction of streams from left to right, the right-most argument between $(j-1, j)$ will be evaluated a total of $O(n^2)$ times. Depending on the argument, this can lead to a noticeable performance drain.

Two solutions present themselves: (i) a more complex evaluation of (non-) terminals or (ii) making use of Bellman's principle. As option (i) requires complex type-level programming, basically determining which argument to evaluate when, and option (ii) has the general benefit of rewriting productions in terms of other productions, let us consider the latter option.

If Bellman's principle holds, a problem can be subdivided into smaller problems that, when combined, yield the same result as solving the original problem, and each subproblem is reused multiple times.

If the above production has the same semantics under an objective function, as the one below, we can rewrite it, and benefit from not having to evaluate the right-most argument more than once.

```
S → char T char                T → string S string
     i  i+1 j-1  j                   i+1     k l    j-1
```

We want to introduce another non-terminal (T) only conceptually, but translation into ADPfusion is actually quite easy. Given the original code

```
f <<< char 'then' string 'then' s 'then' string
      'then' char ... h
```

the new nested version is

```
f <<< char 'then'
      (g <<< string 'then' s 'then' string ... h)
      'then' char ... h
```

This version still yields efficient code and the final `char` argument is evaluated just once. In terms of ADPfusion, bracketing and evaluation of subproductions (`g <<< string 'then' ···`) is completely acceptable, the inner production has type (`DIM2` $\rightarrow \alpha$), variants of which are available by default.

The availability of such an optimization will depend on the specific problem at hand and will not always be obvious. As the only changes are a pair of brackets and an inner objective function, changes are easily applied and a test harness of different input sequences can be used to determine equality of the productions with high certainty – even without having to *prove* that Bellman's principle holds. One particularly good option is to automate testing using QuickCheck [5] properties.

7. Two examples from RNA bioinformatics

In this section, we test the ADPfusion library using two algorithms from the field of computational biology. The `Nussinov78` [29] grammar is one of the smallest RNA secondary structure prediction grammars and structurally very similar to our introductory example of Figs. 1 and 2. The second algorithm, `RNAfold 2.0` [26] tries to find an optimal RNA secondary structure as well.

Both algorithms can be seen as variants of the CYK algorithm [15, Sec. 4.2]. The difference is that every word is part of the language and parsing is inherently syntactically ambiguous: every input allows many parses. By attaching semantics (say: a score or an energy), similar to the sum of digits semantics, the optimal parse is chosen.

We pit ADPfusion code against equivalent versions written in C. The `Nussinov78` grammar and algebra (Fig. 4) are very simple and we will basically measure loop optimization. `RNAfold 2.0` is part of an extensive set of tools in the ViennaRNA package [26]. The complicated structure and multiple energy tables lead to a good "real-world" test.

All benchmarks are geared toward the comparison of `C` and ADPfusion in Haskell. Legacy ADP runtimes are included to point out how much of an improvement we get by using strict, unboxed arrays and a modern fusion framework.

The legacy ADP version of RNAfold is not directly compatible with `RNAfold 2.0` (C and ADPfusion). It is based on an older version of RNAfold (1.x) which is roughly 5% – 10% faster than 2.0.

We do not provide memory benchmarks. For `C` vs. ADPfusion the requirements for the DP tables are essentially the same, while legacy ADP uses boxed tables and always stores lists of results with much overhead.

The Haskell versions of `Nussinov78` and `RNAfold 2.0` have been compiled with `GHC 7.2.2` and `LLVM 2.8`; compilation options: `-fllvm -Odph -optlo-O3`. The `C` version of `Nussinov78` was compiled using `GCC 4.6` with `-O3`. The ViennaRNA package was compiled with default configuration, including `-O2` using `GCC 4.6`. All tests were done on an Intel Core i7 860 (2.8 GHz) with 8 GByte of RAM.

7.1 Nussinov's RNA folding algorithm

The algorithm by Nussinov et al. [29] is a very convenient example algorithm that is both: simple, yet complex enough to make an interesting test. A variant of the algorithm in ADP notation is shown in Fig. 4 together with its CFG. The algorithm expects as input a sequence of characters from the alphabet $\mathcal{A} = \{ACGU\}$. A *canonical basepair* is one of the six (out of 16 possible) in the set $\{AU, UA, CG, GC, GU, UG\}$. The algorithm maximizes the number of paired nucleotides with two additional rules.

Two nucleotides at the left and right end of a subword (i, j) can pair only if they form one of the six canonical pairs. For all pairs (k, l) it holds that neither $i < k < j < l$ nor $k < i < l < j$ and if $i == k$ then $j == l$. Any two pairs are juxtaposed or one is embedded in the other.

The mathematical formulation of the recursion implied by the grammar and pairmax semantics in Fig. 4 is

$$S[i,j] = \max \begin{cases} 0 & i == j \\ S[i+1,j] & i < j \\ S[i,j-1] & i < j \\ S[i+1,j-1]+1 & \text{if (i,j) pairing} \\ \max_{i<k<j} S[i,k] + S[k+1,j] & . \end{cases}$$

As there is only one non-terminal `S` (respectively DP matrix `s`) and no scoring or energy tables are involved, the algorithm measures mainly the performance for three nested loops and accessing one array.

As Fig. 5 clearly shows, we reach a performance within $\times 2$ of `C` for moderate-sized input. The `C` version used here is part of the `Nussinov78` package available online[3].

[3] `Nussinov78` hackage library: `http://hackage.haskell.org/package/Nussinov78`

```
-- signature
nil   :: S
left  :: Char → S → S
right :: S → Char → S
pair  :: Char → S → Char → S
split :: S → S → S
h     :: Stream S → S

-- structure or grammar
                s = (
S →  ε          nil   <<< empty               |||
   | bS         left  <<< base-~~s            |||
   |  Sb        right <<<        s~~-base     |||
   | bSb        pair  <<< base-~~s~~-base
   | S S                  'with' pairing      |||
                split <<<      s+~+s          ... h)

-- semantics or algebra
nil = 0                    pair a s b = s+1
left b s   = s             split l r  = l+r
right  s b = s             h xs = maximum_S xs
```

Figure 4. Top: The signature Σ for the `Nussinov78` grammar. The functions `nil, left, right, pair,` and `split` build larger answers `S` out of smaller ones. The objective function `h` transforms a stream of candidate answers, e.g. by selecting only the optimal candidate.
Center left: The context-free grammar `Nussinov78`. Character `b` $\in \mathcal{A} = \{A,C,G,U\}$.
Center right:The `Nussinov78` algorithm in ADPfusion notation with `base :: DIM2 →Char`. This example was taken from [14]. Compared to the CFG notation, the evaluation functions are now explicit as is the non-empty condition for the subwords of `split`. The `(-~~)` combinator allows a size-one subword to its left (cf. `cThenS` in Fig. 2). Its companion `(~~-)` to the right (`sThenC`). The `(+~+)` combinator enforces non-empty subwords (`nonEmpty`).
Bottom: Pairmax algebra (semantics); maximizing the number of basepairs. In `pair`, it is known that `a` and `b` form a valid pair due to the `pairing` predicate of the grammar.

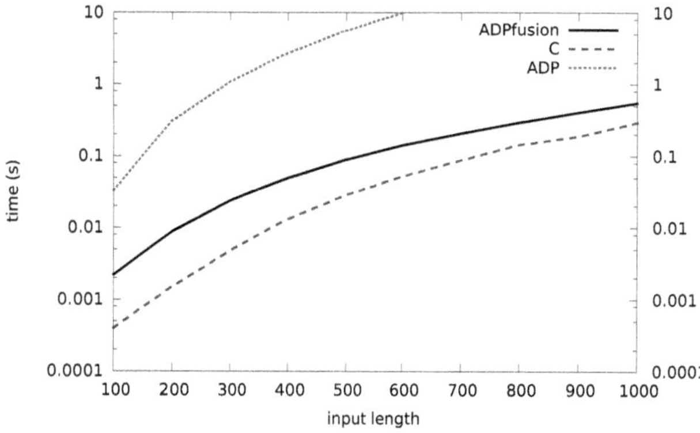

Figure 5. Runtime in seconds for different versions of the `Nussinov78` algorithm. The `Nussinov78` algorithm accesses only one DP matrix and no "energy tables". The comparatively high runtime for the ADPfusion code for small input is an artifact partially due to enabled backtracking.

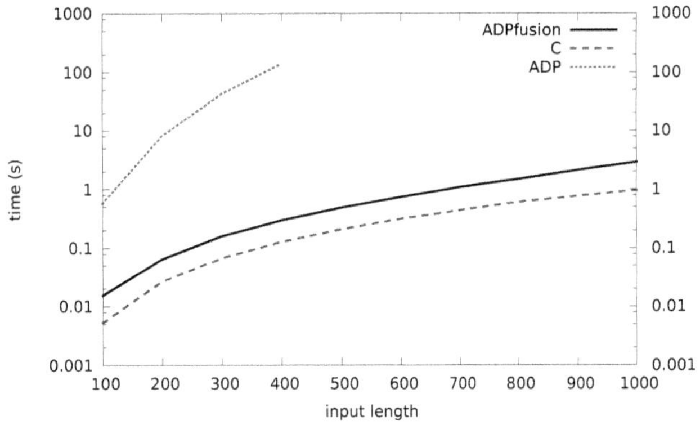

Figure 6. Runtime in seconds for different implementations of the `RNAfold 2.0` algorithm for random input of different length. The highly optimized `C` code is used by the official ViennaRNA package. ADPfusion is the code generated by our library. For illustrative purposes, ADP is the performance of the original Haskell implementation of the older `RNAfold 1.x` code.

An algorithm like `Nussinov78` is, however, not a good representative of recent developments in computational biology. Modern algorithms, while still adhering to the basic principles formulated by Nussinov et al. [29], use multiple DP matrices and typically access a number of additional tables providing scores for of different features. The `RNAfold 2.0` algorithm, described next, is one such algorithm.

7.2 RNAfold

The ViennaRNA package [16, 26] is a widely used state-of-the-art software package for RNA secondary structure prediction. It's newest incarnation is among the top programs in terms of prediction accuracy and one of the fastest. It provides an interesting target as it has been optimized quite heavily toward faster prediction of results. Compared to other programs, speed differences of $\times 10$ to $\times 100$ in favor of `RNAfold 2.0` are not uncommon [26].

The complete ViennaRNA package provides many different algorithms which makes it impractical to re-implement the whole package in Haskell. We concentrate on the minimum-free energy prediction part, which is the most basic of the offered algorithms.

We refrain from showing the ADPfusion version of the grammar. A version of RNAfold using recursion and diagrams for visualization is described in [2] and the ADPfusion grammar itself can be examined online[4].

We do, however, give some statistics. The grammar uses 4 non-terminals, three of which are interdependent while the fourth is being used to calculate "exterior" structures and only $O(n)$ matrix cells are filled instead of $O(n^2)$ as for the other three tables. A total of 17 production rules are involved and 18 energy tables. One production has an asymptotic runtime of $O(n^2)$ for each subword yielding a total runtime of $O(n^4)$. By restricting the maximal size for two linear-size subwords in the grammar to at most 30, the final runtime of RNAfold is bounded by $O(n^3)$. This restriction is present in both the `C` reference version and the ADPfusion grammar where we make use of a combinator that restricts the maximal subword size based on subword sizes calculated by another combinator, thus giving us the required restriction.

[4] `RNAFold` hackage library: `http://hackage.haskell.org/package/RNAFold`

Given inputs of size 100 (nucleotides) or more, ADPfusion code is efficient enough to get within $\times 2 - \times 3$ of the `C` implementation. Fig. 6 shows runtimes for legacy ADP, ADPfusion, and `C` code.

8. Backtracking and algebra products

ADP introduced the concept of algebra products. A typical dynamic programming algorithm requires two steps: a forward step to fill the dynamic programming matrices and a backward or backtracking step to determine the optimal path from the largest input to the smallest sub-problems. For a CYK parser, the forward step determines if a word is part of the language while the backward step yields the parse(s) for this word.

This forces the designer of a DP algorithm to write the recurrences twice, and keep the code synchronized as otherwise subtle bugs can occur. Algebra products "pull" the backward step into the forward step. Considering the case of the optimal path and its backtrace, one writes `(opt ***backtrace)`, where `opt` is the algebra computing the score of the optimal answer, while `backtrace` is its backtrace, and `(***)` the algebra product operation. This yields a new algebra that can be used as any other.

It has the effect of storing with each optimal result the description of how it was calculated or some information derived from this description. This is conceptually similar to storing a pointer to the cell(s) used for the calculation of the optimal result.

The algebra product is a very elegant device that allows for simple extension of algorithms with proper separation of ideas. A backtrace does not have to know about scoring schemes as each answer for the first argument of `(***)` is combined with exactly one answer of the second argument. Adding, say, sub-optimal results requires a change only to `opt` to capture more than one result, while co-optimal results are automatically available from the ADP definition of the algebra product.

The algebra product as used in ADP is, unfortunately, a problematic device to use in practice. While it allows for a simple design of algorithms and removes another source of potential bugs, it comes with a high runtime cost.

Consider an algorithm that calculates a large number of co- or sub-optimal results, like the `Nussinov78` algorithm in backtracking.

Standard implementations calculate the DP matrices in the forward step and then enumerate all possible backtraces within a certain range. The forward step does not change compared to just asking for the optimal result. The backward step, while tedious to get right, only has to deal with one backtrace at a time – unless they all have to be stored. ADP, on the other hand, stores *all* backtraces within its DP matrices. The memory cost is much higher as all answers – and all answers to sub-problems – that pass the objective function are retained within the matrices.

In addition, we can not use strict, unboxed arrays of Ints (or Floats or Doubles) if we store backtraces directly in the DP matrices.

For ADPfusion we prefer to have an explicit backtrace step. As a consequence, the programmer is faced with a slightly bigger task of defining the forward algebra and the backward algebra separately instead of just using the algebra product, but this is offset by the gains in runtime and memory usage. One can even use a version of the algebra product operation in the backward step to keep most of its benefits. In this case, the use of the algebra product becomes quite harmless as we no longer store each answer within the matrices. In terms of absolute runtime, this approach works out favorably as well. The costly forward phase (for RNAfold: $O(n^3)$) is as efficient as possible, while the less costly backtracking (for RNAfold: $O(n^2 * k)$, with k the number of backtracked results) uses the elegant algebra product device.

9. Technical details

9.1 Functional dependencies vs. type families

Type families [3] are a replacement for functional dependencies [21]. As both approaches provide nearly the same functionality, it is a good question why this library requires both: type families and functional dependencies. The functions to extract values from function arguments, collected in the type class `ExtractValue`, are making use of associated type synonyms as this provides a (albeit subjectively) clean interface.

The stream generation system, using the `StreamGen` and `PreStreamGen` type classes, is based on functional dependencies. The reasons are two-fold: (i) the replacement using type families does not optimize well, and (ii) functional dependencies allow for overlapping instances.

The type family-based version[5] of the ADPfusion library does not optimize well. Once a third argument, and hence nested `Boxes` come into play, the resulting code is only partially optimized effecting performance by a large factor. This seems to be due to insufficient compile-time elimination of `Box` data constructors. This problem is currently under investigation.

Using a fixed number of instances, say up to 10, would at best be a stop-gap measure since this restricts the user of the library to productions of at most that many arguments and leads to highly repetitive code.

As functional dependencies allow unlimited arguments, require only overlapping instances, and consistently produce good code, they are the better solution for now even though they are, in general, not well received[6].

9.2 Efficient memoization

The ADPfusion library is concerned with optimizing production rules independent of underlying data structures, lazyness, and boxed or unboxed data types. The author of a DP algorithm may choose the data structure most suitable for the problem and by giving an `ExtractValue` instance makes it compatible with ADPfusion. If priority is placed on performance, calculations can be performed in the ST or IO monad. The `PrimitiveArray`[7] library provides a set of unboxed array data structures that have been used for the algorithms in Sec. 7 as boxed data structures cost performance.

When first writing a new DP algorithm, lazy data structures can be used as this frees the programmer from having to specify the order in which DP tables (or other data structures) need to be filled. Once a proof-of-concept has been written, only small changes are required to create an algorithm working on unboxed data structures.

10. Conclusion and further work

High-level, yet high-performance, code is slowly becoming a possibility in Haskell. Projects like DPH [4] and Repa [22] show that one does not have to resort to unsightly low-level (and/or imperative-looking) algorithms anymore to design efficient algorithms. Furthermore, we can reap the benefits of staying within a language and having access to libraries and modern compilers compared to moving to a domain-specific language and its own compiler architecture.

The ability to write ADP code and enjoy the benefits of automatic fusion and compiler optimization are obvious as can be shown by the improvements in runtime as described in Sec. 7. Furthermore, one can design dynamic programming algorithms with the ease provided by ADP [10] and seamlessly enable further optimizations like strict, unboxed data structures, without having to rewrite the whole algorithm, or having to move away from Haskell.

With this new high-performance library at hand, we will redesign several algorithms. Our Haskell prototype of `RNAfold 2.0` allows us to compare performance with its optimized `C` counterpart. `RNAwolf` [18] is an advanced folding algorithm with a particularly complicated grammar including nucleotide triplets for which an implementation is only available in Haskell. `CMCompare` [17] calculates similarity measures for a restricted class of stochastic context-free grammars in the biological setting of RNA families.

Some rather advanced techniques that have become more appreciated in recent years (stochastic sampling of RNA structures [28] being one recent example) can now be expressed easily and with generality.

The ADP homepage [14] contains further examples of dynamic programming algorithms, as well as certain specializations and optimizations which will drive further improvements of this library. Of particular interest will be dynamic programming problems *not* in the realm of computational biology in order to make sure that the library is of sufficient generality to be of general usefulness.

The creation of efficient parsers for formal grammars, including CYK for context-free languages, is one such area of interest. Another are domain-specific languages that have rule sets akin to production rules in CFGs but do not require dynamic programming.

The ability to employ monadic combinators, which are available in the library, will be of help in many novel algorithmic ideas. We ignored the monadic aspect, but the library is indeed completely monadic. The non-monadic interface hides the monadic function application combinator `(#<<)`, nothing more. This design is inspired by the `vector`[8] library.

Coming back to the title of "sneaking around *concatMap*", we can not claim complete success. While we have gained huge improvements in performance, the resulting library is rather heavyweight (requiring both, functional dependencies and type families, and by extension, overlapping, flexible, and undecidable instances). Unfortunately, we currently see no way around this. As already pointed out in the stream fusion paper [7, section 9], optimizing for `concatMap` is not trivial. Furthermore, we would need optimizations that deal well with partially applied functions to facilitate a faithful translation of ADP into high-performance code.

Right now, results along these lines seem doubtful (considering that the stream fusion paper is from 2007) to become available soon. In addition, our view of partitioning a subword allows us to employ certain specializations directly within our framework. We know of no obvious, efficient way of implementing them within the original ADP framework. The most important one is the ability to observe the index stack to the left of the current combinator making possible the immediate termination of a stream that fails definable criteria like maximal sum of sub-partition sizes.

The code generated by this library does show that we have achieved further separation of concerns. While algebraic dynamic programming already provides separation of grammar (search space) and algebra (evaluation of candidates and selection via objective function) as well as asymptotic optimization by partial tabulation, we can add a further piece that is very important in practice – optimization of constant overhead. While the application of Bellman's principle still has to happen on the level of the grammar and by proof, all *code optimization* is now moved into the ADPfusion library.

The ADPfusion library itself depends on low-level stream optimization using the stream fusion work [7, 25] and further code optimization via GHC [36] and LLVM [24]. Trying to expose cer-

[5] github: branch `tf`

[6] cf. "cons" on overlap: `http://hackage.haskell.org/trac/haskell-prime/wiki/OverlappingInstances`

[7] `http://hackage.haskell.org/package/PrimitiveArray`

[8] `http://hackage.haskell.org/package/vector`

tain compile-time loop optimizations either within ADPfusion or the stream fusion library seems very attractive at this point as does the potential use of modern single-instruction multiple-data mechanisms. Any improvements in this area should allow us to breach the final $\times 2$ gap in runtime but we'd like to close this argument by pointing out that it is now *easy* to come very close to hand-optimized dynamic programming code.

Availability

The library is BSD3-licensed and available from hackage under the package name ADPfusion: `http://hackage.haskell.org/package/ADPfusion`. The git repository, including the type families (`tf`) branch, is available on github: `https://github.com/choener/ADPfusion`.

Acknowledgments

The author thanks Robert Giegerich and the Practical Computer Science group at Bielefeld University (ADP), Ivo Hofacker (dynamic programming), Roman Leshchinskiy (`vector` library, fusion, high-performance Haskell), and his family for letting him design, code and (mostly) finish it during the 2011-12 winter holidays. Several anonymous reviewers have provided detailed and valueable comments for which I am very thankful.

This work has been funded by the Austrian FWF, project "SFB F43 RNA regulation of the transcriptome"

References

[1] R. E. Bellman. On the Theory of Dynamic Programming. *Proceedings of the National Academy of Sciences*, 38(8):716–719, 1952.

[2] A. F. Bompfünewerer, R. Backofen, S. H. Bernhart, J. Hertel, I. L. Hofacker, P. F. Stadler, and S. Will. Variations on RNA folding and alignment: lessons from Benasque. *Journal of Mathematical Biology*, 56(1):129–144, 2008.

[3] M. M. Chakravarty, G. Keller, and S. Peyton Jones. Associated Type Synonyms. In *Proceedings of the tenth ACM SIGPLAN international conference on Functional programming*, ICFP'05, pages 241–253. ACM, 2005.

[4] M. M. Chakravarty, R. Leshchinskiy, S. Peyton Jones, G. Keller, and S. Marlow. Data Parallel Haskell: a status report. In *Proceedings of the 2007 workshop on Declarative aspects of multicore programming*, DAMP'07, pages 10–18. ACM, 2007.

[5] K. Claessen and J. Hughes. QuickCheck: A Lightweight Tool for Random Testing of Haskell Programs. In *Proceedings of the fifth ACM SIGPLAN international conference on Functional programming*, ICFP'00, pages 268–279. ACM, 2000.

[6] T. H. Cormen, C. E. Leiserson, R. L. Rivest, and C. Stein. *Introduction to Algorithms*. The MIT press, 2001.

[7] D. Coutts, R. Leshchinskiy, and D. Stewart. Stream Fusion: From Lists to Streams to Nothing at All. In *Proceedings of the 12th ACM SIGPLAN international conference on Functional programming*, ICFP'07, pages 315–326. ACM, 2007.

[8] R. Durbin, S. Eddy, A. Krogh, and G. Mitchison. *Biological sequence analysis*. Cambridge Univ. Press, 1998.

[9] R. Giegerich and C. Höner zu Siederdissen. Semantics and Ambiguity of Stochastic RNA Family Models. *IEEE/ACM Transactions on Computational Biology and Bioinformatics*, 8(2):499–516, 2011.

[10] R. Giegerich and C. Meyer. Algebraic Dynamic Programming. In *Algebraic Methodology And Software Technology*, volume 2422, pages 243–257. Springer, 2002.

[11] R. Giegerich and P. Steffen. Challenges in the compilation of a domain specific language for dynamic programming. In *Proceedings of the 2006 ACM symposium on Applied computing*, pages 1603–1609. ACM, 2006.

[12] R. Giegerich, C. Meyer, and P. Steffen. Towards a Discipline of Dynamic Programming. *Informatik bewegt, GI-Edition-Lecture Notes in Informatics*, pages 3–44, 2002.

[13] R. Giegerich, C. Meyer, and P. Steffen. A Discipline of Dynamic Programming over Sequence Data. *Science of Computer Programming*, 51(3):215–263, 2004.

[14] R. Giegerich et al. Algebraic Dynamic Programming Website. `http://bibiserv.techfak.uni-bielefeld.de/adp/`, 2004.

[15] D. Grune and C. J. Jacobs. *Parsing techniques: a practical guide*. Springer-Verlag New York Inc, 2008.

[16] I. L. Hofacker, W. Fontana, P. F. Stadler, L. S. Bonhoeffer, M. Tacker, and P. Schuster. Fast Folding and Comparison of RNA Secondary Structures. *Monatshefte für Chemie/Chemical Monthly*, 125(2):167–188, 1994.

[17] C. Höner zu Siederdissen and I. L. Hofacker. Discriminatory power of RNA family models. *Bioinformatics*, 26(18):453–459, 2010.

[18] C. Höner zu Siederdissen, S. H. Bernhart, P. F. Stadler, and I. L. Hofacker. A folding algorithm for extended RNA secondary structures. *Bioinformatics*, 27(13): 129–136, 2011.

[19] P. Hudak, J. Hughes, S. Peyton Jones, and P. Wadler. A History of Haskell: Being Lazy with Class. In *Proceedings of the third ACM SIGPLAN conference on History of programming languages*, HOPL III, pages 1–55. ACM, 2007.

[20] G. Hutton. Higher-order functions for parsing. *Journal of Functional Programming*, 2(3):323–343, 1992.

[21] M. P. Jones. Type Classes with Functional Dependencies. *Programming Languages and Systems*, pages 230–244, 2000.

[22] G. Keller, M. M. Chakravarty, R. Leshchinskiy, S. Peyton Jones, and B. Lippmeier. Regular, Shape-polymorphic, Parallel Arrays in Haskell. In *Proceedings of the 15th ACM SIGPLAN international conference on Functional programming*, ICFP'10, pages 261–272. ACM, 2010.

[23] K. Lari and S. J. Young. The estimation of stochastic context-free grammars using the Inside-Outside algorithm. *Computer Speech & Language*, 4(1):35–56, 1990.

[24] C. Lattner and V. Adve. LLVM: A Compilation Framework for Lifelong Program Analysis & Transformation. In *Code Generation and Optimization, 2004. CGO 2004. International Symposium on*, pages 75–86. IEEE, 2004.

[25] R. Leshchinskiy. Recycle Your Arrays! *Practical Aspects of Declarative Languages*, pages 209–223, 2009.

[26] R. Lorenz, S. H. Bernhart, C. Höner zu Siederdissen, H. Tafer, C. Flamm, P. F. Stadler, and I. L. Hofacker. ViennaRNA Package 2.0. *Algorithms for Molecular Biology*, 6(26), 2011.

[27] M. Mernik, J. Heering, and A. M. Sloane. When and How to Develop Domain-Specific Languages. *ACM Computing Surveys*, 37(4):316–344, 2005.

[28] M. Nebel and A. Scheid. Evaluation of a sophisticated SCFG design for RNA secondary structure prediction. *Theory in Biosciences*, 130:313–336, 2011. ISSN 1431-7613.

[29] R. Nussinov, G. Pieczenik, J. R. Griggs, and D. J. Kleitman. Algorithms for Loop Matchings. *SIAM Journal on Applied Mathematics*, 35(1):68–82, 1978.

[30] B. O'Sullivan, D. B. Stewart, and J. Goerzen. *Real World Haskell*. O'Reilly Media, 2009.

[31] S. Peyton Jones. Call-pattern Specialisation for Haskell Programs. In *Proceedings of the 12th ACM SIGPLAN international conference on Functional programming*, ICFP'07, pages 327–337. ACM, 2007.

[32] E. Rivas, R. Lang, and S. R. Eddy. A range of complex probabilistic models for RNA secondary structure prediction that includes the nearest-neighbor model and more. *RNA*, 18(2):193–212, 2012.

[33] G. Sauthoff, S. Janssen, and R. Giegerich. Bellman's GAP - A Declarative Language for Dynamic Programming. In *Proceedings of the 13th international ACM SIGPLAN symposium on Principles and practices of declarative programming*, PPDP'11, pages 29–40. ACM, 2011.

[34] R. Sedgewick. *Algorithms*. Addison-Wesley Publishing Co., Inc., 1983.

[35] P. Steffen. *Compiling a domain specific language for dynamic programming*. PhD thesis, Bielefeld University, 2006.

[36] The GHC Team. The Glasgow Haskell Compiler (GHC). `http://www.haskell.org/ghc/`, 2012.

Experience Report: Haskell in Computational Biology

Noah M. Daniels Andrew Gallant Norman Ramsey

Department of Computer Science, Tufts University

{ndaniels, agallant, nr}@cs.tufts.edu

Abstract

Haskell gives computational biologists the flexibility and rapid prototyping of a scripting language, plus the performance of native code. In our experience, higher-order functions, lazy evaluation, and monads really worked, but profiling and debugging presented obstacles. Also, Haskell libraries vary greatly: memoization combinators and parallel-evaluation strategies helped us a lot, but other, nameless libraries mostly got in our way. Despite the obstacles and the uncertain quality of some libraries, Haskell's ecosystem made it easy for us to develop new algorithms in computational biology.

Categories and Subject Descriptors D.1.1 [*Applicative (Functional) Programming*]; J.3 [*Biology and genetics*]

Keywords memoization, stochastic search, parallel strategies, QuickCheck, remote homology detection

1. Introduction

Computational biologists write software that answers questions about sequences of nucleic acids (genomic data) or sequences of amino acids (proteomic data). When performance is paramount, software is usually written in C or C++. When convenience, readability, and productivity are more important, software is usually written in a dynamically typed or domain-specific language like Perl, Python, Ruby, SPSS, or R. In this paper, we report on experience using a third kind of language, Haskell:

- We had to reimplement an algorithm already implemented in C++, and the Haskell code is slower. But the Haskell code was easy to write, clearly implements the underlying mathematics (Section 3.1), was easy to parallelize, and performs well enough (Section 3.3). And our new tool solves a problem that could not be solved by the C++ tool which preceded it.
- Higher-order functions made it unusually easy to create and experiment with new stochastic-search algorithms (Section 3.2).
- Haskell slowed us down in only one area: understanding and improving performance (Section 3.4).
- Although the first two authors are computational biologists with little functional-programming experience, Haskell made it easy for us to explore new research ideas. By contrast, our group's C++ code has made it hard to explore new ideas (Section 4).
- The Haskell community offers libraries and tools that promise powerful abstractions. Some kept the promise, saved us lots of effort, and were a pleasure to use. Others, not so much. We couldn't tell in advance which would be which (Section 5.2).

ICFP'12, September 9–15, 2012, Copenhagen, Denmark.

2. The biology

Proteins, by interacting with one another and with other molecules, carry out the functions of living cells: metabolism, regulation, signaling, and so on. A protein's function is determined by its structure, and its structure is determined by the sequence of amino acids that form the protein. The amino-acid sequence is ultimately determined by a sequence of nucleic acids in DNA, which we call a gene. Given a gene, biologists wish to know the cellular function of the protein the gene codes for. One of the best known methods of discovering such function is to find other proteins of similar structure, which likely share similar function. Proteins that share structure and function are expected to be descended from a common ancestor—in biological terms, *homologous*—and thus the problem of identifying proteins similar to a *query sequence* is called *homology detection.*

Computational biologists detect homologies by building algorithms which, given a query sequence, compare it with known proteins. When the known proteins have amino-acid sequences that are not too different from the query sequence, homology can be detected by a family of algorithms called *hidden Markov models* (Eddy 1998). But in real biological systems, proteins with similar structure and function may be formed from significantly different amino-acid sequences, which are not close in edit distance. Our research software, MRFy (pronounced "Murphy"), can detect homologies in amino-acid sequences that are only distantly related. MRFy is available at `mrfy.cs.tufts.edu`.

3. The software

Homology-detection software is most often used in one of two ways: to test a hypothesis about the function of a single, newly discovered protein, or to compare every protein in a genome against a library of known protein structures. Either way, the software is *trained* on a group of proteins that share function and structure. These proteins are identified by a biologist, who puts their amino-acid sequences into an *alignment.* This alignment relates individual amino acids in a set of homologous proteins. An alignment may be represented as a matrix in which each row corresponds to the amino-acid sequence of a protein, and each column groups amino acids that play similar roles in different proteins (Figure 1).

An alignment may contain *gaps*, which in Figure 1 are shown as dashes. A gap in row 2, column j indicates that as proteins evolved, either protein 2 lost its amino acid in position j, or other proteins gained an amino acid in position j. If column j contains few gaps, it is considered a *consensus column*, and the few proteins with gaps probably lost amino acids via *deletions.* If column j contains *mostly* gaps, it is considered a *non-consensus column*, and the few proteins without gaps probably gained amino acids via *insertions.*

Once a protein alignment is constructed, it is used to train a *hidden Markov model.* A hidden Markov model is a probabilistic finite-state machine which can assign a probability to any query sequence. A protein whose query sequence has a higher probability

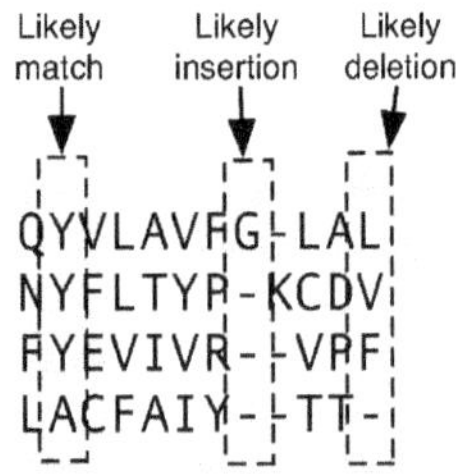

Figure 1. A structural alignment of four proteins ($C = 12$)

is more likely to be homologous to the proteins in the alignment. We write a query sequence as $x_1, \ldots, x_N$, where each x_i is an amino acid. The number of amino acids, N, can differ from the number of columns in the alignment, C.

A hidden Markov model carries probabilities on some states and on all state transitions. Both the probabilities and the states are determined by the alignment:

- For each column j of the alignment, the hidden Markov model has a *match state* M_j. The match state contains a table $e_{M_j}(x)$ which gives the probability that a homologous protein has amino acid x in column j.
- For each column j of the alignment, the hidden Markov model has an *insertion state* I_j. The insertion state contains a table $e_{I_j}(x)$ which gives the probability that a homologous protein has gained amino acid x by insertion at column j.
- For each column j of the alignment, the hidden Markov model has a *deletion state* D_j. The deletion state determines the probability that a homologous protein has lost an amino acid by deletion from column j.

The probabilities $e_{M_j}(x)$ and $e_{I_j}(x)$ are *emission probabilities.*

A hidden Markov model also has distinguished "begin" and "end" states. In our representation, each state contains a probability or a table of probabilities, and it is also labeled with one of these labels:

```
data StateLabel = Mat | Ins | Del | Beg | End
```

We use the "Plan7" hidden Markov model, which forbids direct transitions between insertion states and deletion states (Eddy 1998). "Plan7" implies that there are exactly 7 possible transitions into the states of any column j. Each transition has its own probability:

- A transition into a match state is more likely when column j is a consensus column. Depending on the predecessor state, the probability of such a transition is $a_{M_{j-1}M_j}$, $a_{I_{j-1}M_j}$, or $a_{D_{j-1}M_j}$.
- A transition into a deletion state is more likely when column j is a non-consensus column. The probability of such a transition is $a_{M_{j-1}D_j}$ or $a_{D_{j-1}D_j}$.
- A transition into an insertion state is more likely when column j is a non-consensus column. The probability of such a transition is $a_{M_{j-1}I_j}$ or $a_{I_{j-1}I_j}$.

3.1 Computing probabilities using perspicuous Haskell

Given a hidden Markov model, an established software package called HMMER (pronounced "hammer") can compute the probability that a new protein shares structure with the proteins used to train the model. The computation finds the most likely path through the hidden Markov model. To make best use of floating-point arithmetic, the software computes the *logarithm* of the probability of each path, by summing the logs of the probabilities on the states and edges of the path (Viterbi 1967). The path that maximizes the log of the probability is the most likely path.

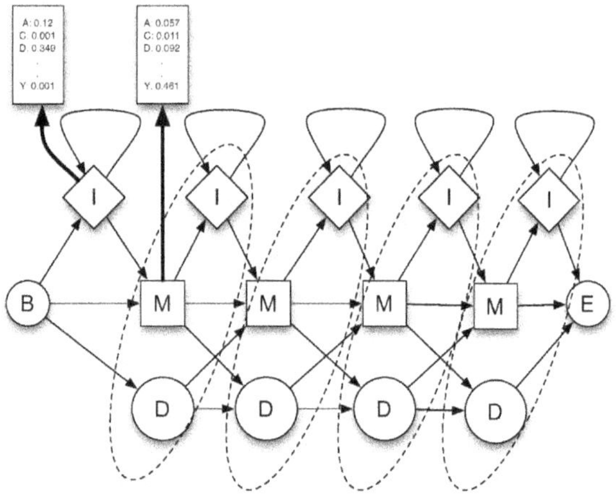

This model has begin and end states B and E, as well as four nodes, each containing an insertion state I, a match state M, and a deletion state D.

Figure 2. A hidden Markov model ($C = 4$)

The computation is specified on the left-hand side of Figure 3. A probability $V_j^M(i)$ represents the probability of the most likely path of the first i amino acids in the query sequence, terminating with placement of amino acid x_i in state M_j. Probabilities $V_j^I(i)$ and $V_j^D(i)$ are similar. The equations are explained very clearly by Durbin et al. (1998, Chapter 5)

To be able to use Haskell, we had to reimplement the standard algorithm for solving Viterbi's equations. Haskell made it possible for us to write code that looks like the math, which made the code easy to write and gives us confidence that it is correct.

Our code represents a query sequence as an immutable array of amino acids. In idiomatic Haskell, we might represent an individual amino acid x_i using a value of algebraic data type:

```
data Amino = Ala | Cys | Asp | Glu | ...    -- not used
```

But our models use a legacy file format in which each amino acid is a small integer used only to index arrays. We therefore chose

```
newtype AA = AA Int
```

Our legacy file format also *negates* the log of each probability, making it a positive number. The negated logarithm of a probability is called a *score.*

```
newtype Score = Score Double
```

Type `Score` has a limited `Num` instance which permits scores to be added and subtracted but not multiplied.

In a real hidden Markov model, each probability is represented as a score. Our code implements a transformed version of Viterbi's equations which operates on scores. The transformed equations are shown on the right-hand side of Figure 3. They minimize the score (the negated log probability) for each combination of column j, amino acid x_i, and state M_j, I_j, or D_j.

A model is represented as a sequence of *nodes;* node j includes states M_j, I_j, and D_j, as well as the probabilities of transitions out of that node. Each node contains tables of emission scores

$$V_j^M(i) = \log \frac{e_{M_j}(x_i)}{q_{x_i}} + \max \begin{cases} \log a_{M_{j-1}M_j} + V_{j-1}^M(i-1) \\ \log a_{I_{j-1}M_j} + V_{j-1}^I(i-1) \\ \log a_{D_{j-1}M_j} + V_{j-1}^D(i-1) \end{cases}$$

$$V_j^I(i) = \log \frac{e_{I_j}(x_i)}{q_{x_i}} + \max \begin{cases} \log a_{M_j I_j} + V_j^M(i-1) \\ \log a_{I_j I_j} + V_j^I(i-1) \end{cases}$$

$$V_j^D(i) = \max \begin{cases} \log a_{M_{j-1}D_j} + V_{j-1}^M(i) \\ \log a_{D_{j-1}D_j} + V_{j-1}^D(i) \end{cases}$$

$$V_j'^M(i) = e'_{M_j}(x_i) + \min \begin{cases} a'_{M_{j-1}M_j} + V_{j-1}'^M(i-1) \\ a'_{I_{j-1}M_j} + V_{j-1}'^I(i-1) \\ a'_{D_{j-1}M_j} + V_{j-1}'^D(i-1) \end{cases}$$

$$V_j'^I(i) = e'_{I_j}(x_i) + \min \begin{cases} a'_{M_j I_j} + V_j'^M(i-1) \\ a'_{I_j I_j} + V_j'^I(i-1) \end{cases}$$

$$V_j'^D(i) = \min \begin{cases} a'_{M_{j-1}D_j} + V_{j-1}'^M(i) \\ a'_{D_{j-1}D_j} + V_{j-1}'^D(i) \end{cases}$$

$$a'_{s\hat{s}} = -\log a_{s\hat{s}} \qquad e'_s(x) = -\log \frac{e_s(x)}{q_x} \qquad V_j'^M(i) = -V_j^M(i)$$

Figure 3. Viterbi's equations, in original and negated forms

e'_{M_j} and e'_{I_j}. These tables are read by function `eScore`, whose specification is `eScore` $s\ j\ i = e'_{s_j}(x_i)$. We place the transition probabilities into a record in which each field is labeled $s\_\hat{s}$, where s and $\hat{s}$ form one of the 7 permissible pairs of state labels:

```
newtype TProb = TProb { logProbability :: Score }
data TProbs = TProbs
  { m_m :: TProb, m_i :: TProb, m_d :: TProb
  , i_m :: TProb, i_i :: TProb
  , d_m :: TProb, d_d :: TProb }
```

These scores are read by function `aScore`, whose specification is `aScore` $s\ \hat{s}\ (j-1) = a_{s_{j-1}\hat{s}_j}$.

Scores can be usefully attached to many types of values, so we have defined a small abstraction:

```
data Scored a = Scored { unScored :: !a, scoreOf :: !Score}
(/+/) :: Score -> Scored a -> Scored a
```

Think of a value of type `Scored a` as a container holding an "a" with a score written on the side. The `/+/` function adds to the score without touching the container. Function `fmap` is also defined; it applies a function to a container's contents. Finally, we made `Scored` an instance of `Ord`. Containers are ordered by score alone, so applying `minimum` to a list of scored things chooses the thing with the smallest (and therefore best) score.

Armed with our models and with the `Scored` abstraction, we attacked Viterbi's equations. The probability in each state is a function of the probabilities in its predecessor states, and all probabilities can be computed by a classic dynamic-programming algorithm. This algorithm starts at the begin state, computes probabilites in nodes 1 through C in succession, and terminates at the end state. One of us implemented this algorithm, storing the probabilities in an array. The cost was $O(|N| \times |C|)$; in MRFy, C and N range from several hundred to a few thousand.

Another of us was curious to try coding Viterbi's equations directly as recursive functions. Like a recursive Fibonacci function, Viterbi's functions, when implemented naïvely, take exponential time. But like the Fibonacci function, Viterbi's functions can be *memoized*. For example, to compute $V_j'^M(i)$ using the equation at the top right of Figure 3, we define `vee' Mat` $j\ i$. The equation adds $e'_{M_j}(x_i)$, computed with `eScore`, to a minimum of sums. The sum of an $a'_{s\hat{s}}$ term and a $V_{j-1}'^s(i-1)$ term is computed by function `avSum`, in which the terms are computed by `aScore` and `vee''`, respectively:

```
vee' Mat j i = fmap (Mat `cons`) $
   eScore Mat j i /+/ minimum (map avSum [Mat, Ins, Del])
 where avSum prev =
         aScore prev Mat (j-1) /+/ vee'' prev (j-1) (i-1)
```

What about the call to ``fmap (Mat `cons`)``? This call performs a computation *not* shown in Figure 3: MRFy computes not only the probability of the most likely path but also the path itself. Function ``(Mat `cons`)`` adds M to a path; we avoid `(Mat :)` for reasons explained in Section 3.3 below.

Function `vee''` is the memoized version of `vee'`. Calling `vee''` produces the same result as calling `vee'`, but faster:

```
vee'' = Memo.memo3 (Memo.arrayRange (Mat, End))
                   (Memo.arrayRange (0, numNodes))
                   (Memo.arrayRange (-1, seqlen))
                   vee'
```

Functions `Memo.memo3` and `Memo.arrayRange` come from Luke Palmer's `Data.MemoCombinators` package. The value `numNodes` represents C, and `seqlen` represents N.

Memoization makes `vee'` perform as well as our classic dynamic-programming code. And the call to `Memo.memo3` is the *only* part of the code devoted to dynamic programming. By contrast, standard implementations of Viterbi's algorithm, such as in HMMER, spend much of their code managing dynamic-programming tables. Haskell enabled us write simple, performant code with little effort. Because the memoized version so faithfully resembles the equations in Figure 3, we retired the classic version.

3.2 Exploring new algorithms using higher-order functions

We use Viterbi's algorithm to help detect homologies in proteins with specific kinds of structure. When a real protein folds in three dimensions, amino acids that are far away in the one-dimensional sequence can be adjacent in three-dimensional space. Some groups of such acids are called *beta strands*. Beta strands can be hydrogen-bonded to each other, making them "stuck together." These beta strands help identify groups of homologous proteins. MRFy detects homologous proteins that include hydrogen-bonded beta strands; using prior methods, many instances of this problem are intractable.

Beta strands require new equations and richer models of protein structure. When column j of an alignment is part of a beta strand and is paired with another column $\pi(j)$, the probability of finding amino acid x_i in column j depends on the amino acid x' in column $\pi(i)$. If x' is in position i' in the query sequence, Viterbi's equations are altered; for example, $V_j'^M(i)$ depends not only on $V_{j-1}'^M(i-1)$ but also on $V_{\pi(j)}'^M(i')$. The distance between j and $\pi(j)$ can be as small as a few columns or as large as a few hundreds of columns. Because $V_j'^M(i)$ depends not only on nearby values but also on $V_{\pi(j)}'^M(i')$, dynamic programming cannot compute the maximum likelihood quickly (Menke et al. 2010; Daniels et al. 2012).

The new equations are accompanied by a new model. Within a beta strand, amino acids are not inserted or deleted, so a bonded

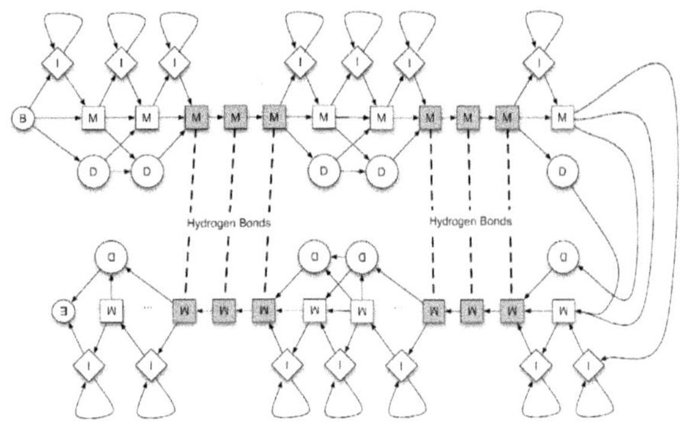

Each shaded node represents a beta-strand position. Nodes connected by dashed edges are hydrogen-bonded.

Figure 4. A Markov random field with two beta-strand pairs

pair of beta strands is modeled by a pair of sequences of match states. Between beta strands, the model is structured as before. The combined model, an example of which is shown in Figure 4, is called a *Markov random field*.

MRFy treats the beta strands in the model as "beads" which can slide along the query sequence. A positioning of the beta strands is called a *placement*. A placement's likelihood is computed based on frequencies of amino-acid pairs observed in hydrogen-bonded beta strands (Cowen et al. 2002). Given a placement, the maximum likelihood of the rest of the query sequence, between and around beta strands, is computed quickly and exactly using Viterbi's algorithm. This likelihood is *conditioned* on the placement.

MRFy searches for likely placements stochastically. MRFy implements random hill climbing, simulated annealing, multistart simulated annealing, and a genetic algorithm. These algorithms share much code, and MRFy implements them using higher-order functions, existentially quantified types, and lazy evaluation.

We describe MRFy's search abstractly: MRFy computes a sequence of *points* in a search space. The type of point is existentially quantified, but it is typically a single placement or perhaps a population of placements. Each point also has a `Score`; MRFy looks for points with good scores.

Ideally, MRFy would use the now-classic, lazy, modular technique advocated by Hughes (1989), in which one function computes an infinite sequence of points, and another function uses a finite prefix to decide on an approximation. But because MRFy's search is stochastic, making MRFy's search modular is not so easy.

To illustrate the difficulties, we discuss our simplest search: random hill climbing. From any given point in the search space, this search moves a random distance in a random direction. If the move leads to a better point, we call it *useful*; otherwise it is *useless*.

```
data Utility a = Useful a | Useless
```

(We also use `Useful` and `Useless` to tag *points*.) With luck, an infinite sequence of useful moves converges at a local optimum.

MRFy's search path follows only useful moves; if a move is useless, MRFy abandons it and moves again (in a new random direction) from the previous point. Ideally, MRFy would search by composing a *generator* that produces an infinite sequence of moves, a *filter* that selects the useful moves, and a *test* function that enumerates finitely many useful moves and returns the final destination. But a generator may produce an infinite sequence of useless moves. (For example, if MRFy should stumble upon a global optimum, every move from that point would be useless.) Given an infinite sequence of useless inputs, a filter would not produce any values, and the search would diverge.

We address this problem by combining "generate and filter" into a single abstraction, which has type `SearchGen pt r`. Type variable `pt` is a point in the search space, and `r` is a random-number generator. `Rand r` is a lazy monad of stochastic computations:

```
data SearchGen pt r =
 SG { pt0     :: Rand r (Scored pt)
    , nextPt  :: Scored pt -> Rand r (Scored pt)
    , utility :: Move pt -> Rand r (Utility (Scored pt))
    }
```

The monadic computation `pt0` randomly selects a starting point for search; `nextPt` produces a new point from an existing point. Because scoring can be expensive, both `pt0` and `nextPt` use *scored* points, and they can reuse scores from previous points.

To tell if a point returned by `nextPt` is useful, we call the `utility` function, which scrutinizes a move represented as follows:

```
data Move pt = Move { older        :: Scored pt
                    , younger      :: Scored pt
                    , youngerCCost :: CCost }
```

The decision about utility uses not only a source of randomness but also the *cumulative cost* of the point, which we define to be the number of points explored previously. The cumulative cost of the current point is also the age of the search, and in simulated annealing, for example, as the search ages, the `utility` function becomes less likely to accept a move that worsens the score.

Using these pieces, function `everyPt` produces an infinite sequence containing a mix of useful and useless moves:

```
everyPt :: RandomGen r
        => SearchGen pt r -> CCost -> Scored pt
        -> Rand r [CCosted (Utility (Scored pt))]
everyPt sg cost startPt = do
  successors <- mapM (nextPt sg) (repeat startPt)
  tagged <- zipWithM costedUtility successors [succ cost..]
  let (useless, CCosted (Useful newPt) newCost : _) =
                      span (isUseless . unCCosted) tagged
  (++) (CCosted (Useful startPt) cost : useless) <$>
                                     everyPt sg newCost newPt
 where costedUtility pt cost =
         utility sg move >>= \u -> return $ CCosted u cost
        where move = Move { older = startPt, younger = pt
                          , youngerCCost = cost }
```

Both `nextPt` and `utility` are monadic, but we can still exploit laziness: from its starting point, `everyPt` produces an infinite list of randomly chosen successor points, then calls `costedUtility` to tag each one with a cumulative cost and a utility. We hope that if you look carefully at how `successors` is computed, you will understand why we separate `pt0` from `nextPt` instead of using a single function that produces an infinite list: We don't *want* the infinite list that would result from applying `nextPt` to many points in succession; we want the infinite list that results from applying `nextPt` to `startPt` many times in succession, each time with a different source of randomness.

Once the successors have been computed and tagged, `span` finds the first useful successor. In case there *is* no successor, `everyPt` also returns all the useless successors. If we do find a useful successor, we start searching anew from that point, with a recursive call to `everyPt`. (Because `everyPt` is monadic, the points accumulated so far are appended to its result using the `<$>` operator.) The most informative part of `everyPt` is last expression of the `do` block, which shows that the result begins with a useful point, is followed by a (possibly infinite, possibly empty) list of useless points, and then continues recursively with another call to `everyPt`.

The rest of the search uses Hughes's classic composition of generator and test function. Because our code is monadic, we use the monadic composition operator =<<, which is the bind operator with its arguments swapped:

```
search :: RandomGen r => SearchGen pt r -> SearchStop pt
       -> Rand r (History pt)
search strat test =
  return . test =<< everyPt strat 0 =<< pt0 strat
```

The `test` function has type `SearchStop pt`:

```
type SearchStop pt =
       [CCosted (Utility (Scored pt))] -> History pt
```

Type `History pt` retains only the useful points. (Internally, MRFy needs only the *final* useful point, but because we want to study how different search algorithms behave, we keep all the useful points.)

The definition of `SearchStop` reveals two forms of non-modularity which are inherent in MRFy's search algorithm. First, we need `Utility`, because if we omit the useless states, search might not terminate. Second, we need `CCosted`, because some of our test functions decide to terminate based either on the cumulative cost of the most recent point or on the difference between costs of successive useful points.

Despite these non-modular aspects, the search interface provides ample scope for experiments. Random hill climbing took 50 lines of code and one day to implement. Simulated annealing required only a new `utility` function, which took 15 lines of code and half an hour to implement. (Hill climbing accepts a point if and only if it scores better than its predecessor; simulated annealing may accept a point that scores worse.) Our genetic algorithm uses very similar functions, except for `nextPt`: recombination of parent placements took forty lines of code and a full day to implement.

We're not entirely happy with the way we're writing all the individual functions. In particular, `SearchStop` functions aren't composable; we can't, for example, combine two functions to say that we'd like to stop if scores aren't improving or if we've tried a thousand points, whichever comes first. Eventually, we'd like to have combinator libraries for `SearchStop` and `nextPt`, at least.

3.3 Performance

At each point in its search, MRFy calls `vee'` several times. Our `vee'` function computes a `Scored [StateLabel]`, that is, an optimal path and its score. But at intermediate points in MRFy's search, MRFy uses only the score. Even though Haskell evaluation is lazy, `vee'` still allocates thunks that could compute paths. To measure the relevant overhead, we cloned `vee'` and modified it to compute only a score, with no path. This change improved run time by nearly 50%.

Could we keep the improvement without maintaining two versions of `vee'`? In Lisp or Ruby we would have used macros or metaprogramming, but we were not confident of our ability to use Template Haskell. Instead, we used higher-order functions. As shown in Section 3.1, `vee'` does not use primitive `(:)` but instead uses an unknown function `cons`, which is passed in. To get a path, we pass in primitive `(:)`; to get just a score, we pass in `\_ _ -> []`. This trick is simple and easy to implement, and it provides the same speedup as the cloned and modified code. But we worry that it may work only because of undocumented properties of GHC's inliner, which may change.

Even with this trick, MRFy's implementation of Viterbi's algorithm is much slower than the C++ version in MRFy's predecessor, SMURF. For example, on a microbenchmark that searches for a structural motif of 343 nodes in a protein of 2000 amino acids using only Viterbi's algorithm and no beta-strand information, MRFy takes 2.32 seconds and SMURF takes 0.29 seconds.

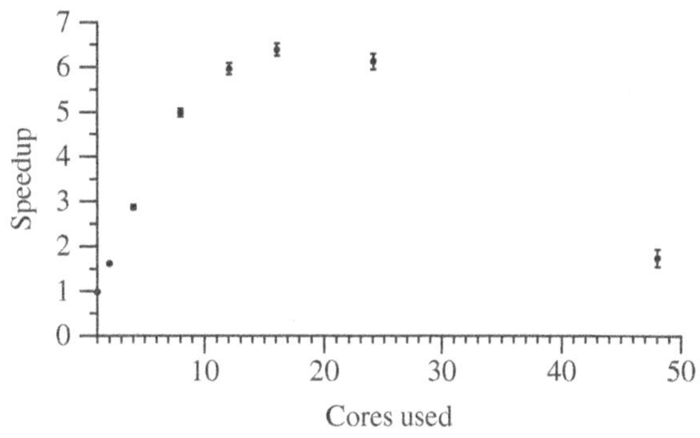

Figure 5. MRFy's parallel speedup on an 8-bladed beta propeller

But MRFy's job is not to run Viterbi's algorithm on large models; MRFy's job is to detect homologies to structures for which both Viterbi's algorithm and SMURF's more complex algorithm are unsuited. MRFy can solve problems that SMURF cannot. For example, we tried both programs on a complex, 12-stranded "beta sandwich" model. The model contains 252 nodes, 97 of which appear in the 12 beta strands. MRFy computes an alignment in under a minute, but SMURF allocates over 16GB of memory and does not terminate even after eight hours.

We also benchmarked MRFy using a model of an "8-bladed beta propeller." The model has 343 nodes, of which 178 appear in 40 beta strands. The segments between beta strands typically have at most 10 nodes. We used a query sequence of 592 amino acids, but each placement breaks the sequence into 41 pieces, each of which typically has at most 20 amino acids. Because MRFy can solve the models between the beta strands independently, this benchmark has a lot of parallelism, which Haskell made it easy to exploit. Using `Control.Parallel`, parallelizing the computation was as easy as substituting `parmap rseq` for `map`. Figure 5 shows speedups when using from 1 to 48 of the cores on a 48-core, 2.3GHz AMD Opteron 6176 system. Errors are estimated from 5 runs. After about 12 cores, where MRFy runs 6 times as fast as sequential code, speedup rolls off. By running 4 instances of MRFy in parallel on different searches, we hope to be able to use all 48 cores with about 50% efficiency.

3.4 Awkward debugging and testing

Our experience writing code and trying new ideas was excellent, as was the ease of parallelizing MRFy. Higher-order functions, memoization, laziness, and parallel strategies really worked. But we also encountered obstacles that prevented functional programming from working as well as we would have liked. The most significant obstacles were in debugging and testing.

We had a hard time diagnosing run-time errors. We expected some run-time errors; our group's legacy file format is poorly documented and hard to deal with. (When beta strands overlap and are doubly paired, even the invariants of the format are unclear.) But using Haskell, we found the errors hard to diagnose. Calls to `trace` littered our code, even when relegated to wrapper functions. We didn't know about the backtrace feature of GHC's profiler, and even after we learned about it, it didn't help: the profiler can be used only on very small test cases, which didn't always trigger the errors. This same limitation affected GHCi's debugger; in GHCi, our `vee'` function is too slow to be runnable on nontrivial inputs. Moreover, GHCi's debugger can set breakpoints only at top-level functions or at specific column/line positions, which made debugging the memoized `vee''` function impractical. In August 2011, Lennart Augustsson said that the biggest advantage of Strict Haskell is getting a stack trace on error, and Simon Marlow said that he may have figured out how to track call stacks properly in a lazy functional language. We can't wait.

Our difficulties with debugging led to internal disagreements. The junior members of our team wanted to apply the debugging skills they had honed through years of imperative programming. But these skills did not transfer well to Haskell. The senior member of the team kept repeating that a proper approach to debugging Haskell code should involve QuickCheck. But mere exhortation was unhelpful.

Only the senior member of our team was able to use QuickCheck easily. In retrospect, we have identified some obstacles that prevented the junior people from using QuickCheck.

- The examples and tutorials we found focused predominantly on writing and testing properties using data types that already implemented class `Arbitrary`. We didn't understand the `Arbitrary` class very well, perhaps because the overloaded `arbitrary` value is not a function. (For programmers accustomed to object-oriented dispatch on *arguments*, it is hard to grasp how Haskell's type-class system can find the proper version of `arbitrary` using only the type of a *value*.)
- Our difficulties were compounded by a weak understanding of monads. We were too baffled by QuickCheck's `Gen` monad to grasp its importance.
- We continually overlooked the critical role of *shrinking*. As a result, on the one or two occasions we did use QuickCheck, the counterexamples were too large to be informative.

Because of these obstacles, we wrote thousands of lines of code without ever defining an instance of `Arbitrary` and therefore without looking hard at QuickCheck. After the fact, we were overwhelmed by the work involved in writing and testing instances of `Arbitrary`. The work got done only when the whole team pitched in to meet the deadlines for this paper.

At the last minute, QuickCheck did find a bug in our implementation of Viterbi's algorithm: we had omitted the score for the transition from the final node of the hidden Markov model to the special "end" state. Without QuickCheck, we probably wouldn't have known anything was wrong.

4. Our previous experience compared

Our Haskell code for hidden Markov models and Viterbi's algorithm solves the same problems as existing C++ code. Other researchers using Haskell may also have to reimplement code, but in computational biology, reimplementing existing algorithms is unremarkable. For example, both SMURF and HMMER also contain new implementations of hidden Markov models and Viterbi's algorithm.

When performance has mattered, members of our group, like other computational biologists, have used C++. To compare our Haskell experience with our C++ experience, we discuss three tools:

- Matt (Menke et al. 2008) is used to create alignments like that shown in Figure 1. It comprises about 12,000 lines of C++. The only external tools or libraries it uses are `zlib` and `OpenMP`, and its initial development took two years.
- SMURF (Menke et al. 2010) is used to detect homologous proteins in the presence of paired beta strands. It comprises about 9,000 lines of C++, of which about 1,000 lines are shared with Matt. It uses no external tools or libraries, and its initial development took a year and a half. It uses multidimensional dynamic programming to exactly compute the alignments for which MRFy relies on stochastic search. As a result, in the presence of complex beta-strand topologies, SMURF is computationally intractable.
- MRFy is used to detect homologous proteins in the presence of paired beta strands; it effectively supplants SMURF. It comprises about 2,500 lines of Haskell, about 500 of which are devoted to tests, QuickCheck properties, and generators. Neither Matt nor SMURF includes test code. MRFy uses several external tools and libraries, of which the most notable are Parsec, the BioHaskell bioinformatics library, and the libraries `Data.MemoCombinators`, `Control.Parallel`, and `Data.Vector`. MRFy's initial development took about three months.

Like much research software, all three tools were written in haste. We have experience modifying the older tools.

We modified Matt to use information about sequences as well as structure. The modification added 2,000 lines of code, and it calls external sequence aligners that we did not write. We thought the modification would take three months, but it took most of a year. Matt uses such data structures as mutable oct-trees, vectors, and arrays. It uses clever pointer arithmetic. The mutable data structures were difficult to repurpose, and the pointer arithmetic was *too* clever: nearly every change resulted in new segfaults.

We had hoped to extend Matt further, with support for partial alignments, which we expected to require only a cosmetic manipulation of the output. But this feature wound up requiring deep information about Matt's data structures, and we had to give up. We believe we could write an equivalent tool in Haskell, with most of Matt's performance, in at most nine months.

Our most painful experience was adding "simulated evolution" to SMURF (Daniels et al. 2012). Although simulated evolution represents a relatively minor enhancement, just understanding the existing code took several months.

We built MRFy quickly, and we expect that higher-order functions will make MRFy easy to extend. Each new addition to MRFy's stochastic search has taken at most a day to implement.

Haskell encourages hasty programmers to slow down. We have to get the types right, which makes it hard to write very large functions. To get the code to typecheck, we have to write type signatures, which also serve as documentation. And once the types are accepted by the compiler, it is not much more work to write contracts for important functions. MRFy is still hasty work. Many types could be simplified; we're sure we've missed opportunities for abstraction; and we know that MRFy's decomposition into modules could be improved. But despite being hasty programmers, we produced code that is easy to understand and easy to extend. Our hastily written Haskell beats our hastily written Ruby and C++.

Looking beyond our research group to computational biology more broadly, our experience with other software is better. Little of it is written in functional languages, but much of the software shared by the community is excellent. MRFy's training component was derived from that of HMMER, and working with the HMMER codebase was pleasant; data structures and their mutators are well documented. There is a BioHaskell library, part of which we use, but it is not nearly as complete as BioPython or BioRuby, which are heavily used in the community. We hope that tools for computational biology in Haskell continue to mature.

5. What can you learn from our experience?

If you are a computational biologist and you are interested in functional programming, you don't need extensive preparation to be productive in Haskell. Two of us (Daniels and Gallant) are graduate students. Daniels has taken a seminar in functional programming, which included some Haskell; Gallant has taken a programming-languages course which included significant functional programming but no Haskell. Ramsey is a professor who has used Haskell for medium-sized projects, but his contributions to MRFy have been limited, mostly to *post hoc* refactoring and testing.

5.1 Obstacles to be overcome

We had quite some difficulty profiling, but we hope that this difficulty may be mitigated by new profiling tools released early in 2012 with GHC 7.4. GHC assigns costs to "cost centers" (Sansom and Peyton Jones 1997), and in GHC 7.0, which we used for most of MRFy's development, cost-center annotations had to be added manually to nested functions. Although these annotations made our code so ugly that we felt compelled to remove them, they did enable us to improve the performance of `vee'` as discussed in Section 3.3. GHC 7.4 provides more sophisticated profiling tools, which we look forward to using. Difficulties using Cabal to enable profiling of installed libraries may remain.

Like other functional programmers, we have found that once we have our types right, our code is often right. But MRFy computes with arrays and array indices, and in that domain, types don't help much. Bounds violations lead to run-time errors, which we have not been able to identify any systematic way to debug. GHC's profiler can provide stack traces, but we found this information difficult to discover, and as noted above, there are obstacles to profiling. We're aware that debugging lazy functional programs has been a topic of some research, but one of the biggest obstacles we encountered to using Haskell is that we have had to abandon our old approaches to debugging.

Ideally we would use QuickCheck to find bugs, but as we mention in Section 3.4, we found obstacles. We have now overcome these obstacles, but we sorely regret not doing so earlier. In light of our experience, we will institute a new programming practice: whenever we introduce a new data type, we will write the instance of `Arbitrary` right away, while relevant invariants are still fresh in memory. When invariants are not enforced by Haskell's static type system, we will write them as Haskell predicates. We can then immediately run QuickCheck on each predicate, to verify that our Arbitrary instance agrees with the predicate. For each predicate `p` we can also check `fmap (all p . shrink) arbitrary`.

5.2 Information that will help you succeed

If you want to use Haskell in your research, we believe that you must have enough experience with functional programming that you can build *all* the code you need, not only the code that is easy to write in a functional language. Implementing Viterbi's equations in Haskell was pure joy. Writing an iterative search in purely functional style was easy. Transforming data in the HMMER file format, *without* using mutable state the way the C++ code does, was difficult.

While the Haskell community offers many enticing tools, libraries, and packages, not all of them are worth using. Some are not ready for prime time, and some were once great but are no longer maintained. The great packages, like `Data.MemoCombinators` and Parallel Strategies, are truly great. But for amateurs, it's not always easy to tell the great packages from the wannabes and the has-beens. And even some of the great packages could be better documented, with more examples.

As in any endeavor, access to experts helps. We would have been better off if our in-house expert had been an enthusiastic student and not a busy professor. But we have been surprised and pleased by the help available from faraway experts on Stack Overflow and on Haskell mailing lists. Although a local expert makes things easier, one is not absolutely necessary.

6. Conclusion

A little knowledge of and a lot of love for functional programming enabled us to carry out a successful research project in a language that computational biologists seldom use. If you *want* to use Haskell—or one of your graduate students wants to use Haskell—you can succeed.

Acknowledgments

Anonymous referees spurred us to think more deeply about laziness and to write more carefully about performance. Josef Svenningsson suggested a correspondence between MRFy's search and stream fusion, which led us eventually to the `Utility` type. Koen Claessen instantly diagnosed an inappropriately strict implementation of the `Rand` monad. We also thank Lenore Cowen, Kathleen Fisher, Ben Hescott, Brad Larsen, and Nathan Ricci.

This work was funded in part by NIH grant 1R01GM080330.

References

Lenore Cowen, Philip Bradley, Matt Menke, Jonathan King, and Bonnie Berger. Predicting the beta-helix fold from protein sequence data. *Journal of Computational Biology*, 2002.

Noah Daniels, Raghavendra Hosur, Bonnie Berger, and Lenore Cowen. SMURFLite: combining simplified Markov random fields with simulated evolution improves remote homology detection for beta-structural proteins into the twilight zone. *Bioinformatics*, March 2012.

Rirchard Durbin, Sean Eddy, Anders Krogh, and Graeme Mitchison. *Biological Sequence Analysis: Probabilistic Models of Proteins and Nucleic Acids*. Cambridge University Press, May 1998.

Sean Eddy. Profile hidden Markov models. *Bioinformatics*, 14: 755–763, 1998.

John Hughes. Why functional programming matters. *The Computer Journal*, 32(2):98–107, April 1989.

Matthew Menke, Bonnie Berger, and Lenore Cowen. Matt: local flexibility aids protein multiple structure alignment. *PLoS Computational Biology*, 2008.

Matthew Menke, Bonnie Berger, and Lenore Cowen. Markov random fields reveal an N-terminal double beta-propeller motif as part of a bacterial hybrid two-component sensor system. *Proceedings of the National Academy of Science*, 2010.

Patrick Sansom and Simon L Peyton Jones. Formally based profiling for higher-order functional languages. *ACM TOPLAS*, 19 (2):334–385, 1997.

Andrew Viterbi. Error bounds for convolutional codes and an asymptotically optimum decoding algorithm. *IEEE Transactions on Information Theory*, 13(2):260–269, April 1967.

You can live to surf the Haskell wave,
but if you slide off the crest, you drown.

A Meta-Scheduler for the Par-Monad

Composable Scheduling for the Heterogeneous Cloud

Adam Foltzer Abhishek Kulkarni Rebecca Swords
Sajith Sasidharan Eric Jiang Ryan R. Newton
Indiana University
{afoltzer, adkulkar, raingram, sasasidh, erjiang, rrnewton} @indiana.edu

Abstract

Modern parallel computing hardware demands increasingly specialized attention to the details of scheduling and load balancing across heterogeneous execution resources that may include GPU and cloud environments, in addition to traditional CPUs. Many existing solutions address the challenges of particular resources, but do so in isolation, and in general do not compose within larger systems. We propose a general, composable abstraction for execution resources, along with a continuation-based meta-scheduler that harnesses those resources in the context of a deterministic parallel programming library for Haskell. We demonstrate performance benefits of combined CPU/GPU scheduling over either alone, and of combined multithreaded/distributed scheduling over existing distributed programming approaches for Haskell.

Categories and Subject Descriptors D.3.2 [*Concurrent, Distributed, and Parallel Languages*]

General Terms Design, Languages, Performance

Keywords Work-stealing, Composability, Haskell, GPU

1. Introduction

Ideally, we seek parallel code that not only performs well, but for that performance to be *preserved under composition*. Alas, this is not always the case even in serial code: implementations of functions f and g may be well-optimized individually, but if $f \circ g$ is run inside a recursive loop, the composition may, for example, exceed the machine's instruction cache. Nevertheless, sequential composition is far easier to reason about than *parallel composition*, which is the topic of this paper.

Historically, there have been many reasons for parallel codes not to compose. First, many parallel programming models are *flat* rather than nested—i.e. a parallel computation may not contain another parallel computation [9, 28]. Moreover, many parallel codes take direct control of hardware or operating system resources, for example by using Pthreads directly. These programs, when composed, result in *oversubscription*, as has famously troubled OpenMP[1] [3].

Yet the rising popularity of work-stealing schedulers (Section 3) is a step forward for composability, at least on symmetric multiprocessors (SMPs). By abstracting away explicit thread management these schedulers enable mutually ignorant parallel subprograms to coexist peacefully without oversubscription, and are now available for a wide range of different languages, including Haskell [26], C++ [2, 19, 32], Java [18], and Manticore [15], as well as many others. New problems arise, however, namely:

1. Multiple schedulers for the same language are difficult to coordinate effectively and in a principled manner (e.g. TBB / Cilk / TPL [2, 19, 32], or even Haskell's sparks [26] and IO threads).
2. Non-CPU resources such as GPUs are competing for attention, and are not treated by existing schedulers.
3. Parallel work schedulers are themselves complex software artifacts (Section 3), typically non-modular [1], and difficult to extend.

The approach we take in this paper is to factor an existing work-stealing implementation into composable pieces. This addresses the complexity problem, but also leads the way to extensibility and interoperability—even beyond the CPU.

We describe a new system, Meta-Par[2], which is an extensible implementation of the Par-monad library for Haskell [25]. The `Par` monad (Section 2) provides only basic parallel operations: *forking* control flow and communication through write-once synchronization variables called *IVars*. The extension mechanism we propose allows new variants of `fork` (e.g. to fork a computation on the GPU), but remains consistent with the semantics of the original `Par` monad, in particular retaining deterministic parallelism.

We present a set of these extensions, which we call *Resources*, that address challenges posed by current hardware: (1) dealing with larger and larger multi-socket (NUMA) SMPs, (2) programming GPUs, and (3) running on clusters of machines. Further, we observe that from the perspective of a CPU scheduler, these Resources have much in common; for example, handling asynchronous completion of work on a GPU or on another machine across the network presents largely the same problem. We argue that Resources provide a useful abstraction boundary for scheduler components, and show that they compose into more sophisticated schedulers using a simple associative binary operator.

Using a composed scheduler, a single program written for Meta-Par today can handle a variety of hardware that it might encounter

ICFP'12, September 9–15, 2012, Copenhagen, Denmark.

[1] OpenMP: A popular set of parallel extensions to the C language widely used in the high-performance computing community.

[2] `http://hackage.haskell.org/package/meta-par`

in the wild: for example, an ad-hoc collection of machines some of which have GPUs while others do not. Hence the *heterogeneous cloud*: mixed architectures within and between nodes.

The primary contributions of this paper are:

- A novel design for composable scheduler components (Section 4).
- A demonstration of how to cast certain aspects of scheduler design—aspects which go beyond multiplexing sources of work—using Resources. One example is adding *backoff* to a scheduler loop to prevent excessive busy-waiting (Section 4.4).
- An empirical evaluation of the Meta-Par scheduler(s), which includes evaluation of a number of recent pieces of common infrastructure in the Haskell ecosystem (network transports, CUDA libraries, and the like), as well as an in-depth case study of parallel comparison-based sorting implementations (Section 6.2).
- The first, to our knowledge, unified CPU/GPU work-stealing scheduler[3] (Section 4.5), along with an empirical demonstration that GPU-aware CPU-scheduling can outperform GPU-oblivious (Section 6.3). With further validation, this principle may generalize beyond our implementation and beyond Haskell.

These results are preliminary, but encouraging. Meta-Par can provide a foundation for future work applying functional programming to the heterogeneous hardware wilderness. The reader is encouraged to try the library, which is hosted on github and released via Haskell's community package manager, Hackage: here, here, and here.

2. The Par Monad(s)

Earlier work [25] introduced a Par monad with the following operations:

```
runPar :: Par a → a
fork   :: Par () → Par ()
new    :: Par (IVar a)
get    :: IVar a → Par a
put_   :: IVar a → a → Par ()
```

A series of fork calls creates a **binary tree of threads**. We will call these *Par-threads*, to contrast them with Haskell's IO threads (i.e. user-level threads) and OS threads. Par threads do not return values—hence the unit type in Par ()—instead they communicate only through IVars. IVars are first class, and an IVar can be read or written anywhere within the tree of Par-threads (albeit written only once).

By blocking to read an IVar, Par-threads can indeed be descheduled and resumed, thereby earning the moniker "thread". Abstractly, IVars introduce synchronization constraints that transform the *tree* describing the structure of the parallel computation into a directed acyclic graph (DAG), as in Figure 1. DAGs are the standard abstraction for parallel computations used in most literature on scheduling [5, 7, 8, 35].

The simple primitives supported by Par can be used to build up combinators capturing common parallelism patterns, and one extremely simple and useful combinator is spawn_, which provides *futures*:

```
spawn_ :: Par a → Par (IVar a)
spawn_ p = do i ← new
              fork (do x ← p; put_ i x)
              return i
```

[3] Though the idea has been discussed [17].

The original paper [25] has many more examples, and explains aspects of the design which we do not cover here, such as the distinction between put_ and put (weak-head-normal-form strictness vs. full strictness), and the reasoning behind this design.

The spawn_ abstraction is sufficient to define divide-and-conquer parallel algorithms by recursively creating a future for every subproblem (a common idiom). We will use mergesort as a running example of this style. Below we define a mergesort on Vectors, a random-access, immutable array type commonly used in high-performance Haskell code.

```
parSort :: Vector Int → Par (Vector Int)
parSort vec =
  if length vec ≤ seqThreshold
  then return (seqSort vec)
  else let n             = (length vec) `div` 2
           (left, right) = splitAt n vec
       in do leftIVar ← spawn_ (parSort left)
             right'   ←         (parSort right)
             left'    ← get leftIVar
             parMerge left' right'
```

This function splits the vector to be sorted and uses spawn_ on the left half, giving rise to a balanced binary tree of work to be run in parallel. A sequential sort is called once the length of the vector falls below a threshold.

2.1 Meta-Par Preliminary: Generalizing Par

In later sections we introduce variations on fork and spawn_ that correspond to alternate flavors of child computations, such as those that might run on a GPU or over the network. Because a scheduler might have any combination of these capabilities, there are many possible schedulers. Therefore, each scheduler will have a distinct variant of the Par monad (a distinct type), so that a subcomputation that depends on, say, a GPU capability cannot encounter a runtime error because it is combined with a scheduler lacking the capability.

Thus we need to take a refactoring step that is common in Haskell library engineering[4]—introduce type classes to generalize over a collection of types that provide the same operations, in this case, multiple Par monads.

```
class Monad m ⇒ ParFuture future m
              | m → future where
  spawn_ :: m a → m (future a)
  get    :: future a → m a

class ParFuture ivar m ⇒ ParIVar ivar m
                        | m → ivar where
  fork :: m () → m ()
  new  :: m (ivar a)
  put_ :: ivar a → a → m ()
```

In the above classes we take an opportunity to separate levels of Par functionality. A given Par implementation may support *just futures*[5] (ParFuture class), or may support futures *and* IVars (ParIVar class). The distinction in levels of capability will become more important as we introduce capabilities such as gpuSpawn and longSpawn (and classes ParGPU, ParDist) in Sections 4.5 and 4.5.2.

In the above class definitions, the type variable 'm' represents the type of a specific Par monad that satisfies the interface (i.e. an *instance*). Some of the complexity above is specific to Haskell and may safely be ignored for the reader of this paper. Namely,

[4] A common example being the PrimMonad type class generalizing over IO and ST—true external side effects and localized, dischargeable ones.

[5] Indeed, we have a scheduler that uses *sparks* [26] and supports only futures. This allows us to compare the efficiency of our scheduling primitives to those built in to the GHC runtime, using the former if desired.

the **ParFuture** and **ParIVar** classes are *multi-parameter* type classes, both parameterized by a type variable **ivar** as well as **m**. This is necessary because two **Par** monads may require different representations for their synchronization variables. Finally, because the type for **ivar** is determined by the choice of **Par** monad, the above includes another advanced feature of GHC type classes: a *functional dependency*, `m` $\rightarrow$ `ivar`. We do not simplify these classes for the purpose of presentation, because they correspond exactly to those used in the released code.

The writer of a reusable library should always use the generic functions, and never commit to a concrete `Par` monad. The final application is then free to decide which concrete implementation—and therefore which heterogeneous execution capabilities—to use. For the remainder of the paper, let us assume that all `Par` implementations reside in their own distinct modules, `Control.Monad.Par.Foo`), each providing a *concrete* type constructor named `Par`, as well as instances for the appropriate generic operations. These are the *schedulers* (plural) in our system, whereas Meta-Par itself is a *meta-scheduler*—not touched directly by users, but instantiated to create concrete schedulers. For readability, we will informally write concrete type signatures, **Par a**, (referring to any valid concrete `Par` monad) rather than the more generic **ParFuture iv p => p a**.

3. Work-Stealing Schedulers

In work-stealing schedulers, each worker maintains a private work pool, synchronizing with other workers *only* when local work is exhausted (the *parsimony* property [34]). Thus the burden of synchronizing and load-balancing falls on idle nodes. Like any parallel scheduler, work-stealing schedulers map work items (e.g. forked Par-threads) onto P *workers*; workers are most often OS threads with a one-to-one correspondence to processor cores.

As a work-stealing algorithm, the original implementation of the `Par` monad [25] is rather standard and even simple. Yet schedulers that "grow up"—for example TBB, Cilk, or the GHC runtime—become very complex, dealing with concerns such as the following:

- Idling behavior to prevent wasted CPU cycles in tight work-stealing loops ("busy waiting").
- Managing contention of shared data structures (backoff, etc.).
- Interacting with unpredictable user programs that can call into the scheduler (e.g. call `runPar`) from different hardware threads or in a nested manner.
- Multiplexing multiple sources of work.

Alas, in spite of this complexity, such schedulers typically have monolithic, non-modular implementations [1, 19, 32]. Regarding work-source multiplexing in particular: a typical work-stealing scheduler is described in pseudocode as an ordered series of checks against possible sources of work. For example, in the widely-used Threading Building Blocks (TBB) package, the reference manual [4], Section 12.1, includes the following description of the task-scheduling algorithm:

```
After completing a task t, a thread chooses its next
task according to the first applicable rule below:
  1. The task returned by t.execute()
  2. The successor of t if t was its last completed
     predecessor.
  3. A task popped from the end of the thread's own
     deque.
  4. A task with affinity for the thread.
  5. A task popped from approximately the beginning
     of the shared queue.
  6. A task popped from the beginning of another
     randomly chosen thread's deque.
```

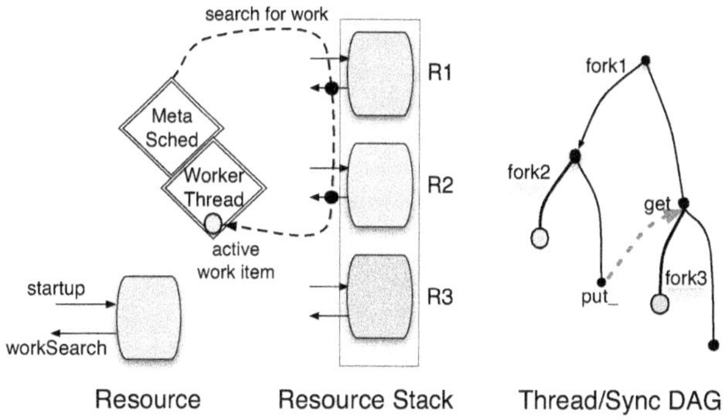

Figure 1. [Left] Meta-scheduling: scan a stack of work sources, always starting at the top. Work sources are heterogeneous, but all work is retrieved as unit computations in the **Par** monad (i.e. **Par ()**). [Right] Work DAGs formed by **forks** and **gets**; the circles at the leaves represent tasks bound for the resource with matching color.

Six possible sources of work! And that is only for CPU scheduling. Rather than *committing* to a list like the above and hardcoding it into the scheduler (the state of the art today), we construct schedulers that are composed of reusable components. For example, a rough description of a distributed CPU/GPU scheduler may look like the following:

1. Steal from CPU-local deque (try N times) *else*
2. Steal-*back* from GPU *else*
3. Steal from network *else*
4. Goto step 1

This resembles a *stack* of resources. In fact, the purpose of this paper is to demonstrate that scheduler composition *need only be a simple associative binary operator.* The familiar `mappend` operation from Haskell's `Monoid` type class then suffices to combine Resources into compound [stacks of] Resources.

4. Meta-Scheduling: The Resource Stack

The scheduler for Meta-Par is parameterized by *a stack of heterogeneous execution resources*, each of which may serve as a source of work. All workers participating in a Meta-Par execution (on all threads and all machines) run a scheduling loop that interacts with the resource stack. Resource stacks are built using `mappend`, where (`a 'mappend' b`) is a stack with `a` on *top* and `b` on the *bottom*. Below, the type `Resource` is used for both singular and composed Resources. We will use "resource stack" informally to refer to complete, composed Resources.

The division of labor in our design is between *schedulers*, *Resources*, and the Meta-Par infrastructure (meta-scheduler).

First, the meta-scheduler itself:

- Creates worker threads, each with a work-stealing deque.
- Detects nested invocations of `runPar` and avoids re-initialization of the Resource (i.e. oversubscription)[6].
- Provides concrete `Par` and `IVar` types that all Meta-Par-based schedulers use and repackage.

[6] This ultimately requires global mutable state via the well-known `unsafePerformIO` with `NOINLINE` pragma hack, both in Meta-Par and for some supplementary Resource data structures. See Figure 2

- This Par provides blocking get operations via a continuation monad, using continuations to suspend Par-threads in the style of Haynes, Friedman, and Wand [16].

Further, each Resource may introduce:

- Additional (internal) data structures for storing work, above and beyond the per-worker thread deques. These might contain work for an external device of a different type than `Par ()`.
- One or more *fork*-like operations appropriate to the resource. These push work into the per-resource data structures.

Finally, each scheduler contains:

- A new `Par` type (a `newtype` as described in Section 2.1),
- a corresponding `runPar`, and
- a composed Resource [stack]

Thus a scheduler is a mere mashup of Resources, re-exporting components of Meta-Par and of constituent Resources. In fact, schedulers can be created on demand with a few lines of code[7]. Typically, each scheduler and each Resource reside their own module. An example module implementing a Resource is shown in Figure 2, and an example module implementing a scheduler is shown in Figure 3.

Because each Resource manages its own data structures, Meta-Par is not strictly *just for work-stealing*. For example, a Resource could choose to ignore Meta-Par's `spawn` in favor of its own operator with work-sharing semantics. Indeed, even the built-in work-stealing behavior can be cast as a stand-alone Resource; however we choose to include it in the core of the system in order to keep the Meta-Par interface simpler.

4.1 Resource Internals

A Resource presents an interface composed of two callbacks: a startup callback, and a work-searching callback.

```
type Startup    = Resource → Vector WorkerState → IO ()
type WorkSearch = Int → Vector WorkerState →
                  IO (Maybe (Par ()))

data Resource = Resource {
    startup    :: Startup,
    workSearch :: WorkSearch
  }
```

The `startup` callback is responsible for performing any work necessary to prepare a Resource, such as spawning worker threads for SMP scheduling, or opening network connections for distributed coordination. A global barrier ensures that no work commences until each Resource in the stack has completed initialization. The `Resource` argument to `startup` ties the knot to make the final composed Resource available when initializing any of its component Resources. `WorkerState` structures store each worker's work-stealing deque, along with certain shared information such as the random number generator used for randomized work stealing.

Each worker may have a single *active Par-thread* currently executing. When that Par-thread is finished or blocks on an `IVar`, the worker first tries to pop from the top of its work-stealing deque, and if no work is found, invokes `workSearch`. The arguments to `workSearch` provide the searcher's ID (just an `Int`) along with the global `WorkerState` vector. The former can be used to look up the local `WorkerState` structure in the latter. The worker expects the `workSearch` to respond either with a unit of work (`Just work`), or with `Nothing`.

Resources, combined with `mappend`, form a *non-commutative* monoid so we can compose them using the `Monoid` type class: [8]

```
instance Monoid Startup
instance Monoid WorkSearch
instance Monoid Resource
```

The `Startup` instance is straightforward, where the empty action does nothing, and composing two `startups` means to run them in sequence with the same arguments. The interesting instance is for `WorkSearch`, which must be composed so that the work-finding attempt runs the second `workSearch` only when the first `workSearch` returns `Nothing`.

```
instance Monoid WorkSearch where
  mempty          = λ_ _ → return Nothing
  mappend ws1 ws2 =
      λwid stateVec → do
        mwork ← ws1 wid stateVec
        case mwork of
          Nothing → ws2 wid stateVec
          _ → return mwork
```

In order to satisfy the axioms of a monoid, the empty Resource `mempty` does nothing—no Meta-Par workers are ever spawned by its `Startup`, no work is ever found by its `WorkSearch`, and so no work can be computed if it is the only Resource. Meta-Par leaves it to non-empty implementations of Resources to decide how many and on which CPUs to spawn worker threads. The Meta-Par module itself, absent any Resources, provides very little. It simply exposes primitives for spawning workers (handling exceptions, waiting for the `startup` barrier, logging debugging info) and running entire `Par` computations with a particular Resource configuration:

```
spawnWorkerOnCPU :: Resource → Int → IO ()
runMetaParIO     :: Resource → Par a → IO a
```

Meta-Par commits to a specific concrete `Par` type (`Control.Monad.Par.Meta.Par`) for its internal implementation and for the construction of new Resources and composed schedulers. This `Par` type allows arbitrary computation via a `MonadIO` instance, which would put the Par-monad determinism guarantee at risk if exposed to the end user. Instead, the privileged `Meta.Par` is wrapped by the schedulers in `newtype Par` types that provide only appropriate instances. For example, the "SMP+GPU" scheduler exports a `Par` monad that is an instance of `ParFuture`, `ParIVar`, and `ParGPU`, but *not* an instance of unsafe classes like `MonadIO`, or even classes for other Meta-Par Resources (e.g., `ParDist`) not included in that particular scheduler.

4.2 CPU Scheduling: Single-threaded and SMP

To show that Meta-Par subsumes the previous implementation of Par-monad, we implement Resources for serial execution and SMP. In section 6.1, we compare the performance against previous results.

The single-threaded Resource is the minimal Resource required for the meta scheduler to execute work. Its `startup` creates a single worker on the current CPU, and its `workSearch` always returns `Nothing`, as the Resource has nowhere to look for more work.

---

[7] However, there is one error prone aspect of scheduler composition. The `newtype Par` may use `newtype`-deriving to derive capabilities such as `ParGPU` corresponding to *only* the resources actually composed. A mismatch here could result in a runtime error when a computation is run on an incompatible scheduler. An alternative would be constructing resource stacks explicitly at the type level (like a monad transformer stack), but this comes with significant complications, including our reluctance to introduce *lift* operations.

[8] For clarity, we use `type` here to present `Startup` and `WorkSearch`, but our implementation uses `newtype` to avoid type synonym instances.

```
module Control.Monad.Par.Meta.Resources.GPU where
...
{-# NOINLINE gpuQueue #-}
gpuQueue :: ConcurrentQueue (Par (), IO ())
gpuQueue = unsafePerformIO newConcurrentQueue

{-# NOINLINE resultQueue #-}
resultQueue :: ConcurrentQueue (Par ())
resultQueue = unsafePerformIO newConcurrentQueue

class ParFuture ivar m ⇒ ParGPU ivar m
                       | m → ivar where
  gpuSpawn :: (Arrays a) ⇒ Acc a → m (ivar a)

instance ParGPU IVar Par where
  gpuSpawn :: (Arrays a) ⇒ Acc a → Par (IVar a)
  gpuSpawn comp = do
    iv ← new
    let wrapCPU = put_ iv (AccCPU.run comp)
        wrapGPU = do
          ans ← evaluate (AccGPU.run comp)
          push resultQueue (put_ iv ans)
    liftIO (push gpuQueue (wrapCPU, wrapGPU))
    return iv

gpuProxy :: IO ()
gpuProxy = do
  -- block until work is available
  (_, work) ← pop gpuQueue
  -- run the work and loop
  work >> gpuProxy

mkResource :: Resource
mkResource = Resource {
  startup = λ _ _ → forkOS gpuProxy
  workSearch = λ _ _ → do
    mfinished ← tryPop resultQueue
    case mfinished of
      Just finished → return (Just finished)
      Nothing → do
        mwork ← tryPop gpuQueue
        fst ‘fmap‘ mwork
}
```

Figure 2. An Accelerate-based GPU Resource implementation module.

```
{-# LANGUAGE GeneralizedNewtypeDeriving #-}
module Control.Monad.Par.Meta.SMPGPU (Par, runPar) where
...

resource = SMP.mkResource ‘mappend‘ GPU.mkResource

newtype Par a = Par (Meta.Par a)
  deriving (Monad, ParFuture Meta.IVar,
            ParIVar Meta.IVar, ParGPU Meta.IVar,...)

runPar :: Par a → a
runPar (Par work) = Meta.runMetaPar resource work
```

Figure 3. A scheduler implementation module combining two Resources.

```
singleThreadStartup resource _ = do
  cpu ← currentCPU
  spawnWorkerOnCPU resource cpu

singleThreadSearch _ _ = return Nothing
```

The SMP Resource offers the same capability as the original implementation of the work-stealing Par-monad scheduler. Its `startup` spawns a Meta-Par worker for each CPU available to the Haskell runtime system. Its `workSearch` selects a stealee worker at random and attempts to pop from the stealee's work queue, looping a fixed number of times if the stealee has no work to steal.

```
smpSearch myid stateVec =
  let WorkerState {rng} = stateVec ! myid
      getNext :: IO Int
      getNext = randomRange (0, maxCPU) rng
      loop :: Int → Int → IO (Maybe (Par ()))
      loop 0 _ = return Nothing
      loop n i | i == myid =
        loop (n-1) =<< getNext
      loop n i =
        let WorkerState {workpool} = stateVec ! i
        in do mtask ← tryPopBottom workpool
              case mtask of
                Nothing → loop (n-1) =<< getNext
                _ → return mtask
  in loop maxTries =<< getNext
```

4.3 CPU Scheduling: NUMA

Modern multi-socket, multi-core machines employ a shared memory abstraction, but exhibit Non-Uniform Memory Access (NUMA) costs. This means that it is significantly cheaper to access some memory addresses than others from a given socket, or *NUMA node*. Unfortunately, even if the memory allocation subsystem correctly allocates into node-local memory, work-stealing can disrupt locality by moving work which depends on that memory to a different node. Thus NUMA provides an incentive for work-stealing algorithms to prefer stealing work from cores within the same NUMA node. Although topology-aware schedulers have been proposed [6], most of the widely deployed work-stealing schedulers [2, 18, 19, 32] are oblivious to such topology issues.

In the Meta-Par SMP setting, workers first try to pop work from their own queues before making more costly attempts to steal work from other CPUs. In the NUMA case, we support analogous behavior: a worker first attempts to steal work from CPUs in its own NUMA node, and only moves on to attempt more costly inter-node steals when no local work is available.

Our NUMA-aware Meta-Par implementation notably is a *resource transformer*, rather than a regular Resource, and demonstrates the *first-class* nature of Resources. Instead of duplicating the work-stealing functionality of the SMP Resource, the NUMA Resource is composed of a subordinate SMP Resource for each NUMA node in the machine. Unlike the SMPs in Section 4.2, which may randomly steal from all CPUs, these subordinate SMP `workSearch`es are restricted to steal *only* from CPUs in their respective node. With these subordinate Resources in place, the NUMA `workSearch` first delegates to the SMP `workSearch` of the calling worker's local node. If no work is found locally, it then enters a loop analogous to the SMP loop that calls all nodes' SMP `workSearch`es at random.

4.4 Another Resource Transformer: Adding Backoff

An essential and pervasive aspect of practical schedulers is the ability to detect when little work is available for computation and back off from busy-waiting in the scheduler loop. Detecting a lack of available work may seem like a primitive capability that must be built into the core implementation of the scheduler loop, but we can in fact implement backoff for arbitrary Meta-Par Resource stacks as a Resource transformer.

The backoff `workSearch` does not alter the semantics of the `workSearch` it transforms. Instead, it calls the inner `workSearch`, leaving both the arguments and the return value unchanged. It does, however, observe the number of consecutive times that a `workSearch` call returns `Nothing` for each Meta-Par thread (a counter kept in the `WorkerState` structure). When little work is available across the scheduler, these counts increase, and the backoff Resource responds by calling a thread sleep primitive with a duration that increases exponentially with the count. When a `workSearch` again returns work for a thread, the count is reset, and the scheduling loop resumes without interruption.

4.5 Heterogeneous Resources - Blocking on foreign work

A key motivation for composable scheduling is to handle different mixes of heterogeneous resources outside of the CPU(s). Working with a non-CPU resource requires launching foreign tasks and scheduling around **blocking operations** that wait on foreign results (or arranging to poll for completion). Existing CPU work-stealing schedulers have varying degrees of awareness of blocking operations. Common schedulers for C++ (e.g. Cilk or TBB) are *completely oblivious* to all blocking operations ranging from blocking in-memory data structures (e.g. with locks) to IO system calls. Obliviousness means that while the scheduler attempts to maintain P worker threads for P processors, fewer than P may be active at a given time.

It is often suggested to use Haskell's IO threads directly to implement Par-threads, as there is widespread satisfaction with how *lightweight* they are. This would appear attractive, as the Glasgow Haskell Compiler (GHC) implements blocking operations at the Haskell thread layer (IO threads) using non-blocking system calls via the GHC event manager [30]. IO threads are even appropriately preempted when blocking on in-memory data structures, namely *MVars*. Unfortunately, GHC's IO threads are not lightweight *enough* for fine-grained parallelism. They still require allocating large contiguous stacks and `Par` schedulers based on them cannot compete [25, 29].

Ultimately, the lightest-weight approaches for pausing and resuming computations are based on *continuation passing style* (CPS). The relationship between CPS and coroutines or threading is old and well known [16], but has increasingly been applied for concurrency and parallelism [11, 20, 21, 33, 37]. In the Par-monad, CPS is already a necessity for efficient blocking on IVars (Meta-Par uses the continuation-monad-transformer, `ContT`). Using continuations, we gain the ability to schedule around foreign work—e.g. to keep the CPU occupied while the GPU computes—for free.

4.5.1 Heterogeneous Resource 1: GPU

Several embedded domain-specific languages (EDSLs) have been proposed to enable GPU programming from within Haskell [9, 24, 36]. In addition, raw bindings to the CUDA and OpenCL are available [13, 27]. Accelerate and other EDSLs typically introduce new types (e.g. `Acc`) for GPU computations as well as a `run` function—much like `Par`, in fact.

In Meta-Par, we provide built-in support for launching Accelerate computations from `Par` computations:

```
gpuSpawn :: Arrays a ⇒ Acc a → Par (IVar a)

-- Asynchronous Acc computation, filling IVar when done:
  do gpuSpawn (Acc.fold (+) 0 (Acc.zipWith ...
```

You might well ask why `gpuSpawn` is needed, given that both `runPar` and Accelerate's `run` are *pure* and should therefore be freely composable. Indeed, they are, semantically, but as discussed in the previous section, we do not want CPU threads to remain idle while waiting on GPU computations. Nor can this be delegated to Haskell's foreign function interface itself, which quite reasonably assumes that a foreign call does actual work on the CPU from which it is invoked!

To avoid worker idleness, we follow the approach of Li & Zdancewic [21], making blocking resource calls only on proxy threads which stand in as an abstraction of the blocking resource. Par-monad workers communicate with these proxies via channels; when a worker would otherwise make a blocking call, it instead places the corresponding IO callback in the appropriate channel, and returns a new `IVar` which will be filled only when the operation is complete. (As usual, reading the `IVar` prematurely will save the current continuation and free the worker to execute other `Par` work.) The proxy runs in a loop, popping callbacks from its channel and executing them. It writes the results to a channel read by the Par-monad workers, who call `put` to fill the `IVar`, waking its waiting continuations with the result value.

As shown in Figure 2, the Accelerate Resource's `workSearch` first checks the queue of results returned by the proxy, and if none are found, attempts to steal unexecuted Accelerate work for execution on a CPU backend in case the GPU is saturated.

4.5.2 Heterogeneous Resource 2: Distributed Execution

We expose remote execution through another variant of `spawn`, called `longSpawn`, and follow CloudHaskell's conventions [14] for remote procedure calls and serialization:

```
longSpawn :: Serializable a
          ⇒ Closure (Par a) → Par (IVar a)
```

In the type of `longSpawn`, the `Serializable` constraint and `Closure` type constructor denote that a given unit of `Par` work and its return type can be transported over the network. A `Serializable` value must have a runtime type representation via the `Data.Typeable` class as well as serialization methods, both of which can be generically derived by GHC [22][9].

To employ `longSpawn`, the programmer uses a Template Haskell shorthand, making distributed calls only slightly more verbose than their parallel counterparts:

```
parVer  = spawn_     (bar baz)
distVer = longSpawn ($(mkClosure bar) baz)
```

In our implementation the `Closure` values contain both a local version (a plain closure in memory) and a serializable remote version of the computation. As with other resources in our work-stealing environment, `longSpawn`ed work is not *guaranteed* to happen remotely, it merely exposes that possibility.

One complication is that the above `longSpawn` requires that the user must further *register* `bar` with the remote execution environment[10]:

```
bar :: Int → Par Int
bar x = ...
remotable ['bar]
```

A bigger limitation is that functions like `bar` above are currently restricted to be *monomorphic*, which makes it very difficult to

[9] Generic serialization routines, however, are frequently much slower than routines specialized for a type, so we provide efficient serialization routines for commonly-used types like `Data.Vector`

[10] Specifically, `remotable` is a macro that creates additional top level bindings with mangled names. The `mkClosure` and `mkClosureRec` macros turn an ordinary identifier into its `Closure` equivalent. Remotable functions must be monomorphic, have `Serializable` arguments, return either a pure or a `Par` value, and only have free variables defined at the top level.

define higher-order combinators like *parMap* or *parFold* which are the bread and butter of the original Par-monad library. We share the hope of CloudHaskell's authors that native support from the GHC compiler will improve this situation, and, if other volunteers are not forthcoming, plan to implement such native support ourselves in the future.

Returning to our running example, a parallel merge sort could be augmented with *both* distributed and GPU execution with the following two-line changes (assuming that `gpuSort` is a separate sorting procedure in the Accelerate EDSL):

```
parSort :: Vector Int → Par (Vector Int)
parSort vec =
  if length vec ≤ gpuThreshold
  then gpuSpawn (gpuSort vec) >>= get
  else let n      = (length vec) ‘div‘ 2
           (l, r) = splitAt n vec
       in do lf ← longSpawn ($(mkClosureRec 'parSort) l)
             r' ←             parSort r
             l' ← get lf
             parMerge l' r'
```

It may appear as though work never reaches the CPU. Recall, however, that `gpuSort` is effectively a *hint*; the work may end up on either the GPU or CPU. Ultimately, it will be possible for a `gpuSort` based on Accelerate to default to an efficient (e.g. OpenCL) implementation when the computation ends up on the CPU[11].

5. Semantics

The operational semantics of `Par` [25] remain nearly unchanged by Meta-Par. The amended rules appear in Appendix A. The only minor extension is that there is more than one $fork$ (e.g. $fork_1, fork_2, ...$) in the grammar, corresponding to the resources R_1, R_2, ... Fortunately, this changes nothing important. The semantics do not need to model the Meta-Par scheduling algorithm (or any other `Par` scheduling algorithm). Rather, execution proceeds inside a parallel evaluation structure in which any valid redex can be reduced at any time. Because these loose semantics are sufficient to guarantee both determinism and deadlock/livelock freedom it is therefore safe for Meta-Par to use an *arbitrary* strategy for selecting between work-sources.

Semantics of Scheduler Composition

To ensure correctness, at minimum we need a single guarantee from Resources: they must be *lossless*—everything pushed by a `fork` eventually is produced by a `searchWork`. Subsequently the following properties will hold:

- monoid laws: scheduler composition is an associative operation with an identity
- commuting Resources in a stack will preserve correctness but may incur asymptotic differences in performance

These hold for any scheduler which is a purely monoidal (`mappended`) composition of Resources as in Figure 2.

Like other work-stealing schedulers, Meta-Par is designed for a scenario of finite work; infinite work introduces the possibility of starvation (i.e. because other workers are busy, given piece of work may never execute). Because `runPar` is used to schedule *pure* computation, fairness of scheduling Par-threads is semantically unimportant—there are no observable effects other than the final value. (And the entire `runPar` completes before the value returned is in weak head normal form.)

[11] Unfortunately, at the time of writing the `accelerate` distribution includes only an interpreter for CPU evaluation of `Acc` expressions.

Time and Space Usage

A precise analysis of scheduler time and space usage is desirable, but is confounded both by (1) Meta-Par being parameterized by arbitrary Resources and (2) by intrinsic difficulty with the powerful class of programming models that include user directed synchronizations (i.e. reading `IVars`) [5, 7, 34].

Nevertheless, while Meta-Par targets a general model, it can *preserve* good behavior of schedulers when certain conditions are met. For example, consider the class of programs that are *strictly phased*. That is, given a resource stack R_1 `‘mappend‘` R_2 `‘mappend‘` R_3, $fork_2$ computations may call $fork_2$, or $fork_1$, but not $fork_3$. In a strictly phased program, all paths down the binary $fork$-tree proceed monotonically from deeper to shallower Resources (i.e. $fork_3$ to $fork_1$). In general, this represents good practice; in a divide-and-conquer algorithm, the programmer should call `longSpawn` before `spawn`.

In such a scenario, as long as the resources themselves manage work in a LIFO manner (a second requirement) the composed Resource stack behaves the same way *as a single, extended stack*. We conjecture that existing analyses would apply in this scenario [34], but do not treat the topic further here.

6. Evaluation

In this section, we analyze the performance of Meta-Par schedulers in several heterogeneous execution environments. First, we compare the performance of the Meta-Par SMP scheduler to the previously published Par-monad scheduler in both a multicore desktop and many-core server environment. Then, we examine the performance of parallel merge sort on a multicore workstation with a GPU. Finally, we compare Meta-Par with a distributed Resource to other distributed Haskell implementations [14, 23].

6.1 Traditional Par-Monad CPU Benchmarks

Our goal in this section is twofold:

- to compare the Meta-Par scheduler to the previously published scheduler [25], which we will call *Trace* (being based on the lazy trace techniques of [11, 21]), and
- to analyze the extent to which our results are contingent upon GHC versions and runtime system parameters, mainly those affecting garbage collection.

The original work [25] studied a set of benchmarks on a 24-core Intel E7450. The benchmarks are all standard algorithms, so we refer the reader to the abbreviated description in that paper, rather than describing their purpose here. In this section we give results for `blackscholes`, `nbody`, `mandel`, `sumeuler`, and `matmult`, while omitting `queens`, `coins`, and `minimax` (which have fallen into disrepair).

We show our latest scaling numbers in Figure 4. These compare the Meta-Par scheduler against the original Par-monad scheduler which does not suffer the overhead of indirection through Resource stacks. The scaling results in Figure 4 come from our largest server platform: four 8-core Intel Xeon E7-4830 (Westmere) processors running at 2.13GHz. Hyper-Threading was disabled via the machine's BIOS for a total of 32 cores. The total memory was 64GB divided into a NUMA configuration of 16GB per processor. The operating system was the 64-bit version of Red Hat Enterprise Linux Server 6.2. SMP shows better scaling on `blackscholes`, but compromised performance on `MatMult` and `mandel`. Overall, we consider the performance of SMP close enough to Trace.

Clusterbench

As with other garbage collected languages (e.g. Java) there are many runtime system parameters that affect GHC memory management and can have a large effect on performance[12]. These are the relevant runtime system options:

- `-A` size of allocation area (first generation)
- `-H` suggested heap size
- `-qa` affinity: pin Haskell OS threads to physical CPUs
- `-qg` enable parallel garbage collection (GC) for one or more generations
- `-qb` control which, if any, generations use a load-balancing algorithm in their parallel GC

Of course, varying all of these parameters results in a combinatorial explosion. Thus most performance evaluations for Haskell experiment by hand, find what seems like a reasonable compromise, and stick with that configuration.

To increase confidence in our results we wanted a more systematic approach. We decided to exhaustively explore a reasonable range of settings for the above parameters (e.g. `-A` between 256K and 2M), resulting in 360 configurations. But when running each benchmark for 5-9 trials (and varying number of threads and scheduler implementation) each configuration requires between 324 and 1000 individual program runs and takes between 10 minutes and two hours. Thus exploring 360 configurations can take up to thirty days on one machine. To address this problem we created a program we call *clusterbench* that can run either in a dedicated cluster or search among a set of identically configured workstations for idle machines to farm out benchmarking work.

We used a collection of twenty desktop workstations, each with an Intel Core i5-2400 (Westmere) running at 3.10 GHz with 4GB of memory under 64-bit Red Hat Enterprise Linux Workstation 6.2. All of these workstations together were able to complete the 360 benchmark configurations in a few days. The results are summarized in Table 5 and were pleasantly surprising. In spite of some past problems with excessive variance in performance in response to GC parameters (in the GHC 6.12 era [29]), under GHC 7.4.1 we see remarkably little impact relative to our default settings, except insofar as high settings of `-H` compromise performance significantly.

6.2 Case Study: Sorting

We analyzed parallel merge sort performance on our "GPU workstation" platform, which has one quad-core Intel W3530 (Nehalem) running at 2.80GHz with 12GB and an NVIDIA Quadro 5000 GPU under 64-bit Red Hat Enterprise Linux Workstation 6.2.

Our first comparison examines performance of three task-parallel (but not vectorized) CPU-only configurations, Figure 6. Each configuration sorts `Data.Vector.Storable` vectors of 32-bit integers, and uses a parallel Haskell merge sort until falling below a fixed threshold, when one of three routines is called:

- **Haskell**: A sequential Haskell merge sort [12].
- **Cilk**: A *parallel* C merge sort using the Cilk parallel runtime.
- **C**: A sequential C quick sort called through the FFI. This is the same sequential code as the Cilk algorithm employs at the leaves of its parallel computation.

The pure Haskell sort does quite well, considering its limitation that while it is in-place at the sequential leaves (using the `ST` monad), it must copy the arrays during the parallel phase of the algorithm. In general, `ST` and `Par` are effects that do not compose.[13]

[12] See Table 2 in [29].

[13] However, in the future we are interested in exploring mechanisms to guarantee that slices of mutable arrays are passed *linearly* to only one branch of a `fork` or the other, but not both.

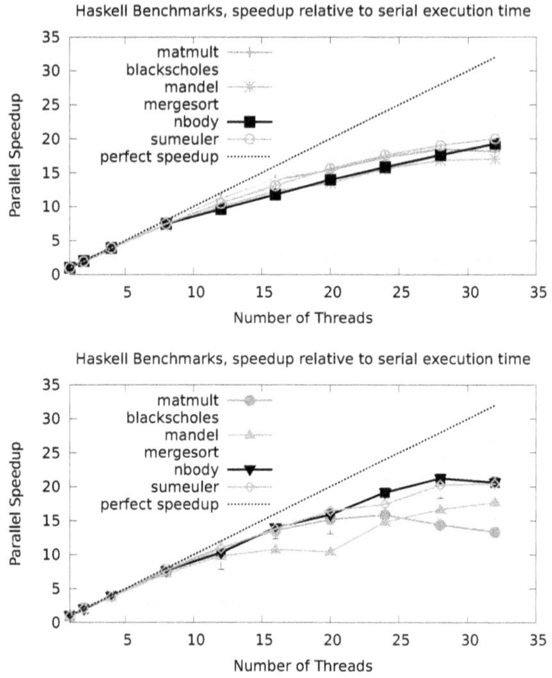

Figure 4. Scaling behavior of original `Par` scheduler (top) vs. Meta-Par SMP scheduler on 32-core server platform. Error bars represent minimum and maximum times over five trials. Mergesort is memory bound beyond four cores. (The pure Cilk version likewise has a maximum speedup less than five.)

threads	1	2	3	4
-	0.00	0.00	0.00	0.00
-qa	-0.05	-0.43	-0.81	-0.97
-qb	0.00	0.00	0.00	0.00
-qb0	-0.16	-0.35	0.14	0.75
-qb1	-0.29	-0.52	-0.21	0.31
-qg	-0.06	-3.34	-7.09	-10.37
-qg0	0.00	0.00	0.00	0.00
-qg1	-0.09	-3.51	-6.96	-9.54
-	0.00	0.00	0.00	0.00
-H128M	5.08	-6.06	-4.91	-5.08
-H256M	6.49	2.22	-3.88	-7.51
-H512M	2.22	-5.85	-9.02	-14.42
-H1G	-8.39	-24.76	-34.51	-42.10
-A256K	-0.07	-0.11	-0.16	-0.17
-A512K	0.00	0.00	0.00	0.00
-A1M	-0.05	-0.08	-0.09	-0.09
-A2M	-0.07	-0.11	-0.14	-0.14

(Speedup/slowdown in percentages.)

Figure 5. Effect of runtime system parameters on performance variation. Each number represents the percentage *faster* or *slower* that the benchmark suite ran given the particular setting of that parameter, and relative to the *default* setting of the parameter (i.e. the 0.00 row). Each percentage represents a geometric mean over all parameter settings *other* than the selected one.

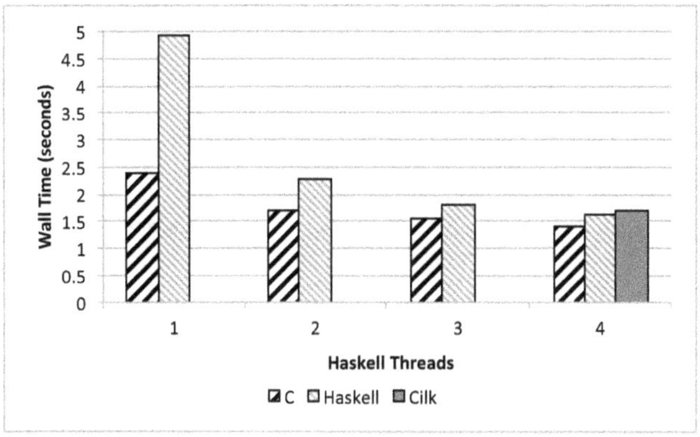

Figure 6. Median elapsed time (over 9 trials) to sort a random permutation of 2^{24} 32-bit integers on the CPU. Parallel phase of the algorithm in Haskell in all cases, below a threshold of 4096 the algorithm switches to either sequential C, sequential Haskell, or Cilk.

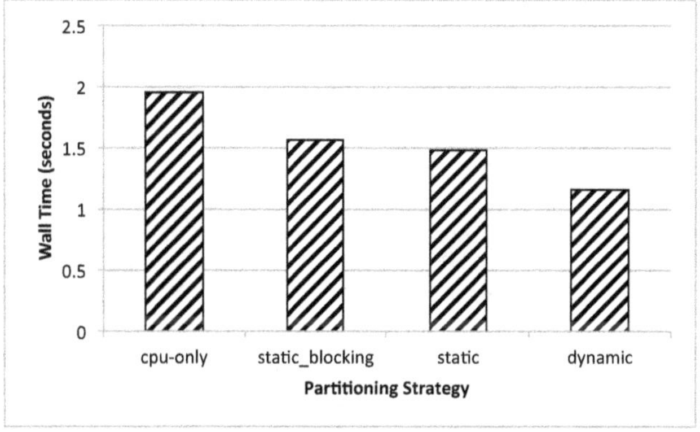

Figure 7. Median elapsed time (over 9 trials) to sort a random permutation of 2^{24} 32-bit integers with 4 threads. For all cases, the CPU threshold was 4096 elements. The GPU threshold was 2^{22} elements for static partitioning, and between 2^{14} and 2^{22} for dynamic partitioning.

We include the parallel Cilk routine for two reasons. First, it provides an objective performance comparison: `cilksort.c` [14]. It is not a *world-class* comparison-based CPU sorting algorithm—that would require a much more sophisticated algorithm including vectorization and a multi-way merge sort at sizes larger than the cache [10] —but it is an extremely good sort, especially for its level of complexity. Second, by calling between Haskell and Cilk, two *unintegrated* schedulers, we explore a concrete example of oversubscription. When running on a 4-core machine, the Cilk runtime dutifully spawns 4 worker threads, oblivious to the 4 Meta-Par workers already contending for CPU resources. The overhead introduced by this contention makes overall performance worse than both pure Haskell and hybrid Haskell/C merge sorts.

6.3 GPU Sorting

Next, to demonstrate the support of Meta-Par for heterogeneous resources, we examine merge sort configurations that add a GPU Resource in addition to the parallel CPU sort of the last section. (We select the version that bottoms out to a sequential C sort routine.)

[14] `http://bit.ly/xrgc8P`

Initially, we selected a sort routine based on Accelerate (and coupled with an Accelerate-supporting Meta-Par Resource). However, due to temporary stability and performance problems[15] we are instead making direct use of the CUDA SDK through the `cuda` package. Using this we call a GPU routine that is an adaptation of the NVIDIA CUDA SDK `mergesort` example that can sort vectors up to length 2^{22}. Since our benchmark input size of 2^{24} is larger than this limit, we always use a divide and conquer strategy to allow subproblems to be computed by the GPU.

We examine three strategies for distributing the work between the CPU and GPU:

- **static_blocking**: Static partitioning of work (50% CPU, 50% GPU) where GPU calls block a Meta-Par worker. This work division was selected based on the fact that our 4-core Cilk (CPU) and CUDA (GPU) sorts perform at very nearly the same level.
- **static**: Static partitioning of work (50% CPU, 50% GPU) with non-blocking GPU calls as described in section 4.5.
- **dynamic**: Dynamic partitioning of work with CPU-GPU work stealing.

In all cases, adding GPU computation improves performance over CPU-only computation. Performance improves further by adding non-blocking GPU calls. The dynamic strategy, representative of the Accelerate Resource implementation described in section 4.5, pairs each spawn of a GPU computation with a CPU version of that same computation, allowing the utilization of both resources to benefit from work stealing. Figure 7 shows that this yields better performance than a priori static partitioning of the work.

6.4 Comparison against other Distributed Haskells

Meta-Par offers Resources for execution on distributed memory architectures. We have prototyped Resources based on different communication backends: (1) `haskell-mpi`, Haskell bindings for the Message Passing Interface (MPI), and (2) `network-transport`, an abstract transport layer for communication that itself has multiple backends (e.g. TCP, linux pipes). All results below are from our `network-transport`/TCP Resource. This results in lower performance than using MPI, but our MPI runs are currently unstable due to a number of bugs.

We evaluated the distributed performance on a cluster of 128 nodes, each with two dual-core AMD Opteron 270 processors running at 2GHz and 4GB of memory. The nodes were connected by a 10GB/s Infiniband network and Gigabit Ethernet. Figure 8 shows a comparison between HdpH [23] and Meta-Par for the `sumeuler` benchmark which involved computing the sum of Euler's totient function between 1 and 65536 by dividing up the work in 512 chunks. The tests were run up to 32 nodes since significant speedup was not observed beyond that for the above workload. The HdpH tests were run with 1 core per node[16], whereas the Meta-Par tests used all 4 cores on the node. Both tests measured the overall execution time including the time required for startup and shutdown of the distributed instances.

As seen in Figure 8, Meta-Par performed nearly 4 times better than HdpH in this test, but HdpH continued scaling to a larger num-

[15] We are working with the Accelerate authors to resolve these issues.

[16] In the original HdpH paper [23] the authors report not seeing further increases in performance when attempting multi-process (rather than multi-threaded) parallelism within each node. Recent versions of HdpH, after the submission of this paper, have added better support for SMP parallelism. But we have not yet evaluated these; our attempt at using HdpH (r0661a3) with multiple threads per node led to a regression involving extremely variable runtimes.

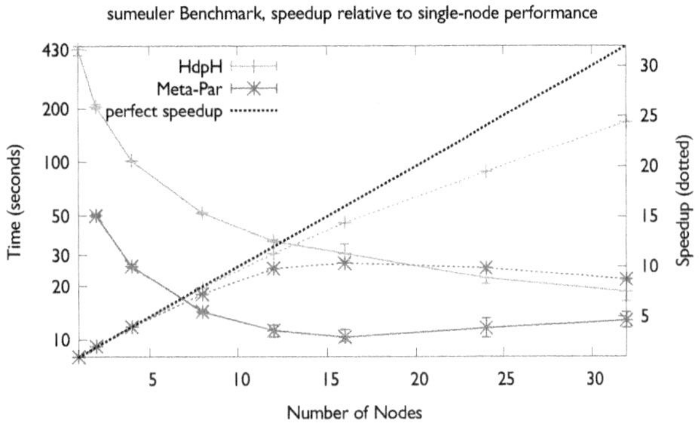

Figure 8. Performance comparison and scaling behavior of Meta-Par (distributed) vs. HdpH.

ber of nodes: 30 rather than 16. The advantage in performance in this case was due entirely to the *composed scheduler*, which mixed fine-grained SMP work-stealing with distributed work-stealing. For our chosen workload, the lower bound in performance was limited by the Meta-Par bootstrap time and the time to process a single chunk sequentially. As a result, no significant speedup was achieved beyond 16 nodes with a best execution time of 9 seconds.

HdpH ran using MPI in this example, and it also uses a more sophisticated system than Meta-Par for global work-stealing in which nodes "prefetch" work when their own work-pools run low, not waiting for them to run completely dry. This helps hide the latency of distributed steals and may contribute to the better scaling seen in Figure 8. There is clearly much work left to be done. Fortunately, HdpH and Meta-Par expose very similar interfaces, and we hope by standardizing on interfaces (type-classes) that it will possible for the community to incrementally develop and optimize a number of (compatible) distributed execution backends for Haskell.

Distributed KMeans

To compare directly against CloudHaskell we ported the KMeans benchmark. We have not yet run this benchmark on our cluster infrastructure, but we have run a small comparison with two workers (on the 3.10 GHz Westmere configuration). Under this configuration CloudHaskell takes 2540.9 seconds to process 600K 100-dimensional points in 4 clusters for 50 iterations. Meta-Par, on the other hand took 175.8 seconds to accomplish the same.

In this case we believe the difference comes from (1) Meta-Par having a more efficient dissemination of the (>1GB) input data, and (2) a high level of messaging overhead in CloudHaskell. In our microbenchmarks, CloudHaskell showed a 10ms latency for sending small messages.

7. Related Work

In the introduction we mentioned the triple problem of scheduler's non-compositionality, complexity, and restriction to CPUs-only. Several systems have attempted to solve one or more of these problems.

For example, the Lithe [31] system addresses the first–the *scheduler* composition problem—by instrumenting a number of different schedulers to support the dynamic addition and subtraction of worker threads. Thereafter *hardware resources themselves* can become first class objects that are passed along in subroutine calls: that is, a subroutine inside one library may receive a certain resource allocation that it may divvy among its own callees. Lithe is focused on composing a-priori unrelated schedulers, whereas Meta-Par focuses on creating an architecture for composable heterogeneity.

In the functional programming context, Manticore [15] also aims at scheduler deconstruction, by providing a set of primitives used to construct many different schedulers. But, like Lithe, Manticore only targets CPU computation. Further, to our knowledge Manticore has not been used to demonstrate advantages of simultaneous use of different scheduling algorithms in the same application (rather than between different applications).

Li, Marlow, Peyton-Jones, and Tolmach's work on lightweight concurrency primitives [20] is a wonderfully clear presentation of an architecture very similar to Meta-Par. The core of their system exposes a spartan set of primitives used by client libraries to implement callbacks, an arrangement much like our Resources. Their work focuses on the lower-level details of implementing Haskell concurrency primitives for CPUs, while Meta-Par extends the higher-level, deterministic Par-monad framework to heterogeneous environments, and it is encouraging to see similar architectures yield good results toward both goals.

CloudHaskell [14] is a library providing Erlang-like functionality for Haskell. CloudHaskell offers a relatively large API in one package (messaging, monitors, serialization, task farming), and in our experiments was high-overhead. We found small messages incurring a 10ms latency on a gigabit Ethernet LAN. For these reasons we ended up basing our own Meta-Par library on lower level communication libraries rather than CloudHaskell.

8. Future Work and Conclusions

While we have achieved some initial results that show strong CPU/GPU and CPU/distributed integration, there remain many areas where we need to improve our infrastructure and apply it to more applications. In the process, we plan to continue to contributing to low-level libraries for high-performance Haskell. (This work has resulted in both `GHC`[17] and `haskell-mpi` bug fixes!) We also will work on Accelerate development until Accelerate CPU/GPU programs can be written and run efficiently in Meta-Par.

We want to ensure that Meta-Par is usable by the community, and ultimately we regard it as a relatively thin layer in an ecosystem of software including GPU and networking drivers, EDSLs, concurrent data structures, and so on. But by integrating disparate capabilities in one framework, Meta-Par opens up interesting possibilities, such as automatically generating code for separate phases of a recursive algorithm (e.g. distributed, parallel, sequential).

[17] Atomic compare-and-swap operations were missing a GC barrier.

References

[1] Code for cilk runtime system. https://github.com/mirrors/gcc/tree/cilkplus/libcilkrts.

[2] Intel Cilk Plus. http://software.intel.com/en-us/articles/intel-cilk-plus/.

[3] Openmp article. http://intel.ly/9h7c7B.

[4] Threading Building Blocks Reference Manual, 2011. http://threadingbuildingblocks.org/documentation.php.

[5] N. S. Arora, R. D. Blumofe, and C. G. Plaxton. Thread scheduling for multiprogrammed multiprocessors. In *Proceedings of the tenth annual ACM symposium on Parallel algorithms and architectures*, SPAA '98, pages 119–129, New York, NY, USA, 1998. ACM.

[6] S. Blagodurov, S. Zhuravlev, A. Fedorova, and A. Kamali. A case for numa-aware contention management on multicore systems. In *Proceedings of the 19th international conference on Parallel architectures and compilation techniques*, PACT '10, pages 557–558, New York, NY, USA, 2010. ACM.

[7] G. Blelloch, P. Gibbons, Y. Matias, and G. Narlikar. Space-efficient scheduling of parallelism with synchronization variables. In *Proceedings of the 9th Annual ACM Symposium on Parallel Algorithms and Architectures*, pages 12–23, Newport, RI, jun 1997.

[8] R. D. Blumofe, C. F. Joerg, B. C. Kuszmaul, C. E. Leiserson, K. H. Randall, and Y. Zhou. Cilk: an efficient multithreaded runtime system. *SIGPLAN Not.*, 30:207–216, August 1995.

[9] M. M. Chakravarty, G. Keller, S. Lee, T. L. McDonell, and V. Grover. Accelerating haskell array codes with multicore gpus. In *Proceedings of the sixth workshop on Declarative aspects of multicore programming*, DAMP '11, pages 3–14, New York, NY, USA, 2011. ACM.

[10] J. Chhugani, A. D. Nguyen, V. W. Lee, W. Macy, M. Hagog, Y.-K. Chen, A. Baransi, S. Kumar, and P. Dubey. Efficient implementation of sorting on multi-core simd cpu architecture. *PVLDB*, 1(2):1313–1324, 2008.

[11] K. Claessen. A poor man's concurrency monad. *J. Funct. Program.*, 9:313–323, May 1999.

[12] D. Doel. The vector-algorithms package. http://hackage.haskell.org/package/vector-algorithms. Efficient algorithms for vector arrays.

[13] M. Dybdal. The hopencl package. http://hackage.haskell.org/package/hopencl. Haskell bindings for OpenCL.

[14] J. Epstein, A. P. Black, and S. Peyton-Jones. Towards haskell in the cloud. In *Proceedings of the 4th ACM symposium on Haskell*, Haskell '11, pages 118–129, New York, NY, USA, 2011. ACM.

[15] M. Fluet, M. Rainey, J. Reppy, A. Shaw, and Y. Xiao. Manticore: a heterogeneous parallel language. In *Proceedings of the 2007 workshop on Declarative aspects of multicore programming*, DAMP '07, pages 37–44, New York, NY, USA, 2007. ACM.

[16] C. T. Haynes, D. P. Friedman, and M. Wand. Obtaining coroutines with continuations. *Computer Languages*, 11(3.4):143 – 153, 1986.

[17] C. Lauterback, Q. Mo, and D. Manocha. Work distribution methods on GPUs. University of North Carolina Technical Report TR009-16.

[18] D. Lea. A java fork/join framework. In *Proceedings of the ACM 2000 conference on Java Grande*, JAVA '00, pages 36–43, New York, NY, USA, 2000. ACM.

[19] D. Leijen, W. Schulte, and S. Burckhardt. The design of a task parallel library. *SIGPLAN Not.*, 44:227–242, Oct. 2009.

[20] P. Li, S. Marlow, S. Peyton Jones, and A. Tolmach. Lightweight concurrency primitives for ghc. In *Proceedings of the ACM SIGPLAN workshop on Haskell workshop*, Haskell '07, pages 107–118, New York, NY, USA, 2007. ACM.

[21] P. Li and S. Zdancewic. Combining events and threads for scalable network services implementation and evaluation of monadic, application-level concurrency primitives. In *Proceedings of the 2007 ACM SIGPLAN conference on Programming language design and implementation*, PLDI '07, pages 189–199, New York, NY, USA, 2007. ACM.

[22] J. P. Magalhães, A. Dijkstra, J. Jeuring, and A. Löh. A generic deriving mechanism for haskell. In *Proceedings of the third ACM Haskell symposium on Haskell*, Haskell '10, pages 37–48, New York, NY, USA, 2010. ACM.

[23] P. Maier, P. Trinder, and H.-W. Loidl. Implementing a High-Level Distributed-Memory parallel Haskell in Haskell, 2011. Submitted to IFL 2011.

[24] G. Mainland and G. Morrisett. Nikola: embedding compiled gpu functions in haskell. In *Proceedings of the third ACM Haskell symposium on Haskell*, Haskell '10, pages 67–78, New York, NY, USA, 2010. ACM.

[25] S. Marlow, R. Newton, and S. Peyton Jones. A monad for deterministic parallelism. In *Proceedings of the 4th ACM symposium on Haskell*, Haskell '11, pages 71–82, New York, NY, USA, 2011. ACM.

[26] S. Marlow, S. Peyton Jones, and S. Singh. Runtime support for multicore haskell. In *Proceedings of the 14th ACM SIGPLAN international conference on Functional programming*, ICFP '09, pages 65–78, New York, NY, USA, 2009. ACM.

[27] T. L. McDonell. cuda. http://hackage.haskell.org/package/cuda. FFI binding to the CUDA interface for programming NVIDIA GPUs.

[28] C. Newburn, B. So, Z. Liu, M. McCool, A. Ghuloum, S. Toit, Z. G. Wang, Z. H. Du, Y. Chen, G. Wu, P. Guo, Z. Liu, and D. Zhang. Intel's array building blocks: A retargetable, dynamic compiler and embedded language. In *Code Generation and Optimization (CGO), 2011 9th Annual IEEE/ACM International Symposium on*, pages 224–235, april 2011.

[29] R. Newton, C.-P. Chen, and S. Marlow. Intel Concurrent Collections for Haskell, March, 2011. MIT CSAIL Technical Report, MIT-CSAIL-TR-2011-015.

[30] B. O'Sullivan and J. Tibell. Scalable i/o event handling for ghc. *SIGPLAN Not.*, 45(11):103–108, Sept. 2010.

[31] H. Pan, B. Hindman, and K. Asanović. Composing parallel software efficiently with Lithe. *SIGPLAN Not.*, 45:376–387, June 2010.

[32] J. Reinders. *Intel Threading Building Blocks: Outfitting C++ for Multi-core Processor Parallelism*. O'Reilly Media, July 2007.

[33] T. Rompf, I. Maier, and M. Odersky. Implementing first-class polymorphic delimited continuations by a type-directed selective cps-transform. *SIGPLAN Not.*, 44:317–328, Aug. 2009.

[34] D. Spoonhower, G. E. Blelloch, P. B. Gibbons, and R. Harper. Beyond nested parallelism: tight bounds on work-stealing overheads for parallel futures. In *Proceedings of the twenty-first annual symposium on Parallelism in algorithms and architectures*, SPAA '09, pages 91–100, New York, NY, USA, 2009. ACM.

[35] D. Spoonhower, G. E. Blelloch, R. Harper, and P. B. Gibbons. Space profiling for parallel functional programs. In *Proceedings of the 13th ACM SIGPLAN international conference on Functional programming*, ICFP '08, pages 253–264, New York, NY, USA, 2008. ACM.

[36] J. Svensson, M. Sheeran, and K. Claessen. Obsidian: A domain specific embedded language for parallel programming of graphics processors. In S.-B. Scholz and O. Chitil, editors, *Implementation and Application of Functional Languages*, volume 5836 of *Lecture Notes in Computer Science*, pages 156–173. Springer Berlin / Heidelberg, 2011.

[37] D. Syme, T. Petricek, and D. Lomov. The f# asynchronous programming model. In *Proceedings of the 13th international conference on Practical aspects of declarative languages*, PADL'11, pages 175–189, Berlin, Heidelberg, 2011. Springer-Verlag.

A. Appendix: Operational Semantics

[Reproduced for convience in largely identical form to [25]]

Figure 9 gives the syntax of values and terms in our language. The only unusual form here is `done` M, which is an internal tool for the semantics of `runPar`. The main semantics for the language is a big-step operational semantics written $M \Downarrow V$ meaning that term M reduces to value V in zero or more steps. It is entirely conventional, so we omit all its rules except one, namely $(RunPar)$ in Figure 11. We will discuss $(RunPar)$ shortly, but the important point for now is that it in turn depends on a small-step operational semantics for the `Par` monad, written: $P \rightarrow Q$. Here P and Q are *states*, whose syntax is given in Figure 9. A state is a bag of terms M (its active "threads"), and `IVars` i that are either full, $\langle M\rangle_i$, or empty, $\langle\rangle_i$. In a state, the $\nu i.P$ serves (as is conventional) to restrict the scope of i in P. The notation $P_0 \rightarrow^* P_i$ is shorthand for the sequence $P_0 \rightarrow ... \rightarrow P_i$ where $i >= 0$.

States obey a structural equivalence relation $\equiv$ given by Figure 10, which specifies that parallel composition is associative and commutative, and scope restriction may be widened or narrowed provided no names fall out of scope. The three rules at the bottom of Figure 10 declare that transitions may take place on any substate, and on states modulo equivalence. So the $\rightarrow$ relation is inherently non-deterministic.

The transitions of $\rightarrow$ are given in in Figure 11 using an *evaluation context* $\mathcal{E}$:

$$\mathcal{E} ::= [\cdot] \mid \mathcal{E} >>= M$$

Hence the term that determines a transition will be found by looking to the left of $>>=$. Rule $(Eval)$ allows the big-step reduction semantics $M \Downarrow V$ to reduce the term in an evaluation context if it is not already a value.

Rule $(Bind)$ is the standard monadic bind semantics.

Rule $(Fork)$ creates a new thread.

Rules (New), (Get), and $(PutEmpty)$ give the semantics for operations on `IVars`, and are straightforward: `new` creates a new empty `IVar` whose name does not clash with another `IVar` in scope, `get` returns the value of a full `IVar`, and `put` creates a full `IVar` from an empty `IVar`. Note that there is no transition for `put` when the `IVar` is already full: in the implementation we would signal an error to the programmer, but in the semantics we model the error condition by having no transition.

Several rules that allow parts of the state to be *garbage collected* when they are no longer relevant to the execution. Rule $(GCReturn)$ allows a completed thread to be garbage collected. Rules $(GCEmpty)$ and $(GCFull)$ allow an empty or full `IVar` respectively to be garbage collected provided the `IVar` is not referenced anywhere else in the state. The equivalences for ν in Figure 10 allow us to push the ν down until it encloses only the dead `IVar`.

Rule $(GCDeadlock)$ allows a set of deadlocked threads to be garbage collected: the syntax $\mathcal{E}[\texttt{get}\ i]^*$ means one or more threads of the given form. Since there can be no other threads that refer to i, none of the `gets` can ever make progress. Hence the entire set of deadlocked threads together with the empty `IVar` can be removed from the state.

The final rule, $(RunPar)$, gives the semantics of `runPar` and connects the `Par` reduction semantics $\rightarrow$ with the functional reduction semantics $\Downarrow$. Informally it can be stated thus: if the argument M to `runPar` runs in the `Par` semantics yielding a result N, and N reduces to V, then `runPar` M is said to reduce to V. In order to express this, we need a distinguished term form to indicate that the "main thread" has completed: this is the reason for the form `done` M. The programmer is never expected to write `done` M directly, it is only used as a tool in the semantics.

$$
\begin{array}{llcll}
 & x, y & \in & \mathit{Variable} & \\
 & i & \in & \texttt{IVar} & \\
\mathit{Values} & V & ::= & x \mid i \mid \backslash x \mid - > \mid M & \\
 & & \mid & \texttt{return}\ M \mid M >>= N & \\
 & & \mid & \texttt{runPar}\ M & \\
 & & \mid & \texttt{fork}_{\texttt{n}}\ M & \\
 & & \mid & \texttt{new} & \\
 & & \mid & \texttt{put}\ i\ M & \\
 & & \mid & \texttt{get}\ i & \\
 & & \mid & \texttt{done}\ M & \\
\mathit{Terms} & M, N & ::= & V \mid M\ N \mid \cdots & \\
\mathit{States} & P, Q & ::= & M & \text{thread of computation} \\
 & & \mid & \langle\rangle_i & \text{empty IVar named } i \\
 & & \mid & \langle M\rangle_i & \text{full IVar named } i\text{, holding } M \\
 & & \mid & \nu i.P & \text{restriction} \\
 & & \mid & P \mid Q & \text{parallel composition}
\end{array}
$$

Figure 9. The syntax of values and terms

$$
\begin{array}{c}
P \mid Q \equiv Q \mid P \\
P \mid (Q \mid R) \equiv (P \mid Q) \mid R \\
\nu x.\nu y.P \equiv \nu y.\nu x.P \\
\nu x.(P \mid Q) \equiv (\nu x.P) \mid Q, \qquad x \notin fn\,(Q) \\[1em]
\dfrac{P \rightarrow Q}{P \mid R \rightarrow Q \mid R} \qquad \dfrac{P \rightarrow Q}{\nu x.P \rightarrow \nu x.Q} \\[1em]
\dfrac{P \equiv P' \quad P' \rightarrow Q' \quad Q' \equiv Q}{P \rightarrow Q}
\end{array}
$$

Figure 10. Structural congruence, and structural transitions.

$$
\begin{array}{rcll}
 & \dfrac{M \not\equiv V \quad M \Downarrow V}{\mathcal{E}[M] \rightarrow \mathcal{E}[V]} & & (Eval) \\[1em]
\mathcal{E}[\texttt{return}\ N] >>= [M] & \rightarrow & \mathcal{E}[M\ N] & (Bind) \\
\mathcal{E}[\texttt{fork}_{\texttt{n}}\ M] & \rightarrow & \mathcal{E}[\texttt{return}\ ()] \mid M & (Fork) \\[1em]
\mathcal{E}[\texttt{new}] & \rightarrow & \nu i.(\langle\rangle_i \mid \mathcal{E}[\texttt{return}\ i]), & (New) \\
 & & i \notin fn\,(\mathcal{E}) & \\
\langle M\rangle_i \mid \mathcal{E}[\texttt{get}\ i] & \rightarrow & \langle M\rangle_i \mid \mathcal{E}[\texttt{return}\ M] & (Get) \\
\langle\rangle_i \mid \mathcal{E}[\texttt{put}\ i\ M] & \rightarrow & \langle M\rangle_i \mid \mathcal{E}[\texttt{return}\ ()] & \\
 & & & (PutEmpty) \\[1em]
\texttt{return}\ M & \rightarrow & & (GCReturn) \\
\nu i.\langle\rangle_i & \rightarrow & & (GCEmpty) \\
\nu i.\langle M\rangle_i & \rightarrow & & (GCFull) \\
\nu i.(\langle\rangle_i \mid \mathcal{E}[\texttt{get}\ i]^*) & \rightarrow & & (GCDeadlock) \\[1em]
 & \dfrac{(M >>= \backslash x.\texttt{done}\ x) \rightarrow^* \texttt{done}\ N, \quad N \Downarrow V}{\texttt{runPar}\ M \Downarrow V} & & (RunPar)
\end{array}
$$

Figure 11. Transition Rules

Nested Data-Parallelism on the GPU

Lars Bergstrom
University of Chicago
larsberg@cs.uchicago.edu

John Reppy
University of Chicago
jhr@cs.uchicago.edu

Abstract

Graphics processing units (GPUs) provide both memory bandwidth and arithmetic performance far greater than that available on CPUs but, because of their *Single-Instruction-Multiple-Data* (SIMD) architecture, they are hard to program. Most of the programs ported to GPUs thus far use traditional data-level parallelism, performing only operations that operate uniformly over vectors.

NESL is a first-order functional language that was designed to allow programmers to write irregular-parallel programs — such as parallel divide-and-conquer algorithms — for wide-vector parallel computers. This paper presents our port of the NESL implementation to work on GPUs and provides empirical evidence that nested data-parallelism (NDP) on GPUs significantly outperforms CPU-based implementations and matches or beats newer GPU languages that support only flat parallelism. While our performance does not match that of hand-tuned CUDA programs, we argue that the notational conciseness of NESL is worth the loss in performance. This work provides the first language implementation that directly supports NDP on a GPU.

Categories and Subject Descriptors D.3.0 [*Programming Languages*]: General; D.3.2 [*Programming Languages*]: Language Classifications—Applicative (Functional) Programming, Concurrent, distributed, and parallel languages; D.3.4 [*Programming Languages*]: Processors—Compilers

General Terms Languages, Performance

Keywords GPU, GPGPU, NESL, nested data parallelism

1. Introduction

Graphics processing units (GPUs) provide large numbers of parallel processors. For example, the NVIDIA Tesla C2050 has 14 multiprocessors, each with 32 cores, for 448 total cores. This card provides over 1200 GFLOPS, far more than the approximately 50 GFLOPS available from a typical Intel quad-core i7 processor. While the GPU cores provide very good integer and floating point throughput, they are very limited compared to a general-purpose CPU. They only achieve peak performance when all cores are executing the same instructions at the same time. This model works well for a wide variety of arithmetically intense, regular parallel problems, but it does not support *irregular* parallel problems — problems characterized by abundant parallelism but that have non-uniform problem subdivisions and non-uniform memory access, such as divide-and-conquer algorithms.

ICFP'12, September 9–15, 2012, Copenhagen, Denmark.

Most GPU programming is done with the CUDA [NVI11b] and OpenCL [Khr11] languages, which provide the illusion of C-style general-purpose programming, but which actually impose restrictions. There have been a number of efforts to support GPU programming from higher-level languages, usually by embedding a data-parallel DSL into the host language, but these efforts have been limited to regular parallelism [CBS11, MM10, CKL+11].

The current best practice for irregular parallelism on a GPU is for skilled programmers to laboriously hand code applications. The literature is rife with implementations of specific irregular-parallel algorithms for GPUs [BP11, DR11, MLBP12, MGG12]. These efforts typically require many programmer-months of effort to even meet the performance of the original optimized sequential C program.

GPUs have some common characteristics with the wide-vector supercomputers of the 1980's, which similarly provided high-performance SIMD computations. NESL is a first-order functional language developed by Guy Blelloch in the early 1990's that was designed to support irregular parallelism on wide-vector machines. NESL generalizes the concept of data parallelism to *nested data-parallelism* (NDP), where subcomputations of a data-parallel computation may themselves be data parallel [BS90, Ble96, PPW95, CKLP01]. For example, the dot product of a sparse vector (represented by index/value pairs) and a dense vector is a data-parallel computation that is expressed in NESL using a parallel map comprehension (curly braces) and a parallel summation reduction function:

```
function svxv (sv, v) =
    sum ({x * v[i] : (x, i) in sv});
```

Using this function, we can define the product of a sparse matrix (represented as a vector of sparse vectors) with a dense vector as:

```
function smxv (sm, v) =
    { svxv(row, v) : row in sm }
```

This function is an example of a nested data-parallel computation, since its subcomputations are themselves data-parallel computations of irregular size.

As described, NDP is not well-suited to execution on SIMD architectures, such as wide-vector supercomputers or GPUs, since it has irregular problem decomposition and memory access. Blelloch's solution to this problem was the *flattening* transformation, which vectorizes an NDP program so that the nested array structures are flat and the operations are SIMD [BS90, Kel99, PPW95, Les05]. This compilation technique allows NDP codes to be run on vector hardware, but it has not yet been applied to GPUs.

In this paper, we describe a port of the NESL language to run on GPUs. Our implementation relies on the NESL compiler to apply the flattening transformation to the program, which produces a vectorized stack-machine code, called VCODE. We use a series

```
function quicksort(a) =
  if (#a < 2) then a
  else let
    p   = a[#a/2];
    lt  = {e in a | e < p};
    eq  = {e in a | e == p};
    gt  = {e in a | e > p};
    r = {quicksort(v) : v in [lt, eq, gt]};
    in r[0] ++ r[1] ++ r[2];
```

Figure 1. NESL implementation of Quicksort, demonstrating irregular parallelism in a divide-and-conquer algorithm.

```
function quicksort' (as) =
  if all(#as < 2) then as
  else let
    ps  = {a[#a/2] : a in as};
    lts = {{e in es | e < p} : p in ps; es in as};
    eqs = {{e in es | e == p} : p in ps; es in as};
    gts = {{e in es | e > p} : p in ps; es in as};
    rs  = quicksort' (flatten ([lts, eqs, gts]));
    in rs;
```

Figure 2. Flattening-inspired implementation of Quicksort, providing a high-level overview of the effect of the code and data transformations.

of code optimizers and libraries to transform this intermediate language for efficient execution on GPUs. This paper makes the following contributions:

1. We demonstrate that a general purpose NDP language, such as NESL, can be implemented efficiently on GPUs. By allowing irregular parallel applications to be programmed for a GPU using NESL, we effectively move the requirement for highly-skilled GPU programmers from the application space to the language-implementation space.
2. We explain the performance requirements of modern GPU hardware and describe the techniques and data structures that we developed to tune the performance of the underlying vector primitives required to implement NDP on a GPU.
3. We demonstrate that our preliminary implementation provides performance better than many of the flat data-parallel languages, which illustrates the potential of this compilation approach.

The remainder of the paper is organized as follows. In the next section, we describe the programming and execution model using quicksort as an example. Then, we provide an overview of GPU hardware and the CUDA language. Section 4 is a detailed description of our implementation and the match between the requirements of NESL on the vector machine and the CUDA language and its associated libraries, focusing on the design decisions required for high performance on GPUs. Since directly implementing the vector hardware model was not sufficient for our performance targets, Section 5 describes additional optimizations we perform. After we introduce several related systems in some depth in Section 6.2, we compare the performance of our system to these systems. Finally, we cover some related work and conclude.

The source code for our implementation and all benchmarks described in this paper are available at: `http://smlnj-gforge.cs.uchicago.edu/projects/neslgpu`.

2. NESL

NESL is a first-order dialect of ML that supports nested data-parallelism [BCH+94]. It provides the ability to make data-parallel function calls across arbitrarily nested data sequences. A standard example of NDP computation in NESL is the quicksort algorithm [Ble96], which is given in Figure 1. The recursive calls to the `quicksort` function lead to irregular parallel execution in general. That is, the compiler cannot know how the data will be partitioned, so it cannot statically allocate and balance the workload.

The NESL compiler supports such irregular NDP computations by transforming the code and data into a representation where nested arrays have been *flattened*. The result of this transformation is *VCODE*, which is code for a stack-based virtual vector machine [BC90]. This language executes in an interpreted environment on the host machine, calling primitives written in the *C Vector Library* (CVL) [BC93]. In this section, we explain the NESL compilation process using quicksort as a running example.

2.1 Flattened quicksort

Figure 2 shows an idealized version of this flattened program in syntax similar to that of NESL. This version is not actually emitted by the NESL compiler, but is helpful for understanding the transformation.

Flattening transforms the `quicksort` function from operating over a single vector at a time into a new version that operates over a nested vector of vectors. In a language such as C, this structure might be represented with an array of pointers to arrays. In the implementation of NESL, however, nested vectors are represented in two parts. One part is a flat vector containing the data from all of the different vectors. The other part is one or more segment descriptors (one per level of nesting). Segment descriptors are vectors that contain the index and length information required to reconstruct the nested vectors from the flat data vector. To cope with the change in representation, the body of `quicksort` must also be changed. Each operation that previously operated on a scalar value is lifted to operate on a vector and vector operations are lifted to operate on nested vectors.

The scalar `p`, which was a scalar value holding the single pivot element from the input vector `a` in the original program becomes the vector `ps`, holding all of the pivots from each of the vectors inside of the nested vector `as`. The vectors that previously held the `lt`, `eq`, `gt`, and `r` vectors from `a` are now turned into nested vectors holding all of the vectors of corresponding elements from the vectors represented by `as`. The termination condition for this function, which was previously that the vector `a` is of length less than 2, becomes a check to ensure that *all* of the vectors in `as` have length less than 2.

The `flatten` operator, which is used to combine the vectors for the recursive call to `quicksort'`, is of type $[[\alpha]] \rightarrow [\alpha]$. It removes one level of nesting by appending the elements of each of the top-level vectors.

2.2 NESL runtime

The output of the NESL compiler is the flattened program translated into a virtual-machine code called *VCODE*. The NESL runtime system can be viewed as consisting of a VCODE interpreter that runs on a CPU and a machine-specific vector library that runs on a device. In some cases, the vector device might be the CPU, but in our case it is the GPU. Because most of the computational load is in the vector operations, performance is dominated by the efficiency of the vector library.

2.2.1 VCODE

VCODE is a stack-based language that is intended to be run on a host computer with vector operations performed on a vector machine. Figure 3 contains a small fragment of the actual VCODE

```
FUNC QUICKSORT_13            function entry
  COPY 1 0                   stack manipulation
  CALL PRIM-DIST_37          function call
  COPY 2 1
  COPY 1 2
  CALL VEC-LEN_13
  CONST INT 2                push the vector [2]
  COPY 1 2
  CALL PRIM-DIST_6
  COPY 1 2
  POP 1 0                    stack manipulation
  < INT                      element-wise integer comparison
...
```

Figure 3. A small section of the over 1500 lines of VCODE corresponding to the original quicksort example. This section is the beginning of the flattened version, which determines whether the lengths of all of the segments passed in are less than 2.

generated by the NESL compiler from the quicksort program in Figure 1. We have annotated some of the instructions with their meaning. There are four categories of VCODE instructions:

Vector instructions. These include both element-wise vector operations (such as the `< INT` in Figure 3) as well as various reduction, prefix-scan, and permutation operations. These operations are executed by the vector device.

Stack instructions. These include various instructions for permuting, copying, and discarding stack elements, and are executed on the interpreter. All references to live data are on the stack and the VCODE interpreter uses these manage space automatically (there are no memory-management instructions in VCODE). Stack values are represented by a device-specific handle to the data paired with type information. Underlying data values are *not* transferred between the CPU and device except when required for I/O.

Control instructions. These include function entries calls, and returns, as well as conditionals and the `CONST` instruction. These instructions are executed on the CPU and do not directly affect the device (except for the `CONST` instruction, which allocates a vector on the device).

Other instructions. VCODE includes instructions for I/O, system initialization and shutdown, and various other miscellaneous operations.

2.2.2 CVL

The C Vector Library (CVL) is a set of C library functions callable from a host machine that implement the VCODE vector operations and is the primary hook between the host machine and hardware on which the program is executing. This library is well-documented in its manual [BC93] and has been ported to many of the high-performance parallel computers of the 1990's. It also has a sequential C implementation for execution on scalar uniprocessors. In this work, we have implemented a version of the CVL library in CUDA.

3. GPU hardware and programming model

Graphics processing units (GPUs) are high-performance parallel processors that were originally designed for computer graphics applications. Because of their high performance, there has been growing interest in using GPUs for other computational tasks. To support this demand, C-like languages, such as CUDA [NVI11b] and OpenCL [Khr11] have been developed for general-purpose programming of GPUs. While these languages provide a C-like expression and statement syntax, there are many aspects of their programming models that are GPU-centric. In this paper, we focus on the CUDA language and NVIDIA's hardware, although our results should also apply to OpenCL and other vendors' GPUs.

A typical GPU consists of multiple streaming multiprocessors (SMP), each of which contains multiple computational cores. One of the major differences between GPUs and CPUs is that the memory hierarchy on a GPU is explicit, consisting of a global memory that is shared by all of the SMPs, a per-SMP local memory, and a per-core private memory. An SMP executes a group of threads, called a *warp*, in parallel, with one thread per computational core. Execution is *Single-Instruction-Multiple-Thread* (SIMT), which means that each thread in the warp executes that same instruction. To handle divergent conditionals, GPUs execute each branch of the conditional in series using a bit mask to disable those threads that took the other branch. An SMP can efficiently switch between different warps, which allows it to hide memory latency. GPUs have some hardware support for synchronization, such as per-thread-group barrier synchronization and atomic memory operations.

3.1 CUDA

CUDA is a language designed by NVIDIA to write parallel programs for their GPU hardware [NVI11b]. It can be viewed as an extension of C++ and includes support for code synthesis using templates. In CUDA, code that runs directly on the GPU is called a *kernel*. The host CPU invokes the kernel, specifying the number of parallel threads to execute the kernel. The host code also specifies the configuration of the execution, which is a 1, 2, or 3D grid structure onto which the parallel threads are mapped. This grid structure is divided into blocks, with each block of threads being mapped to the same SMP. The explicit memory hierarchy is also part of the CUDA programming model, with pointer types being annotated with their address space (*e.g.*, global vs. local).

3.2 Key programming challenges on GPUs

The various features of the GPU hardware and programming models discussed above pose a number of challenges to effective use of the GPU hardware. Our implementation largely addresses these challenges, which allows the programmer to focus on correctness and asymptotic issues instead of low-level hardware-specific implementation details.

Data transfer Communication between the host CPU and GPU is performed over the host computer's interconnect. These interconnects are typically high-bandwidth, but not nearly as high in bandwidth as is available on the card itself. For example, a PCI-E 2.0 bus provides 16 GB/s of bandwidth, but the bandwidth between the NVIDIA Tesla C2050's SMPs and the global memory is 144 GB/s. Therefore, fast GPU programs carefully balance the number and timing of their data transfers and other communications between the host and device.

Memory access Within a GPU kernel, access to the global memory is significantly slower than access to local or private memory. In fact, naive kernels that rely excessively on global memory are often slower than native CPU speeds. Furthermore, GPU global memory performance is very sensitive to the patterns of memory accesses across the warp [NVI11a]. Lastly, the memory characteristics differ between cards, so a kernel that is tuned for one card may not run well on another.

Divergence Threads within a warp must execute the same instruction each cycle. When execution encounters divergent control flow, the SMP is forced to execute both control-flow paths to the point where they join back together. Thus care must be taken to reduce the occurrence of divergent conditionals.

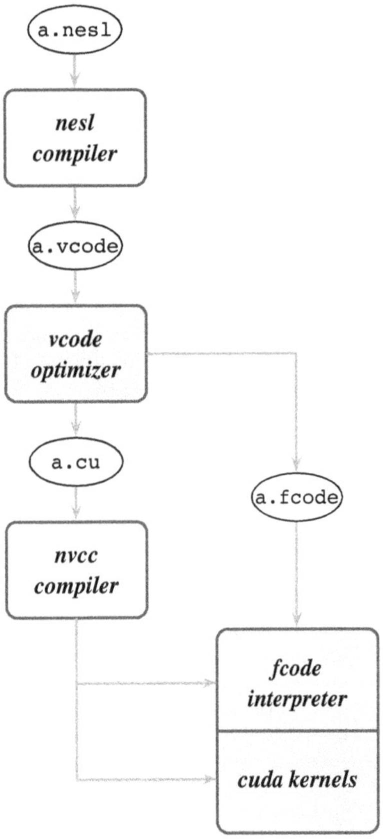

Figure 4. The NESL/GPU toolchain. The shaded portions represent our contributions.

No recursive calls Recursion is not, in general, permitted in GPU kernels.[1] This limitation means that any program with recursive calls must be transformed into a non-recursive one. This can be done by CPS converting and using a trampoline (as is done by the OptiX library [PBD+10]), by explicitly managing the return stack on the GPU [YHL+09], or by managing control flow on the host CPU. Our NESL implementation does the latter.

4. Implementation

Figure 4 shows the structure of our implementation. It takes a NESL program (`a.nesl`) and compiles it to VCODE (`a.vcode`) using the preexisting NESL compiler from CMU. We then optimize the VCODE to produce specialized CUDA kernels (`a.cu`) and fused VCODE (`a.fcode`) for the program. Finally, the code is executed by a modified version of the VCODE host interpreter, using our own CUDA-based implementation of the CVL.

The remainder of this section describes our implementation of the CVL, which consists of over 200 kernel functions, split up into segmented and unsegmented versions of element-wise operations, reductions, scans, permutations, and miscellaneous conversion and management operations. This implementation is the end product of many iterations of design and careful performance profiling. Our implementation passes all of the single-precision NESL regression tests.[2] We leave a discussion of the VCODE optimizer and supporting interpreter modifications to Section 5.

4.1 Implementation basics

CVL uses a fixed-sized heap and performs garbage collection when there is insufficient space remaining for a requested allocation. All data values in our implementation are 32-bits long — `float`, `integer`, and `bool` values. The VCODE interpreter keeps reference counts to track the lifetime of vectors. We augmented each of our CUDA calls with information about opportunities to reuse a source vector for the destination values for cases where they are both the same length and there is no concurrency issue with reusing the storage space. This optimization results in a significant reduction of the maximum memory footprint.

4.2 Segment Descriptors

As mentioned in Section 2, segment descriptors are used in the flattened data representation to describe the original structure of the data. For example, consider the nested vector $[[4], [5, 6, 7], [8, 9]]$. This vector can be represented by the flat data vector $[4, 5, 6, 7, 8, 9]$ paired with the segment descriptor $[1, 3, 2]$, which indicates that the first segment is one element long, the second segment is three elements long, and the third segment is two elements long. Although simple, this representation is terrible for execution of segmented operations on GPUs.

Many kernels need to know for a given thread which segment it is in. Using the representation described above would mean that each thread would be scanning the segment descriptor to determine its segment, which would result in excessive memory traffic. To avoid this problem, we expand segment descriptors to the length of the underlying data vector, with the ith element of the segment descriptor holding the segment number that the ith data element belongs to. For our example, the descriptor is $[1, 2, 2, 2, 3, 3]$. With this representation, each thread has constant-time access to its segment and the access pattern is optimal for global memory bandwidth.

This representation can be further improved. Some kernels, such as the extraction and permutation kernels, need to know how far offset a given segment is within the data, which requires knowing the length of the segment. For example, to extract the second element from the third segment in the data vector, the kernel needs to compute the total number of elements from the first two segments and then add two. Because these operations are common in a large number of kernels, we concatenate the original segment lengths vector to the end of the segment descriptor vector. Returning to this section's example, the full descriptor is $[1, 2, 2, 2, 3, 3, 1, 3, 2]$.

These representation choices are the result of experimentation with three different alternatives. The worst — lengths only — resulted in individual kernel calls taking multiple *seconds*, even after optimization. Using a flags vector increased performance over the lengths-only representation and used less space (since multiple boolean flags can be compacted into single words), but were slower than our final representation because of the need to compute the per-element segment index in many kernels. After settling on this format and carefully tuning each of the different types of kernel calls, those same calls take no more than a couple of hundred microseconds, even on very-large input data. The remaining subsections discuss implementation details and trade-offs in these kernel calls.

4.3 Element-wise kernels

The element-wise kernels perform a unary or binary operation uniformly across the elements of its arguments, independent of

[1] Recursion is supported on some newer cards, but only for kernels that may be called from other kernel functions — not the host.

[2] Our implementation does not yet support double-precision codes.

their nesting structure. These kernels are the only ones that are unaffected by the choice of segment descriptor representation, but they do have the property that they are memory bound, since their inputs and output are stored in global memory. This property means that they are very sensitive to the number of warps per thread block. With too many warps per block, warps will be idle waiting on computing resources, whereas with too few warps per block, the SMP will be idle waiting for memory operations to complete, This problem is the *memory access* challenge discussed in Section 3.2.

We tested block sizes between 32 and 4096 threads and found that blocks of 256 threads (8 warps) provided the best overall performance, by up to a factor of 8. At lower numbers of threads, the blocks were too small to keep the hardware busy, since most of our kernels are memory-bound. Increasing beyond 256 threads per block caused low occupancy rates. At 8 warps per block, this breakdown allows roughly 12 cycles to compute the address and make a request for memory from each thread before all of the memory requests have been issued and the first warp has been filled and is ready to execute. These results agree with those recommended by NVIDIA for memory-bound kernels [NVI11a].

In addition to the basic element-wise vector math operations, there is also an element-wise random number generation operation. While there are many random number generators available for GPUs, we have elected to execute this operation on the host CPU instead. This strategy makes it easier to compare our GPU implementation's results against CPU versions and the extra communication cost is not detrimental to performance, since the benchmarks only use random number generation during initialization.

4.4 Scans and reductions

Scan and reduction operators perform an associative binary operation over an input vector. The reduction operation results in a single value, whereas scan operations produce a vector containing all the intermediate results.

Our implementation uses the Thrust implementation of scan and reduction [HB11], which also supports the segmented scan operation directly. These implementations are based on the work by Sengupta *et al.* that produced efficient versions of the scan primitives tuned for GPUs [SHZO07]. Thrust also allows custom binary operators, so we also provide custom classes implementing the full set of binary operations available in the NESL language. Our segment descriptor format is directly usable as a flag vector for the segmented scan primitives by design.

While Thrust includes a native reduction operator, it does not include a segmented version of reduction. Our segmented reduction is implemented by first performing a segmented inclusive scan and then performing a second kernel call to extract all of the reduction sums. This second kernel call requires the locations of the final, reduced values from each of the segments.

In our initial implementation of this kernel, we computed — per warp — the corresponding offsets for each of the segments. But, this was far too slow on vectors with more than a few thousand segments, as each warp needed to read every element from the lengths portion of the segment descriptor. Now, we perform a prefix sum of the lengths portion of the segment descriptor so that each thread can directly get the resulting value. For example, if we had a thousand segments, each of length 10, in the first version there would be `ceil(1000/32)=32` threads accessing and adding up, on average, half of those numbers. Worse, nearly all of those threads would access the first few elements, resulting in nearly the worst possible GPU memory access pattern. In the final version, we efficiently compute a vector corresponding to each of the offsets for each thread index and both avoid the multiple-access penalty and remove the portion of code from the start of each kernel where every other thread but the first was blocked, waiting for the first to compute all of the offsets for each of the threads in the warp.

In many cases, the segmented scan and reduction operators are called on single-segment vectors (*i.e.*, flat or non-nested vectors). Because of the overhead of creating and initializing extra data structures to handle multiple segments and the extra bounds checking in the segmented operators, we wrote custom implementations of the segmented operations for the single-segment case. These specialized implementations achieve a nearly 20% speedup over the general versions.

4.5 Permutation and vector-scalar operations

Permutation operators shuffle elements from their locations in a source vector to a target vector, sometimes incorporating default values for unmapped or extra elements. Vector-scalar operations extract or replace values in a vector or create a vector from a base value and an optional stride value. When a stride is provided, the resulting vector elements are equal to the sum of the base value and the product of the element index and the stride value.

These operators rely on the segment descriptor information that allows individual threads to avoid each reading the vector of lengths repeatedly. Similar to the previous section, this requirement means that we often perform a `+-scan` of the segment descriptor lengths to provide the per-segment offsets, sometimes for both source and target segment descriptors if they differ and are required. The operations requiring these data are infrequent relative to the cost in both memory and time of always computing these scanned segment lengths, so we do not just maintain both formats.

However, computing indexing information through composition of efficient scan-vector operations is critical for high-performance kernel code. In every case that we tried to compute indexed offsets in a kernel by hand on a per-warp or per-thread basis, there arose input data edge cases that pushed execution times for each of those inefficient kernel calls into the range of seconds.

4.6 Miscellaneous operations

The general facilities of the implementation include memory allocation, windowing, I/O, host/vector hardware data transfer, and timing operators. During the initialization process, we currently only select a single GPU — the one with the estimated highest performance.

There are also library functions that directly implement sorting. These *rank* operations take a vector of numbers and return a vector of integer indices indicating the target index that the corresponding number would take on in a sorted vector. We use the Thrust library's radix sort to implement the rank operations. The segmented rank operation is implemented by multiple invocations of the unsegmented radix sort operation, once per segment. We do not rely on the *rank* operation in any of our benchmark code, but provide it for API compatibility.

The *index* operations are heavily used and fill in vectors with default values. The values are not only constants, but can also support a stride, allowing the value at an index to be a function of an initialization value and a stride factor. Again, this is an operation that benefited from both the new segment descriptor format that provided the index number associated with an element as well as an extra data pass where we generate the offset into the segment of each element. This offset allows the computation of the value at an index to just be a simple multiply and add. Similar to the scan and reduction operators, this operation is frequently called in its segmented form but with a single vector. There is a significant performance gain by optimizing the case of a single segment since all elements share the same stride and index and can be loaded from their fixed location in GPU memory once per warp and shared across all of the threads.

The final operation with an interesting implementation is the creation of a segment descriptor, which is performed even more often than the indexing operation — once per vector, unless the segment descriptor can be reused from a previous vector. Vectors are immutable in the NESL implementation, so segment descriptors are frequently shared and reused in the generated VCODE. Creation of the segment descriptor takes a vector with the lengths of each segment. For example, the vector `[1,3,3]` describes an underlying vector of seven elements divided into three segments. We allocate space for the underlying vector's length plus the length of the segment descriptor. In this case, that would be 10 elements. First, we fill the portion of the vector that is the length of the underlying data vector with zeros. In our example, there would now be a vector of seven zeros. Then, at the location of the start of each segment in the vector, we place the index of that segment. In this case, the beginning of the vector is now: `[1,2,0,0,3,0,0]`. An inclusive `max-scan` carries the segment indices over each of the zero-initialized elements quickly, resulting in: `[1,2,2,2,3,3,3]`. Finally, we copy the original lengths input to the end of the vector for use in the numerous kernels that require it. The final segment descriptor is: `[1,2,2,2,3,3,3,1,3,3]`. This operation is executed as a single kernel invocation.

There are many other more straightforward ways to fill in this data, such as having one thread per element that computes its correct index, but, as in the other examples that required the `+-scan` of the segment descriptor lengths, any kernel implementation that requires a large number of kernel threads to touch the same piece of memory will perform so poorly that an individual kernel call will take longer than the entire remainder of the benchmark.

5. Optimization

A straightforward porting of the NESL implementation to GPUs suffers from some obvious performance issues. The VCODE produced by the NESL compiler is sub-optimal. It includes many trivial utility functions and a significant amount of stack churn. Furthermore, a straightforward port of the CVL library to GPUs requires an individual CUDA kernel invocation for each computational VCODE operation. This property adds significant scheduling overhead and reduces memory locality, since the arguments and results of the operations must be loaded/stored in global memory. For example, consider the following simple NESL function:

```
function muladd (xs, ys, zs) =
    {x * y + z : x in xs; y in ys; z in zs};
```

Figure 5 shows the unoptimized VCODE as produced by the NESL compiler. From this figure, we can see examples of the first two issues. The code includes trivial utility functions (*e.g.*, `ZIP-OVER_8`) and is dominated by stack manipulations; many of which end up computing the identity. In addition, the multiplication is run as a separate operation from the addition, which means that the intermediate result (*i.e.*, the `x*y` value) must be stored in global memory and then reloaded to perform the addition.

To improve performance of our system, we have implemented an optimizer that takes the VCODE produced by the NESL compiler and produces an optimized program in an extension of VCODE that we call *FCODE* (for *Fused vCODE*). As shown in Figure 4, this optimization fits inbetween the NESL compiler and the VCODE interpreter. We describe this optimizer in the rest of this section and discuss its impact on performance in Section 6.4.

5.1 VCODE optimizations

The VCODE optimizer consists of five phases. The first two of these address inefficiencies in the VCODE generated by the NESL compiler. The first phase is the inliner, which visits functions in reverse topological order inlining calls to other VCODE operations.

```
FUNC MULADD1_7            FUNC ZIP-OVER_8
CPOP 2 4                  CPOP 2 2
CPOP 2 4                  CPOP 2 2
CPOP 2 4                  POP 1 1
CALL ZIP-OVER_8           CPOP 1 2
CALL ZIP-OVER_10          CPOP 1 2
COPY 1 3                  CPOP 1 2
CPOP 1 4                  RET
CPOP 1 4
CPOP 1 4                  FUNC ZIP-OVER_10
COPY 1 3                  CPOP 2 3
POP 1 0                   CPOP 3 2
* INT                     POP 1 2
CPOP 1 3                  CPOP 1 3
CPOP 1 3                  CPOP 1 3
POP 1 0                   CPOP 2 2
+ INT                     RET
RET
```

Figure 5. Unoptimized VCODE for the `muladd` function

The inliner does not inline recursive functions and uses a size metric to limit code growth. Our size metric is the number of computational instructions in the function.

Once we have performed inlining, the next phase converts the stack machine code into an expression language with let-bound variables. In this representation, each computation is bound to a unique variable. Continuing with our example, the `muladd` function is represented as follows:[3]

```
function MULADD1_7 (p0, p1, p2, p3)
    let t033 = p1 * p2
    let t034 = t033 + p3
    in
      RET (p0, t034)
```

This conversion has the effect of compiling away stack manipulation instructions (*i.e.*, POP, COPY, and CPOP). When we convert back to the stack machine representation, we are careful to avoid redundant and unnecessary stack operations, so the final result is much more compact. For example, the resulting code for the `muladd` function is:

```
FUNC MULADD1_7
  CPOP 2 1
  * INT
  CPOP 1 1
  + INT
  RET
```

5.2 Fusion

While the VCODE optimizations produce much more compact programs, they do not address the most significant performance issue, which is the use of individual kernel invocations for each computational instruction. For example, in the `muladd` code, a kernel invocation is used to perform the element-wise multiplication on the `xs` and `ys` to produce an intermediate result array. Then a second kernel invocation is used to add the result of the first with the `zs` array. For element-wise operations, this pattern is extremely inefficient, since we incur kernel invocation overhead for relatively small kernels that are dominated by global memory traffic. As has been observed by others, the flattening approach to implementing NDP requires *fusion* to be efficient [Kel99, Cha93]. VCODE does not have a way to express fused operators, so we must leave the confines of the VCODE instruction set and extend the interpreter.

[3] Parameter `p0` is the segment descriptor for the result vector.

Our VCODE optimizer identifies element-wise computations that involve multiple operations and replaces them with synthesized *superoperators*. This approach is similar to Proebsting's superoperators [Pro95] and Ertl's super instructions [Ert01], with the main difference being that we introduce superoperators for any eligible subcomputation, independent of its frequency.

In our implementation, fusion is a two-step process. The first step is the reducer, which replaces variables in argument positions with their bindings. The reducer limits its efforts to element-wise operations and "flat" constants. The reducer also eliminates unused variables and function parameters. After reduction, the `muladd` function consists of a single, multi-operation expression:

```
function MULADD1_7 (p0, p1, p2, p3, p5)
    let t034 = (p1 * p3) + p5
    in
      RET (p0, t034)
```

The second step is to identify the unique fused expressions and to lift them out of the program as superoperators, as is shown in the following code:

```
fused OP0 ($0 : INT, $1 : INT, $2 : INT) =
    ($0 * $1) + $2

...

function MULADD1_7 (x025, x026, x027, x028)
    let x029 = OP0 (x026, x027, x028)
    in
      RET (x025, x029)
```

The two benefits of the fused kernels over the optimized VCODE are reductions in the number of kernel calls and the number of global memory loads and stores. For this example, we reduce the number of kernel calls by four for each dynamic instance of the `MULADD1_7` function and we reduce the number of global loads and stores by one each per element of the argument vectors.

Limitations Our implementation currently fuses only element-wise operations. Fusing map-reduce combinations would further reduce the number of kernel calls and global memory accesses, but we have not yet implemented this feature.

5.3 Code generation

The final phase of the optimizer is code generation, which is responsible for both converting the expression representation back to stack-machine format and generating CUDA C code for the fused superoperators. First, the optimized VCODE is transformed to remove all identified opportunities for fusion with a call to a superoperator. In this example, we produce the following code:

```
FUNC MULADD1_7
  FUSED 0
  RET
```

where the "0" is the ID of the fused operation that is being invoked. Then, we generate custom CUDA kernels for each fused superoperator. The corresponding kernel for the fused operation in this example is shown in Figure 6.

5.4 Calling the custom kernels

Alongside each of these CUDA kernels, we generate both a host C function and a set of data structures. The data structures contain summary information about the kernel, such as its arity, parameter and return types, vector size information, and whether or not last-use input parameters can be reused as the output storage. We have modified the VCODE interpreter to handle fused operators, such as **`FUSED 0`** in the example. When the interpreter hits a fused kernel call it runs code to perform the proper allocations, argument checks, and invoke the kernel through the host C function.

```
__global__ void fused0Kernel (MAXALIGN *data,
  int dst, int s0, int s1, int s2,
  int len, int scratch)
{
  int addr = blockDim.y * blockIdx.y
      + blockDim.x * blockIdx.x + threadIdx.x;
  if (addr < len) {
    int *pDst = (int*)(&data[dst]);
    int *pSrc0 = (int*)(&data[s0]);
    int *pSrc1 = (int*)(&data[s1]);
    int *pSrc2 = (int*)(&data[s2]);

    pDst[address] = pSrc0[addr] * pSrc1[addr]
      + pSrc2[addr];
  }
}
```

Figure 6. Kernel for fused operation `OP0`

6. Evaluation

To evaluate the effectiveness of our approach to implementing NESL on GPUs, we compare the performance of our system to CPU-based systems that use flattening to implement NDP and to GPU-based systems that support flat data parallelism. Specifically, we compare with NESL running on a single CPU, Data Parallel Haskell (DPH) running on 8 cores, Copperhead running on a GPU, and hand-written CUDA code running on a GPU. We choose the best available implementation of each benchmark for each measured system. We take this approach because each platform varies in compiler technology, target hardware, and implementation tuning, resulting in unfair penalties to platforms with different hardware tradeoffs or where benchmark authors were no longer maintaining tuned algorithms for the evolving GPU hardware.

While our implementation does not achieve the level of performance of hand-tuned CUDA programs, our results are better than other high-level NDP and flat data-parallel programming languages. Furthermore, NESL programs are significantly smaller than the corresponding hand-tuned CUDA (typically a factor of 10 smaller) and require no direct knowledge of GPU idiosyncrasies. Thus, we make GPUs applicable to a wider range of parallel applications and a wider range of programmers.

6.1 Experimental framework

Our benchmark platform has an Intel i7-950 quad-core processor running at 3.06GHz, with hyper-threading enabled for a total of eight cores available for parallel execution. Our GPU is an NVIDIA Tesla C2050, which has 14 SMPs, each with 32 cores for a total of 448 cores, and 3GB of global memory. For most experiments, we ran Linux x86-64 kernel version 3.0.0-15 with the CUDA 4.1 drivers, but for one test we used Microsoft Windows 7 (also with the CUDA 4.1 drivers).

We report the wall-clock execution time of the core computation, excluding initialization and result verification times. We exclude the latter, because those times differ widely between different platforms. Each benchmark was run at least 20 times at each size configuration and we report the mean.

6.2 Comparison systems

We compare our NESL/GPU implementation with a number of different systems, which are described in this section. To illustrate the programming models of these systems, we give code for the data-parallel computation of the dot product. In NESL, this code is:

```
function dotp (xs, ys) =
  sum ({ x*y : x in xs; y in ys })
```

```
import Data.Array.Parallel
import Data.Array.Parallel.Prelude.Double
    as D

dotp' :: [:Double:] -> [:Double:] -> Double
dotp' xs ys = D.sumP (zipWithP (*) xs ys)
```

Figure 7. Data Parallel Haskell implementation of dot product

```
from copperhead import *

@cu
def dot_product(xs, ys):
    return sum(map(lambda x,y: x*y, xs, ys))
```

Figure 8. Copperhead implementation of dot product

6.2.1 NESL/CPU

We measured the CPU-based version of NESL running on a single core of our test machine. For these experiments, we ran the output of our optimizer with fusion turned off (*i.e.*, the VCODE after inlining and elimination of redundant stack operations). The CPU version of NESL uses an implementation of CVL that is quite efficient. The code uses macros for loop unrolling and inlining, which exposes multiple adjacent operations that the C compiler optimizes into SSE instructions.

6.2.2 Data Parallel Haskell

Data Parallel Haskell (DPH) also uses flattening in its implementation of NDP [CLPK08]. This extension of the Glasgow Haskell Compiler (GHC) [GHC] implements a subset of the Haskell language with strict evaluation semantics. On a per-module basis, code restricted to this subset and using the appropriate types will be flattened. DPH does not support GPU execution, but it does support parallel execution on multicore systems. For our benchmarks, we report the DPH performance on all eight cores of our test machine.[4] We measured the DPH implementation as of February 2012 and GHC Version 7.4.1.

Dot product in DPH The DPH version of our dot-product example is shown in Figure 7. At its core, the last line is very similar to the NESL code for this example.

6.2.3 Copperhead

Copperhead [CGK11] is an extension of the Python language that provides direct language support for data parallel operations on GPUs. It is limited to element-wise operations and reductions (*i.e.*, it does not support NDP computations). Sources intended to run on the GPU (and optionally also the CPU) are annotated with an `@cu` tag, indicating that only the subset of Python that can be compiled to the GPU may occur in the following definitions. Using a special `places` keyword, those annotated definitions can be executed either on the GPU or CPU.

We are using the Copperhead sources as of February, 2012, available from: `http://code.google.com/p/copperhead/`. These sources are compiled against Python 2.7.1, Boost 1.41, PyCuda 2011.1.2, and CodePy 2011.1. The Copperhead project is still under active development and the compiler is not yet mature enough to implement all of the benchmarks used in this paper.

Dot product in Copperhead The dot-product example is very straightforward to write in Copperhead and appears in Figure 8. The `@cu` annotation on the `dot_product` function tells Copperhead to compile the code to run on the GPU. When the `dot_product` function is invoked, its arguments are converted to CUDA representation and transferred to the GPU. Likewise, the result of the function is transferred back to the CPU and converted to Python representation automatically.

[4] We also measured the performance on four cores without hyper-threading, but found that the eight-core performance was better.

```
#define N (2048*2048)
#define THREADS_PER_BLOCK 512

__global__ void dot (int *xs, int *ys, int *res)
{
  __shared__ int temp[THREADS_PER_BLOCK];
  int index = threadIdx.x + blockIdx.x
      * blockDim.x;
  temp[threadIdx.x] = xs[index] * ys[index];

  __syncthreads();

   if (0 == threadIdx.x) {
     int sum = 0;
     for (int i = 0; i < THREADS_PER_BLOCK; i++)
       sum += temp[i];
     atomicAdd (res , sum);
   }
}

int main(void)
{
  dot<<<N/THREADS_PER_BLOCK, THREADS_PER_BLOCK>>>
    (dev_xs, dev_ys, dev_res);
}
```

Figure 9. Basic CUDA implementation of dot product

6.2.4 CUDA

We also measured hand-coded implementations of our benchmarks to provide a measure of the best possible performance that one might expect for these benchmarks. These implementations represent significant programmer effort, but make very efficient use of the GPU.

Dot product in CUDA Figure 9 gives CUDA kernel code for the dot product. This program performs basic blocking and uses fast shared memory on the GPU, but is slower than the optimized version available in CUBLAS.[5] Even a simple implementation in CUDA of this small example is significantly more complicated and verbose than the code on any of the other platforms.

6.3 Benchmarks

Table 1 summarizes our benchmark results. As would be expected, hand-coded CUDA code outperforms the other implementations on all benchmarks. But the NESL/GPU implementation is the second fastest system on almost all of the benchmarks and also has the shortest programs.

All of the NESL results reported in this section are for programs optimized as described in Section 5. The NESL/CPU programs do not include fused kernel operations because those were implemented only for the NESL/GPU backend.

[5] For our performance experiments, we measured the faster CUBLAS version of dot product.

	Problem Size (# elements)	Lines of code NESL	CUDA	DPH	Copper	Execution time (ms) NESL/CPU	NESL/GPU	CUDA	DPH	Copper
Dot Product	10,000,000	**8**	80	39	31	27	3.0	**< 1.0**	12	710
Sort	1,000,000	**12**	136	52	46	230	259	**3.1**	2,360	230
Black-Scholes	10,000,000	**37**	337	*N/A*	*N/A*	8,662	163	**1.9**	*N/A*	*N/A*
Convex Hull	5,000,000	**25**	*unknown*	72	*N/A*	1,000	283	**269**	807	*N/A*
Barnes-Hut	75,000	**225**	1930	414	*N/A*	22,200	4,502	**40**	10,200	*N/A*

Table 1. Lines of non-whitespace or comment code for the benchmark programs, omitting extra testing or GUI code. Benchmark times are also reported, as the mean execution times in milliseconds (ms). Smaller numbers are better for both code and time.

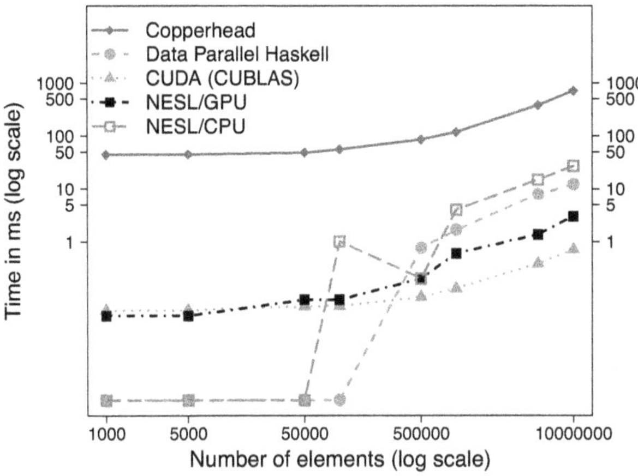

Figure 10. Dot product execution times (ms) for a range of problem sizes. Smaller times are better. Axes are log scale.

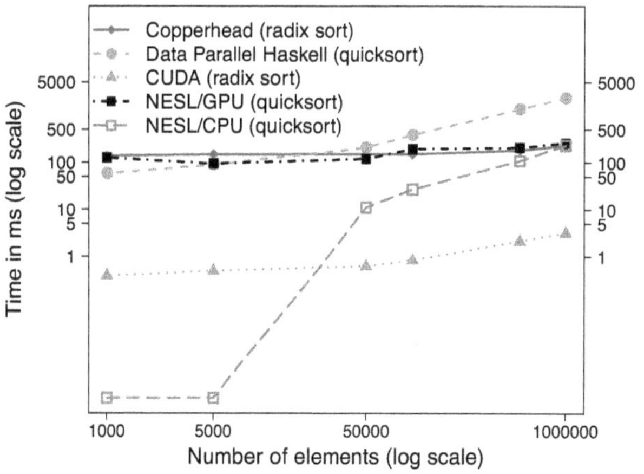

Figure 11. Sorting execution times (ms) for a range of problem sizes. Smaller times are better. Axes are log scale.

6.3.1 Dot product

The dot product of two vectors is the result of adding the pairwise multiplications of elements from each of the vectors. This small benchmark is interesting because it contains one trivial vector-parallel operation (multiplying each of the elements) and one that requires significant inter-thread communication (reducing those multiplied elements to a single value through addition).

In the summary data in Table 1, each vector contains 10,000,000 32-bit floating point. Figure 10 provides a more detailed breakdown for each system across many vector lengths. Because the performance of these systems vary widely, we use a logarithmic scale for the time axis in this plot.

The superb CUDA performance is provided by a highly-tuned implementation of dot product from the CUBLAS library. The NESL/GPU version of dot product also performs well. For vector sizes less than 5,000,000, the NESL/GPU version finishes faster than the finest resolution of the timing APIs. This good performance is owed to the use of a highly-tuned parallel reduction operator for the addition operation and relatively low additional overhead around the element-wise multiplication. The poor Copperhead behavior appears to be related to failing to take full advantage of the parallel hardware.

6.3.2 Sorting

For the sorting benchmarks, we selected the best algorithm for the particular platform, which was quicksort for the CPU (DPH and NESL/CPU) and radix sort for the GPU (CUDA and Copperhead). The one exception is that we measured quicksort for the NESL/GPU platform, since it runs nearly 10% faster than radix sort owing to lower CPU/GPU communication overhead. The sorting benchmarks in Table 1 measure the sorting of a vector of 1,000,000 random integers (the actual vectors differ because of differences in the random-number generation algorithms).

Figure 11 provides a more detailed breakdown for each system across many vector lengths. Copperhead and CUDA both make very effective use of the GPU and scale well across increasing problem sizes. The NESL/CPU version of quicksort performs better than the NESL/GPU version because of the reduced cost of vector operations.

6.3.3 Black-Scholes

The Black-Scholes option pricing model is a closed-form method for computing the value of a European-style call or put option, based on the price of the stock, the original strike of the option, the risk-free interest rate, and the volatility of the underlying instrument [BS73]. This operation is numerically dense and trivially parallelizable. Reported numbers are for the pricing of 10,000,000 contracts.

The NESL/GPU version is able to perform much faster than the NESL/CPU version because of the very aggressive fusion of the dense numeric operations. The CUDA version is a hand-optimized version included in the NVIDIA SDK.

Figure 12 provides a more detailed breakdown for each system across many vector lengths.

6.3.4 Convex Hull

The convex-hull benchmark results shown in Table 1 are the result of determining the convex hull of 5,000,000 points in the plane. While this algorithm is trivially parallel, the parallel subtasks are not guaranteed to be of equal work sizes, providing an example of irregular parallelism. The NESL and DPH codes are based on the algorithm by Barber *et al.* [BDH96]. The convex-hull algorithm

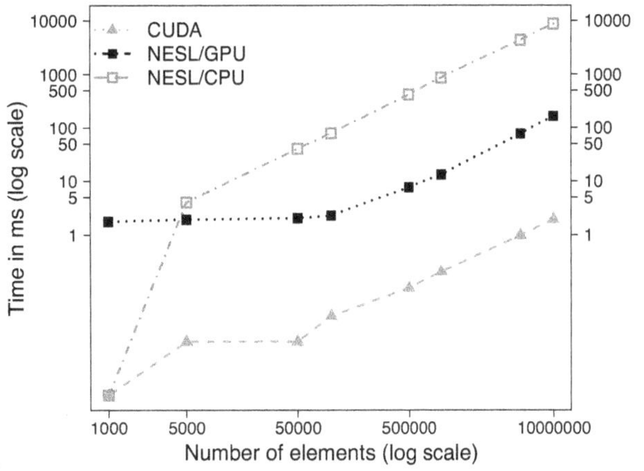

Figure 12. Black-Scholes execution times (ms) for a range of problem sizes. Smaller times are better. Axes are log scale.

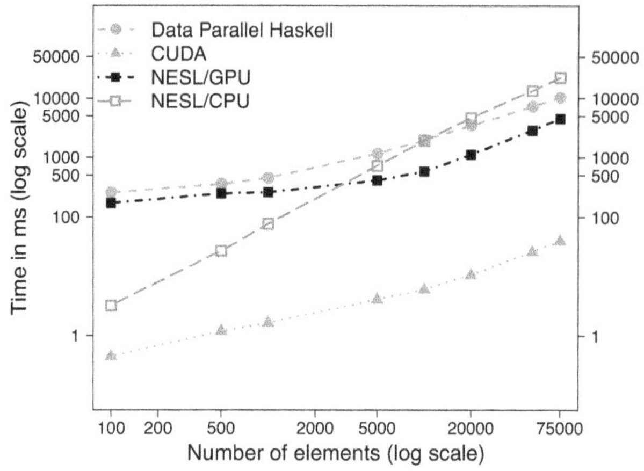

Figure 14. Barnes-Hut execution times (ms) for a range of problem sizes. Smaller times are better. Axes are log scale.

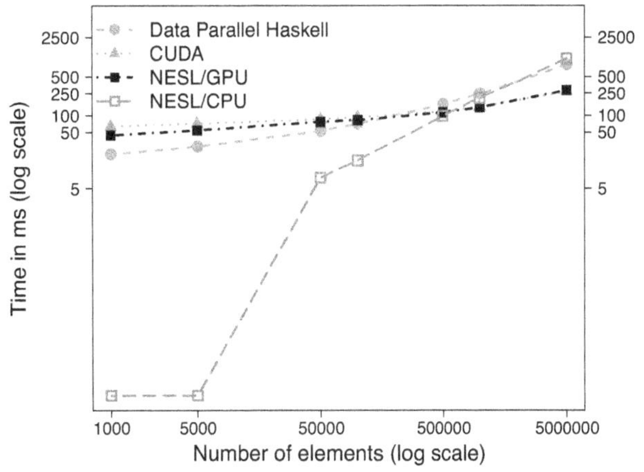

Figure 13. Convex Hull execution times (ms) for a range of problem sizes. Smaller times are better. Axes are log scale.

written in CUDA is from ongoing work at the National University of Singapore [GCN+12]. Their gHull algorithm was originally based on the quickhull algorithm, but has been optimized for better performance on a GPU. Their algorithm also works with points in 3D, but in our testing we constrained it to the 2D case for comparison with these other systems. It performs slightly better than the quickhull algorithm implemented in NESL and run on the GPU. This code was only made available to us in binary form, for execution on Windows, so we measured its performance on our benchmark machine under Windows 7 using the CUDA 4.1 drivers.

Figure 13 provides a more detailed breakdown for each system across many vector lengths.

6.3.5 Barnes-Hut (N-Body)

The Barnes-Hut benchmark [BH86] is a hierarchical N-body problem solver; we measure the 2D version that uses a quadtree to accelerate the computation. Each iteration has two phases. In the first phase, the quadtree is constructed from a sequence of mass points. The second phase then uses this tree to accelerate the computation of the gravitational force on the bodies in the system. All versions of this benchmark shown in Table 1 run one iteration over 75,000 random particles. Figure 14 provides a more detailed breakdown for each system across many vector lengths. The number of iterations is held constant at one.

The CUDA version of Barnes-Hut was implemented by Burtscher and Pingali [BP11]. We use version 2.2 of their source, which was the newest available as of February 2012.

All implementations exhibit roughly the same scalability. While the NESL/GPU implementation is the second fastest implementation, it is still significantly slower than the CUDA version. The NESL/GPU implementation's runtime is split roughly $1/3$ on memory operations and $2/3$ on kernel calls. These memory operations are related to allocations and conditional branches. When there is a conditional statement over a vector, first we perform the conditional check. Then, we sum the number of true elements from that conditional check and then transfer the integer (or integers, for a segmented vector) back from the GPU to the CPU to allocate a memory block of the correct size for each of the true and false elements. After that allocation, we copy the true elements into the true vector and the false ones into the false vector and then execute the clauses of the conditional on the appropriate vectors. These memory transfers back to the CPU and extra kernel calls could be avoided by moving some of the allocation code onto the GPU in a future implementation.

6.4 Effects of optimizations

In Section 5, we described a set of optimizations we perform on the code produced by the NESL compiler. Table 2 compares the execution time for the benchmarks across the optimizations on the NESL/GPU implementation, normalized to the mean execution time of the baseline. In nearly all cases, these optimizations result in improvements.

The one place where there is a decrease in performance is between the optimized and fused versions of quicksort. In the GPU version of quicksort, the vast majority of the remaining time spent in execution after optimization is in segmented sums and reductions that determine the number of elements in each of the less-than and greater-than partitions in order to shuffle them for the recursive calls. Because of this balance of work, the fusion of the element-wise operations that compare elements does not have a large enough effect to increase performance. While the mean execution time is slightly slower under fusion than the simple optimized version for this benchmark, the median of the fused

	NESL/GPU		
	Base	Opt	Fused
Dot Product	1.0	0.95	0.94
Sort	1.0	0.92	0.93
Black-Scholes	1.0	1.0	0.67
Convex Hull	1.0	0.95	0.91
Barnes-Hut	1.0	0.94	0.90

Table 2. Performance benefits from VCODE optimization. Execution times are normalized to the base (unoptimized) strategy, with smaller values being better.

values is lower and a more rigorous statistical analysis shows that the fused version is the same speed as the optimized one.[6]

One benchmark that particularly benefits from fusion and the creation of kernels is Black-Scholes option pricing. This benchmark is numerically dense and our optimizer aggressively reduces the number of kernel invocations, generating several kernels that each turn what would have been more than 10 separate GPU calls into a single call that both performs all of the operations and avoids intermediate writes to global memory.

7. Related Work

To the best of our knowledge, our work is the only example of an NDP language that is compiled for GPUs, so we divide the related work into languages that support (non-nested) data parallelism on GPUs and languages that use flattening to implement NDP on CPUs.

7.1 GPU Languages

The work on languages targeting GPUs is focused on regular data-parallel programs. These languages typically also provide library functions with efficient parallel implementations of `map` and `reduce`. While many of the available languages address some of the issues listed in Section 3.2, none of them address either the recursive call issue or any of the memory, data, and thread issues with respect to irregular data-parallel programs.

Barracuda [Lar11] and Single-Assignment C (SAC) for GPUs [GS06, GTS11], both provide techniques for compiling applicative array languages down to GPUs. Array languages have proven ideally suited for translation to the regular, flat parallelism available on the GPU. While these languages do not support parallelizing over irregular operations, SAC includes a fusion pass that finds operations whose results are based on the same index set and reduces those operations to a single pass generating multiple results. This fusion technique is not supported by our system, but it and other optimizations used in SAC may be useful for optimizing VCODE.

Nikola and Accelerate provide support for compiling operations on flat vectors in Haskell programs to run on GPUs [MM10, CKL+11]. Similarly Copperhead, discussed in more detail in Section 6.2, is a language targeting GPUs based on Python [CGK11]. These languages add `map`, `reduce`, and other high-level operations to significantly ease programming for GPUs and rely on the CPU to handle more complicated control-flow.

OptiX is an embedded domain-specific language and library that supports ray-oriented applications on GPUs [PBD+10]. These applications have a significant recursive component, which OptiX handles by CPS conversion and a trampoline.

[6] The Wilcoxon signed-rank test — appropriate for nonparametric, independent data points — provides 92% confidence that the difference between the two distributions is zero.

7.2 CPU Languages

Data Parallel Haskell (DPH) is the culmination of many years of research into expanding the flattening transformation to handle both more datatypes and higher-order functions [CKLP01, LCK06]. The NESL language does not support datatypes and is only first-order. DPH also supports partial vectorization, which allows portions of a program to remain unflattened [CLPK08]. In NESL, the entire program and all data are flattened. Finally, DPH implements a much wider range of fusion operations to remove the redundant allocations than the implementation presented in Section 5.2.

The Manticore project takes a different approach to nested data parallelism, implementing it without flattening and relying on efficient runtime mechanisms to handle load balancing issues [BFR+10].

8. Conclusion

We have shown that with careful implementation of the library primitives, the flattening transformation can be used on NDP programs to achieve good performance on GPUs. By focusing our performance tuning efforts on the VCODE implementation, we make it possible for a wide range of irregular parallel applications to get performance benefits from GPUs, without having to be hand ported and tuned. While performance does not match that of hand-tuned CUDA code, NESL programs are a factor of 10 shorter and do not require expertise in GPU programming. We hope that this work will be used as a better baseline for new implementations of irregular parallel applications than the usual sequential C programs. Better, of course, would be the integration of these classic compilation techniques for vector hardware into modern programming languages.

8.1 Future work

The most obvious limitation of our approach is that communication with the host CPU is required for allocation of memory. This requirement, as described Section 6.3.5, results in many additional communications between the CPU and GPU merely to provide an address. Moving the memory allocation responsibility into the GPU kernels would remove much of this communication cost. This issue is addressed by the compilation model used by Chatterjee in his work porting NESL to the MIMD Encore Multimax [Cha93]. His implementation included size analysis of programs and full custom C code generation. Some of his techniques may be applicable to improving GPU performance of NDP.

Acknowledgments

Ben Lippmeier provided help understanding the benchmark results and current status of Data Parallel Haskell. Bryan Catanzaro untangled the Copperhead dependency stack and provided insight into its current implementation and performance limitations.

We thank the NVIDIA Corporation for their generous donation of both hardware and financial support. This material is based upon work supported by the National Science Foundation under Grants CCF-0811389 and CCF-1010568, and upon work performed in part while John Reppy was serving at the National Science Foundation. The views and conclusions contained herein are those of the authors and should not be interpreted as necessarily representing the official policies or endorsements, either expressed or implied, of these organizations or the U.S. Government.

References

[BC90] Blelloch, G. and S. Chatterjee. VCODE: A data-parallel intermediate language. In *FOMPC3*, 1990, pp. 471–480.

[BC93] Blelloch, G. and S. Chatterjee. CVL: A C vector language, 1993.

[BCH+94] Blelloch, G. E., S. Chatterjee, J. C. Hardwick, J. Sipelstein, and M. Zagha. Implementation of a portable nested data-parallel language. *JPDC*, **21**(1), 1994, pp. 4–14.

[BDH96] Barber, C. B., D. P. Dobkin, and H. Huhdanpaa. The quickhull algorithm for convex hulls. *ACM TOMS*, **22**(4), 1996, pp. 469–483.

[BFR+10] Bergstrom, L., M. Fluet, M. Rainey, J. Reppy, and A. Shaw. Lazy tree splitting. In *ICFP '10*. ACM, September 2010, pp. 93–104.

[BH86] Barnes, J. and P. Hut. A hierarchical $O(N \log N)$ force calculation algorithm. *Nature*, **324**, December 1986, pp. 446–449.

[Ble96] Blelloch, G. E. Programming parallel algorithms. *CACM*, **39**(3), March 1996, pp. 85–97.

[BP11] Burtscher, M. and K. Pingali. An efficient CUDA implementation of the tree-based Barnes Hut n-body algorithm. In *GPU Computing Gems Emerald Edition*, chapter 6, pp. 75–92. Elsevier Science Publishers, New York, NY, 2011.

[BS73] Black, F. and M. Scholes. The pricing of options and corporate liabilities. *JPE*, **81**(3), 1973, pp. 637–654.

[BS90] Blelloch, G. E. and G. W. Sabot. Compiling collection-oriented languages onto massively parallel computers. *JPDC*, **8**(2), 1990, pp. 119–134.

[CBS11] Cunningham, D., R. Bordawekar, and V. Saraswat. GPU programming in a high level language compiling X10 to CUDA. In *X10 '11*, San Jose, CA, May 2011. Available from `http://x10-lang.org/`.

[CGK11] Catanzaro, B., M. Garland, and K. Keutzer. Copperhead: compiling an embedded data parallel language. In *PPoPP '11*, San Antonio, TX, February 2011. ACM, pp. 47–56.

[Cha93] Chatterjee, S. Compiling nested data-parallel programs for shared-memory multiprocessors. *ACM TOPLAS*, **15**(3), July 1993, pp. 400–462.

[CKL+11] Chakravarty, M. M., G. Keller, S. Lee, T. L. McDonell, and V. Grover. Accelerating Haskell array codes with multicore GPUs. In *DAMP '11*, Austin, January 2011. ACM, pp. 3–14.

[CKLP01] Chakravarty, M. M. T., G. Keller, R. Leshchinskiy, and W. Pfannenstiel. Nepal – nested data parallelism in Haskell. In *Euro-Par '01*, vol. 2150 of *LNCS*. Springer-Verlag, August 2001, pp. 524–534.

[CLPK08] Chakravarty, M. M. T., R. Leshchinskiy, S. Peyton Jones, and G. Keller. Partial vectorisation of Haskell programs. In *DAMP '08*. ACM, January 2008, pp. 2–16. Available from `http://clip.dia.fi.upm.es/Conferences/DAMP08/`.

[DR11] Dhanasekaran, B. and N. Rubin. A new method for GPU based irregular reductions and its application to k-means clustering. In *GPGPU-4*, Newport Beach, California, March 2011. ACM.

[Ert01] Ertl, M. A. Threaded code variations and optimizations. In *EuroForth 2001*, Schloss Dagstuhl, Germany, November 2001. pp. 49–55. Available from `http://www.complang.tuwien.ac.at/papers/`.

[GCN+12] Gao, M., T.-T. Cao, A. Nanjappa, T.-S. Tan, and Z. Huang. A GPU Algorithm for Convex Hull. *Technical Report TRA1/12*, National University of Singapore, School of Computing, January 2012.

[GHC] GHC. The Glasgow Haskell Compiler. Available from `http://www.haskell.org/ghc`.

[GS06] Grelck, C. and S.-B. Scholz. SAC — A Functional Array Language for Efficient Multi-threaded Execution. *IJPP*, **34**(4), August 2006, pp. 383–427.

[GTS11] Guo, J., J. Thiyagalingam, and S.-B. Scholz. Breaking the GPU programming barrier with the auto-parallelising SAC compiler. In *DAMP '11*, Austin, January 2011. ACM, pp. 15–24.

[HB11] Hoberock, J. and N. Bell. Thrust: A productivity-oriented library for CUDA. In W. W. Hwu (ed.), *GPU Computing Gems, Jade Edition*, chapter 26, pp. 359–372. Morgan Kaufmann Publishers, October 2011.

[Kel99] Keller, G. *Transformation-based Implementation of Nested Data Parallelism for Distributed Memory Machines*. Ph.D. dissertation, Technische Universität Berlin, Berlin, Germany, 1999.

[Khr11] Khronos OpenCL Working Group. OpenCL 1.2 Specification, November 2011. Available from `http://www.khronos.org/registry/cl/specs/opencl-1.2.pdf`.

[Lar11] Larsen, B. Simple optimizations for an applicative array language for graphics processors. In *DAMP '11*, Austin, January 2011. ACM, pp. 25–34.

[LCK06] Leshchinskiy, R., M. M. T. Chakravarty, and G. Keller. Higher order flattening. In V. Alexandrov, D. van Albada, P. Sloot, and J. Dongarra (eds.), *ICCS '06*, number 3992 in LNCS. Springer-Verlag, May 2006, pp. 920–928.

[Les05] Leshchinskiy, R. *Higher-Order Nested Data Parallelism: Semantics and Implementation*. Ph.D. dissertation, Technische Universität Berlin, Berlin, Germany, 2005.

[MGG12] Merrill, D., M. Garland, and A. Grimshaw. Scalable GPU graph traversal. In *PPoPP '12*, New Orleans, LA, February 2012. ACM, pp. 117–128.

[MLBP12] Mendez-Lojo, M., M. Burtscher, and K. Pingali. A GPU implementation of inclusion-based points-to analysis. In *PPoPP '12*, New Orleans, LA, February 2012. ACM, pp. 107–116.

[MM10] Mainland, G. and G. Morrisett. Nikola: Embedding compiled GPU functions in Haskell. In *HASKELL '10*, Baltimore, MD, September 2010. ACM, pp. 67–78.

[NVI11a] NVIDIA. NVIDIA CUDA C Best Practices Guide, 2011.

[NVI11b] NVIDIA. NVIDIA CUDA C Programming Guide, 2011. Available from `http://developer.nvidia.com/category/zone/cuda-zone`.

[PBD+10] Parker, S. G., J. Bigler, A. Dietrich, H. Friedrich, J. Hoberock, D. Luebke, D. McAllister, M. McGuire, K. Morley, A. Robison, and M. Stich. OptiX: a general purpose ray tracing engine. *ACM TOG*, **29**, July 2010.

[PPW95] Palmer, D. W., J. F. Prins, and S. Westfold. Work-efficient nested data-parallelism. In *FoMPP5*. IEEE Computer Society Press, 1995, pp. 186–193.

[Pro95] Proebsting, T. A. Optimizing an ANSI C interpreter with superoperators. In *POPL '95*, San Francisco, January 1995. ACM, pp. 322–332.

[SHZO07] Sengupta, S., M. Harris, Y. Zhang, and J. D. Owens. Scan primitives for GPU computing. In *GH '07*, San Diego, CA, August 2007. Eurographics Association, pp. 97–106.

[YHL+09] Yang, K., B. He, Q. Luo, P. V. Sander, and J. Shi. Stack-based parallel recursion on graphics processors. In *PPoPP '09*, Raleigh, NC, February 2009. ACM, pp. 299–300.

Work Efficient Higher-Order Vectorisation

Ben Lippmeier[†] Manuel M. T. Chakravarty[†] Gabriele Keller[†] Roman Leshchinskiy[†]

Simon Peyton Jones[‡]

[†]Computer Science and Engineering
University of New South Wales, Australia
{benl,chak,keller,rl}@cse.unsw.edu.au

[‡]Microsoft Research Ltd.
Cambridge, England
{simonpj}@microsoft.com

Abstract

Existing approaches to *higher-order vectorisation*, also known as *flattening nested data parallelism,* do not preserve the asymptotic work complexity of the source program. Straightforward examples, such as sparse matrix-vector multiplication, can suffer a severe blow-up in both time and space, which limits the practicality of this method. We discuss why this problem arises, identify the mis-handling of index space transforms as the root cause, and present a solution using a refined representation of nested arrays. We have implemented this solution in Data Parallel Haskell (DPH) and present benchmarks showing that realistic programs, which used to suffer the blow-up, now have the correct asymptotic work complexity. In some cases, the asymptotic complexity of the vectorised program is even better than the original.

Categories and Subject Descriptors D.3.3 [*Programming Languages*]: Language Constructs and Features—Concurrent programming structures; Polymorphism; Abstract data types

General Terms Languages, Performance

Keywords Arrays, Data parallelism, Haskell

1. Introduction

Data Parallel Haskell (DPH) is an extension to the Glasgow Haskell Compiler (GHC) that offers *nested data parallelism*. With nested parallelism, each parallel computation may spawn further parallel computations of arbitrary complexity, whereas with flat parallelism, they cannot; so nested data parallelism is vastly more expressive for the programmer. On the other hand, flat data parallelism is far easier to implement, because flat data parallelism admits a simple load balancing strategy and can be used on SIMD hardware (including GPUs). The *higher-order vectorisation* (or *flattening*) transform [17] bridges the gap, by transforming source programs using *nested* data parallelism into ones using just *flat* data parallelism [1, 17]. That is, it transforms the program we want to write into the one we want to run.

Unfortunately, practical implementations, including ours, have had a serious flaw: the standard transformation only guarantees to preserve the parallel *depth complexity* of the source program, and not its asymptotic *work complexity* as well. If our benchmark machines had an infinite number of processors, this would be of no concern, but alas they do not. Nor is this phenomenon rare: while working on DPH we have encountered simple programs that suffer a severe, and sometimes even exponential, blow-up in time and space when vectorised.

This is a well-known problem that arises due to the flat representation of nested arrays in vectorised code [3, Appendix C]. Several attempts have been made to solve it, but so far they have been either incomplete [15], do not work with higher order languages [10], or give up on flattening the parallelism [4, 8] or arrays [18] altogether. In this paper, we will show how to overcome the problem for full-scale higher-order vectorisation. Overall, we make the following contributions:

1. We present the first approach to higher-order vectorisation that, we believe, ensures the vectorised program maintains the asymptotic work complexity of the source program, while allowing nested arrays to retain their flattened form (§4). We only require that vectorised programs are *contained* [2, 18], a property related to the standard handling of branches in SIMD-style parallel programming (§5.6).
2. We identify the key problem of mishandled index space transforms, which worsen the asymptotic complexity of vectorised code using prior flat array representations (§3).
3. We introduce a novel delayed implementation of the central index space transforms (§4) and discuss the pragmatics of achieving good constant factors, in addition to the required asymptotic performance (§6).
4. Finally, we present performance figures for several realistic programs, including the Barnes-Hut n-body algorithm. This supports our claim that our delayed implementation of the index space transforms leads to vectorised programs that operate within the required asymptotic bounds (§7).

The claim that our new approach to higher-order vectorisation is work efficient is supported by experiments with a concrete implementation in GHC — but not yet by formal proof, which we leave to future work. Nevertheless, our work presents a significant advance of the state of the art on a long-standing problem. Achieving good *space* complexity is an orthogonal problem that we discuss in §5.5. A reference implementation of our new array representation is available in the companion technical report [13].

ICFP'12, September 9–15, 2012, Copenhagen, Denmark.

2. The Asymptotic Complexity Problem

We start with an example illustrating vectorisation. The function **retrieve** simultaneously indexes several arrays, the **xss**, each of which is distributed across one subarray of indices contained in **iss**. It returns a nested array of the results and uses nested parallelism — an inner parallel computation (**mapP indexP xss**) is performed for each of the outer ones.

```
retrieve :: [:[:Char:]:] -> [:[:Int:]:] -> [:[:Char:]:]
retrieve xss iss
  = zipWithP mapP (mapP indexP xss) iss
```

Here is **retrieve** applied to two example arrays.[1]

```
retrieve [[A B]   [C D E] [F G] [H]]       (xss)
         [[1 0 1] [2]     [1 0] [0]]       (iss)
    ==>  [[B A B] [E]     [G F] [H]]
```

In the type signature, **[:Char:]** refers to *bulk-strict, parallel, one-dimensional arrays*. Elements of these arrays are stored unboxed, so that demanding any element causes them all to be computed. **zipWithP** and **mapP** are parallel versions of the corresponding list functions, while **indexP** is array indexing — Figure 1 shows these and other typical array operations. The work-complexity of **retrieve** is linear in the number of leaf elements of the array **iss** (seven here), since each is used once for indexing. (Technically it is also linear in the number of sub-arrays in **iss**, since empty arrays in **iss** would still cost.)

The vectorised form of **retrieve** is the following — the accompanying technical report [13] includes the full derivation.

```
retrieve_v :: PA (PA Char) -> PA (PA Int) -> PA (PA Char)
retrieve_v xss iss
 = let ns = takeLengths iss
   in  unconcat iss
        $ index_l (sum ns) (replicates ns xss)
        $ concat iss
```

The type **PA** is a generic representation type that determines the layout of the user-visible type **[::]** in a type-dependent manner [6]. When applied to our example array, the function first concatenates **iss** to yield a flat array of indices, and uses **takeLengths** to get the lengths of the inner arrays of **iss**:

```
ns   = takeLengths iss = [3     1  2    1]
iss1 = concat iss      = [1 0 1  2  1 0  0]
```

The **replicates** function distributes the subarrays of **xss** across the flat indices array. It takes an array of replication counts and an array of elements, and replicates each element by its corresponding count:

```
xss1 = replicates ns xss
     = replicates [3 1 2 1] [[A B] [C D E] [F G] [H]
     = [[A B] [A B] [A B] [C D E] [F G] [F G] [H]]
```

Now we have one sub-array for each of the elements of **iss1**. Continuing on, we use the *lifted indexing* operator **index_l**, which has the following type:

```
index_l :: Int -> PA (PA e) -> PA Int -> PA e
```

Given an array of arrays, and an array of indices of the same length, for each subarray-index pair, **index_l** retrieves the corresponding element of the array. In other words, **index_l** is effectively **zipWithP indexP**, except that it gets the length of the two arrays as an additional first argument.

[1] The concrete syntax for array literals is [:x1, ..., xn:]. To save space, we elide the colon and comma.

```
lengthP      :: [:e:] -> Int
indexP, (!:) :: [:e:] -> Int -> e
concatP      :: [:[:e:]:]      -> [:e:]
mapP         :: (d -> e)       -> [:d:] -> [:e:]
zipWithP     :: (c -> d -> e)  -> [:c:] -> [:d:] -> [:e:]
foldP        :: (e -> e -> e)  -> [:e:] -> e
```

Figure 1. User Visible Array Operators

```
data PA e = PA {length :: Int, pdata :: PData e}
data family    PData e
data instance PData Int      = PInt  (Vector Int)
data instance PData Char     = PChar (Vector Char)
data instance PData (PA e)   = PNested Segd (PData e)
data Segd = Segd {lengths, indices :: Vector Int}
index       :: PA e         -> Int        -> e
index_l     :: Int          -> PA (PA e)  -> PA Int -> PA e
replicate   :: Int          -> e          -> PA e
replicates  :: Vector Int -> PA e         -> PA e
concat      :: PA (PA e)    -> PA e
unconcat    :: PA (PA e)    -> PA e       -> PA (PA e)
```

Figure 2. Baseline Array Representation and Parallel Primitives

Applying **index_l** to our example yields the following:

```
xss2
 = index_l (sum ns) (replicates ns xss) (concat iss)
 = index_l 7 [[A B] [A B] [A B] [C D E] [F G] [F G] [H]]
             [1     0     1     2       1     0     0]
 = [B A B E G F H]
```

Finally, we use **unconcat** to reapply the original nesting structure to this flat result:

```
xss3 = unconcat [[1 0 1] [2] [1 0] [0]] [B A B E G F H]
     = [[B A B] [E] [G F] [H]]
```

In the vectorised function **retrieve_v**, all parallelism comes from the implementation of the primitive flat parallel array operators such as **index_l** and **replicates**. However, simply converting nested parallelism to flat parallelism is not sufficient. We previously implemented **replicates** by physically copying each of the subarrays. With that implementation, suppose we evaluate the following expression:

```
retrieve [[A B C D E F G H]] [[0 1 2 3 4 5 6 7]]
```

In terms of the source program, this expression takes eight steps, one for each index in the second array. However, in the vectorised program, **replicates** will also copy **[A B C D E F G H]** eight times. As we have the same number of characters in the first array as indices in the second array, vectorisation turned a function that performs $O(n)$ work into an $O(n^2)$ function: Disaster!

It turns out that the trouble with **replicates** is just one of a class of problems related to the mishandling of index space transforms during vectorisation. These transforms change the mapping between elements in the source and result arrays, but do not compute new element values. In addition to identifying index space transforms as the culprit, in the next two sections we contribute a novel delayed implementation, which enables vectorised programs to remain within the required asymptotic complexity bounds. What are those bounds? Consider an absolutely *direct* implementation of DPH, in which a value of type **[:a:]** is represented by an ordinary array of pointers to values of type **a**.

> **Complexity Goal:** for the output of vectorisation to have the same *asymptotic work complexity* as the direct implementation, but with much better *constant factors* and *amenability to parallelism*.

3. Baseline Representation of Nested Arrays

A key idea of Blelloch's vectorisation transformation is to flatten the representation of nested arrays, as well as the parallelism itself. More precisely: an array A of sub-arrays $A_0, A_1, \ldots, A_{n-1}$ (each with its own length) is represented by (a) a single long array of data, $D = [A_0, A_1, \ldots, A_{n-1}]$ all laid out in one contiguous block, and (b) a *segment descriptor* that gives the length of each A_i in the data block D. We call A_i the *segments* of A. The idea is to divide the data block D evenly over the processors, and process each chunk independently in parallel. This provides both excellent granularity and excellent data locality, which is intended to satisfy the second part of our Complexity Goal. There is some book-keeping to do on the segment descriptor; generating that book-keeping code is the job of the vectorisation transformation.

Figure 2 gives the representation of nested arrays in Haskell, using GHC's *data families* [5]. An array of type `(PA e)` is represented by a pair `PA n d`, where `n` is the length of the array, and `d :: PData e` contains its data. The representation of `PData` is type-dependent — hence, its declaration as a `data family`. When the argument type is a scalar, matters are simple: `PData Int` is represented merely by a `Vector Int`, which we take as primitive here[2]. Arrays of `Char` are represented similarly. On the other hand, the data component of a *nested array*, with type `PData (PA e)` is represented by a pair of a segment descriptor of type `Segd`, and the *data block* of type `PData e`. The segment descriptor `Segd` has two fields, `lengths` and `indices`. The latter is just the scan (running sum) of the former, but we maintain both in the implementation to avoid recomputing `indices` from `lengths` repeatedly. Each is a flat `Vector` of `Int` values.

Using the example from the previous section, the array `xss1` has type `(PA (PA Char))` and is represented like this:

```
  replicates [3 1 2 1] [[A B] [C D E] [F G] [H]]
  = [[A B] [A B] [A B] [C D E] [F G] [F G] [H]]
------------------------------------------------ (ARRO)
 PA 7 (PNested
  (Segd lengths: [2 2 2 3 2 2  1]
        indices: [0 2 4 6 9 11 13])
  (PChar [A B A B A B C D E F G F G H]))
```

We show the *logical value* of the array above the line, and its *physical representation* below. The representation is determined by the data type declarations in Figure 2. The result array is built with an outer `PA` constructor, pairing its length, 7, with the payload of type `PData (PA Char)`. From the `data instance` for `PData (PA e)`, again in Figure 2, we see that the data field consists of a `PNested` constructor pairing a segment descriptor with a value of type `PData Char`. Finally, the latter consists of a `PChar` constructor wrapping a flat `Vector` of `Char` values.

The process continues recursively in the case of deeper nesting: the reader may care to write down the representation of a value of type `PA (PA (PA Int))`. We will see an example in §4.4.

Now the problem with `replicates` becomes glaringly obvious. The baseline representation of arrays, which was carefully chosen to give good locality and granularity, is *physically incapable of representing the sharing between subarrays in the result* — and losing that sharing leads directly to worsening the asymptotic complexity. It is not possible to simply eliminate the call to `replicates` itself, because this function plays a critical role in vectorisation. In the example from §2, `replicates` distributes shared values from the context of the outer computation (`zipWithP mapP`) into the inner computation (`mapP indexP`). Since we cannot eliminate `replicates`, the only way forward is to change the representation of nested arrays.

[2] It is provided by the `vector` library.

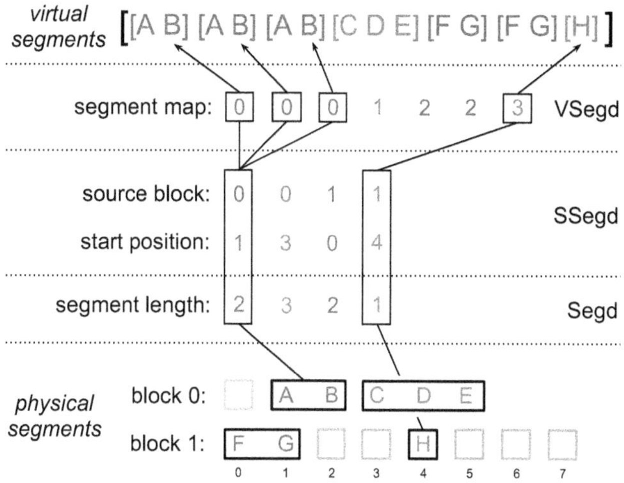

Figure 3. New Array Representation

4. New Representation of Nested Arrays

The new array representation must support all index space transforms that vectorisation introduces, in a way that allows the vectorised program to have the same asymptotic complexity as the original unvectorised program. This is up to *containment* which is discussed in §5.6. In most cases this comes down to having the same complexity as the direct representation, where nested arrays are stored as flat arrays of pointers to more arrays. However, we cannot use this representation as described, because it would lose the granularity and data locality benefits of the baseline segmented representation. We need the best of both worlds.

4.1 Physical, Virtual and Scattered Segments

An example array with the same value as `ARRO` is shown in Figure 3. Our new representation has the following key features:

1. We distinguish between *physical* and *virtual* segments. Physical segments consist of real element data in memory, while virtual segments are defined by mapping onto physical segments. This distinction enables us to define nested arrays with repeated segments without copying element data.
2. The physical segments of a nested array may now be scattered through several data blocks, instead of being contiguous. Although we prefer segments to be contiguous for locality reasons, we must also allow them to be scattered, so that we can filter a nested array without copying element data.

In the example, there are seven virtual segments defined from four physical segments. The physical segments lie scattered in two data blocks. We will see why we need to allow physical segments to lie in separate data blocks in §4.5. The overall segment descriptor is now stratified into three layers: `VSegd` (virtual segments); `SSegd` (scattered segments) and plain `Segd` (contiguous segments). In our terminology, we refer to all of `VSegd`, `SSegd` and `Segd` as "segment descriptors", individually or grouped together. At the bottom layer, `Segd` gives the length of each segment, and would be sufficient to describe the array if all segments were contiguous in a single block. The `SSegd` gives the index of the source data block, and starting position for each physical segment in its block. The `VSegd` provides the mapping between virtual and physical segments. We have elided the `indices` field from the diagram for clarity, but also include this in our new array representation as part of the `Segd`.

```
data PA e = PA { length :: Int, pdata :: PData e }
data family   PData  e
data family   PDatas e
data instance PData  Int  = PInt   (Vector Int)
data instance PDatas Int  = PInts  (Vector (Vector Int))
data instance PData  Char = PChar  (Vector Char)
data instance PDatas Char = PChars (Vector (Vector Char))

data instance PData (PA e)
 = PNested { vsegd :: VSegd, pdatas :: PDatas e }

data instance PDatas (PA e)
 = PNesteds (Vector (PData (PA e)))

data VSegd   -- Virtual-segment descriptor.
 = VSegd { segmap  :: Vector PsId, ssegd :: SSegd }

data SSegd   -- Scattered-segment descriptor.
 = SSegd { sources :: Vector DbId, starts :: Vector Int }
         , segd    :: Segd }

data Segd    -- Contiguous-segment descriptor.
 = Segd  { lengths :: Vector Int, indices :: Vector Int }

type PsId = Int   -- Physical segment Id, indexes 'sources'
type DbId = Int   -- Data block Id, indexes 'pdatas'
```

Figure 4. Definition of the New Array Representation

4.2 The Concrete Definition

The concrete definition of our new array type is given in Figure 4. The data type `PA` is unchanged from Figure 2: a pair of a length and payload. The instances for `PData Int` and `PData Char` are also unchanged. The difference is in the representation of nested arrays:

```
data instance PData (PA a)
  = PNested { vsegd  :: VSegd, pdatas :: PDatas a }
```

The payload is now a `PDatas` (plural) rather than `PData`. Where `PData` represents a single data block, `PDatas` represents a vector of data blocks. We use the type `DbId` (short for data-block identifier) to index this vector of `PData` values.

The `vsegd` field holds the *virtual segment descriptor*. It consists of a vector of physical segment identifiers (`segmap`), and a scattered segment descriptor (`ssegd`). The `segmap` maps virtual segments onto physical segments and corresponds 1-1 with the outer level of the array being represented. In Figure 3, we have seven entries in this map and seven subarrays in the overall nested array.

Each entry in the `segmap` is a *physical segment identifier*, of type `PsId`. A `PsId` is the index of one of the physical segments described by the `SSegd` and `Segd` types. Crucially, the `segmap` can contain repeated use of the same physical segment. In Figure 3 we have used `[0 0 0 1 2 2 3]` to indicate three copies of the first physical segment, one copy of the second, and so on. This is how we represent the sharing defined by `replicates`. Note that we can not just store the replication counts `[3 1 2 1]` directly because we must be able to map virtual segments to physical segments in constant time.

The `SSegd` and `Segd` together describe the physical segments. Together they contain four vectors, *all of the same length*, two of them nested inside the `segd` field. The `sources` vector gives the data block identifier, `DbId`, which is the index of one of the data blocks in the `pdatas` field. The next two, `starts` and `lengths`, give the starting position and length of the physical segment in that data block. Finally `indices` is, as before, a cached copy of the scan (accumuated sum) of `lengths`. Keeping `SSegd` and `Segd` separate is helpful when optimising vectorised code for absolute performance, which we discuss in §6.

Finally, the array representation must obey the following invariants:

1. The lengths of the `sources`, `starts`, `lengths`, and `indices` fields must all be the same.
2. Every `PsId` in the `segmap` must be less than the length of the `sources` field.
3. Each `DbId` in `sources` must be less than the length of the `pdatas` vector.
4. Each element of `starts[i]` must be less than the length of `pdatas[sources[i]]`.
5. The `indices` field is equal to `init (scan (+) 0 lengths)`.
6. All physical segments defined by the `SSegd` and `Segd` types must be reachable from the `segmap`. More precisely, the set of physical segment identifiers in the `segmap` must cover `[0..np-1]`, where `np` is the length of the `starts`, `sources`, `lengths`, and `indices` fields.
7. All `pdata` blocks must be reachable from the `sources` field. More precisely, the set of `sources` must cover `[0..nb-1]`, where `nb` is the length of the `pdatas` vector.

Invariants 1 to 4 are standard well-formedness conditions. Invariant 2 ensures that each physical segment identifier points to a real physical segment. Invariant 3 ensures that each data block identifier points to a real data block. Invariant 5 says that `indices` is precomputed from `lengths`. The reason for this is discussed in §6. Invariants 6 and 7 ensure that the size of the internal structure of the array is bounded by the number of virtual segments, which is necessary for the complexity bound on `append` (§4.5). Invariant 7 is also needed to ensure that the parallel implementation of reductions such as `sum` do not duplicate work (§5.4). However, an implementation may be able to relax these last two invariants in certain cases (§6).

4.3 Replicates again

Now let us implement `replicates` using our new array representation. The start is easy, because the result `PA` array must be built with a `PA` constructor:

```
replicates :: Vector Int -> PA e -> PA e
replicates ns arr = PA (sum ns) (replicatesPR ns arr)
```

The real work is in `replicatesPR`. But now we encounter a slight problem: since the representation of `PData` is indexed by the element type `e`, we require a type-indexed function to operate over `PData` values. That is, we need a type class, with an instance for `Int` and an instance for `(PA e)`:

```
class PR e where
  replicatesPR :: Vector Int -> PData e -> PData e
  ...more methods...

instance PR Int where
  replicatesPR = replicatesI
  ...
instance PR e => PR (PA e) where
  replicatesPR = replicatesPA
  ...
```

The `PR` (Parallel Representation) class is given in Figure 5, and conveniently collects all the necessary primitive operations over arrays. We will see more of them in this section, but `replicatesPR` is one. So, in fact, we lied: the types of `replicates` and `replicatesPR` are overloaded thus:

```
replicates   :: PR e => Vector Int -> PA e    -> PA e
replicatesPR :: PR e => Vector Int -> PData e -> PData e
```

```
class PR e where
emptyPR       :: PData  e
lengthPR      :: PData  e -> Int

replicatePR  :: Int          -> e         -> PData e
replicatesPR :: Vector Int -> PData e -> PData e

appendPR      :: PData  e -> PData e -> PData e

indexPR       :: PData  e -> Int -> e
indexvsPR     :: PDatas e -> VSegd
              -> Vector (Int, Int) -> PData e

extractPR     :: PData  e -> Int    -> Int -> PData e
extractvsPR   :: PDatas e -> VSegd -> PData e

packPR    :: PData  e -> Vector Bool -> PData e
combinePR:: Vector Bool -> PData e -> PData e -> PData e

lengthdPR     :: PDatas e -> Int
emptydPR      :: PDatas e
singletondPR :: PData  e -> PDatas e
appenddPR     :: PDatas e -> PDatas e -> PDatas e
indexdPR      :: PDatas e -> Int -> PData e

------- Utility functions --------
sumV         :: Vector Int -> Int
singletonV  :: e -> Vector e
replicateV  :: Int -> e -> Vector e
replicatesV :: Vector Int -> Vector e -> Vector e
```

Figure 5. Primitive Array Operators

(In what follows we will often omit the "PR =>" context from types to save space.) Now we are ready to implement the two cases. The case for `Int` is straightforward:

```
replicatesI :: Vector Int -> PData Int -> PData Int
replicatesI ns (PInt xs) = PInt (replicatesV ns xs)
```

where `replicatesV` is the `Vector`-level replication operation shown in Figure 5. The interesting case is the one for nested arrays:

```
instance PR e => PR (PA e) where
 replicatesPR = replicatesPA

replicatesPA :: Vector Int -> PData (PA e) -> PData (PA e)
replicatesPA lens (PNested segmap pdatas)
 = PNested (VSegd segmap' ssegd) pdatas
 where segmap' = replicatesV lens segmap
```

With our new array representation, we can apply segmented replicate to an array by using `replicatesV` on the `segmap` field. The element data, `pdatas`, does not need to be copied, and is untouched in the result. Continuing the example from §3, applying `replicates` to the array from Figure 3 yields:

```
  replicates [0 0 1 1 0 0 1] {Figure 3}
= [[A B] [C D E] [H]]
------------------------------------------------ (ARR1)
 PA 3 (PNested
   (VSegd  segmap:  [0 1 3]
   (SSegd sources:  [0 0 1 1]  starts:  [1 3 0 4])
   (Segd  lengths:  [2 3 2 1] indices:  [0 2 5 7]))
   (PChars 0:  [X A B C D E]
           1:  [F G X X H X X X])
```

In fact, the above definition of `replicatesPA` function is not yet complete. Physical segments 0, 1 and 3 are used, but segment 2 is not, which violates invariant 6. We will discuss why this matters in §4.6.

4.4 Plain replicate

Vectorisation also uses a simpler form of replication, which we call `replicate` (singular). The call `(replicate n x)` returns an array of `n` elements, each a (virtual) copy of `x`. This function is introduced when an inner parallel computation uses a shared constant or a free variable that is defined in an outer context. This is essentially the same reason that the more general `replicates` function is introduced, though with plain `replicate` the shared value is used uniformly by all inner computations. We will see an example in §6.1. Note that unlike `replicates`, the result of plain `replicate` has a greater nesting depth than the source element. The interesting case is for nested arrays:

```
replicatePA :: Int -> PA e -> PData (PA e)
replicatePA c (PA n pdata)
 = replicatesPR (singletonV c)
 $ PNested (singletonVSegd n) (singletondPR pdata)

singletonVSegd :: Int -> VSegd
singletonVSegd len
 = VSegd (singletonV 0)
  (SSegd (singletonV 0)    (singletonV 0)
  (Segd  (singletonV len) (singletonV 0)))
```

To perform a `replicate` we simply add a new segment descriptor on top of the old array. This furnishes us with an example array of greater nesting depth:

```
 replicate 2 {Figure 3}
----------------------------------------------- (ARR2)
 PA 2 (PNested
  (VSegd  segmap:  [0 0]
  (SSegd sources:  [0]   starts:  [0]
  (Segd  lengths:  [7] indices:  [0])))
  (PNesteds
   0: PNested
      (VSegd  segmap:  [0 0 0 1 2 2 3]
      (SSegd sources:  [0 0 1 1]   starts:  [1 3 0 4])
      (Segd  lengths:  [2 3 2 1] indices:  [0 2 5 7]))
      (PChars 0:  [X A B C D E]
              1:  [F G X X H X X X])
```

Notice that the cost of `(replicate n x)` is $O(n)$, regardless of how much data `x` contains. With our new representation the complexity of `replicate` is linear in the length of the created `segmap`, which is also the length of the overall array.

4.5 Append

Let us consider another important operation: appending two arrays.

```
appendPA :: PA e -> PA e -> PA e
```

As mentioned in §4.2 we need invariants 6 and 7 to achieve the Complexity Goal here. Append should be linear in the length of the two argument arrays, regardless of how deeply nested they are. This is impossible with the baseline representation from §3 because we would need to copy all elements into a single data block.

With our new representation we do not need to copy array elements. To append two nested arrays we append the two `PDatas` and combine the segment descriptor fields. Although we can simply append the `lengths` and `starts` fields, we need to recompute the `indices`. We also need to increment the entries in the second `segmap` and `sources` field to account for the physical segments and data blocks defined by the first array. For this process to have complexity linear in the length of the two argument arrays, the lengths of their `starts`, `sources`, `lengths` and `indices` fields can be no greater than the length of their `segmap`. To put this another way: the number of physical segments can be no greater than the number of virtual segments. Likewise, the length of the two `PDatas` can be no greater than the `sources` fields. These constraints are implied by invariants 6 and 7. The definition of `appendPR` (the version that works on `PData`) is on the next page.

```
appendPR :: PData (PA e) -> PData (PA e) -> PData (PA e)
appendPR (PNested vsegd1 pds1) (PNested vsegd2 pds2)
  = PNested (appendVSegd (length pds1) vsegd1 vsegd2)
            (pds1 ++ pds2)

appendVSegd ps1 (VSegd sm1 ssegd1) (VSegd sm2 ssegd2)
  = VSegd (sm1 ++ map (+ lengthSSegd ssegd1) sm2)
  $ appendSSegd ps1 ssegd1 ssegd2

appendSSegd ps1 (SSegd ss1 us1 segd1) (SSegd ss2 us2 segd2)
  = SSegd (ss1 ++ ss2) (us1 ++ map (+ ps1) us2)
  $ appendSegd segd1 segd2

appendSegd (Segd ls1 is1) (Segd ls2 is2)
  = let n1 = sum ls1
    in  Segd  (ls1 ++ ls2) (is1 ++ map (+ n1) is2)
```

Here is an example array that we will use in a moment:

```
                  [[K] [] [L M N O]]
---------------------------------------------- (ARR3)
PA 3 (PNested
(VSegd  segmap: [0 1 2]
(SSegd sources: [0 0 0] starts:  [0 1 1])
(Segd  lengths: [1 0 4] indices: [0 1 1]))
(PChars 0: [K L M N O]))
```

Appending the array from Figure 3 with ARR3 above yields:

```
   [[A B] [A B] [A B] [C D E] ...  [K] [] [L M N O]
---------------------------------------------- (ARR4)
PA 10 (PNested
(VSegd  segmap: [0 0 0 1 2 2 3 4 5 6]
(SSegd sources: [0 0 1 1 2 2 2]  starts: [1 3 0 4 0 1 1]
(Segd  lengths: [2 3 2 1 1 0 4] indices: [0 2 5 7 8 9 9])))
(PChars 0: [X A B C D E]
        1: [F G X X H X X X]
        2: [K L M N O]))
```

The data block of ARR3 joins the set of data blocks in the result without any copying.

4.6 Culling Physical Segments

As mentioned in §4.5, we need invariants 6 and 7 to ensure that appendPA has the correct asymptotic complexity. Suppose we wish to append ARR1 from §4.3 to ARR3 above. Invariant 7 is already satisfied, so this part is fine. However, as we produced ARR1 by using a replicates operation with zero valued replication counts, physical segment 2 is no longer reachable from the segmap, which violates invariant 6. To recover this we use the following operations:

```
cullOnSegmap::Vector PsId-> SSegd-> (Vector PsId, SSegd)
cullOnSSegd ::    SSegd   -> PDatas e-> (SSegd, PDatas e)
```

The cullOnSegmap function takes the segmap and SSegd for an array. It filters out the physical segments from the SSegd that are unreachable from the segmap, returning an updated segmap and SSegd. In the result, the number of physical segments is necessarily bounded by the length of segmap. Likewise, cullOnSSegd filters out data blocks in the PDatas not reachable from the sources field of the SSegd. We need this second operation because performing just the first could leave some data blocks unreachable from the sources field, thus violating invariant 7. Culling ARR1 yields:

```
              [[A B] [C D E] [H]]
---------------------------------------------- (ARR5)
 PA 3 (PNested
  (VSegd  segmap: [0 1 2]
  (SSegd sources: [0 0 1]  starts: [1 3 4])
  (Segd  lengths: [2 3 1] indices: [0 2 5]))
  (PChars 0: [X A B C D E]
          1: [F G X X H X X X])
```

All array operators that filter out entries from the segmap need to apply cullOnSegmap and cullOnSSegd to preserve the invariants. For example, the invariant preserving version of replicatesPA is as follows:

```
replicatesPA:: Vector Int -> PData (PA e) -> PData (PA e)
replicatesPA lens (PNested (VSegd segmap ssegd) pdatas)
 = PNested (VSegd segmap' ssegd'') pdatas'
 where (segmap', ssegd')
        = cullOnSegmap (replicatesV lens segmap) ssegd
       (ssegd'', pdatas')
        = cullOnSSegd   ssegd' pdatas
```

We will now sketch how cullOnSegmap is implemented, leaving the full details to the companion technical report [13]. The operation of cullOnSSegd is similar. We start by producing a vector of flags that record which of the physical segments are reachable from the segmap. For ARR1 this is [T T F T]. The flags are calculated by first filling the target vector with the default value F and then using *concurrent writes* to set elements referenced by the segmap to T. Then, we use the flags vector to compute the physical segment identifiers that appear in the result: [0 1 3]. We expand this vector to one that maps between the physical segment identifiers in the result to the identifiers in the source: [0 1 X 2]. The X indicates an unused element, which the implementation can fill with any value. Finally, we use this mapping to permute the segmap, sources, starts and lengths fields of the source array, and then recompute the indices.

The work and space complexity of cullOnSegmap is linear in the length of the segmap being processed and the number of physical segments referenced. Likewise, the complexity of cullOnSSegd is linear in the length of the SSegd and the number of data blocks. This ensures that we do not break the complexity budget of operations such as replicates that make use of these functions.

5. Projection, Concatenation and Reduction

The replicates and append operators described in the previous sections highlight the fundamental features of our array representation. The work efficient implementation of replicates requires that we represent shared segments without copying element data. As replicates may also drop segments, we must handle scattered segments as well. In addition, the work efficient implementation of append requires multiple data blocks with scattered segments as well as the use of the culling operations from §4.6. Culling ensures that the size of the physical representation of an array is bounded by the size of its logical value. We now move on to describe the other operators that we need to support with the new representation when vectorising programs. Happily, we can support them with the correct work complexity without any further extensions.

5.1 Index and Extract

Indexing into a nested array is straightforward. We use the segmap to determine the target segment and then extract (slice) it from its data block. We present this operation for expository purposes only: indexing operators in the source program will be vectorised to lifted indexing, which we discuss in a moment.

```
indexPA (PNested (VSegd segmap
                 (SSegd sources starts
                 (Segd  lengths _))) pdatas) ix
 = PA len (extractPR pdata start len)
 where psegid  = segmap  ! ix
       source  = sources ! psegid
       start   = starts  ! psegid
       len     = lengths ! psegid
       pdata   = indexdPR pdatas source
```

For indexing to be constant time, `extractPR` must be as well. When the returned value is a `Vector Int`, or some other vector of scalars, the `vector` package provides constant time extract by storing a starting index as well as the slice length in the returned `Vector`. To extract a range of subarrays from a nested array we extract their physical segment identifiers from the `segmap` and then cull the other fields to enforce invariants 6 and 7 from §4. For example, extracting the middle two segments from ARR4 yields:

```
                        [[F G] [F G]]
------------------------------------------------- (ARR6)
  PA 2 (PNested
   (VSegd  segmap: [0 0]
   (SSegd sources: [0]     starts: [0]
   (Segd  lengths: [2]    indices: [0])))
   (PInts 0: [F G X X H X X X]))
```

Unfortunately, when `indexPA` returns a nested array, the called `extractPR` instance must cull unused physical segments; hence, the overall indexing operation is not constant time. For this reason, our new array representation cannot perform all operations that the direct pointer based one could within the same complexity bounds. However, this does *not* worsen the complexity of vectorised programs relative to the baseline representation, because only *lifted* index and extract operators are used in vectorised code. We can perform the lifted operations within the required complexity bounds.

Lifted indexing itself is a simple wrapper for the `indexvsPR` function, whose signature is shown in Figure 5.

```
indexlPR :: Int -> PData (PA e) -> PData Int -> PData e
indexlPR c (PNested vsegd pdatas) (PInt is)
  = indexvsPR pdatas vsegd $ zipV (enumFromN 0 c) is
```

The `indexvsPR` function takes a set of data blocks, a virtual segment descriptor, and an array of pairs of virtual segment identifiers and element indices within those segments. As we wish to lookup one element from each segment, we enumerate all the available segment identifiers with `enumFromN`. The `indexvsPR` function itself implements *virtual shared indexing*, it retrieves several elements from some shared data blocks (`pdatas`). It uses the index space transform expressed by the `vsegd` to map the logical view of the array referred to by the segment identifiers and element indices, to the physical view of the array in terms of the `pdatas`. The definition of `indexvsPR` is similar to `indexPR`, though we leave the full details for the technical report [13].

5.2 Concatenation

The central feature of Blelloch's approach to flattening nested parallelism is that it does not need multiply lifted versions of source functions in vectorised code. This is achieved by using the `concat` and `unconcat` operators when vectorising higher order functions such as `mapP` and `zipWithP`. Every source-level application of such a function uses a `concat/unconcat` pair in the vectorised version. An example of this is shown in `retrieve_v` from §2.

With the baseline array representation from Figure 2, both `concat` and `unconcat` are constant time operations. To concatenate an array we simply remove the segment descriptor, and to unconcatenate we reattach it. This is possible with the baseline representation, because the form of the segment descriptor implies that the physical segments lie contiguously in a single, flat data block. The description of the segments consists fundamentally of the `lengths` field, with the `indices` being computed directly from it. There is no scattering information such as the `starts` and `sources` fields of our `SSegd`.

As we have seen, the limitation of the baseline representation is that it cannot represent index space transformations on nested arrays except by copying element data. In our new representation, we encode such index space transforms in the segment descriptor, which avoids this copying. The price we pay is that the physical segments in a nested array are no longer guaranteed to be contiguous, so we cannot simply discard the segment descriptor to concatenate them. Instead, the `concat` function must now copy the segment data through the index space transform defined by the segment descriptor, to produce a fresh contiguous array. This is essentially a *gather* operation. The main job is done by `extractvsPR` from Figure 5, with `concat` itself being a wrapper for it:

```
concat :: PA (PA e) -> PA e
concat (PA _ (PNested vsegd pdatas))
 = let  pdata   = extractvsPR pdatas vsegd
   in   PA (lengthPR pdata) pdata
```

The `extractvsPR` function takes some data blocks, a segment descriptor that describes the logical array formed from those blocks, and copies out the segment data into a fresh contiguous array. Importantly, although both `extractvsPR` and `concat` are now *linear* in the length of the result, this does not worsen the complexity of the vectorised program compared with the baseline representation. The reason is that `concat/unconcat` trick is only needed when vectorising higher order functions such as `mapP`. In terms of the unvectorised source program, `mapP` is at least linear in the length of its argument array, because it produces a result of the same length. The vectorised version of `mapP` is implemented by concatenating the argument array, applying the (lifted) worker function, and then unconcatenating the result. The `concat` and `unconcat` functions can then be linear in the length of this result, because the unvectorised version of `mapP` has this complexity anyway.

Note that the linear complexity of `concat` is independent of the depth of nesting of the source array. To concatenate an array of type `(PA (PA (PA (PA Int))))` we only need to merge the two outer-most segment descriptors. The third level segment descriptors, and underlying `Int` data blocks are not touched. There is an example of this in the accompanying technical report [13].

5.3 Demotion, Promotion and Unconcatenation

The `unconcat` function is defined in terms of generally useful demotion and promotion operators that convert between the different segment descriptor types. We will discuss these operators first before continuing onto `unconcat`. The operators are as follows:

```
demoteVSegd   :: VSegd -> SSegd
demoteSSegd   :: SSegd -> Segd
promoteSegd   :: Segd  -> SSegd
promoteSSegd  :: SSegd -> VSegd
```

Abstractly, demoting a `VSegd` to a `SSegd` or a `SSegd` to a `Segd` discards information about the extended structure of the array, such as how segments are shared or scattered through the store. Going the other way, promoting a `Segd` to a `SSegd` or a `SSegd` to a `VSegd` adds redundant information. In our concrete implementation, many array functions (including `unconcat`) are defined in terms of these operators. The fact that these functions are defined this way is also used when optimising for absolute performance, which we will discuss in §6.

5.3.1 Demotion

Demoting a segment descriptor eliminates fields from its representation. Consider the following example:

```
  virtual segs: [ [B C D] [G] [] [B C D] [E F] [A] ]
 physical segs: [ [A] [G] [B C D] [E F] [] ]
------------------------------------------------ (ARR7)
PA 6 (PNested
 (VSegd  segmap: [2 1 4 2 3 0]
 (SSegd sources: [1 0 1 0 0] starts:   [0 2 1 0 0]
 (Segd  lengths: [1 1 3 2 0] indices:  [0 1 2 4 6])))
 (PChars 0: [E F G] 1: [A B C D]))
```

Here we have shown the virtual segments as described by the VSegd, as well as the physical segments described by the SSegd. Note that the virtual segments need not appear in the same order as the physical segments are defined, which allows us to implement permutation operations on nested arrays by permuting the segmap. Demoting the VSegd to a SSegd pushes the information about sharing encoded by the segmap into the other fields of the segment descriptor. It also forces the entries in the SSegd to appear in the same order as the logical array they define:

```
       [ [B C D] [G] [] [B C D] [E F] [A] ]
-----------------------------------------------------
 (SSegd sources: [1 0 0 1 0 1]  starts: [1 2 0 1 0 0]
 (Segd  lengths: [3 1 0 3 2 1] indices: [0 3 4 4 7 9]))
 (PChars 0: [E F G] 1: [A B C D])
```

To demote the array we have computed new starts, sources and lengths fields by permuting the originals using the segmap. In practice, when we demote a VSegd, we must be mindful of the potential for *index space overflow*. By this we mean that if a nested array consists of many virtual copies of a large sub-array, then the total number of elements in the virtual array may be larger than the address space of the machine, even though all the *physical* data fits within it. In this case the elements of the indices field may no longer fit in a machine word. We will return to this point in §5.4.1. Avoiding index space overflow is the main reason we use an explicit segmap, instead of representing all arrays with the above demoted form (without a segmap).

Continuing on, we demote a SSegd to a Segd by simply discarding the outer SSegd wrapper, along with the sources and starts fields. To represent the same logical array, we must then gather the segment data into a fresh data block, similarly to the extractvsPR function described in §5.1. For our example this produces:

```
       [ [B C D] [G] [] [B C D] [E F] [A] ]
-----------------------------------------------------
 (Segd lengths: [3 1 0 3 2 1] indices: [0 3 4 4 7 9])
 (PChars 0: [B C D G B C D E F A])
```

As with the previous demotion, our nested array still has the same logical value as the original. However, by giving up the sources and starts fields we have lost information about how the segments were originally scattered through the store. This forces us to copy them into a fresh data block to represent the original logical array, leaving us with the old array representation from Figure 2.

5.3.2 Promotion

Promoting an array fills in missing segment descriptor fields with redundant information. To promote a Segd to a SSegd, we reuse the existing indices field for starts and fill the sources with all zeros. This indicates that all physical segments lie contiguously in a single flat array. To promote the SSegd to a VSegd we then enumerate the physical segments in the segmap. Performing both promotions to the demoted array from the previous section yields the following:

```
        [ [B C D] [G] [] [B C D] [E F] [A] ]
------------------------------------------------- (ARR8)
PA 5 (PNested
 (VSegd  segmap: [0 1 2 3 4 5]
 (SSegd sources: [0 0 0 0 0 0] starts:   [0 3 4 4 7 9]
 (Segd  lengths: [3 1 0 3 2 1] indices: [0 3 4 4 7 9])))
 (PChars 0: [B C D G B C D E F A]))
```

Note that promoting a segment descriptor does not change the logical structure of the array, it just fills in redundant fields in the representation. In our concrete implementation the initialisation of the segmap and sources fields with these "boring" values can often be avoided (§6).

5.3.3 Unconcatenation

To unconcatenate an array, we demote the source segment descriptor down to a plain Segd and then re-promote it back to a VSegd, before attaching it to the second array:

```
unconcatPR :: PA (PA a) -> PA b -> PA (PA b)
unconcatPR (PA n (PNested vsegd _)) (PA _ pdata)
 = let  segd    = demoteSSegd  $ demoteVSegd vsegd
        vsegd'  = promoteSSegd $ promoteSegd segd
   in   PA n (PNested vsegd' (singletondPR pdata))
```

We need the demotion-promotion process because the sharing and scattering information in the VSegd is only relevant to the first array, not the second array (of type (PA b)) that we attach it to.

Finally, we can normalise the physical structure of an array by concatenating it down to atomic elements and then unconcatenating to re-apply the nesting structure. This eliminates all unused array elements from the data blocks, which improves locality of reference for subsequent operations, and is useful when writing arrays to the file system. Here is the version for triply nested arrays:

```
normalise3 :: PA (PA (PA e)) -> PA (PA (PA e))
normalise3 arr2
 = let  arr1    = concat arr2
        arr0    = concat arr1
   in   unconcat arr2 (unconcat arr1 arr0)
```

Creating versions of normalise for other degrees of nesting is straightforward. Normalising the doubly nested ARR7 from §5.3.1 yields exactly ARR8 from §5.3.2. Note that if we were to elide the VSegd and SSegd layers, a normalised arrays have the same form as the baseline representation from §3.

5.4 Reduction and Dynamic Hoisting

Consider the following function retsum, which indexes several shared arrays, and adds the retrieved value to the sum of the array it came from. This has a similar structure to retrieve from §2.

```
retsum :: [:[:Int:]:] -> [:[:Int:]:] -> [:[:Int:]:]
retsum xss iss
 = zipWithP mapP
          (mapP (\xs i. indexP xs i + sumP xs) xss) iss
```

Here is retsum applied to some example arrays:

```
retsum  [[1 2]   [4 5 6] [8]]       (xss)
        [[1 0 1] [1 2]   [0]]       (iss)
   ==>  [[5 4 5] [20 21] [16]]
```

The subexpression sum xs duplicates work for every application of the inner function abstraction, because it sums the entire xs array once for each of the integer elements in the result. The result of vectorisation, inlining and simplifying retsum is shown below — the accompanying technical report [13] includes the full derivation.

```
retsum_v :: PA (PA Int) -> PA (PA Int) -> PA (PA Int)
retsum_v xss iss
 = let ns       = lengths iss
       n        = sum ns
       yss'     = replicates ns xss
   in  unconcat iss
        $ add_l n (index_l n yss' (concat iss))
                  (sum_l n yss')
```

In retsum_v, the fact that the original sum expression duplicates work is revealed in the fact that the lifted version (sum_l) is being applied to a replicated array. At runtime, the segments of the first array are replicated according to the lengths of the segments in the second. The intermediate result (replicates ns xss) is on the next page.

```
    [[1 2] [1 2] [1 2] [4 5 6] [4 5 6] [8]]
----------------------------------------------- (ARR9)
  PA 6 (PNested
   (VSegd  segmap: [0 0 0 1 1 2]
   (SSegd sources: [0 0 0]     starts: [0 2 5]
   (Segd  lengths: [2 3 1]    indices: [0 2 5])))
   (PInts 0: [1 2 4 5 6 8])
```

Our `segmap` directly encodes which of the physical segments are being shared. Instead of repeatedly summing segments we know to be identical, we can instead sum the physical segments defined by the `SSegd`, and replicate the results according to the `segmap`. By doing this we actually *improve* the asymptotic complexity of the original program, by avoiding repeated computation that it would otherwise perform. Note that this process depends on Invariant 6 from §4, as we do not wish to sum unreachable physical segments that are not part of the logical array.

Avoiding repeated computation in this way achieves the same result as the *hoisting* or *full laziness* program transformation, but in a dynamic way. In contrast, performing this transform statically at compile-time would yield the following:

```
retsum xss iss
  = zipWithP mapP
          (mapP (\xs. let x = sumP xs
                      in \i. indexP xs i + x) xss) iss
```

However, the GHC simplifier will *not* in-fact perform the above transform, as it does not generally improve performance [16]. Finally, although dynamic hoisting may seem like an opportunistic improvement, perhaps not worth the trouble, failing to perform it has other ramifications, which we discuss in the next section.

5.4.1 Fused Hylomorphisms and Index Space Overflow

A subtle point about the `retsum` example is that if an implementation does not perform dynamic hoisting, it could risk overflowing machine words. This is a general problem with *fused hylomorphisms*, with a hylomorphism being a computation that first builds a structure (like with `replicates`) before reducing it (like with `sum_l`). Although it may be possible to fuse these two operations together so the intermediate structure is never actually created, it is problematic when the index space of that structure is larger than the address space of the machine.

For example, suppose the `xss` array from the previous section contains 10 elements and `iss` contains 500 million. Although this amount of data is easily stored on current hardware, the total number of virtual elements produced by `replicates` would be 5 x 10^9. This number is not representable in a 32-bit word. This problem is acute because the function that defines the intermediate structure (`replicates`) is introduced by vectorisation and does not appear in the source program. Simply telling the user "you can't do that" would be unreasonable.

Managing this problem is the main reason that we include an explicit `segmap` in our array representation. Without the `segmap`, we would instead record each virtual segment separately, like with the first demoted array of §5.3.1. However, in cases of index-space overflow, elements of the `indices` field would become too large to be stored. The `indices` field itself is needed when partitioning the work in the implementation of `sum_l`. We also need the total size of the array, which would again be too large.

Requiring 64-bit array indices and eliminating the `segmap` is an alternate solution, but it is not clear whether this would be better overall. On 32-bit machines, memory traffic to the `indices` field would double because of the larger word size. On all machines, operations such as `replicates` would need to process both the `sources` and `starts` field instead of touching the singular `segmap`. On the other hand, indexing operations would not need to dereference the `segmap`, or maintain invariant 6, but as as we will see in §6 this can often be avoided anyway. The code to maintain this invariant is localised, and very similar to that needed for invariant 7, so it would not be a significant reduction in implementation complexity. For now we choose to keep the `segmap` and leave the quantitative comparison to future work.

5.5 Flattening and Space Usage

In contrast to the problem with replication outlined in §2, flattening nested parallelism can increase the asymptotic space complexity in a way that this paper does not address [14, 19]. For example, suppose we vectorise the following function that takes an array of n points and computes the maximum distance between any pair. The full derivation is in the companion technical report [13].

```
furthest :: PA (Float, Float) -> Float
furthest ps = maxP (mapP (\p. maxP (mapP (dist p) ps)) ps)
```

The flattened version is a hylomorphism that first computes $O(n^2)$ distances before reducing them to determine the maximum. Whereas the unflattened version would run in $O(n)$ space, the flattened version needs $O(n^2)$ space to hold the intermediate vector of distances. Note that vectorisation does not increase the asymptotic *work* complexity, because these distances must be computed anyway.

5.6 Pack and Combine

The `pack` and `combine` functions from Figure 5 are used in the parallel implementation of `if-then-else`. The `pack` function takes an array of elements, an array of flags of the same length, and returns only those elements that have their flag set. This function is used to split the parallel context of `if-then-else` into the elements associated with each branch. It can be implemented in terms of `replicates`, using a replication count of `1` for `True` flags and `0` for `False` flags. We mention it separately because `pack` is the common name for this operation in the literature. The `combine` function takes an array of flags, two arrays of elements, and intersperses the elements according to the flags. For example `combine [T F F T] [1 2] [3 4] = [1 3 4 2]`. This function is used to merge the results of each branch once they have been computed. On a high level, the implementation of `combine` is similar to `append` because the result contains elements from both source arrays, though we leave the implementation to [13].

To achieve our Complexity Goal, both `pack` and `combine` must be linear in the length of the `flags` array. This is because entering a branch in the source program is a constant time operation. In vectorised code, many branches are entered in one parallel step, so the functions that implement this operation must be linear in the number of elements being processed. Achieving this goal with the baseline array representation is not possible, because packing and combining nested arrays requires that we copy element data. In contrast, with our new representation we can simply pack and combine the segment descriptors, leaving the underlying element data untouched. In [1], Blelloch suggested that it would be more efficient to work on *sparse segments*, which we are now able to do.

As mentioned in §1 vectorisation can only preserve the complexity of the source program up to *containment*. This problem stems from the fact that flattening `if-then-else` causes the computations that take each branch to be executed one after another, instead of concurrently. In [18] Riely and Prins give an example recursive function that calls itself in both branches of an `if-then-else`, and where vectorisation worsens its asymptotic complexity independent of considerations of the array representation. Luckily, the containment problem is rarely met in practice. Riely and Prins prove that provided one branch in each `if-then-else` executes with a constant number of parallel steps, the containment problem is avoided. This constraint is met by the base case of most recursive functions. However, their language is first order, so their proof does not automatically apply to ours.

6. Pragmatics

Although our new array representation allows the index space transforms introduced by the vectoriser to have the correct asymptotic complexity, there are several cases where a direct implementation would perform poorly in absolute terms. For example, implementing `promoteSSegd` from §5.3.2 by physically filling the `segmap` with `[0 1 2 ...]` leaves something to be desired. However, in many cases the construction of these fields can be sidestepped using rewrite rules. For example, in our concrete implementation we have the following functions:

```
sum_vs :: VSegd -> PDatas Int -> PData Int
sum_s  :: Segd  -> PData  Int -> PData Int
```

Both of these can be used to implement lifted sum (`sum_l`) by using a simple wrapper. The difference is that while `sum_vs` accepts a full `VSegd` to describe the segmentation of the array, `sum_s` only accepts a plain `Segd`. The implementation of the latter is simpler, as it does not need to worry about the `segmap`, `starts` and `sources` fields that define the sharing and scattering of segments. During code transformation, we apply the following rewrite rule:

```
RULE "sum_vs/promote"  forall segd arr.
      sum_vs (promoteSSegd (promoteSegd  segd))
             (singletondPR arr)       = sum_s segd arr
```

The rule says that to sum the segments of a nested array defined by a promoted `Segd`, we can just use the `Segd` directly. Rules like this one are frequently applicable because the definition of key operations such as `unconcat` and `extractvsPR` explicitly use `promoteSegd` and so on to construct their results. Note that the ability to apply rules such as this depends critically on the split between the `VSegd`, `SSegd` and `Segd` types, and the fact that `indices` field is in `Segd` rather than `SSegd`. Abstractly, the fact that an array is representable with just a `Segd` tells us that all the segments lie contiguously in the store. The fact that it is representable with just a `SSegd` tells us that the number of physical segments matches the number of logical segments, though several entries in the `SSegd` may still point to the same element data.

Another technique we use is to store a lazy, pre-concatenated version of the array in the array structure itself. In our concrete implementation, the `PNested` structure contains two extra fields holding a plain `Segd` and the `PData` corresponding to the concatenated version of the overall array. Every function that constructs an array is responsible for initialising these fields, either with pre-existing concatenated data, such as produced by `extractvsPR`, or a suspended computation that will concatenate when demanded. When a consumer, such as `mapP`, requires a concatenated version of the array, it can use these fields instead of explicitly concatenating the data itself. With this method array consumers avoid repeatedly concatenating (and thus copying) arrays that the producers know are already concatenated.

We use a similar method to avoid some applications of the `cullOnSegmap` function discussed in §4.6. The key point here is that while reduction operations like `sum_l` need invariant 6 to avoid duplicating work, indexing operations are oblivious to unreachable physical segments. In our implementation, we suspend calls to `cullOnSegmap` with lazy evaluation, and also keep an *unculled* version of the `SSegd` in the array representation. If, say, a nested array is packed and then immediately indexed, then the indexing operation uses the unculled `SSegd`, avoiding the need to call `cullOnSegmap` at all.

6.1 Rewrite Rules and Replication

A reader may be wondering why we cannot also use a rewrite rule to eliminate calls to replication operators in the vectorised program, instead of introducing a new array representation. Suppose we vectorise the following function that gathers multiple character values from a shared array called `table`.

```
gather :: [:Char:] -> [:Int:] -> [:Char:]
gather table indices
 = mapP (\ix -> table !: ix) indices
```

The vectorised version is as follows:

```
gather_v :: PA Char -> PA Int -> PA Char
gather_v table indices
 = index_l len (replicate len table) indices
 where len = length indices
```

As per §2, `index_l` is lifted indexing. Note that with the old array representation, this function would have the wrong asymptotic complexity due to the use of `replicate`. However, suppose we had a second version of indexing (`index_s`) that could retrieve elements from a single shared array. This operation is also known as *backwards permutation*.

```
index_l :: Int -> PA (PA a) -> PA Int -> PA a
index_s :: Int ->     PA a  -> PA Int -> PA a
```

Given `index_s`, a seemingly obvious way to optimise `gather_v` is to apply the following rewrite rule:

```
RULE "index_l/index_s" forall c xs ys.
      index_l c (replicate c xs) ys = index_s c xs ys
```

The problem is that this rule improves the asymptotic complexity of the program, which turns out to be a bad thing engineering wise. The left of the rule uses work and space $O(\mathit{length}$ `xs` . length `ys`$)$ while the right uses $O(\mathit{length}$ `ys`$)$. These are different because indexing is a *projection*, which does not inspect all of its input data.

The trouble is that for the rule to fire, the producer (`replicate`) and consumer (`index_l`) of the replicated array must come together during code transformation. If the program is written in a way that prevents this from happening, then `replicate` will not be eliminated. For example, suppose we parameterised `gather` over a function to apply to each index value:

```
gatherFun ::([:Char:] -> Int -> Char)
          -> [:Char:] -> [:Int:] -> [:Char:]
gatherFun fun table indices = mapP (fun table) indices
```

Vectorising this function yields the following:

```
gatherFun_v :: PA (PA Char :-> Int :-> Char)
            -> PA Char -> PA Int -> PA Char
gatherFun_v (AClo fv fl envs) table indices
 = fl c envs (replicate c table) $:^ indices
 where c = length indices
```

When we vectorize higher order functions, the parameter function is represented as an *array closure*. The array closure constructor `AClo` bundles up the closure-converted version of the function (`fv`), the lifted version (`fl`) and the environment that was captured in its closure (`envs`). The lifted application operator (`$:^`) then applies the closure to its final argument `indices`. See [11, 12] for a more detailed explanation. The main point here is that the parameter function `fl` is unknown to the vectoriser. With just the code above, it is impossible to eliminate the `replicate` operation, because we do not know what `fl` will turn out to be.

A tempting hack-around is to force every function in the program to be inlined, and hope that follow on code transformation discovers the true identity of `fl`. We used this approach in our previous implementation of DPH, and it turns out to be a slippery slope to suffering. Small changes in the structure of the source program, or behaviour of the various transforms, can result in a previously well performing program becoming unrunnable due to the changed asymptotic complexity. This approach also does not "fix" recursive programs where the producer and consumer are the same function, as the the same function cannot be inlined into itself indefinitely. An example of such a program is given in §7.2. Our solution is to instead provide a new array representation, that guarantees that even with all follow-on optimisations disabled, the program will still run with the correct asymptotic complexity.

7. Benchmarks

In this section we present several programs where the baseline array representation worsened the asymptotic complexity of the vectorised program. All benchmarks were taken on an Intel i7 QuadCore / 8GB desktop machine. We have opted to present data for the program running in single threaded mode only. We have not finished adapting our parallel stream fusion framework to the new array representation, so parallel speedup is currently dominated by the creation of intermediate arrays such as the "boring" fields described in §5.3.2 and §6. However, all of the underling primitives we use operate on bulk arrays and are amenable to parallelisation.

7.1 Sparse Matrix-Vector Multiplication

This program multiples a sparse matrix by a dense vector and is discussed in [11]. The matrix is represented as an array of rows, where each row is an pair of a column index and the `Double` value in that column.

```
smvm :: [:[:(Int, Double):]:] -> [:Double:] -> [:Double:]
smvm matrix vector
 = let term (ix, coeff) = coeff * (vector ! ix)
       sumRow row       = sumP (mapP term row)
   in  mapP sumRow matrix
```

As `vector` is free in the definition of `term`, with the old array representation it would be copied once for every non-zero element of the matrix. With the new array representation the vector is not copied and it runs with the same asymptotic complexity as an unvectorised reference implementation written with the `Data.Vector` package. The `Data.Vector` version is currently faster than with our new representation because stream fusion [7] does a better job at eliminating intermediate values.

7.2 Tree Lookup

The following microbenchmark exposes the replicate problem in sharp relief. It performs a divide-and-conquer of an `indices` array, while referring to a top level `table`. In the base case, a single index is used to access the top-level table, and the table is rebuilt during the return calls.

```
treeLookup :: [:Int:] -> [:Int:] -> [:Int:]
treeLookup table indices
  | lengthP indices == 1 = [:table !: (indices !: 0):]
  | otherwise
  = let half = lengthP indices `div` 2
        s1   = sliceP 0    half indices
        s2   = sliceP half half indices
    in concatP (mapP (treeLookup table) [: s1, s2 :])
```

As `table` is partially applied to `treeLookup`, with the baseline representation the entire `table` is copied once for every element of `indices`. In the vectorised version the call to `replicate` cannot be eliminated with the rewrite rules discussed in §6.1, because the producer and consumer of the replicated array are in different recursive calls. With our new array representation, the sharing is managed by our `segmap` and the elements of `table` are not copied.

7.3 Barnes-Hut

The Barnes-Hut algorithm performs a two dimensional gravitation simulation of many massive bodies. At each time step, the algorithm builds a quad-tree to partition the space the bodies lie in, and computes the centroid of all bodies in each branch. The tree is then used to compute the force between each body and all the others, approximating the force between distant bodies by using the centroids. Whereas a naive algorithm would use work $O(n^2)$ in the number of bodies, the Barnes-Hut approximation is $O(n.log\ n)$.

With the baseline array representation, the copying replication problem appears at the very top level. Once we have built the quad-tree, we use it to compute the force on each body.

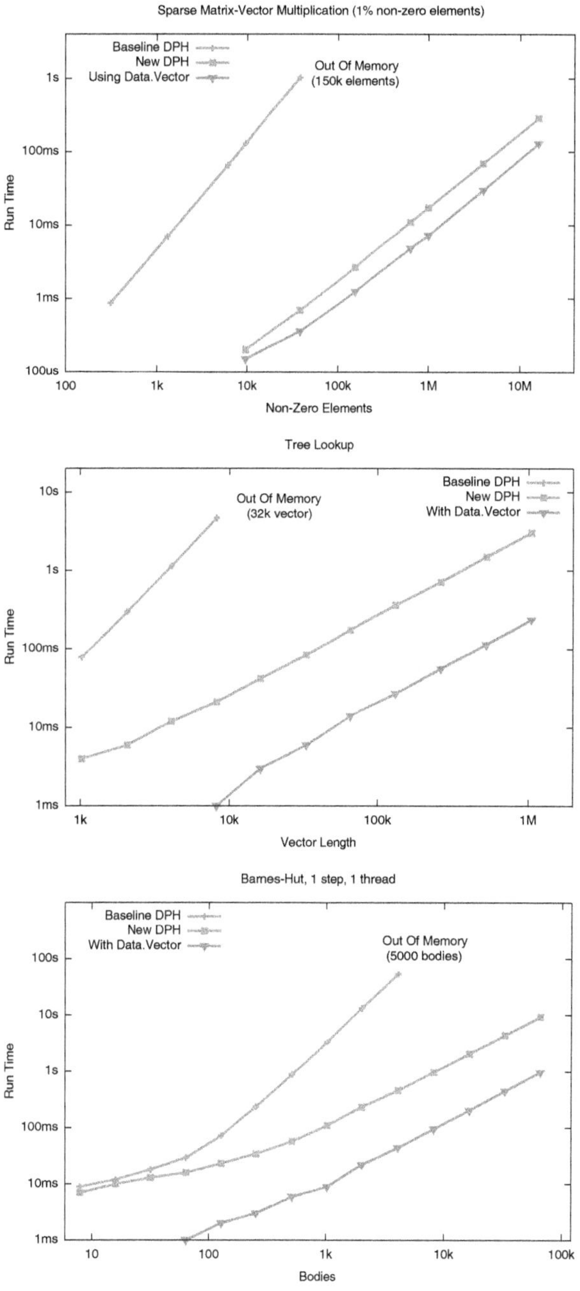

Figure 6. Benchmark Runtime Performance

This is done by the following function:

```
calcAccels :: Double -> Box -> [:MassPoint:] -> [:Accel:]
calcAccels epsilon boundingBox points
 = mapP (\m -> calcAccel epsilon m tree) points
 where tree = buildTree boundingBox points
```

As `tree` is free in the closure passed to `mapP`, it is copied once for every body. As before, with the new array representation the tree is not copied and the program runs with the same asymptotic complexity as an unvectorised reference implementation written with the `Data.Vector` package.

When divide and conquer algorithms such as Barnes-Hut are vectorised, the resulting code increases the nesting level of the source array during the division phase (on the way down) and concatenates the result on the way back up. We refer to such algorithms as *dynamically nested* for this reason. As discussed in §5.2, `concat` normalises the array representation, so the program effectively switches between the old baseline representation and our new scattered representation as it runs.

8. Related Work

Approaches to the implementation of irregular parallelism roughly fall into two categories: thread-based implementations, like Manticore [8] or Ct [9], and those based on flattening. Both have their advantages and drawbacks. With the former approach, scheduling, synchronisation, and granularity control are a concern, as well as a more restricted set of target architectures, though they do not suffer from the complexity problem described in this paper. However, the problem we describe is a fundamental issue for all flattening based approaches, and has been identified and discussed in several publications.

The original first-order flattening transform and array representation shown in Figure 2 was introduced by Blelloch and Sabot in in [1]. In this work the `replicate` function is called `distribute` when applied to scalars and `distribute-segment` when applied to arrays. As a possible extension to the handling of conditionals they suggest operating on sparse segments instead of first eliminating gaps between them with the `pack` operation. This idea is not elaborated further. The single example program they present (Quicksort) only uses `distribute` and `pack` on arrays of scalars, and thus does not suffer problems with asymptotic complexity.

In [2] Blelloch proves that a subset of programs written with the scan-vector instruction set can be vectorised while preserving their asymptotic work and step complexity. Such programs must be both *contained*, and not use indirect memory access, which is equivalent to disallowing functions to have free variables. Appendix C of the NESL manual [3] gives the work complexity of vectorised programs, and states that the contents of free variables is copied across each iteration of the `apply-to-each` (`map`) construct. Finally, in [4] the authors present a provably time and space efficient version of NESL, but the operational semantics is based around fine grained threads instead of SIMD style vectors.

In [15], Palmer et al. address the issue by disallowing partial applications and removing some of the problematic cases using rewrite rules. For Haskell, ruling out partial applications to appear anywhere in a parallel context would be neither desirable nor statically enforceable. The rewrite rules used do not fire if the offending index space transform is applied indirectly as part of another function. This is a general drawback of using rewrite rules, which can be acceptable if the rewriting only leads to a constant improvement, but not in our case, where the failure to identify problematic expressions results in asymptotically worse performance.

In [18], Riely and Prins solve this problem by using vectors of references, but at the time the article was written, there was no implementation, so they could not provide any experimental data as to the absolute performance. To the best of our knowledge, they have not published any further results on this approach. The suggested representation is similar to one of the states our representation can take on, for example, as a result of creating a nested vector by collecting a number of different flat arrays in a nested one. However, the use of purely pointer based representations can lead to poor locality and complicates distribution and load balancing. It also increases garbage collection overhead, as every subarray must be traversed individually. In contrast, our approach aims at keeping the data representation as flat as possible, and only resorts to the partially flattened representation whenever the completely flat representation would lead to worse work complexity.

Acknowledgements This work was supported in part by the Australian Research Council under grant number LP0989507.

References

[1] G. Blelloch and G. W. Sabot. Compiling collection-oriented languages onto massively parallel computers. *Journal of Parallel and Distributed Computing*, 8:119–134, 1990.

[2] G. E. Blelloch. *Vector models for data-parallel computing*. MIT Press, 1990.

[3] G. E. Blelloch. NESL: A nested data-parallel language (version 3.1). Technical report, Carnegie Mellon University, 1995.

[4] G. E. Blelloch and J. Greiner. A provable time and space efficient implementation of NESL. In *ICFP 1996: International Conference on Functional Programming*, pages 213–225, 1996.

[5] M. M. T. Chakravarty, G. Keller, S. Peyton Jones, and S. Marlow. Associated types with class. In *POPL 2005: Principles of Programming Languages*, pages 1–13. ACM Press, 2005.

[6] M. M. T. Chakravarty, R. Leshchinskiy, S. Peyton Jones, G. Keller, and S. Marlow. Data Parallel Haskell: a status report. In *DAMP 2007: Declarative Aspects of Multicore Programming*. ACM Press, 2007.

[7] D. Coutts, R. Leshchinskiy, and D. Stewart. Stream fusion: from lists to streams to nothing at all. In *ICFP 2007: International Conference on Functional Programming*, 2007.

[8] M. Fluet, M. Rainey, and J. Reppy. A scheduling framework for general-purpose parallel languages. In *ICFP 2008: International Conference on Functional Programming*, pages 241–252. ACM, 2008.

[9] A. Ghuloum, T. Smith, G. Wu, X. Zhou, J. Fang, P. Guo, B. So, M. Rajagopalan, Y. Chen, and B. Chen. Future-proof data parallel algorithms and software on Intel multi-core architecture. *Intel Technology Journal*, November 2007.

[10] J. Hill, K. M. Clarke, and R. Bornat. Vectorising a non-strict data-parallel functional language, 1994.

[11] R. Leshchincskiy. *Higher-Order Nested Data Parallelism*. PhD thesis, Technische Universität Berlin, 2006.

[12] R. Leshchinskiy, M. M. T. Chakravarty, and G. Keller. Higher order flattening. In *ICCS 2006: International Conference on Computational Science*, volume 3992, pages 920–928. Springer, 2006.

[13] B. Lippmeier, M. M. T. Chakravarty, G. Keller, R. Leshchinskiy, and S. P. Jones. Work efficient higher-order vectorisation (unabridged). Technical Report UNSW-CSE-TR-201208, University of New South Wales, 2012.

[14] D. W. Palmer, J. F. Prins, S. Chatterjee, and R. E. Faith. Piecewise execution of nested data-parallel programs. In *Languages and Compilers for Parallel Computing, volume 1033 of Lecture Notes in Computer Science*, pages 346–361. Springer-Verlag, 1995.

[15] D. W. Palmer, J. F. Prins, and S. Westfold. Work-efficient nested data-parallelism. In *Proc. of the 5th Symposium on the Frontiers of Massively Parallel Processing*, pages 186–193. IEEE, 1995.

[16] S. Peyton Jones, W. Partain, and A. Santos. Let-floating: Moving bindings to give faster programs. In *ICFP 1996: International Conference on Functional Programming*, pages 1–12, 1996.

[17] S. Peyton Jones, R. Leshchinskiy, G. Keller, and M. M. T. Chakravarty. Harnessing the multicores: Nested data parallelism in Haskell. In *FSTTCS 2008: Foundations of Software Technology and Theoretical Computer Science*, LIPIcs, pages 383–414. Schloss Dagstuhl, 2008.

[18] J. Riely and J. Prins. Flattening is an improvement. In *Proc. of the 7th International Symposium on Static Analysis*, pages 360–376, 2000.

[19] D. Spoonhower, G. E. Blelloch, R. Harper, and P. B. Gibbons. Space profiling for parallel functional programs. In *ICFP 2008: International Conference on Functional Programming*, 2008.

Tales from the Jungle

Peter Sewell
University of Cambridge
Peter.Sewell@cl.cam.ac.uk

Abstract

We rely on a computational infrastructure that is a densely interwined mass of software and hardware: programming languages, network protocols, operating systems, and processors. It has accumulated great complexity, from a combination of engineering design decisions, contingent historical choices, and sheer scale, yet it is defined at best by prose specifications, or, all too often, just by the common implementations. Can we do better? More specifically, can we apply rigorous methods to this mainstream infrastructure, taking the accumulated complexity seriously, and if we do, does it help? My colleagues and I have looked at these questions in several contexts: the TCP/IP network protocols with their Sockets API; programming language design, including the Java module system and the C11/C++11 concurrency model; the hardware concurrency behaviour of x86, IBM POWER, and ARM multiprocessors; and compilation of concurrent code.

In this talk I will draw some lessons from what did and did not succeed, looking especially at the empirical nature of some of the work, at the social process of engagement with the various different communities, and at the mathematical and software tools we used. Domain-specific modelling languages (based on functional programming ideas) and proof assistants were invaluable for working with the large and loose specifications involved: idioms within HOL4 for TCP, our Ott tool for programming language specification, and Owens's Lem tool for portable semantic definitions, with HOL4, Isabelle, and Coq, for the relaxed-memory concurrency semantics work. Our experience with these suggests something of what is needed to make full-scale rigorous semantics a commonplace reality.

Categories and Subject Descriptors F.3.1 [*LOGICS AND MEANINGS OF PROGRAMS*]: Specifying and Verifying and Reasoning about Programs; D.3.1 [*PROGRAMMING LANGUAGES*]: Formal Definitions and Theory

General Terms Design, Languages, Reliability, Standardization, Verification

Keywords Mainstream systems

Acknowledgments

I acknowledge funding from EPSRC grants EP/F036345 and EP/H005633.

ICFP'12, September 9–15, 2012, Copenhagen, Denmark.
ACM 978-1-4503-1054-3/12/09.

Propositions as Sessions

Philip Wadler
University of Edinburgh
wadler@inf.ed.ac.uk

Abstract

Continuing a line of work by Abramsky (1994), by Bellin and Scott (1994), and by Caires and Pfenning (2010), among others, this paper presents CP, a calculus in which propositions of classical linear logic correspond to session types. Continuing a line of work by Honda (1993), by Honda, Kubo, and Vasconcelos (1998), and by Gay and Vasconcelos (2010), among others, this paper presents GV, a linear functional language with session types, and presents a translation from GV into CP. The translation formalises for the first time a connection between a standard presentation of session types and linear logic, and shows how a modification to the standard presentation yield a language free from deadlock, where deadlock freedom follows from the correspondence to linear logic.

Categories and Subject Descriptors F.4.1 [*Mathematical Logic*]: Lambda calculus and related systems; F.4.1 [*Mathematical Logic*]: Proof theory; D.3.3 [*Language Constructs and Features*]: Concurrent programming structures

Keywords linear logic, lambda calculus, pi calculus

1. Introduction

Functional programmers know where they stand: upon the foundation of λ-calculus. Its canonicality is confirmed by its double discovery, once as natural deduction by Gentzen and once as λ-calculus by Church. These two formulations are related by the Curry-Howard correspondence, which takes

propositions *as* types,
proofs *as* programs, and
normalisation of proofs *as* evaluation of programs.

The correspondence arises repeatedly: Girard's System F corresponds to Reynold's polymorphic λ-calculus; Peirce's law in classical logic corresponds to Felleisen's call-cc.

Today, mobile phones, server farms, and multicores make us all concurrent programmers. Where lies a foundation for concurrency as firm as that of λ-calculus? Many process calculi have emerged—ranging from CSP to CCS to π-calculus to join calculus to mobile ambients to bigraphs—but none is as canonical as λ-calculus, and none has the distinction of arising from Curry-Howard.

Since its inception by Girard (1987), linear logic has held the promise of a foundation for concurrency rooted in Curry-Howard. In an early step, Abramsky (1994) and Bellin and Scott (1994) devised a translation from linear logic into π-calculus. Along another line, Honda (1993) introduced session types, further developed by Honda et al. (1998) and others, which take inspiration from linear logic, but do not enjoy a relationship as tight as Curry-Howard.

Recently, Caires and Pfenning (2010) found a twist on Abramsky's translation that yields an interpretation strongly reminiscent of session types, and a variant of Curry-Howard with

propositions *as* session types,
proofs *as* processes, and
cut elimination *as* communication.

The correspondence is developed in a series of papers by Caires, Pfenning, Toninho, and Pérez. This paper extends these lines of work with three contributions.

First, inspired by the calculus πDILL of Caires and Pfenning (2010), this paper presents the calculus CP. Based on dual intuitionistic linear logic, πDILL uses two-sided sequents, with two constructs corresponding to output ($\otimes$ on the right of a sequent and $\multimap$ on the left), and two constructs corresponding to input ($\multimap$ on the right of a sequent and $\otimes$ on the left). Based on classical linear logic, CP uses one-sided sequents, offering greater simplicity and symmetry, with a single construct for output ($\otimes$) and a single construct for input ($⅋$), each dual to the other. Caires et al. (2012a) compares πDILL with πCLL, which like CP is based on classical linear logic; we discuss this comparison in Section 4. (If you like, CP stands for Classical Processes.)

Second, though πDILL is clearly reminiscent of the body of work on session types, no one has previously published a formal connection. Inspired by the linear functional language with session types of Gay and Vasconcelos (2010), this paper presents the calculus GV, and presents a translation from GV into CP, for the first time formalising a tight connection between a standard presentation of session types and linear logic. In order to facilitate the translation, GV differs from the language of Gay and Vasconcelos (2010) in some particulars. These differences suffice to make GV, unlike the original, free from deadlock. (If you like, GV stands for Good Variation.)

Curry-Howard relates proof normalisation to computation. Logicians devised proof normalisation to show consistency of logic, and for this purpose it is essential that proof normalisation terminates. Hence, a consequence of Curry-Howard is that it identifies a fragment of λ-calculus for which the Halting Problem is solved. Well-typed programs terminate unless they explicitly resort to non-logical features such as general recursion. Similarly, a consequence of Curry-Howard for concurrency is that it identifies a fragment of a process calculus which is free of deadlock. In particular, πDILL and CP are both such fragments, and the proof that GV is deadlock-free follows immediately from its translation to CP.

Third, this paper presents a calculus with a stronger connection to linear logic, at the cost of a weaker connection to traditional process calculi. Bellin and Scott (1994) and Caires and Pfenning (2010) each present a translation from linear logic into π-calculus such that cut elimination converts one proof to another if and only if the translation of the one reduces to the translation of the other; but to achieve this tight connection several adjustments are necessary.

Bellin and Scott (1994) restrict the axiom to atomic type, and Caires and Pfenning (2010) omit the axiom entirely. In terms of a practical programming language, such restrictions are excessive. The former permits type variables, but instantiating a type variable to a type requires restructuring the program (as opposed to simple substitution); the latter outlaws type variables altogether. In consequence, neither system lends itself to parametric polymorphism.

Further, Bellin and Scott (1994) only obtain a tight correspondence between cut elimination and π-calculus for the multiplicative connectives, and they require a variant of π-calculus with surprising structural equivalences such as $x(y).x(z).P \equiv x(z).x(y).P$—permuting two reads on the same channel! Caires and Pfenning (2010) only obtain a tight correspondence between cut elimination and π-calculus by ignoring commuting conversions; this is hard to justify logically, because commuting conversions play an essential role in cut elimination. Pérez et al. (2012) show commuting conversions correspond to contextual equivalences, but fail to capture the directionality of the commuting conversions.

Thus, while the connection established in previous work between cut elimination in linear logic and reduction in π-calculus is encouraging, it comes at a substantial cost. Accordingly, this paper cuts the Gordian knot: it takes the traditional rules of cut elimination as specifying the reduction rules for its process calculus. Pro: we let logic guide the design of the 'right' process calculus. Con: we forego the assurance that comes from double discoveries of the same system, as with Gentzen and Church, Girard and Reynolds, and Pierce and Felleisen. Mitigating the con slightly are the results cited above that show a connection between Girard's linear logic and Milner's π-calculus, albeit not as tight as the other connections just mentioned.

In return for loosening its connection to π-calculus, the design of CP avoids the problems described above. The axiom is interpreted at all types, using a construct suggested by Caires et al. (2012a), and consequently it is easy to extend the system to support polymorphism, using a construct suggested by Turner (1995). All commuting conversions of cut elimination are satisfied.

This paper is organised as follows. Section 2 presents CP. Section 3 presents GV and its translation to CP. Section 4 discusses related work. Section 5 concludes.

2. Classical linear logic as a process calculus

This section presents CP, a session-typed process calculus. CP is based on classical linear logic with one-sided sequents, the system treated in the first paper on linear logic by Girard (1987).

Types Propositions, which may be interpreted as session types, are defined by the following grammar:

$A, B, C ::=$	
X	propositional variable
$X^\perp$	dual of propositional variable
$A \otimes B$	'times', output A then behave as B
$A \mathbin{⅋} B$	'par', input A then behave as B
$A \oplus B$	'plus', select from A or B
$A \mathbin{\&} B$	'with', offer choice of A or B
$!A$	'of course!', server accept
$?A$	'why not?', client request
$\exists X.B$	existential, output a type
$\forall X.B$	universal, input a type
1	unit for $\otimes$
$\perp$	unit for ⅋
0	unit for $\oplus$
$\top$	unit for $\&$

Let A, B, C range over propositions, and X, Y, Z range over propositional variables. Every propositional variable X has a dual written $X^\perp$. Propositions are composed from multiplicatives ($\otimes$, ⅋), additives ($\oplus$,$\&$), exponentials ($!, ?$), second-order quantifiers ($\exists, \forall$), and units ($1, \perp, 0, \top$). In $\exists X.B$ and $\forall X.B$, propositional variable X is bound in B. Write $\mathsf{fv}(A)$ for the free variables in proposition A.

Duals Duals play a key role, ensuring that a request for input at one end of a channel matches an offer of a corresponding output at the other, and that a request to make a selection at one end matches an offer of a corresponding choice at the other.

Each proposition A has a dual $A^\perp$, defined as follows:

$$\begin{array}{rclrcl} (X)^\perp &=& X^\perp & (X^\perp)^\perp &=& X \\ (A \otimes B)^\perp &=& A^\perp ⅋ B^\perp & (A ⅋ B)^\perp &=& A^\perp \otimes B^\perp \\ (A \oplus B)^\perp &=& A^\perp \mathbin{\&} B^\perp & (A \mathbin{\&} B)^\perp &=& A^\perp \oplus B^\perp \\ (!A)^\perp &=& ?A^\perp & (?A)^\perp &=& !A^\perp \\ (\exists X.B)^\perp &=& \forall X.B^\perp & (\forall X.B)^\perp &=& \exists X.B^\perp \\ 1^\perp &=& \perp & \perp^\perp &=& 1 \\ 0^\perp &=& \top & \top^\perp &=& 0 \end{array}$$

The dual of a propositional variable, $X^\perp$, is part of the syntax. Multiplicatives are dual to each other, as are additives, exponentials, and quantifiers.

Duality is an involution, $(A^\perp)^\perp = A$.

Substitution Write $B\{A/X\}$ to denote substitution of A for X in B. Substitution of a proposition for a dual propositional variable results in the dual of the proposition. Assuming $X \neq Y$, define

$$\begin{array}{rclrcl} X\{A/X\} &=& A & X^\perp\{A/X\} &=& A^\perp \\ Y\{A/X\} &=& Y & Y^\perp\{A/X\} &=& Y^\perp \end{array}$$

The remaining clauses are entirely standard, for instance $(A \otimes B)\{C/X\} = A\{C/X\} \otimes B\{C/X\}$.

Duality preserves substitution, $B\{A/X\}^\perp = B^\perp\{A/X\}$.

Environments Let Γ, Δ, Θ range over environments associating names to propositions, where each name is distinct. Assume $\Gamma = x_1 : A_1, \ldots, x_n : A_n$, with $x_i \neq x_j$ whenever $i \neq j$. Write $\mathsf{fn}(\Gamma) = \{x_1, \ldots, x_n\}$ for the names in Γ, and $\mathsf{fv}(\Gamma) = \mathsf{fv}(A_1) \cup \cdots \cup \mathsf{fv}(A_n)$ for the free variables in Γ. Order in environments is ignored. Environments use linear maintenance. Two environments may be combined only if they contain distinct names: writing Γ, Δ implies $\mathsf{fn}(\Gamma) \cap \mathsf{fn}(\Delta) = \emptyset$.

Processes Our process calculus is a variant on the π-calculus (Milner et al., 1992). Processes are defined by the following grammar:

$P, Q, R ::=$	
$x \leftrightarrow y$	link
$\nu x : A.(P \mid Q)$	parallel composition
$x[y].(P \mid Q)$	output
$x(y).P$	input
$x[\mathsf{inl}].P$	left selection
$x[\mathsf{inr}].P$	right selection
$x.\mathsf{case}(P, Q)$	choice
$!x(y).P$	server accept
$?x[y].P$	client request
$x[A].P$	send type
$x(X).P$	receive type
$x[\,].0$	empty output
$x().P$	empty input
$x.\mathsf{case}()$	empty choice

In $\nu x : A.(P \mid Q)$, name x is bound in P and Q, in $x[y].(P \mid Q)$, name y is bound in P (but not in Q), and in $x(y).P$, $?x[y].P$, and

$$\frac{}{w \leftrightarrow x \vdash w : A^{\perp}, x : A}\ \mathsf{Ax} \qquad \frac{P \vdash \Gamma, x : A \quad Q \vdash \Delta, x : A^{\perp}}{\nu x : A.(P \mid Q) \vdash \Gamma, \Delta}\ \mathsf{Cut}$$

$$\frac{P \vdash \Gamma, y : A \quad Q \vdash \Delta, x : B}{x[y].(P \mid Q) \vdash \Gamma, \Delta, x : A \otimes B}\ \otimes \qquad \frac{R \vdash \Theta, y : A, x : B}{x(y).R \vdash \Theta, x : A \parr B}\ \parr$$

$$\frac{P \vdash \Gamma, x : A}{x[\mathsf{inl}].P \vdash \Gamma, x : A \oplus B}\ \oplus_1 \qquad \frac{P \vdash \Gamma, x : B}{x[\mathsf{inr}].P \vdash \Gamma, x : A \oplus B}\ \oplus_2 \qquad \frac{Q \vdash \Delta, x : A \quad R \vdash \Delta, x : B}{x.\mathsf{case}(Q, R) \vdash \Delta, x : A \,\&\, B}\ \&$$

$$\frac{P \vdash ?\Gamma, y : A}{!x(y).P \vdash ?\Gamma, x : !A}\ ! \qquad \frac{Q \vdash \Delta, y : A}{?x[y].Q \vdash \Delta, x : ?A}\ ? \qquad \frac{Q \vdash \Delta}{Q \vdash \Delta, x : ?A}\ \mathsf{Weaken} \qquad \frac{Q \vdash \Delta, x' : ?A, x'' : ?A}{Q\{x/x', x/x''\} \vdash \Delta, x : ?A}\ \mathsf{Contract}$$

$$\frac{P \vdash \Gamma, x : B\{A/X\}}{x[A].P \vdash \Gamma, x : \exists X.B}\ \exists \qquad \frac{Q \vdash \Delta, x : B}{x(X).Q \vdash \Delta, x : \forall X.B}\ \forall\ (X \notin \mathsf{fv}(\Delta))$$

$$\frac{}{x[\,].0 \vdash x : 1}\ 1 \qquad \frac{P \vdash \Gamma}{x().P \vdash \Gamma, x : \perp}\ \perp \qquad (\text{no rule for } 0) \qquad \frac{}{x.\mathsf{case}() \vdash \Gamma, x : \top}\ \top$$

Figure 1. CP, classical linear logic as a session-typed process calculus

$!x(y).P$, name y is bound in P. We write $\mathsf{fn}(P)$ for the free names in process P. In $x(X).P$, propositional variable X is bound in P.

The form $x \leftrightarrow y$ denotes forwarding, where every message received on x is retransmitted on y, and every message received on y is retransmitted on x. Square brackets surround outputs and round brackets surround inputs; unlike π-calculus, both output and input names are bound. The forms $x(y).P$ and $!x(y).P$ in our calculus behave like the same forms in π-calculus, while the forms $x[y].P$ and $?x[y].P$ in our calculus both behave like the form $\nu y.x\langle y\rangle.P$ in π-calculus.

A referee suggested, in line with one tradition for π-calculus, choosing the notation $\overline{x}(y).P$ in place of $x[y].P$; but overlines can be hard to spot, while the distinction between round and square brackets is clear.

Judgments The rules for assigning session types to processes are shown in Figure 1. Judgments take the form

$$P \vdash x_1 : A_1, \ldots, x_n : A_n$$

indicating that process P communicates along each channel named x_i obeying the protocol specified by A_i. Erasing the process and the channel names from the above yields

$$\vdash A_1, \ldots, A_n$$

and applying this erasure to the rules in Figure 1 yields the rules of classical linear logic, as given by Girard (1987).

2.1 Structural rules

The calculus has two structural rules, Axiom and Cut. We do not list Exchange explicitly, since order in environments is ignored.

The axiom is:

$$\frac{}{w \leftrightarrow x \vdash w : A^{\perp}, x : A}\ \mathsf{Ax}$$

We interpret the axiom as forwarding. A name input along w is forwarded as output along x, and vice versa, so types of the two channels must be dual. Bellin and Scott (1994) restrict the axiom to propositional variables, replacing A by X and replacing $w \leftrightarrow x$ by the π-calculus term $w(y).x\langle y\rangle.0$. Whereas we forward any number of times and in either direction, they forward only once and from X to $X^{\perp}$.

The cut rule is:

$$\frac{P \vdash \Gamma, x : A \quad Q \vdash \Delta, x : A^{\perp}}{\nu x : A.(P \mid Q) \vdash \Gamma, \Delta}\ \mathsf{Cut}$$

Following Abramsky (1994) and Bellin and Scott (1994), we interpret Cut as a symmetric operation combining parallel composition with name restriction. Process P communicates along channel x obeying protocol A, while process Q communicates along the same channel x obeying the dual protocol $A^{\perp}$. Duality guarantees that sends and selections in P match with receives and choices in Q, and vice versa. Communications along Γ and Δ are disjoint, so P and Q are restricted to communicate with each other only along x. If communication could occur along two channels rather than one, then one could form a loop of communications between P and Q that leads to deadlock.

Observe that, despite writing $\nu x : A$ in the syntax, the type of x differs in P and Q—it is A in the former but $A^{\perp}$ in the latter. Including the type A in the syntax for Cut guarantees that given the type of each free name in the term, each term has a unique type derivation. To save ink and eyestrain, the type is omitted when it is clear from the context.

Cut elimination corresponds to process reduction. Figure 2 shows three equivalences on cuts, and one reduction that simplifies a cut against an axiom, each specified in terms of derivation trees; from which we read off directly the corresponding equivalence or reduction on processes. We write $\equiv$ for equivalences and $\Longrightarrow$ for reductions. Equivalence (Swap) states that a cut is symmetric:

$$\nu x : A.(P \mid Q) \equiv \nu x : A^{\perp}.(Q \mid P)$$

It serves the same role as the π-calculus structural equivalenc for symmetry, $P \mid Q \equiv Q \mid P$. Equivalences (Assoc) permit reordering cuts:

$$\nu y.(\nu x.(P \mid Q) \mid R) \equiv \nu x.(P \mid \nu y.(Q \mid R))$$

It serves the same role as the π-calculus structural equivalences for associativity, $P \mid Q \equiv Q \mid P$, and scope extrusion $(\nu x.P) \mid Q \equiv \nu x.(P \mid Q)$ when $x \notin P$.

Reduction (AxCut) simplifies a cut against an axiom.

$$\nu x.(w \leftrightarrow x \mid P) \Longrightarrow P\{w/x\}$$

We write $P\{w/x\}$ to denote substitution of w for x in P.

$$\text{(Swap)} \quad \dfrac{P \vdash \Gamma, x : A \quad Q \vdash \Delta, x : A^\perp}{\nu x : A.(P \mid Q) \vdash \Gamma, \Delta}\text{Cut} \equiv \dfrac{Q \vdash \Delta, x : A^\perp \quad P \vdash \Gamma, x : A}{\nu x : A^\perp.(Q \mid P) \vdash \Gamma, \Delta}\text{Cut}$$

$$\text{(Assoc)} \quad \dfrac{\dfrac{P \vdash \Gamma, x : A \quad Q \vdash \Delta, x : A^\perp, y : B}{\nu x.(P \mid Q) \vdash \Gamma, \Delta, y : B}\text{Cut} \quad R \vdash \Theta, y : B^\perp}{\nu y.(\nu x.(P \mid Q) \mid R) \vdash \Gamma, \Delta, \Theta}\text{Cut} \equiv \dfrac{P \vdash \Gamma, x : A \quad \dfrac{Q \vdash \Delta, x : A^\perp, y : B \quad R \vdash \Theta, y : B^\perp}{\nu y.(Q \mid R) \vdash \Delta, \Theta, x : A^\perp}\text{Cut}}{\nu x.(P \mid \nu y.(Q \mid R)) \vdash \Gamma, \Delta, \Theta}\text{Cut}$$

$$\text{(AxCut)} \quad \dfrac{\dfrac{}{w \leftrightarrow x \vdash w : A^\perp, x : A}\text{Ax} \quad P \vdash \Gamma, x : A^\perp}{\nu x.(w \leftrightarrow x \mid P) \vdash \Gamma, w : A^\perp}\text{Cut} \Longrightarrow P\{w/x\} \vdash \Gamma, w : A^\perp$$

Figure 2. Structural cut equivalences and reduction for CP

2.2 Output and input

The multiplicative connectives $A \otimes B$ and $A \invamp B$ are dual. We interpret $A \otimes B$ as the session type of a process which outputs an A and then behaves as a B, and $A \invamp B$ as the session type of a process which inputs an A and then behaves as a B.

The rule for output is:

$$\dfrac{P \vdash \Gamma, y : A \quad Q \vdash \Delta, x : B}{x[y].(P \mid Q) \vdash \Gamma, \Delta, x : A \otimes B}\otimes$$

Processes P and Q act on disjoint sets of channels. Process P communicates along channel y obeying protocol A, while process Q communicates along channel x obeying protocol B. The composite process $x[y].(P \mid Q)$ communicates along channel x obeying protocol $A \otimes B$; it allocates a fresh channel y, transmits y along x, and then concurrently executes P and Q. Disjointness of P and Q ensures there is no further entangling between x and y, which guarantees freedom from deadlock.

The rule for input is:

$$\dfrac{R \vdash \Theta, y : A, x : B}{x(y).R \vdash \Theta, x : A \invamp B}\invamp$$

Process R communicates along channel y obeying protocol A and along channel x obeying protocol B. The composite process $x(y).R$ communicates along channel x obeying protocol $A \invamp B$; it receives name y along x, and then executes R. Unlike with output, the single process R that communicates with both x and y. It is safe to permit the same process to communicate with x and y on the input side, because there is no further entangling of x with y on the output side, explaining the claim that disentangling x from y on output guarantees freedom from deadlock.

For output, channel x has type B in the component process Q but type $A \otimes B$ in the composite process $x[y].(P \mid Q)$. For input, channel x has type B in the component process R but type $A \invamp B$ in the composite process $x(y).R$. One may regard the type of the channel evolving as communication proceeds, corresponding to the notion of session type. Assigning the same channel name different types in the hypothesis and conclusion of a rule is the telling twist added by Caires and Pfenning (2010), in contrast to the use of different variables in the hypothesis and conclusion followed by Abramsky (1994) and Bellin and Scott (1994).

The computational content of the logic is most clearly revealed in the principal cuts of each connective against its dual. Principal cut reductions are shown in Figure 3.

Cut of output $\otimes$ against input $\invamp$ corresponds to communication, as shown in rule $(\beta_{\otimes\invamp})$:

$$\nu x.(x[y].(P \mid Q) \mid x(y).R) \Longrightarrow \nu y.(P \mid \nu x.(Q \mid R))$$

In stating this rule, we take advantage of the fact that y is bound in both $x[y].P$ and $x(y).Q$ to assume the same bound name y has been chosen in each; Pitts (2011) refers to this as the 'anti-Barendregt' convention.

Recall that $x[y].P$ in our notation corresponds to $\nu y.x\langle y\rangle.P$ in π-calculus. Thus, the rule above corresponds to the π-calculus reduction:

$$\nu x.(\nu y.x\langle y\rangle.(P \mid Q) \mid x(z).R) \Longrightarrow \nu y.P \mid \nu x.(Q \mid R\{z/y\})$$

This follows from from $x\langle y\rangle.P \mid x(z).R \Longrightarrow P \mid R\{z/y\}$, and the structural equivalences for scope extrusion, since $x \notin \mathsf{fn}(P)$.

The right-hand side of the above reduction can be written in two ways, which are equivalent by use of the the structural rules (Swap) and (Assoc).

$$\begin{array}{lll} & \nu x : A.(P \mid \nu y : B.(Q \mid R)) & \\ \equiv & \nu x : A.(P \mid \nu y : B^\perp.(R \mid Q)) & \text{(Swap)} \\ \equiv & \nu y : B^\perp.(\nu x : A.(P \mid R) \mid Q) & \text{(Assoc)} \\ \equiv & \nu y : B.(Q \mid \nu x : A.(P \mid R)) & \text{(Swap)} \end{array}$$

The apparent lack of symmetry between $A \otimes B$ and $B \otimes A$ may appear unsettling: the first means output A and then behave as B, the second means output B and then behave as A. The situation is similar to Cartesian product, where $B \times A$ and $A \times B$ differ but satisfy an isomorphism. Similarly, $A \otimes B$ and $B \otimes A$ are interconvertible.

$$\dfrac{\dfrac{\dfrac{}{w \leftrightarrow z \vdash w : B^\perp, z : B}\text{Ax} \quad \dfrac{}{y \leftrightarrow x \vdash y : A^\perp, x : A}\text{Ax}}{x[z].(w \leftrightarrow z \mid y \leftrightarrow x) \vdash w : B^\perp, y : A^\perp, x : B \otimes A}\otimes}{w(y).x[z].(w \leftrightarrow z \mid y \leftrightarrow x) \vdash w : A^\perp \invamp B^\perp, x : B \otimes A}\invamp$$

Let $Q \vdash \Delta$ be the conclusion of the above derivation. Given an arbitrary derivation ending in $P \vdash \Gamma, w : A \otimes B$, one may replace $A \otimes B$ with $B \otimes A$ as follows:

$$\dfrac{P \vdash \Gamma, w : A \otimes B \quad Q \vdash \Delta}{\nu w.(P \mid Q) \vdash \Gamma, x : B \otimes A}\text{Cut}$$

Here process P communicates along w obeying the protocol $A \otimes B$, outputting A and then behaving as B. Composing P with Q yields the process that communicates along x obeying the protocol $B \otimes A$, outputting B and then behaving as A.

The multiplicative units are 1 for $\otimes$ and $\perp$ for $\invamp$. We interpret 1 as the session type of a process that performs an empty ouput, and $\perp$ as the session type of a process that performs an empty input. These are related by duality: $1^\perp = \perp$. Their rules are shown in Figure 1. Cut of empty output 1 against empty input $\perp$ corresponds to an empty communication, as shown in rule $(\beta_{1\perp})$:

$$\nu x.(x[].0 \mid x().P) \Longrightarrow P$$

$(\beta_{\otimes\parr})$

$$\dfrac{\dfrac{P \vdash \Gamma, y : A \quad Q \vdash \Delta, x : B}{x[y].(P \mid Q) \vdash \Gamma, \Delta, x : A \otimes B}\,\otimes \qquad \dfrac{R \vdash \Theta, y : A^\perp, x : B^\perp}{x(y).R \vdash \Theta, x : A^\perp \parr B^\perp}\,\parr}{\nu x.(x[y].(P \mid Q) \mid x(y).R) \vdash \Gamma, \Delta, \Theta}\,\mathsf{Cut} \quad \Longrightarrow$$

$$\dfrac{P \vdash \Gamma, y : A \qquad \dfrac{Q \vdash \Delta, x : B \quad R \vdash \Theta, y : A^\perp, x : B^\perp}{\nu x.(Q \mid R) \vdash \Delta, \Theta, y : A^\perp}\,\mathsf{Cut}}{\nu y.(P \mid \nu x.(Q \mid R)) \vdash \Gamma, \Delta, \Theta}\,\mathsf{Cut}$$

$(\beta_{\oplus\&})$

$$\dfrac{\dfrac{P \vdash \Gamma, x : A}{x[\mathsf{inl}].P \vdash \Gamma, x : A \oplus B}\,\oplus_1 \qquad \dfrac{Q \vdash \Delta, x : A^\perp \quad R \vdash \Delta, x : B^\perp}{x.\mathsf{case}(Q, R) \vdash \Delta, x : A^\perp \mathbin{\&} B^\perp}\,\&}{\nu x.(x[\mathsf{inl}].P \mid x.\mathsf{case}(Q, R)) \vdash \Gamma, \Delta}\,\mathsf{Cut} \quad \Longrightarrow \quad \dfrac{P \vdash \Gamma, x : A \quad Q \vdash \Delta, x : A^\perp}{\nu x.(P \mid Q) \vdash \Gamma, \Delta}\,\mathsf{Cut}$$

$(\beta_{!?})$

$$\dfrac{\dfrac{P \vdash ?\Gamma, y : A}{!x(y).P \vdash ?\Gamma, x : !A}\,! \qquad \dfrac{Q \vdash \Delta, y : A^\perp}{?x[y].Q \vdash \Delta, x : ?A^\perp}\,?}{\nu x.(!x(y).P \mid ?x[y].Q) \vdash ?\Gamma, \Delta}\,\mathsf{Cut} \quad \Longrightarrow \quad \dfrac{P \vdash ?\Gamma, y : A \quad Q \vdash \Delta, y : A^\perp}{\nu y.(P \mid Q) \vdash ?\Gamma, \Delta}\,\mathsf{Cut}$$

$(\beta_{!W})$

$$\dfrac{\dfrac{P \vdash ?\Gamma, y : A}{!x(y).P \vdash ?\Gamma, x : !A}\,! \qquad \dfrac{Q \vdash \Delta}{Q \vdash \Delta, x : ?A^\perp}\,\mathsf{Weaken}}{\nu x.(!x(y).P \mid Q) \vdash ?\Gamma, \Delta}\,\mathsf{Cut} \quad \Longrightarrow \quad \dfrac{Q \vdash \Delta}{Q \vdash ?\Gamma, \Delta}\,\mathsf{Weaken}$$

$(\beta_{!C})$

$$\dfrac{\dfrac{P \vdash ?\Gamma, y : A}{!x(y).P \vdash ?\Gamma, x : !A}\,! \qquad \dfrac{Q \vdash \Delta, x' : ?A, x'' : ?A}{Q\{x/x', x/x''\} \vdash \Delta, x : ?A}\,\mathsf{Contract}}{\nu x.(!x(y).P \mid Q\{x/x', x/x''\}) \vdash ?\Gamma, \Delta}\,\mathsf{Cut} \quad \Longrightarrow$$

$$\dfrac{\dfrac{\dfrac{P' \vdash ?\Gamma', y' : A}{!x'(y').P' \vdash ?\Gamma', x' : !A}\,! \qquad \dfrac{\dfrac{P'' \vdash ?\Gamma'', y'' : A}{!x''(y'').P'' \vdash ?\Gamma'', x'' : !A}\,! \quad Q \vdash \Delta, x' : ?A^\perp, x'' : ?A^\perp}{\nu x''.(!x''(y'').P'' \mid Q) \vdash ?\Gamma', \Delta, x : ?A^\perp}\,\mathsf{Cut}}{\nu x'.(!x'(y').P' \mid \nu x''.(!x''(y'').P'' \mid Q)) \vdash ?\Gamma', ?\Gamma'', \Delta}\,\mathsf{Cut}}{\nu x'.(!x'(y).P \mid \nu x''.(!x''(y).P \mid Q)) \vdash ?\Gamma, \Delta}\,\mathsf{Contract}$$

$(\beta_{\exists\forall})$

$$\dfrac{\dfrac{P \vdash \Gamma, x : B\{A/X\}}{x[A].P \vdash \Gamma, x : \exists X.B}\,\exists \qquad \dfrac{Q \vdash \Delta, x : B^\perp}{x(X).Q \vdash \Delta, x : \forall X.B^\perp}\,\forall}{\nu x.(x[A].P \mid x(X).Q) \vdash \Gamma, \Delta}\,\mathsf{Cut} \quad \Longrightarrow$$

$$\dfrac{P \vdash \Gamma, x : B\{A/X\} \quad Q\{A/X\} \vdash \Delta, x : B^\perp\{A/X\}}{\nu x.(P \mid Q\{A/X\}) \vdash \Gamma, \Delta}\,\mathsf{Cut}$$

$(\beta_{1\bot})$

$$\dfrac{\dfrac{}{x[\,].0 \vdash x : 1}\,1 \qquad \dfrac{P \vdash \Gamma}{x().P \vdash \Gamma, x : \bot}\,\bot}{\nu x.(x[\,].0 \mid x().P) \vdash \Gamma}\,\mathsf{Cut} \quad \Longrightarrow \quad P \vdash \Gamma$$

$(\beta_{0\top})$ (no rule for 0 with $\top$)

Figure 3. Principal cut reductions for CP

This rule resembles reduction of a nilary communication in the polyadic π-calculus.

2.3 Selection and choice

The additive connectives $A \oplus B$ and $A \mathbin{\&} B$ are dual. We interpret $A \oplus B$ as the session type of a process which selects from either an A or a B, and $A \mathbin{\&} B$ as the session type of a process which offers a choice of either an A or a B.

The rule for left selection is:

$$\dfrac{P \vdash \Gamma, x : A}{x[\mathsf{inl}].P \vdash \Gamma, x : A \oplus B}\,\oplus_1$$

Process P communicates along channel x obeying protocol A. The composite process $x[\mathsf{inl}].P$ communicates along channel x obeying protocol $A \oplus B$; it transmits along x a request to select the left option from a choice, and then executes process P. The rule for right selection is symmetric.

The rule for choice is:

$$\dfrac{Q \vdash \Delta, x : A \quad R \vdash \Delta, x : B}{x.\mathsf{case}(Q, R) \vdash \Delta, x : A \mathbin{\&} B}\,\&$$

The composite process $x.\mathsf{case}(Q, R)$ communicates along channel x obeying protocol $A \mathbin{\&} B$; it receives a selection along channel x and executes either process Q or R accordingly.

For selection, channel x has type A in the component process P and type $A \oplus B$ in the composite process $x[\mathsf{inl}].P$. For choice, channel x has type A in the component process Q, type B in the component process R, and type $A \mathbin{\&} B$ in the composite process $x.\mathsf{case}(Q, R)$. Again, one may regard the type of the channel evolving as communication proceeds, corresponding to the notion of session type.

$$
\begin{array}{llcll}
(\kappa_{\otimes 1}) & \nu z.(x[y].(P \mid Q) \mid R) & \Longrightarrow & x[y].(\nu z.(P \mid R) \mid Q), & \text{if } z \in \mathsf{fn}(P) \\
(\kappa_{\otimes 2}) & \nu z.(x[y].(P \mid Q) \mid R) & \Longrightarrow & x[y].(P \mid \nu z.(Q \mid R)), & \text{if } z \in \mathsf{fn}(Q) \\
(\kappa_{\wp}) & \nu z.(x(y).P \mid Q) & \Longrightarrow & x(y).\nu z.(P \mid Q) & \\
(\kappa_{\oplus}) & \nu z.(x[\mathsf{inl}].P \mid Q) & \Longrightarrow & x[\mathsf{inl}].\nu z.(P \mid Q) & \\
(\kappa_{\&}) & \nu z.(x.\mathsf{case}(P, Q) \mid R) & \Longrightarrow & x.\mathsf{case}(\nu z.(P \mid R), \nu z.(Q \mid R)) & \\
(\kappa_{!}) & \nu z.(!x(y).P \mid Q) & \Longrightarrow & !x(y).\nu z.(P \mid Q) & \\
(\kappa_{?}) & \nu z.(?x[y].P \mid Q) & \Longrightarrow & ?x[y].\nu z.(P \mid Q) & \\
(\kappa_{\exists}) & \nu z.(x[A].P \mid Q) & \Longrightarrow & x[A].\nu z.(P \mid Q) & \\
(\kappa_{\forall}) & \nu z.(x(X).P \mid Q) & \Longrightarrow & x(X).\nu z.(P \mid Q) & \\
(\kappa_{\bot}) & \nu z.(x().P \mid Q) & \Longrightarrow & x().\nu z.(P \mid Q) & \\
(\kappa_{0}) & & \text{(no rule for 0)} & & \\
(\kappa_{\top}) & \nu z.(x.\mathsf{case}() \mid Q) & \Longrightarrow & x.\mathsf{case}() &
\end{array}
$$

Figure 4. Commuting conversions for CP

Cut of selection $\oplus$ against choice $\&$ corresponds to picking an alternative, as shown in rule $(\beta_{\oplus\&})$:

$$x[\mathsf{inl}].P \mid x.\mathsf{case}(Q, R) \Longrightarrow \nu x.(P \mid Q)$$

The rule to select the right option is symmetric.

The additive units are 0 for $\oplus$ and $\top$ for $\&$. We interpret 0 as the session type of a process that selects from among no alternatives, and $\bot$ as the session type of a process that offers a choice among no alternatives. These are related by duality: $0^\bot = \top$. Their rules are shown in Figure 1. There is no rule for 0, because it is impossible to select from no alternatives. Hence, there is also no reduction for a cut of an empty selection against an empty choice, as shown in Figure 3.

2.4 Servers and clients

The exponential connectives $!A$ and $?A$ are dual. We interpret $!A$ as the session type of a server that will repeatedly accept an A, and interpret $?A$ as the session type of a collection of clients that may each request an A. Servers and clients are asymmetric: a server must be impartial, providing the same service to each client; whereas differing clients may accumulate requests to pass to the same server.

The rule for servers is:

$$\frac{P \vdash ?\Gamma, y : A}{!x(y).P \vdash ?\Gamma, x : !A}\ !$$

Process P communicates along channel y obeying protocol A. The composite process $!x(y).P$ communicates along channel x obeying the protocol $!A$; it receives y along x, and then spawns a fresh copy of P to execute. All channels used by P other than y must obey a protocol of the form $?B$, for some B, to ensure that replicating P respects the type discipline. Intuitively, a process may only provide a replicable service if it is implemented by communicating only with other processes that provide replicable services.

There are three rules for clients, corresponding to the fact that a server may have one, none, or many clients. The three rules correspond to the standard rules of classical linear logic for dereliction, weakening, and contraction.

The first rule is for a single client.

$$\frac{Q \vdash \Delta, y : A}{?x[y].Q \vdash \Delta, x : ?A}\ ?$$

Process Q communicates along channel y obeying protocol A. The composite process $?x[y].Q$ communicates along channel x obeying protocol $?A$; it allocates a fresh channel y, transmits y along x, and then executes process Q. Cut of rule ! against rule ? corresponds to spawning a single copy of a server to communicate with a client, as shown in rule $(\beta_{!?})$:

$$\nu x.(!x(y).P \mid ?x[y].Q) \Longrightarrow \nu y.(P \mid Q)$$

The second rule is for no clients.

$$\frac{Q \vdash \Delta}{Q \vdash \Delta, x : ?A}\ \mathsf{Weaken}$$

A process Q that does not communicate along any channel obeying protocol A may be regarded as communicating along a channel obeying protocol $?A$. Cut of rule ! against Weaken corresponds to garbage collection, deallocating a server that has no clients, as shown in rule $(\beta_{!W})$:

$$\nu x.(!x(y).P \mid Q) \Longrightarrow Q, \quad \text{if } x \notin \mathsf{fn}(Q)$$

The third rule aggregates multiple clients.

$$\frac{Q \vdash \Delta, x' : ?A, x'' : ?A}{Q\{x/x', x/x''\} \vdash \Delta, x : ?A}\ \mathsf{Contract}$$

Process Q communicates along two channels x and x' both obeying protocol $?A$. Process $Q\{x/x', x/x''\}$ is identical to Q save all occurrences of x' and x'' have been renamed to x; it communicates along a single channel x obeying protocol $?A$. Cut of rule ! against Contract corresponds to replicating a server, as shown in rule $(\beta_{!C})$:

$$\begin{array}{l}\nu x.(!x(y).P \mid Q\{x/x', x/x''\}) \Longrightarrow \\ \qquad \nu x'.(!x'(y).P \mid \nu x''.(!x''(y).P \mid Q))\end{array}$$

The type derivation on the right-hand side of rule $(\beta_{!C})$ applies Contract once for each free name z_i in Γ. The derivation is written using the following priming convention: we assume that to each name z there are associated other names z' and z'', and we write P' for the process identical to P save that each free name z in P has been replaced by z'; that is, if $\mathsf{fn}(P) = \{y, z_1, \dots, z_n\}$ then $P' = P\{y'/y, z_1'/z_1, \dots, z_n'/z_n\}$, and similarly for P''.

A referee notes weakening and contraction could be given explicit notation rather than implicit. For instance, we could replace Q by $?x[\,].Q$ in weakening, and $Q\{x/x', x/x''\}$ by $?x[x', x''].Q$ in contraction, yielding

$$\frac{Q \vdash \Delta}{?x[\,].Q \vdash \Delta, x : ?A}\ \mathsf{Weaken}$$

and

$$\frac{Q \vdash \Delta, x' : ?A, x'' : ?A}{?x[x', x''].Q \vdash \Delta, x : ?A}\ \mathsf{Contract}$$

while reduction rules ($\beta_{!W}$) and ($\beta_{!C}$) become

$$\nu x.(!x(y).P \mid ?x[].Q) \Longrightarrow ?z_1[].\cdots.?z_n[].Q$$

and

$$\begin{array}{l} \nu x.(!x(y).P \mid ?x[x', x''].Q) \Longrightarrow \\ \quad ?z_1[z_1', z_1''].\cdots.?z_n[z_n', z_n'']. \\ \qquad \nu x'.(!x'(y').P' \mid \nu x''.(!x''(y'').P'' \mid Q)) \end{array}$$

where $\mathsf{fn}(P) = \{y, z_1, \ldots, z_n\}$.

2.5 Polymorphism

The quantifiers $\exists$ and $\forall$ are dual. We interpret $\exists X.B$ as the session type of a process that instantiates propositional variable X to a given proposition, and interpret $\forall X.B$ as the session type of a process that generalises over X. These correspond to type application and type abstraction in polymorphic λ-calculus, or to sending and receiving types in the polymorphic π-calculus of Turner (1995).

The rule for instantiation is:

$$\frac{P \vdash \Gamma, x : B\{A/X\}}{x[A].P \vdash \Gamma, x : \exists X.B}\ \exists$$

Process P communicates along channel x obeying protocol $B\{A/X\}$. The composite process $x[A].P$ communicates along channel x obeying protocol $\exists X.B$; it transmits a representation of A along x, and then executes P.

The rule for generalisation is:

$$\frac{Q \vdash \Delta, x : B}{x(X).Q \vdash \Delta, x : \forall X.B}\ \forall\ (X \notin \mathsf{fv}(\Delta))$$

Process Q communicates along channel x obeying protocol B. The composite process $x(X).Q$ communicates along channel x obeying protocol $\forall X.B$; it receives a description of a proposition along channel x, binds the proposition to the propositional variable X, and then executes Q.

Cut of instantiation $\exists$ against generalisation $\forall$ corresponds to transmitting a representation of a proposition, as shown in rule ($\beta_{\exists\forall}$):

$$\nu x.(x[A].P \mid x(X).Q) \Longrightarrow \nu x.(P \mid Q\{A/X\})$$

This rule behaves similarly to beta reduction of a type abstraction against a type application in polymorphic λ-calculus, or communication of a type in the polymorphic π-calculus.

2.6 Commuting conversions

Commuting conversions are shown in Figure 4. To save space, these are shown as reductions on terms, without the accompanying derivation trees.

Each commuting conversion pushes a cut inside a communication operation. There are two conversions for $\otimes$, depending upon whether the cut pushes into the left or right branch. Each of the remaining logical operators has one conversion, with the exception of $\oplus$, which has two (only the left rule is shown, the right rule is symmetric); and of 0, which has none.

An important aspect of CP is revealed by considering rule ($\kappa_{\otimes}$), which pushes cut inside input:

$$\nu z.(x(y).P \mid Q) \Longrightarrow x(y).\nu z.(P \mid Q)$$

On the left-hand side process Q may interact with the environment, while on the right-hand side Q is guarded by the input and cannot interact with the environment. In our setting, this is not problematic. If x is bound by an outer cut, then the guarding input is guaranteed to match a corresponding output at some point. If x is not bound by an outer cut, then we consider the process halted while it awaits external communication along x; compare this with the use of labeled transitions in Lemma 5.7 of Caires and Pfenning (2010).

2.7 Cut elimination

In addition to the rules of Figures 2, 3, and 4, we add a rule relating reductions to structural equivalences:

$$\frac{P \equiv Q \quad Q \Longrightarrow R \quad R \equiv S}{P \equiv S}$$

And we add rules that permit reduction under cut:

$$\frac{P \Longrightarrow R}{\nu x.(P \mid Q) \Longrightarrow \nu x.(R \mid Q)} \qquad \frac{Q \Longrightarrow R}{\nu x.(P \mid Q) \Longrightarrow \nu x.(R \mid Q)}$$

We do not add reduction under other operators; see below.

CP satisfies subject reduction: well-typed processes reduce to well-typed processes.

THEOREM 1. *If $P \vdash \Gamma$ and $P \Longrightarrow Q$ then $Q \vdash \Gamma$.*

Proof sketch: Figures 2 and 3 contain the relevant proofs for their rules, the proofs for Figure 4 are similar. □

Say process P is a *cut* if it has the form $\nu x.(Q \mid R)$ for some x, Q, and R. CP satisfies top-level cut elimination: every process reduces to a process that is not a cut.

THEOREM 2. *If $P \vdash \Gamma$ then there exists a Q such that $P \Longrightarrow^* Q$ and Q is not a cut.*

Proof sketch: If P is a cut, there are three possibilities. If one side of the cut uses the axiom, apply AxCut. If one side of the cut is itself a cut, recursively eliminate the cut. In the remaining cases, either both sides are logical rules that act on the cut variable, in which case a principal reduction of Figure 3 applies, or at least one side is a logical rule acting on a variable other than the cut variable, in which case a commuting reduction of Figure 4 applies. Since we support impredicative polymorphism, where a polymorphic type may be instantiated by a polymorphic type, some care is required in formulating the induction to ensure termination, but this is standard (Gallier, 1990). □

This result resembles the Principal Lemma of Cut Elimination (Girard et al., 1989, Section 13.2), which eliminates a final cut rule, possibly replacing it with (smaller) cuts further up the proof tree. Top-level cut elimination corresponds to lack of deadlock; it ensures that any process can reduce until it needs to perform an external communication.

If our goal was to eliminate all cuts, we would need to introduce congruence rules, such as

$$\frac{P \Longrightarrow Q}{x(y).P \Longrightarrow x(y).Q}$$

and similarly for each operator. Such rules do not correspond well to our notion of computation on processes, so we omit them; this is analogous to the usual practice of not permitting reduction under lambda.

3. A session-typed functional language

This section presents GV, a session-typed functional language based on one devised by Gay and Vasconcelos (2010), and presents its translation into CP.

Our presentation of GV differs in some particulars from that of Gay and Vasconcelos (2010). Most notably, our system is guaranteed free from deadlock whereas theirs is not. Achieving this property requires some modifications to their system. We split their session type 'end' into two dual types '$\mathsf{end}_!$' and '$\mathsf{end}_?$', and we

$$\frac{}{x : T \vdash x : T}\ \text{Id} \qquad \frac{}{\vdash \mathsf{unit} : \mathsf{Unit}}\ \text{Unit} \qquad \frac{\Phi \vdash N : U \quad \mathsf{un}(T)}{\Phi, x : T \vdash N : U}\ \text{Weaken} \qquad \frac{\Phi, x' : T, x'' : T \vdash N : U \quad \mathsf{un}(T)}{\Phi, x : T \vdash N\{x/x', x/x''\} : U}\ \text{Contract}$$

$$\frac{\Phi, x : T \vdash N : U}{\Phi \vdash \lambda x.N : T \multimap U}\ {\multimap}\text{-I} \qquad \frac{\Phi \vdash L : T \multimap U \quad \Psi \vdash M : T}{\Phi, \Psi \vdash L\,M : U}\ {\multimap}\text{-E} \qquad \frac{\Phi \vdash L : T \multimap U \quad \mathsf{un}(\Phi)}{\Phi \vdash L : T \to U}\ {\to}\text{-I} \qquad \frac{\Phi \vdash L : T \to U}{\Phi \vdash L : T \multimap U}\ {\to}\text{-E}$$

$$\frac{\Phi \vdash M : T \quad \Psi \vdash N : U}{\Phi, \Psi \vdash (M, N) : T \otimes U}\ \otimes\text{-I} \qquad \frac{\Phi \vdash M : T \otimes U \quad \Psi, x : T, y : U \vdash N : V}{\Phi, \Psi \vdash \mathsf{let}\ (x, y) = M\ \mathsf{in}\ N : V}\ \otimes\text{-E}$$

$$\frac{\Phi \vdash M : T \quad \Psi \vdash N : !T.S}{\Phi, \Psi \vdash \mathsf{send}\ M\ N : S}\ \text{Send} \qquad \frac{\Phi \vdash M : ?T.S}{\Phi \vdash \mathsf{receive}\ M : T \otimes S}\ \text{Receive}$$

$$\frac{\Phi \vdash M : \oplus\{l_i : S_i\}_{i \in I}}{\Phi \vdash \mathsf{select}\ l_j\ M : S_j}\ \text{Select} \qquad \frac{\Phi \vdash M : \&\{l_i : S_i\}_{i \in I} \quad (\Psi, x : S_i \vdash N_i : T)_{i \in I}}{\Phi, \Psi \vdash \mathsf{case}\ M\ \mathsf{of}\ \{l_i : x.N_i\}_{i \in I} : T}\ \text{Case}$$

$$\frac{\Phi, x : S \vdash M : \mathsf{end}_! \quad \Psi, x : \overline{S} \vdash N : T}{\Phi, \Psi \vdash \mathsf{with}\ x\ \mathsf{connect}\ M\ \mathsf{to}\ N : T}\ \text{Connect} \qquad \frac{\Phi \vdash M : T \otimes \mathsf{end}_?}{\Phi \vdash \mathsf{terminate}\ M : T}\ \text{Terminate}$$

Figure 5. GV, a session-typed functional language

replace their constructs 'accept', 'request', and 'fork', by two new constructs 'with-connect-to' and 'terminate'.

A number of features of Gay and Vasconcelos (2010) are not echoed here. Their system is based on asynchronous buffered communication, they show that the size required of asynchronous buffers can be bounded by analysing session types, and they support recursive functions, recursive session types, and subtyping. We omit these contributions for simplicity, but see no immediate difficulty in extending our results to include them. Of course, adding recursive terms or recursive session types may remove the property that all programs terminate.

For simplicity, we also omit a number of other possible features. We do not consider base types, which are straightforward. We also do not consider how to add replicated servers with multiple clients, along the lines suggested by ! and ? in CP, or how to add polymorphism, along the lines suggested by $\exists$ and $\forall$ in CP, but both extensions appear straightforward.

Session types Session types are defined by the following grammar:

$S ::=$	
$!T.S$	output value of type T then behave as S
$?T.S$	input value of type T then behave as S
$\oplus\{l_i : S_i\}_{i \in I}$	select from behaviours S_i with label l_i
$\&\{l_i : S_i\}_{i \in I}$	offer choice of behaviours S_i with label l_i
$\mathsf{end}_!$	terminator, convenient for use with output
$\mathsf{end}_?$	terminator, convenient for use with input

Let S range over session types, and let T, U, V range over types. Session type $!T.S$ describes a channel along which a value of type T may be sent and which subsequently behaves as S. Dually, $?T.S$ describes a channel along which a value of type T may be received and which subsequently behaves as S. Session type $\oplus\{l_i : S_i\}_{1 \in I}$ describes a channel along which one of the distinct labels l_i may be sent and which subsequently behaves as S_i. Dually, $\&\{l_i : S_i\}_{1 \in I}$ describes a channel along which one of the labels l_i may be received, and which subsequently behaves as S_i. Finally, $\mathsf{end}_!$ and $\mathsf{end}_?$ describe channels that cannot be used for further communication. As we will see, it is convenient to use one if the last action on the channel is a send, and the other if the last action on the channel is a receive.

Types Types are defined by the following grammar:

$T, U, V ::=$	
S	session type (linear)
$T \otimes U$	tensor product (linear)
$T \multimap U$	function (linear)
$T \to U$	function (unlimited)
Unit	unit (unlimited)

Every session type is also a type, but not conversely. Types are formed from session types, tensor product, two forms of function space, and a unit for tensor product.

Each type is classified as linear or unlimited:

$$\mathsf{lin}(S) \quad \mathsf{lin}(T \otimes U) \quad \mathsf{lin}(T \multimap U) \quad \mathsf{un}(T \to U) \quad \mathsf{un}(\mathsf{Unit})$$

Here $\mathsf{lin}(T)$ denotes a type that is linear, and $\mathsf{un}(T)$ a type that is unlimited. Session types, tensor, and one type of function are limited; the other type of function and unit are unlimited. Unlimited types support weakening and contraction, while linear types do not. Unlimited types correspond to those written with ! in CP.

Duals Each session type S has a dual $\overline{S}$, defined as follows:

$$\begin{aligned} \overline{!T.S} &= ?T.\overline{S} \\ \overline{?T.S} &= !T.\overline{S} \\ \overline{\oplus\{l_i : S_i\}_{i \in I}} &= \&\{l_i : \overline{S_i}\}_{i \in I} \\ \overline{\&\{l_i : S_i\}_{i \in I}} &= \oplus\{l_i : \overline{S_i}\}_{i \in I} \\ \overline{\mathsf{end}_!} &= \mathsf{end}_? \\ \overline{\mathsf{end}_?} &= \mathsf{end}_! \end{aligned}$$

Input is dual to output, selection is dual to choice, and the two terminators are dual. Duality between input and output does not take the dual of the type.

Duality is an involution, $\overline{\overline{S}} = S$.

Environments We let Φ, Ψ range over environments associating variables to types. Write $\mathsf{un}(\Phi)$ to indicate that each type in Φ is unlimited. As in Section 2, order in environments is ignored and we use linear maintenance.

Terms Terms are defined by the following grammar:

$L, M, N ::=$	
x	identifier
unit	unit constant
$\lambda x.\, N$	function abstraction
$L\ M$	function application
(M, N)	pair construction
$\mathsf{let}\ (x, y) = M\ \mathsf{in}\ N$	pair deconstruction
$\mathsf{send}\ M\ N$	send value M on channel N
$\mathsf{receive}\ M$	receive from channel M
$\mathsf{select}\ l\ M$	select label l on channel M
$\mathsf{case}\ M\ \mathsf{of}\ \{l_i : x.N_i\}_{i \in I}$	offer choice on channel M
$\mathsf{with}\ x\ \mathsf{connect}\ M\ \mathsf{to}\ N$	connect M to N by channel x
$\mathsf{terminate}\ M$	terminate input

The first six operations specify a linear λ-calculus, and the remaining six specify communication along a channel.

The terms are best understood in conjunction with their type rules, shown in Figure 5. The rules for variables, unit, weakening, contraction, function abstraction and application, and pair construction and deconstruction are standard. Functions are either limited or unlimited. As usual, function abstraction may produce an unlimited function only if all of its free variables are of unlimited type. Following Gay and Vasconcelos (2010) we do not give a separate rule for application of unlimited function, but instead give a rule permitting an unlimited function to be treated as a linear function, which may then be applied using the rule for linear function application.

For simplicity, we do not require that each term have a unique type. In particular, a λ-expression where all free variables have unlimited type may be given either linear or unlimited function type. In a practical system, one might introduce subtyping and arrange that each term have a unique smallest type.

The rule for output is

$$\frac{\Phi \vdash M : T \qquad \Psi \vdash N : !T.S}{\Phi, \Psi \vdash \mathsf{send}\ M\ N : S}\ \mathsf{Send}$$

Channels are managed linearly, so each operation on channels takes the channel before the operation as an argument, and returns the channel after the operation as the result. Executing 'send M N' outputs the value M of type T along channel N of session type $!T.S$, and returns the updated channel, which after the output has session type S.

The rule for input is

$$\frac{\Phi \vdash M : ?T.S}{\Phi \vdash \mathsf{receive}\ M : T \otimes S}\ \mathsf{Receive}$$

Executing 'receive M' inputs a value from channel M of session type $?T.S$, and returns a pair consisting of the input value of type T, and the updated channel, which after the input has session type S. The returned pair must be linear because it contains a session type, which is linear.

Gay and Vasconcelos (2010) treat 'send' and 'receive' as function constants, and require two versions of 'send' to cope with complications arising from currying. We treat 'send' and 'receive' as language constructs, which avoids the need for two versions of 'send'. Thanks to the rules for limited and unlimited function abstraction, $\lambda x.\, \lambda y.\, \mathsf{send}\ x\ y$ has type $T \multimap\, !T.S \multimap S$ and also type $T \to\, !T.S \multimap S$ when $\mathsf{un}(T)$.

The operations Select and Case are similar, and standard.

The rule to create new channels is:

$$\frac{\Phi, x : S \vdash M : \mathsf{end}_! \qquad \Psi, x : \overline{S} \vdash N : T}{\Phi, \Psi \vdash \mathsf{with}\ x\ \mathsf{connect}\ M\ \mathsf{to}\ N : T}\ \mathsf{Connect}$$

Executing 'with x connect M to N' creates a new channel x with session type S, where x is used at type S within term M and at the dual type $\overline{S}$ within term N. The two terms M and N are evaluated concurrently. As is usual when forking off a value, only one of the two subterms returns a value that is passed to the rest of the program. The left subterm returns the exhausted channel, which has type $\mathsf{end}_!$. The right subterm returns a value of type T that is passed on to the rest of the program.

Finally, we require a rule to terminate the other channel:

$$\frac{\Phi \vdash M : T \otimes \mathsf{end}_?}{\Phi \vdash \mathsf{terminate}\ M : T}\ \mathsf{Terminate}$$

Executing 'terminate M' evaluates term M, which returns a pair consisting of an exhausted channel of type $\mathsf{end}_?$ and a value of type T, then deallocates the channel and returns the value.

The constructs for Connect and Terminate between them deallocate two ends of a channel. The system is designed so it is convenient to use $\mathsf{end}_!$ on a channel whose last operation is Send, and $\mathsf{end}_?$ on a channel whose last operation is Receive.

Usually, session typed systems make end an unlimited type that is self-dual, but the formulation here fits better with CLL. A variation where end is a linear type requiring explicit deallocation is considered by Vasconcelos (2011).

One might consider alternative designs, say to replace Connect by an operation that creates a channel and returns both ends of it in a pair of type $S \otimes \overline{S}$, or to replace Terminate by an operation that takes a pair of type $\mathsf{end}_! \otimes \mathsf{end}_?$ and returns unit. However, both of these designs are difficult to translate into CP, which suggests they may suffer from deadlock.

3.1 Translation

The translation of GV into CP is given in Figures 6 and 7.

Session types The translation of session types is as follows:

$$\begin{aligned}
[\![!T.S]\!] &= [\![T]\!]^\perp \parr [\![S]\!] \\
[\![?T.S]\!] &= [\![T]\!] \otimes [\![S]\!] \\
[\![\oplus\{l_i : S_i\}_{i\in I}]\!] &= [\![S_1]\!] \,\&\, \cdots \,\&\, [\![S_n]\!], \quad I = \{1, \ldots, n\} \\
[\![\&\{l_i : S_i\}_{i\in I}]\!] &= [\![S_1]\!] \oplus \cdots \oplus [\![S_n]\!], \quad I = \{1, \ldots, n\} \\
[\![\mathsf{end}_!]\!] &= \perp \\
[\![\mathsf{end}_?]\!] &= 1
\end{aligned}$$

This translation is surprising, in that each operator translates to the dual of what one might expect! The session type for output in GV, $!T.S$ is translated into $\parr$, the connective that is interpreted as input in CP, and the session type for input in GV, $?T.S$ is translated into $\otimes$, the connective that is interpreted as output in CP. Similarly $\oplus$ and $\&$ in GV translate, respectively, to $\&$ and $\oplus$ in CP. Finally, $\mathsf{end}_!$ and $\mathsf{end}_?$ in GV translate, respectively, to $\perp$ and 1 in CP, the units for $\parr$ and $\otimes$.

The intuitive explanation of this duality is that Send and Receive in GV take channels as *arguments*, whereas the interpretation of the connectives in CP is for channels as *results*. Indeed, the send operation takes a value and a channel, and sends the value to that channel—in other words, the channel must *input* the value. Dually, the receive operation takes a channel and returns a value—in other words, the channel must *output* the value. A similar inversion occurs with respect to Select and Case.

Recall that duality on session types in GV leaves the types of sent and received values unchanged:

$$\overline{!T.S} = ?T.\overline{S} \qquad \overline{?T.S} = !T.\overline{S}$$

Conversely, the translation of these operations takes the dual of the sent value, but not the received value:

$$[\![!T.S]\!] = [\![T]\!]^\perp \parr [\![S]\!] \qquad [\![?T.S]\!] = [\![T]\!] \otimes [\![S]\!]$$

In classical linear logic, $A \multimap B = A^\perp \parr B$, so the right-hand side of the first line could alternatively be written $[\![T]\!] \multimap [\![S]\!]$. Accordingly, and as one would hope, the translation preserves duality: $[\![\overline{S}]\!] = [\![S]\!]^\perp$.

$$\left[\!\left[\frac{}{x : T \vdash x : T}\ \mathsf{Id} \right]\!\right] z \;=\; \frac{}{x \leftrightarrow z \vdash x : [\![T]\!]^\perp,\ z : [\![T]\!]}\ \mathsf{Ax} \qquad \left[\!\left[\frac{}{\vdash \mathsf{unit} : \mathsf{Unit}}\ \mathsf{Unit} \right]\!\right] z \;=\; \frac{\dfrac{}{y.\mathsf{case}() \vdash y : \top}\ \top}{!z(y).y.\mathsf{case}() \vdash z : !\top}\ !$$

$$\left[\!\left[\frac{\Phi \vdash N : U \quad \mathsf{un}(T)}{\Phi, x : T \vdash N : U}\ \mathsf{Weaken} \right]\!\right] z \;=\; \frac{[\![N]\!]z \vdash [\![\Phi]\!]^\perp,\ z : [\![U]\!]}{[\![N]\!]z \vdash [\![\Phi]\!]^\perp,\ x : [\![T]\!]^\perp,\ z : [\![U]\!]}\ \mathsf{Weaken}$$

$$\left[\!\left[\frac{\Phi, x' : T, x'' : T \vdash N : U \quad \mathsf{un}(T)}{\Phi, x : T \vdash N\{x/x', x/x''\} : U}\ \mathsf{Contract} \right]\!\right] z \;=\; \frac{[\![N]\!]z \vdash [\![\Phi]\!]^\perp,\ x' : [\![T]\!]^\perp,\ x'' : [\![T]\!]^\perp,\ z : [\![U]\!]}{[\![N\{x/x', x/x''\}]\!]z \vdash [\![\Phi]\!]^\perp,\ x : [\![T]\!]^\perp,\ z : [\![U]\!]}\ \mathsf{Contract}$$

$$\left[\!\left[\frac{\Phi, x : T \vdash N : U}{\Phi \vdash \lambda x.N : T \multimap U}\ {\multimap}\text{-}\mathsf{I} \right]\!\right] z \;=\; \frac{[\![N]\!]z \vdash [\![\Phi]\!]^\perp,\ x : [\![T]\!]^\perp,\ z : [\![U]\!]}{z(x).[\![N]\!]z \vdash [\![\Phi]\!]^\perp,\ z : [\![T]\!]^\perp \mathbin{⅋} [\![U]\!]}\ ⅋$$

$$\left[\!\left[\frac{\Phi \vdash L : T \multimap U \quad \Psi \vdash M : T}{\Phi, \Psi \vdash L\,M : U}\ {\multimap}\text{-}\mathsf{E} \right]\!\right] z \;=\;$$

$$\frac{[\![L]\!]y \vdash [\![\Phi]\!]^\perp,\ y : [\![T]\!]^\perp \mathbin{⅋} [\![U]\!] \qquad \dfrac{[\![M]\!]x \vdash [\![\Psi]\!]^\perp,\ x : [\![T]\!] \qquad \dfrac{}{y \leftrightarrow z \vdash y : [\![U]\!]^\perp,\ z : [\![U]\!]}\ \mathsf{Ax}}{y[x].([\![M]\!]x \mid y \leftrightarrow z) \vdash [\![\Psi]\!]^\perp,\ y : [\![T]\!] \otimes [\![U]\!]^\perp,\ z : [\![U]\!]}\ \otimes}{\nu y.([\![L]\!]y \mid y[x].([\![M]\!]x \mid y \leftrightarrow z)) \vdash [\![\Phi]\!]^\perp,\ [\![\Psi]\!]^\perp,\ z : [\![U]\!]}\ \mathsf{Cut}$$

$$\left[\!\left[\frac{\Phi \vdash L : T \multimap U \quad \mathsf{un}(\Phi)}{\Phi \vdash L : T \to U}\ {\to}\text{-}\mathsf{I} \right]\!\right] z \;=\; \frac{[\![L]\!]y \vdash [\![\Phi]\!]^\perp,\ y : [\![T \multimap U]\!]}{!z(y).[\![L]\!]y \vdash [\![\Phi]\!]^\perp,\ z : ![\![T \multimap U]\!]}\ !$$

$$\left[\!\left[\frac{\Phi \vdash L : T \to U}{\Phi \vdash L : T \multimap U}\ {\to}\text{-}\mathsf{E} \right]\!\right] z \;=\; \frac{[\![L]\!]y \vdash [\![\Phi]\!]^\perp,\ y : ![\![T \multimap U]\!] \qquad \dfrac{\dfrac{}{x \leftrightarrow z \vdash x : [\![T \multimap U]\!]^\perp,\ z : [\![T \multimap U]\!]}\ \mathsf{Ax}}{?y[x].x \leftrightarrow z \vdash y : ?[\![T \multimap U]\!]^\perp,\ z : [\![T \multimap U]\!]}\ ?}{\nu y.([\![L]\!]y \mid ?y[x].x \leftrightarrow z) \vdash [\![\Phi]\!]^\perp,\ z : [\![T \multimap U]\!]}\ \mathsf{Cut}$$

$$\left[\!\left[\frac{\Phi \vdash M : T \quad \Psi \vdash N : U}{\Phi, \Psi \vdash (M, N) : T \otimes U}\ \otimes\text{-}\mathsf{I} \right]\!\right] z \;=\; \frac{[\![M]\!]y \vdash [\![\Phi]\!]^\perp,\ y : [\![T]\!] \qquad [\![N]\!]z \vdash [\![\Psi]\!]^\perp,\ z : [\![U]\!]}{z[y].([\![M]\!]y \mid [\![N]\!]z) \vdash [\![\Phi]\!]^\perp,\ [\![\Psi]\!]^\perp,\ z : [\![T]\!] \otimes [\![U]\!]}\ \otimes$$

$$\left[\!\left[\frac{\Phi \vdash M : T \otimes U \quad \Psi, x : T, y : U \vdash N : V}{\Phi, \Psi \vdash \mathsf{let}\ (x, y) = M\ \mathsf{in}\ N : V}\ \otimes\text{-}\mathsf{E} \right]\!\right] z \;=\;$$

$$\frac{[\![M]\!]y \vdash [\![\Phi]\!]^\perp,\ y : [\![T]\!] \otimes [\![U]\!] \qquad \dfrac{[\![N]\!]z \vdash [\![\Psi]\!]^\perp,\ x : [\![T]\!]^\perp,\ y : [\![U]\!]^\perp,\ z : [\![V]\!]}{y(x).[\![N]\!]z \vdash [\![\Psi]\!]^\perp,\ y : [\![T]\!]^\perp \mathbin{⅋} [\![U]\!]^\perp,\ z : [\![V]\!]}\ ⅋}{\nu y.([\![M]\!]y \mid y(x).[\![N]\!]z) \vdash [\![\Phi]\!]^\perp,\ [\![\Psi]\!]^\perp,\ z : [\![V]\!]}\ \mathsf{Cut}$$

Figure 6. Translation from GV into CP, Part I

Types The translation of types is as follows:

$$\begin{aligned} [\![T \multimap U]\!] &= [\![T]\!]^\perp \mathbin{⅋} [\![U]\!] \\ [\![T \to U]\!] &= !([\![T]\!]^\perp \mathbin{⅋} [\![U]\!]) \\ [\![T \otimes U]\!] &= [\![T]\!] \otimes [\![U]\!] \\ [\![\mathsf{Unit}]\!] &= !\top \end{aligned}$$

Session types are also types, they are translated as above.

The right-hand side of the first equation could alternatively be written $[\![T]\!] \multimap [\![U]\!]$, showing that linear functions translate as standard.

The right-hand side of the second equation could alternatively be written $!([\![T]\!] \multimap [\![U]\!])$. There are two standard translations of intuitionistic logic into classical linear logic or, equivalently, of λ-calculus into linear λ-calculus. Girard's original takes $(A \to B)^\circ = !A^\circ \multimap B^\circ$, and corresponds to call-by-name, while a lesser known alternative takes $(A \to B)^* = !(A^* \multimap B^*)$, and correspond to call-by-value (see Benton and Wadler (1996) and Toninho et al. (2012)). The second is used here.

In classical linear logic, there is a bi-implication between 1 and $!\top$ (in many models, this bi-implication is an isomorphism), so the right-hand side of the last equation could alternatively be written 1, the unit for $\otimes$.

An unlimited type in GV translates to a type constructed with ! in CP: If $\mathsf{un}(T)$ then $[\![T]\!] = !A$, for some A.

Terms Translation of terms is written in a continuation-passing style standard for translations of λ-calculi into process calculi. The translation of term M of type T is written $[\![M]\!]z$ where z is a channel of type $[\![T]\!]$; the process that translates M transmits the answer it computes along z. More precisely, if $\Phi \vdash M : T$ then $[\![M]\!]z \vdash [\![\Phi]\!]^\perp,\ z : [\![T]\!]$, where the Φ to the left of the turnstile in GV translates, as one might expect, to the dual $[\![\Phi]\!]^\perp$ on the right of the turn-style in CP.

The translation of terms is shown in Figures 6 and 7. Rather than simply giving a translation from terms of GV to terms of CP, we show the translation as taking type derivation trees to type derivation trees. Giving the translation on type derivation trees rather than terms has two advantages. First, it eliminates any ambiguity arising from the fact, noted previously, that terms in GV do not have unique types. Second, it makes it easy to validate that the translation preserves types.

Figure 6 shows the translations for operations of a linear λ-calculus. A variable translates to an axiom, weakening and contraction translate to weakening and contraction. Function abstraction and product deconstruction both translate to input, and func-

$$\left[\!\!\left[\dfrac{\Phi \vdash M : T \quad \Psi \vdash N : !T.S}{\Phi, \Psi \vdash \mathsf{send}\ M\ N : S}\ \mathsf{Send}\right]\!\!\right] z \quad = \quad \dfrac{\dfrac{[\![M]\!]y \vdash [\![\Phi]\!]^\perp, y : [\![T]\!] \quad \dfrac{}{x\leftrightarrow z \vdash x : [\![S]\!]^\perp, z : [\![S]\!]}\ \mathsf{Ax}}{x[y].([\![M]\!]y \mid x\leftrightarrow z) \vdash [\![\Phi]\!]^\perp, x : [\![T]\!] \otimes [\![S]\!]^\perp}\ \otimes \qquad [\![N]\!]x \vdash [\![\Psi]\!]^\perp, x : [\![T]\!]^\perp \parr [\![S]\!]}{\nu x.(x[y].([\![M]\!]y \mid x\leftrightarrow z) \mid [\![N]\!]x) \vdash [\![\Phi]\!]^\perp, [\![\Psi]\!]^\perp, z : [\![S]\!]}\ \mathsf{Cut}$$

$$\left[\!\!\left[\dfrac{\Phi \vdash M : ?T.S}{\Phi \vdash \mathsf{receive}\ M : T \otimes S}\ \mathsf{Receive}\right]\!\!\right] z \quad = \quad [\![M]\!]z \vdash [\![\Phi]\!], z : [\![T]\!] \otimes [\![S]\!]$$

$$\left[\!\!\left[\dfrac{\Phi \vdash M : \oplus\{l_i : S_i\}_{i\in I}}{\Phi \vdash \mathsf{select}\ l_j\ M : S_j}\ \mathsf{Select}\right]\!\!\right] z \quad = \quad \dfrac{[\![M]\!]x \vdash [\![\Phi]\!]^\perp, x : [\![S_1]\!] \,\&\, \cdots \,\&\, [\![S_n]\!] \qquad \dfrac{\dfrac{}{x\leftrightarrow z \vdash x : [\![S_j]\!]^\perp, z : [\![S_j]\!]}\ \mathsf{Ax}}{x[\mathrm{in}_j].x\leftrightarrow z \vdash x : [\![S_1]\!]^\perp \oplus \cdots \oplus [\![S_n]\!]^\perp, z : [\![S_j]\!]}\ \oplus_i}{\nu x.([\![M]\!]x \mid x[\mathrm{in}_j].x\leftrightarrow z) \vdash [\![\Phi]\!]^\perp, z : [\![S_j]\!]}\ \mathsf{Cut}$$

$$\left[\!\!\left[\dfrac{\Phi \vdash M : \&\{l_i : S_i\}_{i\in I} \quad (\Psi, x : S_i \vdash N_i : T)_{i\in I}}{\Phi, \Psi \vdash \mathsf{case}\ M\ \mathsf{of}\ \{l_i : x.N_i\}_{i\in I} : T}\ \mathsf{Case}\right]\!\!\right] z \quad = \quad \dfrac{[\![M]\!]x \vdash [\![\Phi]\!]^\perp, x : [\![S_1]\!] \oplus \cdots \oplus [\![S_n]\!] \qquad \dfrac{([\![N_i]\!]z \vdash [\![\Psi]\!]^\perp, x : [\![S_i]\!]^\perp, z : [\![T]\!])_{i\in I}}{x.\mathsf{case}([\![N_1]\!], \ldots, [\![N_n]\!]) \vdash x : [\![S_1]\!] \,\&\, \cdots \,\&\, [\![S_n]\!], z : [\![T]\!]}\ \&}{\nu x.([\![M]\!]x \mid x.\mathsf{case}([\![N_1]\!], \ldots, [\![N_n]\!])) \vdash [\![\Phi]\!]^\perp, [\![\Psi]\!]^\perp, z : [\![T]\!]}\ \mathsf{Cut}$$

$$\left[\!\!\left[\dfrac{\Phi, x : S \vdash M : \mathsf{end}_! \quad \Psi, x : \overline{S} \vdash N : T}{\Phi, \Psi \vdash \mathsf{with}\ x\ \mathsf{connect}\ M\ \mathsf{to}\ N : T}\ \mathsf{Connect}\right]\!\!\right] z \quad = \quad \dfrac{\dfrac{[\![M]\!]y \vdash [\![\Phi]\!]^\perp, x : [\![S]\!]^\perp, y : \bot \qquad \dfrac{}{y[\,].0 \vdash y : 1}\ 1}{\nu y.([\![M]\!]y \mid y[\,].0) \vdash [\![\Phi]\!]^\perp, x : [\![S]\!]^\perp}\ \mathsf{Cut} \qquad [\![N]\!]z \vdash [\![\Psi]\!]^\perp, x : [\![S]\!], z : [\![T]\!]}{\nu x.(\nu y.([\![M]\!]y \mid y[\,].0) \mid [\![N]\!]z) \vdash [\![\Phi]\!]^\perp, [\![\Psi]\!]^\perp, z : [\![T]\!]}\ \mathsf{Cut}$$

$$\left[\!\!\left[\dfrac{\Phi \vdash M : T \otimes \mathsf{end}_?}{\Phi \vdash \mathsf{terminate}\ M : T}\ \mathsf{Terminate}\right]\!\!\right] z \quad = \quad \dfrac{[\![M]\!]y \vdash [\![\Phi]\!]^\perp, y : [\![T]\!] \otimes 1 \qquad \dfrac{\dfrac{\dfrac{}{z\leftrightarrow y \vdash z : [\![T]\!], y : [\![T]\!]^\perp}\ \mathsf{Ax}}{x().z\leftrightarrow y \vdash z : [\![T]\!], y : [\![T]\!]^\perp, x : \bot}\ \bot}{y(x).x().z\leftrightarrow y \vdash z : [\![T]\!], y : [\![T]\!]^\perp \parr \bot}\ \parr}{\nu y.([\![M]\!]y \mid y(x).x().z\leftrightarrow y) \vdash [\![\Phi]\!]^\perp, z : [\![T]\!]}\ \mathsf{Cut}$$

Figure 7. Translation from GV into CP, Part II

tion application and product construction both translate to output. The translation of each elimination rule ($\multimap$-E, $\to$-E, and $\otimes$-E) also requires a use of Cut.

Figure 7 shows the translation for operations for communication. For purposes of the translation, it is convenient to work with n-fold analogues of $\oplus$ and $\&$, writing $\in_i$ for selection and $\mathsf{case}(P_1, \cdots, P_n)$ for choice.

Despite the inversion noted earlier in the translation of session types, the translation of Send involves an output operation of the form $x[y].(P \mid Q)$, the translation of Select involves an select operation of the form $x[\mathrm{in}_j].P$, the translation of Case involves a choice operation of the form $\mathsf{case}(Q_1, \ldots, Q_n)$, the translation of $\mathsf{end}_!$ in Connect involves an empty output of the form $y[\,].0$, and the translation of Terminate involves an empty input of the form $x().P$. Each of these translations also introduces a Cut, corresponding to communication with supplied channel. The translation of Receive is entirely trivial, but the corresponding input operation of the form $x(y).R$ appears in the translation of $\otimes$-E, which deconstructs the returned pair. Finally, the translation of Connect involves a Cut, which corresponds to introducing a channel for communication between the two subterms.

The translation preserves types.

THEOREM 3. *If* $\Phi \vdash M : T$ *then* $[\![M]\!]x \vdash [\![\Phi]\!]^\perp, x : [\![T]\!]$.

Proof sketch. See Figures 6 and 7. □

We also claim that the translation preserves the intended semantics. The formal semantics of Gay and Vasconcelos (2010) is based on asynchronous buffered communication, which adds additional complications, so we leave a formal proof of correspondence between the two for future work.

4. Related work

Session types Session types were introduced by Honda (1993), and further extended by Takeuchi et al. (1994), Honda et al. (1998), and Yoshida and Vasconcelos (2007). Subtyping for session types is considered by Gay and Hole (2005), and the linear functional language for session types considered in this paper was introduced by Gay and Vasconcelos (2010). Session types have been applied to describe operating system services by Fähndrich et al. (2006).

Deadlock freedom Variations on session types that guarantees deadlock freedom are presented in Sumii and Kobayashi (1998) and Carbone and Debois (2010). Unlike CP, where freedom from deadlock follows from the relation to cut elimination, in the first it is ensured by introducing a separate partial order on time tags, and in the second by introducing a constraint on underlying dependency graphs.

Linear types for process calculus A variety of linear types systems for process calculus are surveyed by Kobayashi (2002). Most of these systems look rather different than session types, but Kobayashi et al. (1996) presents an embedding of session types into a variant of π-calculus with linear types for channels.

Linear proof search Functional programming can be taken as arising from the Curry-Howard correspondence, by associating program evaluation with proof normalisation. Analogously, logic programming can be taken as arising by associating program evaluation with proof search. Logic programming approaches based on linear logic give rise to systems with some similarities to CP, see Miller (1992) and Kobayashi and Yonezawa (1993, 1994, 1995).

Polymorphism CP's support of polymorphism is based on the polymorphic π-calculus introduced by Turner (1995) and further discussed by Pierce and Turner (2000) and Pierce and Sangiorgi (2000), which uses explict polymorphism (Church-style). In contrast, Berger et al. (2005) introduce a polymorphically typed session calculus that uses implicit polymorphism (Curry-style).

Linear logic as a process calculus Various interpretations of linear logic as a process calculus are proposed by Abramsky (1993), Abramsky (1994), and Abramsky et al. (1996), the second of these being elaborated in detail by Bellin and Scott (1994).

This paper is inspired by a series of papers by Caires, Pfenning, Toninho, and Pérez. Caires and Pfenning (2010) first observed the correspondence relating formulas of linear logic to session types; its journal version is Caires et al. (2012b). Pfenning et al. (2011) extends the correspondence to dependent types in a stratified system, with concurrent communication at the outer level and a dependently-typed functional language at the inner level, and Pfenning et al. (2011) extends further to support proof-carrying code and proof irrelevance. Toninho et al. (2012) explores encodings of λ-calculus into πDILL. Pérez et al. (2012) introduces logical relations on linear-typed processes to prove termination and contextual equivalences. Caires et al. (2012a) is the text of an invited talk at TLDI, summarising the above.

Mazurak and Zdancewic (2010) present Lolliproc, which also offers a Curry-Howard interpretation of session types by relating the call/cc control operators to communication using a double-negation operator on types.

DILL vs. CLL Caires et al. (2012b) consider a variant of πDILL based on one-sided sequents of classical linear logic, which they call πCLL. Their πCLL is similar to CP, but differs in important particulars: its bookkeeping is more elaborate, using two zones, one linear and one intuitionitic; it has no axiom, so cannot easily support polymorphism; and it does not support reductions corresponding to the commuting conversions.

Caires et al. (2012b) state they prefer a formulation based on DILL to one based on CLL, because DILL satisfies a locality property for replicated input while CLL does not. Locality requires that names received along a channel may be used to send output but not to receive input, and is useful both from an implementation point of view and because a process calculus so restricted satisfies additional observational equivalences, as shown by Merro and Sangiorgi (2004). Caires et al. (2012b) only restrict replicated input, because restricting *all* input is too severe for a session-typed calculus. However, the good properties of locality have been studied only in the case where *all* input is prohibited on received names. It remains to be seen to what extent the fact that DILL imposes locality for replicated names is significant.

Additionally, in a private conversation, Pfenning relayed that he believes DILL may be amenable to extension to dependent types, while he suspects CLL is not because strong sums become degenerate in some classical settings, as shown by Herbelin (2005). However, linear logic is more amenable to constructive treatment than traditional classical logic, as argued by Girard (1991), so it remains unclear to what extent CP, or πCLL, may support dependent types.

5. Conclusion

One reason λ-calculus provides such a successful foundation for functional programming is that it includes both fragments that guarantee termination (typed λ-calculi) and fragments that can model any recursive function (untyped λ-calculus, or typed λ-calculi augmented with a general fixpoint operator). Indeed, the former can be seen as giving rise to the latter, by considering recursive types with recursion in negative positions; untyped λ-calculus can be modelled by a solution to the recursion equation $X \simeq X \to X$. Similarly, a foundation for concurrency based on linear logic will be of limited value if it only models deadlock-free processes. Are there extensions that support more general forms of concurrency?

Girard (1987) proposes one such extension, the Mix rule. In our notation, this is written:

$$\frac{P \vdash \Gamma \quad Q \vdash \Delta}{P \mid Q \vdash \Gamma, \Delta}\ \textsf{Mix}$$

Mix differs from Cut in that there are *no* channels in common between P and Q, rather than one. Mix is equivalent to provability of the proposition $A \otimes B \multimap A \parr B$. Systems with Mix still do not deadlock, but support concurrent structures that cannot arise under CLL, namely, systems with two components that are independent. Caires et al. (2012a) consider two variations of the rules for 1 and $\bot$, the second of which is less restrictive and derives a rule similar to Mix.

Abramsky et al. (1996) proposes another extension, the Binary Cut rule (a special case of Multicut). In our notation, this is written:

$$\frac{P \vdash \Gamma, x : A, y : B \quad Q \vdash \Delta, x : A^{\perp}, y : B^{\perp}}{\nu x : A, y : B.(P \mid Q) \vdash \Gamma, \Delta}\ \textsf{BiCut}$$

Binary Cut differs from Cut in that there are *two* channels in common between P and Q, rather than one. Binary Cut is equivalent to provability of the proposition $A \parr B \multimap A \otimes B$. Binary Cut allows one to express systems where communications form a loop and may deadlock.

Systems with both Mix and Binary Cut are compact, in that from either of $A \otimes B$ and $A \parr B$ one may derive the other. Abramsky et al. (1996) provides a translation of full π-calculus into a compact linear system, roughly analogous to the embedding of untyped λ-calculus into typed λ-calculus based on the isomorphism $X \simeq X \to X$.

Searching for principled extensions of CP that support the unfettered power of the full π-calculus is a topic for future work. As λ-calculus provided foundations for functional programming in the last century, may we hope for this emerging calculus to provide foundations for concurrent programming in the coming century?

Acknowledgements For comments and discussions, my thanks to Samson Abramsky, Luis Caires, Marco Gaboardi, Simon Gay, Andy Gordon, Marc Hamann, Jiansen He, Kohei Honda, Luke Ong, Frank Pfenning, Colin Stirling, Michael Stone, Vasco Vasconcelos, Hongseok Yang, Nobuko Yoshida, Stephan Zdancewic, and the anonymous referees.

References

Samson Abramsky. Computational interpretations of linear logic. *Theoretical Computer Science*, 111(1&2):3–57, 1993.

Samson Abramsky. Proofs as processes. *Theoretical Computer Science*, 135(1):5–9, 1994.

Samson Abramsky, Simon J. Gay, and Rajagopal Nagarajan. Interaction categories and the foundations of typed concurrent programming. In *Deductive Program Design, Marktoberdorf*, pages 35–113, 1996.

Gianluigi Bellin and Philip J. Scott. On the pi-calculus and linear logic. *Theoretical Computer Science*, 135(1):11–65, 1994.

Nick Benton and Philip Wadler. Linear logic, monads and the lambda calculus. In *Logic in Computer Science (LICS)*, pages 420–431, 1996.

Martin Berger, Kohei Honda, and Nobuko Yoshida. Genericity and the pi-calculus. *Acta Inf.*, 42(2-3):83–141, 2005.

Luís Caires and Frank Pfenning. Session types as intuitionistic linear propositions. In *CONCUR*, pages 222–236, 2010.

Luís Caires, Frank Pfenning, and Bernardo Toninho. Towards concurrent type theory. In *Types in Language Design and Implementation (TLDI)*, January 2012a.

Luís Caires, Frank Pfenning, and Bernardo Toninho. Linear logic propositions as session types. *Mathematical Structures in Computer Science*, 2012b. Submitted.

Marco Carbone and Søren Debois. A graphical approach to progress for structured communication in web services. In *Interaction and Concurrency Experience (ICE)*, pages 13–27, 2010.

Manuel Fähndrich, Mark Aiken, Chris Hawblitzel, Orion Hodson, Galen C. Hunt, James R. Larus, and Steven Levi. Language support for fast and reliable message-based communication in Singularity OS. In *European Conference on Computer Systems (EuroSys)*, pages 177–190, 2006.

Jean H. Gallier. *On Girard's "Candidats de Reducibilité"*, pages 123–204. Academic Press, 1990.

Simon J. Gay and Malcolm Hole. Subtyping for session types in the pi calculus. *Acta Informatica*, 42(2-3):191–225, 2005.

Simon J. Gay and Vasco T. Vasconcelos. Linear type theory for asynchronous session types. *Journal of Functional Programming*, 20(1):19–50, 2010.

Jean-Yves Girard. Linear logic. *Theoretical Computer Science*, 50: 1–102, 1987.

Jean-Yves Girard. A new constructive logic: Classical logic. *Mathematical Structures in Computer Science*, 1(3):255–296, 1991.

Jean-Yves Girard, Yves Lafont, and Paul Taylor. *Proofs and Types*, volume 7 of *Cambridge Tracts in Theoretical Computer Science*. Cambridge University Press, 1989.

Hugo Herbelin. On the degeneracy of sigma-types in presence of computational classical logic. In *Typed Lambda Calculi and Applications (TLCA)*, pages 209–220, 2005.

Kohei Honda. Types for dyadic interaction. In *CONCUR*, pages 509–523, 1993.

Kohei Honda, Vasco T. Vasconcelos, and Makoto Kubo. Language primitives and type discipline for structured communication-based programming. In *European Symposium on Programming (ESOP)*, pages 122–138, 1998.

Naoki Kobayashi. Type systems for concurrent programs. In *10th Anniversary Colloquium of UNU/IIST*, LNCS 2757, pages 439–453, 2002.

Naoki Kobayashi and Akinori Yonezawa. Acl — a concurrent linear logic programming paradigm. In *International Logic Programming Symposium (ILPS)*, pages 279–294, 1993.

Naoki Kobayashi and Akinori Yonezawa. Higher-order concurrent linear logic programming. In *Theory and Practice of Parallel Programming*, LNCS 907, pages 137–166, 1994.

Naoki Kobayashi and Akinori Yonezawa. Asynchronous communication model based on linear logic. *Formal Aspects of Computing*, 7(2):113–149, 1995.

Naoki Kobayashi, Benjamin C. Pierce, and David N. Turner. Linearity and the pi-calculus. In *POPL*, pages 358–371, 1996.

Karl Mazurak and Steve Zdancewic. Lolliproc: to concurrency from classical linear logic via curry-howard and control. In *International Conference on Functional Programming (ICFP)*, pages 39–50, 2010.

Massimo Merro and Davide Sangiorgi. On asynchrony in name-passing calculi. *Mathematical Structures in Computer Science*, 14(5):715–767, 2004.

Dale Miller. The pi-calculus as a theory in linear logic: Preliminary results. In *Extensions to Logic Programming*, LNCS 660, pages 242–264, 1992.

Robin Milner, Joachim Parrow, and David Walker. A calculus of mobile processes, i. *Information and Computation*, 100(1):1–40, 1992.

Jorge Pérez, Luís Caires, Frank Pfenning, and Bernardo Toninho. Termination in session-based concurrency via linear logical relations. In *European Symposium on Programming (ESOP)*, 2012.

Frank Pfenning, Luís Caires, and Bernardo Toninho. Proof-carrying code in a session-typed process calculus. In *Certified Programs and Proofs (CPP)*, pages 21–36, 2011.

Benjamin C. Pierce and Davide Sangiorgi. Behavioral equivalence in the polymorphic pi-calculus. *Journal of the ACM*, 47(3):531–584, 2000.

Benjamin C. Pierce and David N. Turner. Pict: a programming language based on the pi-calculus. In Gordon D. Plotkin, Colin Stirling, and Mads Tofte, editors, *Proof, Language, and Interaction, Essays in Honour of Robin Milner*, pages 455–494. The MIT Press, 2000. ISBN 978-0-262-16188-6.

Andrew M. Pitts. Structural recursion with locally scoped names. *J. Funct. Program.*, 21(3):235–286, 2011.

Eijiro Sumii and Naoki Kobayashi. A generalized deadlock-free process calculus. In *High-Level Concurrent Languages (HLCL)*, 1998. *ENTCS* 16(3):225–247, 1998.

Kaku Takeuchi, Kohei Honda, and Makoto Kubo. An interaction-based language and its typing system. In C. Halatsis, D. G. Maritsas, G. Philokyprou, and S. Theodoridis, editors, *PARLE*, LNCS 817, pages 398–413, 1994.

Bernardo Toninho, Luís Caires, and Frank Pfenning. Functions as session-typed processes. In *Foundations of Software Science and Computation (FoSSaCS)*, 2012.

David N. Turner. *The Polymorphic Pi-calculus: Theory and Implementation*. PhD thesis, University of Edinburgh, 1995.

Vasco T. Vasconcelos. Sessions, from types to programming languages. *Bulletin of the European Association for Theoretical Computer Science*, 103:53–73, 2011.

Nobuko Yoshida and Vasco T. Vasconcelos. Language primitives and type discipline for structured communication-based programming revisited: Two systems for higher-order session communication. *Electronic Notes in Theoretical Computer Science*, 171(4):73–93, 2007.

Typing Unmarshalling without Marshalling Types

Grégoire Henry
CNRS, PPS, UMR 7126
Univ Paris Diderot
Sorbonne Paris Cité
F-75205 Paris, France
henry@pps.univ-paris-diderot.fr

Michel Mauny
ENSTA-ParisTech
32, boulevard Victor,
F-75739 Paris Cedex 15, France
Michel.Mauny@ensta.fr

Emmanuel Chailloux
LIP6 - UMR 7606
Université Pierre et Marie Curie
Sorbonne Universités
75005 Paris, France
Emmanuel.Chailloux@lip6.fr

Pascal Manoury
Université Pierre et Marie Curie
PPS, UMR 7126 CNRS
Univ Paris Diderot
Sorbonne Paris Cité
F-75205 Paris, France
Pascal.Manoury@pps.univ-paris-diderot.fr

Abstract

Unmarshalling primitives in statically typed language require, in order to preserve type safety, to dynamically verify the compatibility between the incoming values and the statically expected type. In the context of programming languages based on parametric polymorphism and uniform data representation, we propose a relation of compatibility between (unmarshalled) memory graphs and types. It is defined as constraints over nodes of the memory graph. Then, we propose an algorithm to check the compatibility between a memory graph and a type. It is described as a constraint solver based on a rewriting system. We have shown that the proposed algorithm is sound and semi-complete in presence of algebraic data types, mutable data, polymorphic sharing, cycles, and functional values, however, in its general form, it may not terminate. We have implemented a prototype tailored for the OCaml compiler [17] that always terminates and still seems sufficiently complete in practice.

Categories and Subject Descriptors D.3.3 [*Programming Languages*]: Language Constructs and Features—Input/Output; F.3.3 [*Logics and Meanings of Program*]: Studies of Program Constructs—Type structure

General Terms Languages, Safety

Keywords Type-safe marshalling, OCaml

1. Introduction

Marshalling is the process of transforming the memory representation of a value into a linear form, suitable for communication or storage. Unmarshalling is the reverse operation, importing external data as values in a running program. In the context of functional languages with parametric polymorphism, we can distinguish two main categories of verification mechanisms used to preserve type safety when unmarshalling data.

The first category relies on an *ad hoc* external representation of values and a couple of *ad hoc* functions for marshalling and unmarshalling: for a given type the unmarshalling function may either reconstruct a well-typed value or fail if the input is unexpected. This approach suits well the Haskell type-class mechanism which allows the multiple *ad hoc* functions to be hidden behind a unique name. Many Haskell libraries reuse the principles proposed in [14] to automatically derive the (un)marshalling functions from an algebraic type definition. Such libraries also exist in SML [7] or OCaml [21, 26] with less convenient interfaces.

The second category of verification mechanisms relies on the introduction of run-time type representations. In such mechanisms, marshalling primitives are generic functions that traverse the memory graph representing a value, and linearize it as a sequence of bytes. To ensure type safety, a value is usually marshalled together with its type and the unmarshalling primitives will accept to reconstruct the memory graph only when the marshalled type corresponds to the statically expected one. This category include mechanisms based on a `dynamic` type [1, 9, 16]. When the marshalling primitives are used to communicate values between different programs on different hosts, the main difficulty is to choose a common representation for the types [5].

We propose in this paper a third approach, also based on generic (un)marshalling functions but without adding more type information in the external representation than those already required to rebuild the corresponding memory graph. To ensure type safety, the initial idea is to check the *compatibility* of the reconstructed memory graph with the expected type. In other words, we check whether the memory graph may actually represent a value of that type. In a first approach, this can be achieved by recursively traversing the graph and the type together. In a more general way, we have defined an algorithm for checking the compatibility of a memory graph against classical algebraic data types (sums and records), but also against generalized algebraic data types or closures—that may introduce existential types—and against mutable record types or ar-

ICFP'12, September 9–15, 2012, Copenhagen, Denmark.

rays. This algorithm is efficient: it is linear in the size of the graph in presence of monomorphic or polymorphic sharing and quasi-linear in presence of cycles. The proposed algorithm is sound and semi-complete, however, in the most general case, it may not terminates. In practice, we have implemented a prototype tailored for the OCaml compiler that always terminates and seems sufficiently complete.

In section 2, we informally describe the algorithm in terms of graph traversal. In section 3 we define the compatibility relation between a memory graph and a type, then in section 4 we describe the algorithm as a rewriting system and study its soundness and completeness with respect to the previous compatibility relation. In section 5 we compare our proposal with other type-safe (un)marshalling primitives.

2. Type-checking a memory graph: discussion

Our algorithm has been initially conceived for the OCaml runtime which uses a tagged, uniform representation for values. The description of the algorithm will be done for such a representation but in section 4.5 we will discuss how it may be reused in a runtime with different representations for values.

Uniform representation The uniform representation of OCaml runtime values uses a bit tag that allows distinction between an immediate value and a pointer to an allocated value (a memory block). Furthermore, every allocated value has a generic header containing its size and a tag. The tag is a small integer mainly used to discriminate between cases of an algebraic data type (hereafter abbreviated ADT) but there are also some tags reserved for specific allocated values such as character strings, closures or boxed floats[15]. The latter tags specify that the content of the value does not follow the uniform representation and hence should not be traversed by the garbage collector.

More precisely, integers are represented by immediate values and characters are represented by immediate values lower than 256. Records and tuples are represented by allocated values of tag 0. A constant constructor is represented as an immediate value that is the position of the constructor in the corresponding type definition. A non-constant constructor is an allocated value whose tag also depends on the position of the constructor in the corresponding type definition. For example, consider the following list of rational numbers:

```
type Rlist =
| Nil
| IC of Int * Int * Rlist
| FC of Float * Rlist
let l : Rlist = FC (3.14, IC (22, 7, Nil))
```

It is represented by the memory graph in figure 1 where the tags of allocated blocks are represented with a symbolic name instead of an integer.

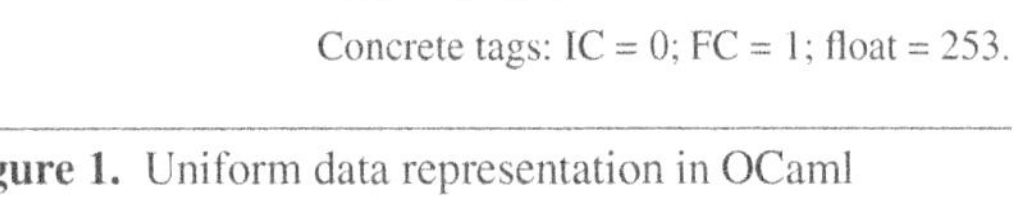

Concrete tags: IC = 0; FC = 1; float = 253.

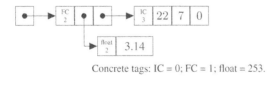

Figure 1. Uniform data representation in OCaml

Generic (un)marshalling primitives With the uniform tagged representation used by OCaml, a marshalling primitive could be implemented with a generic depth-first traversal of the memory graph. And a type-safe unmarshalling primitive could be conceptually split into two steps: a generic function that rebuilds a well formed memory graph, with respect to the invariants assumed by the garbage collector, and a function that traverses the reconstructed graph to check its compatibility with the expected type.

A simple recursive algorithm Checking the compatibility of a well formed graph against primitive data types is simple—an integer should be an immediate value, a float should be an allocated value whose tag is the one specific to boxed float, etc.—and checking the compatibility against a classical ADT is easily achieved with a recursive algorithm that test if the size and the tag of the value correspond to a constructor in the type definition, then deduce the expected type for sub-values and recurse. For example, consider the following parametric definition of list:

$$\texttt{type List}(\alpha) = \texttt{Nil} \mid \texttt{Cons of } \alpha * \texttt{List}(\alpha)$$

A memory graph is compatible with `List(Int)` if and only if:

- it is the immediate value 0 (representing `Nil`), or
- it is an allocated value of tag 0 and size 2 (repr. `Cons`), where:
  - the first element is compatible with `Int`, i. e. its an immediate value,
  - the 2nd element is recursively compatible with `List(Int)`.

This recursive algorithm is extended in section 2.1 to efficiently handle sharing and cycles in the memory graph. In the presence of polymorphic sharing and polymorphic recursion, as introduced respectively by the generalizing `let` and `let rec` constructions[18], this will require to traverse the graph in topological order and to recompute, from all the types expected for a shared value, an approximation of its inferred polymorphic type in the source code. This is the main difference with a classical type inference algorithm: while checking the memory graph corresponding to a program `let` $x = e_1$ `in` e_2, our algorithm traverses e_2—in order to collect all the expected types for x—before traversing e_1.

Section 2.2 describes a simple extension that allows the verification of mutable data, and section 2.3 extends the algorithm to handle generalized algebraic data types (hereafter abbreviated GADT) and function types. This will require the introduction of existential types and the use of unification to instantiate them. This will also complexify the order in which the graph is traversed: the verification of a value against an existential type is postponed until the type is instantiated.

2.1 Topological traversal and anti-unification

In terms of soundness, checking the compatibility of a memory graph with neither cycles nor mutable data could be achieved by checking shared values multiple times, with possibly different expected types. However, given that compilers tend not to introduce more sharing in the memory graph than is explicitly introduced by the programmer with `let` constructions and functional abstractions, those multiple verifications seem redundant. In fact, to obtain a complete algorithm it should be sufficient to check shared values only once with the type of the corresponding variable in the original source code.

In the absence of polymorphic sharing or polymorphic recursion, a shared value in the source code has a monomorphic type. Then, in such a situation, we can assume while checking a memory graph that all the expected types for that shared value are equal to that monomorphic type. Hence, we can obtain an efficient algorithm by marking values with their expected types when traversing them for the first time; and, when checking a previously marked value, only test the equality between the new expected type and the memorized one.

Polymorphic sharing in the absence of cycle In the presence of polymorphic sharing, we can only assume that the original type of a shared value is more general than all the expected types for that value. If we can definitely not recompute the original type, we can still try to recompute a type "minimally more general" than every expected type, hence compatible with this node of the memory graph. With a language based on parametric polymorphism like OCaml, a type that satisfies those conditions is the principal anti-unifier of the expected types [13, 19] (see section 4.2 for a formal definition). Then, in the absence of cycles in the memory graph, we obtain an efficient algorithm by using the following strategy:

- traverse the graph in a topological order, hence collecting all the types expected for a shared value before traversing it,
- check a shared value only once against the anti-unifier of all its expected types.

For example, consider the following values and the corresponding memory graph in figure 2.

type $\texttt{Tree}(\alpha)$ =
| Leaf of String
| Node of $\texttt{Tree}(\alpha) * \alpha * \texttt{Tree}(\alpha)$

let *leaf* : $\forall\alpha.\,\texttt{Tree}(\alpha)$ = Leaf ".."
let *trees* : $(\texttt{Tree(Int)} * \texttt{Tree(Char)})$ =
(Node (*leaf*, 3, *leaf*), Node (*leaf*, 'A', *leaf*))

The set of expected types collected for *leaf* while checking the compatibility of *trees* against the type $(\texttt{Tree(Int)} * \texttt{Tree(Char)})$ is $\{\texttt{Tree(Int)}; \texttt{Tree(Char)}\}$. Their anti-unifier is $\forall\alpha.\,\texttt{Tree}(\alpha)$.

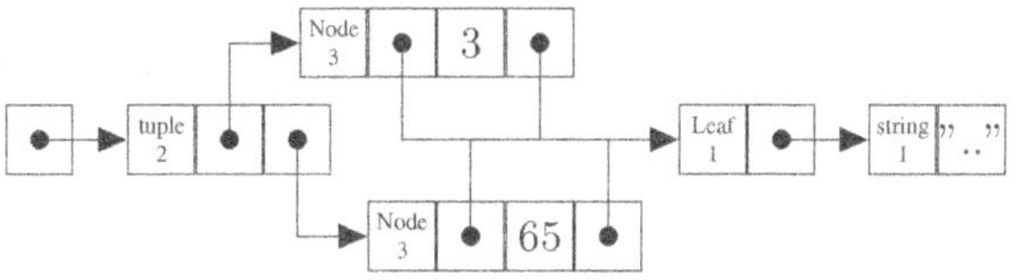

Concrete tags: tuple = Leaf = 0; Node = 1; string = 252.

Figure 2. Sharing in the memory graph

Cycles In an algorithm like ours, which recursively traverses the memory graph and the expected type together, it is not possible to collect all expected types for a value involved in a cycle without traversing that value. Hence, we have to elaborate a specific treatment for such cyclic values. One possibility is to mark them with their expected type when traversing them for the first time; and then, when checking a previously marked value against a type that is not an instance of the memorized one, to recheck the value against the anti-unifier of the two types, while marking the value with the anti-unifier. That process will reach a fixed point: each anti-unification reduces the size of the memorized type[1] and the smallest type is the empty type: $\forall\alpha.\,\alpha$. Hence, the number of iterations for a value is limited by the size of the first expected type.

The proposed process is complete even in the presence of polymorphic recursion but is not easy to implement efficiently. Furthermore, in the absence of polymorphic recursion in the source language, it should not be necessary to check values involved in a cycle twice: the types collected from outside the strongly connected components (hereafter abbreviated SCC) should allow the algorithm to recompute a sufficiently general type for the *roots* of the SCC. Hence, we initially restrict ourselves to monomorphic recursion and in our prototype implementation we apply the following strategy, assuming that the graph has been previously annotated with the number of references towards a shared value:

[1] at least as long as we do not consider recursive type expression.

(a) traverse the graph in topological order using a reference counter and anti-unify all the expected types before traversing a value; if some expected types could not be collected, then the graph contains cycles: proceed with (b).

(b) identify the SCCs and sort them in topological order; for each SCC proceed with (c).

(c) mark the values of the current SCC for which types were collected, anti-unify all the expected types and proceed recursively with (a) for all the marked values, considering the graph reduced to the current SCC.

(d) while checking a previously marked value, fail if the expected type is not equal to the memorized one.

We propose in section 4.4 an extension of that strategy that handles polymorphic recursion.

2.2 Mutable fields

OCaml allows the definition of mutable fields in record types. However, mutability is known only at compile time: the runtime representation of records does not distinguish mutable fields from immutable ones. However, as we traverse a graph and its expected type in parallel, we can add a specific treatment when the expected type requires that a field of the corresponding value has to be considered as mutable. In that case, we check that the expected type for the mutable field is monomorphic, in order to avoid the well-know soundness problem of polymorphic references.

As the mutation of record fields is achieved in-place, the proposed verification for mutable records is only allowed if the checked memory graph could only be manipulated with the verified type. It is the case in the context of an unmarshalling function but it would not be the case in a *cast* function that does not duplicate the memory graph first. Otherwise, if a value with a mutable type is cast into an immutable type, nothing warrants that a mutated value would still be compatible with the checked type.

2.3 Existential types

The simple recursive algorithm described at the beginning of section 2 allows the verification of compatibility of a value against classical ADT. In this section we describe the different difficulties introduced by the existential types of GADT and how our algorithm handles them. In a second step, the mechanisms introduced to handle existential types will be reused for the verification of polymorphic closures.

Unification The version 4.0 of OCaml includes GADTs. Their memory representation is the same as the classical ADTs. In particular, they do not contain witness for existential types. To reconstruct the existential types, the recursive algorithm is extended with a unification mechanism. More concretely, the algorithm proceeds according to the following steps: test if the size and the tag of the value correspond to a constructor in the type definition; unify the expected type with the return type of the constructor; deduce the expected type for sub-values and recurse. For example, consider the following simple type definition:

type $\texttt{T}_1(\_)$ =
| Int : Int $\to \texttt{T}_1\texttt{(Int)}$
| Char : Char $\to \texttt{T}_1\texttt{(Char)}$
| Bin : $\texttt{T}_1(\alpha) * \texttt{T}_1(\alpha) \to \texttt{T}_1(\alpha)$

Checking the compatibility of an allocated value of tag 1 and size 1, representing the constructor Char, against type $\texttt{T}_1\texttt{(Int)}$ will fail while unifying $\texttt{T}_1\texttt{(Int)}$ with the return type of the constructor Char, i. e. $\texttt{T}_1\texttt{(Char)}$. On the contrary, while checking the compatibility of an allocated value of tag 2 and size 2, representing Bin, against type $\texttt{T}_1\texttt{(Int)}$, the unification allows the instantiation of α and the recursive checking of the sub-values against the type $\texttt{T}_1(\texttt{Int})$.

In a more general way, the unification allows the instantiation of the existential types introduced by GADT. For example, consider the following type definition:

$\texttt{type}\ \texttt{T}_2(\_) =$
$\mid \texttt{Int} : \texttt{Int} \to \texttt{T}_2(\texttt{Int})$
$\mid \texttt{Char} : \texttt{Char} \to \texttt{T}_2(\texttt{Char})$
$\mid \texttt{Couple} : \texttt{T}_2(\alpha) * \texttt{T}_2(\beta) \to \texttt{T}_2(\alpha * \beta)$
$\mid \texttt{Fst} : \texttt{T}_2(\alpha * \beta) \to \texttt{T}_2(\alpha)$

While checking the compatibility of an allocated value of tag 3 and size 1, representing `Fst`, against the type $\texttt{T}_2(\texttt{Int})$, the unification leaves the β uninstantiated. Then, the recursive call has to verify that there exists a type β such that the argument of `Fst` is compatible with $\texttt{T}_2(\texttt{Int} * \beta)$. If this argument is the representation of `Couple (Int 1, Char 'A')`, it is decomposed in two independent checks:

- is the representation of `Int 1` compatible with $\texttt{T}_2(\texttt{Int})$?
- is the representation of `Char 'A'` is compatible with $\texttt{T}_2(\beta)$?

The latter will instantiate β as `Char`.

Delayed verification In the presence of existential types, not every memory graph can be verified with a simple recursive algorithm. For example, consider the following type definition of dynamic types reduced to three constant constructors:

$\texttt{type}\ \texttt{Ty}(\_) =$
$\mid \texttt{TBool} : \texttt{Ty}(\texttt{Bool})$
$\mid \texttt{TInt} : \texttt{Ty}(\texttt{Int})$
$\mid \texttt{TChar} : \texttt{Ty}(\texttt{Char})$
$\texttt{type}\ \texttt{Dyn} = \texttt{Dyn} : \alpha * \texttt{Ty}(\alpha) \to \texttt{Dyn}$

Testing the representation of `Dyn (65, TInt)` against the type `Dyn` with the recursive algorithm leads to the following question: is there a type β such that:

- the immediate value 65 is compatible with β, and
- the representation of `TInt` is compatible with $\texttt{Ty}(\beta)$?

There are at least two possible instantiations of β that could satisfy the former part of the question, that is: `Int` and `Char`; but only `Int` would also satisfy the latter part. Hence, while traversing this value, it is important to check the compatibility of `TInt`—and instantiate β as `Int` by unification—before traversing 65. For this purpose, the algorithm must be able to delay the verification of some values until the expected type has been instantiated.

Universal types Some existential types can not be instantiated by unification. Consider the following type definition, similar to $\texttt{T}_2(\_)$ but where the constructors `Int` and `Char` have been replaced by a generic constructor `Const`:

$\texttt{type}\ \texttt{T}_3(\_) =$
$\mid \texttt{Const} : \alpha \to \texttt{T}_3(\alpha)$
$\mid \texttt{Couple} : \texttt{T}_3(\alpha) * \texttt{T}_3(\beta) \to \texttt{T}_3(\alpha * \beta)$
$\mid \texttt{Fst} : \texttt{T}_3(\alpha * \beta) \to \texttt{T}_3(\alpha)$

While checking the compatibility of a memory graph representing `Fst (Couple (Const 3, Const 'A') )` against $\texttt{T}_3(\texttt{Int})$, the test will be reduced to:

- is there a type β such that the immediate value 65, representing the character `'A'`, is compatible with β?

While answering this question on the paper is trivial, our algorithm could not delay the verification anymore nor instantiate β by unification. However, in the same way Goldberg [10] shows that a garbage collector based on type reconstruction can collect values for which it can not reconstruct the type, we can ignore such values without breaking the soundness of the host language. For formalizing this situation in section 3, we will introduce an abstract type, named *universal type*, that is compatible with every memory graph. It will be used at the end of the traversal to instantiate the remaining type variables.

Functional types We now extend the algorithm to allow the verification of closures. We suppose that the compiler is able to provide an association table that stores for each code pointer, the static type of the corresponding lambda-abstraction in the source code and the typing environment required to type the function. For example, consider the following piece of code:

$\texttt{let}\ \mathit{one} : \texttt{Int} = 1$
$\texttt{let}\ \mathit{succ} : \texttt{Int} \to \texttt{Int} = \lambda x.\ x + \mathit{one}$
$\texttt{let}\ \mathit{delayed\_apply} : (\alpha \to \beta) \to \alpha \to \texttt{Unit} \to \beta =$
$\quad \lambda f.\ \lambda x.$
$\quad\quad \texttt{let}\ \mathit{apply} : \texttt{Unit} \to \beta = \lambda().\ (f\ x)\ \texttt{in}$
$\quad\quad \mathit{apply}$

The static type associated to the three named lambda-abstractions *succ*, *delayed_apply*, and *apply* are the following types, where the typing environment is written inside square brackets:

$$\begin{aligned}\sigma_{succ} &= [\mathit{one} \mapsto \texttt{Int}] \to \texttt{Int} \to \texttt{Int}\\ \sigma_{delayed\_apply} &= \forall \alpha\beta.\ [\,] \to (\alpha \to \beta) \to \alpha \to \texttt{Unit} \to \beta\\ \sigma_{apply} &= \forall \alpha\beta.\ [f \mapsto (\alpha \to \beta); x \mapsto \alpha] \to \texttt{Unit} \to \beta\end{aligned}$$

Now consider the following partial application of *delayed_apply* and the corresponding closure in figure 3 where dashed arrows represent code pointers and their associated static types:

$\texttt{let}\ \mathit{dsucc} : \texttt{Unit} \to \texttt{Int} = \mathit{delayed\_apply}\ \mathit{succ}\ 52$

The code pointer of the closure representing *dsucc* corresponds to the code of *apply*. Hence, the static type associated to $dsucc$ is σ_{apply} and while checking the compatibility of $dsucc$ against the type $\texttt{Unit} \to \texttt{Int}$ the exact type of the environment has been lost and must be recomputed by our algorithm:

$$[f \mapsto (\texttt{Int} \to \texttt{Int}); x \mapsto \texttt{Int}] \to \texttt{Unit} \to \texttt{Int}$$

Given this static type information, checking the compatibility of a closure against a functional type could be achieved with a mechanism similar to those introduced for handling GADTs. In our algorithm this is achieved in three steps: instantiate the associated static type schema by replacing universally quantified type variable with existential types; unify the expected type with the instantiated static type; recursively check the environment.

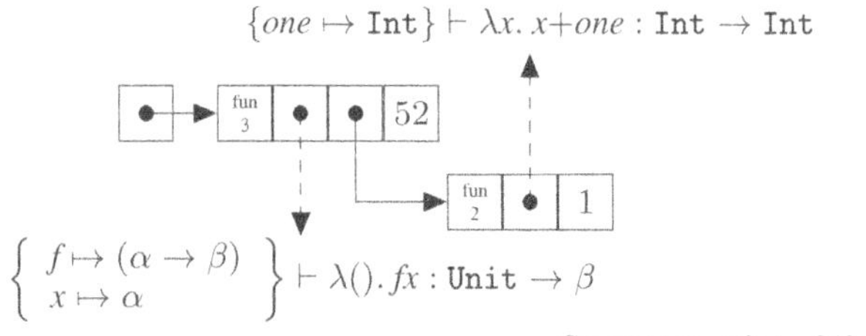

Concrete tags: fun = 249.

Figure 3. Representation of the function $dsucc$

2.4 Existential types in presence of sharing

When we try to implement in the presence of existential types the topological traversal proposed in section 2.1, two facets still require attention: how to anti-unify existential types and how to avoid "deadlocks" between the topological sort and the delayed verification.

Parallel propagation of types When the set of collected types for a shared value contains existential types, it is not always possible to compute their anti-unifier. For example, if the set of expected types contains $\alpha \rightarrow$ `Int` and `Bool` $\rightarrow \beta$ where α and β are existential types, the anti-unifier depends on the future instantiation of α and β: if α is later instantiated in `Int` and β in `Bool`, the anti-unifier is $\forall\gamma.\gamma \rightarrow \gamma$; but if α in instantiated in `Bool` and β in `Int`, it is `Bool` $\rightarrow$ `Int`; and for any other substitutions, it is $\forall\gamma\delta.\gamma \rightarrow \delta$. There is no other choice than to check the compatibility of the shared values against every collected type.

For this situation, we have extended our algorithm to check the compatibility of a value against a set of types and stated that it will accept the value if and only if it is compatible with the anti-unifier of the set. This allows two optimizations. Firstly, given a set, all types must have the same head constructors, otherwise their anti-unifier is the empty type and no value could be accepted; this allows partial instantiation of some existential types. Secondly, the set of types that is computed for sub-values of an allocated value may not contain existential types and it could be simplified by anti-unification.

The same difficulties arise in the presence of cycles: the equality test between the expected types for a marked value and all the possible anti-unifiers of the memorized set of types, is not complete. For example, if the expected type is $\forall\alpha.\,\alpha \rightarrow \alpha$ and the set of memorized types contains $\alpha \rightarrow$ `Int` and `Bool` $\rightarrow \beta$, the test is valid only if α is later instantiated as `Int` and β in `Bool` but is invalid otherwise. In this situation, the test may be postponed until the end of the traversal. At that stage, remaining type variables can be instantiated with the universal type and the set of expected types can be anti-unified.

Explicit decomposition For some specific cases, delaying the verification of a value when the expected type is an existential type does not always allow the collection of all the expected types for shared values. Consider for example the following piece of code and the corresponding memory graph in figure 4:

```
type T = None | Some of (T → Int)
let f : T → Int = λx. match x with
  | None → 0
  | Some g → g None
let h : Unit → Int = delayed_apply f (Some f)
```

Verifying the compatibility of the closure h against the type `Unit` $\rightarrow$ `Int` will be recursively decomposed into the question of knowing if there is an α such that:

- the representation of f is compatible with $\alpha \rightarrow$ `Int`, and
- the representation of `Some` f is compatible with α?

If we try to follow the proposed strategy for graph traversals then the verification is stuck at this step: we can not traverse f to solve the first part of the question until the second expected type for f is collected; and we can not traverse `Some` f to solve the second part until α is instantiated. In such situation, our algorithm *forces* the verification of `Some` f by introducing an existential type for every sub-value of the allocated block representing `Some` f—here it will introduce an existential type β for f—and it memorizes an explicit *constraint* to be solved when α is instantiated: is an allocated value with the tag of `Some` and with a single sub-value of type β compatible with α?

3. A type system for heap values

Before formally describing our algorithm in section 4, we define in this section the syntax of values and the compatibility relation, between the representation of a value in memory and a type, on which the algorithm is based. The syntax of values relies on the

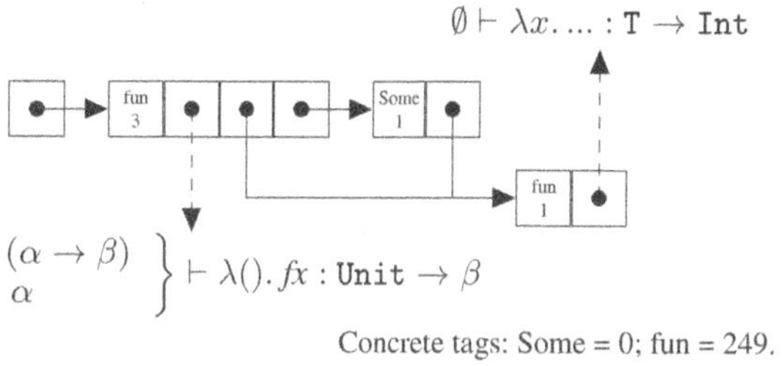

Figure 4. Representation of the function h

notion of heap to allow the explicit description of sharing and cycle. Then, the compatibility relation is defined as a classical type system for heap values. We do not prove in this paper the soundness of this type system with respect to the operational semantics of a programming language. However, our language of values and its type system are very similar to the OCaml ones and we assume their soundness.

Syntax of types and values In order to simplify the formalization of the proposed algorithm while still covering all the situations described in section 2, we restrict ourselves to the following type algebra:

$$\begin{array}{rcll} \tau & ::= & \texttt{Bool} \mid \texttt{Int} \mid \texttt{Unit} \mid (\tau * \tau) \mid \texttt{List}(\tau) \mid \tau \rightarrow \tau & \\ & \mid & \texttt{Ref}(\tau) & \textit{reference} \\ & \mid & \alpha & \textit{type variable} \\ & \mid & \star & \textit{universal type} \end{array}$$

The universal type is a type compatible with every immediate value and allocated block. It is required to instantiate the existential variables that could not be instantiated by unification (see section 2.4). We write $fv(\tau)$ the set of variables of τ and we write $\tau_1 \preccurlyeq \tau_2$ when τ_2 is an instance of τ_1, meaning there exists a substitution θ such that $\theta(\tau_1) = \tau_2$.

A value is represented by a couple (w, μ) where w is a word and μ is a heap. A word w is either an integer or a pointer:

$$\begin{array}{rcll} w & ::= & i & \textit{integer} \\ & \mid & \ell & \textit{pointer} \end{array}$$

A heap μ is a partial function from pointers to allocated values. An allocated value h is either a block containing two words or a closure:

$$\begin{array}{rcll} h & ::= & \texttt{Blk}(w, w) & \textit{block} \\ & \mid & \langle \tau, w \rangle & \textit{closure} \end{array}$$

To simplify the formal presentation of the algorithm, references are represented by blocks of size 2 whose second element is the immediate value 0.

A closure is represented by the static type of the original code (see section 2.3) and a single word w for the environment. We will write $fp(img(\mu))$ for the set of pointers occurring in the image of μ. A value (ℓ, μ) is well defined when $fp(img(\mu)) \cup \{\ell\}$ is included in the domain of μ.

Typing rules A typing environment Ψ is a partial function from pointer to types. Typing judgments for words w and allocated values h are respectively written $\Psi \vdash w : \tau$ and $\Psi \vdash h : \tau$. We will say that a pointer ℓ is compatible with a type τ in an environment Ψ if τ is an instance of $\Psi(\ell)$.

$$\frac{\Psi(\ell) \preccurlyeq \tau}{\Psi \vdash \ell : \tau} \quad \text{[W-LABEL]}$$

The compatibility of an integer with a type is abstracted by a function $Imm(\tau)$ that returns the set of immediate values compatible with τ. It is defined by case analysis on the head type constructor:

$$\begin{array}{rcll} Imm(\texttt{Unit}) & = & \{0\} & [\text{IMM-UNIT}] \\ Imm(\texttt{List}(\tau)) & = & \{0\} & [\text{IMM-EMPTYLIST}] \\ Imm(\texttt{Bool}) & = & \{0;1\} & [\text{IMM-BOOL}] \\ Imm(\texttt{Int}) & = & \{\ldots;-1;0;1;\ldots\} & [\text{IMM-INT}] \\ Imm(\star) & = & \{\ldots;-1;0;1;\ldots\} & [\text{IMM-UNIV}] \\ Imm(\tau) & = & \emptyset & \textit{otherwise} \end{array}$$

$$\frac{i \in Imm(\tau)}{\Psi \vdash i : \tau} \quad [\text{W-INT}]$$

The compatibility of a block $\texttt{Blk}(w_1, w_2)$ with a type uses a function $Arg(\tau)$ that returns the types expected for the components of a block of type τ. It is defined by case analysis of the head type constructor[2].

$$\begin{array}{rcll} Arg(\texttt{List}(\tau)) & = & [\tau\,;\,\texttt{List}(\tau)] & [\text{ARG-LIST}] \\ Arg((\tau_1 * \tau_2)) & = & [\tau_1\,;\,\tau_2] & [\text{ARG-COUPLE}] \\ Arg(\texttt{Ref}(\tau)) & = & [\tau\,;\,\texttt{Unit}] & [\text{ARG-REF}] \end{array}$$

$$\frac{Arg(\tau) = [\tau_1\,;\,\tau_2] \quad \Psi \vdash w_1 : \tau_1 \quad \Psi \vdash w_2 : \tau_2}{\Psi \vdash \texttt{Blk}(w_1, w_2) : \tau} \quad [\text{H-BLK}]$$

A block is compatible with the universal type only if, for each of its components, there exists a type that is compatible with it[3].

$$\frac{\Psi \vdash w_1 : \tau_1 \qquad \Psi \vdash w_2 : \tau_2}{\Psi \vdash \texttt{Blk}(w_1, w_2) : \star} \quad [\text{H-UNIV}]$$

A closure $\langle \tau, w \rangle$ is compatible with a type $\tau_1 \to \tau_2$ if there exists a type τ_{env} compatible with the captured environment and such that $\tau_{env} \to \tau_1 \to \tau_2$ is an instance of the static type of the original code.

$$\frac{\tau \preccurlyeq \tau_{env} \to \tau_1 \to \tau_2 \qquad \Psi \vdash w : \tau_{env}}{\Psi \vdash \langle \tau, w \rangle : \tau_1 \to \tau_2} \quad [\text{H-CLOS}]$$

To prove some intermediate steps of the type verification algorithm, we will have to manipulate partially typed heaps and to distinguish the type hypothesis for the pointers of a heap from the actual type of those pointers. In that case, we will say that a heap μ is partially compatible with type environment Ψ under the hypothesis Ψ', and we will write $\Psi' \vdash \mu : \Psi$, if and only if:

- $dom(\Psi) \subseteq dom(\mu)$
- $fp(img(\mu)) \subseteq dom(\Psi')$
- for all pointers $\ell \in dom(\Psi)$ then $\Psi' \vdash \mu(\ell) : \Psi(\ell)$,
- for all pointers $\ell \in dom(\Psi')$ such that $\Psi'(\ell) = \texttt{Ref}(\tau)$, then τ is closed.

We will say that a heap μ is compatible with an environment Ψ and we will write $\mu : \Psi$ if and only if $\Psi \vdash \mu : \Psi$. We will say that a value (w, μ) is compatible with a type τ if there exists an environment Ψ such that $\mu : \Psi$ and $\Psi \vdash w : \tau$.

4. Rewriting system

The order in which the algorithm described in section 2 traverses a memory graph depends on the structure of the graph but also on the expected types. To formally describe this complex traversal, we used a rewriting system (sections 4.1 and 4.2) inspired from a constraint-based algorithm for ML type inference[20]. In a first step, the set of rewriting rules allows us to prove the soundness and the semi-completeness of the algorithm independently of the traversal order (section 4.3). In a second step, a rewriting strategy allows us to precise the traversal order (section 4.4). In its general form, the algorithm does not terminate, but we show its termination in the absence of cycle, as well as in the absence of existential types. To conclude we propose a variant of the algorithm that always terminates and still seems sufficiently complete in concrete situation.

4.1 Syntax of constraints

Terms of the rewriting system are called *constraints*. They are defined by the following grammar detailed afterwards:

$$\begin{array}{rll} C ::= & \texttt{True} & \textit{trivial constraint} \\ & \mid \texttt{False} & \textit{failure} \\ & \mid C \wedge C & \textit{conjunction} \\ & \mid (\mu, \Phi).\,C & \textit{heap fragment and memorized types} \\ & \mid w : \{\tau\,;\,\ldots\} & \textit{type constraint} \\ & \mid \exists\dot{\alpha}.\,C & \textit{existential quantification} \\ & \mid \tau = \tau & \textit{unification} \\ & \mid \texttt{arg}(\tau) = [\tau\,;\,\tau] & \textit{ADT decomposition} \\ & \mid \Diamond\{\tau\,;\,\ldots\} & \textit{head type constructors homogeneity} \end{array}$$

where Φ is an environment that associates a set of types to a pointer: it allows the memorization of the already checked types for an allocated value. In the rewriting rules, we will write $\Phi \cup \{\ell : \{\tau;\ldots\}\}$ to denote the environment obtained by replacing in Φ the set associated to ℓ by the extended one $\Phi(\ell) \cup \{\tau;\ldots\}$, i.e. the environment $\Phi \oplus \{\ell : \Phi(\ell) \cup \{\tau;\ldots\}\}$.

A type constraint $w : \{\tau;\ldots\}$ represents the set of yet unchecked types for the value w. Hence, the initial constraint for checking a value (w, μ) against a type τ is:

$$(\mu, \emptyset).\, w : \{\tau\}$$

The normal forms will be the constraints `True` and `False`.

The existential quantification $\exists\dot{\alpha}.\,C$ binds a type variable in C. The existentially qualified type variables are syntactically distinguished with an upper dot. The other type variables—that appear in a constraint without being explicitly bound by an existential quantifier—represent empty types. We will call them universal type variables. We will write $fev(\tau)$ (respectively $fuv(\tau)$) the set of existential (resp. universal) variables of a type.

Equalities $\tau_1 = \tau_2$ will be resolved by a unification procedure, that will consider universal variables as fixed types and produce a substitution for existential variables. We will write such a substitution $\dot{\theta}$.

The ADT decomposition $\texttt{arg}(\tau) = [\tau\,;\,\tau]$ and the head type constructor homogeneity $\Diamond\{\tau\,;\,\ldots\}$ are required when forcing the verification of a block against an existential type variable.

The construction $(\mu, \Phi).\,C$ binds the pointer from $dom(\mu)$ into C and into the image of μ. This explicit introduction of the heap in the syntax of constraints will allow in section 4.4 the split of a heap into fragments corresponding to SCCs and the expression of a rewriting strategy based on a topological sort.

4.2 Rewriting rules

Rewriting rules are written $C_1 \gg C_2$, meaning that a constraint C_1 could be rewritten into C_2 in any context. We present progressively the set of rewriting rules, starting with those for handling sharing and cycles. We then present the set of rules allowing the verification of immediate values and allocated blocks, and finally those required for closures and existential types.

[2] On a concrete setting, the function $Arg(\_)$ receives also the tag of the block being checked and returns the types of the components of the corresponding data constructor.

[3] Requiring the existence of types compatible with the components slightly restricts the set of memory graphs compatible with a type. However, it simplifies the algorithm in the situation described in section 2.4 where it is required to force the verification of a block against existential types.

Allocated values

$$(\mu, \Phi').\,(\ell : \{\tau_{1..n}\} \wedge C) \gg \exists \dot{\alpha}_{1..m}.\,\dot{\beta}_{1..m}.\,\left\{\begin{array}{l} \Diamond\{\tau_{1..m}\} \\ \bigwedge_{i=1..m} \texttt{arg}(\tau_i) = [\dot{\alpha}_i\,;\,\dot{\beta}_i] \\ (\mu, \Phi' \cup \{\ell : \{\tau_{1..n}\}\}).\,(w' : \{\dot{\alpha}_{1..m}\} \wedge w'' : \{\dot{\beta}_{1..m}\} \wedge C) \end{array}\right. \quad \text{[R-BLK]}$$

$$\textit{if } \mu(\ell) = \texttt{Blk}(w', w'') \textit{ and } \Phi'(\ell) = \{\tau_{n+1..m}\}$$
$$\textit{and } \{\dot{\alpha}_{1..m}\,;\,\dot{\beta}_{1..m}\} \;\#\; \textit{fev}(\{\tau_{1..m}\}) \cup \textit{fev}(\Phi') \cup \textit{fev}(C)$$

$$(\mu, \Phi').\,(\ell : \{\tau_{1..n}\} \wedge C) \gg \exists \bar{\dot{\alpha}}_{1..m}.\,\left\{\begin{array}{l} \bigwedge_{i=1..m} \tau_i = \dot{\tau}'_i \rightarrow \dot{\tau}''_i \\ (\mu, \Phi' \cup \{\ell : \{\tau_{1..n}\}\}).\,(C \wedge w : \{\dot{\tau}^{env}_{1..m}\}) \end{array}\right. \quad \text{[R-CLOS]}$$

$$\textit{if } \mu(\ell) = \langle \tau^{env} \rightarrow \tau' \rightarrow \tau'', w\rangle \textit{ and } \textit{fv}(\tau^{env} \rightarrow \tau' \rightarrow \tau'') = \bar{\alpha}$$
$$\textit{and } \Phi'(\ell) = \{\tau_{n+1..m}\} \textit{ and } \bar{\dot{\alpha}}_{1..m} \;\#\; \textit{fev}(\tau_{1..m}) \cup \textit{fev}(\Phi') \cup \textit{fev}(C)$$

Parametricity

$$\exists \bar{\dot{\alpha}}_i \bar{\dot{\beta}} \bar{\dot{\gamma}}.\,\overline{\Diamond\{\dot{\alpha}_{1..n}\}} \wedge \overline{\Diamond\{\texttt{Ref}(\tau)\}} \wedge \overline{\texttt{arg}(\dot{\beta}) = [\tau'\,;\,\tau'']} \wedge \overline{i : \{\dot{\gamma}\}} \gg \texttt{True} \qquad \textit{if } \overline{\textit{fuv}(\tau) = \emptyset} \quad \text{[R-UNIV]}$$

Figure 5. Rewriting rules

We let implicit some trivial rules such as associativity and commutativity of the conjunction and commutativity and hoisting of existential quantification. In general, we write constraints in the following form, where overlines denote sets:

$$\exists \bar{\dot{\alpha}}.\,\overline{\tau = \tau} \wedge \overline{\Diamond\{\bar{\tau}\}} \wedge \overline{\texttt{arg}(\tau) = [\tau\,;\,\tau]} \wedge \overline{(\mu, \Phi)}.\,\left(\overline{\ell : \{\bar{\tau}\}}\right)$$

Anti-unification The formalization of the algorithm uses the definition of principal anti-unifiers proposed by Huet [13]. It supposes the existence of a bijection $au(\tau, \tau')$ from the set of distinct couple of types without existential variables to a subset of universal type variables. We write $\tau \curlywedge \tau'$ for the anti-unifier of τ and τ' defined by the following rules of congruence:

$$\begin{array}{rcll} \texttt{Int} & \curlywedge & \texttt{Int} & = \texttt{Int} \\ \texttt{Unit} & \curlywedge & \texttt{Unit} & = \texttt{Unit} \\ \texttt{List}(\tau) & \curlywedge & \texttt{List}(\tau') & = \texttt{List}(\tau \curlywedge \tau') \\ \texttt{Ref}(\tau) & \curlywedge & \texttt{Ref}(\tau') & = \texttt{Ref}(\tau \curlywedge \tau') \\ (\tau_1 * \tau_2) & \curlywedge & (\tau'_1 * \tau'_2) & = ((\tau_1 \curlywedge \tau'_1) * (\tau_2 \curlywedge \tau'_2)) \\ (\tau_1 \rightarrow \tau_2) & \curlywedge & (\tau'_1 \rightarrow \tau'_2) & = (\tau_1 \curlywedge \tau'_1) \rightarrow (\tau_2 \curlywedge \tau'_2) \\ \tau & \curlywedge & \tau' & = au(\tau, \tau') \quad \textit{otherwise} \end{array}$$

Modulo a renaming of the produced type variables, the definition of anti-unification is associative and commutative. Given a set of types $\tau_{1..n}$, we write $\curlywedge\{\tau_{1..n}\}$ for its principal anti-unifier.

Property 4.1. *We have* $(\tau_1 \curlywedge \tau_2) \preccurlyeq \tau_1$ *and* $(\tau_1 \curlywedge \tau_2) \preccurlyeq \tau_2$.

Property 4.2. *If* $\tau \preccurlyeq \tau_1$ *and* $\tau \preccurlyeq \tau_2$, *then* $\tau \preccurlyeq (\tau_1 \curlywedge \tau_2)$.

Sharing The rewriting rule [R-MERGE] allows the merge of two sets of expected types for the same allocated value, while the [R-AUNIF1] allows the simplification of a set of expected types by replacing two of its types by their principal anti-unifier. The latest applies only if the anti-unifier is independent of the future instantiation of existential type variables.

$$\ell : \{\tau_{1..n}\} \wedge \ell : \{\tau_{n+1..m}\} \gg \ell : \{\tau_{1..m}\} \qquad \text{[R-MERGE]}$$
$$w : \{\tau_1\,;\,\tau_2\,;\,\tau_{3..n}\} \gg w : \{\tau\,;\,\tau_{3..n}\} \qquad \text{[R-AUNIF1]}$$
$$\textit{if } \forall \dot{\theta}.\,\dot{\theta}(\tau) = \dot{\theta}(\tau_1) \curlywedge \dot{\theta}(\tau_2)$$

The rewriting rule [R-AUNIF2] allows the simplification of the set of memorized types for an allocated value by replacing two of the types by their principal anti-unifier. As for the rule [R-AUNIF1], it applies only if the anti-unifier is independent of the future instantiation of existential type variables.

$$(\mu, \Phi' \cup \{\ell : \{\tau_1\,;\,\tau_2\}\}).\,C \gg (\mu, \Phi' \cup \{\ell : \{\tau\}\}).\,C \qquad \text{[R-AUNIF2]}$$
$$\textit{if } \forall \dot{\theta}.\,\dot{\theta}(\tau) = \dot{\theta}(\tau_1) \curlywedge \dot{\theta}(\tau_2)$$

The rule [R-REMOVE] allows the removal of type constraints that are instances of previously checked types. More precisely, this rule applies only if, for any substitution $\dot{\theta}$, the anti-unifier of the instantiations of the expected types by $\dot{\theta}$ is an instance of the anti-unifier of the instantiations of the memorized types by $\dot{\theta}$.

$$(\mu, \Phi').\,(\ell : \{\tau_{1..n}\} \wedge C) \gg (\mu, \Phi').\,C \qquad \text{[R-REMOVE]}$$
$$\textit{if } \ell \in \textit{dom}(\Phi')$$
$$\textit{and } \forall \dot{\theta}.\; \curlywedge\{\dot{\theta}(\Phi'(\ell))\} \preccurlyeq \curlywedge\{\dot{\theta}(\tau_{1..n})\}$$

Immediate values The rewriting rules for immediate values simply reflect the function $\textit{Imm}(\tau)$ and state that the verification against an existential type is delayed.

$$i : \{\tau\} \gg \texttt{True} \qquad \textit{if } i \in \textit{Imm}(\tau) \qquad \text{[R-INT]}$$
$$i : \{\tau\} \gg \texttt{False} \qquad \textit{if } \tau \not\equiv \dot{\alpha} \textit{ and } i \notin \textit{Imm}(\tau) \qquad \text{[R-INT-FAIL]}$$

While checking an immediate value against a set of expected types that can not be anti-unified because of existential type variable, it is sufficient to ensure its compatibility against one of the types and to ensure that all the types share the same head type constructor. As the function $\textit{Imm}(\_)$ is defined by case analysis of the head constructor of its type argument, this will ensure that the value is compatible with the anti-unifier of the expected types.

$$i : \{\tau_{1..n}\} \gg \Diamond\{\tau_{1..n}\} \wedge i : \{\tau_1\} \qquad \textit{if } n \geq 2 \qquad \text{[R-INT-SET]}$$

Blocks The rewriting rule [R-BLK] described in figure 5, allows the verification of an allocated block $\texttt{Blk}(w', w'')$. It introduces two existential variables $\dot{\alpha}_i$ and $\dot{\beta}_i$ for each expected type τ_i and ensures that they correspond to the types expected for the arguments of a block of type τ_i, as computed by the function $\textit{Arg}(\tau_i)$. It also generates types constraints $w' : \{\dot{\alpha}_1; \ldots; \dot{\alpha}_n\}$ and $w'' : \{\dot{\beta}_1; \ldots; \dot{\beta}_n\}$.

The explicit introduction of the constraint $\texttt{arg}(\tau_i) = [\dot{\alpha}_i\,;\,\dot{\beta}_i]$ allows the application of the rule [R-BLK] even when the set of expected types only contains existential types variables. This constraint is resolved by the rules [R-ARG] and [R-ARG-FAIL] that simply reflect the function $\textit{Arg}(\tau)$ and state that the verification against an existential type is delayed.

$$\texttt{arg}(\tau) = [\tau'\,;\,\tau''] \gg \tau' = \tau_1 \wedge \tau'' = \tau_2 \qquad \text{[R-ARG]}$$
$$\textit{if } \textit{Arg}(\tau) = [\tau_1\,;\,\tau_2]$$
$$\texttt{arg}(\tau) = [\tau'\,;\,\tau''] \gg \texttt{False} \qquad \text{[R-ARG-FAIL]}$$
$$\textit{if } \tau \not\equiv \dot{\alpha} \textit{ and } \tau \notin \textit{dom}(\textit{Arg})$$

The rule [R-BLK] also adds the set of expected types τ_i in the environment of memorized types Φ. Without specific rewriting strategy, it is possible to start the verification of a block without collecting all the expected types. Then, to handle the situation where a block is checked for the second time (or more), the rule [R-BLK] checks the block against the new expected types *and* the previously checked types. This is required in the presence of existential types to verify that the block is compatible with the anti-unifier of all those types.

Consider the following heap containing two closures and two blocks—it corresponds to the memory graph in figure 4 where the closure's environment has been boxed in an allocated block:

$$\mu = \left\{ \begin{array}{l} \ell_1 \mapsto \langle(\alpha * (\alpha \to \beta)) \to \texttt{Unit} \to \beta, \ell_2\rangle \\ \ell_2 \mapsto \texttt{Blk}(\ell_3,\ell_4) \\ \ell_3 \mapsto \texttt{Blk}(\ell_4,0) \\ \ell_4 \mapsto \langle \texttt{Unit} \to \texttt{T} \to \texttt{Int}, 0\rangle \end{array} \right\}$$

And consider the following type environments that will be used as aliases for memorized types in the rewriting sequence:

$$\begin{array}{lll} \Phi_1 = & \{ \ell_1 \mapsto \{ \texttt{Unit} \to \texttt{Int} \} & \} \\ \Phi_2 = \Phi_1 \cup & \{ \ell_2 \mapsto \{ (\dot\alpha * (\dot\alpha \to \texttt{Int})) \} & \} \\ \Phi_3 = \Phi_2 \cup & \{ \ell_3 \mapsto \{ \dot\alpha \} & \} \\ \Phi_4 = \Phi_3 \cup & \{ \ell_4 \mapsto \{ \dot\beta ;\ \dot\alpha \to \texttt{Int} \} & \} \\ \Phi'_4 = \Phi_1 \cup & \{ \ell_2 \mapsto \{ (\texttt{T} * (\texttt{T} \to \texttt{Int})) \} & ; \\ & \ \ \ell_3 \mapsto \{ \texttt{T} \} & ; \\ & \ \ \ell_4 \mapsto \{ \texttt{T} \to \texttt{Int}; \texttt{T} \to \texttt{Int} \} & \} \end{array}$$

To allow the verification of value of type T, the functions *Imm*(_) and *Arg*(_) are extended with the following cases:

$$\begin{array}{rcl} Imm(\texttt{T}) & = & \{0\} \\ Arg(\texttt{T}) & = & [(\texttt{T} \to \texttt{Unit}) ; \texttt{Unit}] \end{array}$$

A possible rewriting sequence for checking the compatibility of the value (ℓ_1, μ) against the type $\texttt{Unit} \to \texttt{Int}$ begins by checking the closure $\mu(\ell_1) = \langle(\alpha * (\alpha \to \beta)) \to \texttt{Unit} \to \beta, \ell_2\rangle$:

$$\begin{array}{rl} & (\mu, \emptyset).\,(\ell_1 : \{\texttt{Unit} \to \texttt{Int}\}) \\ [\text{R-CLOS}] \gg & \exists \dot\alpha\dot\beta.\ \left\{ \begin{array}{l} \texttt{Unit} \to \texttt{Int} = \texttt{Unit} \to \dot\beta \\ (\mu, \Phi_1).\,(\ell_2 : \{(\dot\alpha * (\dot\alpha \to \dot\beta))\}) \end{array} \right. \\ [\text{R-UNIF}] \gg & \exists \dot\alpha.\,(\mu, \Phi_1).\,(\ell_2 : \{(\dot\alpha * (\dot\alpha \to \texttt{Int}))\}) \end{array}$$

Continue by checking the block $\mu(\ell_2) = \texttt{Blk}(\ell_3,\ell_4)$.

$$\begin{array}{rl} [\text{R-BLK}] \gg & \exists \dot\alpha\dot\beta\dot\gamma.\ \left\{ \begin{array}{l} \Diamond\{(\dot\alpha * (\dot\alpha \to \texttt{Int}))\} \\ \texttt{arg}(\dot\alpha * (\dot\alpha \to \texttt{Int})) = [\dot\beta ; \dot\gamma] \\ (\mu, \Phi_2).\,(\ell_3 : \{\dot\beta\} \wedge \ell_4 : \{\dot\gamma\}) \end{array} \right. \\ [\text{R-}\Diamond] \gg & \exists \dot\alpha\dot\beta\dot\gamma.\ \left\{ \begin{array}{l} \texttt{arg}(\dot\alpha * (\dot\alpha \to \texttt{Int})) = [\dot\beta ; \dot\gamma] \\ (\mu, \Phi_2).\,(\ell_3 : \{\dot\beta\} \wedge \ell_4 : \{\dot\gamma\}) \end{array} \right. \\ [\text{R-ARG}] \gg & \exists \dot\alpha\dot\beta\dot\gamma.\ \left\{ \begin{array}{l} \dot\beta = \dot\alpha \wedge \dot\gamma = \dot\alpha \to \texttt{Int} \\ (\mu, \Phi_2).\,(\ell_3 : \{\dot\beta\} \wedge \ell_4 : \{\dot\gamma\}) \end{array} \right. \\ [\text{R-UNIF}] \gg & \exists \dot\alpha.\,(\mu, \Phi_2).\,(\ell_3 : \{\dot\alpha\} \wedge \ell_4 : \{\dot\alpha \to \texttt{Int}\}) \end{array}$$

Start the verification of block $\mu(\ell_3) = \texttt{Blk}(\ell_4,0)$.

$$\begin{array}{rl} [\text{R-BLK}] \gg & \exists \dot\alpha\dot\beta\dot\gamma.\ \left\{ \begin{array}{l} \Diamond\{\dot\alpha\} \wedge \texttt{arg}(\dot\alpha) = [\dot\beta ; \dot\gamma] \\ (\mu, \Phi_3).\ \left\{ \begin{array}{l} \ell_4 : \{\dot\beta\} \\ \ell_4 : \{\dot\alpha \to \texttt{Int}\} \\ 0 : \{\dot\gamma\} \end{array} \right. \end{array} \right. \\ [\text{R-MERGE}] \gg & \exists \dot\alpha\dot\beta\dot\gamma.\ \left\{ \begin{array}{l} \Diamond\{\dot\alpha\} \wedge \texttt{arg}(\dot\alpha) = [\dot\beta ; \dot\gamma] \\ (\mu, \Phi_3).\ \left\{ \begin{array}{l} \ell_4 : \{\dot\beta ; \dot\alpha \to \texttt{Int}\} \\ 0 : \{\dot\gamma\} \end{array} \right. \end{array} \right. \end{array}$$

Postpone the verification of constraints $\Diamond$ and $\texttt{arg}(\_)$ and continue by checking the closure $\mu(\ell_4) = \langle \texttt{Unit} \to \texttt{T} \to \texttt{Int}, 0\rangle$.

$$\begin{array}{rl} [\text{R-CLOS}] \gg & \exists \dot\alpha\dot\beta\dot\gamma.\ \left\{ \begin{array}{l} \Diamond\{\dot\alpha\} \wedge \texttt{arg}(\dot\alpha) = [\dot\beta ; \dot\gamma] \\ \dot\beta = \texttt{T} \to \texttt{Int} \\ \dot\alpha \to \texttt{Int} = \texttt{T} \to \texttt{Int} \\ (\mu, \Phi_4).\ \left\{ \begin{array}{l} 0 : \{\texttt{Unit}; \texttt{Unit}\} \\ 0 : \{\dot\gamma\} \end{array} \right. \end{array} \right. \\ [\text{R-UNIF}] \gg & \exists \dot\gamma.\ \left\{ \begin{array}{l} \Diamond\{\texttt{T}\} \wedge \texttt{arg}(\texttt{T}) = [\texttt{T} \to \texttt{Int} ; \dot\gamma] \\ (\mu, \Phi'_4).\ \left\{ \begin{array}{l} 0 : \{\texttt{Unit}; \texttt{Unit}\} \\ 0 : \{\dot\gamma\} \end{array} \right. \end{array} \right. \end{array}$$

Conclude by checking the postponed constraints.

$$\begin{array}{rl} [\text{R-}\Diamond] \gg & \exists \dot\gamma.\,(\ldots) \\ [\text{R-ARG}] \gg & \exists \dot\gamma.\,(\dot\gamma = \texttt{Unit} \wedge \ldots) \\ [\text{R-UNIF}] \gg & (\mu, \Phi_4).\,(0 : \{\texttt{Unit}; \texttt{Unit}\} \wedge 0 : \{\texttt{Unit}\}) \\ [\text{R-HEAP}] \gg & 0 : \{\texttt{Unit}; \texttt{Unit}\} \wedge 0 : \{\texttt{Unit}\} \\ [\text{R-AUNIF1}] \gg & 0 : \{\texttt{Unit}\} \wedge 0 : \{\texttt{Unit}\} \\ [\text{R-INT}] \gg & 0 : \{\texttt{Unit}\} \\ [\text{R-INT}] \gg & \texttt{True} \end{array}$$

Figure 6. An example of rewriting sequence

To ensure the compatibility of a block with the anti-unifier of the expected types, it is required to check that all the expected types share the same head type constructor (lemma 4.3). For that purpose, the rule [R-BLK] introduces an homogeneity constraint $\Diamond\{\tau_1 ; \ldots ; \tau_n\}$. This constraint is resolved by the rewriting rule [R-$\Diamond$] where T is a type constructor distinct from **Ref**.

$$\begin{array}{l} \Diamond\{\texttt{T}(\tau_1, \ldots, \tau_n) ; \tau'_{1..m}\} \gg \qquad [\text{R-}\Diamond] \\ \quad \exists \dot\alpha_{(1,1)..(n,m)}.\ \bigwedge_{i=1..m}(\tau'_i = \texttt{T}(\dot\alpha_{(1,i)}, \ldots, \dot\alpha_{(n,i)})) \\ \qquad \textit{if } \dot\alpha_{(1,1)..(n,m)} \# fv(\{\tau'_{1..m}\}) \textit{ and } \texttt{T} \not\equiv \texttt{Ref} \end{array}$$

The homogeneity constraint is also used to ensure that the expected type for a mutable field does not contain any universal variable. The rule [R-$\Diamond$-REF] could not be applied if the type τ contains existential variables.

$$\begin{array}{lll} \Diamond\{\texttt{Ref}(\tau)\} \gg \texttt{True} & \textit{if } fv(\tau) = \emptyset & [\text{R-}\Diamond\text{-REF}] \\ \Diamond\{\texttt{Ref}(\tau)\} \gg \texttt{False} & \textit{if } fuv(\tau) \neq \emptyset & [\text{R-}\Diamond\text{-REF-FAIL}] \\ \Diamond\{\texttt{Ref}(\tau) ; \tau_{1..n}\} \gg & & [\text{R-}\Diamond\text{-REF-SET}] \\ \quad \Diamond\{\texttt{Ref}(\tau)\} \wedge \bigwedge_{i=1..n}(\tau_i = \texttt{Ref}(\tau)) & & \end{array}$$

Closures The rewriting rule [R-CLOS], described in figure 5, allows the verification of a closure $\langle\tau^{env} \to \tau' \to \tau'', w\rangle$. To test the existence for every expected type τ_i of a type τ_i^{env} such that $\tau_i^{env} \to \tau_i$ is an instance of the closure static type $\tau^{env} \to \tau' \to \tau''$, the rewriting rule introduces a unification constraint between τ_i and an instance of $\tau' \to \tau''$ where every type variable has been replaced by an existential type variable. This instance is written $\dot\tau'_i \to \dot\tau''_i$; the corresponding instance of τ^{env} is written $\dot\tau_i^{env}$ and the set of existential variable of $\dot\tau_i^{env} \to \dot\tau'_i \to \dot\tau''_i$ is written $\bar{\dot\alpha}_i$. The unification constraints are resolved using the two following rules.

$$\begin{array}{ll} \exists\bar{\dot\alpha}.\,\tau_1 = \tau_2 \wedge C \gg \dot\theta(C) & [\text{R-UNIF}] \\ \quad \textit{if } \dot\theta \textit{ is the m.g.u of } \tau_1 \textit{ and } \tau_2\textit{, and if } dom(\dot\theta) = \bar{\dot\alpha} & \\ \exists\bar{\dot\alpha}.\,\tau_1 = \tau_2 \wedge C \gg \texttt{False} & [\text{R-NUNIF}] \\ \quad \textit{if } \tau_1 \textit{ and } \tau_2 \textit{ do not unify} & \end{array}$$

As for the rule [R-BLK], when a closure is checked for the second time (or more), the rule [R-CLOS] checks the closure against the new expected types *and* the previously checked types.

Administrative rules To complete the set of rewriting rules there are also four administrative rules that respectively allow the propagation of a failure [R-FALSE], the removal of the trivial constraint [R-TRUE], the removal of heap fragment when there is no more type constraints over the bound pointers [R-HEAP], and the instantiation of the remaining existential variables with the universal type [R-UNIV] (fig. 5).

$$\begin{array}{llll} C \wedge \texttt{False} & \gg \texttt{False} & & [\text{R-FALSE}] \\ C \wedge \texttt{True} & \gg C & & [\text{R-TRUE}] \\ (\mu, \Phi).\,C & \gg C & \textit{if } fp(C) \# dom(\mu) & [\text{R-HEAP}] \end{array}$$

Example A complete example is given in figure 6.

4.3 Rewriting system properties

We have shown that the rewriting system is sound and semi-complete with respect to the relation of compatibility between a value and a type that is defined in section 3.

Theorem 4.1 (Soundness). *If* $(\mu, \emptyset).(\ell : \{\tau\}) \gg \texttt{True}$ *then there exists a typing environment* Ψ *such that* $\mu : \Psi$ *and* $\Psi(\ell) \preccurlyeq \tau$.

Theorem 4.2 (Semi-completeness). *If* $(\mu, \emptyset).(\ell : \{\tau\}) \gg \texttt{False}$ *then there exists no typing environment* Ψ *such that* $\mu : \Psi$ *and* $\Psi(\ell) \preccurlyeq \tau$.

To prove those theorems, we will use two distinct invariant expressed with a notion of constraint satisfiability.

Constraint satisfiability The first notion of constraint satisfiability allows the proof of soundness of the rewriting system. It is parametrized by a substitution $\dot\theta$ for the free existential variables of the constraint and a typing environment Ψ for the free pointers. We write $\dot\theta, \Psi \models C$ when a constraint C is satisfied by $\dot\theta$ and Ψ.

The constraint $\texttt{True}$ is always satisfied and a conjunction $C_1 \wedge C_2$ is satisfied whenever both C_1 and C_2 are satisfied. The constraint $\texttt{False}$ can not be satisfied.

[C-TRUE]
$$\dot\theta, \Psi \models \texttt{True}$$

[C-AND]
$$\frac{\dot\theta, \Psi \models C_1 \qquad \dot\theta, \Psi \models C_2}{\dot\theta, \Psi \models C_1 \wedge C_2}$$

An existential constraint $\exists \dot\alpha. C$ is satisfied by $\dot\theta$ and Ψ if and only if there exists a type τ such that C is satisfied by $\dot\theta$ extended with a substitution $\dot\alpha \mapsto \tau$ and Ψ.

[C-EXISTS]
$$\frac{\dot\theta \oplus \{\dot\alpha \mapsto \tau\}, \Psi \models C}{\dot\theta, \Psi \models \exists \dot\alpha. C}$$

A type constraint $w : \{\tau_{1..n}\}$ is satisfied by $\dot\theta$ and Ψ if and only if under the environment Ψ the word w is compatible with the anti-unifier of the instantiations of $\tau_{1..n}$ by $\dot\theta$.

[C-QUESTION]
$$\frac{\Psi \vdash w : \curlywedge\{\dot\theta(\tau_{1..n})\}}{\dot\theta, \Psi \models w : \{\tau_{1..n}\}}$$

An equality constraint $\tau_1 = \tau_2$ is satisfied by $\dot\theta$ if and only if after instantiation by $\dot\theta$ the types are syntactically equal. In the same way, an ADT decomposition constraint $\texttt{arg}(\tau) = [\tau_1 \,;\, \tau_2]$ is satisfied by $\dot\theta$ if and only if after instantiation by $\dot\theta$ it corresponds to a case of the function *Arg*(_); and a head type constructor constraint $\Diamond\{\tau_{1..n}\}$ is satisfied by a substitution $\dot\theta$ if and only if after instantiation by $\dot\theta$ all the type share the same head type constructor.

[C-EQUAL]
$$\frac{\dot\theta(\tau_1) = \dot\theta(\tau_2)}{\dot\theta, \Psi \models \tau_1 = \tau_2}$$

[C-ARG]
$$\frac{Arg(\dot\theta(\tau)) = [\dot\theta(\tau') \,;\, \dot\theta(\tau'')]}{\dot\theta, \Psi \models \texttt{arg}(\tau) = [\tau' \,;\, \tau'']}$$

[C-$\Diamond$]
$$\frac{\forall i = 1..n, \;\; \dot\theta(\tau_i) = \texttt{T}_1(\tau_i^1, \ldots, \tau_i^m)}{\dot\theta, \Psi \models \Diamond\{\tau_{1..n}\}}$$

[C-$\Diamond$-REF]
$$\frac{\forall i = 1..n, \;\; \dot\theta(\tau_i) = \texttt{Ref}(\tau_i') \qquad fv(\tau_i') = \emptyset}{\dot\theta, \Psi \models \Diamond\{\tau_{1..n}\}}$$

And the satisfiability of a constraint $(\mu, \Phi').C$ is defined by the following rule, where $\Psi' = \curlywedge\{\dot\theta(\Phi')\} \curlywedge \Psi''$ is a type environment such that for all $\ell \in dom(\Psi'')$:

$$\Psi'(\ell) = \begin{cases} \Psi''(\ell) & \text{if } \ell \notin dom(\Phi') \\ (\curlywedge\{\dot\theta(\tau) \mid \forall \tau \in \Phi'(\ell)\}) \curlywedge \Psi''(\ell) & \text{otherwise} \end{cases}$$

[C-HEAP]
$$\frac{dom(\Psi'') = dom(\mu) \qquad \Psi' = \curlywedge\{\dot\theta(\Phi')\} \curlywedge \Psi'' \qquad \Psi \oplus \Psi' \vdash \mu : \Psi'' \qquad \dot\theta, \Psi \oplus \Psi' \models C}{\dot\theta, \Psi \models (\mu, \Phi').C}$$

In other words, a constraint $(\mu, \Phi').C$ is satisfied when:

- there exists a typing environment Ψ' more general than the memorized types, that allows the satisfaction of C, and
- there exists a typing environment Ψ'' compatible with μ under the hypothesis Ψ', such that:
  - $\Psi''(\ell)$ is an instance of $\Psi'(\ell)$ for all pointers ℓ of $dom(\mu)$ for which there are memorized types, and
  - $\Psi''(\ell)$ is equal to $\Psi'(\ell)$ for all the other pointers of $dom(\mu)$.

Soundness The satisfiability of the initial constraint correspond to the relation of compatibility between a value and a type (lemma 4.1) and for each rewriting rule, the satisfiability of the right constraint implies the satisfiability of the left constraint (lemma 4.2). These two lemmata allow the proof of soundness of the rewriting system (theorem 4.1).

Lemma 4.1. $\emptyset, \emptyset \models (\mu, \emptyset).(\ell : \{\tau\})$ *if and only if there exists a typing environment* Ψ *such that* $\mu : \Psi$ *and* $\Psi(\ell) \preccurlyeq \tau$.

Lemma 4.2. *If* $C_1 \gg C_2$ *and* $\dot\theta, \Psi \models C_2$ *then* $\dot\theta, \Psi \models C_1$.

To prove the soundness of the rule [R-BLK], we have to check that the function $Arg(\tau)$ is stable by anti-unification (lemma 4.3).

Lemma 4.3. *If, given a set of types* $\tau_{1..n}$ *sharing all the same head constructor, there exists* τ_i' *and* τ_i'' *such that* $Arg(\tau_i) = [\tau_i' \,;\, \tau_i'']$, *then* $Arg(\curlywedge\{\tau_{1..n}\}) = [\curlywedge\{\tau_{1..n}'\} \,;\, \curlywedge\{\tau_{1..n}''\}]$.

Semi-completeness The first definition of constraint satisfiability allows the proof of semi-completeness of the rewriting system only if we add an extra application condition for the rules [R-BLK] and [R-CLOS] stating that the types to be checked are not instances of previously checked types. However, in presence of existential types such a condition is not the exact negation of the application condition of the rule [R-REMOVE] and some constraint may remain stuck in a non-trivial form. For example, consider the following constraint:

$$C_{stuck} = (\mu, \{\ell \mapsto \{\texttt{Int} \rightarrow \texttt{Int}\}\}).(\ell : \{\dot\alpha \rightarrow \dot\alpha\})$$

We can not decide, without instantiating the variable $\dot\alpha$, whether the expected type $\dot\alpha \rightarrow \dot\alpha$ is an instance or not of the memorized types $\texttt{Int} \rightarrow \texttt{Int}$. We choose not to add this extra condition, allowing the introduction in section 4.4 of rewriting strategies that "unstuck" this constraint by applying the rule [R-CLOS].

To prove the semi-completeness without adding the extra condition to the rules [R-BLK] and [R-CLOS], we introduce a second definition of constraint satisfiability, called strict satisfiability and written $\dot\theta, \Psi \models^{s} C$. The set of strictly satisfied constraints is the subset of satisfied constraints for which the memorized types is actually compatible with the heap. More precisely, it can be defined by replacing the rule [C-HEAP] by the following rule:

[C'-HEAP]
$$\frac{dom(\Psi'') = dom(\mu) \qquad \Psi' = \curlywedge\{\dot\theta(\Phi')\} \curlywedge \Psi'' \qquad \Psi \oplus \Psi' \vdash \mu : \Psi' \qquad \dot\theta, \Psi \oplus \Psi' \models^{s} C}{\dot\theta, \Psi \models^{s} (\mu, \Phi').C}$$

The strict satisfiability of the initial constraint still corresponds to the relation of compatibility between a value and a type (lemma 4.4) and for every rewriting rule, the satisfiability of the left constraint implies the satisfiability of the right constraint (lemma 4.5). Those two lemmata allow the proof of semi-completeness of the rewriting system (theorem 4.2).

Lemma 4.4. $\emptyset, \emptyset \models^{s} (\mu, \emptyset).(\ell : \{\tau\})$ *if and only if there exists a typing environment* Ψ *such that* $\mu : \Psi$ *and* $\Psi(\ell) \preccurlyeq \tau$.

Lemma 4.5. *If* $C_1 \gg C_2$ *and* $\dot\theta, \Psi \models^{s} C_1$ *then* $\dot\theta, \Psi \models^{s} C_2$.

The second notion of satisfiability does not allow the soundness proof of the rule [R-HEAP].

Termination In the presence of cycles in the memory graph, the rewriting system described in section 4.2 may not terminate. One trivial way to create an infinite rewriting sequence is to apply the rule [R-BLK] or [R-CLOS] whenever the rule [R-REMOVE] is applicable. Such infinite sequences are easily avoided by using rewriting strategies that prefer the latter rule over the former; however, it is not sufficient to avoid all infinite sequences as shown by the following example. Consider, the heap[4]:

$$\mu = \{\ell_0 \mapsto \langle \sigma_{apply}, \{f : \ell_0\,;\, x : 0\}\rangle\}$$

Checking the compatibility of μ against the type $\texttt{Unit} \to \texttt{Int}$ will lead to following infinite sequence:

$$\begin{array}{lll} & & (\mu, \emptyset).\,(\ell_0 : \{\texttt{Unit} \to \texttt{Int}\}) \\ \begin{array}{l}[\text{R-CLOS}]\\ [\text{R-UNIF}]\end{array} & \gg & \exists\dot\alpha.\,(\mu, \Phi_1).\left\{\begin{array}{l} \ell_0 : \{\dot\alpha \to \texttt{Int}\} \\ 0 : \{\dot\alpha\}\end{array}\right. \\ \begin{array}{l}[\text{R-CLOS}]\\ [\text{R-UNIF}]\end{array} & \gg & \exists\dot\alpha\dot\beta\dot\gamma.\,(\mu, \Phi_2).\left\{\begin{array}{l} \ell_0 : \{\dot\beta \to \texttt{Int}; \dot\gamma \to \texttt{Int}\} \\ 0 : \{\dot\alpha\} \wedge 0 : \{\dot\beta\,;\,\dot\gamma\}\end{array}\right. \\ [\text{R-CLOS}] & \gg & \ldots \end{array}$$

where:

$$\begin{array}{lll} \Phi_1 & = & \{\ell_0 \mapsto \{\texttt{Unit} \to \texttt{Int}\}\} \\ \Phi_2 & = & \{\ell_0 \mapsto \{\texttt{Unit} \to \texttt{Int}\,;\, \dot\alpha \to \texttt{Int}\}\} \end{array}$$

When applying the rule [R-CLOS] for the second time, and like the constraint C_{stuck}, it is not possible to decide without instantiating $\dot\alpha$ whether $\dot\alpha \to \texttt{Int}$ is an instance of $\texttt{Unit} \to \texttt{Int}$ or not.

If we can not prove the termination of the rewriting system in the general case, we have proved its termination in two specific situations: in the absence of cycle (theorem 4.3) and in the absence of existential types (theorem 4.4) as introduced by GADTs or polymorphic closures. We propose in section 4.4 an extension of the rewriting system that terminates but may not be complete in the presence of cycles and existential types.

Theorem 4.3. *In a heap* μ *that contains no cycle, a constraint* $(\mu, \emptyset).(\ell : \{\tau\})$ *is rewritten in* ***True*** *or* ***False*** *in a finite number of steps.*

Theorem 4.4. *In a heap* μ *that contains no polymorphic closure that may introduce existential types, a constraint* $(\mu, \emptyset).(\ell : \{\tau\})$ *is rewritten in* ***True*** *or* ***False*** *in a finite number of step.*

To prove the termination in presence of cycles, but in the absence of existential types, we defined the size of a constraint and showed that, for every rewriting rule, the right constraint is smaller than the left constraint. More precisely, the size of a constraint is a 6-uple, sorted in lexicographic order, and composed of the number of pointers without memorized type, the number of type constructors in the anti-unifiers of memorized type's sets, the number of type constraints, the number of types in the sets of memorized types and in the sets of types constraints, the number of homogeneity and decomposition constraints, and the number of unification constraints.

[4] This heap may represent *A.loop* in the OCaml program:

```
module rec A : sig
  val loop : Unit → α
end = struct
  let delay f x = fun () → f x
  let loop = delay A.loop ()
end
```

4.4 Rewriting strategy

In order to express precisely the topological traversal of the graph and to enable termination in presence of cycles and existential types, we now add one rewriting rule in order to topologically sort the heap, and two rules dedicated to ensure termination. The two latter rules imply loosing completeness.

Topological sort To express the topological traversal proposed in section 2.1 as a rewriting strategy, the following rule allows the split of the heap in fragments corresponding to SCCs.

$$\begin{array}{lr} (\mu, \Phi).\,C \gg (\mu_1, \Phi_1).\,(\mu_2, \Phi_2).\,C & [\text{R-SORT}] \\ \quad \textit{if } \mu_1 \uplus \mu_2 = \mu & \\ \quad \textit{and } fp(img(\mu_1)) \# dom(\mu_2) & \\ \quad \textit{and } \Phi_i = \Phi_{|dom(\mu_i)} & \end{array}$$

When a heap is decomposed in SCCs, the rules [R-BLK] and [R-CLOS] syntactically forbid to check a value that does not belong to the current SCC. Once a SCC has been checked, it can be removed from the constraints with the rule [R-HEAP].

Monomorphic recursion As shown in section 2.1, when we restrict ourselves to monomorphic recursion, it is not necessary to check an allocated cyclic value twice when the memory graph is traversed in a topological order: it is sufficient to check the equality between the expected type and the memorized one. Hence, we never apply the rules [R-BLK] or [R-CLOS] for previously checked pointers, and we replace the rule [R-REMOVE] by the following rule, that allows the unification of the expected type with the memorized one:

$$\begin{array}{lr} (\mu, \Phi').\,(\ell : \{\tau'\} \wedge C) \gg & [\text{R-FORCEUNIF}] \\ \quad \tau = \tau' \wedge (\mu, \Phi').\,C & \\ \quad \textit{if } \Phi'(\ell) = \{\tau\} & \end{array}$$

This rule is sound (as for lemma 4.2) but not semi-complete (as for lemma 4.5).

If a set of expected types or a set a memorized types could not be simplified by anti-unification, the following rule allows the instantiation of an existential variables with the universal type.

$$\exists\dot\alpha.\,C \gg \exists\dot\alpha.\,(C \wedge \dot\alpha = \star) \qquad [\text{R-FORCEINST}]$$

This rule is obviously not semi-complete, hence it is applied only when no other rules apply.

Polymorphic recursion If we want to accept polymorphic recursion, we may need to check cyclic values several times, and accept that the types expected from inside the SCC be instances of the memorized types. In order to do so, we allow the usage of the rule [R-REMOVE]. Guaranteeing termination may then be obtained by allowing multiple checks of cyclic values (rules [R-BLK] and [R-CLOS]) only when we may anti-unify[5] the expected types with memorized types.

4.5 Type-safe (un)marshalling primitives

We have implemented a prototype of this algorithm for the OCaml compiler. This provides a type-safe unmarshalling function based

[5] Remember that the anti-unifier may not always be computed in the presence of existential type variables.

on the unsafe marshalling mechanism available in the OCaml standard library without changing the external representation of data. The current unsafe (un)marshalling functions of the standard library have the following type signatures, where the type `String` is used as a sequence of bytes:

`val` *marshall* : $\alpha \rightarrow$ `String`
`val` *unmarshall* : `String` $\rightarrow \alpha$

The type-safe unmarshalling function has the following prototype:

`val` *safe_unmarshall* : `Ty`$(\alpha) \rightarrow$ `String` $\rightarrow \alpha$

where `Ty`(τ) is the classical singleton type whose unique value is a runtime representation of the type τ [6, 12].

Adapting our algorithm to other runtimes The compatibility algorithm works on a memory graph where pointers and immediate values can be distinguished. In situations where the runtime does not make such a distinction but still uses an exact garbage collection mechanism that traverse precisely the memory graph, our algorithm remains applicable. We would ask the generic marshalling function to add the necessary information to the external representation of data. Our algorithm would then be applied on an intermediate form of the memory graph.

For checking the compatibility of closures, our algorithm asks the running program to provide the static type of the code pointers being unmarshalled. This has been implented in our prototype.

Note that type-safe unmarshalling of closures allows marshalling unevaluated lazy values.

The OCaml external representation of closures is composed of a raw code pointer and the representation of the environment. Hence, the unmarshalling of a closure can only take place in different instances of the same compiled program. In situations where the runtime uses dynamic loading of code and relinking when unmarshalling closures, we would again delegate this task to the generic unmarshaller, and check type compatibility on the resulting memory graph.

5. Related work

Type-safe (un)marshalling in OCaml When compared to existing OCaml libraries that provide type-safe marshalling mechanisms, our proposal is the first to provide both the ability to communicate safely with un-trusted peers—such as a web browser for an HTTP server—and to handle GADTs and closures with the help of existential type variables. The Deriving library[26] use the Camlp4 preprocessor to generate *ad hoc* functions from data type definitions. As other mechanisms based on *ad hoc* functions we know of, it allows the communication with un-trusted peers but do not handle closures and existential types.

Our proposal does not allow the (un)marshalling of abstract data types introduced by the OCaml module system, whereas the HashCaml [5] compiler or the Quicksilver library [21] do. The HashCaml compiler is an extension of the OCaml compiler, that adds runtime type representations. It contains a safe (un)marshalling mechanism that keeps the type of a value in its external representation. For representing abstract types, it computes a hash of the type definition and of the source code of the associated function. Quicksilver is another Camlp4 based marshalling library that generates *ad hoc* (un)marshalling functions. It allows the user to associate a cryptographic key to each abstract type and to encrypt the external representation of an abstract value.

Polytypic programming Another approach to type-safe serialization is polytypic programming [24]. To motivate a programming language that allows the explicit manipulation and analysis of type expressions in a typed manner, Weirich [25] uses a generic marshalling function that recursively analyzes the type of the value. This typed approach has the obvious advantage of not requiring an external proof of soundness. However, it may not be possible to handle polymorphic sharing with anti-unification of the expected types.

Type reconstruction The idea of traversing a memory graph in parallel with its type has been previously used to build tag-free garbage collectors [3, 4, 10, 23] or to implement debuggers [2]. In these contexts, the memory graph is known to be compatible with the type. Our algorithm may also be used to pretty-print values in a debugger. Our approach has the advantage of being less intrusive and does not require to keep runtime type information in the stack or inside the values.

Interoperability The TypedRacket programming language [22] is a statically typed version of Racket. Both languages share the same runtime and they use dynamic type compatibility checking to make sure that untyped data can be safely imported in typed parts of a program. The main differences with our algorithm is that compatibility checking is based on contracts [8] and checking of functional values is delayed until their application.

6. Conclusion

We have presented a type compatibility checking algorithm for ML-like programming languages, that handles algebraic data types, mutable data, cyclic data, GADTs and closures. We gave a formal description of the problem, and presented the verification as a rewriting system, the algorithm being essentially a particular rewriting strategy.

This systematic approach greatly simplifies the proof of soundness: the soundness of each rewriting rule is proved independently. The naive strategy being incomplete, the presentation as a rewriting system enables the precise identification of where completeness is lost and what step to follow in order to minimize the chances of rejecting correct data in a finite time.

The obtained algorithm is efficient and has been implemented in a prototype version of the OCaml compiler. It needs no type information in the data representation and can be used to import, in a statically typed program, external data built by untyped or differently-typed programs.

References

[1] M. Abadi, L. Cardelli, B. C. Pierce, and D. Rémy. Dynamic typing in polymorphic languages. *Journal of Functional Programming*, 5(1): 111–130, Jan. 1995.

[2] S. Aditya and A. Caro. Compiler-directed type reconstruction for polymorphic languages. In *FPCA '93: Proceedings of the Conference on Functional Programming Languages and Computer Architecture*, pages 74–82, June 1993.

[3] S. Aditya, C. H. Flood, and J. E. Hicks. Garbage collection for strongly-typed languages using run-time type reconstruction. In *LFP '94: Proceedings of the 1994 ACM Conference on LISP and Functional Programming*, pages 12–23, June 1994.

[4] A. W. Appel. Runtime tags aren't necessary. *Lisp and Symbolic Computation*, 2(2):153–162, July 1989.

[5] J. Billings, P. Sewell, M. R. Shinwell, and R. Strnisa. Type-safe distributed programming for OCaml. In *ML'06: Proceedings of the ACM Workshop on ML*, pages 20–31, Sept. 2006.

[6] K. Crary, S. Weirich, and G. Morrisett. Intensional polymorphism in type-erasure semantics. In *ICFP'98: Proceedings of the 3rd ACM International Conference on Functional Programming*, volume 34(1) of *SIGPLAN Not.*, pages 301–312, Sept. 1998.

[7] M. Elsman. Type-specialized serialization with sharing. In *TFP'05: Revised Selected Papers from the Sixth Symposium on Trends in Functional Programming*, pages 47–62, Sept. 2005.

[8] R. B. Findler and M. Felleisen. Contracts for higher-order functions. In *ICFP'02: Proceedings of the 7th ACM International Conference on Functional Programming*, volume 37(9) of *SIGPLAN Not.*, pages 48–59, Sept. 2002.

[9] J. Furuse and P. Weis. Input/output of caml values (in french). In *JFLA'00: Journées Francophones des Langages Applicatifs*. INRIA, Jan. 2000.

[10] B. Goldberg and M. Gloger. Polymorphic type reconstruction for garbage collection without tags. *SIGPLAN Lisp Pointers*, V(1):53–65, 1992.

[11] G. Henry. *Typing unmarshalling without marshalling types (in french)*. PhD thesis, Univ Paris Diderot, 2011. URL `http://tel.archives-ouvertes.fr/tel-00624156/PDF/these.pdf`.

[12] M. Hicks, S. Weirich, and K. Crary. Safe and flexible dynamic linking of native code. In R. Harper, editor, *Workshop on Types in Compilation*, volume 2071 of *Lecture Notes in Computer Science*, pages 147–176. Springer-Verlag, 2000.

[13] G. Huet. *Résolution d'équations dans des langages d'ordre 1,2,..., ω*. PhD thesis, Université Paris 7, 1976.

[14] A. J. Kennedy. Pickler combinators. *Journal of Functional Programming*, 14(6):727–739, 2004.

[15] X. Leroy. Efficient data representation in polymorphic languages. In *PLILP'90: 2nd International Workshop on Programming Language Implementation and Logic Programming*, volume 456 of *Lecture Notes in Computer Science*, pages 255–276. Springer, Aug. 1990.

[16] X. Leroy and M. Mauny. Dynamics in ML. *Journal of Functional Programming*, 3(4):431–463, 1993.

[17] X. Leroy, D. Doligez, J. Garrigue, D. Rémy, and J. Vouillon. *The Objective Caml system release 3.12*, June 2011.

[18] A. Mycroft. Polymorphic type schemes and recursive definitions. In *ISP'84: Proceedings of the 6th International Symposium on Programming*, volume 167 of *Lecture Notes in Computer Science*, pages 217–228. Springer, 1984.

[19] G. Plotkin. A note on inductive generalization. *Machine Intelligence*, 5:153–163, 1970.

[20] F. Pottier and D. Rémy. The Essence of ML Type Inference. In B. C. Pierce, editor, *Advanced Topics in Types and Programming Languages*, chapter 10, pages 389–489. MIT Press, 2005.

[21] H. Sutou and E. Sumii. Quicksilver/OCaml: A poor man's type-safe and abstraction-secure communication library. Unpublished, 2007.

[22] S. Tobin-Hochstadt and M. Felleisen. The design and implementation of Typed Scheme. In *POPL'08: Proceedings of the 35th ACM Symposium on Principles of Programming Languages*, pages 395–406, Jan. 2008.

[23] A. P. Tolmach. Tag-free garbage collection using explicit type parameters. In *LFP '94: Proceedings of the 1994 ACM Conference on LISP and Functional Programming*, pages 1–11, June 1994.

[24] S. Weirich. Higher-order intensional type analysis. In *ESOP'02: Proceedings of the 11th European Symposium on Programming*, pages 98–114, 2002.

[25] S. Weirich. Type-safe run-time polytypic programming. *Journal of Functional Programming*, 16(10):681–710, Nov. 2006.

[26] J. Yallop. Practical generic programming in OCaml. In *ML'07: Proceedings of the ACM Workshop on ML*, pages 83–94, Sept. 2007.

Deconstraining DSLs

Will Jones Tony Field Tristan Allwood

Department of Computing
Imperial College London
{wlj05,ajf,tora}@doc.ic.ac.uk

Abstract

Strongly-typed functional languages provide a powerful framework for embedding Domain-Specific Languages (DSLs). However, building type-safe functions defined over an embedded DSL can introduce application-specific type constraints that end up being imposed on the DSL data types themselves. At best, these constraints are unwieldy and at worst they can limit the range of DSL expressions that can be built. We present a simple solution to this problem that allows application-specific constraints to be specified at the point of use of a DSL expression rather than when the DSL's embedding types are defined. Our solution applies equally to both tagged and tagless representations and, importantly, also works in the presence of higher-rank types.

Categories and Subject Descriptors D.3.3 [*Language Constructs and Features*]: Constraints, Data types and structures, Polymorphism; D.3.2 [*Language Classifications*]: Applicative (functional) languages

Keywords Static typing, constraints, domain-specific languages.

1. Introduction

Embedding a *Domain-Specific Language* (DSL) into a general-purpose programming language provides a simple and effective way to support domain-specific functionality without the need for a custom compiler [1, 14]. Modern functional languages provide particularly powerful host languages for DSLs due in part to their rich type systems which, appropriately exploited, can endow the DSL with important safety properties.

The usual way to enforce type-safety is to add constraints to the data types used to embed the DSL. However, these constraints do exactly what they say: they *constrain* the way the DSL can be used. This is fine when there is a single use, or implementation of the DSL, for example one involving the invocation of a domain-specific library or the generation of code for a specific hardware platform. However, if the intention is to support multiple implementations of the DSL, or to use a particular DSL expression in different ways, then these constraints can interfere in a way that precludes the co-existence of some (and in exceptional cases, all) implementations.

To illustrate the problem, consider the following (rather crude) Haskell embedding of a very tiny expression language comprising polymorphic values, conditionals and equality; we will refer to this throughout the paper:

```
data Exp a where
  ValueE :: a → Exp a
  CondE :: Exp Bool → Exp a → Exp a → Exp a
  EqE   :: Eq a ⇒ Exp a → Exp a → Exp Bool
```

Here we have made use of *Generalised Algebraic Data Types* (GADTs) [24] as supported in the Glasgow Haskell Compiler (GHC). The intention is that the DSL be able to support any set of basic types, provided the arguments to EqE are expressions that are comparable under equality. The corresponding Eq a constraint is the *only* constraint that we want to impose on the DSL.

Let's now see what happens when we try to define a function over DSL expressions that imposes its own 'local' constraint. The function compileSM below implements a compiler for a very simple stack machine that has no support for floating-point arithmetic. To make the function type-safe it needs to enforce the rule that the DSL expression it is given contains only integers and booleans; the booleans False and True will be encoded as the integers 0 and 1 in the usual way. Ignoring unique label generation, we have:

```
compileSM :: Exp a → String
compileSM (ValueE x)
  = "PUSH " ++ show (toInt x) ++ "\n"
compileSM (CondE p t f)
  = compileSM p ++ "CMP #0\n" ++ "BEQ L1\n" ++
      compileSM t ++ "BR L2\n" ++
        "L1: " ++ compileSM f ++ "L2: "
compileSM (EqE e1 e2)
  = compileSM e1 ++ compileSM e2 ++ "EQ\n"
```

Here, toInt is overloaded to work only on Ints and Bools, which we can express using a type class, such as the following:

```
class IntBool a where
  toInt :: a → Int
instance IntBool Int  where toInt = id
instance IntBool Bool where toInt = fromEnum
```

The function fromEnum in Haskell's Enum class converts booleans to integers, as required.

Now we have a problem: compileSM doesn't type check because the use of toInt in the ValueE rule requires that a be a member of the IntBool class. A first thought might be to add a context to the type of compileSM itself to express the IntBool constraint:

```
compileSM :: IntBool a ⇒ Exp a → String
```

However, this doesn't solve the problem, because the a here refers only to the result type of the top-level expression. The Haskell type system has no way of proving that the arguments to EqE carry

ICFP'12, September 9–15, 2012, Copenhagen, Denmark.

the same constraint: the a in EqE's type signature is *existentially* quantified.

The usual solution to this type of problem (see Axelsson et al. [2] and Chakravarty et al. [7] for examples) is to add a constraint to the type of ValueE as follows:

$$\begin{aligned}&\textbf{data}\ \mathsf{Exp}\ a\ \textbf{where}\\&\quad \mathsf{ValueE} :: \mathsf{IntBool}\ a \Rightarrow a \rightarrow \mathsf{Exp}\ a\end{aligned}$$

compileSM now type checks, but the unfortunate effect of the constraint is to restrict *all* uses of the DSL to expressions containing only integers or booleans. For example, the expression ValueE sin, which would have been perfectly valid before we added the constraint, now fails to type check. This was clearly not the intention: what we wanted to do was restrict the set of DSL programs that are compilable with compileSM, not the DSL itself.

Any function over the DSL that imposes a similar constraint will compound the problem, as those constraints will need to be added to ValueE's type as well. In the worst case these constraints may collectively have no types in common, in which case it will be impossible to build a DSL expression at all! Although our motivation in this paper concerns DSLs this is in fact a problem with all data types, not just those that encode DSLs.

In this paper we present two solutions to this problem. The first is presented somewhat as an aside, as it requires nothing more than a relatively simple abstraction over the target implementation platform using similar techniques to that described by Hughes [11]. The problem with this is that it breaks down in the context of higher-rank types, which means that it becomes extremely cumbersome to define the type of a function that uses a given DSL expression in two *different* ways, as in:

$$\begin{aligned}&f :: \mathsf{Exp}\ p\ a \rightarrow \ldots\\&f\ e = \ldots(\mathsf{compileSM}\ e)\ldots(\mathsf{pretty}\ e)\ldots\end{aligned}$$

for example, where pretty pretty-prints a given expression. Assuming that p represents the target platform, typing this function requires instantiating p at the types required by compileSM and pretty simultaneously. Unfortunately, introducing the required higher-rank type *hides* the type p, preventing it from being used to constrain values dynamically. This is explained in more detail in Section 8; the reader might wish to read this section first before continuing with Section 2.

The second solution, which constitutes the main contribution of the paper, takes a completely different approach and solves the restriction problem even in the presence of higher-rank types. The idea is to replace concrete constraints in a data type with *generic constraints* which capture at the *type level* key properties of a DSL expression, such as the primitive object types that it depends upon or the set of DSL operations that are used in its construction. Independently of the DSL data type(s), the constraints imposed by individual functions over the data type are specified separately as *platform* constraints. The trick, which involves some quite subtle type-level reasoning, is to ensure that these platform constraints are compatible with the generic constraints of the given DSL expression at the point where the function is *applied*. This constitutes the main technical challenge of the paper.

The key principle that underpins our idea is that implementation-specific constraints should be imposed at the point of *use* of a data type, not at the point of *definition*, i.e. it embodies the established principle that an interface should be separated from its implementation(s).

Our contributions are as follows:

- We describe a method for imposing generic constraints on data types that avoids the restrictions ordinarily imposed by concrete constraints (Section 2). In the context of a DSL we show how these can be used to impose independent implementation-specific constraints, for example on the types (Section 2.3) and operations (Section 6) supported by a given target platform.
- We show how the idea, which is initially presented in the context of GADTs, can be applied equally to tagless representations (Section 5) and representations involving rank-2 types (Section 5.1).
- We show that both the compile-time and run-time overheads of the scheme are bounded by a constant that is a function of the size of the list of types forming the constraint set, which we expect typically to be small (Section 2.4).
- Our implementation makes use of many of the latest Haskell extensions, including kind polymorphism (Section 6), constraint kinds (Section 3) and promotion (Section 2) and thus serves to document the application of these extensions in a practical setting.

1.1 Motivation

This work has been inspired by our broader efforts to build type-safe embedded DSLs for exploiting heterogeneous multi-core parallelism. Our objective is to be able to target a multitude of platforms with a view to exploiting both control and data parallelism in a type-safe manner. From the typing perspective there are two key challenges: 1. Allowing a variety of platform-specific program analysis (performance modelling, optimisation etc.) and compilation functions to co-exist without restricting the application of the DSL; 2. Allowing the same DSL program to be compilable to multiple platforms in the same context. The latter is particularly important for heterogeneous data parallelism, for example. We do not discuss these issues in any detail in this paper, although the running examples we use throughout have been chosen to illustrate some of the problems that arise in this area.

2. Generic constraints

We now continue with the example of Section 1. The idea is to associate each value of type Exp with a list of types as which represents *symbolically* the types that appear in the expression. Individual, concrete, constraints (such as IntBool) are then replaced with a set of *generic* constraints of the form Elem a as (or, using infix notation, $a \in as$).

For the ValueE constructor, a single generic constraint $a \in as$ captures the notion that the type of object wrapped by ValueE must be an element of the list of types, as. Similarly for the CondE case, which also requires the constraint Bool $\in as$ to cater for the type of the predicate. The EqE case again follows suit, except that it also retains the original Eq a constraint. In many, if not all, cases it may suffice to generate these $(\cdot \in \cdot)$ constraints mechanically, e.g. using Template Haskell [26] (see Section 10.1), but for the time being we decorate the constructor types explicitly:

$$\begin{aligned}&\textbf{data}\ \mathsf{Exp}\ as\ a\ \textbf{where}\\&\quad \mathsf{ValueE} :: (a \in as) \Rightarrow a \rightarrow \mathsf{Exp}\ as\ a\\&\quad \mathsf{EqE} \quad\ :: (\mathsf{Eq}\ a, a \in as, \mathsf{Bool} \in as)\\&\qquad\qquad \Rightarrow \mathsf{Exp}\ as\ a \rightarrow \mathsf{Exp}\ as\ a \rightarrow \mathsf{Exp}\ as\ \mathsf{Bool}\\&\quad \mathsf{CondE} :: (a \in as, \mathsf{Bool} \in as)\\&\qquad\qquad \Rightarrow \mathsf{Exp}\ as\ \mathsf{Bool} \rightarrow \mathsf{Exp}\ as\ a \rightarrow \mathsf{Exp}\ as\ a\\&\qquad\qquad \rightarrow \mathsf{Exp}\ as\ a\end{aligned}$$

Importantly, this definition will suffice for *all* functions defined over the DSL.

A point that is worth making here is that Haskell's type inference engine automatically deletes duplicate constraints. As an example, consider the following expression:

```
eMixed
  = CondE (EqE (ValueE (3 :: Int)) (ValueE (4 :: Int)))
      (ValueE (0.0 :: Float)) (ValueE (3.9 :: Float))
```

The constraint Bool $\in$ as is inferred twice: once when typing the subexpression EqE... which computes the constraints (Eq Int, Int $\in$ as, Bool $\in$ as), and once when typing the conditional CondE... which independently imposes the constraint Bool $\in$ as in addition to Float $\in$ as (the top-level result is an Exp as Float). The Eq Int constraint is trivially satisfied, and so is removed, and the duplicate Bool $\in$ as constraints are collapsed into one. The resulting inferred type for eMixed is thus:

(Int $\in as$, Bool $\in as$, Float $\in as$) $\Rightarrow$ Exp as Float

A key feature is that the constraints list explicitly the types that appear *within* an expression that are not visible simply by looking at the expression's top-level type (Exp as Float in the case of eMixed).

2.1 Aside: type-level lists

At first sight the idea of a list of *types* might seem rather odd, as lists in Haskell are traditionally data types (with kind $\star$). What we need here is the concept of a list itself being a type. Fortunately, a recent extension to Haskell [29] supports the *promotion* of certain values; in particular this allows Haskell's familiar list constructors to be used at the type level. The promotion of the Haskell list type produces:

- A *type* $'[\,]$ and a *type constructor* (:) which may be used for building lists *at the type level*. The quote (′) in the name of $'[\,]$ exists to distinguish it from the traditional list type constructor $[\,]$ (of kind $\star \rightarrow \star$).
- A set of *kinds* $[\kappa]$, each of *sort* $\Box$ (pronounced 'box'). $'[\,]$ thus has kind $\forall\kappa.\ [\kappa]$ and (:) has kind $\forall\kappa.\ \kappa \rightarrow [\kappa] \rightarrow [\kappa]$.

Note that our technique does not rely on Haskell's ability to support type-level lists. We could equally well use the 'pair' and 'unit' type constructors (as in HList [13]), for example (Int, (Bool, ())) instead of $'$[Int, Bool], but choose to take advantage of the rather more convenient list syntax and associated kind safety.

2.2 Picking types

At this point the list of types as is purely symbolic, so if an expression e is typed as $(\tau_1 \in as, \ldots, \tau_n \in as) \Rightarrow$ Exp $as\ \tau$ then the constraints state that as must contain *at least* the types $\tau_1, \ldots, \tau_n$ for e to have type Exp $as\ \tau$, *whatever as happens to be.*

Given a constrained type, one thing we should certainly be able to do is *instantiate* some or all of the types specified in the constraints. Thus, in the same way that we can instantiate a in the type of Haskell's built-in function abs :: Num $a \Rightarrow a \rightarrow a$ to the specific instance abs :: Int $\rightarrow$ Int, for example, so we should be able to do the same for constraints involving $(\cdot \in \cdot)$. We would therefore like all of the following to be valid instantiations for the type of eMixed above:

```
eMixed :: (Bool ∈ as, Float ∈ as) ⇒ Exp (Int : as) Float
eMixed :: Exp '[Bool, Float, Int] Float
eMixed :: Exp '[Char, Bool, Float, Int] Float
```

whilst an attempted instantiation such as

```
eMixed :: Exp '[Bool, Int] Float
```

should fail to type check.

To see how this can be achieved we now develop the implementation of $(\cdot \in \cdot)$ and discuss some possible variations. We remark that, in what follows, considerable care is needed to ensure that we don't inadvertently restrict the ability of DSL designers to use Haskell's operator overloading; we elaborate on this in Section 7.

We have a basic requirement to ensure that a constraint $a \in as$ is only satisfied when the list of types as contains a. The usual approach when dealing with lists is to assert that if the head of as is a then the constraint is satisfied trivially and, if not, to seek evidence that a appears somewhere in the tail of as. The following GADT describes these two cases:

```
data Evidence a as where
  Head :: Evidence a (a : as)
  Tail :: (a ∈ as) ⇒ Evidence a (b : as)
```

This states that if an object of type Evidence a as is Head then a is at the head of the as, and that if it is Tail then a *is* in the list, but is not at the head. Notice that the recursive check into the tail of the list is performed by virtue of the constraint $a \in as$ in the definition of Tail (but see also Section 2.2.1 below). Crucially, therefore, if a is *not* in as then it should be impossible to construct an object which matches the type of either Head or Tail. Thus, if an object has type Evidence a as then it is irrefutably the case that a is in as, for otherwise we have a type error! This is the key property that governs our definition of $(\cdot \in \cdot)$:

```
class a ∈ as where
  evidence :: Evidence a as
```

which can be read: 'a is an element of as and the value evidence is either Head or Tail, depending on where in the list a resides.' There are no other possibilities! Which of the two cases we have is now determined by the instance declarations:

```
instance a ∈ (a : as) where
  evidence = Head

instance (a ∈ as) ⇒ a ∈ (b : as) where
  evidence = Tail
```

Thus, for example, the following:

```
evidence :: Evidence Int '[Int, Char]
evidence :: Evidence Int '[Float, Int]
```

have values Head and Tail respectively, whereas there is no instance of $(\cdot \in \cdot)$ which provides evidence :: Evidence Int $'$[Bool].

Note that it is important that there is no case for $'[\,]$ because we want there to be no evidence that a is an element of $'[\,]$, which is surely a 'lie'! However, it is interesting to see what happens if we try to define such an instance. Rather conveniently, if we attempt the following:

```
instance a ∈ '[] where
  evidence = ...
```

then the only thing we can put on the right-hand side is $\bot$ (or error). Looking at this another way, such an instance can successfully encode the 'lie' that a is an element of $'[\,]$, but the body *cannot* provide the evidence!

2.2.1 Implementation note

A possible variation on the scheme proposed is to replace the constraint $a \in as$ in Tail with explicit evidence of the existence of a in the tail of as as follows:

```
Tail :: !(Evidence a as) → Evidence a (b : as)

instance (a ∈ as) ⇒ a ∈ (b : as) where
  evidence = Tail evidence   -- Note: the two evidences
                             -- have different types.
```

This works in principle, but we must ensure that the Tail constructor is strict in its argument (hence the '!' annotation) in order to force the recursion into the tail of as.

In both approaches, the two instances of $(\cdot \in \cdot)$ shown *overlap*, and may thus only be used when one is recognisably more specific than the other. This means that we may only eliminate $(\cdot \in \cdot)$ constraints when reasoning about lists of *ground* types: there is no way in general for the compiler to know if the type variable a is a member of the list $(b : as)$, i.e. whether a and b are the same type. This is not a serious limitation, however, as the constraints are typically only eliminated at the point where a concrete type must be picked anyway (see Section 10.2).

2.3 Platform constraints

Let us now return to the compileSM function for our simple stack machine. Thanks to compileSM's non-discriminating type, the EqE and CondE cases require no modification from those shown in Section 1. The ValueE clause is less obvious so let's reproduce it here:

```
compileSM (ValueE x)
    = "PUSH " ++ show (toInt x) ++ "\n"
```

From the definition of Exp above, all we know about the type of x (b, say) is that $b \in as$. For this particular implementation we need to establish the fact that b is also either an integer or a boolean, i.e. we need to satisfy the constraint IntBool b before we can invoke toInt.

The key is to look at the type of compileSM itself. There is clearly a *platform-specific* requirement that all types in a given expression must be either Ints or Bools so the place to specify this constraint must be in the definition of compileSM itself:

```
compileSM :: AllIntBool as ⇒ Exp a as → String
```

The idea is for the AllIntBool type class to define a 'wrapper' function, toInt', whose role is to pick the right instance of IntBool (here either the Int or Bool instance); this involves convincing the type checker that such an instance exists. In order to do this toInt' needs to carry with it the list of constrained types as:

```
class AllIntBool as where
  toInt' :: (b ∈ as) ⇒ Proxy as → b → Int
```

What is the role of the Proxy type? On the left of the $\Rightarrow$ we have the constraint that $b \in as$. To be able call toInt' we will need to pass an argument that makes the type as concrete, such that the Haskell compiler can pick the correct instance of AllIntBool. Usually this would involve passing an argument of type as, but as has kind $[\star]$ whereas function arguments must have kind $\star$. The Proxy data type suffices to effect the conversion:

```
data Proxy as = Proxy
```

Before we continue with AllIntBool, it will be useful to complete the compiler in order to see how the proxy value comes into play:

```
compileSM (ValueE x)
    = "PUSH " ++ show (toInt' (Proxy :: Proxy as) x)
        ++ "\n"
```

Let's now build the AllIntBool class instances, beginning with the instance for (:). If a is an instance of IntBool and the list as is AllIntBool then we need to extend the constraint to the list $(a : as)$:

```
instance (IntBool a, AllIntBool as)
        ⇒ AllIntBool (a : as) where
  toInt' _ x = ...
```

The trick is to observe the type of toInt':

```
    (IntBool a, AllIntBool as, b ∈ (a : as))
  ⇒ Proxy (a : as) → b → Int
```

Here, both a and b are *type variables* so in the event that b is at the *head* of the list $(a : as)$, we shall have that $a \equiv b$ and hence IntBool b. In this case, we can therefore apply toInt to x and we are done. If b is in the *tail* of the list $(a : as)$ then we require a proof that $b \in as$, in which case we will proceed by recursion. How do we know whether b is at the head of as? We use the evidence method of the corresponding $(\cdot \in \cdot)$ instance:

```
instance (IntBool a, AllIntBool as)
        ⇒ AllIntBool (a : as) where
  toInt' _ (x :: b)
    = case evidence :: Evidence b (a : as) of
        Head → toInt x
        Tail  → toInt' (Proxy :: Proxy as) x
```

Notice that in the recursive call to toInt' we must reconstruct a new proxy object, as its type must reflect that of the tail of $(a : as)$. This proxy argument is never referred to at the object level; its role is simply to pick the required type instance for AllIntBool.

An instance for '[] is needed because the AllIntBool instance for a : '[] (see above) requires the two constraints IntBool a and AllIntBool '[]. Of course, in this case it *must* be the case that the corresponding evidence is Head for otherwise the type we are looking for would not be in the list; a recursive call to toInt' with argument (Proxy :: Proxy '[]) can therefore never occur. We thus need the '[] instance, but not its associated implementation of toInt':

```
instance AllIntBool '[] where
  toInt' _ (x :: b)
    = seq (evidence :: Evidence b '[]) ⊥
```

Note that we could simply have made the right-hand side $\perp$ but we instead 'call the bluff' of any instance of the form $b \in$ '[]. We have seen earlier (Section 2.2) that the value of any alleged evidence can only be $\perp$; the above code thus explicitly exposes the lie!

2.4 Implementation cost

The process of picking concrete types for each $(\cdot \in \cdot)$ constraint (Section 2.2) incurs a compile-time overhead, as we must ensure that each $(\cdot \in \cdot)$ constraint is satisfied by the given list of concrete types. For example, for the DSL expression e with type $(\tau_1 \in as, \ldots, \tau_n \in as) \Rightarrow$ Exp as a we can impose any type of the form e :: Exp τs a provided each τ_i appears in τs. If τs contains m types then the cost of the static type check is $O(mn)$.

There is also a run-time overhead, however, which depends on how the type classes involved are implemented. In what follows we shall assume the use of a *dictionary transformation* as presented by Wadler and Blott [28] to explain in principle what must happen at run time. Each overloaded function used in a given implementation (e.g. toInt in compileSM) must be invoked at the correct type. This is *not* done by traversing a list of types, however, as no type information is retained at run time. Instead, each constraint in a function's type (e.g. $\mathcal{C} \Rightarrow \ldots$) is translated by the Haskell compiler into an additional argument ($\mathcal{C} \rightarrow \ldots$) that implements a *dictionary* of functions that correspond to a specific instance of the corresponding class (here $\mathcal{C}$). In our example above, the invocation of the functions toInt', evidence and the pattern match on Tail at different types results in the introduction of different dictionaries at runtime. When evidence (whose dictionary corresponds to the constraint $b \in (a : as)$) returns Head the dictionary argument of toInt' so happens, by construction, to contain the required instance of IntBool, i.e. the instance for either Int or Bool.

It is not necessary to understand how the dictionary transformation effects this at run time (see the work of Wadler and Blott [28] for full details), but suffice it to say that the cost of invoking toInt at type τ in the example above is linearly proportional to the index, n say, of τ in the list τs in the imposed type Exp τs a. In short, we do not end up 'searching' for the correct dictionary for τ at run time; instead toInt' is invoked exactly n times whereupon its additional dictionary argument provides the required τ instance of the IntBool class.

2.5 Single expression, multiple use

Let us now consider what happens if we wish to apply several constrained functions to a single DSL expression. Since we have so far only seen the compileSM function, let us introduce a similarly constrained pretty-printer:

```
pretty :: AllShowable as ⇒ Exp as a → String
```

Here the constraint AllShowable as provides a guarantee that every type in as has a textual representation. We might apply both compileSM and pretty to a single expression, for example:

```
f e = ... (compileSM e) ... (pretty e) ...
```

For this to type check, e must be an expression of type Exp as a. The use of compileSM requires the constraint AllIntBool as to be satisfied. Additionally, the use of pretty introduces the constraint AllShowable as. Assuming that no other context is required, f's type will thus be inferred as:

```
f :: (AllIntBool as, AllShowable as) ⇒ Exp as a → ...
```

Note that e's type, Exp as a, makes no reference to either platform – it is completely removed from any implementation. A corollary of this is that e's type is the same at the call sites of compileSM and pretty. If it were not, e would have to be defined as a *polymorphic* argument and f would require a rank-2 type [23, 27]. We shall see later in Section 8 some of the problems that rank-2 types can create, all of which we avoid. Furthermore, we show in Section 5.1 that even when rank-2 types must be introduced, the flexibility of our terms remains unaffected.

3. Higher-order constraints

While AllIntBool is a useful type class, its implementation is both non-trivial and tied to the needs of the compileSM function. Far better would be to write one type class which encapsulates the notion of traversing type-level lists and subsequently *parameterise* it by a particular platform-dependent constraint. Thanks to GHC's recently-added support for *constraint kinds* (based on the work of Orchard and Schrijvers [19]), we can do just that:

```
class All c as where
  ...
```

All's first parameter, c, is a *constraint constructor*. As an example, the idea is that instantiating c to be IntBool will recreate the definition of AllIntBool above. Of course, this will only be the case if toInt' is generalised appropriately. To this end, let's attempt to define a function withElem, say, that abstracts over the result type (Int, in the case of toInt' above) , which must now carry the constraint c b:

```
class All c as where
  withElem :: (b ∈ as) ⇒ Proxy as → (c b ⇒ d) → d
```

Unfortunately, while this is a valid type in the eyes of the type checker,[1] this leads to ambiguous type constraints because of the fact that constraints in Haskell 'float' to the leftmost position in a type. As an example, consider the toInt function above. Its type is IntBool $b \Rightarrow b \rightarrow$ Int, a seemingly perfect fit for the above, which we would like to lead to the type:

[1] Provided that higher-rank types are permitted.

```
withElem :: (b ∈ as) ⇒ Proxy as
         → (IntBool b ⇒ b → Int) → b → Int
```

However, the IntBool constraint is instead floated out to yield:

```
   (b ∈ as, IntBool b)
⇒  Proxy as → (c b ⇒ b → Int) → (b → Int)
```

which leaves an ambiguous constraint c b which the compiler is unable to solve. To mitigate this issue, we transform the constraint c b into a data type which 'traps' the relationship between c and b:

```
data Trap c b where
  Trap :: c b ⇒ Trap c b
```

Pattern matching on a constructor Trap of type Trap c b will bring into scope the constraint c b; similarly one may not create a value of type Trap c b unless the constraint c b is satisfiable. Thus we arrive at:

```
class All c as where
  withElem :: (b ∈ as) ⇒ Proxy as → (Trap c b → d) → d
```

The instances of All are now simple generalisations of the AllIntBool class above:

```
instance All c '[] where
  withElem _ (f :: Trap c b → d)
    = seq (evidence :: Evidence b '[]) ⊥
instance (c a, All c as) ⇒ All c (a : as) where
  withElem _ (f :: Trap c b → d)
    = case evidence :: Evidence b (a : as) of
        Head → f Trap
        Tail → withElem (Proxy :: Proxy as) f
```

Note that the second instance requires Haskell's support for *undecidable instances* [22] as the type system cannot decide whether the constraint expressions c a and All c $(a : as)$ can ever be the same, in which case the type checker will loop. In this case it is easy to see that no instantiation of c can ever satisfy this property, not least because c a makes no reference to as.

To illustrate the use of withElem let's see how the compileSM function above can be defined in terms of an All c as constraint. In this case, withElem's second argument is a function of type Trap IntBool b → String and its job is to show the integer representation of a given b. The constraint that b is an instance of IntBool is now captured by a Trap value of type Trap IntBool b which must be named explicitly in a type signature:

```
compileSM :: All IntBool as ⇒ Exp as a → String
compileSM (ValueE x)
  = "PUSH " ++ withElem (Proxy :: Proxy as) (showInt x)
    ++ "\n"
   where
    showInt :: b → Trap IntBool b → String
    showInt x Trap = show (toInt x)
```

The other two cases are unchanged. Without the explicit type signature, the type of showInt would be inferred as:

```
showInt :: IntBool b ⇒ b → Trap c b → String
```

where the dictionary has an unconstrained (polymorphic) type. We must instead enforce the IntBool constraint on the dictionary itself; in short, we want a specific instance of showInt's principal type that enforces the constraint relationship between IntBool and b.

4. Summary

The basic apparatus we need is now in place, so this is a good point at which to summarise. We have shown that we can shift platform-specific type constraints from a DSL's embedding data type to the corresponding function(s) over that data type using the steps outlined below. At this point we'll assume we're working with tagged representations using GADTs, but we'll see shortly (Section 5) how the approach generalises to tagless representations.

1. Add generic constraints to each constructor's type signature that collectively identify the minimal set of types that must be supported on a given platform in order for the constructor to be used. For example, for a GADT $\mathcal{T}$ with constructor $\mathcal{C}$:

   data $\mathcal{T}$ as a **where**
   $\mathcal{C}$ :: (Eq a, $a \in as$, Char $\in as, \ldots,$ Int $\in as$)
   $\Rightarrow \mathcal{T}$ as $a \rightarrow \mathcal{T}$ as Char $\rightarrow \cdots \rightarrow \mathcal{T}$ as Int

   where as represents *symbolically* a list of types. The key point is that these generic constraints enumerate not only the basic constraints such as Eq a but also constraints on the result type (here Int) and, importantly, existential types that are otherwise invisible outside the type (here a and Char).

2. Make each overloaded function f for which there is a platform-specific implementation a member of some type class $\mathcal{P}$ that encodes the platform constraint, for example:

   class $\mathcal{P}$ a **where** $f :: a \rightarrow \ldots$

   and define appropriate instances for each platform.

3. For a platform function p over the DSL data type $\mathcal{T}$ use higher-order constraint classes such as All to specify the type restrictions imposed on as by p, for example:

   p :: All $\mathcal{P}$ $as \Rightarrow \mathcal{T}$ as $a \rightarrow \ldots$

4. Apply the platform function to a given DSL expression, e, say, by picking a specific type list as, for example,

   p (e :: $\mathcal{T}$ '[Int, Char, ...] a)

   This imposes the platform-specific constraints on e, rather than $\mathcal{T}$. Type-safety is ensured by virtue of the fact that the chosen as must be compatible both with the generic constraints in e's type and the platform constraints encoded in p's type in order for the application to type check.

5. Tagless representations

Up until now, we have focused on a GADT-based representation of DSLs. Tagless representations [5, 21] offer an alternative approach to embedding a domain-specific language using functions rather than data constructors. To illustrate this, let's construct a tagless encoding of our simple expression language using generic constraints:

```
class TaglessExp e where
  valueE :: (a ∈ as) ⇒ a → e as a
  eqE    :: (Eq a, a ∈ as, Bool ∈ as)
         ⇒ e as a → e as a → e as Bool
  condE  :: (a ∈ as, Bool ∈ as)
         ⇒ e as Bool → e as a → e as a
         → e as a
```

Functions over terms in this tagless representation are realised as *instances* of the TaglessExp type class. As an example, the compileSM function above that was previously defined over a GADT must now be recast in terms of a data type and a corresponding TaglessExp instance that defines the valueE, eqE and condE functions. The data type is straightforward and may make use of All:

```
newtype CompileSM as a
  = CompileSM (All IntBool as ⇒ String)
```

There is a small complication with the definition of valueE, which can be seen when we try to define the TaglessExp instance:

```
instance TaglessExp CompileSM where
  valueE x
    = ...
```

At this point we need to construct a Proxy of type Proxy as, but we have no as to refer to. The solution is to define a helper function valueE', whose type signature reaffirms the constraint $a \in as$ on x's type:

```
valueE' :: (a ∈ as) ⇒ a → CompileSM as a
valueE' x
  = CompileSM
      ("PUSH " ++ withElem (Proxy :: Proxy as) (showInt x)
        ++ "\n")
```

showInt is as defined earlier. We can now complete the instance:

```
instance TaglessExp CompileSM where
  valueE x
    = valueE' x
  eqE (CompileSM s1) (CompileSM s2)
    = CompileSM (s1 ++ s2 ++ "EQ\n")
  condE (CompileSM p) (CompileSM t) (CompileSM f)
    = CompileSM $
        p ++ "CMP #0\n" ++ "BEQ L1\n" ++ t ++
          "BR L2\n" ++ "L1: " ++ f ++ "L2 :"
```

A function for compiling an expression to our stack machine can now be built simply by picking the correct instance of the TaglessExp class:

```
compileSM :: All IntBool as ⇒ CompileSM as a → String
compileSM (CompileSM s) = s
```

5.1 Rank-2 types

In contrast with GADT representations, tagless encodings are by construction parameterised by the implementation they target (e). Consequently, invoking multiple implementations of a single expression is not possible with the definitions given so far. Assuming the presence of Pretty, a tagless implementation of a pretty-printer, we may revisit our earlier example:

```
f e = ... (compileSM e) ... (pretty e) ...
```

f will not type check. To see why, assume that the type checker reaches compileSM first, whereupon the type variable e will be instantiated (via unification) to the type CompileSM, associated with the compiler. When the type checker later reaches the application of pretty, the checker will attempt a similar thing for the pretty printer, but will now attempt to unify the types CompileSM (the instantiation of e) and Pretty and that unification will fail. This is the classic limitation of rank-1 types: the type variable e can be instantiated to any type for which there is a corresponding TaglessExp instance, but it cannot be changed once it has been picked.

We may alleviate this problem by giving f a rank-2 type [23, 27], but better would be to close our terms once and for all:

```
newtype AnyTaglessExp as a
  = AnyTaglessExp (∀e. TaglessExp e ⇒ e as a)
```

f may now be rewritten to accept a value of type AnyTaglessExp:

```
f (AnyTaglessExp e) = ... (compileSM e) ... (pretty e) ...
```

A key point to note is that the type being constrained, as, 'escapes' the rank-2 type of AnyTaglessExp. In effect, AnyTaglessExp is equivalent to the Exp GADT introduced earlier.

6. Exploiting kind polymorphism: restricting operations

The previous sections have demonstrated how we may restrict the types of values that are introduced into a computation. We shall see now that we may also bound the *operations* that are used in an expression, thanks in part to GHC's support for *kind polymorphism* [29].

Thus far, the $(\cdot \in \cdot)$ and All type classes have been used to constrain lists of kind $[\star]$. However, their definitions afford them the following, more general kinds (note that Constraint is the kind of type class constraints – Show a or Eq b, for example):

$$(\cdot \in \cdot) :: \forall\kappa.\ \kappa \to [\kappa] \to \mathsf{Constraint}$$
$$\mathsf{All} \quad :: \forall\kappa.\ (\kappa \to \mathsf{Constraint}) \to [\kappa] \to \mathsf{Constraint}$$

Here, as one might expect, κ may be instantiated to *any kind*. What does this buy? Consider extending Exp to record the operations, os say, in addition to the types, that are used in the construction of an expression:

```
data Exp as os a where
  ...
```

We would like to use the $(\cdot \in \cdot)$ type class to constrain os, similar to the way we constrained types using as. We can achieve this by promoting the constructors of a data type such as:

```
data Op = EqOp | CondOp
```

to the type level. The modifications required to Exp are straightforward:

```
data Exp as os a where
  ValueE :: (a ∈ as) ⇒ a → Exp as os a
  EqE    :: (Eq a, a ∈ as, Bool ∈ as, EqOp ∈ os)
            ⇒ Exp as os a → Exp as os a → Exp as os Bool
  CondE  :: (a ∈ as, Bool ∈ as, CondOp ∈ os)
            ⇒ Exp as os Bool → Exp as os a → Exp as os a
            → Exp as os a
```

Note: we would ideally like to be able to promote the consructors of the Exp type itself, as in:

```
data Exp as os a where
  ...
  EqE :: (Eq a, a ∈ as, Bool ∈ as, EqE ∈ os)
         ⇒ Exp as os a → Exp as os a → Exp as os Bool
```

for example. However, Haskell does not allow the promotion of GADTs, as that would require coercions between kinds rather than the rather simpler notion of α-equivalence [29].

Given the modified version of Exp above, we may now pick and choose which operations are permitted in a given implementation. As an example, suppose we wish to generate code for an architecture in which conditional branching is undesirable (Nvidia's CUDA platform, for example). Once again, a type class may be defined to capture the operations that are supported:

```
class CUDACompatible o
instance CUDACompatible EqOp
```

The extension of CUDACompatible over a list os is then handled by the All class:

```
compileCUDA :: All CUDACompatible os
               ⇒ Exp as os a → String
compileCUDA
  = ...
```

(We omit the details of a full CUDA compiler!)

6.1 Combining types and operations

Parameterising Exp by both the types it contains (as) and the operations it uses (os) seems a little cumbersome. Another approach is to use some form of union operation, but at the type level. For example, we can use a promoted version of Haskell's Either type:

```
data Either a b = Left a | Right b
```

With this, Exp can instead be parameterised by a single list, ts, of kind [Either $\star$ Op]; each item of ts will be *either* a type *or* an operation:

```
data Exp ts a where
  ValueE :: (Left a ∈ ts) ⇒ a → Exp ts a
  EqE    :: (Eq a, Left a ∈ ts, Left Bool ∈ ts,
              Right EqOp ∈ ts)
            ⇒ Exp ts a → Exp ts a → Exp ts Bool
  CondE  :: (Left a ∈ ts, Left Bool ∈ ts,
              Right CondOp ∈ ts)
            ⇒ Exp ts Bool → Exp ts a → Exp ts a
            → Exp ts a
```

However, the All family of type classes introduced in Section 3 doesn't fit well with this because All constrains *all* items in a list, whereas we need to be able to constrain either the as (Left) or the os (Right). We must therefore adapt the class by decomposing it into a pair of classes, each designed to constrain one of the types present in the list:

```
class AllLeft c ts where
  withLeftElem  :: (Left a ∈ ts)
                   ⇒ Proxy ts → (Trap c a → d) → d
class AllRight c ts where
  withRightElem :: (Right b ∈ ts)
                   ⇒ Proxy ts → (Trap c b → d) → d
```

If we consider the AllLeft class (the workings of AllRight follow suit), we see that we now need *two* instances for (:) that will begin:

```
instance (c a, AllLeft c ts)
         ⇒ AllLeft c (Left a : ts) where
  ...
instance AllLeft c ts ⇒ AllLeft c (Right a : ts) where
  ...
```

In the first case a type Left a can only be added to the list ts if a satisfies the constraint c. The instance is thus similar to that given in the definition of All:

```
instance (c a, AllLeft c ts)
    ⇒ AllLeft c (Left a : ts) where
  withLeftElem _ (f :: Trap c b → d)
    = case evidence :: Evidence (Left b) (Left a : ts) of
        Head → f Trap
        Tail → withLeftElem (Proxy :: Proxy ts) f
```

As for the second instance, it is in fact simpler – types of the form Right a may be added to the list ts regardless:

```
instance AllLeft c ts ⇒ AllLeft c (Right a : ts) where
  withLeftElem _ (f :: Trap c b → d)
    = case evidence :: Evidence (Left b) (Right a : ts) of
        Tail → withLeftElem (Proxy :: Proxy ts) f
```

Despite the absence of a Head clause in the **case**-statement, this function is total so an attempt to pattern match on Head will be a type error: the compiler knows that the types Left b and Right a will never be unifiable (a fact which Head would contradict).

With these instances in place, we can now reason about types and operations simultaneously. For example, if we have a CUDA-capable GPU which does not support double-precision arithmetic, we might type its compiler thus:

```
compileCUDASP :: (AllLeft SinglePrecision ts,
                  AllRight CUDACompatible ts)
               ⇒ Exp ts as → String
```

Of course, we can generalise this still, to produce a type such as:

```
compileCUDASP :: (All Left SinglePrecision ts,
                  All Right CUDACompatible ts)
               ⇒ Exp ts as → String
```

in which there is once again a single All class. We omit the details of its implementation.

7. Operator overloading

The lists of types discussed in this paper are not so much built as *described* – the presence of a list as is established before being appropriately constrained. A side-effect of this is that every subexpression in a term will be parameterised by the same list as – only the constraints may differ at any given point. Importantly, this is precisely what is required to overload many of Haskell's operators to work with Exp values. As an example, consider the Num type class:

```
class Num a where
  (+), (−), (∗) :: a → a → a
  abs, signum   :: a → a
  fromInteger   :: Integer → a
```

Suppose that we wish to overload the $(+)$ operator on expressions in our DSL. To support this we'll need a new Exp constructor which, in the 'vanilla' GADT of Section 2 might look like this:

```
data Exp as a where
  ...
  AddE :: (a ∈ as)
       ⇒ Exp as a → Exp as a → Exp as a
```

We then seek an instance declaration that allows us to overload the $(+)$ operator in Haskell's Num class, which has type Num $a \Rightarrow a \rightarrow a \rightarrow a$. The required instance now falls out provided we work the $a \in as$ constraint into the instance header:

```
instance (a ∈ as) ⇒ Num (Exp as a) where
  (+) = AddE
```

Extending this procedure appropriately across the Haskell Prelude's wealth of overloadable functions, we see that it is possible to hide much of the machinery of our technique from the end user. In fact, the only evidence will be the need to supply an instantiation for each type-level list accumulated. For example, let us take our example term, eMixed, and make it more palatable:

```
eMixed
  = if 3 ≡Exp 4 then 0.0 else 3.9
```

Here we have used GHC's support for rebindable syntax to overload Haskell's **if**-**then**-**else** expression. The literals 3 and 4 are translated into the applications fromInteger 3 and fromInteger 4 respectively, where fromInteger is a member of the Num class described earlier. In a similar fashion, the floating-point literals are rewritten as calls to the overloaded fromRational function. Haskell's equality operator, $(\equiv)$, is overloadable also, but perhaps ironically is one of a set of operators which do not work nicely with many DSLs. In our case, for example, we would like to implement $(\equiv)$ using the EqE constructor, which has type:

```
(Eq a, a ∈ as) ⇒ Exp as a → Exp as a → Exp as Bool
```

Unfortunately, $(\equiv)$'s type, while overloaded in its arguments (through the Eq class), must always produce a Bool:

```
Eq a ⇒ a → a → Bool
```

We have therefore defined and used an alternative operator, $(\equiv_{\mathsf{Exp}})$, which provides the parametricity we need. For additional convenience we have also specialised $(\equiv_{\mathsf{Exp}})$'s type so that it compares integer expressions only: if its type were to be made more general then we would require type annotations. This is not a problem specific to our technique, however: it is a consequence of the fact that the argument types of EqE (which implements the $(\equiv_{\mathsf{Exp}})$ function) are existential (i.e. they do not appear in the type of its result). Consequently they must be fixed before the type checker is willing to discard the knowledge of their existence. There are alternative solutions to such problems which are common in DSL design, but these fall outside the scope of this paper.

8. The type restriction problem revisited

As we hinted in Section 1 the problem we began with can be solved for the case of rank-1 types using a scheme analogous to that presented by Hughes [11]. The purpose of this section is to outline that solution and to show how it breaks down in the presence of higher-rank types. The idea is to abstract not only over the result type of an expression, but also the target platform itself. By 'target platform' we really mean some abstraction of a specific use of the DSL, although the word 'platform' is particularly appropriate when we think of compiling DSLs.

We first capture the notion that a type a is 'supported by', or is 'typeable on', a particular platform using a type class:

```
class Typeable p a
  valueP :: a → p a
```

We can now use this to specify the constraints on DSL expressions:

```
data Exp p a where
  ValueE :: Typeable p a ⇒ a → Exp p a
  CondE  :: Exp p Bool → Exp p a → Exp p a → Exp p a
  EqE    :: Eq a ⇒ Exp p a → Exp p a → Exp p Bool
```

Here, Exp has been parameterised by a type p which represents the target platform. The ValueE constructor can only be used to lift values whose types are statically known to be representable in the domain of the type p (through the valueP function). Note that while we have once again constrained ValueE's type, the constraint does not tie expressions down to a specific target platform. As an example, compileSM might now be implemented as follows:

```
newtype SM a = SM {fromSM :: Int}

instance IntBool a ⇒ Typeable SM a where
  valueP = SM · toInt

compileSM :: Exp SM a → String
compileSM (ValueE x)
  = "PUSH " ++ show (fromSM (valueP x)) ++ "\n"
```

with the other two cases unchanged. In the ValueE clause, Typeable has taken the role of the IntBool class above whilst valueP is an abstraction of toInt.

So far so good! But let's now build a second function over the DSL in a similar way; here a pretty-printer:

```
newtype Pretty a = Pretty {fromPretty :: String}
```

```
instance Show a => Typeable Pretty a where
  valueP = Pretty · show

pretty :: Exp Pretty a -> String
pretty (ValueE x)
  = fromPretty (valueP x)
pretty (EqE e1 e2)
  = "(" ++ pretty e1 ++ " == " ++ pretty e2 ++ ")"
pretty (CondE p t f)
  = "(if " ++ pretty p ++ " then " ++ pretty t ++
      " else " ++ pretty f ++ ")"
```

This is also perfectly valid and, what's more, it doesn't interfere with compileSM in the sense that neither has restricted the uses of the DSL. However, now suppose that we wish to apply the two functions to the *same* expression, as in:

```
f :: Exp p a -> ...
f e = ... (compileSM e) ... (pretty e) ...
```

Type checking the applications of compileSM and pretty will result in the instantiation of p to two different types, namely SM and Pretty. f will therefore fail to type check. This is exactly the problem we saw in Section 5.1 and is a direct result of representing the target platform in an expression's type.

8.1 Hidden types

As we have seen earlier, the usual solution is to introduce a rank-2 type. Let's first try to attach a quantifier to the expression data type:

```
newtype AnyExp a = AnyExp (∀p. Exp p a)
```

f may now be rewritten to accept a value of type AnyExp a as its argument:

```
f :: AnyExp a -> ...
f (AnyExp e) = ... (compileSM e) ... (pretty e) ...
```

Does this solve the problem? No! Let's see why:

```
AnyExp (ValueE False)
```

The above expression will not type check due to a missing Typeable p Bool constraint in the type of AnyExp. Of course, we can fix this by altering AnyExp's type:

```
newtype AnyExp a
  = AnyExp (∀p. Typeable p a => Exp p a)
```

but this will only get us so far. Let's now consider an application of AnyExp to the eMixed expression given in Section 2, which harbours more than one type of ValueE application:

```
AnyExp $
  CondE
    (EqE (ValueE (3 :: Int)) (ValueE (4 :: Int)))
      (ValueE (0.0 :: Float))
      (ValueE (3.9 :: Float))
```

AnyExp's type provides us with the constraint Typeable p Float, but we also need Typeable p Int. We now have a new problem: the constraint Typeable p a can only be verified with respect to the *top-level* expression type; what the type checker needs is a guarantee that *every* type in the expression is typeable on p. To capture this we need to add a constraint to AnyExp for *every* type that we ever expect to encounter in our DSL, thus:

```
newtype AnyExp a
  = AnyExp (∀p. (Typeable p τ1,
                 Typeable p τ2,
                 ...
                 Typeable p τn) => Exp p a)
```

which is a mess! Worse still, *every* platform must now support *at least* the types $\tau_1, \ldots, \tau_n$ which defeats the purpose of abstracting p in the first place!

Suppose instead, we try to constrain the type of each function over the DSL instead, as in:

```
f :: (∀p. Exp p a) -> ...
```

We encounter exactly the same problem as above, but now the constraints are at least localised to the function:

```
f :: (∀p. (Typeable p σ1,
           Typeable p σ2,
           ...
           Typeable p σm) => Exp p a) -> ...
```

where now $\sigma_1, \ldots, \sigma_m$ is an enumeration of all the types common to the instances of p that f requires for its definition (SM and Pretty in the example above). Once again the need to enumerate all these constraints defeats the purpose of abstracting over the platform.

9. Related work

The separation of interface from implementation is a well understood problem. Dynamically typed languages such as Ruby and Python are very flexible in this respect (particularly with regard to DSL embedding) but offer none of the static guarantees we seek in this paper. In contrast, Scala [18] is a statically typed language designed with DSL embedding in mind. Hofer et al. present a technique for embedding DSLs [10] in Scala which is not unrelated to the tagless encodings [5, 21] discussed earlier. Their scheme does not consider the potential consequences of 'impedance mismatches' between multiple implementations, however.

In the functional programming community, Haskell has shown to be a popular host language for a wide variety of embedded DSLs, many of which have been designed to exploit parallelism [1, 2, 7, 15]. Nikola [15] only supports values of type Float so the issues addressed by this paper do not arise. Accelerate [7] is an example of a more powerful language that has been designed with multiple targets in mind but where the designers have opted to constrain the DSL at the point of definition to identify explicitly a single set of supported types. A number of unpublished articles and mailing list discussions raise the issue of data type restriction as defined in this paper: a few offer solutions similar to the one outlined in Section 8. [2]

Phantom types [14] are an alternative tool which may be used for embedding DSLs in which the underlying representation of the DSL is essentially untyped [8]. This offers the designer flexibility when writing functions such as compileSM, but means that a carefully chosen type-safe interface must be exported to the end-user. In our approach we have chosen not to make such a compromise, though the lists of types we use are themselves phantom types, having no impact on a value's representation. Kiselyov's work on implicit configurations [12] also makes use of phantom types and could be applied in the context of constraining data types, though this has not been investigated. Pantheon [25] and Eden [9] are examples of how Template Haskell [26] may be used effectively to manipulate DSLs at compile-time. While this paper has not focused on compile-time techniques, we discuss some potential opportunities in this domain in Section 10.

Dependently typed systems, such as those exhibited by Agda [17] and Idris [3] have already been shown to be useful in DSL construction [4, 20]. They, and the work on SHE [16] have inspired many of the newly-added Haskell features exploited in this paper. However, as we have already pointed out, we only leverage these features

[2] `http://www.haskell.org/pipermail/haskell-cafe/2011-November/096699.html` discusses a technique which uses constraint kinds, for example.

without depending upon them. HList [13] is a Haskell library for working with type-level lists and provides a far greater range of operations and features than those described here.

10. Future work

10.1 Automatic constraint generation

As hinted at in Section 2, we could add generic constraints to the constructors of a type (or equally, the class methods of a tagless representation) mechanically in many cases. In the case of annotating a GADT, $\mathcal{T}$, of kind $\star \to \star$, for example, a naïve algorithm for doing this might proceed as follows:

- Parameterise all occurrences of $\mathcal{T}$ by a list of types as, giving it the new kind $[\star] \to \star \to \star$.
- For each of $\mathcal{T}$'s constructors, $\mathcal{C} :: \tau_1 \to \cdots \to \tau_n \to \mathcal{T}\ as\ a$, add a constraint $b \in as$ for each τ of the form $\mathcal{T}\ as\ b$.

Template Haskell [26] is an extension to Haskell that provides facilities for compile-time metaprogramming (CTMP), and a tool that could be used to implement the above transformation. More interesting however is the question of whether or not a platform's specification (IntBool and its instances, for example) can be generated from a description of the platform at compile-time. Considering our CUDA example from Section 6, it might be possible to infer that the use of conditional operations should be prevented given some first-class representation of the fact that it is a single instruction, multiple thread (SIMT) architecture.

10.2 Eliminating type annotations

Somewhat frustrating is the need to supply type annotations whenever a list of types is eliminated, viz.:

$$\mathsf{compileSM}\ (\mathsf{ValueE}\ 3 :: \mathsf{Exp}\ '[\mathsf{Int}]\ \mathsf{Int})$$

In the case of compileSM, this burden may be removed by creating a compiler with a more grounded type signature:

```
compileSM' :: Exp '[Int, Bool] a → String
compileSM' = compileSM
```

Such a definition permits the expression compileSM' (ValueE 3) while others such as compileSM' eMixed are rejected as ill-typed. This technique will not suffice for all targets however. Consider a Haskell evaluator for our GADT expressions:

```
evaluate :: Exp as a → a
evaluate (ValueE x)     = x
evaluate (EqE e1 e2)    = evaluate e1 ≡ evaluate e2
evaluate (CondE p t f) = if evaluate p
                            then evaluate t
                            else evaluate f
```

In this case there are an infinite number of types we could instantiate as to. This is particularly annoying when, given a principal type, there is a mechanical translation from its list of $(\cdot \in \cdot)$ constraints to a minimal satisfying list of types. For example, the type:

$$(\mathsf{Int} \in as, \mathsf{Bool} \in as, \mathsf{Float} \in as) \Rightarrow \mathsf{Exp}\ as\ \mathsf{Float}$$

may always be instantiated to:

$$\mathsf{Exp}\ '[\mathsf{Int}, \mathsf{Bool}, \mathsf{Float}]\ \mathsf{Float}$$

Each constraint of the form $a \in as$ results in the type a being added to the list of types we shall pick. We can encode this type-level function directly, using either GADTs or GHC's support for *type families* [6]:

```
type family Satisfying (c :: Constraint) :: [⋆]
type instance Satisfying (a ∈ as)     = '[a]
type instance Satisfying (a ∈ as, c) = a : Satisfying c
```

However, using such a family proves impossible without a type annotation due to the issues involved in 'trapping' type classes mentioned in Section 3 (see the case for Trap). Furthermore, we would then have to convince the compiler that the type Satisfying c really does satisfy the constraint c. We expect that such a process is non-trivial but it merits further investigation.

10.2.1 Making use of metaprogramming

If we are willing to ask for the compiler's help, Template Haskell provides a function reify which allows one to obtain information about an identifier at compile-time. This includes an ADT representation of the identifier's type, from which we can surely implement the translation realised as a type family above. Moreover, since such an instantiation would occur during type checking, the compiler would be able to verify whether or not the types picked satisfy the constraints being eliminated. However, due to some of Template Haskell's practical limitations, such as not being able to reify names defined in the same module (see the work of Sheard and Peyton Jones [26] for more information), we have not yet implemented such functionality. A key point also is that reify can only operate on *named* values. In this respect it would be beneficial to have something similar to C++'s `decltype` operator, which is capable of returning the declared type of an arbitrary expression.

11. Conclusions

We have presented what is essentially a design pattern for the type-safe separation of an interface from multiple implementations. Each implementation may enforce different typing requirements and restrictions on a data type without limiting other uses of the same type. Interestingly, in some situations we are able to support an element of re-use that would ordinarily require the introduction of a rank-2 type, for example when applying multiple functions to the same DSL expression. This turns out to be useful when building DSL compilers for exploiting heterogeneous data parallelism, for example, where we may need to implement a DSL program on more than one target architecture. When there is a need for higher-rank types, for example to support the same type of re-use in a tagless DSL representation, our method applies equally well. The idea of imposing only generic, rather than concrete, constraints on a data type thus has a number of advantages.

Somewhat as an aside, we have also found many of Haskell's latest type features, in particular first-class constraints and type promotion, to be very useful, although, as we have noted, it is possible to achieve the same effect without them.

References

[1] L. Augustsson, H. Mansell, and G. Sittampalam. Paradise: A Two-Stage DSL Embedded in Haskell. In *Proceedings of the 13th ACM SIGPLAN International Conference on Functional Programming*, ICFP '08, pages 225–228, New York, NY, USA, 2008. ACM. ISBN 978-1-59593-919-7.

[2] E. Axelsson, K. Claessen, M. Sheeran, J. Svenningsson, D. Engdal, and A. Persson. The Design and Implementation of Feldspar - An Embedded Language for Digital Signal Processing. In *Proceedings of the 22nd Symposium on Implementation and Application of Functional Languages*, Lecture Notes in Computer Science, pages 121–136. Springer-Verlag, 2010. ISBN 978-3-642-24275-5.

[3] E. C. Brady. IDRIS – Systems Programming Meets Full Dependent Types. In *Proceedings of the 5th ACM Workshop on Programming Languages Meets Program Verification*, PLPV '11, pages 43–54, New York, NY, USA, 2011. ACM. ISBN 978-1-4503-0487-0.

[4] E. C. Brady and K. Hammond. Scrapping your Inefficient Engine: Using Partial Evaluation to Improve Domain-Specific Language Implementation. *ACM SIGPLAN Notices*, 45(9):297–308, September 2010. ISSN 0362-1340.

[5] J. Carette, O. Kiselyov, and C. chieh Shan. Finally Tagless, Partially Evaluated: Tagless Staged Interpreters for Simpler Typed Languages. *Journal of Functional Programming*, 19:509–543, September 2009. ISSN 0956-7968.

[6] M. M. T. Chakravarty, G. Keller, S. Peyton Jones, and S. Marlow. Associated Types with Class. In *Proceedings of the 32nd ACM SIGPLAN-SIGACT Symposium on Principles of Programming Languages*, POPL '05, pages 1–13, New York, NY, USA, 2005. ACM. ISBN 1-58113-830-X.

[7] M. M. T. Chakravarty, G. Keller, S. Lee, T. L. McDonell, and V. Grover. Accelerating Haskell Array Codes with Multicore GPUs. In *Proceedings of the 6th Workshop on Declarative Aspects of Multicore Programming*, DAMP '11, pages 3–14, New York, NY, USA, 2011. ACM. ISBN 978-1-4503-0486-3.

[8] C. Elliott, S. Finne, and O. de Moor. Compiling Embedded Languages. *Journal of Functional Programming*, 13(3):455–481, 2003. ISSN 0956-7968.

[9] K. Hammond, J. Berthold, and R. Loogen. Automatic Skeletons in Template Haskell. *Parallel Processing Letters*, 13(3):413–424, September 2003. ISSN 0129-6264.

[10] C. Hofer, K. Ostermann, T. Rendel, and A. Moors. Polymorphic Embedding of DSLs. In *Proceedings of the 7th International Conference on Generative Programming and Component Engineering*, GPCE '08, pages 137–148, New York, NY, USA, 2008. ACM. ISBN 978-1-60558-267-2.

[11] J. Hughes. Restricted Data Types in Haskell. In *Proceedings of the 1999 Haskell Workshop*. University of Utrecht, Technical Report UU-CS-1999-28, October 1999.

[12] O. Kiselyov and C. chieh Shan. Functional Pearl: Implicit Configurations–or, Type Classes Reflect the Values of Types. In *Proceedings of the 2004 ACM SIGPLAN Workshop on Haskell*, Haskell '04, pages 33–44, New York, NY, USA, 2004. ACM. ISBN 1-58113-850-4.

[13] O. Kiselyov, R. Lämmel, and K. Schupke. Strongly Typed Heterogeneous Collections. In *Proceedings of the 2004 ACM SIGPLAN Workshop on Haskell*, Haskell '04, pages 96–107, New York, NY, USA, 2004. ACM. ISBN 1-58113-850-4.

[14] D. Leijen and E. Meijer. Domain-Specific Embedded Compilers. In *Proceedings of the 2nd Conference on Domain-Specific Languages - Volume 2*, DSL'99, pages 109–122, Berkeley, CA, USA, 1999. USENIX Association.

[15] G. Mainland and G. Morrisett. Nikola: Embedding Compiled GPU Functions in Haskell. In *Proceedings of the 3rd ACM Haskell Symposium*, Haskell '10, pages 67–78, New York, NY, USA, 2010. ACM. ISBN 978-1-4503-0252-4.

[16] C. McBride. Faking It: Simulating Dependent Types in Haskell. *Journal of Functional Programming*, 12:375–392, July 2002. ISSN 0956-7968.

[17] U. Norell. *Towards a Practical Programming Language based on Dependent Type Theory*. PhD thesis, Department of Computer Science and Engineering, Chalmers University of Technology, SE-412 96 Göteborg, Sweden, September 2007.

[18] M. Odersky, P. Altherr, V. Cremet, B. Emir, S. Maneth, S. Micheloud, N. Mihaylov, M. Schinz, E. Stenman, and M. Zenger. An Overview of the Scala Programming Language. Technical Report IC/2004/64, EPFL Lausanne, Switzerland, 2004.

[19] D. A. Orchard and T. Schrijvers. Haskell Type Constraints Unleashed. In *Proceedings of the 10th International Symposium on Functional and Logic Programming*, Lecture Notes in Computer Science, pages 56–71. Springer-Verlag, 2010. ISBN 978-3-642-12251-4.

[20] N. Oury and W. Swierstra. The Power of Pi. In *Proceedings of the 13th ACM SIGPLAN International Conference on Functional Programming*, ICFP '08, pages 39–50, New York, NY, USA, 2008. ACM. ISBN 978-1-59593-919-7.

[21] E. Pašalić, W. Taha, and T. Sheard. Tagless Staged Interpreters for Typed Languages. In *Proceedings of the 7th ACM SIGPLAN International Conference on Functional Programming*, ICFP '02, pages 218–229, New York, NY, USA, 2002. ACM. ISBN 1-58113-487-8.

[22] S. Peyton Jones, M. Jones, and E. Meijer. Type Classes: Exploring the Design Space. In *Proceedings of the 1997 Haskell Workshop*, 1997.

[23] S. Peyton Jones, D. Vytiniotis, S. Weirich, and M. Shields. Practical Type Inference for Arbitrary-Rank Types. *Journal of Functional Programming*, 17:1–82, January 2007. ISSN 0956-7968.

[24] T. Schrijvers, S. Peyton Jones, M. Sulzmann, and D. Vytiniotis. Complete and Decidable Type Inference for GADTs. In *Proceedings of the 14th ACM SIGPLAN International Conference on Functional Programming*, ICFP '09, pages 341–352, New York, NY, USA, 2009. ACM. ISBN 978-1-60558-332-7.

[25] S. Seefried, M. M. T. Chakravarty, and G. Keller. Optimising Embedded DSLs Using Template Haskell. In *GPCE '04*, volume 3286 of *Lecture Notes in Computer Science*, pages 186–205. Springer-Verlag, 2004. ISBN 3-540-23580-9.

[26] T. Sheard and S. Peyton Jones. Template Meta-Programming for Haskell. *SIGPLAN Notices*, 37:60–75, December 2002. ISSN 0362-1340.

[27] D. Vytiniotis, S. Weirich, and S. Peyton Jones. Boxy Types: Inference for Higher-Rank Types and Impredicativity. In *Proceedings of the 11th ACM SIGPLAN International Conference on Functional Programming*, ICFP '06, pages 251–262, New York, NY, USA, 2006. ACM. ISBN 1-59593-309-3.

[28] P. Wadler and S. Blott. How to Make Ad-Hoc Polymorphism Less Ad Hoc. In *Proceedings of the 16th ACM SIGPLAN-SIGACT Symposium on Principles of Programming Languages*, POPL '89, pages 60–76, New York, NY, USA, 1989. ACM. ISBN 0-89791-294-2.

[29] B. A. Yorgey, S. Weirich, J. Cretin, S. Peyton Jones, D. Vytiniotis, and J. P. M. aes. Giving Haskell a Promotion. In *Proceedings of the 8th ACM SIGPLAN Workshop on Types in Language Design and Implementation*, TLDI '12, pages 53–66, New York, NY, USA, 2012. ACM. ISBN 978-1-4503-1120-5.

Explicitly Heterogeneous Metaprogramming with MetaHaskell

Geoffrey Mainland
Microsoft Research
gmainlan@microsoft.com

Abstract

Languages with support for metaprogramming, like MetaOCaml, offer a principled approach to code generation by guaranteeing that well-typed metaprograms produce well-typed programs. However, many problem domains where metaprogramming can fruitfully be applied require generating code in languages like C, CUDA, or assembly. Rather than resorting to add-hoc code generation techniques, these applications should be directly supported by *explicitly heterogeneous* metaprogramming languages.

We present MetaHaskell, an extension of Haskell 98 that provides modular syntactic and type system support for type safe metaprogramming with multiple object languages. Adding a new object language to MetaHaskell requires only minor modifications to the host language to support type-level quantification over object language types and propagation of type equality constraints. We demonstrate the flexibility of our approach through three object languages: a core ML language, a linear variant of the core ML language, and a subset of C. All three languages support metaprogramming with open terms and guarantee that well-typed MetaHaskell programs will only produce closed object terms that are well-typed. The essence of MetaHaskell is captured in a type system for a simplified metalanguage. MetaHaskell, as well as all three object languages, are fully implemented in the `mhc` bytecode compiler.

Categories and Subject Descriptors D.3.3 [*Software*]: Programming Languages

General Terms Languages, Design

Keywords Metaprogramming, open terms, type systems, quasiquotation, linear languages

1. Introduction

Large bodies of widely-used scientific code, such as FFTW3 [14], ATLAS [40], and SPIRAL [29], are built using ad-hoc, custom code generators. Though code generators provide a certain kind of abstraction, allowing one program to express many different, specialized versions of a function, the implementer is typically consigned to a "`printf` purgatory" in which program fragments are represented as arrays of characters and the primary form of composition is string splicing.

ICFP'12, September 9–15, 2012, Copenhagen, Denmark.

Languages such as MetaML [37] and MetaOCaml [35] provide metaprogramming environments on the other end of the spectrum—they guarantee that well-typed metaprograms produce well-typed object programs. However, these languages focus on homogeneous metaprogramming, in which the metalanguage and object language are identical. This makes them less suited for applications that must generate code in some other object language. Ideally programmers could write type safe metaprograms and have flexibility in choosing an object language.

We take a step towards the goal of type safe heterogenous metaprogramming with MetaHaskell. We make the following contributions:

- A type system for an idealized metalanguage/object language pair that guarantees that well-typed metaprograms only ever produce closed object language terms that are well-typed. Object terms may contain free variables, and these free variables may be used polymorphically. To our knowledge, no other metaprogramming language allows free variables to be used polymorphically.
- MetaHaskell, a extension of Haskell 98 implemented in the `mhc` compiler that provides modular type system support for metaprogramming with multiple object languages.
- Three object language "plug-ins;" a core ML language, MiniML, a linear variant of the core ML language, Linear MiniML, and C♭. C♭ is a subset of C that is expressive enough to serve as a target for type safe, heterogeneous, run-time code generation which we demonstrate with a compiler for regular expression matchers.
- A methodology for converting a base language and type system into an object language and type system suitable for metaprogramming.

The rest of the paper is organized as follows. We give an overview of MetaHaskell through several small examples in Section 2. In Section 3 we outline our goals for a heterogeneous metaprogramming language. A simplified type system that captures the features of MetaHaskell that are relevant to metaprogramming is described in Section 4 along with the type system of MiniML, a small ML-like language. In Section 5 we show that our framework can accommodate even a substructural object language with little trouble. C♭, a C-like object language, is described in Section 6 in the context of a regular expression compiler that performs run-time code generation. We give some further details of our implementation in Section 7. Section 8 describes related work, and we conclude and describe future work in Section 9. The `mhc` compiler, which implements MetaHaskell and the object languages described in this paper, is publicly available.

2. MetaHaskell Basics

Syntactically, MetaHaskell builds on the quasiquotation feature of GHC [22]. Quasiquotation provides syntactic convenience when working with fragments of abstract syntax—instead of writing an inscrutable mess of constructor applications to build the abstract syntax tree representation of a term, the programmer can write the same term using concrete syntax. Given a quasiquoter, exp, that parses a "core" Haskell language, we can write the classic staged power function as follows.

```
power :: Int → Exp → Exp
power n x
      | n ≡ 0      = ⟦exp|1⟧
      | n ≡ 1      = ⟦exp| $x⟧
      | even n     = square (power (n ‘div‘ 2) x)
      | otherwise = ⟦exp| $x ∗ $(power (n − 1) x)⟧
  where
    square :: Exp → Exp
    square x = ⟦exp| $x ∗ $x⟧
```

The power function takes an integer n and an abstract syntax tree x and returns a new abstract syntax tree representing x raised to the power n. The syntax ⟦**exp**|·⟧ is a quasiquote. At compile time, the argument between the brackets is passed as a string constant to the quasiquoter exp which returns a Haskell expression represented using GHC's internal Haskell AST data type. The effect is just as if the programmer had written the equivalent Haskell term directly, but the syntax is usually much more pleasant. The quasiquoter will often support antiquotation, written here using the syntax $(...). Internally, exp parses the antiquotation as a Haskell expression and splices the result into the abstract syntax tree in place of the antiquotation. Antiquotation support is purely the responsibility of the quasiquoter, but its inclusion makes the mechanism vastly more useful.

We have used quasiquotation for the purposes of code generation in past work in the context of sensor networks [25] and GPUs [24]. It is also used to support quasiquotation of perl and Ruby-style interpolated strings, regular expressions, parser grammars [15], and JavaScript [3] among other applications. Though quasiquotation provides syntactic convenience and some type safety since it supports terms represented using algebraic data types instead of strings, the terms it produces are still fundamentally untyped. There is nothing to stop the programmer from passing the power function a value of type Exp that represents a *string* expression. A Haskell program containing this call to power will happily type check only to generate an ill-typed core Haskell term at run-time.

We would like to do better. Rather than building a Haskell term of type Exp, our quasiquoter should build a Haskell term with a more accurate type. Ideally, it would build a term with a type that is somehow isomorphic to the type the quoted term has *in the type system of the quoted language*. That is, when we quote a term in core Haskell, it should receive a core Haskell type suitably lifted to Haskell. MetaHaskell allows quasiquoters to reflect object language types into the Haskell type system. We can write the same power function, now with more accurate types.

```
power :: ∀γ.Int → ⟦exp|γ ▷ Int⟧ → ⟦exp|γ ▷ Int⟧
power n x
      | n ≡ 0      = ⟦exp|1⟧
      | n ≡ 1      = ⟦exp| $x⟧
      | even n     = square (power (n ‘div‘ 2) x)
      | otherwise = ⟦exp| $x ∗ $(power (n − 1) x)⟧
  where
    square :: ∀γ.⟦exp|γ ▷ Int⟧ → ⟦exp|γ ▷ Int⟧
    square x = ⟦exp| $x ∗ $x⟧
```

Only the type signatures have changed. Although we have written them out explicitly here, these types appear exactly as they would be inferred by MetaHaskell. As well as expressions, object language types can be quoted. The type ⟦**exp**|γ ▷ Int⟧ is the type of code that, in any type environment γ, has type Int. That is, object terms can be polymorphic in their typing environment. Note that we quantify over γ at the *metalanguage* level. We discuss this further in Section 4.

MetaHaskell quasiquoters provide strong typing of object language terms by plugging in to the metalanguage's type system. In all object languages we describe, object language types are refinements of Haskell types. For example, in the case of power, we refined the Haskell type Exp of abstract syntax trees. The run-time representation of a quasiquoted object term is just the corresponding abstract syntax term with an unrefined type. This means that, at run-time, we can convert an object language term to its abstract syntax representation via a safe erase function defined in terms of unsafeCoerce.

```
erase :: ∀γ, α.⟦exp|γ ▷ α⟧ → Exp
erase = unsafeCoerce
```

2.1 Safe run-time code generation

Strongly typed quasiquotation guarantees that only well-typed object language terms will be constructed, at least up until the point of erasure, but we can use it for more than just generating abstract syntax. Consider again our power function, but imagine instead that we wish to generate a specialized version of the power function at run-time as MetaOCaml would allow. MetaHaskell includes support for the C♭ object language, a restricted form of C, as well as a quasiquoter for C♭ functions that instead of producing a value whose run-time representation is an abstract syntax tree, produces a pointer to an actual compiled function. A code-generating version of the power function, cpower, can be written as follows. As with power, the type signatures for both go and cpower are not necessary as they would be inferred by MetaHaskell as shown.

```
cpower :: Int → FunPtr (CDouble → IO CDouble)
cpower n
    ⟦cfun|double pown (double x)
          {double r;
           $stms:(reverse (go n))
           return r;
          }⟧
    )
  where
    go :: ∀γ.Int → [⟦cstm|{double x; double r} γ ▷ void⟧]
    go n | n ≡ 0      = [⟦cstm|r = 1.0⟧]
         | n ≡ 1      = [⟦cstm|r = x; ⟧]
         | even n     = ⟦cstm|r = r ∗ r; ⟧:go (n ‘div‘ 2)
         | otherwise = ⟦cstm|r∗= x; ⟧   :go (n − 1)
```

We note several aspects of MetaHaskell that are newly illustrated by cpower. First of all, ⟦**cfun**|·⟧ takes a quoted function and returns a FunPtr—the type of foreign function pointers in Haskell's foreign function interface—indexed by the Haskell translation of the quoted function's type. That is, because the quoted function `pown` has the C♭ type `double (*)(double)`, the index to FunPtr is its translation, CDouble → IO CDouble. This is in contrast to power, which returned a value with an object language type. Because ⟦**cfun**|·⟧ performs run-time code generation and therefore requires the quoted function to be closed, attempting to quote an open C♭ function using ⟦**cfun**|·⟧ results in a compile-time error.

Also in contrast to the core Haskell quasiquoter, C♭ provides quasiquoters for *multiple* syntactic categories. We use the ⟦**cstm**|·⟧ quasiquoter to build up the body of the `pown` function via recursive calls to go. The ⟦**cstm**|·⟧ quasiquoter *does* return a value with an object language type—the type of the quoted C♭ statement. The type of go reflects the fact that it returns a list of statements, each of which is valid in a type environment where the variables `x` and `r` have type `double`. The implementation of cpower uses C♭'s ability to antiquote lists of statements to build the body of `pown`.

2.2 Why not GADT's?

This seems like a lot of trouble to go to when GADTs [41] suffice to write the power function. A quasiquoter has three basic jobs. First, it provides concrete syntax for an object language. Second, it embodies a decision procedure that provides a type—which may be an object language type—for the quoted term (and its antiquotations). Third, it must reflect the type provided by the decision procedure into the host language.

The first job is no different from that performed by quasiquoters as implemented in GHC—it is a purely syntactic task. We argue that the second job—performing type inference on object terms—is useful even when object language types have a strong encoding in the metalanguage's type system, i.e., when the encoding is injective. For example, although GADTs can encode open lambda terms [1], dealing with the structural rules required to work with such terms involves a great deal of bookkeeping—exactly the sort of bookkeeping that a type inference procedure automates. Furthermore, it is not clear how often an object language's type system has a strong encoding in Haskell with GADTs. Consider the following MetaHaskell term.

$$\mathsf{polyopen} = [\![\mathbf{exp}|(\mathsf{f}\ 1, \mathsf{f}\ \mathsf{True})]\!]$$

This MetaHaskell term, which uses the free variable f polymorphically, has the following type.

$$\forall \alpha, \beta, \rho, \gamma . [\![\mathbf{exp}|\{\mathsf{f} :: [\mathsf{Int} \to \alpha ; \mathsf{Bool} \to \beta]\,\rho\}\gamma \rhd (\alpha, \beta)]\!]$$

This type states that the quoted term is valid in any type environment that contains at least a binding for f, that the binding for f must have at least *both* the types $\mathsf{Int} \to \alpha$ and $\mathsf{Bool} \to \beta$, and that in such an environment the quoted expression has type (α, β). We give further details in Section 4, but suffice to say that inference is tricky and the appropriate GADT encoding for such a type is not immediately obvious. However, even if our host language were a language like Coq, which in this case would ensure a strong embedding of the object language type system, we would still like to have access to the decision procedure embodied in the object language quasiquoter and a framework for object language integration.

3. Design Goals

Before proceeding, we outline our design goals for a heterogeneous metaprogramming languages. In what follows we primarily use small, idealized object and metalanguages. Rather than utilizing the concrete MetaHaskell syntax seen in Section 2, we use MetaML-like syntax for quotation and antiquotation. For example, in the following expression, the body of the lambda is a quotation containing the antiquoted term f 1.

$$\lambda f \to \langle\!\langle (\mathtt{g}\ 1, \tilde{\ }(f\ 1)) \rangle\!\rangle$$

- **Syntactic support:** The programmer should be able to write object terms using the object language's syntax.
- **Antiquotation:** The metalanguage should allow abstraction over object language sub-terms. That is, object terms should be able to contain antiquoted sub-terms.
- **Heterogeneity:** The metalanguage should provide support for multiple object languages in the same overall framework. Ideally, support for new object languages can be added to the metalanguage in a modular way that require little or no modification of the metalanguage implementation.
- **Type soundness:** Well-typed metaprograms should only generate well-typed object terms.
- **Type inference:** The metalanguage should be able to infer the types of object terms without excessive programmer burden. Annotations on the level of those that Haskell requires for, e.g., impredicative instantiation, are reasonable. If the object language's type checker can infer the type of an object term, then the metalanguage's type inference engine should be able to infer the type of the same object term when it appears in a metaprogram.
- **Open object terms:** The metalanguage should permit object terms with free variables. Ideally, inference for open object terms would not require additional programmer annotations. This would allow us to quote object language fragments like the C expression $\langle\!\langle \mathsf{sin}\ (\mathsf{x}) \rangle\!\rangle$, where both sin and x are free.
- **Subterm typability:** If an object term is well-typed, then any of its sub-terms, when appearing in isolation, should also be well-typed.
- **Subterm abstractability:** We want the property that, at the metalanguage level, we can perform β-abstraction over object language sub-terms. That is, we want to be able to abstract over any sub-term of an object term, apply the abstraction to the abstracted sub-term, and have the new application be well-typed. Obviously we want preservation to hold, so if this application is well-typed, then it has the same type as the original term, which we would recover via β-reduction. For example, we want it to be the case that the metalanguage term

$$\langle\!\langle \underline{\mathtt{let}}\ \mathtt{f} = \lambda\mathtt{x} \to \mathtt{x}\ \underline{\mathtt{in}}\ (\mathtt{f}\ 1, \mathtt{f}\ \underline{\mathtt{true}}) \rangle\!\rangle$$

is equivalent to the metalanguage term

$$(\lambda e \to \langle\!\langle \underline{\mathtt{let}}\ \mathtt{f} = \lambda\mathtt{x} \to \mathtt{x}\ \underline{\mathtt{in}}\ \tilde{\ }e \rangle\!\rangle)\langle\!\langle (\mathtt{f}\ 1, \mathtt{f}\ \underline{\mathtt{true}}) \rangle\!\rangle$$

This is slightly different from *subterm typability* which only requires that any object language sub-term be typeable in isolation, not that an object language term be β-abstractable. In particular, there is difficulty with abstracting over a sub-term that appears in the right-hand side of a recursive let binding which we discuss in Section 4.1.

- **Fresh name generation:** The metalanguage should provide facilities for generating fresh names for use in object terms. That is, we want to be able to `gensym` names that are guaranteed not to occur in any object language term so we can avoid unintended variable capture when generating code.
- **Hygiene:** The programmer should have the ability to require that free variables appearing in an antiquote be used hygienically. For example, consider the term:

$$\langle\!\langle \underline{\mathtt{let}}\ \mathtt{x} = \ldots\ \underline{\mathtt{in}}\ \tilde{\ }(f\ \langle\!\langle \mathtt{x} \rangle\!\rangle)) \rangle\!\rangle$$

Here `x` appears free in the argument to f, which appears in an antiquotation and is some metalanguage function that manipulates object language fragments. We would like the programmer to be able to reason about this fragment without knowing the implementation details of f. In particular, the programmer should not have to know what object language context f might place its argument in in the process of building a new object language term—even if that context might bind a variable named `x`. We want hygiene—the `x` appearing in $\langle\!\langle \mathtt{x} \rangle\!\rangle$ should always refer to the `x` bound by the top-level $\underline{\mathtt{let}}$, not to any `x` that might be bound in the term constructed by f in which $\langle\!\langle \mathtt{x} \rangle\!\rangle$ may find itself.

- **Object term elimination:** The programmer should be able to eliminate as well as introduce object language terms. That is, we want to be able to use the metalanguage to perform intensional analysis of object terms while retaining full object term typing.

MetaHaskell make substantial progress in providing these desirable features: it provides syntactic support, antiquotation, heterogeneity, type soundness, inference, open terms, and subterm typability. We have not addressed hygiene, fresh name generation, or object term elimination. Ideas for making further progress are outlined in Section Section 9.

4. A Type System for Heterogeneous Metaprogramming

MetaHaskell consists of Haskell 98 plus extensions for heterogeneous metaprogramming—it is a rather large language. As such, in this section we describe the type system not of full MetaHaskell, but of MiniMeta, a simplified version of MetaHaskell that nonetheless contains all the type system features essential to MetaHaskell's support for metapgrogramming. Jointly, we present the type system for MiniML, an ML-like object language.

4.1 MiniML: Object Language Essentials

Two of our object language design goals are to support open terms and antiquotation, e.g., object language terms in which we have abstracted over a sub-term, as in the term $\lambda x \rightarrow \langle\!\langle \tilde{}x + \mathtt{1} \rangle\!\rangle$. Both requirements present difficulties.

The presence of free variables means that we no longer face a type inference problem, but a *typing* inference problem. The difference between the two is that given a term, *typing* inference must produce a typing context as well as a type, whereas type inference need only produce a type. Although ML does have the principal type property, it *does not* have principal typings. We can see this by considering the (open) object language term $\mathtt{x}\ \mathtt{x}$ [1]. We could give this term one of the following two typings

$$\{x : \forall a.a\} \vdash \mathtt{x}\ \mathtt{x} : \forall a.a$$
$$\{x : \forall a.a \rightarrow a\} \vdash \mathtt{x}\ \mathtt{x} : \forall a.a \rightarrow a$$

The former derivation provides more because the term has type $\forall a.a$, but it requires more than the latter derivation because it can only occur in a typing environment where x has type $\forall a.a$. Neither derivation is more general than the other.

Shao and Appel [33] partly addressed the issue of typing open terms in solving the *smartest compilation* problem. They present an algorithm to infer the minimal import interface required by a compilation unit. In essence they are inferring a minimal context, i.e., a typing. Jim [16] connects smartest compilation to the typing problem and gives a more explicit presentation of a typing inference algorithm. ML's lack of principal typings will not hinder us because we will allow contexts to include more types than can appear in the expression language. The algorithm presented by Shao and Appel [33] collects constraints on variable instantiations and then "matches" them against the poltype inferred at the variable's binding site. The algorithm presented by Jim [16] uses intersection types to represent what are morally the same constraints, a technique we will reuse for MiniML.

Open terms present difficulties, but at least it is syntactically apparent which variables are free in an open term. An object language term containing an antiquotation is not so well-behaved. After all, what are the free variables in the term $\langle\!\langle \tilde{}x + 1 \rangle\!\rangle$? It is apparent that we must somehow express joint constraints on the context of a quotation and the contexts of its constituent antiquotations.

[1] This example is taken from Jim [16].

Term variables		$\in$	$\mathtt{x}, \mathtt{y}, \mathtt{z}, \mathtt{f}, \mathtt{g}, \mathtt{h}$
Type variables		$\in$	$\mathtt{a}, \mathtt{b}, \mathtt{c}$
Extension variables	ρ		
Row variables	γ		
Expressions	$\mathtt{e}$	::=	$\mathtt{i} \mid \underline{\mathtt{true}} \mid \underline{\mathtt{false}} \mid \mathtt{x} \mid$
			$\bullet_i \mid \lambda\mathtt{x}.\mathtt{e} \mid \mathtt{e}_1\ \mathtt{e}_2 \mid$
			$\underline{\mathtt{let}}\ \mathtt{x} = \mathtt{e}_1\ \underline{\mathtt{in}}\ \mathtt{e}_2$
Types	τ	::=	$\underline{\mathtt{int}} \mid \underline{\mathtt{bool}} \mid \tau_1 \rightarrow \tau_2 \mid \mathtt{a}$
Type schemes	σ	::=	$\forall\bar{\mathtt{a}}.\tau$
Type environment schemes	ξ	::=	$\bigwedge[\tau_i]\xi \mid \sigma \mid \rho$
Type environments	Γ	::=	$\{\mathtt{x}_i : \xi_i\}\Gamma \mid \bot \mid \gamma_{\#\bar{\mathtt{x}}}$
Context environments	Δ	::=	$\{\bullet_i : \Gamma_i \rhd \sigma_i\}$

Figure 1: Object language syntax

The syntax of MiniML is given in Figure 1. We use a typewriter font to distinguish MiniML terms from metalanguage terms. Its differences with respect to a standard ML-like language are highlighted. The only change in the syntax of expressions is the presence of *contexts* for antiquotations, $\bullet_i$. Although our concrete syntax inlines antiquotations into quotations, antiquotation is really an abstraction/application pair. For example, the quasiquote $\lambda x \rightarrow \langle\!\langle \tilde{}x + 1 \rangle\!\rangle$ desugars into $\lambda x \rightarrow \langle\!\langle \bullet_1 + 1 \rangle\!\rangle\ x$. A syntactically valid MiniML term will only contain sequentially and distinctly numbered contexts, although there is no constraint on which permutation of context numbering is chosen—in practice the parser numbers the contexts sequentially in parse order.

We represent contexts using Rémy's extensible records [30, 31]. This is a natural way to express the joint constraints between quasiquotation contexts and their antiquotations. Extensible records use *row variables* to represents "the rest" of the fields in a record, allowing expressions to be polymorphic in the records they manipulate—only the fields that are accessed are required to be present, but the record may also contain additional unreferenced fields that are represented by the row variable. Similarly, row variables allow our object language terms to be polymorphic in "the rest of" their context. This form of polymorphism is permissible because our object language allows weakening. MiniML's type environments, Γ, use Rémy's record type, including row variables with lacks constraints of the form $\gamma_{\#\bar{\mathtt{x}}}$. A lacks constraint specifies which variables (record labels) may not appear in the record extension associated with the row variable that it annotates.

Type environments do not bind variables to type schemes, but to *type environment schemes*. A type environment scheme is either a polytype or an *extensible* intersection type. Extensible intersection types type free variables in open terms. For example, the quotation

$$\langle\!\langle (\mathtt{f}\ \mathtt{1}, \mathtt{f}\ \underline{\mathtt{true}}) \rangle\!\rangle$$

has the type

$$\forall \mathtt{a}, \mathtt{b}, \rho, \gamma. \boxed{\{\mathtt{f} : \bigwedge[\underline{\mathtt{int}} \rightarrow \mathtt{a}; \underline{\mathtt{bool}} \rightarrow \mathtt{b}]\,\rho\}\,\gamma \rhd (\mathtt{a}, \mathtt{b})}$$

Note that quoted terms are metalanguage terms, so this type is a metalanguage type. In this type we have quantified over the object language typing variables $\mathtt{a}$, $\mathtt{b}$, ρ, and γ, but the quantification is

$$\boxed{\Gamma; \Delta \vdash_{\Box} e : \sigma}$$

$$\frac{}{\Gamma; \Delta \vdash_{\Box} i : \underline{\texttt{int}}}\ \textsc{ObjInt} \qquad \frac{}{\Gamma; \Delta \vdash_{\Box} \{\underline{\texttt{true}}, \underline{\texttt{false}}\} : \underline{\texttt{bool}}}\ \textsc{ObjBool}$$

$$\frac{\texttt{x} : \bigwedge[\tau_1 \dots \tau_n]\,\sigma \in \Gamma}{\Gamma; \Delta \vdash_{\Box} \texttt{x} : \sigma}\ \textsc{ObjVar}$$

$$\frac{\texttt{x} : \bigwedge[\tau_1 \dots \tau_i \dots \tau_n]\,\rho \in \Gamma}{\Gamma; \Delta \vdash_{\Box} \texttt{x} : \tau_i}\ \textsc{ObjFreeVar}$$

$$\frac{\Gamma, \texttt{x} : \tau_1; \Delta \vdash_{\Box} e : \tau_2}{\Gamma; \Delta \vdash_{\Box} \lambda\texttt{x}.\texttt{e} : \tau_1 \to \tau_2}\ \textsc{ObjAbs}$$

$$\frac{\Gamma; \Delta \vdash_{\Box} \texttt{e}_1 : \tau_1 \to \tau_2 \qquad \Gamma; \Delta \vdash_{\Box} \texttt{e}_2 : \tau_1}{\Gamma; \Delta \vdash_{\Box} \texttt{e}_1\ \texttt{e}_2 : \tau_2}\ \textsc{ObjApp}$$

$$\frac{\Gamma; \Delta \vdash_{\Box} \texttt{e}_1 : \sigma \qquad \Gamma, \texttt{x} : \sigma; \Delta \vdash_{\Box} \texttt{e}_2 : \tau}{\Gamma; \Delta \vdash_{\Box} \underline{\texttt{let}}\ \texttt{x} = \texttt{e}_1\ \underline{\texttt{in}}\ \texttt{e}_2 : \tau}\ \textsc{ObjLet}$$

$$\frac{\Gamma; \Delta \vdash_{\Box} \texttt{e} : \sigma \qquad \texttt{a} \notin \mathrm{ftv}(\Gamma) \cup \mathrm{ftv}(\Delta)}{\Gamma; \Delta \vdash_{\Box} \texttt{e} : \forall \texttt{a}.\sigma}\ \textsc{ObjGen}$$

$$\frac{\Gamma; \Delta \vdash_{\Box} \texttt{e} : \sigma \qquad \sigma \le \sigma'}{\Gamma; \Delta \vdash_{\Box} \texttt{e} : \sigma'}\ \textsc{ObjInst}$$

$$\frac{\bullet_i : \Gamma_i \rhd \sigma_i \in \Delta}{\Gamma_i; \Delta \vdash_{\Box} \bullet_i : \sigma_i}\ \textsc{Anti}$$

Figure 2: Declarative typing rules for MiniML

done at the metalanguage level. The type of the object language term is enclosed in a box when it appears in a metalanguage type to distinguish it as an object language type. We further discuss these details in Section 4.2, but for now the germane aspect of this type is the extensible intersection type assigned to `f` in the typing environment, $\bigwedge[\underline{\texttt{int}} \to \texttt{a}; \underline{\texttt{bool}} \to \texttt{b}]\,\rho$. This type says that `f` must have both type $\underline{\texttt{int}} \to \texttt{a}$ and type $\underline{\texttt{bool}} \to \texttt{b}$, but that it may also have additional types in the typing environment, indicated by the extension variable ρ. Extension variables serve the same function in extensible intersection types as row variables serve for extensible records.

Context environments, Δ, provide typings for contexts, of the form $\Gamma \rhd \sigma$, that specify both an environment Γ and a polytype σ. The declarative type system for MiniML is given in Figure 2 along with the corresponding subsumption relation in Figure 3; we again highlight the differences with respect to the standard declarative rules for an ML-like language. The rule for typing contexts, Anti, requires that the environment component Γ_i of a context's typing in the context environment Δ must exactly match the Γ_i in the derivation where the context $\bullet_i$ occurs. This directly implies that any bound variable that scopes over $\bullet_i$, as well as any variable that occurs free *anywhere* in the quotation in which $\bullet_i$ appears, must be present in Γ_i. These free variables may be used at additional types in the expression "plugged in" to the context due to the extension variable ρ, and this expression may also use additional free variables that do not appear explicitly in Γ due to the row variable γ. As we explain in Section 4.2, the type variables ρ and γ are instantiated at the metalanguage level whenever a quotation is applied to an antiquotation.

$$\boxed{\sigma \le \sigma'}$$

$$\frac{\beta_i \notin \mathrm{ftv}(\forall\overline{\alpha}.\tau)}{\forall\overline{\alpha}.\tau \le \forall\overline{\beta}.[\overline{\alpha \mapsto \tau'}]\tau}$$

Figure 3: MiniML type subsumption relation

Type environment schemes have the form $\bigwedge[\tau_i]\,\sigma$, where σ is a polytype, or $\bigwedge[\tau_i]\,\rho$, where ρ is an extension variable, and in both cases the intersection may be empty. Though the polytype form of type environment schemes is not strictly necessary for the declarative rules, it is a technical device for the benefit of the algorithmic rules, which we do not present here, allowing them to substitute a polytype σ for an extension variable ρ in the typing rules for binders. A type environment scheme $\bigwedge[\tau_i]\,\sigma$ is therefore only well-formed when σ can be instantiated to each of the τ_i in the intersection. A variable `x` with a type environment scheme $\bigwedge[\tau_1 \dots \tau_n]\,\sigma$ must therefore have type σ according to ObjVar. A variable that occurs free is expected to have a type environment scheme $\bigwedge[\tau_1 \dots \tau_n]\,\rho$ and may have any type τ_i, $1 \le i \le n$, according to ObjFreeVar.

There is a subtlety with generalization: the rule ObjGen must look for free type variables in both Γ and Δ. Consider the following term

$$\lambda x \to \langle\!\langle \underline{\texttt{let}}\ \texttt{y} = \lambda\texttt{z} \to \texttt{z}\ \tilde{}x\ \underline{\texttt{in}}\ (\texttt{y}\ (\lambda\texttt{u} \to 1), \texttt{y}\ (\lambda\texttt{v} \to \underline{\texttt{true}})) \rangle\!\rangle$$

Because `z` will appear in the Δ used to type the context $\bullet_1$ (where $\tilde{}x$ occurs), we cannot generalize `y`, so this term cannot be typed. To see why this must be the case, imagine applying this lambda to the expression $\langle\!\langle \texttt{z}\ 2 \rangle\!\rangle$

In general, the presence of an antiquotation in the right-hand-side of a binding prevents generalization. This means that our extended language does not satisfy the *subterm abstractability* goal defined in Section 3. If we also added type ascription, then a type signature would suffice in this case to assign `y` a polymorphic type.

4.2 MiniMeta: Object Language Type System Integration

MiniMeta integrates support for using MiniML as an object language. Though we present it here in a setting where MiniML is the only supported object language, we will shortly point out the type system features that are necessary to support MiniML and show that they are general enough to also support a variety of other object languages. In Section 4.4 we give a more detailed qualitative description of the process for transforming a base language's syntax and type system into a suitable object language syntax and type system.

The syntax of MiniMeta is given in Figure 4. Quotations, of the form $\langle\!\langle \texttt{e} \rangle\!\rangle$, are the only non-standard expression syntax. We have also already seen object language typings, of the form $\boxed{\Gamma \rhd \sigma}$. The third novel aspect of MiniMeta is that it allows quantification over types by object language type variables (a), object language row variables (γ), and object language extension variables (ρ).

Quantification must be done at the metalanguage level if there is any hope of connecting typing constraints on quotations to constraints on their constituent antiquotations. Consider the term

$$\lambda x \to \langle\!\langle (\texttt{f}\ 1, \tilde{}x) \rangle\!\rangle$$

The metalanguage binds x, which must have an object language typing (we will show the typing rules shortly). There are no constraints on the type of x, so we will simply use the type variable

Term variables		$\in$	x, y, z, f, g, h
Type variables		$\in$	a, b, c
Quantification variables	ω	$::=$	$a \mid \mathsf{a} \mid \rho \mid \gamma$
Expressions	e	$::=$	$i \mid \mathsf{true} \mid \mathsf{false} \mid x \mid \lambda x.e \mid e_1\ e_2 \mid \mathsf{let}\ x = e_1\ \mathsf{in}\ e_2 \mid \langle\!\langle \mathsf{e} \rangle\!\rangle$
Types	ν	$::=$	$\mathsf{int} \mid \mathsf{bool} \mid \nu_1 \rightarrow \nu_2 \mid a \mid \boxed{\Gamma \rhd \sigma}$
Type schemes	φ	$::=$	$\forall \overline{\omega}.\nu$
Type environments	Θ	$::=$	$\{x_i : \varphi_i\}$

Figure 4: MiniMeta syntax

$$\boxed{\Theta \vdash e : \varphi}$$

$$\frac{}{\Theta \vdash i : \mathsf{int}}\ \textsc{Int} \qquad \frac{}{\Theta \vdash \{\mathsf{true}, \mathsf{false}\} : \mathsf{bool}}\ \textsc{Bool}$$

$$\frac{x : \varphi \in \Theta}{\Theta \vdash x : \varphi}\ \textsc{Var}$$

$$\frac{\Theta, x : \nu_1 \vdash e : \nu_2}{\Theta \vdash \lambda x.e : \nu_1 \rightarrow \nu_2}\ \textsc{Abs} \qquad \frac{\Theta \vdash e_1 : \nu_1 \rightarrow \nu_2 \quad \Theta \vdash e_2 : \nu_1}{\Theta \vdash e_1\ e_2 : \nu_2}\ \textsc{App}$$

$$\frac{\Theta \vdash e_1 : \varphi \quad \Theta, x : \varphi \vdash e_2 : \nu}{\Theta \vdash \mathsf{let}\ x = e_1\ \mathsf{in}\ e_2 : \nu}\ \textsc{Let}$$

$$\frac{\Theta \vdash e : \varphi \quad \omega \notin \mathrm{ftv}(\Theta)}{\Theta \vdash e : \forall \omega.\varphi}\ \textsc{Gen} \qquad \frac{\Theta \vdash e : \varphi \quad \varphi \leq \varphi'}{\Theta \vdash e : \varphi'}\ \textsc{Inst}$$

$$\frac{\Gamma; \{\bullet_i : \Gamma_i \rhd \sigma_i\} \vdash_{\square} \mathsf{e} : \sigma}{\Theta \vdash \langle\!\langle \mathsf{e} \rangle\!\rangle : \overline{\boxed{\Gamma_i \rhd \sigma_i}} \rightarrow \boxed{\Gamma \rhd \sigma}}\ \textsc{Quote}$$

Figure 5: Declarative typing rules for MiniMeta

$$\boxed{\varphi \leq \varphi'}$$

$$\frac{b_i, \mathsf{b}_j, \rho_k, \gamma_l \notin \mathrm{ftv}(\forall \overline{\omega}.\nu)}{\forall \overline{\omega}.\nu \leq \forall \overline{b}\, \overline{\mathsf{b}}\, \overline{\rho}\, \overline{\gamma}.[\overline{a \mapsto \nu'}, \overline{\mathsf{a} \mapsto \nu''}, \overline{\rho \mapsto \xi}, \overline{\gamma \mapsto \Theta}]\nu}$$

Figure 6: MiniMeta type subsumption relation

b to represent this type. However, we do know that the typing environment of x's object language typing must include `f` at least at the type $\underline{\texttt{int}} \rightarrow \mathsf{a}$ for some a. Furthermore, x may also use free variables other than `f`, and in fact may use `f` at other types, but whatever these uses may be, they will *also* occur in the quotation $\langle\!\langle$(f 1,$\tilde{\ }x$)$\rangle\!\rangle$ where x occurs as a sub-expression. We use type variables ρ and γ to represent these shared uses of the environment. The full expression therefore has the type

$$\forall \mathsf{a}, \mathsf{b}, \rho, \gamma. \boxed{\{\texttt{f} : \bigwedge[\underline{\texttt{int}} \rightarrow \mathsf{a}]\,\rho\}\,\gamma \rhd \mathsf{b}} \rightarrow \boxed{\{\texttt{f} : \bigwedge[\underline{\texttt{int}} \rightarrow \mathsf{a}]\,\rho\}\,\gamma \rhd (\mathsf{a}, \mathsf{b})}$$

MiniMeta's typing rules appear in Figure 5. Although we have not explicitly kinded the four varieties of type variables in our presentation, morally they do have different kinds as shown by the subsumption relation given in Figure 6.

Object language types are just types in our metalanguage. A term with an object language type, e.g., a quasiquotation, can appear in a program, and an object language type can be used to instantiate a type variable a. However, object language type variables that appear in metalanguage types, name a, ρ, and γ, serve only as *evidence*—no values will ever have a type with an object language kind.

Quotations are typed with the QUOTE rule. This rules makes use of the object language judgment to type the quoted object language term and results in an arrow type with as many arguments as there are contexts in the quotation. Recall that the typing environment for contexts must "match up" exactly with the typing environment in the derivation where the context occurs. This means that for the abstraction introduced by a quotation to be applied, the ith applicand—an antiquotation—must have precisely the type $\boxed{\Gamma_i \rhd \sigma_i}$. This may be unsettling because it seems to place too many restrictions on Γ_i. However, it is only unsettling because we are not used to encountering polymorphic environments. Just as a classic polymorphic function like cons allows us to build a list at many types, row and extension variables allow us to use a typing polymorphically and therefore use an object term *at many typings*. We use an object term at many typings the same way we would use cons at many types—by instantiating its type variables within the metalanguage. That is, metalanguage instantiation lets us "match up" the Γ's in object language types.

4.3 Hygiene

Although we listed hygiene as one of our goals in Section 3, MiniML and MiniMeta are unhygienic, a rather undesirable feature. Kim et al. [20] allow programmer control over hygiene by introducing hygienic lambda abstraction, λ^{*}, that performs capture-avoiding substitution on the abstraction before it is applied. We believe this extension could be incorporated easily into our system: instead of elaborating to abstract syntax trees, quasiquoted expressions would elaborate to computations in a name-generating monad. Assuming that computations in our name-generating monad were run via runQ, the erase function would then be defined as

$$\mathsf{erase} :: \forall \gamma, \alpha. [\![\mathbf{exp}|\gamma \rhd \alpha]\!] \rightarrow \mathsf{Exp}$$
$$\mathsf{erase} = \mathsf{runQ} \circ \mathsf{unsafeCoerce}$$

We note that our desire for subterm abstractability is incompatible with hygiene. However, providing both hygienic and unhygienic binding forms also allows the programmer to choose between subterm abstractability and hygiene on a case-by-case basis.

4.4 Crafting an Object Language

Our metalanguage and object language seem to be tied together intimately. This raises two related questions: how easily can a new object language be integrated into MiniMeta, and how does one transform a base language—a language, like core ML, without support for antiquotation and without a typing inference procedure—into an object language suitable for integration.

There are four points of integration between MiniMeta and MiniML.

1. Syntactic support for quoting object language terms and object language types.

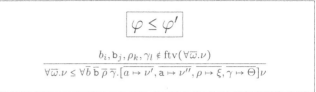

2. Type system support for object language types appearing as terms in metalanguage types.
3. Quantification over object language type variables in metalanguage types.
4. Passing type equality constraints from the metalanguage's type checker to the object language.

Importantly, MiniMeta knows nothing about the term structure of either MiniML types or MiniML terms—object language expressions and object language types are both completely opaque to the metalanguage. Syntactic support for quasiquotation is straightforward, as the object language parser need only produce an object language term and a list of antiquotations which the metalanguage parser then handles. The object language must provide hooks for working with object language type variables, but this can be done in a generic way. Similarly, the metalanguage type checker can simply pass equality constraints between object language types to the object language type checker without requiring any knowledge of the structure of these types. We claim that the metalanguage is largely agnostic with respect to the form of the object language and its types and that integrating new object languages requires few changes to the metalanguage and its type system, and we back up this claim in Section 5.

More difficult is the question of how, in general, to convert a base language and its type system into an object language. The syntactic portion of the problem is easy—just add support for antiquotation to the object language. Even the type "inference" problem is not too hard if we simply require all free variables and contexts to be fully annotated. However, this seems somewhat draconian and we have three examples of object languages that do not require such an annotation burden but still provide inference—MiniML, Linear MiniML, and C♭—so we expect there to be a general method for providing inference even in the presence of free variables and antiquotation.

Given a base language to convert to an object language, it is clear that we must first solve the *typing* inference problem for the base language. During *type* inference, bindings are known, and uses of a binding generate constraints that are immediately resolved using the binding's definition. For languages based on Hindley-Milner, this immediate resolution is performed using unification. To move from type inference to typing inference, the type system must be extended so that it can capture these constraints *in a type*. For MiniML, these constraints are captured by an extensible intersection type. A typing is then a pair of an environment, which maps free variables to types that accurately reflect the constraints imposed by the uses of the free variables, and a type.

Typings are not quite enough to get us where we want to go because we must also address the issue of antiquotation. It is useful to think of an object language quotation as representing an entire class of base language syntax trees formed by substituting a base language expression for each of the contexts, $\bullet_i$, in the quotation. But each object language quotation must be paired with a typing derivation that parameterizes the base language derivations for the same class of base language expressions that the quotation represents. Furthermore, these term/derivation pairs must be constructed in such a way that when they are composed—that is, when an object language term is "plugged in" to a context and its corresponding derivation is "plugged in" to the parent derivation—the resulting object language term/derivation pair still consists of a valid representative of an entire class of base language term/typing derivations.

Consider a variant of MiniML that did not allow antiquotation. For such a language, intersection types alone would be enough to provide typings—there would be no need for either extension variables or row variables. This wouldn't be a particularly useful language—after all, how would one ever construct a closed term from an open term without antiquotation. However, the point of proposing such an object language is to make the observation that we could represent entire classes of base language derivations using object language types that do not make use of row or extension variables. The need for row and extension variables arises in MiniML *because of antiquotation*. Unlike derivations for our hypothetical antiquotation-free variant, MiniML derivations have "holes" where the derivations for antiquoted terms must eventually be plugged in.

The process for constructing the object language MiniML from a core ML base language consisted of the following steps

- Modify the term structure of expressions to allow object language expressions to represent entire classes of base language expressions by adding support for antiquotation.
- Extend the base language type system so that types can represent the constraints a term's use of free variables imposes on those variables' types.
- Extend the base language type system so that object language derivations represent classes of derivations where sub-derivations, corresponding to antiquotations, are left free. For MiniML this required adding row and extension variables to represent typing environment constraints shared by a derivation and its free sub-derivations.

We conjecture that only type systems that can be written in a syntax-directed form are suitable for use in an object language as quotations consists of terms and derivations whose holes "line up" in a one-to-one correspondence.

In the following two sections we support our claim that MiniMeta represents a general metaprogramming framework that can support many object languages by describing two additional object languages, a linear variant of MiniML and a C-like language.

5. A linear object language

The type system we have presented is expressed for a pair of languages: a metalanguage and a *specific* object language. It is natural to ask whether or not the type system fragment associated with the metalanguage can be adapted to other object languages, and if so, how difficult this might be. In particular, one might expect that because we expend so much effort on context manipulation, supporting an object language with a substructural type system would be particularly challenging. In this section we demonstrate that although implementing the type checker for a linear object language is non-trivial and requires some novel techniques, integrating it into the metalanguage takes almost zero effort—essentially the only change to the metalanguage that is required is to allow quantification over a newly-kinded type variable.

Our linear language, Linear MiniML, is a variant of MiniML that adds two new binding constructs: a linear **let** binding and a linear λ binding. Its syntax is shown in Figure 7 with the differences with respect to MiniML highlighted.

Many existing presentations of substructural type systems annotate types with use notations that capture, e.g., when variables are used in a linear [38] or unique (in the sense of uniqueness typing) [12] way. While one could imagine using a version of our previous object language's type system extended with such annotations to type open terms, there is a complication that makes this approach a non-starter: antiquotation. The difficulty with antiquotation is that it is not syntactically obvious which variables will be used by a term that is substituted into a context $\bullet_i$, much less which variables it will use linearly!

Term variables		$\in$	$\mathtt{x}, \mathtt{y}, \mathtt{z}, \mathtt{f}, \mathtt{g}, \mathtt{h}$
Type variables		$\in$	$\mathtt{a}, \mathtt{b}, \mathtt{c}$
Extension variables	ρ		
Row variables	γ		
Use variables	υ		
Expressions	e	::=	$\underline{\mathtt{true}} \mid \underline{\mathtt{false}} \mid \mathtt{x} \mid \bullet_i \mid$
			$\lambda\mathtt{x.e} \mid \lambda^1\mathtt{x.e} \mid \mathtt{e}_1\ \mathtt{e}_2 \mid$
			$\underline{\mathtt{let}}\ \mathtt{x} = \mathtt{e}_1\ \underline{\mathtt{in}}\ \mathtt{e}_2 \mid$
			$\underline{\mathtt{let}}^1\ \mathtt{x} = \mathtt{e}_1\ \underline{\mathtt{in}}\ \mathtt{e}_2 \mid$
			$(\mathtt{e}_1, \mathtt{e}_2) \mid$
			$\underline{\mathtt{case}}\ \mathtt{e}_1\ \underline{\mathtt{of}}\ \{\ (\mathtt{u}, \mathtt{v}) \to \mathtt{e}_2\ \}$
Types	τ	::=	$\underline{\mathtt{int}} \mid \underline{\mathtt{bool}} \mid \tau_1 \to \tau_2 \mid$
			$\tau_1 \multimap \tau_2 \mid \mathtt{a} \mid (\tau_1, \tau_2)$
Variable use sets	ζ	::=	$\upsilon \mid \{\overline{\mathtt{x}}\} \mid \mathbb{1} \mid \mathbb{0} \mid$
			$\zeta_1 \cap \zeta_2 \mid \zeta_1 \oplus \zeta_2$
Type schemes	σ	::=	$\forall\overline{\mathtt{a}}.\tau$
Environment schemes	ξ	::=	$\bigwedge[\tau_i]\xi \mid \sigma \mid \rho$
Type environments	Γ	::=	$\{\mathtt{x_i} : \xi_i\}\Gamma \mid \bot \mid \gamma_{\#\overline{\mathtt{x}}}$
Context environments	Δ	::=	$\{\bullet_i : \Gamma_i \rhd \sigma_i\}$

Figure 7: Linear object language syntax

Consider the following term, in which **z** is a *linear* binding, i.e., it must be used linearly in the body of the **let**

$$\lambda x \to \langle\!\langle \underline{\mathtt{let}}^1\ \mathtt{z} = \underline{\mathtt{true}}\ \underline{\mathtt{in}}\ \tilde{\ }x \rangle\!\rangle$$

Unfortunately we have abstracted over the body of the let, so we must somehow figure out how to assign x a type that reflects the fact that it must use the (free) variable **z** linearly.

Our approach to solving this problem is to construct a typing judgment that tracks two sets of disjoint variables that are free in the expression under judgment: those that are use linearly and those that are not used linearly. These sets of variables must contain not just object language variables, such as **z**, but also *metavariables* υ, that themselves represent sets of variables. These metavariables will allow us to quantify over sets of variables. Our typing judgment has the following form, where ζ^1 is the set of variables used linearly by $\mathtt{e}$ and ζ^ω is the set of variables that $\mathtt{e}$ does not use linearly.

$$\Gamma; \Delta \vdash_{\square} \mathtt{e} : \sigma|_{(\zeta^1, \zeta^\omega)}$$

We claim that our previous quotation of a linear term has the type

$$\forall a, \gamma, \upsilon^1, \upsilon^\omega. \boxed{\{\mathtt{z} : \underline{\mathtt{bool}}\}\gamma \rhd a|_{(\upsilon^1 \oplus \upsilon^1 \cap \{z\} \oplus \{z\}, \upsilon^\omega)}} \to \boxed{\gamma \rhd a|_{(\upsilon^1 \oplus \upsilon^1 \cap \{z\}, \upsilon^\omega)}}$$

Though we will shortly show that we can infer this type automatically, we make no claims regarding its readability or programmer-friendliness, so we will walk through our claim carefully. We use the set operations intersection, $\cap$, and symmetric difference, $\oplus$, to represent sets of variables. Our type quantifies over two *variable use metavariables*, υ^1 and υ^ω. The type of the binder should not look entirely foreign; it says that the binder is an object language term that is only valid in a type environment that must at least contain a binding for **z** at type $\underline{\mathtt{bool}}$ and that in such an environment it has the type α. However, its type also places a constraint on the set of variables that the binder must use linearly—we claim that the constraint requires that **z** is a member of this set. To see this, let us calculate the intersection of $\upsilon^1 \oplus \upsilon^1 \cap \{\mathtt{z}\} \oplus \{\mathtt{z}\}$ with the set containing just the variable **z**

$$\begin{aligned}(\upsilon^1 \oplus \upsilon^1 \cap \{\mathtt{z}\} \oplus \{\mathtt{z}\}) \cap \{\mathtt{z}\} &= \upsilon^1 \cap \{\mathtt{z}\} \oplus \upsilon^1 \cap \{\mathtt{z}\} \oplus \{\mathtt{z}\} \\ &= \{\mathtt{z}\}\end{aligned}$$

A similar calculation shows that the result of applying the lambda is an object expression that is guaranteed not to use a free variable **z** linearly.

The typing rules for our linear language are given in Figure 8. They utilize join ($\sqcup$) and meet ($\sqcap$) operators, defined in Figure 9, for combining the two variable use sets according to whether two subexpressions execute in sequence ($\sqcup$) or as alternatives ($\sqcap$) (note that set union and set difference can be expressed in terms of $\cap$ and $\oplus$). We see both mixing operators at work in rule LINIFTHENELSE. The variable uses of e_2 and e_3, the **then** and **else** branch, respectively, of an **if** expression, must be combined so that only those variables that are used linearly in both branches are judged to be used linearly in the body of the **if** expression; this is the job of the meet ($\sqcap$) operator. In contrast, only those variables that are used linearly in *either* the scrutinee of the **if** expression, e_1, or the body, may be judged to be used linearly by the **if** expression as a whole; this is the job of the join ($\sqcup$) operator.

The standard abstraction rule, LINABS, is unsurprising. The application rule, LINAPP, must take care to recognize that because the λ being applied is not guaranteed to use the variable it binds linearly, a variable used linearly by the argument cannot be guaranteed to be used linearly by the application as a whole. Linear abstraction, LINABS^1, is like LINABS but with an additional side condition requiring that the variable it binds is present in the set of variables used linearly by the body of the λ^1. Application of a λ^1-binding is judged by LINAPP^1 to use linearly any variables that are used linearly by the argument since the λ^1-binding is guaranteed to only use its argument linearly. The other rules follow similarly.

As Kennedy [19] observed in the setting of labels for extensible records, variables sets with the union and symmetric difference operators form a Boolean ring with $\mathbb{0}$ being the empty set and $\mathbb{1}$ the set of all labels. Amazingly, unification over Boolean rings is decidable and unitary [2, 26]. MetaHaskell includes the linear language in Figure 7 as an object language, and the object language's type checker uses Boolean unification to provide type inference.

Coming up with a type system and corresponding inference procedure for our linear language required some thought—we could not simply reuse an existing language as-is. Although we provided a qualitative description of how to go about converting a language and type system to a form suitable for use as an object language in Section 4.4, one has to expect that adding support for *typing* inference (in contrast to just type inference) as well as antiquotation to an existing language will require some non-trivial amount of work. However, adding support for our linear object language required only a few, small changes to the metalanguage in three areas:

1. The MetaHaskell parser was changed to recognize quoted Linear MiniML expressions and types.
2. The algebraic data type representing object language type metavariables was extend with a constructor for the Linear MiniML metavariables that can be quantified at the metalanguage level, i.e., ρ, γ, and υ.

$$\boxed{\Gamma;\Delta \vdash_{\Box} e : \sigma|_{(\zeta^1,\zeta^\omega)}}$$

$$\frac{}{\Gamma;\Delta \vdash_{\Box} \{\underline{\mathtt{true}},\underline{\mathtt{false}}\} : \underline{\mathtt{bool}}|_{(\varnothing,\varnothing)}}\ \textsc{LinBool}$$

$$\frac{\mathtt{x} : \bigwedge[\tau_1 \ldots \tau_n]\,\sigma \in \Gamma}{\Gamma;\Delta \vdash_{\Box} \mathtt{x} : \sigma|_{(\mathtt{x},\varnothing)}}\ \textsc{LinVar}$$

$$\frac{\mathtt{x} : \bigwedge[\tau_1 \ldots \tau_i \ldots \tau_n]\,\rho \in \Gamma}{\Gamma;\Delta \vdash_{\Box} \mathtt{x} : \tau_i|_{(\mathtt{x},\varnothing)}}\ \textsc{LinFreeVar}$$

$$\frac{\begin{array}{c}\Gamma;\Delta \vdash_{\Box} \mathtt{e}_1 : \underline{\mathtt{bool}}|_{\overline{\zeta}_1} \\ \Gamma;\Delta \vdash_{\Box} \mathtt{e}_2 : \tau|_{\overline{\zeta}_2} \qquad \Gamma;\Delta \vdash_{\Box} \mathtt{e}_3 : \tau|_{\overline{\zeta}_3}\end{array}}{\Gamma;\Delta \vdash_{\Box} \underline{\mathtt{if}}\ \mathtt{e}_1\ \underline{\mathtt{then}}\ \mathtt{e}_2\ \underline{\mathtt{else}}\ \mathtt{e}_3 : \sigma|_{\overline{\zeta}_1 \sqcup (\overline{\zeta}_2 \sqcap \overline{\zeta}_3)}}\ \textsc{LinIfThenElse}$$

$$\frac{\Gamma, \mathtt{x} : \tau_1;\Delta \vdash_{\Box} e : \tau_2|_{(v^1,v^\omega)}}{\Gamma;\Delta \vdash_{\Box} \lambda\mathtt{x}.\mathtt{e} : \tau_1 \to \tau_2|_{(v^1 \setminus \mathtt{x},\, v^\omega \setminus \mathtt{x})}}\ \textsc{LinAbs}$$

$$\frac{\Gamma;\Delta \vdash_{\Box} \mathtt{e}_1 : \tau_1 \to \tau_2|_{(u^1,u^\omega)} \qquad \Gamma;\Delta \vdash_{\Box} \mathtt{e}_2 : \tau_1|_{(v^1,v^\omega)}}{\Gamma;\Delta \vdash_{\Box} \mathtt{e}_1\ \mathtt{e}_2 : \tau_2|_{(u^1,u^\omega) \sqcup (\varnothing,\, v^1 \cup v^\omega)}}\ \textsc{LinApp}$$

$$\frac{\Gamma, \mathtt{x} : \tau_1;\Delta \vdash_{\Box} e : \tau_2|_{(v^1,v^\omega)} \qquad \mathtt{x} \in v^1}{\Gamma;\Delta \vdash_{\Box} \lambda^1\mathtt{x}.\mathtt{e} : \tau_1 \multimap \tau_2|_{(v^1 \setminus \mathtt{x},\, v^\omega)}}\ \textsc{LinAbs}^1$$

$$\frac{\Gamma;\Delta \vdash_{\Box} \mathtt{e}_1 : \tau_1 \multimap \tau_2|_{(u^1,u^\omega)} \qquad \Gamma;\Delta \vdash_{\Box} \mathtt{e}_2 : \tau_1|_{(v^1,v^\omega)}}{\Gamma;\Delta \vdash_{\Box} \mathtt{e}_1\ \mathtt{e}_2 : \tau_2|_{(u^1,u^\omega) \sqcup (v^1,v^\omega)}}\ \textsc{LinApp}^1$$

$$\frac{\Gamma;\Delta \vdash_{\Box} \mathtt{e}_1 : \sigma|_{(u^1,u^\omega)} \qquad \Gamma, \mathtt{x} : \sigma;\Delta \vdash_{\Box} \mathtt{e}_2 : \tau|_{(v^1,v^\omega)}}{\Gamma;\Delta \vdash_{\Box} \underline{\mathtt{let}}\ \mathtt{x} = \mathtt{e}_1\ \underline{\mathtt{in}}\ \mathtt{e}_2 : \tau|_{(\varnothing,\, u^1 \cup u^\omega) \sqcup (v^1 \setminus \mathtt{x},\, v^\omega \setminus \mathtt{x})}}\ \textsc{LinLet}$$

$$\frac{\begin{array}{c}\Gamma;\Delta \vdash_{\Box} \mathtt{e}_1 : \sigma|_{(u^1,u^\omega)} \\ \Gamma, \mathtt{x} : \sigma;\Delta \vdash_{\Box} \mathtt{e}_2 : \tau|_{(v^1,v^\omega)} \qquad \mathtt{x} \in v^1\end{array}}{\Gamma;\Delta \vdash_{\Box} \underline{\mathtt{let}}^1\ \mathtt{x} = \mathtt{e}_1\ \underline{\mathtt{in}}\ \mathtt{e}_2 : \tau|_{(u^1,u^\omega) \sqcup (v^1 \setminus \mathtt{x},\, v^\omega)}}\ \textsc{LinLet}^1$$

$$\frac{\Gamma;\Delta \vdash_{\Box} \mathtt{e} : \sigma|_{\overline{\zeta}} \qquad \mathtt{a} \notin \mathrm{ftv}(\Gamma) \cup \mathrm{ftv}(\Delta)}{\Gamma;\Delta \vdash_{\Box} \mathtt{e} : \forall \mathtt{a}.\sigma|_{\overline{\zeta}}}\ \textsc{LinGen}$$

$$\frac{\Gamma;\Delta \vdash_{\Box} \mathtt{e} : \sigma|_{\overline{\zeta}} \qquad \sigma \le \sigma'}{\Gamma;\Delta \vdash_{\Box} \mathtt{e} : \sigma'|_{\overline{\zeta}}}\ \textsc{LinInst}$$

$$\frac{\bullet_i : \Gamma \rhd \sigma|_{\overline{\zeta}} \in \Delta}{\Gamma;\Delta \vdash_{\Box} \bullet_i : \sigma|_{\overline{\zeta}}}\ \textsc{LinAnti}$$

Figure 8: Declarative typing rules for the linear object language

3. The algebraic data type representing object languages types was extended with a construct for Linear MiniML typings, and the metalanguage unification procedure was modified to pass equalities between Linear MiniML types to the Linear MiniML solver.

In total, these changes amounted to a few tens-of-lines of code. Both the metalanguage type system presented in Section 4 and its implementation in the context of MetaHaskell are flexible enough to easily incorporate a variety of object languages, even substructural languages.

$$(u^1,u^\omega) \sqcup (v^1,v^\omega) = \left((u^1 \setminus v^\omega) \oplus (v^1 \setminus u^\omega),\, u^\omega \cup v^\omega \cup (u^1 \cap v^1)\right)$$
$$(u^1,u^\omega) \sqcap (v^1,v^\omega) = \left(v^1 \cap u^1,\, u^\omega \cup v^\omega \cup (u^1 \oplus v^1)\right)$$

Figure 9: Variable use operators

6. Regular Expression Compilation in C♭

One of the original motivations for this work grew out of our experiences using Haskell to generate code for C-like languages in Flask [25] and Nikola [24]. Projects like FFTW [14], ATLAS [40], and SPIRAL [29] show that there are many practical applications for code generation, but that these applications require targeting C-like languages. In this section we describe C♭, a pared-down version of C meant to demonstrate that the MetaHaskell approach to heterogeneous metaprogramming is flexible enough to support these languages.

Although the code generating applications we have cited, with the exception of Nikola, are used in an off-line fashion to generate libraries for later linking with application code, we believe that on-line code generation is also useful. In general, settings where profile-guided optimization [7] is beneficial may also be candidates for run-time code generation. A more concrete application that we believe would benefit from run-time code generation is network packet inspection and processing which often includes a component that performs some kind of evaluation of a decision tree constructed from pattern matching rules. The organization of branches in such a decision tree could easily be optimized given knowledge about the distribution of packets. In practice, this distribution will change over time, and we would like to recompile our pattern matcher periodically to adapt it to the new packet distribution. If rules are added or removed as the packet inspection is executing, there is even more reason to desire run-time code generation.

We present a simple example in this vein: a regular expression compiler that generates executable binary code from a regular expression represented as a string. Because we take advantage of MetaHaskell's support for C♭ as an object language, we don't have to include regular expression compilation as a primitive as .NET does with `RegexOptions.Compiled`. Instead, we can implement our own regular expression compiler as a library without sacrificing type safety.

Figure 10 shows the DFA compilation stage of our regular expression compiler written to use GHC's `QuasiQuotes` language extension (we have elided the other stages suchs as regular expression parsing and NFA to DFA conversion). The function `dfa2c` has type `DFA` → `C.Func`; it produces an abstract syntax tree representation of a C function that implements the DFA given to it as an argument. This version is not type safe—we have no guarantee about the type of the generated code, although we do at least know that the genrated code will be syntatically correct. However, we can use MetaHaskell to write the same function and gain type safety.

The type-safe version of the DFA compiler, written in MetaHaskell, is given in Figure 11. We have elided some code that is unchanged with respect to the previous version—all that has changed is the type signatures. Furthermore, these signatures are exactly the types inferred by the C♭ object language inference engine and could themselves be elided. Note that the use of the free variables `state` and `accept` in the quotation in the body of `trans2c` is propagated to the type of the quoted C♭ statement in the body of `state2c`.

Although we could have defined an erasure function, as we did with MiniML, to convert a quoted C♭ function definition to its corresponding abstract syntax, this would not have allowed us to maintain type safety when generating compiled code. The $[\![\mathbf{cfun}|\cdot]\!]$ quasiquoter, in addition to elaborating a quoted function

```
dfa2c :: DFA → C.Func
dfa2c (DFA start states) =
    [[cfun|int matches (char * s)
        {
          int state   = $int:(fromIntegral start);
          int accept  = $int:(if daccept startState
                                then 1
                                else 0);
          while (*s != 0) {
            switch (state) {
              $stms:(map state2c (map snd states))
            }
          }
          return accept;
        }]]
  where
    startState :: DFAState
    startState = fromJust (lookup start states)

    state2c :: DFAState → C.Stm
    state2c (DFAState i accept trans) =
      [[cstm| case $int:(fromIntegral i):{
            switch (*s+) {
              $stms:(map trans2c trans)
              default:return 0;
            }
            break; }]]

    trans2c :: (Char, DLabel) → C.Stm
    trans2c (c, next) =
      [[cstm| case $char:c:{
              state  = $int:(fromIntegral next);
              accept = $int:(if daccept nextState
                               then 1
                               else 0);
              break;
            }]]
      where
        nextState :: DFAState
        nextState = fromJust (lookup next states)
```

Figure 10: DFA compiler in GHC

to a Haskell term representing a FunPtr, must also incorporate a type function that translates C♭ types to Haskell FFI types. The other delta with respect to MiniML and Linear MiniML is C♭'s support for quoting and antiquoting multiple syntactic categories: functions, statements, and expressions can be quoted, and statements, lists of statements, expressions, and various constants can be antiquoted.

7. Implementation

MetaHaskell is implemented in `mhc` which supports Haskell 98 plus MetaHaskell extensions. It includes a type checker that elaborates to FC_2 [39], a bytecode compiler, and a bytecode execution engine. Every MetaHaskell program can in fact be erased to a plain Haskell program, so it would take little effort to modify `mhc` to output pure Haskell.

In essence, an object language quasiquoter consists of a parser, a quasiquote type checker, and a unification procedure for object language types. The parser converts a quasiquote into a pair consisting of the quote itself and a list of antiquotations, each of which is then parsed by `mhc` as a MetaHaskell expression. The quasiquote type

```
dfa2c :: DFA → FunPtr (CString → IO CInt)
dfa2c (DFA start states) = ...
  where
    startState :: DFAState
    startState = ...

    state2c :: DFAState
            → [[cstm|{ int accept; int state; char * s}'γ ▷ void]]
    state2c (DFAState i accept trans) = ...

    trans2c :: (Char, DLabel)
            → [[cstm|{ int accept; int state}'γ ▷ void]]
    trans2c (c, next) = ...
```

Figure 11: DFA compiler in MetaHaskell

checker takes a quote and the Haskell expressions representing the elaborations of its antiquotes and returns the type of the quote, the types each of its antiquotations must have, an elaborated Haskell term representing the quote, and the type of the elaborated term. `mhc` then checks that the antiquotations have the types specified by the quasiquoter. The `mhc` type inference engine passes equality constraints between object language type to the object language's type inference engine.

Although the type inference engines for MiniML and Linear MiniML required a fair amount of work, incorporating them into `mhc` took comparatively little effort, as we detailed for Linear MiniML in Section 5. The C♭ object language reused a great deal of code from the `language-c-quote` package on Hackage [23]. We also reused much of the code from MiniML for inferring type environments, and as C♭ is not polymorphic, type inference was otherwise straightforward. The run-time code generation feature of C♭ is implemented via unsafePerformIO by calling out to `gcc` to compile a function into a shared library and then dynamically loading the shared library. This use of unsafePerformIO by the erasure of a [[**cfun**|·]] term is rendered safe by the extra type information carried by the un-erased term.

8. Related Work

There are a large number of type systems designed explicitly for metaprogramming. We attempt to describe the major players and their important features here. Most of these systems are multi-stage—they support arbitrary nesting of quotation and antiquotation. Stages are typically numbered by the quotation nesting level at which they occur, so programs without any quotations exist entirely at stage 0. All systems are homogeneous, so the object language and the metalanguage are identical. Some of these type systems support "open code" in the sense that quoted terms at stage n may contain free variables, but in all system but one, these free variables must be bound in a previous stage $m < n$. The use of variables bound in stage m by stages $n > m$ is called *cross-stage persistence*. Cross-stage persistence and support for multiple stages make sense for homogeneous metaprogramming languages, but they seem significantly less important in the heterogeneous setting; support for cross-stage persistence would require providing a meaningful translation of values from one language to the other, and multiple stages would require that the object language, which is different from the metalanguage, also be a metaprogramming language.

Mini-ML$^\Box$ [10, 11] and its corresponding core calculus, $\lambda^\Box$, support staged computation but not open code. In contrast, $\lambda^\bigcirc$ [9] supports cross-stage persistence, but it does not provide a way to express (in the type system) the fact that a particular term is closed. Nanevski [27] adds support for intensional analysis to $\lambda^\Box$.

λ^{α} [36] classifies open code terms by their environment. Calcagno et al. [5] show that inference for λ^{α} is not possible and give a subset, λ^{i}_{let}, for which inference can be performed. As with $\lambda^{\bigcirc}$, a free variable must be bound in a previous stage. $\text{MiniML}^{\text{meta}}_{\text{ref}}$ [4] adds support for computational effects.

Chen and Xi [8] develop λ^{+}_{code} and show that it can be embedded in a language with GADTs. Neither polymorphic object terms nor open object terms are supported. We believe that the combination of quasiquotation and GADTs in Haskell would serve to implement all the features of λ^{+}_{code}.

A prototype implementation of λ^{+}_{code} exists, and λ^{i}_{let} is essentially the language supported by MetaOCaml. None of these systems support explicitly heterogeneous code. However, Eckhardt et al. [13] describe *implicitly* heterogeneous metaprogramming in which the meta- and object languages are both MetaOCaml, but a subset of object language terms can be translated—or *offshored*—automatically to C. Though offshoring cannot handle all MetaOCaml terms, it is capable of handling non-trivial examples [34]. In contrast, our system supports explicit metaprogramming in multiple object languages. We also provide a path to adding heterogeneous metaprogramming support to an existing language through relatively minor language extensions, whereas offshoring must be built on an existing homogeneous metaprogramming language.

The work most similar to ours is Kim et al. [20]. They support open code, inference, and effects for the polymorphic lambda calculus. Like us, they use extensible records to provide principal typings for their multi-stage homogenous metaprogramming language. Unlike MiniML, their system does not support polymorphic uses of free variables, so they cannot type the term

$$(\lambda e \rightarrow \langle\!\langle \underline{\texttt{let}}\ \texttt{f} = \lambda \texttt{x} \rightarrow \texttt{x}\ \underline{\texttt{in}}\ \tilde{\ } e \rangle\!\rangle) \langle\!\langle (\texttt{f 1}, \texttt{f}\ \underline{\texttt{true}}) \rangle\!\rangle$$

because the free variable `f` is instantiated at two different types in the object term $\langle\!\langle (\texttt{f 1}, \texttt{f}\ \underline{\texttt{true}}) \rangle\!\rangle$. They can, however, type the β-reduced form, $\langle\!\langle \underline{\texttt{let}}\ \texttt{f} = \lambda \texttt{x} \rightarrow \texttt{x}\ \underline{\texttt{in}}\ (\texttt{f 1}, \texttt{f}\ \underline{\texttt{true}}) \rangle\!\rangle$. Rhiger [32] shows how to support open code and inference, but in a simply-typed setting. Nanevski et al. [28] give a foundational account of the kind of modal type system needed to support languages metaprogramming, but they ignore the practical issue of inference. Kim et al. [20] describe an inference algorithm, but they do not provide an implementation.

A significant body of work addresses practical metaprogramming issues in the context of MetaOCaml [6, 17, 18, 21, 34]. We are very interested in adapting ideas from the MetaOCaml community to our setting, particularly those related to efficient object language code generation described by Swadi et al. [34] and Kameyama et al. [18].

9. Conclusions and Future Work

MetaHaskell provides a modular framework for supporting type safe heterogeneous meatprogramming with multiple object languages. Although two of the object languages we describe, MiniML and Linear MiniML, required novel type system features to support antiquotation and open terms, integrating then into MetaHaskell as object languages required little work. Our framework accommodates even exotic languages with substructural type systems. We also provide a methodology for constructing an object language and its type system from a base language that does not support metaprogramming.

MetaHaskell meets many of the goals outlined in Section 3. It provides syntactic support, antiquotation, heterogeneity, type soundness, inference, open terms, and subterm typability. Although it seems we cannot in general provide subterm abstractability, we believe annotations are an acceptable solution. We have not addressed fresh name generation or hygiene, but we expect that hygiene can be provided as outlined in Section 4.3.

Our language only allows construction of type safe object language terms. Intensional analysis of the terms is only possible by first calling a function like erase to yield an abstract syntax tree, losing type information in the process. Maintaining types while allowing intensional analysis of object terms requires moving to a dependently typed language. An intermediate solution that we plan to implement in MetaHaskell is a partial function check that, given an abstract syntax tree and an object type, will check that the term represented by the abstract syntax tree has the specified type and cast the AST to an object term of that type.

Although we do not describe them here, we have both a syntax-directed and an algorithmic version of the declarative type system for MiniML given in Figure 2. We are in the process of proving progress and preservation, as well as soundness and completeness of the algorithmic system. We use Rémy's unification algorithm [31], which is decidable and unitary, to unify typing contexts, and we use a similar algorithm to unify our extendable intersection types. Our inference algorithm for Linear MiniML is not complete because the type system does not quantify over linearity; inference always makes the assumption that a free variable applied to an argument is not a linear function.

We also plan to translate our work to a dependently typed setting, like Coq. Although embedding an object language in Coq will not require modifications to Coq's type system since a strong embedding of the object language's type system should be possible, our techniques for constructing object languages and providing inference will still be useful. Furthermore, the modifications we made to Haskell's type system to support metaprogramming will provide guidance as we encode object language types in Coq.

Acknowledgments

We are grateful to Greg Morrisett for his early support and helpful discussions. Dimitrios Vytiniotis helped clarify our thinking about generalization in the presence of antiquotation and suggested a greater focus on developing a methodology for constructing object languages from base languages. Claudio Russo and Nick Benton provided useful feedback on drafts of this paper. Andrew Kennedy brought Boolean unification to our attention.

References

[1] Robert Atkey, Sam Lindley, and Jeremy Yallop. Unembedding domain-specific languages. In *Proceedings of the 2nd ACM SIGPLAN Symposium on Haskell (Haskell '09)*, pages 37–48, Edinburgh, Scotland, 2009. ACM.

[2] Franz Baader and Tobias Nipkow. *Term Rewriting and All That*. Cambridge University Press, 1998.

[3] Gershom Bazerman. jmacro, jul 2011.

[4] Cristiano Calcagno, Eugenio Moggi, and Tim Sheard. Closed types for a safe imperative MetaML. *Journal of Functional Programming*, 13(03):545–571, 2003.

[5] Cristiano Calcagno, Eugenio Moggi, and Walid Taha. ML-Like inference for classifiers. In *In European Symposium on Programming (ESOP '04)*, volume 2986 of *Lecture Notes in Computer Science*, pages 79—93, 2004.

[6] Jacques Carette. Gaussian elimination: A case study in efficient genericity with MetaOCaml. *Science of Computer Programming*, 62 (1):3–24, sep 2006.

[7] P. P. Chang and W.-W. Hwu. Inline function expansion for compiling c programs. In *Proceedings of the ACM SIGPLAN 1989 Conference on Programming language design and implementation*, PLDI '89, page 246–257, New York, NY, USA, 1989. ACM. ISBN 0-89791-306-X.

[8] Chiyan Chen and Hongwei Xi. Meta-Programming through typeful code representation. *Journal of Functional Programming*, 15(06): 797–835, 2005.

[9] R. Davies. A temporal-logic approach to binding-time analysis. In *Proceedings of the 11th Annual IEEE Symposium on Logic in Computer Science*, page 184. IEEE Computer Society, 1996.

[10] Rowan Davies and Frank Pfenning. A modal analysis of staged computation. In *Proceedings of the 23rd ACM SIGPLAN-SIGACT symposium on Principles of programming languages*, pages 258–270, St. Petersburg Beach, Florida, United States, 1996. ACM.

[11] Rowan Davies and Frank Pfenning. A modal analysis of staged computation. *Journal of the ACM (JACM)*, 48:555–604, may 2001. ACM ID: 382785.

[12] Edsko de Vries. *Making Uniqueness Typing Less Unique*. PhD thesis, Trinity College, Dublin, Ireland, 2008.

[13] Jason Eckhardt, Roumen Kaiabachev, Emir Pašalić, Kedar Swadi, and Walid Taha. Implicitly heterogeneous multi-stage programming. *New Gen. Comput.*, 25(3):305–336, 2007.

[14] Matteo Frigo and Steven G Johnson. The design and implementation of FFTW3. *Proceedings of the IEEE*, 93(2):216–231, 2005. Special issue on "Program Generation, Optimization, and Platform Adaptation".

[15] Hideyuki Tanaka. peggy, feb 2012.

[16] Trevor Jim. What are principal typings and what are they good for? In *Proceedings of the 23rd ACM SIGPLAN-SIGACT symposium on Principles of programming languages*, pages 42–53, St. Petersburg Beach, Florida, United States, 1996. ACM.

[17] Yukiyoshi Kameyama, Oleg Kiselyov, and Chung-chieh Shan. Closing the stage: from staged code to typed closures. In *Proceedings of the 2008 ACM SIGPLAN symposium on Partial evaluation and semantics-based program manipulation*, pages 147–157, San Francisco, California, USA, 2008. ACM.

[18] Yukiyoshi Kameyama, Oleg Kiselyov, and Chung-Chieh Shan. Shifting the stage: staging with delimited control. *Journal of Functional Programming*, 21(06):617–662, 2011.

[19] Andrew J. Kennedy. Type inference and equational theories. Technical Report LIX/RR/96/09, LIX, Ecole Polytechnique, 91128 Palaiseau Cedex, France, sep 1996.

[20] Ik-Soon Kim, Kwangkeun Yi, and Cristiano Calcagno. A polymorphic modal type system for lisp-like multi-staged languages. In *Conference record of the 33rd ACM SIGPLAN-SIGACT symposium on Principles of programming languages*, pages 257–268, Charleston, South Carolina, USA, 2006. ACM.

[21] Oleg Kiselyov and Walid Taha. Relating FFTW and Split-Radix. In *Embedded Software and Systems*, pages 488–493. 2005.

[22] Geoffrey Mainland. Why it's nice to be quoted: Quasiquoting for haskell. In *Haskell '07: Proceedings of the ACM SIGPLAN Workshop on Haskell*, page 73–82, New York, NY, USA, 2007. ACM.

[23] Geoffrey Mainland. language-c-quote, 2010.

[24] Geoffrey Mainland and Greg Morrisett. Nikola: embedding compiled GPU functions in haskell. In *Proceedings of the third ACM Haskell symposium on Haskell*, pages 67–78, Baltimore, Maryland, USA, 2010. ACM.

[25] Geoffrey Mainland, Greg Morrisett, and Matt Welsh. Flask: Staged functional programming for sensor networks. In *Proceeding of the 13th ACM SIGPLAN International Conference on Functional Programming (ICFP '08)*, page 335–346, New York, NY, USA, 2008. ACM.

[26] Urusula Martin and Tobias Nipkow. Boolean unification—The story so far. *Journal of Symbolic Computation*, 7(3–4):275—293, apr 1989.

[27] Aleksandar Nanevski. Meta-programming with names and necessity. In *Proceedings of the seventh ACM SIGPLAN International Conference on Functional Programming*, pages 206–217, Pittsburgh, PA, USA, 2002. ACM.

[28] Aleksandar Nanevski, Frank Pfenning, and Brigitte Pientka. Contextual modal type theory. *ACM Transactions on Computational Logic (TOCL)*, 9:23:1–23:49, jun 2008. ACM ID: 1352591.

[29] Markus Püschel, José M. F. Moura, Bryan Singer, Jianxin Xiong, Jeremy Johnson, David Padua, Manuela Veloso, and Robert W. Johnson. Spiral: A generator for Platform-Adapted libraries of signal processing alogorithms. *International Journal of High Performance Computing Applications*, 18(1):21—45, feb 2004.

[30] Didier Rémy. Type inference for records in natural extension of ML. Research Report 1431, Institut National de Recherche en Informatique et Automatisme, 1991.

[31] Didier Rémy. Syntactic theories and the algebra of record terms. Research Report 1869, Institut National de Recherche en Informatique et Automatisme, Rocquencourt, BP 105, 78 153 Le Chesnay Cedex, France, 1993.

[32] Morten Rhiger. First-class open and closed code fragments. *In Proceedings of the Sixth Symposium on Trends in Functional Programming*, 2005.

[33] Zhong Shao and Andrew W. Appel. Smartest recompilation. In *Proceedings of the 20th ACM SIGPLAN-SIGACT symposium on Principles of programming languages*, pages 439–450, Charleston, South Carolina, United States, 1993. ACM.

[34] Kedar Swadi, Walid Taha, Oleg Kiselyov, and Emir Pasalic. A monadic approach for avoiding code duplication when staging memoized functions. In *Proceedings of the 2006 ACM SIGPLAN symposium on Partial evaluation and semantics-based program manipulation*, PEPM '06, page 160–169, New York, NY, USA, 2006. ACM. ACM ID: 1111570.

[35] Walid Taha. A gentle introduction to multi-stage programming. In Christian Lengauer, Don S. Batory, Charles Consel, and Martin Odersky, editors, *Domain-Specific Program Generation*, volume 3016 of *Lecture Notes in Computer Science*, page 30–50. Springer, 2003.

[36] Walid Taha and Michael Florentin Nielsen. Environment classifiers. In *Proceedings of the 30th ACM SIGPLAN-SIGACT symposium on Principles of programming languages*, POPL '03, page 26–37, New York, NY, USA, 2003. ACM.

[37] Walid Taha and Tim Sheard. Multi-stage programming with explicit annotations. In *Proceedings of the 1997 ACM SIGPLAN symposium on Partial Evaluation and Semantics-Based Program Manipulation (PEPM '97)*, pages 203–217, Amsterdam, The Netherlands, 1997. ACM.

[38] Philip Wadler. Is there a use for linear logic? In *Proceedings of the 1991 ACM SIGPLAN symposium on Partial evaluation and semantics-based program manipulation*, PEPM '91, page 255–273, New York, NY, USA, 1991. ACM. ISBN 0-89791-433-3.

[39] Stephanie Weirich, Dimitrios Vytiniotis, Simon L. Peyton Jones, and Steve Zdancewic. Generative type abstraction and type-level computation. In *Proceedings of the 38th ACM SIGPLAN-SIGACT symposium on Principles of programming languages (POPL '11)*, Austin, TX, 2011.

[40] R. Clint Whaley and Antoine Petitet. Minimizing development and maintenance costs in supporting persistently optimized BLAS. *Softw. Pract. Exper.*, 35(2):101–121, 2005.

[41] Hongwei Xi, Chiyan Chen, and Gang Chen. Guarded recursive datatype constructors. In *Proceedings of the 30th ACM SIGPLAN-SIGACT symposium on Principles of programming languages - POPL '03*, pages 224–235, New Orleans, Louisiana, USA, 2003.

A Generic Abstract Syntax Model for Embedded Languages

Emil Axelsson
Chalmers University of Technology
emax@chalmers.se

Abstract

Representing a syntax tree using a data type often involves having many similar-looking constructors. Functions operating on such types often end up having many similar-looking cases. Different languages often make use of similar-looking constructions. We propose a generic model of abstract syntax trees capable of representing a wide range of typed languages. Syntactic constructs can be composed in a modular fashion enabling reuse of abstract syntax and syntactic processing within and across languages. Building on previous methods of encoding extensible data types in Haskell, our model is a pragmatic solution to Wadler's "expression problem". Its practicality has been confirmed by its use in the implementation of the embedded language Feldspar.

Categories and Subject Descriptors D.2.11 [*Software Architectures*]: Languages; D.2.13 [*Reusable Software*]: Reusable libraries; D.3.2 [*Language Classifications*]: Extensible languages; D.3.3 [*Language Constructs and Features*]: Data types and structures

Keywords the expression problem, generic programming, embedded domain-specific languages

1. Introduction

In 1998, Philip Wadler coined the "expression problem":[1]

> "The Expression Problem is a new name for an old problem. The goal is to define a datatype by cases, where one can add new cases to the datatype and new functions over the datatype, without recompiling existing code, and while retaining static type safety (e.g., no casts)."

This is not just a toy problem. It is an important matter of making software more maintainable and reusable. Being able to extend existing code without recompilation means that different features can be developed and verified independently of each other. Moreover, it gives the opportunity to extract common functionality into a library for others to benefit from. Having a single source for common functionality not only reduces implementation effort, but also leads to more trustworthy software, since the library can be verified once and used many times.

[1] http://www.daimi.au.dk/~madst/tool/papers/expression.txt

ICFP'12, September 9–15, 2012, Copenhagen, Denmark.

Our motivation for looking at the expression problem is highly practical. Our research group has developed several embedded domain-specific languages (EDSLs), for example, Lava [5], Feldspar [3] and Obsidian [8]. There are several constructs and operations that occur repeatedly, both between the languages and within each language. We are interested in factoring out this common functionality in order to simplify the implementations and to make the generic parts available to others. A modular design also makes it easier to try out new features, which is important given the experimental state of the languages.

In addition to the requirements stated in the expression problem, a desired property of an extensible data type model is support for generic traversals. This means that interpretation functions should only have to mention the "interesting" cases. For example, an analysis that counts the number of additions in an expression should only have to specify two cases: (1) the case for addition, and (2) a generic case for all other constructs.

Our vision is a library of generic building blocks for EDSLs that can easily be assembled and customized for different domains. Modular extensibility (as stated in the expression problem) is one aspect of this vision. Support for generic programming is another important aspect, as it can reduce the amount of boilerplate code needed to customize interpretation functions for specific constructs.

This paper proposes a simple model of typed abstract syntax trees that is extensible and supports generic traversals. The model is partly derived from Swierstra's *Data Types à la Carte* (DTC) [18] which is an encoding of extensible data types in Haskell. DTC is based on fixed-points of extensible functors. Our work employs the extensibility mechanism from DTC, but uses an application tree (section 2.2) instead of a type-level fixed-point. Given that DTC (including recent development [4]) already provides extensible data types and generic traversals, our paper makes the following additional contributions (see also the comparison in section 10):

- We confirm the versatility of the original DTC invention by using it in an alternative setting (section 3).
- Our model provides direct access to the recursive structure of the data types, leading to simpler generic traversals that do not rely on external generic programming mechanisms (section 4).
- We explore the use of explicit recursion in addition to predefined recursion schemes (sections 5, 6 and 7), demonstrating that generic traversals over extensible data types are not restricted to predefined recursive patterns.

Our model is available in the SYNTACTIC library[2] together with a lot of utilities for EDSL implementation (section 9). It has been successfully used in the implementation of Feldspar [3] (section 9.1), an EDSL aimed at programming numerical algorithms in time-critical domains.

[2] http://hackage.haskell.org/package/syntactic-1.0

The code in this paper is available as a literate Haskell file.[3] It has been tested using GHC 7.4.1 (and the `mtl` package). A number of GHC-specific extensions are used; see the source code for details.

2. Modeling abstract syntax

It is common for embedded languages to implement an abstract syntax tree such as the following:

```
data Expr1 a where
  Num1 :: Int -> Expr1 Int
  Add1 :: Expr1 Int -> Expr1 Int -> Expr1 Int
  Mul1 :: Expr1 Int -> Expr1 Int -> Expr1 Int
```

`Expr1` is a type of numerical expressions with integer literals, addition and multiplication. The parameter `a` is the type of the *semantic value* of the expression; i.e. the value obtained by evaluating the expression. (For `Expr1`, the semantic value type happens to always be `Int`, but we will soon consider expressions with other semantic types.) Evaluation is defined as a simple recursive function:

```
evalExpr1 :: Expr1 a -> a
evalExpr1 (Num1 n)   = n
evalExpr1 (Add1 a b) = evalExpr1 a + evalExpr1 b
evalExpr1 (Mul1 a b) = evalExpr1 a * evalExpr1 b
```

The problem with types such as `Expr1` is that they are not extensible. It is perfectly possible to add new interpretation functions in the same way as `evalExpr1`, but unfortunately, adding new constructors is not that easy. If we want to add a new constructor, say for subtraction, not only do we need to edit and recompile the definition of `Expr1`, but also all existing interpretation functions. Another problem with `Expr1` is the way that the recursive structure of the tree has been mixed up with the symbols in it: It is not possible to traverse the tree without pattern matching on the constructors, and this prevents the definition of generic traversals where only the "interesting" constructors have to be dealt with. We are going to deal with the problem of generic traversal first, and will then see that the result also opens up for a solution to the extensibility problem.

2.1 Exposing the tree structure

One way to separate the tree structure from the symbols is to make symbol application explicit:

```
data Expr2 a where
  Num2 :: Int -> Expr2 Int
  Add2 :: Expr2 (Int -> Int -> Int)
  Mul2 :: Expr2 (Int -> Int -> Int)
  App2 :: Expr2 (a -> b) -> Expr2 a -> Expr2 b
```

Here, `Add2` and `Mul2` are *function-valued symbols* (i.e. symbols whose semantic value is a function), and the only thing we can do with those symbols is to apply them to arguments using `App2`. As an example, here is the tree for the expression $3 + 4$:

```
ex1 = App2 (App2 Add2 (Num2 3)) (Num2 4)
```

What we have gained with this rewriting is the ability to traverse the tree without necessarily mentioning any symbols. For example, this function computes the size of an expression:

```
sizeExpr2 :: Expr2 a -> Int
sizeExpr2 (App2 s a) = sizeExpr2 s + sizeExpr2 a
sizeExpr2 _          = 1
```

[3] http://www.cse.chalmers.se/~emax/documents/axelsson2012generic.lhs

```
*Main> sizeExpr2 ex1
3
```

However, even though we have achieved a certain kind of generic programming, it is limited to *a single type*, which makes it quite uninteresting. Luckily, the idea can be generalized.

2.2 The `AST` model

If we lift out the three symbols from `Expr2` and replace them with a single symbol constructor, we reach the following syntax tree model:

```
data AST dom sig where
  Sym  :: dom sig -> AST dom sig
  (:$) :: AST dom (a :-> sig) -> AST dom (Full a)
                              -> AST dom sig
infixl 1 :$
```

The `AST` type is parameterized on the *symbol domain* `dom`, and the `Sym` constructor introduces a symbol from this domain. The type `(:->)` is isomorphic to the function arrow, and `Full a` is isomorphic to `a`:

```
newtype Full a   = Full {result :: a}
newtype a :-> b = Partial (a -> b)
infixr :->
```

As will be seen later, these types are needed to be able to distinguish function-valued expressions from partially applied syntax trees.

The `AST` type is best understood by looking at a concrete example. `NUM` is the symbol domain corresponding to the `Expr1` type:

```
data NUM a where
  Num :: Int -> NUM (Full Int)
  Add :: NUM (Int :-> Int :-> Full Int)
  Mul :: NUM (Int :-> Int :-> Full Int)

type Expr3 a = AST NUM (Full a)
```

`Expr3` is isomorphic to `Expr1` (modulo strictness properties). This correspondence can be seen by defining smart constructors corresponding to the constructors of the `Expr1` type:

```
num :: Int -> Expr3 Int
add :: Expr3 Int -> Expr3 Int -> Expr3 Int
mul :: Expr3 Int -> Expr3 Int -> Expr3 Int

num     = Sym ∘ Num
add a b = Sym Add :$ a :$ b
mul a b = Sym Mul :$ a :$ b
```

Symbol types, such as `NUM` are indexed by *symbol signatures* built up using `Full` and `(:->)`. The signatures of `Num` and `Add` are:

```
Full Int
Int :-> Int :-> Full Int
```

The signature determines how a symbol can be used in an AST by specifying the semantic value types of its arguments and result. The first signature above specifies a terminal symbol that can be used to make an `Int`-valued AST, while the second signature specifies a non-terminal symbol that can be used to make an `Int`-valued AST node with two `Int`-valued sub-terms. The `Num` constructor also has an argument of type `Int`. However, this (being an ordinary Haskell integer) is to be regarded as a parameter to the symbol rather than a syntactic sub-term.

A step-by-step construction of the expression $a + b$ illustrates how the type gradually changes as arguments are added to the symbol:

```
a, b :: AST NUM (Full Int)

Add                 :: NUM (Int :→ Int :→ Full Int)
Sym Add             :: AST NUM (Int :→ Int :→Full Int)
Sym Add :$ a        :: AST NUM (Int :→ Full Int)
Sym Add :$ a :$ b :: AST NUM (Full Int)
```

We recognize a fully applied symbol by a type of the form `AST dom (Full a)`. Because we are often only interested in complete trees, we define the following shorthand:

```
type ASTF dom a = AST dom (Full a)
```

In general, a symbol has a type of the form

```
T (a :→ b :→ ... :→ Full x)
```

Such a symbol can be thought of as a model of a constructor of a recursive reference type T_{ref} of the form

```
T_ref a → T_ref b → ... → T_ref x
```

Why is `Full` only used at the result type of a signature and not the arguments? After all, we expect all sub-terms to be complete syntax trees. The answer can be seen in the type of `(:$)`:

```
(:$) :: AST dom (a :→ sig) → AST dom (Full a)
                           → AST dom sig
```

The `a` type in the first argument is mapped to `(Full a)` in the second argument (the sub-term). This ensures that the sub-term is always a complete AST, regardless of the signature.

The reason for using `(:→)` and `Full` (in contrast to how it was done in $\texttt{Expr}_2$) is that we want to distinguish non-terminal symbols from function-valued terminal symbols. This is needed in order to model the following language:

```
data Lang a where
  Op1 :: Lang Int → Lang Int → Lang Int
  Op2 :: Lang (Int → Int → Int)
```

Here, $\texttt{Op}_1$ is a *non-terminal* that needs two sub-trees in order to make a complete syntax tree. $\texttt{Op}_2$ is a function-valued terminal. This distinction can be captured precisely when using `AST`:

```
data LangDom a where
  Op1' :: LangDom (Int :→ Int :→ Full Int)
  Op2' :: LangDom (Full (Int → Int → Int))

type Lang' a = AST LangDom (Full a)
```

Without `(:→)` and `Full`, the distinction would be lost.

2.3 Simple interpretation

Just as we have used `Sym` and `(:$)` to construct expressions, we can use them for pattern matching:

```
eval_NUM :: Expr3 a → a
eval_NUM (Sym (Num n))       = n
eval_NUM (Sym Add :$ a :$ b) = eval_NUM a + eval_NUM b
eval_NUM (Sym Mul :$ a :$ b) = eval_NUM a * eval_NUM b
```

Note the similarity to $\texttt{evalExpr}_1$. Here is a small example to show that it works:

```
*Main> eval_NUM (num 5 'mul' num 6)
30
```

For later reference, we also define a rendering interpretation:

```
render_NUM :: Expr3 a → String
render_NUM (Sym (Num n))       = show n
render_NUM (Sym Add :$ a :$ b) =
    "(" ++ render_NUM a ++ " + " ++ render_NUM b ++ ")"
render_NUM (Sym Mul :$ a :$ b) =
    "(" ++ render_NUM a ++ " * " ++ render_NUM b ++ ")"
```

A quick intermediate summary is in order. We have shown a method of encoding recursive data types using the general `AST` type. The encoding has a one-to-one correspondence to the original type, and because of this correspondence, we intend to define languages only using `AST`, without the existence of an encoded reference type. However, for any type `(ASTF dom)`, a corresponding reference type can always be constructed. So far, it does not look like we have gained much from this exercise, but remember that the goal is to enable extensible languages and generic traversals. This will be done in the two following sections.

3. Extensible languages

In the quest for enabling the definition of extensible languages, the `AST` type has put us in a better situation. Namely, the problem has been reduced from extending recursive data types, such as $\texttt{Expr}_1$, to extending non-recursive types, such as `NUM`. Fortunately, this problem has already been solved in Data Types à la Carte (DTC). DTC defines the type composition operator in Listing 1, which can be seen as a higher-kinded version of the `Either` type. We demonstrate its use by defining two new symbol domains:

```
data Logic a where -- Logic expressions
  Not :: Logic (Bool :→ Full Bool)
  Eq  :: Eq a ⇒ Logic (a :→ a :→ Full Bool)

data If a where      -- Conditional expression
  If :: If (Bool :→ a :→ a :→ Full a)
```

These can now be combined with `NUM` to form a larger domain:

```
type Expr a = ASTF (NUM :+: Logic :+: If) a
```

A corresponding reference type (which we do not need to define) has all constructors merged at the same level:

```
data Expr_ref a where
  Num :: Int → Expr_ref Int
  Add :: Expr_ref Int → Expr_ref Int → Expr_ref Int
  ...
  Not :: Expr_ref Bool → Expr_ref Bool
  ...
  If  :: Expr_ref Bool → Expr_ref a → Expr_ref a
                                    → Expr_ref a
```

Unfortunately, the introduction of `(:+:)` means that constructing expressions becomes more complicated:[4]

```
not :: Expr Bool → Expr Bool
not a = Sym (Inj_R (Inj_L Not)) :$ a

cond :: Expr Bool → Expr a → Expr a → Expr a
cond c t f = Sym (Inj_R (Inj_R If)) :$ c :$ t :$ f
```

```
data (dom₁ :+: dom₂) a where
  Inj_L :: dom₁ a → (dom₁ :+: dom₂) a
  Inj_R :: dom₂ a → (dom₁ :+: dom₂) a

infixr :+:
```

Listing 1: Composition of symbol domains (part of DTC interface)

```
class (sub :<: sup) where
  inj :: sub a → sup a
  prj :: sup a → Maybe (sub a)

instance (expr :<: expr) where
  inj = id
  prj = Just

instance (sym :<: (sym :+: dom)) where
  inj          = Inj_L
  prj (Inj_L a) = Just a
  prj _         = Nothing

instance (sym₁ :<: dom)
      ⇒ (sym₁ :<: (sym₂ :+: dom)) where
  inj          = Inj_R ∘ inj
  prj (Inj_R a) = prj a
  prj _         = Nothing

-- Additional instance for AST
instance (sub :<: sup) ⇒ (sub :<: AST sup) where
  inj         = Sym ∘ inj
  prj (Sym a) = prj a
  prj _       = Nothing
```

Listing 2: Symbol subsumption (part of DTC interface)

The symbols are now tagged with injection constructors, and the amount of injections will only grow as the domain gets larger. Fortunately, DTC has a solution to this problem too. The `(:<:)` class, defined in Listing 2, provides the `inj` function which automates the insertion of injections based on the types. The final instance also takes care of injecting the `Sym` constructor from the `AST` type. We can now define not as follows:

```
not :: (Logic :<: dom)
    ⇒ ASTF dom Bool → ASTF dom Bool
not a = inj Not :$ a
```

The `prj` function in Listing 2 is the partial inverse of `inj`. Just like `inj` allows one to avoid a nest of $\texttt{Inj}_L$/$\texttt{Inj}_R$ constructors in *construction*, `prj` avoids a nest of injection constructors in *pattern matching* (see section 3.2). The instances of `(:<:)` essentially perform a linear search at the type level to find the right injection. Overlapping instances are used to select the base case.

The remaining constructs of the `Expr` language are defined in Listing 3. Note that the types have now become more general. For example, the type

```
(⊕) :: (NUM :<: dom)
    ⇒ ASTF dom Int → ASTF dom Int → ASTF dom Int
```

[4] Here we override the `not` function from the `Prelude`. The `Prelude` function will be used qualified in this paper.

```
num :: (NUM :<: dom) ⇒ Int → ASTF dom Int

(⊕) :: (NUM :<: dom)
    ⇒ ASTF dom Int → ASTF dom Int → ASTF dom Int

(⊙) :: (NUM :<: dom)
    ⇒ ASTF dom Int → ASTF dom Int → ASTF dom Int

(≡) :: (Logic :<: dom, Eq a)
    ⇒ ASTF dom a → ASTF dom a → ASTF dom Bool

condition :: (If :<: dom)
          ⇒ ASTF dom Bool
          → ASTF dom a → ASTF dom a → ASTF dom a

num              = inj ∘ Num
a ⊕ b            = inj Add :$ a :$ b
a ⊙ b            = inj Mul :$ a :$ b
a ≡ b            = inj Eq  :$ a :$ b
condition c t f = inj If  :$ c :$ t :$ f

infixl 6 ⊕
infixl 7 ⊙
```

Listing 3: Extensible language front end

says that (⊕) works with *any* domain `dom` that contains `NUM`. Informally, this means any domain of the form

```
... :+: NUM :+: ...
```

Expressions only involving numeric operations will only have a `NUM` constraint on the domain:

```
ex₂ :: (NUM :<: dom) ⇒ ASTF dom Int
ex₂ = (num 5 ⊕ num 0) ⊙ num 6
```

This means that such expressions can be evaluated by the earlier function $\texttt{eval}_{NUM}$, which only knows about `NUM`:

```
*Main> eval_NUM ex₂
30
```

Still, the type is general enough that we are free to use $\texttt{ex}_2$ together with non-numeric constructs:

```
ex₃ = ex₂ ≡ ex₂
```

The class constraints compose as expected:

```
*Main> :t ex₃
ex₃ :: (Logic :<: dom, NUM :<: dom) ⇒ ASTF dom Bool
```

That is, $\texttt{ex}_3$ is a valid expression in *any language* that includes `Logic` and `NUM`.

3.1 Functions over extensible languages

The evaluation function $\texttt{eval}_{NUM}$ is closed and works only for the `NUM` domain. By making the domain type polymorphic, we can define functions over open domains. The simplest example is `size`, which is completely parametric in the `dom` type:

```
size :: AST dom a → Int
size (Sym _)  = 1
size (s :$ a) = size s + size a
```

```
*Main> size (ex2 :: Expr3 Int)
5
*Main> size (ex3 :: Expr Bool)
11
```

But most functions we want to define require some awareness of the symbols involved. If we want to count the number of additions in an expression, say, we need to be able to tell whether a given symbol is an addition. This is where the prj function comes in:

```
countAdds :: (NUM :<: dom) ⇒ AST dom a → Int
countAdds (Sym s)
    | Just Add ← prj s = 1
    | otherwise        = 0
countAdds (s :$ a)     = countAdds s + countAdds a
```

In the symbol case, the prj function attempts to project the symbol to the NUM type. If it succeeds (returning Just) and the symbol is Add, 1 is returned; otherwise 0 is returned. Note that the type is as general as possible, with only a NUM constraint on the domain. Thus, it accepts terms from any language that includes NUM:

```
*Main> countAdds (ex2 :: Expr3 Int)
1
*Main> countAdds (ex3 :: Expr Bool)
2
```

We have now fulfilled all requirements of the expression problem:

- We have the ability to extend data types with new cases, and to define functions over such open types.
- We can add new interpretations (this was never a problem).
- Extension does not require recompilation of existing code. For example, the NUM, Logic and If types could have been defined in separate modules. The function countAdds is completely independent of Logic and If. Still, it can be used with expressions containing those constructs (such as ex_3).
- We have not sacrificed any type-safety.

3.2 Pattern matching

The encoding we use does come with a certain overhead. This is particularly visible when doing nested pattern matching. Here is a function that performs the optimization $x + 0 \rightarrow x$:

```
optAddTop :: (NUM :<: dom) ⇒ ASTF dom a → ASTF dom a
optAddTop (add :$ a :$ b)
  | Just Add     ← prj add
  , Just (Num 0) ← prj b   = a
optAddTop a = a
```

(This function only rewrites the top-most node; in section 6.2, we will see how to apply the rewrite across the whole expression.) Note the sequencing of the pattern guards. An alternative is to use the ViewPatterns extension to GHC instead:

```
optAddTop
  ((prj→ Just Add) :$ a :$ (prj→ Just (Num 0))) = a
optAddTop a = a
```

While view patterns have the advantage that they can be nested, doing so tends to lead to long lines. For this reason, it is ofter preferable to use a sequence of pattern guards.

4. Generic traversals

We will now see how to define various kinds of generic traversals over the AST type. In this section, we will only deal with fold-like traversals (but they are defined using explicit recursion). In sections 5 and 7, we will look at more general types of traversals.

According to Hinze and Löh [9], support for generic programming consists of two essential ingredients: (1) a way to write overloaded functions, and (2) a way to access the structure of values in a uniform way. Together, these two components allow functions to be defined over a (possibly open) set of types, for which only the "interesting" cases need to be given. All other cases will be covered by a single (or a few) default case(s).

We have already encountered some generic functions in this paper. For example, size works for all possible AST types, and countAdds works for all types (AST dom) where the constraint (NUM :<: dom) is satisfied.[5] For size, all cases are covered by the default cases, while countAdds has one special case, and all other cases have default behavior.

An important aspect of a generic programming model is whether or not new interesting cases can be added in a modular way. The countAdds function has a single interesting case, and there is no way to add more of them. We will now see how to define functions for which the interesting cases can be extended for new types. We begin by looking at functions for which *all cases* are interesting.

4.1 Generic interpretation

The interpretation functions $eval_{NUM}$ and $render_{NUM}$ are defined for a single, closed domain. To make them extensible, we need to make the domain abstract, just like we did in countAdds. However, we do not want to use prj to match out the interesting cases, because now all cases are interesting. Instead, we factor out the evaluation of the symbols to a user-provided function. What is left is a single case for Sym and one for (:$):

```
evalG :: (∀a . dom a      → Denotation a)
      → (∀a . AST dom a → Denotation a)
evalG f (Sym s)    = f s
evalG f (s :$ a) = evalG f s $ evalG f a

type family   Denotation sig
type instance Denotation (Full a)    = a
type instance Denotation (a :→ sig) =
                a → Denotation sig
```

The Denotation type function strips away (:→) and Full from a signature. As an example, we let GHCi compute the denotation of (Int :→ Full Bool):

```
*Main> :kind! Denotation (Int :→ Full Bool)
Denotation (Int :→ Full Bool) :: *
= Int → Bool
```

Next, we define the evaluation of NUM symbols as a separate function:

```
evalSymNUM :: NUM a → Denotation a
evalSymNUM (Num n) = n
evalSymNUM Add     = (+)
evalSymNUM Mul     = (*)
```

[5] One can argue that these functions are not technically generic, because they only work for instances of the AST type constructor. However, because we use AST as a way to encode hypothetical reference types, we take the liberty to call such functions generic anyway.

Because this definition only has to deal with non-recursive symbols, it is very simple compared to $\texttt{eval}_{NUM}$. We can now plug the generic and the type-specific functions together and use them to evaluate expressions:

```
*Main> evalG evalSym_NUM ex_2
30
```

Our task is to define an extensible evaluation that can easily be extended with new cases. We have now reduced this problem to making the $\texttt{evalSym}_{NUM}$ function extensible. The way to do this is to put it in a type class:

```
class Eval expr where
  eval :: expr a → Denotation a

instance Eval NUM where
  eval (Num n) = n
  eval Add     = (+)
  eval Mul     = (*)

instance Eval Logic where
  eval Not = Prelude.not
  eval Eq  = (==)

instance Eval If where
  eval If = λc t f → if c then t else f
```

Now that we have instances for all our symbol types, we also need to make sure that we can evaluate combinations of these types using `(:+:)`. The instance is straightforward:

```
instance (Eval sub_1, Eval sub_2)
      ⇒ Eval (sub_1 :+: sub_2) where
  eval (Inj_L s) = eval s
  eval (Inj_R s) = eval s
```

We can even make an instance for `AST`, which then replaces the `evalG` function:

```
instance Eval dom ⇒ Eval (AST dom) where
  eval (Sym s)   = eval s
  eval (s :$ a)  = eval s $ eval a
```

Now everything is in place, and we should be able to evaluate expressions using a mixed domain:

```
*Main> eval (ex_3 :: Expr Bool)
True
```

4.2 Finding compositionality

One nice thing about `eval` is that it is completely compositional over the application spine of the symbol. This means that even partially applied symbols have an interpretation. For example, the partially applied symbol `(inj Add :$ num 5)` evaluates to the denotation `(5 +)`. We call such interpretations *spine-compositional*.

When making a generic version of $\texttt{render}_{NUM}$ we might try to use the following interface:

```
class Render expr where
  render :: expr a → String
```

However, the problem with this is that rendering is not spine-compositional: It is generally not possible to render a partially applied symbol as a monolithic string. For example, a symbol representing an infix operator will join its sub-expression strings differently from a prefix operator symbol. A common way to get to a spine-compositional interpretation is to make the renderings of the sub-expressions explicit in the interpretation. That is, we use `([String] → String)` as interpretation:

```
class Render expr where
  renderArgs :: expr a → ([String] → String)

render :: Render expr ⇒ expr a → String
render a = renderArgs a []
```

Now, the joining of the sub-expressions can be chosen for each case individually. The following instances use a mixture of prefix (`Not`), infix (`Add`, `Mul`, `Eq`) and mixfix rendering (`If`):

```
instance Render NUM where
  renderArgs (Num n) [] = show n
  renderArgs Add [a,b] = "(" ++ a ++ " + " ++ b ++ ")"
  renderArgs Mul [a,b] = "(" ++ a ++ " * " ++ b ++ ")"

instance Render Logic where
  renderArgs Not [a]   = "(not " ++ a ++ ")"
  renderArgs Eq [a,b] = "(" ++ a ++ " == " ++ b ++ ")"

instance Render If where
  renderArgs If [c,t,f] = unwords
      ["(if", c, "then", t, "else", f ++ ")"]
```

Although convenient, it is quite unsatisfying to have to use refutable pattern matching on the argument lists. We will present a solution to this problem in section 6.

The instance for `AST` traverses the spine, collecting the rendered sub-terms in a list that is passed on to the rendering of the symbol:

```
instance Render dom ⇒ Render (AST dom) where
  renderArgs (Sym s)  as = renderArgs s as
  renderArgs (s :$ a) as = renderArgs s (render a:as)
```

Note that the case for `(:$)` has two recursive calls. The call to `renderArgs` is for traversing the application spine, and the call to `render` is for rendering the sub-terms. The `Render` instance for `(:+:)` is analogous to the `Eval` instance, so we omit it. This concludes the definition of rendering for extensible languages.

```
*Main> render (ex_2 :: Expr Int)
"((5 + 0) * 6)"
```

The functions `eval` and `render` do not have any generic default cases, because all cases have interesting behavior. The next step is to look at a function that has useful generic default cases.

4.3 Case study: Extensible compiler

Will now use the presented techniques to define a simple compiler for our extensible expression language. The job of the compiler is to turn expressions into a sequence of variable assignments:

```
*Main> putStr $ compile (ex_2 :: Expr Int)
v3 = 5
v4 = 0
v1 = (v3 + v4)
v2 = 6
v0 = (v1 * v2)
```

Listing 4 defines the type `CodeGen` along with some utility functions. A `CodeGen` is a function from a variable identifier (the result location) to a monadic expression that computes the program as a list of strings.[6] The monad also has a state in order to be able to generate fresh variables.

Listing 5 defines the fully generic parts of the compiler. Note the similarity between the types of `compileArgs` and `renderArgs`. One difference between the `Compile` and `Render` classes is that `Compile` has a default implementation of its method. The default method assumes that the symbol represents a simple expression, and uses `renderArgs` to render it as a string. The rendered expression is then assigned to the result location using `(=:=)`. The instances for `AST` and `(:+:)` are analogous to those of the `Render` class. Finally, the `compile` function takes care of running the `CodeGen` and extracting the written program.

The code in Listings 4 and 5 is *completely generic*—it does not mention anything about the symbols involved, apart from the assumption of them being instances of `Compile`. In Listing 6 we give the specific instances for the symbol types defined earlier. Because `NUM` and `Logic` are simple expression types, we rely on the default behavior for these. For `If`, we want to generate an if statement rather than an expression with an assignment. This means that we cannot use the default case, so we have to provide a specific case.

A simple test will demonstrate that the compiler works as intended:

```
ex4 = condition (num 1 ≡ num 2) (num 3) ex2

*Main> putStr $ compile (ex4 :: Expr Int)
v2 = 1
v3 = 2
v1 = (v2 == v3)
if v1 then
   v0 = 3
else
   v6 = 5
   v7 = 0
   v4 = (v6 + v7)
   v5 = 6
   v0 = (v4 * v5)
```

5. Implicit and explicit recursion

So far, our functions have all been defined using explicit recursion. But there is nothing stopping us from defining convenient recursion schemes as higher-order functions. For example, the `AST` instances for `renderArgs` and `compileArgs` (see section 4) both perform the same kind of fold-like bottom-up traversal which can be captured by the general combinator `fold`:

```
fold :: ∀dom b . (∀a . dom a → [b] → b)
               → (∀a . ASTF dom a    → b)
fold f a = go a []
  where
    go :: ∀a . AST dom a → [b] → b
    go (Sym s)  as = f s as
    go (s :$ a) as = go s (fold f a : as)
```

Note, again, the two recursive calls in the case for `(:$)`: the call to `go` for traversing the spine, and the call to `fold` for folding the sub-terms. Despite the traversal of the spine, `fold` should not be confused with a "spine fold" such as `gfoldl` from Scrap Your Boilerplate [11]. Rather, we are folding over the whole syntax tree, and `go` is just used to collect the sub-results in a list. This way of using ordinary lists to hold the result of sub-terms is also used in the Uniplate library [15] (see the `para` combinator).

[6] Thanks to Dévai Gergely for the technique of parameterizing the compiler on the result location.

```
type VarId      =  Integer
type ResultLoc  =  VarId
type Program    =  [String]
type CodeMonad  =  WriterT Program (State VarId)
type CodeGen    =  ResultLoc → CodeMonad ()

freshVar        ::  CodeMonad VarId
var             ::  VarId → String
(=:=)           ::  VarId → String → String
indent          ::  Program → Program

freshVar        =  do v ← get; put (v+1); return v
var v           =  "v" ++ show v
v =:= expr      =  var v ++ " = " ++ expr
indent          =  map ("    " ++)
```

Listing 4: Extensible compiler: interpretation and utility functions

```
class Render expr ⇒ Compile expr where
  compileArgs :: expr a → ([CodeGen] → CodeGen)
  compileArgs expr args loc = do
      argVars ← replicateM (length args) freshVar
      zipWithM ($) args argVars
      tell [loc =:= renderArgs expr (map var argVars)]

instance Compile dom ⇒ Compile (AST dom) where
  compileArgs (Sym s) args loc =
      compileArgs s args loc
  compileArgs (s :$ a) args loc = do
      compileArgs s (compileArgs a [] : args) loc

instance (Compile sub1, Compile sub2)
      ⇒ Compile (sub1 :+: sub2) where
  compileArgs (InjL s) = compileArgs s
  compileArgs (InjR s) = compileArgs s

compile :: Compile expr ⇒ expr a → String
compile expr = unlines
             $ flip evalState 1
             $ execWriterT
             $ compileArgs expr [] 0
```

Listing 5: Extensible compiler: generic code

```
instance Compile NUM
instance Compile Logic

instance Compile If where
  compileArgs If [cGen,tGen,fGen] loc = do
    cVar ← freshVar
    cGen cVar
    tProg ← lift $ execWriterT $ tGen loc
    fProg ← lift $ execWriterT $ fGen loc
    tell $ [unwords ["if", var cVar, "then"]]
       ++ indent tProg
       ++ ["else"]
       ++ indent fProg
```

Listing 6: Extensible compiler: type-specific code

As a demonstration, we show how to redefine render and compile in terms of fold:

```
render₂ :: Render dom ⇒ ASTF dom a → String
render₂ = fold renderArgs

compile₂ :: Compile dom ⇒ ASTF dom a → String
compile₂ a = unlines
           $ flip evalState 1
           $ execWriterT
           $ fold compileArgs a 0
```

Here, renderArgs and compileArgs are only used as algebras (of type (dom a → [...] → ...)), which means that the Render and Compile instances for AST are no longer needed.

Despite the usefulness of functions like fold, it is important to stress that our traversals are by no means restricted to fold-like patterns. We can fall back to explicit recursion, or define new custom recursion schemes, whenever needed. As an example of a function that does not suit the fold pattern, we define term equality. The generic code is as follows:

```
class Equality expr where
  equal :: expr a → expr b → Bool

instance Equality dom ⇒ Equality (AST dom) where
  equal (Sym s1)    (Sym s2)    = equal s1 s2
  equal (s1 :$ a1) (s2 :$ a2) =
      equal s1 s2 && equal a1 a2
  equal _ _ = False

instance (Equality sub₁, Equality sub₂)
    ⇒ Equality (sub₁ :+: sub₂) where
  equal (Inj_L s1) (Inj_L s2) = equal s1 s2
  equal (Inj_R s1) (Inj_R s2) = equal s1 s2
  equal _ _                   = False
```

And, once the generic code is in place, the type-specific instances are trivial; for example:

```
instance Equality NUM where
  equal (Num n1) (Num n2) = n1 == n2
  equal Add      Add      = True
  equal Mul      Mul      = True
  equal _ _               = False
```

We see that term equality comes out very naturally as an explicitly recursive function. Expressing this kind of recursion (simultaneous traversal of two terms) in terms of fold is possible, but quite tricky (for a general method, see the generic version of zipWith in reference [12]). In section 7, we will see another example where explicit recursion is useful.

6. Regaining type-safety

The use of a list to hold the interpretation of sub-terms (used by, for example, renderArgs and fold) has the problem that it loses type information about the context. This has two problems:

- The algebra function can never know whether it receives the expected number of arguments (see the refutable pattern matching in implementations of renderArgs).
- All intermediate results are required to have the same type and cannot depend on the type of the individual sub-expressions.

We can make the problem concrete by looking at the local function go that traverses the spine in fold:

```
go :: ∀a . AST dom a → [b] → b
go (Sym s)   as = f s as
go (s :$ a) as = go s (fold f a : as)
```

Now, consider folding an expression with Add as its top-level symbol: fold f (Sym Add :$ x :$ y), for some algebra f and sub-expressions x and y. This leads to the following unfolding of go:

```
go (Sym Add :$ x :$ y) []                 =
go (Sym Add :$ x)      [fold f y]         =
go (Sym Add)           [fold f x, fold f y]
```

In this sequence of calls, go is used at the following types:

```
go :: AST dom (Full Int)                  → [b] → b
go :: AST dom (Int :→ Full Int)           → [b] → b
go :: AST dom (Int :→ Int :→ Full Int) → [b] → b
```

We see that the type of the term gradually changes to reflect that sub-terms are stripped away; the number of arrows (:→) determines the number of missing sub-terms. However, the type of the list remains the same, even though its contents grows in each iteration. This is the root of the problem with fold. What we need instead is a list-like type—we will call it Args,—indexed by a symbol signature, and with the property that the number of arrows determines the number of elements in the list.

With such a list type, the go function will get a type of this form:

```
go :: ∀a . AST dom a → Args a → ...
```

Specifically, in the last recursive call in the above example, go will have the type:

```
go :: AST dom (Int :→ Int :→ Full Int)
   → Args     (Int :→ Int :→ Full Int)
   → ...
```

The first argument is an expression that is missing two sub-terms, and the intention is that the second argument is a two-element list containing the result of folding those particular sub-terms.

6.1 Typed argument lists

A definition of Args that fulfills the above specification is the following:

```
data Args c sig where
  Nil  :: Args c (Full a)
  (:*) :: c (Full a) → Args c sig
                     → Args c (a :→ sig)
infixr :*
```

Here we have added a parameter c which is the type constructor for the elements. The elements are of type c (Full a) where a varies with the position in the signature. Each cons cell (:*) imposes an additional arrow (:→) in the signature, which shows that the number of elements is equal to the number of arrows. Here is an example of a list containing an integer and a Boolean, using Maybe as type constructor:

```
argEx :: Args Maybe (Int :→ Bool :→ Full Char)
argEx = Just (Full 5) :* Just (Full False) :* Nil
```

The reason for making the elements indexed by Full a rather than just a is to be able to have lists with expressions in them. It is not possible to use (ASTF dom) as the type constructor c because ASTF is a type synonym, and, as such, cannot be partially applied. But because the elements are indexed by Full a, we can instead use (AST dom) as type constructor. Lists of type Args (AST dom) are used, for example, when using recursion schemes to transform expressions as we will do in the following section.

6.2 Type-safe fold

We are now ready to define a typed version of `fold`:

```
typedFold :: ∀dom c
  . (∀a . dom a → Args c a → c (Full (Result a)))
  → (∀a . ASTF dom a        → c (Full a))
typedFold f a = go a Nil
  where
    go :: ∀a . AST dom a → Args c a
                         → c (Full (Result a))
    go (Sym s)  as = f s as
    go (s :$ a) as = go s (typedFold f a :* as)
```

Note the close correspondence to the definition of the original `fold`. The `Result` type function simply gives the result type of a signature:

```
type family   Result sig
type instance Result (Full a)    = a
type instance Result (a :→ sig) = Result sig

*Main> :kind! Result (Int :→ Full Bool)
Result (Int :→ Full Bool) :: *
= Bool
```

The `Args` list ensures that the algebra will always receive the expected number of arguments. Furthermore, the elements in the `Args` list are now indexed by the type of the corresponding sub-expressions. In particular, this means that we can use `typedFold` to transform expressions without losing any type information. As a demonstration, we define the function `everywhere` that applies a function uniformly across an expression. It corresponds to the combinator with the same name in Scrap Your Boilerplate [11]:

```
everywhere :: (∀a . ASTF dom a → ASTF dom a)
           → (∀a . ASTF dom a → ASTF dom a)
everywhere f = typedFold (λs → f ∘ appArgs (Sym s))

appArgs :: AST dom sig → Args (AST dom) sig
                       → ASTF dom (Result sig)
appArgs a Nil       = a
appArgs s (a :* as) = appArgs (s :$ a) as
```

The algebra receives the symbol and its transformed arguments. The general function `appArgs` is used to apply the symbol to the folded arguments, and `f` is applied to the newly built expression.

We can now use `everywhere` to apply `optAddTop` from section 3.2 bottom-up over a whole expression:

```
*Main> render (ex₃ :: Expr Bool)
"(((5 + 0) * 6) == ((5 + 0) * 6))"
*Main> render $ everywhere optAddTop (ex₃::Expr Bool)
"((5 * 6) == (5 * 6))"
```

For the cases when we are not interested in type-indexed results, we define a version of `typedFold` with a slightly simplified type:

```
newtype Const a b = Const { unConst :: a }

typedFoldSimple :: ∀dom b
  . (∀a . dom a → Args (Const b) a → b)
  → (∀a . ASTF dom a                → b)
typedFoldSimple f =
    unConst ∘ typedFold (λs → Const ∘ f s)
```

Using `typedFoldSimple`, we can finally define a version of `Render` that avoids refutable pattern matching (here showing only the `NUM` instance):

```
class Render_safe sym where
  renderArgs_safe ::
      sym a → Args (Const String) a → String

instance Render_safe NUM where
  renderArgs_safe (Num n) Nil = show n
  renderArgs_safe Add (Const a :* Const b :* Nil) =
      "(" ++ a ++ " + " ++ b ++ ")"
  renderArgs_safe Mul (Const a :* Const b :* Nil) =
      "(" ++ a ++ " * " ++ b ++ ")"

render_safe :: Render_safe dom ⇒ ASTF dom a → String
render_safe = typedFoldSimple renderArgs_safe
```

7. Controlling the recursion

All generic recursive functions that we have seen so far have one aspect in common: the recursive calls are fixed, and cannot be overridden by new instances. The recursive calls are made in the instances for `AST` and `(:+:)`, and these are not affected by the instances for the symbol types. To have full freedom in writing generic recursive functions, one needs to be able to control the recursive calls on a case-by-case basis. This can be achieved by a simple change to `typedFold`: simply drop the recursive call to `typedFold` and replace it with the unchanged sub-term:

```
query :: ∀dom a c
  . (∀b . (a ~ Result b)
      ⇒ dom b → Args (AST dom) b → c (Full a))
  → ASTF dom a → c (Full a)
query f a = go a Nil
  where
    go :: (a ~ Result b)
       ⇒ AST dom b → Args (AST dom) b → c (Full a)
    go (Sym a)  as = f a as
    go (s :$ a) as = go s (a :* as)
```

In `typedFold`, the function `f` is applied across all nodes, which is why it is polymorphic in the symbol signature. In the case of `query`, `f` is only used at the top-level symbol, which is why we can allow the constraint `(a ~ Result b)` (the scope of `a` is now the whole definition). This constraint says that the top-most symbol has the same result type as the whole expression. By reducing the required polymorphism, we make `query` applicable to a larger set of functions. We note in passing that `typedFold` can be defined in terms of `query`, but leave the definition out of the paper.

One example where `query` is useful is when defining generic context-sensitive traversals. As a slightly contrived example, imagine that we want to change the previously defined optimization `everywhere optAddTop` so that it is performed everywhere, except in certain sub-expressions. Also imagine that we want each symbol to decide for itself whether to perform the optimization in its sub-terms, and we want to be able to add cases for new symbol types in a modular way.

Because we need to be able to add new cases, we use a type class:

```
class OptAdd sym dom where
  optAddSym :: sym a → Args (AST dom) a
                     → AST dom (Full (Result a))
```

(The need for the second parameter will be explained shortly.) The idea is that the class method returns the optimized expression given the top-level symbol and its sub-terms. However, we do not want to use `optAddSym` as the algebra in `typedFold`. This is because `typedFold` traverses the expression bottom-up, and when the function is to join the results of a symbol and its sub-terms, it is already too late to decide that certain sub-terms should remain unoptimized. Rather, we have to let `optAddSym` receive a list of *unoptimized* sub-terms, so that it can choose whether or not to recurse depending on the symbol.

We can now use `query` to lift `optAddSym` to operate on a complete syntax tree:

```
optAdd :: OptAdd dom dom ⇒ ASTF dom a → ASTF dom a
optAdd = query optAddSym
```

Before we define instances of the `OptAdd` class we need a default implementation of its method:

```
optAddDefault :: (sym :<: dom, OptAdd dom dom)
              ⇒ sym a → Args (AST dom) a
                      → AST dom (Full (Result a))
optAddDefault s = appArgs (Sym (inj s))
                ∘ mapArgs optAdd
```

This function calls `optAdd` recursively for all arguments and then applies the symbol to the optimized terms. The `mapArgs` function is used to map a function over an `Args` list:

```
mapArgs :: (∀a . c1 (Full a) → c2 (Full a))
        → (∀a . Args c1 a    → Args c2 a)
mapArgs f Nil       = Nil
mapArgs f (a :* as) = f a :* mapArgs f as
```

In the optimization of `NUM`, we make a special case for addition with zero, and call the default method for all other cases. The optimization of `Logic` uses only the default method.

```
instance (NUM :<: dom, OptAdd dom dom)
      ⇒ OptAdd NUM dom where
  optAddSym Add (a :* zero :* Nil)
    | Just (Num 0) ← prj zero = optAdd a
  optAddSym s as = optAddDefault s as

instance (Logic :<: dom, OptAdd dom dom)
      ⇒ OptAdd Logic dom where
  optAddSym = optAddDefault
```

Now, to show the point of the whole exercise, imagine we want to avoid optimization in the branches of a conditional. With the current setup, this is completely straightforward:

```
instance (If :<: dom, OptAdd dom dom)
      ⇒ OptAdd If dom where
  optAddSym If (c :* t :* f :* Nil) =
    appArgs (Sym (inj If))
            (optAdd c :* t :* f :* Nil)
```

This instance chooses to optimize only the condition, while the two branches are passed unoptimized.

The instance for `(:+:)` concludes the definition of `optAdd`:

```
instance (OptAdd sub1 dom, OptAdd sub2 dom)
      ⇒ OptAdd (sub1 :+: sub2) dom where
  optAddSym (Inj_L a) = optAddSym a
  optAddSym (Inj_R a) = optAddSym a
```

The purpose of the second parameter of the `OptAdd` class is to let instances declare constraints on the whole domain. This is needed, for example, to be able to pattern match on the sub-terms, as the `NUM` instance does. As a nice side effect, it is even possible to pattern match on constructors from a different symbol type. For example, in the `If` instance, we can pattern match on `Num` simply by declaring `(NUM :<: dom)` in the class context:

```
instance (If :<: dom, NUM :<: dom, OptAdd dom dom)
      ⇒ OptAdd If dom where
  optAddSym If (cond :* t :* f :* Nil)
    | Just (Num 0) ← prj t = ...
```

8. Mutually recursive types

Many languages are naturally defined as a set of mutually recursive types. For example, the following is a language with expressions and imperative statements:

```
type Var = String

data Expr a where
  Num  :: Int → Expr Int
  Add  :: Expr Int → Expr Int → Expr Int
  Exec :: Var → Stmt → Expr a

data Stmt where
  Assign :: Var → Expr a → Stmt
  Seq    :: Stmt → Stmt → Stmt
```

The purpose of the `Exec` construct is to return the contents of the given variable after executing the imperative program. `Assign` writes the result of an expression to the given variable. In the `AST` model, it is not directly possible to group the symbols so that only some of them are available at a given node. However, it is possible to use type-level "tags" to achieve the same effect. In the encoding below, the types in the symbol signatures are tagged with `E` or `S` depending on whether they represent expressions or statements.

```
data E a   -- Expression tag
data S     -- Statement tag

data ExprDom a where
  NumSym  :: Int → ExprDom (Full (E Int))
  AddSym  :: ExprDom (E Int :→ E Int :→Full (E Int))
  ExecSym :: Var → ExprDom (S :→ Full (E a))

data StmtDom a where
  AssignSym :: Var → StmtDom (E a :→ Full S)
  SeqSym    :: StmtDom (S :→ S :→ Full S)

type Expr_enc a = ASTF (ExprDom :+: StmtDom) (E a)
type Stmt_enc   = ASTF (ExprDom :+: StmtDom) S
```

For example, `ExecSym` has the signature `(S :→ ...)`, which means that its argument must be one of the symbols from `StmtDom`, since these are the only symbols that result in `Full S`. Because the tags above reflect the structure of the `Expr` and `Stmt` types, we conclude that $\texttt{Expr}_{enc}$ and $\texttt{Stmt}_{enc}$ are isomorphic to those types. Following this recipe, it is possible to model arbitrary mutually recursive syntax trees using `AST`.

9. The SYNTACTIC library

The abstract syntax model presented in this paper is available in the SYNTACTIC library, available on Hackage[7]. In addition to the `AST` type and the generic programming facilities, the library provides various building blocks for implementing practical EDSLs:

- Language constructs (conditionals, tuples, etc.)
- Interpretations (evaluation, equivalence, rendering, etc.)

[7] http://hackage.haskell.org/package/syntactic-1.0

- Transformations (constant folding, code motion, etc.)
- Utilities for host-language interaction (the `Syntactic` class [2, 16], observable sharing, etc.)

Being based on the extensible `AST` type, these building blocks are generic, and can quite easily be customized for different languages. A particular aim of SYNTACTIC is to simplify the implementation of languages with binding constructs. To this end, the library provides constructs for defining higher-order abstract syntax, and a number of generic interpretations and transformations for languages with variable binding.

9.1 Practical use-case: Feldspar

Feldspar [3] is an EDSL for high-performance numerical computation, in particular for embedded digital signal processing applications. Version 0.5.0.1[8] is implemented using SYNTACTIC. Some details about the implementation can be found in reference [2]. A demonstration of the advantage of a modular language implementation is given in reference [16], where we show how to add monadic constructs and support for mutable data structures to Feldspar without changing the existing implementation.

As a concrete example from the implementation, here is a functional for loop used for iterative computations:

```
data Loop a where
  ForLoop :: Type st ⇒
      Loop ( Length                  -- # iterations
         :→ st                       -- initial state
         :→ (Index → st → st)        -- step function
         :→ Full a )                 -- final state
```

The first argument is the number of iterations; the second argument the initial state. The third argument is the step function which, given the current loop index and state, computes the next state. The third argument is of function type, which calls for a way of embedding functions as `AST` terms. SYNTACTIC provides different ways of doing so, but the nice thing—and a great advantage of using SYNTACTIC—is that the embedding of functions is handled completely independently of the definition of `ForLoop`.

Feldspar has a back end for generating C code. It is divided in two main stages: (1) generating an intermediate imperative representation (used for low-level optimization, etc.), and (2) generating C code. It is worth noting that the first of these two stages uses the same basic principles as the compiler in section 4.3.

10. Related work

Data Types à la Carte [18] (DTC) is an encoding of extensible data types in Haskell. Our syntax tree model inherits its extensibility from DTC. Bahr and Hvitved [4] show that DTC supports generic traversals with relatively low overhead using the `Foldable` and `Traversable` classes. Our model differs by providing generic traversals directly, without external assistance. Given that instances for said type classes can be generated automatically (as Bahr and Hvitved do), the difference is by no means fundamental. Still, our method can generally be considered to be more lightweight with slightly less encoding overhead. The original DTC paper only considered untyped expressions. Bahr and Hvitved extend the model to account for typed syntax trees (as all trees in this paper are). This change also lets them handle mutually recursive types in essentially the same way as we describe in section 8.

[8] http://hackage.haskell.org/package/feldspar-language-0.5.0.1

The DTC literature has focused on using recursion schemes rather than explicit recursion for traversing data types. Although examples of explicit recursion exist (see the `render` function in reference [18]), the combination of explicit recursion and generic traversals appears to be rather unexplored. In this paper we have shown how to support this combination, demonstrating that generic traversals over extensible data types are not restricted to predefined recursive patterns.

Lämmel and Ostermann [13] give a solution to the expression problem based on Haskell type classes. The basic idea is to have a non-recursive data type for each constructor, and a type class representing the open union of all constructors. Interpretations are added by introducing sub-classes of the union type class. This method can be combined with existing frameworks for generic programming.[9] One drawback with the approach is that expression types reflect the exact structure of the expressions, and quite some work is required to manage these heterogeneous types.

Yet another method for defining fully extensible languages is *Finally Tagless* [7], which associates each group of language constructs with a type class, and each interpretation with a semantic domain type. Extending the language constructs is done by adding new type classes, and extending the interpretations is done by adding new instances. In contrast to DTC and our model, this technique limits interpretations to compositional bottom-up traversals. (Note, though, that this limit is mostly of practical interest. With a little creativity, it is possible to express even apparently non-compositional interpretations compositionally [10].)

There exist a number of techniques for *data-type generic programming* in Haskell (see, for example, references [11, 14]). An extensive, though slightly dated, overview is given in reference [17]. However, these techniques do not qualify as solutions to the expression problem, as they do not provide a way to extend existing types with new constructors. Rather, the aim is to define generic algorithms that work for many different types. *The spine view* [9] is a generic view for the Scrap Your Boilerplate [11] style of generic programming. The `Spine` type has strong similarities to our `AST` type. The main difference is that `Spine` is a *one-layer* view, whereas `AST` is a complete view of a data type. This means that the `Spine` type is not useful on its own—it merely provides a way to define generic functions over other existing types. It should be pointed out that the one-layer aspect of `Spine` is a *good thing* when it comes to ordinary generic programming, but it does mean that `Spine` alone cannot provide a solution to the expression problem. So, although `Spine` and `AST` rely on the same principle for generic constructor access, they are different in practice, and solve different problems.

Another use of a spine data type is found in Adams' Scrap Your Zippers [1], which defines a generic zipper data structure. The `Left` data type—similar to our `AST`—holds the left siblings of the current position. Just like for `AST`, its type parameter specifies what arguments it is missing. The `Right` data type—reminiscent of our `Args`—holds the right siblings of the current position, and its type parameter specifies what arguments it provides. This similarity suggests that it might be possible to implement a similar generic zipper for the `AST` type.

Outside the Haskell world, an interesting approach to implementing EDSLs is Modelyze [6]. The Modelyze language is specifically designed to be a host for embedded languages. It has built-in support for open data types, and such types can be traversed generically by pattern matching on symbolic applications in much the same way as our `countAdds` example (section 3.1). However, generic traversals

[9] See slides by Lämmel and Kiselyov *"Spin-offs from the Expression Problem"* http://userpages.uni-koblenz.de/~laemmel/TheEagle/resources/xproblem2.html.

require resorting to dynamic typing (for that particular fragment of the code), which makes the approach slightly less type-safe than ours.

11. Discussion

In this paper we have focused on the `AST` model and the basic principles for programming with it. To remain focused, we have left out many details that are important when implementing an embedded language but still not fundamental to the underlying syntax model. Such details include how to deal with variable binding and syntactic annotations. The SYNTACTIC library has support for these aspects (with varying degree of stability), but it is important to stress that all of this extra functionality can be implemented on top of the existing `AST` type. So while SYNTACTIC is still developing, the `AST` model appears to be rather mature.

One important aspect of extensible syntax that we have not treated in this paper is the ability to ensure that certain constructs are present or absent at certain passes in a compiler. Bahr and Hvitved have demonstrated how to do this with Data Types à la Carte, using a desugaring transformation as example. The example is directly transferable to our model.

Our experience with implementing Feldspar has shown that, while the resulting code is quite readable, developing code using SYNTACTIC can be quite hard due to the heavy use of type-level programming. In the future, we would like to look into ways of hiding this complexity, by providing a simpler user interface, and, for example, using Template Haskell to generate the tricky code. However, we do not expect these changes to affect the underlying `AST` type.

Our syntax tree encoding imposes a certain run-time overhead over ordinary data types. Although we have not investigated the extent of this overhead, we have not noticed any performance problems due to the encoding in the Feldspar implementation. Still, the performance impact should be investigated, as it may become noticeable when dealing with very large programs.

12. Conclusion

Our goal with this work is to make a library of generic building blocks for implementing embedded languages. Any such attempt is bound to run into the expression problem, because the library must provide extensible versions of both syntactic constructs and interpretation functions. The `AST` model provides a pleasingly simple and flexible basis for such an extensible library. Its distinguishing feature is the *direct* support for generic recursive functions—no additional machinery is needed. For extensibility, some extra machinery had to be brought in, but the overhead is quite small compared to the added benefits. Even though our model comes with convenient recursion schemes, it is by no means restricted to fixed traversals. The user has essentially the same freedom as when programming with ordinary data types to define general recursive traversals.

Acknowledgments

This work has been funded by Ericsson, the Swedish Foundation for Strategic Research (SSF) and the Swedish Basic Research Agency (Vetenskapsrådet). The author would like to thank the following people for valuable discussions, comments and other input: Jean-Philippe Bernardy, Koen Claessen, Dévai Gergely, Patrik Jansson, Oleg Kiselyov, Anders Persson, Norman Ramsey, Mary Sheeran, Josef Svenningsson, Wouter Swierstra and Meng Wang. The anonymous reviewers also helped improving the paper.

References

[1] M. D. Adams. Scrap your zippers: a generic zipper for heterogeneous types. In *Proceedings of the 6th ACM SIGPLAN workshop on Generic programming*, WGP '10, pages 13–24. ACM, 2010.

[2] E. Axelsson and M. Sheeran. Feldspar: Application and implementation. In *Lecture Notes of the Central European Functional Programming School*, volume 7241 of *LNCS*. Springer, 2012.

[3] E. Axelsson, K. Claessen, G. Dévai, Z. Horváth, K. Keijzer, B. Lyckegård, A. Persson, M. Sheeran, J. Svenningsson, and A. Vajda. Feldspar: A domain specific language for digital signal processing algorithms. In *8th ACM/IEEE International Conference on Formal Methods and Models for Codesign (MEMOCODE 2010)*, pages 169–178. IEEE Computer Society, 2010.

[4] P. Bahr and T. Hvitved. Compositional data types. In *Proceedings of the seventh ACM SIGPLAN workshop on Generic programming*, WGP '11, pages 83–94. ACM, 2011.

[5] P. Bjesse, K. Claessen, M. Sheeran, and S. Singh. Lava: Hardware Design in Haskell. In *ICFP '98: Proceedings of the Third ACM SIGPLAN International Conference on Functional Programming*, pages 174–184. ACM, 1998.

[6] D. Broman and J. G. Siek. Modelyze: a gradually typed host language for embedding equation-based modeling languages. Technical Report UCB/EECS-2012-173, EECS Department, University of California, Berkeley, Jun 2012.

[7] J. Carette, O. Kiselyov, and C.-c. Shan. Finally tagless, partially evaluated: Tagless staged interpreters for simpler typed languages. *Journal of Functional Programming*, 19(05):509–543, 2009.

[8] K. Claessen, M. Sheeran, and B. J. Svensson. Expressive array constructs in an embedded GPU kernel programming language. In *Proceedings of the 7th workshop on Declarative aspects and applications of multicore programming*, DAMP '12, pages 21–30. ACM, 2012.

[9] R. Hinze and A. Löh. "Scrap Your Boilerplate" Revolutions. In *Mathematics of Program Construction*, volume 4014, pages 180–208. Springer, 2006.

[10] O. Kiselyov. Typed tagless final interpreters. In *Lecture Notes of the Spring School on Generic and Indexed Programming (to appear)*. 2010.

[11] R. Lämmel and S. P. Jones. Scrap your boilerplate: a practical design pattern for generic programming. In *Proceedings of the 2003 ACM SIGPLAN international workshop on Types in languages design and implementation*, TLDI '03, pages 26–37. ACM, 2003.

[12] R. Lämmel and S. P. Jones. Scrap more boilerplate: reflection, zips, and generalised casts. In *Proceedings of the ninth ACM SIGPLAN international conference on Functional programming*, ICFP '04, pages 244–255. ACM, 2004.

[13] R. Lämmel and K. Ostermann. Software extension and integration with type classes. In *Proceedings of the 5th international conference on Generative programming and component engineering*, GPCE '06, pages 161–170. ACM, 2006.

[14] J. P. Magalhães, A. Dijkstra, J. Jeuring, and A. Löh. A generic deriving mechanism for Haskell. In *Proceedings of the third ACM Haskell symposium on Haskell*, Haskell '10, pages 37–48. ACM, 2010.

[15] N. Mitchell and C. Runciman. Uniform boilerplate and list processing. In *Proceedings of the ACM SIGPLAN workshop on Haskell workshop*, Haskell '07, pages 49–60. ACM, 2007.

[16] A. Persson, E. Axelsson, and J. Svenningsson. Generic monadic constructs for embedded languages. In *23rd International Symposium on Implementation and Application of Functional Languages, IFL 2011*, volume 7257 of *LNCS*, 2012.

[17] A. Rodriguez, J. Jeuring, P. Jansson, A. Gerdes, O. Kiselyov, and B. C. d. S. Oliveira. Comparing libraries for generic programming in Haskell. In *Proceedings of the first ACM SIGPLAN symposium on Haskell*, Haskell '08, pages 111–122. ACM, 2008.

[18] W. Swierstra. Data types à la carte. *Journal of Functional Programming*, 18(4):423–436, 2008.

Experience Report: a Do-It-Yourself High-Assurance Compiler

Lee Pike
Galois, Inc.
leepike@galois.com

Nis Wegmann
University of Copenhagen
niswegmann@gmail.com

Sebastian Niller
Unaffiliated
sebastian.niller@gmail.com

Alwyn Goodloe
NASA
a.goodloe@nasa.gov

Abstract

Embedded domain-specific languages (EDSLs) are an approach for quickly building new languages while maintaining the advantages of a rich metalanguage. We argue in this experience report that the "EDSL approach" can surprisingly ease the task of building a high-assurance compiler. We do not strive to build a fully formally-verified tool-chain, but take a "do-it-yourself" approach to increase our confidence in compiler-correctness without too much effort. *Copilot* is an EDSL developed by Galois, Inc. and the National Institute of Aerospace under contract to NASA for the purpose of runtime monitoring of flight-critical avionics. We report our experience in using type-checking, QuickCheck, and model-checking "off-the-shelf" to quickly increase confidence in our EDSL tool-chain.

Categories and Subject Descriptors D.2.4 [*Software/Program Verification*]: Reliability

General Terms Languages, Verification

Keywords embedded domain-specific language, compiler, verification

1. Introduction

The "do-it-yourself" (DIY) culture encourages individuals to design and craft objects on their own, without relying on outside experts. DIY construction should be inexpensive with easy-to-access materials. Ranging from hobbyist electronics[1] to urban farming to fashion, DIY is making somewhat of a resurgence across the United States.

We see no reason why DIY culture should not also extend to compilers, and in particular, to high-assurance compilers. By *high-assurance*, we mean a compiler that comes with compelling evidence that the source code and object code have the same operational semantics.

High-assurance compilers development has traditionally required years of effort by experts. A notable early effort was the CLI Stack, of which a simple verified compiler was one part [17]. The CLI Stack was verified by the precursor to the ACL2 theorem prover. The most recent instance is CompCert, which compiles a subset of C suitable for embedded development to machine code for a number of targets [16]. CompCert is formally verified in the Coq theorem-prover—indeed, CompCert is written in Coq's specification language. While CompCert achieves the highest levels of assurance, generating the evidence comes at a steep price, since it relies on manually interacting with a theorem-prover. Neither the CLI Stack nor CompCert are DIY projects: building them requires relatively esoteric skills that combine interactive theorem-proving and multiple engineer-years of verification effort.

In this experience report, we argue that by leveraging functional languages and off-the-shelf verification tools, we can accumulate significant evidence of correctness at a fraction of the cost and without the specialized know-how required by interactive verification approaches.

The case-study of our approach is the Copilot language and toolset, developed by Galois, Inc. and the National Institute of Aerospace under contract to NASA. Copilot is a stream language for generating embedded C-code software monitors for system properties. Copilot itself is not comparable to a verified compiler like CompCert: Copilot back-ends stop at the C level, where CompCert starts. Verifying C semantics against the semantics of a machine model is extraordinarily difficult. Still, for high-level languages, we can do much better than the status quo.

Specifically, we employ three not-so-secret weapons from the functional languages and formal methods communities in our work.

1. *Embedded DSLs*: We implement Copilot as an embedded domain-specific (EDSL) language [15] within Haskell.
2. *Sub-Turing complete languages*: Copilot is targeted at embedded programming, therefore we focus on the class of programs that are computable in constant time and constant space.
3. *A verifying compiler*: CompCert typifies a *verified compiler* approach in which the compiler itself is proved correct. A *verifying compiler* is one that provides evidence that a specific compilation is correct [19]. We borrow from this second approach. (We emphasize that this report is about assurance of the EDSL compiler itself, not about the functional correctness of programs written in the EDSL.)

While the approaches we describe are known within the functional programming and formal methods communities, the purpose of this experience report is to demonstrate the engineering ease in putting them to use. In particular, the EDSL approach is well-known for quickly prototyping new languages, but the reader should have some level of skepticism that they are appropriate for high-assurance development; we hope to dispel that skepticism. Furthermore, there is nothing special about the Copilot language with respect to assurance. We hope to convince the reader that the approach we have taken can be applied broadly to new language design.

Outline. In Section 2, we briefly introduce Copilot (we assume some familiarity with Haskell syntax). The heart of the report is Section 3 in which we describe our "lessons learned" for easily

[1] This even includes full-featured unpiloted air vehicles! See `http://diydrones.com/`.

ICFP'12, September 9–15, 2012, Copenhagen, Denmark.

generating evidence of correctness. We briefly mention related work in Section 4, and make concluding remarks in Section 5.

2. The Copilot Language & Toolset

From 2009-2011, NASA contracted Galois, Inc. to research the possibility of augmenting complex aerospace software systems with *runtime verification* (RV). RV is a family of approaches that employ *monitors* to observe the behavior of an executing system and to detect if it is consistent with a formal specification. A monitor implementation should be simple and direct and serve as the last line of defense for the correctness for the system. The need for aerospace RV is motivated by recent failures in commercial avionics and the space shuttle [11].

Our answer to the contract goals was Copilot, an EDSL to generate embedded monitors.[2] The Copilot language itself, focusing on its RV uses for NASA, has been previously described [20]. We will very briefly introduce Copilot in this paper; our focus is more specifically about compiler correctness.

One research challenge of the project was phrased as, "Who watches the watchmen?" meaning that if the RV monitor is the last line of defense, then it must not fail or worse, introduce unintended faults itself! Nonetheless, because the primary goal of the project was to implement an RV system and to field-test it, few resources were available for assuring the correctness of the Copilot compiler. Our approach was born out of necessity.

Copilot's expression language. In the following, we briefly and informally introduce Copilot's expression language. One design goal for Copilot is to use a familiar syntax and model of computation; doing so is a first step in reducing specification errors. The Copilot language mimics both the syntax and semantics of lazy lists (which we call *streams*) in Haskell. One notable exception though is that operators are automatically promoted point-wise to the list level, much like in Lustre, a declarative language for embedded programming [12]. For example, the Fibonacci sequence modulo 2^{32} can be written as follows in Haskell:

```
fib :: [Word32]
fib = [0,1] ++ zipWith (+) fib (drop 1 fib)
```

In Copilot, the equivalent definition is the following:

```
fib :: Stream Word32
fib = [0,1] ++ (fib + drop 1 fib)
```

Copilot overloads or redefines many standard operators from Haskell's Prelude Library. Here is a Haskell and equivalent Copilot function that implements a latch (flip-flop) over streams—the output is the XOR of the input stream and the latch's previous output. For example, for the input stream

```
T, F, F, T, F, F, T, F, F, ...
```

`latch` generates the stream

```
F, T, T, T, F, F, F, T, T, T, ...
```

In Haskell, `latch` can be defined

```
latch :: [Bool] -> [Bool]
latch x = out x
  where
  out ls   = [False] ++ zipWith xor ls (out ls)
  xor n m  = (n || m) && not (n && m)
```

and then in Copilot (`xor` is a built-in operator for Copilot):

```
latch :: Stream Bool -> Stream Bool
latch x = out
  where out = [False] ++ x `xor` out
```

[2] Copilot source code is available at `http://leepike.github.com/Copilot/` and is licensed under the BSD3 license.

The base types of Copilot over which streams are built include Booleans, signed and unsigned words of 8, 16, 32, and 64 bits, floats, and doubles. Type-safe casts in which overflow cannot occur are permitted.

Sampling. Copilot programs are meant to monitor arbitrary C programs. They do so by periodically *sampling* symbol values. (Copilot samples variables, arrays, and the return values of side-effect free functions—sampling arbitrary structures is future work.) For a Copilot program compiled to C, symbols become in-scope when arbitrary C code is linked with the code generated by the Copilot compiler. Copilot provides the operator `extern` to introduce an external symbol to sample. The operator types a string denoting the C symbol.

Copilot can be interpreted as well as compiled. When interpreted, representative values are expected to be supplied by the programmer. For example, the following stream samples the C variable `e0` of type `uint8_t` to create each new stream index. If `e0` takes the values `2, 4, 6, 8, ...` the stream `ext` has the values `1, 3, 7, 13, ....`

```
ext :: Stream Word8
ext = [1] ++ (ext + extern "e0" interp)
  where interp = Just [2,4..]
```

We make the design decision to build interpreter values for external values into the language. (If the user wishes not to provide interpreter values, the constructor `Nothing` can be used.)

Sampling arrays and functions is similar (for space constraints, we omit an example of function sampling). For example, the following stream samples an array with the prototype `uint32_t arr[3]`:

```
arr :: Stream Word32
arr = externArray "arr" idx 3 interp
  where idx :: Stream Word8
        idx    = [0] ++ (idx + 1) `mod` 2
        interp = Just (repeat [0,1,2])
```

The interpreter takes a list of lists to represent possible array values.

Effects. Copilot has exactly one mechanism for output called *triggers*. For example, consider the following example trigger:

```
trigger "trig" (fib `mod` 2 == 0)
  [ arg fib, arg (latch fib) ]
```

A trigger has a guard that is a Boolean-valued Copilot stream, and a list of arguments, which are Copilot expressions. A trigger is *fired* exactly when its guard (stating that the current value from the `fib` stream is even in this case) is true. A trigger's implementation is a C function with a `void` return type that takes the current values of the trigger arguments as arguments. For example, given the definition of `fib` and `latch` above, the prototype of the C-function implementing the trigger `trig` defined above is

```
void trig(uint32_t, bool);
```

The definition of a trigger is implementation-dependent and up to the programmer to implement.

Copilot's toolchain. Copilot's toolchain is depicted in Figure 1, which we highlight here; assurance-relevant aspects of the toolchain are covered in more detail later. Copilot is deeply embedded in Haskell. A Copilot program is reified (i.e., transformed from a recursive structure into explicit graphs via observable sharing [10]) and then some domain-specific type-checking is done. At this point, we have transformed the program into the "core" language, an intermediate representation. The core package contains an interpreter ($\sim$300 LOCs) as well as a custom QuickCheck engine and test harness for testing interpreter output against one of the back-ends

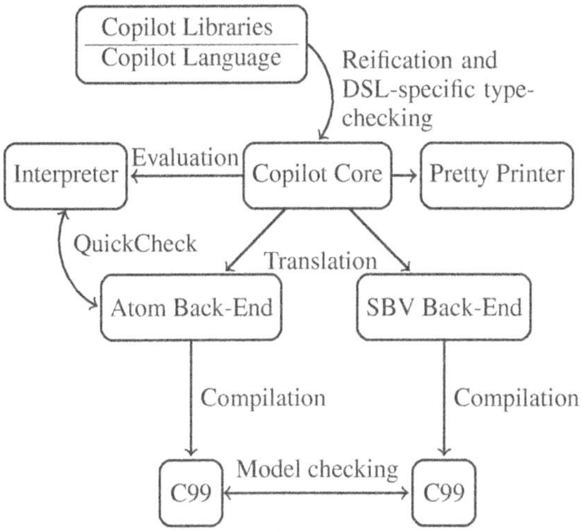

Figure 1. The Copilot toolchain.

The back-ends translate a Copilot core program into the language of another Haskell-hosted EDSL for code generation. We use the Atom[3] [13] and SBV[4] packages for code generation, both of which generate a subset of C99 embedded code that is constant-memory and nearly constant-time. Atom is an EDSL originally designed by Tom Hawkins at Eaton Corp. for synthesizing real-time embedded control systems from high-level specifications. The language provides scheduling constructs, obviating the need for a real-time operating system when cooperative scheduling is sufficient. Symbolic Bit Vectors (SBV) is an EDSL developed by Levent Erkök. The primary focus of SBV is to express and reason about bit-level Haskell programs. In particular, the language provides tight integration with satisfiability modulo theories (SMT) solvers (e.g., Yices [8]) for automatic proofs and to check for satisfiability. The EDSL also contains a C-code generator which we use. Other features of the language include test-case generation and automated synthesis.

We use the recent Safe Haskell compiler extensions to implement Copilot [23]. Copilot's language package is explicitly *Trustworthy Haskell*, as there is a single instance of `unsafeCoerce` to implement observable sharing. Copilot's core language is written in *Safe Haskell*.

A separate package generates a driver for the CBMC model-checker [6], which we use to check the equivalence between the C code generated by each back-end.

3. Lessons Learned: Quick and Easy Correctness Evidence

In the following, we describe some "lessons-learned" in quickly and easily building assurance into an EDSL compiler.

Lesson: Turing-complete macros, small, Turing-incomplete languages. C-like languages treat macros as a second-class feature—they are just textual substitution. Lisp-like languages take the converse approach, treating macros as a first-class datatype, so macros are on par with (Turing-complete) programming. These are two extremes, but they largely represent the status of macro programming.

EDSLs, however, treat meta-programming as first-class, and programming as second-class! The difference in emphasis of EDSLs is because the embedded language is a datatype within its host language (we assume a deep-embedding of the DSL [10]). The difference affects how one programs using an EDSL. Practically, one spends very little time directly using the operators of the EDSL itself but rather, one generates EDSL programs using combinators from the host language.

Embedded system programming, with time and memory constraints, does not require the full power of a general-purpose Turing-complete language [4]. But a Turing-complete *macro language* affords benefits in code-reuse and library development. With an EDSL, one can have his cake and eat it too: Arbitrarily complex combinators over the EDSL can be written, but then a simple core language can be reasoned about.

Reasoning about the correctness of sub-Turing-complete languages is easier than general-purpose languages. For example, a verifying compiler for a cryptographic DSL leveraged the ability to automatically generate measures to formally prove termination of programs written in the language [19]. Conversely, Sassaman *et al.* argue that a principal origin of insecurity in computer systems is due to Turing-complete (or more generally, too powerful) data-description languages [21].

```
data Expr a where
  -- Constants
  Const :: Type a -> a -> Expr a
  -- Stream constructors
  Drop  :: Type a -> Int -> Id -> Expr a
  -- Let expressions
  Local :: Type a -> Type b -> Name -> Expr a
        -> Expr b -> Expr b
  Var   :: Type a -> Name -> Expr a
  -- Operators
  Op1   :: Op1 a b -> Expr a -> Expr b
  Op2   :: Op2 a b c -> Expr a -> Expr b -> Expr c
  Op3   :: Op3 a b c d -> Expr a -> Expr b
        -> Expr c -> Expr d
  -- Externals
  ExternVar
    :: Type a -> Name -> Maybe [a] -> Expr a
  ExternFun
    :: Type a -> Name -> [UExpr]
    -> Maybe (Expr a) -> Maybe Int -> Expr a
  ExternArray
    :: Integral a => Type a -> Type b
    -> Name -> Int -> Expr a -> Maybe [[b]]
    -> Maybe Int -> Expr b

-- Untyped streams
data UExpr = forall a. UExpr
  { uExprType :: Type a
  , uExprExpr  :: Expr a }
```

Figure 2. The core Copilot expression language abstract syntax.

The core language of Copilot is both small and unpowerful: as noted, only programs requiring a constant amount of space can be written in Copilot. In Figure 2 is the generalized abstract datatype (GADT) [22] that is the abstract syntax for Copilot expressions in the core language. There are constants, the "drops" stream constructor (dropping a finite number of prefix list elements), let-expressions within Copilot for user-defined expression sharing, external program inputs, and unary, binary, and ternary operators. One final data type, `UExpr` contains existentially-typed streams that are used in argument lists. Everything else is syntactic sugar or specific operators. (The operational semantics of Copilot, given by an interpreter function over the `Expr` datatype, is about 200 LOCs.)

Despite the small size of the core language and the lack of computational power, with Haskell's parametric polymorphism and

[3] `http://hackage.haskell.org/package/atom`, BSD3 license.

[4] `http://hackage.haskell.org/package/sbv`, BSD3 license.

standard library combinators, we can enjoy the benefits of code reuse and abstraction in building libraries while maintaining a terse core language. For example, in our fault-tolerant voting library, the Boyer-Moore linear-time Majority Vote algorithm [3] is written as a Haskell function that gets expanded at compile-time into a Copilot program. Libraries for bounded linear-temporal logic, regular expressions, bounded folds, bounded scans, etc. are similarly just Copilot macros.

The idea that the macro language can be arbitrarily complex is obvious to the functional languages community, but it is a disruptive one to the embedded languages community, particularly for safety-critical systems. Typical declarative languages for embedded systems design, like Lustre [4], are not polymorphic (polymorphism is limited to a small set of pre-defined operators, like **if-then-else**).

Lesson: multi-level type-checking. Type-checking is the first defense against incorrect programs. We used a two-layer approach: let the host language enforce types where possible, and write a custom checker for type-checking that falls outside of the host language's type system. In this way, we rely on Haskell to do most of the heavy lifting.

We use GADTs to represent both the front-end abstract syntax and the core language. The use of parameterized datatypes makes the probability of unanticipated type-casts low. There are only two cases during which we escape Haskell's type system, which may lead to incorrect type-casts.

The first case is when a back-end pretty-prints C code. The correctness of such code can be determined by inspecting a small number of functions and class instances.

The second case arises during the translation from the core abstract syntax into the back-ends, which are themselves EDSLs embedded in Haskell. Both the core language and the back-ends make use of polymorphic functions and class constraints. As a matter of software engineering, we do not want Copilot's core functions to be dependent on the classes introduced in the back-ends—doing so would require modifying functions and datatypes defined in the core with new class constraints for each time a new back-end is added!

Therefore, we use the ideas of type-safe dynamic typing to translate from the core language to the back-end languages without relying on compiler extensions or unsafe functions [2]. The basic idea is to create witness functions that we pattern-match against. For example, for the class `SymWord` ("Symbolic Word") in the SBV back-end, we create the following instance datatype and an instance function mapping Copilot types to `SymWord`s:

```
data SymWordInst a = SymWord a => SymWordInst

symWordInst :: Type a -> SymWordInst a
symWordInst t =
  case t of
    Bool   -> SymWordInst
    Int8   -> SymWordInst
    ...
```

where `Type` is a phantom type containing concrete representations of Copilot's core types.

```
data Type :: * -> * where
  Bool    :: Type Bool
  Int8    :: Type Int8
  ...
```

Then during the translation, we pattern-match. For example, in translating the addition operator, we translate from Copilot's `Add` constructor in the core language to SBV's addition operator `+`:

```
transBinaryOps op = case op of
  Add t -> case W.symWordInst t of
                   W.SymWordInst ->  (+)
  ...
```

The upshot is that we have created potentially partial translation functions, but type-incorrect translation is not possible.

In addition to type-checking provided by Haskell, we perform a small amount of custom type-checking (~250 LOCs). The two classes of custom type-checking are (1) causality analysis and (2) type-checking external variables (arrays and functions). Causality analysis ensures that stream dependencies are evaluated strictly. Strict dependencies are necessary when we are sampling variable values in real-time from the external world. For example, the following Copilot stream equations fail type-checking since `y` initially depends on values from the variable `x` before any values have been generated:

```
x :: Stream Word8
x = extern "ext" Nothing
y = drop 2 x
```

We also check at compile-time that streams are productive; for example, the stream definition `x = x` fails type-checking.

In addition, external variables are just strings with associated types. Therefore, we must check that the same string is not given two different types or declared to be of two different kinds of symbols (e.g,. a global variable vs. a function symbol). For example, the following two expressions, if they appear in the same Copilot program, fail type-checking:

```
x :: Stream Word8
x = extern "ext" Nothing

y :: Stream Word16
y = extern "ext" Nothing
```

Lesson: cheap front-end/back-end testing. QuickCheck [5] testing is so easy to implement and so effective that no EDSL compiler should be without it. QuickCheck can of course be used for unit testing during compiler development, but we use it to generate regression tests for the semantics of the EDSL by comparing the output of the interpreter against the Atom back-end (we plan to implement QuickCheck testing against the SBV back-end in the future).

We generate a stand-alone executable that for a user-specified number of iterations,

1. generates a random Copilot program,
2. compiles the Copilot program to C,
3. generates a **driver.c** file containing a **main** function as well as values for external variables,
4. compiles and links an executable (using *gcc*),
5. executes the program,
6. and compares its output to the output from the Copilot interpreter.

Weights can be set to determine the frequency of generating the various Copilot language constructs and streams of different types.

There are at least two approaches to generating type-correct programs. First, we can generate random programs, then filter ill-typed programs using the type-checker. Second, we can generate type-correct programs directly. We take the second approach. Generating type-correct programs is not difficult in our case: as described already, because Copilot's abstract syntax is parameterized by Haskell type variables, type-correct expression generation is straight-forward. We need only to ensure the small number of domain-specific type rules are also satisfied.

The benefit of generating type-correct programs directly is that if the generator is implemented correctly, every generated program is type-correct and will be tested. The danger, however, is that the generator may be too strict, omitting some type-correct programs from being generated and tested.

With the standard options, we generate, compile, test and pretty-print to standard output about 1,000 programs per minute. It is easy to let the QuickCheck test generator run continuously on a server, generating some million and a half programs per day (in practice, bugs, if present, tend to appear after just 10s or 100s of generated programs). The kinds of bugs we have caught include forgotten witness for the Atom back-end and the "out-of-order" bugs in which the interpreter output stream values *before* sampling variables. A "non-bug" we discovered was disagreement on floating-point values between GHC's runtime system (executing the interpreter) and *libc*. We solved this problem by just checking that floating point values are within some small constant range, noting that pathological cases may cause differences outside of a constant range without violating the IEEE floating-point standard.

Lesson: cheap back-end proofs. The verified compiler approach assumes that the compiler itself is within the *trusted computing base* (TCB)—the software that must be trusted to be correct. Consequently, it requires a monolithic approach to verification in which the compiler is verified. But what if the compiler can be removed from the TCB? Doing so can reduce the difficulty of providing assurance evidence.

This is our motivation for a proof approach of the back-ends. Recalling Figure 1, Copilot has two back-ends that generate C. We leverage the open-source model-checker CBMC to prove the equivalence of the code generated by each back-end [6]. CBMC uses C as its specification language. In our work, we use CBMC. CBMC can prove memory-safety properties, such as no division by zero, no not-a-number floating-point errors, and no array out-of-bound indexes. It can also prove arbitrary propositional formulas given in the body of `assert()` functions.

To prove equivalence between the two back-end outputs, we automatically generate a driver program that executes both back-ends for one step, compares their outputs, takes another step, compares their outputs, and so on for a user-specified number of iterations. The generated driver is of the form

```
for (i = 0; i < RNDS; i++) {
  sampleExterns();
  atom_step();
  sbv_step();
  assert(   atomStr_0 == sbvStr_0
        && atomStr_1 == sbvStr_1
        && ... );
}
```

For sampled variables (arrays, functions), we use CBMC's built-in model of nondeterminism to model arbitrary inputs to Copilot programs. CBMC proves the two programs are memory-safe and have equivalent semantics for a finite number of user-specified iterations (`RNDS`).

Model-checking works "out of the box" in our case because both back-ends generate simple code (e.g., no non-linear pointer arithmetic, no function pointers, no loops) in the state-update functions. This use of formal methods emphasizes the lesson about simple, Turing-incomplete languages from Section 3.

A proof of correspondence on the C code reduces the trust required in the Atom and SBV back-ends. Assuming the model-checker is sound, incorrectly-generated code will be claimed to be equivalent only if bugs with the same effects appear in both back-ends. In addition, memory-safety errors, even if they appear simultaneously in both programs, will be caught.

That said, one must still trust the C compiler—CompCert [16] would be a good point in this case. Furthermore, Copilot programs are expected to be executed forever (i.e., they are programs over infinite streams), which mimics the behavior of embedded software. CBMC symbolically unrolls programs either completely if possible or to a user-specified depth; it does not perform an inductive proof, so currently, we only show equivalence up to a user-set bound (`RNDS` in the code-snippet above). Using a model-checker with induction (e.g., k-induction via SAT [14]) would strengthen the assurance case. Finally, note that this use of model-checking takes the verifying rather than verified-compiler approach: model-checking is done for *each* program compiled.

The kinds of bugs we have caught mostly include incorrect ordering of functions in the generated C (e.g., sampling external values after computing next-state values for streams). Because we do not yet have a QuickCheck testing infrastructure between the interpreter and the SBV back-end, we get a transitive argument that the SBV back-end is equivalent to the Atom back-end, which has evidence of matching the interpreter through the use of QuickCheck. From an evidence perspective, model-checking the back-ends reduces the required trust in the Haskell compiler/interpreter, since we check the generated artifacts. Ideally, we would have the power of an EDSL without having to trust the runtime system of the host language.

Lesson: a unified host language. Our last lesson is one obvious to the functional programming community, but novel in safety-critical languages. EDSLs are intrinsically immune to whole classes of potential compiler bugs. For example, because a separate parser, lexer, tokenizer, etc. are not necessary, EDSLs do not suffer from these front-end bugs. This assumes that the host language's front-end does not contain bugs, which for a stable well-used host language, is more likely than for a new DSL front-end.

We enjoyed two other advantages. First, translating between EDSLs in the same host language was type-safe and relatively easy since the two back-ends we use were existing EDSLs. Translating from Copilot into a back-end is a matter of converting from one abstract syntax datatype into another, never leaving the host language.

Second, the host language serves as more than a macro language: it serves as a partial build system. For example, consider the case of generating distributed Copilot programs to be run on networked processors, where we want to parameterize inputs based on the processor identifier. With an EDSL, this is no more difficult than parameterizing the `compile` function. In our experiments with NASA, we did just this to build fault-tolerant monitors [20].

4. Related Work

Our experience report builds on research in disparate fields including functional programming and EDSL design, compiler verification, and embedded safety-critical languages. In this section, we provide just a few pointers into the literature that inspired us.

Some might believe that compilers are generally bug-free (even if specific programs are buggy). Work at the University of Utah has dispelled this myth [24], having uncovered hundreds of bugs in C compilers like *gcc*, *clang*, and even the (unverified) front-end of the CompCert compiler [16]. Compiler verification is still important. Our work does not address C compilation directly, but it does reduce the risk of encountering bugs in C compilers by constraining the language to a small subset of well-defined C.

FeldSpar is an EDSL in Haskell designed for digital signal processing designed by Ericsson and Chalmers University [1]. FeldSpar's architecture and implementation is similar to Copilot's and could integrate the assurance approaches we have described. Researchers at the University of Minnesota have also built a family of DSLs tailored for safety-critical embedded system modeling [9]. The host language was designed so that new DSLs can be specified using attribute grammars. It appears the purpose of the language is primarily for modeling, so the work does not address compilation, and consequently does not address compiler correctness issues. Finally, Filet-o-Fish is a related DSLs framework for operating system development [7]. The authors emphasize compiler assurance as we do, also using an interpreter to provide an operational semantics and using QuickCheck for testing.

An alternative to the EDSL approach is to take a functional language and augment it with sufficient evidence to be used directly in safety-critical contexts, such as avionics development. A consortium did just that with OCaml, rewriting the SCADE code generator [18]. Qualifying the software required substantially reducing OCaml's runtime system and garbage collector, extensive testing, and providing "traceability" of requirements. From a formal verification perspective, the requirements are lightweight (the main direct evidence for correctness is testing).

5. Conclusions

Despite our experience, EDSLs are not a panacea. Copilot suffers the same problems that many EDSL implementations do. Error messages from the Haskell compiler are not domain-specific. There is no graphical development environment (common in embedded systems development). Large Haskell expressions are easy to generate, which can be expensive to interpret or compile. Copilot does not currently have a highly-optimizing back-end.

Regarding our approach to compiler assurance, there are some weaknesses. First, since the interpreter and back-ends are built on the core language, bugs in translation from the front-end will affect all the targets. While QuickCheck tests the executables against the interpreter, the model-checker only proves properties about (its interpretation of) the C source semantics. CompCert would obviously be a good choice to compile C, then. Finally, as noted in the introduction, we have focused here on evidence of correct compilation, but our implementation does not necessarily help ensure a specific program meets its specification. These shortcomings point to future research efforts.

In summary we hoped to make two points in this report: first, that EDSLs are a viable approach for building high-assurance compilers, and second, that strong evidence can be generated with little work or expertise. With the EDSL, you do not have to write your own front-end, most type-checking is done for you, and today's off-the-shelf model-checkers are capable of checking real programs.

But don't take our word for it; do-it-yourself.

Acknowledgments

This work was supported by NASA Contract NNL08AD13T. We wish to especially thank the following individuals for advice on our work: Ben Di Vito, Paul Miner, Eric Cooper, Joe Hurd, and Aaron Tomb. Robin Morisset worked on an earlier version of Copilot. Nis Wegmann and Sebastian Niller completed this work while they were visiting researchers at the National Institute of Aerospace.

References

[1] E. Axelsson, K. Claessen, M. Sheeran, J. Svenningsson, D. Engdal, and A. Persson. The design and implementation of Feldspar - an embedded language for digital signal processing. In *Implementation and Application of Functional Languages*, volume 6647 of *LNCS*, pages 121–136. Springer, 2011.

[2] A. I. Baars and S. D. Swierstra. Typing dynamic typing. In *Intl. Conference on Functional Programming (ICFP)*, pages 157–166. ACM, September 2002.

[3] R. S. Boyer and J. S. Moore. MJRTY: A fast majority vote algorithm. In *Automated Reasoning: Essays in Honor of Woody Bledsoe*, pages 105–118, 1991.

[4] P. Caspi, D. Pialiud, N. Halbwachs, and J. Plaice. LUSTRE: a declarative language for programming synchronous systems. In *14th Symposium on Principles of Programming Languages*, pages 178–188, 1987.

[5] K. Claessen and J. Hughes. QuickCheck: A lightweight tool for random testing of Haskell programs. In *ACM SIGPLAN Notices*, pages 268–279. ACM, 2000.

[6] E. Clarke, D. Kroening, and F. Lerda. A tool for checking ANSI-C programs. In *Tools and Algorithms for the Construction and Analysis of Systems (TACAS)*, LNCS, pages 168–176. Springer, 2004.

[7] P. E. Dagand, A. Baumann, and T. Roscoe. Filet-o-Fish: practical and dependable domain-specific languages for OS development. In *Proceedings of the Fifth Workshop on Programming Languages and Operating Systems (PLOS '09)*, pages 1–5. ACM, 2009.

[8] B. Dutertre and L. D. Moura. The Yices SMT solver. Technical report, SRI, 2006.

[9] J. Gao, M. Heimdahl, and E. Van Wyk. Flexible and extensible notations for modeling languages. In *Fundamental Approaches to Software Engineering (FASE)*, volume 4422 of *LNCS*, pages 102–116. Springer Verlag, March 2007.

[10] A. Gill. Type-safe observable sharing in Haskell. In *Proceedings of the 2009 ACM SIGPLAN Haskell Symposium*, September 2009.

[11] A. Goodloe and L. Pike. Monitoring distributed real-time systems: A survey and future directions. Technical Report NASA/CR-2010-216724, NASA Langley Research Center, July 2010.

[12] N. Halbwachs and P. Raymond. Validation of synchronous reactive systems: from formal verification to automatic testing. In *ASIAN'99, Asian Computing Science Conference*. LNCS 1742, Springer, December 1999.

[13] T. Hawkins. Controlling hybrid vehicles with Haskell. Presentation. *Commercial Users of Functional Programming* (CUFP), 2008. Available at `http://cufp.galois.com/2008/schedule.html`.

[14] T. Kahsai, Y. Ge, and C. Tinelli. Instantiation-based invariant discovery. In *3rd NASA Formal Methods Symposium*, volume 6617 of *LNCS*, pages 192–207. Springer, 2011.

[15] D. Leijen and E. Meijer. Domain specific embedded compilers. In *Domain-Specific Languages Conference*. USENIX, 1999.

[16] X. Leroy. Formal verification of a realistic compiler. *Communications of the ACM*, 52:107–115, July 2009.

[17] J. S. Moore, editor. *Special Issue on System Verification: Journal of Automated Reasoning*, volume 5, 1989.

[18] B. Pagano, O. Andrieu, T. Moniot, B. Canou, E. Chailloux, P. Wang, P. Manoury, and J.-L. Colao. Experience report: using Objective Caml to develop safety-critical embedded tools in a certification framework. In G. Hutton and A. P. Tolmach, editors, *International Conference on Functional Programming (ICFP)*, pages 215–220. ACM, 2009.

[19] L. Pike, M. Shields, and J. Matthews. A verifying core for a cryptographic language compiler. In *Proceedings of the 6th Intl. Workshop on the ACL2 Theorem Prover and its Applications*, pages 1–10. ACM, 2006.

[20] L. Pike, S. Niller, and N. Wegmann. Runtime verification for ultra-critical systems. In *Proceedings of the 2nd Intl. Conference on Runtime Verification*, LNCS. Springer, September 2011.

[21] L. Sassaman, M. L. Patterson, S. Bratus, and A. Shubina. The Halting problems of network stack insecurity. *;login: The USENIX Magazine*, 36(6), December 2011.

[22] T. Schrijvers, S. Peyton Jones, M. Sulzmann, and D. Vytiniotis. Complete and decidable type inference for GADTs. In *International Conference on Functional Programming (ICFP)*, ICFP '09, pages 341–352. ACM, 2009.

[23] D. Terei, S. Marlow, S. P. Jones, and D. Mazières. Safe haskell. In *Proceedings of the Haskell Symposium*, 2012.

[24] X. Yang, Y. Chen, E. Eide, and J. Regehr. Finding and understanding bugs in C compilers. In *Programming Language Design and Implementation (PLDI)*, pages 283–294. ACM, 2011.

Equality Proofs and Deferred Type Errors
A Compiler Pearl

Dimitrios Vytiniotis Simon Peyton Jones
Microsoft Research, Cambridge
{dimitris,simonpj}@microsoft.com

José Pedro Magalhães
Utrecht University
jpm@cs.uu.nl

Abstract

The Glasgow Haskell Compiler is an optimizing compiler that expresses and manipulates first-class equality proofs in its intermediate language. We describe a simple, elegant technique that exploits these equality proofs to support *deferred type errors*. The technique requires us to treat equality proofs as possibly-divergent terms; we show how to do so without losing either soundness or the zero-overhead cost model that the programmer expects.

Categories and Subject Descriptors D.3.3 [*Language Constructs and Features*]: Abstract data types; F.3.3 [*Studies of Program Constructs*]: Type structure

General Terms Design, Languages

Keywords Type equalities, Deferred type errors, System FC

1. Introduction

In a compiler, a typed intermediate language provides a firm place to stand, free from the design trade-offs of a complex source language. Moreover, type-checking the intermediate language provides a simple and powerful consistency check on the earlier stages of type inference and other optimizing program transformations. The Glasgow Haskell Compiler (GHC) has just such an intermediate language. This intermediate language has evolved in the last few years from System F to System FC (Sulzmann et al. 2007; Weirich et al. 2011) to accommodate the source-language features of *GADTs* (Cheney and Hinze 2003; Peyton Jones et al. 2006; Sheard and Pasalic 2004) and *type families* (Chakravarty et al. 2005; Kiselyov et al. 2010); and from System FC to System $F_C^{\uparrow}$, a calculus now fully equipped with *kind polymorphism* and *datatype promotion* (Yorgey et al. 2012).

The principal difference between System F and System $F_C^{\uparrow}$ is that, together with type information, System $F_C^{\uparrow}$ carries *equality proofs*: evidence that type equality constraints are satisfied. Such proofs are generated during the type inference process and are useful for type checking System $F_C^{\uparrow}$ programs. However, once type checking of the $F_C^{\uparrow}$ program is done, proofs – very much like types – can be completely (and statically) erased, so that they induce no runtime execution or allocation overhead.

Proof assistants and dependently typed languages (Bove et al. 2009; Norell 2007; The Coq Team) adopt a similar design with statically erasable proofs, including ones that go beyond equality to more complex program properties. However, there is one important difference: in proof assistants the proof language *is* the computation language, always a side-effect free and terminating language that guarantees logical consistency of the proofs. On the other hand, in System $F_C^{\uparrow}$ the computation language includes partial functions and divergent terms. To ensure logical consistency, $F_C^{\uparrow}$ keeps the equality proof language as a syntactically separate, consistent-by-construction set of equality proof combinators.

In this paper we investigate the opportunities and challenges of blurring the rigid proof/computation boundary, without threatening soundness, by allowing "proof-like" first-class values to be returned from *ordinary* (even divergent or partial) computation terms. We make the following contributions:

- The proofs-as-values approach opens up an entirely new possibility, that of *deferring type errors to runtime*. A common objection to static type systems is that the programmer wants to be able to run a program even though it may contain some type errors; after all, the execution might not encounter the error. Recent related work (Bayne et al. 2011) makes a convincing case that during prototyping or software evolution programmers wish to focus on getting *part* of their code right, without first having to get *all* of it type-correct. Deferring type errors seems to be just the right mechanism to achieve this. Our new approach gives a principled way in which such erroneous programs can be run with complete type safety (Sections 3 and 5).
- The key to the almost effortless shift to proofs-as-values is based on a simple observation: System $F_C^{\uparrow}$, with the recent addition of kind polymorphism (Yorgey et al. 2012), already allows us to *define within the system* an ordinary first-class type for type equality (Section 4). As such, we can have ordinary values of that type, that are passed to or returned from arbitrary (even partial or divergent) terms. Moreover, deferring type errors aside, there are other compelling advantages of proofs-as-values in an evidence-passing compiler, as we outline in Section 6.
- Most functional programmers think of types as static objects, with zero run-time overhead, and they expect the same of proofs about types. Treating type equality proofs as values seriously undermines this expectation. In Section 7 we address this challenge and show how the optimizer of GHC, with no changes whatsoever, can already eliminate the cost of equality proofs – except in corner cases where it would be wrong to do so.

ICFP'12, September 9–15, 2012, Copenhagen, Denmark.

Everything we describe is fully implemented. As far as we know, GHC is the first, and only, widely-used optimizing compiler that manipulates first-class proofs. We describe this paper as a "pearl" because it shows a simple and elegant way in which the apparently-esoteric notion of a "proof object" can be deployed to solve a very practical problem.

2. The opportunity: deferring type errors

Suppose you type this Haskell term into the interactive read-eval-print prompt in GHCi:

```
ghci> fst (True, 'a' && False)
```

This term does not "go wrong" when evaluated: you might expect to just get back the result *True* from projecting the first component of the pair. But in a statically typed language like Haskell you get the type error:

```
Couldn't match 'Bool' with 'Char'
In the first argument of '(&&)', namely 'a'
```

This behaviour is fine for programs that are (allegedly) finished, but some programmers would much prefer the term to evaluate to *True* when doing exploratory programming. After all, if the error is in a bit of the program that is not executed, it is doing no harm! In particular, when refactoring a large program it is often useful to be able to run parts of the completed program, but type errors prevent that. What we want is to defer type errors until they matter. We have more to say about motivation and related work in Section 8.

As we shall see, System $F_C^{\uparrow}$ allows us to offer precisely this behaviour, *without giving up type safety*. Here is an interactive session with `ghci -fdefer-type-errors`:

```
ghci> let foo = (True, 'a' && False)
Warning: Couldn't match 'Bool' with 'Char'
ghci> :type foo
(Bool, Bool)
ghci> fst foo
True
ghci> snd foo
Runtime error: Couldn't match 'Bool' with 'Char'
```

Notice that:

- The definition of *foo* produced a warning (rather than an error), but succeeds in producing an executable binding for *foo*.
- Since type checking of *foo* succeeded it has a type, which can be queried with `:type` to display its type, (*Bool*, *Bool*).
- The term *fst foo* typechecks fine, *and also runs fine*, returning *True*.
- The term *snd foo* also typechecks fine, and runs; however the evaluation aborts with a runtime error giving *exactly the same error* as the original warning.

That is, the error message is produced lazily, at runtime, when and only when the requirement for *Char* and *Bool* to be the same type is encountered.

2.1 How deferring type errors works, informally

GHC's type inference algorithm works in two stages: first we *generate* type constraints, and then we *solve* them (Vytiniotis et al. 2011). In addition, inference elaborates the Haskell source term to an explicitly typed $F_C^{\uparrow}$ term, that includes the types and proofs ("evidence" in GHC jargon) computed by the constraint solver.

In the previous example, during type inference for the sub-term `'a'` && *False* we generate a type equality constraint, written $Char \sim Bool$. Usually the constraint solver would immediately reject such a constraint as insoluble, but with `-fdefer-type-errors` we take a different course: we generate "evidence" for $Char \sim Bool$, but ensure that if the (bogus) evidence is ever evaluated it brings the program to a graceful halt. More concretely, here is the $F_C^{\uparrow}$ term that we generate for *foo*:

$$\begin{array}{l} foo = \textbf{let}\ (c : Char \sim Bool) = error\ \texttt{"Couldn't..."} \\ \qquad\quad \textbf{in}\ (True, (cast\ \texttt{'a'}\ c)\ \&\&\ False) \end{array}$$

The elaborated *foo* contains a lazy binding of an evidence variable *c* of type $Char \sim Bool$ to a call to *error*. The latter is a built-in Haskell constant, of type $\forall a\ .\ String \to a$, that prints its argument string and brings execution to a halt.

When we evaluate *fst foo* the result is *True*; but if we evaluate *snd foo*, we must evaluate the result of (&&), which in turn evaluates its first argument, *cast* `'a'` *c*. The cast forces evaluation of *c*, and hence triggers the runtime error. Note that the exact placement of coercions, and thus which errors get deferred, depends on the internals of the type inference process; we discuss this in more detail in Section 5.4.

There is something puzzling about binding variable *c* with the type $Char \sim Bool$. The evidence variable *c* is supposed to be bound to a proof witnessing that *Char* and *Bool* are equal types, but is nevertheless bound to just a *term*, and in fact a crashing term, namely *error*! How can we then ensure soundness, and how can we get statically erasable proofs? It turns out that the type $Char \sim Bool$ is almost but *not quite* the type of a proof object. To explain how this works, we move on to present some more details on GHC's typed intermediate language, System $F_C^{\uparrow}$.

3. The $F_C^{\uparrow}$ language

System $F_C^{\uparrow}$ is a polymorphic and explicitly typed language, whose syntax is given in Figure 1. Our presentation closely follows the most recent work on $F_C^{\uparrow}$ Yorgey et al. (2012), and we will not repeat operational semantics and type soundness results; instead, we refer the reader to Yorgey et al. (2012) for the details.

A quick glance at Figure 1 will confirm that the term language *e* is mostly conventional, explicitly-typed, lambda calculus, with let-bindings, literals (*l*), data constructors (*K*), and case expressions. In addition, the language includes type *and kind* polymorphism: type ($\Lambda a{:}\eta\ .\ e$) and kind ($\Lambda\chi\ .\ e$) abstractions, and type ($e\ \varphi$) and kind ($e\ \kappa$) applications, respectively. Some motivation for kind abstractions and applications comes from previous work but, as we shall see in Section 6.2, kind polymorphism will play a key role here as well.

The distinctive feature of $F_C^{\uparrow}$ is the use of *coercions*, γ. A coercion γ of type $\tau \sim_{\#} \varphi$ is nothing more than a *proof of type equality* between the types φ and τ. Contrary to the notation used in Section 2.1 and in previous presentations of System $F_C^{\uparrow}$ notice that we use symbol $\sim_{\#}$ instead of $\sim$ for coercion types, and $Constraint_{\#}$ rather than *Constraint* for their kind – this is for a good reason that will become evident in Section 4.2.

The term ($e \triangleright \gamma$) is a *cast* that converts a term *e* of type τ to one of type φ, when $\gamma : \tau \sim_{\#} \varphi$. Once again, this is deliberately different than the *cast* term that appeared in Section 2.1, as we discuss in Section 4.2. The only other place where a coercion γ may appear in the term language is in an application ($e\ \gamma$), so coercions are not first-class values. Dually, one can abstract over such coercions with a coercion abstraction $\lambda(c{:}\tau \sim_{\#} \varphi)\ .\ e$.

Terms

e, u	$::=$	$x \mid l \mid \lambda x{:}\sigma . e \mid e\ u$	
	$\mid$	$\Lambda a{:}\eta . e \mid e\ \varphi \mid \Lambda \chi . e \mid e\ \kappa$	Type/kind polymorphism
	$\mid$	$\lambda c{:}\tau . e \mid e\ \gamma$	Coercion abs/app
	$\mid$	$K \mid \textbf{case}\ e\ \textbf{of}\ \overline{p \to u}$	
	$\mid$	$\textbf{let}\ x{:}\tau = e\ \textbf{in}\ u$	
	$\mid$	$e \triangleright \gamma$	Cast
p	$::=$	$K\ \overline{c{:}\tau}\ \overline{x{:}\tau}$	Patterns

Types

$\varphi, \sigma, \tau, \upsilon$	$::=$	a	Variables
	$\mid$	H	Constants
	$\mid$	F	Type functions
	$\mid$	$\varphi_1\ \varphi_2$	Application
	$\mid$	$\varphi\ \kappa$	Kind application
	$\mid$	$\forall a{:}\eta . \varphi$	Polymorphic types
	$\mid$	$\forall \chi . \tau$	Kind-polymorphic types

Type constants

H	$::=$	T	Datatypes
	$\mid$	$(\to)$	Arrow
	$\mid$	$(\sim_\#)$	Primitive equality type

Kinds

κ, η	$::=$	$\chi \mid \star \mid \kappa \to \kappa$	
	$\mid$	$\forall \chi . \kappa$	Polymorphic kinds
	$\mid$	$Constraint_\#$	Kind of static proofs

Coercion values

γ, δ	$::=$	c	Variables
	$\mid$	$\gamma_1\ \gamma_2$	Application
	$\mid$	$\langle \varphi \rangle$	Reflexivity
	$\mid$	$\gamma_1 ; \gamma_2$	Transitivity
	$\mid$	$sym\ \gamma$	Symmetry
	$\mid$	$\ldots$	Other coercion forms

Environments

Γ, Δ	$::=$	$\cdot \mid \Gamma, bnd$	
bnd	$::=$	χ	Kind variable
	$\mid$	$a : \eta$	Type variable
	$\mid$	$c : \sigma \sim_\# \varphi$	Coercion variable
	$\mid$	$x : \sigma$	Term variable
	$\mid$	$T : \forall \overline{\chi} . \overline{\kappa} \to \star$	Data type
	$\mid$	$K : \forall \overline{\chi}\ \overline{(a{:}\eta_a)} . \overline{\tau} \to T\ \overline{\chi}\ \overline{a}$	Data constructor
	$\mid$	$\ldots$	Type families etc.

Notation

$T\ \overline{\kappa}\ \overline{\tau}$	$\equiv$	$T\ \kappa_1 \ldots \kappa_m\ \tau_1 \ldots \tau_n$
$\overline{\alpha} \to \alpha$	$\equiv$	$\alpha_1 \to \ldots \to \alpha_n \to \alpha$
		for α either κ or τ
Γ_0	$\equiv$	initial (closed) environment
	$\ni$	$(\sim_\#) : \forall \chi . \chi \to \chi \to Constraint_\#$

Figure 1: Syntax of System FC (excerpt)

$$\boxed{\Gamma \vdash^{tm} e : \tau}$$

$$\frac{(x{:}\tau) \in \Gamma}{\Gamma \vdash^{tm} x : \tau}\ \textsc{EVar} \qquad \frac{(K{:}\sigma) \in \Gamma_0}{\Gamma \vdash^{tm} K : \sigma}\ \textsc{ECon}$$

$$\frac{\Gamma, (x{:}\sigma) \vdash^{tm} e : \tau \quad \Gamma \vdash^{ty} \sigma : \star}{\Gamma \vdash^{tm} \lambda x{:}\sigma . e : \sigma \to \tau}\ \textsc{EAbs} \qquad \frac{\Gamma \vdash^{tm} e : \sigma \to \tau \quad \Gamma \vdash^{tm} u : \sigma}{\Gamma \vdash^{tm} e\ u : \tau}\ \textsc{EApp}$$

$$\frac{\Gamma, (c{:}\sigma) \vdash^{tm} e : \tau \quad \Gamma \vdash^{ty} \sigma : Constraint_\#}{\Gamma \vdash^{tm} \lambda c{:}\sigma . e : \sigma \to \tau}\ \textsc{ECAbs}$$

$$\frac{\Gamma \vdash^{tm} e : (\sigma_1 \sim_\# \sigma_2) \to \tau \quad \Gamma \vdash^{co} \gamma : \sigma_1 \sim_\# \sigma_2}{\Gamma \vdash^{tm} e\ \gamma : \tau}\ \textsc{ECApp}$$

$$\frac{\Gamma \vdash^{k} \eta \quad \Gamma, (a{:}\eta) \vdash^{tm} e : \tau}{\Gamma \vdash^{tm} \Lambda a{:}\eta . e : \forall a{:}\eta . \tau}\ \textsc{ETAbs} \qquad \frac{\Gamma \vdash^{tm} e : \forall a{:}\eta . \tau \quad \Gamma \vdash^{ty} \varphi : \eta}{\Gamma \vdash^{tm} e\ \varphi : \tau[\varphi/a]}\ \textsc{ETApp}$$

$$\frac{\Gamma, \chi \vdash^{tm} e : \tau}{\Gamma \vdash^{tm} \Lambda \chi . e : \forall \chi . \tau}\ \textsc{EKAbs} \qquad \frac{\Gamma \vdash^{tm} e : \forall \chi . \tau \quad \Gamma \vdash^{k} \kappa}{\Gamma \vdash^{tm} e\ \kappa : \tau[\kappa/\chi]}\ \textsc{EKApp}$$

$$\frac{\Gamma, (x{:}\sigma) \vdash^{tm} u : \sigma \quad \Gamma, (x{:}\sigma) \vdash^{tm} e : \tau}{\Gamma \vdash^{tm} \textbf{let}\ x{:}\sigma = u\ \textbf{in}\ e : \tau}\ \textsc{ELet} \qquad \frac{\Gamma \vdash^{tm} e : \tau \quad \Gamma \vdash^{co} \gamma : \tau \sim_\# \varphi}{\Gamma \vdash^{tm} e \triangleright \gamma : \varphi}\ \textsc{ECast}$$

$$\frac{\begin{array}{l} \Gamma \vdash^{tm} e : T\ \overline{\kappa}\ \overline{\sigma} \\ \text{For each branch } K\ \overline{x{:}\tau} \to u \\ \quad (K{:}\forall \overline{\chi}\ \overline{(a{:}\eta_a)} . \overline{\sigma_1 \sim_\# \sigma_2} \to \overline{\tau} \to T\ \overline{\chi}\ \overline{a}) \in \Gamma_0 \\ \quad \varphi_i = \tau_i[\overline{\kappa/\chi}][\overline{\sigma/a}] \\ \quad \varphi_{1i} = \sigma_{1i}[\overline{\kappa/\chi}][\overline{\sigma/a}] \\ \quad \varphi_{2i} = \sigma_{2i}[\overline{\kappa/\chi}][\overline{\sigma/a}] \quad \Gamma, \overline{c{:}\varphi_1 \sim \varphi_2}\ \overline{x{:}\varphi} \vdash^{tm} u : \sigma \end{array}}{\Gamma \vdash^{tm} \textbf{case}\ e\ \textbf{of}\ \overline{K\ \overline{(c{:}\sigma_1 \sim_\# \sigma_2)}\ \overline{(x{:}\tau)} \to u} : \sigma}\ \textsc{ECase}$$

Figure 2: Well-formed terms

The syntax of coercions themselves (γ in Figure 1) includes coercion variables, constructors for reflexivity, transitivity, and symmetry, as well as other constructors (such as lifting type equalities over data constructors) that we do not need to discuss in this paper.

The well-formedness judgement for terms appears in Figure 2 and is mostly conventional. In particular, the rules for coercion abstraction and application (ECABS and ECAPP) mirror those for terms (EABS and EAPP). The rule for case expressions (ECASE) is also standard but notice that it allows us to bind coercion variables, as well as term variables, in a pattern.

3.1 Types, kinds, and kind polymorphism

The type language of System $F_C^{\uparrow}$ includes variables and constants, type and kind application, as well as the type of type-polymorphic values ($\forall a{:}\eta . \varphi$) and the type of kind-polymorphic values ($\forall \chi . \tau$). The type constants H include data constructors (T), and the function constructor ($\to$) as well as the equality constructor ($\sim_\#$). The well-formedness judgement for types appears in Figure 3.

What should the kind of $\sim_\#$ be? We mentioned previously that we would like to classify any type $\tau \sim_\# \sigma$ as having kind $Constraint_\#$, but the kind of τ and σ can be *any* kind whatsoever. This indicates that $\sim_\#$ should be given the *polymorphic* kind:

$$\forall \chi . \chi \to \chi \to Constraint_\#$$

This kind, made valid because the syntax of kinds κ includes kind polymorphism, is recorded in the initial environment Γ_0 (bottom of Figure 1). Well-formedness of kinds ($\Gamma \vdash^{k} \kappa$), for this presentation, amounts to well-scoping, so we omit the details from Figure 3. As a convention, we write $\tau \sim_\# \varphi$ to mean $(\sim_\#)\ \kappa\ \tau\ \varphi$ in the rest of this paper, where the kind κ of τ and φ is clear from the context.

Finally, notice that well-formed arrow types[1] are allowed to accept an argument which is either $Constraint_\#$ or $\star$, to account for coercion or term abstraction, but may only return $\star$, hence disallowing any functions to return a value of type $\tau \sim_\# \varphi$. However, as we will

[1] For simplicity of presentation we do not include a binding for $(\to)$ in the initial environment Γ_0, hence only allowing fully applied arrow types, unlike Haskell.

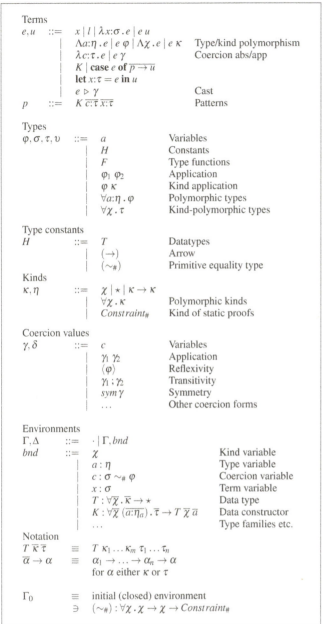

$$\boxed{\Gamma \vdash^{ty} \tau : \kappa}$$

$$\frac{(a:\eta) \in \Gamma}{\Gamma \vdash^{ty} a : \eta}\ \text{TVAR} \qquad \frac{(T:\kappa) \in \Gamma}{\Gamma \vdash^{ty} T : \kappa}\ \text{TDATA}$$

$$\frac{\Gamma \vdash^{ty} \tau_1 : \kappa_1 \quad \Gamma \vdash^{ty} \tau_2 : \star \quad \kappa_1 \in \{\star, \mathit{Constraint}_\#\}}{\Gamma \vdash^{ty} \tau_1 \to \tau_2 : \star}\ \text{TARR}$$

$$\frac{\Gamma \vdash^{ty} \tau_1 : \kappa_1 \to \kappa_2 \quad \Gamma \vdash^{ty} \tau_2 : \kappa_1}{\Gamma \vdash^{ty} \tau_1\ \tau_2 : \kappa_2}\ \text{TAPP} \qquad \frac{\Gamma \vdash^{ty} \tau : \forall \chi . \kappa \quad \Gamma \vdash^{k} \eta}{\Gamma \vdash^{ty} \tau\ \eta : \kappa[\eta/\chi]}\ \text{TKAPP}$$

$$\frac{\Gamma, (a{:}\eta) \vdash^{ty} \tau : \star \quad \Gamma \vdash^{k} \eta}{\Gamma \vdash^{ty} \forall a{:}\eta . \tau : \star}\ \text{TALL} \qquad \frac{\Gamma, \chi \vdash^{ty} \tau : \star}{\Gamma \vdash^{ty} \forall \chi . \tau : \star}\ \text{TKALL}$$

$$\boxed{\Gamma \vdash^{co} \gamma : \sigma_1 \sim_\# \sigma_2}$$

...

$$\boxed{\Gamma \vdash^{k} \kappa}$$

...

Figure 3: Well-formed types and coercions

see in Section 4, a function can well return terms *that contain* such coercions.

3.2 $F_C^\uparrow$ datatypes with coercions

In $F_C^\uparrow$, coercions can appear as arguments to data constructors, a feature that is particularly useful for representing generalized algebraic datatypes (GADTs) (Peyton Jones et al. 2006). Consider this *source* Haskell program which defines and uses a GADT:

```
data T a where
  T1 :: Int → T Int
  T2 :: a   → T a

f :: T a → [a]
f (T1 x) = [x+1]
f (T2 v) = []
main = f (T1 4)
```

In $F_C^\uparrow$, we regard the GADT data constructor T_1 as having the type:

$$T_1 : \forall a . (a \sim_\# \mathit{Int}) \to \mathit{Int} \to T\ a$$

So T_1 takes three arguments: a type argument to instantiate a, a coercion witnessing the equality between a and *Int*, and a value of type *Int*. Here is the $F_C^\uparrow$ version of *main*:

$$\mathit{main} = f\ \mathit{Int}\ (T_1\ \mathit{Int}\ \langle \mathit{Int} \rangle\ 4)$$

The coercion argument has kind $\mathit{Int} \sim_\# \mathit{Int}$, for which the evidence is just $\langle \mathit{Int} \rangle$ (reflexivity). Similarly, pattern-matching on T_1 binds two variables: a coercion variable, and a term variable. Here is the $F_C^\uparrow$ elaboration of function f:

```
f = Λ(a : ⋆). λ(x : T a).
      case x of
        T1 (c : a ~# Int) (n : Int)
             → (Cons (n+1) Nil) ▷ sym [c]
        T2 v → Nil
```

The cast converts the type of the result from $[\mathit{Int}]$ to $[a]$[2]. The coercion $\mathit{sym}\ [c]$ is evidence for (or a proof of) the equality of these types, lifting c (of type $a \sim_\# \mathit{Int}$) over lists ($[c]$, of type $[a] \sim_\# [\mathit{Int}]$), before applying symmetry. We urge the reader to consult Sulzmann et al. (2007) and Weirich et al. (2011) for more examples and intuition.

A final remark: we will be presenting and discussing a number of $F_C^\uparrow$ programs in the rest of the paper. For readability purposes we will sometimes omit type or kind applications in $F_C^\uparrow$ terms when these types or kinds are obvious from the context, making the syntax appear less verbose.

4. Two forms of equality

In Section 2 we sketched how to use type-equality evidence to support deferred type errors, using $\sigma \sim \tau$ as the type of equality evidence. Then in Section 3 we introduced our intermediate language, System $F_C^\uparrow$, in which explicit coercions of type $\sigma \sim_\# \tau$ represent evidence for the equality of two types. The distinction between $(\sim)$ and $(\sim_\#)$ is crucial: it allows us to to marry a sound, erasable language of proofs with the potentially-unsound ability to have terms that compute proofs, as we discuss in this section.

4.1 The tension

Types have a very valuable property that programmers take for granted: they give strong static guarantees, but they carry *no run-time overhead*. This zero-overhead guarantee is formally justified by an *erasure* property: we can erase all the types before running the program, without changing the result.

Can we offer a similar guarantee for coercions? Yes, we can. System $F_C^\uparrow$ is carefully designed so that coercion abstractions, coercion applications, and casts, are all statically erasable, just like type abstractions and applications.

But this statement is manifestly in tension with our approach to deferred type errors. Consider once more the $F_C^\uparrow$ term

```
let (c : Char ~ Bool) = error "Couldn't match..."
in snd (True, (cast 'a' c) && False)
```

Obviously we cannot erase the binding of c and the cast, leaving *snd* (*True*, 'a' && *False*), because the latter will crash. So it seems that insisting on complete erasure of equalities kills the idea of deferring type errors stone dead!

4.2 The two equalities

We now present our resolution of this tension. We have carefully maintained a distinction between

- $(\sim_\#)$, the type of primitive coercions γ in $F_C^\uparrow$, which are fully erasable, and
- $(\sim)$, type of evidence generated by the type inference engine, which cannot be erased.

However $(\sim)$ is not some magical built-in device. Rather, we can define it as a perfectly ordinary GADT (like the one we have already seen in Section 3.2), thus:

```
data a ~ b where
  Eq# :: (a ~# b) → a ~ b
```

[2] We informally use Haskell's notation $[\tau]$ for the type list of τ, and *Cons* and *Nil* as its constructors.

This definition introduces a new algebraic data type constructor $(\sim)$, belonging in the T syntactic category of Figure 1. It has exactly one data constructor $Eq_{\#}$, whose (important) argument is a *static equality proof*. Readers familiar with proof assistants or type theory will immediately recognize in the definition of $(\sim)$ the type used traditionally in such systems to internalize *definitional equality* as a type (e.g. `refl_equal` in Coq).

Like $(\sim_{\#})$, the data type $(\sim)$ is polymorphically kinded:

$$\begin{array}{l} \sim \; : \forall \chi \, . \, \chi \to \chi \to \star \\ Eq_{\#} : \forall \chi \, . \, \forall (a:\chi)\,(b:\chi) \, . \, (a \sim_{\#} b) \to (a \sim b) \end{array}$$

As with $\tau \sim_{\#} \sigma$ we usually omit the kind application in $\tau \sim \sigma$ as a syntactic convenience.

The key point is that if $\gamma : \sigma \sim_{\#} \tau$, then a value $Eq_{\#}\ \gamma$ is an ordinary term, built with the data constructor $Eq_{\#}$, and having type $\sigma \sim \tau$. Given the GADT $(\sim)$ we can define the function *cast* that takes such a term-level equality witness and casts a value between equivalent types:

$$\begin{array}{l} cast : \forall (a\, b : \star) \, . \, a \to (a \sim b) \to b \\ cast = \Lambda (a\, b : \star) \, . \, \lambda (x : a) \, . \, \lambda (eq : a \sim b) \, . \\ \qquad \mathbf{case}\ eq\ \mathbf{of}\ Eq_{\#}\ (c : a \sim_{\#} b) \to x \triangleright c \end{array}$$

Each use of *cast* forces evaluation of the coercion, *via* the **case** expression and, in the case of a deferred type error, that is what triggers the runtime failure.

Just as *cast* is a lifted version of $\triangleright$, we can lift all the coercion combinators from the $(\sim_{\#})$ type to $(\sim)$. For example:

$$\begin{array}{l} mkRefl :: \forall \chi \, . \, \forall (a : \chi) \, . \, a \sim a \\ mkRefl = \Lambda \chi \, . \, \Lambda (a : \chi) \, . \, Eq_{\#}\ \chi\ a\ a\ \langle a \rangle \\ mkSym :: \forall \chi \, . \, \forall (a\, b : \chi) \, . \, (a \sim b) \to (b \sim a) \\ mkSym = \Lambda \chi \, . \, \Lambda (a\, b : \chi) \, . \, \lambda (c : a \sim b) \, . \\ \qquad \mathbf{case}\ c\ \mathbf{of}\ Eq_{\#}\ c \to Eq_{\#}\ \chi\ b\ a\ (sym\ c) \end{array}$$

The relationship between $(\sim)$ and $(\sim_{\#})$ is closely analogous to that between *Int* and $Int_{\#}$, described twenty years ago in our implementation of arithmetic in GHC (Peyton Jones and Launchbury 1991). Concretely, here is GHC's implementation of addition on *Int*:

$$\begin{array}{l} \mathbf{data}\ Int = I_{\#}\ Int_{\#} \\ plusInt :: Int \to Int \to Int \\ plusInt\ x\ y = \mathbf{case}\ x\ \mathbf{of}\ I_{\#}\ x' \to \\ \qquad \mathbf{case}\ y\ \mathbf{of}\ I_{\#}\ y' \to I_{\#}\ (x' +_{\#} y') \end{array}$$

An *Int* is an ordinary algebraic data type with a single constructor $I_{\#}$ (the '#' is not special; it is just part of the constructor name). This constructor has a single argument, of type $Int_{\#}$, which is the type of *unboxed integers*, a honest-to-goodness 32-bit integer value just like C's *int*. Finally $(+_{\#})$ is the machine 32-bit addition instruction. We may summarise the relationships thus:

- A value of type *Int*, or $\sigma \sim \tau$, is always heap-allocated; it is always represented by a pointer to the heap-allocated object; and the object can be a thunk.
- A value of type $Int_{\#}$, or $\sigma \sim_{\#} \tau$ is never heap-allocated; and it cannot be a thunk. There is no bottom value of type $Int_{\#}$, or $\sigma \sim_{\#} \tau$; we say that they are *unlifted types*.
- The *plusInt* function lifts the primitive addition $+_{\#}$ from $Int_{\#}$ to *Int*, by explicitly evaluating and unboxing its arguments; and the function *mkSym* works in just the same way.

The main difference between *Int#* and $a \sim_{\#} b$ is that the fomer is represented by a 32-bit unboxed value, whereas the latter has a structure that is *irrelevant* for the execution of a program, and can be represented by a zero-bit value, or entirely erased — it comes to the same thing in the end.

5. Type inference and deferral of type errors

With $F_C^{\uparrow}$ in hand we can now explain in more detail the mechanism of deferring type errors. We begin by sketching a little more about the type inference process.

5.1 Type inference by constraint generation

GHC's type inference algorithm works in two stages (Vytiniotis et al. 2011):

- Step 1: traverse the syntax tree of the input Haskell term, generating *type constraints* together with an *elaborated term*[3] in System $F_C^{\uparrow}$.
- Step 2: solve the constraints, creating $F_C^{\uparrow}$ bindings that give evidence for the solution.

For example, consider the term *show xs*, where $xs : [Int]$, and $show : \forall a \, . \, Show\ a \Rightarrow a \to String$. In Step 1 we generate:

$$\begin{array}{rl} \text{Elaborated term:} & show\ [Int]\ d_6\ xs \\ \text{Constraint:} & d_6 : Show\ [Int] \end{array}$$

The elaborated term looks much like the original except that *show* is now applied to a *type argument* $[Int]$ (corresponding to the "$\forall a$" in *show*'s type) and an *evidence argument* d_6 (corresponding to the "$Show\ a \Rightarrow$" in its type). The constraint is given a fresh name, d_6 in this example, which is mentioned in the elaborated term. Afficionados of Haskell's type-class system will recognise d_6 as *show*'s dictionary argument: it is simply a tuple of functions, the methods of the *Show* class.

When Step 1 is complete, the constraint solver solves the generated constraints, producing *evidence bindings*:

$$d_6 : Show\ [Int] = \$dShowList\ Int\ \$dShowInt$$

Here the solver has constructed a dictionary for $Show\ [Int]$, using the dictionary-construction functions that arise from the instance declarations of the class *Show*:

$$\begin{array}{lcl} \$dShowInt & : & Show\ Int \\ \$dShowList & : & \forall a \, . \, Show\ a \to Show\ [a] \end{array}$$

Finally, the evidence bindings are wrapped around the term in a **let** to make an executable term:

$$\begin{array}{l} \mathbf{let}\ d_6 = \$dShowList\ Int\ \$dShowInt \\ \mathbf{in}\ show\ [Int]\ d_6\ xs \end{array}$$

5.2 Equality constraints

This is all quite conventional. Somewhat less conventionally (but following the French school of type inference (Pottier and Rémy 2005)) GHC generates *equality constraints* as well as type-class constraints. We simplified the *show* example; in reality GHC generates the following:

$$\begin{array}{rl} \text{Elaborated term:} & show\ \alpha\ d_6\ (cast\ xs\ c_5) \\ \text{Constraints:} & d_6 : Show\ \alpha \\ & c_5 : [Int] \sim \alpha \end{array}$$

When instantiating *show*'s type in Step 1, the constraint generator does not yet know that it will be applied to the type $[Int]$, so instead it creates a fresh unification variable α, and uses that to instantiate *show*'s type. Later, when checking *show*'s argument x, it must ensure that *show*'s argument type α is equal to the actual type of *xs*, namely $[Int]$. It ensures this (eventual) equality by generating

[3] In reality we first generate an elaborated term by decorating the Haskell source term, and *then* desugar it, but we will ignore that extra step here.

an *equality constraint* $c_5 : [Int] \sim \alpha$, again with an arbitrary fresh name c_5 which names the evidence for the equality. Lastly, in the elaborated term, we use the cast term *cast xs* c_5 to convert *xs* into a term of type α. Notice that c_5's type $[Int] \sim \alpha$ uses the boxed equality $(\sim)$ rather than the primitive $F_C^{\uparrow}$ equality $(\sim_{\#})$ (Section 4.2).

In Step 2, the constraint solver has a little extra work to do: as well as solving the constraints and giving bindings for the evidence variables, it must also produce bindings for the unification variables. In our running example, the solution to the constraints looks like this:

$$\begin{array}{rcl} \alpha &=& [Int] \\ c_5 : [Int] \sim \alpha &=& mkRefl\,[Int] \\ d_6 : Show\,[Int] &=& \$dShowList\ Int\ \$dShowInt \end{array}$$

The solver decided to eliminate α by substituting $[Int]$ for α, the first of the above bindings. The equality c_5 now witnesses the vacuous equality $[Int] \sim [Int]$, but it must still be given a binding, here *mkRefl* $[Int]$. (Recall that *mkRefl* was introduced in Section 4.2.)

Actually, as a matter of efficiency, in our real implementation the constraint generator solves many simple and immediately-soluble equalities (such as $\alpha \sim [Int]$) "on the fly" using a standard unification algorithm, rather than generating an equality constraint to be solved later. But that is a mere implementation matter; the implementation remains faithful to the semantics of generate-and-solve. Moreover, it certainly cannot solve *all* equalities in this way, because of GADTs and type families (Vytiniotis et al. 2011).

5.3 Deferring type errors made easy

In a system generating equality proofs using the $(\sim)$ datatype, which has values that can be inhabited by ordinary terms, it is delightfully easy to support deferred type errors. During constraint generation, we generate a type-equality constraint *even for unifications that are manifestly insoluble.* During constraint solving, instead of emitting an error message when we encounter an insoluble constraint, we emit a warning, and create a value binding for the constraint variable, which binds it to a call to *error*, applied to the error message string that would otherwise have been emitted at compile time. And that's all there is to it.

It is worth noting several features of this implementation technique:

- Each $F_C^{\uparrow}$ term given above *is a well-typed* $F_C^{\uparrow}$ term, even though some are generated from a type-incorrect Haskell term. Of course it can fail at run-time, but it does so in a civilized way, by raising an exception, not by causing a segmentation fault, or performing (&&) of a character and a boolean. You might consider that a program that fails at runtime in this way is not well-typed, in Milner's sense of "well typed programs do not go wrong". But Haskell programs can *already* "go wrong" in this way — consider (*head* [ ]) for example — so matters are certainly no worse than in the base language.

  In short, *we have merely deferred the type errors to runtime; we have not ignored them!*

- Deferring type errors is not restricted to interpreted expressions typed at the interactive GHCi prompt. You can compile any module with `-fdefer-type-errors` and GHC will produce a compiled binary, which can be linked and run.

- There is no reflection involved, nor run-time type checking. Indeed there is no runtime overhead whatsoever: the program runs at full speed unless it reaches the point where a runtime error is signalled, in which case it halts. (This claim assumes the optimisations described in Section 7.)

- The technique makes elegant use of laziness. In a call-by-value language, a strict binding of *c* in Section 2.1 would be evaluated by the call *fst foo*, or even when *foo* is bound, and it would obviate the entire exercise if that evaluation triggered the runtime error! Nevertheless, the idea can readily be adapted for call-by-value, by simply making $(\sim)$ into a sum type:

  $$\begin{array}{l} \textbf{data}\ a \sim b\ \textbf{where} \\ \quad Eq_{\#}\ :: (a \sim_{\#} b) \to a \sim b \\ \quad Error :: String \quad \to a \sim b \end{array}$$

  Now, the "evidence" for an erroneous type constraint would be an *Error* value, and evaluating that is fine. We simply need to adjust *cast* to deal with the *Error* case:

  $$\begin{array}{l} cast = \Lambda(a\,b : \star)\,.\,\lambda(x : a)\,.\,\lambda(eq : a \sim b)\,. \\ \qquad \textbf{case}\ eq\ \textbf{of} \\ \qquad\quad Eq_{\#}\ (c : a \sim_{\#} b) \to x \triangleright c \\ \qquad\quad Error\ s \to error\ s \end{array}$$

- The technique works uniformly for *all* type constraints, not only for equality ones. For example, in Section 5.1, suppose there was no instance for *Show* $[Int]$. Then the constraint d_6 : *Show* $[Int]$ would be insoluble, so again we can simply emit a warning and bind d_6 to an error thunk. Any program that needs the evidence for d_6 will now fail; those that don't, won't.

- We can defer all *type* errors in terms, but not *kind* errors in types. For example, consider

  $$\begin{array}{l} \textbf{data}\ T = MkT\ (Int\ Int) \\ f\ (MkT\ x) = x \end{array}$$

  The type *Int Int* simply does not make sense – applying *Int* to *Int* is a kind error, and we do not have a convenient way to defer *kind* errors, only type errors.

5.4 The placement of errors

Since many different parts of a program may contribute to a type error, there may be some non-determinism about *how delayed* a deferred type error will be. Suppose that *upper* : $[Char] \to [Char]$, and consider the term:

$$upper\ [True, \texttt{'a'}]$$

There are two type incompatibilities here. First, the boolean *True* and character `'a'` cannot be in the same list. Second, the function *upper* expects a list of characters but is given a list with a boolean in it. Here is one possible elaboration:

$$\begin{array}{rl} \text{Elaborated term:} & upper\ [cast\ True\ c_7, \texttt{'a'}] \\ \text{Constraints:} & c_7 : Bool \sim Char \end{array}$$

But the program could also be elaborated in another way:

$$\begin{array}{rl} \text{Elaborated term:} & upper\ (cast\ [True, cast\ \texttt{'a'}\ c_8]\ c_9) \\ \text{Constraints:} & c_8 : Char \sim Bool \\ & c_9 : [Bool] \sim [Char] \end{array}$$

In this case, type inference has cast `'a'` to *Bool* using c_8, so that it can join *True* to form a list of *Bool*; and then cast the list $[Bool]$ to $[Char]$ using c_9 to make it compatible with *upper*. The two elaborated programs have slightly different runtime behaviour. If the term is bound to *tm*, then *head* (*tail tm*) will run successfully (returning `'A'`) in the first elaboration, but fail with a runtime error in the second.

We might hope that the type inference engine inserts as few casts as possible, and that it does so as near to the usage site as possible. In fact this turns out to be the case, because the type inference engine uses the (known) type of *upper* to type-check its argument, expecting the result to be of type $[Char]$. This idea of "pushing down" the expected type into an expression, sometimes called *bidirectional* or *local* type inference (Pierce and Turner 2000), is already implemented in GHC to improve the quality of error messages; see Peyton Jones et al. (2007, Section 5.4) for details. Although it is a heuristic, and not a formal guarantee, the mechanism localises the casts very nicely in practice.

Nevertheless, the bottom line is that the dynamic semantics of a type-incorrect program depends on hard-to-specify implementation details of the type inference algorithm. That sounds bad! But we feel quite relaxed about it:

- The issue arises only for programs that contain errors. Type correct programs have their usually fully-specified semantics.
- Regardless of the precise placement of coercions, the elaborated program is type correct. This is not a soundness issue.
- The imprecision of dynamic semantics is no greater a shortcoming than the lack of a formal specification of the precise type error message(s) produced by a conventional type inference engine for a type-incorrect program. And yet no compiler or paper known to us gives a formal specification of what type errors are produced for a type-incorrect program.

That said, it is interesting to reflect on approaches that might tighten up the specification, and we do so in Section 9.

5.5 Summary

There are many reasons why evidence-based type elaboration, using constraint generation and subsequent constraint solving, is desirable (Vytiniotis et al. 2011):

- It is *expressive*, readily accommodating Haskell's type classes, implicit parameters, and type families.
- It is *modular*. The constraint *generator* accepts a very large input language (all of Haskell), so it has many cases, but each case is very simple. In contrast, the constraint *solver* accepts a very small input language (the syntax of constraints) but embodies a complex solving algorithm. Keeping the two separate is incredibly wonderful.
- It is *robust*: for example it does not matter whether the constraint generator traverses the term left-to-right or right-to-left: the resulting constraint is the same either way.
- Neither the constraint generator nor the solver need be trusted; a very simple, independent checker can type-check the elaborated $F_C^{\uparrow}$ term.

To this list we can now add a completely new merit: it is dead easy to implement deferred type errors, a feature that is desired by many Haskell programmers.

6. Discussion

Now that we have discussed type inference in more detail, we pause to reflect on our design choices.

6.1 Evidence uniformity

We've seen that deferring type errors provides a good motivation for treating coercions as term-level constructs. But there is another way in which treating coercions as values turns out to be very convenient. In the Haskell source language, *equality constraints* are treated uniformly with *type-class constraints* and *implicit-parameter constraints*; anywhere a class constraint can appear, an equality constraint can appear, and vice versa. Class constraints and implicit-parameter constraints definitely cannot be erased: by design their evidence carries a runtime value. Treating some constraints as non-erasable values and others (the equalities) as type-like, erasable constructs, led to many annoying special cases in the type inference and source-to-$F_C^{\uparrow}$ elaboration of Haskell programs.

The most troublesome example of this non-uniformity arises when treating Haskell's superclasses. Consider the declaration

$$\textbf{class}\ (a \sim F\ b, Eq\ a) \Rightarrow C\ a\ b\ \textbf{where}\ldots$$

Here $Eq\ a$ is a superclass of $C\ a\ b$, meaning that from evidence for $C\ a\ b$ one can extract evidence for $Eq\ a$. Concretely this extraction is witnessed by a field selector:

$$sc_2 : C\ a\ b \to Eq\ a$$

which takes a dictionary (i.e. record of values) for $C\ a\ b$ and picks out the $Eq\ a$ field. In just the same way one should be able to extract evidence for $a \sim F\ b$, which suggests a selector function with type

$$sc_1 : C\ a\ b \to (a \sim F\ b)$$

Before we distinguished $(\sim)$ and $(\sim_{\#})$ we could not write this function because there simply is no such function in $F_C^{\uparrow}$; indeed the type $C\ a\ b \to (a \sim_{\#} F\ b)$ is not even well kinded in Figure 3. There is a good reason for this: dictionaries can be recursively defined and can diverge (Lämmel and Peyton Jones 2005), so the selector function may diverge when evaluating its arguments – but the type $a \sim_{\#} F\ b$ cannot represent divergence, because that would be unsound.

The tension is readily resolved by $(\sim)$; the type of sc_1 is well formed and its definition looks something like this:

$$\begin{aligned} sc_1 = \Lambda ab\,.\,\lambda(d : C\ a\ b)\,.\\ \textbf{case}\ d\ \textbf{of}\\ MkC\ (c : a \sim_{\#} F\ b)\ (eq : Eq\ a)\ldots \to Eq_{\#}\ c \end{aligned}$$

This accumulation of infelicities led us to the two-equality plan, and in fact we had fully implemented this design even *before* we ever thought of deferring type errors. Now, we get the ability to defer errors regarding type unification, missing class constraints, and implicit parameters, all in one go.

6.2 Why kind polymorphism is important

We have mentioned that both equalities $(\sim_{\#})$ and $(\sim)$ are kind-polymorphic, but we have not yet said why. Right from the beginning Haskell has featured kinds other than $\star$, such as $\star \to \star$. During type inference, when unifying, say, $\alpha\ \beta \sim Maybe\ Int$, the inference engine — or, more precisely, the constraint solver — must decompose the equality to give $\alpha \sim Maybe$ and $\beta \sim Int$. The former equality is at kind $\star \to \star$, so it follows that the $(\sim)$ type constructor itself must be either (a) magically built in or (b) poly-kinded. And similarly $(\sim_{\#})$.

Solution (a) is entirely possible: we could add $\sigma \sim \tau$ and $\sigma \sim_{\#} \tau$ to the syntax of types, and give them their own kinding rules. But there are unpleasant knock-on effects. The optimizer would need to be taught how to optimize terms involving $(\sim)$. Worse, it turns out that we need equalities between equalities, thus $(\sigma_1 \sim \tau_1) \sim (\sigma_2 \sim \tau_2)$, which in turn leads to the need for new coercion combinators to decompose such types.

There are many other reasons for kind polymorphism in $F_C^{\uparrow}$ (Yorgey et al. 2012), and once we have kind polymorphism we can readily make the equality type constructors kind-polymorphic.

6.3 What the Haskell programmer sees

A salient feature of Haskell's qualified types (type classes, implicit parameters, equality constraints) is that the type inference engine fills in the missing evidence parameters. So if f has type

$$f :: (Num\ b, a \sim F\ b) \Rightarrow a \rightarrow b \rightarrow b$$

then given a source-language call $(f\ e_1\ e_2)$, the type inference will generate the elaborated call $(f\ \sigma\ \tau\ d\ c\ e_1\ e_2)$, where σ and τ are the types that instantiate a and b, and d and c are evidence terms that witness that $Num\ \tau$ holds and that $\sigma \sim F\ \tau$, respectively.

One might wonder whether one can (in Haskell) also write

$$g :: (a \sim_{\#} F\ b) \Rightarrow a \rightarrow b \rightarrow b$$

and have the above evidence-generation behaviour. No, you cannot. The whole point of the $(\sim)$ type is that it can be treated uniformly with other evidence (bound in letrec, returned as a result of a call), whereas $(\sim_{\#})$ cannot. So in the source language $\sigma \sim_{\#} \tau$ is not a type constraint you can write before the "$\Rightarrow$" in a Haskell type, and have it participate in constraint solving. The entire constraint generation and solving process works exclusively with well-behaved, uniform, boxed constraints. Only when constraint solving is complete does $(\sim_{\#})$ enter the picture, as we discuss next.

7. Optimizing equalities

We now have a correct implementation, but it looks worryingly expensive. After all, the constraint generation/solving process may generate a program littered with coercion bindings and casts, all of which are invisible to the programmer, have no operational significance, and merely ensure that "well typed programs don't go wrong". Yet each will generate a heap-allocated $Eq_{\#}$ box, ready to be evaluated by *cast*. Happily, almost all of these boxes are eliminated by existing optimizations within GHC, as this section describes.

7.1 Eliminating redundant boxing and unboxing

The fact that we have defined $(\sim)$ as an ordinary GADT means that is fully exposed to GHC's optimizer. Consider a Haskell 98 program that turns out to be well typed. The constraint generator will produce many constraints that are ultimately solved by reflexivity, because the two types really are equal. Here is a typical case of an elaborated term:

$$\textbf{let}\ (c : Char \sim Char) = mkRefl\ Char$$
$$\textbf{in} \ldots (cast\ e\ c) \ldots$$

(Recall that *mkRefl* and *cast* were defined in Section 4.2.) As it stands, the **let** will heap-allocate a thunk which, when evaluated by the *cast*, will turn out to be an $Eq_{\#}$ constructor wrapping a reflexive coercion $\langle Char \rangle$. All this is wasted work. But GHC's optimizer can inline the definitions of *mkRefl* and *cast* from Section 4.2 to get

$$\textbf{let}\ (c : Char \sim Char) = Eq_{\#}\ \star\ Char\ Char\ \langle Char \rangle$$
$$\textbf{in} \ldots (\textbf{case}\ c\ \textbf{of}\ Eq_{\#}\ c' \rightarrow e \triangleright c') \ldots$$

Now it can inline c at its use site, and eliminate the case expression, giving

$$\ldots (e \triangleright \langle Char \rangle) \ldots$$

Remembering that primitive casts $(\triangleright)$ can be erased, we have eliminated the overhead. Moreover, the optimizations involved have all been in GHC for years; there is no new special purpose magic.

What happens when a deferred type error means that a cast cannot, and should not, be erased? Consider once more the $F_C^{\uparrow}$ term

$$\textbf{let}\ (c : Char \sim Bool) = error\ \texttt{"Couldn't match..."}$$
$$\textbf{in}\ snd\ (True, (cast\ \texttt{'a'}\ c)\ \&\&\ False)$$

Now, simply by inlining *cast* and c, the optimizer can transform to

$$snd\ (True, (\textbf{case}\ error\ \texttt{"..."}\ \textbf{of}\ \{Eq_{\#}\ c \rightarrow \texttt{'a'} \triangleright c\})\ \&\&\ False)$$

After inlining (&&), and simplifying **case**-of-*error* to just a call of *error*, both standard transformations in GHC's optimizer) we get

$$snd\ (True, error\ \texttt{"..."})$$

Even erroneous programs are optimized by removing their dead code! The point is this: by exposing the evaluation of coercions, we allow the *existing* optimizer transformations to work their magic.

7.2 Equalities and GADTs

Let us reconsider the GADT example given in Section 3.2:

$$\textbf{data}\ T\ a\ \textbf{where}$$
$$T_1 :: Int \rightarrow T\ Int$$
$$T_2 :: a \quad \rightarrow T\ a$$

There we said that the constructor T_1 is typed thus:

$$T_1 : \forall a\,.\,(a \sim_{\#} Int) \rightarrow Int \rightarrow T\ a$$

That is true in System $F_C^{\uparrow}$. But the Haskell programmer, who knows only of the type $\sigma \sim \tau$, considers T_1 to have this type:

$$T_1 :: \forall a\,.\,(a \sim Int) \rightarrow Int \rightarrow T\ a$$

It would be perfectly sound to adopt the latter type for T_1 in the elaborated program; for example, function f from Section 3.2 would be elaborated thus:

$$f = \Lambda a\,.\,\lambda(x : T\ a)\,.$$
$$\textbf{case}\ x\ \textbf{of}$$
$$T_1\ (c : a \sim Int)\ (n : Int)$$
$$\rightarrow cast\ (Cons\ (n+1)\ Nil)\ (mkSym\ [c])$$
$$T_2\ v \rightarrow Nil$$

Since an argument of type $a \sim Int$ has a lifted type with a boxed representation, it would take up a whole word in every T_1 object. Moreover, since c is bound by the pattern match, the **case** expression in *mkSym* will not cancel with an *Eq#* box in the binding for c. This is not good! What has become of our zero-overhead solution?

The solution is simple: we desugar GADTs to contain *unlifted*, rather than *lifted*, equalities. We can do this in such a way that the Haskell programmer still sees only the nice well-behaved $(\sim)$ types, as follows. First, in the elaborated program the type of T_1 is:

$$T_1 : \forall a\,.\,(a \sim_{\#} Int) \rightarrow Int \rightarrow T\ a$$

However, the elaborator replaces every source-language call of T_1 with a call of a constructor wrapper function, *T1wrap*, defined like this:

$$T1wrap : \forall a\,.\,(a \sim Int) \rightarrow Int \rightarrow T\ a$$
$$T1wrap = \Lambda(a : \star)\,.\,\lambda(c : a \sim Int)\,.\,\lambda(n : Int)\,.$$
$$\textbf{case}\ c\ \textbf{of}\ Eq_{\#}\ c_1 \rightarrow T_1\ c_1\ n$$

The wrapper deconstructs the evidence and puts the payload into T_1 where, since it is erasable, it takes no space.

Dually, a source-program pattern match is elaborated into a $F_C^{\uparrow}$ pattern match together with code to re-box the coercion. So our function f is elaborated thus:

$$f = \Lambda a\,.\,\lambda(x : T\ a)\,.$$
$$\textbf{case}\ x\ \textbf{of}$$
$$T_1\ (c_1 : a \sim_{\#} Int)\ (n : Int)$$

$$\rightarrow \textbf{let}\ c = Eq_{\#}\ c_1 \quad \text{-- Re-boxing}$$
$$\quad \textbf{in}\ cast\ (Cons\ (n+1)\ Nil)\ (mkSym\ [c])$$
$$T_2\ v \rightarrow Nil$$

Now the earlier optimizations will get rid of all the boxing and unboxing and we are back to nice, efficient code. The technique of unboxing strict arguments on construction, and re-boxing on pattern matching (in the expectation that the re-boxing will be optimized away) is precisely what GHC's `UNPACK` pragma on constructor arguments does. So, once more, coercions can hitch a free ride on some existing machinery.

7.3 How much is optimized away?

We have argued that the boxing and unboxing, introduced in the elaborated program by the type checker, will largely be eliminated by standard optimizations. But not always! Indeed that is the point: the main reason for going to all of this trouble is to handle smoothly the cases (deferred type errors, recursive dictionaries) when equalities cannot, and should not, be erased. But still, one might reasonably ask, can we offer any guarantees at all?

Consider a type-correct Haskell program that contains (a) no equality superclasses, and (b) no functions that take or return a value of type $\sigma \sim \tau$, apart from GADT constructors. This includes all Haskell 98 programs, and all GADT programs. After typechecking and elaboration to $F_C^{\uparrow}$, suppose that we inline every use of *mkRefl*, *mkSym*, etc, and the GADT constructor wrappers. Then

- Every use of a variable of type $\sigma \sim \tau$ will be a case expression that scrutinises that variable, namely the unboxing **case** expressions in *mkRefl*, *mkSym*, etc, and GADT constructor wrappers.
- Every binding of an evidence variable of type $\sigma \sim \tau$ will be a **let** whose right hand side returns a statically-visible $Eq_{\#}$ box.

By inlining these **let**-bound evidence variables at their use sites, we can cancel the **case** with the $Eq_{\#}$ constructors, thereby eliminating all boxing and unboxing. To illustrate, consider once more the elaboration of function f at the end of the previous subsection. If we inline *mkSym* and *cast* we obtain:

$$f = \Lambda a.\,\lambda(x : T\ a).$$
$$\quad \textbf{case}\ x\ \textbf{of}$$
$$\qquad T_1\ (c_1 : a \sim_{\#} Int)\ (n : Int)$$
$$\qquad\quad \rightarrow \textbf{let}\ c \ = Eq_{\#}\ c_1\ \textbf{in} \quad \text{-- Re-boxing}$$
$$\qquad\qquad \textbf{let}\ c_2 = \textbf{case}\ c\ \textbf{of}\ Eq_{\#}\ c' \rightarrow Eq_{\#}\ (sym\ [c'])$$
$$\qquad\qquad \textbf{in case}\ c_2\ \textbf{of}$$
$$\qquad\qquad\quad Eq_{\#}\ c_2' \rightarrow Cons\ (n+1)\ Nil \triangleright c_2'$$
$$\qquad T_2\ v \rightarrow Nil$$

The right hand side of c_2 comes from inlining *mkSym*, while the "**case** c_2..." comes from inlining *cast*. Now we can inline c in "**case** c...", and c_2 in "**case** c_2...", after which the cancellation of boxing and unboxing is immediate.

When does this *not* work? Consider exception (b) above, where a programmer writes a function that is explicitly abstracted over an equality:

$$f : \forall a\,.\,F\ a \sim Int \Rightarrow [F\ a] \rightarrow Int$$
$$f\ x = head\ x + 1$$

The elaborated form will look like this:

$$f : \forall a\,.\,F\ a \sim Int \rightarrow [F\ a] \rightarrow Int$$
$$f = \Lambda a.\,\lambda(c : F\ a \sim Int).\,\lambda(x : [F\ a]).$$
$$\quad head\ (cast\ x\ c) + 1$$

Since c is lambda-bound, there is no $Eq_{\#}$ box for the *cast* to cancel with. However we can perform the same worker/wrapper split to this user-defined function that we did for constructors, thus

$$f : \forall a\,.\,F\ a \sim Int \rightarrow [F\ a] \rightarrow Int$$
$$f = \Lambda a.\,\lambda(c : F\ a \sim Int).\,\lambda(x : [F\ a]).$$
$$\quad \textbf{case}\ c\ \textbf{of}\ Eq_{\#}\ c' \rightarrow fwrk\ c'\ x$$

$$fwrk : \forall a\,.\,F\ a \sim_{\#} Int \rightarrow [F\ a] \rightarrow Int$$
$$fwrk = \Lambda a.\,\lambda(c' : F\ a \sim_{\#} Int).\,\lambda(x : [F\ a]).$$
$$\quad \textbf{let}\ c = Eq_{\#}\ c'\ \textbf{in}\ head\ (cast\ x\ c) + 1$$

Now in *fwrk* the boxing and unboxing cancels; and dually we are free to inline the wrapper function f at its call sites, where the unboxing will cancel with the construction. This worker/wrapper mechanism is precisely what GHC already implements to eliminate boxing overheads on strict function arguments (Peyton Jones and Santos 1998), so it too comes for free. There *is* a small price to pay, however: the transformation makes the function strict in its equality evidence, and that in turn might trigger a deferred error message slightly earlier than strictly necessary. In our view this is a trade-off worth making. In our current implementation the worker/wrapper transform on equalities is only applied when the function really is strict in the equality; we have not yet added the refinement of *making* it strict in all equalities.

7.4 Summary

In short, although we do not give a formal theorem (which would involve formalizing GHC's optimizer) we have solid grounds, backed by observation of optimized code, for stating that the uniform representation of equality evidence can be successfully optimized away in all but the cases in which it cannot and should not be eliminated, namely for deferred type errors and functions that must accept or return term-level equalities (such as selectors for equality superclasses). Of course, introducing and then eliminating all these boxes does mean a lot more work for the compiler, but this has not proved to be a problem in practice.

8. Related work

8.1 Relation to hybrid and gradual typing

Hybrid type checking (Flanagan 2006) refers to the idea of deferring statically *unproved* goals as runtime checks. Achieving similar effects, but arriving from the opposite end of the spectrum *soft typing* tries to elimiminate statically as many runtime checks as possible (Wright and Cartwright 1997). There are two differences compared to our approach: First, in hybrid type checking typically only unsolved goals will be deferred whereas insoluble ones will be reported statically. In our case, insoluble and unsolved goals will be deferred. Second, unsolved goals will be deferred as *checks* in hybrid type systems, whereas they will remain errors in our system: Our treatment of coercions does not *replace* static type errors by runtime checks, but rather *delays* triggering a static error until the offending part of the program is evaluated, at runtime. For instance, consider the following program, which contains a static error but is compiled with `-fdefer-type-errors`:

$$f :: \forall a\,.\,a \rightarrow a \rightarrow a$$
$$f\ x\ y = x\ \&\&\ y$$

There is a static error in this program because f is supposed to be polymorphic in the type of its arguments x and y, which are nevertheless treated as having type *Bool*. At runtime, even if we evaluate the application of f on arguments of type *Bool*, such as *f True False* we will get a type error "Couldn't match type a with *Bool*", despite the fact that the arguments of f *are* of type *Bool* at runtime. In contrast, a truly dynamic type-check would not trigger a runtime error.

In the context of GHC, there is no straightforward way to incorporate runtime checks instead of error triggers at runtime, unless dynamic type information is passed along with polymorphic types. Though systems with dynamic types and coercions have been studied in the literature (Henglein 1994), we have not examined this possibility.

There is a large body of work on interoperating statically and dynamically typed parts of a program, often referred to as *gradual typing* (Ahmed et al. 2011; Siek and Taha 2006; Siek and Vachharajani 2008; Tobin-Hochstadt and Felleisen 2006). Typically, statically insoluble goals will be reported statically (Siek and Taha 2006), whereas insoluble goals which perhaps arise from the potential interoperation of dynamic and static parts of the program will be wrapped with runtime checks. The main problem in gradual typing is to identify how to assign blame in case of a contract violation (or a dynamic type error). We have seen in Section 5.3 that non-determinism in the dynamic placement of the type error may well exist. Consequently it might be an interesting avenue to explore if ideas from gradual typing could help us specify a more predictable "blame assignment" for these deferred type errors. Note finally that previous work on type error slicing (Haack and Wells 2004) has focused on identifying parts of a program that contribute to a type error and would be potentially useful for reducing this non-determinism both for static error messages and for better specifying the dynamic behaviour of an erroneous program.

8.2 Deferring type errors

DuctileJ is a plugin to the Java compiler that converts a normal Java program to one in which type checking is deferred until runtime (Bayne et al. 2011). The authors provide an extensive discussion of the software engineering advantages of deferring type errors, under two main headings.

- During *prototyping*, programmers often comment out partly written or temporarily out-of-date code, while prototyping some new part. Commenting out is tiresome because one must do it consistently: if you comment out *f* you must comment out everything that calls *f*, and so on. Deferring type errors is a kind of lazy commenting-out process.
- During *software evolution* of a working system it can be burdensome to maintain global static type correctness. It may be more productive to explore a refactoring, or change of data representation, in part of a software system, and test that part, without committing to propagating the change globally.

We urge the reader to consult this excellent paper for a full exposition, and a good evaluation of the practical utility of deferring type errors both during prototyping and for software evolution.

Note however that although our motivations are similar, our implementation differs radically from that in DuctileJ. The latter works by a "de-typing" transformation that uses Java's runtime type information and reflection mechanisms to support runtime type checks. This imposes a significant runtime cost – the paper reports a slowdown between 1.1 and 7.8 times. In contrast, our implementation performs no runtime reflection and runs at full speed until the type error itself is encountered. The DuctileJ de-typing transformation is also not entirely faithful to the original semantics — unsurprisingly, the differences involve reflection — whereas ours is fully faithful, even for programs that involve Haskell's equivalent of reflection, the *Typeable* and *Data* classes. To be fair, many of the DuctileJ complexities go away because Haskell is a simpler language than Java. Further, GHC already implemented (the quite advance features of) kind polymorphism, coercions, and unboxing, which allowed us to piggyback `-fdefer-type-errors` onto the existing compiler implementation with very little effort.

Deferring type errors is also a valuable tool in the context of IDE development. In an IDE it is essential to provide feedback to the programmer even if the program has errors. The Visual Basic IDE uses a hierarchy of analysis to provide gradually more functionality depending on the type of errors present (Gertz 2005). For instance, if there are type errors, but no parse errors, smart indentation and automatic code pretty-printing can already be applied. However, more complicated refactorings require type information to be available. Some IDEs use error-correcting parsers to be able to provide some functionality in the presence of parsing errors, but a type error will require a correction by the user before the IDE can offer functionality that depends on the availability of types. Deferring type errors allows the compiler to complete type checking without fixing the type errors, allowing for a Haskell IDE to remain functional even for programs that do not type-check.

8.3 Proof erasure

Coq (The Coq Team) uses a *sort-based* erasure process by introducing a special universe for propositions, *Prop*, which is analogous to our $Constraint_{\#}$ kind. Terms whose type lives in *Prop* are erased even when they are applications of functions (lemmas) to computational terms. This is sound in Coq, since the computation language is also strongly normalizing. Extending the computation language of $F_C^{\uparrow}$ proofs or finding a way to restrict the ordinary computation language of $F_C^{\uparrow}$ using kinds in order to allow it to construct *primitive* equalities is an interesting direction towards true dependent types for Haskell.

Irrelevance-based erasure is another methodology proposed in the context of pure type systems and type theory. In the context of Epigram, Brady et al. (2003) presented an erasure technique where term-level indices of inductive types can be erased even when they are deconstructed inside the body of a function, since values of the indexed inductive datatype will be simultaneously deconstructed and hence the indices are irrelevant for the computation. In the Agda language (Norell 2007) there exist plans to adopt a similar irrelevance-based erasure strategy. Other related work (Abel 2011; Mishra-Linger and Sheard 2008) proposes erasure in the context of PTSs guided with lightweight programmer annotations. There also exist approaches that lie in between sort-based erasure and irrelevance-based erasure: for instance, in *implicit calculus of constructions* (Miquel 2001) explicitly marked static information (not necessarily *Prop*-bound) does not affect computation and can be erased (Barras and Bernardo 2008). In $F_C^{\uparrow}$ the result of a computation cannot depend on the structure of an equality proof, by construction: there is no mechanism to decompose the structure of a coercion at all at the term-level. Hence a coercion value needs no structure (since it cannot be decomposed), which allows us to perform full erasure without any form of irrelevance analysis.

This idea – of separating the "computational part" of a proof-like object, which always has to run before we get to a zero-cost "logical part" – is reminiscent of a similar separation that A-normal forms introduce in refinement type systems, for instance (Bengtson et al. 2008) or the more recent work on value-dependent types (Borgstrom et al. 2011; Swamy et al. 2011). This line of work seems the closest in spirit to ours, with similar erasure concerns, and there is rapidly growing evidence of the real-world potential of these ideas – see for instance the discussion and applications reported by Swamy et al. (2011).

9. Future work and conclusions

Error coercion placement This paper has been about an *implementation* technique that uses first-class proof-like objects to allow for deferred type errors with very low overhead. A natural next step would be towards a declarative specification of the "elaboration" process from source to a target language which specifies the placement of the deferred error messages on potentially erroneous sub-terms. Recent related work on coercion placement in the context of coercive subtyping is the work of Luo (2008) and Swamy et al. (2009); these would certainly be good starting points for investigations on a declarative specification of deferring type errors. The canonical reference for coercion placement in a calculus with type-dynamic is the work of Henglein (1994), but it seems somewhat disconnected from our problem as we do not have currently any way of dynamically passing type information or executing programs that contain static errors but are safe dynamically.

In general, this problem seems very hard to tackle without exposing some of the operation of the underlying constraint solver. In the other direction, a principled approach to deferring type errors might actually provide *guidance* on the order in which constraints should be solved. For instance, when solving the constraints $C_1 \cup C_2 \cup C_3$ arising from the expressions e_1, e_2, and e_3 in the term **if** e_1 **then** e_2 **else** e_3, we might want to prioritise solving the constraint C_1. In this way, if an error is caused by the interaction of the expressions e_2 or e_3 with e_1, we would still be able to execute the condition of the branch e_1 before we emit a deferred type error for e_2 or e_3. Otherwise we run the danger of the term e_2 or e_3 forcing some unification that makes constraint C_1 insoluble, giving rise to an earlier error message (during evaluation of the condition term e_1). However, it is not clear what should happen when C_2 and C_3 have a common unification variable, and there is freedom in deferring either one, for instance. Therefore this problem is certainly worth further investigation.

The equality type Internalizing definitional equality ($\sim_\#$) as a type ($\sim$) is pretty standard in languages with dependent types (Licata and Harper 2005). For example, programming with first-class equality witnesses is sometimes convenient to avoid shortcomings of implementations of dependent pattern matching.

Recent work on higher-dimensional type theory (Licata and Harper 2012) goes one step further to show that the ($\sim$) datatype can be *extended* with yet another constructor for term-level isomorphisms between types. Interestingly the usual definitional equality inference rules apply for this extended equality type. Moreover they show that the term language can be equipped with an equational theory that is rich enough, so that types enjoy canonical forms. Of course the language they address is simpler in some respects (no partiality or divergence, no polymorphism), nor is there a reduction semantics. In a real compiler, being able to extend the ($\sim$) datatype with true computational isomorphisms and maintain soundness and providing a transparent treatment of these isomorphisms with minimal programmer intervention is an interesting direction for future research.

Conclusions In this paper we have proposed a simple and lightweight mechanism for deferring type errors, in a type-safe way that requires no program rewriting, and preserves the semantics of the program until execution reaches the part that contains a type error. We have shown that this can be done in an entirely safe way in the context of a typed intermediate language, and in fact without requiring any modifications to System $F_C^\uparrow$ or the compiler optimizer. This work is fully implemented in GHC, where it has in addition greatly simplified the implementation of type inference and elaboration of Haskell to $F_C^\uparrow$.

Acknowledgments

Particular thanks are due to Etienne Laurin, who suggested to us the idea of deferring type errors (GHC Trac ticket 5624), although his implementation was very different to the one described here. We thank Stephanie Weirich and Brent Yorgey for their detailed comments and suggestions, and the ICFP reviewers for the helpful feedback.

This work has been partially funded by the Portuguese Foundation for Science and Technology (FCT) via the SFRH/BD/35999/2007 grant, and by EPSRC grant number EP/J010995/1.

References

Andreas Abel. Irrelevance in type theory with a heterogeneous equality judgement. In *Foundations of Software Science and Computational Structures, 14th International Conference, FOSSACS 2011*, pages 57–71. Springer, 2011.

Amal Ahmed, Robert Bruce Findler, Jeremy G. Siek, and Philip Wadler. Blame for all. In *Proceedings of the 38th annual ACM SIGPLAN-SIGACT Symposium on Principles of Programming Languages*, POPL '11, pages 201–214, New York, NY, USA, 2011. ACM. ISBN 978-1-4503-0490-0. doi: 10.1145/1926385.1926409.

Bruno Barras and Bruno Bernardo. The implicit calculus of constructions as a programming language with dependent types. In *Foundations of Software Science and Computation Structure*, pages 365–379, 2008. doi: 10.1007/978-3-540-78499-9_26.

Michael Bayne, Richard Cook, and Michael Ernst. Always-available static and dynamic feedback. In *Proceedings of 33rd International Conference on Software Engineering (ICSE'11)*, pages 521–530, Hawaii, 2011.

Jesper Bengtson, Karthikeyan Bhargavan, Cédric Fournet, Andrew D. Gordon, and Sergio Maffeis. Refinement types for secure implementations. In *Proceedings of the 2008 21st IEEE Computer Security Foundations Symposium*, pages 17–32, Washington, DC, USA, 2008. IEEE Computer Society. ISBN 978-0-7695-3182-3.

Johannes Borgstrom, Juan Chen, and Nikhil Swamy. Verifying stateful programs with substructural state and Hoare types. In *Proceedings of the 5th ACM Workshop on Programming Languages meets Program Verification*, PLPV '11, pages 15–26, New York, NY, USA, 2011. ACM. ISBN 978-1-4503-0487-0.

Ana Bove, Peter Dybjer, and Ulf Norell. A brief overview of Agda — a functional language with dependent types. In *TPHOLs '09: Proceedings of the 22nd International Conference on Theorem Proving in Higher Order Logics*, pages 73–78, Berlin, Heidelberg, 2009. Springer-Verlag.

Edwin Brady, Conor McBride, and James McKinna. Inductive families need not store their indices. In Stefano Berardi, Mario Coppo, and Ferruccio Damiani, editors, *TYPES*, volume 3085 of *Lecture Notes in Computer Science*, pages 115–129. Springer, 2003.

Manuel M. T. Chakravarty, Gabriele Keller, and Simon Peyton Jones. Associated type synonyms. In *ICFP '05: Proceedings of the Tenth ACM SIGPLAN International Conference on Functional Programming*, pages 241–253, New York, NY, USA, 2005. ACM.

James Cheney and Ralf Hinze. First-class phantom types. CUCIS TR2003-1901, Cornell University, 2003.

Cormac Flanagan. Hybrid type checking. In *Proceedings of the 33rd ACM SIGPLAN-SIGACT Symposium on Principles of Programming Languages*, POPL '06, pages 245–256, New York, NY, USA, 2006. ACM. doi: 10.1145/1111037.1111059.

Matthew Gertz. Scaling up: The very busy background compiler. *MSDN Magazine*, 6 2005. URL `http://msdn.microsoft.com/en-us/magazine/cc163781.aspx`.

Christian Haack and J. B. Wells. Type error slicing in implicitly typed higher-order languages. *Science of Computer Programming*, 50:189–224, March 2004. ISSN 0167-6423.

Fritz Henglein. Dynamic typing: syntax and proof theory. *Science of Computer Programming*, 22:197–230, June 1994. ISSN 0167-6423.

Oleg Kiselyov, Simon Peyton Jones, and Chung-chieh Shan. Fun with type functions. In A.W. Roscoe, Cliff B. Jones, and Kenneth R. Wood, editors, *Reflections on the Work of C.A.R. Hoare*, History of Computing, pages 301–331. Springer London, 2010. doi: 10.1007/978-1-84882-912-1_14.

Ralf Lämmel and Simon Peyton Jones. Scrap your boilerplate with class: extensible generic functions. In *Proceedings of the 10th ACM SIGPLAN International Conference on Functional Programming*, ICFP '05, pages 204–215, New York, NY, USA, 2005. ACM. doi: 10.1145/1086365.1086391.

Daniel R. Licata and Robert Harper. A formulation of dependent ML with explicit equality proofs. Technical Report CMU-CS-05-178, Carnegie Mellon University Department of Computer Science, 2005.

Daniel R. Licata and Robert Harper. Canonicity for 2-dimensional type theory. In *Proceedings of the 39th annual ACM SIGPLAN-SIGACT Symposium on Principles of Programming Languages*, POPL '12, pages 337–348, New York, NY, USA, 2012. ACM. doi: 10.1145/2103656.2103697.

Zhaohui Luo. Coercions in a polymorphic type system. *Mathematical Structures in Computer Science*, 18(4):729–751, August 2008. ISSN 0960-1295. doi: 10.1017/S0960129508006804.

Alexandre Miquel. The implicit calculus of constructions: extending pure type systems with an intersection type binder and subtyping. In *Proceedings of the 5th International Conference on Typed Lambda Calculi and Applications*, TLCA'01, pages 344–359, Berlin, Heidelberg, 2001. Springer-Verlag. ISBN 3-540-41960-8.

Nathan Mishra-Linger and Tim Sheard. Erasure and polymorphism in pure type systems. In Roberto Amadio, editor, *Foundations of Software Science and Computational Structures*, volume 4962 of *Lecture Notes in Computer Science*, pages 350–364. Springer Berlin / Heidelberg, 2008.

Ulf Norell. *Towards a practical programming language based on dependent type theory*. PhD thesis, Department of Computer Science and Engineering, Chalmers University of Technology, September 2007.

Simon Peyton Jones and John Launchbury. Unboxed values as first class citizens in a non-strict functional programming language. In *FPCA91: Conference on Functional Programming Languages and Computer Architecture*, pages 636–666, New York, NY, August 1991. ACM Press.

Simon Peyton Jones and André Santos. A transformation-based optimiser for Haskell. *Science of Computer Programming*, 32(1-3):3–47, September 1998.

Simon Peyton Jones, Dimitrios Vytiniotis, Stephanie Weirich, and Geoffrey Washburn. Simple unification-based type inference for GADTs. In *Proceedings of the 11th ACM SIGPLAN International Conference on Functional Programming*, pages 50–61, New York, NY, USA, 2006. ACM Press. ISBN 1-59593-309-3.

Simon Peyton Jones, Dimitrios Vytiniotis, Stephanie Weirich, and Mark Shields. Practical type inference for arbitrary-rank types. *Journal of Functional Programming*, 17(01):1–82, 2007. doi: 10.1017/S0956796806006034.

Benjamin C. Pierce and David N. Turner. Local type inference. *ACM Transactions on Programming Languages and Systems*, 22(1):1–44, January 2000. ISSN 0164-0925. doi: 10.1145/345099.345100.

François Pottier and Didier Rémy. The essence of ML type inference. In Benjamin C. Pierce, editor, *Advanced Topics in Types and Programming Languages*, chapter 10, pages 389–489. MIT Press, 2005.

Tim Sheard and Emir Pasalic. Meta-programming with built-in type equality. In *Proc 4th International Workshop on Logical Frameworks and Meta-languages (LFM'04)*, pages 106–124, July 2004.

Jeremy G. Siek and Walid Taha. Gradual typing for functional languages. In *Scheme and Functional Programming Workshop*, pages 81–92, September 2006.

Jeremy G. Siek and Manish Vachharajani. Gradual typing with unification-based inference. In *Proceedings of the 2008 symposium on Dynamic languages*, DLS '08, pages 7:1–7:12, New York, NY, USA, 2008. ACM. doi: 10.1145/1408681.1408688.

Martin Sulzmann, Manuel M. T. Chakravarty, Simon Peyton Jones, and Kevin Donnelly. System F with type equality coercions. In *Proceedings of the 2007 ACM SIGPLAN Workshop on Types in Language Design and Implementation*, pages 53–66, New York, NY, USA, 2007. ACM.

Nikhil Swamy, Michael Hicks, and Gavin M. Bierman. A theory of typed coercions and its applications. In *Proceedings of the 14th ACM SIGPLAN International Conference on Functional Programming*, ICFP '09, pages 329–340, New York, NY, USA, 2009. ACM. ISBN 978-1-60558-332-7.

Nikhil Swamy, Juan Chen, Cedric Fournet, Pierre-Yves Strub, Karthikeyan Bharagavan, and Jean Yang. Secure distributed programming with value-dependent types. In *Proceedings of the 16th ACM SIGPLAN International Conference on Functional Programming*, ICFP'11, pages 266–278. ACM, September 2011. doi: 10.1145/2034773.2034811.

The Coq Team. *Coq*. URL `http://coq.inria.fr`.

Sam Tobin-Hochstadt and Matthias Felleisen. Interlanguage migration: from scripts to programs. In *Companion to the 21st ACM SIGPLAN Symposium on Object-Oriented Programming Systems, Languages, and Applications*, OOPSLA '06, pages 964–974, New York, NY, USA, 2006. ACM. doi: 10.1145/1176617.1176755.

Dimitrios Vytiniotis, Simon Peyton Jones, Tom Schrijvers, and Martin Sulzmann. OutsideIn(X): Modular Type inference with local assumptions. *Journal of Functional Programming*, 21, 2011.

Stephanie Weirich, Dimitrios Vytiniotis, Simon Peyton Jones, and Steve Zdancewic. Generative type abstraction and type-level computation. In *Proceedings of the 38th annual ACM SIGPLAN-SIGACT Symposium on Principles of Programming Languages*, POPL '11, pages 227–240, New York, NY, USA, 2011. ACM. ISBN 978-1-4503-0490-0.

Andrew K. Wright and Robert Cartwright. A practical soft type system for scheme. *ACM Transactions on Programming Languages and Systems*, 19(1):87–152, January 1997. ISSN 0164-0925. doi: 10.1145/239912.239917.

Brent A. Yorgey, Stephanie Weirich, Julien Cretin, Simon Peyton Jones, Dimitrios Vytiniotis, and José Pedro Magalhães. Giving Haskell a promotion. In *Proceedings of the 8th ACM SIGPLAN Workshop on Types in Language Design and Implementation*, TLDI '12, pages 53–66, New York, NY, USA, 2012. ACM. doi: 10.1145/2103786.2103795.

A Traversal-based Algorithm for Higher-Order Model Checking

Robin P. Neatherway
University of Oxford
robin.neatherway@cs.ox.ac.uk

C.-H. Luke Ong
University of Oxford
luke.ong@cs.ox.ac.uk

Steven J. Ramsay
University of Oxford
steven.ramsay@cs.ox.ac.uk

Abstract

Higher-order model checking—the model checking of trees generated by higher-order recursion schemes (HORS)—is a natural generalisation of finite-state and pushdown model checking. Recent work has shown that it can serve as a basis for software model checking for functional languages such as ML and Haskell. In this paper, we introduce *higher-order recursion schemes with cases* (HORSC), which extend HORS with a definition-by-cases construct (to express program branching based on data) and non-determinism (to express abstractions of behaviours). This paper is a study of the *universal HORSC model checking problem for deterministic trivial automata*: does the automaton accept every tree in the tree language generated by the given HORSC? We first characterise the model checking problem by an intersection type system extended with a carefully restricted form of union types. We then present an algorithm for deciding the model checking problem, which is based on the notion of *traversals* induced by the fully abstract game semantics of these schemes, but presented as a goal-directed construction of derivations in the intersection and union type system. We view HORSC model checking as a suitable backend engine for an approach to verifying functional programs. We have implemented the algorithm in a tool called TRAVMC, and demonstrated its effectiveness on a test suite of programs, including abstract models of functional programs obtained via an abstraction-refinement procedure from pattern-matching recursion schemes.

Categories and Subject Descriptors D.2.4 [*Software Engineering*]: Software/Program Verification; F.3.1 [*Logics and Meanings of Programs*]: Specifying and Verifying and Reasoning about Programs

General Terms Algorithms, Verification

Keywords Model-checking, Higher-order Programs

1. Introduction

Over the past decade, model checking and its allied methods have been applied to program verification with great effect. For first-order, imperative programs, highly optimised finite-state and pushdown model checkers (such as SLAM [2] and BLAST [3]) have been successfully applied to bug-finding, property checking and test case generation. Building on theoretical results on the model checking of *higher-order recursion schemes* (HORS) [6, 16], Kobayashi [8] has sparked a growing interest in the development of an analogous model checking framework for higher-order, functional programs.

A HORS is a kind of higher-order grammar, which can be viewed as a mechanism for generating a possibly-infinite, ranked tree. HORS model checking is concerned with the problem of deciding whether the tree generated by a given HORS satisfies a given property and, when the property is expressed by a formula of the modal mu-calculus (equivalently, an alternating parity tree automaton), then the problem is known to be decidable [16]. Since they can equally well be viewed as a closed, ground-type term of the simply-typed lambda calculus with recursion and uninterpreted first-order constants, HORS are a natural home for models of higher-order computation. Indeed, HORS model checking is a smooth generalisation of finite-state and pushdown model checking (finite-state programs and pushdown systems/Boolean programs are captured by order-0 and order-1 HORS respectively).

HORS model checking is, inherently, an extremely complex problem. Ong [16] has shown that the modal mu-calculus model checking problem for order-n recursion schemes is n-EXPTIME (i.e. tower of exponentials of height n) complete. Even for the purposes of safety verification (model checking against properties expressible as *deterministic trivial tree automata* (DTT)), the problem is $(n-1)$-EXPTIME complete [11], which is still formidably complex. Hence, the feasibility of HORS model checking as a verification technology is predicated upon the ability to design decision procedures that hit the worst-case complexity only in pathological cases.

That such algorithms are possible was demonstrated by Kobayashi's *hybrid algorithm*, presented in [7], which solves the safety verification problem. In an attempt to avoid the hyper-exponential bottleneck, the algorithm closely analyses the actual behaviour of the HORS as it is evaluated, generating the ranked tree. The hybrid algorithm builds a graph to record the trace of this computational behaviour and from the graph derives guesses at proofs which witness the satisfaction of the property. The algorithm is implemented in the TRECS tool [9], which has been shown to perform remarkably well in a variety of applications.

However, whilst HORS allow for the expression of higher-order behaviour very naturally, they lack two important features which, we believe, are highly desirable in a convenient abstract model of *functional programs*. The first is a case analysis construct, with which one can express program branching based on data; the sec-

ICFP'12, September 9–15, 2012, Copenhagen, Denmark.

ond is non-determinism[1], with which one can express abstractions of behaviour. In this paper, we present a class of structures called *higher-order recursion schemes with cases* (HORSC) which extend HORS in both these directions, allowing grammar rules to be non-deterministic and incorporating a finitary case analysis construct.

Example 1. The *Risers* program from Mitchell and Runciman [14] provides an interesting example of a program with partial pattern matching that cannot crash:

$$\begin{array}{l}\mathsf{risers}\ [\,] = [\,]\\ \mathsf{risers}\ [x] = [[x]]\\ \mathsf{risers}\ (x : y : etc) = \mathbf{if}\ x \le y\ \mathbf{then}\ (x : s) : ss\ \mathbf{else}\ [x] : (s : ss)\\ \quad \mathbf{where}\ (s : ss) = \mathsf{risers}\ (y : etc)\end{array}$$

A natural abstraction that might be selected by an automated approach is to the finite domain $\{\mathsf{Nil}, \mathsf{Cons}_1, \mathsf{Cons}_2\}$ (for lists of length 0, 1 or more and 2 or more respectively). Using non-deterministic choice for the **if** statement and a case construct operating on the finite domain yields:

$$\begin{array}{l}\mathsf{risers}\ xs \rightarrow \mathsf{case}(xs, \mathsf{Nil}, \mathsf{Cons}_1, \mathsf{ifthenelse})\\ \mathsf{ifthenelse} \rightarrow \mathsf{cons}\ (\mathsf{destruct}\ (\mathsf{risers}\ \mathsf{Cons}_1))\\ \mathsf{ifthenelse} \rightarrow \mathsf{cons}\ (\mathsf{cons}\ (\mathsf{destruct}\ (\mathsf{risers}\ \mathsf{Cons}_1)))\\ \mathsf{destruct}\ xs \rightarrow \mathsf{case}(xs, \mathsf{error}, \mathsf{Nil}, \mathsf{Cons}_1)\\ \mathsf{destruct}\ xs \rightarrow \mathsf{case}(xs, \mathsf{error}, \mathsf{Nil}, \mathsf{Cons}_2)\\ \mathsf{cons}\ xs \rightarrow \mathsf{case}(xs, \mathsf{Cons}_1, \mathsf{Cons}_2, \mathsf{Cons}_2)\end{array}$$

The pattern match error is preserved – it occurs in the case where an empty list is destructed under the assumption that it has length at least one. Furthermore, the safety of the original program has been preserved in the abstraction to HORSC-like syntax.

Our central contribution is an algorithm to decide the model checking problem of HORSC against DTT. Our algorithm is inspired by the game-semantic analysis (in particular, the notion of *traversals*) behind the original decidability proof of Ong [16] for the model checking problem for HORS. The technical machinery of game semantics is not required for this algorithm, but here we offer a brief overview for the interested reader. Game semantics [5] is a way of giving meanings to programs by viewing computation as a game between Proponent (whose point of view is the program) and Opponent (whose point of view is the program context). The type of a program $M : \theta$ is interpreted as an arena $[\![\theta]\!]$, and the program is interpreted as a Proponent strategy, $[\![M]\!]$, for playing in the arena $[\![\theta]\!]$. Inspired by the success of the hybrid algorithm, we aim to search for proofs in a way which is guided by an analysis of the behaviour of the HORS but, rather than evaluating the HORS and analysing its traces, we analyse the *traversal* induced by its game semantics.

The standard method to evaluate such a λ-term is by β-reduction but, because of the nature of substitution, β-reduction *deforms* the syntactic structure of the term and information about the computation that took place can be lost in the reduct. The game semantics of the simply-typed λ-calculus gives rise to a method of evaluating a term M by *traversing* its computation tree, $\lambda(M)$, which is a slightly souped-up version of its abstract syntax tree. In contrast, evaluation by traversal leaves the structure of the term in question intact.

Example 2 (Traversals over recursion scheme $\mathcal{G}_1$). Let $a : o$, $b : o \rightarrow o$ and $c : o \rightarrow o \rightarrow o$ be terminal symbols. Consider the recursion scheme $\mathcal{G}_1$ given by the following recursive definition of functions, $S : o$ and $F : o \rightarrow o$, viewed as rewrite rules:

$$\begin{array}{rcl} S & \rightarrow & F\ a\\ F\ x & \rightarrow & c\ x\ (F\ (b\ x))\end{array}$$

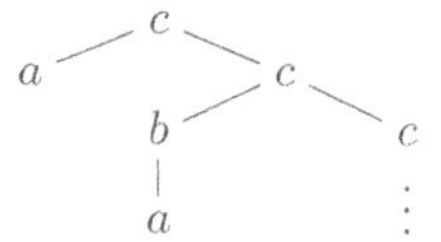

Unfolding from S, we have

$$S \rightarrow F\ a \rightarrow c\ a\ (F\ (b\ a)) \rightarrow c\ a\ (c\ (b\ a)\ (F\ (b\ (b\ a)))) \rightarrow \cdots$$

thus generating the infinite term $c\ a\ (c\ (b\ a)\ (c\ (b\ (b\ a)))\ (\cdots))$. Define the tree generated by $\mathcal{G}_1$, $[\![\mathcal{G}_1]\!]$, to be the abstract syntax tree of the infinite term, as shown above (on the right).

The computation tree $\lambda(\mathcal{G}_1)$ is the underlying tree in Figure 1 whose nodes are labelled by symbols λ, λx, @, a, b and c. We will not give the rules that define the traversals over a computation tree. Instead, we illustrate how traversals compute the paths in $[\![\mathcal{G}_1]\!]$ that are labelled $c \cdot a$ and $c \cdot c \cdot b \cdot a$ respectively. The path $c \cdot a$ in $[\![\mathcal{G}_1]\!]$ corresponding to the traversal over $\lambda(\mathcal{G}_1)$ from the root to (1), jumping to the segment that starts from (1), namely, $\lambda \cdot @ \cdot \lambda x \cdot c \cdot \lambda \cdot x \cdot \lambda \cdot a$. The path $c \cdot c \cdot b \cdot a$ in $[\![\mathcal{G}_1]\!]$ corresponding to the traversal over $\lambda(\mathcal{G}_1)$ from the root to (2), jumping to the segment that starts from (2) and which ends at (3), and jumping to the segment that starts from (3); namely, $\lambda \cdot @ \cdot \lambda x \cdot c \cdot \lambda \cdot @ \cdot \lambda x \cdot c \cdot \lambda \cdot x \cdot \lambda \cdot b \cdot \lambda \cdot x \cdot \lambda \cdot a$. Let $\Sigma = \{ a, b, c \}$. Note that the Σ-projection of the two traversals are the two paths in $[\![\mathcal{G}_1]\!]$.

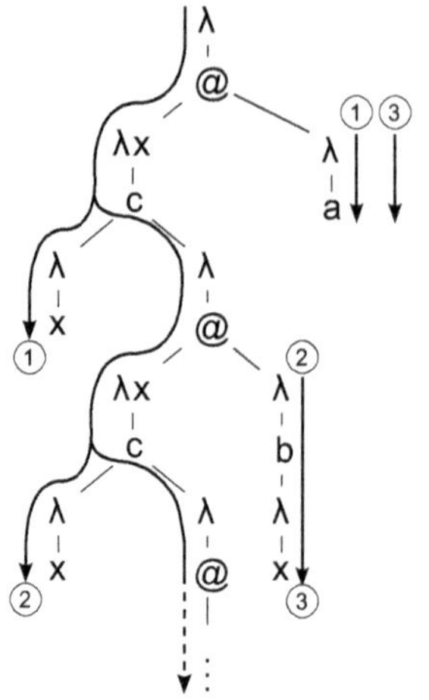

Figure 1. Traversals in $\lambda(\mathcal{G}_1)$ (Example 2)

An insight of Kobayashi, which has been instrumental in the design of practical model checking algorithms, is that the HORS model checking problem can be characterised as a problem of type inference in a certain intersection type system. By this characterisation, searching for a proof that a given HORS satisfies a given property is reduced to searching for a typing for the given HORS in the type system induced by the given property. We show that the HORSC model checking problem also has an elegant, type-theoretic characterisation, but that the combination of higher-order functions, case-analysis and non-determinism lead one to consider a system of intersection *and union* types. Since we want to minimize any increase to the size of the search space of typings (which, by the characterisation, act as potential witnesses to property satisfaction), we have carefully constructed a type system in which union types can occur only in a restricted fashion. In particular, unions are only ever allowed over a subset of the ground types.

[1] In fact, there is no requirement for HORS to be purely deterministic by definition, but the type theory on which the model checking tools are built has only been properly developed for deterministic HORS.

In light of this type-theoretic characterisation, we present our model checking algorithm as a goal-directed construction of a typing derivation. (For reasons of exposition, we suppress the game-semantic origin and interpretation of the algorithm, but present a formal account of the correspondence in the long version of the paper) The ultimate aim is to show that the start symbol S of the HORS is typable by a type representing the initial state of the property automaton q_0, so the initial goal is to find a typing environment Γ such that $\Gamma \vdash S : q_0$. In our type system, we are allowed to take for Γ the environment that consists of the single typing $S : q_0$, but only if we are able to show that the definition of S (by a production rule in the HORS) respects this typing. Hence, following the type system, the algorithm is obliged to spawn a subgoal (itself a typing judgement) according to the definition of S. In general, to solve a goal the algorithm simply attempts to construct a typing derivation according to the rules of the type system, but, where this construction involves making additional assumptions (such as in the typing derivation for $S : q_0$ as above) an obligation is incurred to justify these assumptions. Since discharging such obligations can sometimes require "jumping back" to refine previously completed typing derivations, the construction is not a straightforward bottom-up exercise in tree building. In fact, the pattern of construction (precisely, the sequence of calls to the *Close*−-procedures of Algorithm 1) follows exactly the game-semantic traversals over the corresponding computation tree.

Based on an empirical evaluation, the traversal algorithm is several orders of magnitude faster than Kobayashi's linear-time algorithm GTRecS [10]. Although it does not quite match Kobayashi's hybrid algorithm (which is generally up to an order-of-magnitude faster), the traversal algorithm is still remarkably fast and practical, in view of the worst-case asymptotic complexity of the problem, which is $(n-1)$-EXPTIME complete [11].

Outline The rest of the paper is organised as follows. We introduce higher-order recursion schemes with cases in Section 2, and recall some standard definitions from the literature. In Section 3 we describe an intersection and union type system used to characterise the model checking problem for HORSC, before going on to describe a type inference algorithm in Section 4. Section 5 presents the empirical evaluation of our methods and algorithms, with a discussion of related work in Section 6, followed by our conclusion and further directions in Section 7. Note: a long version of the paper is available [15], which contains proofs and additional material.

2. Higher-Order Recursion Schemes with Cases

We introduce a new class of structures, *higher-order recursion schemes with cases* and their model checking problem, and agree on familiar definitions of Σ-labelled trees and deterministic trivial tree automata.

Recursion Schemes with Cases

Let D be a set of *directions* (e.g. $D = \{1, 2, \cdots, m\}$). A *D-tree* (or simply *tree*) is a prefix-closed subset T of D^*. Let Σ be a ranked alphabet. A *Σ-labelled tree* is a function $t : dom(t) \to \Sigma$ such that $dom(t)$ is a tree. We refer to elements of $dom(t)$ as *nodes* of t.

In what follows, we refer to simple types as *kinds* (reserving the word *type* for intersection types, to be introduced shortly) and define the set of kinds by $\kappa ::= d \mid o \mid \kappa \to \kappa$ where o is the kind of Σ-labelled trees, and d is the kind of a finite domain for definition by cases. As usual, the *order* of a kind is the maximum nesting of an arrow on the left, that is: $ord(o) = 0$ and $ord(\kappa_1 \to \kappa_2) = \max(ord(\kappa_1)+1, ord(\kappa_2))$. We use β and β_i to range over ground (i.e. order-0) kinds.

Definition 1. A *(non-deterministic) higher-order recursion scheme with cases* (HORSC) is a quadruple $\mathcal{G} = \langle \Sigma, \mathcal{N}, \mathcal{R}, S \rangle$ where

(i) Σ is an alphabet of well-kinded terminal symbols (ranged over by f, g, a, b, etc.) with kinds drawn from those of order at most one. Further Σ contains a distinguished subset of d-kinded symbols, $\mathcal{B} = \{\mathsf{b}_1, \ldots, \mathsf{b}_n\}$; and if $f \in (\Sigma \setminus \mathcal{B})$ then f has return kind o i.e. $f :: \beta_1 \to \cdots \to \beta_m \to o$ where $m \geq 0$.

(ii) $\mathcal{N}$ is an alphabet of kinded non-terminal symbols (ranged over by F, G etc.).

(iii) $\mathcal{R}$ is a set of rewrite rules of the form $F x_1 \cdots x_m \to e$ where $F :: \kappa_1 \to \cdots \to \kappa_m \to \beta$ with $\beta \in \{d, o\}$, each $x_i :: \kappa_i$ is drawn from a countably infinite set of variables and $e :: \beta$ is a (well-kinded) applicative *term* generated from the following grammar

$$e ::= x \mid f \mid F \mid e_1\, e_2 \mid \mathsf{case}(e, e_1, \ldots, e_n)$$

where n is the cardinality of $\mathcal{B}$, $x \in \{x_1, \ldots, x_m\}$, $f \in \Sigma$ and $F \in \mathcal{N}$. When a term contains no occurrence of a variable x, we say that it is *closed*. The kinding rule for the case construct is: if $s :: d$ and each $t_i :: \beta$ (base kind) then $\mathsf{case}(s, t_1, \ldots, t_n) :: \beta$; the other kinding rules are standard. We consider $\mathcal{R}$ to be a function defined by:

$$\mathcal{R}(F) := \{\lambda x_1 \cdots x_m.e \mid F\, x_1 \cdots x_m \to e \in \mathcal{R}\}$$

When $\mathcal{G}$ is deterministic, that is, for each $F \in \mathcal{N}$, $\mathcal{R}(F)$ is a singleton, we abuse notation and identify $\mathcal{R}(F)$ with its only member.

(iv) $S \in \mathcal{N}$ is a distinguished 'start' symbol of kind o, and $\mathcal{R}(S)$ is a singleton set. By abuse of notation we write $S \to \mathcal{R}(S)$ for the unique rule for S.

The (call-by-name) reduction relation of the HORSC $\mathcal{G}$, written $\to_{\mathcal{G}}$ (or simply $\to$ whenever $\mathcal{G}$ is understood), is a binary relation over closed, ground-kinded terms, defined by induction over the following rules.

$$\frac{\lambda x_1 \ldots x_m.t \in \mathcal{R}(F)}{F\, s_1 \ldots s_m \to t[\overline{s}/\overline{x}]} \qquad \frac{1 \leq i \leq n}{\mathsf{case}(\mathsf{b}_i, s_1, \ldots, s_n) \to s_i}$$

$$\frac{s \to s'}{C[s] \to C[s']}$$

where the (one-holed) contexts are defined as follows:

$$\begin{array}{rcl} C & ::= & [\,] \mid C\, s \mid s\, C \mid \mathsf{case}(C, t_1, \ldots, t_n) \\ & \mid & \mathsf{case}(s, t_1, \ldots, t_i, C, t_{i+2}, \ldots t_n). \end{array}$$

We refer to (closed, ground-kinded) terms of the shape $F\, s_1 \ldots s_m$ or $\mathsf{case}(\mathsf{b}_i, s_1, \ldots, s_n)$ as *redexes*. Note that whenever $s \to s'$, there are unique C and Δ such that $s = C[\Delta]$ and Δ is the redex contracted (i.e. $\Delta \to \hat{\Delta}$ and $s' = C[\hat{\Delta}]$).

Write $\Sigma^\perp$ for the alphabet Σ extended with symbol $\perp$ of arity 0. Given a term t, we define $t^\perp$ for the (finite) $\Sigma^\perp$-labelled tree defined inductively by (i) $(f\, s_1 \ldots s_n)^\perp := f\, s_1^\perp \ldots s_n^\perp$ (ii) $t^\perp := \perp$ if t is of the form $F\, s_1 \ldots s_n$ or $\mathsf{case}(s, t_1, \ldots, t_n)$. With respect to the standard approximation ordering $\sqsubseteq$ (defined by the compatible closure of $\perp \sqsubseteq t$ for all t), the set of $\Sigma^\perp$-labelled trees is a complete partial order. The *tree language generated by* $\mathcal{G}$, written $[\![\mathcal{G}]\!]$, is defined to be the set of $\Sigma^\perp$-labelled trees of the form $\bigsqcup_{i \in I} t_i^\perp$ where I is a prefix of ω, and $\langle t_i \rangle_{i \in I}$ is a maximal (possibly infinite) sequence of closed, ground-kinded terms satisfying:

(outermost) The term $t_0 = S$ and for each $i \in I$, $t_i \to t_{i+1}$ is an *outermost* reduction (i.e. the redex contracted is not a subterm of another redex in t_i)

(fairness) Every outermost redex is eventually contracted i.e. for each $i \in I$ and each outermost redex Δ in t_i, there exists $i' \geq i$ such that Δ is contracted in $t_{i'} \to t_{i'+1}$.[2]

Example 3. The HORSC $\mathcal{G}_2$ is specified by terminal symbols $\mathsf{b}_1 :: d$, $\mathsf{b}_2 :: d$, $zero :: o$, $succ :: o \to o$ and $pred :: o \to o$; non-terminal symbols $S :: o$, $H :: d$ and $G :: (o \to o) \to o$, start symbol S and rules:

$$\begin{array}{lcl} S & \to & \mathsf{case}(H, G\ succ, G\ pred) \\ H & \to & \mathsf{b}_1 \\ H & \to & H \\ G\ g & \to & g\ zero \end{array}$$

It computes the single, finite tree which, when written as a term, is denoted $succ\ zero$ i.e. $[\![\mathcal{G}_2]\!] = \{\, succ\ zero \,\}$.

Remark 1. HORSC extends Kobayashi's *recursion schemes with finite data domains* (RSFD) [13] in several ways: (i) The b_is of HORSC are terminals, but the d_is of RSFD are *data* (distinct from variables, terminals and non-terminals). (ii) In RSFD the return kind of both non-terminals and the case construct must be o. There is no such restriction in HORSC. (iii) RSFD does not handle non-determinism.

A consequence of (i) and (ii) is that in RSFD, the first argument of the case construct must be an atomic datum d_i or a variable. In contrast, the first argument of a case construct in HORSC is an arbitrary term of kind d i.e. any term which may reduce to an element of $\mathcal{B}$ or otherwise diverge. For example, the HORSC $\mathcal{G}_2$ is not a RSFD, since it is non-deterministic, and contains a case construct that has a non-terminal as the first argument.

Deterministic Trivial Tree Automata

We use a simple form of automata over infinite trees to specify properties of the tree languages of HORSC.

Definition 2. A *deterministic trivial tree automaton* (DTT) is a quadruple $\mathcal{A} = \langle \Sigma, Q, \delta, q_0 \rangle$ where

(i) Σ is a ranked alphabet;

(ii) Q is a finite set of states containing an initial state q_0;

(iii) $\delta : Q \times \Sigma \rightharpoonup Q^*$ is a (partial) transition function such that if $\delta(q, a) = q_1 \ldots q_n$ then n is the arity of a.

A Σ-labelled tree t is *accepted* by a DTT $\mathcal{A}$ just if there is a Q-labelled tree r, called a *run-tree* of $\mathcal{A}$ over t, satisfying:

(i) $dom(r) = dom(t)$;

(ii) $r(\epsilon) = q_0$;

(iii) for every $\alpha \in dom(r)$, $(r(\alpha), t(\alpha), r(\alpha\,1) \cdots r(\alpha\,m)) \in \delta$ where m is the arity of $t(\alpha)$.

Thus a run tree of $\mathcal{A}$ over t is an annotation of the nodes of t with states that respects δ such that the root is annotated q_0.

Example 4 (A DTT $\mathcal{A}_1$). Take the ranked alphabet Σ of Example 2; $[\![\mathcal{G}_1]\!]$ is accepted by $\mathcal{A}_1 = \langle \Sigma, \{q_0, q_1\}, \delta, q_0 \rangle$, where $\delta : (q_0, c) \mapsto q_1 q_0, (q_1, b) \mapsto q_1, (q_1, a) \mapsto \epsilon$. Thus $\mathcal{A}_1$ accepts a Σ-labelled tree t if, and only if, a and b are seen only on the left of a c.

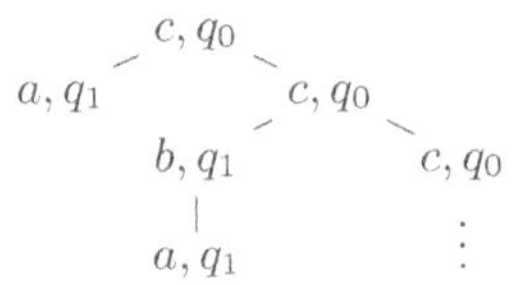

Universal HORSC Model Checking Problem

Let $\mathcal{A} = \langle \Sigma, Q, \delta, q_0 \rangle$ be a DTT. Define the DTT $\mathcal{A}^\perp := \langle \Sigma^\perp, Q, \delta', q_0 \rangle$ by $\delta' := \delta \cup \{\, (q, \perp, \epsilon) \mid q \in Q \,\}$ (so that $\mathcal{A}^\perp$ will accept any subtree labelled $\perp$ from any state).

Given a HORSC $\mathcal{G}$ and a DTT $\mathcal{A}$, we say that the tree language $[\![\mathcal{G}]\!]$ is *universally accepted* (respectively *existentially*) by the DTT $\mathcal{A}$ just if every (respectively some) element of the tree language $[\![\mathcal{G}]\!]$ is accepted by $\mathcal{A}^\perp$. The *Universal HORSC Model Checking Problem for DTT* is to check whether the language $[\![\mathcal{G}]\!]$ is universally accepted by $\mathcal{A}^\perp$. Henceforth, we will refer to this problem simply as the *HORSC Model Checking Problem*.

3. An Intersection and Union Type System

We wish to characterise the HORSC model checking problem as a kind of type inference problem in an intersection type system. In doing so, we not only establish decidability, but also rephrase the question of acceptance as one of bounded search – which is much better understood algorithmically.

Well-Kinded Types

We introduce an intersection and union type system parameterised by a DTT $\mathcal{A} = \langle \Sigma, Q, \delta, q_0 \rangle$ with $\mathcal{B} \subseteq \Sigma$. First we define the set of *well-kinded types* simultaneously with a kinding relation on types, which is defined by induction over the following rules:

$$\frac{q \in Q}{q\ ::\ o} \qquad \frac{B \subseteq \mathcal{B}}{\bigvee B :: d} \qquad \frac{\theta_i :: \kappa_1 \text{ (for all } i \in I) \quad \theta\ ::\ \kappa_2}{(\bigwedge_{i \in I} \theta_i) \to \theta\ ::\ \kappa_1 \to \kappa_2}$$

Any expression σ such that $\sigma :: \kappa$ is derivable in the above system is a well-kinded type. For example, given $Q = \{q_0, q_1\}$, the expressions $q_1 \to q_0$ and $((q_1 \to q_1) \wedge (q_0 \to q_0)) \to q_0$ are *well-kinded types* while $(q_0 \wedge (q_0 \to q_1)) \to q_1$ is not. Note that there are only finitely many well-kinded types of each kind. We write Type for the collection of well-kinded types. Henceforth, we will say type to mean well-kinded type.

We write $\bigwedge_{i=1}^k \theta_i$ for $\bigwedge\{\theta_1, \cdots, \theta_k\}$, and $\top$ for $\bigwedge \emptyset$; similarly we write $\bigvee_{j=1}^l \mathsf{b}_{i_j}$ for $\bigvee\{\mathsf{b}_{i_1}, \cdots, \mathsf{b}_{i_l}\}$and $\perp$ for $\bigvee \emptyset$; further we write $\bigvee\{\mathsf{b}_i\}$ simply as b_i. Note that intersection is only allowed on the left of an arrow; and union is only defined on a subset of $\mathcal{B}$.

Type System

We now present the type system itself. Intuitively, a typing for a term t describes the tree generated by t. For example, the typing $a : q_0$ indicates that the trivial tree a is accepted from state q_0. Intuitively a term has an intersection type if it generates a tree that is acceptable from *every* state in the intersection; a term has a union type if it generates a singleton tree b_i for some i. For example, the typing $\lambda x.s : (q_0 \wedge q_1) \to (\mathsf{b}_0 \vee \mathsf{b}_1)$ says that we have a function

[2] Note that if $s = C[\Delta] \to C[\Delta]$ and Δ is outermost, and Δ' is a different outermost redex in s, then Δ' occurs in C i.e. Δ has a unique residual in $C[\Delta]$.

that takes a tree accepted from both q_0 and q_1 as an argument and returns a tree $s[t/x]$ that is either b_0 or b_1.

A *type environment* (typically Γ) is a finite set of *type bindings*, which are pairs $\xi : \tau$ where ξ is a non-terminal symbol or a variable, and τ is a type. Note that non-terminal symbols and variables are treated in the same way by the system; and different types may be bound to the same symbol in an environment.

A *judgement* is a triple, written $\Gamma \vdash_{\mathcal{A}} t : \theta$, in which Γ is a type environment, θ is a type and t is a λ-term with case construct. A judgements is valid just if it can be derived in the following system:

$$\frac{\theta \text{ is well-kinded}}{\Gamma, x : \theta \vdash_{\mathcal{A}} x : \theta}\ \textsc{Var}$$

$$\frac{\delta(q, a) = q_1 \cdots q_n}{\Gamma \vdash_{\mathcal{A}} a : q_1 \to \cdots \to q_n \to q}\ \textsc{Term}$$

$$\frac{\Gamma \vdash_{\mathcal{A}} s : (\bigwedge_{i \in I} \theta_i) \to \theta \qquad \Gamma \vdash_{\mathcal{A}} t : \theta_i \quad (i \in I)}{\Gamma \vdash_{\mathcal{A}} s\, t : \theta}\ \textsc{App}$$

$$\frac{\Gamma, x : \theta_1, \ldots, x : \theta_n \vdash_{\mathcal{A}} t : \theta \qquad x \notin \Gamma}{\Gamma \vdash_{\mathcal{A}} \lambda x.t : (\bigwedge_{i \in \{1,\ldots,n\}} \theta_i) \to \theta}\ \textsc{Abs}$$

$$\frac{\Gamma \vdash_{\mathcal{A}} t : \bigvee_{i \in I} \mathsf{b}_i \qquad \Gamma \vdash_{\mathcal{A}} t_i : \theta \quad (i \in I)}{\Gamma \vdash_{\mathcal{A}} \mathsf{case}(t, t_1, \ldots, t_n) : \theta}\ \vee\text{-}\textsc{Elim / Case}$$

$$\frac{\exists i \in I \cdot \Gamma \vdash_{\mathcal{A}} t : \mathsf{b}_i}{\Gamma \vdash_{\mathcal{A}} t : \bigvee_{i \in I} \mathsf{b}_i}\ \vee\text{-}\textsc{Intro / Union}$$

$$\frac{}{\Gamma \vdash_{\mathcal{A}} \mathsf{b}_i : \mathsf{b}_i}\ \textsc{Base}$$

Note in particular the final three rules, which cover the addition of case to the term language. In $\vee$-ELIM each possible typing for t requires a proof of typability of the corresponding t_i. The disjunction can only be eliminated here, ensuring that disjunction types cannot be used in other contexts. A canonical typing derivation will reserve the $\vee$-INTRO rule to be used immediately before BASE, delaying the choice of which member type of the disjunction to choose as late as possible. Each $b \in \mathcal{B}$ can be typed by a singleton disjunction of a type of the same name.

Characterisation

Following Kobayashi [8, 12], we characterise the HORSC model checking problem in terms of the existence of certain type environments that are appropriate to the scheme that we are checking.

Definition 3. Fix a HORSC $\mathcal{G}$ and a DTT $\mathcal{A}$. We say that a type environment Γ is $\vdash_{\mathcal{G},\mathcal{A}}$*-complete*, written $\vdash_{\mathcal{G},\mathcal{A}} \Gamma$, just if

(i) $dom(\Gamma) \subseteq \mathcal{N}$

(ii) $\Gamma \vdash_{\mathcal{A}} S : q_0$

(iii) for each $(F : \theta) \in \Gamma$ and for each $\lambda\overline{x}.t \in \mathcal{R}(F)$ we have $\Gamma \vdash_{\mathcal{A}} \lambda\overline{x}.t : \theta$.

Intuitively, a type environment Γ is $\vdash_{\mathcal{G},\mathcal{A}}$*-complete* whenever it contains enough well-kinded typings for the non-terminal symbols in $\mathcal{G}$ so that S can be typed with q_0, but not so many that some are inconsistent with the behaviour of their defining rules.

Theorem 1 (Characterisation). *Given a HORSC $\mathcal{G}$ and a DTT $\mathcal{A}$, $[\![\mathcal{G}]\!]$ is accepted by $\mathcal{A}^{\perp}$ if, and only if, there exists a $\vdash_{\mathcal{G},\mathcal{A}}$-complete type environment.*

Given a HORSC $\mathcal{G}$ and a DTT $\mathcal{A}$, the number of non-terminal symbols in $\mathcal{G}$ and the number of well-kinded types is finite. It follows that the problem of the existence of a $\vdash_{\mathcal{G},\mathcal{A}}$-complete type environment is decidable. However, the size of the search space is hyper-exponential in the largest order of the kind of any non-terminal symbol. Thus, in the following section we describe an algorithm which is able to explore this vast expanse in a goal-directed way, which, we will argue in Section 5, gives good performance in practice.

Remark 2. In fact, since the data types in HORSC are finite, the model checking problem can be shown to be decidable by reduction, via determinisation and a Church-style encoding of constants as projection functions, to an instance of the HORS model checking problem. However, such a transformation is known to increase the order and arity of the non-terminal symbols and so is not palatable from a practical point of view.

Example 5 (A typing for $\mathcal{G}_1$). We can see that $\Gamma_1 = \{S : q_0, F : q_1 \to q_0\}$ is $\vdash_{\mathcal{G}_1,\mathcal{A}_1}$-complete, hence, thanks to Theorem 1, $[\![\mathcal{G}_1]\!]$ is accepted by $\mathcal{A}_1$.

4. The HORSC Model Checking Algorithm

Our approach to deciding the HORSC model checking problem exploits the characterisation by the intersection and union type system as stated in Theorem 1. Given a HORSC $\mathcal{G}$ and a DTT $\mathcal{A}$, the decision procedure seeks to construct a $\vdash_{\mathcal{G},\mathcal{A}}$-complete type environment.

Fix $\mathcal{A} = \langle \Sigma, Q, \delta, q_0 \rangle$. Consider a term $t_0\, t_1 \ldots t_n$ (where t_0 is atomic) which is expected to produce a tree of type q, the canonical example being the term $\mathcal{R}(S)$ and the type q_0. This can be viewed as a typing judgement $\vdash t_0\, t_1 \ldots t_n : q$. Our goal is to construct a derivation for it. After n (bottom-up) applications of the APP rule, a subgoal $\vdash t_0 : \theta$ is generated where $\theta = \alpha_1 \to \cdots \to \alpha_n \to q$ and the α_i are type variables that are as yet undetermined. The values they take on will depend on how t_0 uses its arguments, and we can explore this in a syntax-directed manner.

- Suppose t_0 is a terminal symbol. Since $\delta(q, a)$ is unique, all α_i will be fully determined, yielding n further subgoals, which are judgements of the form $t_i : \alpha_i$ to prove.
- Encountering a non-terminal, say $t_0 = F$, requires us to assume that $F : \theta$ and to build new derivations showing that $s : \theta$ for all $s \in \mathcal{R}(F)$. Bear in mind the characterisation of the problem by $\vdash_{\mathcal{G},\mathcal{A}}$-completeness (Theorem 1).
- In case the symbol t_0 is a variable (i.e. a formal parameter), we must ensure that the corresponding *actual* parameter has the necessary return type.

The use of type variables (such as α_i above) captures the connection made by term variables between typing derivations and enables us to detect the situation where a typing derivation is redundant. A type variable is instantiated to a set of type expressions (call *open types*) which may themselves contain type variables. A derivation need not be explored further when two derivations both aim to show $\mathcal{R}(F) : \theta$, one of which is already complete. We use a restricted system of union types to represent non-deterministic choices in the argument to a case term, which is illustrated in the following example.

Example 6 (Building a derivation for $\mathcal{G}_2 \vDash \mathcal{A}_2$). We consider a simple DTT $\mathcal{A}_2 = \langle \{succ, pred, zero\}, \{q_0, q_1\}, \delta, q_0 \rangle$ where δ is the map: $(q_0, succ) \mapsto q_1, (q_1, zero) \mapsto \epsilon$. Starting with the

$$\dfrac{\dfrac{}{\vdash_{\mathcal{A}} \mathsf{b}_1 : \mathsf{b}_1}\textsc{Base}}{\vdash_{\mathcal{A}} \mathsf{b}_1 : \beta}\vee\textsc{-Intro} \qquad \dfrac{\dfrac{\dfrac{}{\{g : \alpha_1\} \vdash g : \alpha_2 \to q_0}\textsc{Var}}{\{g : \alpha_1\} \vdash g\ zero : q_0}\textsc{App}}{\vdash \lambda g.g\ zero : \alpha_1 \to q_0}\textsc{Abs}$$

$$\dfrac{\dfrac{}{\Gamma^o \vdash_{\mathcal{A}} H : \beta}\textsc{Var} \quad \dfrac{\dfrac{}{\Gamma^o \vdash_{\mathcal{A}} G : \alpha_1 \to q_0}\textsc{Var} \quad \Gamma^o \vdash_{\mathcal{A}} succ : \alpha_2 \to q_0}{\Gamma^o \vdash_{\mathcal{A}} G\ succ : q_0}\textsc{App}}{\Gamma^o \vdash_{\mathcal{A}} \mathsf{case}(H, G\ succ, G\ pred) : q_0}\vee\textsc{-Elim}$$

Table 1. Examples of pre-derivations ($\Gamma^o = \{H : \beta\}$)

initial goal of showing $S : q_0$, it immediately becomes necessary to build a derivation rooted at $\vdash_{\mathcal{A}} \mathcal{R}(S) : q_0$. Since the right-hand side of S

$$\mathcal{R}(S) = \mathsf{case}(H, G\ succ, G\ pred)$$

is a case construct, we assume that $H : \beta$ where β is a fresh type variable and proceed to explore $\mathcal{R}(H)$ to find which members of the finite domain $\mathcal{B}$ it can reduce to. This leaves us with the derivation

$$\dfrac{\dfrac{}{\{H : \beta\} \vdash_{\mathcal{A}} H : \beta}\textsc{Var}}{\{H : \beta\} \vdash_{\mathcal{A}} \mathsf{case}(H, G\ succ, G\ pred) : q_0}\textsc{App}$$

and two further derivations to build, which are rooted at the following, corresponding to the respective right-hand sides of H:

$$\emptyset \vdash_{\mathcal{A}} H : \beta \qquad\qquad \emptyset \vdash_{\mathcal{A}} \mathsf{b}_1 : \beta$$

where β is instantiated to $\bigvee \emptyset = \bot$ initially, avoiding the need to show any typings for the choice terms in the case construct. As usual, $\bot$ represents nontermination, which is exactly the situation that would prevent the case from reducing to any choice term. If the exploration of the scrutinee (here H) ever reduces to a b_i then β will be updated accordingly. Notice that taking the type environment to be $\Gamma = \{S : q_0, H : \beta\}$ in the sense of Theorem 1, the derivations to ensure that the right-hand sides match the typings are already in place, although as yet incomplete. To build a derivation rooted at the right-hand judgement we use the $\vee$-INTRO and BASE rules (see the derivation on the left in the top row of Table 1). This requires β to contain b_1, causing an additional obligation to type the first choice term ($G\ succ$) of the case construct.

To complete this example, we aim to build a derivation rooted at this new judgement

$$\{H : \beta\} \vdash_{\mathcal{A}} G\ succ : q_0.$$

In order to apply the APP rule (in a bottom-up fashion), we introduce another type variable, α_1. Dually to the use of $\vee$-ELIM, α_1 is initially instantiated to $\bigwedge \emptyset = \top$, again avoiding the need to prove any typing for $succ$ at this time. Exploring the right-hand side of G (top-right in Table 1), as for H, we find a use of the variable g. Looking at the typing rules, we find that this typing must be justified by the VAR rule, which requires "enlarging" α_1, and just as before, after adding the new type to α_1, the use of the APP rule to "close" the judgement $\{H : \beta\} \vdash_{\mathcal{A}} G\ succ : q_0$ is no longer valid. We must add an extra judgement for the operand (see the lower derivation in Table 1), which in turn can be justified by the TERM rule. This captures informally how we build up the typing derivations. Notice that if we take Γ to be the union of all non-terminal type bindings in the various derivations then (i) $dom(\Gamma) \subseteq \mathcal{N}$; (ii) $\Gamma \vdash_{\mathcal{A}} S : q_0$; (iii) If all judgements are closed then for each $F : \theta$ in Γ, each $t \in \mathcal{R}(F)$, we have $\Gamma \vdash_{\mathcal{A}} t : \theta$. Clearly if the tree language generated by the HORSC is finite, then all judgements will eventually be closed following this approach. However in general we require a more complex termination condition.

Open Types, Instantiation and Reification Maps

We now formalise the method introduced in Example 6. First we introduce *open types*, which represent intersection types using type variables. An open type has the form $\alpha_1 \to \cdots \to \alpha_n \to \beta$ where each variable α_i ranges over finite sets of intersection types, and $\beta \in Q \cup \mathcal{P}(\mathcal{B})$. Given an instantiation map (to be defined shortly), open types are a representation of types. Assume, for each kind κ, a countably infinite set A_κ of type variables. The set $\mathbb{P}_\kappa$ of *open types* of kind κ is defined by recursion over κ as follows (we use $\theta^o, \theta^o_1, \cdots$ to range over $\mathbb{P}_\kappa$).

$$\mathbb{P}_o := Q \qquad \mathbb{P}_d := \mathcal{P}(\mathcal{B})$$
$$\mathbb{P}_{\kappa_1 \to \kappa_2} := \{\, \alpha \to \theta^o \mid \alpha \in \mathsf{A}_{\kappa_1}, \theta^o \in \mathbb{P}_{\kappa_2} \,\}$$

Let $\mathsf{A} := \bigcup_{\kappa \in Kind} \mathsf{A}_\kappa$ and $\mathbb{P} := \bigcup_{\kappa \in Kind} \mathbb{P}_\kappa$. We say that a function $\Theta : \mathsf{A} \to \mathcal{P}(\mathbb{P})$ is an *instantiation map* if it is (i) *finite*: there exists a finite subset C of A such that Θ maps every element of $(\mathsf{A} \setminus C)$ to $\emptyset$, and (ii) *kind-respecting*: for each kind κ, Θ restricts to a function from A_κ to the set $\mathcal{P}_{\mathrm{fin}}(\mathbb{P}_\kappa)$ of finite subsets of $\mathbb{P}_\kappa$.

Instantiation maps $\Theta : \mathsf{A} \to \mathcal{P}(\mathbb{P})$ are used to reify open types. Given such a map, we derive from it a kind-indexed family of maps on open types, $\widehat{\Theta}_\kappa : \mathbb{P}_\kappa \to \mathit{Type}_\kappa$ with $\kappa \in Kind$, as follows:

$$\widehat{\Theta}_o(q) := q, \qquad \widehat{\Theta}_d(B) := \bigvee B$$
$$\widehat{\Theta}_{\kappa_1 \to \kappa_2}(\alpha \to \theta^o) := \left(\bigwedge\nolimits_{\theta^o_1 \in \Theta(\alpha)} \widehat{\Theta}_{\kappa_1}(\theta^o_1)\right) \to \widehat{\Theta}_{\kappa_2}(\theta^o)$$

Note that for each $\alpha \in \mathsf{A}_{\kappa_1}$, $\Theta(\alpha)$ is a finite subset of $\mathbb{P}_{\kappa_1}$. The map $\widehat{\Theta}_\kappa$ is well-defined by structural induction on κ. We define $\widehat{\Theta} : \mathbb{P} \to \mathit{Type}$ by $\theta^o \mapsto \widehat{\Theta}_\kappa(\theta^o)$ for $\theta^o \in \mathbb{P}_\kappa$, and call it the *reification map*.

Example 7. Let $\kappa = ((o \to o) \to o) \to o \to o$, and take $\theta^o = \alpha_1 \to \alpha_2 \to q_1$, an element of $\mathbb{P}_\kappa$. Let Θ be the instantiation map: $\alpha_1 \mapsto \{\alpha_3 \to q_2, \alpha_4 \to q_1\}$, $\alpha_2 \mapsto \{q_1\}$, $\alpha_3 \mapsto \emptyset$, $\alpha_4 \mapsto \{\alpha_5 \to q_0\}$, $\alpha_5 \mapsto \{q_0\}$. Then

$$\widehat{\Theta}(\theta^o) = \bigwedge \{\top \to q_2, (q_0 \to q_0) \to q_1\} \to q_1 \to q_1.$$

Open types are used to build up intermediate information about the necessary typings of non-terminal symbols while keeping the relation between these different types explicit in the mapping. This relationship would be lost using concrete types.

For notational convenience we use some further conventions. We use the superscript 'o' to mean *open* (in the sense of containing variables). Thus open types are ranged over by $\theta^o, \theta^o_1, \cdots$; similarly, *open-type environments* are ranged over by $\Gamma^o, \Gamma^o_1, \cdots$. The reification map $\widehat{\Theta}$ is extended to open-type environments Γ^o where it proceeds point-wise. Let $J = \Gamma^o \vdash t : \theta^o$ be an *open-type judgement*. We write $\widehat{\Theta}(J)$ to mean the judgement $\widehat{\Theta}(\Gamma^o) \vdash_{\mathcal{A}} t : \widehat{\Theta}(\theta^o)$. Further, let Δ be a finite tree whose nodes are labelled by open-type judgements (such as typing derivations). We write $\widehat{\Theta}(\Delta)$ to mean the tree that is obtained from Δ by replacing each judgement J by $\widehat{\Theta}(J)$.

Recall that a typing derivation is a tree whose nodes are labelled by judgements; each such judgement is justified by a rule if it labels an internal node, or by an axiom if it labels a leaf node. Informally a *pre-derivation* is a finite tree whose nodes are labelled with open-type judgements. In a pre-derivation, a judgement that occurs at a leaf-node is said to be *closed* if there is a line above it; otherwise it is said to be *open*. A pre-derivation that has no open judgements is said to be *closed*; otherwise it is *open*. We write D for the set of pre-derivations.

The Model Checking Algorithm

The algorithm proceeds by growing a tree $\mathcal{D}$ and an accompanying instantiation map Θ. Each node n of $\mathcal{D}$ is associated with a type binding of the form $(F, s : \theta^o)$ where F is a non-terminal, $s \in \mathcal{R}(F)$ and θ^o is an open type; and n represents the subgoal of building a derivation for the judgement $\Gamma^o \vdash s : \theta^o$ for some open-type environment Γ^o. In the process of constructing such a derivation (in a bottom-up fashion), new derivation subgoals may be created, which are represented by the spawning of new nodes (corresponding to the subgoals); and Θ is updated. The root node is associated with the binding $(S, \mathcal{R}(S) : q_0)$ (recall that we write $S \to \mathcal{R}(S)$ for the unique rule for S), and it represents the original goal, namely, to build a derivation for $\cdots \vdash \mathcal{R}(S) : q_0$.

Formally, a *state* of the algorithm is a pair $(\mathcal{D}, \Theta)$ where $\mathcal{D}$ is a $((\mathcal{R} \times \mathbb{P}) \times \mathsf{D})$-labelled tree, and Θ is an instantiation map. Each node n of $\mathcal{D}$ is labelled by a quadruple, $\mathcal{D}(n) = (F, s : \theta^o, \Delta)$, such that the judgement at the root of the pre-derivation Δ has the form $\Gamma^o \vdash s : \theta^o$ for some term $s \in \mathcal{R}(F)$ and open-type environment Γ^o. Observe that (F, s) uniquely identifies a rule from $\mathcal{R}$. Henceforth we shall refer to Δ as the *pre-derivation* of n, and the triples $(F, s : \theta^o)$ and $(F, s : \widehat{\Theta}(\theta^o))$ respectively as the *open-type binding* and *reified-type binding* of n.

Given a state $(\mathcal{D}, \Theta)$, a node of $\mathcal{D}$ is said to be *closed* if its pre-derivation Δ is closed (and we shall see—Lemma 1—that it follows that $\widehat{\Theta}(\Delta)$ is a valid type derivation of $\vdash_{\mathcal{A}}$); otherwise, the node is *open*. The function open, when applied to $\mathcal{D}$, returns the set of judgements J that is currently open (in some open pre-derivation of $\mathcal{D}$).

The top loop of the algorithm is shown in Algorithm 1 and follows the ideas outlined in Example 6. As mentioned earlier, we must start with the open judgement $\emptyset \vdash \mathcal{R}(S) : q_0$ and this informs the initialisation. (W.l.o.g. we assume that $\mathcal{R}(S)$ is a singleton set.) The *open* judgements, $\Gamma^o \vdash s : \theta^o$, are then closed in turn by application of the appropriate rule (as implemented by one of the six *Close*– procedures), depending on the shape of s.

Termination of the loop depends on the existence of a *complete cut* of a certain initial subtree of $\mathcal{D}$. Fix a state $(\mathcal{D}, \Theta)$. Define

$$\mathcal{D}^{\mathrm{cl}} := \{\, n \in dom(\mathcal{D}) \mid n \text{ and all its } \mathcal{D}\text{-ancestors are closed} \,\}.$$

Thus $\mathcal{D}^{\mathrm{cl}}$ is the largest initial subtree of $\mathcal{D}$ consisting only of closed nodes.

Let t be a Σ-labelled tree. As usual a subset $C \subseteq dom(t)$ is a *cut* of t just if for every maximal path B of t, $B \cap C$ is a singleton set. Let C be a cut of $\mathcal{D}^{\mathrm{cl}}$. We write $n \prec C$ to mean that n is an ancestor of some element of C (read: n is an *interior node* of C); and $n \preccurlyeq C$ to means that $n \prec C$ or $n \in C$.

Definition 4. We say that a cut C of the tree $\mathcal{D}^{\mathrm{cl}}$ is *complete* if for every $c \in C$, either c is a leaf-node[3] of $\mathcal{D}$, or there is an interior node of C that has the same reified-type binding as c.

(Observe that $\mathsf{open}(\mathcal{D}) = \emptyset$ if, and only if, every node of $\mathcal{D}$ is closed. Hence, if $\mathsf{open}(\mathcal{D}) = \emptyset$, the set of its leaf-nodes is a complete cut; note that $\mathcal{D}$ is finite.)

Algorithm 1: Model Checking

```
input  : HORSC 𝒢 = ⟨Σ, 𝒩, ℛ, S⟩, DTT 𝒜 = ⟨Σ, Q, δ, q0⟩
output: Whether 𝒢 ⊨ 𝒜, with a witness
𝒟 :=
singleton tree with label (S, ℛ(S) : q0, ∅ ⊢ ℛ(S) : q0)
Θ := {α ↦ ∅ | α ∈ A}
while 𝒟^cl does not have a complete cut do
    foreach (Γ° ⊢ s : θ°) as J ∈ open(𝒟) do
        if s = t u then CloseApp(J)
        if s ∈ 𝒩 then CloseNonTerm(J)
        if s ∈ V then CloseVar(J)
        if s ∈ ℬ then CloseUnion(J)
        if s = case(t, t̄) then CloseCase(J)
        if s ∈ Σ then try CloseTerm(J) with
                              Trace s → return (NO, s)
    end
end
return (YES, 𝒟)
```

Procedure *CloseNonTerm*

```
input  : J = Γ° ⊢ F : θ° in pre-derivation Δ
// θ° = α1 → ··· → αn → β
foreach Γ°1 ⊢ s : θ°1 in pre-derivation Δ do
    Γ°1 := Γ°1 ∪ {F : θ°}
end
J :=  ─────────────
       Γ° ⊢ F : θ°
foreach λx1 ... xn.s ∈ ℛ(F) do
    Add a fresh node, labelled (F, λx1 ... xn.s : θ°, J'), as
    the rightmost child of the node of 𝒟 containing J where
            {xi : αi | 1 ≤ i ≤ n} ⊢ s : β
    J' :=  ─────────────────────────────
              ∅ ⊢ λx1 ... xn.s : θ°
end
```

Example 8 (Completion of analysing $\mathcal{G}_2$ against $\mathcal{A}_2$)**.** We will now look at the completed data structures, continuing from Example 6. Δ_1, Δ_2 and Δ_3 are the pre-derivations explored in the previous example, with Δ_2, Δ_3 and Δ_4 being required to prove Δ_1, as can be seen from $\mathcal{D}$ in Table 2. Tracing the computation from Example 6 to this state is left as an exercise to the reader. In this case, the open *pre-derivations* Δ_5 and Δ_6 trivially have the same reified-type binding as Δ_3 and Δ_4 ($H, H : \mathsf{b}_1$ and $H, \mathsf{b}_1 : \mathsf{b}_1$). As a

[3] which means that $\emptyset \vdash s : \widehat{\Theta}(\theta^o)$ is valid (since c is closed and thanks to Lemma 1, page 8), where $(F, s : \theta^o)$ is the open-type binding of c

Procedure *AddDer*

input : Type variable α, open type θ^o

`// Find intro. of` α `in pre-derivations of` $\mathcal{D}$

if $\exists\,!\, J' = \dfrac{\overline{\Gamma^o \vdash t : \alpha \to \theta_1^o} \quad \cdots}{\Gamma^o \vdash t\ u : \theta_1^o}$ **then**

  $J' := \dfrac{\overline{\Gamma^o \vdash t : \alpha \to \theta_1^o \quad \Gamma^o \vdash u : \theta^o} \quad \cdots}{\Gamma^o \vdash t\ u : \theta_1^o}$

else $(\theta^o = b_i)$

  $\exists\,!\, J' = \dfrac{\overline{\Gamma^o \vdash t : \alpha} \quad \cdots}{\Gamma^o \vdash \mathsf{case}(t, t_1, \ldots, t_n) : \theta_1^o}$

  $J' := \dfrac{\overline{\Gamma^o \vdash t : \alpha \quad \Gamma^o \vdash t_i : \theta^o} \quad \cdots}{\Gamma^o \vdash \mathsf{case}(t, t_1, \ldots, t_n) : \theta_1^o}$

end

$\Theta := \Theta[\alpha \mapsto \Theta(\alpha) \cup \{\, \theta^o \,\}]$

Procedure *CloseApp*

input : $J = \Gamma^o \vdash t\ u : \theta^o$

$J := \dfrac{\Gamma^o \vdash t : \alpha \to \theta^o}{\Gamma^o \vdash t\ u : \theta^o}$ (α fresh)

Procedure *CloseVar*

input : $J = \Gamma^o \vdash x : \theta^o$

$J := \dfrac{}{\Gamma^o \vdash x : \theta^o}$

$AddDer(\Gamma^o(x), \theta^o)$

Procedure *CloseTerm*

input : $J = \Gamma^o \vdash a : \theta^o$

`//` $\theta^o = \alpha_1 \to \cdots \to \alpha_n \to q$

if $(q, a) \notin \delta$ **then**

  raise (Trace ⟨counter-example trace⟩)

else $(\delta(q, a) = q_1 \ldots q_n)$

  $J := \dfrac{}{\Gamma^o \vdash a : \theta^o}$

  foreach $i \in \{1, \ldots, n\}$ **do**

    $AddDer(\alpha_i, q_i)$

  end

end

Procedure *CloseCase*

input : $J = \Gamma^o \vdash \mathsf{case}(t, t_1, \ldots, t_n) : \beta$

$J := \dfrac{\Gamma^o \vdash t : \beta}{\Gamma^o \vdash \mathsf{case}(t, t_1, \ldots, t_n) : \theta^o}$

Procedure *CloseUnion*

input : $J = \Gamma^o \vdash \mathsf{b}_i : \beta$

$J := \dfrac{\overline{\Gamma^o \vdash \mathsf{b}_i : \mathsf{b}_i}}{\Gamma^o \vdash \mathsf{b}_i : \beta}$

$AddDer(\beta, \{\mathsf{b}_i\})$

result the environment $\Gamma = \{S : q_0, G : (q_1 \to q_0) \to q_0, H : \mathsf{b}_1\}$ is guaranteed to be a witness to $[\![\mathcal{G}_2]\!] \vDash \mathcal{A}_2$.

Correctness

First we observe that Algorithm 1 never gets stuck: every open judgement is matched by one of the six rules (corresponding to the six *Close-* procedures). We formulate it as an important invariant of the algorithm.

Lemma 1 (Invariant). *Let $(\mathcal{D}, \Theta)$ be a state of the algorithm, n be a node of $\mathcal{D}$, and $\mathcal{D}(n) = (F, s : \theta^o, \Delta)$ where the judgement at the root of the pre-derivation Δ is $\Gamma^o \vdash s : \theta^o$ (where $s \in \mathcal{R}(F)$).*

(i) Every internal judgement (respectively closed judgement) of $\widehat{\Theta}(\Delta)$ is an instance of a rule (respectively axiom) of $\vdash_{\mathcal{A}}$. Hence, if n is closed then $\widehat{\Theta}(\Delta)$ is a valid type derivation, witnessing $\widehat{\Theta}(\Gamma^o) \vdash s : \widehat{\Theta}(\theta^o)$.

(ii) Let $\Gamma^o = \{\, F_1 : \theta_1^o, \ldots, F_l : \theta_l^o \,\}$ and for each i, $\mathcal{R}(F_i) = \{\, s_{i1}, \ldots, s_{ir_i} \,\}$. Then $\bigcup_{i=1}^{l} \{\, n_{i1}, \cdots, n_{ir_i} \,\}$ is the set of successor nodes of n, where $\mathcal{D}(n_{ij}) = (F_i, s_{ij} : \theta_i^o, \Delta_{ij})$ for each i.

Proof. (Sketch) Given $(\mathcal{D}, \Theta)$ we prove that each of the six rules (corresponding to the six *Close-* procedures) preserve these properties. □

Lemma 2. *Let $(\mathcal{D}, \Theta)$ be a state of the algorithm. Suppose there is a complete cut C of $\mathcal{D}^{\mathrm{cl}}$. Define Ξ to be the set:*

$$\Xi := \{\, F : \widehat{\Theta}(\theta^o) \mid \exists n \,.\, n \preccurlyeq C \wedge \mathcal{D}(n) = (F, s : \theta^o, \Delta) \,\}$$

Then $\vdash_{\mathcal{G},\mathcal{A}} \Xi$ (in the sense of Theorem 1).

Proof. Take $n \preccurlyeq C$ with $\mathcal{D}(n) = (F, s : \theta^o, \Delta)$. We need to show that there exists $\Gamma \subseteq \Xi$ such that $\Gamma \vdash_{\mathcal{A}} s : \widehat{\Theta}(\theta^o)$, for *every* $s \in \mathcal{R}(F)$. We may assume that $n \prec C$; for if not, since C is a complete cut, there is some interior node n' of C that has the same reified-type binding as n; and so, we take n' instead of n. Since n is a node in $\mathcal{D}^{\mathrm{cl}}$, by Lemma 1, for some $\Gamma^o = \{\, F_1 : \theta_1^o, \ldots, F_l : \theta_l^o \,\}$, we have

$$F_1 : \widehat{\Theta}(\theta_1^o), \ldots, F_l : \widehat{\Theta}(\theta_l^o) \vdash_{\mathcal{A}} s : \widehat{\Theta}(\theta^o)$$

where the set of successors of n is $N = \bigcup_{i=1}^{l} \{\, n_{i1}, \ldots, n_{ir_i} \,\}$, with $\mathcal{D}(n_{ij}) = (F_i, s_{ij} : \theta_i^o, \Delta_{ij})$ for each $s_{ij} \in \mathcal{R}(F_i)$. If $N = \emptyset$, we are done. Otherwise, take an arbitrary successor of n, say, n_{11}. Since C is a cut, $n_{11} \prec C$ or $n_{11} \in C$. If the latter, since C is complete, there is an interior node of C that has the same reified-type binding as n_{11}. Thus there is a subset N' consisting of interior nodes of C such that the set of reified-type bindings of nodes in N coincide with the set of reified-type bindings of nodes in N', and we are done. Now take $s' \in \mathcal{R}(F)$. By assumption, $s' \preccurlyeq C$, using the same reasoning as before, we can show the desired result.

□

Theorem 2 (Correctness). *Let $\mathcal{G} = \langle \Sigma, Q, \delta, \mathcal{R}, S \rangle$ be a HORSC and $\mathcal{A}$ a DTT.*

(i) If Algorithm 1 returns YES then $\mathcal{A}$ accepts $[\![\mathcal{G}]\!]$.

(ii) If Algorithm 1 returns NO then $\mathcal{A}$ rejects $[\![\mathcal{G}]\!]$.

(iii) Algorithm 1 terminates on every input.

$$\mathcal{D} = (S, \mathsf{case}(H, G\, succ, G\, pred) : q_0, \Delta_1) \longrightarrow (G, \lambda g.g\, zero : \alpha_1 \to q_0, \Delta_2)$$

$$\longrightarrow (H, H : \beta, \Delta_3)$$

$$\longrightarrow (H, \mathsf{b}_1 : \beta, \Delta_4) \longrightarrow (H, H : \beta, \Delta_5), \; (H, \mathsf{b}_1 : \beta, \Delta_6)$$

$$\Delta_1 = \dfrac{\dfrac{}{\Gamma^o \vdash_{\mathcal{A}} H : \beta}\,\textsc{Var} \qquad \dfrac{\dfrac{}{\Gamma^o \vdash_{\mathcal{A}} G : \alpha_1 \to q_0}\,\textsc{Var} \quad \dfrac{}{\Gamma^o \vdash_{\mathcal{A}} succ : \alpha_2 \to q_0}\,\textsc{Term}}{\Gamma^o \vdash_{\mathcal{A}} G\, succ : q_0}\,\textsc{App}}{\Gamma^o \vdash_{\mathcal{A}} \mathsf{case}(H, G\, succ, G\, pred) : q_0}\,\vee\textsc{-Elim}$$

$$\Delta_2 = \dfrac{\dfrac{\dfrac{}{\{g : \alpha_1\} \vdash g : \alpha_2 \to q_0}\,\textsc{Var} \quad \dfrac{}{\{g : \alpha_1\} \vdash zero : q_1}\,\textsc{Term}}{\{g : \alpha_1\} \vdash g\, zero : q_0}\,\textsc{App}}{\vdash \lambda g.g\, zero : q_0}\,\textsc{Abs}$$

$$\Delta_3 = \dfrac{\dfrac{}{\vdash_{\mathcal{A}} \mathsf{b}_1 : \mathsf{b}_1}\,\textsc{Base}}{\vdash_{\mathcal{A}} \mathsf{b}_1 : \beta}\,\vee\textsc{-Intro} \qquad \Delta_5 = H : \beta \vdash_{\mathcal{A}} \mathsf{b}_1 : \beta$$

$$\Delta_4 = \dfrac{}{\vdash_{\mathcal{A}} H : \beta}\,\textsc{Var} \qquad \Delta_6 = \vdash_{\mathcal{A}} H : \beta$$

$$\Theta = \{\alpha_1 \mapsto \{\alpha_2 \to q_0\}, \alpha_2 \mapsto \{q_1\}, \beta \mapsto \{\mathsf{b}_1\}\} \qquad \Gamma^o = \{G : \alpha_1 \to q_0, H : \beta\}$$

Table 2. A terminating state $(\mathcal{D}, \Theta)$ of the algorithm with input $\mathcal{G}_2$ and $\mathcal{A}_2$ (Example 8).

Remark 3 (Round). We organise the computation of the while-loop in Algorithm 1 into *rounds*. In each round, for each $J \in \mathsf{open}(\mathcal{D})$ we apply the appropriate *Close-* procedure repeatedly to the judgement that is opened up, until we reach a non-terminal. Thus at the end of each round, the open judgements (if any) are all non-terminals.

Proof. (i) follows from Lemma 2.

(ii) It suffices to show that given a state (Δ, Θ), for every judgement $\Gamma \vdash t : \theta^o \in \Delta$ with q as the result type of θ^o, we can construct a term t' that is a subterm of some u such that $S \to_{\mathcal{G}}^* u$; further if there is a run tree r, then $r(\beta) = q$ where $u(\beta) = t'$. Intuitively this means that for every such judgement determines a path in a runtree. (iii) Let $\mathcal{N} = \{ F_1, \ldots, F_m \}$ where $F_1 = S$, and let N be the product of the number of rewrite rules and the total number of types (of the relevant kinds) of $\mathcal{G}$. Using our standard notion of round (Remark 3), the open nodes of a state tree $\mathcal{D}$ are necessarily leaf nodes. To show termination of the algorithm (in case of a yes-instance), we aim to exhibit a state tree such that every path in it is either sufficiently long to guarantee a recurrence of a reified type binding, or it ends in a closed node. To this end, we systematically compute all traversals. For each traversal, we keep on extending it until we reach a closed node, or it has induced a path in the state tree of length greater than N. Termination of such a computation of traversals is a consequence of [16, Lemma 14 (long version)]. An alternative argument from first principles is Lemma 3, which is proved in the long version of this paper. $\square$

Correspondence with Traversals

The computation of the algorithm can be represented by a possibly infinite tree, called *justified judgement tree*, which is defined to be a (justified) tree of judgements (i.e. the nodes are labelled by judgements; we shall refer to a node by its label) such that J' is a *successor* of J just if the execution of the call $Close\Xi(J)$ (where the suffix Ξ, which is one of Abs, $NonTerm$, Var, $Term$, $Case$ and $Union$, is determined by the head symbol of the term in J) constructs the open judgement J' either in the same pre-derivation as J or in a new pre-derivation. Thus each path in the justified judgement tree represents a sequence of judgements that are successively closed by one of the four $Close\Xi$ procedures. The judgement tree is *justified* in the sense that some nodes have a pointer back to an ancestor node. In the long version of this paper, we show that the justified judgement tree and the *traversal tree* (in the sense of [16]) are isomorphic with respect to both the successor and pointer relations.

Theorem 3 (Correspondence). *(i) There is a bijective map Φ from maximal paths in the traversal tree to maximal paths in the computation tree. (ii) Further, for every maximal path π, the Σ-projection of π to Σ coincides with the Σ-projection of $\Phi(\pi)$.*

Lemma 3. *If a traversal is well-founded (in the sense that there exists $N \geq 0$ such that all paths that are induced in the state tree have length less than N) then it is finite.*

Optimisations

A crucial optimisation is *Actual Parameter Revisit Avoidance.* Fix a node n with open-type binding $F : \theta^o$, and a variable x that occurs more than once in $\mathcal{R}(F)$. Suppose at state $(\mathcal{D}, \Theta)$, the open judgement $J_2 = \Gamma^o \vdash x : \theta_2^o$ in the pre-derivation of n (call it Δ) is chosen and $Close Var(J_2)$ is called with $\Gamma^o(x) = \alpha$ and $\theta_0^2 = \beta_1 \to \cdots \to \beta_n \to q$. Suppose at an earlier state, a judgement of the form $J_1 = \Gamma^o \vdash x : \theta_1^o$ with $\theta_1^o = \alpha_1 \to \cdots \to \alpha_n \to q$ was closed (and let J_1 be the first such), and so, we have $\theta_1^o \in \Theta(\alpha)$. Then we optimise as follows.

(i) When executing $AddDer(\alpha, \theta_2^o)$ as called by $Close Var(J_2)$, do not search for J' nor update it (using the notation of the procedure $AddDer$), instead, after executing $\Theta(\alpha) := \Theta(\alpha) \cup \{ \theta_2^o \}$, perform: for each i, $\Theta(\beta_i) := \Theta(\alpha_i)$; and for each $\theta'^o \in \Theta(\beta_i)$, call $AddDer(\beta_i, \theta'^o)$.

(ii) Subsequently, every call to $AddDer(\alpha_i, \theta'^o)$ automatically triggers a call to $AddDer(\beta_i, \theta'^o)$, for $i \in \{ 1, \cdots, n \}$.

To see why the optimisation is sound, consider $AddDer(\alpha, \theta_1^o)$, which constructs a new open judgement $\Gamma_1^o \vdash u : \theta_1^o$ (say). Eventually for some $i \in \{ 1, \cdots, n \}$, $AddDer(\alpha_i, \theta'^o)$ is called, which performs the update $\Theta(\alpha_i) := \alpha_i \cup \{ \theta'^o \}$ with control then returning the original pre-derivation Δ, seeking to prove a typing

θ'^o for the ith-argument (of the first occurrence) of x. Let this sequence of calls to a *Close* procedure between $AddDer(\alpha, \theta_1^o)$ and $AddDer(\alpha_i, \theta'^o)$ be Υ_{i,θ'^o}. Now consider a call to $CloseVar(J_2)$ which calls $AddDer(\alpha, \theta_2^o)$, and which constructs a new open judgement $\Gamma_1^o \vdash u : \theta_2^o$ (say). Note that for each i and θ'^o, Υ_{i,θ'^o} determines a corresponding sequence of calls to a *Close* procedure between $AddDer(\alpha, \theta_2^o)$ and $AddDer(\beta_i, \theta'^o)$. The optimisation removes such call sequences for each i and θ'^o (but not their effects). Our experiments (see Section 5) demonstrate that the optimisation results in close to an order-of-magnitude improvement for HORS of orders 4 or higher.

Translated into the language of traversals, the optimisation says that if the traversal reaches a variable x with state q, instead of jumping to the actual parameter of x, one can immediately traverse downwards with state q' to the i-child of x, provided the traversal has visited another occurrence of x before with state q and subsequently visiting its (the earlier occurrence's) i-child with state q'.

The *canonical types* optimisation aids with the critical part of a *complete cut* (and thus termination) is finding two nodes with the same concrete type bindings. We can increase the chance of finding two such nodes using subtyping to yield canonical types. Given any intersection type $\bigwedge_{i \in I} \theta_i \to \theta$ it is sufficient to consider instead $\bigwedge_{j \in J} \theta_j \to \theta$ where $J \subseteq I$ and for all $k \in I \setminus J$, there exists some $j \in J$ such that $\theta_j \leq \theta_k$ (where $\leq$ is standard intersection type subtyping). Intuitively, this θ_k may be removed because θ_j already places a stronger requirement on a parameter to this function. Any typing tree that uses $x : \theta_k$ could therefore be replaced with one that uses $x : \theta_j$ instead. Removing these redundant types during reification of open types allows us to consider a smaller space of *canonical types*.

At a lower-level, *reification caching* was introduced to handle the relatively expensive calculation of $\widehat{\Theta}$ as the requirement to search for a cut after each round of operation led this to dominate the runtime of the algorithm. By caching the result of $\widehat{\Theta}$ for each α and maintaining a dependency mapping (such that if $\alpha' \in \widehat{\Theta}(\alpha)$ then α depends on α') we can avoid the majority of Θ lookups while preserving correctness by invalidating cache entries in the transitive closure of the dependencies for any α that we update.

Finally, an unguided execution of the algorithm can yield a vast number of subgoals very quickly. Every time a terminal symbol of arity n is encountered, the number of subgoals rises by $n - 1$. To address this, our implementation uses a search guided by the termination check. While searching for a *complete cut* using a breadth-first search of $\mathcal{D}$, any subtree rooted at a node with a type binding already seen is not explored, and any open judgements within this subtree are not expanded at this time. This focuses the attention of the algorithm on areas of the tree that could not currently form part of a *complete cut*. In the extremal case, all open judgements are contained in such subtrees, and the algorithm terminates.

5. Empirical Results and Evaluation

We have constructed TRAVMC, an implementation of Algorithm 1 presented in Section 4. The implementation, and all the examples presented here, can be accessed through a web interface at http://mjolnir.cs.ox.ac.uk/horsc/. For comparison we have considered not just HORSC, but also standard HORS, which can be handled by our algorithm as a degenerate case.

Instance	O	S	R	H	G	T	T_B	T'
example2-1	1	2	Y	2	1	34	0	33
fileocamlc	4	21	Y	8	1680	60	23	718
fileocamlc2	4	22	Y	7	1980	58	18	918
fileorder5-2	5	30	Y	109	–	201	167	–
filewrong	4	11	N	0	–	86	47	85
flow	4	7	Y	1	3	32	0	32
g35	3	11	Y	–	136	–	–	–
g41	4	8	Y	–	608	55	15	–
lock2	4	11	Y	10	–	64	23	132
m91	5	25	Y	39	–	429	381	–
order5	5	9	Y	5	–	62	8	46
order5-variant	5	11	Y	12	–	47	7	317
stress	1	13	Y	29	3	187	133	180

Table 3. HORS MC comparison

HORSC	O	S	R	T	T_H
checknz	1	27	Y	46	36
checkpairs	1	86	N	53	93
filepath	1	369	Y	1950	–
filter-nonzero	4	49	N	74	156
filter-nonzero-1	4	69	Y	1756	–
last	1	60	Y	71	45
map-head-filter	2	110	N	62	116
map-head-filter-1	2	190	Y	1080	1538
map-plusone	4	39	Y	83	161
map-plusone-1	4	49	Y	296	860
map-plusone-2	4	63	Y	4144	–
mkgroundterm	1	108	Y	179	96
risers	1	165	Y	113	127
safe-foldr1	2	145	Y	450	625
safe-head	2	106	Y	71	56
safe-init	2	235	Y	209	288
safe-tail	2	154	Y	88	74
RSFD	**O**	**S**	**R**	**T**	**H**
gap_id	3	26	Y	248	15
homrep	4	12	Y	1767	7
merge_addr	1	7	Y	52	1
mult	1	5	Y	52	1
remove_b	2	7	Y	54	2
xhtmlm-drop-a	1	33	Y	1252	146
xhtmlm_id	1	33	Y	996	64
xhtmls-remove-meta	1	13	Y	277	9
xhtmlf_id	1	51	Y	–	456

Table 4. HORSC MC results

HORS Model Checking

For HORS, we have used a benchmark suite containing a number of examples from the literature, along with some fresh examples. The columns "O", "S" and "R" in the table indicate the order, number of rules and result of the example respectively. The "H" and "G" columns contain timing data (in milliseconds) for Kobayashi's hybrid (TRECS version 1.32) and game-based algorithms (GTRECS version 0.10[4]). Those labelled "T" or "T_B" (resp. "T′") are for the algorithm introduced in this paper with (resp. without) the *Revisit Avoidance* optimisation at order 1, the subscript B indicating a 'batch' processing mode. Where an algorithm did not terminate within 10 seconds this is indicated by "–".

[4] We did not have access to a GTRECS binary, as a result experiments were carried out through the author's web interface. Timings are not directly comparable, but indicative.

Table 3 shows that for most examples TRAVMC performs approximately an order of magnitude slower than the current version of TRECS. However, given the immature state of our implementation, we believe that this gap may be crossed given careful optimisation. For the very rapid examples (around 100ms and below), we found that the runtime was dominated by the first round of expansion. We believe that this is JIT overhead tied to our use of F# on .NET (both TRECS and GTRECS are implemented in OCaml). This is supported by our batch mode experiment, which saw all examples processed consecutively by a single invocation of the model checker, avoiding the repeated startup overhead commonly associated with JIT compilers and reduced the runtime by around 50ms consistently. One area where we believe significant speedups may be gained are in extending the *Actual Parameter Revisit Avoidance* optimisation to orders 2 and above. Although some savings are still made at higher orders in the current implementation, the amount of work which is potentially avoided can be increased exponentially by extending the optimisation to each order. Furthermore, in order to keep the cost of checking the termination condition low, it is currently somewhat conservative, but it is possible that a more thorough procedure, if carefully engineered, could potentially detect termination earlier. Exploring this trade-off could provide substantial benefits.

It is worth noting that both TRECS and TRAVMC could handle almost all of the examples without trouble, implying that further work on more taxing examples is needed to better understand where each algorithm breaks down. One direction in which both algorithms struggled is a set of examples introduced by Kobayashi [10] known as $\mathcal{G}_{n,m}$. When checked by the hybrid algorithm, these examples require $\mathcal{O}(\mathbf{exp}_n(m))$ expansions to obtain type information for non-terminals at the bottom of a hyper-exponential tree. Our new algorithm's performance improved markedly due to the *Revisit Avoidance* optimisation, checking $\mathcal{G}_{4,1}$ even faster than Kobayashi's linear-time algorithm GTRECS, although higher values of n and m resulted in timeouts. We believe the speedup will be lifted to higher values of n with a full implementation of the *Revisit Avoidance* optimisation.

Such examples display the power of GTRECS fully and it is encouraging to note that TRAVMC seems to be able to handle some such recursion schemes. In more realistic cases, TRAVMC outperforms GTRECS by several orders of magnitude.

HORSC Model Checking

For HORSC, we have generated some examples as the output of an abstraction procedure based on earlier work [17]. The abstraction procedure operates on a *pattern-matching recursion scheme* (PMRS), which can be thought of as an instance of a simply-typed programming language with higher-order, recursive functions and pattern-matching over algebraic data-types. The abstract models that are produced are not strictly HORSC, since they can have patterns on the left-hand side of grammar rules which include free variables (though such variables are not allowed to appear on the right-hand side of grammar rules), so they are first put through a translation which is detailed in the long version of this paper. For some examples (those with numbers appended) we performed refinement of the abstraction and here we give the timings for each round of model checking. See Table 4, where the columns are labelled as before.

In order to evaluate the usefulness of a primitive case analysis construct, which is afforded by HORSC, we have compared the results of checking these HORSC model checking instances with corresponding HORS encodings (using TRAVMC in both cases). In each case, the HORS encoding of the HORSC is obtained by determinising and modelling the constants as projection functions. Unavoidably, this raises the order and arity, and hence worst-case complexity significantly (see Remark 2). The time to check the original instance is given in column "T" and to check the encoding can be seen in the column "T_H". For some examples, particularly the simpler ones, checking HORS is fast enough, but as the size and order of the example increases, this approach breaks down. We believe that this offers a compelling argument for the introduction of HORSC.

Pattern-match safety An important verification problem in functional programming is that of ensuring that partial pattern matches never receive one of the missing cases and so are 'safe'. Pattern-match safety is reducible to reachability, and the results for these can be seen at the top of the table. One simple example is the list-processing function *last*, which assumes that its input is a non-empty list. The CATCH tool [14] targets this verification problem, and we have used some of the same examples: the *Risers* program and *Safe* and *FilePath* libraries, which contain partial pattern matching that we verify to be safe. The input HORSC is in both cases rather large, but the algorithm still terminates quickly.

A more complex example uses *filter* to remove empty lists from the input before invoking *head* on the remaining lists (*map-filter-head*). The *mkgroundterm* program contains a counting function that sums the values of constants within a ground term. By guarding the input to this partial function (by removing variables), we are able to prove that the program is safe.

Output term While pattern-match safety reduces to reachability, we can check more interesting properties such as verifying some structure of the output of a function. The *filter-nonzero* example uses *filter* with a *nonzero* function and verifies that the output list contains no element equal to zero. For the *map-plusone* example, we add one to all elements of an input list of naturals and verify again that the output list contains no zeroes.

RSFD Kobayashi, Tabuchi and Unno model check *recursion schemes with finite data domains* (RSFD) as part of their work [13]. RSFD form a sub-class of HORSC in which there are additional typing restrictions on the scrutinee appearing in each case analysis. Since each RSFD can be viewed as a HORSC, our tool is also able to solve the RSFD model checking problem. We have compared the performance of our tool (column "T") versus the TRECS (version 1.32) tool of Kobayashi *et al.* (column "H") in the second part of Table 4. The data reveals that, perhaps unsurprisingly, the specialist RSFD checker is more efficient in all examples. Indeed, the particular additional restrictions imposed in the definition of RSFD make the class particularly appealing from an algorithmic point of view, though one which is not expressive enough for our purposes. However, even at higher orders or with a large number of automaton states, our tool can solve almost all the example instances.

6. Related Work

MSO Model Checking Problem The MSO model checking problem for order-n recursion schemes was first proved to be decidable (with optimal complexity of n-EXPTIME) by Ong [16]. His proof used game semantics to reduce the model checking problem to the solution of parity games over *variable profiles*. To date, three other proofs are known, employing different methods to build appropriate parity games. Hague et al. [4] constructed configuration graphs of collapsible pushdown automata; Kobayashi and Ong [12] used intersection types; and Salvati and Walukiewicz [19] appealed to Krivine machines. For the restricted class of *trivial automata* (but for the full hierarchy of HORS), Aehlig [1] gave a decidability proof based on a novel finite semantics for simply-typed lambda calculus. Kobayashi's proof of the same result, which was based on intersection types [8], used a similar idea.

Practical Model Checking Algorithms for HORS As discussed in the Introduction, the first practical model checking algorithm for HORS against trivial automata was Kobayashi's *hybrid algorithm* [7], which was implemented in the model checker TRecS [9]. There are important differences between the hybrid algorithm and our traversal algorithm. The hybrid algorithm extracts intersection types by partial evaluation of the HORS followed by an over-approximation; whereas the traversal algorithm (following game semantics) harvests *variable profiles* from the traversals in game semantics. Secondly the hybrid algorithm uses a loop—each iteration being a greatest fixpoint construction starting from a seed type environment—which will eventually compute a $\vdash_{\mathcal{G},\mathcal{A}}$-complete type environment in case $(\mathcal{G}, \mathcal{A})$ is a yes-instance. In contrast, the traversal algorithm builds a $\vdash_{\mathcal{G},\mathcal{A}}$-complete type environment "from below".

Kobayashi's FoSSaCS'11 algorithm [10] is inspired by game semantics, even though the formal development of the algorithm is purely type-theoretic, and no concrete relationship with game semantics is known. A notable feature of the algorithm is its simplicity, which consists of two fixpoint constructions, first least then greatest. Thanks to Rehof and Mogensen's optimisation [18], a consequence of the fixpoint design is its linear-time complexity in the size of the HORS, assuming that the other parameters are fixed. The main innovation of the algorithm lies in the least fixpoint computation. Given a candidate type environment Γ, for each subset $\Gamma_1 \subseteq \Gamma$, and each $F : \theta \in \Gamma$, more "expansive" versions of Γ_1 and θ, namely, Γ' and θ' (satisfying $\Gamma_1 \preceq_O \Gamma'$ and $\theta \preceq_P \theta'$) respectively, are selected such that $\Gamma' \vdash \mathcal{R}(F) : \theta'$. (The expansive relations $\preceq_O$ and $\preceq_P$ represent Opponent and Proponent moves respectively.) The type environment that is constructed in the next iteration consists of Γ extended by $\Gamma' \cup \{ F : \theta' \}$, for all $F : \theta$ and for all such Γ' and θ'. Our traversal algorithm may be viewed as a process of approximating a (canonical) $\vdash_{G,\mathcal{A}}$-complete type environment from below. There are however two differences. First the successive approximants are not related by containment. Secondly, our algorithm selects just one such pair of Γ' and θ', as determined by the traversal development.

7. Conclusions and Further Directions

We have presented a practical algorithm for the universal model checking problem for higher-order recursion schemes with cases (HORSC) against deterministic trivial automata. The algorithm is based on *traversals*, and is induced by the fully abstract game semantics of the recursion schemes, but presented as a goal-directed construction of derivations in an intersection and union type system. We view HORSC model checking as a suitable backend for an approach to verify functional programs (presented as *pattern-matching recursion schemes*) via an abstraction-refinement procedure. Preliminary experiments with our tool implementation TravMC indicate that the algorithm performs remarkably well on a number of small but realistic examples generating schemes with hundreds of rules. We hope to explore the scalability of our approach by verifying larger examples of pure functional programs from the literature.

8. Acknowledgements

We would like to thank our reviewers for their helpful comments on the first version of this paper. We would also like to thank Naoki Kobayashi for his assistance when benchmarking against his tools, and for offering an automated approach for performing the translation from HORSC to HORS (see Section 5).

References

[1] Klaus Aehlig. A finite semantics of simply-typed lambda terms for infinite runs of automata. *Logical Methods in Comp. Sci.*, 3(3), 2007.

[2] Thomas Ball, Rupak Majumdar, Todd D. Millstein, and Sriram K. Rajamani. Automatic predicate abstraction of C programs. In *PLDI*, pages 203–213, 2001.

[3] Dirk Beyer, Thomas A. Henzinger, Ranjit Jhala, and Rupak Majumdar. The software model checker blast. *STTT*, 9(5-6):505–525, 2007.

[4] Matthew Hague, Andrzej S. Murawski, C.-H. Luke Ong, and Olivier Serre. Collapsible pushdown automata and recursion schemes. In *LICS*, pages 452–461, 2008.

[5] J. M. E. Hyland and C.-H. Luke Ong. On full abstraction for PCF: I, II, and III. *Inf. Comput.*, 163(2):285–408, 2000.

[6] Teodor Knapik, Damian Niwinski, and Pawel Urzyczyn. Higher-order pushdown trees are easy. In *FoSSaCS*, pages 205–222, 2002.

[7] Naoki Kobayashi. Model-checking higher-order functions. In *PPDP*, pages 25–36, 2009.

[8] Naoki Kobayashi. Types and higher-order recursion schemes for verification of higher-order programs. In *POPL*, pages 416–428, 2009.

[9] Naoki Kobayashi. http://www-kb.is.s.u-tokyo.ac.jp/~koba/trecs/, 2009.

[10] Naoki Kobayashi. A practical linear time algorithm for trivial automata model checking of higher-order recursion schemes. In *FOSSACS*, pages 260–274, 2011.

[11] Naoki Kobayashi and C.-H. Luke Ong. Complexity of model checking recursion schemes for fragments of the modal mu-calculus. In *ICALP (2)*, pages 223–234, 2009.

[12] Naoki Kobayashi and C.-H. Luke Ong. A type system equivalent to the modal mu-calculus model checking of higher-order recursion schemes. In *LICS*, pages 179–188, 2009.

[13] Naoki Kobayashi, Naoshi Tabuchi, and Hiroshi Unno. Higher-order multi-parameter tree transducers and recursion schemes for program verification. In *POPL*, pages 495–508, 2010.

[14] Neil Mitchell and Colin Runciman. Not all patterns, but enough - an automatic verifier for partial but sufficient pattern matching. In *Haskell '08: Proceedings of the first ACM SIGPLAN symposium on Haskell*, pages 49–60. ACM, September 2008.

[15] Robin P. Neatherway, C.-H. Luke Ong, and Steven J. Ramsay. A traversal-based algorithm for higher-order model checking. Long version, available from: http://mjolnir.cs.ox.ac.uk/papers/traversal.pdf, 2012.

[16] C.-H. Luke Ong. On model-checking trees generated by higher-order recursion schemes. In *LICS*, pages 81–90, 2006. Long version (55 pp.) http://www.cs.ox.ac.uk/people/luke.ong/personal/publications/ntree.pdf.

[17] C.-H. Luke Ong and Steven J. Ramsay. Verifying functional programs with pattern matching algebraic data types. In *POPL*, pages 587–598, 2011.

[18] Jakob Rehof and Torben Æ. Mogensen. Tractable constraints in finite semilattices. *Sci. Comput. Program.*, 35(2):191–221, 1999.

[19] Sylvain Salvati and Igor Walukiewicz. Krivine machines and higher-order schemes. In *ICALP (2)*, pages 162–173, 2011.

Functional Programs that Explain their Work

Roly Perera
University of Birmingham & MPI-SWS
rolyp@mpi-sws.org

Umut A. Acar
Carnegie Mellon University & MPI-SWS
umut@cs.cmu.edu

James Cheney
University of Edinburgh
jcheney@inf.ed.ac.uk

Paul Blain Levy
University of Birmingham
P.B.Levy@cs.bham.ac.uk

Abstract

We present techniques that enable higher-order functional computations to "explain" their work by answering questions about how parts of their output were calculated. As explanations, we consider the traditional notion of program slices, which we show can be inadequate, and propose a new notion: trace slices. We present techniques for specifying flexible and rich slicing criteria based on partial expressions, parts of which have been replaced by holes. We characterise program slices in an algorithm-independent fashion and show that a least slice for a given criterion exists. We then present an algorithm, called *unevaluation*, for computing least program slices from computations reified as traces. Observing a limitation of program slices, we develop a notion of *trace slice* as another form of explanation and present an algorithm for computing them. The unevaluation algorithm can be applied to any subtrace of a trace slice to compute a program slice whose evaluation generates that subtrace. This close correspondence between programs, traces, and their slices can enable the programmer to understand a computation interactively, in terms of the programming language in which the computation is expressed. We present an implementation in the form of a tool, discuss some important practical implementation concerns and present some techniques for addressing them.

Categories and Subject Descriptors D.2.5 [*Software Engineering*]: Testing and debugging—Tracing; D.3.4 [*Programming Languages*]: Processors—Debuggers

Keywords program slicing; debugging; provenance

1. Introduction

Many problem domains in computer science require understanding a computation and how a certain result was computed. For example, in debugging we aim to understand why some erroneous result was computed by a program. This goal of understanding and explaining computations and their results often runs against our desire to treat a computation as a black box that maps inputs to outputs. Indeed, we lack rich general-purpose techniques and tools for understanding and explaining computations and their relationship to their outputs. One such technique is program slicing, which was first explored in the imperative programming community.

Originally formulated by Weiser [27], a *program slice* is a reduced program, obtained by eliminating statements from the original program, that produces the behavior specified by a *slicing criterion*. A slice is called *static* if it makes no assumptions on the input—it works for any input—and *dynamic* if it works only for the specified input. Originally defined to yield *backward slices*, which identify parts of a program contributing to a specific criterion on the output, slicing techniques were later extended to compute forward slices. Since it pertains to a specific execution, and explains the relationship between a computation and its result, dynamic backward slicing is considered more relevant for the purposes of understanding a computation. In this paper, we consider dynamic, backward slicing only. While primarily motivated by debugging and program comprehension, other applications of slicing have also been proposed, including parallelization [4], software maintenance [5], and testing [3]. For a comprehensive overview of the slicing literature, we refer the reader to existing surveys [26, 28].

While slicing has been studied extensively in the context of imperative languages, there is comparatively less work in functional languages. Slicing techniques developed for imperative programs do not translate well to the functional setting for two reasons. First, in the functional setting, higher-order values are prevalent; it is not clear whether slicing techniques for imperative programs can be extended to handle higher-order values. Second, functional programs typically manipulate complex values such as recursive data types, whereas slicing techniques in imperative programs often perform slicing at the granularity of variables, which is too coarse a grain to be effective for functional programs.

Reps and Turnidge [21] present slicing technique for functional programs. Their techniques compute static slices, however, and apply only to first-order functional programs; they also do not preserve the semantics of strict functional programs. Biswas [6] considers strict, higher-order functional programs and proposes slicing techniques with a single form of criterion: the entire output of the program. Ochoa, Silva, and Vidal [19] present techniques that allow more flexible criteria but which only apply to first-order, lazy functional languages. To the best of our knowledge, the problem of slicing of strict, higher-order functional programs with rich criteria has remained an open problem.

In this paper, we develop techniques for computing program slices for strict, higher-order functional programs based on rich slicing criteria and propose techniques for more powerful examinations of computations via trace slices.

ICFP'12, September 9–15, 2012, Copenhagen, Denmark.

To enable expressing rich queries on the computation, we consider two forms of slicing criteria: partial values and differential partial values. We define a *partial value* as a value where some subvalues are replaced by a *hole*, written □. Intuitively, a partial value discards parts of a value that are of no interest to the user. For example, the partial value `(□,2)` specifies a pair where the first component is of no interest; the partial value `cons(□,cons(2,□))` specifies a list where the first element and the second tail are of no interest. While partial values help throw away parts of a value that are of no interest, they may not always be used to focus on a specific part of a value, because the "path" to the part of interest cannot be replaced by a hole, e.g., we cannot focus on the second part of a tuple without specifying there being a tuple. To make it possible to focus on parts of a value, we define *differential* partial values, which can highlight subvalues of interest. For example the differential partial value `cons(□,cons( 2 ,□))` specifies a list where the second element is of interest.

For slicing criteria consisting of (differential) partial values, we define *program slices* in an algorithm-independent way and show that least program slices exists (Section 3). We define a *partial program* as a program where some subexpressions are replaced by holes and give an operational semantics for partial programs (expressions). We call a partial program a *program slice* for a partial value if executing the partial program yields that partial value as an output. We then exhibit a family of Galois connections between partial programs and partial values which guarantees the existence of a least program slice for a given partial value.

Our characterization of program slices shows that it is possible to compute least program slices but does not provide an algorithm that does so. To efficiently compute least program slices, we develop an *unevaluation* algorithm (Section 4). Unevaluation relies on traces that represent an evaluation by recording the evaluation derivation as an unrolled expression. Our use of traces are inspired by self-adjusting computation [1], but we structure them differently to enable their use in computation comprehension. Given a slicing criterion, our unevaluation algorithm uses the trace to "push" the criterion, a partial value, backward through the trace, discarding unused parts of the trace and rolling the remaining parts up into a least program slice for the criterion.

Our program slices can give valuable explanations about a computation, but as with any slicing technique, they can lose their effectiveness in complex computations. Intuitively, the reason for this is that each expression in a program slice must subsume the many different behaviors that the expression exhibits in an execution. Indeed, even though program slices were motivated by debugging, they are of limited assistance when the bug involves different execution paths along the same piece of code, which a program slice cannot distinguish. For example, we show how program slices become ineffective when trying to understand a buggy mergesort implementation (Section 2.3).

Motivated by the limitations of program slices, we introduce the concept of *trace slicing* (Section 5). As the name suggest, the high-level idea is to compute a slice of a trace for a given slicing criterion by replacing parts of the trace that are not relevant to the criterion with holes. We call the resulting reduced trace a *partial trace*; a partial trace *explains* a partial value (slicing criterion) if the trace contains enough information to unevaluate the partial value. We then present a trace-slicing algorithm for computing the least partial trace which explains a given partial value. When computing a least trace slice, it is critical to compute least slices of any higher-order values; our trace-slicing algorithm defers to unevaluation to do this.

When used in combination, our techniques can offer an interactive and precise approach to understanding computations. The user can execute a program with some input and then compute a (least) program slice for a desired slicing criterion. If interested in understanding the computation in more depth, the user can then ask for a trace slice, which will present a precise description of how the computation has unfolded, eliminating subtraces that do not contribute to the slicing criterion, and highlighting those that contribute. Since the trace slices reflect closely the program code itself, the user can read the trace slice as an unrolled program. Explanations are expressed in the same programming language as the computation itself.

We present a tool, Slicer, that enables interactive trace exploration for source code written in an ML-like language that we call TML (Transparent ML). Slicer itself is implemented in Haskell and takes advantage of the lazy evaluation strategy of Haskell to avoid constructing traces except when needed. Inspired by Haskell's laziness, we present a technique for trading space for time by a form of controlled lazy evaluation that can also be used in the context of strict languages.

Our contributions include the following:

1. Techniques for specifying flexible slicing criteria based on differential and partial values.
2. An algorithm-independent formulation of least program slices.
3. An algorithm, called unevaluation, for computing least slices of strict, higher-order functional programs.
4. The concept of trace slices and an algorithm for computing them.
5. Proofs of relevant correctness and minimality properties.
6. The Slicer tool for computing and visualizing program and trace slices.

Proofs that are omitted due to space restrictions can be found in the companion technical report [20].

2. Overview

We present an overview of our techniques considering examples with increasing sophistication. All the figures presented here were produced by our tool, Slicer. Slicer accepts programs written in TML and allows them to be executed and queried by using partial values to generate partial programs and traces. Slicer enables visualizing partial programs and traces in an interactive way, allowing the programmer to "browse" them. By default, Slicer prints out the outermost nesting level of traces and hides the deeper levels under ellipses written as "...". The user can click on ellipses to see the hidden contents. This invites the user to think of the execution of an expression as an "unrolling" of that expression. Slicer can also display the (partial) value associated with a step in the computation, which is a feature that we often utilize; such partial values are printed in shaded (gray) boxes.

Slicer prints holes, written as □ throughout the formalism, as ⊞, because the user can ask for what is hidden behind the hole to be displayed.

2.1 Example: List Length

Consider using the standard `length` function to compute the length of a list with three elements:

```
let fun length xs =
      case xs of
        Nil -> 0
        Cons(x,xs) -> 1 + length xs'
in length (Cons(1,Cons(2,Cons(3,Nil))))
```

To understand the computation, we ask Slicer to compute the partial slice for the result 3, which is shown in Figure 1. The interesting point about the program slice (Figure 1(a)) is that the elements of input are all replaced by a hole, because they do not contribute to the output. This is consistent with our expectation of `length` that its output does not depend on the elements of the input

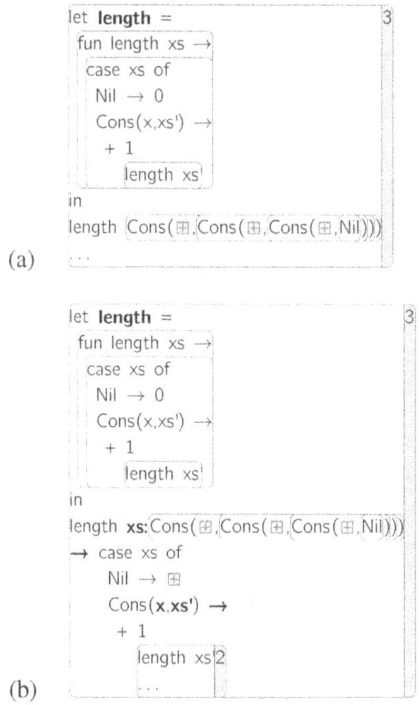

Figure 1. (a) slice of `length`; (b) expanded by one step

list. The slice also illustrates that all of the function `length` is relevant to the output, i.e., all branches were exercised to compute the result. To see the trace slice for the actual computation, we unroll the ellipses at the end of the program slice. The trace slice, shown in Figure 1(b) following the expression slice of `length`, illustrates how the result is actually computed, throwing away subtraces not contributing to the result. The trace slice is an unrolling of the `case` expression constituting the body of `length`, leading to a recursive call which returns 2.

2.2 Example: List Map

Consider applying the standard list primitive `map` to increment each element of the list `Cons(6,Cons(7,Cons(2,Nil)))` by one:

```
let fun map f xs =
      case xs of
        Nil -> Nil
        Cons y -> Cons (f (fst y), map f (snd y))
in map (fn x => x + 1) (Cons(6,Cons(7,Cons(2,Nil))))
```

After performing this computation in Slicer, we can ask for a trace slice with the partial value `Cons(⊞,Cons(8,⊞))`. Figure 2(a) shows the trace slice computed by Slicer. (Please ignore for now the shaded green boxes.) The trace slice starts with a slice of the definition of `map`, where the `Nil` branch is a hole. This indicates that the `Nil` branch was unused – indeed, the partial value does not end with `Nil` but with a hole. The trace slice continues with the application of `map` to the increment function and the input list, where parts of the input are replaced with holes. What is interesting here is that the way the list argument to map has been sliced shows that both the first `Cons` cell, without the head, and the second `Cons` cell, without the tail, contribute to the partial result. Indeed, making changes to any of these elements could change the parts of the result relevant to the criterion.

The partial trace for the partial value `Cons(⊞,Cons(8,⊞))` enhances our understanding of how the second element was computed. To understand how exactly the second element, 8, is computed from the input, we ask Slicer to isolate it by using as a slicing criterion the differential partial value `Cons(⊞,Cons( 8 ,⊞))`. Slicer returns a trace slice where parts contributing directly to the

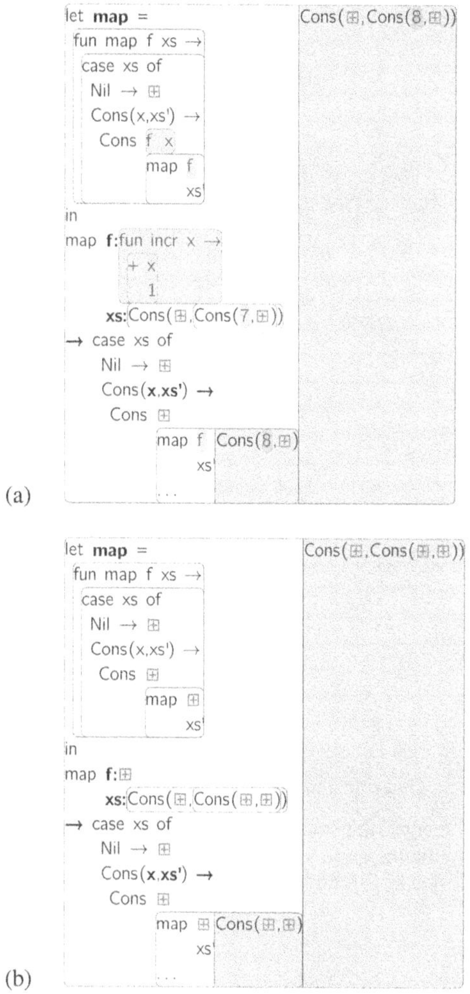

Figure 2. Slice of `map incr [6,7,2]`

second element are also highlighted in green, as shown in Figure 2(a). The highlighted parts show that the second element is computed by applying the increment function to the second element.

We generate differential trace slices by taking advantage of a monotonicity property of partial traces. Consider two partial values u, v where v is greater than u in the sense that v replaces with actual values some holes of u. As we show in Section 5, the trace slice for v is greater in the same sense than the trace slice for u. This property allows us to compute the delta between two partial traces which have a common structure in this way by performing a trace traversal. To compute the differential trace slice for `Cons(⊞,Cons( 8 ,⊞))`, we compute the delta between the trace slice for `Cons(⊞,Cons(8,⊞))` and then trace slice for `Cons(⊞,Cons(⊞,⊞))`. It is this difference that is highlighted in Figure 2(a). For the purposes of comparison, we show the trace slice for `Cons(⊞,Cons(⊞)))` in Figure 2(b). Note that the green highlighted parts are exactly those parts that are holes in the trace (b) that are not holes in the trace (a).

2.3 Example: Mergesort

Our final example is merge sort, an algorithm that significantly restructures its input to produce an output in a way that can be difficult to understand. We consider a buggy implementation and describe how Slicer can help us locate the bug. Our implementation is entirely standard: it splits non-singleton lists into two, sorts them

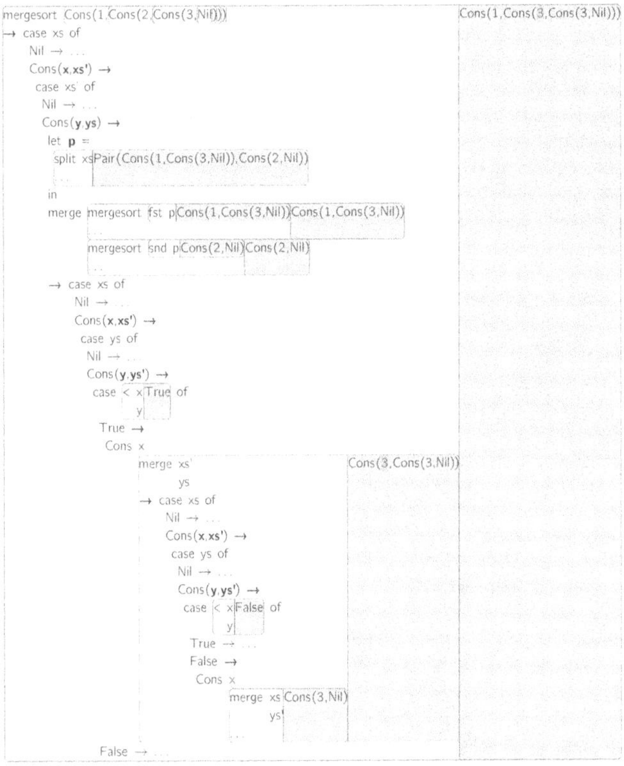

Figure 3. Outermost merge phase of mergesort.

recursively, and merges the results to produce the sorted output list. The bug is in the merge function: the "else" branch should be `Cons(y, ...)` instead of `Cons(x, ...)`. Here is the buggy code for `merge`:

```
fun merge xs ys =
  case xs of
    Nil -> ys
    Cons (x,xs') ->
      case ys of
        Nil -> xs
        Cons (y,ys') -> case x < y of
                          True -> Cons(x,merge(xs',ys))
                          False -> Cons(x,merge(xs,ys'))
```

When used to sort the list `Cons(1,Cons(2,Cons(3,Nil)))` the buggy merge sort returns the list `Cons(1,Cons(3,Cons(3,Nil)))`. To identify the bug, we slice the trace with respect to the differential value `Cons(1,Cons( 3 ,Cons(3,Nil)))` isolating the second element. Unfortunately, the program slice computed by Slicer provides no information. This is an example where program slices are not, and cannot be, precise enough, even though they are least slices for the supplied criterion. We therefore inspect the actual trace slice. Figure 3 illustrates the outermost level of the trace slice including the outermost level of the merge function. As the figure illustrates, Slicer highlights precisely the offending statement of the `merge` function in the trace showing where the 3 in the output comes from `Cons` statements in the `False` branch of the `merge` function, the buggy expression.

3. A Characterisation of Program Slicing

Before we discuss traces and their role in calculating program slices, we formalize our notions of slicing criteria and program slices in the setting of a typed, call-by-value reference language with familiar functional programming constructs such as recursive types and higher-order functions. We formulate the problem of computing least (minimal) dynamic slices under flexible criteria in an algorithm-independent fashion and show that least dynamic slices exist.

Types	τ	$::=$	$1 \mid b \mid \tau_1 + \tau_2 \mid \tau_1 \times \tau_2 \mid \tau_1 \to \tau_2 \mid \mu\alpha.\tau \mid \alpha$
Contexts	Γ	$::=$	$\bullet \mid \Gamma, x : \tau$
Expressions	e	$::=$	$x \mid () \mid c \mid e_1 \oplus e_2 \mid \texttt{fun}\ f(x).e \mid e_1\ e_2$
		$\mid$	$(e_1, e_2) \mid \texttt{fst}\ e \mid \texttt{snd}\ e \mid \texttt{inl}\ e \mid \texttt{inr}\ e$
		$\mid$	$\texttt{case}\ e\ \texttt{of}\ \{\texttt{inl}(x_1).e_1; \texttt{inr}(x_2).e_2\} \mid$
		$\mid$	$\texttt{roll}\ e \mid \texttt{unroll}\ e$
Values	v	$::=$	$c \mid (v_1, v_2) \mid \texttt{inl}\ v \mid \texttt{inr}\ v \mid \texttt{roll}\ v$
		$\mid$	$\langle \rho, \texttt{fun}\ f(x).e \rangle$
Environments	ρ	$::=$	$\bullet \mid \rho[x \mapsto v]$

Figure 4. Reference language: abstract syntax

3.1 The reference language

The syntax of the reference language is given in Figure 4. Types include the usual unit, sum, product and function types, plus iso-recursive types $\mu\alpha.\tau$, type variables α, and primitive types b. Variable contexts are defined inductively in the usual way. Expressions include the unit value $()$, standard introduction and elimination forms for products, sums and recursive functions, `roll` and `unroll` forms for recursive types, primitive constants c, and applications $e_1 \oplus e_2$ of primitive operations. The typing judgments $\Gamma \vdash e : \tau$ for expressions and $\Gamma \vdash \rho$ are given in Figure 6; the latter means that ρ is a well-formed environment for Γ. The signature Σ assigns to every primitive constant c the primitive type $c : b \in \Sigma$, and to every primitive operation $\oplus$ the argument types and return type $\oplus : b_1 \times b_2 \to \tau \in \Sigma$.

Evaluation for the reference language is given by a conventional call-by-value big-step semantics, shown in Figure 5. The judgment $\rho, e \Downarrow_{\mathsf{ref}} v$ states that expression e evaluates in closing environment ρ to value v. Values include the usual forms, plus closures $\langle \rho, \texttt{fun}\ f(x).e \rangle$. The choice of an environment-based semantics is deliberate: environments will be helpful later when we want to record an execution as an unrolling of the program syntax. As usual $\hat{\oplus}$ means $\oplus$ suitably interpreted in the meta-language.

Evaluation is deterministic and type-preserving. We omit the proofs, which are straightforward inductions.

Lemma 1 (Type preservation for $\Downarrow_{\mathsf{ref}}$). *If* $\Gamma \vdash e : \tau$ *and* $\Gamma \vdash \rho$ *and* $\rho, e \Downarrow_{\mathsf{ref}} v$ *then* $\vdash v : \tau$.

Lemma 2 (Determinism of $\Downarrow_{\mathsf{ref}}$). *If* $\rho, e \Downarrow_{\mathsf{ref}} v$ *and* $\rho, e \Downarrow_{\mathsf{ref}} v'$ *then* $v = v'$.

The language used in our examples and implementation can be easily desugared into the reference language just described.

3.2 Characterizing program slices

In an imperative language, a program can often be sliced by simply deleting some of its statements. This approach is unsuitable for functional languages, which tend to be expression-based. We therefore introduce a new expression constructor $\Box$ called *hole*, which inhabits every type, and use holes to represent deleted sub-terms of an expression or value. For example we can "slice" the expression $\texttt{inl}\ (3 \oplus 4)$ by replacing its left sub-expression by $\Box$, obtaining $\texttt{inl}\ (\Box \oplus 4)$. The additional syntax rules are given at the top of Figure 7.

Introducing $\Box$ into the syntax gives rise to a partial order $\sqsubseteq$ on expressions. This follows immediately from the standard construction of expressions as sets of odd-length paths, where a *path* is an alternating sequence $\langle k_0, n_0, \ldots, k_{i-1}, n_{i-1}, k_i \rangle$ of constructors k and child indices n. In order to represent an expression, a set of such paths must satisfy two properties characteristic of "tree-

$\boxed{\rho, e \Downarrow_{\mathsf{ref}} v}$

$$\frac{}{\rho, x \Downarrow_{\mathsf{ref}} \rho(x)} \qquad \frac{}{\rho, c \Downarrow_{\mathsf{ref}} c} \qquad \frac{\rho, e_1 \Downarrow_{\mathsf{ref}} c_1 \quad \rho, e_2 \Downarrow_{\mathsf{ref}} c_2}{\rho, e_1 \oplus e_2 \Downarrow_{\mathsf{ref}} c_1 \hat{\oplus} c_2}$$

$$\frac{}{\rho, \mathtt{fun}\ f(x).e \Downarrow_{\mathsf{ref}} \langle \rho, \mathtt{fun}\ f(x).e \rangle}$$

$$\frac{\rho, e_2 \Downarrow_{\mathsf{ref}} v_2 \quad \begin{array}{c}\rho, e_1 \Downarrow_{\mathsf{ref}} v_1 \\ \rho'[f \mapsto v_1][x \mapsto v_2], e \Downarrow_{\mathsf{ref}} v\end{array}}{\rho, e_1\ e_2 \Downarrow_{\mathsf{ref}} v}\ v_1 = \langle \rho', \mathtt{fun}\ f(x).e \rangle$$

$$\frac{\rho, e_1 \Downarrow_{\mathsf{ref}} v_1 \quad \rho, e_2 \Downarrow_{\mathsf{ref}} v_2}{\rho, (e_1, e_2) \Downarrow_{\mathsf{ref}} (v_1, v_2)} \qquad \frac{\rho, e \Downarrow_{\mathsf{ref}} (v_1, v_2)}{\rho, \mathtt{fst}\ e \Downarrow_{\mathsf{ref}} v_1}$$

$$\frac{\rho, e \Downarrow_{\mathsf{ref}} (v_1, v_2)}{\rho, \mathtt{snd}\ e \Downarrow_{\mathsf{ref}} v_2} \qquad \frac{\rho, e \Downarrow_{\mathsf{ref}} v}{\rho, \mathtt{inl}\ e \Downarrow_{\mathsf{ref}} \mathtt{inl}\ v} \qquad \frac{\rho, e \Downarrow_{\mathsf{ref}} v}{\rho, \mathtt{inr}\ e \Downarrow_{\mathsf{ref}} \mathtt{inr}\ v}$$

$$\frac{\rho, e \Downarrow_{\mathsf{ref}} \mathtt{inl}\ v_1 \quad \rho[x_1 \mapsto v_1], e_1 \Downarrow_{\mathsf{ref}} v}{\rho, \mathtt{case}\ e\ \mathtt{of}\ \{\mathtt{inl}(x_1).e_1; \mathtt{inr}(x_2).e_2\} \Downarrow_{\mathsf{ref}} v}$$

$$\frac{\rho, e \Downarrow_{\mathsf{ref}} \mathtt{inr}\ v_2 \quad \rho[x_2 \mapsto v_2], e_2 \Downarrow_{\mathsf{ref}} v}{\rho, \mathtt{case}\ e\ \mathtt{of}\ \{\mathtt{inl}(x_1).e_1; \mathtt{inr}(x_2).e_2\} \Downarrow_{\mathsf{ref}} v}$$

$$\frac{\rho, e \Downarrow_{\mathsf{ref}} v}{\rho, \mathtt{roll}\ e \Downarrow_{\mathsf{ref}} \mathtt{roll}\ v} \qquad \frac{\rho, e \Downarrow_{\mathsf{ref}} \mathtt{roll}\ v}{\rho, \mathtt{unroll}\ e \Downarrow_{\mathsf{ref}} v}$$

Figure 5. Reference language: call-by-value evaluation

$\boxed{\Gamma \vdash e : \tau}$

$$\frac{}{\Gamma \vdash () : 1} \qquad \frac{}{\Gamma \vdash x : \tau}\ x : \tau \in \Gamma \qquad \frac{}{\Gamma \vdash c : b}\ c : b \in \Sigma$$

$$\frac{\Gamma \vdash e_1 : b_1 \quad \Gamma \vdash e_2 : b_2}{\Gamma \vdash e_1 \oplus e_2 : \tau}\ \oplus : b_1 \times b_2 \to \tau \in \Sigma$$

$$\frac{\Gamma, f : \tau_1 \to \tau_2, x : \tau_1 \vdash e : \tau_2}{\Gamma \vdash \mathtt{fun}\ f(x).e : \tau_1 \to \tau_2} \qquad \frac{\Gamma \vdash e_1 : \tau_1 \to \tau_2 \quad \Gamma \vdash e_2 : \tau_1}{\Gamma \vdash e_1\ e_2 : \tau_2}$$

$$\frac{\Gamma \vdash e_1 : \tau_1 \quad \Gamma \vdash e_2 : \tau_2}{\Gamma \vdash (e_1, e_2) : \tau_1 \times \tau_2} \qquad \frac{\Gamma \vdash e : \tau_1 \times \tau_2}{\Gamma \vdash \mathtt{fst}\ e : \tau_1}$$

$$\frac{\Gamma \vdash e : \tau_1 \times \tau_2}{\Gamma \vdash \mathtt{snd}\ e : \tau_1} \qquad \frac{\Gamma \vdash e : \tau_1}{\Gamma \vdash \mathtt{inl}\ e : \tau_1 + \tau_2} \qquad \frac{\Gamma \vdash e : \tau_2}{\Gamma \vdash \mathtt{inr}\ e : \tau_1 + \tau_2}$$

$$\frac{\Gamma \vdash e : \tau_1 + \tau_2 \quad \Gamma, x_1 : \tau_1 \vdash e_1 : \tau \quad \Gamma, x_2 : \tau_2 \vdash e_2 : \tau}{\Gamma \vdash \mathtt{case}\ e\ \mathtt{of}\ \{\mathtt{inl}(x_1).e_1; \mathtt{inr}(x_2).e_2\} : \tau}$$

$$\frac{\Gamma \vdash e : \mu\alpha.\tau}{\Gamma \vdash \mathtt{unroll}\ e : \tau[\mu\alpha.\tau/\alpha]} \qquad \frac{\Gamma \vdash e : \tau[\mu\alpha.\tau/\alpha]}{\Gamma \vdash \mathtt{roll}\ e : \mu\alpha.\tau}$$

$\boxed{\Gamma \vdash \rho}$

$$\frac{}{\bullet \vdash \bullet} \qquad \frac{\Gamma \vdash \rho \quad \vdash v : \tau}{\Gamma, x : \tau \vdash \rho[x \mapsto v]}$$

$\boxed{\vdash v : \tau}$

$$\frac{}{\vdash () : 1} \qquad \frac{}{\vdash c : b}\ c : b \in \Sigma$$

$$\frac{\Gamma \vdash \rho \quad \Gamma, f : \tau_1 \to \tau_2, x : \tau_1 \vdash e : \tau_2}{\vdash \langle \rho, \mathtt{fun}\ f(x).e \rangle : \tau_1 \to \tau_2} \qquad \frac{\vdash v_1 : \tau_1 \quad \vdash v_2 : \tau_2}{\vdash (v_1, v_2) : \tau_1 \times \tau_2}$$

$$\frac{\vdash v : \tau_1}{\vdash \mathtt{inl}\ v : \tau_1 + \tau_2} \qquad \frac{\vdash v : \tau_2}{\vdash \mathtt{inr}\ v : \tau_1 + \tau_2} \qquad \frac{\Gamma \vdash v : \tau[\mu\alpha.\tau/\alpha]}{\Gamma \vdash \mathtt{roll}\ v : \mu\alpha.\tau}$$

Figure 6. Reference language: typing judgments

hood": prefix-closure, and deterministic extension. Prefix-closure means that if a path is in the set, then each of its prefixes is in the set; deterministic extension means that all paths agree about the value of k_i for a given position in the tree.

The partial order $\sqsubseteq$ is simply the inclusion order on these sets. For example, that $\mathtt{inl}\ (3 \oplus \square)$ and $\mathtt{inl}\ (3 \oplus 4)$ are related by $\sqsubseteq$ comes about because the sets of paths that comprise the two expressions are similarly related:

$$\underbrace{\overbrace{\begin{array}{l}\langle \mathtt{inl} \rangle, \\ \langle \mathtt{inl}, \mathbf{0}, \oplus \rangle, \\ \langle \mathtt{inl}, \mathbf{0}, \oplus, \mathbf{0}, 3 \rangle\end{array}}}_{\mathtt{inl}\ (3 \oplus \square)} \sqsubseteq \underbrace{\overbrace{\begin{array}{l}\langle \mathtt{inl} \rangle, \\ \langle \mathtt{inl}, \mathbf{0}, \oplus \rangle, \\ \langle \mathtt{inl}, \mathbf{0}, \oplus, \mathbf{0}, 3 \rangle, \\ \langle \mathtt{inl}, \mathbf{0}, \oplus, \mathbf{1}, 4 \rangle\end{array}}}_{\mathtt{inl}\ (3 \oplus 4)}$$

(The child indices are shown in bold to avoid ambiguity.)

Clearly, an expression smaller than a given expression e is a variant of e where some paths have been truncated in a way which preserves prefix-closure. It is e with some sub-expressions "missing", with the absence of those sub-expressions indicated in the conventional syntax by the presence of a $\square$. It is natural to talk about such a truncated expression as a *prefix* of e, and so we denote the set of such expressions by $\mathsf{Prefix}(e)$.

Definition 1 (Prefix of e). $\mathsf{Prefix}(e) = \{e' \mid e' \sqsubseteq e\}$

What is more, the set $\mathsf{Prefix}(e)$ forms a finite, distributive lattice with meet and join denoted by $\sqcap$ and $\sqcup$. To see why, consider two prefixes e_1 and e_2 of e. We can take their meet $e_1 \sqcap e_2$ by taking the intersection of the sets of paths that comprise e_1 and e_2; intersection preserves prefix-closure and deterministic extension, and so yields another prefix of e which is the greatest lower bound of e_1 and e_2.

Dually, we can take the join $e_1 \sqcup e_2$ by taking the union of the sets of paths comprising e_1 and e_2. Set union will not in general preserve deterministic extension (consider taking the union of $\mathtt{inl}\ 3 \oplus 4$ and $\mathtt{inl}\ 3 \oplus 5$, for example) but it does so whenever the two expressions have compatible structure. Here, e_1 and e_2 do have compatible structure because both are prefixes of e. And so union also yields a prefix of e, in this case the least upper bound of e_1 and e_2, as illustrated by the following example:

$$\underbrace{\overbrace{\begin{array}{l}\langle \mathtt{inl} \rangle, \\ \langle \mathtt{inl}, \mathbf{0}, \oplus \rangle, \\ \langle \mathtt{inl}, \mathbf{0}, \oplus, \mathbf{0}, 3 \rangle\end{array}}}_{\mathtt{inl}\ (3 \oplus \square)} \sqcup \underbrace{\overbrace{\begin{array}{l}\langle \mathtt{inl} \rangle, \\ \langle \mathtt{inl}, \mathbf{0}, \oplus \rangle, \\ \langle \mathtt{inl}, \mathbf{0}, \oplus, \mathbf{1}, 4 \rangle\end{array}}}_{\mathtt{inl}\ (\square \oplus 4)} = \underbrace{\overbrace{\begin{array}{l}\langle \mathtt{inl} \rangle, \\ \langle \mathtt{inl}, \mathbf{0}, \oplus \rangle, \\ \langle \mathtt{inl}, \mathbf{0}, \oplus, \mathbf{0}, 3 \rangle, \\ \langle \mathtt{inl}, \mathbf{0}, \oplus, \mathbf{1}, 4 \rangle\end{array}}}_{\mathtt{inl}\ (3 \oplus 4)}$$

Finally, we note that the greatest element of $\mathsf{Prefix}(e)$ is e itself, and the least element is $\square$.

3.3 Slicing with respect to partial output

We now have a way of representing programs with missing parts: we simply replace the parts we want to delete with appropriately typed holes. What we need next is a way of saying whether the missing bits "matter" or not to some part of the output. We will do this by enriching the base language with rules that allow programs with holes in to be executed.

The intuition we want is that if we encounter a hole during evaluation, then we had better be computing a part of the output that was also unneeded. In other words, $\Downarrow_{\mathsf{ref}}$ is free to consume a hole, but only in order to produce a hole. We capture this informal notion by extending the $\Downarrow_{\mathsf{ref}}$ rules with the additional rules for propagating holes given in Figure 7. Hole itself evaluates to $\square$, and moreover for every type constructor, there are variants of the elimination rules which produce a hole whenever an immediate sub-computation produces a hole. From now on, by $\Downarrow_{\mathsf{ref}}$ we shall mean the extended version of the rules.

$$\begin{array}{lll} \text{Expressions} & e ::= & \ldots \mid \Box \\ \text{Values} & v ::= & \ldots \mid \Box \end{array}$$

$\boxed{\Gamma \vdash e : \tau}$

$$\ldots \qquad \frac{}{\Gamma \vdash \Box : \tau}$$

$\boxed{\vdash v : \tau}$

$$\ldots \qquad \frac{}{\vdash \Box : \tau}$$

$\boxed{\rho, e \Downarrow_{\mathsf{ref}} v}$

$$\ldots \qquad \frac{}{\rho, \Box \Downarrow_{\mathsf{ref}} \Box} \qquad \frac{\rho, e_1 \Downarrow_{\mathsf{ref}} \Box}{\rho, e_1 \oplus e_2 \Downarrow_{\mathsf{ref}} \Box}$$

$$\frac{\rho, e_1 \Downarrow_{\mathsf{ref}} c_1 \qquad \rho, e_2 \Downarrow_{\mathsf{ref}} \Box}{\rho, e_1 \oplus e_2 \Downarrow_{\mathsf{ref}} \Box} \qquad \frac{\rho, e_1 \Downarrow_{\mathsf{ref}} \Box}{\rho, e_1\ e_2 \Downarrow_{\mathsf{ref}} \Box} \qquad \frac{\rho, e \Downarrow_{\mathsf{ref}} \Box}{\rho, \mathtt{fst}\ e \Downarrow_{\mathsf{ref}} \Box}$$

$$\frac{\rho, e \Downarrow_{\mathsf{ref}} \Box}{\rho, \mathtt{snd}\ e \Downarrow_{\mathsf{ref}} \Box} \qquad \frac{\rho, e \Downarrow_{\mathsf{ref}} \Box}{\rho, \mathtt{case}\ e\ \mathtt{of}\ \{\mathtt{inl}(x_1).e_1; \mathtt{inr}(x_2).e_2\} \Downarrow_{\mathsf{ref}} \Box}$$

$$\frac{\rho, e \Downarrow_{\mathsf{ref}} \Box}{\rho, \mathtt{unroll}\ e \Downarrow_{\mathsf{ref}} \Box}$$

Figure 7. Additional rules for partial expressions

Since evaluation can produce partial values, clearly environments may now map variables to partial values. This gives rise to a partial order on environments. Specifically, we overload $\sqsubseteq$ so that $\rho \sqsubseteq \rho'$ iff there exists $\mathrm{dom}(\rho) = \mathrm{dom}(\rho')$ and $\forall x \in \mathrm{dom}(\rho).\rho(x) \sqsubseteq \rho'(x)$. For any Γ, we will write $\Box_\Gamma$ for the least partial environment for Γ, viz. the ρ such that $\rho(x) = \Box$ for every $x \in \mathrm{dom}(\Gamma)$. Again, the set $\mathsf{Prefix}(\rho)$ forms a finite distributive lattice where the join $\rho \sqcup \rho'$ is the partial environment $\{x \mapsto \rho(x) \sqcup \rho'(x) \mid x \in \mathrm{dom}(\rho)\}$, and analogously for meet.

It follows from the inductive definition of environments that environment extension with respect to a variable x is a lattice isomorphism. Suppose $\Gamma \vdash \rho$ and $\vdash v : \tau$. Then for any x, the bijection $-[x \mapsto -]$ from $\mathsf{Prefix}(\rho) \times \mathsf{Prefix}(v)$ to $\mathsf{Prefix}(\rho[x \mapsto v])$ satisfies:

$$(\rho' \sqcap \rho'')[x \mapsto u \sqcap u'] = \rho'[x \mapsto u'] \sqcap \rho''[x \mapsto u''] \qquad (1)$$

and similarly for joins.

Now suppose $\rho, e \Downarrow_{\mathsf{ref}} v$ and some partial output $u \sqsubseteq v$. We are now able to say what it is for a partial program $(\rho', e') \sqsubseteq (\rho, e)$ to be a "correct" slice of (ρ, e) for u. The idea is that if running (ρ', e') produces a value u' at least as big as u, then (ρ', e') is "correct" in the sense that it is at least capable of computing the part of the output we are interested in. We say that (ρ', e') is a *slice of* (ρ, e) *for* u.

Definition 2 (Slice of ρ, e for u)**.** Suppose $\rho, e \Downarrow_{\mathsf{ref}} v$ and $u \sqsubseteq v$. Then any $(\rho', e') \sqsubseteq (\rho, e)$ is a *slice of* (ρ, e) *for* u if $\rho', e' \Downarrow_{\mathsf{ref}} u'$ with $u' \sqsupseteq u$.

This makes precise our intuition above: a slice for partial output u is free to evaluate holes as long as the resulting holes in the output are subsumed by those already specified by u, the slicing criterion.

3.4 Existence of least slices

We have defined what it is to be a slice for some partial output u. Now let us turn to the question of whether there is a unique minimal slice for u. We shall see that introducing holes into the syntax, and then extending evaluation with hole-propagation rules, induces a family of Galois connections between partial programs and partial values and that this guarantees the existence of least slices.

Suppose a terminating computation $\rho, e \Downarrow_{\mathsf{ref}} v$. Evaluation has several important properties if we restrict the domain of evaluation to just the prefixes of (ρ, e), which we will write as $\mathsf{eval}_{\rho,e}$. The first is that $\mathsf{eval}_{\rho,e}$ is total: the presence of a hole cannot cause a computation to get stuck, but only to produce an output with a hole in it. Second, $\mathsf{eval}_{\rho,e}$ is monotonic. Third, $\mathsf{eval}_{\rho,e}$ preserves meets. Since this third property implies the second, we just state the following.

Theorem 1 ($\mathsf{eval}_{\rho,e}$ is a meet-preserving function from $\mathsf{Prefix}(\rho, e)$ to $\mathsf{Prefix}(v)$)**.** *Suppose* $\rho, e \Downarrow_{\mathsf{ref}} v$. *Then:*

1. *If* $(\rho', e') \sqsubseteq (\rho, e)$ *then* $\mathsf{eval}_{\rho,e}(\rho', e')$ *is defined: there exists* u *such that* $\rho', e' \Downarrow_{\mathsf{ref}} u$.
2. $\mathsf{eval}_{\rho,e}(\rho, e) = v$.
3. *If* $(\rho', e') \sqsubseteq (\rho, e)$ *and* $(\rho'', e'') \sqsubseteq (\rho, e)$ *then* $\mathsf{eval}_{\rho,e}(\rho' \sqcap \rho'', e' \sqcap e'') = \mathsf{eval}_{\rho,e}(\rho', e') \sqcap \mathsf{eval}_{\rho,e}(\rho'', e'')$.

Technically, $\mathsf{eval}_{\rho,e}$ is a *meet-semilattice homomorphism*. Using this property for the cases that involve environment extension, we can now prove Theorem 1:

Proof. Part (2) of Theorem 1 is immediate from the definition of $\Downarrow_{\mathsf{ref}}$. For parts (1) and (3), we proceed by induction on the derivation of $\rho, e \Downarrow_{\mathsf{ref}} v$, using the hole propagation rules in Figure 7 whenever the evaluation would otherwise get stuck, and Equation 1 for the binder cases. □

Finally we are ready to show that a least slice for a given v exists and give an explicit characterisation of it by considering a basic property of meet-semilattice homomorphisms. Every meet-preserving mapping $f_* : A \to B$ is the *upper adjoint* of a unique Galois connection. The *lower adjoint* of f_*, sometimes (confusingly) written $f^* : B \to A$, which preserves joins, inverts f_* in the following minimising way: for any output b of f_*, the lower adjoint yields the smallest input a such that $f_*(a) \sqsupseteq b$. Extensionally, the lower adjoint satisfies $f^*(b) = \bigsqcap\{a \in A \mid f_*(a) \sqsupseteq b\}$.

Corollary 1 (Existence of least slices)**.** *Suppose* $\rho, e \Downarrow_{\mathsf{ref}} v$. *Then there exists a function* $\mathsf{uneval}_{\rho,e}$ *from* $\mathsf{Prefix}(v)$ *to* $\mathsf{Prefix}(\rho, e)$ *satisfying:*

$$\mathsf{uneval}_{\rho,e}(u) = \bigsqcap\{(\rho', e') \in \mathsf{Prefix}(\rho, e) \mid \mathsf{eval}_{\rho,e}(\rho', e') \sqsupseteq u\}$$

Proof. Immediate from Theorem 1. □

So for any terminating computation $\rho, e \Downarrow_{\mathsf{ref}} v$, there is a total function, which we call $\mathsf{uneval}_{\rho,e}$, from partial values to partial programs which, for any $u \sqsubseteq v$, yields the least slice of (ρ, e) for u. Extensionally, $\mathsf{uneval}_{\rho,e}(u)$ is the meet of all the slices of (ρ, e) for u. This smallest slice is, in the parlance of the slicing literature, a *dynamic* slice: it pertains to a single execution, namely $\rho, e \Downarrow_{\mathsf{ref}} v$.

But the fact that $\mathsf{uneval}_{\rho,e}$ is uniquely determined by $\mathsf{eval}_{\rho,e}$ does not give us an efficient algorithm for computing it. We will turn to this in the next section.

3.5 Differential slices

As discussed in Section 2, the difference between two slices can be useful for diagnosing the cause of a problem. To focus on a partial subterm of a partial value, we can use a pair $\Delta(u, v)$ where $u \sqsubseteq v$. Here, the inner part u shows the context and the outer part v shows the additional part of the value that we are more interested in. Given an algorithm for computing least slices $\mathsf{uneval}_{\rho,e}$, we can then simply define the differential slice as $\mathsf{diff}_{\rho,e}(\Delta(u, v)) = \Delta(\mathsf{uneval}_{\rho,e}(u), \mathsf{uneval}_{\rho,e}(v))$. Thus, differential slicing is straightforward once we have a slicing algorithm.

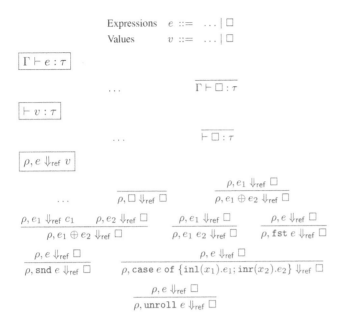

Traces $T ::= \square \mid x \mid c \mid T_1 \oplus_{c_1,c_2} T_2 \mid (T_1, T_2)$
$\mid \texttt{fst}\ T \mid \texttt{snd}\ T \mid \texttt{inl}\ T \mid \texttt{inr}\ T$
$\mid \texttt{case}\ T\ \texttt{of}\ \{\texttt{inl}(x_1).T_1; \texttt{inr}(x_2).e_2\}$
$\mid \texttt{case}\ T\ \texttt{of}\ \{\texttt{inl}(x_1).e_1; \texttt{inr}(x_2).T_2\}$
$\mid \texttt{fun}\ f(x).e \mid T_1\ T_2 \triangleright f(x).T$
$\mid \texttt{roll}\ T \mid \texttt{unroll}\ T$

Figure 8. Syntax of traces

4. Program Slicing as Backwards Execution

In Section 3, we showed that for an arbitrary prefix v of the output of a computation, there is a least dynamic program slice. To calculate the least slice for v, we could in principle consider every prefix of the program, and take the meet of those large enough to compute v. Clearly such an approach would not lead to a practical algorithm. Instead what we would like to do is somehow infer backwards from unneeded parts of the output to unneeded parts of the input. To this end, we record, as a trace, certain information during execution to allow the computation to be "rewound" by an *unevaluation* algorithm that given slicing criterion (a partial output) reconstructs a the least partial program that evaluates to a result consistent with that criterion.

4.1 Abstract syntax

Figure 8 gives the abstract syntax of traces, which closely mirrors that of expressions. We will explain the trace forms in more detail when giving the tracing semantics in Section 4.2 below. Traces also include a hole form $\square$; as with expressions, this induces a partial order on traces, which we again denote by $\sqsubseteq$, and a lattice $\mathsf{Prefix}(T)$ of prefixes of a given trace T. The typing rules for traces are given in Figure 9; the judgment $\Gamma \vdash T : \tau$ states that T has type τ in Γ. When we are not concerned with τ but only with Γ, we sometimes write this as $\Gamma \vdash T$. The only potentially surprising typing rule is for application traces, where T may be typed in an arbitrary Γ' extended with bindings for f and x. Note that if $\Gamma \vdash T : \tau$ and $S \sqsubseteq T$, then $\Gamma \vdash S : \tau$.

The Slicer implemention associates every trace node with a value, as shown in our examples earlier, but this is not necessary in order to compute slices, so we omit the value annotations from the formalism.

4.2 Tracing semantics

We now define a tracing semantics for the reference language presented earlier. The rules, given in Figure 10, are identical to those for $\Downarrow_{\mathsf{ref}}$, except that they construct a trace as well as a value. Tracing evaluation for an expression $\Gamma \vdash e : \tau$ in environment ρ for Γ, written $\rho, e \Downarrow v, T$, yields both a value $v : \tau$ and a trace $\Gamma \vdash T : \tau$ describing how the value was computed.

Before explaining what the trace records, we dispense with a few preliminary properties. Where the proofs are straightforward inductions or closely analogous to those for the reference language they are omitted. First, tracing evaluation is deterministic:

Lemma 3 (Determinism of $\Downarrow$). *If $\rho, e \Downarrow v, T$ and $\rho, e \Downarrow v', T'$ then $v = v'$ and $T = T'$.*

The tracing semantics and the reference semantics agree on values:

Theorem 2. $\rho, e \Downarrow_{\mathsf{ref}} v \iff \exists T. \rho, e \Downarrow v, T$

Tracing evaluation is both type-preserving and, when domain-restricted to the prefixes of a terminating computation (ρ, e), a meet- and join-preserving function. For the latter property, we do not state a theorem since we will use the reference semantics where possible in what follows.

$\boxed{\Gamma \vdash T : \tau}$

$$\frac{}{\Gamma \vdash \square : \tau} \qquad \frac{}{\Gamma \vdash () : 1} \qquad \frac{}{\Gamma \vdash x : \tau}\ x : \tau \in \Gamma$$

$$\frac{}{\Gamma \vdash c : b}\ c : b \in \Sigma$$

$$\frac{\vdash c_1 : b_1 \quad \begin{array}{c}\Gamma \vdash T_1 : b_1 \\ \Gamma \vdash T_2 : b_2\end{array} \quad \vdash c_2 : b_2}{\Gamma \vdash T_1 \oplus_{c_1,c_2} T_2 : \tau}\ \oplus : b_1 \times b_2 \to \tau \in \Sigma$$

$$\frac{\Gamma, f : \tau_1 \to \tau_2, x : \tau_1 \vdash e : \tau_2}{\Gamma \vdash \texttt{fun}\ f(x).e : \tau_1 \to \tau_2}$$

$$\frac{\Gamma \vdash T_2 : \tau_1 \quad \begin{array}{c}\Gamma \vdash T_1 : \tau_1 \to \tau_2 \\ \Gamma', f : \tau_1 \to \tau_2, x : \tau_1 \vdash T : \tau_2\end{array}}{\Gamma \vdash T_1\ T_2 \triangleright f(x).T : \tau_2}$$

$$\frac{\Gamma \vdash T_1 : \tau_1 \quad \Gamma \vdash T_2 : \tau_2}{\Gamma \vdash (T_1, T_2) : \tau_1 \times \tau_2} \qquad \frac{\Gamma \vdash T : \tau_1 \times \tau_2}{\Gamma \vdash \texttt{fst}\ T : \tau_1}$$

$$\frac{\Gamma \vdash T : \tau_1 \times \tau_2}{\Gamma \vdash \texttt{snd}\ T : \tau_2} \qquad \frac{\Gamma \vdash T : \tau_1}{\Gamma \vdash \texttt{inl}\ T : \tau_1 + \tau_2} \qquad \frac{\Gamma \vdash T : \tau_2}{\Gamma \vdash \texttt{inr}\ T : \tau_1 + \tau_2}$$

$$\frac{\Gamma \vdash T : \tau_1 + \tau_2 \quad \Gamma, x_1 : \tau_1 \vdash T_1 : \tau \quad \Gamma, x_2 : \tau_2 \vdash e_2 : \tau}{\Gamma \vdash \texttt{case}\ T\ \texttt{of}\ \{\texttt{inl}(x_1).T_1; \texttt{inr}(x_2).e_2\} : \tau}$$

$$\frac{\Gamma \vdash T : \tau_1 + \tau_2 \quad \Gamma, x_1 : \tau_1 \vdash e_1 : \tau \quad \Gamma, x_2 : \tau_2 \vdash T_2 : \tau}{\Gamma \vdash \texttt{case}\ T\ \texttt{of}\ \{\texttt{inl}(x_1).e_1; \texttt{inr}(x_2).T_2\} : \tau}$$

$$\frac{\Gamma \vdash T : \mu\alpha.\tau}{\Gamma \vdash \texttt{unroll}\ T : \tau[\mu\alpha.\tau/\alpha]} \qquad \frac{\Gamma \vdash T : \tau[\mu\alpha.\tau/\alpha]}{\Gamma \vdash \texttt{roll}\ T : \mu\alpha.\tau}$$

Figure 9. Typing rules for traces

Lemma 4 (Type preservation for $\Downarrow$). *If $\Gamma \vdash e : \tau$ and $\Gamma \vdash \rho$ with $\rho, e \Downarrow v, T$, then $\vdash v : \tau$ and $\Gamma \vdash T : \tau$.*

With these properties in mind, we can explain the tracing evaluation judgment. The idea is that tracing evaluation equips every value with a trace which describes how it was computed, where the trace takes the form of an unrolling of the original expression, akin to inlining the definition of functions into every call site.

Least elements are preserved, so the trace of the expression $\square$ is the trace $\square$. The trace of a variable x is the corresponding trace form x; in general the trace of $\Gamma \vdash e : \tau$ is not closed but is instead also typed in Γ. The traces of other nullary expressions are just the corresponding nullary trace form. For non-nullary forms, such as projections, pairs, and `case` expressions, the general pattern is to produce a trace which looks like the original expression except that any executed sub-expressions have been inflated into their traces. For example a trace of the form $\texttt{case}\ T\ \texttt{of}\ \{\texttt{inl}(x_1).T_1; \texttt{inr}(x_2).e_2\}$ records the scrutinee and the taken branch unrolled into their respective executions. The non-taken branch e_2 is kept in the trace to be consistent with our notion of a trace as an unrolled expression.

Primitive operations are special because they are black boxes: we have no information about how their outputs relate to their inputs. For subsequent slicing, we therefore record not only operand traces, but also the values of the operands. This allows the unevaluation algorithm to proceed through a primitive operation into the operand computations. Alternative approaches to primitives are discussed in Section 4.3 below.

The main point at which traces diverge from expressions is with function calls. An application trace $T_1\ T_2 \triangleright f(x).T$ records not only the evaluation T_1 and T_2 of the function and argument, but also the evaluation T of the function body, which may contain free occurrences of f and x. The notation $f(x).T$ denotes that f and x are re-bound at this point in the trace.

$\boxed{\rho, e \Downarrow v, T}$

$$\frac{}{\rho, \square \Downarrow \square, \square} \qquad \frac{}{\rho, x \Downarrow \rho(x), x} \qquad \frac{}{\rho, c \Downarrow c, c}$$

$$\frac{\rho, e_1 \Downarrow c_1, T_1 \qquad \rho, e_2 \Downarrow c_2, T_2}{\rho, e_1 \oplus e_2 \Downarrow c_1 \hat{\oplus} c_2, T_1 \oplus_{c_1,c_2} T_2} \qquad \frac{\rho, e_1 \Downarrow \square, T_1}{\rho, e_1 \oplus e_2 \Downarrow \square, \square}$$

$$\frac{\rho, e_1 \Downarrow c_1, T_1 \qquad \rho, e_2 \Downarrow \square, T_2}{\rho, e_1 \oplus e_2 \Downarrow \square, \square}$$

$$\frac{}{\rho, \mathtt{fun}\ f(x).e \Downarrow \langle \rho, \mathtt{fun}\ f(x).e \rangle, \mathtt{fun}\ f(x).e}$$

$$\frac{\begin{array}{c}\rho, e_1 \Downarrow v_1, T_1 \qquad \rho, e_2 \Downarrow v_2, T_2 \\ \rho'[f \mapsto v_1][x \mapsto v_2], e \Downarrow v, T\end{array}}{\rho, e_1\ e_2 \Downarrow v, T_1\ T_2 \rhd f(x).T}\ v_1 = \langle \rho', \mathtt{fun}\ f(x).e \rangle$$

$$\frac{\rho, e_1 \Downarrow \square, T_1}{\rho, e_1\ e_2 \Downarrow \square, \square} \qquad \frac{\rho, e_1 \Downarrow v_1, T_1 \qquad \rho, e_2 \Downarrow v_2, T_2}{\rho, (e_1, e_2) \Downarrow (v_1, v_2), (T_1, T_2)}$$

$$\frac{\rho, e \Downarrow (v_1, v_2), T}{\rho, \mathtt{fst}\ e \Downarrow v_1, \mathtt{fst}\ T} \qquad \frac{\rho, e \Downarrow \square, T}{\rho, \mathtt{fst}\ e \Downarrow \square, \square} \qquad \frac{\rho, e \Downarrow (v_1, v_2), T}{\rho, \mathtt{snd}\ e \Downarrow v_2, \mathtt{snd}\ T}$$

$$\frac{\rho, e \Downarrow \square, T}{\rho, \mathtt{snd}\ e \Downarrow \square, \square} \qquad \frac{\rho, e \Downarrow v, T}{\rho, \mathtt{inl}\ e \Downarrow \mathtt{inl}\ v, \mathtt{inl}\ T}$$

$$\frac{\rho, e \Downarrow v, T}{\rho, \mathtt{inr}\ e \Downarrow \mathtt{inr}\ v, \mathtt{inr}\ T}$$

$$\frac{\rho, e \Downarrow \mathtt{inl}\ v_1, T \qquad \rho[x_1 \mapsto v_1], e_1 \Downarrow v, T_1}{\begin{array}{c}\rho, \mathtt{case}\ e\ \mathtt{of}\ \{\mathtt{inl}(x_1).e_1; \mathtt{inr}(x_2).e_2\} \Downarrow \\ v, \mathtt{case}\ T\ \mathtt{of}\ \{\mathtt{inl}(x_1).T_1; \mathtt{inr}(x_2).e_2\}\end{array}}$$

$$\frac{\rho, e \Downarrow \mathtt{inr}\ v_2, T \qquad \rho[x_2 \mapsto v_2], e_2 \Downarrow v, T_2}{\begin{array}{c}\rho, \mathtt{case}\ e\ \mathtt{of}\ \{\mathtt{inl}(x_1).e_1; \mathtt{inr}(x_2).e_2\} \Downarrow \\ v, \mathtt{case}\ T\ \mathtt{of}\ \{\mathtt{inl}(x_1).e_1; \mathtt{inr}(x_2).T_2\}\end{array}}$$

$$\frac{\rho, e \Downarrow \square, T}{\rho, \mathtt{case}\ e\ \mathtt{of}\ \{\mathtt{inl}(x_1).e_1; \mathtt{inr}(x_2).e_2\} \Downarrow \square, \square}$$

$$\frac{\rho, e \Downarrow v, T}{\rho, \mathtt{roll}\ e \Downarrow \mathtt{roll}\ v, \mathtt{roll}\ T} \qquad \frac{\rho, e \Downarrow \mathtt{roll}\ v, T}{\rho, \mathtt{unroll}\ e \Downarrow v, \mathtt{unroll}\ T}$$

$$\frac{\rho, e \Downarrow \square, T}{\rho, \mathtt{unroll}\ e \Downarrow \square, \square}$$

Figure 10. Tracing semantics: call-by-value evaluation

Finally the hole propagation rules, which apply when for example a scrutinee evaluates to $\square$, always produce a hole trace.

4.3 Program slicing via unevaluation

We are now able to define a deterministic program slicing algorithm, called *unevaluation*, which utilises the information in a trace in order to run a computation backwards and recover a prefix of the original program. The definition is given in Figure 11. For a value $\vdash v : \tau$ and trace $\Gamma \vdash T : \tau$, the judgment $v, T \Downarrow^{-1} \rho, e$ states that T can be used to unevaluate v to partial environment $\Gamma \vdash \rho$ and partial expression $\Gamma \vdash e : \tau$. Later we will show that these side-conditions are satisfied whenever T is produced by tracing evaluation to v (Theorem 4 below) or by slicing another trace with respect to v (Theorem 7, Section 5).

A key part of the definition which for convenience is omitted from Figure 11 is as follows. Every time a rule takes the join of two values or environments there is an implicit side-condition requiring that the joins exist. For example, the application rule has a side-condition stating that $v_1 \sqsubseteq v_1'$ and $\langle \rho, \mathtt{fun}\ f(x).e \rangle \sqsubseteq v_1'$ have a least upper bound, plus another side-condition stating that ρ_1 and ρ_2 have a least upper bound.

$\boxed{v, T \Downarrow^{-1} \rho, e \text{ where } \Gamma \vdash T : \tau}$

$$\frac{}{\square, T \Downarrow^{-1} \square_\Gamma, \square} \qquad \frac{}{v, x \Downarrow^{-1} \square_{\Gamma.x \mapsto v}, x}\ v \neq \square$$

$$\frac{}{c, c \Downarrow^{-1} \square_\Gamma, c} \qquad \frac{c_2, T_2 \Downarrow^{-1} \rho_2, e_2 \qquad c_1, T_1 \Downarrow^{-1} \rho_1, e_1}{v, T_1 \oplus_{c_1,c_2} T_2 \Downarrow^{-1} \rho_1 \sqcup \rho_2, e_1 \oplus e_2}\ v \neq \square$$

$$\frac{}{\langle \rho, \mathtt{fun}\ f(x).e \rangle, \mathtt{fun}\ f(x).e' \Downarrow^{-1} \rho, \mathtt{fun}\ f(x).e}$$

$$\frac{\begin{array}{c} v, T \Downarrow^{-1} \rho[f \mapsto v_1][x \mapsto v_2], e \\ v_2, T_2 \Downarrow^{-1} \rho_2, e_2 \qquad v_1 \sqcup \langle \rho, \mathtt{fun}\ f(x).e \rangle, T_1 \Downarrow^{-1} \rho_1, e_1 \end{array}}{v, T_1\ T_2 \rhd f(x).T \Downarrow^{-1} \rho_1 \sqcup \rho_2, e_1\ e_2}\ v \neq \square$$

$$\frac{v_2, T_2 \Downarrow^{-1} \rho_2, e_2 \qquad v_1, T_1 \Downarrow^{-1} \rho_1, e_1}{(v_1, v_2), (T_1, T_2) \Downarrow^{-1} \rho_1 \sqcup \rho_2, (e_1, e_2)}$$

$$\frac{(v_1, \square), T \Downarrow^{-1} \rho, e}{v_1, \mathtt{fst}\ T \Downarrow^{-1} \rho, \mathtt{fst}\ e}\ v_1 \neq \square \qquad \frac{(\square, v_2), T \Downarrow^{-1} \rho, e}{v_2, \mathtt{snd}\ T \Downarrow^{-1} \rho, \mathtt{snd}\ e}\ v_2 \neq \square$$

$$\frac{v, T \Downarrow^{-1} \rho, e}{\mathtt{inl}\ v, \mathtt{inl}\ T \Downarrow^{-1} \rho, \mathtt{inl}\ e} \qquad \frac{v, T \Downarrow^{-1} \rho, e}{\mathtt{inr}\ v, \mathtt{inr}\ T \Downarrow^{-1} \rho, \mathtt{inr}\ e}$$

$$\frac{v, T_1 \Downarrow^{-1} \rho_1[x_1 \mapsto v_1], e_1 \qquad \mathtt{inl}\ v_1, T \Downarrow^{-1} \rho, e}{\begin{array}{c} v, \mathtt{case}\ T\ \mathtt{of}\ \{\mathtt{inl}(x_1).T_1; \mathtt{inr}(x_2).e_2\} \Downarrow^{-1} \\ \rho_1 \sqcup \rho, \mathtt{case}\ e\ \mathtt{of}\ \{\mathtt{inl}(x_1).e_1; \mathtt{inr}(x_2).\square\} \end{array}}\ v \neq \square$$

$$\frac{v, T_2 \Downarrow^{-1} \rho_2[x_2 \mapsto v_2], e_2 \qquad \mathtt{inr}\ v_2, T \Downarrow^{-1} \rho, e}{\begin{array}{c} v, \mathtt{case}\ T\ \mathtt{of}\ \{\mathtt{inl}(x_1).e_1; \mathtt{inr}(x_2).T_2\} \Downarrow^{-1} \\ \rho_2 \sqcup \rho, \mathtt{case}\ e\ \mathtt{of}\ \{\mathtt{inl}(x_1).\square; \mathtt{inr}(x_2).e_2\} \end{array}}\ v \neq \square$$

$$\frac{v, T \Downarrow^{-1} \rho, e}{\mathtt{roll}\ v, \mathtt{roll}\ T \Downarrow^{-1} \rho, \mathtt{roll}\ e}$$

$$\frac{\mathtt{roll}\ v, T \Downarrow^{-1} \rho, e}{v, \mathtt{unroll}\ T \Downarrow^{-1} \rho, \mathtt{unroll}\ e}\ v \neq \square$$

Figure 11. Slicing rules: unevaluation

Unevaluation traverses the trace and folds it back into an expression from which the unneeded bits have been discarded. As with evaluation, least elements are preserved, which simply means that "holes map to holes": unevaluating the value $\square$ produces the expression $\square$ and $\square_\Gamma$, the least environment for Γ. Unevaluating the trace of a variable x with v yields x as an expression and the least environment for Γ mapping x to v, which we write as $\square_{\Gamma.x \mapsto v}$.

The general pattern for non-nullary trace constructors is that the traces of the sub-computations are unevaluated and the resulting partial environments joined. For example we unevaluate a pair trace with a pair (v_1, v_2) by unevaluating the respective components with v_1 and v_2 and joining the results. When binders are involved, the fact that traces are typed allows us to safely extract partial values for the bound variables. For example with a `case` trace for `inl`, the selected branch is unevaluated, producing a partial environment of the form $\rho_1[x \mapsto v_1]$, where v_1 is a partial value which is then injected into the sum type and used to slice the scrutinee.

Unevaluating the application of a primitive operation retrieves the values c_1 and c_2 previously cached in the trace and uses those to unevaluate the arguments. We treat all primitive operations as strict in both operands; it would be straightforward to extend the semantics and slicing rules to accommodate non-strict operations. There are also alternatives to the caching approach. One is to require that every primitive operation provide its own adjoint slicing operation, although this places additional burden on the implementer.

The application rule is the most interesting. For a trace $T_1\ T_2 \rhd f(x).T$, we unevaluate T to obtain a slice e of the original function body, plus an environment $\rho[f \mapsto v_1][x \mapsto v_2]$ where ρ is a slice of the environment in which the closure was captured, and v_1 and v_2 are slices describing the usage of f and x respectively inside T. Since T contains all recursive uses of the function, v_1 (which is a partial closure) captures how much of f was used below this step of the computation. We then join v_1 with $\langle \rho, \texttt{fun}\ f(x).e\rangle$ to merge in information about the usage of the function at the present step, and use it to unevaluate T_1.

4.4 Correctness of tracing evaluation

Unevaluation is deterministic, which is again a straightforward induction, relying on the $v \neq \square$ side-conditions in Figure 11:

Lemma 5 (Determinism of unevaluation). *If $v, T \Downarrow^{-1} \rho, e$ and $v, T \Downarrow^{-1} \rho', e'$ then $(\rho, e) = (\rho', e')$.*

Not every well-typed trace T can be used to unevaluate a value v of the same type. First, T might have some strange (but well-typed) structure that could never be produced by evaluation, so that the required joins do not exist. Second, T might have the right structure, but also some holes, and not enough trace is available to unevaluate v. So a key property of T with respect to v is whether it is able to guide the unevaluation of v. When T has this property, we say that it *explains* v. We can think of the unique (ρ, e) such that $v, T \Downarrow^{-1} \rho, e$ as the "explanation" of v which T produces. Note that there is not a unique trace which explains v.

Definition 3 (T explains v). For any value v and trace T, we say that T *explains* v iff there exist ρ, e such that $v, T \Downarrow^{-1} \rho, e$.

The key correctness property of tracing evaluation is as follows. If evaluating a program yields v and T, then T explains v. Before proving this, we first show that a trace T of v where $v, T \Downarrow^{-1} \rho, e$ gives rise to a monotonic function $\mathsf{tr\text{-}uneval}_{v,T}$ from $\mathsf{Prefix}(v)$ to $\mathsf{Prefix}(\rho, e)$. In fact $\mathsf{tr\text{-}uneval}_{v,T}$ also preserves meets and joins, but monotonicity is sufficient here.

Definition 4 ($\mathsf{tr\text{-}uneval}_{v,T}$). Suppose T explains v. Then define $\mathsf{tr\text{-}uneval}_{v,T}$ to be $\Downarrow^{-1}$ domain-restricted to $\{(u, T) \mid u \sqsubseteq v\}$.

We omit the v subscript when it is clear from the context that the argument to $\mathsf{tr\text{-}uneval}_{v,T}$ is a prefix of v.

Theorem 3 (Monotonicity of explanation).
Suppose T explains v. Then:

1. *For any $u \sqsubseteq v$, $\mathsf{tr\text{-}uneval}_T(u)$ is defined.*
2. *If $u \sqsubseteq u' \sqsubseteq v$ then $\mathsf{tr\text{-}uneval}_T(u) \sqsubseteq \mathsf{tr\text{-}uneval}_T(u')$.*

Proof. See Appendix (supplementary material). □

Monotonicity means that smaller values have smaller explanations. Now we establish that tracing evaluation to v does indeed produce a trace able to explain v. Moreover, unevaluation after evaluation is deflationary: explanation of values are smaller than the programs which compute them. We state and prove these simultaneously. Again, we drop the ρ, e subscript from $\mathsf{tr\text{-}eval}_{\rho,e}$ when it is clear from the context that the argument is a prefix of (ρ, e).

Theorem 4 (Explanations are program prefixes).
Suppose $\rho, e \Downarrow v, T$. Then T explains v. Moreover, for any $(\rho', e') \sqsubseteq (\rho, e)$:

$$\mathsf{tr\text{-}uneval}_T(\mathsf{eval}(\rho', e')) \sqsubseteq (\rho', e')$$

Proof. See Appendix (supplementary material). □

4.5 Correctness of unevaluation

As we sketched in Section 3, the intuition is that a slice, or explanation, is "correct" if it can evaluate to at least the slicing criterion. We now show that we compute slices which have this property.

First we make the following observation. If we are able to unevaluate v with T, then for any trace U of a sub-computation of T which was used to unevaluate an intermediate value $u \neq \square$, we must also have had $U \neq \square$, since otherwise unevaluation would have got stuck. But dually, we can also observe that if U were used to unevaluate an intermediate value $u = \square$, then U was discarded in its entirety. In fact whenever T suffices to unevaluate v, any larger trace is equally good:

Lemma 6. *Suppose S explains v. Then any $T \sqsupseteq S$ explains v. Moreover, for any $u \sqsubseteq v$, we have $\mathsf{tr\text{-}uneval}_S(u) = \mathsf{tr\text{-}uneval}_T(u)$.*

Proof. See Appendix (supplementary material). □

It is also useful to have a lemma which composes some of our previous observations.

Lemma 7. *Suppose $\rho, e \Downarrow v, T$ and $(u, S) \sqsubseteq (v, T)$. If S explains u then $\mathsf{tr\text{-}uneval}_S(u) \sqsubseteq (\rho, e)$.*

Proof.
Suppose $\rho, e \Downarrow v, T$ and $(u, S) \sqsubseteq (v, T)$ where S explains u. Then:

$$\begin{array}{lll} & \mathsf{tr\text{-}uneval}_S(u) & \\ = & \mathsf{tr\text{-}uneval}_T(u) & (T \sqsupseteq S \text{ and Lemma 6}) \\ \sqsubseteq & \mathsf{tr\text{-}uneval}_T(v) & \text{(Theorem 3)} \\ \sqsubseteq & (\rho, e) & \text{(Theorem 4)} \end{array}$$

□

Theorem 5 (Correctness of $\Downarrow^{-1}$). *Suppose $\rho, e \Downarrow v, T$. If $(u, S) \sqsubseteq (v, T)$ and S explains u then $\mathsf{eval}(\mathsf{tr\text{-}uneval}_S(u)) \sqsupseteq u$.*

Proof. See Appendix (supplementary material). □

4.6 Computation of least slices

It is now easy to see that the unevaluation of u is the smallest program slice large enough to evaluate to u. Moreover, any program slice as large as the unevaluation of u is large enough to evaluate to u:

Corollary 2 (Computation of least slices). *Fix a terminating computation $\rho, e \Downarrow v, T$. For any $u \sqsubseteq v$ and $(\rho', e') \sqsubseteq (\rho, e)$ we have:*

$$u \sqsubseteq \mathsf{eval}(\rho', e') \iff \mathsf{tr\text{-}uneval}_T(u) \sqsubseteq (\rho', e')$$

Proof. For the $\Longrightarrow$ direction, suppose $\rho', e' \Downarrow u', S$ with $u' \sqsupseteq u$. Note that $S \sqsubseteq T$ and $u' \sqsubseteq v$ by monotonicity.

$$\begin{array}{rll} \mathsf{tr\text{-}uneval}_T(u) = & \mathsf{tr\text{-}uneval}_S(u) & (S \sqsubseteq T, \text{Lemma 6}) \\ \sqsubseteq & \mathsf{tr\text{-}uneval}_S(u') & \text{(Theorem 3)} \\ \sqsubseteq & (\rho', e') & \text{(Theorem 4)} \end{array}$$

For the $\Longleftarrow$ direction, suppose $\mathsf{tr\text{-}uneval}_{v,T}(u) \sqsubseteq (\rho', e')$. Then:

$$\begin{array}{rll} \mathsf{eval}(\rho', e') \sqsupseteq & \mathsf{eval}(\mathsf{tr\text{-}uneval}_T(u)) & \text{(Theorem 1)} \\ \sqsupseteq & u & \text{(Theorem 5)} \end{array}$$

□

5. Trace Slicing

As discussed in Section 2, program slices omit information that can be essential for understanding how a program computed a result. Indeed, it is common that distinct criteria on the output (for example picking out different elements of a list) yield the same program slice. This is often because the program is computing some aggregate property of its input, such as an average or total order.

In this section, we show how given a trace T which explains v, we can calculate a least prefix S of T which still preserves

$$\boxed{v, T \searrow \rho, S \text{ where } \Gamma \vdash T : \tau}$$

$$\frac{}{\Box, T \searrow \Box_\Gamma, \Box} \qquad \frac{}{v, x \searrow \Box_{\Gamma.x \mapsto v}, x}\ v \neq \Box \qquad \frac{}{c, c \searrow \Box_\Gamma, c}$$

$$\frac{c_2, T_2 \searrow \rho_2, S_2 \qquad c_1, T_1 \searrow \rho_1, S_1}{v, T_1 \oplus_{c_1,c_2} T_2 \searrow \rho_1 \sqcup \rho_2, S_1 \oplus_{c_1,c_2} S_2}\ v \neq \Box$$

$$\frac{}{\langle \rho, \mathtt{fun}\ f(x).e \rangle, \mathtt{fun}\ f(x).e' \searrow \Box_\Gamma, \mathtt{fun}\ f(x).\Box}$$

$$\frac{\begin{array}{c} v, T \searrow \rho[f \mapsto v_1][x \mapsto v_2], S \qquad v, T \Downarrow^{-1} \_, e \\ v_2, T_2 \searrow \rho_2, S_2 \qquad v_1 \sqcup \langle \rho, \mathtt{fun}\ f(x).e \rangle, T_1 \searrow \rho_1, S_1 \end{array}}{v, T_1\ T_2 \rhd f(x).T \searrow \rho_1 \sqcup \rho_2, S_1\ S_2 \rhd f(x).S}\ v \neq \Box$$

$$\frac{v_2, T_2 \searrow \rho_2, S_2 \qquad v_1, T_1 \searrow \rho_1, S_1}{(v_1, v_2), (T_1, T_2) \searrow \rho_1 \sqcup \rho_2, (S_1, S_2)}$$

$$\frac{(v_1, \Box), T \searrow \rho, S}{v_1, \mathtt{fst}\ T \searrow \rho, \mathtt{fst}\ S}\ v_1 \neq \Box \qquad \frac{(\Box, v_2), T \searrow \rho, S}{v_2, \mathtt{snd}\ T \searrow \rho, \mathtt{snd}\ S}\ v_2 \neq \Box$$

$$\frac{v, T \searrow \rho, S}{\mathtt{inl}\ v, \mathtt{inl}\ T \searrow \rho, \mathtt{inl}\ S} \qquad \frac{v, T \searrow \rho, S}{\mathtt{inr}\ v, \mathtt{inr}\ T \searrow \rho, \mathtt{inr}\ S}$$

$$\frac{v, T_1 \searrow \rho_1[x_1 \mapsto v_1], S_1 \qquad \mathtt{inl}\ v_1, T \searrow \rho, S}{\begin{array}{c} v, \mathtt{case}\ T\ \mathtt{of}\ \{\mathtt{inl}(x_1).T_1; \mathtt{inr}(x_2).e_2\} \searrow \\ \rho_1 \sqcup \rho, \mathtt{case}\ S\ \mathtt{of}\ \{\mathtt{inl}(x_1).S_1; \mathtt{inr}(x_2).\Box\} \end{array}}\ v \neq \Box$$

$$\frac{v, T_2 \searrow \rho_2[x_2 \mapsto v_2], S_2 \qquad \mathtt{inr}\ v_2, T \searrow \rho, S}{\begin{array}{c} v, \mathtt{case}\ T\ \mathtt{of}\ \{\mathtt{inl}(x_1).e_1; \mathtt{inr}(x_2).T_2\} \searrow \\ \rho_2 \sqcup \rho, \mathtt{case}\ S\ \mathtt{of}\ \{\mathtt{inl}(x_1).\Box; \mathtt{inr}(x_2).S_2\} \end{array}}\ v \neq \Box$$

$$\frac{v, T \searrow \rho, S}{\mathtt{roll}\ v, \mathtt{roll}\ T \searrow \rho, \mathtt{roll}\ S} \qquad \frac{\mathtt{roll}\ v, T \searrow \rho, S}{v, \mathtt{unroll}\ T \searrow \rho, \mathtt{unroll}\ S}\ v \neq \Box$$

Figure 12. Trace slicing

the "explanatory power" of T with respect to v, in that S retains sufficient information to unevaluate v. Least slices can provide more specific information about which parts of the computation contribute to a part of the output. The missing proofs can be found in the companion technical report [20].

The judgment $v, T \searrow \rho, S$, defined in Figure 12, states that slicing $\Gamma \vdash T : \tau$ with respect to a partial value $\vdash v : \tau$ yields partial environment $\Gamma \vdash \rho$ and partial trace $S \sqsubseteq T$. As with unevaluation, there are side-conditions, which we omit from the figure for convenience, on the rules which take joins, asserting that the joins exist.

The rules are similar in flavour to those for unevaluation, but sub-computations are sliced, rather than unevaluated back to expressions. The significant differences are in the function and application cases. For function traces, we produce the least environment for Γ and the least function trace smaller than T, namely $\mathtt{fun}\ f(x).\Box$. For application traces, we both slice *and* unevaluate T: we slice to obtain a *trace* slice S for the function body, and we unevaluate to obtain *expression* slice e for the function body, so that it can be merged into v_1 and used as the slicing criterion for T_1. Unevaluation of the function body also yields a partial environment, but it is identical to the one obtained by slicing, so we disregard it. (See Theorem 6 below.)

5.1 Correctness of trace slicing

Trace slicing is deterministic. The proof is a straightforward induction, relying on the $v \neq \Box$ side-conditions in Figure 12.

Lemma 8. *Suppose $v, T \searrow \rho, S$ and $v, T \searrow \rho', S'$. Then $\rho = \rho'$ and $S = S'$.*

If T explains v then we can slice T with v. Moreover the partial environment we obtain is the one we would obtain via unevaluation:

Theorem 6. $v, T \Downarrow^{-1} \rho, e \implies \exists S. v, T \searrow \rho, S.$

Proof. Straightforward induction on the derivation of $v, T \Downarrow^{-1} \rho, e$. The only non-trivial case is the application rule, because we invoke the $\Downarrow^{-1}$ judgment from the $\searrow$ judgment. Then we use that $\Downarrow^{-1}$ is deterministic (Lemma 5). □

The key correctness property of trace slicing with v is that it yields a partial trace able to explain v. Moreover, the resulting trace is smaller than the original trace:

Theorem 7 (Correctness of trace slicing)**.** *If $v, T \searrow \rho, S$ then S explains v and $S \sqsubseteq T$.*

The fact that slicing produces a smaller trace means that if we can slice T with v, then it must be that T explains v. By determinism the judgments agree on environments.

Corollary 3. $v, T \searrow \rho, S \implies \exists e. v, T \Downarrow^{-1} \rho, e.$

Proof. Suppose $v, T \searrow \rho, S$. Then S explains v and $S \sqsubseteq T$ by Theorem 7. But if $S \sqsubseteq T$, then T also explains v by Lemma 6. Then there exist ρ', e such that $v, T \Downarrow^{-1} \rho', e$. But then $\rho = \rho'$ by Theorem 6 and the fact that $\searrow$ is deterministic (Lemma 8). □

5.2 Computation of least trace slices

When we slice T with v to obtain S, although S may be strictly smaller than T, by Lemma 6 the program slice obtained by unevaluating v with S is the same as would be obtained by unevaluating with T. But S is the canonical explanation of v compatible with T, in that it is the least prefix of T which still explains v:

Theorem 8 (Trace slicing computes the least trace explaining v)**.** *Suppose $v, T' \searrow \rho, S$, and any $T \sqsubseteq T'$ that explains v. Then $S \sqsubseteq T$.*

6. Implementation and Tracing Strategies

We have completed a prototype implementation, in Haskell, of our slicing techniques, as a tool that we call Slicer. As with most dynamic program slicers or debuggers, Slicer records a trace of the computation, consuming space linear in the number of execution steps of the program. Slicing and debugging information is often so critical that programmers routinely pay the space and time cost of recording the trace. We briefly outline two strategies for controlling tracing costs and present preliminary experimental results.

Our first strategy relies on Haskell's lazy evaluation to construct the trace lazily, which is possible because the trace is not needed until it is sliced. Since slicing can throw away a portion of the trace, laziness may successfully avoid the redundant work of building the parts thrown away. Our second strategy, which we call *delayed* tracing, is a form of controlled laziness. It takes advantage of the fact that, in our design, a trace is essentially a recursive unfolding of an expression. This makes it possible to reduce the size of a trace dramatically by substituting it with the expression that generated it. When the trace is needed during slicing, we rerun the expression to generate the full trace, but after slicing, retain only the slice. Delaying thus pushes the cost of tracing from a run to slicing, and can thus be helpful in the cases where slices are small or computed interactively on demand. For comparison we also implemented a third strategy, *eager*. The three strategies are summarised below:

- The *eager* strategy involves adding strictness annotations to the datatype for traces, along with *seqs* used for implementing our eager evaluation semantics in Haskell, so that the trace is completely constructed before we begin slicing it.

Test Eval(s) Slice/Trace	Strategy	Trace(s)	Slice(s)	Total (s)
`sort` 0.07 447K/500K	eager lazy delay	0.17 0.12 0.01	0.48 0.21 0.38	0.65 0.33 0.39
`rbtree` 0.29 1.55M/1.61M	eager lazy delay	0.88 0.66 <0.01	2.41 1.31 2.48	3.29 1.97 2.49
`rbtree-len` 0.29 9K/1.61M	eager lazy delay	0.9 0.67 <0.01	0.02 0.04 0.01	0.92 0.71 0.01
`vec-sum` 0.13 20/220K	eager lazy delay	0.16 0.13 <0.01	<0.01 <0.01 <0.01	0.16 0.13 <0.01

Table 1. Comparison of eager, lazy and delayed tracing strategies. Times are in seconds. Eval is the time to evaluate without tracing, and Trace and Slice are the additional time needed for tracing and slicing respectively. Slice/Trace is the ratio of number of nodes in the trace slice to the full trace.

- The *lazy* strategy uses Haskell's default lazy evaluation order for the traces. This still has a runtime cost, because thunks are constructed that capture intermediate values that may ultimately be needed to reconstruct parts of the trace.
- The *delayed* strategy uses a new trace form called a *delay* to record the current environment and expression instead of the full trace. We insert delays during evaluation at function calls when a given recursion depth is exceeded. When we encounter a delay trace during during slicing, we run the expression with tracing enabled, which may lead to a trace with additional delays. In our prototype implementation, we make no attempt to avoid multiple evaluations of an expression. We use an initial depth bound of 10, which doubles during re-tracing so that we collect more detailed traces as we get closer to our goal.

Table 1 shows preliminary timing measurements for eager, lazy and delayed tracing. The programs involved are `sort`, which mergesorts a list, `rbtree`, which builds a red-black tree from a list, `rbtree-len`, which builds a pair of a red-black tree and the length of a list, and `vec-sum`, which does a vector addition of two lists. The list lengths are 1000 for `sort`, `rbtree`, and `rbtree-len` and 10000 for `vec-sum`. For `vec-sum` and `sort`, we slice the first element of the result list, for `rbtree` we slice the root value, and for `rbtree-len` we slice the second (length) component of the result. The trace slices for `vec-sum` and `rbtree-length` are small compared to the full trace, while for the other two examples, the trace slice is almost as large as the original trace. We used GHC 6.12.1 with optimization level -O2 running on a MacBook Pro (2.8 GHz Intel Core Duo, 4GB RAM).

The timing results show that the lazy strategy successfully reduces tracing costs compared to eager by around 30%. Slicing costs are also reduced, though, so the total overhead of tracing and slicing is almost 50% less than the eager strategy. Delayed tracing almost eliminates initial tracing costs, and when the resulting slice is small, the slicing cost is also negligible. When a slice is close to the full trace, however, delaying is more expensive than lazy slicing, because expressions may be re-evaluated multiple times in our prototype implementation. Preliminary memory profiling suggests that lazy uses much less memory for both tracing and slicing on the benchmarked programs than eager, while delay usually uses less memory for both tracing and slicing in all examples except tree, often by more than an order of magnitude.

These measurements are consistent with the brief conceptual discussion of the strategies, suggesting that a careful implementation that uses lazy and delayed tracing can further reduce overhead.

7. Related Work

We mentioned in the introduction some of the related work from the large literature on program slicing and related techniques; here we discuss more closely-related work, as well as other related work on provenance, debugging, and execution indexing.

Program slicing. Biswas's [6] and Ochoa *et al.*'s [19] work are the closest to our program slicing techniques. The main difference between Biswas' work and ours is that we support more flexible slicing criteria that permit arbitrary portions of the output to be thrown out or selected—Biswas considers only slicing with respect to the entire output. Ochoa *et al.* present techniques for computing slices under more flexible slicing criteria, but consider only first-order lazy programs. Our techniques appear to be the first where flexible criteria can be used in a strict, higher-order setting. We also realize a limitation of program slices and propose computation slices as a fine-grained techniques for understanding computations.

In terms of technique, Biswas' and Ochoa *et al.*'s approach both rely on labelling parts of the program and propagating the labels through execution to determine which parts of the program contribute to the output. Both can be viewed as constructing an execution trace: Biswas constructs an implicit trace by propagating labels through the execution and Ochoa *et al.* construct an explicit trace in form of a redex trail [23] so that expressions that are lazily evaluated can be identified. Our techniques also rely on construction of a trace, but our traces reflect closely the syntax of expressions. This allows us to "unevaluate" trace slices back to expressions and to handle higher-order programs in a simple way.

Provenance. Provenance concerns the auditing and analysis of the origins and computational history of data. Provenance is a growing field with applications in databases [8, 9, 13, 14], security [10, 25] and scientific workflow systems [7, 12, 22]. The techniques employed sometimes rely on traces but have to date mainly been developed for languages of limited expressiveness (e.g., monotone query languages) rather than general-purpose languages and often without proper formal foundations. Provenance extraction seems to be an important future application area for language-based tracing and slicing techniques. Some efforts in this direction include Hidders et al. [15], who model workflows using a core database query language extended with nondeterministic, external function calls, and partially formalize a semantics of *runs* which are used to label the operational derivation tree for the computation. Recent work on security and provenance [2] by some of the present authors is also based on big-step techiques similar to those presented here. The authors present a "disclosure slicing" algorithm similar to our trace slicing algorithm, which ensures that a trace retains enough information to show how an output was produced. However, that work does not investigate program slicing or unevaluation, and is unable to slice higher-order values.

View ML [24] has similar high-level goals to ours but is technically quite different to our approach. VML allows the programmer to define special functions called *views* that carry some intensional information in the form of a datatype constructor with arguments showing how parameters were set. These can later be inspected or pattern-matched. This is a useful form of user-defined provenance, but is distinct from that provided by detailed tracing. On the other hand, views could provide a mechanism for abstraction/granularity control with larger traces, potentially addressing some of the issues of scale that we leave as future work.

Debugging. Debugging techniques often involve tracing. The problem of scale – in terms of both resource usage and human cognitive capacity – has received some attention in this area. Nilsson's "piecemeal" tracing for lazy languages [18] builds a trace in the form of an evaluation-dependency tree, but allows the trace to be started at selected, suspected functions, akin to setting a breakpoint in a traditional debugger. Claessen *et al.'s* work on Hat [11], based on redex trails, explores efficient storage and visualisation techniques and demonstrates that trace-based approaches are feasible for large, multi-module programs. Both these systems also support the declaration of "trusted" components for which no internal trace is recorded.

Execution monitoring. An alternative to tracing is the *execution monitoring* of Kishon and Hudak [17]. A generic instrumented interpreter provides observation events to a *monitor*, which can use this information to calculate various properties of the execution. This has the advantage of avoiding creating large intermediate data structures like traces or redex trails. A disadvantage is that it is not possible to manipulate or transform the view of execution after the fact, short of building an explicit trace as we do.

Execution indexing. Execution indexing is a technique, sometimes implemented using execution monitoring, for setting up a correspondence or alignment between the execution traces of two different runs of a program. Recent applications of execution indexing include a form of differential slicing [16]. Their differential slices differ from ours in supporting comparison of distinct runs, unlike our technique which only allows two slices of the same computation to be compared. However, these techniques have been developed only for imperative languages.

8. Conclusions

We often treat computation as a "black box", but debugging, comprehension and analysis problems require breaking this abstraction and looking inside the box. Opening the box exposes a great deal of useful information to the programmer but also presents several implementation and user-interface challenges. In this paper, we focused on foundations. We presented a novel algorithm-independent characterisation of the problem of calculating a least dynamic program slice, showed how to support fine-grained differential slicing criteria in the presence of higher-order functions, and showed how to slice reified computations, or traces, as well as programs. Our techniques, realised in our tool Slicer, enable the user to interact with a computation and understand it in terms of the programming language the program was expressed in.

The main challenge that lies ahead for our approach is scaling it to large programs. In the present paper, we briefly described techniques for reducing the overhead of tracing by delaying tracing until it is needed for slicing. Previous work in the area of functional debugging has explored several complementary techniques which may be of use in making trace-based approaches more scalable, including piecemeal construction of traces, "trusted" components for which tracing is disabled, and offline storage. Investigating the applicability of these and other techniques we defer to future work.

References

[1] U. A. Acar. *Self-Adjusting Computation*. PhD thesis, Department of Computer Science, Carnegie Mellon University, May 2005.

[2] U. A. Acar, A. Ahmed, J. Cheney, and R. Perera. A core calculus for provenance. In *Proceedings of the First Conference on Principles of Security and Trust (POST)*, pages 410–429. Springer, 2012.

[3] J. R. Allen, K. Kennedy, C. Porterfield, and J. Warren. Conversion of control dependence to data dependence. In *POPL*, pages 177–189. ACM, 1983.

[4] D. C. Atkinson and W. G. Griswold. Implementation techniques for efficient data-flow analysis of large programs. In *ICSM*, pages 52–61. IEEE, 2001.

[5] T. Ball and S. Horwitz. Slicing programs with arbitrary control-flow. In *Proceedings of the First International Workshop on Automated and Algorithmic Debugging*, pages 206–222, London, UK, 1993. Springer-Verlag.

[6] S. Biswas. *Dynamic Slicing in Higher-Order Programming Languages*. PhD thesis, University of Pennsylvania, 1997.

[7] R. Bose and J. Frew. Lineage retrieval for scientific data processing: a survey. *ACM Comput. Surv.*, 37(1):1–28, 2005.

[8] P. Buneman, J. Cheney, and S. Vansummeren. On the expressiveness of implicit provenance in query and update languages. *ACM Transactions on Database Systems*, 33(4):28, November 2008.

[9] P. Buneman, S. Khanna, and W. Tan. Why and where: A characterization of data provenance. In *ICDT*, number 1973 in LNCS, pages 316–330, 2001.

[10] A. Cirillo, R. Jagadeesan, C. Pitcher, and J. Riely. Tapido: Trust and authorization via provenance and integrity in distributed objects. In *ESOP*, volume 4960 of *LNCS*, pages 208–223, 2008.

[11] K. Claessen, C. Runciman, O. Chitil, J. Hughes, and M. Wallace. Testing and tracing lazy functional programs using Quickcheck and Hat. In *In 4th Summer School in Advanced Functional Programming, number 2638 in LNCS*, pages 59–99. Springer LNCS, 2003.

[12] S. B. Davidson and J. Freire. Provenance and scientific workflows: challenges and opportunities. In *SIGMOD*, pages 1345–1350, New York, NY, USA, 2008.

[13] J. N. Foster, T. J. Green, and V. Tannen. Annotated XML: queries and provenance. In *PODS*, pages 271–280, 2008.

[14] T. J. Green, G. Karvounarakis, and V. Tannen. Provenance semirings. In *PODS*, pages 31–40, 2007.

[15] J. Hidders, N. Kwasnikowska, J. Sroka, J. Tyszkiewicz, and J. Van den Bussche. A formal model of dataflow repositories. In *DILS*, volume 4544 of *LNCS*, pages 105–121, 2007.

[16] N. M. Johnson, J. Caballero, K. Z. Chen, S. McCamant, P. Poosankam, D. Reynaud, and D. Song. Differential slicing: Identifying causal execution differences for security applications. In *IEEE Symposium on Security and Privacy*, 2011.

[17] A. Kishon and P. Hudak. Semantics directed program execution monitoring. *J. Funct. Prog.*, 5(4):501–547, 1995.

[18] H. Nilsson. Tracing piece by piece: affordable debugging for lazy functional languages. In *Proceedings of the 1999 ACM SIGPLAN international conference on Functional programming*, pages 36–47, Paris, France, Sept. 1999. ACM Press.

[19] C. Ochoa, J. Silva, and G. Vidal. Dynamic slicing of lazy functional programs based on redex trails. *Higher Order Symbol. Comput.*, 21(1-2):147–192, 2008.

[20] R. Perera, U. A. Acar, J. Cheney, and P. B. Levy. Functional programs that explain their work. Technical Report MPI-SWS-2012-003, Max Planck Institute for Software Systems, July 2012.

[21] T. Reps and T. Turnidge. Program specialization via program slicing. In O. Danvy, R. Glück, and P. Thiemann, editors, *Partial Evaluation*, volume 1110 of *LNCS*, pages 409–429. Springer-Verlag, 1996.

[22] Y. Simmhan, B. Plale, and D. Gannon. A survey of data provenance in e-science. *SIGMOD Record*, 34(3):31–36, 2005.

[23] J. Sparud and C. Runciman. Complete and partial redex trails of functional computations. In *IFL 1997*, number 1467 in LNCS, pages 160–177. Springer-Verlag, 1998.

[24] E. Sumii and H. Bannai. VMλ: A functional calculus for scientific discovery. In Z. Hu and M. Rodrguez-Artalejo, editors, *Functional and Logic Programming*, volume 2441 of *Lecture Notes in Computer Science*, pages 290–304. Springer Berlin / Heidelberg, 2002.

[25] N. Swamy, B. J. Corcoran, and M. Hicks. Fable: A language for enforcing user-defined security policies. In *IEEE Symposium on Security and Privacy*, pages 369–383, 2008.

[26] F. Tip. A survey of program slicing techniques. *J. Prog. Lang.*, 3(3), 1995.

[27] M. Weiser. Program slicing. In *ICSE*, pages 439–449, 1981.

[28] B. Xu, J. Qian, X. Zhang, Z. Wu, and L. Chen. A brief survey of program slicing. *SIGSOFT Softw. Eng. Notes*, 30:1–36, March 2005.

Author Index

NOTES

www.ingramcontent.com/pod-product-compliance
Lightning Source LLC
Chambersburg PA
CBHW080147060326
40689CB00018B/3887
* 9 7 8 1 4 5 0 3 1 0 5 4 3 *